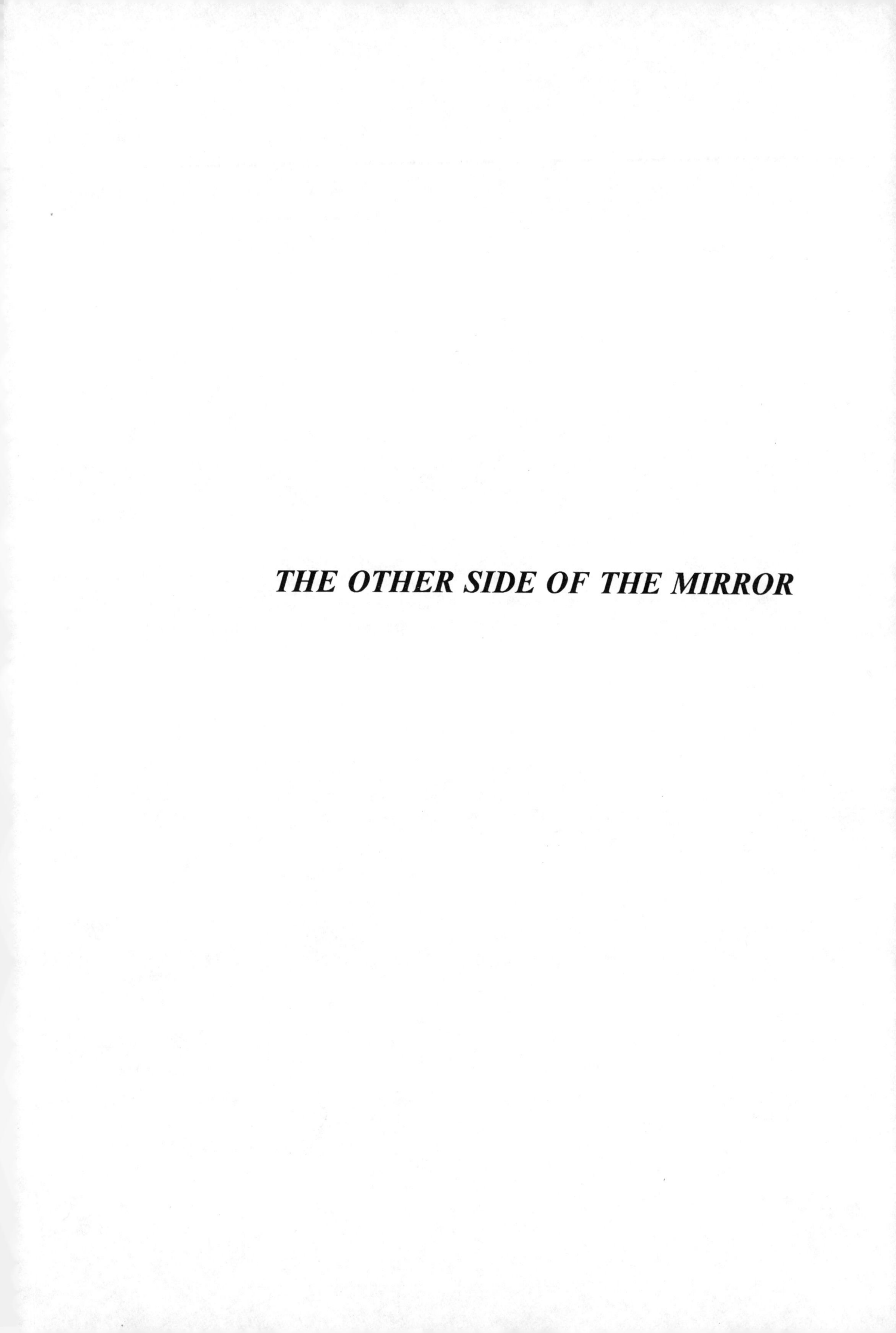

THE OTHER SIDE OF THE MIRROR

THE OTHER SIDE OF THE MIRROR

Mariah Hourihan, Editor

THE INTERNATIONAL SOCIETY OF POETS

The Other Side of the Mirror

Copyright © 1996 by The International Society of Poets
as a compilation.

Rights to individual poems reside with the artists themselves.
This collection of poetry contains works submitted to the Publisher by individual authors who confirm that the work is their original creation. Based upon the authors' confirmations and to the Publisher's actual knowledge, these poems were written by the listed poets. The International Society of Poets does not guarantee or assume responsibility for verifying the authorship of each work. Address all inquiries to Jeffrey Franz, Publisher, 45c Joseph Wilson Estate, Millstrood Road, Whitstable, Kent CT5 3PS.

All rights reserved under International and Pan-American copyright conventions. No part of this book may be reproduced, stored in a retrieval system or transmitted in any form, electronic, mechanical, or by other means, without written permission of the publisher.

ISBN 1-57553-117-8

Printing and Binding by
BPC Wheatons Ltd, Exeter, UK

Editor's Note

Alexander Pope, a prominent poet and critic in the eighteenth century, famously characterized successful poetry as

> ... Nature *to Advantage drest,*
> *What oft was* Thought, *but ne'er so well* Exprest.

(Pope, *An Essay on Criticism*)

In one admirable couplet, Pope identifies the fundamental challenge to any poet: to represent imagination, emotion, and experience in lines, stanzas, and cantos; to cast one's words, like a net, onto the page and to capture life between the letters. Anyone who has sat in a garden and attempted to pen even a few lines of poetry, knows the difficulty of rendering a yellow daffodil onto a white page with black ink. To do it well is an even greater challenge and requires an exceptional command of language, shrewd observation, and imagination. *The Other Side of the Mirror* is a collection of works by poets who are meeting this challenge.

One such poet is Mr. Harry West. In his aptly named poem "Words", he creates a lively carnival of language. His five stanzas, like circus tents, house displays of colourful acrobatics as Mr. West playfully juggles and turns his utterances, often playing off well-known expressions:

> *Argued, shouted, wise and foolish - whispered in friendly ear;*
> *Fired in anger, tied in knots - twisted, laughed, and shed with tear.*
> *Padded out for boring speeches - spoken for the sake of Pete!*
> *Bitter, sweet, scrawled and neat - daubed on walls along the street.*

Using both internal and external rhymes, as well as a steady rhythm of eight beats per line, Mr. West skillfully injects the poem with vitality and animation.

Another effective but very different poem is "S A D Winter" by Leslie Stiles. In remarkably precise language, the poet draws an exquisitely detailed winter scene. Every word is important and is employed to its full potential:

> *Blackened leaves on sagging stems are comforted by diadems,*
> *cold fashioned from the night before as winter's mantle covered more*
> *than gravel paths . . .*

The imagery is exceptionally innovative and evocative:

> *Skeletons cling to spidered beech, menacing rose thorns*
> *fill the breach, darkly defiant, awaiting springwood, static*
> *aggression with no velvet hood.*

As the poem continues, one senses a building emotional urgency. Rose thorns are described as "menacing" and rain drops as "hazard's dank drummers" and "purveyors of pain". In the third stanza, anxiety is increased further with the appearances of words like "alert", "retreat", and "shield". This sense of emotional crisis is best explained by the title of the poem: "S A D Winter". Seasonal Affective Disorder, abbreviated S.A.D., is a medical condition in which the change of seasons can affect one's mood and energy level. The dark, cold winter days leave those suffering from the disorder feeling extremely weary and depressed; more simply, sad. With the promise of Spring however, comes the assurance of better health and good cheer:

> *. . . but Pandora's box may lift the heart, as dawn*
> *and dusk grow more apart, for spirits may soar high to sing*
> *when bursting burgeons herald Spring.*

"S A D Winter" is a carefully composed piece that sublimely depicts a landscape which succeeds in being both physically and psychologically threatening.

Nature poses another threatening circumstance in Michael O'Reilly's poem "Night Crossing". This circumstance however, is rather more tragic: the loss of a loved one to cancer. Mr. O'Reilly poignantly expresses the exhausting emotional limbo that results from slow battle with terminal disease:

> *I wake to find myself*
> *exactly half way*
> *between last night and*
> *touching you.*

The persona's sense of life suspended "half way between" is reinforced by the form of the poem. In this first stanza, one sentence runs through four lines, breaking in seemingly unnatural places. Open space exists between words, isolating them, and leaving thoughts lingering in the air, never quite completed.

The flowers by the bedside, like both the persona and subject, weaken and fold under the strain, "beneath a litany of false alarms. / that are halfway between burning down and coming true." Helpless, overwhelmed, and holding on for life, it is a "season of falling satellites, the internal bleeding / of unwritten poems, forest-fires for no reason" as the persona waits "for news of all of these, and cannot sleep".

As the poem draws to its close, so does the subject's life:

> *you are listing, now, unsure*
>
> *if it is my hand in yours or yours in mine*
>
> *if your pulling away will leave my falling behind.*

The form of these last three lines, separated by additional spacing, visually represents the subject's pulling away. The fusing of poetic form and subject in "Night Crossing" also underscores the union expressed between the persona and subject. He cannot rest easily until she is whole again and they are one, until she puts her arms around him "like a bay" and he can "tide in and out of" her. However, she will not be whole again and their union inevitably dissolves, as the poem literally ends in pieces.

Another impressive poem is Steven Howards' "Bruises of Love", which explores the potentially destructive passion of two star-crossed lovers in a divided community. The poet evokes the dark and violent world in which his relationship with an Irish woman is considered taboo. Together, they try to escape from their "lives in the shrapnel" and the affair has the excitement of high-speed joyriding:

> *A golden St. Christopher hangs 'round the neck*
> *With bruises of love, in this burnt twisted wreck*
> *Of a car in a lay-by, the city streets left*
> *In the rough blur of speed and the thrill in the theft*

The impending social consequences of their actions hover above them like an impending traffic accident or the prognostication of disease:

> *Cold soberness waiting somewhere in the light*
> *Where the morning will slowly infect what is night*

There are may other interesting poems to note as well. "A Terminal Case" by Jean Watson is a sobering snapshot of one rich man's demise. Robert Morris paints a disturbing, haunting portrait of the modern American Indian in "Gambling Shop U.S.A". Families are disappointed when rain falls on their "Day Out", in a superbly descriptive piece by Peter Keegan. And Lilian Kelly depicts the essence of the harvest season in the fleeting descent of leaves in "Autumn in All Five Seconds".

So many of the works included in this anthology will delight you with their wit, talent, and creativity. Unfortunately I lack the space to mention the many remarkable poems here, but I encourage you to peruse your copy of *The Other Side of the Mirror*. I am confident you will be rewarded, as I was, by discovering the myriad successful and skillfully-crafted works among these pages.

The Other Side of the Mirror is the culmination of the efforts of many talented and dedicated individuals. I would like to thank the editors, assistant editors, customer service representatives, data entry, administrative staff, post production personnel and all of those who brought their respective talents to bear on this project.

Mariah Hourihan, Editor

Featured Poetry

Be Your Saviour

Liken your emotions
to the petals of the cherry blossom
and with baited breath
wait for the gentle whisper
  of the breeze

Liken your anger
to the crashing moan of the wave
with the turn of the tide
  they disappear

But for your sanity
liken your whole existence
to the infinite rays of the sun
be the source of life and energy
  to your loved one
and with the blast of your light
make the shadows in your life history.

Georgina Laverse

The Foxglove And The Bee

Flower bells hanging
on a green spike,
coming out in sequence
starting with the bottom first;
each flower blushed purple
full open and inviting

Any wandering bee into them.
And when enticed
the bees appear to be in ecstasy
buzzing as they thrust
deep into the flower

Before shyly backing out.
The pattern of attraction locked
away in the shape of a developing seed;
ready to repeat itself once more
when the time is ripe again
for the foxglove and any roving bee.

George B. Burns

A Poem Called Life

When you come into this world, you know nothing at all,
You're chubby and bouncy, you're content with all.
Then you become school age, in the world of exams,
You study and learn, your teachers' demands,
Then you are older, and wiser it seems,
At last a teenager with exciting dreams.
You go to dances, you're carefree and wild,
Gone are the school days gone is the child.
Then you fall in love, with the one of your dreams,
The world is your oyster, your plans and your schemes.
You marry your loved one, then after a while,
The patter of small feet makes it all worthwhile
Now you're a parent raising daughters and sons,
a happy family, so good and so true.
Life has been so kind to you.
But comes the time, the kids leave the nest.
You have seen them through, and done your best.
Now you're alone, but memories remain, and if you could
You'd do it all again. So in your rocking chairs
You sit hand in hand waiting for the promised land.

Hilda Hoad

Wasting Away

You live on cigarettes and not a lot more,
you've lost all your friends they all think you're a bore
you're obsessed with your weight and nothing they say
will get through to you that you're wasting away.
You're a different person all angry and cold,
you're killing yourself but you just won't be told.
Don't waste your life on a misplaced ideal
admit you need help, that you're problem is real.

Gemma Dawkins

On The Outside

When the darkness comes your shrouded in pain;
you're lost for words, can't explain;
why does it keep happening again?
Your heart aches so much, but you can't say why;
there's no answer, but there's plenty reason to cry.

From our hearts, from our soul;
if there's a reason, any reason at all;
You must look inside before you stumble and fall;
I'll be your brother, I'll be your friend;
On me you can always depend.

You talk to me of broken hearts and broken dreams;
It's all so distant, or so it seems;
but tomorrow's the beginning not the end;
your emotions are for real, so never pretend;
out of the darkness, out of pain,
you'll learn to live again.

Graeme Stirton

An Invitation To Live

I accept with trepidation
Your kind invitation,
With heavy heart and sweated brow
How can I accept the fact
The people one grew up to love
Are not my flesh and blood.
How can one pay the debt of love

But it is to those I say
Rewards are not too far away.
It is in one grasp
The rewards of patience
So I gladly accept now with no trepidation
Your kind and generous invitation
To be born of kindly things
And love and life itself.

Heather Atkinson

Expression

Take a look at your expression,
Your inner being does portray;
Do you go on quite regardless,
Irrespective of what it may say;

To look at your expression,
Is the window of your soul,
Does it show spite, or aggression,
Or tear tracts in the mould!

Is the framework upright, and honest,
The pane made of love and care,
The latch of understanding,
When to others, you would stare!

Are your features loving, and giving,
Does God's sunlight enter through;
Tell me!, what shall others interpret
In your expression, when they look at you?

Esther J. Armstrong

Giving Up

Giving up is easy so they say,
You just keep busy all the day,
But what do you do in the middle of the night,
When you lie awake and the craving starts to bite?
You toss and turn around in your bed,
And a voice keeps whispering in your head
Why not get up and have a smoke?
Believe me friend it's no joke,
You try counting sheep but they won't stay still,
Perhaps you'd better take a pill:
No wait: I have the answer, just what you need,
Try counting the money you save by not smoking the weed.

Diana Bean

Perfect Romance

Let's walk along the sandy shores
Your hand in mine, mine in yours
The sand so soft beneath our feet
You hold me close, then our lips meet.

Let's go down closer by the sea
That blue stretch of eternity,
Let's feel the spray upon our hair
It hits my cheek, you kiss me there.

Let's lie down on this golden bed
And count the stars above our head,
The moon is watching from above
It's starting new, just like our love.

Let's hold each other, skin to skin
And let our love making begin,
Now I am yours and you are mine
As our bodies and our hearts entwine.

Alison Carnon

Ophelia

Pale lady with long flowing hair
your face held no great beauty
but your loveliness was fair.

A vision of colour with such grace
flowers adorned your gown instead of lace.
Crown of blossoms woven with care
Kissing your face as they fell from your hair

Your Lord demanded and then in madness,
you were denied
No longer adored, but cast aside.
So lost in love, no one could save
brought you to this.
A watery grave.

Anne Stead

Grandpa

I saw you lying in the hospital bed,
Your face all pale and white,
Having suffered a massive heart attack,
You gave me such a fright.

I thought I had lost you,
The Grandfather dearest of all,
You've been around for ever,
Like an oak tree, sturdy and tall.

You look at me as though nothing has happened,
Yourself you even scorn,
You hug me, kiss me, joke with me,
Like an oak tree and his young acorn.

Like all living things on earth,
I know your life must end,
But left behind will be my broken heart,
Which when you're gone, will never mend.

Ginnie M. Thomson

Yesterday

Give me a yesterday instead of a tomorrow,
Yesterdays were happy
Tomorrow full of sorrow.
Yesterday had sunny days
Tomorrow's full of rain,
Please give me back
My yesterdays,
And I can smile again.
All my friends belong to
Yesterday
Who will I have tomorrow
I close my eyes and think
Again.
If I didn't have tomorrow
How would I have yesterdays.

Annette Brookes

Dedication To My Son

You brought me joy, you give me happiness
Your eyes filled with a ray of sunshine
You are my son the special gift of life from God.
You are here to keep, me going
You are like a diamond the precious stone
to be taken care of and treasured.
Though you're only four, four years of
happiness you have brought unto me
four years of your broad smile
never a dull moment with you, that
special little person loved by so many.
I can simply say son you are the very
best and that no one can ever fill your space.
For you are the son I always wanted
keep on smiling,
keep on shining
Most of all keep on being you.

Jacqueline Warrington

The Game Of Life

Will you reach the finishing line. Will
you win the race? Though battered and
bruised by life's cruel twists of fate.
Will you find your second breath before it's too late?

All too soon the race will end, and the
finishing flag comes down. Will you cheer with
jubilation, or throw in the towel, and end your
days with a frown?

Sometimes we're slow to get started,
and seem to lose our way. But it's up to
you if you win or lose. Through disappointments
and setbacks try to win the day.

When we reach the finishing line tired
and out of breath. Will you manages to
raise a smile, thankful you've manage to
make the last mile? Then say," it was
worth it, I'd do it again, though it's
certainly a struggle when you play life's game".

Catherine Hardie

J'Daddy's Girl'

She says, Daddy come home, 'Oh' what do you do,
You scream at the heavens, as your heart breaks in two,
She can't see the reason, why Daddy's not there,
And Mummy's unhappy, so she cuddles her bear.

As she gets older, she'll think long and hard,
About the fun and games in her back yard,
You know she'll cry and that hurts too.
Because Daddy can't do what she wants him to do.

To run, to her Dad, with out-stretched arms,
A walk on the ceiling, before a bedtime yarn.
The story to tell, would be happy, not sad,
When she would wake up one morning
With her mum, and her dad.

Derek James

Rider In A Storm

Behind the dark doors of a brilliant mind
You were locked and chained
Through endless corridors you ran.
Exploring depth and height head
 heavy from sight.
Words made senseless patterns
But the world could not fathom
 your beauty
Screaming for release from your
endless thoughts, galloping faster
 than speed!
Unable to regain walking pace
In a race to infinity, a remarkable
man who didn't fit into life's strait-
jacket. A head of this time.

Glynis Saupe

Charlie

You sat and listened to me cry,
You sat and heard me laugh,
You sat there through a lonely night,
When nothing would go right.

For years you were a part of me,
We saw some ups and downs,
You know more about me,
Thorns and many crowns.

Little one you were so brave,
No one could threaten me,
You'd show your teeth and give a growl,
You showed your love for all to see.

A place is empty in my heart,
A tear is shed each day,
for a special dog called Charlie,
These words I have to say.

I had to say Good-bye my friend
I had to let you go,
Your pain and hurt, it had to end,
I love and miss you so

June Groome

Once Is Gone

It upsets me to think
you many never see beauty such as this.
You might have once, but no more.
Everything moves as one.
Golden grain sways from side to side.
Thorned bushes shudder as wind develops.
Long grass is toppled,
while the wind makes its mark.
Grey day, where the sun shines through clouds,
brightens a page where words scroll.
The sun dies behind the mountains,
only to resurrect at dawn.
I wish you could too,
but your time has gone.

Jennifer Boyle

Our Wedding

When you walked down the aisle all dressed in white,
You made me feel as high as a kite,
Your teeth were all white your cheeks all rosy.
You stood beside me and I felt all cosy,
When he read you your vows you said them with ease,
You looked at me and I was so pleased,
You may kiss the bride he said with a smile,
I was so happy my grin stretched a mile,
Click, click, click, all smiling in time.

We arrived at the reception in a Rolls Royce car,
It seemed a long time but we never travelled far,
We all sat down to a hot meal and at long last we never had a bill,
Ten O'clock came and we had to go.
We kissed our goodbyes the end of our show,
These our my thoughts of that special day,
You dressed in white and me in striped grey.

Jamie Keith Boyle

Ode To Alan Donald

This is my poem to you my dear Alan Donald,
you like trains, both real and scale modelled,
you love all kinds of trains, as young people do,
as an intercity 125 arrives at a tunnel, it goes through,
when you travel on any train, it can be a bumpy ride,
connecting doors in the middle, and windows on the side,
all these trains go fast, and they sometimes go slow,
when your own train is expected to be due, no one knows,
four feet eight inches, all the way to the top of your head,
you are even the same height, as you lie down in your bed,
as I now bring this poem of yours up to the final end,
all these fine words, especially for you Alan, I do send.

Josephine Teresa Elliott

For Thelma

No-one can deny your pain and suffering.
You inspired the hearts of everyone you knew.
For your weakness, which was always so apparent.
Stood abated, as your faith came shining through
I can draw on the example that you were to me,
How you stood the test with such great fortitude.
For you knew the Lord was always there beside you
As you prayed to Him for strength to be renewed.
Yes, He knew of all the pain that you were bearing
And decided it was time for you to go
To be with Him, were you can share forever,
The home prepared because He loves you so.

Joyce Hopkins

Loved Ones

What do you think, just lying there,
You haven't a penny, or a care,
You've had your breakfast,
Of toast and beans,
The next meal you think,
Is an eternity, it seems,
You have your partner by your side,
Neither a lover nor a bride,
You are neither awake nor asleep,
As you guard your domain, laid in a heap,
Are you waiting for someone
To knock on the door,
So you can offer a shoe
Or a big hairy paw,
There's one thing for sure,
I've known from the start,
I love you, my dogs,
With all of my heart.

Eileen P. Byne

The Seven Ages Of Life

Life is like a mountain slope,
You have to work hard to reach the top.
In infancy the path is good,
No worries or cares to block the road.
A schoolboy next you have to be tough,
The mountain slope is rocky and rough.
Still going upwards, teenager is next,
The climb's getting harder,
Which path should you take?
As an adult you think you can cope,
The climb's still rough, but you've got hope.
Parenthood with its doubts and fears,
The climb can be good or reduce you to tears
The climbing upwards you're nearing the top,
You're old and you're weary and ready to stop.
Until at last you're up on high,
You've climbed life's mountain,
And reached the sky.

Glenis Perkins

"My Friend"

If I could have my way
Your life would be like a summers day
You'd wake up every morning and look up at skies
Of blue, with a garden filled with flowers
Covered in morning dew.
The birds would all be singing some happy
Tunes for you, and family and friends would fill
Your day with laughter and happiness all the way.
You'd have no grief or suffer pain, only happy
Memories would remain to the ones who always loved you,
They know you have given your all and been
There to pick them up when they fall, and before
This summer day comes to an end, I want you to
Know, you are my very best friend.

Jean M. Judd

Look Who's Talking!!!

Children they amuse me, but constantly confuse thee?
You don't know where you've got them, indeed
they changed faster then, one, two three!
Take my young niece Lisa, 'Contrary' soul is she.
She's twelve, and twenty, in the mind... A handful she can be.
And then there's Ben, my nephew. He's so miserable consistently
moans. My poor sisters, at 'wit's end'. "Such whining why?"
She groans.
Then there's Sarah, next house but one, six, a real bully.
She bites the kids, and pulls their hair. God help them, when
she's developed fully!!! My other sister. She has twins.
Identicals, not the word. Not a freckle separates - such similarity,
is quite absurd! Now my 'friend' Karen, there's a one.
She's two 'kids,' eight and three.
I swear to God, if they were mine, "such monsters".! I would flee!!!
As I've stated. I believe this baby bearing, is overrated. I don't
see, why the need! You have to get up in the night, make bottles,
sort out temperature and then sit, and feed!! Sorry, not for me!
No patience. 'Free and single.' I'm ten now, when I grow up,
"that's what I want to be"!!! "Free" - "Me"!!!

Andrea Lewis

Thank You

Thanks Annette for all those years of keep fit,
You certainly made us work hard you git,
What with side bends to improve our waists,
And those hip thrusts, yea, they were great.

Then there were those doggy lifts,
Just one mention and we all had a fit,
As for the exercises for our tummies
After those we felt like crash test dummies.

Those leg exercises they made us cringe,
As for some of our legs, definitely wanted a hinge,
Out of all the keep fit classes, we thought you the best,
Because you certainly taught us how to stretch.

Even so you're a very nice lady to know,
And in summer time now our figures we can show,
So please let us thank you now,
Before you take your final bow.

Irene Partridge

Lottery Fever

Money won't buy happiness, nor will it buy health
You can't buy time to stay here no matter what your wealth
But there are many lovely things which we can have for free
The glory of a sunset, the beauty of a tree.
The galaxy of stars at night against a velvet sky
Bird song in the morning, a river flowing by.
The happy sound of laughter from children as they play
Love and understanding which help you through each day.
So don't waste time in dreaming of your numbers coming right
You cannot buy a rainbow or the silver moon so bright
Just count your many blessings, be grateful for each day
For time is of an essence and will quickly slip away.

Cynthia M. Crisp

The Snowdrop

Little flower so clean and bright
You really are a welcome sight
In these winter days so bleak
We had a pleasant surprise this week.
The snow had melted and you appeared
So beautiful, and our lives were cheered
You herald spring and warmer days
God does work in mysterious ways!
If you survive then so can we
In spite of grief and misery
Let us thank God for little things
Like you, and all the joy you bring.

Julia Mcall

A Day Out In The Car

Isn't it wonderful to own a car
You can travel to the shops or decide to go far.
A day at the seaside, that would be great.
So mum says, to bed now you kids, or you'll get up too late.

At seven in the morning, everyone's up with haste.
Mum shouts out, don't forget to put the cap, on the toothpaste.
The kids pack up, their bucket and spade.
There's a lunch box of sandwiches, freshly made.

The dogs are coming as well, it's a full load.
Everyone's ready, and the cars on the road.
Dad's not happy were now in a traffic jam.
Out come the sandwiches, there's cheese, egg, or ham.

We approach the sea front, dad says, at last we're here.
Mum's really excited she wants to go on the pier.
Dog's are playing on the beach, all sand in their coat.
Kids are building sand castles, complete with moat,

Come on says dad, let's go round the fair.
But mum wants to relax in her deck chair.
It's been a lovely day out, that's now at an end.
Time has come for us, our way home to wend.

Doreen Sharp

Deliberation

Allow your mind to be cautious
Yet your heart to be kind
There are many sweet tongues
To fool the incautious mind

Be sure of yourself, the decisions you make
Do not be impulsive, you will make mistakes
Do not make decisions in a confused state of mind
You will question "How could I have been so blind?"

Don't regret the things that have caused you pain
For the knowledge within that pain will always remain
For who could have taught you in words
The wisdom you have learned in life
Only each and every person who put you through strife

Though you have cried many tears and felt much pain
There need not be anyone to blame
Don't forget your pain or the wisdom you gained.
Or you will go through the process again
For life is a process which goes on and on
Until you learn where you are going wrong.

Grace Oleghe

Mine Caravette

Mine mobile home was deigned to roam,
Yet somewhere to rest mine head,
No corner turned is no ambition yearned
In seeking the setting sun

Oh give to me the open road,
Shade not the sun nor rain,
Caress mine eyes with travelling skies,
This eases my longing pain.

Mine caravette gives happiness, far beyond it's heart,
Poetry in motion, revealing devotion,
Contains a living soul, no shackled mind
Will ever find the peace it imparts.

A dawning vista, encamped in a distant place,
Enjoying life's, unhurried, placid pace,
Fragrances to torment a gourmet tongue,
Open fraternity tuned to song.

Oh give to me the open road
Shade not the sun nor, rain,
Swathe mine eyes with travelling skies
This heals my longing pain.

Bryan Spalding

Rusky

Yer coat feels smooth and soft as silk
Yer teeth and whiskers white as milk
I've yet tae meet ane o' yer ilk, aristocrat
Yer bodie's sleek as golden silk, sophisticat'

Yer e'en like liquid amber mead
Licht up wi' love, or is it greed?
Whenever ye require a feed, lean meat, nae fat
Puss ye'll get everything ye need, yer a tam cat

Ye purr and wheedle round my feet
In the early mornin' when we meet
Yer affection nearly mak's me greet, but then I sigh
For when I meet ye in the street ye'd pass me by

Yer fickle heart's an irritation
Ony open door's an invitation
Tae lock ye in's a great temptation, tak' care I micht
O' "Rusky" whar' in a" creation do ye ga'e at nicht?

Ye've claws like daggers, when they're oot
And yer juist too fond o' trailin' aboot
But that'll stop without a doubt, as well it micht
We're ga'en tae ha'e ye seen aboot next Thursday nicht.

Elizabeth M. Mitchell

Colours

Colours are a joy to see; red and blue and green.
Yellow, mauve, black and white, and all those in between.
A shimmering sea of silver or Adriatic blue,
A golden field of sunflowers; gardens of myriad hue.
The seasons bring us colours; winter snows all white,
Then comes the spring, green and gold; a truly wondrous sight.
Summer is the 'rainbow', enhanced by gentle rain,
Another feast of colours when autumn comes again.
Amber, yellow fawns and red,
All shades of brown when leaves are shed.
Then those of us with eyes to see,
Thank GOD for painting all this scenery.

Hazel M. Birch

Night

The stillness of the night
Wraps her arms around me
As ivy creeps around a tree.
The moon shines so bright,
What an earthly night
To bring yonder, such a sight!
Naked,
In the moonlight
Do lovers stir,
Their vision a blur,
For the aftermath brings sweet slumber.
Slumber is far from my eyes
As I ponder the stars
And the planet Mars:
How they gleam,
Deliciously so and decidedly so,
Spread out through the sky.
Ah! What a night!

Anela Das

Phases (Love's Touch Burns)

Touching love, that blast the miles away,
With undiminished phases hard and great,
They detour from a well established fate.

Glowing hearts a burning, come to stay,
The fire melts the tortured wait,
And burns away inside of love's last play.

I still can feel the warmth today,
As love's touch burns away at fate,
And Valentines will pave the way,
Of undiminished phases, never late.

Most dreams end but this might never
Phases that may last for ever.

Andrew Hearn

If

If I should no new morning see,
Would I very soon forgotten be.
Is there something I have not done
To remember with kindness when I am gone.
Have I at any time not striven
A bring a smile, or new hope given.
To the stranger passing by,
Did I not hear his anxious sigh.
Have I not helped to bring a smile
To anyone in time of trial.
A helping hand stretched out to reach
To put in practice what I preach.
Was there help I refused to give
Was mine the only life to live?
Could my life so empty be
That I forever refuse to see
The other persons point of view,
And only my own selfish way pursue.
If I should no new morning see,
O may this not be said of me.

Betty Bolderbergs

Our World

It's nice to sit in silence sometimes, and think of this wonderful world.
all types of people, colour and race, millions and billions with a different face,
Language spoken in many tongues, the miracle of birth in this massive throng,
So many religions and cultures are found,
Each country and citizen with duty bound.
Our seas, oceans and beautiful rivers,
Protect their livestock and keep pure for ever.
Our luscious forests a home for all, birds and creatures, do hear their call.
The habitation of plants and trees, the singing of birds, the hum of the bees,
The swamps and rushes the sun and rain,
Enhance the dwellings of all in name.
This great inheritance all children will share.
If green pastures and forests are handled with care.

Fay Fleck

A Stroke Of What

Invalidity, disability, what does it all mean,
Words I'd heard in passing are now an everyday scene.
To someone who was active and forever on the go
It's take your time, hold on, slow down, steady, whoah

The doctor said you've had a stroke, a stroke of what said I,
When I realized my body couldn't move, I began to cry,
The tears I cried would fill a brook, a never ending stream,
And a voice inside said stop it, you cannot change what's been.

The only thing I now can do, is make the best of what I've got,
For each arm and leg I use some poor souls have not.
To try to readapt is perhaps the hardest thing to do
What once, accomplished unaided now sometimes takes two.

I've started to sew tapestries, a pastime I do enjoy
It takes time to get started then how that needle flies.
I also like writing poetry, so far I've written quite a few,
But will they ever be published this answer lies with you.

Dorothy Howse

"Cats"

Their feline spirit is always there
When you're feeling down and through.
The rub of their noses on your palm,
gives you feelings of love and honour.
Their wide eyes and cherub noses,
Spy the frisky birds.
Their striking personality is there to be friend.
Ginger, brown, black and grey
every cat is different,
for every owner knows,
their cats own mischievous ways.

Alyson Morrison

Only Four

My Granddad had a shed full of
wondrous things, and when he said "let's
look in the shed" my four year old feet had wings.

Now Grandma she was very quiet
not always well I think, her skirts
came night down to the ground over
which she wore an apron, on one foot
she had a very large boot can't
think why she had to have that on!

Although they lived in quite a big
house they never went upstairs, what's up
there I used to wonder a mystery for
sure but little girls they didn't ask and I was only four.
Out in the garden there were trees
apple plum and pear, and all the veggies you could name,
they all grew there.

Pram loaded up home we would go with food for the coming
week, lucky us even with a war on we had enough to eat!

Gwen Lammas

Dancing On The Titanic

With your heart in your mouth, you step from the house,
Wondering what you're breathing today.
As you lift up your eyes, you're blind to the skies.
You feel your mind go drifting away.

You know you've got to pull your shirt-sleeves down
  as far as you can
'Cause you don't want to find yourself getting an unhealthy tan.

You check your cholesterol, because after all
You never know the time of your life.
Don't make love any more - that's another closed door
For who knows who may have infected your wife?

Passive smoking leaves you choking so you stay in your bed.
Don't you sometimes think that maybe you'd be better off dead?

There's a sign on your lead-free motor saying "This car is alarmed."
That's no surprise 'cause you're s**t-scared
That we're going to come to harm
'Cause we're all dancing on the Titanic, fiddling while Rome burns.
Everybody's up in arms but no-one ever learns.

You use recycled paper to wipe your backside clean.
You've changed your washing powder -
  now you're feeling really green.
Your dog's a vegetarian while the cows are eating sheep
And nightmares of Creutzfeldt and Jakob haunt you in your sleep.

Brian D. Johnston

Without You

As I gaze into your eyes,
wondering what secrets they hold
dark brown and hazy,
no expression is told

Reaching for the picture,
I try to understand; my anger, my loss, my sadness, my fear
The feelings I hide...tucked right up inside
the memories I have...some good and some bad

I wonder "Just why?"
"Oh God; Oh Mighty, why oh why?"
I can't smile, I can't cry
I can't live, I can't die
All I can do is try and try

The pain will not go, the memories will stay
Now I know what I must do to make them proud of me today
I'll eat, I'll drink, I'll live and I'll sleep
The memories in my heart forever will beat

Until the day it's time for me, to join them there wherever they may be
The breeze, the wind, the ocean, the sea...If that is them,
that is me.

Becky Armbruster

A Birds Eye View

Looking down upon the world, from high up in the sky,
Wondering what life's all about, and trying not to cry,
Knowing it's a journey, full of heartache and despair,
Giving us a reason for not wanting to be there.

Then we feel emotions swelling up inside,
Love, joy and anger, and a few more besides,
Patiently waiting, to explode once more,
Into something beautiful, waiting at the door.

Everyday and every night, living in this world,
There's a lamp to guide us, deep within our soul,
Pursuing righteousness, Love and prosperity,
Being generous to the needy, and glowing within you and me.

What happened to self discipline and understanding? (It flew
  out the door),
A lot of cruelty and greed came in, asking for more and more,
Giving us a reason to try again to learn to live,
The way it was intended, and trying hard to forgive.

Will we ever fathom out the right road in life?
It's the quality of our journey, that's important to drive out strife,
We will smother evil with good, and hate with love,
But,......No where......is secure,......as I see it from above.

Joan Yvonne Matthews

Mystical Forest

There I walk through the woods, filled with a fog so mystical,
without warning I cry,
I sense the magic of centuries that have gone by.
I feel I know this place, yes I know it so well,
and although I am only there in my mind, I've been there before,
in body, in another time, I can tell.
I walk some more, I feel the spirit of the trees welcome me,
treating me like a lost friend, they were glad to see.
And I was equally glad to be there, breathing in the magic air,
those trees were so beautiful, even though they were bare.
I wanted to stay there in this place I felt was mine,
but I was called back to my own time.
I will return again I'm sure, to the trees so tall,
I know I will because the magic will call.
And each time I return from this mystical place,
I will be filled with love and wisdom, for the problems of my own
time I have to face.

Gordon Tibbitts

Reflections Of Youth

As I sombrely walk amidst green meadows in sunshine,
with wings so colourful and fragile, butterflies pass me by,
and all that I have encountered through childhood,
floods back in my mind's eye,
of children's dancing shadows, moving around so fast,
trying to catch the duplicate of oneself,
that the sun's golden rays have cast.

When days of adolescence were carefree,
and hours of play were bliss,
when years of aging were so far away,
these are all the things I miss.

My knowledge of life is stored in the pages of memory,
another chapter in my existence it turned,
the legacy of life carries on through my children,
and all the wonders of life I have learned.

Time seems to pass by so quickly,
the years of time for some take their toll,
and as I approach my final chapter in life,
I believe that I have reached my goal!!!

Beverley Hesketh

Oh Beautiful Angel

My angel, oh beautiful angel
With wing's glistening up above,
My angel, oh beautiful angel
A Goddess of beauty and love.

The way your hair sparkles in sunlight
The way that you glow in the night,
No evil could ever surpass me
For with each dawn, you bring a new light.

My angel, oh beautiful angel
Your heart is so full of love,
My angel, oh beautiful angel
For you are my peaceful dove

My angel, oh beautiful angel
Your laughter makes my day,
Your smile is like a shooting star
Shining bright to lead the way.

So go back to the heaven's, my angel
Your beauty's to much for just me,
Go back to the heaven's my angels
And shine for the whole world to see.

Alan David White

James

Your eyes are such a fascinating feature
You surreptitiously walk like a gentle creature
I wonder if you are a human at all
Or another being that took a fall
It seems you don't belong with us
To communicate is too much fuss
We fill your mind, stimulate your brain
So that you may one day talk the same
We teach you things, the lessons are few
We've learnt much more from encountering you
You fill our hearts with just a smile
Content with assuming that you're happy? For a while
Where are you now, that vacant stare
Tells us you've gone off somewhere.
Fingers twisted, sounds of elation
Or are they screams of frustration?
We reach out for you, but all in vain
Are we the mad ones and you the sane
You can't get out. We can't get through.
If only we knew the little you.
You're here with us, yet all alone,
　one day we'll find your place, your home.

Gaynor Atkins

"Awakening From Escapism"

Up the hill I go,
With troubled heart and soul, removed from all society.
On the summit, thoughts and memories come flooding back.

No longer am I standing on the hill.
But on rocks on a wild deserted beach.
The sun before me a massive fireball,
Slowly sinking into the briny horizon,
Casting a myriad of colours across the sky.
I feel at one with myself, serene and peaceful.

Suddenly, a movement brings me back.
With a feeling of pure delight, I spy the rabbit.
Its two doleful eyes watching, watching,
So beautiful and soft, so gentle.
Its grey fur blowing in the wind.

The rabbit stands in a small clearing,
Surrounded by harsh and unfriendly brambles.
Thorns protrude at every angle.
There is nothing soft about its surroundings.
The rabbit seems out of place.
Then all becomes clear. The rabbit and I, are one and the same.

Christine Shaw

Silent Thoughts

The thinking of mankind is strange
With thoughts of a various range
They can be pleasant, sad or gay
With silence deep we do not say
The secret ones we do not share
Sometimes pretending they are not there
With hurting pain we still can't explain
The thoughts that penetrate our brain
The fear of escape in thought so dense
Or rejection of the consequence
We keep it tight and tighter still
But hoping that we will fulfil
The silent thoughts that are only ours
That tremble with Almighty powers
Because of silence and there to remain
To keep and cherish and to attain
The thought that never would come true
Is the silent thought just for you.

June H. G. Shaw

Coming Year

Do I look forward to the coming year
With those I love and for them I care
Wondering if it will be the same
Or will it be a year of shame
Some want a world of peace
But go wrongly about it to say the least
"Said" peaceful people using force for a cause
Are just as bad as those making tools for wars
Should be not try to find a peaceful cure
With words deeds and acts for sure
To really care for our fellow beings
So as to live out our life's innings
In it build a better way on earth
So we can say to ourselves that's what it's worth
For instead of war and aerial flares
Make tools for growing crops and plough shares
So to all people on earth show that you care
And make my dreams come true in the coming year

Ernest Webb

The Race Is On

The race is on the gallop of the horses as each one runs by
With tails outspread behind him his eyes look straight ahead.
As his jockey strokes his head, "come on now my beauty
we'll soon be home and dry, but first of all
I need you now so just give it a try."
With nostrils all a flaying and foam around the jaws you give
one more jerk and run, soon the cup is yours.
The sound it's like a battle as everyone does cheer, but most
of all it's over when you hear them roar.
You beat the fillies to the ground even the black
could run behind you no more
So there my beauty now you've won.
Thank you for what you've done.

Elizabeth A. Wilkinson

Spring

When bright yellow daffodils stand on parade
With tulips like soldiers of a deep crimson shade
Cover all the land with a beautiful hue
It is spring and it all looks so new

The lambs in the field are only just born
The birds in the trees waking at dawn
The call of the cuckoo tells us it's spring
What a joy to hear him sing.

White and pink blossom looking like snow
New buds forming ready to grow
Seeds are sown in the freshly dug ground
The sweet scented air of spring all around

Baby chicks all fluffy with down
Gardens look pretty with lawns freshly mown
Looking at the land and what it can bring
You can tell it is ready for spring.

Julie Taylor

Love's Orbits

Rocket-like, love zooms from the soul
With such power it needs no hole
Yes how it's out to do some good
Surely as trees are made of wood

Because it's all around the world
It's time its secrets were unfurled
As it hones in on its target
Unique new forces now are set

A chain reaction makes a start
Right in the centre of the heart
All at a swiftly moving pace
Like runners in a relay race

Dispense some love for it is true
Other love will return to you
You've heard it makes the world go round
Yes, well its spring is fully wound

Now really it's not used enough
And that can make the going tough
So exploit this heavenly gift
Then lots of troubles we could shift.

Harry C. Derx

Autumn

Summer is ending the trees are sighing
with sadness for the dying year,
wild geese fly in straight lined grace
to their distant suns then my heart
will grieve with the falling golden leaves.
As the last leaf clings so must I to
youth and warmth and life, yesterday's
spring will come no more, the days we
used to know will soon be out of sight
beneath the softly falling snow.
Sleeping snowdrops below the copper
leaves will bring a hope renewed
remembering the sunlit hours that only
summer can bring, returning swallows and
nestlings cry the golden bells of the
daffodils will once more teach my heart to sing.

Catherine Neale

Circle Of Love

I hold in my hand, a circle of gold
With pride in my voice, I whisper sixty-nine years old
That's now long since I bought it
For my wife's finger then to fit
I remember the day that I put it there
For my dear lady wife, always to wear
She was so very proud of that golden ring
She made up a ditty, about it to sing
I can only remember words just a few
But I'll try to say, a few then to you
"A gold circle of love, on my wedding day
A gold band on my finger and there it will stay
The loveliest thing that I ever did see
A circle of love, from you dear to me
Fast on my finger forever to stay
And no one shall ever, take it away"
But when my wife died, I took that ring
But that ditty she sang, I could not sing
Now this circle of gold I hold in my hand
Will be hers once again, in that promised land

Charles Serbert

Half A Life

Ours are the wandering vagrant souls,
With no aspirations, no directions, no ideas.
Where do we go?
What should we do?
People like us have no life, no identity -
We merely borrow from those that do,
Whilst we search endlessly for a purpose we know not exists.

Janine Pickles

The Old Maid's Lament

I've had a long and dreary life,
With nought but worry, toil and strife;
Problems great and troubles rife,
    Oh dear!

I rose up early every day,
And worked and slaved for little pay;
I never had a holiday,
    Oh dear!

In those days I was smart and quick,
But now I feel so weak and sick,
Can't get along without my stick,
    Oh dear!

My clothes are getting old and frayed;
The fuel bills are still unpaid;
It's hard to be a poor old maid,
    Oh dear!

Now you young girls, take my advice;
When asked to wed, don't say 'No' twice;
Don't be old maids at any price,
    Oh dear!

Hilda Womack

"I Remember"

I remember the house where I lived as a kid
with my three brothers Jack, Ernie and Syd
It was an old house, with two up and two down
Not many yards from Darlaston town.

My mum worked hard and so did dad
The money was scarce, and times where bad
Mum had a struggle rearing four boys
The heartaches, the pressures, but also the joys.

I remember the stairs, so dangerously steep
also the bedroom where us lads used to sleep
The ceiling was bulging and in quite a mess
Probably due to the age I would guess.

Maims and dads bedroom was just as dreary
But it was somewhere to sleep when tired and weary
I wondered why we stayed there in a way
I supposed it was a small rent we had to pay.

Downstairs you could say was far from bright
With just an old oil lamp to get some light
But how well I remember the old black grate
All nice and polished, in a lovely old state.

Harold Platt

Otters

Otters are such beautiful creatures
With many distinguishing features
Once hunted and chased by man.
Virtually until almost extinct
Now instead they hunt mink.
Otters persecuted and slaughtered
When never should they have oughted
Continuing over hundreds of years
Alas, almost too late man realized the fears
That if they continued to hunt
This ever so graceful mammal
They would no more be
Thankfully now their numbers increasing
Each and every year breeding unceasing
Let's hope that man has learned
Was all the otters yearned
To be felt in peace on river banks
Now with the grace of God and thanks
They are so many fold
Living their lives in peace and dying old.

Ivan Keeling

Death Of My Love

Dark and empty, my life seems so bleak,
your voice has grown silent, your lips cannot speak.
The sweet words of love, you would always repeat,
as in each other's arms we lay, our passion replete.
A day full of sunshine, my heart leapt for joy,
how I remember the time, when girl met boy.
Long summer days, hand in hand we'd spend walking,
cold winter evenings, at home we'd spend talking.
Times with our friends, and times on our own,
even when apart, we were not quite alone.
There was always a cord, that bound us together,
we felt so strong, we could live forever.
My lover and I, we shared so much,
how I long for the warmth of your tender touch.
I miss your soft laughter, your warm loving gaze,
these things I will cherish, the rest of my days.
So much in love, my heart full of pride,
my heart now lies broken, I feel empty inside.
I mourn your passing, it fills me with pain,
you are locked in my heart and there you'll remain.

Colette McCullough

Lee

Tenth of June you entered the world,
You made us cry with joy,
You looked so small but perfect,
Our number three little boy.

Days flew by so very quickly,
Our own little King,
Then new year's eve you went so pale,
The doctor we rushed to ring.

You then went to another hospital far,
Our hearts all a flutter,
We sat with you night and day,
Many prayers we did mutter.

Three weeks passed you still laid there,
Not saying or moving at all,
We cried and cried so very much,
You looked so ill and small.

The day finally came and you came home,
We were all a little afraid,
We would watch you every move,
The world complete you have made.

Debbie Gregson

The Mistress

Enchantingly, young, and tall, standing there in the sun-light
  With her swinging shiny hair glinting bright
Smiling with dewy love filled eyes
  Into his middle-aged steel-blue gaze - was this wise?
He in his large country house with pool, enticing her to live with him
  Where he could kiss her every limb
So his mistress she became - was it on a whim, was this a clever thing?
  All went well till dreadful day
He clutched at his chest and died - nothing could hold his life at bay
  The will was read in cold and formal tones
The Wife smirked at her toy-boy - she held no bones
  As she heard the words: to my Wife and family I leave my entire estate
To Lilly I bequeath the lurcher dog - because to her he can relate
  And for her life the beach hut at Southend-on-Sea
No home and none to commiserate with thee
  A sudden icy coldness clenched her heart
She knew then he never loved her and she must depart
  They found her body washed up on a beach
The stranger who found her said 'Oh God she looks such a peach, why did she do this'?
  A warning: is being a mistress worth the risk!

Ann Hill

Street Walking

Treading the dark dank lonely street
With heavy heart and dragging feet
Trying to look towards the sky
Hoping to see a sparrow fly
Searching looking through the mist
Wondering if these things exist
  Thinking
Was it only yesterday
We trod this street a different way
With heart aglow and feet a-flight
The sky so sunny warm and bright
The birds all singing their sweet song
Surely that was not so long
  Hoping
Things will change when we reach the bend
The cold dark lonely street will end
The birds will sing the sun will shine
And lightened feet will skip the line
The heart will lose its heavy fears
As we turn away from the street of years

Dorothy Riley

"Winter Sadness"

The field stands white
with frost, and the bitter
wind has become my companion.
On the horizon I watch a fox
whose injuries have reduced her
near to death.

Slowly she crawls close to the
ground, rubbing her blood stained
belly upon the earth. But the frost
does not want to hold or nurse her, and
still she lies, her soul now gliding toward
the afterlife. Droplets of crimson blood seeps
like a stream gently from the fresh carcass, whilst
the savage wind softly kisses its breath across the
vixens thick fur.

Winter has arrived, and so to has darkness,
which comes in the shape of man's savage lust
for wildlife destruction. And for myself now
stood over the foxes body, I shed sombre tears
of spirit sorrow.

Jeffrey Woods

The Young Man

To Kevin

His heart beats in harmonic motion
With friends, near the close to a party.
Quiet music rotating on a mulled red
Then the warmth of empathy

They are his friends, with whom
Life is a compliment at every hour:
Talking to create a shrine for kinship;
He will not sleep this night

Why does the moon smile
And say "Touch that star over there,
Tomorrow you will wean on God
Then kindness will be your scar?"

Kismet may let the earth spin for ever!
Enemies, perhaps, allowing an easy path
To the mountain of dreams which yields
Letting him be himself like Socrates

In opposition his heart could bellow
In a theatre of uncertainty.
Then a lady would emerge to touch him,
And imprison his heart in quiescence.

Graham Morris

Thoughts Of Spring

Their heads are bells without the chimes
with elegant stems so proud and high.
We know that Spring approaches
when fields of yellow catch our eye.

Beeping beneath the woodland trees
they are a joy for us to behold.
What beauty greets us on our walks
though the March winds are blowing cold.

Life is too short to ignore simple things
that can give us so much pleasure.
The flowers, the lambs, birds making nests,
are memories all to treasure.

In the countryside here we are fortunate
this bounty is there for us to see.
The daffodil fields are all around us
and nature's wonders all are free.

When our lives are feeling troubled
and material needs are rated high.
Just be thankful for the memories
and special thoughts of Spring days gone by.

Elizabeth Brace

Corfe Castle

Oh Castle, oh Castle, of stone you were built,
With boulders and limestone, and bonded with silt,
You withstood the ravages of tempest and storm,
Until under Cromwell, you were left forlorn.
Your portals asunder, your magazine spent,
Your roof tumbled in, your bastion rent,
As onwards destroying, Cromwell's men went.

On ramparts and battlements the brave men of old,
Stood shoulder to shoulder, withstanding the cold,
With cauldrons of oil, and slings full of rocks,
Defending the castle, against insurgents and Celts,
With quivers of arrows attached to their belts.
The Castle stood proudly, surrounded by moat,
Till the advent of gunpowder and guns, when you broke.

The battle was brave and many men fell,
Defending the Castle they knew, oh so well,
The walls fell asunder, the ramparts were breached,
As broadsides of cannon balls were released.
The nobles and servants, ladies and all,
Died there, defending their Castle wall.

Janet McKinney

A Night In Blackpool

I hope you enjoyed Blackpool tonight
With all those big bright dazzling lights
Little Faye said there's postman Pat
Stevie shouts look there's his cat
Lynn's excited when she sees the tower
Mark says let's go in and spend an hour
But Carol wants to walk awhile
Right along the Golden Mile
Stuart's excited when he sees the fair
Steve said let's leave the kids there
When little David shouted look Mam
Is that really a Blackpool tram
Too soon it was time to say goodbye
To those big bright lights
And the tower in the sky
Louis Tausaud's and all its horror
We'll tell everyone come tomorrow
The kids are tired time to go
To make sure we keep up
With the traffic flow.

June Metcalf

To Silently Tread

To silently tread in this green peaceful land
With all nature's treasures and gifts there at hand
Snowcapped mountains, green valleys and streams
This green perfect land is my soul and my dreams

Walking over the hills and far, far away
Why put off till the morrow what you can enjoy today
This garden of Eden with flowers of every hue
From wild red poppies to tiny bells of blue

The sun and rain giving equity to this earth
Ensuring this land with green colour from birth
The panoramic view its beauty to behold
Watching nature's fingers divulge and unfold

Breathe deeply the air and feel the peace
The tranquil clouds glide, as all troubles cease
The trees with their blossoms floating down on the breeze
Help render your body and mind all at ease

Christine Atkinson Higham

A World Of War

Will the bombs and shells ever stop falling?
Will help ever reach the needy who are calling?
Will the people in this world ever sort themselves out?
That I admit I very much doubt.
Coz people don't know right from wrong
And if there was peace it wouldn't last long.

If only people could see and understand
Fighting need not go on throughout the land
And maybe when the New Year begins
These murderers may discover all their sins.

Maybe at last peace may come
And the soldiers need not get a call
To leave their families to go and fight
To witness the bloodshed and the terrible sight
Of all the bodies scattered around
Lifeless, dead and just heaped on the ground.

So please if you can spare a minutes thought
And think about the people who are trapped and caught.

Amanda Davison

Garden Of Mercy

In a garden's pensile slumber,
neath a pool of rippled air,
complex feathered ferns develop
E'en before the sun is near.
Dancing 'neath a crippled willow,
Each fair frond surmounts the branch
Never still above the brackens
Inodorous arm of brown,
sewn with earths own thread of perfume
Embroiled when the storm poured down.

Susan E. Spencer

If You Could Look into My Heart

If you could look into my heart,
I'll tell you what you'd find.
No cross, no words, no bitter sweet,
But just a rose sublime.

It's white, with many petals,
Each deal, holds for you,
A love that's strong and pure,
A love forever true.

And if some day you take this rose,
And crush it, in your hand.
Though petals fall, roads grow dark,
I still will understand.

This message, husband, comes to say,
Now that we're far apart.
Please take this rose and plant it dear.
Deep within your heart.

Patricia Beech

Ghosts And Things

Grey shapes floating not touching the ground,
Wistful and winsome they hover around.
Spine chilling shivers creep up your back,
No substance or form just limp and slack.
Eerie and nerve wracking as they pass by,
Gone in a flash when you blink your eye.

White shapes reminding you of a dove,
Daintily dancing in the air above.
Teasing and friendly in a haunting way,
Catching your eye as they elegantly sway.
Curtains drape windows of mullioned glass,
Moving gently when ghosts pass.

Reminders of family now long gone,
Ghosts from the past merge into one.
In your dreams they silently appear,
Filling thoughts of loved ones held dear.
Joy and happiness are the memories they give,
Urging you onwards as your life you live.

Jean Mary Osborne

The Fisherman

The fisherman walks along the shore
Wishing he were here once more,
To kick the sand and smell the salt
Loose the weed when it got caught
Around the line, the weights and hooks
Just as written in fishing books.
Whooshing waves and breaking foam
Brings many a wandering traveller home
How good to catch the biggest bream,
Truly, an enthusiasts dream,
The sport, the play the anglers net
Exhilarated, tired and wet
Now he dreams and thinks once more
Of days and nights spent on the shore
As he lies in slumber deep
Resting in eternal sleep.

Ann Lloyd

The Comedian

Backstage I hear you, a tough crowd.
Will you break or will I?
Your laughter is my fix - I AM an addict,
Your laughter is my pleasure,
I take it as a trophy, a sign of my worth.
Stepping onto the spot, panic rises with the curtain.
Not a sound.
My hands sweat, brain races, muscles tighten.
Heart doesn't beat.
Eyes focus, throat clears, lips move -

Deliver a line, your mouth crinkles.
The next line. You smile. My blood flows.
The next. You laugh. I am alive.
Your laughter continues, I am on a roll
I must keep it going, hold your attention in my hand -

One last laugh so loud it deafens.
The curtains drops. The laughter stops.
Something dies.

Emma Collins

Marriage

Marriage, it's that blissful state,
where the bride has the privilege of being late.
Under the thumb when you're out of line,
in the dog house is a very bad sign.
Kitchen pans and oven gloves,
burnt offerings and soggy clothes.
Mother-in-law with deadly stealth,
watches your pockets and your health.
Yes, marriage is that blissful state.
I'LL BET NOW, YOU JUST CAN'T WAIT?

Catherine Nutt

The Flame

For all the love we used to share,
I try not to shed a tear,
Things seem so unfair,
As memories start to appear.
The blazing flame burnt you,
You were so close to me,
I thought we'd make it all the way,
But you paid the fee.
In my mind I say lots of crazy things,
When standing by your grave,
Remembering when you looked at me
And said "Be brave."
Your smile has gone,
You're no longer here,
All the screams have died down,
There is no more fear.
My grief is so strong,
Since we are apart,
All I have are my memories
And a broken heart.

Emma Dugmore

Amaryllis

Wild primrose turns to yellow ochre reflection in your face so fair
With a golden honey highlight in your wild orchid melanin hair
Flower trumpets fanfare the Lily's arrival with a sunlight blessed
    fandango
As Amaryllis treads a dainty winding path through the
    mellifluous meadow
Candy floss pink dress caressed by a gentle warm Sirocco
Daffodil diaphanous maiden with a delicate buttercup tread
Cinchona daughter dancing between Narcissus flower heads.

Her head sways as Amaryllis chants the chorus of a favourite song
Melodious voice creating diadrom caresses upon green leaves with
    diapase sound
A cadence stimulates diadelphous action on sun warmed
    spring-tinged ground.
Buds open in harmonious outreach in celebration of nature's rebirth
She stays on the windward side of Winter as snowdrop trees melt
    between silver birch
Standing to Calvary attention bereft of cicatrice intervention
Declination to pick as the amative lady crouches to envelop the
    amaranthine convention.

Jon Wilde

Time Was My Friend

What have I done with the days of my youth.
Why was I so blind to the naked truth
Why did I choose to ignore what I knew
Love truly is blind for I loved only you.

You shattered my dreams when you strayed from love's way
I can never forgive what you told me that day
All my life I'll remember till the day that I die
And the wound just won't heal
    and the tears just won't dry
The pain is still hurting for the love that has flown
But I never owned it, your love was your own
And eyes that are weeping and blinded by tears
Can't see that the anguish
    will fade with the years.

Harsh words of bitterness spoken in the past
Causes pain and breaks the heart but doesn't last
For time heals the hurt and time is kind and true
Time was my friend, for I've stopped loving you.

Janet McCran

My Man

My friends all ask the same thing
Why do you stay with a man who abuses you
Why do you stay with a man who treats you badly

Is it fright that makes you stay. Oh No, I'm not frightened you see
Then why stay with him, when he treats you so badly

One hundred times a day, my head tells me to leave him
Pack my bags and go, but my heart refuses to listen

When I look into his eyes, I see no hatred, I feel I stand before the stars

When I look at his lips, I hear no harsh words
I just want to touch and kiss them tenderly

When I look at his hands, I see no fists that hurt me so
I just see the hands that caress me and makes me feel whole

My head tells me to leave, my heart tells me No
He might be the death of me, but still I stay
My heart will not let me walk away
Ask any woman in my position and I am sure this is what they will say:
In time I hope he will change.

Glenda Smith

The Willow Wand

On weeping tree
why are you so?

You that grows in such splendour
and you're boughs so heavily laden?
Why not rejoice in your beauty?
Shake off you burdens stretch your breaking back.
For sure you are worthy.

Fountain of the earth - you flourish
green tears you cry - unseasoned
They fall to nourish stale, crumbling clods.
That guzzle piggishly.

When your boughs are empty - all your tears are spent,
You'll bear their burdens silently
Lull the land to sleep.

In spring you touch your toes
Summer fringe your skirts,
In autumn, sweet willow, you will sleep
And winter the willow wand weeps

Fiona Haswell

Lady Of The Night

Oh beautiful lady of the night,
Whose brilliant aurora is ever bright,
Your fingers stretch with shafts of light,
Oh beauteous wonder of the night.

The scudding clouds which dim your beams,
Go quickly by as if unseen,
You shine so bright deep in the night,
Your light forever burning bright.

So many wonders of this earth,
A planet of your universe,
The human race so small so slight,
Pays wondrous homage to your light.

Joined with the sun you play your role,
The rise and fall of tides control,
The many hearts you've lifted high,
Your sensuous light makes lovers sigh.

So wondrous lady shining bright,
Whose soft sweet beams caress the night,
Shine brightly on into the night,
'Til comes the sun with morning light

Brian Kenneth Williams

Carnage

"They're back!" Screamed the news flash, "Breach of cease-fire shocks whole world,"
Many dead and injured, man from 4th floor window hurled,
Blue flash, massive explosion, emergency red alert,
Bomb wreaks havoc in the city, over a hundred hurt.

The blast ripped buildings wide apart, shattered windows to deadly silvers,
People torn limb from limb, other shaking with fearful shivers,
Caught up in mass hysteria, and screaming a piercing sound,
Through a pall of choking dust, devastation all around.

Many staggered blindly, drenched with blood in the dark of night,
A mum-to-be in agony, is her unborn child alright?
Heroes shepherd the wounded, irrespective of age or creed,
New victims of old hatred, for which there is no need.

Condemn this breach of cease-fire, the control of which we lack,
Unspoken fear of what is here, sad memories flooding back,
The full horrific history of how innocents are maimed,
The unsuspecting public at whom carnage is aimed.

They cannot win by bullet or bombs, this band of desperadoes,
For every one of their flint hearts, we have a hundred heroes,
Explosive caches we will destroy, the gunfire made to cease,
Tirelessly and endlessly we're wedded to bring peace.

Beryl Taylor

True Friends

I have two pals called Iris and Diane
Who take me out, once a week if they can
We've tried all the world's local cuisine
From Mexican fried rice to Italian Chicken Supreme
Their loyalty and trust leave me in no doubt
If I needed help I'd just have to shout
For twenty odd years my problems they've shared
Two silent listeners when others neither worried or cared
At one time problems seemed such a lot
But never once did they say shut up, you clot
When we were a lot younger we tried aerobics to keep fit
But now I've got a full time convincing them we're too old for these tricks
As middle age spread, grey hairs and wrinkle abound
Let's hope for along time us three pals stay around
To wine, dine and natter; on things big and small
To see all the kids we love grow strong and tall
But when we go to the big restaurant in the sky
For us there'll be no two veg and meat pie
For when we finally say au revoir, to us will be served
Champagne, smoked salmon and caviare

Jean Thomas

Who Cares For The Children

Children, welcome to an adult world,
who gives you warning,
who helps you in your fight against fate,
more pain in the world than you'll ever guess
and yet you blunder forth unguided,
why don't we warn our children -
    against love.

It will break their hearts and may devour their souls.
Shouldn't our children be taught on the important things,
    when adults are a-fool in love,
    what chance have children?

Fate can be guided if warned against
if experience were to be taught as well as gained
we could learn thricefold
and our children would reap the harvest we sow.
So why don't children go into the world pre-armed,
lust warned against, the traps of vice known,
so at least when their sprung
they would be so knowingly.
If knowledge is a sin, what of ignorance?

Cliff Homewood

Charles

Now here is a man so brave and true
Who fought for his country as most men do,
But when he came back from the jaws of hell,
This is the story he had to tell,
How young men died and fought in vain
Please God don't let it happen again.
He worked and slaved for his family,
And prepared them all for their destiny
We thank you Dad for giving us hope,
And showing us the way to cope.
We're proud to have a Dad like you,
And hope you feel the same way too.
We thank you Lord for everything,
Especially for our Dad.
Florence Tooth

A Passion Liberated

A warmth of touch, melting snows of apprehension
whispering tenderness, communicating content admiration.
Caressing smooth tones, exciting, rousing emotions
yearning, hungry, subtly grazing a harvest of beauty.
Charging of atoms, releasing torrents of feeling, desire,
a liberation of energy concealed within.
Winds of passion subside, calming oceans of joy
quietly sweeping the shores of exultation.
A gentle breath stirs, submerged in tranquillity
silent words, thundering volumes of love.
Longing for tenderness, time an enemy, marching on
with minds as one we are together yet alone.
George W. Knox

The Old Churchyard

I walk upon the hallowed ground
  while people stare askance
  with no conception of the truth
  that contact made by me with those
  who lie beneath the grass
  is dedicated reverence and love;
  as I may wish some day
  that feet will walk across my grave,
  not deviate with chilly awe,
  respectful of my sad decay.

Though cold within the small stone church,
  I sit down in a pew and think
  of those who in bygone days
  beguiled away with roving eyes
  The hours of tedious sermons preached
  on heaven and hell. And now they know
  what's to be known - which may be
  naught, who can tell. But to their
  ghosts, if there be ghosts, I give this
  hour and wish them well.
Gertrude Arbuthnot Somerville

Just Care

People pass by, with a look in their eye,
Which says "God, what a pitiful sight".
It is I, with their eye, that they pity, despise,
Do you wonder what is my plight?

I am hungry and cold, mentally old,
My home is a bench in the park.
I wander the streets with aching sore feet
From dawn until it gets dark.

I am battered by rain, the cold causes pain,
I am dirty and shabbily dressed.
If only they knew, those people so few,
How I'd just like to be like the rest.

But see with those eyes, not pity, despise,
But someone who once was like you.
And care, do not stare, reach out, unaware
Of the hope that you give to a few.
Graine Lloyd

I Thank You Lord

Thank you Lord for giving me strength
which helps me carry the burden of
everyday living.

Thank you Lord for giving me understanding
that I may understand life on Earth has also
pains, frustrations and loneliness.

Thank you Lord for being so compassionate
help me stop and think when there's
anger in my heart.

Thank you Lord for giving me confidence
which helps me build my life when I'm in trouble.

Thank you Lord for giving me love
which made me realise that I could give love in
return,
in spite of the wickedness in this world.

Thank you Lord for being so kind and gentle
that you only look on the goodness of men
and not on his faults and weaknesses.

Thank you Lord for all the guidance
which helps me find the way to peace, happiness
and be close to your heart.
Haydee Stanton

The Silent Enemy

The disturbing silence of the unknown,
Which erodes the edges of sanity
Like an empty space in the darkness of our minds.
It becomes the enemy for which we have no answer.
Like a ship groping its way on a fog bound course.
The silence is a nightmare of a hidden force.

The walls which surrounds us are no protection from the unseen fear.
Of what? An animal on the prowl,
Creatures weaving their patterns over and over again;
another human being who would wish us well or, a force of evil?
Come the dawn.
The sun shines through the morning mist.
The darkness of the night fades away
They bring sanity and serenity
To start another day.
Dorothy Pimblett

Our Worshipful Master

Command with courtesy is Sid's pedigree
Whether first or second or third degree:
Master of ritual, Worshipful twice,
Yet always available for advice!
To any masons, whether younger or old 'uns,
He sets an example so high it emboldens
And makes you strive to make the connection
Between "The blue book" and true perfection.
How does he do it? It sounds quite banal
Wearing the pathway by the canal;
And he's told us before - it gave me a shock -
All this learning is early, before 8 o'clock!
Without more ado, let's ensure that he's cheered,
A Worshipful Master who's truly revered.
I ask you, Brethren, let your glass not be hid,
Let's toast our Worshipful Master Sid!
John H. Birkett

Tribute to Macmillan Nurses

In the darkest hour of the endless night,
  When no one at all seems to care,
When the pathway of life is shrouded in mist,
  Macmillan Nurses will be there.

When the howling storm has raged to a peak,
  And no more worries can you bear,
When the river of time finally sweeps you away,
  Macmillan Nurses will be there.
David Almond

Solitude

Oh! powerfully winged gull in flight
Wherefore art thou bound?
heading for the sunset bright,
Across the rippling sound.
Tinged golden is thy rounded breast,
A silent symmetry.
Are you flying at God's behest?
Are you alone like me?
Standing in the pale twilight,
I watch you gracefully skim
The shawl of dark that heralds the night,
And gaze at the day's last rim.
Sun's glinting halo lingers
Where skies do reach the deep,
Rosy tenacious fingers
Around the horizon creep.
I stand alone at the edge of night,
Alas I see no more -
The dark has robbed me of my sight,
but memories will endure.

Eileen Hughes

Armageddon

What of Armageddon? It's the last great battle men say
where the forces of good and evil must meet on the last great day
then the winds and the sea will be raging with foaming gaping jaws
and we all will be running and hiding locking and barring our doors,
with thunder and lightning cracking across rolling angry skies
women and children screaming no one hearing there cries,
grown strong men struck helpless with fear,
watching the angels of good and evil draw near,
angels waiting for combat holding their heads on high
calmly awaiting instructions from their spirit leaders near by,
all this within focus on the human eye,
scoff and laugh if you must the choice is yours
not one will be safe outside or indoors,
only the ones who've live in good ways, have the smallest chance
 In those last few days
  so think of LOT, and remember NOAH,
   they took the same chance long years before.

Jean A. Smith

Memories

I would like to go back to the place I was born,
Where the coaltips looked down like the mountains of morn.
Three rows of houses one hundred each side,
Three hundred toilets - not very wide.
Lots of pale children, thin short and tall.
Next door's cat was used as a ball.
No washing machines, tellys, spin driers or cars,
Our only game was counting the stars.
We were told Father Christmas had lost his way
That his reindeers were hungry and had run out of hay.
Where Easter eggs were round stones painted white.
Fish and chips were a wonderful sight!
But we had lots of friends, love and much more than that
We all had each other and next door's bloomin' cat!

Dorothy Taffetsauffer

Lost Priorities

Left alone staring at the mystic of the tide
with all its anger, its strength and pride.
The party has gone but somehow not,
as if the whole world has lost its plot.

People are dazed, confused and lost
in the importance of possessions, power and cost.
Time has the power and money the aim
People now play a different game.

Trees are still standing and the oceans are free
but all is destroyed so rapidly.
Life has the power not money or oil
Richness is gained from air and soil.

Abi Waller

Death At Peckfield (1984)

"Desolation is the word that describes the scene,
Where once proud buildings stood,
Hives of hard work;
Underground, bodies blackened with coal dust,
Sweat glistening on smiling faces
Of a tough breed of men,
Hewing the coal from the unyielding earth;
The work hard and demanding.
On mind and body alike.
And now?
The wheels that once took miners down into the depths
Are still - ghostly
There's not much left on the surface.
The old engine house and a shed,
The pit-head baths have gone,
The slag heaps grassed and over-grown,
And in the village
Houses for sale,
Miners' houses!"

Geoff H. Phillips

'Longings'

Give me the strength to look towards the skies,
Where love and beauty there may fill my eyes,
And wipe away the sorrow and the tears,
That seem to linger on throughout my years.
My hopes, my dreams as yet are unaspired
And sometimes when I'm jaded, lost and tired -
I wonder if my God has heard my prayer
And knows the longings deep within I bear;
but then I feel the love and strength within
The whispered voice that says, 'Please don't give in'.
I lean upon that rock of faith that through the years has grown
And take the comfort of God's hand and know I'm not alone.
And then for all such souls as mine together then we pray
That we may find the answers to the prayers we say each day.
Maybe the hopes and dreams we have are not for us to gain,
But just a lesson in this life to understand the pain;
But God in all His mercy will not let us hope in vain,
He will help us journey onwards towards our inner aims.
And one day when the time is right our cross He'll take away,
And in our outstretched arms He'll place the longings of today.

Christine Locke-Hart

For We Have Warred Too Long

Come, take my hand, for we have warred too long.
Where is the need? desire? once mutual - gone.
The lustful path we strode now dark and strewn with weeds
and yes-to-days or no-todays implanted bitter seeds.
Could we be brave and honest? just we two,
sweep aside what's past and start anew?
Could we two walk and talk? (without wild claims of who said what,
or who did this because) Could that be so? Why not?
Come, take my hand, for we have warred too long.
A silent war, no words were spoken - none.
In mute contempt we plagued each others lives,
disturbing each the other's peace of mind.
Should we be brave and honest? - just we two.
To wipe us both form mind, No, me! No you?!
If I had choice to voice I'd say, "I cared and feel no shame
and so it will remain". What thought are yours? - the same?
Come, take my hand,
for we have warred, and we have warred, too long.

George Doyle

Bluebell Wood

In Bluebell Wood I was a child
With heart so light and spirit free
In Bluebell Wood I laughed and smiled
The world was a magical place for me.

In Bluebell Wood I felt so young
I had no worries to bring me down
In Bluebell Wood I danced and sang
Until the leaves turned from green to brown.

Sharon Griffin

"The Park Is Closing"

O'er the Park, Night softly falls,
With his bell the Keeper calls
To everyone within his sight,
"The Park is closing for the night."

From the Playground every child departs;
It doesn't take a lot to fill their hearts!
Their minds are full of simple things
Like roundabouts, climbing-frames and swings.

From the Lake the boats are all called in,
Though many children think it is a sin!
But not until the last child has gone
Will come again the Moorhen, Duck and Swan.

There's silence now where once was laughter gay;
The Keeper, thoughtful, homeward makes his way,
But with tomorrow's sun a new day will begin
As through the open gates the crowds pour in.
John H. E. Rendall

Dance Of Autumn

Rich is Autumn, and slow to turn.
With leaves lined golden,
Colours that burn.
Although red they're no longer molten.
But brittle and dry.
Rustling as taffeta, swirling by
To where the wind blows them.
Taking the chance.
To stay awhile longer,
Having one last dance.
Before winter arrives,
Interrupting her rhythm.
Stripping her bare.
Taking the colour out of her hair.
Spoiling her beauty, her crowing glory.
Of russet, and gold as burnished copper.
Jacqueline Savage

The Graveyard Shift

Are there stories written amongst gravestones
Where bodies lying silent
Speak
To those who listen carefully.
Murderers and thieves
Poets, heroes, cowards
All lie here
And amidst their silent conversation
A thousand tales
Lie unrevealed.
And if just once the poet,
Storyteller, bard,
Could discern that barely whispered sound
Then should such books be written
as would astonish all the world.
For if the truth be stranger still than lies
Then these massed dead could tell
The strangest tales of all.
Charles Acheson-Crow

My World

How can the sky fall
when it looks so blue?
How can I live without hope of what's new?
The shadows of doubt
like the bars of a cage,
the boundaries within which burn my fear and my rage.

Softly, like raindrops
each misery calls,
wrapping my heart in its terrible walls.
Then something special
from nowhere appears,
dissolving the heartache, diminishing tears.
Emma Edge

Baby's Sunbeam

A sunbeam peeps into the room
Where baby lies asleep.
It flies away and then returns
For just another peep.

It wanders through the golden curls,
And round the chubby face.
Along the dainty coverlet
Trimmed with silken lace.

The baby stirs, and brighter glows
That tiny golden gleam.
"I wish those eyes would open"
Sighs the little sunbeam.

Then two sparkling eyes of blue
Gaze upward in the light,
And see an impish sunbeam
Dancing with delight.

A step is heard, and baby tries
In vain a sound to make.
Then Mummy's voice, so clear and bright.
"Ah! baby is awake!"
Ellen May France

Forty Foot

I was born in a village called Forty Foot, a mile along the drove,
Where a little old thatched cottage stood, about one hundred years old.
The old brown paint was cracked and dry, but as cosy as can be,
When the family got together, around the range for tea.
We had candles and an oil lamp, and no carpets on the floor,
All we had was linoleum, and a mat right near the door.
There wasn't any bathroom, to lay and soak for hours,
But an old tin bath to wash in, no such luxury as showers.
Carbolic soap to wash with, was the perfume of the day,
No sprays or anti-perspirants, or things for tooth decay.
Cod liver oil and brown medicine, was the cure of all ills,
No matter what was wrong with you, including spots and chills.
The toilet was down the garden path, in the dark was hard to find,
There wasn't any mod cons, just the wooden kind.
With a seat and a bucket and a latch upon the door,
Sometimes had to be emptied, twice a week or more.
I know it sounds archaic to you, but after all you see,
I'm glad it happened in those days, to a little girl like me.
Dorothy Smith

Friend

A friend is somebody towards whom one wishes to express goodwill.
When you are with him that's how good you feel.

An encounter with a friend can happen at any time
And when you meet him,
The impression you have is fine.
Just for you he was waiting.

You speak, cry, laugh, sing, ask, keep silent
The friend is there with you.
Hearing, crying, laughing,
Singing, answering, keeping silent too.

When the friend hears your good and bad news
You feel all the bad things fall down.
And there's no such thing
You feel lie you're wearing a crown.

When the friend talks, the words seem made of light
It seems you are listening to the voice of your heart.
When you suffer he suffers with you,
Without saying a single a word,
He makes you understand the world.
Ana Maria De Souza Carter

Discover Peace

Walk with me for peace is but a step away
When you are troubled take my hand
Let me guide you through the darkest day
To where the waves gently wash the sand

Walk with me to where the sunbeams dance
Upon the sparkling sea that laps the shore
Leave your fears behind and take a chance
On finding joy and happiness once more

Stand beside me when the night time falls
Face the darkness with no need to hide
Break away from all the towering walls
That you have kept your troubles locked inside

Follow me and let me lead you where
Blue skies resound with joyous birds in song
A thousand flower perfumes fill the air
And lift your heart on summer days so long

Let us be together through the years
Give me time before you turn and run
To take you far away from all your fears
And drive away the rain to greet the sun

Gwen Bagley

Daughter

I watched you grow I cared for you,
I often wondered if you knew.
How I worried as you grew,
and if what I chose was right for you;

There are no books with sets of rules,
there are no helpful workman's tools
I can only be a guiding light
as a torch will guide you in the night.

But through the times of bad behaviour
a mother's love will never waiver
and when you feel down on your luck,
I'll be there to pick you up.

The path of life is never straight,
and often full of things we hate
but these trials will make you strong
and teach you all the rights from wrongs.

One day you will be wife and mother too,
and remember what I said to you,
your watchful eye will guide them through,
and you will feel the love and pride as I have for you

J. C. S. Waite

The Puddles Of Life

Looking back through the times gone by.
When we lingered to say goodbye.
The sun-kissed sand, we wrote our names.
We laughed out loud, played silly games.
The rainy days we splashed in puddles.
Cold nights inside, kisses and cuddles.
Sweet Christmas cards, your, "I love you."
Valentine's heart, with just, "Guess who?"
Our wedding day, promises to keep.
The honeymoon night, we fell asleep.
Your happy tears for a baby boy.
Then a little girl to bring more joy.
The pride inside to see them grow.
Their teenage years, then time to go.
Life's autumn days, that soon flew by,
Now you have gone I must not cry,
For looking back through times we had,
I'll remember you and I'll feel glad.
Someday I know we'll meet again,
And splash in puddles in the rain.

Jim Dolbear

We Never Said Goodbye

She shall not wither like a rose in Autumn
when the clutch of death comes like a sting
or dip her wings to touch the night
when the wind no longer sing.
She shall not fade or bruise her colour
when the swallow flies to seek the Sun
or stand like poignant shadows in the shade
as evening come.
She will not leave behind a tear
that the rain shall wash away
or stare like empty branches in the silence of the day.
When I pause to breathe of life
in a moment that goes by
as the swallows ventures home
in the twilight of the sky;
We never said goodbye.

Errol Heibner

Our Future Gone

Bare trees, bare trees,
Where are all your leaves?
Gone Sir, gone Sir for we are all diseased.

No more buds or green leaves Sir,
To dance in the teasing wind.
Seasons are just a dream Sir,
Our beauty now gone.

The acid rain that came Sir,
Has killed us one by one.
Now we stand here dead Sir,
Never to reach the sun.

Bare trees, bare trees,
Where are all your leaves.
Gone Sir, gone Sir,
For we are all diseased.

Josephine Ann Waring

The Seasons Poem

Spring brings the sun,
When the children have fun,
Paddling in the pool,
Where it is nice and cool.

Summer brings the birth of baby calves,
Mums and dads cut dinner in halves,
Baby lambs are so sweet,
You would kiss them if you meet.

Autumn brings colourful leaves on trees,
And we say "goodbye" to bees.
Say goodbye to the pool,
Where it used to be nice and cool.

Winter brings snow,
Water flows down rivers, fast and slow,
Winter brings scarves, gloves and hats,
Snowy boots on the mats.

Julie Gray

A Dying Love

What became of that imperishable love we shared?
When our eyes would speak for hours and we'd
smile and laugh without reason. When my heart burnt
for you like the sun embraces the scorching plain.
Indomitable, that feeling that so flooded my
days and kept me company in the cavernous recesses
of dreamland.
But that was then and this is now, and you're a
stranger to me. And as much as it hurts I
Find myself slowly turning from that radiance
that for so long melted me at first sight. Your
softness has gone my love, and like the winter
comes to slaughter the last colours of autumn,
you stare with a vacant indifference.

Dean Parkin

It's A Dog's Life

Off to the woods to have some fun
When they let me off I run and run.
Is there a squirrel or fox to follow
Or a muddy puddle in which to wallow.

They can't keep up, I'm running faster,
Hold on a minute is that my master,
He's telling me it's time to go
I wish he wouldn't walk so slow.

I hope I haven't got too dirty
If I have he tends to get so shirty.
Oh! Please don't put me in the shower
O.K. - I'm going you've got the power.

Now here I am all clean and bright
Mind you I gave him quite a fright,
I shook myself - when I was soapy,
I'll teach him to think I'm dopey.

I've opened the door, I think I'm out,
Oh! listen to the family shout
Where's my dinner, I need to eat,
Now I'm off to bed to rest my feet.

Doreen Cave

The Four Seasons

I love the spring
When the little birds sing
The buds begin to peep
And the willow starts to weep
I love the spring

I love the summer
When the days get warmer
The long lazy days
The early morning haze
I love the summer

I love the autumn
When tumbling down the leaves come
The children don their wellies and mittens
And with rosy cheeks prance around like kittens
I love the autumn

I love the winter
When the logs start to splinter
On a fire that's glowing
While outdoors the wind's blowing
I love the winter

Jennifer Morbey Myatt

Invisible

Cloudy days and nights, restless sleep, lonely nights
Will I ever see will there ever be
A night of warmth, a day of happiness
My days are long the hours too slow

I spend my days gazing out the window
a living world. People smiling, traffic passing by
I feel invisible, nobody can see me does any one know I'm alive
I'm trapped between these four walls
Just bad memories. Suffering and pain.
Surrounded by pictures of people I've loved and lost
I often wish I was somewhere, someone else
Or that I was a bird, I could spread my wings and fly

But still I'm lying here in the darkness
I can hear nothing only my thoughts
Waiting for the next light
Looking out the window
but I won't give up without a fight

Joannah Townsend

Mystical

Down between the rolling hills,
Where magic forests grow.
Snow-kissed purple mountains rise,
Where nature's wine does flow,
Into the caves where mermaids live,
Whose teardrops fall as gifts,
Where dragons breathing smoke and flames,
Turn the tears to mist,
Up it swirls along the ground,
And lightly through the trees,
Then gently drops an Angel's kiss,
That moistens all the leaves,
Then wafting gently on its way,
It finds a spider's web,
And makes a jewelled necklace,
On a single silken thread,
Then out across a waving sea,
It slowly leaves the land,
Placing crazy patterns,
On the pebbles in the sand.

Brian John Nye

My Heart And I

I thank the Lord I'll always know what lies beyond the final glow,
when setting sun and dusky skies give way to countless
    twinkling eyes.
For this is when the night discovers the mystic rights of covert
lovers, and blesses them with conscious sleep, thus, they alone
    their secrets keep.

Safe in the arms of one you love, no other power can rise above
the elemental need for touch, and words that mean so very much.
Alas, too soon the dawn will break, and with it, dreamers must awake
and hasten back to separate lives, possessed of husbands,
    work or wives.

I pray my dreams will one day be precursors of reality,
with little need to hide away for fear of what the world may say.
When open hearts may then reveal the love no other dream
    can steal.

James E. Ingram

The Morning After The Night Before

For Sarah Parker - always a free spirit

Last night I went to bed
Wi' thoughts o' man o' moors a swimming in me head,
His eyes combing the wet, tufty turf,
His heart, drinking in nature wi' a greedy thirst.

Slumped over City desk I see him still,
Heroic shoulders framed against the shrouding clouds,
His gaze, liquid, like the turbulent river,
Races wi' every gusting wind that tugs and blows.

Static, mortgage - cuffed, within my City prison,
My spirit soars wi' shared knowledge and empathy wi' yourn,
And though a life away here in EC3,
I know I am free, because we are as one,
thee and me.

Helen Drummond

Untitled

She at table, lunching there,
With companions, dark and fair,
Why oh why must I but stare,
At her, midst all others.

Work over, she hurries to the train,
I ease forward, then back again,
She'll not turn round, me to see,
She walks as one possessed,
Yet not possessed of me.

In olden days, portraits were painted,
Head, shoulders, dividing line of burst.
Such a perfect posing model,
She would make an artist's brush.

Doreen Davis

In Search Of Sanctuary

What crafted artistry shall we find,
when oft' we seek the perfect place.
Far along life wandering mind,
A wondrous World of charm and grace?

A journey through a century,
could not divulge the secret home,
Of which we search for sanctuary,
Until we decide no more to roam.

The fire of life, cheers and enhances,
A cloud of dreams spills from its flame.
Like lovers cacooned in warm embraces,
So our sorrows are harnessed in the frame.

The concept of a broader canvas,
Excites our mind, drawing us inside.
To follow where we know we trespass,
Until we prove our right to abide.

Christine Trayford

Loneliness

Loneliness is when your heart feels down,
when no-one seems to come around.
Friends are few and smiles are rare
the calendar always seems so bare

You check the phone just one more time
you never know with faulty lines
Convince yourself that someone soon
will come and fill your empty room.

The weekends are long and very slow
there's so many places I could go
But on my own it wouldn't feel right
so here's to another lonely night.

If someone took the time to care
my whole world, with them I'd share
But for now I'll stay alone
waiting by the telephone

If you could see inside my mind
you'd find a person oh so kind
One day I'll find someone that's true
maybe I won't, maybe it's you

Cheryl Audrey Sellers

Gillingham, Dorset, 1996

I grew up in Gillingham Town
When meadows lush and green,
To the river's banks came rolling down,
Where the Stour meets the Shreen.

A public library now's been raised,
A superstore and all
And petrol pumps where cattle grazed,
Advanced the urban sprawl.

Bay, Wyke, Peacemarsh, Commonmead,
Roll's Bridge and Wavering Lane;
'Developed' with indecent speed
Won't be the same again.

The softened vowels of Dorset's speech
Once everywhere you'd hear;
Not now, it's raucous cockney screech
That grates upon the ear.

Oh! Town where Alfred quelled the Danes
And King John hunted too;
Of character not much remains,
What have they done to you?

Derek Gatehouse

Am I My Brother's Keeper?

Am I my brother's keeper? Questioned Cain that fateful day
When in jealousy and temper he did his brother slay,
And that great and age old question, uttered first in Eden's land
With the passing of the ages is still heard on every hand

Am I my brother's keeper? Is his life my concern?
Should I care about his problems or my heart with pity burn?!
In estimates and calculations, say what is the price
Of the tears of starving children, as they plead for grains of rice?

The affluent and greedy ignore the weakling's cry
They revel in their plenty, while the hungry waste and die
Agitators and dictators rise with dreams of domination
And always leave within their train a scene of devastation

With bullets, bombs, and missiles, they wield their mighty power
While the victims of aggression in dust and ashes cower.
As we view the devastation, can we calmly stand aloof
To the desperate need of others or with conviction face the truth?

Yes! I am my brother's keeper, for in love we should be one
By the mercy of the Father and the travail of His Son
Yes! I am my brother's keeper and must to him outreach
The hand of aid and justice, one for all and all for each

Arthur Aston

Adulthood

I watch the stars and ocean, the clouds and the moon,
When I was young I never took into account
That it could end so soon.
So look up to the heavens and hold that final thought,
If I could paint a picture, it would come to nought.

If I could write a love song, I surely would've by now.
As I grow I become an effigy of that faceless man in the crowd.
So these are the days when we start to wonder,
Holding onto all we ever knew,
For what we learn now, will mean nothing
In this asylum called adulthood.

I used to play at soldiers, the battles I always won.
It was so simple then, in boyhood,
Where have all the heroes gone?
Oh yes, these are the days when we bloody wonder
Still holding onto all we ever knew.
For what we learn now, will mean nothing
In this asylum called adulthood.

Colin John Leamon

Memories

This is a poem of days gone by
When I was a child and pit heaps reached the sky
There they stood like mountains high,
With miners' homes in long rows near by
I remember our village as it was then
The miners' pride and joy, and every one was busy,
And everyone was busy as each new day passed by
There were butchers and bakers, fishmongers too
Coal wagons, wheel barrows with everything for you
Also I remember when a siren used to blow
Then home came all the miners from that dirty pit below
Caps tilted on the sides of their heads
And faces very black, with eyes that seemed to twinkle
And white teeth that would flash
They would be very tired in those great heavy boots.
With knee pads fastened 'round their legs
When up those streets they trudged.
Yes there's lots I can remember,
And always I'll be proud, that I had the privilege
To live at that time, when our village was miners' ground.

Ellen Walt

Tribunal Day

When you look at me what will you perceive
When I say my back is bad will you believe
All the pain that I go through
Or will it mean absolutely nothing to you
Like sometimes when I cannot do my hair
This is almost too much to bear
I know this is pure vanity
But it means such a lot to me
Will you say that I can work
Pull yourself together and do not shirk
Or will you listen, who can tell
Look at me, believe and know full well
That I am different from the crowd
And my appeal should be allowed
Very soon I will know
Wish the time wouldn't go so slow.

Beryl Simmons

When

When songbirds sing at early dawn
When gardeners start to cut the lawn
When new blooms blossom there's great scent
When helping hands are lent

When shadows fall o'er hill and dale
When crying stops from killer whale
When full moon rises in the east
When family gathers for evening feast

When night time falls we rest our head
When we lie down in comfy bed
When good books are often read
When peace at last love words are said.

Eileen Lawton Edwards

Alone!

Who am I? I do not know
what should I do? Where should I go?
I'm flying high, high in the sky
I wonder if I'm going to die
Am I dreaming or is this true?
Will somebody wake me and ask "Who are you?"
Help me! Help me! Help me please!
I'm begging on my hands and knees.
I'm alone with my candle in my hand
Flying over this beautiful land.
My white, wax candle is so bright
It's shedding lots and lots of light
My white, wax candle stands so tall
But when it melts it shrinks so small
The smoky smell that comes from
You and lots of other candles too
but everything has to die
So I want to say my last
  GOODBYE!

Hayley Trow

Faith

When the rain pours down and drowns the earth
When the snow hides the flowers and curtails their birth
When the ice stills the flow of the waters of life
You must have faith

When the people lose interest and appear unkind
When casual actions unnerve the mind
When life seems empty and your spirit wanes
You must have faith

When the day seems long and the night so dark
When sleep will not come or the ache leave your heart
When your body is cold and fear fills your soul
You must have faith

If you have faith your loneliness is shared
Your step will be lighter, you found someone who cared
The world opens wide and sets you free
Because you had faith

Josephine Dunlop

To A Soldier

Oh soldier why are you so far away
When all I want is for you to stay
To hold my hand and be by my side
To get in our car and go for a ride
Hold you in my arms all night long
Talk to you laugh with you sing you a song
Oh why are you so far away.

Oh soldier why are you so far away
When all I want is for you to stay
To play with our children when you come home
Making sure we are never alone
To cook your dinner and mend your socks
To go out for long country walks
Oh why are you so far away.

Oh soldier why are you so far away
When all I want is for you to stay
To walk by the sea under the sun
To laugh and play and go for a run
To wake in the morning and see you there
Out of the war safe with all of us here.

Dorothy Barnes

Second Love

I walked alone; I didn't care if the world just passed me by.
What was there to live for? Who with, where and why?
I walked alone; I had no love as far as I could see.
He was my world, but he had been taken away from me.

Then, when I thought there was no one who could really care;
I looked across a road - and you were standing there.
I didn't know at the time what thoughts went through your mind
All I saw was someone who was handsome, good and kind.

Feelings warm and tender went through me once again.
I knew inside my heart you could ease my pain.
We spoke awhile; holding hands we slowly walked.
It was fun. Just before you left, we talked.

Was this right? The answer I do not know.
My feelings told me I could not let you go.
Now we know we love each other, memories only will remain.
But with your love beside me I'll never walk alone again.

Jacqueline Hanson

The Greatest Robbery Of All

Your mother's gone, she passed away,
What was that? What did he say?
Not my mother, so sweet and so kind,
He's just gone crazy, he's out of his mind.

My mother wouldn't go, without saying goodbye,
Please say it's not true, please don't make me cry,
He won't take it back, he says it's the truth,
It can't be, I tell him, show me the proof!

He says that he's sorry, there's nothing he can do,
How would you feel if it happened to you?
I thought a mistake, that she would be back,
But now I know the truth, it is now a fact.

My mother has gone, that cannot be changed,
I must have gone crazy, and maybe deranged,
For the rest of my life, she won't be there,
To kiss or caress, or my problems to share.

How could a child of six years cope?
My whole life echoed - there isn't any hope,
But as time passes and eases the pain,
Hope and joy can enter life once again.

Anne Teasdale

"Hope Reborn"

What of destiny my little one,
What of life before us now.
Will fate cruelly snatch away
This hold I have on yesterday
Will the rages of another war
Some day claim your tender years,
And witness once again my bitter tears,
Leaving my life empty as before.
Will you, my darling, seek your sweet revenge
And follow in your father's steps.
Another war, another life.
Neither then a mother or a wife.
Or will you one day hold your infant son,
And spare his mother endless sorrow?
For you alone my child can change tomorrow.
Through in this wicked world what's done is done,
I pray that in my ageing years
I once again can smile, and say
"These tears belong to yesterday,
and maybe now this war at last is won."

Christine Banner

Humanity

With failings all, with virtues strong
With actions - invariably wrong.
Whose eyes to sunlight open wide,
Whose deeds create a nightmare fright,
Like children crying in the night.

Whose venom ire spits out its hate,
Which with compassion swift abates;
With viscous blow strikes down its kind,
With deep regrets within the mind.

Who can with God so deep aspire,
And yet with evil, long conspire,
And place its hand with loving care
On childish head beyond compare,
Then strike it down with fearsome war,
Then reason out - What for, What for?

Which crawls from out primeval past
With gaze on stars, from first to last;
Whose hate, whose hate, will never last.

Humanity!
With failings all, with virtues strong.

Fred Alston

Life's Enigma

Life's at its prime, love's dream is so sweet.
We marry and start a new home in the street

Work is a daily acceptable drill,
Then home to relax with my wife and young Phil.

We budget our earnings, the mortgage is paid,
We enjoy what life offers, so why be afraid?

For twenty odd years as the family grew,
We paid all our dues and we both remained true.

But slowly we noticed the labour force fall,
And we wondered who next would go to the wall.

A gold watch presented for service well done
Was treasured but left us with...'What is to come?'

One day as we stood in our place in the queue,
We were handed our wages...the last we all knew.

But bewildered and stunned we hastened on home
And wondered how best we should make the news known.

The wife...bless her willingness, worked to relieve,
We struggled on bravely so the kids should achieve.

But now in our thirties with debts round our ears
We are facing a crisis worse than our fears.

Frances V. Bailey

Inner Thoughts

When I've had a busy day and go upstairs to bed -
What a wonderful feeling it is for me to rest my weary head;
To push my feet as far as I please
And gradually make myself at ease
So that aches and pains are banished and my book waits to be read.

But sometimes after my first deep sleep I become quite wide awake,
And have to write down all my thoughts before the dawn should break.
Many subjects, many themes,
Many hopes and many dreams
Are written down and noted for future verse to make.

By writing down my hopes and fears I learn what can I do
To solve my problems and perhaps help others solve theirs too.
Troubles shared and plans discussed
With a person you can trust
Oils the wheels of life and pulls us through.

Bessie Martin

No Tomorrows?

Where do you go when there's nothing to live for
What do you do when the world's all at war
When people are killing and people are dying
When children are starving and mothers are crying

Do you know what to do when your brain is awash
With spirits and drugs and you just want more cash
To drown out your memories and kill your tomorrows
And try not to remember all of your sorrows

I know where to go and I know what to say
Because all my tomorrows are really today
The Lord will provide what I need to survive
He will comfort my sorrows and help me to live

So turn to our God with a heart open wide
Don't turn your face or e'en try to hide
For his love conquers all from the small to the tall
If you let him come in he will succour us all

Fiona Higgins

To Nicky, Happy Christmas

At Christmas the situation is tricky
what do you buy for a girl like, Nicky?
She's nice, she's a pet, she is really a honey
But what do you buy that don't cost much money,
I'll buy her a record, or some nice earrings,
But maybe she's already got all those things,
I'll have to sit down and have a good think,
I know - I'll buy her something to drink.
no - that wont do, she's far too young,
I'd buy her some scent, but she might not like the pong.
I've got it, - striped stockings the kind with the toes in,
I'll have to go now or the shops will be closing
So I'll put on me Wellies and have a look round
But on second thoughts
 I'll just send her five pound.

Eva Parker

Still Water Brook

We danced to our goal like horses in foal.
We feared no-one and no-one would come.

The trees glowed with their eerie stare;
We bedded the night it was just for a dare.

The brook water shone and came alive-
With the still air around us we wanted to dive.

We found the eye of the hurricane in that still
pool calm; the magic was there, it was time to embalm.

Hitting that magical glow- when dived below.
The moon was our lighthouse, it shone so bright:
behold our brave world, it was a still water's night.

Justin J. Dyson

Years Of Change

The twentieth century's in its waning years,
What are our hopes? what are our fears?
As we look back on the years that have passed,
Which of memories and achievements will last.

Many wars and conflicts and strife.
Death for many, for others life.
Great benefits in medicine have been discovered,
Some diseases wiped out, many more uncovered.

Man has made space craft to go to the moon,
Will we go there for holidays soon?
Discoveries in science have made our lives better
But we can't make the weather drier or wetter!

What can we look forward to in century twenty-one?
What can we do? What must be done?
Will governments learn to live in peace?
Will all war and conflict cease?

What for our children does the future hold?
They'll grow up as new discoveries unfold.
Will they do their best to make life worthwhile
That mankind may live in a better style?

Jean Goddard

Looking Into The Future

I'm just wondering, in the years far ahead
What exactly will be called "appropriate" for our daily bread
The environment is being so badly polluted
What's going to be safe, our palates to be suited.

We've already been shocked by mad cow disease
And left to wonder if it's safe to eat mince and peas
It's also been said, we're at risk if we eat eggs
That these battery hens would taste better running around on their legs.

Now the seas are polluted with lots of poisonous waste
What's this going to do to the fish and its taste
That's if there are any fish left for you and me
As the EEC countries appear to be clearing the sea

I saw a film in the '30's (that was in my youth)
I thought at the time, too ridiculous for the truth
The idea that we would no longer enjoy a mixed grill
That we would in fact simply just swallow a pill
sadly I look forward with much dismay
It seems a three course meal of three pills is on its way.

Helen M. Johnson

Welcome To 1996

Christmas has gone and January is here,
We've spent our spare cash on Sherry and Beer,
The bills are now due, think 'lectric the first
The meter's like me - has a hell of a thirst.

The Gas bill comes later, of this there's no doubt,
It's NEVER this much - it can't be you shout,
Oh! Yes it is, remember how cold
That spell last November - you just wouldn't be told.

The House Insurance due next, we mustn't forget
The contents as well - it's gone up - you bet!
But it's got to be paid what ever we do
In case we get flooded by burst pipes too.

That reminds me the Water bills next to be paid,
You can bet they'll be pinching any money we've saved
I think that's the lot, as far as I know
Oh! What about food - now that is a blow

Ah! Yes - the T.V. Licence - just cannot be paid
The reminder arrived just today in the Mail,
That's solved all our problems, I'll turn it on now
At least we'll be fed when we land up in JAIL!!!

Hazel Bryan

Do You Ever Have Days...?

All was well, when I awoke.
Well my alarm didn't ring,
Just managed a choke!
I drew back the curtains to see outside,
My dad was giving my pony a ride!
Rubbing my eyes, I climbed downstairs
Mum had set the table on top of the chairs!
"What's wrong?" I shouted, with all my might
"Nothing" said Mum, everything's all right!
The school bus came, but no Mr. Higgs,
Instead it was driven by a family of Pigs!
And just down the road, where Sarah now lives,
I saw her mum in a terrible tiss...
For under her mat, instead of the floor,
She found herself staring, at her own front door!
Are there days that you know
When things just aren't right?
When you turn on the tele, to turn off the light!
If you notice those days, and they're looking so bleak,
Leave your head on the pillow, and sleep for a week!

Jacqui Gillingham

The Balance Of The Scales

The recipe for a good life is the balance of the scales.
Weighing the good and bad things? We find it never fails.
Children often cause concern as well we may recall.
Imagine how empty life would be if we had none at all.

Disappointment lurking at hand, another set-back we say.
Still, better luck tomorrow there's always another day.
Unhappiness for no real reason, tis then when we wait for a sign.
Just a kind word or gesture and there we are up on cloud nine.

Sorrow and trouble surround us, a happy day ne'r to be found.
Comes a light at the end of a tunnel as friends all rally around.
Death of a love one will numb us, but notice how much people care.
Bereavement cards through the letter-box make it easier to bear.

Harsh words that come from a dear one will hurt us now and then.
Just a smile and, 'sorry, I love you' and it's all forgotten again.
Take a calm sea or rough sea, a ship on the ocean sails.
God sees that our life is evenly weighed, the balance of the scales.

Barbara Davies

Grandad And Me

We play at conkers grandad and me
We went and collected them from the chestnut tree
We took them home and baked them hard
This makes them strong and no holds are barred,
We each have three goes to break them from the string
Grandad is having his very last fling
For he's still a boy and sure wants to win
He wants to see the conker fall from the string,
He grits his teeth and hits it so hard
Mine now has a very big scar,
Grandad looks at it says I nearly did it that time
That's what you think the conker's still mine
I'll show you how to do it young man
I'll break your conker with only one hand,
With one last blow mine falls to the floor
That's it grandad I don't want to play any more
I hope you are happy now you've beaten me
For you're forty nine and I'm only three.

Chris Gardner

Jacqui Vision

Life is like a door with a heavenly mansion with many rooms
We try one, close the other only to wonder why we bother.
Life is a building built on love and understanding.
Remembering every stone that's laid,
the building must be concrete
Solid all around
Its contents full of love, peace and joy.
And angels all around, keeping you sound.

Jacqui Frank

Sirens Of The Night

Planes are flying overhead, houses are in dark,
We sit in silence of the night, and then the sirens start.

The dugout in the garden, is the next place we can go,
So we hurry up the garden path, with some blankets and my poe.

In a candlelit shed, we are both under cover,
Mum singing softly, "The White Cliffs of Dover".

The fighter planes pass over, the sirens sound again,
When will this war be over, it's driving me insane.

Mum's tired eyes looked at me, and caringly she said,
"Come on now, back to the house, let's both go to our bed".

We gathered up the blankets, but not my little poe,
We ran down the garden path, and then indoors we go.

I ran to my bedroom, and took off my clothes,
I said my prayers, and then blew my nose.

I gazed out of the window, into the night,
and thought to myself. "Why do men have to fight".

They fight for king and country, they fight for peace not war
If it wasn't for the forces, England would be no more.

So don't forget that special year 1945
V.E Day the 8th of May and England did survive.

Brenda J. Shipman

Sixty

Roy Rogers and I were buddies, riding a back street range.
We shared sherbet dabs a penny,
but then I was only ten.

She was beautiful, my taste buds were alive
in velvet coffee kisses on a South Coast sea wall.
It was plenty for me at twenty.

My new son ate worms and his word was mud.
Blond curly hair and blue eyes.
He was my flesh and blood.
We had reached thirty.

Now forty and at the hour glass' waist.
With three kids and a mortgage,
life was headlong, quick, poste haste.
Ah! Forty.

Here is fifty! There it goes!
Then fifty-one and so on.
Two, three, four etcetera.
Grown kids and I am a grand-dad to five.
It's good to be alive.

Sixty???

Bryan Smith

The Skies

I love the sky - because of what it is,
What is it? What is beyond the blue?
A heaven - a heavenly place
Where the God of love
Waits to embrace - you?
Heaven yes - for I believe is such.

The skies - cloudy sometimes - grey perhaps
Sunny blue or inky black
Until stars begin to peep -
Then the moon walks in her silver sheen
To weep for us on this poor unfriendly world.

On this earth men differ
War or no war they always bicker
They claim land, sea and sky -
Nay no one can ever claim the high.

Love and beauty are
represented in the skies
If one takes time to realize.

June Mimms

Jesus' Love

Babe of Heaven; You came down to Earth;
we rejoice at Your Holy Birth.

No one can take away from us,
the Gift that you have given to us.
With Your tiny Hands You lift us up
to Your Father in Heaven above.

The Wonder and the Beauty
of such a Gift to us...
I hold in awe so very very much.
The Shepherds and the Wise Men
witnessed the Miracle, You brought
to us with Your Father's Love.

Your Mother Mary, Wife of Joseph
took all this in her stride.
The Stable she did accept with Grace.
The Ox and Ass kept watch over Your Tiny Frame.

At the very Moment of Your Birth,
You began the Work of our Redemption.
You kissed everyone, everywhere,
all over the World; for all time.

Anne E. Ball

No Regrets

As surely as the spring sun's warm and the winter weather rages
We must experience all life offers in all its different stages.
First seeing life through an infant's eyes, all innocence and pure
Then comes the intensity of youth with all our passions raw.

Now as a wife and mother we take on a different role
To raise a healthy, happy family is our ultimate goal.
These years pass much too quickly, full of hard work and pleasure
We store up all our memories like jewels that we shall treasure.

Our families are now grown, and gone their separate ways
And we are fast approaching the autumn of our days.
Now we're growing old and getting 'long in the tooth'
And like a thief in the night we've been robbed of our youth.

Now if you look in the mirror and see only signs of the passing years
Which fills you full of sadness and brings you close to tears,
Then your feelings are truly selfish, pointless and very cold
And you should remember those denied the privilege of growing old.

So live each day to the full as if it were your last
Then none of it will you have wasted when your time has passed.
Not for us sorrow and regret when our time comes to depart
But we can reflect upon our lives with pleasure and a thankful heart.

Deborah Bennington

Growing Up

When first we come into this world all innocent and free
We live cocooned in love and care given by our family
Their patience and protection seem to strengthen as we grow
And all their time is taken teaching us all that they know.

We benefit from all they've learned, their years of ups and downs
We get to understand them, smiles and laughter tears and frowns
We take their love for granted, ever present always free
While inside their hearts they're wondering what we'll turn out to be.

We start our education at about the age of five
We're happy and receptive and glad to be alive
But by the age of fourteen often school becomes a bore
We can't wait to start earning - we don't want to learn no more.

If we are very lucky, we might land ourselves a job
At first it's quite a novelty - but novelties wear off
Soon, filled with disillusion after five years maybe ten
We'd gladly give up working to go back to school again.

Our families offer sympathy, but only smile and say
'Wait til you've worked as long as us and have the bills to pay'
And soon we find out for ourselves how wise their words had been
But we weren't really listening when we were just sixteen.

Barbara C. Parker

We All Need Heroes

On foreign soil, with our sights set high,
We faced the dark legions.
Forward boys came the command
And we cried aloud as one, God is on our side.
Charging under grey skies
Forward to the jaws of hell we went,
Facing the cannons of raging fire.

As the night's darkness crumbles away
And the morning mist fades,
His body is broken
But he now lies content
'Good-bye,' his last words, 'remember me to God'
And slips into perpetual darkness.

And in that high hour in which he lived and died
He remembers what the man had said.
The words still linger on,
You will be set among the stars
We all need heroes
Heroes... heroes...
We all need heroes
Clarence A. Smith

"No Tears Were Shed At Kohima"

We were the ones who brought you grief
We died in a battle that was beyond belief
We were the ones who bore the pain
And we were buried in the monsoon rain
"No tears were shed at Kohima"

Our bodies are buried, but we are not there
We are the raindrops in the midnight air
We are the weather so warm and fair
We are the breeze that rustles your hair
"No tears were shed at Kohima"

We are the stars in the midnight skies
The Christmas delight in a small child eyes
We are the pillows where you lay your head
We are the vision at the foot of your bed
"No tears were shed at Kohima"

You could not go to see our Graves
The resting place of the young and brave
It will not be safe they always say
Yet because of the likes of us
They enjoy their freedom today "No tears were shed at Kohima"
John Done

Fires Of Life

We used to light fires in the woods up by me.
We didn't see the beauty in a living, breathing tree.
Life was much simpler then, we didn't have to think,
we'd just do what we wanted eat, play and drink.

Yet life was an imposing teacher and we had to learn,
that we couldn't always be kids and watch everything burn.
We'd have to grow up and become like the rest,
throw fists in anger and be put to the test.

For life seems an act once childhood has faded,
and the roles to me seem tired and jaded.
That's why I can't be bothered about life,
for it cuts down your dreams with a purpose sharpened knife.

If I had a choice I would return to the fire,
and I'd pile on my old life as the flames grew higher.
Then I'd sit there and laugh like a child playing games,
happy watching it all go up in flames.
Helen Slater

The Pacific's Cry

We dream the same dream,
We breath the same air,
We flow down life's same stream,
So why don't we care?

We smell the same scent,
We view the same pleasant sight,
We share the same birth event,
So why do we argue and fight?

We experience the same love,
We want the same out of life,
We believe in 'someone' above,
So why inflict misery and strife.

What is the point, the point of it all,
As killing adds up the body score,
Of babies, of victims, thousands fall,
In the name of any 'bloody war'.
Frank Grant

Regret

Why is it with those most dear.
We always hurt them first.
It is with things we always fear.
That brings out all that's worst.

To think in silence when alone.
Those hasty words and temper spent.
Would it be wise to write or phone.
We only know that we repent.

The moment comes it may pass by,
Our hearts are full but words come slow.
It's useless now to sit and cry.
The first word comes, it is 'Hello'

The torrent then of words flows fast
The heavy heart its burden lays.
Relief, and sadness comes at last.
The ones we love must know our ways.

Perhaps they listen with their heart.
Maybe in time their feelings mend.
We do not want to be apart.
Along life's pathway that we wend.
Beatrice Wootten

Dance Of The Seasons

Not a sound in the night as I quietly write
Watching the seasons dance by my sight
From the birth of spring and the blossoming summer
To the gusty autumn and the wintry slumber

The buds on the trees and the flowers in bloom
The blushing bride and the anxious groom
Soft breeze as the leaves are gently shaken
The songs of the birds say that spring has awakened

The golden glory of a summers day
The warmth of the sun as I quietly lay
Upon emerald green grass or silver white-sand
On a far off shore of a distant land

Then dramatic autumn with its wind and rain
Throws liquid diamonds to my window pane
Lifting up leaves in a bee-like swarming
All multi-coloured and richly warming

Snowflakes falling without a sound
Ephemeral footprints upon the ground
Streets cushioned in glistening white
Winter comes and then bids you good-night
Clare Savage

The Best

The premiership, division one,
Watching football is such fun,
But watching teams like York and Hull,
Can make you bored- they are so dull,
Blackburn Rovers, Tottenham,
Are really fab and not so dumb.

Alan Shearer is the best,
He can't be compared to the rest,
He plays his game at Ewood Park,
In every match he makes his mark.
In every match you can bet,
He'll get a goal into the net.

Blackburn, Arsenal, Spurs, and Stoke,
All are great and not a joke,
Man. United, Bolton too,
Are not so good, they're doggy-do,
Alan Shearer's still the best,
Take him on; forget the rest.

Jessica Western

My Dearest Dream

At six years old my dearest dream,
was to own a telephone I had seen.
In a Shop window laden with toys,
everything for girls and boys.
The Red Shiny Telephone seemed to say,
"I will belong to you someday".

On my way to school I would always stop
and gaze with longing at the shop.
My only fear while on the way,
was that it was sold yesterday.
Yes, there it was still waiting for me,
but it would cost sixpence a lot of money.

I could not believe my eyes one day,
for lying there in a little courtway,
was a small bright sixpence on the ground
the only thing I had ever found.
Now I can have my telephone,
but first must run all the way home.

I must tell Mum how lucky I'd been
and about the telephone I had seen.
She looked at the sixpence in my hand,
and shaking her head said "you must understand,
that fourpence will buy a loaf of bread"
so that is what Mum bought instead.

My dearest dream stayed on the shelf,
for never again could I bring myself
to pass that shop it would cause such pain,
No I never went that way again.
Finding that sixpence it would seem,
was the end of my wonderful wonderful dream.
The lesson I learned was not to waste time
in dreaming of things that can never be mine.

Hilda E. Laurence

Up From The Deep

Nessy the monster slowly creeps
Up from the bottom, up from the deep
Neck arched long in elegant grace
The last of the species of his race
Two black eyes with beady stare
Look balefully round, with eyes that glare
From his mouth a forlorn tone
As if to ask, why am I alone
No friend or mate to share his time
Getting old, near the end of his line
His tired body once big and strong
Now everything seems to be going wrong
He glides along more slowly now
His aching body moving somehow
Taking one last look at the clear blue sky
He returns to the deep, to sleep, to die.

Jean Aldridge

When Will It Happen

What kind of a world is it today?
Was this the way He wanted it to be?
Starvation, pollution, homelessness, selfishness and greed,
Everyone out for their own selfish needs.

Murderers, evil, sadness and unhappiness,
Is this the way things are to be.
Did You make this world for this to happen?

One day it will happen,
People will scream they won't know what has happened,
For people are scared, they don't want to know,
That this old world will certainly 'GO'!

There will be no more pain,
Their lives will never be the same,
But to live on forever you have to believe,
That He will come again at the end.

If you believe, you will live on to see,
This new and beautiful planet,
The way it was meant to be.

Julie Synott

A Passage On Earth

Why do I see an old, old man
walking alone in the hills
slowly retracing the steps of his life
his vision of peace to fulfil

Why do I dream of a dark wooden cross
abandoned and terribly old
Its powerful secrets withheld from below
will never be free to be told

Why do I cry at the futility
at the way that my heart is alone
to take all your worries and cast them away
leaves me broken and cold like a stone

So why do I see?, for no prophet am I
is it part of some strange fantasy
perhaps it's a vision of my future span
just a dream of my own destiny

Why then are we living, then why are we dead
our passage through time little worth
when you consider this vast universe
containing our small Spaceship Earth.

Claire Roberts

The Storm Of Memory

The wind that howled then and now
Wakes me up, leaves me in turmoil
So wicked, so cruel, brings dread to my world
It haunts me like a hollow tree
Through me, over me, shaking me passionately
What can I do
But let the sea of thought calm
Rest my soul
My feelings deep
Oh but it howls, it groans
Captures my very own
Self being
Keeps me prisoner to the whistling whirl
Of leaves and branches
My leaves and branches
My very own anticipations
Regrets
Of what's been and past
The storm of memory.

Amanda Henderson

The Classroom

The classroom stands, still and quiet,
Waiting for the hoards to come.
The bell rings and they enter,
A large, loud, rambling riot.

The teacher calls their names,
In alphabetical order.
They answer then they leave,
Through the portal where they came.

Soon the English group arrive,
They all sit in their places.
A hushed whisper fills the room,
Just like a buzzing beehive.

Other lessons throughout the day,
Leave the classroom in a mess.
The cleaner comes into the room,
And groans with much dismay.

The hoover is struck dumb,
As the cleaner's work is finished.
The classroom stands, still and quiet,
Waiting for the hoards to come.
  Emma Sharp

Sweet-Heart Be Mine

S - is for some-one special to me,
W - is for wishing we will always be.
E - is for like eternity when I have to wait,
E - is excepting you're going to be late.
T - is true love between you and I,
H - is happiness which can never die.
E - is the energy you seem to give,
A - is affection you shower me with.
R - is romance between us two,
T - is for trust I find in you.

B - is the beauty I see in your eyes,
E - is the emotion I can't disguise.

M - is the moment I first fell in love,
I - is the image of you I'm thinking of.
N - is the nearness we feel when apart,
E - is for the entrance to the door of your heart.

 "Our love should last forever,
  no matter what's at stake,
  what we are sharing together,
  let no-man try to break".
   John Carman

Sam

There was a man named Samuel Knox
Very well known for his smelly socks
Now he's gone but not forgotten
His heart was good but his feet were rotten

Sam had a dog whose name was Rover
Then one day he just keeled over
Gone to where all dead dogs meet
All because of Sam's smelly feet

Feet it seems are a source of strife
For Sam once had a lovely wife
She outlived Sam, which is quite a mystery
When you consider Sam's feet's history

Children now you all take care
Brush your teeth and comb your hair
Wash your back and your belly
Or like Sam you'll end up smelly

This is the end of my little ditty
I'm sure you'll think - oh what a pity
But when it comes to social misfits
You should read my tale of Sam's wife's armpits.
  Fred Manning

The Love in Life

Love is a poem alive in our ears,
Verses and rhymes throughout the years.
Friendship and love, sorrow and tears,
These are what everyone hears.

A bird on the wing
A horse on the hoof
A lady so coy,
Slightly aloof.

My friends, my verse of life and love
  is written for you
with feeling and sorrow
  for maybe there will be
    No tomorrow
Life is short, of that I'm sure,
If I knew God
  I'd make it more.
   David Drewett

Happy Days

Happiness is something that's with me every day
Upsetting thoughts that come to mind are simply sent away
By remembering the happy things that have been in my life
Like forty five years of marriage to really a wonderful wife
My children growing up so fast and the things they used to do
Their children staying with us and the days out at the Zoo
Now we're getting on a bit, in fact we're O.A.P.s
Needing specs and manmade teeth, and weak and aching knees
But all that is forgotten when a grandchildren comes to say
"Granddad can you mend this? It got broken yesterday"
So out comes glue or toolbox and thoughts of yesteryear
When the cry was "Daddy mend it, I'll leave it over here"
What happy times that we can share when children are so small
Full of energy and love and have no cares at all
We now have a great grandchild who's just a few weeks old
I'm looking forward to the time when I can have a hold
Then later on when she can walk and come and sit with me
There'll be another happy moment as she dandles on my knee
And after that, if I'm still here, I hope she'll come and say
"Great grandad can you fix this? It got broken yesterday"
  Henry Scarisbrick

Come Home Today

Each and every day arrives,
Upsetting many peoples lives.
Many just cry all the day,
Hoping that the police will say.
Your child has been found,
Safe and sound.
But they dread them to say,
We found your child dead today.

Your life is meant to be full of gladness,
And not all full of sadness,
Your family is still alone,
So please just pick up the phone.
All you have to say,
Is you will be home some-day.
What I am trying to say,
Is please come home, now, today.
  Christina Borley

Think...

Children in Africa with hungry eyes,
Trying to drive away the flies.
Left deserted all alone,
With no food, water or a home.
Homeless people on the streets,
Rummaging in bins for things to eat.
People with no clothes to wear,
Helpless eyes watch and stare.
While we're in our homes comfy and snug,
Think of the people with no one to love.
  Anna Louise Firth

A Christmas Mystery

I saw a lonely figure once
upon a Christmas night,
It took me by surprise in fact
it gave me quite a fright.

I did not speak I did not dare
my heart did miss a beat
all I could do was stand and stare
who could this stranger be?

A moonlit sky with wispy clouds
a few stars here and there
the pavements laced with frozen snow
a stillness filled the air.

My grandma told me long ago, of strange things she had seen
What purpose did this figure serve
where had this stranger been?

Then all at once the church clock struck,
It was the midnight hour I blinked my eyes and shook myself
no more the need to cower.
Was this the spirit of Christmas, who had come to let us know
Good will to All, Peace on Earth was it FRIEND or FOE?.

Elizabeth M. Ransom

Sonnet To Symbiosis

This afternoon a chaffinch on the hedge,
Untroubled, this, then that way cocked his head.
It seemed, as I had, he had sensed the pledge
That Spring, with lightest step, will shortly tread
The year, trailing her fingers greenly through
Bush and tree and dark, expectant earth,
Renewing life. And so it was that you
Touched my life's winter, bringing it rebirth.
I know you, as I know that you know me.
No one demands, each gives what each can give.
Two lives in balance, tuned in harmony,
Each held in trust - the only way to live.
So, through the winter starkness of the thorn,
I saw the marvel of my world reborn.

Brian Travis

An Ode To The Undead

Death is darkness, tranquil, peaceful.
Until you are brought back. A Vampire, a lich eternal damnation.
I see the burning hatred and envy for living things in your eyes
and I sympathize.
You know you could kill with a single move,
savouring the cool red waters. Making the living taste your pain.
How I would like to be you, never dying already dead.

Andrew Faulds

"Me"

Just turn around, and you're not there.
Turn around and say we care.
Some say it with flowers, "that is nice."
The sweet smell is refreshing to entice.
To clear the air.
Oh what do we do, where do we go.
Shall we, or shall we not
"Oh what a dilemma"
The fields are green, the trees are too,
Just sit there, and feel a new
Sweet smell,
To clear the air.
Are we seeing from time to time, the awkward
child, or is it me.
Misled, misguided, or is it to be,
What to do, who to see.
Just wait till morning, the sun may shine,
To clear the air
Take a breath, feel anew
Out with the old, on with the new, 'oh' a posy would be nice.

Elaine Marshall

The Mission

I will stride the path in death's shoes.
Until the mission I conclude,
Till the mission I conclude.

No sorrows or regret.
Death is my mission,
My mission is met.

The enemy is before me, around me
And yet no fear will I have.

My mission is met, death is my mission,
My mission is met.

The night will bring so much death,
So many horrors born,
On a river of blood called duty,
By men who compassion, as I scorn.

The life I have, wasn't mine to choose,
But death will always be the shoes that I walk in;
I will stride the path in death's shoes.

Until the mission I conclude,
Till the mission I conclude,
Death is my mission, my mission is met.

Alistair James Kelly

The Search

We search, yet know not what we seek.
Unfathomable depths and distant hills
Guard jealously the secrets of the past.
We listen for the sounds our ears deny us
Unwritten music stirs our loins with deep desire
And words unspoken challenge all we know.
We study what we cannot comprehend
And know that all experience comes to naught
Unless our wrongs and fears are swept away.
Our lives and loves, infinitesimal in time and space
And yet significant like sand upon the shore
Have meaning and importance none can know,
As contribution to the greater whole.
Our little scraps of life pass on
In time of no beginning and no end,
Transmuted into dust of past and future hope,
Each speck essential in the master plan
Of universal space, of worlds unknown, of different spheres,
Unending in incomprehensible shades,
Yet still a vital link with life, and joy, and hope.

Doreen M. Hill

Dakota Hills

Pretty little girls with long golden locks,
unassumingly, collecting buckets of bullocks.
Set in North Dakota's rugged hills, begins the battle,
the skilled cowboys round up some 300 cattle.

The women folk arrive with van loads of brunch,
eat and drink now, you won't stop for lunch.
The branding will carry on until the last calf's injected,
Had its ear tabbed, branded and castrated.

Deafening bellows made by their mothers,
heavy with their creamy udders.
Breathless from their chase over the hills, into pens, now await,
for their offspring, like mothers outside a school gate.

Lassoed by their spindled legs, then dragged though dust.
Met by four strong men, held down firmly, appears a must.
The red hot irons brand your rump, they say it only stings.
A sharp knife cuts your private parts, then pulled out like strings.

The smell of burning hair and flesh-nauseates, its mouth foams,
tongue stretched out with choking moans.
De-horned with red hot pokers, whites of eyes full of fear and pain,
Soon the nasty men will let you go, to roam the Dakota Hills again.

Deborah Lockwood

Words

Linger on the tips of tongues and disappear off tops of heads;
Turn up when you least expect them, sometimes even in our beds.
Hot and cold and warm and tender, spoken nicely on the News.
Nagging, bragging, forged for wagging - playing hide and
 seek in clues.

Argued, shouted, wise and foolish - whispered in friendly ear;
Fired in anger, tied in knots - twisted, laughed, and shed with tear.
Padded out for boring speeches - spoken for the sake of Pete!
Bitter, sweet, scrawled and neat - daubed on walls along the street.

Chalked and talked and educated - used by Sir and Miss for teaching;
Guessed and blessed, full of jest - close to heart and so far-reaching.
Long and short, loose and taut - describing all those complex things;
Fill blank pages, cards and rages - and the bag the Postman brings.

Read from cups with patterned tea leaves, crystal balls and
 in the stars,
toffee-nosed and hoity-toity - slurred and blurred and sworn in bars.
Searching, bending, truth and mending - broken hearts and
 soothing nerves;
witty, gritty, sitting pretty - drooling over female curves.

In the Bible, slander, libel - cheered and chanted, sung at Match;
Taken out of mouth and context - down to earth and up to scratch.
Cooling ardour, quenching thirsts - fill with knowledge empty holes;
Answer all the burning questions - light the fires in poets' souls.

Harry West

Moulding

Rise above your tears and smile,
Try to run that extra mile,
Got to be first in the queue,
Strive to find the slimmer you.

Why is society hell-bent,
On making us so discontent?

What to eat, what to wear,
Be 'cholesterol aware',
Fight back, bite back, win the game,
Put your neighbour's lawn to shame.

Stop your pale skin from browning,
Help us, save us, sinking, drowning,
Swirling, spinning, twist your arm,
Pull the plug. Breathe. Sigh. Relief. Calm.
Independence. Stop the chain reaction.
Finally find some satisfaction.

Think. Feel. Consider. Care.
Look around, enjoy the air.
Don't dwell upon trouble and strife,
Stretch out your arms, embrace your life.

Julie Maynard

A Valentine's Dream

I guess the beginning is a good place to start
to tell you what I feel, what's in my heart
The thing is I think you're just the most
And in my estimation none comes close
You must be at least a 10 out of 10
I haven't seen the like, since I don't know when
You're pretty clever, happy and kind
Boy was I lucky to meet you
What a find
Sometimes I think it's a shame you're so far away
But I'm counting the time till you're here with me
day by day.
I often pray to the Lord, to bring what he wants to
happen and to pass
That's about all what I wanted to say
To tell you one thing on this Valentine's day
I hope you don't think this poem is too corny
But I really do love you
Heaps and heaps baby

Dawn Benson

Microscope

I looked through the microscope
Trouble was large green and menacing
Scorching breath and swishing tail
Full of sound and fury.

I took a walk
The path a forest of dark trees
High branches that hid the sky
And I heard the sigh
of wind in winter.

The shapes ahead twisting
to grotesque images.
But the way led to a leafy glade
And beyond the shade sun filtered in.
Spring follows winter
As surely as there are two views to life.
With the naked eye trouble is a caterpillar
Slow moving of little significance.

Freda Grieve

No Escape

Trapped in a bubble spinning around
Trapped in a body trapped on the ground
Trapped in an era heading for doom
Trapped like a con in an eight by eight room

Trapped in a time in a town in a class
Trapped on the dole in a queue with the mass
Trapped in a marriage poverty stricken
Trapped in a stew which the multitudes thicken

Trapped like a fox as the dogs start to rip
Trapped like a rat in a sinking ship
Trapped with an illness destiny knocks
Trapped very soon in a funeral box.

Art B. Brady

Cobwebs Of Time

Misty mornings, cobwebs clinging,
Trace a pattern in the sky
Drops of water softly falling
Drop to earth and there to lie
Shadows moving - scurrying, hurrying,
Owls hooting - prepare to die
Winds are blowing, leaves are stirring
Noises made and something sighs
Daylights breaking, all earth's awakening
Is this the time, the end is nigh.

Janet A. Mitchell

A Pleasant View From A Window In School

There in the distance beyond, the reservoir,
Towers the grey steeple of a church
Emerging from the green canopy of trees.
Shimmering amongst the branches, yellow lights
the misty-munkey haze of evening. It's a wintry day.

There is a inner feeling of fear,
Far below the dimly lit street, life goes on.
The water within seems so cold but clear,
It flourishes the mind with cool thoughts,
yet it's so remote to the unsuspecting.
The different speeches of birds which flock there
it seems an oasis to them.
Green grass embanks the reservoir, the stillness of the
water calms, the hurried mind so clear and still.
The hovering speeches of birds convene and depart
in slowness of motions a sight to behold.
A pleasant view those maestros of the air
Ducks, geese, graceful swans, swam.
A symphony of sound to hear.

Cornell W. Jacobs

"An Ending"

Blue veined pale hands, poker grasping,
Tortured breath with effort rasping,
Stirring long dead coals.

Shawl drawn taut around frame skeletal
To vainly curb cruel fingered cold,
No flame thrown cabaret of shadows
To salve the mind from winters woe,
Sinking down with joints protesting,
Momentum irreversible,
Deep armchair at last relenting
To couch her in its pseudo glow.

Blue veined pale hands
Uncovered by harsh winters sun,
No longer crave for warmth or succour,
For their warm days; are done.

Alan Beech

Untitled

Today, I've reached the depths of my despair.
Today could see the end of all things fine and free.
If he won't call or write to-day,
I could see the end of what I laughingly call - my sanity.

SOMEHOW I got through it - that dark and dreadful night.

SOMEONE pulled me on and outward - just far enough to see the light.

SOMEWHERE there is an answer to the unanswerable of now.

SOMETHING will guide me to it and show me why...

Then, I'll know how...

Iris Curtis

A Poem In Mind

These modern times to find the rhymes
To write each little poem
The only way to do these things
Is when you're all alone

To tease your mind of all its thoughts
That does not give you rest
You try to ask it right out loud
Come on and do your best

As years go on it's getting old
It stops and tries to bare
The little thought it cast aside
The thought that was despair

So little mind you've done your best
The time has come to take a rest
Just, relax, and ease the pain
By thinking more you'll never gain.

James Robinson

"Spring Time"

I look forward, every year,
    To when springtime, comes around,
For it makes me really happy,
    Seeing snowdrops, peeping through the ground

Everything, that's been, sleeping in winter,
    Suddenly, springs to life,
Which clears away, your winter blues,
    And all, your worries, and the strife.

I love to see, the new buds,
    Growing on the trees
Also watching, all the clothes, I've washed,
    Blowing in the breeze.

But a day in the country,
    Is where, I really long to be,
For a field, of new born lambs, is still,
    A joy, for me, to see.

Jean Hendrie

A Rose

A rose in the early morning spreads her petals slowly
to welcome the rising sun. Morning dew shimmers catching
the bright rays throwing rainbows out towards the dawn
and the beginning of a new day.

Jan P. Carmichael

Creation

God sent a tiny child like me,
To walk His earthly plane,
To see His world in all its beauty,
To feel the gentle falling rain.

To see the flowers in all their glory,
To feel the warmth of the glowing sun,
To see the twinkling stars up in the heavens,
The light of the moon when day is done.

To see His mighty rolling oceans,
The majestic mountains standing tall,
To scan the wild and windswept moors,
To see life both great and small.

To hear the morning bird song,
Like a chorus fill the air,
To be in awe and wonder,
Of the God who put them there.

To grow up kind and caring,
And to love my fellow man,
To thank the Lord for this my life,
And always do the best I can.

Jean Little

First Child

Your invitations are sent, and accepted with pleasure
To the wedding of your darling little treasure
You think now they have gone, the house will be quiet
But sorry to say, you are in for a riot.
Fasten your seat belts prepare for a shock,
For the next thing is a maternity frock.
Nine months of waiting for a boy or a girl.
Puts your head and feet in a bit of a whirl.
But when it arrives, things only get worse,
A screaming baby, and a head fit to burst.
Don't bother to polish or wash the floors,
Remember that babies have sticky paws.
Up with your feet, enjoy life while you can
For very soon you will be Gramp and Gran
Gone will be your peaceful, quiet nights of bliss
Instead you'll get the best thing on earth, a grandchild's kiss.

Alice Dyer

The Change Of Life

You can go from the Creme de la Creme
To the lowest of the low
In the time it takes
a Daffodil to grow.

You can have no knowledge of anything
To learning something new
In the time it took
to fall in love with you.

You can lose your hair and grow old
Long before you're ready to
But not too late for me
to give this band of gold to you.

You can have a ready made family
A growing boy and girl
But the little one we have made
will be more precious than a pearl.

You can adjust your life, to suit your needs
As we have done before
But I never would have believed
how much to you, I hopelessly adore.

Alan Mansfield

Earth Rape

Can God forgive
Desecration of Mother Earth
Slowly dying from the pollution
Chemicals and misuse of fertile lands
Governments dictate
Yield to the dollar
But for what?
Children of generations to come
Will inherit what's left
Education and thought
Is what's needed
For this is political rape
Action is needed
For we all suffer
We may ignore and not care
But the problems remain there
Slow suffocation, skies of grey
Politicians lie with smiles
Everybody help, save our earth
Respect, enjoy, care...
Robert Wlodarz

Fanny Winifred Florence

She awoke to the early kiss of dawn
To the flickering rays of a Winter's solstice morn
Rays that squeezed through the woven chintz
Dense with heady dust, particles of mince
Like a babe leaving its mothers womb
She slid out from under the covers and crossed the room
This wee small child scantily clad, and frail
Climbed upon the window box and pulled herself up by the rail
The cold Winter's morn welcomed her with delight
Enveloped and fondled that poor little mite
So that soon she was shivering, shaking with cold
But was driven on with a determination so bold
Like an inquisitive hen she dabbled and drew
With her small finger so cold and now blue
O'er the frosted pattern on the window of feathers
Now disclosing a peephole; a sight of the weather
In wonderment she gazed upon the small backyard
A view so beautiful in white bridal garb
As she gazed upon the scene transfixed in wonder
It began to snow again regardless of those under
Daphne Porter-Lovell

The Far-Off Land

I want to go back to that far-off land,
To the far-off land of my youth.
Where life was so easy to understand
Where my days were all beauty and truth.

Oh! Let me go back to that wondrous clime,
When the sun shone the whole day long;
When I basked in the light of my golden prime
And my thoughts were all gladness and song.

Take me back, take me back to that wave-beat shore,
To blue seas edged with golden sands;
To my childhood home and those days of yore
To the best of all beautiful lands.

I would fain toss aside my knowledge of life
And in innocence skip through each day;
And in fancy forget that sadness and strife
Have been with me for much of the way.

Then in dreams let me go to that distant land
To those cloudless, elusive skies
To my wonderful far-away, far off land
Lying wait for my shuttered eyes.
Jessie Edwards

A Treasure Chest In The Sky

The clouds festooned with gold auroras stand,
thread with rose and silver as if by magic wand;
A treasure chest in the sky,
with sun as gold and rainbows flying by.

Sunset is but reflection of a space diamond,
twinkling with tiny stars, as jewelled band;
or, to arise on the morrow as glorious topaz,
blazing from the treasure chest in the sky.
Anita Fellowes

So I Failed Myself

So I failed myself, I kept my true feelings hidden
To tell you that I love you, I did not dare
I was alien to love, thought it was forbidden
Your feelings for another to openly declare.
For I am that duckling, who won't turn beautiful swan
And how could a goddess like you fall for me
Little did I know that one day you'll be gone
Leaving me with just a golden memory.
Tell you I couldn't, I was filled with fear
I knew not what reaction to expect
If insulted you would not let me near
Thus if not love, better than hate is respect

But you are my only love, this promise I make
The place you have in my heart no-one else may take.
Balall Maqbool

The Human Way?

Why do men look to war
To solve disputes evermore?
Why? Because man has a fear
Of losing that which is so dear.
They see not that their loss is more.
They care not for rich or poor.
For them, to blast and kill is "right",
Disregarding others' plight.
It is "politics," they all say.
A means of getting their own way.

Man still tries to struggle on
And seldom to rely upon
A tender heart and kind concern.
Why will we never learn?
We are just as raw
As before
When jungle life was our won't
With no one there to say, "don't":
Then, We slaughtered all in our way
Much as we do - even today.
Jean O'Donnell

The Joy of Life

If as a child we had the foresight
To see what the fates held in store,
Would we tremble at our future plight?
Would we be rich, famous or poor

It would be wrong, of that I'm certain
We should live each day as our last
And if we daily face the final curtain
Then our joy will be unsurpassed

There will be a richness in our living
We will meet people good and kind
We won't be takers we will be giving
And the rat race will lag behind

Far better if we looked backward
To those distant childhood days
Would our life prove its own reward?
Or be just one meaningless haze
John Allen

Secret Love

What can I do or say to thee
to show thee how I feel
For thou art everything to me
I find it so unreal.

Thy face invades my every dream
Thy voice is constant in my sleep
Mine eyes are moist whene'er you're seen
and in thy presence I want to keep

Thee close to me for all to see
This love which gives such pain
Within my heart yet comforts me
When we are far apart and then again
When thou looks at me
I'm everything and more I'd ever dreamed I'd be.

Jeanne Jones

Untitled

Was it just a dream of yesterday
to see you standing by my side?
Is it yet to come?
Or did it fly right past?
Or maybe someone just turned me around.

Did you ask me once not to turn away
from our dreams of yesterday?
Did you tell me once that you'd wait for me?
or did that dream just blow away?

Am I holding on tight wishing things were right?
Was it me that destroyed our dreams?
Scared of reaching out too fast
did I push right past
our dream of a lonely day?

Where you standing there with your dreams to share
then I only reached for one?
Did the rest blow away on a windy day?
or did you burn them in the sun?

Jo Mason

Forever Young

You miss her now your loving wife
To sleep she fell she lost her life.
Her face aglow, with love and youth
To you her heart her soul her truth,
Strong and handsome her one and only
Old and frail you're oh, so lonely
Shared feelings and emotions.
You together never needed love potions.
your sight now gone,
But who will mind,
For up in heaven
it's her you'll find
Together again,
Forever young.

Gina Hughes

Anger Wanger

He wants to tell you he is angry, but he can't.
Walking innocently down the street, when it prods, prods him in his
stomach in a place he cannot reach.
It strikes him on the head like a raindrop made from glass, it whips
his feet from under him, pushing him to the ground.
It is not his fault, it is not my fault, it is not anybody's fault.
F*** this element of doubt I must rationalize, after all I have a son.
Something must be done with this anger-wanger.

If you have trouble unravelling your thoughts then I will give you
a clue. Imagine they're on a calm sea and you can be there too.
A cool soft breeze will blow away the troubles of your mind,
and the warmth of the sun will touch your heart and make you
   feel kind.

Charles Baker

Now You Are Grown Up

Now you are all married and moved away, there are a few
things I want to say. I was still young when small and I don't
think you were much trouble at all.

Except when Stuart cut his head and Alison thought the rabbit
hadn't been fed. She put her finger in the cage and ran to me
in an awful rage.

When I looked to see what she had done I found that her
finger tip had gone, so off to hospital we would go where the
name of 'Bruce' they soon got to know.

Stuart would fall and cut his knees and not always through
climbing trees! One Friday night Alison stood on a ball, we all
knew she would have a fall.

She fell off and broke her arm, and was very quick at raising
the alarm! So off to hospital again we sped where she ended
up in a hospital bed.

To have it in plaster was her aim but alas this time it never
came. So next time she got it right and broke her ankle one
swimming club night.

Life was hectic, life was fun, and we tried each year to take
you to the sun. We lost the twins in Folkestone by the sea
and Alison was lost in Rimini.

Then on that awful day in May God came and took your Dad
away, I know you miss him, I miss him too but I've tried to
make it up to you.

You've been so good in the past two years helped me through
the sorrow and the tears. Now you are married, life starts
again think of the sunshine, not the rain.

I'd like to say thanks for all you've done; life without you all
would be no fun in the whole wide world there just couldn't
be, a Mum who is as proud as me!

Carole Knowles

Our Joe

When in doubt our thoughts return
To sadness, loss and woe,
We should, but remember of all the times
Of love and laughter with our Joe

My heart is filled with sadness too,
And loss beyond compare,
For he was my childhood friend,
A brother, truly loyal, most rare.

But the hurt has vanished now
And in my heart there still remains,
A living Joe, an Uncle too,
To keep for ever on this plane.

I can't help but miss him so
And tears are easy to fall and flow.
But I am thankful to have known,
A super human like our Joe.

Carolanne Burch

A "Moving" Thought

Sheltered housing is a boon
To older folk who need less room
The flats are cosy, snug and warm
Wardens check on us each day
Making sure that we're okay
And none of us have come to harm.
There is a laundry room nearby
Where we can wash or tumble-dry.
Or hang our clothes on the whirligigs
Where breezes blow and dances jigs
If company is what you need
The common room is there, indeed
To meet good friends and have a blather
Or let your worries share, whatever
If privacy and peace is what you crave for
Just say goodnight and close your door.

Isabella Rugg

Today

I worked and toiled and scrubbed all day.
To make my home all bright and gay.

I walked and ran, I laughed all day.
The hours they seemed to fly away.

I wrote, I drew, I painted all day.
Smiling faces on models of clay.

I sifted the earth and planted all day.
I rested, watching the leaves gently sway

The sun came out, a bright new day.
The children all came out to play.

Scurrying feet, pass my door each day
I wonder if any will pause and stay

The earth is grey, no sun today,
No one is coming down my way.
Frances Percival

Christmas In A Distant Land

Now is the time in a distant land,
To listen to the sounds of a Christmas band
Now is the time, to tie the calf, head high
To the wall despite its painful cry
No hay under foot, no water to hand
Cry... cry... calf, in this distant land.
No mother is near though you are so young.
Born to be fattened for the human tongue.
But hist; of your suffering, no charge
Is made, unable to move: Fed the wrong diet,
But hush now, tis Christmas. We don't want to know
We have our merry making to do!
So stand there, die there. Poor little thing...
While we at home, of angels sing.
Goodbye little calf, while I'm drinking my soup,
My tears will flow, no-one will know why....

Because I am part of the human race,
I am part of this national disgrace.
Daphne J. Grant

Multiple Sclerosis (MS)

I'd like to run but show me how
To go on walks, but not far now
I'd like to do these things once more
My mind is willing but my body's slower.

MS, MS dominates my life
But you still have to be a mother and wife
Does anyone really understand
There's no perfect days in the MS land.

If I sit down and take a break
My legs start twitching they really ache
You're hot, you're cold, you can't sit still
You've got MS but you're not ill.

People look but can they tell
You're walking funny but look so well
You're stable now but will it get worse
Will someone lift this MS curse.

Some day I hope they find a cure
Yet all this research, I'm not so sure
Alas tomorrow another day
With all the same problems to get in my way.
Alan Brammah

Methinks

Thou may'est mock to think me dim,
Though thou the one who torts in sin,
Thou laughs whilst I in silence dwell
Thou can'st not read me
Nor I tell.
Irene Grant

Poet's Reward

The poet has but little chance
To gain the riches sought by men
His riches are the fireflies' dance
And not the gold they count by ten

He hears the babble of the brook
And writes a verse unknown to them
The richest gem is in his book
Was found in some secluded glen

He travels far and in the end
Is laid to rest in an unknown grave
The lines which took so long are penned
Alas are lost as the receding wave.

The poet has received a gift
Lost by many men
Their power at last became too swift
Their evil made them lose again.
James MacNab

The Big Blow - October 1989

You mighty wind, in gusts did blow
To fright us mortals here below
Your strength doth bring us to our knees
Blow down our houses and our trees

You bring the clouds so full of rain
To flood our valley and our plain
Our flowing rivers owe you no thanks
They flow so fast and burst their banks

You toss our ships about at will
And buckle plates that are made of steel
Have you no thought for sailors brave
Who sail the seas in search of trade

You do all this and even more
Knock down our sea walls, invade our shores
Toss small craft high and dry
And make us puny humans cry

You have had your fun, you've played your game
And then steal off from whence you came
A gentle breeze now stirs the grass
At peace at last now you have passed.
Frederick G. Hayward

Remember

I woke one day in forty-five
To find that I was still alive.
There was no need more bombs to drop;
No need to fly another op.

But where was Rex, and where was Bob?
They hadn't found another job.
Their bones were scattered far and wide;
For us they had been crucified.

They hadn't lived to celebrate
That day for which we had to wait
Six long years of war time horror
With no regard for youth's tomorrow.

"Let's build the peace," the wise men cried.
"Let's erect plaques to those who died.
Remember what the young men did
To counteract the fascists' bid.

How true the facts made evident,
Revealing evil government.
But Rex and Bob will never see
They gave their lives for victory.
Eric Broad

Woodland By Night

Out in the woods your hear hooting of owl.
To feed his family goes out on the prowl.
Fox moving quietly crosses to the furrow.
Patiently settles himself by rabbit's burrow.
Searching the landscape eyes sharp as a bird,
Stag keeping guard protecting his herd.
Near the big houses are family cats,
Though they're well fed they are looking for rats.
Whatever the weather it is always the same,
Come sun to shine, snow hail or rain.
Whether big cloud has shut out all light,
Or if the moon is up there shining bright.
Night in the woodland is always same as in day.
Animals hungry in search of their prey.
The gentle river goes rippling along.
Asleep amid rushes a snowy white swan.
Nightingales singing so sweet and mellow.
Trees spread their branches like mantles below.
Moon shines like a queen in the velvet sky,
Her courtiers the stars which are twinkling on high.

Barbara Goode

Hope For Our Earth

Now we have the time to 'stand and stare,'
To drink in the beauty of each day.
Time to think about this earth, and care.
Watch sunrise, sunset, and find time to pray.

We hurried through our lives at breakneck speed,
Enjoyed the freedom of this bounteous earth.
To years a-flying by, we paid no heed.
Oh youth, slow down. See life for what it's worth.

Why were we so careless all those years?
Of our precious earth, our heritage?
They'll try to save us and allay our fears.
They care now, those of a younger age.

We cannot turn the clock back to repair what we have done.
Nor must we spend time grieving, looking far behind.
But rather, help the young to right our wrong,
To make a safer world for all mankind.

Beatrice Mackay

A Better Man Than Me

Within this life, we are simply what we wish to be, free
perhaps to do what we would hold to be the core of want, not
the cant we hear in some places, nor the hypocrisy of other
faces who do not understand the truth of feeling between two people.

But, where, oh where is the time we spent amidst our yearning,
our learning of a love without the fear. It's not here.

Sadly now the banishment of this man for whilst he can with
all denizens and friends, sail around the bends and curves that
life is famous for, he has decreed another door - to close.

And yet 'tis the pity of it all were generations yet to come not
to see and feel the reality of something lost by the way, seen
in youth and then felt once more in later days when the man
had no right. But he had to fight!

So now the end! Tend not the tear that falls when looked
upon in gracious thought. It is not fraught with salient
wishes, just that we will not feed the fishes of the seas again.

Amen, Farewell - to fight and lose, this I understand by mine
own hands not being on the oars. A cause lost to better reasons.

Simply to a man for all the seasons

John A. Johnson

What Is Love?

Life is strange, yet wondrous in hindsight,
To choose and do what is wrong or right,
Our plans we make, yet never see through,
Are often put to one side because of you.

The 'LOVE' word is so strong yet used so free,
Caress and touch used mostly in place of thee,
Whether it's lust or not, is so hard to foretell,
The person must search deep and turn to the wishing well.

Is it for life or just a bus stop call?
Does anyone really know at all?
Trust, truth and respect should always prevail,
Else the Just cause is lost and love will fail.

So the tale to tell is, is it worth it to try,
Or be left wondering until the day we die?
To love and cherish, honour and keep,
Until our great Lord takes our soul to keep.

Denise Alison Dye

Moments Are Precious

I cherish every moment we have chance
to be together.
It can be a rare occasion sometimes.
But it's nice to remember forever.
Those precious little moments we spend as a family.
These are the times I cherish in my heart happily.
It maybe a walk on a hillside or just a stroll down a lane
A ride on our bicycles or just a drive in the rain.
But the love that binds us together.
Seems to carry on forever.
Its roots seem to grow deeper, into a solid ground.
And I thank God above, for the love we have found.
For no storms can shake our branches.
No seas wash us apart.
For the love is strong between us and
will flourish in our hearts.

Janet Cross

Friends

When it comes to say goodbye,
To all your friends,
For all of time,
It's hard to say a last goodbye,
And go your separate ways,
No-one knows,
Who you are,
What you do,
Or where you go,
But your friends know all your dreams,
You never know if you will meet again.
When or where at what time,
You'll say you'll keep in touch,
You do for a little while,
But as your life goes on,
School days are a distant theme,
To where there is no return,
Except for an odd picture or two,
To bring an old smile.

Jodi Perkins

Untitled

Dearest Sweetest Marianne,
    Try to imagine if you can,
what special joy, and purpose you inspire,
with just that special look, and pretty smile,
Like a stream where dappled sunlight plays,
    A frosty surface where the moonbeams stray,
    A wood where songbirds scream with sheer delight,
your tinkling laugh, and dance so sweet and slight,
When bed time comes and you begin to mime,
Telling us "the-very-last-time"
A thing of beauty was created thus,
When you were sent to Mummy - and to us

Iris J. Brown

The Listener

I am the listener, the agony aunt,
To all my friends at school.
They come to me with their problems,
And I'm sure I've seen them all.

What they don't seem to realize,
Is that I still hurt inside.
When I'm upset and lonely,
I can only run and hide.

My best friend she listens,
To all my day's events.
But I'm sure she's not that interested,
Well, that is what I sense.

My mum on the other hand,
Listens to what I say.
She is there already listening,
Every minute of every day.

My mum, she makes me happy,
When I am feeling low.
It is to my loving mum,
That my happiness is owed.
Gemma Fossett

Letting Go - With Love

Maternal intrusion, lending confusion
to a novice in the adult world
letting go, restless fingers slip through mine
stand in the shadows, just within reach

Coping with changing, her life re-arranging
discarding childish ways
let her grow, slowly finding her own way
watch from a distance, but stay within sight

Emotional chess game, with joy and pain
clever moves or chances taken
does she know the rules and how to play
advise then back away, still within ear shot

The bond we share, will not alter or wear
with times passing circles
and yet, it was so much simpler then
when I was the player, not the spectator
Gail Morgan

A Fool's Dream

"Who watches me in my sleeping hour?" I said,
"'Tis lonely" replied the silver coined head,
That hung against the black satin sky, without the need of thread.

"What makes you shine so holy bright, against the coldness
 black of night?"
I asked by thought to the silver glint;
Looking to the light.

"I hover here with all my might, without the need of wings
 for flight."
Said the wise old 'Punch'-like face.
"But how do you shine so bright?"

"I know the secrets of God's insight, and understand the
 strange twilight."
Replied the mystic smile of mouth.
"But how do you shine so bright?"

"Why do you care how I shine so bright, when I'm willing to tell the
 secrets of the night?"
Returned the glowing angel face.
"Yes but, HOW do you shine so bright?"

"Fool, I steal the shining every night, of the beam of brilliant sunlight,
 Reflecting wisdom down to common man,
 Yet still you ask of me, sans sight."
Julian Crichton Dodd

Return To The Omega Tree

Fifty credits paid
Times four.
Then through the arboretum door,
Conducted tours, of what used to be,
The remnants of the omega tree.
A glass fronted room
Empty and bare,
The final beech had once stood there.
Rotted wood, perspex decayed
Placed on view in a sanctuary made.
To the ignorance of mankind.
We left.
Above the entrance was a notice,
A reminder,
Words, once spoken, by Oppenheimer?
"I have become death, the destroyer of worlds."
Chris Gibbons

The Meadow

I walked through the meadow, through the colourful flowers
Time had passed by, I'd been there for hours
The sun smiled down, it was looking at me
I knew this was the place that I wanted to be
The birds in the trees, all singing their song
I knew this feeling couldn't be wrong
This feeling I had as I sat in the sun
What a day, it's really been fun
I'm sad to go, I feel such sorrow
Maybe I'll come back again tomorrow
Julie Rivers

Pointing The Way

The Christian proudly guards the Gate
Tightly shut against the rest.
It opens not to Muslims' fate
Or Buddhist meditation blest.

The Power looks down upon the scene
And points a finger in dismay,
"Surely all humans must have been
Through this same Gate that points the way?"

The Guard looks up and hears the voice,
And murmurs sadly "Nay, not so,
Not all that come can have the choice,
Only the saved may come and go."

The POWER is vexed and questions why
So many mortals turned away;
The Guard looks up towards the sky
"Ask HIM", he said, "who holds the sway".

The lightning flashed, the gateway's wide,
Shows the way for those encumbered:
"Harass not those who had to hide
And pass all creeds without being numbered!"
Edward O'Neill

Beauty Beneath

I dreamt one night I had sailed away,
To a sunny island with a sandy bay,
The trees were green and the sky blue,
But all of this couldn't stop me thinking of you.

The sun was your smile to light my way,
The sky was your eyes that had something to say,
The trees were your hair blowing in the wind,
And the sand was your heart where all my hopes were pinned.

I awoke from my dream and fumbled around,
To find that I was asleep on the ground,
The lapping of water filled my ears,
And only then did my eyes fill with tears.

I was on an island it wasn't a dream,
But my handsome lover wasn't all that I'd seen,
No muscles surrounded him, no confidence beamed,
But he was the reality of the person that I dreamed.
Joanne Austin

The Golden Hinde

I visited Padstow harbour on a warm summers night
Tied up at the quayside a magnificent sight
It was a replica of the Golden Hinde
Sir Francis Drake's sailing ship, a wonderful find
I paid an entrance fee of just two pound
Went aboard to look around
What would it have been like in days of old
In perilous seas and temperatures so cold
Around the world it had sailed with glory
Returning with treasure and many a story
History surrounded me at every turn
So much to discover, so much to learn
Sailors of a bygone age
Hardship and valour for a pitiful wage
Above me the masts soaring high into the sky
As I stepped off the gang plank to a seagull's cry
Memories linger of that warm summers night
The Golden Hinde - a magnificent sight.

Brenda M. Hadley

Death Of A Rose

Today I traced my childhood haunt
Through wood and field and spinney I'd jaunt,
To see the newts and frogs in reeds
And blow the dainty dandelion seeds.
I'd smell the air where I found
A fragrant rose upon a mound
Of meadow flowers of pink and blue
Swaying in a shower of dew;
But when I neared all I could see
Was bricks, dust and machinery
That polluted the ponds and meadowland
For reasons of progress I understand.
Kicking a brick from its dewy bed
Revealed a severed buttercup head;
Overcome by indignation
Shocked by this vile stagnation;
Hoping it might just expose
The remnants of that fragrant rose.

Debbie J. Keach

War

Children suffer on this earth,
Through war and hunger from their birth.

To see them helpless in their plight,
Because their country choose to fight.

Damaged minds from all their pain,
Their tears flowing down like rain.

The horrors show upon their face,
Of happiness there is no trace.

Children's laughter ringing out,
That's what this world should be about.

Children's happy smiling faces,
It makes no difference what their race is.

A precious gift they are you see,
The futures theirs they hold the key.

This awful thing that war has done,
There is no glory with a gun.

Jayne Pearce

Sands Of Time

At the fountain of knowledge I would gladly kneel
To find those words I really feel
But those sands of time have played their part
Each grain a memory implanted in my heart
A look, a kiss, a touch of hands
All preserved in those grains of sands
Precious they all shall be
and remain immortal just to me
Until that final breath of wind shall set them free
and for all eternity.

Aubrey Henstock

Untitled

Materialisation of dreams and desires
through the forest around us within the barbed wires
there's good luck and good fortune
for peace and good will
take in all that surrounds you
as long as there's still
something to take,
I keep playing the fool
and my friends I upset
when I'm kind and then cruel
which I truly regret,
try to help and I share
but I guess I'm abusive
I've loved and not cared
and been far too protective
I still run away,
but I'd soon stand my ground
and I've lived for the day
almost every year round

Dryden Sykes

In All Of These

Shall I wander as a child
Through summer days, benign and mild,
Softly, softly treading down
Fields of gold and thistledown.

Shall I journey through the night,
And mark the stars so deep and bright,
See the moonlight's tender glow
Shine soft, mysterious below.

Shall I walk beside the sea,
The dry warm sand delighting me,
And watch the flowing tide begin,
The tumbling waves come rolling in.

Shall I savour love's caress,
Or friendship's hand in dire distress,
Know nothing yet can be compared
With sweetness of a loving shared.

Shall the magic of the earth,
The joy of love's and friendship's worth
Ever fail to comfort me,
Restore my faith in life to be.

John A. Gilroy

"Departure From San Francisco"

The evening sun casts shafts of light
Through golden gate across the bay.
Seagulls and cormorants in flight
Take leave of this departing day.

A rapturous time has passed
Mid sunny hill-top streets.
In cable-cars that lurched
Through acrobatic feats.

Where fishermen hang their nets
And moonlit vessels sway,
Now lovers walk and sigh
As sleepless children play.

Through Chinatown the dazzling shops,
With pageantry of old,
Recall a bygone Age
To a race reborn to California's fold.

Farewell then, 'Frisco town
Your alluring spell I break.
Your golden sun to see
A whole new day before you 'wake.

Brian Harris

The River

The river winds through cities and towns,
Through country villages and over downs,
It has no troubles, or no worry,
It never, never needs to hurry,
It hears church bells when they ring,
And sees all that nature has to bring,
The birds in full song and in flight,
The nocturnal creatures of the night,
It's seen the wars and the strife
That men can bring in their short lives
It's seen the countryside, they rend and tear.
I'm sure the river must despair.

John Green

Thoughts Of You Dad

Rushing rivers in my mind, bring back thoughts I'd soon forget.
Thoughts of when I was a child, being a brat all the time.
Never did as I was told, I was daring, I was bold.
Looking for attention you see, I thought no one cared for me.
But now I'm older I can see, why my dad had scolded me.
If I could turn back the tides of time, I would make his life more fine
I would have told him that I cared, I still think of him often
in my prayers.

So if you're listening to me Dad, I didn't mean to make you sad.
All I know is you're not here, and it's hard to hold back the tears,
So when it's time for me to go, I hope you're waiting by my door.

Jean Jones

A Poem For James

To me, you are a mirror of myself, the reflection of my
thoughts and emotions, the lost piece that now can be found.

When I am with you, I get the answers I need to hear,
you understand my thoughts, give me a chance to be myself,
and not someone people expect me to be!

To others I am a lost spirit, but to you, I am the part of
yourself you have been searching for.

We are so very different, but so in tune our minds, my
words are spoken by you before they even question my lips.

I do care, the more time I spend with you, the more
I realize. But perhaps my heart wasn't ready to feel?

It isn't until you think you have lost something, that
you realize how much it really means.

Without You I am not complete.
Without Your love, I can't be free.
Free my heart, let me learn to really love you

When I can, we will be together
MIND BODY AND SOUL

Giselle Rowe

Hands Together

Nothing could be finer than what we have here today
Thought and love shine out as we look at each display
Many hours of hard work but worth it in the end
To see the look of pleasure on the faces that attend

What could hold more beauty than the colourful array
Of flowers that adorn the church on this special day
Splendour, glory, sheer delight you must agree
Set amidst these stones walls so decoratively

Which of things are better made than those which have been done
With love and care and patience by each and every one
Hands have worked for many hours to bring forth such a store
Of needle, thread and wool work and many items more

Nowhere else could hold all the treasure that you see
Gathered here around us, magnificently
Than this house of GOD that's filled with joy
For man and woman girl and boy

So feast your eyes let them wander where they may
And remember GOD is with us and what we have here today

Janet Bell

To Maud, A Caution

Don't go in the garden, Maud
'Though the ice and the snow is now thawed
Remember last year? It caused many a tear
When you found yourself heavily floored.

Stay out of the garden, Maud
Does the memory not strike a chord?
In a comatose state, you became "Keyhole Kate"
In the micro-surgery ward.

Resist the temptation, dear Maud
Take a tip from your Master and Lord
You may skid on the stones, and rebreak your bones-
A mishap I just can't afford.

Stick to the conservatory, Maud
With your humerus brittle and flawed;
Another such slip, could well shatter your hip-
An incident to be deplored.

Remember the 'vino' you poured?
Which you drank of your own sweet accord?
Alleviate my anxiety, and act with propriety
And if go out you must, GO ABROAD!

Gerald M. King

Untitled

Come deceptions of each kind:
Those of gulls who whirl through
Frail snowfall taste of
Sea's spiced breath upon my window,
Then ease themselves upon tumbling,
With senseless cry celebrating
This world's terror;
Those of thin thrush, sick
With cold, balanced on bare stick,
Piping of neglected hedges thick
With rose and cream-lipped honeysuckle.
Old crows, thrown like scraps away
In this grey hour of day,
Make your tuneless cry your only song,
Bring forth your unsteady young,
Come deceptions of Springkind.

George Sims

Why

Sometimes I wonder why.

Why are people ever brought into this world,
this world of hate, mistrust and violence.

But why should this be? - Maybe we made this world what it is?

The hate from people having a different coloured skin,
or even a different language.
The mistrust in not trusting or believing our own people.
The violence brought about by hate and mistrust.

But what happened to love and peace? - Will this ever be?

With country against country,
person against person,
and all for the love of war and power,
one person with power,
the power to press that button or say that word,
and innocent loving people,
who would never harm anyone - die.

Why in this world should someone have that right.
In this world where everyone is equal,
but of course,
some are more equal than others!

Faye Adams

Live Each Day

There is comfort in the knowledge that you've walked this way before.
Contentment is in the familiar and the dear.

There is sadness if the need to look behind shadows the beauty of the moment.
Regret and loneliness live uneasily together.

There is wisdom in the need to glance behind but look toward the road ahead.
Peace and joy may lie in the unexpected.

Josephine Lister

What A Dream!

Can I really justify this weekly due
This rental?
Yes, rental it could be on hi-fi or TV!
Of course I can.
I smoketh not cannabis nor pot
Although I do indulge the nightly tot.
This amount could feed a third world child
Could even put clothes upon his back
The very thought does really make me wild
I demand my money back!
No, better not because this very week
The prizes and the splendour that I seek
May come my very way
And with them I could pay
For what?
Thrice nightly tot?
Luxury for life, no more hard work, no strife
What a dream, oh what a scheme
Will it ever go away?
'Fraid not, lottery fever's here to stay.

Barbara McGannan

"A Wedding Present From The Heart"

As this is your special day,
This note with love is sent to say,
Now you are one, instead of two,
You've taken your vows, and said 'I do'.

You've built a home and life together,
Which God be willing, will last forever,
With all best wishes we hope and pray,
That only good things will come your way.

May your children be happy, bright and healthy,
May you never want and always be wealthy,
Above all always look after each other,
To Andrea my sister and Andrew my brother.

You've found in each other a piece of your soul,
And now your together, you'll reach every goal,
So to Andrew and Andrea, husband and wife,
Hope you feel like today for the rest of your life.

Joanne L. Smith

Where Do I Stand?

I feel I don't fit in my slot,
This key has jagged edges.
I try to mould and fill my plot,
Yet everywhere a piece catches.
I pretend to be who I am not,
This game is hard I sit on the bench.

I feel no one has accepted me,
I try another image, to my disappointment
I'm stranded in a choppy sea,
They stab my back, I apply the ointment.
I want to be who I'm destined to be
To find myself I make an appointment.

Heather Slade

The Cry Of The Tempest

For some a deity designed, for others nature's trick
   This globe within a cooling state, made home for nature's quick
The turbulence of ocean beds, gave rise to mountains high
   And from its seas a cell was born, to fill its lands and sky.

Was all this glory thus gone by designed to be foreclosed
   Some say a man of God came down to save believers' souls
A minute of the world's own time was only gone before
   Destruction came within the wake of mankind's human call.

Didactic nations sat on chairs to alleviate the poor
   The world's resources all spread out dire warnings to ignore
The seal was set the will too late, what was important then
   Became as in a foolish dream to nature's diadem.

The warming of the earth became, not as a summer's day
   That lays its gentle hand on land, but as an angry fray
The ice that lay on earth's great crust as on a holy head
   Ran into seas already filled to dedicate the dead

When all was over and tempestuous seas again in quietude
   Did Phoenix from the ashes rise its nature to renew?

Joan G. Ratliffe

'Can We Win?'

We must be fools in life today,
To allow so few to rule their way.
They tell us how to live and die,
The few in power who think they are higher,
For years and years we let them have power,
Maybe one day it will be our hour.
They send us to war to fight and kill,
We don't know why and never will.
The powerful live, the meek are killed,
Can you read where this is willed?
How can we win in this wicked world,
But to stand together and not be fooled.
We live in this world to toil and feed,
But the ones at the top are filled with greed.
We say we are free to say what we please,
But 'Big Brother' is listening so don't be at ease.

Edward Harris

Loving

Remember on this 14th day
your love is held for all of time.
A heart of pure blood so red and deep
and given to me so I may keep
more precious than gold and diamond
with warmth of life so fresh, so crisp.

You light my way, you hold me safe.
you keep me living. You pull me back.
When people try to suffocate my being
seeing your eyes focused on mine
removes all pretence and lies.
Kiss my tears, pull me close.
Until our maker takes us home

Paula J. Coe

Untitled

I met you on the tech wall
your hair was shining and soft,
I said hello but you never spoke at all.
We met some days later as
We passed along the street,
You lifted your head and smiled
at me and I whispered can we meet.
That was four years ago
and we are still together.
I will never forget only just
remember.

Mark Phair

You

My heart I gave you a long time ago.
You've kept it as safe as the drifting snow,
Many times when we've been pushed to the edge
You've kept our love as fast as a wedge.

We've never been blessed with loads of money.
You've just had a way of keeping everything sunny
When my thoughts have started to go grey.
You've been there to push them away.

When we've been looked upon as though we've committed
  a scandal,
You've held me close under the magic glow of a candle.
As we rest, and I hold onto you tight
You softly lean over and kiss me good night.
   Samantha Hopton

Untitled

Just one more word, you'll be in my head
You've got me thinking of the things you said
Just one step closer and I'll feel like giving in
Your breath feels so warm upon my skin
Just one more click and you'll turn the key
And I'll be right where you want me to be
Just one more kiss and I'll be on my knees
Begging for your love, please
Just one more touch, and I'm ready to fall
You have me now you're over the wall
Just one more move and our souls will meet
With your arms around me I admit defeat
Just one more thing that's left to do
And that is for me to seduce you.
   Kelly Gibson

Old Age

So you're running out of puff,
You're getting old and done enough.
Sit back now watch others race
And remember times when you'd keep pace.
Your teeth sit smiling in their glass
The days of chewing steak is past.
Your hair is grey, that's what is left,
It just hangs limp it's lost its zest.
Your limbs all ache, your bones all creak,
There's corns upon your tired feet.
Your glasses sit there on your nose,
You need them now to read the prose.
It's hard to hear when people speak
It's muffled up, the sounds are weak.
Your mind still works, but not as well
You forget some things, and on others dwell.
You reminisce when you'd jump and run
And wish again that you were young.
But age must come to one and all,
Giving you wisdom to teach the fool.
   Yvonne Butchart

Special Days

You saw me through my baby days
You saw one through my crazy day
My crazy days were special days
Of boys, dancing Liverpool Night Clubs
Liverpool Beatles, Mostly now a haze.

Then come my censor days of training,
nursing, marriage, babies and blues,
you were there, always there, you would
say go run, you, no you can go on

Then with one last wave, Mum
you were gone, never to be seen
again, you died, you died, and
I have tried and tried to go on
I did, I did, I went on and on,
now I am the one who sees my brood,
through all their crazy days
   Ronnie Seddon

Of Robert Graves, Singer Of The Sacred Song

It does not matter that you journey on;
Your truth is stored in verse and prose and song;
And intimations, far beyond this life,
Of what you knew, transcending human strife.

In you welled up the truths of ancient time,
Forming in ranks again, line upon line,
To show us how to right our very wrong;
To help the speechless birds to rise in song.

You lived and wrote among these olive trees,
Striding the limestone rocks to cala seas
To plunge within the salt sea womb of time,
To say aloud what others only mime.

You came to tea so very many times
To tell of what you read between the lines;
For poets' truth must turn the world from wrong,
And you have raised again the sacred song.
   Martin Tallents

The Bouquet Within

You are the curling, thrusting vine
Your strength has no limits,
Yet delicate fruits are sheltered
By your capable, tender leaves.
Before your harvest
No one knew the secret of the fruit
Plucked from sturdy branches
Which stoically pushed forth again
I know the secret,
Your wine flows into me, the vessel
for your liquid beauty.
And you are sealed secure within
Your richness mellowing through the years
Your flavour safe with me
   Rita Taylor

A Mother's Bond

Beyond the skies, I call you, "Mum",
your spirit always near.
I miss your touch, your warm, embrace
The smile that never left your face.
Through all my pain I've suffered since,
I felt your closeness there.

My joy that now I've found in love,
So special warm and true.
I wish you too were here with me,
On the day I say "I do".
My tears of joy, my laughter too.
The day will hold the presence of you.
The future now ahead will be,
A family bond, "which you gave me."
   Linda Hilton

Daffodils

You stand majestic in the sun
your slender body skyward thrust
Your hands a-begging by your side
your head, a golden crust.

The crinkled collar upon your neck
your quiet downward gaze
Your family all around you still
in brightly coloured haze.

A warm breeze blows through your hair
the rain your eyes does fill
Too soon the winter weather storms
your family cruelly chills

Autumn leaves are not too far
from trees on nearby hills
The sun then soon will warm again
the heart of daffodils.
   A. J. Morrison

The Unlucky Ghost

You read my mind and traced my palm.
Your parting words broke my calm.
When the crystal ball shattered
no prediction mattered.
Stars cannot guide you to the coast,
you cannot touch the unlucky ghost.

Missing in a lost world, strange beliefs don't set you free.
Your superstitious sadness casts a shadow over me.
Still no nearer to the coast,
you cannot reach the unlucky ghost.

Your father was a sailor, buried unknown at sea.
He left you swimming hard to be free.
Still no sighting of the coast,
still no grasp of the unlucky ghost.

Dawn revealed another side of you.
Dawn revealed another side of you.
Unseen destiny to meet, I questioned death
as I ghosted down the deserted street.
Cast out of your warm bed, only sadness to boast,
abandoned to fate like an unlucky ghost.

Paul D. Harris

Sunless Days

When your heart is beating fast,
your mind, it wanders to the past,
all that's lost from yesterday.
Goodbye my friend so far away.

The love we had has gone for good,
you never knew or understood,
what life was like for me inside,
and how I felt, just like a child.

You took great pride in teaching me
the things in life which were meant to be,
it's such a shame you never said
what was soon to lie ahead.

Pamela Sinclair

In 1930

In 1930 I bought a radio and a gramophone.
Your faded photograph sought me from the mantle,
Surrounded by dreams I was never alone.
Too tired to sleep, too sleepy to wake
The pain of my loss would ache and ache.
Trying to remember your eyes laughing, your smile
Visiting that foreign place I would be happy for awhile.
Smoke a woodbine, a glass of stout,
   Heave coal upon the fire
(Never let it go out)
You are dead these score of years
And I have lived too long.
Too long on memories, woodbines, silent screams.
In 1930 I bought a radio and gramophone.
I locked your faded photograph away in a drawer
I listened to the radio, played the gramophone
In the twilight of the day I was always alone.

C. M. Lorn

Ghosts

You sneaked up behind me, and dealt me a blow.
You left me alone with nowhere to go.

Years we had - wasted - now down the drain.
Sitting alone in my sadness and pain.

Memories around me go round in my head.
Driving me mad, I stare at our bed.

Laughter replaced by the tears and the shame.
Look at me needing you again and again.

And though I never believed in ghosts.
I know that you will now make the most.
Of laughing about me as you lay in our bed -
with your lover on my side, now that I'm dead.

Wayne Learmond

"White Horse"

"Come ride the white horse", the horse dealer cried,
"You'll have a great trip" he casually lied,
"The first ride is free", those words did the trick,
He rode off on her back but after felt sick
The horse ran to heaven and hell with his soul,
He was no longer the master, the horse had control.
When the journey was over the horse brought him back.
To a new hell of earth, where he needed more smack,
He found the horse dealer, and begged him for more,
His pride, and ten pound it cost him to score.
Fixed up once more, to the heavens he rode,
He tried chasing the dragon, but it cost him much gold.
White horses cost plenty, his money had all gone
He stole to feed his habit, but knew it was wrong,
In my world, white horses are not allowed in,
He shivered, grew sick and his body turned thin,
So if you ride the white horse please ride it well,
'Cos the white horse called heroin will take you to hell!

D. C. Richardson

The Mysterious Sea

It's like a mirror flat and calm
You'd never think it could do you harm
One minute so gentle clear and cold
Lapping the shore in its gentle hold
It carries us gently, as we swim and glide
But also has secrets it chooses to hide
Tales have been told as its fury unfurls
Huge waves with white horses riding its curls
Beneath its surface new worlds to be found
All sorts of creatures beneath it abound
It offers to anyone bothered to look
An alien lifestyle in every nook
There's treasure to search for from times gone by
Where ships and their crew were sunk there to die
It's a powerful force we must always respect
Not for a moment be allowed to neglect
It allows us to visit far flung places
To learn of their people and study their faces
Just tarry awhile when you happen to be
And gaze and reflect the power of the sea.

Rhona Peel

My Grandma

I wish you were here with me once again.
You were my Grandma and I was your friend.
We'd walk through the fields picking flowers each day.
For our kitchen table, I'd help you display.

Though now those days are far left behind.
The memories still linger clear in my mind.
Of days when we really did have so much fun.
Of days when my Grandma and I were as one.

Oh Grandma I need you, it gets harder to bear.
These days are much longer now you are not there.
Your smile can no longer light up my heart.
Since God sent His angel to tear us apart.

Why did you answer His call right away?
Couldn't you have stayed for just one more day?
To give me a chance to show love that's true.
Oh Grandma I miss you, do you miss me too?

D. Williams

Inspiration

You must have a hope to inspire you,
You must have a path to pursue.
You must have an object to work for
And a plan and a purpose in view.

You must have a sense of direction
Though swiftly the years may depart.
But you'll always have something to live for
If you have a dream in your heart

Steven Burgin

Emptiness

I am the lock, you are my key,
You stared into my eyes, said you really loved me.
Did it have to end, I don't know why.
For many months I cried and cried.

They say love is blind, but I knew you so well,
I just didn't realise you'd put me through hell.
I've lost my appetite, my throat is dry,
I know it's over, this is no reason why.

You just couldn't cope, you could give me no hope,
But what will I do in this world without you?
I'm empty so miserable, lost, all alone.
You don't even write, you don't even phone.

There's nothing left, there's no future for me,
Will my heart ever mend, now this is the end?
I see you, I want you, I miss you near.
As I write my eyes are flooding with tears.

Loneliness of being without you envelopes my world.
I ache inside, thinking, wondering, wanting,
How long can I last, when I feel out cast,
I'm lost without you near.

Suzanah L. Shaw

Lament Of The Killers

You kill mine then I must kill yours.
You say those who died are justified
While their lovers cry away bitter hours.
You hate me because you are right.
I hate you because you are wrong
And on a pool of blood the sun dawns its warming light.
But there is no warmth in this troubled land of sorrows.
The heart and soul have been ripped out
And all that's left are fearful tomorrows.
The rain cries tears of pity on my Black Rose
While the thorns of the Rose bring tears of pain.
We are the thorns, the killer in this weeping isle.
How long more must we breed indifference and hate
As yet more blood drowns the voice peace?
Would you down your weapons at my demise? Would I at yours?
Who will lay flowers on our graves?
The souls we stole from this earth had no choice like us my
    living enemy.
We must seize upon the challenges our times present.
Our two peoples want change, a change only you and I can give.
And then, we can really call ourselves friends and men.

Martin Higgins

Pastimes

'There you are',
you said,
as you handed me the box,
then walked away
into the kitchen
to make the tea.

Unfamiliar prints, reprints, passports, enlargements.
A voyeur of fading black and white smiles,
focusing on overexposed family or friends,
the glossy girls posing and other unknowns caught
unaware,
there you are
in almost everyone
I see you
differently.

'Alright?'
Now your face is a blur in the doorway shadow
and I snap shut the box.

Sarah Blease

Hopes For The Future

To mend the pieces of a broken heart
You really don't know where to start
You realize that you won't die
Now it's time to smile not cry.

I hope to soon go back to school
Instead of always feeling a fool
I need to get my confidence back
Because this is something I dearly lack

I seem to plan what we will do
Today, tomorrow and next year to
Never thinking we could be so strong
The time that's past has felt so long

I've sat for years only feeling sorrow
Thinking there would be no tomorrow
At last I've started to see the light
And now the future is looking bright

E. C. Thomas

A Valentine Of Hope

I watch you darling from a far,
You really are my guiding star,
I see you walking down the street,
Every step you take you look so neat and sweet.

I don't mind, you being grey or a little fat.
As long as you'll come and share my front door mat.
No one could call me old, yet my mind does wander off.
But with you beside me I'd be your ever loving toff.

I suffer from arthritis and my knees will hardly bend,
But with you to give them massage they soon would quickly mend.
Some days I lose my teeth, and my glasses too
But that would never happen, if you'll come to see me through.
I'm healthy I'm frisky and I'm only ninety-seven.
So Darling, please be my Valentine before I pop to heaven.

E. Willmott

The Face Of A Clown

Life is like a circus ring
You paint your face laugh and sing
No one knows how you feel deep down inside
Their only along for the ride
You put the powder and paint on your face
Then go and pretend to the human race
They see you as being happy and gay
But they don't see you at the end of the day
When all worn out you end in tears
Left with your grief and your fears
What does your future hold
Loneliness left out in the cold
All the times you sit and weep
All the nights you don't sleep
But you put on your face of a clown
Don't let people see your down
If only people could see inside
But that would only hurt your pride
You would rather cry alone
In the privacy of your own home

I. Turner

Only 40

So you now are 40, who ever would have guessed.
You look so young and line free and always look your best.
You have reached the time in life when all experiences
have been had.
There is still a lot to look forward to, so no need for feeling sad.
There's false teeth and grey hair and sagging bits to name
but a few.
But these things are a long way off knowing you as I do.
So when your zimma frame goes back again because it's faulty
You'll look back and think how good it was to be just only 40!

G. Chambers

Sad World

I looked at the sea, and the sea saw me, and it seemed to say, could
You help me please, I used to be clean and clear and gleam, but now
You have made me a dirty thing.
I looked at the sky, and the sky saw me, and it seemed to say could
You help me please? I used to be fresh and pure and light and now
You have made me a deadly sight.
I looked wildlife, and wildlife saw me, and it seemed to say, please
Go away our species were many and large and free, and now we are
Few and some unseen.
I looked at man, but he didn't see me, profit, position, stupidity,
And greed, no rational philosophy can he heed.
Kenneth Bishop

My Children

My children, when you were born
You gave quality and meaning, to my life
Your love meant everything to me
You were my source of joy and hope for the future
You inspired me and made me dare to be who I am
You made my life a warm and happy place to be.

And now my children, our lives will take a different path
You will learn people don't always say what they mean
For the road is never straight, and never as it seems
As you start your own adventures in life
Remember these words and realise all your dreams.

May you fly with the eagle and learn to be free
May you swim with the dolphins as they flee captivity
May you ride a wild pony, see the beauty through their eyes
May you hunt with the tiger and learn to survive
May you sing with the skylark, let there music caress your ears
And, may you walk in God's footsteps for the rest of your years.
Maureen Gentry-Evans

You Cared

There's a place set apart for people like you,
You ease the cares of others in everything you do,
I think it was your destiny,
To walk the path you're bound,
If help was ever needed,
Then help was always found.

Nothing was too big for you,
You'd find a way around,
There's lots of folk about,
Who have reason to be glad,
For they found in you,
A quality not everybody has.

And when one day, you leave this earth,
To live on high above.
You'll be held in high esteem,
You showed the greatest love,
Because you cared.
May Hemmings

The Road Of Dreams

As I walk on the road breathing its air,
my mind free from troubles, my mind ... where,
People walk past with nothing to say,
they're doing their thing, their own way,
It's hard to explain the way that I feel,
It's like walking up an endless hill,
I watch the birds fly freely, way up in the sky,
What is it that I'm feeling, please tell me why.
People stop and look at the girl,
Is she thinking heaven or thinking hell,
They cannot see what is on her mind,
and these answers they cannot find,
the girls getting tired, the road has no bends
She's lost in her dreams, the road never ends
She falls to her knees, she wants to be free
but what is she thinking, no one can see...
except the road of dreams.
Teresa Jane Thorn

A Different World I See

Life's lived at such a fast pace, everywhere you go
You can't keep up you're older, so only can go slow
Today there's so much pressure, you feel you can't relax
Maybe you should rest now! Watch a film, oh no!! Not Mad Max
This world's gone very high tech, I really am quite dim
Or so my children tell me, as my telly I try to tune in
So many little buttons that tell me what to do
On something called a C.D.!! I'm feeling really blue
Go do a bit of shopping, drat. It's raining so taking a brolly
Well that's a cheek I must say! A pound to use a trolley!!
I think I'll go bingo, haven't been there for some years
Oh no! I don't believe it, another of my fears
No balls that go round slowly, it's so fast, oh! I can't keep up
He's stood there pressing a button, what chance of any luck?
Go home, settle for some music!! That's not a very nice verse!!
Maybe I misheard him? No I didn't, he really does curse
Watch Telly, relax, just forget it! Oh no this can't be true
At this time of night, oh how could they? I'm watching
  something blue!!
Well some cocoa, a biscuit, my bedtime, I feel tired, am really worn out
But tomorrow I'll be up bright and early, there's so much I must
  learn more about
Sylvia Robson

My Dearest Friend

Memories of all the happy times we've shared
You and I forever entwined by an ethereal ribbon of friendship

Daily I thank my lucky stars above for the
Enduring support and love that we share with each other
As soon take away my very breath, as to lose you
Remnants of our lives always with each other
Everlasting as the golden firmament, the precious gift we share
Secure in the knowledge that nothing will ever change
Truly soulmates who will always journey together

Friendship is such a little for such a huge emotion
Reaching out to find inadequate words to express the heart
Inspired thoughts of you take me through life's turmoil
Endowing rays of sunshine, like golden stars to light my way
Nothing can divide or take away such heartfelt joy
Dearest friend, I thank you for being there, for being you.
Rosemary Atherley

Senses

Deep, deep, to the depths I plunge, my soul I feel is lost.
Yet! In the darkest hour moves a glow from a creature in the dust
Its body, it is covered with slime and gunge and muck
Yet! Never faltering it struggles to escape this man made schmuk
Once free its pursuit follows the life that it was given
My lesson learned I now must give without the condescension
The gifts I have I must learn to use with thanks for what I've got
Sight, smell, taste and feeling, not forgetting my fading hearing
Combined pleasures undreamed of when I was down and out
Senses, once taken for granted these I must not flout
Passions rise, when music heard, stirs memories from deep within
My body aches for longing of those times not to return
Can I now retire, my body fading fast
just once more to enjoy my senses to the last.
C. R. Crockett

Remember Me

So brief was the time we spent as one,
yet eternity it will seem to me,
for even upon my death,
will it never cease to be.

Now upon this day my friend we part,
so fair thee well, keeper of my heart,
now once again I say to thee, remember,
even in death,
remember me.
Paul Anthony Woods

Awakening

A man awakens screaming, it's the middle of the night.
Yesterday he turned forty, yet he sees no end in sight.

He spent his whole life searching for something he'll never find.
When all he ever needed was right there inside his mind.

He's always focused outward never thought to look within
when there deep down inside him was everything he'd need to win.
You see if he'd looked inside himself, right there inside his soul
he would have found the strength there to achieve his every goal

We need a zest for living a life ablaze just like the sun.
So if your life seems empty, don't give up, you can do it, go build a better one.

Know as he lays there shaking, sweat dripping from his head
he feels a new beginning and a end to all this dread

His mind it starts a racing a review of all his life
from the day that he was born, and that day he meet his wife
he starts to look inside him a peek and nothing more,
but once you've had a peek there, you can't relock the door

His life he sees is not over, in fact, it's just begun,
and from that day and forever he blazes like the sun.
Paul Foley

Mango Love

Let we go down by de ravine and pick some mango,
Yellowy green and soft to touch
Dis tropical boy love mango so much.
We'd lime all day beneath those trees
Smoke a spliff and wonder
If we'd ever leave dis tropical sun
For a foreign shore
Where mango trees would be no more.
The lazy days and Island ways
Soon led us to another place
Where apple trees on a winter's morn
Hung with ice where fruit was borne;
No burning sun no humid heat
No mango trees from beneath to eat.
"I love you like a mango" she heard him say
And laughed aloud (as was her way)
But deep within dat tropical soul
He held her close and laughed the most
For even in a land so cold
Mango love had taken hold.
Nicholas Edwards

My Wife

My wife has asked me to
write a line, so easy, so easy that
is fine. We sit on a Sunday, it's
our lazy day, the rest of the
week she grafts for pay. Always
on the go, always on the move,
we listen the music cos we like
the groove. Paying the bills, this
is no sweat, with a wife like
mine I never fret. Often a
wince, but never a moan, this is
the wife I love in our home.
She is the one, that is the best,
all of the models they're second best
I hereby come to the end of my
line, devoted to my wife she's so fine.
D. G. Wilkinson

The Wonder Of Life

At birth we only know a small amount,
When we are five and learning how to count
Beginning to wonder of science, beauty all about.
As we grow, senses and brain cells mature,
Thinking of careers, family and the future,
Caring, creating and doing our best,
Then we can finally go for a rest.
J. Wilson

Eternally Yours

Far away on a craggy hill,
wrapped in cold lonely and still,
stands a figure looking out to sea,
I know that she waits for me.

She comes through the night,
her lonely heart aches,
hoping and praying,
until the dawn breaks.

For the sea is so cruel,
it took her true love,
so now she comes here,
my lonely white dove.

I call her name, she turns to me,
for she can hear but cannot see,
the time has come our arms entwine,
the lonely white dove is forever mine.
S. M. Smith

The Fete

The day was fine, we held our breath
Would it last forever,
Or would the rain come down again
On everybody's efforts.
Books and cakes were put on stalls.
Tombola drums were ready.
Floating ducks, toboggan runs
To keep the children happy.
The people came at twelve o'clock
They gathered round in clusters
And the children laughed as they swung high
And coconuts went tumbling.
Teddy-bears sat and winked their eyes
As if to say "come win me."
Balloons with tags, went flying high
To see which went the furthest.
"Hurrah" we cried, as money mounted,
And stalls were emptied quickly.
Our charities were helped today,
And everyone said..."Thank You."
R. M. Lamberth

"A Typical Week"

Mondays are always distressing
Work is highly depressing
Tuesdays aren't much better
And you haven't got any fitter
Wednesday, the middle of the working week
The weekend, you're longing to seek
Thursdays come, you've nearly made it through
But you still have some work to do
Fridays are always worth waiting for
The night out, you've been longing for
Saturdays are very sporting occasions
The night times are full of persuasions
Sundays are always for getting over the booze
Ready for the Monday morning blues.
Paul Goddard

Winter

Winter is cold and bare, trees stand tall
with nothing to wear.
The grass is short, unable to grow
just appearing above the snow.
The frost is sparkling fresh and bright
especially in the moon lit night.
The rain is falling to the ground
often making quite a sound.
The fog is thick and silent to you
won't see much in front of you.
The wind does blow with nothing to show.
I know Winters been but it will also go.
Pauline Taylor

'A Poet's Dream'

I have an ambition, to write a book of poetry
Words to show all those hurtful people, what I now see
It would be a book of inspiration
Dedicated to all those people, in every nation

For I have lived an emotional time
I'll show all these faces, the story that's mine
A story about love walking out the door
Then finding a love, that's forever more

I'm calling a chapter, 'The River-The Dance'
Every page I'm writing, while I have a chance
Yes, I've found this river, river of love
The dance I've been on, I've had enough

For friends like my words, I don't know why
Because I just think about the love I found, my life gone by
They said I should send a poem, enter a competition
Maybe they're right, the thoughts I have of poetry as 'my mission'

D. A. Morley

Coma

I was sitting by the fireside

Dreaming of the past
Wondering where my life had gone
And why my life had passed so fast
I am slipping slowly into dream-world
I think I've slipped too far
but someone is pushing me further
As if I'm being pushed up a steep hill in a car
I see the light ahead of me
but people are calling me back
But I feel I cannot turn around
I feel I cannot get back on the right track
I get slowly pushed towards the light
and into another place
this place is full of strangers
I long for a friendly face
Then suddenly I realize
I'm in my flesh no more
I'm full of spirit and of soul
I don't need to worry for evermore for I have reached my final core.

Mhairi Mitchell

Life's Looking - Glass

Through the looking-glass of life I peer,
Wondering, where I go from here?
My life, so far, has seemed so bleak,
Struggling hard, from week to week;
I ask myself "if there's any hope"?
For, with this life, I cannot cope;
I look into those tiny eyes,
Listening to children's bitter cries,
For happiness, love and affection,
All the world gives them is rejection,
I really want to do much more,
So many obstacles in life's law.

Michelle Moore

A Child

Never still, never quiet,
Wondering, questioning,
Finding dull things of new interest,

Quickly caressing and playing a game,
Innocent, loving, amusing,
Always a dreamer on a magic Island;

A child, a dear child -
The pain of bringing you into the world
Was worth the happiness your presence
brought to us
O child, dear child you are a miracle
itself.

Wendy Watson

Night Time

The darkness is upon us
The moon becomes our guide,
The stars pleasing to the eye,
A breath of fresh air becomes a yawn.
Thousands of lights burning bright
A cry of a restless child that calls for the comfort,
Of its mothers touch

A shriek of a tom cat injured by only its pride
Off in the distance the drone of nightclubs
And people sharing a laugh.
The scurrying door mouse whose lost its path.
The singing of a drunk who's bottled up too much.

Night time is upon us and we should not stir.
We dream of things that happen when they do not occur
So close your eyes, lay your head to rest.
For tomorrow's another day but night time's the best

Sandra Dyer

Different Worlds

Down in the bush where nobody sees,
Within the foresty outback of trees,
   Where Boogie-men's children run as they please,
That's what's down in the bush.

The scary things that give you a fright,
The singing and dancing all through the night,
   The music that plays on until morning light,
That's what's down in the bush.

We'll sit by the river and hear what they say,
And see what they do on a hot sunny day,
   We'll sail down the river that floats far away,
And see what's down in the bush.

They hunt in the forest looking so bold,
The clothes that they wear make them look cold,
   The words which they speak is a language so old,
That's what's down in the bush.

Maybe they're not magic, but clever and wise,
Because they don't have world wars and their spies,
   And they don't have a government telling them lies,
That's what's down in the bush!

Michelle Wilson

Beautiful

I observed his movements as he became wrapped
   within his own world.
His legs tapped and bounced as his body turned and twisted.
His shoulders curved over then back and from one side to the other.
While above them, dancing whisks of brown hair
   trembled softly upon his warm neck.

His arms weaved like wild snakes of both vicious and calm,
The obscure depth of his black velvet cuffs engulfing
A silken sea of shimmering sleeve, that transposed
   into crests of moonlit waves.
The contours of his caressing hands glided effortlessly
   through a tide of rhythm,
His fingers, spiders of endless energy, surrendering
   his heart to the expanse beneath them.

But the power of all his emotions radiated from
   and through his beautiful face,
As he passionately and gradually nuzzled his way
   into his beloved, gargantuan world.
Eyes full of pounding love slept softly, while
   their brows waved slenderly, tenderly speaking.
His lips sealed with a satisfied smile, glowed in
   the air of his melting soul.
He was hopelessly and devotedly in love,
   in a world, with the music.

A. T. Lias

My Brothers

I remember you both as babies.
With your black hair and big dark eyes,
I remember you both as toddlers,
Two happy smiling little guys.
  We spent our childhood together,
Fought and plated as sibling do.
Through it all I loved you my brothers,
And I knew that you loved me too.
  We grew up and went our separate ways,
Though our paths would often cross,
I took for granted we had a lifetime,
No inkling of my coming loss.
  Now it's too late and you're both gone,
I wish that you could have stayed,
I think of the hours we spent talking,
I think of the years that we played.
  Now I look at my son so much like one,
My daughter so much like the other,
And I know I still have you in my heart.
My dear little baby brothers.
  Susan Langley

What England Means To Me

England oh England how beautiful you are
With your fresh green fields
and your snow covered mountains
Farms and Hamlets also villages to see
Big cities with the power of industry
Like an artist of days gone by
Has painted a picture and framed it with
gold for me
The silver streams glittering in the sun
The golden sands kissed by the sea
England oh England
That is what you mean to me
  Kerry Ann Hodgkins

West Yorkshire County

West Yorkshire county is a lovely land
with trees and fields and a lot of lambs.
The springtime season is a fresh new start
when the crocus flowers and the tulip parts.

West Yorkshire county is a lovely land
when it's raining in April the thunder bangs.
And when it has stopped the sun shines through
and the birds start singing just for you.

West Yorkshire county is a lovely land
with the May day gala and a morris band.
Dancing in the street having a gay old time
with a glass of beer and drinking wine.

West Yorkshire county is a lovely land
in the summer meadows and the forest bands.
This warm season is the best you will find
for the DALES summer colours are just divine.
  I. Titmarsh

Transmigration

Life springs forth
Wonder and amazement abound
With linguistic skills this magic fades

In Summer love
The hormonal surge
Now demigod's, we shape to their needs

Autumn Son matured
Fulfilled or distant
The wise remain open

The fall to Winter hastens
Eternity beckons
In final sleep mystery resides
  R. G. Kitching

Illusion

They came like Thieves in the Night
With the mission of putting things Right
But Thirty years On
The job is far from being Done

When they Came
Everything was in Shame
Morale was Down
Everybody wore a Frown

"Please be Calm
We mean nobody any Harm,
We have come to put things Right"
Said the Fighting man of Might

Thank God! for the Fighting Man
But it was a flash in the Pan
For within the twinkling of the Eye
The idle years rolled By

Yes! Thirty years On
It's back to square One
  Sammy A. Adeyemi

The Bruises Of Love

A golden St. Christopher hangs 'round the neck
With the bruises of love in this burnt, twisted wreck
Of a car in a lay-by, the city streets left
In the rough blur of speed and the thrill in the theft
Of the skin and the metal, the ways that we've grown
In the soft Irish accent of you and the stone
Cold of soberness waiting somewhere in the light
Where the morning will slowly infect what is night
In our fingers, I want you, I ache as you talk
Of your childhood, your body the paleness of chalk
On a black, scratchy board in a classroom but this
Is the way you undress me, the way that we kiss
For our lives in the shrapnel, not feeling what comes
In the chill of this dark or the edges it numbs
From our senses, now touched by the dryness of rain
On our tongues to be burnt in slow colours of pain.
  Steven Howard

Spring Time

Delicate colours, covering twigs that winter left bare,
With sweet scented blossom, filling the air
Spring flowers showing, making their debut,
Adding fragrance and beauty, down each avenue,
Bluebells and snowdrops, enhancing the woods,
Branches on trees, spreading out with buds,
Already transforming, into beautiful leaves.
Soon to be changing, into all shades of green
A lark is soaring, above in the sky.
The hawk is gliding, searching with his keen eye,
Unsuspecting prey, scurrying on the ground.
Hoping to get back, before they are found.
The sun is shining, just over the hill.
Little birds looking for crumbs on the windowsill.
How fortunate are we, to hear the birds sing.
And also thank nature, who gave all these things.
  Margaret F. Curran

Untitled

Unstanched flows the crimson brook
With none to think or care of dams.
Or such mere irrelevancies.
All the globe it moistens
Trickling ever onwards with aimless ease, until,
In unnoticed quiet, it vanishes forever.
Sinking into sand and dust enduring.

Then expressionless features must twist with agony,
Tortured screams must shred the silence
And remorseless visions will pierce the dark of blindness,
As tormented anguish distorts all to pure pain -
Cruelly choking that limpid flow of release.
  Yvonne Parsons

Truth's Tapestry

Would that I too might make my mark
With poets pen upon this page
To weave upon this tapestry
The very essence of the thoughts
Which flow across the age!

A skein of truthfulness, unsullied
By the ingenuity of thought,
By strands and threads of conjured practice.
Allow the needle to find its course,
Its pattern and its matrix.

What beauty, ah! What ecstasy.
Alas! what truth the stitches would create
Within this frame of life now wrought,
With no protection from the glare
Of stark reality.

What colour thread the needle eye would take?
What form would this expression make?
And once his eye had rested there,
Would man but stare,
But never shed a tear.

Kelvin S. Thomas

The Cat

Sneaky hunter of the night
With padded paws you creep
By day it is a bird in flight
Now a tiny mouse asleep.

You love warm places
Sun and hearth
To follow your traces.
I would loose my path

You hide in the trees
And under the bush
Chase all moving leaves
Dashing out with a rush.

Weird noises bellow through the night
As with other cats you fight
When you are cruel with your prey
You catch them and just want to play

I scold you for the things you do
Your gorgeous eyes just stare me through
To win me over yet again
So all my scolding was in vain.

H. Compston

In Past, Our Love Lies Lost

When I was young you gave me hope,
Within my heart you melted frost,
Where'er I went you followed strong
In past, our love lies lost.

For decades half you dedicated,
Heart and soul without a cost,
The more you gave, the more I hated,
In past, our love lies lost.

And when I cried you cried with me
And when I laughed you shone with glee,
The quilt of all the misery,
In past, our love lies lost.

I stayed a child, did not mature.
Enough to handle one so fine.
You were too good, I was so weak,
In past, our love lies lost.

The clock it only does advance,
My heart forever, back to frost,
My life there is no second chance.
In past, our love lies lost.

Norm Elliott

A Lesson in Life

As I lay here thinking of you,
With my life - what should I do?
Throughout my dreams you're always there,
But until we're together, my life I cannot bear.
As I pray for our day to be bright,
And not for it to end in a fight.
I must write this on your 1st birthday,
Because I've got so many words to say.
The time together was so short,
But a lesson in life had to be taught.
Every day since, I've paid the price,
All I want is to see your smiles.
My darling son I love you so.

Samantha O'Brien

The Legend Of The "Forget Me Not" And The Middles Ages Dumb Blond

The knight in shining armour strode
With maid beside the pond
He bent to scoop the flowers of blue
Which matched the maiden blond.

He slipped and fell full length to drown
Sinking beneath the mire
His arms thrust high
His lips did cry, "Forget me not" "Mariah."

How sweet of him to tell me
What they're called, at such a time
The maiden thought, a smile appeared
Remembering he had style.

Her happiness endured this way
As life gently passed above
No mention of the brave young man
Who gave his life for love.

Throughout her life she often said
When e're these flowers she saw
On good authority I've been told
"Forget Me Nots" they're called.

Keith Arbie Johnson

Beauty In Prowl

He prowls in splendour like a king,
With head in stately grace and pose,
And stealthy step which treads to bring,
All manly might with movement froze,
In majesty in beauteous cling,
As manifest in combat throes.

The strength of muscle set to show,
All supple spring and heaving mass,
Which ripples through each mortal flow,
And raises above all with dash,
With lips that seal a pristine row,
That subtle bares with prey in clash.

The glory of his eyes of green,
Like grassy leas as rolling laid,
And clearest gaze that blinks in preen,
Which captures all and then puts paid,
To thoughts of flight when ever seen,
As once beheld can never fade.

A. A. Hopkins

Untitled

What of my tomorrow
what's in store for me
shall I find my happiness, peace reality.
Will there be hope and joy
one can never say
for I am here this moment
This moment is today

P. Burroughs

Time To Love

She was the alarm no man could turn down
With hands so soft, and a face so brown.
An hourglass figure - my heart did once stop.
The clock had struck twelve: tick-tock, tick-tock.

There followed twelve chimes of desperate yearning,
And twelve moments of erotic day-dreaming.
For minutes my weakened limbs trembled in fear,
For months I could watch this woman so dear.

The charms were numerous on my fabulous date,
And for a split second, the time was just 'rate'.
I would ask to snooze on her lap by the lamp,
And time would always be on our hands...

And the time would always be on our hands.
Philip Gaunt

"Christmas Time"

The howling wind that blows so strong,
With force that even drifts the snow,
To form or block mans passage along,
The paths or tracks that lead to home.

To home with warmth and family love,
The glow of embers in the heart,
The flame that dances in the grate,
Throw dancing shadows on ceiling above.

The Winters blizzard, icy and cold,
That blows and chills, both young and old,
Through crevices, nooks and crannies to,
And even keyholes the cold blows through.

The warmth within the family home,
Is one of happiness, love and joy,
At this the special time of year,
When all you love is so very dear.

The family ties are so very strong,
With love and hope we won't go wrong,
So blow Winters rage, for we are warm inside,
Against the elements that persist outside.
B. H. Brown

Marigold

When I was only eight, Nature Walks in Bradley Woods,
with dear Miss Bown, who had the gift to fill our minds,
that I still remember all she taught me now at eighty-one.
Not to disturb the common Adder and young worshipping the
sun on crumbled rock a bed of blending twigs like twine
Mauve Violets, Bee Orchids, Yellow Rattle, rose like leaves on
Eglantine. The day that's been a memory through the years of
growing old Goblin Green of Marsh Mud, guarding enamel
Yellow Marigold. Bemused, forgetting my new boots, the
grown ups thought my ankles weak into sludge and mud,
hands enfolding wet sappy stems of the flowers I seek.
A treasure of Golden king Cups for my mother, who did not
even mention the mud encrusted boots with laces, crumpled
frock, her whole attention was on the golden offering in my
hand, and the magic in my eye.
Now the years have gone, I am eighty-one, but to the child of
eight I never say goodbye.
B. H. Bucknell

The Flower Of Life

One day I saw a flower, growing in the ground,
With dirt and filth and rubbish, scattered all around,
How can this thing of beauty, live in such disgrace,
I'll have to move it at once I thought, to a better place,
I bent down and I picked it up, and held it in my hand,
But the petals drooped and wilted, and I couldn't understand,
I should have left this thing of beauty, left it where it grew,
And moved the things around it, and yet I never knew,
But isn't this the world today, we never stop to think,
We pluck the things of beauty, until they are extinct,
Why can't we leave them growing, as nature world have them do,
And move the things around them, for the sake of me and you.
J. R. Hayward

September Days

And what think thee, young Cuthbert, of summer passing by
With corn stacked thick on sultry fields, and orchards laden high.
Think not thee to stir thyself, to gather nature's gifts
Wherein the savour fruitfulness on winter's chilly nights.

The squirrel he doth labour all thro' a summer's night
His gatherings to keep hidden in hollows out of sight.
But thou, young Cuthbert, waste the hours in senseless lazy pose;
Think not that others'll pity thee, when hunger hits thy nose.

Out upon the moorland vast, the heath is purple-dyed,
And sheep do graze and scratch to fill each ravenous inside;
Their woollen coats to thicken, 'gainst winter's icy blast.
But thou, sly wretch, will not stir to stop a certain fast.

September mellows, till Michaelmas time be come,
And barns be filled, coppage stacked, and all be rightly done.
But it be not due to folks like he, a slothy feckless rake.
His days are sun filled, squandered, and no give, but all take.

Oh, harvest moon in velvet sky, with scented woodfire smoke;
With ale a-flowing, lanterns glowing, and many a jester's joke.
We merry shall be who've toiled so hard to off-set winter's chill,
But Cuthbert's thrashed with leathern strap and banished to treadmill.
J. G. Scott

The Holly Bush

Golden King and Silver Queen stand stately by the lawn,
With berries red and leaves so green, they greet each wintry morn.
The Silver Queen, one day she died, amid the snow and frost,
His leaves the Golden King did hide for the Silver Queen he'd lost.

No more berries were produced among Golden King's green leaves,
The beauty there was soon reduced, and the King was left bereaved.
The winter days turned into spring, with Golden King still alone,
Hoping that the summer would bring some life where the
Queen had grown.

Summer days began to fade and autumn loomed up ahead.
Where was his Queen whom God had made? Why was she
still lying dead?
Suddenly amidst all the soil, a shoot of green was seen,
Giving off an air so royal, it had to be his Silver Queen.

She grew so stately and so fair, the Golden King was proud,
For once again they both could share a love that blossomed
to the crowd.
United now they both did stand where clearly they could be seen,
With freshness new from God's land, stand Golden King and
Silver Queen
G. Reynolds

The Desert

Resting in my armchair
with a second cup of tea,
I look out on the scene today
and this is what I see.

There are dew drops on the thirsty leaves
everywhere is fresh.
The morning sun throws shadows
that seem to stretch and stretch.

The buildings once so square and clear
away across the space;
Now blend as hills a-rolling
on life's long busy race.

All is far from peaceful,
tranquil and evergreen.
For the sun is fast arising
destroying all I've seen.

Out there the dusty desert
takes on its arid shape.
All my glistening dewdrops
begin to look a fake.
Pamela A. F. Smith

A Wish Come True

'Twas on a mystery tour, that this Cottage, caught their eyes
With a sale sign, in the garden, (TO THE BEACH) was just a mile
They memorized the places, as they travelled in the bus
And began to count up what they'd need, there surely was enough.

For years, this ageing couple, had been longing for a place
Where they could while away the hours, and enjoy a steady pace
They imagined, seeing dew upon the grass, at early dawn
Then relaxing, in a deck chair, in the middle of the lawn.

They pictured in their mind's eye, lovely roses round the door
With lots of pretty flowers blooming, and plenty room for more
Some poultry, would be nice to keep, in a cree, just by the hedge
And a garden, at the back as well, where they could grow some veg.

Together, they went to the Bank, they'd help without a doubt
Excitement grew as they planned and packed, both eager to move out
Just looking to the future, and forgetting about the past
To own this lovely Cottage, was a dream come true at last.

F. E. Schurmann

China Dreams

When I reach the gates of heaven, will I find you waiting there
  with a hand stretched out to greet me, and a smile to show you care.
Will you know how much I've loved you, or will I merely find
  that the times I thought I felt you close, were only in my mind.
We did not meet in this life, and yet, sometimes I'm sure
  that you're the one true love I've known from many lives before.
The first time that I saw you, and looked into your eyes
  I saw the soul I'd searched for through a hundred different lives.
But even as I found you, fate once again stepped in
  as the Lord recalled your soul to Heaven to live once more with him.
Leaving me to wonder if another time will come,
  when our souls will come together, and our hearts will beat as one.
Or was it wishful thinking, were you just a china dream?
  A carefully created image upon the silver screen.
There is no way of knowing, I'll just have to wait and see,
  when I reach the gates of heaven, if you'll be waiting there for me

L. Wardle

My House Is A Nut House

My house is a nut house,
with a cat a dog and a friendly mouse,
that's a nut house.
Two gold fish, two hamsters and even a wood louse,
that's a nut house.
With my mum and dad screaming down my ear,
as if I couldn't hear.
That's what I call a nut house.
My sister stepping on my toes and my brother
pulling on my nose.
That's what I call a nut house.
The wood louse ate my bed so I have
know where to lay down my sleepy head.
That's what I call a nut house.
My house and I mean my house,
  It's a nut house.

Michelle Lees

Bag Lady

Saw you sitting there, all alone,
with no one to care.
Empty bottles around your feet,
Hands in your hair,
A whole world, in just one stare,
Expressions of despair.
Years of life, love, laughter and misery.
Memories in brown paper bags,
This heart cried out, but was chased away.
The only friends left in the world,
Pigeons in the square, Empty bottles
around your chair.
Past caring, Past sharing,
Just waiting for the day
that you don't have to wait for
anymore.

Sylvia Edwards

"Jimmy"

Many dogs we have had - some naughty
  wilful, but never bad,
We have loved them all, one by one,
Until their time on earth was done,

But the sweetest most loving dog of all,
  has finally answered the good Lord's call,
Our dear little Jimmy, dear little friend,
little Jack Russell has finally reached
the end - of his time on earth.

How we miss you Jimmy dear, but in
our hearts you are ever near,
As you lie in the garden buried close
we thank you for all the happiness and fun,
Your gay, merry nature brought to everyone,
Goodnight Jimmy a kiss for you -
We'll meet again when we too, are through.

Lucy Bass

Will You

My love
Will you come chase summer butterflies with me
and watch the swallows fly into the sunset

Walk along quiet Autumn beaches
and listen to the waves caress the shore

Walk through snow covered Winter meadows
and trace crazy patterns in the snow with our footsteps

Walk through the woods in Springtime
and search for the new bracken fronds

Will you walk through the seasons in love with me
to our own Paradise
Of twin hearts, twin minds, twin souls

P. Skeates

A Sense

If the care is deep within, then heart and soul
Will be torn from the torso.
Compress it, deny it, refuse its existence and life
Will be one miserable nightmare.

Conform to standards, don't rock the boat, a norm
Existence, accept the inevitable, smile with self esteem.

Close pure pupil, arrogance an ignorance.
Wear the mask of content, hypocrisy condoned
Vanity self styled.

Material are meaningless, happiness born not
Made, joy be the artery of life, the bubbling
Cells fused in the intensity of self sacrifice.

Martin S. Lownds

Poor Misguided Fools

Why punish the murdered or the terrorists?
Why punish the molester or the rapist?
They are only poor misguided fools
From broken home, so they break the rules.

Thieves run riot. Vandals run free.
They're the scourge of people like you and me.
They are only poor misguided fools
That are out of work, so they break the rules.

Women and children live in fear
Of sex offenders set free here.
Offenders? Only misguided fools,
Social misfits, so they break the rules.

Judge and "do-gooders" are afraid, today,
To make all of our criminals pay
For breaking our country's rules.
Or are they just poor misguided fools?

Warren L. Baker

Happy 50th Birthday

Twenty four hours are in one day,
Why do we not notice Life slipping away,
The minutes tick-tock, around goes the clock.

Supple and young, I'm laughing and gay,
Why do I not notice life slipping away
Goodbye my sweet youth, as I face the truth.

Middle age dawns, I'm 50 today.
Why did I not notice life slipping away
Welcome old age, the pain and the cramps,
Have I got time to laugh and to dance?

Forget about age, forget about woe,
Life is so precious I'm not really to go.
I have lots to see, and loads to do
So I'm hoping my message gets home to you.
Live life to the full, have fun and romance
Do not go to your grave unable to dance.

G. Haverty

Life

School to work to pension to grave,
Why do we live this life God gave.
I've seen friends and family pass away,
Throughout generations I wish they could stay.

But why do we come? And why do we go?
It's pointless life, and it's full of woe.
The rich and the poor, happy and sad,
I look at the rest and it makes me feel glad.

No job no money no hope for me,
All that I have is all what you see.
So why am I here I wish I knew,
How did we get here, just out of the blue?

No one knows why or where we came from,
But all of a sudden we die and we're gone.
But now it's time to stop guessing and get on with my life,
Face all the troubles and all of the strife.

Sabrina Ramm

Angry Heart

I can't understand the way I feel inside,
Why do I do wrong and put my love aside,
How can I begin, to love the one within,
How can I explain, all this anger caused by pain.

Sometimes in my life, I look towards my memories,
Sometimes in my life, I feel an emptiness deep inside,
Sometimes in my life, I am confused with all the strain,
How can I explain all this anger caused by pain.

Memories of love, can be of good times and of bad,
Memories of love, something I once had
I can't understand, my soul is lost but to be found,
How can I explain all this anger caused by pain.

To find love is to be loved,
To be loved is to see love,
Words cannot explain, I am the one to blame,
For all this anger caused by pain.

M.J.J. Gillen

My Cornwall

Spring flowers all around me bloom,
With balmy skies, no Winter gloom.
On towering, mighty cliffs I stand,
Breeze caressed with a gentle hand.
Below the sea is calm and warm,
With rippling waves from a distant storm.

I feel the Sun, and smell the sea.
There's no-where else I would rather be
This magic place that ends our land,
A beauty and majesty so grand.
No wonder that I've ceased to roam,
Never-more to leave my Cornish home.

P. T. Crocker

Never Had The Chance

She was put there as if by magic,
Why did it have to end so tragic?

Her time was yet so short, in her mother's womb,
She never had the chance, to let her little life bloom.
So many questions the mother did ask,
Like why didn't He let my little baby's life last,
Why was it her He chose to take?
And leave my heart here willing to break,
Is it some sort of punishment He's giving me?
For my little baby, the world did not see,
In her cot she did not lie.
Nobody had the chance to hear my baby cry,
The loss of her will always be there,
Why did He take her it was so unfair,
from her Mummy's tummy, she was took,
She never had the chance, to get a look
At the world, especially her mother,
Or at her dad, her sister or brother,
I don't understand why she had to go,
and the answer, well, no one will ever know.

Sharon Bain

Sadness

Willow weep, and let your boughs trail gently in the flowing stream.
Why are you sad? and does your grief stem from reality or fading dream?
Like myriad tears your leaves dip down and kiss the water's brow.
Oh, willow weep, but keep your sorrow secret any how.

Mayhap in years gone by you were a happy vibrant tree,
Your branches reaching up to touch the sky so readily.
But life's long span of years on you have taken toll;
and wearily you bent down low to shed your soul.

But you are, after all, a glory to behold,
Your twiglets with their leaves cascade down, fold on fold.
And like a maid bent o'er her looking-glass to preen,
You live to see yourself reflected, in the dimpling stream.

Susan C. Johnson

The Dream Of Autumn

I dream a dream of colourful trees
Whose rustling sound my ears do please
Of babbling brooks
And the cawing of rooks
As they rise with the wind and yield
And fly above the fresh ploughed fields

This is my dream of autumn
Where bushes hang heavy with winter crops
And the rain off the leaves gently drops
Here I could go walking
Just me and my loved one talking
Planning our lives just me and her.

As we watch the leaves of autumn stir
In the cool caressing autumn air
This is a dream we both share
A few hours alone just me and her

Rudi Moss

Norfolk Broads

Vistas of drifting clouds and wide blue sky,
Whose lambent light illumines changing scenes
From coastal cliff and Breckland waste, to streams
That widen into Broads where herons fly
With heavy beat, above white sails that die
In failing breeze. An ancient willow leans,
Age-wearied, into water; sunlight gleams
Low on the surface of reflected sky.
Distant, the Church towers, ancient and sublime
Sentinel the marsh where cattle graze
Or, moulded into mounds, pass idle time
Cud-chewing grass, while evenings' haze
Envelops all in shrouds, which ghostlike climb
To mark the ending of the autumn days.

A. A. Gray

...All I Can Do Is Wring My Hands and Write Poetry

You, my love are shining tree
whose branches reach for the furthest dream,
for the deepest thoughts and the highest hopes,
for the spurned love of humanity.

You, my love are ringing stone
that's washed away by the powers of the earth
to reveal its inner loveliness
to the world, in the dust that it soon becomes.

You, my love are a crying dog
that faithfully waits for its master's voice
to release him from his misery
with joyful, hopeful, homecoming cry.

You, my love are a laughing man
cut down by the wicked, unsuspected
death that stalks among us now
to raze to the ground who it searches for.

I, my love am a grieving book
telling tales of hope and love and death,
betrayed by the ones I relied upon,
missing you too soon, now all hope is gone.

Margaret Ross

A Mother

A Mother is a caring friend.
Who will listen to your problems with no end.
She will always be there for you
For she certainly will pursue
Only what's best and in your interest.

She'll show you lots of love.
Keep you from harm.
Always remain calm, even if she shouldn't.

Most of all, she'll be able to recall
What you did as a child.
To her, you'll always be her baby
Although she knows that definitely, not may-be
You'll grow into an adult.

A mum is always best.
There's definitely no contest.
She'll always love you more and more.
And you can always be sure
She'll be there for you
Every time.
Mothers really are divine.

K. L. Freudenberger

Dispensation

What hand applies the brake upon each past or present hour,
Who sets in motion seasons in submission, standing by,
Who opens heaven's floodgates, limits rainfall to a shower
Hand paints the sinking sunsets in a technicoloured sky
What call commands such constancy of tidal ebb or flow
Who lifts the sunken seed up to the lingering light of day
Who talks unto the thunderclap, be silent I've said no
Sends birds migrating off with songs of hope upon their way,
Who carries consolations thro' life's turbulence of trials
Floodlights the fall of night time with a silvery moonlit shine
Who turns believer's tears into a wealth of winning smiles
None but a loving heart of care with promises divine,
Who speaks to all who search for truth with honesty at heart
You'll doubtless find those joys God keeps in mind to give away
A treasure more than gold or silver safely set apart
A tearless morn, one final dawn, real freedom's everlasting day

Ron Mulcahy

What Is Christmas?

Who made Christmas? Who made me?
Who is Jesus? Is He the Key?
The Key to life, the Key to you?
The One that is there in everything you do.
If it wasn't for Him, we would not be free
We would not be sitting here, seeing what we see.

The reason we have Christmas is because of Him
Because He was a gift from God, our Blessed King.

We all give presents at Christmas time
And celebrate, with turkey and wine.
But does everyone know, exactly why
It is there every year until we die?

I shall leave you now with this thought in your head
It is something to think about, when you are lying in bed.
Just ask yourself one little thing
Is Christmas because of Jesus, the forgiver of sin?

Matthew Davis

Remembrance Day

Sleep on in peace you brave and valiant dead,
Who gave your lives for us. We owe you more
Than just a small white cross beside your head
To mark your grave upon some foreign shore.
You, who dug trenches deep and dark as hell
And from them fought, until your foes gave
You mortal wounds; then, to an explosive knell,
Mingled your blood within your self-dug grave.

What's left behind by those who gave their lives
Their Motherland, their friends, a mourning few,
Your comrades, brothers, sisters, mothers, wives,
And some left children - some they never knew.
And who are these who, dauntless, played their part?
Our common men and women - England's heart.

J. A. Blakely

The Sea

The sea laps gently upon the sandy shore
Whispering its secrets behind empty cockleshells
Each waves as it breaks tells a little more
But pebbles remain unmoved by what the tide reveals

The sea bounces playfully around the pier
Gurgling incoherently as ripples spills their tittle-tattle
Both ebb and neap disclose what's happened there
Yet still the pebbles wait while the waters prattle

The sea is restless now as it dashes on the rocky beach
And the surf is howling take notice of me
The wind combed rollers increasing the sea's reach
The pebbles begin to speak and the story is repeated endlessly

The sea lashes blindly at the old sea wall
Spray leaps into the air to tell the land, the fathoms tale
But Davy Jones' locker is so mighty, moody and all
And as the pebbles clash angrily, no one listens, it's all to no avail

A. Booth

The Beauty Of Nature

The beauty of Nature is there to behold
Whether we're young or whether we're old
Take a walk in the country and there to see
Creatures and flowers, the green of the trees
In Winter the landscape can sometimes be drear
But then a Sunset can make us feel near
To the ruler of all things, our Creator who made
All of these wonders we witness today
Each season has something to offer us all
The grey white of winter, the bronze of the fall.
In spring there is brightness, the scent of the flowers
Followed by summer with long golden hours

R. A. Worbey

Winter's Day

The water freezes on the pond
While wind blows through bare trees.
And pretty girls wear long dark skirts
To keep warm lovely knees

Cars make cold reluctant starts
Along the smoke choked roads
While lorries grumble noisily
Against their heavy loads

The old, push curtains to one side
And peer outside with dread
Youngsters snuggle in the sheets
And beg to stay in bed

Dad puts on his heavy socks
Mother her winter boots
They then put straw on the garden
To protect the fuchsia roots

The water freezes on the pond
No doubt that it will thaw
And fuchsias, shoes, and lovely knees
Come into view once more.
Stanley J. Whitehouse

Soldiering On

Life goes along its pre-mapped path
While we lead our separate lives
We are not apart through choice my love
And neither of us has died,
The children grow up without you,
eventually you'll come home,
Nothing can stand still my love
And all too often, I feel alone.
We cannot map our futures,
Just live from day to day,
Each time I learn to know you.
You have to go away.
Our love is full of miss you's
And signed with "All my love"
A hit and miss situation,
That we cannot rise above.
patiently I'll wait for you.
And when you finally came back
We'll spend some time together my love,
before again, your kit has to be packed
Mandy Short

Tramp

Watch me wandering down these lisping lanes
While cold winds cough and penetrate my veins
With sighs of solitude
  Breezes intrude
Upon the warmth of my coat. Destitute
and cold, they wrap about a lantern's wick
The rain beats down like a blind man's stick
Lashing at a face which it cannot see
The cold... the cold! This cold might set me free
I cough... spit
  The lights have a fit
As they wrestle in a sordid gutter.
Meindert Aits Jr.

When You Have Tried

When you have tried the booze
When you have tried the fags
When you have tried the gambling
When you have tried the jail
When you have tried sex with many partners
When you have tried the pills
When you have tried the drugs
When you have tried the clairvoyant
When you have tried the psychiatrist
When you have tried the Samaritans and
When all these things have failed
Try God.
Sheila Lucy Wills

Always Now

If in your hand you held the finger of time
Which way would you take it,
Backward to obliterate the pain of the past,
Forward to deter the heartache of the present,
Hold it still and silent on a chosen day
That each day remains the same,
Or let it uninterrupted move toward paths unknown
With knowledge mirrored from past and present
Vastly stored to conquer the present tomorrow.
Fear not the seeming speed of happiness
That stems so briefly the move of nightmare hours,
For does not time give space between each happening.
Tomorrows come in the guise of the present today,
To live through it, is that so formidable.
Laura McNeeney

The Four Seasons Of Life

I saw a daffodil today
Which means that Spring is on its way
Crocuses and blue-bells hue
Makes my life feel a-new.

Summer comes with all its glory
Uplifts my heart to tell this story
Roses, pansies, columbine
One look, to know, these joys are mine

In the Autumn of my years
No time to shed salty tears
Changing seasons on this isle
To seek elsewhere, be not my style

When Winter's here, I'll warm my toes
Sip the nectar from the sloes
Recall my life with greatest worth
Be thankful for my time on earth.
Maureen Weitman

A Seafarer's Lament

I wandered melancholy along the lonely shore.
Where you and I had laughed and romanced before.
The lights were dancing on the sea
The waves lashing endlessly against the quay.
Out of the misty rain a ship comes into view
Like the one that took me away from you.
It also took my soul, my dreams and my heart.
That finally shattered and tore my world apart.
Like the sun going out on my life's tide
Fearing that you and I could no longer abide
For never to hold you near again
Would only bring me anguish and pain
For amongst the flotsam and jetsam on life's rough sea
The wreckage of our love floats away from me,
As I walk along the old creaking pier
Without the one I love and cherish so dear.
My thoughts flood back to the warm Summer nights.
When we shared the stars and held each other tight
But that was all light years away
From this night so dark, damp, dull and grey.
Tony Holmes

Saturday Night Knows All About Reduction

Drive out
Where there's nowhere to go
From with to where to what
Enjoy
Me meagre
Malign
You no longer exist
Lover
Possible I'm
Potency
Overwhelm me
Overwhelmed me
Tim O'Neill

Sandscript

When the starlight traced the water
Where the wrinkled ripples kiss
There I saw your shadow falter
Near the lip of the abyss.

Then the moon rays - vesper candles
Whispered lace onto the shore
And the imprint of your sandals
Textured - out the dappled floor.

While the night air, scorpion-smarting
Turned in circles from your throat
And pain dulled into aching
As you quick-stepped to the boat,

Then the damp sand felt my limpness
And the salt spray shuddered shock
As I glimpsed the angel whiteness
Of your sail beyond the rock...

...Now, when starlight traces water
Across empty harbour floors
I can see your shadow, father,
Write my name upon the shore.

Ruth Joy Cowell

Switzerland

Switzerland oh Switzerland
Where the mountains and peaks
stand so high, and so grand,
they look so immense, untouched by hand,
the shapes seem to change
on that mystical range,
with the colours of day
or the eventide ray,
Now it's the place to be,
cause the air is so pure and free,
It's my favourite place,
See that smile on my face,
When my work gets me down
Never put on a frown
Just get myself into gear
Cow bells ring in my ear
To that dear land of fame
with the magical name
Switzerland.

Patricia Murray

The Sea Cat

Sleek and agile
With a heart of metal
She stands at the quay
In all her fine fettle!

Fully laden
Away she glides
away from Stranraer
Down Loch Ryan side!

Calmly down the loch
She goes; Purring happily
But round the Mull
See the sea in all its terrible ferocity!

Now the cat
fights and scratches:
The human cargo
Are sick, in batches.

In the calm of the lough
Belfast in sight
The cat can relax
It's won another North Channel fight!

Prue McCullough

Well Of The Dead

Upon a moor of forest spread, stands a cairn near the Well of The Dead.
Where the Clan did meet in full battle cry, saluting those about to die.
Shoulder to shoulder they would go, treading softly breathing slow.
Crossing bog and bubbling stream, on towards an impossible dream.

The English stood holding ground, sighting cannon until target found.
With cannon primed and full of lead, waiting for those who will soon be dead.

Cannon roar, and swirling smoke, the Clan surged forward full of hope.
Blown to pieces, defiant in death, they surged on with baited breath.

They never reached the English line, as history tells us time after time.
The ground stained red with drying blood, where the brave Scots once stood.
No cowards wore a tartan that day, no matter what the English might say.
A legend was born like no other before, of the men who died on Culloden Moor.

Michael Yarwood

Ode To Spring

The day is dull, and trees stand stark along the country lanes
Where is the light? That warm sunlight that cheers amid the gloom
Winter is upon us - the earth is cold and hard
Long dark nights that last till dawn, and start again at noon
How long it seems since soft winds blew, and brought warm summer rains
Humming bees and butterflies toiled in the warm hot sun
Gathering their harvest. Each and every one
Soon soft will fall like petals the virgin snow, like down
From darkened skies, that loom above, to cover all around
To warm the cold, cold, earth below like a thistle eider down
Then sleeping life beneath the soil will rouse and start to rise
To push its way up through the ground, its aim to face the skies
Then all the colours long so faint like rainbows will explode
Painting fields, then banks and trees, with green, and blue and mauve
All around the clumps of trees as far as eye can rove
Just like shafts of golden sunlight there between the glades
The hedge rows, then the gardens are filled with dancing maids
Above the trees a black bird sings at the start of day
A tender song so clear and sweet, enjoy it while you may

Priscilla Curry

"Promises"

Promises kept, promises broken, promises never fulfilled.
Where is the freedom and release?
Where is the steadfast love?
Where is the closeness, the wholeness, the joy?
And my own promises?
Tossed aside, ignored, forgotten.
Irreverently abused, half-heartedly made.
Behind walls of ice, mountains of deceit.
What promises can I then keep?
What promises can I then make?
And who will promise me what I cannot return?
There is a surrounding darkness, a clutching fog
No way in - no way out.

Oriel Wilson

'Life'

Life can sometimes get you down
Try to smile, don't wear a frown,
For in the midst of life you'll see
There's faith and hope inside of thee,
No matter what we say or do
The sun will always come shining through,
Live for today, and do your best
the gift of life will take care of the rest.

Margaret Dove

Europhile? Not I!

Oh England, dear England,
Where have you gone now?
Oh England,. great nation,
So sad and so bowed.

Wherefore the woodlands of which I once knew?
Bathed in bright sunshine where Primroses grew.
Whereto that cold stream; a gurgle, a trickle?
From which I fished Bream; a wriggle, a tickle.

Gone too is the pride in this nation, so dear.
No Dunkirk no Flanders, no Churchill's two fingers.
What 'Tommy' in khaki, which sailor's bell-bottoms?
Whose chest is puffed out to the strains of the Anthem?

Once proud Kingdom-state, laid low by decline.
Abused and neglected by a generation of mine.
No longer our flag; respected, revered.
Political correctness, the banner, I fear!

This child born in England; so proud and so strong,
Now sees this fine country grow hateful and wrong.
A true island fortress is England no more,
Ne'erless, I'm no 'Euro; just an old English bore!
   Robert Giles

"Good Sleep"

Oh carry me forth good sleep to lands unseen
Where golden sands creep silently to sea,
And tall palms rock gently to a warming
Breeze.
Oh carry me forth good sleep towards that dream
Where stormy clouds are ne'er seen,
Or pain of heart be felt
And time means naught.
Aye carry me forth good sleep on thy wings
That I be ready for the coming day,
To sit in pastures green
And take pleasure of that scene.
Yes I have seen and understood good sleep
The earth, the water, the rushing wood,
Where nature fills my dreamy eye and sense
To make me happy forever hence.
Oh take me forth good sleep to further dreams
Towards the realm of heaven,
Where angels dwell on fluffy clouds
And God awaits in his house.
   Thomas D. Green

Pigsties

People say the pig is a dirty animal
When you work with them you really cannot fail
To see they keep a perfect sty
They never mess where they eat or lie
Coats all white and shiny a delight to see
Lying there so comfortably cosy as can be
On a Sunday morning, some people came from town
I didn't know they were coming, wanted to look around
I showed them the farrowing houses each with a sow and litter
The weaner pens with fifty growing fitter
The fattening pens where they get their daily portion
The boer pens you entered with caution
When they had finished looking round they said they never knew
That pigs could look as clean as that, and it isn't just a few
There was about three hundred of varying age and size
What it must take to feed them all and clean out all those sties
When they were getting in their car before they drive away
They thanked me for my trouble and it really made my day
"You shouldn't call it pigsties" the lady said
"Just say four star hotel for pigs instead"
   A. F. Childs

Gardens

Gardens are beautiful heavenly places,
Where flowers and shrubs bloom all
Seasons of the year.
Birds sing sweet music high in the tree
Tops, a joy for the people who live so near,
Spring sees new life begin there,
Summer most things are full grown and in bloom
Autumn the time comes to harvest the fruit.
The leaves turn to golden bronze and brown.
Winter they fall to the ground and lay there,
Then the trees look so stark and so bare,
All except one and that is the holly bush
Ever green and lovely with its red berries,
To shelter the birds in the bleak midwinter
To sing us sweet music when spring comes again
   Olivia Belgin

Egypt

You stand in the afterglow on the same spot,
Where earlier the sun had sucked the sweat from your pores.
Now the stillness surrounds,
A breeze sifts through clothes chilling the skin.
Rising murmurs skim the hissing wind
Whisperings of long ago, a people mourning,
The passing of their king

You watch the painted procession
Radiating gold, turn towards the horizon.
Your gaze rises to the monoliths
Erected in their honour,
Silhouetted against an orange moon.
The incantations of long dead pharaohs
Surrounding you.

The lapping of the river against the banks
Brings reality.
The river boat blazes white light,
More murmurings this time
People in a party mood
Ancient kingdoms forgotten.
   R. J. Soper

With Eternal Love

Where do we turn,
Where do we go,
Now that you've left us and gone.
We've shed tears like streams,
And all had sad dreams,
That kept us awake for so long.
But like birds of a feather,
We will stick together,
And remember all the good that you've done.
So look down from the skies,
See the tears in our eyes,
As we ask the Lord to "Bless You".
   Roman Pobihun

Little Children

My home stands in a park
Where all around are trees
I work hard and do my best
For people I like to please
My grandchildren like to come and play
giving their mums a rest for the day
wiping noses and changing a nappy
I don't mind as long as their happy
Then tucked up in bed without a care
A hug, a cuddle and a kiss
Is something you should never miss
They soon fall asleep
With dolly and ted
in their little cosy bed
Now there in the land of dreams
With creamy cakes and pink ice creams.
   Sue Sims

"The Bide Tryst"

Remember in the days of dawn,
Whenever in the new spring morn,
You'd walk with me beside the stream,
Wherein we'd see the jewels gleam.

Remember how the birds would sing,
We'd watch them flying on the wing,
We'd see them show the colours true,
And shades and tints of every hue.

Remember how the trees would speak
As 'neath their boughs their shade we'd seek.
They seemed to whisper of our plan,
To spread the word of God to man.

Remember how we planned this day,
When destiny would have its way.
The time has come, the way is clear
For you to know, and see, and hear.

Megan Price

Problems

How bad do you feel when you go round the bend
When your minds in a muddle and you're at your wits end
Hearing eveyone's problems though yours are much greater
So sort theirs out first as yours must come later

Is there a solution I'm not so sure
Money would help but it isn't a cure
Do you scream and shout till your problems subside
Or bottle it up and keep it inside

These are reflections all mirrored within
When will it end why does it begin

You put on a show when people are there
So they never know because they'll never care

Malcolm Sargeant

My Head

It is the weirdest sensation to suddenly realise you are alive,
When you know your time has passed and you should have died,
Trusting your head again is the hardest to do,
You can take s*** from others and walk right on through,
But it is a never ending nightmare when your own head lies to you.

I am like a different person now
Because some of me is still dead.
I have lost imagination and wonder at the things loved ones said,
And sadly, the splendour and awe
That used to dance in my head.

I must bury a much loved one,
An old skin I now shed,
I miss him so badly, he owned half this head.
There must be a reason why I am not dead
Something's not finished, something not said.

I hope it comes back or at least visits now and again,
It guided me through darkness and helped shield me from pain
I long for its touch like warm summer rain,
Please call again as I feel I've been tamed
As they've erased half my name.

Nick John Foulsham

"Reflecting"

Fifty years have gone past,
What have we learned, as we hear of
another bomb blast,
Wars still being fought, people still
getting killed,
Watching the news still leaves one chilled.

Will we never learn, whatever, our creed,
To love our neighbour, and forget the greed,
Is it too much to ask, will we never be heard,
Just ordinary folk, spreading the word.

Margarita Reeve

That Old Feeling

What do you see lass, what do you see
When you are looking at me
A really old woman whose heart has been broken
A crabby old woman not very wise
Who's always got very sad eyes
Whose life has been hard till the end
Looking for comfort and friend ship that's true
Not knowing what day she'll learn something new
She brought up her children all on her own
Her husband he left her to cope on her own
She worked so hard from morning till night
Her feet were so crippled the pain in her head
All she wanted was to rest in her bed
Now she is older she lives on her own
The body it crumbles your bones start to ache
Just like jelly wobbling on a plate
Life is so hectic for a old woman like me
Wishing I was young again to live my life so free
What I would give now to do it all again
Instead of people looking and saying I sent she insane

S. Ramsay

Man's Environmental Folly

This earth of ours, must seem a beautiful place,
when viewed by aliens from outer space!
The land looks rich, the oceans blue,
The atmosphere seems fresh, with a tint of hue!
But not for long, will this be the case,
thanks to the stupidity of the human race!

The lush rain forest, greedy man is now set to plunder,
with no care for the environment, or habitat being torn asunder!
When all the trees are gone, will there be rain? Or thunder?
As the world looks on helplessly, in amazement and wonders,
Why the climate's changed from here, to down under!
The question is, will we survive? Or will we flounder?

The effects of global warming, will surely grow,
and melt the polar caps of ice and snow!
To raise the level of the ocean floor,
and cause destruction, death and much more woe!
The ones who suffer most, will be the poor,
while the greedy will always ask for more
And the rich don't care how they make their dough!
But will man survive? I really don't know!

Victor E. Lobo

Mother

To the light you will go,
where it leads to I don't know.
No one could take your place,
for you had an angel's face.
we'll meet again one summer day,
for this to God I will pray.

When I'm all alone,
I will listen for the phone,
that you might call me,
to tell me that you are free.

Your soul will always be with me,
through the lands and through the sea.
I will come to see you where you are,
no matter how near or far,
for you are not alone
for this is your home.

Vince Carrozzino

The Grandchild

I was having a bad day, feeling distraught
When out of the blue good news was brought
hello mum, you had better sit down
I have news to tell, you are going to be a nan
The months went by very fast
the day of the birth was here at last.
When the phone rang, it's a boy,
I was so excited and full of joy
All my troubles seem very slim
When he is in my arms and I cuddle up to him
I have to pinch myself to know it's real
this little child is so ideal
I look at him and I feel in awe
and can't wait for the day when I have some more
I pray to God for him to have good health
And hope he prospers and has wealth
this little person so perfect is he
he means the whole world to me.
Mrs. R. A. Rolls

Widow's Lament

How long does one grieve
when one's beloved leaves
how can the mind and body sustain
the overwhelming and consuming pain
desolate and lonely I go home to weep
but in my heart I have memories to keep
of the brightness and joy he bought into my life
I was his soulmate his lover his wife

I still have a function a role to play
though sadness and loneliness are here to stay
but the light in the dark is my knowing
he will wait for me with love overflowing
his arms outstretched his face I'll see.
When that eternal golden light comes to enfold me.
M. Wilkinson

The Stillness Reigns Supreme

There's a moment of Time in every Day
When peace will reign supreme
Like the stillness that before the rain
Comes late upon the scene.
Or when the Buzz stops and the
Pollen is draw from a flower
By a wandering Bee.
When the Horse drinks and the
Muzzle is dipped into a nearby steam.
When the weather is Hot and the swifts will scream
With an electrifying Burst of speed
But just before they swerve - they glide.
And the Stillness reigns supreme.
J. S. Games

A Little Child's Dream

Is there a valley in the sky
  Where flowers bloom and wild birds cry?

Will there be no more tears and pain
  But golden sunshine, gentle rain?

Will we see pets who've gone before
  Birds and fish, our dog and more?

I trust them to Your gentle care
  To share the joys and pleasures there.

When I'm a worn and tired old man
  I'd like to go there if I can.

And so, dear Lord, I pray to Thee
  Save a place up there for me.
Leslie Thompson

The War Years

Born and bred a brummie, it was totally different then,
When I recall my childhood, way back when I was ten.
Destruction was all around us, at a time when our land was at war,
I remember the air raid shelters, with a makeshift bed on the floor.

Little back houses we lived in, with a mantle we used for a light,
You could hear every word that was uttered, when we were tucked in at night.
We used the wash-house on Mondays, with soap suds a flying galore,
Us kids used to swing on the mangle, that's what we thought it was for

Everyone carried a gas mask, not a light was supposed to be shown,
overhead the air-raid warning, would be sounding all over the town.
Men were called up in the forces, women went to work on the land,
Those in the factories, turned out by the thousands, everyone lending a hand.

Food was scarce, for we were rationed, queuing for hours was our lot,
Down at the wharf, we foraged for coal, but slack was all we got.
But I want to forget the war years, the blackout, the bombs and the fear,
For the loss of so many who didn't return, is a cross we all have to bear.

We can now look back at things that have past, and remember loved ones who died,
We must think of the present, and live for today, our memories locked deep inside.
For things have changed and now we're at peace, a new generations took hold,
Yesterday has gone for ever, and we of the war years are old.
Lyn Harper

To My Son

What can I say, what can I do?
When I know that you
Are suffering too, beyond belief,
What can I do to give relief?

I pray to God, oh how I pray,
That He will give to you this day,
The strength and will to overcome,
The thought that you have wrongly done.

You could not know what was to be,
God is the only one to see,
I know you cannot understand,
But you must be guided by His hand.

Reach out to Him, kneel and pray,
Let out all you have to say,
He will hear and comfort you,
That is all you have to do.

The turmoil now within my heart,
Is really tearing me apart,
If I could bear this pain for you,
My son, I would so gladly do.
D. Jackett

Untitled

That dreaded time has come once more
We've just said our goodbye's
Again I had to hide the tear's
And stop them falling from my eyes

I feel so sad and lonely
When we have to be apart
But I know if you see me crying
It would only break your heart

We both know it's hard at times
But your duties they have to be done
And when there finally finished
Back home again you'll come
P. O'Donnell

Enigma

Turn back the page of yesterday
When I knew not what morrow bring
Let words I said be words to say
And I not tempt the sorrowing
That haunts the paths of haste
Turn back the pages one by one
Till each tomorrow no mark leave
That foolish deeds be left undone
And nought I do bring cause to grieve
Nor rue tomorrow's waste

Turn back the page of youth's fine dream
That we not see where future lies
Or tears that swelled the crystal stream
Where heartbreak waits and first love dies
On banks of innocence
Better now the future accept
And leave tomorrow's page unturned
What purpose served if tears are wept
For streams long dry and bridges burned
In flames of penitence.

Richard Davies

Ode To The Sun

In fancy I think of days gone by,
When from my window I'd see the sky,
At eventide, when days was done,
Such beauty I'd see with the sinking sun.
Departing in its cloak of gold,
Another country to enfold.
Alas, no more I see, the sky at night,
The sky scrappers hide it from my sight.

Margaret Docherty

"Penfriends"

"It's rather wonderful I think,
when friends are made by pen and ink.
A piece of paper, blue and white,
someone decides that they will write.
To someone they have never seen,
who lives where they have never been
a pen becomes a magic wand,
as two strangers start to correspond.
Not strangers long, but soon good friends
with each new letter and new trends.
Such a pleasure to exchange views,
And hear about the different news.
Two friends who live quite far apart
though who can gladden each other's heart.
It's truly marvellous I think.
That friendships can spring from pen and ink.

G. Dickinson

The Wall

Did you see their happiness, did you hear them call
When east met west again, beside the Berlin Wall
Did you see them weeping experience their joy,
But did we all remember a young and dying boy.

The wall was a stark reminder of a political disease.
Of unrelenting leaders, of a country on its knees.
Of families long separated, home life torn apart
Living in a country with no loving, with no heart.

Many tried to breach the wall, reaching ever high
Border guards just shot them, leaving them to die.
Their only crime was wishing for a life among the free
The things we take for granted, the likes of you and me.

So in the sudden euphoria, and it was wonderful to see
do not forget the deaths it caused, trying to be free.
All the frightened faces, watch them how they run
screaming as they fell down, the last sound heard,
"The Gun"

Nan Berry

The Loss

The life I had ended that bright July morning,
When death came without any warning.
No time to tell him I loved him and without him I would die,
Not even time to say goodbye.
Life goes on and must be endured even though your hearts aches
And you are filled with pain.
One day it will all be over and we will be together again,
Let that day come soon I pray,
I feel now that I have lost my way.

Raye Bamford

The Four Seasons

A favourite time of year is spring
when birds start to mate and sing
Frolicking lambs are such a delight
Emerging flowers a pretty sight

Summer months are far too hot
It's not easy finding a shady spot
And jumping into the swimming pool
The only way to keep cool

Autumn at last with a cool breeze
Temperature has dropped a few degrees
Beautiful shades of greens and browns
In meadows and grassy downs

Winter comes with an icy blast
And howling gales follow fast
Snow turns to sleet and icy rain
Time to look forward to spring again

Marion Beata Gunnell

Parents

I'm sure like me you often feel
When all is said and done
The job of raising kids today
is not an easy one.

I'm glad you're there beside me
To counsel and advise
And help me find the answers
To their never-ending "why's"

I'd be lost without your shoulders
So much broader than my own
To lean upon when problems
Seem to big to solve alone.

As long as were together
We can weather storm and strife
And take in our stride the ups and downs
That go with family life.

Patricia Dixon-Jones

Time On Your Mind

On this here cool and long single day,
when a month's a year and it's not yet May.
Clearly time's not fading fast,
when every second just seems to last.
I'll get you yet, I'll get you for sure,
the one sad fact, none of us pure.
Time is changing, and here you are at thirty,
wanting and waiting even speaking rather curtly.
Just feeling as if time has doubled on itself,
not going nowhere and affecting everyone's health.
Don't look back for a better future,
when the future comes to us for nurture.
Feeding minds in time for supper,
underhand manners just gets the upper.
It's funny how when time stands still,
and you have aged thirty years against your will.
Where did you go, can you please come back,
I've sure missed out, because while looking for you,
the boat in my mind floated out to sea, and the only
one to miss it was me.

Michelle Crawford

Seasons

Summer, autumn, winter or spring.
Whatever the weather I love to sing.
Winter snow flurries, heavy frost and high winds.
Much chaos on the roads it often brings
In the spring, I love to walk through the daffodils.
Across the meadows and over the Hills
Comes summer with the sun shining so bright.
The Hedgerows in bloom what a wonderful sight.
Autumn time brings forth the fall.
With no leaves on the trees at all.
The wind blowing in my hair.
My happiness is without a care.
For the sheer joy of living are very good reasons.
To the happy and contented with all of the seasons.
Rachel Jarvis

My Best Friend's Secret

My friend is ill and I'm trying to find out
What my friend's little secret is all about
I peeped around the door to look in his room
Hearing loud sounds of his moans and groans

I promised him faithfully, "I won't say a word
And to cross my heart I am honest as my word."
After a while we were discussing his problem
A boil on the bum was a great big protrusion

The doctors been, some pills he did leave him
And sound advice: he should sit on a cushion
For a time we played but it was just no good
A boil on the bum gave such pain when he moved

Boils are so painful if get them on your front
But a big boil on the back it is surely no fun
He did not cry much as he showed me the sight
This boil on his bum gave me a horrible fright

It took three days for the boil to disperse
That great big boil to him was a terrible curse
Take my advice if you have a boil on your bum
Have plenty of cushions having boils is no fun
G. P. Standard

The Joy Of Spring

The beauty of the countryside,
What joy, that she can bring,
The trees, the plants, the rivers.
The splendour of what is spring,
The flowers that bloom in all their glory,
The sunlight high above,
The power, the peace, the beauty,
All this is what I love,
The insects in the undergrowth,
The raindrops on the leaves,
The butterflies in the meadows,
And the birds among the trees,
Their songs of love as they sing,
That travel in the wind,
To walk the path of natures life,
And the love of natures spring.
A. W. Dodd

The Future

Little children, so trustful and true,
What has this world in store for you?
Will the forest be green,
And snow on the mountains white?
Will the winds be fragrant for your delight?
Will the white clouds be there
And the sky, oh so blue?
Will flowers abound, rivers and fish be true?
Will oceans be fresh and fruit still divine
And animals live all the time?
Will your health be as healthy or better than today,
Or will these things all fade away?
Rosalind Sparkes

Malignant Melanoma

At seventy six years from my birth I did no longer care,
what happened to this planet Earth, since I would not be here.
The threat of nuclear war seemed past tho' some testing still goes on,
With luck this planet might well last, till I am dead and gone.

Global warming so say most, will raise the level of the sea.
But though I live right on the coast I do not feel this threatens me.
The ozone layer is more thin, from CS gases in our sprays.
This thinner layer now lets in more harmful ultra-violet rays.

Since reaching my three score and ten I am more philosophic,
Such problems are for other men, however catastrophic.
I felt this opting out was right, but little did I know,
That ozone layer damage would deal a deadly blow.

A melanoma so they said, through lying in the sun.
In a few months I could be dead, unless something was done.
They cut the cancer from my skin and tests confirmed malignancy,
And one week later I went in, for further surgery.

They say I have recovered well, in spite of all my fears,
And on this earth I now could dwell, at least a few more years,
So after many painful weeks, I take a different view
Ask not at whom pollution strikes, pollution strikes at you.
Lionel James Hampshire

Them And Me

People passing by and stopping, some will even stare
What do they know, do they really care?

Just another drop-out, a social outcast, a disease
They don't understand, did they hear my pleas?

Childhood memories filled with sadness, pain, and fear
Alcohol and abuse, then having to face the shame.

Fantasies of seaside trips, holding hands, laughing and
having fun. Fantasies of love and warmth not yet begun.

Fantasies - that's all that mattered until reality
caught up and left them shattered.

What do they know, what do they care -
"Excuse me sir, do you have some money to spare?"

Why do they have to stop and leer, why can't
they stop and think, why I am here?

I don't want their cruel remarks, or looks of pity,
I just want "them" to understood "me" and cardboard city.
Priscilla Andrews

Looking At Things

As I look through the window from above,
What can I see
The light of the day
Which God has made,
my neighbours garden on either sides
Both with flowers and watering ponds.
Golden fishes moves within
little statues lay around.
It's such a beautiful site to see.

As I look from side to side and all around,
Joey my cat who walks along the garden path,
The flying birds and bees pass by,
Singing and humming as they go by,
So just stay for a little while
In the stillness and with peace
See the wonderful things
God has laid before our eyes
realise now how wonderful God is
This makes my life more wonderful and worthwhile.
So this is why I try to pray each day of my life.
Veronica J. Greenfield

Memories

Whatever happened to innocence? Where did it go?
What became of the childhood games we used to know?
The ha'penny rope from an orange box with which we used to skip,
The hoops we merrily rolled downhill; the spinning top and its whip.
Hopscotch played with a broken tile on neatly chalked-out squares,
In streets where lorries and motor cars were things which were almost rare!
Mud pies made in boot-polish tins, with daisies to decorate,
Marbles played on the way to school, which sometimes made us late.
Yet these are all gone, like the days of our youth, and computers are now the rage?
But do today's children derive as much joy as we did in that golden age?
We had no knowledge of sex and drugs, no fear of violent crime,
For these were bred in the future, in a rather more "prosperous" time.
Yes, we were poor as the world may view but we never lacked love and care,
And those who had more than others did were willing enough to share.
Yet every age has its problems as time goes on and we see
How some of the things we lacked in our day have come with prosperity.
But have we bartered the precious things, like childhood's simple joys
For the knowledge of what we were best without, which comes with more modern "toys"?
Such as "Video nasties" and books and films showing violence, sex and crime,
And is it too late to turn back the clock to that happier, innocent time?

G. M. Adshead

Life!

As one life ends another begins,
What are we all here for?
We live day to day wondering why?
Why do we live only to die?

Life is what you make it so they say,
Mine would be different if I had my way!
Life hasn't been easy or terribly kind,
But I'm hoping one day I'll find,
The reason we're here all of mankind.

Is there really life after death?
Deep down it's what we all wonder,
That when one life has gone there's another beneath
Or do we fade into the yonder.

Well I'll guess I'll just have to wait and see
Nobody ever comes back to tell you
Is your spirit really set free?
Or is this all there is for you and me?

Cave

Bill

Us kids would often have a grin,
When on the street we spotted him.
Bill dearly loved a pint of beer,
Then his legs would act so queer.

We kids loved Bill, he was so kind.
We often teased him, he didn't mind.
He'd look at us in a certain way,
How lovely to be young he'd say.

Bill was born according to God's plan,
A very lowly, a very humble man.
He'd keep the streets of our town so clean
That never a spot of rubbish was seen.

A man in our town committed a sin.
Bill was the only one who had pity for him,
And so from the pit of depression and shame,
He helped him to rise and start again.

Last Sunday morn as the clock struck seven,
Bill's lovely spirit went back to heaven.
God had some special plan in view,
Bill was the one God picked to see it through.

S. Fryer

The Beach

We walk along the empty beach,
Wet glistening stones lay at our feet.
We behold the clouds and breathe the sky,
As hand in hand my Son and I,
Walk on the beach.

Gulls sweep down and dip and sway,
Like screaming Valkryies of another day,
As if this were the best way to annoy,
The inner peace of man and boy,
Who walk the beach.

Majestic waves pound on the run,
To break along the beach and some,
Froth white among a creamy foam,
As my Son and I we turn for home.

This beach and sky, this gift to men,
Will remain to Eternity till when,
No man or son together be,
To marvel at God's gifts we see,
These will have passed beyond the reach,
Of Man and Boy who walk the beach.

B. J. Hart

Lost Love

And all those precious hours of sweet content
were they, alike your winsome heart, just lent
to fashion a heaven for a happy phase
in the soul of one, now, fallen from grace
grasps tight the past 'ere it quickly fades away
as horizon holds the last feint rays of day
loathe to let its beauty fade beyond recall
amid the deepening shadows of even's darksome pall?

The tree that bears our names in hearts
will stand a hundred years.
Grass that felt and heard our love
soaks up the bitter tears.

The lane we wandered hand in hand
now a lonely solitary walk.
Trees and hedges echo back
our fervent secret talk.

Summer, fall and winter
All their changes bring
And if time is really healing
Perchance - another spring!

R. Gillings

Agent's Calling

Footsteps on the path, I hear
Well, it could be my Kleeneze gear
It's Thursday night, it's six o' clock
And I hope it's all in stock

One sink strainer, a packet store
Even a draught excluder for the door
No 'Nesting Cats' well that's a shame
Who on earth will take the blame

Chase up Bristol and give them hell
Satisfy the agents sell

Thank you son, goodbye, good luck
but don't forget the 'Cookie Duck'

Call me sometime, I'll be home
but cancel please the Garden Knome

In five or six, "yes" that'll do
Nice talking to yah, with kind regard
But I'll be back, cos' times are hard

Noreen Tomkins

How Rich Am I?

Today is my birthday, you might say, "so what?"
Well I'm just reflecting, on good things I've got.
Jewels, there are many, diamonds and pearls,
but none can compare, with my beautiful girls.
Julie and Debi, gosh how they shine!
I really feel lucky, just knowing they're mine.
And who keeps these treasures, all safe and sound.
The chest in which precious things can be found?
Dave, he's my husband, lover and friend
It's his heart of gold that I'll love to the end.
So I sit here today, a young fifty four
My reflections are over, I now know for sure!
Money means, riches, power and wealth.
Treasure means
   Husband, Daughters and Health!
Pauline Jones

Measure

What would you like me to tell you today?
Well here is the measure of what I would say.
You can measure in furlongs and fathoms and things,
In poles and in perches in spite of no wings.
In gallons and bushels, in rood and in yard,
You can measure in metric it isn't too hard.
In hectare and acre and even in cubic,
(I wonder whatever happened to Rubik?)
We measure in inches, we measure in miles,
But the way that we're feeling is measured in SMILES.
Lillie Hodson

And The Rain Came Down

The sun came up beyond the Imphal plain
weak rays withering in the monsoon rain,
that cleansed the dead and soothed their
endless pain.

Kohima's freed, the Japs have fled, along this
road of endless hate, we follow with a common goal
into the sun and to the end and loved ones who await.

The thoughts we shared were soldiers' thoughts,
of going home ere it's too late, remembering too
when all is done, the one you killed!
A mother's son!
C. Kendrick

To A Nasty Morning When We Have To Go To Work

One early morning, an October day
We woke to the sound of wind and driving rain
Time to rise and make our weary way
Oh How we wished to stay beneath the counterpane

No word was spoken, as I could recall
As we searched our way through coats for our rain attire
Not one single fly upon the wall
Oh How we longed to stay by a cosy fire

Eventually we dared to venture out
To seagulls wheeling across the sky
To the hissing noise of cars as they sped about
As we picked our way through puddles with a heavy sigh

No bird was singing from a tree
No flowers to dance and say hello
No buzzing from a bumble bee
Just the bang of a gate swinging to and fro

Would we ever see the breaking of the dawn
How dark it was like the middle of the night
Would we never feel the rays of Mr. Sun
Still - no one could deny the lights were bright
E. D. Mitchell

Jamie

Now when the catkins blow
We will remember Jamie,
Small martyr of our evil days.
And when the snowdrops grow
an innocence, then will we grieve
For Jamie - little victim of our time
Smiling through the news
In all its ghastly truth -
That little boys can be so cruel
And silence his small voice forever.

Then as we stood - heads bowed
In biting winds, and heard the
Unfamiliar prayers,
Would we - when sunny crocus
Starred the grass - another cold and windy day
Remember Jamie?
And resolve that no more innocents
Shall ever fall sad prey
To wicked cruelty
And our neglectful ways?
Polly Wates

Jack

His name was Jack de'vere he was a friend and very dear,
We were sergeants and hell we've been through,
He saved my life more than once, as I did for him but only once,
We joined together, passed together, and also joined the same
   squadron together,
One day as we were primed to go,
His engine blew and he was left alone,
We shot up into the blue, at 15,000 ft it was not cool,
We got amongst the bombers late, and got a call to remake,
As we flew over the field, below was craters that looked like hell,
We got a call to land elsewhere, because Jerry had blasted it there,
We got back to the field next day,
I was told Jack had died in a very brave way,
He'd saved the lives of three very scared WRAF's,
By using his body as a wrap,
My friend is flying high in the sky,
While I'm left here just to cry, .
T. J. Cox

He Said He Loved Me!

He said he loved me, which I thought was grand.
We walked together, hand in hand.
We kissed by day. We kissed by night.
We cuddled up by candlelight.
We talked about everything.
Summer, Autumn, Winter, Spring.
When he said he loved me, I danced on air.
My knees went weak. I started to stare,
into his eyes of gentle blue.
I said I loved him too.
So why did he leave me and go away?
I still don't know. Not even today.
He said he loved me. I believed him so.
Why oh why, did he have to go?
Sharon Lydia Rowe

The Sleepers

It rained in the night.
Wet pavements and streets reflected the light
From lamps and shop windows.

And a cold wind blew
Chasing papers and cans noisily through
Gutters across into doorways
Where the sleepers are.

An occasional car
Homeward bound
Contributes its sound
And is gone.

Whilst the sleepers sleep on...
V. R. Mitchell

Serving Time

I have served my time since the day,
We vowed our love, and together we'd stay.
I often wondered how our love grew,
Through the pain, and the fear, nobody knew,
Competing, with another, I could have fought back
But a drink in a glass was your fatal trap.
How could my lover change in such little time,
Become wicked, hateful, and commit such a crime.
Your anger, you always would centre on me,
With the morning, came sorry, I love you, the pleas.
The cuts and the bruises they soon would heal,
But it's the hurt deep inside, you could never feel
I'd look at you sleeping through my blooded tears,
And wish your life over to stop all my fears.
Once again I jump to a key in the lock
My heart thumps, fears return, then comes the shock
It's not you standing there with that look I recall
But our son, he staggers, and slumps to the floor.
Can history repeat such a cruel, wicked crime
Is another love about to, start serving time.

Yvonne Stewart

Independence

You showed me all the kingdoms of the world.
We vowed fidelity, lifelong devotion.
But you have gone, and I can please myself,
Grow flowers, paint a picture, write a novel.
And maybe, sometime in the distant future,
I'll straighten out the chaos in the kitchen.

Phyllis Fountain

"Life On The Dole"

When times are low, no work, no pay
We think what's the point, to each new day
The skies are grey instead of blue
and luck seems to follow the same chosen few.
Try to look further than your own desires
Thinking of others can stir up the fires
There's always someone worse off than you
You may not think it but I assure
you it's true
We can all give a smile, help
others in some small way,
To give us a point to each new day.

Sue Hurwood

Our Son

You have the hair of strawberry blonde
we of you are very fond,
a little bouncing baby boy
to give a family so much joy.
Our days now nice and you are sweet
but oh! the nights when you won't sleep
they tire us out but we keep trying
to stop you from always crying.
We know through life we will have fun
because you are our loving son.

Kate Meldrum

Double Take

Russet red, gold green leaves, dampened by evening dew.
Walk in solace, peace, such stillness.
A sound, standstill, look, listen, heart beats, fast, faster, louder
Look eyes straining, searching, searching, nothing to mar the view.
Fear! Don't move, eyes reflecting in the sun, heart beats even louder.

Then! Life bursts forth, with such speed, no athlete could match,
With the grace of a ballerina, white bob reflecting in the sun.
Clears hedge, ditch, away to freedom. In my throat my breath I catch.
My heart slows, and fills with joy as I watch the deer run.

Cooper

Water At Stream

Water, water, what makes you so clear?
Water, water, you look so nice here
Water running down the stream
Where do you go after this lovely scene

Bye, love to see you again
Bye, love to see you again.

I go down stream to that lovely spot
That lovely spot where all of us go
Where, O where is that my dear friend
Tell me, tell me where do you go?

Bye, love to see you again
Bye, love to see you again

Down to Cuckmere Haven Sir
Down to the lovely deep blue sea
There I find me some new friends
Oh, Ok, I'll see you again

Bye, love to see you again
Bye, love to see you again

S. Richardson

It Could Not Get Worse

She sat in her chair, rocking to and fro
Propelled by the gentle touch of her toe,
A mother of four, a child on her knee,
Wondering what the next meal would be.
And where would it come from, she did not know
With no food in the house, and no money to show,
No credit for her at the shop on the corner
And a letter had just come, with a final order
Pay the electric bill or it would be cut off
And no coal for the fire, if that wasn't enough
Her husband out of work for over a year
How much more of this could she bear
It could not get worse, it had to get better,
Oh well she thought, better open the other letter.
It looked as formidable as did the first.
But I'm sure it couldn't be any the worse.
She read the small print, and nearly dropped to the floor.
I've won $500 in this month's premium draw.
She had cashed her few bonds and kept only one
You have got to have hope, for life to go on.

Catherine Bryan

Dear Mother

You deserted me when I was three,
Was it Daddy or was it me?
You never called, you never wrote,
Not even hello on a little note.

Where have you been all my life?
Are you someone else's wife?
What's the matter, what went wrong?
Twenty years is far too long.

You missed all things important to me,
Did you know I have a family?
You're now a granny, I wonder if you knew,
But then again, they'll never know you.

You may be my mother, but I don't know you,
You've never been there for me to talk to,
You don't even know a thing about me,
That really hurts but you just can't see.

Maybe someday we'll eventually meet,
In my dreams or in the street,
To be quite honest, I don't give a damn,
Until then dear Mother, I'm happy as I am.

Sarah Li

The World Today

The gentle pace of yesteryear, seems far away today,
We now, forever, live in fear,
and only the victims pay.
Whilst villains, sneer, and glower,
because they are set free.
To carry on, their mindless power,
and live, with villainy.
Where are the happy care free days,
When man's home, was his castle.
Not a place for thieves, and thugs.
Who cause so much stress, and hassle.
Where is the integrity, the kindness and the caring.
Which we all, once took for granted,
along with a wealth of learning.
So when the sunbeams fade away,
and shadows seem to fall,
let us remember, the good old days,
or are they, beyond recall.

A. Chamberlain

"Peace At Last"

We think of you, and smile,
We loved you for a very long while!
Your face appears
Our eyes fill with tears!
We see you in the clouds
We hear you on the sea!
We sometimes see you in a crowd
You're still with us; you see!
Our memories of you, will never die
They grow more precious, as time goes by!
As we get older, although we're apart
You'll always hold a place in our hearts!
We remember good times, as well as the bad
Forever we'll be your "Mum and Dad".
Your pains are over! All troubles past
Sleep peacefully dear son, you've found "Peace at last"

R. Ninnis

The Old Ford

At eventide we strolled along,
We listened to the skylark's song
Summers's here he seemed to say
Tomorrow will be another day.

Hand in hand or arms entwined
We never stopped to look behind.
We were all enhanced with each other's love,
We did not see the turtle dove.

At last we reached the water's edge,
Each other's love we did pledge,
We saw the glistening water's flow
There's a trout - where did he go?

But now I go there all alone
Because my lover has gone home
So when I feel upset and bored
I still visit, that Old Ford.

Bethany Jade

Country Wind

Eat and lay, eat and lay,
We know not of a night and day,
Cast us to the wily fox
Better fate than our coffin box,
A hostile cage, forsaken tomb
Of fetid air and death, no room
To brood, no farmyard fair
For us, no summer sun or country air.
Eat and lay, eat and lay,
Plumage plucked as senses stray.
Tiers of poultry, sardine-tinned,
To you, the smell on a country wind.

Sue Richards

World War II

When Hitler attacked - nearly everyone in sight
We knew too, we were in for a fight...
And the Americans came over in '42
Because they knew there was a job to do.

Thousands of our Forces took a chance...
By invading the coast of Northern France.
Fierce fighting ensued... every inch of the way,
With battles by night as well as by day...
Triumphant at the end, with the German War won...
Winston Churchill made a speech and declared 'WELL DONE!'

Then to the Far East we were sent -
To India and Burma we reluctantly went...
We chased the Jap from Assam to Rangoon,
In temperatures topping 100 (F.) at Noon.
The Japanese were retreating fast...
And, as those tedious days passed...
...A 'plane was approaching high in the sky,
With a bomb to drop - and thousands to die...
Many thousands of people will cry..
And millions, will forever, ask why...

Mrs. G. F. Ratcliffe

Please Forgive

Please don't cry little children
We hear your tears, everywhere
Try to forgive mankind
Always to late to the rescue
With your little tummies swollen
Pain and sorrow in your hearts
We can not blot out all your bad memory's
But maybe bring about a new birth
Where starving and bad memory's
Will never live
So that your new birth
Will sing and laugh again
Please forgive

B. Moreton

Willing Workers

We travelled around looking, a job for us
We even used the resort's free bus,
A job to find me we're ready and itching
A hotel bedroom, bar or even the kitchen.

We visited France, Portugal and even Spain
Austria, Switzerland and then France again,
We found our visits were at the wrong time
Even the smallest of countries called Liechtenstein

We saw all the sights like hills, trees and flora
Including 4,000 Metres UP in Andorra,
With no work around we began to bend
So to England for help we had to send.

T. C.

Dream

A dream is of hope of day to day life.
We dream happy thoughts but will those dreams come right.
   Give me a picture of everyday life.
Fill it with love to a bright shining light.
Look at the night at the stars shining bright.
Daze to the moon or the sky of the night.
Think of those moments coming alight.
   One fluffy cloud and in it is a wishful
Through will we dream forever or not.
   Do we carry our dreams forever
To a new life or do we forget in one single fight.
   Dreams are with us as one keep to our hearts
    for everyone.

M. Jackson

Bully

Along the roadways on the awkward linen-backed map,
was familiar handwriting. Unexpected.

The hand of someone uncomfortable with language.
Hesitant, the pen had moved up and down
above the paper more than
it had touched its surface.
Making uncertain marks as if doubtful of his ability
to create recognizable letters
or to form the familiar shapes
which make words.

The pen just brushed the surface,
the ball in its tip
revolved but picked up minimal ink.
Curly, fanciful, writing,
heavily slanted to the right,
like his opinions.

The apathetic ink,
in fine loops and fanciful capitals,
merely rested on the surface.
No impression.
   Sheila Gorman

Deep In Thought

Browse through the "daily's" read what's happening,
Wars, battles, bombs and personal attack,
Navy ships, submarines, jets and army tanks,
Heavily responsible for reducing the ranks,
Someone's little boy or girl, won't be coming back.

Turn a page, there must be more to life,
Violence, murders, cruelty and rapes,
Death, destruction, pestilence and disasters,
Scarred forever, never the same, the victim-
Someone's brother, sister, mother or father.

Throw it down - pick it up - turn another page,
Vendettas, fights, muggings and thieves.
Stabbings, abuse, injustice and disease,
Turn another page, begin to fill with rage,
Racialism, arson, blackmail, more of the same.

Rip it up, screw it up, finally discard it -
Whatever happened to love, respect for each other,
Where is the sense, the love, the joy,
Friendships gone, love versus hate, brother against brother,
If this is the news - God help us all.
   K. C. Curtis

Tip-Toe

Tip toeing - along the sand
Warm - ticklish - soft
Sand golden in colour
Washes over tiny feet...

Sprays of sea salt touches one's nose
Smells oh so fresh - so sweet - so clean
Sea gulls are singing to the Gods of nature
As the sun raises - setting on the horizon...

Tip toeing - along the sand
Shells and pebbles
Beckoning to be touched - yearning to be seen
In the palms of my hands they sparkle - like crystals...

Echoes of the waves - powerful against my ears
Roars - proudly
Like a deep blue magical carpet
Oh - how the sea dances...

I watch - as the sun goes down
Leaving a rich warm glow - over the horizon
Not wanting to break the spell
I tip toe gently - along the sand...
   Sylvia E. James

Kitty

Cute little Kitty all covered in fur
Warm little Kitty with the gentle purr
Sweet little Kitty just lying there
All curled up in the fire-side chair

Sleepy little Kitty all snuggled up tight
Lazing in the glow from the fire light
Pretty little Kitty all fluffy and soft
Should be catching mice up in the loft

I wanted to move Kitty from her cosy seat
So I sneaked upon Kitty and tickled her feet
Poor little Kitty woke with such alarm
That she jumped off the chair and scratched my arm

I'm sorry little Kitty for frightening you
It's something Mummy told me not to do
So sleep little Kitty you'll come to no harm
I'm only sitting watching you while nursing my arm
   Shona Dunlop

Life At Its Best

Have you ever had the feeling, of being all alone,
Wanting to share your problems, in the quiet of your home,
Yearning to laugh at moments, when life is at its best,
Joking with a partner, or even with a guest.

Taking a few moments, to think about the times
Remembering the old days, when worrying was a crime;
I never like to look back at how I use to be,
My life now is so fruitful, a son, a daughter makes three.

We are so very happy, a family, we are one,
Sharing our lives together, a pleasure it's become.
To sit around at meal times, discussing all our days
Solving each others problems, and offering our praise.

We argue when we're tired, mornings just don't suit,
So we move around the kitchen, all remaining mute.
We have our different interests, thank goodness that we do,
It keeps us individual and interesting too.

For us there is no age gap, (or so I'd like to think!)
Without the love we offer, our hopes would truly sink.
So when I start to think about, how quiet it would be
Peaceful times, but loneliness...oh no! It's not for me!
   Karen Smith

Chasing My Thoughts

I wonder why - I wonder why my thoughts must run along and
wait not to be harnessed or set in train, but go careening off
In another new vein, and so on, just to the Junction.

Is this just dreaming? building castles and domes, as fresh thoughts
come along, and jostle or roam, away from the forerunners of
Reason and Logic

I'll follow this one - no that, says my heart, but this one will
bring satisfaction
Alas and alack, I must not get slack, since time marches on
and will not tolerate any treason
So away with you now, and make the most of the view
and take every time some good reason.

But my heart says 'Let be', and my head gives assent, so off
on a joyful ride of nonsense I'm bent
This way and that they lead me astray - creeping in here, then,
away oh, away. What a dance - what a flutter, first a sunbeam,
then a shutter, closed down - no way, - no where - no how.

"Follow me" whispers humour - "yes do!" calls out guile
"Just come with us both - we will amuse you a while"
Then Hither and Thither - like bright lights flashed along to
give some little meaning to life, some sweet song, the why,
and the wherefore, we'll leave for today, and saunters along
in mild disarray
Until - we reach - a Synapse.
   J. Smith

Silence Is Golden

Away from the traffic
Walking through a pathway in the countryside
Smelling and breathing in the fresh air
Having a peaceful moment
Not a sound of noise
From surrounding cities
Looking beyond the hill and trees
Hearing the whistling of the birds
Perching on the branches
Watching every creature
Roam across the fields and skies
With a sheet of a turquoise blue sky
In the heavens above
With no noise at all
Silence - no hassle - no rushing about
To wherever we go
'Tis golden
A moment's peace
Within the Creator's creation
Marilyn Clevett

Lovers in the Spring

Lovers meeting, lovers greeting,
Walking hand in hand,
Birds are singing, hearts are winging,
Into wonderland,
Sun is shining, arms entwining,
Lips are pressing, lips caressing,
Time is standing, understanding,
Lovers in the spring,

Time drifts by in a golden haze,
Two hearts in love, dream of future days,
Anything is possible, everything is clear,
Warm and tender thoughts, hiding all their fears.

Cool evening breezes blowing,
Shadows growing long,
Sweet dreams are fading,
Sadness sings its song,
Parting is a sorrow,
Tears are very near,
Goodbye, until tomorrow,
Quiet whispers you can hear...
K. L. Pusey

My Thoughts, Watching Seagulls In Eastbourne

We shouldn't laugh at the birds and bees the way they
walk then fly for they are only a good example of how
we live and survive, when the world began and they were
food for man, the fear had not subsided yet, so the
only way on a worrying day was to take off and fly away.

I'm looking for examples for how we are today, and what
we do when life gets hard to take the pain away, we
do take off and fly away and we usually go to Spain,
we take a package holiday to smooth away our pains.

For others who can't afford to fly it's usually on a
train, they buy a ticket to London and never come back
again, so we shouldn't laugh at the birds and bees.
Their smarter than you think, for they can fly and hover
high, the troubles down below, so rise above your
heartaches and wait until they go.
Kenneth Harris

A Dirge Of Winter

The black crow and the white gull wheel in the leaden winter sky,
Trying to escape the unforgiving frozen ground,
No tasty carrion or festering rubbish
Greet the hungry gaze of the scouring eye.
Upward and outward the scavengers roam,
Food must be found before returning home.
Their harsh unremitting call
Emptily echoes around the snowy pall.
Black feathers, white feathers, colour matters not.
As the frozen birds fall to the ground,
Snow makes an impartial shroud.
Mary Osborne

A Morning's Wind

The man stands on the street corner of his life
Waiting for the new day's bus to take him to his work,
'Hell', he thinks, 'It's an awful windy day today',
And he is glad it's a June wind and not a January's.
The wind blows an empty carton along the pavement
Until a bush reaches out and captures it.
The carton wants to skip and dance in the morning's wind,
But the bush won't let it go:
And the man thinks, 'The work won't let me go'.

The wind rolls the bus down the street,
And the carton calls to the wind and the wind sets it free.
And the man thinks, 'If the wind blows me under the bus
I, too, will be free'.
But he boards the bus and sits in the back seat
And calls to the wind through the window,
'You keep your freedom - I like it this way'.
And the wind blows the sky spider's spinnings from the sun
And laughs at the morning's joke!
Roy Orpwood

Life's Reflections

Life is like a waking dream
Visions of the future
Remain to be seen

With each new day
We learn some more
As if to open, a closed door

We look and listen all around
And marvel at every sight and sound

People of every walk of life
They all share trouble and strife

Good times, bad times
Highs and lows
The years pass by
That's how it goes

Each year passes faster than the last
What was the future is now the past

Make the most of every day
For they are never here to stay
S. P. Davis

Last Leaf

Autumn leaves are falling fast and winter rushes on,
Very few withstand the blasts that usher it along.

Soon, too soon and all forlorn
  on some forsaken tree
A last lone orphan of the storm
  will hang precariously.

No longer in its emerald green,
  no longer firm and crisp,
Its shrivelled form will now be seen
  a brownish golden mix.

So too, the millions world war one
  enrolled within its ranks.
The years pronounce their season gone,
  dim eyed and shrunken shanks

Once button bright and in their prime
  they marched to fife and drum,
But in the withering blasts of time
  they perish one by one.

So where is he who will outrun these veterans of the past-
  Survive a countdown - three, two, one - and be proclaimed the last?
G. H. Alexander

My Gentle Friend

You're a very gentle person,
very caring through and through
I hope I'll never hurt you, like so many others do.

Your gentle ways, they please me
It's unusual to find, a man who is so caring so loving and so kind.

You're so thoughtful and considerate
Your manners are superb
A rare and beautiful quality
in a man who's had to learn

Some people take advantage of your nature and your ways
They think you're soft and use you
But, they're numbering their days.

For friends like that
You'll do without, don't need their wicked ways
For goodness prevails it always will
You'll win at the end of the day.

Don't ever change, my gentle friend
It's a pleasure knowing you
I hope we'll be friends for a long long time
As I trust that you do too.

M. Little

Mothers

We tend to think we're not worth much,
Us mothers, we have no skill,
Well, no 'O' or 'A' level passes to prove we fit the bill.
But we don't do a bad job, let's face it,
We make quite a good cup of tea,
We vacuum, dust and polish, for one and all to see.
There's the washing to do and the beds to make
And woe betide if weave not baked a cake.
Have you fed the cat? Taken the dog for a walk
What have you done Mum apart from talk?
Is the dinner ready, did you iron my shirt,
There's another voice calling, out for a skirt.
The phone is ringing, there's a knock at the door.
Mum, will you fetch little Johnny at four
And Mum while you're out will you pop to the shop
I really won't have time to stop
Amidst all the hustle and bustle of life
And sad account of constant strife
I lift up my eyes and see Gods face
And thank him for his saving grace.

Ruth Attwood

Old Cob Wall

Old cob wall have fell at last
us knowed he might, a good while past
great grandad, he built thicky wall
with maiden earth, and oaten straw,
he built them in the good old way
and there he stood, until today
but wind and rain and frost and snow
have all combined together, to lay him low
us propped him up, with stones and 'ood
us done our best, but twernt no good
he lived a bit, and then a lot.
and at the finish
down he squat

F. T. H. Pratt

To A Dead Son

My wish is to walk on the path by the burn,
Under the trees, with those I love and they children again
Running and laughing and going on ahead, ever to return
Crying "see, look what I've found" joyous come sun come rain

What foolishness is this? My children all are grown.
Time cannot come again, once it has fled.
And one, whose happy years too soon have flown,
To whom, when young, a golden boy
All life was pleasure and each day was joy,
He - he is dead.

J. M. Thomas

Easter

They called Him "King" as he passed by
Upon the little colt,
And spread their clothes and leaves of palms
At every stop and halt.

What empty words, what false delight
Did sear that tender heart
All this, and Calvary's awful pain
Which thorns and nails impart.

His body lay in Joseph's tomb
In death, now all alone
But angels came on that third day
And rolled away the stone.

Then Mary, she who washed His feet
With tears and ointment rare
Was weeping at the tomb, and thought
She saw the gardener there.

What joy - when He whom she had loved
So softly spoke her name
For lo! Upon that Easter day
Her Lord had risen again.

Muriel B. Thorneloe

Choices.....

When I look back in years to come
Upon my toils today in your employ
Will I be smugly counting out the sum
Of men's spirits it was my duty to destroy?

When I sit back at evening time and smoke,
My pension banked, my limited future sure,
Will I admire the commercial master stroke
Or will the friendless mist lose its allure?

When death approaches fast, then will I need
Redemption, will I feel I've sinned?
Or will I justify it as some others greed
And leave this mortal coil just as thick-skinned?

To trample or be trampled seems the choice
Blood spilt to pay the millstone mortgage
In dreams will I awake to hear an old friends voice
But turn too late to save the flaming bridge?

Can I still exorcise the beast or must I pay
For my misguided corporate impropriety?
I no longer wish to invest another day
In the crumbling Empire Building Society.

Stephen Leeves

The Dry Temptress

She dances high with cruel intent,
Upon ballrooms watery element.
To lure and tantalize the trout,
Their certain downfall bring about.
Hidden beneath her pretty skirt,
A dagger sharpened there doth lurk.
Skid and skate and bob and prance,
A Jezebel the beguiled to lance.
How can they not befall her spell,
When she her charms doth ply so well.
Seal fur gown and furnace wrap,
Lace of wing and bustle dap.
Her hackle points like thistle down,
Summer ballerina without a frown.
For all her wiles and mystique spice,
A spotted suitor she fails entice.
And now her waltz is all played out,
No besotted lover no foolish trout.
Her one chance gone to commit a crime,
Now chase her escort latent line.

R. J. Charlesworth

New Zealand, Land Of The Long White Cloud

O'land apart, flung recklessly
Upon a sea of boundless waste,
Warmed by tropic suns, fanned cool
With breezes from ice capped regions chaste.

Endowed by nature with such gifts,
Clothed you in a growth to yearn,
Through the centuries, an evergreen laced
Filigree of bush and fern.

Mighty Kauri, a thousand years thy span,
Monarch o'er giant bush clad land,
Lowly pungas unfold their fronds,
As in obeisance, beneath you stand.

Long beaked birds the bush to haunt,
To pluck the berries and pry
The insect from its niche, with stately Moa
And Kiwi small, their evolution try.

Depths off shore with bounty stocked
Fresh waters, virgins pure with endless font,
Roar, cascading fall, past hill and plain,
The sun a God, their ceaseless want.

K. W. Carter

Fatherhood Dawns

I watch your face my love, as I hand to your our child.
Unguarded mixed emotions in your eyes, although you smile.
A boy yourself until this day, you now hold in your arms
Another life, who looks to you to shield her from all harm.
Your hands so large and work-worn, hold her tiny being
With love and gentle tenderness for this miracle you are seeing.
I know what you are thinking, you were hoping for a son,
A lad to be best friends with, to talk to and have fun.
But look, her eyes are open, she is gazing up at you,
Taking in your features and frowning, wondering who
This tall and serious man is, cradling her with care.
But instinct from the dawn of time has made her well aware
Of the power of a woman, from the moment she sets eyes
On the man she means to captivate, to love her 'till he dies.
She smiles, she flirts, her little hand reaches out and up to you
She wants your heart forever, and you give it - happy to
You kiss those chubby fingers, and tears well in your eyes,
To you she is the loveliest, an angel from the skies.
I know now, from this moment, this is how it's going to be
Daddy's girl forever more, a family now, we three.

E. June Hope

The Quiet Life

Grant me an ordinary day, Lord,
  Uneventful and mundane,
No dramas or crises please, Lord,
  Then You won't hear me complain.
I've had my fill of excitement, Lord,
  Now it's the quiet life for me -
Some people would be bored, I guess,
  But that's something I'll never be.
Just let me wake to a nondescript day,
  To my own unvaried routine.
I'm quite content with monotony, Lord,
  For there's nowhere I haven't been....
I've experienced life's go-getting action,
  Its fast-lane, and mind-boggling highs,
But I'll settle for mediocrity, Lord,
  Now I'm older and much more wise.
I don't want to be an Old Swinger, Lord,
  And cavort in ridiculous gear,
I just want my comfortable slippers now....
  And a rise in my pension each year.

Pearl Williams

This Land Is Real

Who stood here once
Under oak and elm?
Those ancient trees,
Their names not even whispered among these beeches' leaves
Were the canopy, the roof,
The life on lives played out in this land,
In this very place;
Upon this very sod of dirt.
Kings, warriors, great men
Are celebrated here in works of earth:
Their names are forgotten;
Wives, mothers, real women
Are immortal here in the toil that built those earthworks:
Their toil is forgotten.
This land is real:
Those that walked it, have become it.

Oliver Arditi

A Dickensian Jaunt

After an evening's jollification,
under a dimly lit light.
A stagnation of previous elation,
festered in an intense whirlpool
of enchantment.
Suddenly, out of this concoction
of gloom, Dickensian delights
emanated from an inspired mind.

Dickens, himself came and caricatured
the evening, in style.
They were not hard times, nor the
worst of time, just the best of times.
Pip became a gentleman, and scholar,
as like to myself, in a contemporary way.

Charles, dear fellow, I must
be going, some time today.

Lee Morton

Multiple Sclerosis

Many long days and nights pass by,
Undeniable although we try.
Loved and remembered they will say,
Tomorrow or the next day.
Impatient we may be,
People we love we will never again see.
Lies we say to ease the pain,
Energy they lose, but never gain!

Sanctuary with our memories,
Calmness as I carry on with my studies.
Labelled at birth are we,
Everybody is given a different key.
Rules I slash with a knife,
Observer, am I of human life.
Secrets kept and broken,
Insights and omens.
Sadness, anger and all the rest put us
  all through a vital test!

Lisa Marie James

I The Candle

The dimly-lit candle shone brightly
Trying to give out its light.
Strong winds flicked about the weak flame
Yet the flame continued to fight.
As the winds grew ever stronger
The candle battled through
But the more the winds determined
The more the candle blew.
The candle gave up hope
The winds came ever stronger
The wind at last had won because
The flame could last no longer.

Louise Whitfield

"Fading Moments"

Decades gone by, my final years,
Uncertain departure, my wandering fears:
Would I be alone, the darkness to see,
Or would it be shared, with company!

My feelings go back, to younger days,
When life was calm, happy in many ways,
When boyhood challenge, my only goal,
Then with a blink, back to this old man's soul!

Life I've lead, flashes by, like a flicker screen,
Sad and happy moments, yet again I've seen.
Then a brief pause, to relate to time,
Remembering these passing hours are mine!

It's said I'll be free to roam,
The spirit world, an open dome:
And look upon from heights above,
To those I leave behind and love!

Steve Lloyd

Dirt To Dust

Some mournful unknowns gaze at his angelic remains.
Unblemished soul, or so he claimed.
His ashes cast on Slieve Gallions high,
Even in death he fills my life,
Like the mountain's shadow that darkens our town,
He clouds my memories, my thorny crown.

Oh man of cloth my youth was simple.
You used blind faith to invade my temple.
From creation to cremation your existence bent
With twisted fulfilment without repent.
Now I bow my head with humble content,
Your reign is over, Lord's tolerance spent.

Stephen Martin

Trapped Within

Please help me, let me out!
Unable to tell you what my life's about.
Although I'm trapped I'm still all there,
Will somebody please show me they care.

It's difficult, I can't express;
I get myself in such a mess.
People don't understand, they think I'm dumb;
I wish more could love me, just like Mum.

I wish I could be like the rest,
Then I'd show them who's the best.
They wanted me to be locked away!
If it wasn't for Mum, I'd be there today.

So here's a plea to all who read,
Your love I do so desperately need.
Help me through my trouble and strife;
After all, it wasn't me that chose my life!

Robert Pitman

Ghostly Manifest

It sails on Ebony waters,
Upon the stormy seas.
A Ghostly Ship from long ago,
Whose rigging is snatched by the breeze.

Thrown here and there in the rollers
Scattering a motley crew.
Whose sharp knives are slashing
A monster,
From the depths of the Sea,
— That he knew.

This Sea in a misty manifest,
Disappears in a broiling foam.
Leaving us to Wonder the truth of it
As we sail for away,——
To home.

Sue Williams

The Locket

"We've a present for you Nan"
Two voices shout in Glee
'Pon my soul' Nan gives a shout
It's Bethan and Amy.
Close your eyes Nan
And count one, two, three,
Open them up quickly
And a present you will see.
Tears glisten in Nan's eyes
That prompt the girls to say.
Don't you like your present Nan.
Whatever could she say
She took the girls in her arms
And gave them each a kiss
Holding them very close
She gently told them this
Her heart would forever
Remember this glad day
Her two small granddaughters called to say
We love you Nan. Happy Birthday.

E. M. Nevins

Bridle Path To Wendens Ambo

I know a path, a winding pathway,
Twisting, turning, corkscrew-wise.
I would walk, then hide in hedgerows
waiting - for the sun to rise.

Sunbeams weak, then growing stronger
pierced the gloom, through ill spaced trees,
Swallowing up that smoke like ribbon
of mist, swirled upward by a breeze.

Bridle path to Wendens Ambo,
Somewhere there, a signpost said,
Secluded here, I'd wait for hours
'twas silent, was the whole world dead?

Was it fear that set me dreaming,
Childhood heartaches blur mine eyes?
Never once, saw I those horses
Loom, - then vanish, o'er the rise.

Vanished are the years of living,
Now I gaze towards the sun,
Crying softly, ever hoping,
The best of life - is yet to come.

Mary Rhodes

Our Brother

Dear brother Melvin so close to our heart
Twelve years younger not many years apart

Not so very far away in thought or in mind
A very nice man to know and very very kind

Memories of yesteryear of sweet summer days
Now so many lost, in our autumn haze

Of prams pushed, of cinema trips
Of hands held, small hands, tight grips

Of scarlet fever of hospital trips
Of sad face of trembling lips

So much adored by nurses there
Loved that sweet face, that blond hair

18 months old in bed with a bottle
Miniature whisky, I thought mum would throttle

That dear face drunk as a coot
Too young to say, hangover a beaut

Love unspoken by sisters two
But from the heart fast and true

J. Webb

What Is Life

Life is a time warp between two spheres. A speck of light in a dark
tunnel, you enter the tunnel at conception and travel through slowly,
steadily growing, until the time is right for you to emerge into the light.
The processes and tasks are set before you and step be step,
stage by stage - you will work your way through them.
Sometimes the path will be steep and hard to climb sometimes the
Journey will come easy, and as you progress, you will find the
level of happiness you require. You will take hold of life with
both hands at this time. Later in your life you will look back
and remember all the good times. When things are bad look
forward and remember things must get better, as the sun
always rises and darkness fades away.
Then when twilight comes you will be at a time of life when
your life is ready for the next assessment.
The final assessment may come quickly or come slowly.
And as you re-enter the tunnel, the light will fade away and all
will be dark.
Then you will wait for the time when you again enter the
tunnel and life begins again.
Kathryn Stewart

Pawn

Go ahead make the next move
Try and bring me down
But don't forget in your hasty rush
That I once wore your crown.

And don't forget you're dispensable
Just a pawn in their game
And remember throughout your selfish ploy
You're nothing but a name.

The knights may swarm around you
And defend their favoured queen
But as easily as they built you up
They'll destroy your little dream.

And remember that you caused all this
When you've fallen by the gate
And when you try to regain your dream
I'll smile and say Check-mate.
Lucy Kirwan Crofts

Dream Of Dusky

Little friend as I lay sleeping, just a night or two ago,
Troubled thoughts of you came creeping, was I right to let you go?
It seemed that angry people shouted, people who could never know
The torment that I suffered daily, all because I love you so.
And in my dream I stumbled madly on and on to where you lay,
Needing comfort oh so badly, my little friend had gone away.
On my face I fell crying, by your grave so dull and grey
And my heart was loudly pounding, like a drum at break of day.
Then a purring sound came near me, velvet fur touched my hair
Louder, LOUDER came the singing and I knew that you were there.
In your way you'd come to tell me all was well where you had gone,
That I should no more be troubled, that I had not done you wrong.
All my doubts were put behind me as I saw you on your way,
Your pain and suffering gone forever, could I wish for you to stay.
Brushing by my face once more, walking proudly like a queen
A touch of comfort from your paw, the sweetest cat I've ever seen.
I can only thank you dearly for the comfort that you give,
Memories of you will be near me, for so long as I may live.
A. V. Painter

All Gold

Twilight years have descended,
Treasures of life must be remembered.
I see his face, and feel his hand,
Years ago I accepted his gold band.
He worked hard, trod many roads,
All for family, carrying heavy loads.
He took what came, said it was fate,
He bore no malice, never any hate.
Made every day count of his precious life,
I was proud and happy to have been his wife.
G. R. Davies

The Negative Help Line

A friend tells a friend she is having
trouble at home
'aren't we all' comes the swift reply
She then tells another about the pain in
her bones
'aren't we all' the friend replies
Her eyes are red with tears from stress
aren't we all under stress says another
who claims she has had it from here to here
what a miserable world it is today
to suffer in silence
Is the only way
Even if you say
You are waiting for God
Aren't we all, is all they can say
Nan Hawkins

Artistry In Perfection

The moon silently glides making her lone journey.
Trees like etchings in their starkness,
their bare branches seemingly grotesque.
She turns fields into silver pools and dark lanes becomes
    silver ribbons.
Mountain peaks take on the appearance of iced cakes,
Whilst, in the valleys, silver owls search for silver mice.
Passing over the towns and cities their structures are softened
    their lights are as nothing.
Even their sordidness becomes enhanced by her magical beams.
She touches the ocean dramatically, crests of rippling brilliance
    contrast with the darkened valleys of water.
On she journeys - artistry in perfection.
Marjorie McGrath

Thoughts Of Summer

Walking down a country lane
trees budding incandescently profane
I thought of barmy summer days ahead.

Birds chirping through the forest dense
blue bells shaking their merry bells hence
of rivers flowing in depths of murky green
and mother swans with their cygnets proudly seen
Gliding along with less cares than I
who can only look on whilst breathing a sigh.

For all the glory of a summer's day
peaceful and harmonious I watch as I lay
down in the meadow green where no eyes can pry
no better place the wind whispering nigh
than God's green earth this land. This England
so fair and abundantly grown.
In nature's chest her treasures shown
To rich and poor alike no distinction there.
A kaleidoscope of colour in birds of the air
trees tall and shapely to shade us we share
whilst the skies to affinity laid bare.
J. Oung

The Earth, The Sea, And The Sky

Man pollutes the earth, the sea, and the sky.
Until it's no longer beautiful to the naked eye.

He pumps into the air gas and fume.
Until over all of us the cloud will loom.

Into our rivers and streams go waste.
He does all of this without any haste.

Into the earth man keeps on ripping.
And mankind just keeps on further slipping.

We will murder our earth with waste and pollution.
For the sake of our children is there no solution.

Will man never learn the lesson why.
He can't continue to pollute the earth, the sea, and the sky.
Paul Andrew Lomas

Granny

As I laid the flowers down, I could here a silent sound.
Treasured memories always last, a gift you gave me in the past.
You sat me on your knee that night, hugged and kissed and
　held me tight.
You told me that you would always be there, and that I should
　never ever be scared.

Then you lay there in your bed, you held my hand and then you said.
You told me of your future plans, as you laid and held my hands.
I thought that day would never be, you were slowly slipping
　away from me.
Suddenly your eyes were closed, where you went nobody knows.

The flowers I hold again I lay, the tears fall down as I stand
　and pray.
Please God turn back the time, and bring back someone who
　was mine.
Just one more day to tell you, I love you in every way.
I know this cannot come true, all I want is to get through.

Please will you here my cry.
I love you Granny.
Why did you.
Die?

Louise Brown

"The Wind Maiden"

Softly she blows through dean and dale
Touching all that grows
She fills the plume of the smallest sail
Distributes the winter snows

Giant oaks bow within her path
White clouds race in fear
The earth lays flat in the aftermath
If her temper is severe

She screams and howls on a stormy night
Lashing this fragile land
Her tempest cools with morning light
As she shows her caring hand

Without her oh were would we be
Plagued by flies and dust
Living with a stagnant sea
So abide with her we must

W. C. Parry

Untitled

To stand on the shore and watch the sea,
Tossing pebbles and sifting sand,
Washing stones and shaking shells,
The thin divide between sea and land.

To hear the tide smash over the rocks,
Leaving pools and showering spray,
Collecting debris left by man,
Garlands of seaweed fall in disarray.

The awesome might of the ocean wave,
Heaving swell and surging tide,
Angry rollers and shimmering surf,
Dark deep waters, its secrets hide.

There are times it can be so quiet and still
Gently lapping, peacefully calm,
Inviting us in to play and swim,
Denouncing all thoughts of danger and harm.

Oh what countless changes of moods,
Hidden depths, jekyll and hyde,
Fishermen work, explorers sail,
All wise men will respect the tide.

C. M. Wallwork

Heartbreak

Tomorrow I shall tell him this,
Tomorrow I shall show him that,
And he'll be pleased to learn of this,
And very likely laugh at that.

Tomorrow I am seeing him,
Tomorrow's only hours way,
The hours pass,
And it's Today.

Today he said goodbye and left,
All my tomorrows went with him,
It seems he's found another love,
Some other eyes have beckoned him.

This day will pass, the hours roll
Another day to take its place,
Another night, another day,
Full of empty hours to face.

Yesterday I told him this,
And yesterday I showed him that,
He didn't want to hear of this,
And never even looked at that.

R. M. Smith

Glasnost

We have a chance of peace
Today, if we listen to the openness way.
It's been a long time in coming, but now it's here we have no fear.
If other countries did the same,
I feel it would, ease the pain.
If openness is here to stay,
the bad things would, begin to pay.

Glasnost it means the openness way.
Glasnost I hope it's here to stay.
Glasnost I hope you're on
your way. 'Glasnost?'

We have a chance of peace today
If we listen to the openness way
We know this land will get on
Fine if we listen to the openness
Line, you out there public and press
begin to think openness.

Glasnost, it means the openness way.
Glasnost, I hope it's here to stay.
Glasnost, I hope you're on your way glasnost.

Thomas Murphy

Everything

I love to walk among the trees during Autumn and the Spring
To witness the beginning and the end of everything
The trees and leaves have such beauty, so picturesque to see
This is the perfect setting, the trees, the leaves, and me
In life and death the colours are so vivid to the eye
But now the leaves are falling, golden and to die
Those that still remain aloft attached to trees so high
Form a galaxy of rainbows in a foreground to the sky
Autumn leads to Winter and then comes early Spring
The time of a new beginning, yet the end of everything
The Autumn leaves of golden brown now blackened and quiet dead
Are shrouded by the new life beginning overhead
Soon the trees will break their bud, a vision to be seen
Fantasies of colours all soon to turn to green
An inner sky so beautiful, so innocent and pure
Creating an umbrella over the leaves of yesteryear
I tread this path on leaves of old, the ones I admired before
And I know that those above me still are doomed to this same floor
Yet this will not occur until Autumn and this is early Spring
This is the New Beginning, YES! This is EVERYTHING.

D. H. Hydon

The Valley Of The Shadow

Sorrow: Can one define the depths
to which the mind and senses dive?
Sadness, heavy, dulling the sight
and sounds of life.
Negative thoughts abound, not lifting,
carrying the soul through anguish
unwanted and unsought.

And yet - the subconscious seeking
a reason to escape.
An inner longing to emerge again
into the sunrise.
A rebirth into a new dawn
holding the promise of reprieve
from misery.

Sorrow: A crucifixion of the soul?
No, more a stepping-stone
along the well worn path to victory,
for even Jesus wept.

Margaret Bradley

The Place

Saints and kings journeyed to this place
To watch the Severn ebb and flow.
Men of valour and one ambition
To defeat the common foe.

Two travellers took shelter near this place
From the estuary's biting winds.
Their talk was of the Holy Land
And the cleansing of man's sins.

Many noble knights gathered at this place
To sing the victors song,
Before following their Lord and master
Into the kingdom of Avalon.

Two brothers raced across this place
To cast their boat on the turning tide.
Their mission to preach new sermons
On the Celtic countryside.

A warrior was buried in this place
To add intrigue to the tale.
This secret place, where innocence alone may find,
The mystic Holy Grail.

Steve Gibbins

Dreams

I am seized with a longing to do great things,
To travel the earth and voyage the sea.
To make music, and dance, and join in the rings
of those who are famous, and gone before me

My castles I build, and the seas I explore,
For music and dance, I am given encore!
I travel the earth, then awake!! And once more
My dreams are exactly the same as before!

Norah McComick

True Love

To be near someone and feel secure,
To touch someone that you adore,
To look into their eyes and see
And know, that look is just for me.

To be together for fifty years
To face together all hopes and fears
To disagree, then make amends,
And know that we are still best friends.

To call someone my dearest dear,
To know that they are always near,
To have a bond of real devotion,
That's love the only true emotion.

P. Carr

All Journeys Start With The First Step

You may take a journey, by land sea or air,
to visit some far distant land,
It may be London, Paris, or Rome,
or the deserts with their hot burning sand.

The exciting difference in tongue, food or dress,
the tales you can tell when you're home,
how it broadens the mind of the traveller,
When the true routes to you have been shown.

The Bible itself comes into its own,
When you're travelling the journey of life,
from start to finish the views are just fine,
they fill up the potholes of strife.

You may take a journey in history or thought,
but one thing you must never forget,
no matter how far the distance you go,
It starts with the very first step.

E. R. Buckland

Lottery Fever

Saturday's here, I'm on a high,
to the shop I must go
lottery ticket to buy.
I rush to town and stand in a queue,
each person wondering,
will it be you.
I purchase my ticket then shop for food,
now I am ready and in the mood.
I must get home now, mustn't be late,
they draw the numbers at two past eight.
My ticket has a family share,
each member hoping to be a Millionaire.
It's eight O two and the numbers fall,
Oh God, let me have them all.
The draw is over, adrenalin high,
my ticket I check, then I have a good cry.
My excitement over, new numbers to seek,
ready to do it again next week.

Sheila Saele

Is This Too Much To Ask?

How wonderful this life would be if peace were ours to give,
To take away the suffering, give the homeless a place to live,
If cure's could be found for all disease with no broken bones to mend,
No broken hearts, no war or unrest, just life in peace till the end,
A simple life to live and be free without poverty, crime or care,
Equality, love and friendship, life unbiased, divided and fair,
Our children are born every hour, everyday so innocent and naive,
They look to their elders with trust and respect and what they learn
they believe. If evil and hate and the torment of life is what's seen
then it starts to infest. Surely goodness and love and all that is
right are the things we can teach children best
Destruction, extinction will beckon us all, unless we start facing
the facts. The miracle of life to mere mortals is precious, is this
too much to ask?

Linda Carter

What A Wonderful Way To Live

What a wonderful way to live
To stretch out one's hand to a friend;
To give with the heart
To make a fresh start
What a wonderful way to live.

What a wonderful way to live
To sit by a mountain stream
To hear a lark sing
Or church bells ring
What a wonderful way to live.

What a wonderful way to live
To walk barefoot on the shore,
Just treading the sand
In some distant land
What a wonderful way to live.

R. Dallimore

Great Expectations

I want to take you on a special trip,
To show you Cornwall's lovely countryside
The village where I spent my childhood days
And always hoped to live there till I died.
My Cornish memories return each spring,
The magic beauty that is everywhere,
Oh hills and dales and narrow winding lanes,
Where daffodils spill perfumes on the air.
You will enjoy a wander through the woods,
To gather bluebells that will match your eyes,
Then sit and watch the tranquil cattle graze,
As overhead a large white sea-gull flies.
We'll go to a regatta on the coast,
A gay event that everyone enjoys,
Then come back to this quiet peaceful spot,
Away from all the merriment and noise.
Then in this timeless setting, I have hopes
That our relationship will thrive again,
Forget our quarrels which will be dispelled,
Like brilliant sunshine after heavy rain.

K. M. Worne

Christian Unity

Unity is what we need, to join together to sow the seed,
To show the world what God can do, expressing faith, with joy and hope
A friendly smile, a gift to love, from our heavenly Lord above.
Who gave His life, that we might be, a living example for all to see.

So as we strive to show the lost, we acknowledge His death upon that cross
To save us sinners, like me and you, and give Him our all in what we do
For the torture He suffered, the blood that He shed.
Yet His love was sufficient, as the words were read.
It's finished they cried, but that was not all
For He rose victorious after the fall.
So we give Him our thanks, and centre our thoughts,
Throughout this new year to give Him our all

V. B. Holley

My Wish

If I had a wish fulfilled, it would surely be,
To set all impoverished people free,
Free from hunger, want and fear,
To fill their lives with hope and cheer,
To take away all their pain,
And watch them slowly smile again,
To do away with wars and strife,
Just let the people live their life,
Hopelessness is the thought that no one cares,
So let them know that someone hears,
I haven't much to offer, just simple words I know,
But from a tiny acorn, a giant oak will grow.

Val Matthews

Shades Of Wonder

A wonder sight, a joyous feeling,
to see the changes of the season.
Sun glinting through the trees,
reflects the autumn of the leaves.
Colours so alight with wonder,
time goes...sit, stare, ponder.

Leaves that once were new and green.
Now glow with gold, brown and red.
Fall crisp and crunch beneath you feet.
Like soft and comfort creature beds.

Land of colour, so vivid, so real,
Mesmerized by the high that I feel,
Days ahead are filled with dreams,
Life... is never as it seems!

Kelly Philpott

My Love

Love is what some people just can't understand,
To me it's a dream, a mysterious land.

The one I love is sensitive and kind,
A man like him is near impossible to find.

What can I do? Seems to be my query,
Thinking so much can often make me weary.

Inside my head is a cold hovering mist,
The door to my answers, is closed like a fist.

I have never felt this way before,
But I know it's real, impossible to ignore.

I always hope that he feels the same,
But staying just good friends is my real aim.

Although I know my feelings are not returning,
My love stays as true as a fire burning.

Love is strange, painful if true,
It haunts my life, is it the same with you?

Natalie Glenister

Progress, My Foot!

They're demolishing old Windsor road,
to make way for progress, they say,
so they're flattening the old community hall
and anything else in the way.

Old Johnson's bake house is no longer there,
gone is the fresh smell of bread.
Just a big pile of rubble stands in its place
and the glass underfoot where you tread.

The old cobbler's shop is derelict now,
what's left there is only a shell.
Just dusty remains of the cobbler's bench
and the rusty remains of the bell.

The little old houses now broken and gone,
they were once someone's great joy and pride.
With door knockers gleaming and curtains so white,
now the paintwork has all cracked and dried.

The old fish and chip shop's the only thing left,
soon that will be bulldozed away.
To make way for the new hypermarket that's planned,
but just think of the progress, they say.

Shelagh Prout

Rainbow's End

When small, wished rainbows I could climb,
To lands enchanted, far through time,
Fairy castles in the air,
Magic, wonder, everywhere,
Through coloured hues would then descend,
My home being at the rainbow's end.

Years quickly passed and older grown,
Loving wife, with children of our own,
A tear near shows, when rainclouds nigh,
Hear excited tiny voices cry,
Come daddy, a rainbow o'er the land,
We stand and gaze, there hand in hand,
In their eyes joy, upon each face,
Memories, time will ne'er erase,
They ask, is there a crock of gold?
I smile, and say, so I was told,
I sigh, and think, thank God so true,
Your mother's love, her love for you.

J. L. Ord

Awareness

What can we do for future generations,
To save their World and pave a better way?
Environmentalist keep bravely trying.
Hoping threat of global warming's kept at bay!
Our precious Earth is surely worth the striving
Of all mankind that's blessed with life to breath?
For years we've wasted Nature's own resources
A 'Throw away' decade that makes one seethe.
Past strife torn wars when folk all pulled together,
As fighting forces kept our country free!
Ennoblement indeed! And not forgotten.
'Tis our very Planet now, must rescued be
What e'er the funding Space projects may harness?
Could well be used this time to save our Earth!
To nurture, heal and save the World that's bred us.
Space exploration's had its money's worth!
From scientific facts this Solar system
Can't pull another Planet from its sleeve.
Our Life Force won't exist on any other!
Unite! World wide .. this fight we 'must' achieve.
Peggy Geraldine Oates

Sad World

Why is it we are cruel, unjust and unkind?
To other peoples pain, we are so blind
We live in violence, darkness and hate
Leaving our lives to the hands of fate
We tend to kill each other in cold blood
Like ripping the head off a newly formed bud
Such lack of respect and sense of self worth
With not thought at all to the miracle of birth
So afraid to go out at night all alone
Because of what some people have now become
As for crime, there never seems to be an end
Always lives and possessions we have to defend
Many hearts are filled with sorrow and dismay
At how our world is becoming today.
Sheryl Roach

Reflections

When I was a lad in the 50's I grew,
To open doors and friendship I knew,
To watch the old ladies all scrubbing their steps,
Then be sent down the street to borrow sugar from Bet's,
Which was well overdue from the week before,
As we owed it to Flow who just lived right next door.
Four hovis loaves for a penny I got,
A farthing a piece and that was a lot,
We played pitch and toss up side Nellie's old shed,
The youngest of course stood look out for Ned P.C. that is.
Keith Glenn

Friends Like You

A decision by the head or compelled by the heart
To move away from this place could tear my life apart
Another chapter in my life, another page to turn
Another mountain yet to climb, another lesson to learn

But as this chapter meets its end and the new one does begin
I'll meet again new friends to be, my heart again will sing
And the sun will shine once more upon my saddened face
In this strange then hostile world but now familiar place

With God's hand clenched in mine I'll enjoy this part of life's time
I'll live for each minute, and my times will be fine
I won't be sad, I won't regret, with loving memories, I'll never forget
My dearest closest friends, who were once yet
Strange people in unfamiliar places
At the beginning of a chapter with unfriendly faces

I know we won't see each other every day along the street
But I pray through life once again my friend that we will surely meet
But if never we do my darling, or when a chapter ends
I always will remember, old days, old times, old friends

Precious friends are a gift in life, often received without thanks
Michael P. Burgess

The Good Samaritan

There once was a man travelling from Jerusalem
   to Jericho who was set upon by thieves
They robbed him and left him for dead. There
   he lay all alone on a road with no palm to lift up his head.

In due course of time a priest travels by,
   his eyes avoided the scene. No help did he
propose but on the opposite side goes and
   the man still lies in between.

A Levite appears, no aid to unload but he
   too clearly steers to the opposite side of the
road. But compassion and love appears in
   the midst, from a Samaritan travelling that lie.
He went up to him, poured oil and wine on
   his wounds and bandaged the injured boy.

Gently he lifted him on to his own mount,
   and took him to the inn that was near; to the
innkeeper next day, the Samaritan gave pay,
   with instructions he makes very clear. "Look
after him the Samaritan cried and on my journey back this way,
I'll make good any expense that he has implied."
D. Lawrence

Speed

My thoughts are not coherent enough to warrant me being around to interpret them,
the phone cuts off before you get there, and the opposition always seems one step ahead,
running for a bus AND MAKING it, beating time.

Driving home at dusk and beating the dark, speed is a competition with your mind and the elements.

Speed is avoiding the ghosts of your past life from hounding you,
treading water before the boat arrives
speed is an accelerant, a fire for the brain;
with pain and time it can be measured, with sensation enjoyed
if I was younger I would be quicker, but I am not
if I were older I would slow down, but want it to be so
Watches are good inventions, especially sundials
they aid us and enable us to mark the inevitable passage of time
speed is a programme of events following a pre-programmed course
it has a will of its own, governed only by the user's imagination.
By the time you read this poem I shall be gone, only direction lacking and a thirst for knowledge, if you overtake me on the way please lend a helping hand.
Martin John Holloway

Nightmare

Walking.
Walking with nowhere to go.
Empty spaces, dark shadows,
Wells with no water, down below.

Footsteps.
Footsteps behind you walking slow.
Short taps, but loud.
Sounds with faint echoes.

Darkness.
Darkness shining out from everywhere.
Eyes open, seeing nothing.
A sense of foreboding in the air.

Emptiness.
Emptiness creeping out from the shadows.
Screaming loud, unheard.
No other way to go.

Alone.
Alone without a friend.
As the power gets closer,
So does life's end.
Nisha Shah

This Day And Age

Was it worth, all the trouble and pain.
To get someone born, into this day and age.
With no future for him, as he grows.
With overrun schools, and teachers so few.
No milk at playtimes.
And little to eat.
With you out of work.
And me, rushed off my feet.
With hand-me-down clothes, because money's so tight
With no for an answer, when the kids want a treat.
The money we have, we need for the meat.
The bailiff comes knocking, he wants the telly.
The milkman's stopped calling, because of his bill
We hide from the rent man.
We need the money for bread.
We must have been crazy, off our heads.
To have one more mouth, that needs to be fed.
So all we can offer
The one thing, we have.
And that's the love, from a mum and a dad

Patricia Ann Prescott

Technicolour Death

Thirst for knowledge, deep hunger, pain
To gaze upon your mortal remains
Never knowing, one day, I would see you like this
Dipping my toe in the grisly abyss.

The vision of you in full colourama
Unable to sit up and tell them to stop
They pulled, poked and tore at charred dreams all around you
Unaware and just cursing about how it was hot.

All suited and booted,
Another days work
They laid the blame on you
Before it was light.

Wrapped up and finished
And given a number
As you lay contorted
In a horrific slumber.

The stars all went out
And the moon just refrained
So still and so silent
With tears in the rain.

Terry Foulsham

This Room

I love this room
To gaze out of the window and see the world rushing by,
People bustling, people hard and cruel,
Red-grey walls, grey roofs, grey roads
But here I am content. Beauty in this room
An island of warm colours and quietness
Safe from cruel people and a grey world.
Here there is peace and warmth where no-one can hurt us.

So much has happened to us in this room
I have found you, you have shown me sweetness
I have tasted the honey-taste of joy
We have held each other close
I have heard the ripple of your laughter
And known pride that I could please you.

You are not here now
Nor am I certain that I will ever be here with you again
But my heart is full
I have memories and I dream of joys to come
I have this room.

Veg Truman

Unseen Lodger

Your black velvet cape has waited overlong
to flutter and settle, gently, darkly
on a life that's sung its last song;———
For many years it was a song for Europe
-No, - even more, a hymn to the world.

The music's gone, the lyrics no more,
The rhythm of life's gone out the door,

No reason I should look for you
Maybe you floated down some time ago.

All joy and pleasure, - interest too
You've blanketed, - (and smothered like
a cot - death child, - no breath of hope
or life to come), many a year since.

You've flat-shared, - lived here rent free
- Uninvited tenant, - but bound to show eventually,

Prepare the grave, stoke up the fire
Await the lighting of the byre.

Rick Sassi

Freedom's Sacrifice

I have a passion to return once more
to fields of red, ravaged by a forgotten war
where red poppies drift and sway.
To remind us all of yesterday.

Now verdant and clean
dull and obscene
a burial ground of men unknown
no grave nor cross shown.

I have a passion to go back there
where life's dream once shone fair
where men lay bleeding in the mire
consumed by battle fire.

A fight for freedom we are told
young men never to grow old
giving a life because they cared
for family and friends they will never share.

Pointless beyond belief
the only legacy — grief.
White crossed fields of green
can never tell of horrors they have seen.

A. A. Foreman

War's Own Ghost

Clinging mud gripping feet
Hampering our bloody retreat
Shells exploding all around
Men writhing in agony on the ground
Gas gas spreading fast
Colourless odourless then it's past
Missing limbs a bloodied vest
No one getting any rest
Stretcher bearer goes out the cry
Some are saved but many die
Now is it the writing that scares us the most
Or is it perhaps war's own ghost

James H. Barrass

The Race

I've run a hard race,
  to get to the place,

The place I'm searching for,
  as I climb higher
I also acquire my self with the
  knowledge I face,

What is the goal? Where is the line?

The finish the end of the race?
Will I reach it through pain,
on some other chain
  of events that I still have to face.

Marion Hewlett

Those Happy Little Yuletide Faces

'Tis the season to be jolly.
Hanging mistletoe, and sprigs of holly.
Santa Claus is coming, say children cries.
He has a big sleigh with reindeer, and he eats mince pies.

Their watching little eyes do peer.
Through jack frost windows, left unclear.
Those little faces start to yawn.
Excited, for 'tis almost morn'.

Waking, to find their stockings overflowing.
They quickly open gifts, with faces happily glowing.
Toys, books, games, with a selection of confection.
Dolls and teddies, always cuddled with affection.

Christmas lunch after morning prayer.
Too excited for eating Christmas fare.
Come on now children, is every mother's plea.
More surprises, but good you all must be.

A treat to see a panto', and big top too.
With lots of sweets to suck and chew.
Children, with sticky little fingers from liquorice laces.
Have those happy little Yuletide faces.

Carol Lidster-Wood

My Grandfather Clock

A grandfather clock now stands in my hall,
Handsome and proud, beloved by us all,
A gift from my father, I hold him so dear,
He decided to buy it to give us some cheer.
Dad took ill at Christmas, oh what a fuss,
He just had to come down and stay with us,
Even the dog did not like it out of his house,
No fun this, he was a quiet as a mouse.
Though I was good to them both, this wasn't their home,
But they were getting better and they weren't alone.
At 82 years at age Dad still has a lot to do
He could show us young folk a thing or two.
Working hard at Bayview, a fan of East Fife,
This was his hobby for most of his life
Forlorn and dejected he looked out at the snow—
What could I do? Where could he go?
He straightened his back, a sparkle came to his eyes
He ordered the clock and I got a surprise.
So wherever I am and I hear a "tick tock"
I think of my Dad and my grandfather clock!

Alexandra Pollock

The Rook's Nests

Elm trees great stately trees
Green leaves rustle and quiver
Down by the glen
Where rooks build their nests
On the bank of the meandering river.
Elm trees great stately trees
Giant arms sway in the evening breeze.
Rooks they quarrel, twirl and cry.
Over their rickety nests they fly
Watching them flutter.
"How do they know?"
Whose nest is whose as they fly to and fro,
must go my way
I've captured nature's display
Rooks, cawing, performing, dramatically
Black wings flapping violently,
Caw, Caw, stay clear
No trespassers wanted here
Tenement of the rooks.

Frances Gibson

Colours Life Unseen

Green are the hills that surround me
Green as far as the eye can see.
The grass, the mountains, the trees and all,
Green they are until the fall.

Blue is the river free to be
Flowing, flowing endlessly
So pure, so clear, so far yet so near
The river flows south to the sea.

White are the clouds that bless the sky
Drifting and floating way up high
Formed by the river that flows to the sea
Above the green hills that surround me
These are the things we ignore you see
But to me they are life and eternity.

Claire Hemmings

Seize The Day

Seize the day, in both hands, take it,
Grasp the passing seconds, together we can make it,
Sufficient unto the day is the evil thereof,
Seize the day and ponder.

Seize the day, the opportunities be second best,
This is the moment, life, and is blessed,
Sufficient unto the day, the dangers thereof,
Seize the day, succumb not to idle dreams.

Seize the day who knows what of tomorrow,
Jewels and wealth may only bring sorrow,
Sufficient unto the day is the love of a loved one,
Seize the day, cherish it as a friend.

Seize, is to take possession of by warrant or right,
To grasp, tender, yet with all one's might,
Seize is to lay hold of forcibly, suddenly or eagerly snatch,
For to miss it, is to miss it, there's no turning back.

Seize the day, do not like an idol seize,
Live a life, give a life that blossoms as tree's,
Think for yourself, be your own kind,
Rest not in others for your destiny to find.

John White

The Curtain Closes

In all our lives, we have troubles and strife
good times and bad, I guess everyone's had
yet we must endeavour to be kind to each other
our father, our mother, our sister, our brother
the time that we're lent, should be carefully spent
doing our best for our families and friends.
A kind word, a thought, a pat on the head
a tender embrace, before we're tucked into bed
a sweet gentle kiss would not go amiss
for showing our love, means doing all this.
Why should we wait, for a much later date
to tell our beloved ones, they're looking just great
and then, the curtain closes, carnations, chrysanthemums
and roses, those flowers, those tears, oh those
wasted years, they're not coming back they're gone, it's too late
so while there is time, if you can't talk just mime
and hold the ones close that you love the most
they may be your children, your parents, your mate
tell them you love them, yes right now don't wait
for maybe tomorrow, you could be too late.

June Williams

Autumn

Leaves falling off trees
children playing in them
adults sweeping leaves away
all the nuts are falling off the trees
squirrels are collecting them off
the ground
putting them into storage for the
winter months

Charlene Gibson

My Friends

Big green eyes gleaming at me.
Golden fur so smooth and silky.
Innocent face just like a seal.
A little whimper when he's lonely.
   That's my friend.

Round button eyes, so small and black.
Little pink nose so small and sweet.
Short brown fur soft and smooth
Long white, whiskers twitching all the time.
   That's my friend.

Long grey ears, with pink insides
Little round face so sweet and mild.
Hopping round all day long.
Sweet and innocent also strong.
   That's my friend.

All of my pets are my friends.
My dog is called Jackson.
My rabbit is called Rupert.
My hamster is called Sukie.
   And these are my friends.
Aimee Fegan

No Longer

Whate'er you up to on Friday night?
Going up town, a few pubs or a club
I wish, I'll be avoiding town tonight
Rest is what I need, a peaceful night

That never happens, never here on the streets
The freezing, restless streets that peace can't find
It's easier to avoid hospital in pairs
But who to trust, if anyone

Come 3 am they might tax my only blanket
But others would do worse, as always
Someone cops a kicking, they'll never see the morn
If they rough it, the cold'll help them die.

Two weeks ago I'd be clubbing with mates
No longer, I'd be happy with a warm bed
Sometimes I wish I'd not see the morn
It'd be simple, my knife here, even there

I'm glad to see the dawn, gives me hope for the day
Suicide ain't worth it, I'll beat this
Soon it'll be clubs and pubs again
Despair aside I hope it'll be the streets no longer.
Jamie Williams

Sleeping Autumn

The shafts of golden sunlight filtered through the old bronze foliage, glistening like newly cast raindrops after a storm. It reached every corner except the very darkest ones. Verdant fir trees; standing tall and proud; were ready to take their place as the rulers of the tree kingdom during the winter months. They stood towering above the sleeping Oak and Ash, feeling distinguished and honourable.
As leaf by leaf fell to their dooms, they uncovered the tree's nakedness, and showed the treasures held so secretly within their depths during the summer. Woodland ferns; maroon, beige, fawn and bright terracotta; looked up with great respect at the colossal giants above them, their every frond quivering in the October breeze, gently dancing some unknown dance.
The crisp morning air was almost silent. It was no longer filled with glorious bird songs and tiny wing-beats. There was only the rustling foliage to keep it alive, keep it awake for the following year, the following new Spring.
Anne-Marie Fowler

Life Is A Dream

Life is a dream
   Full of happiness ahead
From a babe in the cradle
   To the elderly in bed
A child takes its first steps 123
   Then learns about the treasure of that old oak tree
The flowers that dance
   In and out of the field
And the sun that beats down
   Of that you must shield
Then school you must go
   To learn how to read
Next - top of the class
   Now you'll be able to lead
You'll lead to a happiness
   Now you're the elderly in bed
Life is a dream
   Full of happiness ahead.
Joyce Evans

Time

The time of your life, is time to give thanks,
for the contentment we have together.
The time to laugh, and time to listen, with
time to remember that time is also a great healer,
then it is time to take a walk,. to eat, and it's time
to care, not forgetting when it's time to plan a holiday.
There's so much time in our lives, we are apt to
forget one great time to say our prayers to give
thanks for this time we have in this beautiful world
Dorothy Jane Lewis

A Chance

Suddenly! The world was mine
given a chance (though past my prime)
"A job!" To earn a decent wage
No more to hunt or 'curb' my rage
When offers of work go sailing by
Because they need a younger guy
At last, all's well (or so I thought)
I worked and did as I was taught
By all accounts now I was "In"
Working, money in my "Bin"
The boss walked in the other day,
Things are 'Bad', I heard him say
Although I'd like to keep you on
I'm afraid it's 'Friday', my old son,
The 'Scrapheap', that's my place I feel.
The state will pay for my next meal.
Endless forms, I'm in a 'Trance'
Please God, give me another chance.
Don Chaplin

Zippy (Time)

I have a cat called Zippy
From the cat and dog home she came
Two days to go, then be condemned
Or she would not have had a name.
Five years the joy she brought to me
Then she started being sick. Oh no I said this cannot be
But with a sad look, I got a lick,
Now she has got so much thinner,
And sometimes doesn't eat her dinner.
Her kidneys are bad and other things too
Sorry to say this poem is true
I just didn't want her to go forever
Tomorrow to the vet she goes but I'll never
Forget this fur ball that brought so much joy
Though my heart will break I'll feel at rest
Knowing that Zippy has had the best.
Now, no pain for her forever.
But my house will never never.
Be the same without her running about
She'll always be remembered without a doubt.
Dolores Giordano

For Safety Exists Not In Memory, But Sleep

Now I doubt
Ghost words between the lines,
I would make fear afraid
by distance, time
the distance is too far.
Not near, no one, take me home.
One dream draws conception, One dies.

Beyond April air discolours not visions,
Treasured sorrows, comfort of shadows
Fraying and adrift, fading inside
the man with the girl upon
his knee sees his eyes
only on her on her face.
Lullaby of waking birds,
To the hum and the sledging of sleep.
Chain slept bundled in sheets
And mystery, dance with the pulse
too soon too soon, words fall from the page,
They vanish or freeze awaiting the warmth,
To melt this snowdrop's fear.
Amy Parsons

Shark The Medieval Killer

From the very darkness of Hell she came.
Gliding like some Medieval sword striking silently.
But with such great force, that with one huge
terrifying ripping bite.
Her prey is ejected from the water,
seldom living beyond the first strike.

There seems an almost Primeval execution in her every movement.
Her appearance like some hugely armoured Knight.
Her dorsal fin the plume that glides through the water
Identifying to all about her of her clan like status.
A true Samurai Warrior if ever there was.

But of all that was war like about her.
The one thing that held me there be easily within
deaths gaping jaws.
Was her eyes.
If before deaths final strike there is something
that is more frightening than death itself then it's the eyes.

To look into death, yet see nothing except the untelling
darkness of Hell, is a Medieval death.
James Thomas Hopkins

The Prisoner

The day before yesterday, I was a child,
Frustrated by the bald injustice
Of never being taken seriously.
If people thought me older, then I smiled,
So thrilled at my perceived maturity.

And now that some few years have passed,
God help the fool who adds some on,
(Especially since I often now subtract)
And all the years of wisdom I've amassed
I lose, astonished by this lack of tact.

My outside shows time's wear, but strange I've found
That inside nothing changes.
Joy and love and pleasure still combine
To make me want to dance around,
And all my past emotions still are mine.

It's sad when May just sees you as September.
It makes me mad, I'm still the same inside.
My heart's so young, how sad that they can't see.
I feel the way I always can remember.
Age is just a number - but I'm still me.
Angela Cummins

My Two Legged Friends

Doesn't anyone realise that Jack
 Frost came last night
He's frozen everything solid, hard, cold and white
I can't get the worms the soil is all ice
The berries are sparse, hard, just not very nice
The water bowl is now like a skating rink
I discovered this when I went for a drink
But I've got to be patient and
 keep a look out
My friends always feed me, but there's
 a sly cat about
My friends treat me, my family and
 friends well
We get seeds, nuts and fruit, but we must
 listen for the cat's bell
We get water to drink and some to wash in
All this and more, from our dear friend Colin
He never forgets us, his wife sees to that
And he goes wild at the sight of
 that black and white cat
Elizabeth Parker

Pride

From today, my life will be different,
from today, I become self contained.
For if I do not react with emotion,
then no-one will know I feel pain.

From today, my life will be different,
from today, the veil drops from my eyes.
For no more will I live with illusions,
but with truth, where reality lies.

Gone are the days when my face reveals all,
gone are the days of remorse.
Gone are the days when I grovel for love,
from today, my head is held tall.
Barbara E. Roberts

The Spirit

What compels our humanity in life to succeed
From hence of our birth after the planted seed?
No miracle doth plan our future fate,
Success will abound by following the right trait.
The Spirit of goodness, understanding and love,
Thoughts for others with arms stretched abreast,
Qualifications to pass the test.
Human from is only a shell,
Listen attentive our Spirit will tell.
The master of self is the ultimate aim,
Endeavour to achieve and experience the gain.
Only a short time doth life dwell
Why make it be a living hell?
Don't nurture the evils to achieve your goal.
Better to deny and save the soul.
Edward King

"Heart's Desire"

A warm blush of elation, emerges,
From a virgin corner of her heart.
To celebrate this ultimate love,
Would destroy his marital realm.
For she must stoically endure,
Bearing witness to his spouse's demands,
For his husbandly affections.
Smiles conceal her festering, wounded pride.
No man has commanded her so completely.
She begs for freedom, from this forbidden coupling.
Their fated love remains unfulfilled,
Whilst he scorns his hearts desire.
Her waiting game must terminate soon,
When true love conquers all.
Elizabeth G. Holmes

A Poem For Christmas

Soon will be Christmas, children excited,
friends to see, family united.
The sound of laughter fills the air,
Santa sits, in his rocking chair.
Sit by the fire, brandy to sip,
Presents wrapped, must keep tight lipped.
Can't wait to see, the children faces,
full of joy, no effort was wasted.
A wonderful time, full of emotion,
When we show, our love, and our devotion.

Joanna Rayner

"The Four Seasons"

New growth is forming on hedgerows and trees
Freshly mown grass, you can smell on the breeze.
Green are the meadows, lovers' hearts start to sing
Little lambs frolicking. You know it is Spring.

Warm days are here. Holidays in the sun.
Parks full of children, all having fun.
Insects and birds fill the air with their murmur.
Most plants in full bloom. You know it is summer.

Flowers are fading, there's a nip in the air.
Leaves are all falling, soon the trees will be bare.
Dark nights drawing in, colder weather to come.
Gathering chestnuts. You know it's Autumn.

Snow on the ground, the frost shining bright.
Children on sledges, a Christmas card sight.
Like slivers of glass, frozen icicles splinter.
People skate on the pond. You know it is Winter.

Frances Jefferies

Metal Jam

People populated metal boxes,
Fresh from nocturnal cull of foxes.
Stand in shimmering lines abreast,
On their horns they do their best.

A million billion plastic cones,
Separate my metal clones.
Traffic management has come of age,
And helps to fester roads that rage.

Make-up done, hair is checked.
Mobile phones stand erect.
Pretty face may strike a chord,
But mostly people dull and bored.

I never saw the one that got me,
I heard no sound, nor made no plea.
A wrench of steel as cars entangle,
Crushing bone as bodies mangle.

And as I fell into a dream,
In the distance there came a scream,
"He's dead, he's dead, he's f***ing dead."
"Oh my God, look at his head."

David Scurr

Springtime

I like Spring for its delights,
For the wonder and glory of innumerable sights,
For new born life upon the earth,
For the happy ring of children's mirth,
For the welcome Spring breezes that whisper and say -
"Winter has gone and left us today".
For clouds of softest white and blue,
For flowers and plants of every hue,
For trees all freshly dressed in green
Where little creatures play and nest unseen.
For the gentle warm rain that April brings
Giving rebirth to all living things.
This Season of miracles, beauty and fullness,
Is God's Springtime of gladness!

Audrey Millership

For You My Son

I could write a novel with the tears I've cried,
Freeze the ocean, with my coldness inside.
I could walk through fires and feel no pain.
That's how much I long to see you again.

I would travel the world all by myself,
Just living off my lost wealth.
I would run the very quickest mile.
Just to see your last smile.

I wish I could hear your voice once more.
Or you coming through that door.
I know my longing is in vain
How I long to hear your laugh out loud again.

My heart is pounding, my head ready to burst.
This grief I feel is the worst.
Your last moments of life. You did enjoy
My love for you is eternal, my very special, special boy

Barbara Kitchener

The Handiwork Of God

Potter, Potter, mixing, turning,
    forming clay to useful shape.
Ready now for heat and burning,
    ready next for content take.
Oils and water, seed for dying,
    needs of man, his life to make.

Potter, Potter, shaping, moulding,
    dextrous fingers touching sure.
Beauty shows to eye beholding
    history hidden, so demure
All the richness of the crafting,
    down the ages, simple, pure.

God the Potter, metamorphism
    each in turn transformed in Christ.
The willing person, not neglectful,
    Spirit formed in holy tryst.

Our task to work with God the Potter
    as men entrusted with the part,
The words of God, the servant's song,
    God's glory in the human heart.

Charles J. Henderson

The Game

The children playing in the park
force his wrinkled face to smile
Laughing as they play their game
He stops to watch them for a while

His mind drifts back to years gone by
back to when he played that game
Although updated through the years
It still looks pretty much the same

He'd love to play the game again
although he'd be a bit too slow
He knows his bones are much too old
but still he'd like to have a go

Out from his breast he pulls the time
it opens with a little flick
round and golden on a chain
It closes with a little click

Across the park he slowly moves
no one sees him walk away
as no one noticed when he stopped
to watch the game he used to play.

Dominic McCallion

76

Waiting

Waiting!
For what, I do not know.
Until when, I do not know.
Waiting!
As all people are waiting for death;
For the minute of disappearing.
Waiting!
My ghost, which frights me,
That is what I know, I am waiting for.
Waiting!
In the open space.
In the endless view of self and existence.
Waiting!
For nothing to happen.
For the elimination of occurrences.
Waiting!
Until the sun will never shine anymore.
But I remain waiting.
Aladdin Ayesh

The Gateway

A gateway to peace I found today
For those who are troubled and have gone astray,
It offers you freedom, it offers you love
And the chance to return from the path you have trod.

The gateway is open, will you chose to go through
To a new way of life that is waiting for you?
The road is not easy the going is tough
And at times you may say "No Lord, I've had enough".

But think again friend, what can you lose?
Just a miserable lifetime on drugs or the booze,
Sure it's good at the time friend, gets rid of the pain
But tomorrow it all just comes back once again.

But with hearts full of courage, of hope and of love
And a strong helping hand from our father above,
It's never too late to try to regain
The life that you thought you had lost once again.

There are people all around you who love you and care
Who are willing to help you to find your way there,
The gateway is open, will you chose to go through?
We are waiting my friend, it's all up to you.
Catherine S. Anderson

The Little Fish

The water ripples the fish await
for Steve to cast his hooked-on bait
Hiding in shadow, skimming the bottom
under the leaves that float from autumn
Where has it landed, that little hook
They peeked from the leaves to have a look
Ah! They see it! A shimmering light,
"Come on" he's saying "take the bite"
The little fish on his way upstream
nears the danger we try and scream!
Look out! Look out! You're on your way
torn from the water and there you lay.
The fish have all scattered, full of dismay
Can't you see you've made his day
Steve's packing up, where can he be?
He's taken that little fish home for tea!
Alison Murray

Silent Partners

For all the seconds that lay ahead
For all the minutes we could have said
For all the hours we never talked
For all the days we silent walked
For all the weeks we can't atone
For all the months we spent alone
For all the years we gave a sigh
For all the love that passed us by
For all the time we wondered why
Chris Bird

Ode To A Dentist

My dentist died and how I cried,
For only he knew I was terrified,
Of needles and drills and little pink pills,
In glasses of water which always spills,
All over my trembling knees.

No, he did not die - I told you a lie;
He merely retired (but that would not scan).
So I penned these few lines to a very nice man,
Who always put me at my ease.

He's a farmer now, with sheep and a cow;
And rides, of course, on a lovely big horse.
He's ever so happy, has a dog that's snappy,
But I don't think it has any fleas!

I wonder if their teeth ache or decay?
If they did; I suppose, at the end of the day,
His opportunity he'd seize.
Perhaps he'd revert to his old profession
And treat his beasts to a dentistry session.

I miss him a lot, but just have to smile
When I picture his creatures with beautiful, perfect teeth.
Jean M. Senior

Abandoned Love

The heart breaks, snapped in two
for I'll never again see you.
Tears flow as the heart cries,
for the breaking of emotional ties.
The hands tremble, the body shakes
as the pain becomes too much to take.
Sobs echo around the empty room,
breaking the silence of the emotional tomb.
No more will I feel your tender touch
for you I know, that is too much.
Your love and warmth I have now lost,
the heat of passion has turned to frost.
Your loving touch withered and died,
from your icy stare I could not hide.
We will laugh, kiss and hug no more,
my arms lay empty, my heart-strings sore.
You used me then cruelly tossed me aside
I just wanted to crawl away and hide.
But no matter what you took from me,
you couldn't strip me of my dignity.
David Mathers

I Go To Church On Sunday

I am sure I am a Catholic and practising one at that
For I go to church on Sunday meet folks and have a chat
I do not love my Neighbour for most of them are black
the old and infirm are the states concern and I do not care a rap
But I go to church on Sunday.

I like the juicy stories the slander and the crap
Calumny and detraction are neatly spread in wrap
I like to do to others not what they do to me
But what to my own benefit is milk and honey to me

There are the ten Commandments but these seem obsolete
What harm if I should covet my neighbours' wife or meat
I like to have my comforts that wealth or stealth can buy
If this is neigh impossible then violence is my line
But I go to church on Sunday.

I have no time for clerics the sanctimonious chaps
who say they spread God's gospel but neatly lay a trap
to take from me my money my pleasure and my sap.
But I go to Church on Sunday.

But I'm sure I am Catholic and practising one at that
For I go to Church on Sunday
an hour or less that's that
Edmund G. Wambeek

"My Friend Sally"

I prayed to the Lord, for the Lord knew my need.
For a friend and companion, my burden to ease.
To change my lifestyle from fear and doubt.
From staying indoors to venturing out.

When I first met Sally, I knew from the start.
That she'd hold a special place in my heart.
For the good Lord had sent her at my request,
To brighten my future, to ease my distress.

As I stroll to the office or on my way home.
She's always with me, I'm never alone.
My confidence grows with her by my side.
She's given me hope, and restored my pride.

She never complains about what I wear
Nor passes comment on how I do my hair.
Yet if I was threatened or ever in need.
She'd show me she was a true friend indeed.

I realize more than ever that the good Lord answers prayers
For His ways are not ours, but He loves us and He cares.
That's why my friend is special, so wonderful and kind,
For Sally is a guide dog, and I am totally blind.

Bob Harrison

The Resurrection Of A Music Hero

The lone throne is my metaphor
For a decaying hero's stone.
The position has no meaning,
Its purpose is unknown.

Towering high above the rock pile,
It has known, it has seen, it still hears.
The granite colour, like His stature,
Has worn throughout the years.

I can witness all curious youth
Hide behind the passion or pain,
But I can only dream the future,
And wish my king could reign again.

Claire Alison

Godspeed And Rest You Well

Travel silently along the northern passage.
Follow the brightest star.
To a land that little is known about
Except that it is very far.

Awake in this glorious place
Where race and colour become one.
There you will find eternal peace
When your journey's done.

Those that you leave, love you sincerely.
Each one of us
Will miss you dearly.
But comfort with memories of you.

Goodnight Grandad.
God go with you.
Sleep long and soundly dear.
The next time you listen to music.
It will be an angels harp you hear.

Ian Cain

Night Garden

The nights dark blanket throwing itself over the sun.
Familiar objects disappear and strange mysterious shapes
cast their shadows over me.
Glistening stars and the crescent moon try to brighten
the lonesome night.
Whistling wind rushing through the trees.
A twig snaps and I try to see the hidden danger.
Thin grey clouds sweep across the moon.
Everything goes black.
Reaching my house, a burst of security sweeps round me.
Safe at last.

James Oliver Robinson

"Tigger's Tale"

My cat tigger is only six months old,
fluffy and round, with fur like spun gold,
a ginger tom who is oh, so bold.

Not so was this kitten when he came to me,
knotted fur, thin body, and a Pregnant flee,
a tiny kitten, who looked so forlorn,
who really wished he'd never been born,

I start my campaign to get him better,
that's why I wrote to "Cat Protection" a letter,
to get him to eat was such a chore,
kit-e-kat, choosey, all were a bore.

Whiskas, I tried on the advice of the vet,
success, every flavour, he leaves none and yet,
although my kitten has grown full of glee,

Please can you advise me?
How to get rid of that flee!??

Barbara Read

Ode To The Lonely Valentine

Soft lilting strings pierce the silence,
    flickering candles dance in the night.
The scent of Romance fills the air
    and the warmth of completeness surrounds.
My eyes open to the barren horizon,
    the solitude of my existence clear.
Tears trickle down from my eyes,
    the frozen void in my heart aches.
I search along the roads of Fate
    for the love of my destiny, my life.
I pray that the darkness goes
    and the golden light returns.
For now, I patiently wait to find
    the eyes, the smile and the love
    of my true Valentine!

David Czuba

Memories

Old logs burning on an open fire,
Flames that flicker into different shapes,
Mournfully I stare at the glowing embers,
Memories of the past dance in the flames.

Stir once more the coal-hot embers,
Fondly remembering yesteryear's friends,
Ghostly figures from a bygone era,
Phantoms created in a minds eye appear.

Tousled heads and smiling faces,
Sweating and laughing in a leafy glade
Children sporting, running and leaping
Dancing and flickering in the fiery flame.

Dancing youths chasing moonbeams,
Cascading light from the log flame brings,
Stirs the memory like the glowing embers,
Flickers, then crumbles to dust so grey.

An old man's memories are like the logs,
Grey and crumpled, as are the embers,
Mind swept clean of nimble thoughts,
Flickering and dying as he remembers.

Joseph Chapman

The Grey Lady

A lonely figure, breathless in the night
Fading, silently, softly out of sight
Re-appearing so tantalizing and bewildering in the mind
Gliding gracefully, this ghostly apparition needs no place to hide.
The air is still; no time to breathe
Your heart lurches and your chest begins to heave
Like a touch of death upon your skin
The sudden cold makes you shudder within
You question your thoughts about the 'Grey Lady' being true
But her presence is known only to the Chosen Few.

Caroline Purser

"Private Agony"

The words in my head I can't get them out
Feels like my mind's bursting
Lying in here screaming the silent shout
Listening to next door's bodies thrusting

So much emptiness and pain
Knowing tomorrow will be the same
It's just yesterday again, again, and again
Will I ever go outside and tell the world my name.

Will somebody give me a drink or pills
Just to watch these images twist and bend
These four walls - no cheap thrills
Will anything make this torture end.

Andrew McLintock

Good Summer's Night

Summer's night, warm summer's night
Feels like a time-bomb just ticking away.
The warmth of the night, makes the mood seem right
As they search for words to say.
Summer's night, wild summer's night
Shooting stars, city lights glowing in the dark
Temperatures rising, blood pumping fast
Deep sighs break the silence
As they make the moments last
Moving closer together, their hearts pound a beat
Making soul music, in the night-time heat
Twisting and turning, cries of emotion
Bodies are burning, then the final explosion
Young lovers, lay holding
Good summer's night over
Dawn's fast approaching.

David Armstrong

Nun

In grass and sand and tears I slept
Feeling the weight of a million bright stars
Upon the fragile tent of my eyelids which
Shield but reveal the barrierless sky
And I was small, compressed to a speck.

In velvet night and fear I slept
Yet always wishing for greater release
to jettison emotions I never wanted;
Always reaching for purpose in peace

Gill Norfolk

The Walk

Turn the key open the door,
Feel the fresh air,
You couldn't ask for anything more.

My boots crunch and crackle on the road
Arms swinging to and fro,
Creature noises using their own code.

Hours and minutes are no more,
All around the sounds of peace,
The memories and thoughts I'd had before.

Confront the hill bend the knees,
Upward slowly reaching the top,
Take in the view it's easy to please.

Turn around must go back,
Heading downward follow the way,
Move along the familiar track.

Approach the house once again,
The path awaits leading me in,
Back to face the problems and the strain.

Donna McSorley

Upwards to Mussoorie

A place way up among the hills,
Far, far beyond the city's roar.
The trav'ler's heart with joy is filled
With thoughts of what might be in store.

From Derra Duhn, the road is steep
And climbs around the mountain edge.
The driver needs great care to keep
Along that narrow winding ledge.

And further up bazaars are sprawled
Along the ever-winding road.
And goods of ev'ry kind are hauled
By coolies, stooped beneath their load.

The "sacred cow" is left to roam
On pathway or on busy street.
And langurs make these parts their home,
And help the picture to complete.

Barbara Haynes

Who Wants To Be A Millionaire

Lots of money, presents a giving,
Fancy cars and high class living.
We all can dream and dream we do,
We've all been there, me and you.
Those of us, that is, who do not have
Such luxuries and wealth.

But what we have we give and share,
And struggle by, the way we do.
Month by month, throughout the year,
Yet still we dream and dream we do,
Imagining all sorts of things
That maybe one day could be true.

Who knows what each new day will bring,
Laughter, tears, love and joy
Good news, bad news, another ploy of
Different ways of turning those dreams
Into reality.
No one can say it will never be,
Because one day, just wait and see.

Angela Slee

Eyes

Eyes to see beautiful things about you
Eyes that see sadness too
The gift of sense, so precious, so dear
Pray, never loose sight of these

Eyes that light up with happiness
And eyes that shows tears of joy
Eyes that are downcast with sadness
Ever sorrowful, who knows why?

Whatever the mood of our eyes
May they always speak for themselves
Show happiness, show pity, show sadness
For their expression, will be without doubt

Betty Millar

Is Time A Healer?

You went away and left us,
Even though we were so young,
Our hearts were left all broken,
When our lives should have just begun.

Many years have past now,
But you're missed an awful lot,
A Father so devoted,
Who won't easily be forgot.

You gave us most of your time,
That time we will always treasure,
Cos for us, you were our Hero,
And up to you, no other could measure.

Jean Kelly

Visions On A Golden Sea

Life can only mirror, the reflections that we see;
Experience and tribulations, designed to set us free.
Day by day, as seasons come and go;
Our minds expanding, enabling the spirit to grow.
But how do we assimilate all that life can give,
Happiness is the key, which is the recipe to live.
No book can hold all the answers or show us the perfect path;
Pills and potions can soothe the pain, humour can make us laugh.
Many will advise us on the solutions to all our ills,
Anxieties and stresses, are the only maladies that kills.
Friends are in name only, their actions speak louder than words;
False hopes and promises, like the wind, are only for the birds.
To think that we have found the answer is foolish to say the least,
For a life without humility is akin to bread without the yeast.
To learn life's bitter lessons can only increase our wealth;
For the stature of respect is the recipe for eternal health.
We each possess an inner strength the ability to love,
These gifts beyond our earthly sights, come, only from above.
Life's vision may sometimes be, a mystery to a soul like me,
But I still hold deep in the inner self, a vision on a Golden Sea.

David F. Manley

Life

Is there anything in this life of mine,
Except for hate, war and crime?
People talk of love, peace and joy,
but all I see is murderous ploy.
Do you carry a knife around with you?
Do to others what they do to you.
Another person dead, shot in the head,
Are you safe in your very own bed?
I watch the news late at night,
Someone else has started a fight.
Is there hope in this life of mine,
of a world without crime.
We're killing our families, our lives, our friends,
Tell me now, will it ever come to an end?

Becky Bennett

Moonlight Tears

Moonlight tears are falling on the silver sand
Ever since you left me for another's arms
Washed by the gentle ebb tide drifting from the shore
Moonlight tears are falling for I'll see you no more

Moonlight tears are falling as I sip my drink alone
At the little corner table we used to call our own
And as the candle flickers my heart is full of pain
Moonlight tears are falling for I'm not see you again

Moonlight tears are falling like tender drops of rain
As memories still linger of walks down lover's lane
So darling please return and take away these fears
Then summers golden sunshine will dry the moonlight tears.

Hugh Todd

The Sea Of War

The green wave of jealous passion
Embraced all with the kiss of death
As it settled in the smoggy air.
The tide guttering the gasping men,
In solid emerald clouded gas
Immersed and swept the drowning bodies
Of men, seeking the glory that they never found.
But neither the glory nor the passion flared
Inside the crystal grains of silicon;
The bass and bedded thoughts in every man
Were now on living through this onslaught of drudgery.
The sea of war upon them,
The tides of death had no escape.
The innocent minds warped by the spray
Of blood writhing within demolished bodies.
War, the sea of hatred -
A violent storm of destruction.
The raging tide of death,
uncontrollable by man.

Helen Richards

Free Spirit

The clock is chiming in the hall,
Evening shadows start to fall,
Sounds of barking, scratching, bangs against the wall,
Leashes hanging, chains jangling, ready for a walk.

The Master's coming, here we go,
Mother and Son, the Springers, bobbing to and fro.
There's just the two dogs now,
Once there were three.

The Father of Moss and Holly's pal,
His name was Todd, a lovely dog,
He went to sleep last year,
His spring now is free.

There they go the pair, racing, stopping, listening,
Sniffing out a lair,
Rolling in the puddles, it seems without a care,
They race across the meadow, the wind in their fur.

Do they know something? Is it their king?
Running and racing with them, in the wild wind.

Joyce May

It's The Losing Game

I dread to hear the night rain, tap in constant rhythm on my pane,
Evening seems so empty now, and everything in life remains
 the same.
The same old lonely evenings, with nothing much to say -
Count right from wrongs, keep writing songs, with words that
 spell the pain -
It's the losing game.

I spend some time to limbo, dazed and somewhat blinded by the dark,
Mind goes back a few years, as we walked together - lovers in
 the park.
Those long cool summer evenings, when flames of love were high -
Those days are gone, though life moves on - keep flowing like
 the pain
It's the losing game.

I heard the open voices, change to silent whispers in the shade,
Time goes by, the truth be know - then all the silent whispers start
 to fade.
The act of love's deceiving - the lessons hard to learn,
I paid the price, throwing the dice, the cost I know by name -
It's the losing game.

It's the losing game, didn't know the time of day to quit, and
 draw the line.
Had a chance to make amends - take a journey on the wings of love.
Instead I bought a one-way ticket, for the midnight train -
And ended up the wrong side of the track - to play the losing game.

David Kendall Jones

The Land I Love

I love this land where I was born
Especially when I see the dawn
The birds they play and sing with glee
As the sun's rays glitter through the trees
And flowers open in bright array
Once more to greet another day.

I lay and bask in the morning light
And watch the swallows in soaring flight
To admire the beauty of his land
Where lovers walk hand in hand
Unaware of nature's strife
As young plants springs to life.

It is a time I dread the most
As I arise to the morning post
To leave this beauty far behind
Back to the city and all its grime
Yet to think of the pleasure I have taken
From this land where I awakened.

Danny Gordon Foster

Storm Warning

The dark is rising,
Enveloping the world in impenetrable obscurity.
Unilluminated we await the rapid approach
of the storm.
Unleashed from the heavens
A threatening rumble advances.
Immense shadows are torn
By the light that streaks the sky.
Banshees screech through the air;
Powerful blasts of shrieking wind;
Whipping and chilling those who seek to pass
Encircled in a bitter embrace.
sheets of rain
Harassing the streets with disruptive torrents;
colliding upon the pavement.
As abruptly as it began, it ended.
Tranquillity returns.
Emma Overton

Voice Of A Storm

Beneath October skies lies a blanket all around
Enveloping like a shroud, a mantle on the ground
Looking towards the heather - clad moor, that I know so well by day
Seems sullen and indifferent, now the light has gone away

I listen to the whistling wind as it echo's through the trees
Dreaming of tempestuous nights, when sailors brave the seas
An angry clap of thunder suddenly sonorous to my ears
I await a play of lightning flash, to alleviate my fears

As I stroke the open fire, and huddle closer to the grate
Watching, incandescent flames dance, while others lie in wait
A violent fall of crashing rain, drums against my window sill
Creates an electrifying background, no one can stop at will

Once more I am plunged into darkness, except for a ghostly white light
Obscuring the half-hidden moon, that has suddenly come into the night
An icy cold chill hangs now in the air, and abruptly fills the room
Lupine echo's scream at the darkness, afraid, I am now filled with doom

I sense from my darkened dominion, that the storm has calmed and now gone
The raging elements now vanquished, I await now Only For Dawn
The dancing flames are now fading, but my memories I now have to keep
I saw farewell to a now silent night, as the world awakes from its sleep
Angela Donovan

Mystical Dreams

Mystical dreams and magical sights,
Enchanted woodlands, moonlit nights,
When fairies appeared on gossamer wings,
To dance with the stars and all living things.
Dragons, castles, kings and queens,
Love conquered all in a princesses dreams,
Wizards, witches, stories untold,
Mysterious happenings in days of old.
The end of a rainbow, though far from reach,
Was laden with gold, our elders did teach,
These magical dreams they soon disappear,
As life brings maturity with the passing of years.
Harshness of reality, violence and strife,
Muggings and hatred, the sad loss of life,
But deep in your heart, somewhere in your mind,
Though life can be cruel, if you look hard you'll find,
Like childhood dreams of fanciful flight,
Love conquers all, so never lose sight,
Of dragons, castles, kings and queens,
Rainbows and fairies and mystical dreams.
Denise Campbell

The Lost Soul

The moon was still, the night was dark.
Echoing winds, a distant bark.
Eerie woodland with persons nil.
Was it haunted? I wonder still.

The silence strong, my body weak,
Confusing thoughts, I need to sleep.
I must go far. I must get there.
Must I carry on? Do I care?

Passion, lust, infatuation -
Vast crime of the congregation.
With open wounds and scars soul deep,
Shattered moments too hurt to keep.

Alone I struggle. Find the gate.
They're coming fast and I'm the bait!
Waiting, waiting - till lights dim low
And voices fade and silence grows.

There! Broken, rusty, hid by trees.
Unlock the door - quick! Set me free.
Freedom of thought, no cruelty,
A perfect world of unity.
Doris Sanviti

Children At Easter

Out the door and up the hill
Easter bunnies - daffodils
Gaily jumping - swaying laughing
Heralding a new awakening
Children running round with glee
Easter eggs to roll you see

Yellow ribbons pure white socks
Peep here and there between the rocks
Racing, scrambling who'll be first
To roll their egg down craggy hill
Mustn't break it - choose your course
So carefully before you roll

Oh; the joy of racing after
Coloured eggs and little sisters
Mum and Dad and Aunty Bee
All at home preparing tea
Sponge cakes, cream, and apple dumplings
Easter's super - even Church time...
Christian S. Mitchell

Karen's Song

A golden brightness pervaded
Early morning of late September,
The rainy days have virtually faded
Save my childhood days to remember.

Autumn sunlight thus incomparable
To remind us of such a Sunday afternoon,
When in anticipation of the closing fall
For me it came but not a moment soon.

Such beauty being September sunrise
Like no other time of our year,
Treasure the smile seen in her eyes
Loveliness like Southern skies: I need her here.

It was indeed a year to remember
A glorious evening, a stillness just like this
When the sweetest air dreamed me into slumber
Whence I did not awake at times I will wish.
David Cooper

Untitled

Memory is a lonely lane, I so often travel
down, now in paradise, because it puts me
closer to you
John Holloran

On Imaginary Wings

An urge of anticipated awareness, engulfs my reverie.
Eagerly awaiting the encroaching effect, your smile bestows on me.

Your closeness like a gentle breeze, infused with the fragrance
    of a flower.
Hauntingly caressing my adoration, so bewitching is its power.

My heart surrenders completely, as each magical moment brings.
An aspiration to an inspiration, that's borne, on imaginary wings.

I admire the warmth of your character, your hair of shining gold.
Could I beseech an acquaintance, your beauty to behold.

This masquerade of fortitude, upheld against foolish pride.
Banished now from my secret thoughts, for no longer can I hide.

This feeling I have for you Darling - I always will.
Shall remain so until forever, my heart is completely still.

Dennis Earl

Grandchildren

My grandchildren, how I love them,
Each one a jewel in my diadem.
No lustrous pearl or ruby rare, could
With the beauty of each compare.
Different, each one their own,
I recognise each smile or frown.
Beauteous, clever, well I should know,
Just like their Dads were, long ago.
When they visit, I can't believe
These miniature creations are part of me.
I marvel at each one in turn,
So many things from them I learn.
Some day, some one may see
In each one, a bit of me,
And those precious jewels of mine,
Will radiate a love divine.

Gwyneth Tilley

"Generations Of Love"

The both claimed my heart from the moment of birth,
Each day that goes by increases its worth,
Watching them grow, my daughter and son
fills me with pride at things they have done.
The love and the caring for others they show
I'm proud I'm their mother, it gives me a glow.
But alas, time goes by and adults they become,
Oh well, dear me, I think my job's done.
But it's no time to mope or to be alone,
along comes a dog, who claims my affection,
to be petted and loved and walked to exhaustion.
And just when I've cracked it, the daily routine,
along comes a baby, my granddaughter, by Pauline.
The joy, to be wanted, just fills me with love.
I now shower affections on baby and dog,
"Here comes Granma, the loveable mug",
Both know how to win me, one look with those eyes,
A wag of a tail, a hug or a kiss,
I'm gone, given in, how can they miss!!

Irene Machon

"Lucy"

Although I sit here in a world of my own,
Do not ignore me,
or leave me alone,
A kind word,
a gentle touch,
to someone like me, they mean,
oh! So much,
Remember this as you live your
life well,
Some day, you will grow old,
and might be like me....
as well.

Erica Gordon

V.E. Day Remembered

Over land and through the trees
Driven by an angry breeze
Blown along to death's door
They came with hearts sore

Thinking of a time past
That left scars to last
No amount of time
Can remove damage done in life's prime

You hear men stand and call
About the poor souls that did fall
But what about those that survived?
Countless numbers who were deprived?

The lesson into the pages of history burned
But has anything been learned?
Or do we seek to hide
The memories we can't abide?

Will it always be the same
When everyone points the finger of blame?
Or when nationalities' bubble does burst
Will we again drink blood to quench our thirst?

John Wynn

Rescue

May day distress call, coast guard's received
Drifting tanker in stormy seas
Passed on message to lifeboat station
Lifeboat men briefed, on location

Launched down the slipway with a splash
Headed out to sea, lifeboat made a dash
Pitched and tossed on giant waves
Some tanker crew, lifeboat men saved

Lifeboat men lifted, survivors from the sea
Wrapped them in blankets, gave them tea
Air rescue service, hovered overhead
Winched up those, nearly dead

Rescue service with survivors, returned to land
Ambulance crews waited to give a hand
Police took over, for investigation
Visited hospitals for information

Rescue services all work together
Whatever the hazards or the weather
They are dedicated to mankind
Our gratitude, we keep in mind.

Frank Prosser

The Valley Of Roe

It's pixies they say beat the bodhrans at night,
dressed in bright oil-cloths and dancing quite sprite;
and I've also heard tell that with string and with bow,
they can play a fine tune in the Valley of Roe.

For there's an old sacred stone high up in the Roe,
where humanoid creatures like us never go;
cause there's ancestral ghosts even pixies never see,
that are guarded in the moonlight by howling banshee.

Now some men have dared to view the sacred stone,
and dance with the pixies in the land they call home:
but the ancestral ghosts have inflicted these men,
by blinding their eyes so they can never see again.

Even then some ignore this and summon a guide,
and pay copious amounts for a clear eye by their side;
but the ghosts keep a journal and a second time round,
these men are deprived of the beauty of sound.

So friend if you wander toward the Valley of Roe,
be careful of the path or the trail you choose to go;
If you value the sight and the sound you possess,
let the pixies play peaceful; let sleeping ghosts rest.

Brian Frazer

Deep Silent River

Silent river that ripples
Down to the endless sea
Your calm clear waters slip
Beneath the willow tree

What melodies you must have heard
As you flow along your way
What mysteries you hold. What secrets
Forever and a day

How many lovers sit beside you
in the summer time?
Their feeling for you will never be
Half as strong as mine

For was it not you that took my love
On a storm-racked Winter's day
You snatched her from your swollen banks
And carried her away

Oh, silent river you've become
Such a part of me
That one day I'll go along with you
To the open, endless sea.

James Ferguson Cunningham

Did He Understand?

I killed a squirrel today,
Don't shrug your shoulders and say
"But accidents happen."
You were not there to see the despair
Of the one that came back and sat by the body.
I walked to him,
Uncomprehending he stared at me.
He sat immobile
Of fear there was no trace,
Perhaps he read the distress in my face.
"I'm so sorry," I said.
Uncomprehending he stared at me,
I didn't know what else to say.
Choking with remorse,
I muttered something about cars and speed and force.
Uncomprehending he stared at me.
With a flick of his lovely tail he was gone,
To who knows where
To who knows what.
Leaving me wretched.

Janice M. Ottley

Dear Bob

Dear Bob,
Don't know how to start and say
The words I have for you today
Thought our wedding anniversary
Would be a good time
So darling here goes
Another rhyme.

Nearly ten years
Just you and me
And never a thought of making it three
Career girl I was and had to be.
So sit still Bobby and hold tight
because the news well it just might
not be quite what you want to hear
but it just happened
We've used no gear!!

Hope my message has sunk in -
go on have anther gin,
trust you're not feeling down and glum
At the thought of wiping our baby's bum

Felicity Janet Broomhall

Twilight Moments

The warm air whispered its comforting voice as I sat alone,
Diamonds illuminated the heavenly blanket with their
radiant smile.
Natures aroma flowed like the purest stream,
Its music sang with innocent passion.
Nobody but my mind for company,
I gaze into eternity.
I see beauty,
I see elegance,
I see no more.

Adam Critchley

Home Sweet Home

Very oft' mind we do recall, when we were four, consummate all.
Domicile together, harmoniously content; familiar, comfortable,
consistent.
But the two we had borne were of a mind, so frightful together,
the quarrelsome kind;
Then miserable apart, no verbal interaction, as each missed
the other, drove us to distraction.
As they matured their paths were diverse; each with their own
they began to disperse.
She with the wanderlust, he with his familiar boundaries of
home, nowhere spectacular.
She the gregarious, always extrovert; he the singular and
quietly introvert.
Their kindred love of each was apparent, despite their vast
differences of temperament.
But when she flew the nest one day for another, he was for a
while like an unrequited lover.
However her brother he was, his thoughts just sensuous (not
sensual mind), his affection indeciduous.
Following times together, and times apart, their family ties a
binding stalwart, his independence on home became more
tenuous; nothing strenuous.
Now two streets apart they continue their lives, as independents
in constant drive to be of each so more deserving, now they
are grown siblings worth preserving.
We miss them both, loving each no less, and 'tis strange a
remark for us to express;
For when they were home we wanted them out, and now they
are gone we feel without.
But our bond is intact, stronger than ever; the web we have
woven, will stay forever;
All but a gasp, a moment of breathlessness, preserved in
memories of happiness.

Jennifer Wright

Ode To A Patient

Welcome to this place of rest
Doctors and nurses doing their best
In treating everyone, so it won't be so sad
And making your stay not at all bad.

Now you are here and have acquired a bed
Ignore the T.V. and put the radio on instead
Place the earpiece to your ear
And your hospital DJ's voice will appear.

There's music shows, interviews and chat,
Who was the Beatles' lead singer?
Now we all should know that.
Was it Paul? No it was John
Even Ringo took lead in some of their songs.

So enjoy your stay, the best way you can
And we wish you to get better by far
I'll leave you now with our one little phrase
We are only here because you are.

Bill McAusland

For Such Is Life

A little child's been battered
Do you see this pretty flower?
A young girl's raped and murdered
See that bird has built a bower
Some youths go on the rampage
See that tumbling waterfall
A bomb explodes and shatters
Did you hear the cuckoo call?
A whirlwind flattened half a town
Can you feel that gentle breeze?
An earthquake tears asunder
See how firm and tall those trees
For such is life, like threads upon a loom
We, need the darker colours to make the bright ones bloom
We need to walk amongst the thorns
To find joy when the path is clear.
If clouds were never in our life
The sun would not bring cheer
So as each day and year go by with happiness and strife
We must accept what fate may bring, for truly such is life.

Jean Donaghue

Inner Thoughts

Do you look at the skies, see the clouds pass by?
Do you look at some trees wondering why they're so high?
Does the wonder of all make you stand and think?
Would you miss all this if you stopped to blink?
Do you stand in wonder and look in awe?
Do you think to yourself, what is all this for?
Do you have an answer to what you ask?
Do you say this creation was quite a task?
Do you often relax and close your eyes?
Do you open them up and look in surprise?
Do you wonder why there is rain and sun?
Do you wonder why the World was begun?
Do you really find concern for life?
Do you find there are lots of stress and strife?
Do you manage to cope with every day?
Do you find it easy to go on your way?
Are you really alone with what you ask?
Do you feel like a clown who wears a mask?
If you find all these answers, please do tell
For all these questions are mine as well.

Ena Andrews

Snowfall

Falling aimlessly from the sky.
Dissolving but not yet to fade away.
Pure and clean.
Allowing only, the reflection of light
To cascade through your transparent features.
Your crystallized appearance slowly transforming,
But only rapidly to be met up by your counterparts.
Nothing can stand in your way only to diminish
On a bright summers day.

Angela Dinham

Hope

A helpless earth at the mercy of man,
Cruelty, corruption and greed rule this precious land,
Man is the judge if to thrive or perish,
No more leaving it to mother nature to cherish,
In our hands animals tree's and plants are dying,
Can't we hear and see their crying,
Are conscience, love, compassion words now so remote
Re-education and transformation our only hope.

Julie Hope

Autumn Leaves

Softly blows the Autumn breeze
Dislodging all those colourful leaves
Leaves of yellow, green and brown
Now unattached come floating down

Covering the ground like a new carpet laid
As the trees discard their Autumn shade
And stand there naked, never shy
Like bony fingers pointing to the sky

Standing there with arms unfold
To greet the winters icy cold
And sleep, until Spring calls anew
When young fresh buds will then burst through

Meanwhile the leaves that fell below
Disintegrate beneath the Winter's snow
And nourish the earth from whence they came
So their Mother tree may bloom again

And so they go from green to rust
Then back to mother earth they must
From old to new, from new to old
Autumn leaves, your story's told.

Gilbert H. Waudby

Untitled

We pollute the oceans with toxic waste
Destroy the forests in our haste
Kill the animals through pure greed
Over populate the land with our seed
How much longer will this go on
Until nothing is left
For our children to live upon
We fight wars for lands we do not need
Let millions starve that we could feed
The world cannot go on in this way
For our children will be the ones to pay
Let's stop and think before it's too late
Stop the greed stop the hate
Let people be free with enough to eat
Walk down in safety the loneliest street
What a world we could live in
If we would only care
Learn to help each other learn to share
Black or white let us see
What we we're born as and meant to be

Ernest Myers

Night Raids 1940

Dedicated to the Ack-Ack Gunners of the Battle of Britain

The low clouds of night cloak the drowsy land.
Slowly the earth grows cool, and breezes blow;
Soft breezes, pouring their subtle music through
The trembling leaves, in homage to the hidden moon;
And only the tensing faces of a few sleepless men
Portend the coming thund'rous hours of hell.

Far to the southeast, probing fingers point;
Bright flashes in the coral glow forewarn.
The hard throbbing hum of the eagles of death
Echoes in the strained ears of waiting men.
Then Hell lets loose in cataclysmic might
And men live, in the last hour of their life.

In the east the probing fingers pale and die-
Pale and die, as the night gives way to dawn:
Sicken and fall exhausted, as haggard men
Lurch from their battle-posts to sleep or die.
Gone to their loathsome lairs the tattered eagles:
Dead in the morning light their prey lies.

James Harvey

Our Dreams

We wonder in our minds about life all the time,
Decisions we have to make speak to us with fear.
Can we progress our crazy emotional thoughts of wondering
what life will create for us.

It's sad you know that life is so cruel for deciding for us,
we people don't always make the rules.
Our bodies change in many ways, grow stronger or simply
deteriorate.

Selfish sadness can occur.
Repeated words we sometimes discuss, hearing our echoes
in minds of gloom.
Sad thoughts prolong in our hearts, we are doomed.

Just one day make our dream come true, for
Thomas and Julia to reach out and be part of
life's happier world.

Happy our babies would be with us.
Strength to wisdom,
love to joy.
Cherished moments as life fulfils,
in our new-born loved creation.

Julia Litterick

Thinking Back, Looking Forward

Where have you gone to, the days of my childhood,
days filled with sunshine and laughter and tears.
Christmas and birthdays and long carefree holidays
where have you gone to, that decade of years.

Where have you gone to, the days of my teen years,
each day a high peak of hope, or despair,
each disappointment hurting so deeply,
each wish fulfilled was joy beyond compare.

Where have you gone to, the days of my family,
husband and children such overflowing hours,
our time was made up of so many emotions
the days slipped together like sunshine and showers.

Then when our children were passing their teen years
their pressures were mine, I felt them once more.
To get too involved or to skim over lightly?
Just like reading a book that I'd once read before.

Now with grandchildren entwined in our circle
a new generation to lengthen the line.
God grant them the wisdom and quiet understanding
to help them accept what will come in their time.

Bertha Logie

The Seasons of the Year

Spring is here, sheep bear lambs,
Daffodils are growing
Days are getting longer.

Summer is now here, the days are long,
And I am having fun, skipping, running, and
swimming in the sun

Autumn is here, days are getting short,
Leaves are falling to the ground, and I
Am having fun, kicking the leaves.

Winter is here, the plants are asleep,
Bare trees are covered with snow,
Rabbits are in their burrows,
And there's a snow man in the fields.

Spring is here again,
Sheep that were lambs, bare lambs
Daffodils are growing.

Charlotte Edgar

"Jaunt To A Diverse World"

A jaunt to a diverse world can be revealing and bewildering but,
D id you know that I, and many fellow brothers have reached this
    treasured place.
I nherited from our ancestors, we have been employed to play a
V ibrant part in caring for this circular matter of green and blue
    shades.
E ndless problems seem to weave our monotonous lives, but
    perseverance
R egardless of your race can determine the final prerogative.
S ense the plants, inhale the air, view the environment
    scrupulously for
E nvy in the minds of mankind can abolish the goodness.

W e as individuals of the creator must unite in faith to,
O verthrow the tight grip that evil has on the mighty throne.
R adiate your inner self of purity amongst the nations and strive for,
L ove to maintain its dignity. Keep the torches burning in the
    darkness.
D ifferenciations in our lifestyles can puncture our soul, but take to
your heart with cherished memories that this is our world.

Edward Rajendram

The Good Husbandman

He prunes His vine
    Cutting out all dead wood
     Our Divine Father
      The Good Husbandman.

It is to make us fruitful

    But not the ones who doubt!

His vision

    That His Vineyard
      Shall see new green shoots sprout
       And bear good fruit,
        Because He loves his Son

      Our Divine Father
       The Good Husbandman!

Dan Pugh

Blood Out Of A Stone

I had a good job, a personal loan,
credit cards and a mobile phone,
but now the job's gone, and I'm in despair,
the credit cards and loan's still there.

When things were good, with a great credit
rate, you all wanted to 'help', you couldn't
wait, now there's no money, you're baying
for blood, my credit rates gone, it's no good.

Must I die, penniless and alone?
Remember creditors, one and all, you can't
get blood out of a stone!

Jacqueline Drake

Five Miles From Stanley

As I lie here upon my bed,
Chilling thoughts went through my head,
Port Stanley I could hear the cry,
O Lord is this where I must die.
I think of home and those I leave,
O Lord help them not to grieve.
I don't feel bitter or full of pain,
I would come back and fight again,
To those who'd say we died in vain,
With needless heart and mindless brain.
I'd say these words, I will not lie,
We'd love to live and not to die.
I died for these Falklands mine,
So never part thee ARGENTINE.
The few last words that come to me,
God bless you all, Remember me.

Aubrey Abram

Deo Volente

Serenity lies mirrored in the sun lit water,
Creating tranquil images that no man could alter.
Meandering light beams portray reflective dreams,
Replenishing forgotten memories like trickling streams.
Whispering gentle breezes sense my inner being,
Nature cradles me with all that I'm seeing.
Perfect perception of all that should be.
Absorbed by the peace I clutch this near to me.

Beside me I see you in a raging storm of fear,
My soul rises out to find you peace and calm.
Reach to me from the darkness ascend from harm.
From childhood to Adult and now aged too,
You've placed hope in me to guide you through.

Now your eyes well with much confused emotion,
Have I lost you, am I drifting alone on my ocean?
Look to me find my peace, it will be all right,
Come from the shadows we will share the light.
With me now your smiles embrace mine,
Our souls in harmony and peace entwine.
Together we look on the water ready to move on.

Ann Wood

France V Rest Of World XI (Winter 1995)

Whistle blows, heavy duty fireworks
crackle round the stadium.
Burning tricolour, long way from home.

National stars, dressed in blue,
unstoppable, play the local unknowns.
World newspapers backing the humble islanders.

Different story at the Parc des Princes,
one game left off the fixture list,
preferring the away games, secluded.

Trouble before the match.
Threats of abandonment.
Carrying on,
despite protests from Rest of World.

Half time, three missed chances
for the French attack.
Storming through the strong Row defence.
Must score in the second half.

Alan Dobbie

The Wire Fence

Bounded by strong, grey-green lichened wood
Cracked and weathered, but still standing erect.
The grey-green stout pliable wire twists and turns between
   the spaces
As if to free itself from the rusty staples.
Here a beautiful tessellation of rhombi,
There an act of sabotage creating an untidy web.
Here an interwoven delight of patterned tidiness,
There a gaping hole despoiling the regularity.

Then comes the hurricane tearing apart the orderliness.
The wires tangle, bend, pull, push.
They gape and contort in a frenzy to comprehend,
Pulled all ways to appease the universe,
Desperately trying to regain shape, harmony, conformity.

But holding on, stretched to breaking point,
A pair of pliers gently eases back the stress and strain,
Completes the symmetry once again.
The fence stands erect and proud and whole -
A boundary between order and chaos.

Jenny G. Stephens

Memories Of A O.A.P.

When I could pedal umpteen miles on a bike
Could jump a fence, and a dyke
I could walk for miles, without a rest
And still have a lot of energy left
A short spell of work, makes me ache, and sweat
So I take it easy, try not to do anything I'd regret
Now I have less energy, and getting old
I once had lots of hair, now I'm nearly bald
I tend the garden, trying to do my best
But now I have to keep stopping for a rest
Preparing the garden, is now hard to do
I keep stopping for a drink, of a well known brew
These days I can't drive very far
I only go for short distances in the car
I belong to a trebles twenty club
I go on their trips, which are very good
I can enjoy the scenery, which I never did
And it only costs me, just a few quid

George E. Woollard

Water Of Will

Confusion, constraints, conditions compared
Contradictions, complaints, collisions and cares
Coughs and colds, ageless and aged
Contamination grown old, the cageless encaged

Construction, conduction, compress and contain
Conjure, creation, crazy and sane
Caught in the crossfire, climbing the beam
Trying to choose, to catch the clean

Crossing the bridges, comparing notes
Swimming the c's, hoping we float
Communication, connection, cans and cant's
Compassion our compass, aim full chance

Dominic Brumwell

May Time

Where bluebells bloom, with May flower white,
Complemented with changing light.
Cherry blossom in pink profusion.
Heavenly halo's, in joyous confusion
Dancing tulips, as if in fun, florets open
Paying homage to the sun
Leafy green and fresh with dew,
From winters sleep, trees born anew
This changing scene on a sunny day
Natures display for the month of May

James Simpson

Flight Of Fantasy

A lone tit twitters from a noiseless nest,
companions flown, life's new-born guests.
Deserted now, afraid to fly,
alone and cold - not knowing why. Just weakly crying.

Night's mantle beckons death's dark claim.
This tiny bird now lying lame
whose nourishment from mother's beak
has ceased. Rejected. Nature's freak. No longer trying.

Small sad dejected eyes just stare
up skyward pleading, 'someone care!'
A loosening grip on life's short pleasure
s'all this might has had to treasure. Yet watchful, prying.

Her task accomplished mother's flown,
with brood all hatched, their wings full-grown.
One half-forgotten unprotesting
mouth to feed lies meekly resting. So close to dying.

O thrill, rejoice - triumphant sleep
delivered new-found strength to keep
fresh hope alive. One final try
then weaving, soaring through a cloudless sky. Finally
flying?

Jean Roberts

What Is Silence

The tutor had spoken
Close your eyes and listen to silence
Silence, a thought of peace
No intrusion from the outside world
Alas no, the ticking clock
The water gurgling in the pipes
Breathing of different intensities
Restless feet at this new experience
How long you think before it ends
But it does not end
The silence without vision is not
Only awareness of different noises
Your eyes open again
Is there really silence
Life goes on
David Suddards

Metal Heart Valve

Night comes dark and quiet, and I hear it then
"Click! Click!" in the mysterious depths of blood and muscle it lurks there,
And life flows through metal, mingling with living tissue
Pushing the red flood to perform its ordained action.
Deep hidden and secret in my heart, but known to me
This alien substance "Click! Clicks!" and I know I am alive;
Living and functioning, moving easily
The more grateful because of remembered pain.
Will the night come, when, with flesh grown old,
I shall hear "Click! Click!" and say despairingly
"Stop! Stop! Let me rest, it is time"?
Will the "Click! Click!" still thunder in my throat
Until I silently beg "No! No! No more, no more"?
But with the morning morbid thoughts subside,
And I rise and live with joy. "Click! Click!"
Jane Turnbull

Seasons

The same old things to do each day
Chores and daily things
Indoor and outdoor seems the same
But each season sings
Winter has it snow and frost
Hail winds and rain
Shortened days leisure hours
Trees without their leaves
Spring comes with flowers breaking forth
From the dew drenched sod
Ploughing fields telling the corn
Trees begin to bud
Days begin to lengthen
lambs in fields gamble and play
Summertime comes to greet
Time for making hay where children play
Autumn collecting fruit and grain.
Harvest fields what are we growing
Wheat or tares, we love a loving God who cares
George Camp

Spring

Spring is here once again,
But still the wind stays cold.
But our hearts are warm and gay.
As we see the lambs at play
The cuckoo's cry is loud and bold,
but I think he feels the cold
The blackbird shouts from treetop high,
To let us know spring is nigh.
So hurry with those warm soft days.
Of summer skies with tranquil ways.
Gladys Austin

Our World

What is our world coming to today?
Children no longer have places to play.
Fields and open spaces disappear.
Houses and skyscrapers appear.

Roads and motorways intervene.
Trees and flowers are no longer seen.
The streets are littered with rubbish and cans.
The roads are blocked with cars, lorries and vans.

Fog and pollution fill the air,
There is a solution, but how many care?
Drugs, crime and alcohol,
Put together take their toll.

Robberies, murder, muggings and rape.
From which there seems to be no escape.
Hostilities and war,
Are certain to kill more.

Our planet is slowly dying,
While many keep trying,
Others just stand by and stare.
Because they simply don't care.
Janet Warren

"Prophecy"

He who travels, walks alone;
Cast adrift in a life unknown.
Time falls away, away from he,
Eons pass and hopes burn free.
We yearn for hope, Verus Amor,
Still it recedes, obscured by tears
Of sorrow. We stand alone,
Battling this tide of rising odds.
Striving for some end - purity, to
A life deplorable, abject decree.
Don Quixote sought to reach
A dream, a hope, some impossible chance.
Some dreamers still do try to seek
That light, such light that never grants
More than a vision - a vision true,
An immortal eye watches over you.
So to every man in every land,
To every person, rich or poor.
Let your hearts guide you all,
For if divided you stand, divided you'll fall.
John M. L. Bolton

Fond Memories Of You

I see you in the morning mist.
Caress you in the Summer rain.
And when you turn to smile at me,
The sun comes shining out again.
You look so pretty standing there
With glistening raindrops in your hair.

We stroll together hand in hand,
Happy in our 'Wonderland'.
Sea-birds call, migrants fly
'Til tiny specs against the sky.
A blackbird on its maiden flight,
Plummets down into the light.

We pause to watch - time passes by.
We are so happy, you and I.
Lost in thought we wend our way,
And plan to come again some day.
Back we turn, through fields, passed briar,
Home to tea before the fire.

And then, content, we dream our dreams
Enwraped within the firelight's gleams.
Betty Edna Keeler

"Windows"

Mary, Mary - look into my eyes, what do you see?
Can you see the shadows of the years,
Hidden by tears, or in your heart Mary
Can you see me?

You never saw me Mary, not the real me,
You saw your prince, the one of your dreams - not me,
You saw what you wanted Mary,
I was everything you wanted me to be.

Go behind my eyes Mary, see what you will find,
Our life together has not made me blind,
I still see clearly despite my rainy eyes,
Go behind my eyes Mary - you may be surprised.

I see things different Mary, different from you,
You think those eyes are just for looking through,
Dig deeper Mary, see what you will find,
Those eyes you look in to, are just windows of my mind.

Maybe it's better Mary, for you not to find,
What goes on in this old mind,
Let things stay the same Mary, they are done,
and in your eyes we'll live our life as one.

John Flaherty

Inheritance

What can we give to the children? What is ours to give?
Can we donate this tired old earth as a place in which to live?
It is ours to tend and care for but not to possess and destroy.
Can we give this world to the children like a broken toy?

Can we give this earth to the children with its smoke and dust
    and grime?
Can we continue to degrade until we run out of time?
It is ours to do as we please with, but not to pollute and destroy.
Can we give this world to the children like a broken toy?

How can we help the children to cherish this planet of ours?
Let us act now before it's too late and speak to those with powers,
Just as Noah in his tiny ark saved creatures that the flood
    would destroy.
I don't want to give my children a broken toy.

I would like to give to the children a world that's clean and bright,
With flowers and trees and good clean air and no pollution in sight.
So let them inherit a rainbow - that sign of hope and joy.
Please don't give the children a broken toy.

Barbara Harrison

Friends

Two friends who live quite far apart,
can gladden each others heart,
can nourish too each others mind,
with goodly thoughts in letter kind.
Who could think that when we first met,
we would have a friendship as good as this,
we tell each other secrets,
and phone every day,
no one could ever take this friendship away,
friends stick together,
friends are always there,
if you get in trouble your friends will see you through,
two friends who live quite far apart,
can gladden each others heart,
can nourish too each others mind,
with goodly thoughts in letter kind.

Joe Knight

Lovers Here-After

Let silence cocoon what might have been,
Bringing forth a butterfly, made of our dream.
To fly, on gossamer wings to heavens gate,
There to alight, there to wait.
Returning our dream, when God sets us free,
To indulge in love for eternity.

Howard Davis

To A Snowdrop

Fair lady of the woodland,
Clothed is snowy white,
Dancing 'neath the rustling trees,
A truly lovely sight.
As February breezes chase
Dark clouds across the sky,
You bravely lift your graceful head,
And winter's chill defy.
Your green stalks pierce the mossy ground,
Mocking both rain and snow,
And in the gloomy leafless glade
You cast your gentle glow.
Just a little snowdrop,
So delicately fair,
Renewing faith, restoring hope,
To those who see you there.
Fair lady of the woodland,
Sweet harbinger of spring,
Thanks be to God who made you,
For all the joy you bring.

Jenny Porteous

The Cuckoo

O! Thou harbinger of spring, sweetly singing on the wing,
Calls to us in sunny weather, o'er the willows gorse, and heather,
The cuckoo like an orphan reared, a trend in bird life not revered,
All aliens to parental care, makes mating love a passing flair.

Brooding and fondling not their part, or hatching clutch to
    warm her heart,
No fledglings, charm the parent breast, of a fond mother in her nest,
Deprived of brotherhood and joy, some unsuspecting bird employ,
To foster an ungainly chick, an unnatural, and disturbing trick.

Devoid of all bird like propriety, feathered drop outs of society,
With selfish habits so absurd, who could commend the cuckoo bird?
Those cuckoo clocks upon the wall, echo the vagrant's plaintive call,
Still during spring my ear I'll strain, to hear that mellow call
    again.

From far off lands he will arrive, some further treachery to contrive,
Although the truth to you I bring, still! He's the harbinger of
    spring,
Now during the merry month of May, that hooting call we hear
    all day,
Yes something enticing about that call, may justify his visit
    after all.

Alexander Hill

Lovelorn!

A Another grunt and then two sighs
C Comes from my loved one's chair.
R Reclining there, he does not speak.
O Oh, I am in despair.
S "Shut up" I'd yelled two hours ago.
S "Shut up" I'd screamed out loud.
W Why did I lose my temper then?
O Oh, see how he is cowed.
R Relaxed, he sleeps; forgets it all.
D Dementia shields him from recall.

A Awake, he stirs and looks at me.
H "Hallo, so who are you?
A And what has happened to my wife?
P Perhaps you know her too."
P "Perhaps" I say, as tears flow down.
Y You see he does not know
W We've been together forty years,
O Or that I love him so.
R "Rosa my love", he says to me,
D "Dear Rosa, is it time for tea?"

Evelyn Golding

On A Winter's Day

Our glorious realm is now subdued
by pallid Winter's light,
with Nature struggling in the grip
of seemingly perpetual night.

There is a longing at this time
to beautify the windblown scene,
To sweep away dull Winter's day
And tarry in one's thoughts - to dream.

To dream of warmer days to come
and propagate sweet thoughts of flowers,
When lyrical birds of every hue
do congregate in leafy bowers.

Until that time of future bliss -
surrounds us lovingly,
The cloak of Winter hides the promise
- of nature's - ingenuity.
David John Harvey

My Flowers

I've always loved my flowers, in a garden full of life
But when my daughter sent a basket of flowers
For a Mother's Day loving thought, several years ago
Little did she know how from this, a hobby would grow and grow.

I love arranging flowers for friends and strangers too
Weddings are so joyful, colours all so bright
Or to celebrate a baby born; flowers in yellow, pink, blue or white.
Sad times need God's flowers, crosses, posies, wreaths and spray
Not to mourn a loved one but to celebrate their life.

Husbands ask for bouquets to show their love for someone special
Others ask for certain shapes or flowers, for a memory they share,
Whatever I am asked for I always try to do my best
To please young or old and leave their thoughts to do the rest!
Doreen Fay

Tears Of Love

They say that crying is a shame, and that our hearts are sad,
But truly tears are signs of love that some have never had.
They tell of special feelings, we have for special ones,
No matter if their dads or mums, daughters, friends or sons.

While standing by a sick child's bed, I stroke that fevered brow,
When will this raging fever end? What will I do, and how?
Just then my tears begin to fall with love for that dear one,
But those dark clouds will flee away and soon will shine the sun.

The dew drops on a tender rose,
Are tears from heaven I suppose.
They touch and heal some wounded flower,
Like tears I've shed at midnight hour.
For a dear loved one sad and sore,
Whose health I pray God will restore.
And life though dark will soon be bright,
A gift bestowed by God's great light.

Some say a man should never cry, that weakness is his lot,
"He is a weakling," some will say, "he, little sense has got."
But even if he's ten feet tall, with lion heart and more,
If tears are shed from honest hearts shows that there's love in store.
James McIlhatton

Forgotten Dream's

If only, I could capture, my best dream's,
But, they vanish o' so quickly, to me it seem's,
That as I awaken, to the light of day.
My favourite one's, grow dim, then fade away.
While some are nightmare's, and, best left behind.
So many, bring me happiness, so I find,
It nice, to store them deep within my heart.
For in them dear, you play, an important part
and, many thing's I hope will come to be,
In my dream's of you, become reality.
June P. Power

Within The Web Of A Spider

The Bustle of the harbour sells essentials to us all
But those who have the gift of wealth
Prepare the traps in which we fall
To crawl out, deeply injured, to struggle, one more day
Caught, just like a hunted fox, for its fur, for fun, some say
And the hustle of the harbour brings goods to those in need
Is sold, with false emotion
That feeds a guilty need for greed.
To those who know no better but whose hunger must subside
Whose poverty is walked upon and then is cast aside
And left to feel their lives stand still
Within the threads of the spider's web,
Whose sinking boat won't stay afloat
To spurn the tides of debt.
But this need is more than money
It's a chance to use your hands
To build the sound foundations, to bring fruition to life's plans
For that golden opportunity
Or a dream that says pretend
That we're all rich and famous - and have influential friends.
Alan Glendinning

"On My Own"

For thirteen years she was my life
But then she went away;
So many things I felt inside
But had no chance to say.

She guided me on my true path
And taught me right from wrong;
Her gentle touch could soothe all pain
For that I do so long.

I close my eyes and smell at times
The scent she always wore;
And when I need to feel her close
Her apron's in my drawer.

When I was sick she'd comfort me
New jigsaws she would buy;
Her laughter rang through every room
And on her face a smile.

I only knew her as a child
Not even in my teens;
But now I hear my mother's voice
Only in my dreams.
Janine Riggs

"Fruits Of Labour"

I'm a socialist, I vote 'Labour',
  Do as I say, not as I do
I want to be poor like my neighbour,
  But that's not so easy, it's true.
I believe all men should be equal
  Taking equal shares from the pool
I hope that there won't be a sequel
  To umpteen years of Tory rule.
All things common, I say we must share
  That's money, goods, straight down the line,
So riches divide, in manner fair -
  But only after I've got mine!
I'll take up the red flag for the cause
  And Tory values now disown,
It's time to arise, and without pause
  Take from the rich their juicy bone.
When 'Labour' tread the halls of power
  How will they earn a rich acclaim
Will this then be their noblest hour,
  Or just 'all change' but still the same?
Barry Sheffield

Untitled

I think I know a thousand words
But none of them are really mine
And whatever I say it's been said before
At least a thousand times
So how am I supposed to let you know
How much it really means
To have you in my life

You can touch my skin
But never know how I really feel
You can watch my face
But never see what's in my heart
You can hold my body
But never grasp the size of love
You can listen to my voice
But never hear the tune of my song

I can talk and talk
For a thousand days
But never find the words to tell
How much it really means
To have you in my life.

Eva Larsen

The Wall

I am found guilty of murder
But it was not me.
But now I am in prison,
Shut up in a cage
There's not much I can do.

The walls surround me
I am by myself.
The chalk on the walls
Grow in much bigger quantities
It grows gloomier as time wears on.
Twenty six years in prison
Soon be out, in a week.

Dark and gloomy and terrifying
I sit on my bed
While I wait for my food
I thought I would stay in there forever.

Christine O'Brien

Untitled

'Known Unto God' is writ upon the stone,
And I lie dead beneath.
Forget not, ye who walk above,
I had but youth -
And scarcely time to live and love.

Bill Dungate

Neglect

The house is old with much to give.
But it needs love if it's to live
A paintbrush here, a duster there.
Rooms that are lived in, not left bare.
Doors once proud and just a little worn.
Now hang abandoned hinges torn.
The windows, its eyes, once happy and bright
Now broken and too dull to let in light.
The paint once gleaming with love and care
Now cracked and dirty, rough and bare.
Where once carpets and furniture stood.
Now only bare floor boards of splintered wood
Spiders and mice roam every empty room
Not a single light to dispose of gloom.
Gardens pretty and lovingly planted with seed
Now jungles of brambles, chocked with weed
How sad that houses like people grow old then die
Left with only memories and echoes of days gone by
To think that this was once a joyful place
Dedicated to caring for the human race

Jamie D. Dolbear

Time To Live

Time is money, it has been said
But is this true when you're almost dead
When you look back and begin to consider
Were you in life, to be the highest bidder

Did more money improve your life
And were you happy with your wife
These are the questions that one must ask
For life is short and soon goes past

It's not the things that you've acquired
That will bring you pleasure when you've retired
It's not the money on reserve
That will provide the memories that you deserve

No happiness, is based on simpler things
Experiences that life will bring
If you allow the time to see
All in life that's there for free

Christopher Meadows

Hurt

You held me close, so very near, whispering lies into my ear.

You told me you were only mine,
but in other arms you did entwine.

The pain you caused by holding her,
Was far too much for me to bear.

My heart, my love, was truly yours,
But still you searched, opening other doors.

Did you not think of me at all?
When into other arms you did fall.

Was it so easy to put me aside?
To cause a rift so deep, so wide.

When you now hold me late at night.
Does her vision enter your sight.

You gave her your body without a thought,
For extra pleasure hotel rooms you sought.

Now though I try to banish my fear,
The pain through my heart sears and sears.

Like a red hot knife it plunges and twists,
Her face still haunts me through love's mists.

What can I do? What can I say? love is blind, for peace I pray.

Janina Boyce

Smack

The first time it may be for kicks,
but then it takes a hold,
it may be started when you're young,
but now you won't grow old.

It makes you steal to feed your need,
it grips you like a fire,
you might say you're in control,
but you'd just be a liar.

It's pushed in schools and on the street,
to young and old as well,
they think that when they start it,
the feeling is just well,

They think that they control it,
but control is what they lack,
it's the drug that's in control of them,
that's the curse of taking smack.
In Memory of W.R.Gardner, A True Friend

Ian K. Cooper

My Love

You never know when you'll find your partner
But I now that I've found mine
You won't find them just over night
It will take a very long time.

When you find your true love you will know
Even though no one will tell you so.

Now I've got him I won't let him go.
Well build our future together,
I know in my heart this was meant to be.
And I know we'll be together forever
He is so special to me he's the most important thing in my life,
If he ever left me it would cut me like a knife

There's just one thing that I want to do.
And that is to say that "I love you"
Janet Bayliss

"Captain Pepper" (Rules The Waves)

Sam Pepper was a pirate — blood-thirsty brigand of the sea
but his map of buried treasure lead some crew to mutiny
He was fearless and aggressive and to cross him wasn't wise
You could see his temper boiling — like bloodshot kettles in his eyes

Words flew swift from Pepper-lips — as fast as any hare
so angry and so grisly and as fierce as any bear
"Halt there, stand avast — withdraw you scurvy knaves,
I'll hang you from the yardarm — keel-haul you though the waves!"

As tight as bosuns bootstraps — Pepper spoiled for the fight
he ranted with his fist until his knuckles bared white
Armed with loaded flintlock — Sam held the mob at bay
his 'first-mate' drew his cutlass at the ready for the fray

The rabble backed-up slowly but, 'one seadog' stood alone
"Hand me here your treasure map or I'll cut you to the bone!"
Sam Pepper squeezed the trigger — Black Patch fell upon the deck
blood ran free and crimson — from a hole drilled in his neck

The mob withdrew from mutiny
the crew sang out a loud "Hooray!"
"Set-sail for Treasure Island!"
"Aye-aye," I heard them say.....
Barry Howard

Tears Of Sorrow

Stand at my grave and weep if you must
But do not weep for what you have lost

I'll be beside you each lonely hour
Each step you'll take no fall will follow

I'll guide you through I'll guard your life
I'm here to hold your hand at night

My warmth your support your worries are mine
Just talk to me hear me smile me a smile

So stand at my grave and weep tears of sorrow
But know I'll be with you for all your tomorrows
Iride Cerbelli

Temptation

And then, she appeared;
but I was young, I couldn't ask
- ashamed I supposed.
But later, she appeared again.
I desired, but the beautiful vision
passed and never offered a glance back.
Then I grew old, and fulfilled my inner duties
but now, greyness about,
she appear again,
young and fresh.
I gaze and yearn
Gary Higginson

Words Of Comfort

"It's for the best," they say;
　But best for whom?
"She's been ill for a long time;"
　Is that meant to comfort?
"She'd lost a lot of weight;"
　Do they think I hadn't noticed?
"She wouldn't have wanted to go on;"
　But how do they know?
"She's out of pain now;"
　So that'll ease my pain?
"You've been a good daughter;"
　But was I good enough?
"Have a good cry, let it all out;"
　Do my tears wash my feelings away?
"Just remember the good times;"
　Then will the dull ache go?
"She was a lovely person;"
　Should I need reminding?
"She was proud of you, you know;"
　Yes I know, I do know.
Brenda Thompson

The Winter Sun

The crimson red sun, breaks through the cold dark night.
Burning the snow; with its flame red glow.

The snow-clad lands, lie untouched from before.
Hugging the land; with its caressing hands.

The snow reflects, with the sparkles of diamonds.
A priceless sight; that lasts till night.

The sun-dyed snow, fades from orange to pink.
A wonderful hue; too good to be true.

The awesome sun, has finally vanished.
Dark sky to follow; but returning tomorrow.
Iain R. Brown

The Rose

The stem is so strong, it's a foundation for growth,
Built sturdy to serve its purpose.
The thorns shaped like a arrowheads to be spiteful to those
　who touch
A warning to show that it cares and protects from harm.
The leaves are shiny and crisp each one cut by nature's hand,
The leaves are tattered and torn, wind swept and worn
The buds like a child growing in faith awaiting its time
When it shall awake like a cygnet changing into a swan.
The petals are like silk and velvet to touch so delicate and elegant,
The scent so pleasant it drifts through the air with grace
The red roses colour is as deep as the blood that the soldiers
　once shed
The yellow rose shines golden as the sun and the gentle
　breeze move it
The corn swaying in the field glows like a buttercup put under
　the chin
The white rose is pure and gentle dressed in its wedding gown
Its elegance made known and wears a dewdrop for a crown.
The rain flows, caresses like teardrops, they stain as they fall
From the petals, raindrops, glisten like diamonds and pearls
As the sun chuckles, hiding behind white fluffy clouds.
Diane Cooper

The Listener

Brown eyes,
Black hair
Warm as he nestles against me
and I pull him close,
Whispering to him, telling him about
My stressful day.

He doesn't comment, just shifts slightly
and shows his understanding
by nudging my hand
With his black, wet nose.
Chris Nolan

'The Measure Of A Man'

I sit and wonder over the cruelty I have seen, I close my eyes to the brutality that has been is this the man that would light up the way? The architect that would lead us to the dawning of a new day? Shakespeare once wrote "what a piece of work is man" I feel he would strike his words if he could see what I can!

What is the measure of a man who destroys his own kind? Is his mind jaded or is he just blind? Who cries for the women and children that die for this brave new world of dreams? Not the killers, only the mothers and fathers, it seems.

I huddle in a corner trying not to hear the screams, but they assail me from all sides like a torrent of horrific dreams. How many more children must you make pay? Before you finally realize this is not the right way, for an instant I ask that you set aside your mask and focus your energies on the real task.

What is the measure of a man who would kill for an ideal? What is the measure of a man who can no longer feel? And who will kill if you finally achieve that which you believe? The mothers left crying perhaps, the ones that still grieve

Maybe it all ends when one person throws away his gun and in turn, the leaders realize the peace process has begun, they will pause to consider their religious cause, and each side will abandon their fruitless wars.

This I would ask in the name of those that have died. For all those still grieving, for those that have cried...

Dedicated to all the souls lost in a fruitless war
Joe Warren

"Nesta"

Near human thought
Bright sparkling eyes
A bark with no bite
Some meaningful sighs
A tail to show love, a 'hand' for to hold
A friend ever trusting, a warmth against cold
A panther like run, and a kitten type purr
Were presented to us wrapped in black velvet fur

Our little black beauty
Ever patient and kind
You have gone from our sight
But not from our minds
You are here in our hearts, as always you'll be
A dearly loved member of our family.

Dawn Swales

In The Jungle

Shadowy figures camouflaged amongst the trees
Bright, flashing eyes peering periodically through the leaves

A low guttural growl
Instills in us immediate fear
In the distance, a blood - curdling howl
Hidden dangers seem forever near
The snap of a twig, a rustle in the bush
With uneasy minds, we venture on
An eerie silence now pervades the air
Someone speaks they are told to hush
Upon our leader's face then appears an icy stare
Slowly his hand reaches for his gun
We feel an urge to begin to run,
but we wait, we listen, our mouths dry with fear
Whatever it is, is now very near
Then everything changes, noises return
What our leader viewed, we will never learn
For when asked what it was that he saw
His face drains of blood.
He can't speak any more!

Jacqueline M. Eldridge

The Chase

Thundering hooves, the sound of baying hounds,
Bright coats, bright sun, a scene pictorial - gay
But in the copse the Vixen hears the sound
And panic stricken tries to run away.

Now every muscle strains, on freedom bent,
The artifice of men and dogs defied,
Too late, the hounds have found the scent,
And join the chase with loud incessant cry.

They trap their prey where once she freely ran,
Her cubs impatient, waiting, doomed to die,
And on the ground the dignity of man
In shame, dishonour, degradation lies.

The baying hounds are gone, the hunter sleeps,
And in the evening stillness - Nature weeps.

Annabel F. Barnes

Parting

Uncertain joy, certain sorrow
Bright as the dawn of a new tomorrow
I gave to you my love unbounded
But for myself, my hopes are grounded.

I gave you all I had to give
And while you stayed I hoped to live
On you I poured my deep devotion
Oh really have you any notion —

What harm your parting does my heart?
Have I really played my part
Or am I groping in the dark
An arrow falling short of mark?

Depart and finally leave this place
Once gone, don't turn and show your face
Do not stay and see me grieve —
Get out, go now, but please, don't leave!

Helen Grierson

Perpetual Soul

Conceal your youth within me,
Bleed away my thickening blood.
Flowing out of pulsating veins,
Strong enough to render even the most enchanting waterfall to shame.
And cave in upon its own mystical soul.
As the potent sapphire prevailing sky,
Pours its honour to my aging time.
The strong yet some how weakening light of gallant day.
Drops to bearing knees in defeat,
Pending to the destruction of resolute night.
As if to descend a black canvas,
Over a raging fire.
Or to cool the burning sun with a fist of ice.
Replace my blood with the melted ashes.
Destroy the mould in which my soul is caged.
Banish the ashes and the characteristic quality remains.
The sun battles through in explicit armour shining in gold.
So I continue my resonant plea,
Conceal your youth within me.

Elizabeth Jayne Dolman

Untitled

One sweet day, when time comes to pass
before that moment
When your dreams, aspirations, hopes
can be lived, sweet is the gift
cherish that moment
to know what it means
before it happens, to fill a yearning
is to know, how lucky you are
happiness is never in a box
never concealed behind doors
too heavy to open
but it's also never buyable
it floats along on the spirit of life.

Gary S. T. Cairns

Why?

Those solemn sounds; full of despair;
Black is the sky; death fills the air;
Rivers of blood; lands all laid bare;
Why was this done?
Why, tell me why?

Those solemn sounds; full of despair;
Time and again, we've heard them before,
As each generation, march off to war;
Why must this be?
Why, tell me why?

Those solemn sounds; full of despair;
Make yesterday's idealists, today's bitter realists,
Tomorrow's fatalists, but never defeatists;
Why is this so?
Why, tell me why?

Those solemn sounds; full of despair;
The wheel of life turns round, we always hear this sound;
These sounds are nothing new; this sense of de-ja vu:
For we know the reason why -
That man, was born to die.
John Cord Mather

Before Mankind

There was a time when the air was clear
Before mankind came on the scene
When animals of all kinds were free to roam
When war and destruction were words unknown
It was when forests grew wild and free
And there was no pollution in the sea
Clear water running in the stream
But now all of this is just a dream
Because one fateful day some time ago
The Earth was dealt a deadly blow
A brand new species reared its head
And filled the world with fear and dread
From that day on the world was changed
The way things were was re-arranged
The species in question was lacking grace
And came to be known as the human race
Has the damage the species caused gone too far?
Or is there someone watching from a distant star?
If there is such a race with the power to lead
Please give us the guidance we so badly need.
John O'Dowd

Patterns

Trees! Leaning against a darkling sky,
Bending and swaying in the bitter wind;
Rough lace, rustling and sighing,
Trimming the edge of Winter's robe.
Stately lady of cold days and frozen nights.

Stark, black, reaching ever upwards,
Giving promise of the buds of spring,
When delicate and fragile tracery
Opens to our ever hopeful eyes
The joys of light and fresh new birth.

Soft greens against the blue of sky.
Birds sing and nestlings flutter still.
The scent of flowers rises to the canopy above,
Summer is here and spreading overhead
Are branches covered by her joyous dress.

Before our drowsy eyes, the pictures change.
Heavy with fruit and humming bees that lull
The senses into mild stupor, we lift our glance
And draped in gold and rust and brown,
Autumn appears, most gracious One of all!
Joan S. Smith

Poetry In Perpetual Motion

Basically due to a totally physical disability
Being house-bound is an horrendously personal indignity
Though I venture forth in adversity - confident in self-perceptibility
Modestly testing my artistic ability - ever constructively occupied
in some creativity, in all manner of expressivity - thus minimizing
the intensity of endurability its pressures so taxing - involving
muscular spasmodic immobility
A challengeable prospect - yet not am I as such - an entire wreck
of humanity but that of a conscious being - inspired with inner
strength and vitality - the ability to change the scenic view - by
way of variation - still I travel far beyond the realms of human
expectation to further higher places - those transpired - by the
gift of imagination - where - entranced - I journey on into temporal
temptation. En route - wholly by means of visual transportation
Through the heavenly wonders of transcendental meditation
However else am I to make known this supreme realization
Or indeed how else am I to acclaim my soul's salvation.
Eleanor Haydon Sanderson

Quench This Thirst

It's said that the longest of journeys
Begins with that first timid step,
And if I step toward you, I wonder,
Would you stand firm, arms open wide
To my love?
Or would you take flight into the night?
Would you let our eyes meet, our lips touch,
Would you allow my fingertips to trace my love
Onto your body?

Let me lose myself in your mystery.
Your loveliness.
Let my soul meander through your desire for me,
Moving gently and kindly on
The paradise of your existence.
Quench this thirst of my need for you
With your body and soul and being,
Eyes meeting, lips touching,
As my fingertips trace my love
Onto your body.
Barbara Hopwood

Hardy's Time

You were old Father Time
    Before you were young,
Born of an ill-matched pair;
    You talked and behaved like no other child,
You didn't ask to be there.

You never knew a kid's laughter,
    There never were times you were glad
And like those who begot you, your parents,
    You lived in a world that was sad.

If Hardy had had his own children
    He'd never have conceived such as you;
Some children die before they grow up,
    You aged before you were two.

With Jude down to his last penny
    You went...and took Sue's tiny pair
Because as you said 'we're too menny'
    ...That was the hardest to bear.
Ivan Bennett

To My Husband

I live but for my love
and in my love.
That love is you.
If there's a heaven above
and God be love -
Let it be true! -
I'll be forever you and you'll be me
throughout our life, and all eternity.
Ella May

Feelings

When dark clouds gather overhead,
And threaten all that you hold dear,
Don't stand aside, for you must fight,
Until those clouds all start to clear,
Stand firm and strong, when you feel weak,
When sadness takes that lonely hold,
Think of the good times, the happy days,
When rainbows held those pots of gold,
Just persevere, and at the end
Through love, your rainbow will reappear,
And happiness will still be yours,
Togetherness is all that's dear.
Judith Wilson

Before The Journeymen Came

He camped atop the tallest tree each season
before it was felled,
singing loud his warnings and welcomes
to those that understood.

For hours I would watch him circling
While she did all the work,
his nest was well feathered and he knew it
though he could never span the ways of the long-pig.

Flying high and looking fearsome
in his jet-black suit,
as if he were a raven, on leave
from the Tower of London.

I'll never find out if he found out
but it's sure he's gone for good,
so I shall remember my fair-weather friend
the blackbird, and Little Wood.
Alan Marston

Thirty Years Of Love

I never knew that love could be like this
Before I saw the wonders of your smile
I thought that only books could hold such bliss
as I do feel, when with you for a while.
Each tender dream I held within my heart
Of what my love when blossomed full would be,
was but a part of all the love I give
When I'm with you, my heart's raging sea
of fiery actions, wondrous tenderness,
one moment I'm a flame the next quite calm
You hold the key to all my untold thoughts
You make the raging sea then lull the storm.
Would that I could with words of simple mean,
tell you of all the gentleness I feel,
or with an action thought and yet not done
if I could say it then I would with will.
Ah but my darling, in my heart I know,
that though no word or action could convey
but part of all my longings and desires,
I'll love you just a little more each day.
Jan Wheeler

Sun Worship

Oh wonderful, beautiful, radiant sun
Another day has just begun.
Your first streak of light
Heralds the dawning
It's going to be a lovely morning.
Soon you will be shining through
When the night sky turns to azure blue.
Up you rise in carmine pink
Enough to make an artist think.
Through the day you're always there
Showing us how much you care
Making all the flowers grow
Twilight comes and down you go.
Bathed in gold and gleaming bright
You fade away into the night.
Dorothy Parsons

A Union A Summer's Night

Glory unto thee, beneath the stars, I lay
Beauty made known to me.
She looks down with a starry-eyed gaze.

I feel the lovingness of
thy warm gentle embrace.
Oh, how I long to touch,
The smooth contours of thy face.

Thou who art, so dear to me
I would, gladly take thee for a bride.
Thy love, means that much to me.
To be forever by my side.

Thou art, like a dream.
Who sparkles Emerald light.
Thou art but a dream.
A balmy summer's night.
Gordon Treuge

A Soldier's Return

The soldier home for the rest of his days
be it beau geste
collapse in the heat, weak heart beat,
a soldier's retreat by golly we were beat,
by an army elite,
one soldier's return look at the burn
stop and return,
to home his eyes would roam
the secrets of a soldier is to get bolder
the winter colder, the winter war,
if we knew it well, in a cell,
if time could tell.
John Bain

"Day Out"

Heavily tattooed arms pushing conveys of prams
Babes screaming for the beach
While groups of raging toddlers follow on
The flip flops slap through grubby pavements
As the dirt ingrained toe nails lead the march
Blue veined legs they throb and boil
Under duress of these large breasted mothers
claps of thunder echo
from the pains of the one stray child
His screams pollute the air
And foul Language is there to share
Pursed lips push hard through a stench of warm brown Ale
She oozes through the open door of these men's second
homes
Where rusty necks get oiled and brain cells are born again
Now cigarette ash hits the frail baby's head
As the fuming drug stick glows it's burning grey and red
slowly filtering its way to the culprit clammy hand
The tribe abruptly stuck in mud clad oily sand
The tome is coarse with faces strained
Their day of pleasure never gained.
Jonathan Keegan

The Busy Stream

Silver glides the valley stream.
Beneath a ridge where tall pines dream
Threading velvet silent combs.
Past an ancient church with leaning tombs.
Here the willows cast their shade
Flickering sun rays through the glade
Running across the meadow crystal clear
A chance to sparkle on the weir.
Tumbling over the slimy rocks
Causing squeals and wetting socks.
Past golden barley and yellow corn
A dive under and bridge from the vicars lawn.
Behind lie hazy watchful hills
Ahead the river and boating thrills.
George Smith

The Alphabet Poem

A is for apple which all of us eat
B is for bobble to keep our hair neat
C is for cry which we do when we're sad, D is for door which we slam when we're mad
E is for envelope which we send with a letter, F is for flu and we hope we get better
G is for giant which stands very tall, H is for hard just like a wall
I is for ice which is very slippy, J is for jewels which are very pretty
K is for kind which you are if you're nice, L is for lolly which is made of ice
M is for mild which isn't very strong, N is for night which is 12 hours long
O is for old which isn't very new, P is for point which is an action you do
Q is for quiver which you do when you're cold, R is for rubbish with grime and with mould
S is for sugar which is nice and sweet, T is for toffee which is a very nice treat
U is for umbrella which will stop the rain, V is for virus which may cause you pain
W is for whisky which is very strong, X is for xylophone which will play a song
Y is for year which is 12 months long, Z is zero otherwise known as none
Alison Lawson

Darkened Destiny

There's a darkened destiny where flowers never grow,
Away from love and laughter, the happiness we know.
To hear a child's voice crying out in despair,
There's a darkened destiny somewhere out there.
Magic mountains, misty meadows and rivers running deep,
Fantasies, a fairy tale, the tired eyes that never sleep.
No pain, no aching heart, no cure for blistered skin,
A crumpled weakened body, the spirit trapped within.
While others squeal in delight,
No one hears the lonely plight
Of the little one left behind
Lost, crippled, deaf and blind.
Sweet prisoner, child of love does penance for time,
Searching for the answers, but love was the only crime
Fated by the seeds that we sow,
In that darkened destiny where flowers never grow.
Claire Olite Pratt

The Last Milk Train

Out on the Moors there was mist and rain,
Awaiting the passing of the early Milk Train.
At the Station, a-puffing, and blowing it stood
And, in just a few minutes it very sadly would
For the very last time - depart a.m. at 4:30
Hissing, and clanking, with smoke so dirty.

At the Canal, the first crossing gates
Old Fred does stand and patiently waits
Train is never late, it's on its way.
Returning a little later on in the day.
The train is now approaching at quite a rate
Fred steps over and opens the gate.
The train slows over the crossing and comes to a stop.
The driver leans out: "Ow do Pop?".
"Last one then Fred," says he
"From Glastonbury to the Sea.
It may well be - "Shanks Pony' from now on
As this line is now sadly finished - gone!"
Off chuffed the train, Glastonbury Tor to the rear.
Fred nodding: "Tis a very sad day for all of us here."
Graham F. Ratcliffe

Autumn

Twisting, twirling, tumbling, turning,
autumn leaves all red and gold,
from their branches fierce winds pluck them
scattering them o'er wood and wold.

Bonfires burning, brightly burning,
fireworks soar and rend the air,
happy children pile on firewood
burn Guy Fawkes without a care.

Ducking, darting, dashing, daring,
leaves are tumbling, swirling round,
how I love to watch them churning
thickly carpeting the ground.

Creeping, crawling, chasing, chiding,
autumn winds and chilly pier,
boldly coloured trees and woodland,
golden season of the year.
Jeanne Martin Tammas

Through the Window

I stare through the window
at what, I do not know
The leaves are falling from the trees
floating just like snow,
There is no sound
at least none I can hear,
My body starts to shiver
is there something that I fear,
My mind is filled with many thoughts
none matter, Of that I have no doubt,
perhaps this is the end for me
surely I should shout,
I try to say a few words but
there's nothing to come out,
I watch the leaves fall like the snow
and realise this would be,
The memory that I take away
and the last thing that I see.
Graham Mills

What A Player

A footballer one day, was chosen to play
At Wembley in front of the queen.
He arrived at the ground, and was amazed when he found
He'd been picked for a girls' netball team.

He did his best to stay cool, but he felt such a fool
As he curtsied to the queen in his skirt.
When the whistle did blow, he stood scratching his jaw
And the crowd shouted, "Have a go Bert."

When he received his first pass, from a big buxom lass
The elastic snapped in his briefs.
The crowd stood and roared, even the queen did applaud
Then Bert tripped and broke his false teeth.

At the end of the game, the fans chanted his name
Even the queen stood and raised her two thumbs.
In the papers the next day, one sporting headline did say
"Poor Bert: all knickers and gums."
Bak Diabira

Love

One thing I want is love,
because when you are, you're like a dove.
Flying high in the sky,
You will never want to die.
Remembering what the other persons said,
Reciting it inside your head.
In your mind you're all a-daze.
Just going through a love faze.
Emma Sears

"Mum"

I'm off to work now, no-one cares,
At the T.V. screen they sit and stare,
Is it me, or the age of technology?
They couldn't careless, until they miss me!

Usually when they come home for tea,
They say (regardless of what I'm doing) "What's for me?"
Not, "How are you Mum, how's been your day?"
"You're here all day, doing nothing "they say!"

When I ask "How was school?"
All I get is "Alright" you are thinking "Fool!"
But when it comes to getting your homework done,
It's "Help, I don't know how to do this, Mum!"

My job is full of hard work and stress.
And because I smile and usually say "Yes"
To anything you need. You know when to mope,
When you ask for something and I say "Nope".

Have you ever thought how tired I get?
After a day at work, there's more at home I bet!
Just remember when you have a daughter or son,
There's no one else ever like your Mum!

Denise Bracey

Remember

My darling, do not weep for me
At the setting of the sun.
Look towards the future,
Be strong for both our sons.

My body now lies with others,
Broken by the war.
I shall not be returning
As comrades reach home once more.

My soul, now lies in heaven
With my father up above,
But my heart, will always be with you
My sweet and precious love.

The bloody fight is over,
The fire and thunder subside.
Peace will now be with you all,
There is no need to hide.

So I ask you, do not weep for me
At the setting of the sun.
Just remember those who gave their all,
With the silence of the guns.

Janice Mary O'Neil

Road Of Dreams

I stare through the windscreen
At the future ahead,
In the distance I'd left, the past is red.
No change in the lights of this tragic life.
The drive is gone, no longer I belong.

Before me I see the future's road
As a horizon of hope, so far, yet still
So near it seems in the scope of my dreams.

Memories of the past are now fading fast.
Memory cuts, deep scars I'd hidden
Panic stricken, my soul frost bitten.
Memories of pain, despair, I'd bared.
As I once ceased to move in the past's traffic queue.

The journey is long, on the road of dreams
Frozen years thaw, as the sun bursts beams
The warmth of the future, on the road of dreams

Jason O'Donnell

Saudian Mountain Echo

Here in the heights of the Hijaz
at al-Shafa, the curing place,
shouts shunt through fissures of rock
seeking an echo.

But Echo who loved Narcissus
lacked a voice of her own:
'Is anyone here?' he called;
'...here?' she echoed alone.
So he shunned his echoed voice
to become beloving of his beloved image.

In these Hijaz hills
the cure is in the shout
for nerve-ragged exiles from the towns.

The harsh and sharded peaks
of these majestic hills
an alembic of primal being.

But after the shout most must go
to home or hotel
where the mirrors are.

Alan Frederick-Smith

The Sea Changes Its Moods As We Change Ours

The sea changes its moods,
As we change ours.
One day it is calm and gentle,
And the next angry and wild.
As it pounds against the sea walls,
Sending spray into the air,
and batters the ships upon the sea.
The sea changes its colour,
From blue to grey to green.

As I walk along the beach,
Leaving footsteps in the sand,
The seagulls screeching overhead,
Flying, floating in the sky.
The waves lapping in and out,
Gently caress my feet,
And as I sit upon the beach,
I feel completely at peace.

Edwina Ann Kernot

Lottery Fever

Lottery fever's everywhere you turn,
As we all try for dreams beyond compare.
Money for nothing, not what we can earn,
But will we be happy, even if we share?

At least good causes gain from our weak wills,
Bringing joy and happiness to others.
But can we spend, and hide those unpaid bills?
Ignoring all that sound advice from mothers.

Should opera gain when others feel the need?
Contentious issues leading to excess.
Surely powers that be will have to heed,
Strong calls to give a share to N.H.S.

Politicians say the lottery is a winner,
And so it is if moderation reigns.
But could the first prize be a little thinner?
Ensuring more of us enjoy the gains.

Millennium funds will swell to help ensure
We celebrate in style a brand new age,
With peace we hope for ever will endure,
Mankind no longer in a rage.

Arthur H. N. Dyke

Ploughing Match

Hope a Ploughing Match site has been found
As November is about to come round
The secretary will be letting the ploughman know
So on match day they will have been told where to go

As they start to arrive, man and machine
Looking very smart, polished and clean
Won't be long till given the word to begin
With each ploughman wishing to win

Now it's time to put up the feering poles
With a bit of luck a plot without ruts and holes
The stewards are on the move having a look
Making sure the ploughman have kept to the rule book

After ploughing away for most of the day
It's the one time of year you won't get a pay
time has come for the judges view
And hope it's been shining down on you

If you have not been good enough to have won
It's the taking part that counts and a bit of fun
Give the winners a loud cheer
Come back and try again next year.
George Main

Sarajevo Child - Spirit Of Innocence

It was beautiful in the Springtime, in the Summer and the Fall
As I wondered where my friends were and why they didn't call,
I roamed from room to room in my Sarajevo home
My parents they had gone away and left me all alone,
So I wandered down the cobbled streets to where I used to play
Though no friends were there to greet me on this bright and
    sunny day,
On passing by the school yard, no laughter met my ears
It had never looked so desolate in all my living years,
I crossed the empty street, to where the sweet shop used to be
To find twisted iron and fallen stone staring back at me,
Continuing to the churchyard it was there I stood aghast
For amidst the withered flowers, I found my friends at last,
I searched amongst the headstones and finally I cried
One read, "Anna Baracova," for in that war, I'd died.
James H. Dalton

Is Anybody There?

"Is anybody there?" I shouted out loud
As I walked in through the front door,
There was nothing but silence as I stood there and listened
Though I'd heard a loud thud I felt sure.

I called out again, "Is anyone there?"
But only my heart I could hear,
I walked through the hall and into the kitchen,
By now I was shaking with fear.

I felt sure there was somebody waiting for me
And would pounce with gun, stick or knife,
And all on my own I would not have a chance
To win in a fight for my life.

The kitchen was empty, Oh what a relief,
I sat down, my legs all a-tremble,
Then I heard it again and quickly looked round
From my seat at the large kitchen table.

And then how I laughed as I realized where
A mind filled with scared thoughts can lead,
For with a loud thud from a flap in the door
Came the cat I had come here to feed.
Audrey Harris

I Just Wanted To Be Healthy

A jealous feeling rushes through me,
As I see the girl next door running,
Her legs moving swiftly on the grass;
She's so healthy.

And there's me sitting in a wheelchair,
Longing to run, longing to jump,
Wheels as the only form of transport;
Nothing to rely on except my wheels.

I turn away, I can't stand it anymore,
Everything seems so helpless since the accident,
I still get flashbacks now and again;
That was the worst day of my life.

I was six years old, on a sunny day,
I only wanted to cross the road,
Instead, they took my legs; amputation was the result;

Now, nine years on, I'm totally dependent,
People take pity on me, because I'm not like them,
I never know who my real friends are;
Because people always look down on me;

I just wanted to be healthy; like everybody else.
Jodie Isaac

Life

As I tread the green grass of the valleys
As I brush past the wind in the air
I feel that it's good to be living,
Although I'm not a millionaire.
Simple things in life are more pleasing.
Without them what would one do,
Like people saying good morning,
Or someone saying I love you.
Life is too short to quarrel, argue, bicker or fight.
For life doesn't last forever.
Our days are soon turned into night,
When time is near we look back and say,
God you can take us, we've done good in our own way,
Our eyes start to close, our hearts stops to beat.
We're ready for you o Lord to meet
In heaven as on earth we will do our best,
Once that our soul has been laid down to rest
So let us make life as happy as we can.
For we have only a very short span.
Barry Kenyon

The Empty Nest

The scattered toys, enhance the noise
As children play 'round my feet
In bed I can't lie, 'cause a baby will cry
There's no time to rest or to sleep

I dream of the space when the children have flown
A welcoming peace and some rest
Today dawn's anew, for that dream has come true
My last child's vacated the nest

The tick of the clock envelops the block
Why? I never heard it before!
The floor shines bright, not a shoe is in sight
And I stare at the silent door

My memories flow to the time long ago
When my home like a merry-go-round
Through the cries and the noise, opaque were the joys
Yet they're treasured, in gold now are bound

When perplexed don't say, "Not another day"
Though the house be full of commotion
For the child will depart, leave a hole in your heart
Carefree, but adrift in the ocean.
Dorothy Carey

"CONTENTMENT"

My little kitchen's small and clean
As bright as many that I've seen
It has a window large and clear
With lovely views all through the year
I see birds flying to their food
In Spring they feed their tiny brood
And so my kitchen gives me fun
From daybreak 'til my work is done.
My lounge I love, it suits me well
It's neither up to date nor swell
It's large enough to seat my friends

So time goes by and daylight ends.
Then to my bedroom's welcome rest
It's then I think that room is best
A nice warm bath is ready too
And then I sleep the whole night through.
So I am thankful every day
Whilst in my little home I stay
And praise the Lord on high above
For blessing me with all this love.

Joyce Newby

Heaven Sent

There's nothing as sweet
As a garden that's neat.
And the early morning dew on the lawn.
And the silvery trail
From a slug or a snail
On the footpath and doorstep at dawn.

There's nothing so bright
As a full moon at night.
For it lights all the rooftops so high.
And jupiter and mars
And the rest of the stars.
Shine like jewels in the black of the sky.

No, there's none to compare
With the beauty so rare.
That nature spreads out through the land.
And it's given with love
From our Father above.
All made by His wondrous hand.

Elizabeth M. Hughes

Across The Way

The friendly old tree looks neglected and sad - for Winter's here.
Arrayed in all its Summer glory
It told a very different story.
Of jubilant birds and sun-kissed leaves
Thrilled to be swayed by the whimsical breeze.
Of folk finding shade from the heat of the day.
And kind, happy voices of children at play.

Now, stripped of beauty it looks cold and forlorn yet not alone.
Between dark branches drooping and bare
An age-old church waits loyally there,
Screened by the tall tree's pageantry,
Now its grey-stoned tower stands brave and free.
Weathering the storm, yet remaining the same,
A symbol of hope, 'til it's Summer again!

Anne Langford

Who's The Clever One

I'm growing daily inside Mum's tum,
and only I know my head from my bum,
she pushes, and pats, trying to guess what is what,
though only I know my head from my bot.

I pinch with my fingers, and kick with my toes,
I'm paying her back, though she doesn't know,
I hear her shout, "I think I've got 'em",
but what she thinks are my knees, is really my bottom,

Never mind Mum, when I'm out, you will see,
Which way up, I'm really meant to be.

Debbie Loftus

In Your Midst

Forever pulled between the two extremities,
Are you the controller or the controlled?
Shake those branches of life, take a chance and search yourself.
Find the true meaning in your life, it is precious.

In the midst of quiet confusion, lay peace and harmony.
Give in to time, look deep inside and discover truth.
We all hold our memories, locked tightly, encased.
Be courageous, be gentle, keep believing in you.

For in the midst of us all are beauty and love.
Beauty and love from the innocence we share,
Where as children we played, laughed and cried.

I am in the midst of it all, searching for my place.
Life is a jigsaw of pieces, some fit, some will never.
Once you discover where you fit, lock the key and hold it forever.

Carol Goodfellow

Tapestry Of Life

The words we speak every day of life,
Are woven in a tapestry of dark or light,
Dark is the weave on the day we grieve,
Or evil thoughts from within us leave.

Bright is the sight of happier times
When words of love bubble out like chimes,
A kind word here, to banish tears,
Or comfort someone's needless fears

We cannot see as each day goes by
Just what scene would catch the eye.
But all unseen the sights unfold
Proving our words either dross or gold.

So let us think and still our mind
Before we let out words unkind
Not only will we hurt our friend,
But think how we mar the picture's end.

The tapestry of life is in our hands
We can decide what shade the strands
Let's paint the pictures golden bright,
With words of kindness, love and light.

Edith Steele

Now The Black Days Are Gone

My hands once chapped, and stained with black,
Are now, silk smooth, and clean.
The lumps of coal, gone from the hearth,
Where cosy flames had been.

No soot, no dust, no clouds of smoke,
Men toiled, and died, to mine.
Hot water spurts from out the taps
Where 'COLD', had reigned sublime.

Oh, how I toiled, the hours that spoiled,
Back bent, with tongs and shovel.
Soot prints on doors, and up the walls,
and the fires 'GONE OUT', for my trouble.

A clank, a whir, SALVATION stirs,
Central Heating, suits me FINE.
If you want a 'REAL FIRE',
Then make it yourself.
I've got TIME to relax with mine.

Heather Overfield

The Old Tree

Once a noble tree you stood,
Alone and proud at the edge of the wood,
But now your broken limbs stand stark,
Bared of leaf, twig and bark,
And yet there is something in your plight,
That still makes you an awesome sight,
Dead for all to see,
A broken, twisted old tree.

Elspeth Wells

Valhalla

Those our fallen comrades, who now fly the silent skies,
Are linked with us eternally, and none can break the ties
Of Brotherhood and Comradeship, built up tight and strong,
By dangers shared, a common cause of right over wrong.
Those evenings in the Arctic gloom, spent round a cosy fire,
The yarns we swopped, the songs we sang, with many a desire
To break the loneliness, which bound us closer still.
Your names are often on our lips, Taffy, Norman, Bill,
And a ghostly host of others, are flying with us yet,
To aid their earthly brothers, that they may not forget.
This time our fallen comrades must not have died in vain,
The hope they had of eternal peace be kept living in our brain,
A future for their loved ones, free from want and woe,
That "Never again" a voice of truth, not a thing of show.
So pass the torch, Oh Brother, that we may carry on,
To keep alight the flame of glory that you, our comrades, won.
Edward William Nichols

Memories

The treasured memories of life,
Are far more vivid after the loss of loved ones,
What is this life that is taken for granted,
We are taught by our parents from childhood,
To love one another, care and share always,
We are told also that God is watching over us,
When looking back on life we remember so much,
Good and bad times, sad and happy times,
Yet this love, care and sharing we are taught,
Help so much through illness, death and sometimes poverty.
This life span being shorter for some than others,
As life being uncertain, but death being sure,
What is this life that is taken for granted,
Memories of families growing over the years,
Unforgettable friends increasing with life,
Neighbours always there for the unexpected in life,
Looking back on memories such as these,
Surely are the richest of treasures,
Anyone could possibly attain in life.
Barbara Jean Smiles

Gardens Of Suburbia

Suburban gardens seen from train
Are boring when there's been some rain.
But on a brighter sunny day
One sees them in a different way.
Patio doors are opened wide
And chairs and tables set outside.
With pensioners in shorts, a-doze,
And washing lines with sun bleached clothes.
A cat lies sleeping 'neath the trees
Dreaming of butterflies and bees.
Delphiniums stand blue and tall.
A clematis adorns a wall.
Lawns are strewn with slides and swings,
Bicycles and other things.
Like dolls and prams and ball and bat,
And grandmother's discarded hat.
Each one varies in its style
As one views them mile by mile.
Suburban gardens without rain.
Are fascinating seen from train.
Anne S. M. Gwynn

Daphne Pope

Don't like sitting around all day,
Always ready to help in some way,
People can say what they like to me,
Hard to upset the best way to be,
No love, no money to call my own,
End of the day so will go back home,

Past times I have quite a few,
Organ playing, and dancing are just two,
Puzzle books each week I buy,
Even though I don't win I do at least try.

Daphne Pope

Mother's Day...

Cup of coffee,
"Another one",
Well, my chores are nearly done,
I've sorted the washing,
Even pegged it out,
I've listened to my kids scream and shout,
Cup of coffee,
"Another one",
Get off, give it back, that's mine,
That's it, I've had enough,
I think it's time,
Cup of coffee,
"Another one",
Now their music's blaring,
I've got a throbbing head.
Right you kids
"GET IN YOUR BED",
Cup of coffee,
Oh no, not another one!!
Anita Spraggs

A Hospital Day

As I lay in my hospital bed,
Another miserable day lies ahead.
Doctor's and nurses rushing around,
Their feet hardly ever touching the ground.
Trolleys rackling to and fro,
Up and down the corridor, they go.
Temperatures taken, and the rounds are done,
What next! A needle in the bum.
Then they say, "Have you been to the toilet today?"
If not, it's a suppository right away.
Then on top of that you try to face a meal,
It doesn't give you much appetite, I can reveal.
Visiting time comes around, after an hours time,
And you pretend to look good and say you feel fine.
By this time nurse has done her rounds again,
And ask you "Do you want anything for the pain?"
Then comes the long and weary night,
A night cap to drink, then out goes the light.
It's all in the course of a day I suppose,
But I'd rather be at home, warming my toes.
Gwen M. Lycett

The First World War (The Great War)

A grey dawn breaking, no sun in the sky
Another charge, o'er the top we rush
Toward the invisible enemy we fly
Sudden screaming then unearthly hush.

In the carnage, a whispered prayer or sigh
Closely our comrades lay around
Dear God, when will it be our turn to die
And we stare sadly towards those on the ground.

Tired, wet and wounded we return without haste
Our minds and our bodies shattered
Uncomprehending this terrible waste
Of precious youth all around scattered.

Once more to Hell and beyond we've been
Through foul mud and murderous fire
Trying to master an enemy unseen
Slaughtered as we crossed the deep mire.

We are homesick for church bells, green fields or the sea
Family life or a talk with a friend
We are defending our beloved country
And pray we're still here at the end.
James Redpath

I Wonder

I look and ponder what you think, the thoughts inside your mind,
And wonder why or if and when some space for me you'll find.
Within your heart, your hopes, your dreams, your plans may
   include me,
Or is this dream too much to pray, a boat adrift at sea?

We love, we cling, we share as one and yet we are as two,
You hide behind a face, a front, as others would see you.
But as you breathe, a sigh, a dream, you are as no-one knows,
A warmth, a love, a smile, it's you that through the darkness shows.

You have to live as those dictate a normal life should be,
To save the pain of others, in turn you must hurt me
But would I change or risk that I might lose the one so near,
To being all I need of life, though tinged by sadness tears?

Change not the person that you are but merely how you care,
To show to others how you feel, the truth with all to share.
I know that this can never be but as long as hope survives,
To you I'll stay devoted, today, all of our lives.

Bill Stewart

Sorcery And Blades

Within a realm of evil, an infernal Serpent dwelt,
And with each passing nightfall, its empire grew and swelled.
Mephistopheles incarnate, the dark hearted king of Hell,
Cut a swath throughout the land, and kingdoms of light fell.
Till a warrior Mage, armed with sorcery and blades,
Fought the Dragon to a standstill and tried to force him back
to Hades.
And though he battled with cunning and might,
His strength began to falter as he fought into the night.
And as the tempest filled sky gave way to dawn,
To deal the final blow in person, Satan took on human form.
He raised his hands in perverse prayer, and blew a Kiss of Thunder,
And the Mage's home of gleaming spires was smashed and
torn asunder.
Armageddon had come in an unearthly fire,
And the land bore the stench of a funeral pyre.
Somehow the Mage stood last and alone,
And sword in hand, he swore to make him atone.
And though in his heart, he felt all may be lost,
He'd fight the fight and damn the cost.
Until the Dark One was punished for his unholy crime,
And bound in Hell till the end of time.

Ian Thomas

The Changing World

Well, the changes that I have seen in the past fifty years
and the way the world is going brings you close to tears.
Drugs, sex and violence all common day things,
stress, when you are busy and the telephone rings.
Meanings for words which change overnight,
council tax bills that give you a fright.
Children not being able to play outside
in fear they might be abducted and taken for a ride,
sex offenders in prisons living like kings
costing tax payers money and all sorts of things.
Road rage, senseless people taking chances with their lives,
gangs of youths, out for trouble wielding their knives.
Young lads with rings in their ears and long greasy hair,
girls with studs in their noses, making other people stare
kids not happy unless they own a computer and games,
no respect for teachers and calling them names.
The good old days, that's the sort of things my gran would say,
but she survived during war time and on very little pay.
What will the world be like in another fifty years?
Full of laughter and excitement or just full of fears?

Jill V. Weightman

Don't Despair

If pain becomes a way of life
And when you move it's like a knife
Don't let despair take hold of you.
There's lots of things that they can do.

They'll give you pills to put it right
That keep you wakeful half the night
They'll take x-rays and do their best
When all you want to do, is rest.

They'll take your blood like vampires too
Then tell you, you're anaemic too
But never mind, the good they do
Is worth a spot of blood or two.

So you must try to carry on
And hope this time the pain has gone
But if you find the going slow
There is one thing that you will know.
You're not alone to bear this ill.
If they can help you, yes, they will

Hazel Hill

Feed The Bird's

I love to feed the bird's each day
And watch my feathered friend's
They seem to know what time it is
At four they all descend
They only have my scrape's of bread
To them it mean's a lot
So I place it on their table
To show I hav'nt forgot
They always pay me back each day
With their singing, it's a treat
To know you're helping feathered friends
Just make your day complete
So if you have a piece of bread
Please feed it to the bird's
To them it could mean much in life
As they cannot ask in words
Remember as the winter comes
It's hard to find the food
So help those little creature's
They'd ask you if they could

Dinah Holt

Untitled

I had a word with God last night
   and told Him how I feel.
   I told Him Dad was dying
   he was very very ill.

I asked Him not to take him
   He already had my mum,
   how much more heartache
   would I have to come,

And with His words he lifted me
   He told me do not weep,
   your father's not in pain my child
   he will only be asleep,

And when he wakes his heart will sing
   all life will be as one,
   he will stand at the gates of heaven,
   and be there with your mum

Coral Gibson

My School

My school is bold and bright
all the people wear blue and white,
we start the day at nine o'clock
have eight subjects all mixed up.
At twelve we have lunch
we all sit down in a bunch
four more subjects follow, and at
three twenty five we are free till tomorrow.

Caroline Lemon

Guess?

It takes millions of years to make diamonds
and thousands die searching for gold.
But of all things created - just one's five star rated
so I'm spreading the news, next to you diamonds lose...
You're a jewel in a star - studded line up
more precious than sapphire and spice.
A star on a high flying banner
not perfect, just human, just nice!
You're the water of life in a desert
a breeze cooling planets of fire.
The warmth on a snow covered mountain
the object of dreams and desire.
You're the sunniest day in the summer
a breath of fresh air in the spring
the past and the present, the future
a Queen in the eyes of a King.
You're the reason men put pen to paper
the world's at your feet - you're the best.
But most of all angel - you're first in the...
bathroom - but always the last to get dressed!   Guessed?
James West

The Deep

I sank slowly down, down to the bottom of the ocean.
And there I lay drained of all emotion.
This was the very bottom, this was surely the end.
All around me there was wreckage and death could only be my friend.
Then in these murky depths I saw that there was life.
Another soul was groping round, I sensed his agony and strife.
The water cleared a little, I saw his face and knew it well.
His hands reached out and so did mine and we said goodbye to hell.
We floated up a little and though the water wasn't clear
We knew we had each other, there was nothing left to fear.
Now I held a dream so dear, it was all a dream could be.
Then just when the way seemed clear to bring it to reality
It floated off one foggy night to vanish forever from my sight.
I was left alone to wonder why - why should there be this sorrow
The only thing I know for sure, it gave me my to-morrow.
Freda Larter

Spring Cleaning (Or "When A Housewife's Fancy Lightly Turns To Dust")

The children off to Aunty Maud's (they're better off out of the way),
And suddenly hubby has discovered a very "Important Match" to play.
The curtains down, the lampshades too, you're covered all in grime,
And a long lost friend decides to call. It happens every time.
With apron on and oldest clothes, in the middle of cleaning the hob,
You drink a hasty cup of tea, whilst sizing up the job.
The chimney man arrives to sweep and underneath his mask
You spy a smile (you hope it is). You're friend leaves- very fast.
Ten hours later, nearly done just hanging up a curtain,
Nearly at the end of one, your legs and arms are hurtin',
Hubby comes back, and offers help. You smile like it's out of fashion
He says "sit down and leave it to me,"
And wonders why you bash him!
Gabrielle Anne Taylor

Spent Age

The days come and the days go,
   And so we spend our age
     Like a copper penny rolling along
We hope to find our goal.

We long for tomorrow
   For brighter things - forgetting
     We're spending age - the most
Valuable thing, in the whole of our life
Yet we spend it everyday.

But then to live - our age is spent
Let's spend it with good feelings
And when we land our goal our age,
Will sparkle like - a golden sovereign.
Daisy Anne Borge

Christmas

Christmas opens her heart
And softly calls me in
Christmas calls me again
I hear her despite the din
Of commercial calling at Christmas
By pushers and sellers of tat
And those who would make a fast buck from us all
Must they use Christmas for that?

May the spirit of Christmas open your heart
Let the Child from the stable come in
May the Spirit of Christmas come to you again
Letting peace and tranquillity in
May the spirit of Christmas be ours evermore
'Til its mysteries we all can explain
May the spirit of Christmas stay in our hearts
And save us from suffering and pain.
David W. Bradley

"Silence"

The moon comes up, the lights go out
And silence reigns supreme,
The mole steps out on velvet foot
From his daytime dream,
Blinded by his depths domain
He cannot see above
The owl whose wing is void of noise
And talons out of glove,
With wings enveloped for the race
And eyes targeted down
The owl descends his fall from grace
Upon the mammal's gown.
The aim on graduated scale
The downward rated scheme
The flurry the shriek the shrill the kill
Then silence reigns supreme.
Douglas Blackham

Starry Eyes

I look into the sky at night,
And see the stars so shiny bright
I try to count them, one by one
It gives me hours of countless fun,
I find it all too much a task
And to myself, a question ask.
Does any person really know
How many stars, up there do glow?
They look as though to wink at me
This, fills my heart with so much glee
I put in them my fullest trust,
And leave behind my earthly lust.
For to me, this massive galaxy
Is part, of my eternity
The ones I know, are just a few
Like Venus, Mars and Saturn too.
I stop, and yes! I look again
At the stars above in their domain,
Who made this beauty that I view?
I think 'twas God above, don't you?
Ronald H. Holloway

Love Just Ain't Enough

Just like a whirlwind he twisted me round
And swept me off my feet
Like the beach at low tide
He dried me out
Sneezed droplets of water onto my face
That tasted like the ocean on my lips
He unbuilt my wall and let himself in
Just like the demolition man
Then he burgled my heart without
A thought
And took what he considered his.
Charlotte R. Watson

Oor Rabbie

Today's the day Oor Rabbie died
And Frein's awe ower the country cried
Fae local meenisters and even preisties
Who took the news tae the timourus beasties.

Each person and animal took it hard
Oan heerin the news ay thur favourite bard
In memory a statue they hud built
Beneath it lay his favourite kilt.

Even today oan a poetic card
The words of Scoatland's learned bard
An still the moose speaks ay his name
An sties beneath Oor Rabbie's hame.

So if today oan the Ayrshur coast
You see yi sense the spirit it's Rabbie's ghost
The beasties around ur feeling hearty
Oor Rabbie's the guest at the beasties' party.

John D. McConnachie

The Black Dog

When I awake from fitful sleep
And feel him standing there
When I first open up my eyes
And see his empty stare
I know the day is grey and dull
The sun all cloaked in cloud
I feel the weight of winter's pull
And feel the lonely shroud.

As selfish thoughts pass through my mind
I cry out to my shame
Go growl around some other soul
And ease the mental strain.

Whose fiendish master is this cur's
Not sent by God's permission?
I fear his name is Satan
And the black dog's name...Depression.

Christophe J. Whelan

No Beauty Queen

No beauty queen is she, to turn men's heads
And draw wolf-whistles from the lips of boys.
Modestly dressed, in low-heeled shoes she treads
Her sober way, and shuns coquettish ploys.
Her deep-blue eyes express both warmth of heart
And purity of mind. Girls such as she
Are nature's own; for what beautician's art
Can glamorize the soul's integrity?
No beauty queen. But look into her eyes,
And in those candid depths you may discern
That innocence which is its own fair prize
A prize that worldly ones too often scorn.
No beauty queen. But oh, to her alone
I'd offer up my heart to be her throne.

John Clark

A Poem For Remembrance Day

Do not despair for things that might have been,
And do not weep for memories never born.
But be yourself with courage evergreen,
And make each day a bright crown to be worn.

Remember those who gave their lives for yours,
And those for whom tomorrow never came.
Who died alone on crowded foreign shores,
And oft without the dignity of name.

Do not forget today is yours my son,
And you can help to shape the years ahead.
May God unite you and your fellow men,
To make your lives a tribute to the dead.

Daphne Weaver Impressed Memory

Prostrate beneath a vivid blue sky
And pitiless sun
The painted desert, in silence lies,
Home, to creatures seldom seen or heard.
Opalescent, its triassic rocks
Spewn from volcanoes in shaded stratas
And fashioned by flash flood, frost and dust
Creates a moonscape - strange, unreal.
A vibrant panorama for a lonely juniper
That stands, dead, gnarled and blackened.
Whilst petrified wood and fossil bones
Relics of an ancient past
Tell of dinosauric times
And petroglyphs and silent ruins
Whisper of the enigmatic Anasazi
Who made this burning land their home.
Enveloped in pervading silence the desert thunders
Of man's mortality and ceaseless combat
'Gainst timeless nature's awesome might.

Jennie Barker

My Hearts Holds The Key

I have a cupboard in my heart, which has a special key,
And on the shelves, I stove my jars, with labels on to see,

There's one with CHILDHOOD happiness, times so full of fun,
When you were there to watch me close, to walk and jump and run.

There's one with ADOLESCENCE of I time I was unsure,
Not knowing what's to happen next, but you were there to cure.

There's one with MARRIAGE, a time of love, you taught me all you knew
Happy times in this for me, were only but a few.

There's one with CHILDREN, of my own, I only have the one,
And he so special in my heart, my darling little son.

There's one with MIDDLE AGE a time some people dread,
But this for me was wonderful, my wings at last I spread.

To do the things you taught me, to be good and kind and true,
I promise I will do my best to follow all these through.

There's a jar remains still empty in the cupboard in my heart,
It's the one without a label, it's when we had to part.

Yet one day I will fill it before my time is done.
And leave it as a parting gift, for my very special son.

Ann Austin

The Clock Of Life

The clock of life is wound just once
And no man has the Power.
To stop that clock, or wind that clock
Beyond its present hour.

The hands of time are destiny set
The Rotating wheel is real - and yet
We all branch out this way and that
But *God* keeps His plans for us, under *HIS* HAT.

That patch of grass that looks so green
Beware - all is not what it may seem.
So take good stock of all that you've done
You may find yet life's Race you've won.

But before the clock winds itself down,
Put on a smile instead of a frown
And count your gain in the love of good friends
Before life's clock stops; and your journey ends.

Janet Robertson Jones

102

Imagination

Where do I go when I am in the dark, all alone
And my mind is at ease and it starts to roam
Which endless Corridors of the imagination do I find
Sometimes it is too much and I'll leave it behind.
I can hear footsteps from People of the past
And I see places and countries, very empty and vast
I dive into the very deep pools of my soul
I drift into darkness and I feel I will fall
The darker side of my being emerges
But my heart is blind, it seeks and searches
Thoughts chase each other, like hungry hounds
Nothing there to embrace me, no light, no sound,
my eyes are closed, like gates in the night
And nothing has colour, not black, nor white,
my thoughts they travel, through universe and space
I have got no body, no limbs, no face,
I am a sphere, a dot, with eternal brain
My ideas surround me, they want to remain
I am united with everything there is, I'm not alone
Time does not matter, all worldly things have gone.
   Ingrid Bockmann

Untitled

The seas that kiss the sands,
and leave with sweet caress,
Have known the anguish of what it is
To love and feel neglect,
The debris which floats along,
drifts. Like rejected love.

The living highs and lows are
like sunlight in the water.
One moment bright, and clear
With naught to mar sweet content.
The scudding clouds cast
their shadows on the water.

The rush of time and tide
gathers, as if sweet embrace,
Whirlpools of ecstasy reflects in the race.
The tender touch of the soft sand,
leaves sculptured patterns, as if done by hand.

The plaintive cry of the gulls
drowns the senses, and gently lulls
The all-embracing waves entwine
the fronds of seaweed in their grasp.
They endure their pain in silent sorrow
Bleak rocks witnesses the horror.
   Alexandrina D. MacGregor

Barriers Built

I built a wall, no-one could see
And it was there, between men and me
It was built carefully and with pride
A haven safe, where I could hide
No more was my love being used
It would never keep any man amused
It stood for years, proud and strong
That was until you came along
A look from your eye, it started to shake
A kiss from your lips, it started to quake
A gentle touch from your hand
Bricks and mortar turned to sand
You knocked it down without a sound
It now lies dead upon the ground
I stand before you without my protection
And can only pray for no rejection.
   Ann-Marie Wegehaupt

The River Flows On

The river... flows on
And in the rippling waters I hear a song
A song, that we sung
By the river, when we were so young
Though the river, may forget
Our love is a memory that lives with me yet
Romance was new, with you I drifted along
But the river, flows on

I hoped and prayed our love would never end
But the break-up was waiting just around the bend

And now... as I stand
By the river, and see young lovers
Go hand in hand
My eyes are dim with tears
They're singing our song
But the river... that lonely river
Yes the river...
Flows on.
   Dennis P. Watson

Untitled

I don't know how to thank you
    and I wouldn't know where to begin
but since I have been going out with you
    you have made me laugh and sing
you chased away the rain clouds
    and brushed down the cobwebs too
now and again I wonder
    if all of this is true
before you walked into my life
    I was sad and blue
I use to sit in my lonely room
    just thinking of someone like you
and now those days have gone
    hoping they will never return
now that I've got you
    to you I will always be true.
   Anthony Clarke

Silver Wolf

Drifting through the dream-time in distant wooded land
Amid white pine and cedar grown on iridescent sand
The moon, but thirty times the size I remembered it to be,
Hung ominously overhead, her presence luring me
I sat inhaling deeply the greenest, freshest air
The ferns before me parted and a silver wolf stood there
With eyes of blazing amber-gold he watched me for a while
Then sat down proud and beautiful, I thought I saw him smile
"Listen to the moon my child, she has her lessons too
Learn to use her rhythms, let the cycles start anew
Love the shadow she creates as well you love the light
I am the moon-dog of your soul, the hunter in the night
I walk with you each path in life, fear not to be alone
Daughter of the moonlight, you are my flesh and bone"
   Jane Spicer

Going Home

Put your arms around her Lord
and cuddle her with care
   Gently whisper in her ear and let
her know you're there
   Tell her on earth her work is done
she did a good job as wife and mum
   Once she knows her loved ones are near
she'll put out her arms and lose all her fear
   She'll quietly walk beside them
and give family and friends a wave
   And now dear Lord you'll have to help
the ones on earth to be brave.
   Betty Crawford

Untitled

Have you ever looked at a tree,
And considered what you are seeing,
What you see is a living thing
The same as a human being.
Just let your mind run riot
As you stand and watch it grow
This tree could have been a sanctuary
For someone long ago
I wonder if a tree can think
As it reaches for the sky
I wonder what it could tell us
If it could speak like you and I
I wonder if in many years
Someone who thinks like me
Will stand near here and say to himself
Have you ever looked upon a tree

Albert Charles Brookes

The Passing Of Innocence

The politicians rant about another new dawn
And Churchmen chant of a path well worn
While you and I scavenge on the ground
For a grain of truth, never to be found

Yesterday has gone with the passing seasons
And tomorrow maybe feared for different reasons
So live the now, the minute and the hour
And let the future, all our dreams devour

This life is not the treasure that we thought
And on inspection, not the purchase that we bought
When young at heart we trusted and believed
Only to find that promises deceived

So ignore the jesters at the seat of power
And forget the message from the holy tower
And live your life from day to day
And a new tomorrow be your reason to pray

John Fitzpatrick

Ellan Vannin's Revenge

She rose from the water, long, long ago
And captured his heart, holding him, so
Year after year a pilgrimage he made
Now much later with heart and soul paid
Rest my dear dad in the land of your dreams

She called and she beckoned with arms outstretched wide
Took my Dad home, to be by her side
He's resting now in the land that he loved
Surrounded by the islands beauty
Caught for all time
On that wild and lovely hillside
Overlooking the Irish Sea
Sleep on dear Dad, in the land that you love.

Hilary M. Crossley

Agedness

I know that I am growing old,
And can't always remember what I am told.
Time goes by so quickly though,
If this is Tuesday where did Monday go?
In my thoughts I'm still twenty-one,
Until there is a job to be done.
My back is not as straight, and my joints creak,
What once took me a day, now takes me a week.
Hills seem like mountains, and I get out of puff,
And going upstairs is getting quite tough.
My hearing is not so good neither my sight.
But! Apart from all that I'm alright.

Cecil Andrew

Hope

All races of the world tire of hate
and billions strive to change their fate.
Condemn useless killing and hunger too;
to hope gives precious life to many not few.

Every colour and creed yearn to love;
destroy the warlords and release a gentle peace dove.
Observe the beauty of birds o'er majestic beast
and wondrous golden sunrises in the mystic east.

Espy the lively dragonfly darting o'er frog spawn;
gossamer cobwebs shimmering in the dawn.
Delight in such sights enhance one's being
with hope in God's gift of bright eyes seeing.

Frosty snowflakes melt on warm skin;
youngsters squeal as whipping tops spin.
Disaster and grief must still be borne
but hope will persist as wind in a storm.

One day in the future; we hope quite soon;
men's lives we'll secure as sure as the moon.
We'll banish despair and aggressive fire
and hope will vanquish all hatred and ire.

Derek D. Hulme

'Behold A Vision'

When the leaves turn yellow and red and gold
And bare their branches, a new scene to unfold
The shimmering crystals of ice and snow
Hanging gently on boughs, shedding diamonds below
They whisper in moonlight, glistening and serene
As dawn breaks we herald God's beauty and sheen.

The magnificent tree stands firm and bold
Spreading limbs so stealthy, a marvel to behold
How can she bare all the ice and the frost
The clogs lakes, stops traffic, and lives sometimes lost
What runs through her veins to withstand all the trauma
Of the gales and storms, the cold and the warmer.

When seasons change and young buds do appear
From her branches once covered by an icy veneer
Watch the colours that form into pale green and pink
As blossoms burst into bloom and bees stop to drink
And her branches are polished and ready to bear
All the fruits of the season, the apple, the pear
Was this magnificent creation once covered in frost
Did I imagine the scene - was it a vision, now lost?

Celia Phillips

Too Much Peace And Quiet

When the kids were boisterous and young
And all the breath used in the lung
At night when they were all in bed
I yearned for time to forge ahead
When they no longer need so much attention
Not when I'm about to draw my pension
I visualized so much peace and quiet
Tranquillity after all the riot
But time is one thing we can't re-wind
Fast forward now I really find
If only I could sit and read
Or listen to their every need
It wasn't that bad mending socks
Or ironing all those little frocks
I wasn't lonely that's for sure
Or waiting for a knock on the door
If only I could have foreseen
How very lucky I had been!

Mollie Barnett

Reflecting Mother Nature

The image before stares back in vain,
an identical picture of blackness and pain.
Deep roads of time, interlock and wind
past each soul socket of hell, unrefined.

Lost within, where nobody sees,
time whirls past, and beauty flees.
Who ever you are, one thing's for sure
she misses no-one, marks beauty pure.

Cheeks once smooth, shining through,
gone the rose and morning dew.
Blackness veils the sky at night,
as youth heads a speedy flight.

The map will mature, with each new day,
beauty robbed, replaced with decay.
A slow process we all think,
but what happened to those roses pink?

As I look at you each morning new,
I stare at me, reflecting too.
A worn out face, for all to see,
taken from her to belong with me.

Debra Stone

Grandad

When you become a grandad, you must be very wise,
Always try to be truthful, and never tell any lies.
You sit there in your armchair, your slippers on your feet,
You close your eyes for a little while, you try to be discreet,
Your hair was once quite dark, it now has turned quite grey,
You feel the cold, you're now quite old, your youth has past away.
You reminisce about the old days, when you were just a boy,
The things you did, the games you played, that brought you such joy.
Sweets would cost a penny, you will often say,
No television, or computers, we never had them in my day.
You try to answer questions, and lend a helping hand,
But it's all beyond you, you just don't understand.
In your youth life was simple, though people were very poor,
You would make ends meet, do without and would not ask for more,
So as you look at life, each day, has something new,
One good thing being a grandad, your grandchildren are so proud of you.

June Thelma Pears

The Two Of Us

There were two of us, my sister and I
Always together since we were knee high
We were very close, never argued as such
I thought she was wonderful, and I loved her so much
She radiated happiness, and brought such joy to me
Always the comedian, her quips mad me laugh endlessly
We had a double wedding, sons six weeks apart
Which brought us even close than we had been at the start
My marriage didn't work out, and often I was in despair
But always through the bad times, my sister, she was there
Then I met someone else, and life was sweeter once more
and my new love, and my sister, shared a special rapport.
Then one day my sister found a lump on her breast
They sent her to the hospital that she might have a test
cancer was diagnosed, and though she fought all the way
one day the Angels took my sister home to stay
I was heartbroken, could not bear to see her die
for we could not be parted, not my sister and I
Words can't describe how I miss her, and though I always will
I know deep down inside me, there are two of us still.

Anne Williams

The Fridge

Oh why is a fridge
Always full when it needs
  defrosting
  yet it's empty when it needs doing
  when the switch is off
  the butter melts the milk is sour
and the food is off
  the water runs the floor gets wet
  the only thing one can do is
  clear the fridge
  wipe it dry
  Switch it on and fill it up.
I like it when the milks cold
but not when the butter is hard.

Janet Poulsen

Dear Pen

My secret friend and paper too, my listener,
always close to hand, when my heart begins to whisper.
Strange thoughts and sorrows, feelings,
tears my eyes won't cry, when voice
begins to fail me, my pen is standing by.
The speaker of my heart, my pen
and paper, what a team, receives my
words, not judging, unflinching if they scream.
When others just won't listen, or refuse
to understand, always there is you pen,
ever close to hand.
When insomnia should strike me, or my
love just turn away, even should it die,
as I would then, each day.
comforting to me, when no one else may care,
you, for me, my pen,
always, you are there.

John Andrew Merrick

A ROSE

A rose, a full blossomed bud. Growing
alone on an overgrown shrub.
Holding its face to be kissed by
the sun, before the wind blows and
Its petals are gone. Just for a
while its glory is seen, its perfume
lingers where once it had been.
Now the stem and thorns are left.
The rose that once was, is now
Only "a hip" - brightly coloured
And full of seeds, shaking its
head in the breeze. The rose
lives on, its story is told -
Tinted in dreams with pale,
Pale gold.

Aileen Andrews Jordan

Humanity

Killing and fighting and crying too,
All these are caused by me and you.
Stopping all this is stopping yourself,
This is all caused by politics and wealth.

Every day goes by when we forget about others,
People are just like our sisters and brothers.
We should treat individuals with respect,
This is a concept which will reflect.

Mankind were put here for a very good reason,
not to commit things like arson and treason.
We have our boundaries and our borders,
we must all abide by others orders.

Angela Zarrabi

The Sprotborough Deer

Here lies the Sprotborough Deer
All satin and Platingnum Deer
Antlers bound with twisted gold
In the coldest morn or Summer's heat
Are ever heard its mythical feet
Hoof to bough and bough to sky
Nothing escapes that wise ancient eye
In Hearn's great forest lost from mortal hen
Where Gods debate the ways of men
A silver streak, a golden gleam
Of the Sprotborough Deer, great kings do dream
Eddie Carter

Untitled

Here is the moment, the word, the happening
all at once you feel your whole soul sharpening
First the fist that hits you in the guts
The tear at your heart that you know you just must
Escape- but where, no turning back.
The chill of the fear as it creeps up your back,
The taste of the vomit, the knocking of knees
Can this be happening, be real, God please
The eyes they start twitching, the feeling of pain,
There is no relief, no redemption again
But eventually you see him, the anecdote, the cure
Slowly he surfaces, steadfastly, sure
His beard is weathered, his eyes have seen much
His mantle is covered by the tears of such
Who have known only time can alleviate pain
And welcome you back to normality again.
Anne Morgan

Loneliness

All alone, no-one seems to care,
All around me people seem to share,
The spirit of life and friendship so dear,
The say "come on now you've nothing to fear",

A day, a week, a month, a year,
always alone with no-one you can share,
a secret of the most important kind,
a partner is the only thing to find,

Waiting and searching for an elusive love,
as fresh and bright as a turtle dove,
Times running out, oh, what would you do,
To hear the sweet words "I really love you",

No one to phone, no one to write,
No one to visit it's not looking bright,
There's no one to blame just myself,
a lonely young man just left on the shelf.

It's now the end of another day,
There really doesn't seem to be a way,
and no one can tell me the reason why,
everyone only wants to say Goodbye.
Dave Howells

Sad To Leave

She gazed out across the bay tonight,
At the lights from the fishing boats below;
Felt the gentle, loving breeze lift her hair, caress her shoulders
Felt the longing grow.....

Looking behind her at the lemon groves
At the red-tiled rooves, and the winding track
That would begin her journey home,
She dreaded going back.

"I'll never come here again" she sighed,
As she walked away in sorrow,
Turning away from the tranquil sea,
From his world, she'd tried to borrow:
The loveliest place she had ever seen,
A country that held so many charms,
And a beauty she'll miss as long as she lives -
More than she'll miss her lover's arms.
Gaelyn Jolliffe

Better Times

Gone are the derricks along the Tyne
Alas no more the sight
of proud ships, as stalwart men
Salute the ships of the line.

Gone are the pit head wheels and heaps
And men all black with grime
Now not just the women weep
At these supposedly better times

The docks are still and empty now
The heaps all grassed and treed
The ponies stand in the harsh daylight
Bewildered at being freed.

The search for work is long and hard
It's soul destroying too
Sorry, you're too old or you're too young
We have no place for you.

What happen's next the people cry
No prospects for our men
These hungry mouths must still be fed
Better times! Now or THEN
Charlotte Anne Norman

Memories (Of A Visit To Scotland)

The hills, green and purple, looming black
Against a sky dotted with fleecy cloud,
Bear with charm and dignity
Their age-long secrets, silent, proud.

Tinkling, streams, cascading gaily in their headlong flight,
Weave jagged patterns on the wooded slopes,
Nature's music reminding us
That life is full of sweetness, joy and hopes.

Below, the water, rippling blue and cool,
Softly laps the shingle, while gannets,
flying high, circle, hover, then
Swoop upon the foam-flecked crests.

Here and there a boat stands out in sharp relief
With gleaming sails against the far off shore,
A small dull-grey ship
Smoothly glides seaward and is seen no more.

Dusk falls and in the distance, twinkling lights
Flash like jewels scattered by nature in her haste..
Silence steals upon us all around,
And soon a veil of darkness sweeps the lonely waste.
Cora Woodfield

The Four Seasons

Spring, when bulbs and buds are peeping out for us to show t
    that once again
God has awakened the earth from sleeping, and it's good to
    see the April rain.
Daffodils like shafts of sunlight, waving gently in the breeze
Crocus, purple, gold and white, growing underneath the trees.

Summer, such joy to see the sun, brightening the beauty of
    the world,
Holidays and all good times begun, flowers and trees are all unfurled.
Birds a-twittering in the branches, in and out the shady hedgerows
Sweetest songs in all the world, mingling with the breeze that blows.

Autumn with its rusts and browns, trees now shedding falling leaves
Bringing with it smiles and frowns, swallows in and out the eaves.
How sad to hear the merry notes of birds beginning to wane,
O how we dearly long to hear those cheerful lovely songs again.
A little sad, perhaps we weep, but know that we must pause to think
That even flowers and trees must sleep, but they again will
    surely wake.

Winter with its icy blasts, crispy white a carpet lies,
Summer sun and warmth is past, sounds of weak unhappy cries.
Frost and snow and bleak winds blowing, down on bended
    knees we pray,
And as we wonder and ponder time is going,
And soon the spring will once again be on its way.
Doris Vellam

"Millennium And Next Century"

Often I wonder, as I view, "progress",
   After this world, has years of, excess;
Will scientists, more marvels, consummate?
   Or will it end, disintegrate?

Men have left earth, - The moon have found,
   Landed indeed, on eerie ground;
But what was found, after all the strain?
   Did they return, - with added brains?

All that money; what was gained?
   What discovered, what obtained?
A few rocks, picked up, excessive danger,
   Did a weird echoing, greet the strangers?

Certain, things, should quietly reside,
   Better lie dormant, better to hide,
Would mortals, flattered with wealth,
   Realize the danger to life, home, health?

Countries, poverty stricken, on this earth,
   Millions die, short life, also at birth;
Yet "easy" help, is thrown away,
   While scientists dream up, another, affray.

Federick T. B. Wills

A Call To Youth

Our time has seen a thousand horrors flung
Across the earth like tentacles of fire
That clutched bewildered youth and bound him fast;
Yet did he strive, and striving did not tire,
For age rememb'ring
Helped him in the fray
With constant might, that only right should live
And always stay.

Can youth and inexperience be strong
When age-old evil seeks with clutching hand
To rend his freedom and destroy his faith,
To steal his own, his home, his native land?
A stubborn spirit
Drives him, when reviled,
To quell the evil which he knows: (yet knows not -
He a child).

Thus youth emerges strengthened from his task:
But let him not forget that evil still
Pervades the world in many a hidden guise;
So must he strive again, unfailing, till his sons in turn
Can carry on the fight,
And then their sons, for peace throughout the world
And ever right.

Cynthia Beck

-Look:-Listen:-And Visualize.

The song of the skylark, sings at dawn,
   Across the air, is swiftly borne
It brings such joy, to all that hear;
   That earthly troubles seem to disappear
A tiny speck against the sky;
   A symphony compose on high:
Lift up your eyes, send forth a prayer
That!, This great joyfulness is yours to share.

The violets, just nestling there,
   The daffodils, and bluebells fair:
The stately trees, with arms outstretched
   Each wearing, there beautiful summer dress.
The butterflies, and the busy bees;
   Surely you have noticed these?
   Put aside your earthly care:
Stop - and gaze; and become aware
That!, this joyfulness, is yours to share.
-This- most beautiful clean country air,
This:- England fair.

F.N.M. Truscott

Wealth And Wishes

Wishing for the things in life
Abundant wealth could bring,
We should wish for health in measure
And work for things that we can treasure,
Thankful for family and friends
As we journey to life's end.

Money cannot buy the sky,
A bird that sings
That nature brings,
The sea the waves
That beauty craves,
The trees and breeze
The snow that falls,
We have it all.

All things come to those who strive
Happiness to survive,
True success is the cream
Wealth and wishes are the dream.

Ivy E. Baker

Another And Another...

Another corpse, under the rubble,
Another country, deep in trouble,
Another building, hit by a bomb,
Another life, simply gone.

Another knife, found covered in blood,
Another body, faced down in the mud,
Another purse, missing 50p
Another madman, roaming free.

Another missile, launched into the sky,
Another young child, playing nearby,
Another environment, smelling diseased and vile,
Another innocent life, thrown onto the pile.

Another orphan, alone in the world,
Another grenade, still being hurled,
Another tear, rolls down his cheek,
It can't get much worse, it's reached its peak!

Areej Raheem

We Sit Together In The Park

We sit together in the park
And talk of the past as heaven
"I am eighty-two" she says
And I am eighty seven

They had forgotten the bad old times
The rays of autumn sun had blurred their vision
"I am eighty-two" she says
And I am eighty seven

The night sky in all its beauty
The empty bench uneven.
And the wind whispers
"I am eighty two" she says,
And I am eighty-seven.

Joan Cashford

Whales

Hunted down by man,
Afraid of being caught,
They live a life of fear,
The song I hear,
Is soft and sad,
There crying out for help.
We should have listened,
We should have stopped,
Now there gone,
It's all our fault.
No longer will they roam the seas,
No longer can they live at ease.
These mammals deserve the right to live.
STOP NOW!
Before it's too late.

Jennifer McLeish

Rare Things in My Life

I'm sat here thinking, of the good days we've had,
Come on let's face it, none of them bad!
I often look back on the years I've gone through
Wondering how I managed, of course, without you,
You're that wonderful person, with the true heart and mind
I must say myself, you are a rare kind.
So thoughtful, so honest, without any lies.
That's why we're together, with no ties.
So honest and stable, your love never crumbles
I hope in our lifetime, it never tumbles.
You're a package, a parcel, like a dream come true.
Wrap it all up, to say, "I love you,"
I couldn't do without you, I felt that from the start
I've never felt this way, nor has my precious heart
It beats just for you, just like a china clock,
You have to be careful, not to break or knock
Your love keeps me going through every single day
Knowing how to cope, knowing what to say.
You're that dream, you're a miracle that's come true
You're a wonderful man, "May God Bless You"

V. J. Goddard

Life!

The same old things! I hear you say
Come on! It's going to be fine today
Give a grin, show them pearly whites
You'll see, your mood will be alright
Give yourself credit, where credit's due.
Though others may fail to do the same for you
Don't let the little things get you down
Treat yourself later, go shopping, down town
To like yourself and do your best
Is harder than any mathematical test
Don't let your confidence slip away
Concentrate, keep within it, make yourself stay
Stride by stride out of the dark tunnel
Emotion comes seeping like smoke from a funnel
Love yourself, you will not go wrong
Contentment within, soon comes along.

Maria Finch

The Colours Of My Life

The carousel goes round and round
Colours fall down to the ground,
All the colours of my life
Happy moments, times of strife.
Red, yellow, mauve and green
All the colours I have seen.
Brown, orange, purple, blue
All the things I've tried to do.
Pink, turquoise, grey and white
Things I've done and thought were right.
Colours warm and colours cold,
Colours dull and colours bold,
I see them all before me where
They're on the ground just lying there.
If I could catch the colours all
As from the carousel they fall,
Then I could start my life again
Be full of hope instead of pain.

Avril D. Lampard

Winter's Depth

North wind, how icy your breath doth blow,
Chilling deep into the body's soul.
The sharpness of your frost, a silent sword,
Strikes anger into the barren earth's core.
Oh Summer Sun how far thy be,
The warmth and goodness that shines on me.
The tranquil silence of your night,
Incites deep slumber till early light,
And then the breaking of the dawn,
Heralds a new start, refreshed and restored.

Shirley Jean Burtonshaw

S A D Winter

Blackened leaves on sagging stems are comforted by diadems,
cold fashioned from the eve before, as winter's mantle covered more
than gravel paths, now crusted white, whilst restless corms
defy the blight; can't wait their call from suns unseen:
Attempt to gild the earth with green.

Skeletons cling to spidered beech, menacing rose thorns
fill the breach, darkly defiant, awaiting springwood, static
aggression with no velvet hood.
Rangy witch-hazels unsheathe the flaxen claw, those less than
robust succumb before thaw; snow-laden conifers half shield
the rest, with late autumn ericas very hard pressed to weather
the spears of the next daunting rain;
hazard's dank drummers:
Purveyors of pain.

No languid alert from banded dove as steel-eyed kestrels hunt above;
scuts retreat from fallow field, with hawthorned margins
nature's shield. A creaking hinge on tipsy gate does nothing more
than animate the down-cast frame of one-time sprite, assuming
weeds for filched sunlight; but Pandora's box may lift the
heart, as dawn and dusk grow more apart, for spirits may soar
high to sing when bursting burgeons herald Spring.

Leslie G. Stiles

The Wind In The Play Ground

He stood by the door with an anxious look,
Clutching his satchel with hands that shook,
He shuffled his feet and twisted his tie.
Trying his hardest, not to cry,
I tried to convince him that school was fun
And hoped his confidence I had won:
But I knew in his hurt, bewildered mind
He believed his mother, was being unkind.
Yet how could I tell this small boy of four
That in letting him go, I loved him more?
How could I possibly make him see
His life held adventures, that excluded me?
We set off together, my small son and I,
My smile reassuring, his eyes asking "why?"
His taut little fingers pulled hard at my coat,
And a lump like a rock pile invaded my throat,
Then down by the school gate, he saw boys he knew;
They called him... he followed, his laughter rang through!
I wanted to call him, to wave last good byes,
But the wind in the play ground blew dust in my eyes.

N. F. Medcalf

The Whole World

Oh holiday in Crete
Clinging together
like a food chain
In the sea
The rain polka-dots us.

I turn to my partner
Who holds me and our child
I say
You have your whole world
in your hands.
Yes, and I have your whole world in mine.

Like seaweed
Like droplets in the ocean
Like a school of fish
Like links in the coral reef
We are integral
We hold and balance
And juggle
Each others lives
Each others worlds in our hands...

Stella Kandinsky

A Winters Reign

Winter prepares to open her gates
Clinging mist crawls and suffocates
As the smothering fog with its clammy hands
Draws its curtain across the lands.

And nature in all her wondrous spite
Has bled the trees of all their fight
As she pillaged the leaves of their summer shroud
Of which they'd once been so humbly proud.

Perilous rain clouds, swollen and doomed
Drowning the ego of all that once bloomed
The wind gathers strength in a frenzied furore
The turbulent rage of a winter war.

As night brings with her the glacial cold
The ice has spread her crock of gold
The aura of daybreak revealing its lust
At the earth that glitters with champagne dust.

And now standing tall the modest trees
She's painted them all with icicle leaves!
No, winter will never be falling from grace
She has the beauty of her other face.

Rebecca Partlett

A Wish From A Tree To David

And now that my arms are heavy with leaves
I can lend you messages dancing with love
I twirl in the sun and my heart gently heaves
Sighs of delight as I look down from above.

As I cradle the breeze and rustle my arms
I can help you to learn in such beautiful ways
The shapes of my voice that will fill you with calm
To put peace in your heart and light in your days.

You have grown up so fast since my arms were all bare
You laugh and you sing and you fill life with fun
Was it me, this old tree, that made you aware
You don't have to be fall to be warmed by the sun

So now that I've watched you slowly unfold
I can bow low over you and whisper with pride
Happy Birthday my friend, who is just two years old
May you always be safe with me by your side.

Brenda Mason

Victims Of War

Millions live with shattered innocence - daily terror - stifled hopes.
Children raped - their bodies tortured - terror holes outside of hell.
Forced submission - freely given - for fear reprisals would be worse.
Such are the reports we're hearing - round the word - as daily news.
Victims - crippled - maimed and slaughtered - abandoned - traumatized and starved.
Helpless orphans - left to wander - sniper's targets - refugees.
Ruthless plots of evil warlords - totally devoid of love.
Heinous - heartless - hateful - hellish- such can be their devilish plans.
Plans to take the young and weakest - pick them off and break morale.
Break the very heart of nations - calculated strategy.
Open graves - with nameless victims - deeper wider - swallowing whole.
No-one speaking words of comfort - telling them how much they're missed.
No-one giving flowers or parties - remembering their precious lives.
No such words of loving memory - on the headstones of these graves.
Can it be - these words describe the world we live in - in our times?
Modern man - with such potential - with eyes to see - and yet so blind.
Blind to all the cruel suffering - hardened to the very core.
Regardless of the devastation - believing they are in control.
Rule - destroy - diffuse and conquer - intimidate - and terrify.
Mutilate and maim and murder - only ruins left - to testify.

Stella Clare Mitchell

Let's Think Again

What have we done to our wonderful world
Chemicals, pollution, disease, the lot.
When are we going to open our eyes
And let this terrible destruction stop.

Governments argue as wildlife dies
Forests disappear before our eyes,
Waters are stagnant as never before
Please God help us! We can take no more.

We crop spray this, and crop spray that
Blowing the ozone layer apart.
Creatures die in horrific pain
Covered in oil as government's gain.

People say "But this is progress"
Me, I think it's a disastrous mess.
Think of your children if not for yourself
Let's think again, and see some sense.

Bunty Macleod

The Lonely Soul

The hectic town and the crowds of people,
Central, the lonely soul.
The noise is deafening and the atmosphere neurotic,
But still, this lonely soul.
The chaos, the chatter, the sound, the sight.
And yet, the lonely soul.
The day monotonous, with each melancholy note,
And there, the lonely soul.
Every person caught up in their own little act,
And so, the lonely soul.
To the stage they take and perform their scene,
Goes on, this lonely soul.
Their existence goes on no matter who or when,
And thinks, this lonely soul,
"When will I be rid of this frantic survival?"
"You can't" this lonely soul does pond.
"Ah well", he sighs. So on it grinds,
But central, the lonely soul.

Lesley Robinson

Dereliction

How I have loved you,
Cefn Coch;
how my heart sailed on Summer's whispered breath
and how my soul danced among fragile snowflakes
drifting from the chill sky of dark midwinter.

Now sad and silent, no more the footsteps fall
upon oaken stair.
No longer, in verdant acres, the gentle whisper
of a precious friend.
Gone now coloured Autumn's crackle,
beneath impatient hooves.
Almost all alone at last
but for the silent sheep and Crychan larch,
Cefn Coch.

No greed can ease the distant longing of a soul
or the breaking of a heart
shattered to a nothingness.
Where once comfort and passion beckoned,
emptiness now fills
a hollow of regret.

A. M. Jones

"War Time Thought 1945 Burma"

L is for Liverpool the last that I saw of a place
  called Blighty that I long for.
O is Overseas that keeps us apart, but still you
  are with me locked in my heart.
V is for Victory we hope will bring peace and hasten
  the day when again we will meet.
E is for Everlasting my thoughts to be true and
  always my England I'M thinking of you.

D. R. Blackwell

"Self Portrait At The Easel"

The arch of body stood in frame, calls mine,
Caught between amorous dancer and saint.
A stance of indecision carved in paint,
Stripped to the waist, his Christ-sad face in line.

I shun the quick, prisoned row of glare bovine
and catch, through the pallid room, your cleft of mind.
Breathe the day you seized by hand. All combined
To challenge God in dye ghostly divine.

You are held, pale and saved before our faces
almost a martyr rumoured in shifting places.

Your artist's simulacrum can regain.
It stills time's derelict struggle, opaque,
Holding the artist ripe in earthly pain
as the body dies, a disillusioned fake.

Richard Alltoft

Among The Trees

In woodland glade, where sunlight gleams
casts molten gold upon the mossy ground,
Spring is now awakened from her dreams,
whilst peeping violets abound.

Bedecked in gowns of jewelled green
young saplings grow so strong and trued
with heads held high and so supreme,
they reach towards the sky of blue.

Swaying gently in the breeze
with rhythm, as a dancer moves
gracefully and then with seeming ease.
What living happiness it proves.

Fronds and foliage drape down
to skirt the trunks of darker hue.
Demure perhaps, but who is there to frown
for in such splendour, what is there to rue?

Pamela J. Hickman

Carpet Of Spring Time

Daffodils strewn the paths and lanes
Caressing the earth like a carpet of Springtime,
I walk with ease through meadows green
With joy in my heart and peace of mind.

I feel the fresh morning breeze stroking my face
Gently gliding through my hair,
And the sound of new life being born
Can be heard everywhere.

I watch a squirrel hop from stock to stow
And far across the village green,
A sky lark flies within my midst
And joyfully sings her sweet refrain.

As I walk through country, town and vale
Endless beauty unfolds,
Of primrose hedges, blue-bell lawns
Leaping deer and frolicking fawns,
And I within the midst of it all wonder in awe
At the splendid sights and my heart takes a picture.

Selena Pearce

"Can I Have Some Money Mam"

Can I have some money Mam?
Can I, can I, please.
I need to have some money Mam,
I'll get down on my knees!
I need to buy essential things
Like toys, chocolate and candy,
I'll just die if I can't have these things,
So money would be handy.
I need to pay my swimming fees,
My tennis and football too,
And don't forget your birthday's soon,
And I need a present for you.

Linda Ives

"The River Of Life"

Thought provoking, changing, flowing
Caressing the banks of denial,
The banks of disdain,
The banks of stricture,
Shaping momentary commitment;
Nothing dare stand before this destructive enigma,
This striving enlightenment,
This eternal duress of universal harmony.
Its carriage boundless, its role ever fluid, liquid, sober,
Dynamic in eternal deliverance,
yet intolerable in the life of the incubus,
Its wraith in growth, its reverence in eternity.
Its entreat hidden within the confines of proscribed epoch,
Its ancestry intertwined within purpose itself,
With mortality, with impetus and virtue akin,
With respect to one holy prominence,
One supremeness, One ever watching nobleman,
Cavalier of the battlefield,
Sovereign of all that contemplate existence.

M. Sheehan

Autumn All In Five Seconds

The masculine wind with style and panache
captured the leaves and fashioned a sash
breathed them together spiralled their tips
a master of flight his invisible lips
selecting the brown, some freckled with violet
a puce woven plume rewarding the pilot
the orange, the gold, the edges of pearl
all colours rotating completing the swirl
exchanging directions an instant in length
a whirlwind crescendo exploding in strength
hues of confusion, resplendent profusion
a rainbowed brocade - an earth bound cascade
completely unbraided free and unaided
sheer beauty in movement as gravity beckons
To begin and be done all in five seconds
arriving to rest with mere blush of sound
a Jacob's coat blanket covered the ground
this field of wild flowers spread in wide girth
embracing the perfume of sweet mother earth.

Lilian Mary Kelly

Innocence

Mr Tree, oh Mr Tree,
Can't you see we mean no harm,
When were climbing on your branches,
Tearing at your arms.
We don't mean to rip your leaves off,
Or even make you weep,
We're just children playing war games,
Even when we sleep.
Your arms are like our weapons,
Each fruit a harmful bomb.
Our parents battle all the time.
It really can't be wrong.
We can't go to our playground,
They say that there's a man.
But Mr Tree, you'll save us,
If we climb, high as we can.

A. Smith

The Magic of Spring

As winter comes with all the snow
Can spring be far behind?
For soon we'll see the flowers grow
To bring us peace of mind.
No longer we will sit and shake
While the cruel winds do blow
For soon the land will come awake
And the earth begin to grow.
The birds will sing, the sun will shine
The trees will come unfurled
So just have patience until you find
All's right with our lovely world.

Phyllis Haines

110

Steam Freight

Steam train thunders down the track
Cab is cobalt, boiler in black,
Smart looking loco for hauling freight
People stare by the crossing gate.
Flat car, box car, petrol tanks,
Huge steel girders stacked in ranks,
Open trucks piled high with coal
The power station is their goal.
Huge wheels driving it passes by,
Acrid smoke assails the eye,
Ruddy firebox all aglow
Steam jets hissing down below.
Con rods thrusting full of power,
Cinders rain down in a shower,
A moment later the train is past,
All that remains is the whistle's blast.
B. Wilson

To The Anglers

Fishermen sit for hours and days,
by the reservoir bank he wades
the water hardly moving by
reflecting images from the sky.

Knee deep in water they stand
a silent dedicated band,
to stand like herons through the day
leaving their families far away.

Watching his float with the wish
to catch the ever wary fish,
he walks away with peace of mind
how I envy people of his kind.

Tomorrow he will be a better man
not minding wind, cold and rain,
he tells the story of the one that got away
at the end of a quiet peaceful day.

His wife fed up with being left alone
has taken up the rod, reel and line,
now fishing is better with a beer,
good company and food to share.
R. F. Brown

Anniversary

In a world where life is never seen
By one and all the same
Where many folk go many ways
They play their different games
The only game that gets us all
The universal glove
Is the game where every fool
Does gladly fall in love
We fall in love with sympathy
We fall in love with fun
It causes many heartaches
Though very few do run
And of all the loves that there can be
Yours should hold no fears
As why define that word called love
Let's just say forty years
Raymond Walker

Andy

I may seem strange when you're far away!
But you're in my thoughts every second of every day!
I know you now like never before!
And find so hard to love you more!
But I promise you that I will try!
From this moment until the day I die!
For now you have won my greatest part!
Not just my love, but the whole of my heart!
S. Weekly

Friedreichs Ataxia

I lie dormant for many a year,
But when I awaken you may well fear.
For I am the defeater of many a good fellow,
Crippling them slowly and being totally unmellow.

The public are blind and ignorant to the effects of me,
And find it easier to ask somebody, does he take sugar in his tea.
Even the people I infect,
Are never quite sure what evil trick I shall do next.
No badness shall I save,
Until I put my host into an early grave.

Then when his body is overcome,
Shall I leave him in peace, my deed is done...
Stephen Russell Marsh

An Ode To Mothers

Mothers are just human, that's what we all believe
But we have so much to thank them for when we, at last, break free
Love begins within their bodies, when first we are conceived
And continues, if we're lucky, until this life they leave

Between, they are our saviours in every move we make
Their love is insurmountable, as every ounce we take
They teach and guide and cherish us, no matter what we do
Their feelings governed greatly by our needs their whole life through

It's a skill that's bred within them, the art of motherhood
Not something that they've time to study, even if they could
No, it's all performed quite naturally with endless love and care
Their supremacy rewarded by our just being there

So perhaps we should remember, when thinking we're the best
That our mothers are the ones that have really stood the test
And thank them for their life-long work, and total dedication
By rewarding them, when we can, with deserved appreciation
Pat Watson

Revelation

Ah! That there could be a time
But time is for the stronger,
For time goes fast, leaves us behind
Then time, it is, no longer.

Ah! That there could be a love
But love is for the foolish,
For love soon dies and gives us time
To know that love does punish.

Ah! That there could be a life
But life is for the sadist,
For life has time to give us love
Then reaps a bitter harvest.

Ah! That there could be a dream
But dreams are for the childish,
For dreams of love and life are gone
When dreams have time to perish.

Ah! That there could be a death
But death is for the living,
For death it knows no love nor dreams
Just time, for life, forgiving.
Valerie J. Melham

Politics

Conservatives are all Talk and Preamble,
But it's ours and the Nation's future they gamble.
What care we for a mere penny off Tax,
We want restored those things that we lack,
Care for the Sick, a Good Education
For children, the backbone of the Nation.
Question Time in the Commons, shouts of derision,
As the party tries to outdo opposition.
The Lords are no better, the laws are Effected
By a gathering of people not even elected
To office by Vote of Consent,
I think it is time that all of them went.
We need Leaders with strength and the Might
To abolish the wrongs and put everything right.
But we will have to wait for a General Election,
Then make sure when we choose our selection
They care for the Country, be Honest and Fair.
That leaves only one choice, OUR TONY BLAIR.

B. R. Bass

Thank You

I've had a super life really,
but there's more to life than death.
I'll still be watching over you,
of that, you must not fret.
But it was I who did the choosing,
when I received your call.
I came with the strict instruction,
to bring joy and happiness to all.
The walks we had, the sticks I've chased
and the secrets that I have shared.
But now there's an empty place in all our lives,
and I know how much you've cared.
So if you need a pal again, don't wait
for all we 'best friends,' require;
is a name, a feed, affection,
and a place beside the fire.
Now I have gained the greatest accolade,
it took twelve years to accomplish that.
Now I can REST IN PEACE and say,
"Thank you; GOD BLESS you MATT."

Matt Matthews

Epitaph

They wring their hands in mock despair,
As wars breakout here and there.
Yet still they sell to the world their arms,
Then salve their consciences with religious balms.
Wise men ponder to their selves to wonder why 'tis so,
Yet as any child will know -
You cannot have a snowball fight -
When there isn't any snow.

C. P. Baker

Addiction

A fire burns in the grate,
But the house is cold.
Someone still lives within the grey walls,
But loneliness pervades the air.
The stranger still waits on the stair.
The stranger you can never know, yet you understand him well;
Both friend and enemy at once,
His existence in the shadows conceals the talisman and traitor.
Seek out his familiar company.
Curse his damning soul that sucks the breath of life,
The stifling embrace that brings the painful pleasure of release.
But to where?
More strange familiarity awaits.
Another dark corridor,
And still the house is there,
Holding you prisoner in its eternal emptiness.

Kevin Cooper

The System

They say it's for the people
But that's one massive lie,

They keep the truth hidden
and torture the ones who defy,

They take a sadistic delight
in hearing you scream through the night,

All they want is power, and money,
but with that they wont go far,

This system is going to crumble
and replaced with another one,

Will this system be the same
or perhaps a better one.

Paul A. Haydock

Endurance

The hardships of life - show in my face,
But - that to me, is no human disgrace;
Simple tasks, for me - that once were,
Prove awkward now, but I've learned to bear;
Life shows its sorrows - I must admit,
To all those disabled, especially, who are confined to everyday sit;

Or like me, one of the many who also have to be fed,
Then - tucked safely, each night into bed;
We just have to be contented with what life to us can offer,
And sincerely remember kindly, the people who truly suffer;
Yes - I am tucked into bed, but can I peacefully sleep?
With a clear conscience - yes, but not before a good weep;

So - what do I do, or where do I go?
Although I am human, I'm confined to be slow;
Now - why should I worry, or why should I care?
Because, I'm proud to be classed as one of the few rare;
They, say that you've got to be cruel to be kind, so I've heard,
But, honestly - I think it's better, if they don't say a word.

Malcolm Stewart

My baby

Kelly-Anne is not an angel, no child could ever be
But she's my darling daughter,
And means the world to me.
She's growing up before my eyes
The time is going so fast,
I wish I could stop the clock,
And make her childhood last.
Before I know it she'll be twenty-one,
With all though's childhood play days gone.
I'll have to keep a picture,
In my mind and in my heart,
of my darling baby daughter.
From the very start.
I hope She'll always need, and want me in her life,
for I know that if she didn't,
It would cut me like a knife.
I feel so proud, when I look at her,
and know she's part of me,
She's everything I wanted,
a child of mine to be.

Tracy Weaver

50 Today

They tell me I'm fifty today
But I don't believe a word they say
I'm so handsome, young, and strong
How can so many years have gone?
My hairs still on top, my teeth are okay
I cannot be fifty today!

I look in the mirror and what do I see?
Middle aged spread, that can't be me!
My hairs not grey, it must be the light.
I'll get the optician to check my sight.
No way am I fifty today!

H. Launchbury

112

My Unborn Child

"It's good that 'he's' active", the midwife has said
but she is not with me, when I am lying in bed.
The twisting and turning, once more I feel sick,
it all seemed worthwhile, when I felt the first kick.

My creation is growing, but making me white
The aches in my back that go on through the night,
but how great the bonding between mother and child
I cannot describe, for it drives me so wild.

The feeling of love, for this baby that's growing
Is so overwhelming, like a red river flowing.
Then the pain disappears when I see the proud face
of the father who still wants me to embrace.
My body has changed, but the love has not gone.
It makes us feel special and helps us be strong.

Our creation of love that is magic and pure
Wipes out all the pain, that I have to endure.
For us as proud parents, are ready to share
Our love with our child, who will always be there.

I love you my child, my angel of love
On the day that you're born, may the sun shine above.

Tarah Melmoth

Lost Love

I always vowed that I'd not weep and would my smile and
　courage keep
But now it's time to say goodbye the tears unbidden in my eye
Cloud my vision, blur my sight, my heart is full and now the light
Is gone from life, and I must bring reality to everything.

Yet I've secret dreamer's life within my thoughts away from strife
And there my heart remembering becomes a joyful, dancing thing.
For now my dearest love has gone I relive the memories, one by one.

Uncaring Fate can be unkind but one cannot change its
　course I find,
Caught fast in the hand of Destiny for what it has written, has to be,
And now I'm just so very glad for all the loving time we had.

Snatched from arms my Love lies sleeping,
My lips smile now, my heart's still weeping.

Kristie Mullen

My Hero

If only it was possible,
But no, it's most improbable,
To think a man as nice as he,
Should bother with a girl like me.

I'm just an ordinary girl
Whereas his life is one long whirl,
Of parties, dinners, dances, dates,
The girl he dates is my pet hate.

He's tall and handsome, with dark hair,
Good-looking, oh so debonair,
I go to dances, just to see
If he will deign to dance with me.

I'm hoping that one day he'll see
That I can dance, perhaps one day
He'll ask me out, and walk my way.

If only it was possible,
Oh please, let's hope it's probable.

Nancy Gilbert

Christmas Visitor

I'd expected Father Christmas,
But it wasn't him at all.
Instead I found a burglar,
Standing in the hall.

"You've got me bang to rights," he said,
"But now I must be leaving".
Then he dropped his sack on the floor and fled,
And I got done for receiving.

G. Barrie

A Pile Of Bricks

I stood beside the pile of bricks
But kept an open mind.
If Modern Art did this for kicks,
Had I been left behind?

Across the room stood Aphrodite,
Carved in marble, Ancient Art,
A work in which the great Almighty
Surely must have played a part.

How many hours did it take,
And how much was the sculptor paid?
How many pieces did he break
Before, at last, he had it made?

Probably, that ancient master
Hadn't learned the tricks.
He could have earned his living faster
If he'd simply just used bricks.

But where, then, would we be today
Without Art from the past?
And will this silly pile of clay,
Like Elgin's marbles, last?

Roland Harvey

My Valentine

My dearest it's not the sound of drums you hear
But it's the beating of my heart while you are away I miss you dear
I count each minute while we are apart.
There is nothing so sure I have to give my love
But my heart so true, and me alone
There is nothing in the world I need sweetheart
Than for you to be mine in our arms to hold.

In your eyes I see my world so clear
Your face lights up the room from every end
With your smile so warm my sadness disappears
Each teardrop's a pearl, a pure and precious gem.
It is you can unlock the door to my heart
Only you holds the key to my dreams
Oh "Darling it seems like a lifetime when we are apart
When we're together, Oh "the excitement, fills every gland like
　sunbeams

If I could have a wish come true oh no I don't want gold.
I'd wish you always by my side, I feel the flames of passion
　standing next to you
"Oh" tell me, tell me, sweet tender love, say you'll be my valentine
Please stay with me forever in the love garden until we both
grow old

Sylvia Wright

Hidden Feelings

Hidden feelings I have many of these,
But they're locked in my heart, my soul and my dreams.

Many a time I've wanted to bellow them out,
But if they're mistaken, I'll have many doubts.

So many feelings, I'm confused as a worm,
Can't keep them much longer,
As my inside will burn.

There's so many hidden causes there's no-one to trust,
So I don't tell a soul,
And that is a must.

Why cause havoc when I'm only a thing,
I'm a bubble in air,
A bubble with wings.

Now my feelings have poured out,
I'm feeling much better,
There's no need to shout.

So a cuddle from me,
And a cuddle from you,
Will make this bubble,
Feel no blue.

Lara Goodwin

Reconciliation

Can any cause justify dismemb'ring humans
Blown to pieces in callous contempt
Of another's life of joyous fulfilment,
Shattered in an instant of hellish resentment?

It's not to reason why, the orders have stated,
Just do the deed and skedaddle fast
From the scene you dare not stay yourself to see
The horror you know it's most certainly to be.

Conscience has no place to weaken your evil plan,
Your fill of hate that subdues all else
Cannot be justified by ruthless terror:
The evil you do can be seen in your mirror.

The answer is clear, goodwill must surely return
And nightmare enmity flee the scene,
Humanity must all argument embrace
To ensure agreement with harmonies' good grace.

HUMANITY makes it paramount to decide
To overcome all dissenting claims,
And bring happiness back to those professing
"We are all God's children requiring HIS blessing".
Stella O'Neill

The Candle

You stand tall and straight.
But I'll soon change that,
as I hold the lighted match to your wick,
you fight, not wanting to change.

But the flame starts, small and yellow,
and you try to hold it back.
But the flame and I win.

The flame dances now,
as if to let you know it has won.
It changes colour as if changing its dress,
pink-blue, blue-yellow, and purple.

And you start crying large tears of wax,
that run down your sides.
Drying up as they get out of reach of the flame.
I see the change I made in you,
and find a change in me you made.
As quietly now I watch at peace,
your dancing flame, and the shadows you make,
as though you are glad of the change in you.
As I am glad of the change in me.
C. A. Stevens

Lonely

You walk on by and leave me to cry
but I don't understand, why even though I do my best to try.

When you're around me, you treat me like dirt:
But when you're with my friends, you turn around and flirt
Even though it hurts you still carry on and treat me like dirt

I let the days go by and try to let my feelings die
You make it clear that you don't care and leave me crying in despair
Every time I try to let go, my feelings come back and show
Every time I try, I can never let go, something in your eye
  captures my soul.

Why can't you treat me the same and stop
looking at me as if I'm to blame
You always let my feelings glow up in a lonely burning flame

You scattered my dreams and scattered my life,
Broke my heart and tone me apart but I still have those special
  feelings for you
I love you
Nomana Yusuf Khwaja

I Only Knew You for a While

I only knew you for a while,
but how I loved to see you smile.
I long to see your smiling face,
and feel your loving, warm embrace,
every night I go to sleep,
I know therefore I must not weep,
for now you have gone to a better place,
but in my heart is an empty space.

Late at night I hear your voice,
maybe I still have no choice,
and in your house I know it is bare,
because I will not find you there.
When I see your smiling face,
I know my world is a brighter place,
for in the end this much is true,
my dear old Dad I miss you.
A. J. Hudson

A Love Story

I know I'll never be a poet worthy of the name,
But hope these lines will show how much I love you just the same.
I think about you constantly and mostly with great joy
For you're the one I chose to love when you were just a boy.

We married and had babies such a long, long time ago.
The babies have had babies now: how quickly they all grow!
We take care of each other still as we have done for years.
I comfort you, and when I'm blue you wipe away my tears.

Because we are together every moment of the day
I must confess that there are times I'd like to get away.
But what on earth would life be like without you by my side,
To share the daily happenings, to listen and to guide?

I need you near to grumble at, to say when I look good.
I need you to remember things when I do not, but should.
So though we drive each other mad at times, that's just our way.
We need and want and love each other every single day.
(Hooray!)
Una Barnes

Untitled

Mother dear we loved you so,
But God decided it was time to go,
He took you up to the heavens above,
Where you would get, just as much love,
God decided you needed rest.
And we all know, God knows best,
So rest you'll get with the angels above,
But you will still have all out love.
You worked so hard you did your best,
So now you have been laid to rest.
Because God above knows what to do,
You will get all, of God's love too.
You'll be missed so much but we'll get by
Because we know you're up there in the sky
God took you up to the heavens above,
Where he will give you all his love.
N. P. Goymer

Healing Hands

Can you explain why some hands can heal
Bringing help and hope to those who are ill,
Is it faith, skill and love
With deft guidance from above?
Or is it the fusion of two spirits
Both concentrating to their limits?
Does a bolt from the Astral Blue
Send a current coursing through
Those minds - those hands?
Are they tuned by Ethereal Bands?
Is the Great Physician supervising
When healing hands are vitalizing.
But perhaps we are never meant to know
Too much of the psychic here below.
Wilfred Purton

Treachery Of Man

The wonders of life are amazing
But don't always turn out amusing
Nature is prodigal with her gifts to mankind.
So of all animals man never lacked behind.
Yet, in man's life want remained a common feature.
It was, in the past, and will be in future.
Soon enough one had greed emanating from wants.
And till today it has remained on man's descendants
Today you find a man sow with great labour.
And tomorrow it is reaped by his neighbour.
The peasant is disparaged by a man of affluence.
For over the majority of men he has great influence.
Upon his fellow man. He inflicts pains
In a brutal bid to achieve gains
It never occurs to him to practice being chaste
For to him virtue and probity are nothing to chase
It really is a sight that brings about pity
To watch man live in such absurdity.

Maria Ibolo

Through the Eyes of Our World

Crying through hunger,
But does anyone hear,
Screaming in pain,
But nobody cares.

So many children brought into this world,
Gives us the love that's so urgently needed,
But little do they know, the world's all wrong,
Sordid and corrupted through no fault of their own.

They're the soul of this life,
But so helpless and weak,
Kept caged like animals,
When laid down to sleep.

As daylight appears for a bright new day,
Children awake for the same routine,
Some are at the bottom, while others may be gifted,
Yet through lack of resource, they'll stay in the pits.

Samantha Stanton

"Paradox".

The sun shone
But because the warmth and brightness it gave
Was comforting -
I climbed into a dark cave.

The roof over my head
And the walls surrounding me
Gave me shelter and protection -
So I slept outside.

With food I wasn't hungry
So I fasted;
And when I was thirsty
I spat out the water I'd drunk

I had friends - but I wanted enemies
I got love - but I needed indifference
I trusted no-one, but couldn't understand
Why no-one trusted me.

So I ran and ran and ran
Only to find
That I hadn't moved.

Pippa Jarman

No Feast Of Love

No feast of love 'tis but a myth,
A lovely shadow which we grasp and hold for a little while,
And when it fades, it leaves behind a silken chain
Which binds us to those dreams of yesterday
And the only companion left within our hearts is constant pain.

Winifred Jack

Fateful Omen

Omnipotent silver moon,
Burdensome, sinister, indication of doom,
Darkness looms, fateful and ancient,
In the dark recesses of this, my room.

I am the oddity that makes you stare,
My idiosyncratic ways attack your sensibilities,
The crumbling defences of your mind evoke
disturbing dreams,
The underbelly of society scratches at your
mask of sanity.

You repress all that is repellant,
Your endeavours survive upon prejudiced recollections,
The tower of the opinionated is sucked into the ground,
All around you I watch your world burn,
Dark, fateful omen, I smile as you frown.

Lorraine Rivers

Two Faces Of Loch Ness

The tempest rose in its attempt to rage
Built up the waves to a turmoil
A sight to behold in its fury and fire
Steep banks aglow with blackened soil

Rain sliced through out of darkened cloud
By the jetty the boat rocked all alone
No man nor beast ventured into the fray
In all directions the waters were blown

Then skyward bound a glimmer appeared
A shining light already to balm
The echoes of storm were fading away
Waters were stilled so serene, so calm

Two faces of Ness with its power to change
Never ceases to amaze those that behold
Its myths and monsters in the mystery of time
Past lives and secrets to be left untold

M. L. Smith

Never Too Late

Blow out the candle on the moon,
bring back the bright warm day,
open the door to earths cocoon,
and hide the stars away.

Persuade smooth hands, collect the veil
that showers us with rain,
tuck it beneath the green pigtail,
that covers GODS domain.

Beckon the wind to cleanse soiled lakes,
create a barrier wall,
keep pure the water man partakes,
new confidence install.

Remove bad microbes from all seeds,
buried in the past,
purify misguided deeds,
that we may sow at last.

New ideals to save our world
from poverty and sin,
Straighten all edges crudely knurled,
let sincerity begin..

Ray Griffiths

Till Dawn

When night enshrines a tired world
And Heaven's lights are lit.
The beauty of tranquillity is seen at last -
To flit from star to star.
Which like diamonds on a Satin tray,
Dazzle eyes that peer into this wilderness of precious stones.
The moon, shining like an emerald, gives gentle light -
To those who travel through the night.
And as this beauty dies away,
There dawns once more another day.

W. G. Hall

'Wish Upon A Star'

When one cold dark winter's night, the stars were shining
  clear and bright,
I made a wish on every star, on constellations near and far,
I closed my eyes and wished so hard, upon a dream in which
  you'd starred
Yet here I am alone and blue, I'm waiting here but where are you?

I'm desolate, my heart laid bare, a barren place, cos you're not there.
I'm desperate, please hear my plea, and end this constant misery.
Will I, can I, live alone, live my lifetime on my own,
A jigsaw with a missing piece, I'll tell my beating heart to cease.

I feel I've lost the will to live, there's nothing left no more to give,
I've worshipped you, revered your name, I used my wish you
  never came,
Now I know, it's not to be, you'll never share your love with me
But am I strong enough to bear, knowing that you'll never care.

Olive McCanaan

Nightmare

Running,
Break through the snatching branches that catch and tug.
Faster,
Dry leaves crackle and crumple crisply,
Have to run, have to get away, escape,
Scream,
He's getting closer, hear his voice break the silence.
Lights,
In the distance through the murky mist they gloom,
Fall,
He reaches me, clasps my arm, I can't get away
Sharp, pierce my skin, thickly pours then covers me,
Pain, in an instant gone, left with his stare,
I feel no more, my skin is cold, dead,
Empty.

Louise Woods

Daddy's Home

Supper's on the table, tin bath is by the fire
bread baking in the oven, what more could man
desire, than a loving wife and children, to
comfort and admire now Daddy's home.
  The little rag-a-muffins are playing in
the street, kids with dirty faces, no shoes
upon their feet, nothing in the bread bin
nothing on the hearth, but the little ring-a-muffins
come running of the path, now Daddy's home.
  Daddy was a miner, tunnelling for coal
up to his waist in water, digging like a mole
to "keep the home fires burning" keep the
wheel a-turning, now Daddy's home,
Daddy's home, Daddy's home.

Margaret Smith

Extra Sensory Perception

Through earth space drag thought falls,
Brain - diffused, pad-borne, time-logged.
Drifting 'twixt sensation and concept,
Seeking the frigid strata of precipitation.
Dispatched by palpitants anxiously expectant
Awaiting the answer
In a paper-bound cypher - world
By mortal time's slow drift, atrophied,
Minds seek minds, through cosmic thought,
Pure thought, ether-borne,
Short circuiting earth - space,
Scorning coarse static,
Contacted, assimilated, acknowledged
To the split second,
By eager minds attuned
To the oscillations compentrant.
Unexpectedly initiating
A facility for experience
In the fourth dimension of the world.

R. Wood

Enduring Love

How sweet this long enduring love of ours,
Born so long ago in days of innocence,
How tender still the glances passed between us,
Joyous shared moments filled with loving memories.

How great your enduring kindness and goodness,
In whose reflected glory I have lived so long
Protected and enriched in all life's moments,
The world so warm a place because of you,
I thank you for this enduring joy
And pray that it may last forever

Margaret Riddell

Beautiful Creation

Fluffy bundle as white as snow
born into a world you do not know
your home is vast and full of peace
little do you know this will all soon cease
your velvet brown eyes look up to see
an image of something, what can it be
an arm is raised
your eyes look on
with one sharp blow your life is gone
around your body on the pure white snow
a crimson web creeps very slow
All that's left of a beautiful creation
and for this
man should suffer eternal damnation

S. A. Greaves

Windsurfers

Windless frowns look on disconsolately,
Bored boards are toying the undulating sea.
Youth's bootied feet feed the hungry sand
Handsome, healthy, wholesome patient little band.

Deep and purposeful their forced repose
Choice of sail size each reluctant to disclose.
Now should they try a six point nine sail -
Lazy surf mammals can at last move their tails.

Mercurial Mistral stirs awake!
Rig, up hauling, down hauling, out hauling, break.
Idling gear they speed to transform
Templed veins, hooked and harnessed, they mount the foam.

Sodden sails their adrenalin whips
They carve jibe a forward loop with thrusting hips.
Lustless snoring sea now arousing
The grasping wind tweaks his swells - its sperm spilling.

Bronzed bodies boomeranged back to shore
Quickly turning, a barrel roll to try for.
Bobbing, twisting in adoration,
Ecstaticly slide into oblivion.

Victoria Burnett

The Miracle Design

The human body's a temple not built by man
Blood, water and bones, but no known brand
Even a story in the palm of the hands-
Yet, by the power of the spirit, it stands

It is said, this body is one, yet many members
And in olden times it was put out for tenders
But can it be explained this marvel body venture
Why there should be only two in the gender

Behind the "seen" is a more powerful "unseen"
All religions pay homage to this colourful scene
No matter bodies of black, white, yellow, brown or cream
All agree when in good health works a dream

Some scientists say it's from fishes, others apes,
But over thousands of years this bodies no fake.
Even the wonders of the animals of powerful make
Have not the gift, the spoken word, in their wake.

J. R. Laird

Lost Light

It's dark inside.
Blood, thick, flowing,
lethargy induced by its potions.
Escape the dark!

Essence of life electrically charged, distorted.
Messages chemically transmitted, confused.
Rationality obscured, denied.
Escape the dark!

Bright light of hope, ambition, love,
extinguished by life.
Is life extinguished?
Seek the light!

Endless dark inside.
Where is the light?
Light of life, light of death.
Which way to the light?

T. Harris

Space - The Final Frontier

Space the final frontier; vast, dark, commanding fear.
Black holes, quasars, pulsars too;
Moons of many, moons of few.
Supernovas, galaxies galore, all those things and much, much more.
From the furthest galaxy, to the nearest asteroid;
Trillions of stars, within a void.
Comprehension of distance unknown;
A universe forever grown.
Comets, meteors, planets as well, how many there are I cannot tell.
One thing I know for sure - in the empty, full, lonely, still;
In the FINAL FRONTIER I shall live - I WILL

Peter Edwards

Known Warriors, Unknown Graves, Rangoon Memorial, Myanmar Formerly Burma

Where they lay they died,
bits of kit may show
someone was there a time ago.
Blasted, no time to call,
missing, no trace at all.
Identity discs, one wonders,
how long would they be able to tell
who fed that lonely place.
Friends moved on, an ever faster pace.
Sepoy, private, corporal, Naik
captain, Havildar, all the same,
warriors in the bloody game.
Others who came back, wrote to tell
of exhaustion, sickness, fear,
of battles large and skirmish small,
about their comrades who answered the call.
The names are there upon the wall.
What of the enemy? yes, they too have a wall.
A tomb in Westminster, recalls this missing host.
It's the loneliness, one thinks about most.

E. D. Bates

My Kitchen

In my kitchen there's lots of food,
beside the oven where my mum is stood.
She cooks and bakes in here all day
without a single word to say.
The colours in the kitchen took quite some time,
We've got gadgets and gizmos of all shades of lime.
We've got a washing machine, fridge and tumble drier.
When we use it our bill goes higher and higher.
We've got central heating in all our rooms
With all different types off smells and fumes.
At the end of the day in the peace and quiet
There's nothing left but for my mum to diet.

Tracy Bathgate

Environment

Clouds scudding across a clear, blue, sky
Birds, few and many, free, flying by
Fish gaping bubbles in the river, slow moving
We snooze on grass, lazing, carefree and proving
In the heyday of youth we'd no thought for the morrow
Now the scene looks so damaged, we reflect with some sorrow...
We scorched down the road, exhaust belching, rubber burning
Left lots of litter before home returning
To destroy all our waste, throw more logs on the fire,
Just to live for the moment, pause not to aspire
To a thought for the future, to a World going on
To all of us working and dwelling upon
The need to take care, learn and teach, to conserve
And to all work together, forgetting reserve
So that I, now I'm aging will depart, well content
With no fears for the future of our ENVIRONMENT.

F. J. Harrison

Spring Time

Daffodils open their trumpets
Birds begin to sing
Little baby lambs are born
It is the sign of spring

Bulbs are now beginning to shoot
Everything nice and green
Crocuses showing their pretty colours
Purple, yellow and white
A nice sight to be seen

Don't forget our feathered friends
It's nesting time again
'Mother birds looking for food
to feed her young
Yes even in the pouring rain
But oh how lovely when you look around
Everywhere smells so fresh, so green
I'm glad it's the sign of spring

Sharyn Waters

Every Child Is Special (C)

Tiny feet take tiny paces,
Big bright eyes search wide open places,
With arms stretched out, you try to run,
Oh! my darling little one.

Your love so warm, your heart so free,
Your trust complete, in all of thee,
But why, Oh why, must we destroy
The Lords hard work, that girl, that boy?

What makes us change from sweet to sour,
Whom told you that you have the power,
To destroy that child, so full of grace,
To leave such scars, upon their face.

No-one did, this I can say,
Give you that right in any way,
So why not take another look
And leave that past behind.
Just shower them with love instead,
For the sake of all man kind.

Linda Archer

Buried Love

Lay down your arms sweet lover
 and we will fight no more.
 Lay down your head sweet lover
while I bury you under the floor.
And I'll walk on you for years
and I'll sit with you at my feet
and no more the sting of my tears.
And never another you'll beat.
I'll never be fancy but by God I'll be free,
from you, your kind and the things done to me.

Susan Howarth

San Francisco

A penny seat - in childhood days - to watch the screen in full amaze.
Bewitched by scenes of Yankee glamour - would only seem to make me clamour
FOR SAN FRANCISCO

This boyhood dream would grow within - the scrapbooks there for filling in. The news reports on crystal set - the deep down fear I'd never get TO SAN FRANCISCO
The teenage T.V. would bring it nearer - ever closer, ever nearer, like Tony Bennett in words apart - like him I left my heart
IN SAN FRANCISCO

In later life the feeling stays - though other things and other ways - have made my wish seem far away - and yet I'd love to go one day
TO SAN FRANCISCO

So tramcar ride and Alcatraz - the seaside wharf and all it has will always haunt me so it seems - I'll only get there in my dreams
TO SAN FRANCISCO

But half a mo - what's this I see - my friends have read this poetry it looks as if I'm on my way - at last to see the bay
IN SAN FRANCISCO

Tom Guy

Sunset

The sun sits on the brow of the hill,
Before it takes its final bow,
Before it goes down, the tall trees standing guard.
The streams wobbling on somewhere or nowhere - who cares?
This scene somewhere is enacted every even
Created by God for man to see how
Beautiful is his earth.

The sun, the hill the trees
All there forever:
The streams still wobbling on somewhere
Or nowhere - who cares?
This scene made by God for man to see how
Beautiful is earth.

The sun gone now behind the hill,
Has left the trees standing tall,
And streams still wobbling on
Somewhere or nowhere who cares?
This scene will be the same for all tomorrows.
For man to see how beautiful is his earth.

W. L. Stokes

Count Your Blessings - One To Nine.
The Percentage Good - You Are...Doing Fine.

ONE - is that you're sound and healthy,
better by far than just being wealthy.

TWO - is that wealth has its uses - True,
and should you have both, then Good Luck to you.

THREE - is for happiness, the wanting to sing,
without which the other two, don't mean a thing.

FOUR - is the love of fathers and mothers,
and the give and take of sisters and brothers.

FIVE - is for friendship, close and sincere.
If you have such, then hold them most dear.

SIX - that your work is also a pleasure.
Not all are that lucky, so count it a treasure.

SEVEN - is to appreciate the joy one can derive,
from simple daily happenings, like the fact that you're alive.

EIGHT - at the end of the day is to find,
sleep taking over with complete peace of mind.

NINE - is for the good things you'll always remember.
So count your blessings one by one from January to December

Miki Fingret Harris

Ivy Cottage

Ivy cottage is so called
Because thick green ivy creeps up its walls,
Pretty front garden small and neat
Tiny trimmed lawn, rickety wooden seat;
Wild flowers grow under windows of leaded pane
A memory of childhood daisy chain,
Rugged front door of solid oak
With polished brass knocker rapped my many folk;
Whimsical dwelling with little sitting room cosy
Cheery coal fire to make everything rosy,
Lovely ruched curtains floral and bright
Cushions that almost match but not quite;
A well aged striped sofa invites you to sit
Pine dresser holds crockery some chipped just a bit,
Hand made rag rugs on a floor of wooden blocks
A couple of simple plants in Terracotta pots.
Wherever I travel or wherever I roam
My heart abides with Ivy Cottage my beloved little home.

Patricia D. Brewin

Going Fishing

It isn't so much that I mind
   being left all alone from morning till night-
   (though I don't think it's right!)

It isn't so much that I mind
   trying to find - ham bread rolls and kind,
   the night before
   in order to ensure
   his peace of mind.

It isn't so much that I mind
   the shrill of the alarm waking me from my warm
   and peaceful sleep,
   the noisy way he tries to creep
   around the house like an elephant mouse.

It isn't so much that I mind
   the shunting of cars around in the drive,
   the cheerful shouts when his pals all arrive
   so eager to get away
   for the day.

It's just that I wish he'd bring home some fish!

M. Parker

"A Mother's Love"

A Mother's love can never be replaced, and I found that out too late.
because my mother has died, and gone through St. Peter's gate.
No longer will I feel her arms around me, or her hand upon my face.
Her cold body lies in the ground, her soul went to another place.
I wish I could turn the clock back, and return the love she gave.
But that is no longer possible, for she is buried in her grave.
The cancer that killed my mother, made her end her days in pain.
Gave me the unhappy decision, never to take life for granted again.
But death has a way of leaving you, with so much more than regret.
Please, please mum forgive me, for treating you with such neglect
The tears keep running down my face and everyone turns away from my sorrow.
They keep telling me that it's natural, and that I will feel better tomorrow.
Even sleep eludes me, so there's nowhere I can find relief
My days and nights are so long, filled with such terrible grief
For guilt has a way of making you face up to the awful truth
that I should have known better, as I am no longer in my youth
The sad lesson that I have learned, my life begun in my mother's womb
And that part of my life has ended, when she was lower'd in her tomb.

L. McDonagh

Sonnet

Dispossessed and wandering astray,
Bereft of hope and lost in pain,
Which direction when there's no right way?
Hopeless defeatism; waiting in vain.
Suffering silently, harrowed in hell,
Fortune told and fate instilled,
Depression leaves an empty well,
With what can this dark void be filled?
Until cohesion requires I depart,
None shall know my destiny,
For searching soul and bleeding heart
conceal the future cunningly.
   Eleventh hour may cause delay,
   but ecstasy shall have its day.
    H. J. Appleby

Life As A Dream

Beneath the darkness,
Beneath the love,
Beneath the skies
And beneath the above,
you'll never find reality,
It's all just a fantasy,
Imagination,
our life is just a dream.
Nothing the truth,
Nothing a lie,
a time will come when we'll all have to die
But we'll still be dreaming tomorrow.
We'll never say goodbye
to a life that's full of beauty
a life that's just a dream,
a light of a tunnel,
something of a beam.
   Karlene Vardy (Age 11)

Nature

In all its splendour, the sun has set,
Behind the hills, beyond the west,
Its beaming rays light up the sky,
As dark night clouds come floating nigh.
And as we gaze across the sea.
The water glistens peacefully.

All through the night, the dark clouds stay,
Then as morning dawns, they fade away.
And once again the sun it shines,
Giving life to every kind
Of flowers, and fruit and all the trees
And everyone, including me.
And as the birds begin to sing,
We thank thee Lord, for everything.
   Margaret-Anne Carmichael

Fools Of Fate

Have the world's people,
Been spectators on their own decline.
They've polluted the atmosphere,
And now they're running out of time.
While they look and stair and wait.
When the planet is uninhabitable.
It will certainly be too late.
If with this policy the people do persist.
Then all the natural beauty of this world,
They certainly will have missed.
When it is a barren rock.
And they've killed themselves with hate,
No one will know they did exist.
They will have been the fools of fate.
   F. C. Pelton

Within

Behind this pale facade I call my face,
behind the hooded eyes and shadowed brow,
inside this husk of flesh, of blood, of bone,
obscure behind this shallow front I dwell.

My inner self, my fleeting thoughts, my fears,
my doubts, my hopes, my secret loves, my dreams,
all stored, unique to me, behind this wall.
Unseen by other eyes remote I keep.

I laugh at others quips, I tell of love,
I cry when others cry and share their pain,
but empty is that temple where I live
and desolate when at last back home I creep.

For here there are no jesters or no swains,
no wisdom bides nor faith in any god,
but only me with all my lonely truths;
cold in a charnel house forlorn I grieve.
   Peter John Gibson

Grandad Wondering

Force one eye open, is it morning, it looks dark,
Bet they'll have found the upturned seats in Chuff Head's Park
"In loving memory of wonderful William Alderk,
Who never knew what it was to be out of work."
"It's them young vandals with nothing better to do
than be a nuisance swapping drugs and sniffing glue."
Fat lot of good stuffing your brains with GCE's
and wearing that bloody uniform to suit them if you please
Write a good letter with the right C.V.
and see what sort of reply it brought to me.
MY mum's shouting like hell, get out of bed,
You are driving me right out of my head.

No Dad, "Shacked up with that tart," she says. No money,
No sex just now and that isn't funny.
"Do you feel like a man now you've reached seventeen,
Cos if you do you can come with me. I'm not an old Queen."
"Piss off you pervert and stick to your mates.
In any case how do I know you haven't got Aids?"

I could live in Buckingham Palace with Princess Di,
and be faithful, and happy and I don't tell a lie.
   Brian H. Keyworth

Meandering

I dreamed the sun on a better Day
Beckoned me to stray.
Light of heart, my spirits soar;
Nature keeps an open door.
Flowers smile, to them I talk,
As over the beaten track, I walk
A plaintive cry, to my ear ascends
As around a corner, my path wends.

A flurry of white, I see
Two pleading eyes look up at me.
Little lamb trapped in a Bramble tree.
I release it gently, set it free
But little lamb, beside me lingers.
"Ah!" Now it's sucking at my fingers,

It's mother! Where is she?
Little Lamb. Save from harm.
I'll carry you to a nearby Farm.
I gently stroke the fleecy down
Then slowly awakening, turn around,
To feel a pillow; beneath my hand.
   Winfred Ollier

Scream Of A Caged Foetus

Every face I see belongs to me.
  But is not mine.

Voices: Sad silk unhallowed whispers,
infant cold and indian summer fresh.
Rancid they are of lost foetus dreams.

In my inner eyed void of vampired memory,
they suck me to wrinkled impotent wisdom,
sneer at me with all the smiles I never smiled.
Mocking with deceitful innocence.

I am now wombed within the crypt of age,
cushioned tight in hard adulthood.

With eyes gentled by insightful convictions
  I can caress the sun without blindness.
But I cannot scream my past away.
  I cannot bleed without pain.

A. E. S. Gamage

If Only

I am rich beyond compare
At last - this money's come to me
I'll never have another care
For I have won the Lottery!

I'll buy a house, a sleek new car
Give a sum to charity
Fly away to places far
Nothing but the best for me.

Designer clothes to enhance my tan
Complemented by gold jewellery
Maybe now I'll get a man
That's a possibility.

It will be nice to spend and spend
Splash out on everything I see
Hope it won't come to an end
Though that's a probability.

The alarm goes off, oh, I could scream
I wake up to reality
To find it all has been a dream
But I'm the same, still poor old me!

Sylvia Hume

A Welcome To Spring

The sun is rising through the trees
Away beyond the hill.
A thing of beauty to behold
Almost if time has stood still.
  A ball of fire appears on high
With fluffy white clouds around
The morning is chilled, the air
is clear. And frost upon the ground.
  Bulbs are just peeping
Through the earth
Birds now beginning to sing
Another new year - another new day
Can I sense the feeling of spring!

D. S. Moss

Ever Green

The colour of beauty, the world all around
A certain intensity as many cross the ground
Life itself revolves around green, from a tree
  to human's envy
As symbol of youth, eternal dreams
The word's of a song love, ageless and evergreen
A momentary escape from reality
Always special just remain green.

Sarah Pratley

Untitled

When I was a teeny, I dreamed of Bliss
At beautiful face, an ardent kiss
Faces came and faces went, but not the face of my intent.
Then on a spring morn that face appeared
Fresh and handsome was what I saw
Then from my eyes the mist hand cleared.
We knew at once that love was there
We also knew we would make a pair
But love was born when our eyes had met
But not for long, the war was on
He went to sea, I sang his favourite song.
But it was not the war that claimed my love
Nor was it forces from above
But the one who gave him birth, claimed him all the time
It was then I knew he would never be mine
That love is till at the bottom of my heart
Never, never, never will be apart.

O. Wright

The Gunfighter

He was dressed in black, this man so tall and gaunt
Astride a mighty black stallion
Two irons of death strapped to his side
He rode, like a shadow through the night

From town to dusty town he rode
A craving, deep within his heart
To find the man, who he knew was waiting
To free his tormented soul

Then, before him his nemesis stood
A figure straight from hell
Crouching, like some demon beast
Hungry for the kill

Two guns barked, fingers of death reaching, clawing
Then the pain deep within his chest
He smiled, for he knew now at last
His tormented soul was free

His victor stooped
And gently closed the sightless eyes
For he knew out there his nemesis awaited
And he too in the dust would lie.

V. J. Ledley

Winter Night

Winter can be a lovely time
As we watch the leaves, they fall
Soon the snow will come and cover all
With a blanket of pure white
It brightens up the night.

The stars they twinkle up on high
In a dark blue sky
The moon is like a great big cheese
There is a bite of freshness in every breeze

The winter primrose starts to bloom
So helps to keep away the gloom
And the holly berries glow so red
All the other trees have gone to bed

Then the rabbits scurry round
Finding any fruit that lies on the ground
Back to their burrow they will run
For old Mr Fox may a-hunting come
The Night is still, there is no sound
Everyone has gone to ground
And the Lord's Presence is all around.

F. W. McConaghey

Twisted, How Sad

Some people may think she is nice
As she cleverly hides behind her false disguise.
Beyond face value - too deep for some to see
Yet it is painfully obvious to me - a person oozing with insincerity.

No need for her to voice her opinion of me.
I am well aware, captured by her startled stare
Vicious thoughts portrayed in that piercing glare.

I despise her.

Her method to question is a mastered art, practised meticulously, very smart.
Behind the abrupt shocking approach lies a devious mind, weaving to find
Things to twist in her malicious mind.

It is not difficult as to reason why she revels and survives on her ability to pry.
Creating self importance - a hunger to be on top
Feeding this need by destroying anyone she can knock.

I despise her.

Through my observation I can only conclude
She must be so sad - to be so rude.
Riddled with hatred and jealousy
Blaming her discontent on people such as me.

She despises herself. I pity her.

Lucy Anderson

Life

Life is long, or so it seems
As we travel down its pathways,
Learning all there is to know,
Travelling through the maze

As we grow up we have no cares,
In our small world we're glad,
Our family and friends are all around,
To teach us good from bad

When we are grown, reality dawns
As we learn to give and share,
We learn of love and heartache,
To laugh, to cry, to care,

The crying hurts, the laughter is fun,
To care gives us so much pleasure,
Giving is good, sharing is joy,
To love is a feeling to treasure.

Sylvia Lowther

Untitled

They said it would become easier
as time goes on
now we have drugs, violence and
the atom bomb
People living their lives on the dole.
Destroying their hearts minds and
their very soul.
Looking for jobs that aren't even there.
Filling their bodies with mind numbing despair
Bills rising day by day.
Trying to keep control on very little pay.
Murder muggings everyday scenes
God help the kids growing within their teens.
Do-gooders all around, court's a sham
nobody seems to give a damn
justice seems for a few
if you've no money you can't afford to sue.
Fighting wars on foreign ground
Believing everything in England
is safe and sound.

L. Barnes

Friend To Friend

Very often I think of the good times we've spent,
And the little favours, exchanged, that were well meant
Now though far apart, these things to me occur,
As I realise that life passes in ever increasing blur,
And time fritters away, quickly, day by day,
Yet these thoughts have I, but have been unable to say.
Now as I sit here with my memories and thoughts,
I now know that friendship can never be bought.
For you I have the greatest love and respect,
And I shall always be grateful for this friendship we did select.
That you've remained friends in any hour of my need,
Is I'm quiet sure more than just a good deed.
The affection I feel in my heart for you,
Is what I feel and is honest and true.
There are different affections, such as for a brother,
A sister, a wife and naturally your mother.
But the affection of our friendship is very unique,
And is never affected by feelings of pique.
My heart and soul lie open as you can see,
And I'm very humbled to know that you feel the same of me.

I. Bate

The House

I lay at night, in the single bed
because the double is too painful for my head.

The bedroom is so silent and bare
Where the one I love used to brush her hair.

The garden once so beautiful is now overgrown
If you listen you can hear the flowers groan.

The house is without sounds
My love for her knows no bounds.

The house no longer has her smell
I now live in a life of hell.

The stairs are silent of her steps
She really is the very best.

The house is full of her ghost
Oh God, I miss her the most.....

Paul A. Lee

Drummin Row

In Drummin Row I remember well
As the evening kissed the night
The yearlings would graze in the bulia field
while my Da smoked a home rolled light
Sitting on the fence down by the gate
In the softness of dusk I'd see his shape
On an old oak table his dinner would wait
While he drank the last of the light.

There by the gate where the wild roses grew
Ma would come out and she'd call to him
He'd lay down his smoke alongside his cares
I remember him there, still see him there, in Drummin Row

The thorns have captured the bulia field
Against wind and rain the gate has yielded
The yearlings are fed in a bright iron shed
Cry a tear for Drummin Row

But somewhere out there I know he sits
Pinching the end of his rolled cigarette
For as long as I live he'll guard my space
And keep alive Drummin Row

Kevin Hart

Holy Interlude

Could a face pervade such weakness and such strength?
At once?
Eyes all manner of sad and happy lines,
The mouth and nose,
Quite non-descript and satisfactory,
Set just so above the reverend clothes.

That in the house of God,
His cool white sanctuary,
The wafting cleansing frankincense
Swirls in wisps,
And dance in sunlight shafts,
From high arched windows,
To touch the prayers a whispered from the lips.

A kingdom held in loving ecstasy,
Quietude transcending hearts within,
To gently pass throughout an age,
From past to now,
Conjoining them in rhythm, time and space.
In universal glory we are stilled.

Y. L. D. Mullins

Within My Mind

In the realms of my sanity
As I witness the Borders of creation
Through an hourglass of pain
My mind expands beyond the vale of time

To the crossroads of decision
Only then can I understand - the seal of reality
The plane of my emotion, transcends through the realms of consciousness
Where peace descends upon me and I am one with God

Every thought that I have witnessed, as I cried
Through the barrier of hate - Had meaning
Because Love was my destiny and love never fails.

Love the true meaning of our existence
Is the only way to Freedom - so dream on with me
The light of our protector will be yours - forever
Then suffering will be but a distance memory - we had to endure.

To understand the truth - that has always been ours
From the beginning -
To where we are now;
Will be with us forever.

Raymond Alcock

The Come-Uppence

"Come away from that lady" a mum said to her little boy
As she yanked his arm which caused the lad to drop his little toy.
I wondered if she thought he'd catch something nasty from me,
Though I don't have a contagious disease, just MS you see.

I didn't like the look of this and decided to ask her why?
She looked all embarrassed, and then the lad began to cry.
I wondered if I'd done something, did I run over his little toe?
She grabbed his hand before rushing off, and now I'll never know.

I saw the same woman months later, and she didn't look too fine,
Poor woman had broke her legs and was in a chair just like mine.
Well her face really was a picture when a little lad went up to her
And cheekily shouted, "Ear Mrs., why are you in that wheelchair?"

I thought of the time that she had sneered, pulling her boy away
Instead of just explaining and saying that talking to me was okay.
Well she looked awful flustered, poor woman didn't know what to do.
I thought of going and rescuing her then thought, well, would you?

Shirley Brown

The Skulls Of Chichen Itza

Metallic clanging
As the bell speaks
Its death cry
The jungle in its cruelty
Shivers at man's bestiality
Whilst the animals, silent
Watch the drama play
A child, blue painted
Head held sigh
Leads the stream of silent men
And by the lake the altar waits
Stone cold as the hearts of the priests
Once more the bell speaks
Reverberating, hollow, deep
The golden knife held high
Arc's a flashing pathway
And a child dies
The lake accepts the sacrifice
And the Gods sigh - why.

H. T. Lawson

Mother Earth

Mother Earth what have we achieved?
   As millions of dead on you now bleed,
   We didn't have the time, we just could not wait,
   So now it is too late.

Mother Earth your trees are dead,
   Crystal waters now run red,
   It wasn't much of a shock,
   If only we could turn back the clock.

Mother Earth can you ever forgives us?
   You were one of our first loves,
   After our stupid greed,
   Giver of life you are what we now need.

Mother Earth you will never be the same again,
   For those that remain,
   Teach them not to repeat what we have done,
   Help the innocent now that the guilty ones have gone.

Mother Earth,
It was you that gave birth,
   You were pure until we came along,
   You were right and we were wrong.

Robert Avery

Reflections

I wonder where the years have gone
As I sit by the window each day.
I try to remember things from the past,
But they seem to slip away.
Who is that girl in the photograph
That sits in the frame on the shelf?
Hand in hand with that nice young man,
Is that a photo of myself?
If that is me, then that man must be
My husband of so many years;
And the time we have spent together
Has been touched with joy and tears.
Joy for the children that came along,
Tears when they all left home,
Joy again for our grandchildren
And for the promise - no more to roam.
But now as I sit by the window
I know I'll never be alone
My husband sits there on the other side,
We are just like Darby and Joan.

Mary Plucinski

Quiet Days

My life is filled with quiet days,
as I sit alone with my thoughts and memories.
My heart aches as music plays,
I picture the girl I love and remember
her special loving ways.

So far away in time is she,
But always on my mind.
Oh quiet days you torture me,
Why be so unkind?

I long to be with her again,
Where happiness I'll find,
But quiet days are all I have, to reflect
on the life I had.

Quiet days, oh quiet days,
You leave me, oh so sad.
Norman Renwick

Did You See

Did you see me escape into the darkness
as I ran beneath the moon.
Did you see me escape into the darkness
as I ran free from my room.

Did you see me running through the meadow
with the shadow that escaped with me there.
Did you see the colourful halo around the moon
were you really that awake and aware.

Did you see the silver mountain tops
in the moonlight bright.
Did you hear an angel singing
when I ran free that night.

Did you ever hear the bluebell ring
as the fairies danced in glee.
Did you hear the frogs sweet melody
as the pixies sang to me.

Did you follow pixie and fairy
through the forest of the night.
To that wonderful place seen so rarely
in a meadow where flowers bloom in moonlight.
Kenneth M. Allan

To...

I see your face and dare to smile,
As I look at you for a short while,
Fond memories of us fly by,
Whatever happened to you and I?

I wish we were together once more,
So I could wade in our love galore,
Taste happiness and feeling again,
Since you've gone, there's nothing but pain.

I watch you slowly walk away,
And dream again of us one day.
Together in perfect harmony,
Together in love, just you and me.
Susannah Higham

Sleep

The motionless ride begins
as we set sail in mind's eye
no place for decisions
as we take comfort in our lie
another world on the same ground
with no sharp edges to be found
as we wait patiently to begin
the colours surround us
and the music is within
now at ease with all around
a beating tempo without a sound
but soon to return without being hurled
I open my eyes back to my own world.
Stephen Squires

Peace

Not even a bird breaks their silence
As they lie there so peaceful below
Though the leaves on the trees they do flutter
Not a sound do they make as they blow
It's so quiet, I only hear heartbeats
Going faster than ever before
Beating right from the hearts of their loved ones
As they gently place flowers in a bowl
Not a breath or even a teardrop
Can disturb them from sleep so divine
Such peace can only be granted
To us when life's race is run
Peace be thine, peace be mine as we know it
Here on earth, as we both struggle on.
Margaret Clarke

Untitled

Follow, follow cried the swallow,
as he sped out of the sun.

I followed, followed,
and soon began to run.
Green were the trees that we passed,
and now that we were flying fast.

I looked below at the land,
and saw a mist touch it like a hand.

And there I saw through these eyes,
a body that I recognized.

Broken, broken left unspoken, alone and lost
my body lay caressed now by frost.

And through mine eyes now streaming,
a light did come bright and beaming.

Upon this ray a voice did say, now that
your choice is made follow, follow me.
S. Townsend

The Fox And The Hound

Running faster, out of breath,
as fast as I can, before my death,
the pound of feet, the barks of joy,
the thunder of horse's, the breath of man,
I'm running as fast as I can.

Through bushes and fields over fences, by trees
I stumble and fall, I hurt both my knees
I fear for my life, as I hear man
but I'm still running as fast as I can.

The sound of the horn, so far yet so near
I run through the woods, and frighten the dear,
they hear the horn too, and run with fear
I too am running as fast as I can

A sharp piercing pain, shoots through my body,
So cold as blackness surrounds me
'No longer am I running'!!!
Pauline Hickford

"My Shopping"

To the supermarket I did go.
Armed with a trolley, cash ready to flow.
Meats, vegetables spices and rice.
And all the sweets, which really are nice.
Tea, coffee, mush peas
Biscuits and cakes, all of these.
A toasty loaf, marmalade too.
This is my breakfast, not for you.
'Round once more, to make sure.
Pick up the toothpaste I nearly forgot
Talcum powder that's the lot
Through the checkout, pay and pack
That's for the week, won't be back.
E. Lightfoot

Immortality

My future stretched before me
As far as the eye could see
No footprints yet upon its path
No sign so far of me

One day I hoped to leave my mark
So other men would know
That in my brief and worthless life
Some imprint there would show

I struggled hard my whole life through
For a sign that could be seen
To leave a mark with all mankind
To prove that I had been

I failed to see the obvious
As by my side they played
The children I had given life
This was the mark I'd made

My family are my epitaph
The sign I'd found at last
To leave behind me in this world
To show that I had passed
Rita Spicer

Flight Of Glory

The clouds over which I hover
As far as the eye can see
Are never ending plains of
Snowcapped mystery

A flight of glory fills the sky
The brilliance dazzling the eye
The sheer elation of the flight
Brings joy and gladness come what might

One feels no movement we float in space
Peace settles in on breathless haste
The sight and sound can titillate
The soul beguile and captivate

This glory that can elevate
The heart and mind to emulate
All the beauty and delight
That brings me joy

This thrill of the glory here in space
Is gone
And in its place
A world again...
V. M. Coote

An April Evening

East blows a cold yet lazy chilling wind
as evening's dying sun sets in the west
and coalescent clouds of white and grey
Drift into faded azure banked so high.

Proud in the churchyard oaks the mocking Crows
Croaking aside non-euphemistic Rooks
Rendering limp and rough harmonious tones
O'er moss encrusted lichen covered slabs.

Now chimes the parish clock for all to hear
Whilst smaller birds twitter their shrill "goodnights"
Within the creepers on the church-tower walls
Ne'er frightened by the sonorous gongs therein.

Amidst the Primrose clumps and Daffodils
Scuttles the Fieldmouse home to covering earth
As languid strolls a mowking Blackberry Cat
Dreaming of conquests through the coming night.

Settle long day, now acquiesce you Rooks
Give away to shrieking-warbling-hooting Owls
Now yield to spirits in their still demesne
Rest all but them; pray anger-not these ghosts!
R. A. Irving

The Beast

I wonder if you the public care,
As at me you stand and stare,
And as to your warm beds you go
Do you think I stand out in the rain and snow?
Well, at night, like locusts to a feast
Men swarm over me, for I'm a beast,
They feed and water me and keep me warm,
For tomorrow before the public I have to perform.
The morning comes, cold and bright,
I stand before you a glorious sight.
Unlike my ancestors, I'm not noisy or flash
As past towns and cities, I dash.
I'm now speeding along, I'm free again
For I'm an inter-city high speed train.
R. W. Lambord

The Rose Of Love

The Rose of love has many a thorn,
As any a wise man will surely warn,
But love is also soft and sweet,
Say many a pen on a poet's sheet.
For he has not lost his love so fine,
Or never, loved a woman like mine.
Her soft red lips and her hazel eyes,
Hid a cruel mind and a web of lies,
But I have been bitter and not very fair
I hope you find a love you can share.
For mine is just one sorry tale,
I hope you are happy and your love won't fail.
Spare no thought for my twisted views
For I have lost and had a lot to lose.
S. Youngs

16th Of June

A shooting star, a wish come true
The morning dew, I think of you
A dream, the sun beams on a rainy day
Our birthdays collide in May
Four golden hair
The Nottingham Fair.

His heart is filled with sorrow
Hoping he'll die tomorrow
He wanted her by his side in the church nave
But instead she lies in a lonely grave
Her beloved is alone
And very far from home.

But she doesn't worry
And he won't hurry
But they'll be together soon
In the shadow of the moon
On the 16th of June.
Clifford Smissen

D.I.Y

I hate it when you buy something new.
And you build it yourself with nails and glue.
You read the instructions follow plan A.
"Why doesn't it fit" inside you will say.
This bit goes here that bit goes there.
"That doesn't look right" you sit back and stare.
It's winding you up, it's making you mad.
You start to get angry and shout for your Dad.
You screw up the plans and start from scratch.
"I'll make it fit, I'll make it match".
You hammer and bang and build your own way.
It's the five minute job that takes you all day.
You tighten the screws and fit the last shelf.
You finish the job quicker if you do it yourself.
"No plans no instructions just common sense"
Michael J. Nicklinson

King Arthur And The Knights Of The Round Table

As darkness fell across the land,
Arthur stood with excaliber in hand,
To you my knights of the round table,
We must battle for good, as we are able,
To cleanse this land of evil deed,
For my subjects cry out and bleed.
Merlin man of wisdom and charm
Did say we would be free from harm.
For the battle is just and right,
I am a godly king and you are fearless knights
So let us battle through this long night
So evil cannot hide, it will have to fight.
Then when the sun glows upon this land
Once more we will stand hand in hand
And to the round table we will meet
To talk of evil and its great defeat.
For this realm of which I am king
Will be free form evil my subjects will sing
And when seasons have past and my subjects are able
They will praise king arthur and the Knights of the Round Table.
Pat Russell

Silent Whispers

Silent whispers in the night
are you still here 'though out of sight?
Is it true what people say
you are really not so far away

I call your name in restless sleep
they say that memories are ours to keep
I fool myself you are still here
when it's hard to face another year

My confidante, my special friend
I know not why a life must end
So many questions fill my mind
a heart that aches deep down and cries

I visualize a special place
somewhere that's warm with a peaceful pace
I focus on your motherly smile
and imagine I'm with you for a while

Dear mother, my friend your love still glows
and within us all that love will grow
In sons and daughters, their families too
but a piece of my heart now dwells with you.
Maralyn Timmins

Flamborough Memories

The early memories that I most treasure
Are of natural beauty, sea and sun.
A world apart from man-made pleasure
Of bingo, discos and fairground fun.

I thrilled to see those cliffs so white
And the moody sea so often changing.
Sometimes a tranquil blue delight,
Sometimes a thundering monster raging.

Seagulls nesting are a wondrous sight.
A thousand birds screech and sing
As they swoop and wheel in precision flight
Bringing food to their hungry offspring.

In the tiny houses fishermen lived and died.
Hard-working, honest folk with tenacity and skill.
What a catalogue of stories those little dwellings hide.
Tales of triumph and of tragedy but never loss of will.

On Sunday evenings the chapel would fill.
Fishermen sang hymns, their faith to impart.
I hear their deep rich voices still
As they pull at the strings of my heart.
R. J. Thurlby

The Light Is Getting Darker

The lights at the end of the tunnel
Are getting darker as the world starts to die
I wish you could say how you're feeling
As you see your own world say goodbye

You wanted life to be nicer
As you made each living thing
But the world turned cruel and horrid
And you didn't know what each day would bring

Listen and hear what I am saying
The world is in need of you
Can't you save the world one more time
Because we don't know what to do

I know this isn't what you wanted
Or what you planned to achieve
But we know if we keep trying
And if we start to believe

We know that you will help us
Get away from this world of hate
I know that we've destroyed it
I hope it's not too late
Louise Holgate

Concord

With style and grace she came down from the sky
Approaching the runway for her first try
At landing, but she was far too high
The beautiful, beautiful, concord

She circled the airport and then disappeared
Gone for ever so everyone feared
But soon she was back and everyone cheered
The beautiful, beautiful, concord

She taxed the runway about half a mile
Then turned and came back as if in single file
And I swear on her face she was wearing a smile
The beautiful, beautiful, concord

She stood there majestic like a queen in a gown
As the steps were placed by her, and people walked down
And she gleamed in the sunlight like jewels on a crown
The beautiful, beautiful, concord

Then after a while her engines were heard
And she took to the sky like a beautiful bird
Somewhere down on the ground someone whispered these words
Goodbye my beautiful concord
Maureen Sylvia Medley

Untitled

Some thoughts for the New Year
Another year, another page
To turn in life's history,
With hope, or apprehension
We wonder - what will be?
A year with better hopes of peace
In a world, all torn with strife?
Will nations come together
Share the good things of life?
We in our small corners each can do our part
In growing plants, and flowers,
To gladden someone's heart.
We'll have our disappointments
Success, and failures too
But, working in with nature
Such lovely things can do.
Another year, another chance
To make our lives worth while,
To do our part, however small
And do it, with a smile.
M. Watts

My Taff

She phones me before she's about to depart
Another long drive for my loving Sweetheart
She says at 2am "I'll be there around ten"
Four fifty miles here - the same back again

She arrives Friday morn for the weekend
A few days of fun we don't want to end
But come Monday morning the tears start to flow
Cos it's that time again and she has to go

This goes on for years - those round-about trips
For a weekend of fun and a goodbye kiss on the lips
Enough is enough so we name the day
We decide to get married - Wales - 29 May

Our friends and family travel from far and wide
To see me finally marry my beautiful bride
It turned out to be the best day of my life
When my beautiful bride became my beautiful wife

We set up home in Scotland - Cardenden - Fife
My Taff and I for the rest of our lives
Two years of marriage - then came our pride and joy
Our bond was sealed with a new baby boy.

Pete Munn

The Meaning Of Life

Today, as I gaze outside at the clouds,
Another day passing at speed,
I wonder why life is so meaningful, yet,
How does one want to proceed?

My childhood recollection as I grew up,
"Oh yes, that's want I want to do!"
Yet now that I've grown to a fine young adult,
Those dreams haven't turned out to be true.

One gets older and wiser, settling down as one wants,
With the stress and the trouble and strife,
But as I soldier on with the weekly routines,
Tell me what is the meaning of life?

This is strange to me as I contemplate,
Not usually having a minute to spare,
Could I possibly find the answer to that,
A simple question - do I dare?

So I think I'll snap out of this moment of time,
And pursue my life's dreams on the way,
Thanks for your time, it was a pleasure, and so
I'll get on and enjoy the day!

A. M. Kilcommins

'Me'

I have a passion quick to rise and
Anger quick to burn,
A temper I can not disguise and
Patience slow to learn.
Yet swiftly does the flame die out,
And swifter still remorse
Constricts my heart. Oh! Without doubt
This is the harder course!
Why is it then my love grows slow
Where other feelings flare?
Why have I not the sense to know
That I should show I care?
And why do I, without a thought,
Those careless comments make?
Nor say I'm sorry when I ought, when
It is my mistake?
Why do I hide my caring side and let
The rough fly free?
It's nought to do with mannish pride.
It's just me being me!

C. R. Jones

Little Bird

A little bird flew down to peck,
    at crumbs upon the ground.
Nervously she glanced about,
    listening for a sound.
She nibbled fast and furious,
    to satisfy her hunger.
Then soared away to rooftop tall,
    not waiting any longer.
I stood there by my window,
    transfixed by works of nature.
Wondering what would life be like,
    in the not to distant future.
It intrigued me as I watched and stared,
    turning over in my mind.
What if we could be like birds,
    contented, free and kind.
Alas just like that little bird,
    so nervous and unsure.
Our world is soured in many ways,
    no longer safe and pure.

Patrick Grant

The Bonding

Some day I will be weak
and you will be strong
Will you then help me along

Comb my hair
Take me to the Loo,
Pull the chain, wipe the seat,
As I did for you.

Kiss the wrinkles
on my face,
Say goodbye when
my last breath I take.

Will you say "God Bless You Mum"
'Thanks for a job well done'.
Or will you feel guilt and sorrow too
that you did nothing for me,
When I needed you.

Do not fret, for I am your mother
my love for you is complete
We will forgive one another,
Our bond is unique.

Nancy Jackson

Life

I sit and ponder of life gone past
And wonder what there is that lasts.
There is life at home, with school and friends
Then all too soon it comes to an end.
Soon there is work and pressures each day
With no-one listening to what workers say.
Life as a wife and mother with so many friends
All of a sudden it comes to an end.
Now there is life alone in my house
At times it is quiet, not even a mouse.
My garden is full of different hues
And people will listen to my different views.
In control of my work it brings me such joy
The love of my children, a girl and a boy.
Life seems to have settled, it is time to look back
To look at life's venture while stroking my cat.
With the learning and loosing all over the years
There's only one thing that brings me to tears,
The love of my life is with me no more
What has the millennium now got in store?

Moira Baker

Through The Year

The north east wind is blowing
and winters in the air;
the open fire is glowing
and the trees are looking bare.

But Spring will soon be coming
and the trees will bud anew;
the daffodils will be blooming
and the birds will bill and coo.

The little lambs will dance and skip,
then summer's on it's way;
the time for all to take a trip,
on our annual holiday.

The holidays are over
and the nights are drawing in;
the sun is getting lower
and the days are getting dim.

Autumn now is ruling firm
and the leaves are turning gold;
the north east wind will soon return
and the winter; dark and cold.

T. B. Fozzard

A Soldier's Prayer

I saw him fall beneath a hail of lead,
And watched his white face turning to the skies,
No need to feel his heart I knew him dead,
For only death could leave those staring eyes.

I saw much more, across those endless miles
There in a little cottage, knowing not,
I saw a wife with soothing tones and smiles
The child he never knew place in his cot.

And then I saw a broken bleeding heart,
Pierced with a sword of anguish, forged by man,
A happy life's foundations torn apart,
A life of pain and misery began.

And then this curse called war I understood,
For in its nakedness it stood revealed,
And in my heart I voiced a prayer to God,
And never more sincere had I appealed:

That he would let the dawn-light soon appear,
To guide us back to peacefulness again,
That he would undertake to dry each tear,
And, in his heart's great mercy, ease our pain.

P. J. Shaw

Musing On A Summer's Day

I saw the clouds form in the sky and gently drift along,
And watched a blackbird choose a perch from which to sing his song;
I marvelled at the purity of notes which filled the air,
And longed to feel such joy as this, and in his praise to share.

A spider spinning skilfully was next to catch my eye,
Its web was intricate and neat exposed against the sky;
Repairing strands so carefully not one link did it miss,
I wished I could pick up life's threads with patience such as this.

A field of corn stretched way ahead as far as I could see,
Then fleeting rain beat down its stems and spoilt its majesty;
But when the sun poured out its warmth it soon regained its crown,
I prayed that I might find such strength when I am beaten down.

A rainbow formed against the clouds reflected from above,
I felt that God was close at hand revealing all His love;
I opened up my heart to Him and cares all slipped away,
Tranquillity surrounded me as I knelt down to pray.

Maureen A. Barrenger

Lake Land Visit

Have you ever been to Lake Land.
And walked the fells and dales.
And viewed with all its splendour.
The lakes with yachts and sails.

The long and winding road they call
The kirk stone pass.
Rolling hills and pastures, all covered
By green grass.
Just listen to the water's fall, all
Trickling, down the stream,
While, angler's sit idly by, as if life's
One big dream.

The calmness that is Conniston, all
Tranquil and serene,
Resting, place of Cambell, end of a
Brave man's dream.

Not forgetting Ulls Water, the lake
That seems so still.
And of course a visit to.
Words worth's daffodil.

R. J. Duffy

If Only

Oh, make me thinner, God, and grow my nails long
And turn my hair to copper,
Make me taller by two inches
And make my rival come a cropper

He would love me if only I could cook,
If I knew about Shakespeare, too
If I understood the rugby league
And regularly cleaned the loo

If my wit was a wow! at parties,
And I made him look the very best of hosts,
Oh, God, if this were all the truth
Then he would love me the most

But it's not the truth, I'm five feet two
And my favourite snack is chips
I haven't read Romeo and Juliet
And I regularly burn the dinner

Perhaps he'll love me for my brain
Or at least my sense of humour,
But I hear she's tall, I hear she's blonde,
Well, God, that's the rumour.

Margaret Moonie

My Child

If you look behind her beautiful eyes
And travel beyond that enchanting smile
You'll discover a piece of her that has died
For she's not perfect I'm told, 'my child'
But she's perfect to us, my family and I
Her brother and sister love her dearly
No hints of resentment or unjustified "Why?"
Just an unconditional love shown clearly
Her arms move this way and her legs go that way
As she struggles to point out a word
For she cannot walk and few words can she say
But she fights on until she's heard
I wish I could give her my arms for play
Or just see her, once, run in the park
To hold an ice-cream or have friends to stay
But all I can give her is my heart
Why do I fret? For she's far from sad
A beautiful child with a love for fun
With a loving brother, and sister, and dad
And a very proud mum

Stephanie Cave

All I Need

Just to lay on the grass, and gaze up to the sky.
And to look from a hill top, down to the sea.
To sit on the sand, to hear the seagulls cry.
To lean on the wind, and to wander born free.
To climb a high tree, and listen to the breeze.
This is the call of nature, and is all I need.
But with sadness or laughter, just to live at ease.
So who needs tension, in this world who indeed.
To live life gently, on the crest of time.
On this lonely planet, we call the earth.
And to stroll with nature, through a life sublime.
This is all I need, whatever the cost is worth.

C. A. Beard

Shadows

I see your shadow everywhere,
and though it may be peaceful in repose,
or faithful still to my mood and whim.
I can find no peace, no solace, only the empty space you have left.
I am filled with your soft breath, your melting eyes.
Behind which are constant, the secret thoughts and dreams we shared,
when it seemed only you and I existed.
My hands long to touch again your soft brow.
To feel your simple understanding.
Though the short space in time we shared will disappear,
as did your footprints in the soft sand as you ran.
I will remember, and those memories will heal the pain
and the loneliness of my bereavement.
For now the loss of you lays heavy on my heart,
and the memories too painful to recall.
So if I sigh when I glimpse you shadow, forgive my human tears
For I have not yet learned the secret of Joy and Sorrow.

Sandra Congleton

Memories Of A Beloved

When I sit alone at night
And think of many things
About my little dog
His joyful leaps and springs

His eyes would follow mine
Which ever was my mood
If I was happy so was he
He'd never think to brood

Closely followed, his life to mine
His trust would never wither
His eyes would light with joy
To mention walks or dinner!

His twelve year span it's now long gone
And when I think of time
Will he be waiting there for me
His afterlife with mine?

Arthur Tattersdill

Happiness

Happiness comes from those we love.
And they are lent from Him above.
Sometimes life seems hard but we must
Do our best, and lend a hand where it's
Needed most, you don't have to be
A really good host.
Just give a smile and help with pride
As we walk through life side by side.
As time passes by and day turns to night.
We can then close our eyes and whisper good night.
On in our slumber we may dream of wealth
But better than that a clean bill of health
But make the most of what you spend.
Before to dust you do descend.
Sharing our happiness with those who pass by.
Before we return to our home in the sky.

D. Hoyle

When

When the guns of war are silent
And there's joy throughout the world
When we see a bright tomorrow
With the flags of peace unfurled
When the Christian and the Moslem
Kneel side by side in prayer
And ask one God's forgiveness
For sins they both declare
When swords are turned to plough-shears
And shells are falling rain
And lands we knew as deserts
Are filled with golden grain
When winters wrath in tempered
By a summers cooling breeze and leaves no longer scatter
From autumn's dying trees
When every meadow glistens
In a spring time dewy frost and sounds of discontentment
In blue-bell chimes are lost

When all these things surround us and the scriptures have been told
We will understand the story of the "Lamb Inside The Fold"

E. Salter

Our Family Tree

You were the roots to anchor us all,
And the trunk, so strong straight and tall.
The wood inside so good and true,
we are the boughs that branched out of you.
The leaves, your crowning glory,
your children and grandchildren.
Each year more leaves grow, and so it goes on
Each one a part of you.
But now you have gone, chopped down before your prime.
An empty space left, were once you stood,
your branches and leaves spread far and wide.
But wait, some seedlings are sprouting,
your great-grandchildren
A new generation, and a new life
All from you, the strong root stock.

Patricia M. Freeman

Queensland Trees

Oh lovely Jacaranda, I see you in my dreams,
And the pretty Oleander, so bright in the sun's beams.
The graceful Frangipani, perfume lingering in the air,
No other fragrance in the world with it can compare!
The stunning Flame and Tulip trees, their brilliance caught my eye,
Their petals almost luminous against the cloudless sky.
Then there's the Poinciana, with its rich abundant spray
Of drooping blood red blossoms, that take your breath away.
Sweet radiant Poinsettia, you took me by surprise,
The Christmas flower of England, right there before my eyes!
Miles and miles of Pine trees, giant paperbarks so tall,
Like regiments of soldiers waiting for the battle call!
Long and slender Palm trees swaying gently on the sands,
Travellers Palms with crowns of leaves like friendly open hands,
I close my eyes and see those trees so far across the sea.
Oh lovely Jacaranda! In my dreams you'll always be!

Sheila Dowling

The Black Rose

As the black rose blooms in the summer
And the bright summer sun shines through
You can smell the fresh air around you
As your toes touch the morning dew

But the black rose won't stay for ever
For in the autumn it just disappears
It will come back again with petals so dark
And the other flowers shall grow in fear

For the black rose is full of beauty
So dark with a mystery to tell
As you walk by the flowers in the morning
All you can feel is the black rose's smell

Katie Holgate

The Flowers Won't Sway Any More

The flowers won't sway any more
And the grass shall not grow again
For the people on earth have destroyed it
There cannot be life without grain

The flowers won't sway any more
Peoples lives have been threatened again
There cannot be joy without sorrow
And there couldn't be peace without pain

So the flowers won't sway any more
The waters are black now not blue
The sky is all cloudy with smoke
And it's the fault of me and you

So the flowers won't sway any more
We could have stopped this if we tried
But we were intent on just killing
And that's why so many have died

Sarah Holgate

Faces On Cracked Blue Tiles

These bushes roar at the wind for more, as we scream up into the rain and the cracked bells tone, over the village moans, now that time has gone away. We are young as we've always been, just locked behind these smiles that are just creases worn and pieces torn, off faces on cracked blue tiles

In a room of cracked windows but without doors, in a house of what would be. There's a broken pain edge by running blood and a cut man who should be free. There's a screwed up man who could turn the key and let the violence forth, who's been to South and East and West and now must head for north.

Who's angry now that he's been pushed, by forces that he cannot see. Who's turned his face once, from the snow and ice, and thinks that he now should be free. And then life's circle came around, to an older and wearier guy, reflecting the memories of younger times, but without the reasons why.

He cannot buck this ring of fate as it circles one more time so he rips the edge with a jagged knife and gives a feral whine and a curse, a curse so profound the that it smells and tastes, cauterizing the lips that speak and withering the whispers of what might have been, on the still unborn cherub's cheek

The times that have passed but were held within, are now a heavy weight left to carry by one who's forgotten, just what they're for, and now has no time left to tarry. And as they all pour forth from the splits and rents, of my soul's cracked and battered door a voice inside has quietly cried, what's it all about? Is it happening again once more?

T. M. Howe

Present

When the apple tree shows her white
and the cherry turns to pink,
will I be there to savour the sight
will they make me stop and think.

Will I listen to the song of the mating bird
will I stand in the chilly pleasant here,
will I clasp in my hand, the hand I have missed
will the thoughts in her heart be so fair.

Or shall I wander about the world that I know
looking ever for that I cannot find,
while this being of me, shrinks to a stone
and my feelings are hidden so profound.

If I cannot stay then I will roam
seeking happiness in graft and in toil,
for there will be nothing left in me
nothing left to spoil.

I will listen to the birds with ears gone deaf
and I will see the daffodil shadow,
I cannot say what my future will be
but for me there will be no tomorrow.

N. Lowe

Sleeping Monsters

Mum read me a tale from the book on the shelf,
and take me away from the thoughts of myself,
Mum, read me of monsters and things from the deep,
and mum, don't stop reading till I'm fast asleep.
please tell me the tale of the boy dressed in blue,
and the mother and children who lived in a shoe.
and tell me again of little bo-peep
for I see them too, when I'm fast asleep.

Mum read me a tale from the book on the shelf,
and take me away from the thoughts of myself,
and read the words soft so I soon drift away,
to the land where the giants and the green goblins play,
Mum tell me the tale of the girl with the hood
of the wolf, whom we know, was up to no good,
and don't let your voice show emotions for me,
for, when you tell me stories, I also can see.

Mum tell me of rainbows, and colours of grass,
Mum tell me of rain, as it runs down the grass,
Mum tell me of light, as glints of the sea,
Mum tell me, why is it, that I cannot see?

Robert Stephen

Freedom

The stars sing in the sky
And the moonbeams sparkle in your eyes
Baby, I hear you laughing
I hear you crying
As you look to the sky

The sun shines on the other side
Shooting beams across the sky
Rainbows follow you
Wherever you go
Wherever you lie down

Breath the breath of light
Into your heart, into your life
Shining from your beauty
Beating from your soul

Sweet songs, dancing butterflies
Spread those wings
And see you fly
Diamonds last forever
Diamonds never die

R. M. Fricker

"Memories"

It was V. E. night when we first met,
And springtime days I remember yet,
That one magic week that began it all,
The joy I knew, I still recall.

And then you had to go away
I felt so lost, my world was grey
Each day that passed brought no joy,
Till I could see my soldier boy.

But all the waiting was worthwhile
One evening you called and I could smile,
The joy was back within my heart.
And our life together had its start.
We've had our ups, we've had our downs
We've had our joys and our frowns
And now in the autumn of our life
I am so glad to be your friend and wife.

Looking from autumn back to spring
I would not change a single thing.

Olive Scoffham

Dirge To A Scottish Blackbird

You should have lived a hundred years ago
And slept in moonlit peace, your quiet hours
And waking, preened your mirrored beauty in the limpid pool.
Happy, your dappled-sunlight flight,
Your tree top ecstasy of flute-like song
And beneath you,
A world of flowered glory and the shining grass.
There would be patchwork fields and ribboned lanes
And far, the shimmering sea
and sounds about you, of meadow-voices and the ripening corn
And insect-hum of summer noon, beneath your branched throne.
Later, evening and the twilight and the following hush of night.
An owl, winging across your quiet moon,
Then, silence and the distant stars —
Yours, for all your precious years.

But you never knew that time,
You were born too late,
Amidst rush and noise and speed and hate
And you have paid the price in blood,
Dead, in the roadway.

Mary Ann Pilsel

I Can't Believe You've Gone

Silently two tears fell as peacefully you slipped away,
And silently I have grieved for you.
I still can't believe you've gone,
That the strong, silent support is no longer there.

I remember our laughter together,
The way you worried over your girls,
The generosity, you knew no other way;
It can't be true that you're not there.

You did grumble and moan a lot, but
You did enjoy your pint and cigarette,
Your holidays and the sun,
Cream teas, ice creams and steak nights.

I can't believe you've gone;
I've got the photographs on the side,
I make believe you are still here;
I miss you; simply, I want my Dad back.

But you and I had some time together, before the end,
You wanted to make sure I was settled,
That I was happy, and would be taken care of.
Thank you Dad for your approval, for your unfailing love.

Sandra Coates

Tearful Eye

A tearful glance moved to the right
And shone the crystal leaves,
That hung so light and delicate
Upon the ghostly trees.

A tear drop fell to freeze on ice
A glistening frozen stream,
That seemed to change with winter moon
To give a sharp bright beam.

The stones seemed glass to tearful eye
So pure and white with frost,
So soft and smooth and precious now
With all their darkness lost.

The moss lay flat as ancient lace
So stiff and fragile lay,
That tearful eye put out his hand
To feel its webby spray.

The frost had come and snow would fall
And tearful eye would go,
For tearful eye was pure born rain
That soon would freeze with snow.

J. Byrne

Winter

If you look around on a winter's day
And see what nature's brought our way
You find the fields are bare and brown
And trees have shed their leafy gown
The wind moans softly, full of woes
And frost touches our fingers and toes
Snow falls silently over the ground
Floating gently, not making a sound
Birds sit outside our door and wait
For the crumbs we give them off our plate
They have ceased to sing their morning song
As the days are short, and darkness long
Our gardens are drab no colour at all
Just ivy clinging on the wall
The garden tools have been put away
And children stay indoors to play
A little mouse will creep inside
Because he wants somewhere to hide
Until the spring arrives to say
That winter time has passed away

J. Dale

Life

It took God six days to make heaven and earth
And put beautiful things in our universe
He gave us the dark and also the light
Put stars in the sky, made them twinkle at night
He gave us warm weather, created the rain
To help grow the food, the wheat and the grain
The sun and the moon shining bright in the sky
And the beautiful clouds as they go drifting by
He put down green fields and filled them with trees
To give us clean air and help us to breathe
The sound of the birds, the dove and the lark
Singing their song as they fly in the park
He gave us the oceans, He gave us the seas
The howl of the winds, the cool evening breeze
The warm summer days, the buzz of the bees
The cold winter nights when the earth starts to freeze
He taught us all laughter and mixed it with tears
To love one another as we go through the years
He gave woman a husband and gave man a wife
But most precious of all, He gave everything life.

G. Ruck

Life Is Unfair

With others we like our own lives to compare,
And often conclude that life's very unfair;
We've tried much harder, but they've fared much better;
Why keep in credit, when it pays to be debtor?

The workers who were hired at day-hour eleven
Seem like death-bed conversions who sneak into heaven;
They've taken things easy and in life were contented;
It seems so unfair - we grossly resent it.

One baby is born into wealth that is blinding,
Another is born into poverty grinding;
One's healthy with parents who put salvation first,
Another's a freak with alcohol cursed.

Life is unfair, we keep on repeating;
Virtue seems always to be self-defeating.
Even Jesus the sinners and tax-thieves he greeted;
The more effort we make, the more we feel cheated.

No matter how bad my position might be,
There's always somebody who's worse off than me;
The man with no socks on the public park seat
Met there a child who was born with no feet.

Thomas F. Murray

The Kiss

A desperate darkness stalked my weary soul
And night - dead night - lived on, forever on.
No trace of light from stars or moonbeams shone.
I had no wish for life, I had no goal.
The icy tendrils of my past had clutched
The last remaining vestige of contented life
In stranglehold of terror and of strife.
In deep despair my heavy heart was touched.

Then through the fog and rain I saw your face.
Sad eyes revealed that you too had known pain.
But when you smiled you caused my blood to race,
You raised my heart from death where it had lain.
    All thoughts of night and death I did dismiss.
    You saved me - with a simple single kiss.
Michael Pattwell

Valentine's Day Poem

I will always love you,
    And my love will be true.
My cold, tired arms,
    Need help from your charms,
I think about your love,
    It can be as quiet as a dove.
When I am sad you cheer me,
    When it is you, I'll cheer thee!
I hope you'll not break my heart,
    If so, you'll tear me apart!
Please think of me in what you do,
    I shall be thinking always of you.
Tell me a secret, don't tell me a lie,
    This way our love will never die!
Maria Mountcastle

Indian Prayer

"My ears heard the wind across the plain,
and my eyes saw my people were in pain,
so I rode from my tribe for a day,
then I stopped, looked to heaven and began to pray."

"Oh Lord, the buffalo have fled from my tribe,
and already we have children who have died.
our clothes they are worn like this land,
no longer can we grow crop in this sand,
and the winter, it will be upon us soon,
I know this I have watched the sun and moon.

The skins of our tee pees are not strong,
in the cold our weakened skins will not last long,
and we cannot make another move 'til spring,
now my people's voices do not lift to sing.

Please God won't you help us make it through,
I fear we cannot make it without you..."

"And then I heard the sound of many feet,
drumming on the ground a heavy beat.
I looked across the plain and saw the herds,
and I knew that God had listened to my words."
  A. G. L. Milne

Untitled

We came across that house beyond the bend,
and stole behind the dark and blackened door.
Upon the floor a dark and sloping end,
a greening slime beyond a broken claw.
Aha I cried, at last I see the bright
and jewelled stones that mother told to me
(old lady withered black but inner sight)
A stone can talk and tell a world to be.
Yet now I look upon the silver frame
of open doors and dangling city lights
and jewels long turned to stone; in aim
a show of brass domain. The hidden sights.
We see but less today - the outside laws
Where heart, and I, seen. Not the dutiful cause
  Orde

Save Those Children

The sound of wars
And motor-cars
Are all so very common.
But what about the other things
We seem to have forgotten?

The sound of children crying
As they watch their people dying
Through drought and war
And famine
As they ask what is their sin.

The sad and lonely children
The cold, forgotten children
Those starving, thirsty children;
Who for them, life is very trying.
Meanwhile, we keep on buying.

Buying presents for ourselves
Like pretty garden elves.
While those children in the Third World
Would give anything to move from the brink;
Just to have some food and drink.
  Wendy L. Schofield

Once More

I want to smell the sea once more as I first did when I was four
and run my hands through sun-baked sands and watch the
    seagulls dive and soar.

I want to hear those songs of fun and youthful dreams of twenty one
and pick a girl and dance to bands and kiss and love till the
    morning sun.

I want to taste that wine with Kate that filled my world at twenty
eight and sit and talk on river strands of life and love and
    dreams and fate.

I want to see my sons alive as I last did at fifty five
in blue and off to foreign lands against an evil foe to strive.

I want to hold my wife to me as I last did at eighty three
and kiss her eyes and take her hands and promise her we'll
    always be.

I want to be myself again no longer old and racked with pain.
I want to walk and hear and see, and feel the sun and touch
    the rain.

But I know I'll never smell sea or sup a wine or dance at tea
and never hear the sound of love or hold my wife or Jack or Lee.

I'll never again be fifty four and see my sons walk through the door
and never kiss my wife again; though I'd sell my soul if I
    could once more.
  Roger Powell

'Whispering Park'

The swirling biting winds crack my lips
as I celebrate and contemplate.

Haunting winds protrude their melodic harmonies
and the birds amour their crackling dawn.

Sweeping leaves make patterns
swaying like a boat and syncopating
softly along the turgid grass.

Oh! How I long for those hazy balmy evenings
Where the sun beams and rusts the grass and bony soil
and people wander aimlessly to the toil.

A speckled thrush bares his all
and a rusty rook swoops before a fall.

As I meander to the distance
the trees outstretch their arms
Welcoming me to their Psalms
It's Sunday and I disappear, to church
without any fear.
  Nigel Robinson

Untitled

You breathed the life into my soul
and made me one that made me whole
but as I grew and made my way
You put me down and made me pay
my life to you was just a game
why do I feel then that I'm to blame
your physical pain and mental abuse
made me feel worthless and of little use
you called me stupid for so many years
is it any wonder I have so many fears
but now I know you can hurt no more
because when it comes to you I've
closed the door.
there are still some times when I do feel sad
after all you're supposed to be my dad

S. Dutton

Alfie's Poem

You stuck needles in me
and made me cry
You had to tell my Mum that
I might die
But through it all you worked so hard
For the ones that have been
lost we are sad
However long or short my life
I will walk tall because you
gave me the greatest gift of all.
My life.

Nikki Merry

Life

He stands in the doorway impatiently waiting
 And looks at his watch in dismay.
How long will she be - has she stood him up,
 What's causing this dreadful delay.

As he looks up the street, with troubled blue eyes,
 He spies her long golden hair,
She runs to him quickly, his arms open wide,
 At last his loved one is here.

Once more he is waiting but he's not alone,
 His Best Man is stood by his side,
People all standing - the doors open wide,
 Sweet music plays "Here comes the Bride."

Now he's with strangers, there's no-one he knows,
 They're all looking tired and drawn.
The door opens quietly - the nurse comes to him,
 Says "Don't worry, your new son is born."

Long years have passed and good ones they were,
 Now they are both old and grey.
They sit and talk quietly of all they have done,
 As they wandered down life's golden way.

Maureen Lake

Untitled

When I was young, I wanted so to learn all things,
and play every musical instrument
but it was not to be.

I grew and longed to be of use to all humanity,
I'd heal the sick and comfort them,
but it was not to be.

I wed and had a family, and still I yearned to be
a foster mum to lonely kids,
but it was not to be.

How swiftly has my life sped by
I cannot believe it's true
that I am now too old to be of use
to anyone but you.

Marjorie Rose Doron

A New Awakening

The dawn crept in, I rubbed my eyes
And looked around in faint surprise
Did I scent magic in the air
A lovely feeling sweet and rare

What could it be, I tried to think
Just bordering upon the brink
Of dreaming and reality
What could it be, this mystery

"I know today's a special day
I know that's why I feel this way"
And yet I really did not know
Exactly why or how 'twas so

Then suddenly, I heard a sound
Leapt from my bed with one great bound
For I had heard a blackbird sing
"Of course today's the first of spring"

G. Freeman

Love Is....

You are like a caged wild bird: Beautiful, elusive and sad.
And like that cherished bird as much I love you
It is kinder to set you free, but with your freedom comes my tomb.
I have given you your life and lost my own.
Possibly you may not return.
In my heart I have always known that you would never stay.
I have loved so much for so long that part of me
Will never be the same.
I will exist but not live. I will eat but not taste.
And I will care but not love.
I have given all of myself to you and will never again be whole
Unless you return.
My love, like your wedding band is eternal.
With no beginning and no end.
Wear it with the knowledge that no matter where you are in the world
I will always be by your side
And I will always love you.

Shelley Wilson

Going Home

Oh, I tread the same old road,
And journey to my first abode;
My heart carries such a load
Of memories I have bestowed.

The same old house, the same old places,
Now missing, the dear familiar faces;
So quiet now, the laughter gone,
Remembering times now bye-gone.

With heavy heart my mind goes back,
To lots of things I now regret;
No smiling welcome at the gate,
As my weary steps I trace.

My words and thoughts cannot be spoken,
Relationships now long since broken;
Memories now flood my mind,
My roots I cannot leave behind.

Marian Brodie

A Soldier's Thoughts Of Home

I sit upon the sands of time
and in my hand, I see your face
for in this picture you're with our children
I wish I was with you, instead of this place
I may not be there to ease your pain
or wipe your tears, whenever you cry
but my children are there to ease and comfort you
and my heart never left, when I waved to you goodbye
I cannot kiss you or hold you in my arms
but our candle of love, will, forever burn
and my thoughts of you and my children will be
in that eternal flame, until, I return

Robert Sibbald

Sweet Memory

A little shiver in the poplar leaves above my head
and I was there again, in mind, though open eyed.
The long dry grass beneath my feet felt like the sand
And I could hear the murmur of the tide.
    And he was there
I could see the stones which banked up to the slope,
and upwards, heather, golden gorse, and blue blue sky.
The footmarks in the sand, some half awash from gentle waves.
The sea so green, and calm, in my mind's eye.
    And he was there

Two white gulls were circling, wheeling over head.
Somewhere a distant buzzard gave its mewing cry.
Wet seaweed lying in the shadowed hollow of a cave.
All time stood still, the breeze was just a sigh.
    And he was there

So many years ago - it's very different now.
The bay is filled with people, children, noise - no peace.
But I can see the past, and feel its calm of old.
Sweet memory, like my love, will never cease.
    And he'll be there.
    Margaret Leigh-Spencer

Sea Change

Under a sky of polished steel the earth is iron grey
And high above like bits of rag the clouds are blown away.
A chill wind deals ruthlessly with sea birds that remain
And their top notes are missing now from winter's low refrain.

The gloom has turned the sullen bay to a sheet of hammered tin
And fishermen with knowing eye have brought their vessels in.
To piling shaped like rotten teeth their rimy ropes are tied,
Their sodden hulls pulled parallel by the suck of the ebbing tide.

A sense of rot is in the air, the stench of mud and damp;
And all around the fishy smell of some primordial swamp.
What devilish blacksmith at his forge a day like this had made?
What anger with the human race has tempered such a blade?

But now a breeze on sandalled feet blows inland from the sea
And slaps a wave of silver spray against the glistening quay.
A raucous flock of geese returns from its long winter flight
And suddenly the hills beyond are touched with glowing light.

And now the bay is burnished bronze, the sky like melting gold
And all around is light and warmth where once was dark and cold.
What loving artist in his loft has dipped his brush in flame
And painted for the human race this masterpiece to frame?
    J. M. Bergin

Not Good Friday

I woke up late, so I missed my train
And got soaking wet in a downpour of rain
On the way home, I slipped on the kerb
This really is becoming absurd
Guess what, there was something more
Because when I got to my front door
I could not find the key to put in the lock
This came as a nuisance and a shock
As inside the house was my spare key
I was therefore not exactly jumping with glee
I had to gain entry by breaking a pane of glass
I was jolly glad a policeman did not pass
I then started to prepare my evening meal
And then what happened seemed quite unreal
I turned on the T.V. to see my favourite soap
But for sound or picture there wasn't a hope
Why oh why has everything gone wrong today
I then realised to my utmost dismay
It's Friday the thirteenth, I should have guessed
That everything most certainly could not be at its best
    M. A. Walters

About Welsh Chapels

The people are mostly chapel, in the village where I live
And go there to sing and pray, and to listen to a sermon
Quite often they nod (Forgive them God) for your man's long winded.
For chapel's mostly serve the working people who are tired out.

There's various types and sizes; small and squat and tall
But none so tall as Central Hall in Tonypandy town
Nor so sad as solemn sold Salem, complete with Graves Academy
First one on the scene of Nonconformists keen dissenters.

And there's Trinity (there's divinity for you) majestic.
Employs the Laity-some gaiety and variety
(We go there to collect our Christmas Bonus from the council)
On the Community, to supplement us poor pensioners.

Must take a look at Ebeneezer on the hill; ancient stock
Where country folk used to flock on a Sunday: Mostly farmers.
Words are not available, for me to be able to convey
The passion of Cymanfa Ganu (Festival of Singing).
Glory, Glory, Glory,
Hallelujah.
Amen.
    F. S. Cole

The Snowflake

The water droplets come together,
And form a little star,
They make a small shape that's as light as a feather,
It starts to move, but not very far.

The small flake sways to and fro,
Following many others,
Settling down, making a sheet of snow,
A bed with silky, white covers.

Before they melt, they look to the sky,
A small little snowflake, precious as a gem,
Then they melt, left to die,
With the sky smiling upon them.
    Katie O'Brien

A Lover's Wish

I want to wrap you in my warmth
And fill your life with love
To give each day a reason
For doing the things you love
To hold you in my arms
And give you everything you need
Is all I've ever wanted
And it's all I'll ever need
When I look into your beautiful eyes
I can see the person deep inside
How I wish you could be mine
To love and care for till the end of time
Oh how happy I would be
If I could say these words to thee
But I must keep them locked inside me
Because my darling, you are not free
    Sue Melia

Blue-Sea-Storm

Spirits arise off from shore arousing clouds of joy
and fear.
Clouds consuming spirits
of hatred,
and despair.
But down below child laughs
and adult tempers flair.
Rhythmic beat of thunder
sets a cast mighty blows and rivers begin to flow.
    Nicholas Maloney

My Granddaughter

I wish I was very small again
And do the things I use to do then.
Hopscotch on the pavement
Missing lines on the squares
And going up two at a time on the stairs.

I loved liquorice fountains and aniseed balls,
And running and jumping on little low walls.
I'd fill in the holes on all writing matter
And oh! To have treacle on lots of warm batter.
I'd entice all the stray cats to follow me home
But after some milk they'd just up and roam.
I wanted a puppy, a pony as well
A scooter, a bike with a whopping great bell.

But now I'm full grown and an example must set
And all the things mentioned I really could get
But I'd really rather be small and have someone matey
The person I'd choose - well it's my darling Katie.

W. Peacock

Woodland Walk

Wild orchids stand in cardinal style
And daffodils bob, weave in single file

Primroses curtsy, with celestial calm
While bluebells gather, in chorus lines of charm

Wild teasel sways, in rhythm to the ladies smock
And sweet scented woodruff of my mother's frock

A cowslip sighs, a tear shed for the summer past
A wild rose kissed, by dew in the morning mist at last

Through the tall melilot the gentle breeze spoke
Scarlet pimpernel, weather guide, to country folk

Rest harrow, of my Hampshire downs
where my love, of the countryside, was found

Ka Pawsey

Sometimes

Sometimes the mists of mental angst thicken
and clarity and sureness gets lost in a welter of blurred edges
and distorted perspectives.
The superficial memories all seem of bad and of stress filled times,
it is a winding corkscrew that leads down.
The only hope is that although the clouds obscure the sun
I still believe that it's there.
And how ever bad the storm, it does end
and we carry on, 'cause that's what we do

C. P. Mayers

"Paradise Lollipop Foundation"

The mustard layered lollipop lady, battered
and beaten though baked in beauty, is
idolized by child and driver alike. Cycling
to provide, her worn shoes slip on the wet
peddles of the swelling tires, condemning
the illuminated school queen to the illusion
of the bobby on the bike or Bunty riding
down the lane. Paradise is too far, like a
three minute mile on square wheeled roller
blades. I chased its warm glow for two years
the mustard yellow offset with white was
just a bottle and an arm away. I was McEvil
McManhole on a Honda Goldwing, not a four
year old on the back of a knackered old push
bike Well maybe I was, but it was in
adulation that I sat there watching her work.
She was the guardian angel of the road, I
was the viewer. Company, love and smiles
the content of my unreached paradise.

Paul Fraser

Ten

Being Ten is awful, I have to wash my plate,
And be in bed by half-past nine, I'm told off if I'm late.
Being Nine was better, I never washed a crock,
But then again, I had to be, in bed by Nine-O'-Clock.

I much preferred it being Eight, with nowhere much to go,
But then again, Mum wouldn't let me play out in the snow.
I miss now being Seven - and all that childish glamour,
Although, back then, my Dad would never, let me use his hammer.

Being Ten is not so bad, although it's sometimes dull,
But playing-out and going to school, makes my life rather full.
It's better now, it's fair to say, than being Six or Five,
Because I can now swim a bit and learning now to dive.

Being Ten is nearly good, as far as being Ten goes,
For now I go to parties and to all the school discos.
Of being Four and being Three, I don't recall a lot.
And as for being Two and One - I slept, then, in a cot.

Being Ten is brilliant, that's what I've always said,
And I will say it all night long until I go to bed.
And if you think that strange, or if you think it's funny,
Being Ten is brilliant, 'cause I have more POCKET MONEY.

Kevin Sawyer

Live Life Not In The Shadows

Follow your heart where it leads
And be happy to enjoy the voyage
Your dreams may hold the future
So dwell not on the past

Keep your smile and your charm
And keep the hope in your heart
That our rainbow is still somewhere
Within your grasp and understanding

Fear not of mysteries to come
Or truths to face; yet with an open mind
Fill yourself with joy, not doubt,
To compete for peace with me

Live life not in the shadows
Live life not for, or because;
But as is: as was; and as will be
Live for the road to tomorrow

Be safe in the Understanding
That where ever or how ever you go
You are not alone; and in your search
Know that I will always be there.

Tim Dickeson

Fulfilment

Another year's almost turned full cycle
And Autumn's scents fill the air,
Crispy leaves swirl all around us,
Gnarled tree branches stretch gaunt and bare.
But Harvest is a time of fulfilment,
Once again, God has blessed the seed,
Sent soft spring rain and summer sunshine
To provide all the food that we need.
Fruits have been picked from the orchards,
Crops and grain gathered from the soil,
Man meets his responsibility
Knowing wants must be met by his toil.
This earthly pattern can teach us
Whatever we sow we must reap
And talents must be nurtured to ripeness,
The Shepherd must be proud of His sheep.
Then when deep winter brings its rest
And life has briefly gone from the earth,
Having put our trust in the Lord above,
We await Spring's triumphant rebirth!

Pat Heppel

My Hero

My boyfriend is clever
And as sweet as can be.
He is tall dark and handsome
And tidy like me.

We talk and chat and laugh a lot
And can both run reasonably fast,
My old boyfriend just sits and stares at me,
But he is all in the past.

Our birthdays share the same month,
And I think we were made to be -
But one little detail I am worried about
Is why won't he go out with me?
Vicki Allum

Mother

The weather is getting colder.
And your feelings are too
You don't seem to understand me
Like you used to do
The hardest thing I've found
Is your lack of trust in me
We all make mistakes and I'm no different,
So why can't you let the past just die!
I've got a new life now, with someone
 who loves and trust me to.
I know you don't like our plans
But it's my life now you know,
I plan to live it the way I want
Regardless of what you think.
I hope you will be happy for us,
But that may be too hard a task for you
nevertheless you're still my family
so how could I forget you.
Sarah Jones

Lost Love

As soft light fades on tree and flower
And all is hushed in the twilight hour,
I stand alone by the orchard wall
For there, sometimes, my name you call,
As stillness threads through every bough
You sometimes come to me, somehow,
My lovely one from days of yore
Where once my golden ring you wore,
I see the clear pools of your eyes
Where every morn my sun would rise,
And as your face once more I see
Your very presence so fills me,
That my senses reel and, fleetingly
Soar with the night o'er vale and lea,
Till a fox's call from a distant dell
Floats on the air to break the spell,
And then a different mood I don
My heart sinks low, for you are gone,
And there, as night replaces day
I slowly turn... and walk away.
A. Webb

"Nostalgia"

As we are straying dreamily,
Along the lanes of memory.
It is the thought of home that start,
The deepest yearning of the heart.
For home is where our hearts belong,
A word, a picture, or a song,
Can strike a chord that brings to mind,
The things that we have left behind.
A strange power binds us, to our own,
And when were exiled and alone.
There comes this feeling sharp as pain.
The yearning to be home again.
L. W. Jenkins

Magic

Hush and listen! The moon is up
And a nightingale raises his song.
The stars like diamonds gleam in the sky;
All these things to the night belong.

Night-scented flowers quicken the air,
The wind is sleeping, the earth is still,
And the nightingale's lovely music
Has for background a murmuring rill.

Silver and black is our workaday world,
Black and silver, mysterious, new.
On the lawn flash myriad diamonds -
Every blade is hung with dew.

A fox like a shadow crosses the path,
Bent on hunting, with cubs to raise.
The moon was once Diana the Huntress,
And the ancients gave her praise.

Small things rustle in bush and tree,
An owl drifts past like blowing snow.
He has supped and is homeward bound
To the hollow tree where the bluebells grow.
J. M. Perrot

Please Come Play

I wake to the sound of laughter, so tinkling and so sweet,
And a little voice that murmurs, "You see she's not asleep."
A kiss as soft as thistledown falls then upon my head.
And a voice so soft and wistful says "Please get out of bed."

"The sun is shining Grandma, and I want to show to you
A little bird upon the tree, and see the sky's so blue.
Take me to the beach Grandma, and we can paddle in the sea,
Oh, I do love you Grandma, please, please, come play with me."

Life is like the seasons, it changes with each passing year
And how I love this autumn time when he is with me here.
We walk to the beach together and I watch him through the day,
And it's "Come and help me Grandma. Oh. Please, oh, please
 come play."
J. Proctor

Dead Happy

May beads of sweat be upon my brow
and a broad smile across my face.
Let the Devil himself be there when I take my bow
and quit the human race.

May the taste of good times be on my tongue
and my behaviour leave a notorious trace.
Let my wayward soul be proud of the things that I've done
so I can exit this world with grace.

May my funeral dirge be a screeching wail
and they speak of me with disgrace.
Let me leave behind rumours and evidence for many a tale
to show none of my time went to waste.

May there be no strange experience left to achieve
and no wild adventure for which to chase.
Let me laugh at them all when I leave;
Epitaph:- 'Bored of this place.'
Roger Phillips

Untitled

Guns are emptied and reloaded
And secret notes, are carefully coded.
Intercepted codes, decoded.
Outrageous modes and myth exploded
Land and time become eroded
Mother Earth is overheated
Lessons past it seems repeated.
Many things are overrated
And messages become belated
Some people by their blood related
And time run out becomes outdated
To their end my poem's fated.
Phillip D. Jude

The Old Oak Tree

I can't believe I'm sitting here,
Amongst its branches - high, with fear.

That little acorn fell long ago,
And buried by squirrel, who ran to and fro.

What stories it could tell,
Of old history in the dell,

Plague and fire, flood and war,
For this old tree, it's never been a bore.

Leaves shed, five hundred times or more,
Laying many a carpet, on the woods floor.

How many more years can it stand,
And watch the seasons lay their magic hand.

My end, will come some day,
Buried amongst its roots, I wish to lay.
Tony Dixon

First Love

In this dimly lit room, I see your face
Amongst faces lit up by your presence
Your very being enchants them, I think
Your charm and wit, no-one could replace.

Time is endless, as I watch you
But only a minute has passed and I am bewitched.
I pray you'll notice me, feel the same
These feelings of love I never new.

You look up and I blush and yet
The room is dark, you may not see
That I am trembling, my heart pounding
Someone like you, I have never met.

The moment has come, you've made a move
Our eyes meet and I am lost to you
This moment feels like forever
I'll always remember you, MY FIRST LOVE.
K. Farr

When I Die

When I die, I want you to care,
Although dying isn't fair,
But when I die, please be strong,
Because your the one that has to carry on.

When I die, I want you to be there,
For my children who'll find life hard to bear,
When I die, you'll need inner strength,
You'll have to explain at great length.

When I die, I want you to cope,
Without you, my children have no hope,
When I die, I don't want you to cry,
Or to sit around asking yourself why.

When I die, I want it to be clear,
For the love I held for you so dear,
For the life I had so happy, so full,
And for my children I'd leave so beautiful.
Michelle E. Halls

Frustration

Reap the whirlwind,
Accept your fate,
There's nothing you can change,
You're following a script.
Like walking through a crowd,
Your path is always there, though
   sometimes hard to find.
You cannot gain control
You're no more than the mental
   images in the fantasies of the gods.
Pete Cape

Take Me Home

Fishing of Greenland in a force 11 gale
An unprotected gutting knife stuck up in the pound board
Going to call the watch below at midnight
I felt a sharp pain my right index finger saved by the bone
We could not go in because of the ice
From November to May would be far too long
So suffer I must until I reach home
Stretching straining through the water shuddering to be free
Impact of heavy waves sending shivers stem to stern
Great waves as high as edifices
Coming at us with a silent roar
Breaking over her bow a great white mist
From force six imminent a squall
Raging hurricane giant waves roll
Through thick fog ice temperatures low
She guided me through all of these and kept me safe
Freezing Arctic Circle the elements all
After all the hard toil tireless days
She would take me home my family would greet
That is the Corsair I knew
Philip Hilton

'Walking Behind Me'

I look over my shoulder and what do I see,
An adorable puppy one step behind me.
She's black and velvety with big soulful eyes
A bundle of lovingness, and attention she vies,
She whimpers and begs and lifts up her paw,
The most beautiful dog that I ever saw.
I adore her already and I cannot ignore her - and yet,
What shall I do? - She is another's pet!
I close my eyes and walk on a pace,
But I cannot shut out her sad little face
I hesitate, then look around - and all of a sudden
Her feet leave the ground - and with a leap and
A bound, she is soon in my arms,
Displaying to me, the extent of her charms.
This feeling between us is something I'm sure,
I cannot let her go, to be, alone anymore.
She nestles against me and such a friend she will be
This little black pup who has just claimed me!
Vera Crouch

My View

Through the window from chair I look,
And all that I can see,
Is God's dear world, the trees and sky,
Just looking in on me.

The sound of children in the street,
So happy in their play,
And then unhappy humans,
Telling them to go away.

The roofs of flats are all around,
Tell me that friends are near,
I wonder if the view they see,
Is somehow quite so clear.

The sky is blue, the evening warm,
A plane sours high above,
To somewhere else in God's dear world,
To happiness and love.

The silence is broken, a soft miaow,
As a friend climbs on my knee,
I'll feed him now and leave the chair,
And leave God's scenery.
Kathleen Brice

A Bird's Eye View

Above the rig the sea birds fly
Alpha! Alpha! They seem to cry.
On sooty therms with smoke filled eyes
They watch as Piper Alpha dies,

A kaleidoscope of twisted steel
Acrid smell as paint doth peel
Fractured risers glowin' red.
Gushing oil from ocean bed,

They can not perch on handrails hot.
Or feed from disposed galley pot
Searing heat drives them away
Oh! what a very tragic day.

The sea birds fly towards the shore
On Piper Alpha they'll perch no more
Death, destruction they leave behind
A disastrous day for all mankind
   J. Massey

The Retired Tailor

As I was walking all alone,
along the river side.
I met a man a poor old man.
Too old and cold to talk
I said Hello but not a sound came,
from his purple lips.
Then all of a sudden I heard a voice say
If you would only take me home,
and put me in a bed,
And give me just a little to eat,
and a needle and thread.
I would sew and I would darn, merrily pass the day,
And I would not forget this deed you so heartily pay.
I took him home quite soon,
and there he had a rest,
He told me that he'd travelled far,
North, South, East and West,
He told me not to sew my clothes, nor to darn my socks.
He told me it would be a pleasure,
and he would do them at his leisure.
   Lavinia Johnson

Longing For Home

If one could just retrace their steps.
Along the path of time.
I'd return to that old village
To those dear friends of mine.
To gaze out from the far off hills,
To the village there below.
Is one of the best things ever
This saddened heart of mine could know.
I'm told that where one's heart is,
there! One's home should also be!
If that is true one thing I know,
This country is not home to me,
For my thoughts and heart are not here.
In this village dull and grey.
No! I left them at the south downs
On the day I moved away!
   K. C. Wood

Winter's Chill

Winter winds are blowing cold,
All the trees are bare and bold,
Suddenly the sky turns grey,
As I look across the way,
Then the snowflakes start to fall,
As I watch beyond the wall,
Everywhere is glistening white
It's going to be a cold, cold night,
Little birds come closer by,
So feed them, so that, they won't die,
A crumb or two will help them out
While the winters chill's about.
   Vera Sutton

Such A Wonderful Life

Never rush a new beginning
Allow yourself time to experience beauty and enchantment
   be nice to strangers
Don't let past emotions cloud inspirational judgements on a new
   friendship, laugh at rain clouds
Let the radiating warmth of your inner smile, light up the
   dimmest day, predators abound
Fly above the dark predilection to consume oneself with envy
   know yourself
Enjoy others comfort and loving and fill them with the
   same satisfaction
Hold babies and know the true meaning of life
   watch sunsets
And learn a small part of the complex organism that we call
   the universe
Love life
And let your love spread to all parts of your friends and family
Strive to be better
And watch the world that we live and love in become a
Better place because of that striving
   Sammy J. Rae

The Lighthouse

A flash of light, the thunder cracked,
All trapped in time with the lighthouse call.
On land the broken trees could hold no longer,
Fall to the ground on buckling frame.
At sea then swirling torrent rebounding wash,
Surge upon the spine of man's own beacon.
All might and lunging challenge,
Comes crashing down thereon.
The charge of battle rising force,
Wailed constant thrust attack from all around.
Here rage and power of eternal sweeping motion,
Lay claim to territory in its domain.
Distant chants, murmurs of grinding echoes
Split with charging fire, sees final assault grow near.
Advance the war cry calling,
Towards the steadfast column of glowing form.
With pounding gulps, the seas own throat could swallow not,
And hastens retreat through anger's passing rage.
The strength and stature made proud by its own being,
Withholds its foe and remains to fight another day.
   Steven M. Mochrie

Moths

The leaded window open, to move the dancing candle flame
And the first months of summer suicidal came.
A new breeze chattered in its May bud tenderness
Sending water lilies sailing as she turned to undress
And the long night awakened, we soared on powdered wings
Circling our tomorrows in the weary months of spring
chasing shadows slipping, creatures of the candle on
a night. Light ride. Dipping weaving fluttering through
The golden needle's eye. In our haystack madness
Butterfly stroking on a spring tide high. Life is too short as the
lemming said. As the candles burned and the moths were wed.
We will all burn together as the wick
grows higher. Before the candle's dead.
The leaded window open to move the dancing
candle flame, and the first moths of summer suicidal
came to join in worship of the light that never dies
in a moment's reflection of two moths spinning in her eyes
   R. Cordell

Love

Unfurled from a chrysalis of passions deep,
A butterfly wing of emotion,
Which may alight you, to cherish and keep.
Grasp it not; lest its wings shall be broken.

The love you emit is given away.
It soars on unfettered wing.
Demand not its echo, your heart to re-pay.
'Tis a fragile, intangible thing.
   G. Lewin

Land Of My Heart

Walk through the country, and see
All the greenery, as far as, can be
The streams and the rivers
Flowing so proud.
When you walk, in the country
Between England towns

The cathedrals, I visit, that's true,
So, old, so beautiful, they'll last for you
The town's and the villages
They look so grand.
When you are in England.
You'll understand.

I will return one day
To this hand, I dream about, every day
Over the oceans, over the seas
Back to this land,
Where, I'm longing to be
England, 'Oh' England
Land of my heart.

Leslie Anthony Compton

Connections

Evolutions all around
All our wishes to be found
So much love
So much hate
Thank heavens the harvest spiders at the gate.

Life is true.
Life is blue
But for what heavens do we do?

Life is so weak
Love is so strong
Thank heavens I know where we belong.

Riddles and rhymes are all the chimes to
our philosophies of today.

A picture puzzled.
A puzzled picture.
To fit in place its simple links, the puzzled picture gives.
No muzzled mouths to say our vows
The puzzled picture of gifts.

Kay Lower

Winter In The Wood

Death hangs over the wood,
All is still and quiet.
Leaves as if commanded
one by one drift down
to fill the dark, dank ground.

Yellow, Red, Brown, Purple,
A carpet stiff and deep,
But soon the leaves decay
as winter takes its toll.

The earth slumbers in its nest
Waiting to hear the voice so sweet,
that calls and wakes it from its rest.

Wake, stretch, come alive,
Spring is here to reap
the rewards within the fold.
As the new tree's peep with tender
shoots from underneath the mould.

M. C. Williams

At Home Is Where I Belong

When you said goodbye
All I could do was cry
Went to a mountain top
Jumped, and learnt to fly

Flying through the air
escaping from despair
I didn't want to stop
Trying to find someone to care

Looking down I found a crowd
I smiled and felt proud
I was searching too hard
At home, I was safe and sound

Falling into the arms of friends
On whose love I can depend
I now feel good and strong
My heart is on a mend

At home is where I belong
All the stupid things that went wrong
Everything can be sorted
That's why I wrote this poem

Neil Cox

'An Accident Of Consequence'

Jumping on clouds, dancing in rain.
After that morning never again.
After a instant your body feels so bare.
Thinking why me, life's cruel and unfair.

The question you ask are hard to make.
The tears you shed are hard to fake.
From that moment your life hangs by a thread.
Hoping for life but wishing you're dead.

As you lie there all silent and still.
Remember your life your dreams and your will.
Scream, shout, bang let out all your rage.
If not you'll be imprisoned like a bird in a cage.

It's hard to accept that your life has changed.
Being crazy with boredom and becoming deranged.
When you're alone don't be afraid to shed a tear.
Don't lock yourself away where no one will hear.

Walk through the darkness and into the light.
Approach the future with vision and sight.
Open the cage door and you too would agree.
It's better to be living, breathing and free.

P. D. Breeden

Alexandra Park

In Oldham, once a famous cotton-mill town,
Alexandra Park wears her own natural gown.
With trees whose branches reach far into the sky,
their restless leaves dancing like a winking eye.

Spring decks their feet with colours supreme
when flowers appear as in a beautiful dream.
Come dawn, dewdrops glisten and sparkle like jewels,
softly dripping and evolving as fairy-like pools.

In summer, pink and white blossoms garland the trees,
then float gently around in a soft warm breeze.
Birds in their nests, with their young up high
singing a merry note, teaching them to fly.

Autumn signifies change as cold winds blow,
leaves turn gold, knowing it's time to go.
As gales snatch them away from what was their home,
they settle, forming carpets, soft as honeycomb.

Winter is here, the trees are now bare,
knotted branches spread like witches' black hair
North winds blow, spreading a snowy-white gown
like an ice queen decked out with a shimmering crown.

Nellie Ingham

Embankment Observation

She placed her agonized face
Against the Embankment wall
And suddenly appeared tranquillity
Her eyes became loving
Her lips became tender
All the agony and tension vanished
What had she found in that aged wall?
Had its coolness abated her fever?
Had it opened her mind to lost love?
I will never know
For almost within seconds
Her face was ravaged
Once more with anguish
That lovely peace was gone
And she strode away.
R. C. Beeching

School Days

To school we go to listen and learn
    All about the world and life
All about the ups and downs
    The happiness and strife.

Enjoy it whilst you are young.
    It doesn't last forever,
For when you leave and have to work
    It's entirely a different endeavour.

At sixty years you can retire
    And dream of days gone by
You then will realise school was great
    And that you'll not deny.
Vera R. Morris

A Memory Of The Promenade

Tell me, who would have thought I would find you,
After searching so long and so hard.
Who would think it would be of all places
In a chemists on Deal's promenade.

I had visions of lakes soft with moonlight
So I really just was not prepared
For a bolt of forked lightning to strike me
In a chemists on Deal's promenade

You were beautiful, all I had dreamed of.
Your companion was really 'on guard'.
She could feel the sparks crackling between us.
In the chemists on Deal's promenade.

I can still see your eyes and eyelashes,
And your mouth, (if I concentrate hard).
I can still smell your brown leather jacket,
In the chemists on Deal's promenade.

Well,...I gathered the hands of my babies.
And without any word of regard,
I turned round and walked out of the doorway
Of the chemists on Deal's promenade.
M. D. Coe

I'm Thinking Of Leaving Home

I'm thinking of leaving home,
Across the Irish Sea inviting.
There's a world out there I do not know.
Is there something that I'm missing?

What keeps me here,
I frequently think.
Ah, forget about,
Lets have another drink.

Well, it's getting late,
Time to hit the old abode.
Damn, it's raining outside,
Well alright, one more for the road.
Sean Mulhern

Christianity

It came to Britain from the East,
accepted far and wide
as the true faith for everyone,
and for it good men died;
we took it North, we took it South,
we took it further West, -
then took it back towards the East,
where men had lost their zest!
We spread the Glory far and near,
we backed it up with sword and spear!
We backed it up with cannon's roar,
bullets gas and bombs, what's more!
Our methods have made many grieve,
but, - none can say we don't believe!
Noel Egbert Williamson

To My Dearest Mother
In Loving Memory Of My Father

The emptiness felt deep inside creates a great yearning
A yearning that was once fulfilled by the warmth of your love
A love that is locked in the depths of my heart
But can no longer be felt by your embracing arms
Only memories.........

I gaze to the sky to look for answers
The clouds do not see my gaze
I stare......and wonder
When I feel you near...is it real?
Or just the yearning......

I see beautiful things every day
the sun, the birds, the flowers....you
Yes I close my eyes and see you.....Beautiful you.
I smile at the life we had together
Then I shed a tear at the loneliness I feel.

I know a love as deep as ours is destined to join together again
As though we never parted.
Until that day my darling
I devote my life to those who care...and love
the way we taught them.....together.
Sue Dalby

Untitled

I'm a fake, a clown,
A worthless hero,
Here for other people's tragedies,
To pick up the pieces of their broken souls,
Sail them along the high sea's of death,
You see death is not gloom,
It's a sea of green, fully in bloom,
No hostility here, just the lapping
of the waves,
Fully in bloom,
Lonely is my work, but many friends
I have,
They come and go as they please,
No thoughts, no games,
Turmoil, disgrace, worries and troubles,
It doesn't matter,
You have an eternity to be forgiven.
Paul Reynolds

Diamonds

Diamonds glitter in the snow,
A sight more precious you will never know,
Facets of brilliance as we pass,
Glittering over peeping grass,
The beauty of a snowy scene,
Heavenly quiet and serene,
Open your eyes to the beauty there,
Of snowy diamonds everywhere,
God gave us beauty such as this,
Too wonderful to ever miss.
Sheila H. Westwood

"The Spirit Of The Sea"

The depths of the oceans,
   A wondrous place.
The movement of plant life,
   A wide open space.
The swimming of the wild life,
   A rich and splendid thing.
Why does man devastate all that nature can bring.

The boats that we sail,
   across the oceans so wide,
Are but for man a coming of tides.
We sail through the rivers the locks and the dykes,
That takes us to oceans that flow through the nights.

We sit and we watch the oceans so blue,
   As a ship in the night draws me closer to you.
I can and think of no place I'd rather be,
   Then sailing the oceans for all eternity.

We put on are wetsuits to go down to the depths,
   To find out the cold and the wet.
The sharks and the flat-fish the squid and the crad,
   Are some of the wonders that man has but grabbed.

But heed the warning the oceans have said,
   For if man does not, the oceans will be dead.

C. B. A. J. Sowden

The Force

An aura of light, emblazoned with colour,
A warm, enfolding cloud.
A mantle of love that fits like a glove,
A stature, upstanding and proud.

A presence of energy, vibrant and solid,
A feeling of life, and of living.
A glow in the dark, a flame or a spark,
Never taking, always giving.

The breath of life we take without thought.
The haven always there.
A place to eat, for friends to meet,
An all embracing care.

A boundless spirit, engulfs and surrounds,
Dependable, always there.
The love never ends, it echoes and sends
A silent whispered prayer.

What is this powerful, passionate force
Passing from one to another?
The caring and sharing, the grinning and bearing,
- Simply, the love of a mother.

Gillian B. Clamp

Fantasies

Beyond the realm of fantasy
A true existence lies,
But who, not I will dwell upon
Its false and frail disguise.

I'll cling to strands of silver thread,
Watch for shooting stars, listen to stories old,
Follow rainbows to their very end
And one day find that pot of gold.

I'll remember Easter bunnies
Tooth fairies, brownies and Imps,
God-Mothers with their magic wands,
Santa Claus and water nymphs.

Wicked witches, Leprechauns,
Goblins, Gnomes and Giants tall.
Friendly Ghosts, Gruesome Ghouls,
Pixies, Sprites and Elfins, small.

Fairy tales and nursery rhymes
Come to mind so readily,
So who, will you come join me
Within the realm of fantasy.

Penny Williamson

Paradise

Paradise, some people say,
A tropical island far away.
Sun-drenched day, and sunset nights,
Maybe even pleasure flights.

No more worries, but peaceful days.
Soaking up, the sea in waves.
But is this really paradise,
Or just a dream, I had last night.

Sun shining through the window panes,
I wake up, from, a sleep again.
In pain, and troubled, I'll put on the mask,
So nobody can see, the trouble of past.

As I get ready, to start my day,
This is heaven on earth I say.
Paradise is life itself,
Whether poor, or rich in wealth.

So whether in pain, worry or strife
Just remember, paradise is life.

Patricia Jesson

My Sarajevo

Under a hill it came to be
A time of sorrow 'twas our town
And when we saw the sun not once
For a long time still.

Our hearts were sad for many a morn
When men were born of my town.
Our people fared as well they will
Into a darkness like no dawn
Of a time stood still.

All for what we ask dear Lord
We hope for peace and love of our town.

Men will come and ask what may
Because of courage they will say rise
Up and begin again until.

The one thing is lost, and the other is gained,
You are of courage, and not to blame.

We in our town are Sarajevo.

A. C. Loader

A Wealth Of Music

From conception, my environs encompassed
a throbbing beat.
It sought to share the sanctuary of my
amniotic reach.
I'd turn and roll, kick and swim to the
rhythm from within.
Roll again and dance with vigour to the
strains of a violin.

A sweet voice without sang songs of love
as my haven was caressed.
Vibrant melody embraced my being; filled
me with delight.
Joy an gladness, an overture a greeting
at my birth.
Thrived on the poise of the voice I loved.
Music was her wealth.

This innate nirvana, thence dictates my life
my fate.
Only with lovers of harmony do I feel loved,
warm, safe.

Margaret Dennison

Terrorists

No contest this, when, hidden out of sight
A 'thing' that those who know call a 'device'.
No contest this of manly vigour
To plant a 'thing' whose aim is to disfigure.
No animal, the lowest of the low,
To such an act allow itself to bow.
You evil ones who like to say you're men,
Come out and let us look upon you then.
Will we see sons and brothers, husbands, fathers,
No, not such ones but rather,
Demonic, inhuman creations of the Devil.
Happy in their ghastly work and revel
In causing chaos, misery and strife,
And love the taking of another life.
   Sheila M. Robins

Untitled

The streets I roam around my home
A teardrop in my eye
For things have changed so much since I
grew up there as a boy

The house I lived in as a child
Is there no more I see
The people too are strangers now
There's no one there for me

The place seems different now somehow
My friends are far away
I feel so lonely standing here
I want to walk away

I'll go back where I came from
My memories I'll write down
I'll keep them safe within my heart
A stranger in my home town
   Rita Masterson

My Special Moment

On holiday in Menorca last September,
A special moment, I will always remember.
All by myself, in the deep blue sea.
No-one around me, content as anyone could be.

Soft classical music passing over my head.
A wonderful experience, over waters to tread.
Swimming, floating, walking on air.
Little wonder a time to stop and stare.

This special moment will remain forever.
The experience felt, always to treasure.
Feeling at last, a sense of inner peace.
As if God was with me, such release.

Very sad this moment had to come to an end.
Only once in a lifetime, not able to extend.
Warm waters, blue sky, sweet music, such charm.
Perhaps never again, will I feel this calm.
   Laura Walmsley

Suddenly, At Home.

There; back then.
A span of years my father used to speak of.
Some lads who used to knock about a bit together.
Whoever turned up; often it involved a ball;
Sometimes a bit more structured:
Bank holidays of films and football.
The eight twenty-eight Victoria, perhaps;
Leicester Square and White Hart Lane,

Not on the sports page now I find them,
Or smilingly, paired outside a church.
Now one is gone, the first of whom I've heard;
Ten or so years too soon, by Bible lore.
Yet they're the lucky ones,
Who fall at once to nature's bullet;
Suddenly, at home.
   Paul Wiley

Our Song

A song of the time you spent with me.
A song that bring back find memory
A song that fills a place in my heart.
A song to remember when we are apart.

Sing me a song, like you used to do
give me a promise and make it come true
Take from me whatever you will
Always remember that I love you still

Sing me our song you remember it well
The words of which only you can tell
Roll back the years with a melody
Our song you song for me.

Our song is a bond between us to keep
Always to remember as we fall asleep
Whatever the new day was to bring
It's our song I hope you will sing
   William Banks

The Household Gavalry

He stands there in all his splendour
A soldier of the crown
Breastplate glinting in the sunlight
Not a smile on his face nor a frown.

Helmet in place sword adjusted
Ready to obey the command
Astride his mount to the sentry box
To the sound of the marching band.

Spectators travel from around the world
To watch this glorious scene
Queen Mary called them tin soldiers
They are blues and royals to our queen.

Just a trot from Knightsbridge to Whitehall
A tradition for years handed down
They are the household Gavalry
The soldiers of the crown.
   Vera Ewers

One For The Birds

For one whole week I couldn't hear
All the sounds you hear each day
I could see the children as they play
But the sounds they made were far away
Maybe they were singing, and was the sound so sweet
As the sounds I heard before of children in the street
The sound of the wind, the sound of the rain
Splashing so hard against the big window pane
The cats, the dogs, the planes, the trains
And the voice of a D.J. yelling love is strange.
All these things I wanted to hear
Theses things and so many more
But for one week of my life God decided
For this once, he would just close the door
And when it opened up again
The first thing that I heard
Was a song so sweet and beautiful
Sung by one very little bird.
   Sheila J. Burton-Pye

Lonely Boy

I look at you and want to be
a running wave on the sea
to come crashing down on the shore
never ending always more

You are so vast clear and blue
Oh lonely sea I am like you
all alone there is no other
no loving friend sister or brother

Oh lonely sea take me with you
to a sunny land that's green and blue
were children play and scream with joy
were every child has a toy.
   C. Bray

Natures Beauty (Missing You)

Not a cloud in sky on a bright summer day,
A soft gentle breeze caused the tree tops to sway.

A bird on a branch rings its chews with zest,
Fledglings full grown and long since flown the nest.

A spiders web which glistens in the bright rays of light,
Hides a dark deadly secret for small insects in flight.

The sun overhead with such radiance and power,
Helps small shoots to grow and closed buds to flower.

Marigolds and Daisies in cheerful array,
Open their leaves to the worth of the day.

Bright coloured blooms entice bees to alight,
The plunder of nectar their never ending plight.

But for all natures beauty which she's willing to share,
One flower is missing with which no other can compare.
A flower of such beauty it's an honour to behold,
A flower after nature had created broke the round.

A flower that brings joy and smiles to one's face,
A flower where in my heart there will always be a place.
Peter McKay

After The Storm

A silence fills the tear-stained heavens,
A slanted shaft of rippling light
Falls gently on the weeping bough,
Rejoicing in its new-found might;
A swirl of wings, a sudden trill,
A lark released from fear's alarm
Soars upward to immensity
To flight again in Nature's calm:
Then hope revives, and all things rise
To counter lightning's vivid power,
And peace dispels the ravaged hour.
W. H. Hodkinson

Love

If I could have a mother, a real and loving brother
  a sister and father as well,
I'd jump for joy and tell the world
  but this is just a dream,
I pray to God that I be seen in places with my mother.
But neither any one of them would come
I'd have to hide and cover
  So not to be discovered.
That these things are just another,
of my silly, silly dreams.
Lynne Michelle Bevans

'A Cornish Band'

With the gold of evening twilight
A summer day is on the wane
The country air - filled with music
It's our village band in sweet refrain

Sweet refrain of music I still remember
A test piece of yesteryear
Rendered with pride and dedication
Through practice - perfection for all to hear.

Each one playing in full accord
Eyes upon music and band master - overlord.
Instruments were gleaming, rendering that sweet refrain
In time - with attentive motion, their test piece yet again.

They travelled to London crystal palace band contest and took part
One for all, all for one, they played with courageous heart
Swept aside, other contestants, to score top in their class.
Gaining full marks for distinction, no other did surpass.

Returned home to their village, "champions of the west"
Earned an accolade of victory, hailed as Cornwall's best.
After many years I still remember those sounds of sweet refrain
From those instruments of special bandsmen (St. Dennis) is the name.
R. M. A. Best

Snapshots

Snapshots of people: snapshots of events:
A single shutter action as the retina accepts
The information.

A polaroid opinion; a polarized choice of thought;
"I like him"; "I hate him": a whole personality caught
In a snapshot.

He reminds me of someone, someone from way back at school.
I remember that guy was a bit of an idiot, and I guess this guy is thesame kind of fool,
And I dismiss him,

Because it's life in the nineties, no time for procrastination:
Instant judgements, instant access, instant results, instant attention, instant gratification,
And I want it now.

And so we compile whole albums of snapshots; we call it our live's and it dictates who we are.
Like pixels on a screen, like grains on a photograph: like pieces of a jigsaw, each snapshot forms a part of who we'd like to be.

But a snapshot is just paper; two dimensions with no depth.
And we end up like that snapshot, pinned on a corkboard with all the rest
That someone else dismissed.
Steve Marsh

"Mud In Your Eyes"

The cast of nations performs its illusions,
a show that's spiced with riddles, confusions,
a confederation in creation.
To a new beginning, to brotherly ties,
let's drink a toast: - "mud in your eyes."

Plans are proposed in halls of power,
signatures, treaties ignored by 'the hour,
symbolic handshakes - Europe shall rise'!
To nations united in half-truths and lies,
here is a toast: - "mud in your eyes."

The phoenix is reborn from the fire,
transformed to an eagle soaring higher and higher.
To unlock the future we must turn to the past
when a prophet spoke: "Rome shall not last,"
"your lots have been cast."

  To the New World Order, the '*beast*' soon to rise,
  to control all our fates until Yeshu' arrives,
  "fill the cup - bottoms up - mud in your eyes."
Sigvard Von Brevern

Oh Why Can't I Remember

Why can't I remember all those early days?
I remember our neighbours and their names,
My mates at school are clear in my mind,
The teachers who cared, not many I know,
Our back yard, my own football pitch,
The box room for me and our kid in bunks,
Did we really have a jerry on the landing?
Saturday morning I went to the rent office,
Which side of the road do I stand for the bus?
A rota for washing up; is it my turn again?
My mum's baking; ah the smell,
My dad peeling veg' at the kitchen sink,
I remember the dolly peg in the back yard.
So many things spring to mind,
But so many things I can't understand,
Did we ever have Christmas dinner?
What did I get for my birthdays?
Did we ever go out for a picnic?
Oh why can't I remember?
K. Homer

142

Alcohol Clever

If you ever caught me sober, you would see
A shivering, shy, nobody
With maybe one or two words (to break the ice).

I am glad you declined at closing time;
Waking to the real me would be
The saddest sight to see.
Still, when I stared into your eyes I saw
You and I, a dimly lit room and a meaning to life!

Just serve me a pint of personality,
Then stay on your side;
My company would drain the shine in your eyes.
Stephen J. Michaux

The One That Got Away

Gunboots, stick, dog and cap, don't really know
when we'll be back, rain or shine we'll be there
wood or field tracking the hare.

There he dashes striving to stay alive, the chain
gets taut as the dog starts to pull his anger
Increases like a raging bull.
Slip the noose and away he goes excitement as he
is freed from his master's gallows

Frantically the dog dashes across the field,
ears pinned back eyes peeled, gracefully he runs
as if running on air faster and faster goes
the frightened hare.

Over fields and under hedgerows past a game keeper
Shooting crows, but the hare he hides and gets
away, escaping from the dog for another day.
Glyn D. Askey

Sharks

A killer instinct born and bred
a ruthless savage inside their head
Such placid creatures calm and still
Waiting for the chance to go in for the kill

Domineering the waters in their motionless state
Survival for others is left up to fate
A magnificent statue of power and size
Long slender bodies, lifeless black eyes

To look in their eyes no reflection is seen
Dark and empty, somehow serene
Then a sense of fear as their eyes roll back
No escaping its jaws as it goes in for attack

A shrill cry of pain, the final echoing sound
Only blood now remaining can be seen all around
Then the shark swims on, no remorse does he feel
Just wanders the sea waiting to catch his next meal.
Ruth Anderson

Baby No More

You said that you should be my "first,"
What made you think that's your right?
Yes it's true - 'you brought me up,'
But that doesn't mean "I'm Yours" at night!
It doesn't allow you to comment,
Or to touch me whenever you feel,
It doesn't allow you to 'ground me'
Just because I don't want to reveal
You tried your emotional blackmail
You made me feel so full of guilt
You made me ashamed and unworthy,
You destroyed all the friendship we'd built.
I still have the hang-ups inside me
I still feel the guilt and the shame
I still feel the fear of you - "father"
You're a 'dad' to me only in name!
Diana Lansdown

A Place.....

There's a place beyond this world
A place where there is peace
A place where
Our souls can be released

A place where everything's calm
A place where we can be free
Free from any harm

A place where there are no worries or fears
A place no need for tears

A place where we don't fight
A place where
We don't fear the night

We can't drive there
Or be flown
If we go there
We go alone
Pembe Suleyman

Another Day

The North wind blows. A web is spun.
A pig is slaughtered. A marathon is run.
Men at work. Children at play.
Women a wash. Another Day.
Night draws in, darkness shrouds.
Drift into sleep, like shapeless clouds.
Dawn a breaks, another day.
A baby is born, a pensioner old.
The baby is warm, the pensioner cold.
Years roll away, a decade gone.
Same old story, life goes on.
A baby peaceably lies, a pensioner forlornly dies.
Another day.
Print put to paper, seeds prepared to sow.
Men at work high, Women at home low.
A glider silently passes, an argument overheard.
Cancer is diagnosed, a song from a bird.
ANOTHER DAY
A. H. Chaplin

My Father

Imagine a man - a man so fine,
A man who did all he could
A man who cared for his fellows
Who tried to do only good.

He only ever did his best
For his wife and family too
He worked and toiled from dawn 'til dusk
Whatever there was, he would do

He was always there when needed
Always had time to hear
Whenever I was worried
he chased away every fear

I really miss my father
The best friend I ever had
I consider that I've been lucky
To have had the Best - My Dad
Wendy Watson

To My Wife

At last, my soul and I have found
A kindred spirit with which to play.
One who makes no great demand,
But loves us truly, day by day.
We in turn devotion true, give
Without thought, to you,
Our friend, our lover, all that's fine.
You, a person most divine, beautiful,
Wise beyond your years,
Nearly bring us both to tears
When we remember how we searched,
But found not the comfort
That now is ours.
Ron Stuart

A Brief Account Of The Life Of My Black Labrador In 'Doggerel'

'Jock' was his name.
A more loyal, faithful friend
None could make claim.
His coat was shiny and black as jet
"In fine condition", said the vet.
Oh how he loved his walk!
I do declare,"That dog did all but talk."
As a puppy he would chew and play.
To find a jumper without a hole made my day!
As a young strong dog Beecraigs Country
Park was his haunt
And there he'd lay chase to rabbit and deer
Which both outstripped him I fear.
Then from the forest he would emerge
tongue out stretched and panting for breath.
Was it all worthwhile? I do declare, "That dog did smile."
'Jock' grew old sixteen a great age we were told.
His sight grew dim and hard of hearing he became.
But without complaint he bore his lot, a shining example to
those of us who cannot.
May Park

A Special Place

It's only a village, not large but not small
A number of houses, some tiny some tall
Some very old, and others quite new
A hotchpotch of buildings, it may seem to you
A church and a chapel, two schools and two pubs
A community hall and two or three clubs
Playing fields for the children, two swings and a slide
Fields to run in and places to hide
Also a factory, but that's different too
Birds in our village have a pink hue
A library, I forgot, where people can meet
Just a few shops, well, we have to eat
One main street, with three different names
A few side roads and quite a few lanes
But it isn't the buildings that make this place warm
A special place this, blessed by above,
filled with people who care and give love
to all those who need it, sad and afraid
by whom the foundations of this village were made
A long time ago and still carry on and may it
continue for years to come
Molly Bailey

Bonfire Night

I'll never forget that spectacular sight
A night in November, the sky filled with light.
'Twas a feast for the eye, a panoramic display.
The place where it came from was not far away.

Drawn ever closer by the welcoming glow
My pace grew quicker, as I knew I must go.
I was soon at the scene, it didn't take long.
I saw a huge fire, in the midst of a throng.

I could feel the excitement as the flames grew taller.
Making all of those watching, appear very much smaller.
Suddenly, what seemed from out of the ground.
Rocket's streaked skywards as I looked up spellbound.
The air was warm from the heat of the ashes.
The spell instantly broken by loud 'Thunder Flashes'
There were children with sparklers eyes gleamed with delight.
As Catherine wheels' spun to illumine the night.
My mind filled with memories going back through the years.
To childhood days - of laughter and tears.
For me this day. I will always remember.
As one of the happiest, the fifth of November.
G. W. Dobson

The Sea

The sea is a raging torrent,
A murderer
Who fills hearts with fear and sheet terror.
She shoots man down.
Her waves will attack him and force him to withdraw,
sinking, drowning
To become part of the furnishings in the home the sea provides.

God sends storms to fight the sea.
They'll fight a battle,
The water struck by lightning,
And the heavens will shout abuse at the sea for all the lives
she has taken.

Serene, soothing, singing.
After the war the sea will calm,
Hide her head in shame.
Sea birds will sing a victory chorus.
Glorious and gracious in their lap of honour,
And ships will sail to destinations to celebrate the harmony
and tranquillity.
Loved ones wave goodbye, not knowing if sea fever break on
the dawn.

But peace will be broken
When the sea strikes again.
Laura Mackay

Untitled

My life was set up so cosily,
A Mum, a Dad and my own family.
The day of dread it had arrived,
My lovely Dad had gone and died.

The world just fell around my ears,
As I remembered some wonderful years.
There were the good times and the bad,
I don't know which ones made me sad.

Time heals everything they all say,
So I live life from day to day.
Being told to always stay strong,
Makes me think that mourning's wrong.

The hurt and anger were robbed from me,
So as not to upset my own family.
What about me? did anyone care?
That maybe I needed my Daddy there.

Five years on, I still feel numb,
Life's not the same with just a Mum.
I know I shouldn't feel this hate,
But why did he die aged forty eight?
Maureen Rolfe

Rainbows Who Knows?

Rainbows that ask our parts of the earth, every colour God
gave us to see is up there, so don't look up and take a
rainbow for granted, or the sea, or a sunset, or anything
planted. Rainbows who knows?
At the end of a rainbow there's a pot of gold, and a cloud has
a silver lining, or so we're told. It starts with the rain, just like
the tears, then the sun smiles down and a rainbows appears.
Rainbows who knows?
Rain is water made from the clouds, wind, who knows where it
comes or goes? A miracle in itself untold. Rainbows who knows?
The earth, the sun, the moon, the stars, our life itself, our
beings our souls. Not black and white but colourful tones.
Rainbows who knows? These beautiful colours arched in the
sky, you know pretty soon
they'll fade and die. These magical colours of a lovely
rainbow, just where do they come from? and where do they
go? Rainbows who knows?
I know why the rainbows appears up above, it's a sign from
God, of peace and love. When the flood came Noah built an
ark to save the believers, the honest, the truthful, the brave.
An ark upside down is to let us all know, just what the
meaning is of a beautiful rainbow.
Rainbows now you all know.
J. Gates

A Mother's Love For Her Sons

There is no price upon this list
A mother's love is a priceless gift
There's an endless list of wants and needs
Demands to be met and endless books to read.
Sleepless nights and tiring days
Washing, Ironing and putting away
Cooking and cleaning when I've got the time
I wouldn't swap this life of mine
My sons to me have been a pleasure
Endless memories I have to treasure
Nursery days and school days too.
I've seen quite a few
Never at a loss for things to do.
Untold pride I have in the four of you.
Meg Turnbull

Look...Because You Can

An abused, disused quarry,
A painting that's a waste of paint,
An unkempt, uncared for garden,
A cottage that's no longer "quaint".

A building that has no character,
A statue that does nothing but stand still,
You've seen these and many other things,
Yet there's people who never will.

So don't moan about a view being boring,
To say something's ugly is unkind,
Try to imagine how it doesn't look,
Through the eyes of someone who's blind.

So take stock and count your blessings,
Don't judge by the cover of the book,
Everything has a point of beauty,
If you only care to look.
Leslie Newell

Lockerbie

A Scottish Hillside silent at night,
A moon in its heaven so full to their plight.
What should have been a joyful journey this night,
ended in tragedy and burst like a kite.
No telling what lay ahead for these souls,
as on to that plane they joyfully strolled.
Just thirty minutes from their last take off,
Approaching the Scottish hillside aloft.
But then all at once an almighty bang
in flames and in tatters, the screams they cry out.
Below in oblivion Lockerbie lays, unknown
the destruction that is coming its way.
The sky rains with fuel alight and white hot.
The plane plunges through houses and leaves not a trace,
the families left homeless is this God's good grace.
The homecoming lost, the people stand bravely
their sorrows to bear,
and the moon in its heaven ever brightly
it glares.
Thomas Allan Liddle

Ham Richmond Surrey

A quiet village near a park,
A century old church completes its mark,
in a peaceful corner amidst the trees.
Across from a house where an author sees.
and writes about his loving cats
This is the village of Ham.

Walk down Ham Street in the morning dew.
and on to Ham House, there you will find,
the former home of the Dysarts,
Full of wondrous treasures to behold,
Surely a tribute to the days of old.
Yes indeed, come to Ham.
No nicer village is known to man.
M. Phillips

"Harsh Reality"

Illusions, false belief, a mind that has gone
A mind that is no longer my own haunts me
Reality hands out another swift blow
Plato's illusions, his reality, his beliefs become my own.
using them to hold on to dear life, yesterday took them away
stunning me, leaving me distraught,
leaving me alone - death's prey
torn, wounded
disillusioned, petrified, dazed
to go, to stay
the feared decision I cannot make
My mind is no longer my own
my soul is alien to me
my limbs are borrowed
my heart no longer beats
my breath is choking
life is passing me by
Dead I am
but I still feel the pain of living
It is Hell.
Mary Laverse

Into My Mind

A glance, a smile, those tender eyes,
A look of caring you can't disguise.
A gentle whisper, so soft your touch,
Your open arms, I need so much.

A wish to reach into my mind,
Embrace the heart that you will find.
These feelings that I can't control,
But eyes shine through and mark the soul.

A trace of love along the way,
Steps from the shadows, here to stay,
To firmly hold a hand so tight.
Reaches to, the still of night.

A hope, a dream in thoughts gone by,
To hold these memories within a sigh.
A spoken word, the warmth that glows,
Settles as rain upon a rose.

My love, at last I've found a way,
To capture dreams and know they'll stay.
Surrendering, my heart is still,
I love you now, I always will.
Steve A. Welland

Watergate Bay In Winter

Picture if you can what lies before my eyes,
A long cold beach now lashed by Winter rain,
With anger showing in the sullen skies,
This beach that once with joyous laughter rang.
Now silent, save for wind and rain,
Which drives upon this Cornish beauty spot,
The sun that shone, has had to wane,
And leave dull beauty in its place.
The wind intensifies in strength,
The waves in Summer that caressed the golden sand,
Now try so hard go to any length,
To pull the soft and yielding sand into the deep.
The tide was on the ebb, now on the flow,
Still pounds against the rocks within the sea,
But the sea with all its power can never go,
Across the cliffs high ageless crags.
Into the green of Cornish countryside,
Or touch the fields when blessed with golden corn,
Within the realm of ocean it must bide,
And bring much pleasure on this Winter time.
D. J. Breden

Bitterness

I sometimes wonder just how long,
   a lonely man can live.
Especially when that lonely man,
   has so much love to give.
He fell in love so long ago,
   and gave away his heart.
And then he found the girl he loved,
   was just a snobbish tart.
She left him flat cause he was poor,
   she wanted wealth's esteem.
She took her hook and went away,
   and broke a lover's dream.
So now this man lives all alone,
   there's no one there to care.
And he can't find another love,
   for she is always there.
He compares the girls he meets to her,
   and they just will not do.
And now he knows he'll spend his life,
   alone till it is through.
    J. M. Thomas

'Alone'

There she sat all alone
A little soup gently simmering on her stove
Reflecting in her dreams of days gone by
trying very hard not to cry.

So cold so cold so very cold
Frost glittering like silver on the outside road
Keep her self warm she must try to do
In tattered clothes she has nothing new

On the fire the last piece of coal
She is so weary in heart and soul
Out of the window she see's a star
So big and bright but so very far

Nearer and nearer it seems to come
Making her aged body seem very numb
With outstretched hand she tries to touch
She wants to follow so very much.

And as it gathers her up in it arm
She at last feels the calm
No more hardship no more pain
No more cold snow or rain
    Pauline Chambers

The Kiss

The wind howls through the rigging of the yachts moored on the sea,
A high pitched wailing desolate sound that's like the pain in me.
I walk the dogs along the green, the night around so dark
Lit only by the yellow neons bordering the park.

I sit down on the hard park bench and look out to the sea
And in my mind I see you there walking across to me.
No words are ever spoken, no need for them you see
For you know what is needed and you send your thoughts to me.

I now can feel your fingers the closeness of your touch,
I lay my head upon your shoulder loving you so much
I touch your face so lightly, you turn to me and smile
Your arm goes round my shoulders in the old familiar style.

Your hazel eyes are shining in the way that makes me weak,
Your lips are barely moving but I know the words you speak
We both arise together, entwined within the kiss
The touching of your fingers makes my heart beat all amiss.

I hear the dogs are barking, I turn my head to see,
No more my ghostly lover, no more my heart set free.
I find I'm sitting all alone just staring out to sea
There's nothing there but cold dark air, the dogs, the night and me.
    Penny Waters

Who Am I

I look in the mirror, what do I see?,
A haunting reflection that's definitely not me,
Those eyes filled with sadness, depression and pain,
A heart that talks through them, says "please not again."

The face is a stranger, who can it be?
It's my image reflected but definitely not me,
The emotions and feelings I try so hard to hide,
Just won't please my wishes and stay locked inside.

They fight to the surface, ignoring my plea.
How will the world know, that's definitely not me,
My soul cannot appear, if only it would,
Then perhaps I would see me as I should.

A dark, brooding feeling what will be, will be,
I cannot accept that, it's definitely not me,
For always and ever, now 'till I die,
God, answer my question...who am I?.
    Pamela Goulding

Storm In The Night

The silence of the night is broken by
A flash of lightning and rumblings in the sky
A light goes on, a baby cries,
Its sleep disturbed where ere it lies.

The wind and lashing of the rain.
The hooting owl is quiet again
The passing clouds reflect no light
The moon and stars they hide in fright

The air is cool refreshed by rain
The sparkling raindrops that remain
On trees and grass and window panes
Are like shiny diamonds on roads and lanes.

The nodding flowers of brightest hue
The rising sun and all is new
A summer shower, a rainbows arc
The sweet singing of the lark.
    Pamela Clifford

Treasures

To hold in my heart a pearl beyond price,
A gem that so glistens, it makes me feel nice,
A rare thread of gold in my bosom I'll hold,
And blend it with silver to fashion and mould.

A rainbow of colours to paint our sad world,
With beauty and love, and the song of a bird.
A blue summer sky to reach by and by,
No more sad tears, adieus, or goodbye.

A shower of raindrops, so fresh and so pure,
That brings in its wake a garden, a flower.
A breeze to caress and a joy to possess
With a life that is full of happiness.
    Magdalen Rhys

Heaven Sent

He stands there, oh so alone so distraught, tired.
Watching the sea listening to the
waves crashing against the rocks.
Taking deep breaths as he slowly
walks along the beach, now and again.
Looking back at his footsteps in the wet sand.
Oh the life without her is so empty.
His thoughts keeping him away from
others who now occupy the beach their
laughter didn't even penetrate his shell
Oh to be with her now would be such heaven.
As he walks down the endless path.
Thinking of only himself and his feelings
and so unaware of a hand that
lightly caresses his, she had been
there all the time because heaven
was so lonely without him.
    Sandra D. Dolman

Wild, Wild, Leaves

In autumn, leaves come tumbling fast,
A golden carpet on the grass;
Sometimes the wind, engulfed in force,
Wields such leaves on a wild, wild, course.

Crisp and dry, they prance in delight,
Swept by the wind throughout the night,
Rustling in corners, eerie sounds,
Under low bushes to nestle down.

Swirling, turning, to gutters high,
Blocking the drains, to cause a sigh;
Verandas, doorsteps, they rendezvous,
Alcoves, ledges, they favour too.

A change of scene, when winds blow sharp,
The last brown leaf glides from the bark,
Earth is covered with nightly frost,
Stiff and frozen, the game is lost.

Rays of sun, through the lofty trees,
Cast ghostly shadows on dead leaves.
Soon, they'll all be swept away,
Left on the compost, to decay.
G. M. Wareing

Hostage

Huddled in this filthy cell ensconced in apathetic hell
900 notches on the wall, on servile hands and knees we crawl
intimate with lice we grope in vain to God for strength to cope
as vermin scurry to and fro at least they're free to come and
go our captors watch us like a hawk yet politicians smile and
talk nitpicking pawns of nothingness are static in this game of
chess while kings and bishops more or less let rooks devour
their pound of flesh then condescendingly appear to swop
like cattle at a fair one of us for two of them, it's bargain time
in Bethlehem point-scoring Arab versus Jew, the notches now
are 942 prostrate we lie in dirt and squalor while Arab oil and
US dollar fluctuate with each release proclaiming scalps
instead of peace untried yet guilty of the crime of being in
wrong place wrong time teacher, journalist or priest now
manacled like common beast fettered to some strange bedfel-
low exchanging smiles of ultra yellow all for one and one for
all, one thousand notches on the wall not knowing is the
greatest pain, the hopelessness, the mental strain despair will
raise its ugly head, monotonously each noon we're fed a daily
bowl of humble pie and ponder if the end is nigh the clock of
life ticks slowly by and I keep asking myself, why?
Margaret Cogan

Divination

A heart is an opening to a conscience.
A sailor sails a current isn't elementary, life is a swirling
Alley, mine can be.

Our globe has a guardian, he's a guide across the Millennium,
I'll locate one figure waiting still and graceful too.

Imagination can picture dramas seen through glass spheres.
Round and round
It seems like I'm being taken away from it all. Nothing? Can
This be holy? Can someone belong? Can you encase a
Mother-of-pearl so gently,
I would instinctively.

A cherry tree waits carefree, to be picked, waits for Angel V.
Her snowy white hands, unblemished and beautiful. Written
Is a covenant scrawled, it's hidden in a vault for Angel V.

When she came, my time become known, when she goes,
Where she wants to, the time does not matter.

Moments will lapse as rainfall falls, the dawn returns, a delight
To a songbirds song, Angel V entertain me on a stringed harp,
My memory will recall.
Vishal Patel

The Forest Of Fang

In the forest of Fang lived a troll and his gang;
a despicable, horrible bunch.
They'd lurk behind stones and gnaw on the bones
of the victims they'd caught for their lunch.

One day to the wood, came a woman so good
that she shimmered and shone full of light.
The trolls saw her aura, and fell down before her;
they wished themselves safe out of sight.

As she drew near, they cowered in fear;
they hoped that she would go away.
Their own acts of spite, filled them with fright,
for they guessed it was their turn to pay.

The glow in her eyes, took them quite by surprise,
and froze them all stiff to the spot.
They wanted to run, but the deed it was done;
they wished they could flee but could not.

To this day they stand, a ring hand in hand,
though the forest has long passed away.
Upon a bleak hill, you can see them still,
a circle of stones to this day.
Tom Beall

"Camalorn"

Whilst dancing on a moonlit beach, an elfin form I saw,
a goblin stood within a cave, nestling on the shore.
As I looked into this eyes, they emitted a shining light,
a force then captured me, which I fought with all my might.

The goblin stood and looked, into the sky forlorn,
he asked me if I knew the way to the land of "Camalorn."
"Camalorn," you may have heard is a land of fairies and elves,
this is where they have to go in order to find themselves.

This being so I told the elf I did not know the way,
but asked him if he could answer me a riddle I'd been asked that day.
So thus I spoke the riddle, "why does the spring fall in May?"
And back he answered clearly, "because the earth was built
that way!"

So agreeing with him, this was the only answer to be found,
I pointed to a little track that lay printed on the ground.
Follow this track my elfin friend, the one that is so worn,
and you will most assuredly find your land of "Camalorn."
Rachael Piper

The Daily Paper Reflections On The Mirror

I take up my paper and what do I see?
A cartoon depicting a naughty M.P.
The P.M., I'm afraid, will throw him out on his ear,
Leaving his seat in The Commons all clear.

Now members be assured you too will be out,
If the new line of "Basics" you flout.
So don't let the temptation of sin come near,
For it could bring the end of a promising career.

I turn to the stars, just over the page
To see what's said for Capricorn, by the sage.
They promise me wealth, it must be in Heaven,
For now I've reached the age of Seventy - Seven.

Now for the crossword, the joy of the week,
With pen and Thesaurus, the words I seek,
And when the completed solution I find,
Oh! What a treat and I'm so satisfied.

I turn to the Scratch Word and what have I found,
I've Won! I've Won! - The Amount Of A Pound.
P. Muter

On Freshfield Beach

A soulless solitude that only the lonely could bear.
A beauty, barren, visible only to the heart that cares.
A brindled beach of stony sand,
where the sky meets the sea that embraces the land.
A merciless wind whips the hair from my face,
blows visions through my mind of a far away place.
It bears now my soul for all nature to see,
a homecoming for the world weary.
Transformed to the ethereal, nature and I now one,
in search of kin, a wind whipped spirit without a home.
But who but I can see the beauty, barren,
that sets the soul soaring higher than heaven.
Who but the sad lonely soul, embraced only by the wind.
Susan Aiton

The Gentle Countryside

Balloons gliding through the clouds,
A ballet up on high.
In unison a graceful dance,
Their stage, the open sky.

High trees through which the sun is seen,
Small birds on branches sitting.
The quiet breeze move leaves of green,
They touch in gentle greeting.

Winding roads and country lanes,
A farmhouse lonely standing.
Shadows fall on window panes,
A distant church clock chiming.

Natures' tapestry all around,
Just look and you will see.
Stop a while, now you have found,
Peace and tranquillity.
Mary F. Hodgetts

The Terrace

Voices visible in freezing sky
sounds of loyalty raised on high
eleven red shirts on the pitch
the twelfth a mass on the terraces.
The whistle blows the games afoot
the chants begin, but in the gut
not fear not hope
but excitement grows
expectation starts to flow
from one to ten and then to all
emotions rise and quickly fall
with one ear one voice ten thousand feet
the terrace lives but once a week.
Tim Mercer

Skywatch At Sunset

The sun illumines by its rays
A multitude of pearl-white clouds,
Diffuses rose and sapphire blue
And muted mauve in a taffeta sky.

Shadows fly across the earth
Beckoning to approaching night.
A brilliant sky, peach-painted,
Reflects the purple clouds which hang
Suspended above the burning horizon.
Suddenly the firmament flares in golden hue
Leaving an aureole of mellow brightness
To encircle the earth with comforting arms.
Gentle evening shadows fall.
The golden sun sinks low.
The darkening dusk draws nearer still;
Surrounds the orange glow.

The tender touch of sunset is no more.
The earth is plunged in darkness
Encompassed by the velvet sky
And night has come.
Margaret Kunzlik

Suddenly!

As a child - I could run up stairs
Soon to school - Mum and Dad care's

Later a letter - ohms by name
In the army - a different game

Time's gone - then I'm out
Job's I need - I would shout

Seem's like yesterday - indeed true
Now as quick - my pensions due

So to young reader's - heed this text
Before you know it - you'll be next

Use every second - to good avail
Ignore me - your turn to wail!
D. McCarthy

Beyond The Dream... Dreamchild

Through eyes that can still see magic. Sail on waves of dreamsleep
Sorrows melt away as unspoken words are heard,
In the infinite fathoms of your mind.
Echoes resound inside a bursting heart and
Spirit you away to places of auspicious awe
Pagan, wild and free.
Wondrously lost, within the untouched essence of your sanity, that
Which is your soul.

Oh, to be so blessed and unblemished,
So pure of thought.
Pity those with deadpool eyes reflecting forgotten dreams,
Who know only the envy of the mystery.

Tendril mists disguise a world, evanescent and surreal
They draw you into dreamscape to another time concealed
A unique and special realm, winds of time could not erase
Spellbinding is this fantasy, this world out with this place

Grow with the mystery as it evolves in only you. Pagan, wild and free
Enveloped in the secret, you will find your place to be.
The enigma is your destiny, to such enchantment you were born
Reach towards the magic, to your hallowed Avalon.
Lorraine Smith

The Book Of Life

The book of life, has so much to offer
   Sometimes I wonder, who was the author
For during our lives, we all will discover
   To enjoy it the most, we first have to suffer
As to appreciate the joy of happiness
   We first must experience the sad
And to know in life what is good
   We first must be thought what is bad
Then it's up to ourselves to get it right
   As there are no rehearsals to make it bright
And right at the start of this book we've been given
Written in stone, our lives are for living
Keith Fraser

Dreams

Every night I tend to dream,
Sometimes nightmares make me scream.
Scary, scary is each one,
Awake each morning, they are gone.
Dreams of good times, dreams of tears,
Light through the curtains, ease my fears.
Days are long, the nights are cold,
Dreams of young and dreams of old.
Dreams of fame and dreams of money,
Dreams of jokers, they are funny.
The morning comes around so fast,
My greatest dreams they don't last.
Remember those that gave us pain,
Till the night time comes round again.
Katie Hanson

To Remember Them

The battle field is silent now where once the
Sound of heavy fire could be heard and the
screams of dying men as they fell in silent
sleep now only poppies of red grow to show where they
fell so we must remember man's inhumanity to man.

Remember those that came back battled scarred
from the depth of hell to keep us safe from
harm and let no man take up arms and go
against his fellow men so that there will be
no more man's inhumanity to man.

So let only peace for years to come and let
the pen and not the sword fight our battles
now war has been wow so least we forget
man inhumanity to man.
Michael R. J. Randle

Killykeen Forest Park

What peace is found by the waterside,
Somewhere to think, somewhere to hide
Amongst the trees, so tall, erect,
Their mirror image, lakes reflect.

A "wee" log cabin by the lake,
Where birds their special music make
While squirrels leap from roof to ground
And scurry swiftly, without sound.

The sound of silence, loud and clear,
Is balm unto the deafened ear,
The sky so blue without a cloud,
Far away from the madding crowd.
Rita O'Rourke

Trees

Looking through my window pane.
Sometimes I wonder why,
The snow the wind, and falling rain,
Just seem to pass us by.
The birch, oak, and poplar high,
Spread their boughs to reach the sky,
The falling rain, and icy snow,
Make them shimmer with a glow,
So here and there, against the light
A leaf is seen, still clinging tight,
Old and spent, yet feeling this
That life is just, too good to miss
And so upon the boughs will cling
The leaves that long, to meet the spring
Marshall Jones

Life

What is life I wish I knew
Sometimes happy sometimes blue,
Some people old and babies new
Make this life for me and you.

Too much sorrow and tales of woe
Of death and hunger as we all know,
Starving millions despair and pain
There's nothing out of life to gain.

Unemployment rises high
Under privileged fade and die,
They turn to drink and drugs to hide
All the pain they feel inside.

To change the world to a better place
Would mean an eternal human race,
Eternal race it can't be done
So one and all must battle on.

All the fighting war and crime
I've seen enough in my lifetime,
A life that's free of all these things
Is what the ideal world would bring.
Kerry Allison

"Red"

Red is a colour, that everyone knows,
Sometimes dull, in appearance shows,
But then it can be, shiny, or even bright,
Never simply red, there's dark or light.

It can indicate a lot as a known colour,
In a lipstick, can make the mouth look fuller,
It can be harsh, as a traffic light stop,
Or even flustered, as a traffic duty cop.

A sign of anger, we are all aware,
The colour of danger, for all to take care,
Sometimes welcomed, sometimes a dread,
Because overdue bills, they come in red.

Red can be flattering, in clothes that's worn,
Even beautiful, when the sun rise does dawn,
So vital too life, in blood, we all need,
But blood money, well that's just, pure greed.

So red is red, what more can you say,
It's a part of our life, in every way,
Not given a thought, to what it really means
Like the yellows, browns, or even the greens.
Pauline Davenport

Barrie's Friend

Down our street there's a man who makes baskets,
Something that nowadays you very rarely see.
He works all alone, in a hut, on a green
and doesn't go home 'til it's time for tea.

He's very, very deaf and you have to write the orders
on some pieces of white paper that he keeps handy by.
Although he's very lonely, you never hear him grumble;
he's working much to hard to ever ask the reason why.

I think he's very glad that I go to visit him,
I write him little letters and I watch him with the cane.
Making shopping baskets, cat baskets, dollies cots and other things.
Wet it, weave it, hammer it and then begin again.

He told me that he's sixty seven, has ten fine children
and he's very soon retiring to Brighton by the sea.
So he said to tell my mother, "You'd better get your order in
if you want to buy some wickerwork from me."
Ruby E. Kennedy

The Summer Breeze

Smoothly, gently blows the breeze
Softly whispering through the trees
Fluttering petals, scattering leaves
Touching grasses, caressing trees.

Puffing at clouds to make haste
She has no time to idly waste
Ruffling feathers of birds on the wing
Carrying echoes of the songs they sing

Swirling past the weather vanes
Whispering round the window panes
Upwards, onwards she calmly billows
Rustling through the weeping willows

Aspen leaves shiver and quiver
As she darts hither and thither
The silver birch bends and sighs
As she glides across the skies

Then as gracefully as she came
She quietly slips away again
Gently, trembling through the trees
Smoothly, softly sweet summer breeze.
Pamela Frances Williams

My Love

When I met you I knew I'd found,
Someone I always wanted to be around
You made me laugh, when all I'd done was cry,
And instead of crawl I began to fly,
You are my friend, my lover too,
My love, I owe so much to you,

I have you more than you could know,
How much is sometimes hard to show,
You are my life and all my dreams,
I hope you know just how much this means,
To have you here to share my life,
I will be so proud to be your wife.

And so my promise will always be,
To stand beside you for all to see,
To share your joys and all your fears,
And hold you close if you shed your tears
The good and bad times will come and go,
but through it all our love will show,
that you and I will be together,
With all our love forever and ever.

Valerie Pattinson

Lost Love

Your love distant, fire has gone
Some-one else hears love's sweet song
Your lips have kindled another flame
Your voice now whispers another's name
Will you ever set me free
To love another such as thee

Your smile sweet, kisses that melt
Another man's gain, for me not felt
Your way gentle, weaves its spell
Your love words, to another tell
Will you ever set me free
To love another such as thee

Your love true, to me return
For your kisses my lips burn
Your smiling face, matched by few
Your sweet heart, my chances blew
Will you ever set me free
To love another such as thee.

Pearl Powell

The Golden Leaf

Some leaves turn to gold, some turn to rusty brown
Some lay in the sun, settling on the ground.
It's winter now, soon to be spring.
Happy flowers blooming, smiling faces they bring.
But there's one thing missing that don't lay in the sun
Missing from the colours of the rose that's just sprung.
It's not the same without it for nature feels it too.
There's a golden leaf missing and it's always going to be you.

Amy

Faces

Faces faces all around
Some are happy
Some are sad.
Some are different through no fault
of their own.
But please don't ignore them when
they are alone.
We look, we stare at those we
see who don't look like you and me.
But they are human in every way
they have a heart as well today.
They feel, they see the looks they get.
But they have hearts that carry neglect.
Next time you're out and you look and stare.
Look beyond the surface and see what's there.
A heart with feelings just like us.
So don't be cruel don't make a fuss.

H. Botterill

From The Heart...

Echoes in an empty room
softly whispered in a silent tomb,
shadows play across the mind
don't look back, just seek and find...

Words just sometimes aren't enough,
when decisions made, seems life's so tough,
emotions can't come into force
practicalities make you stay on course...

Thoughts and feelings sometimes break through
fleetingly three - now still just two,
but decisions made were for the best
mind and body must stand this test...

What love created it can do again,
when times are calmer, serene and more sane,
so gently push fingers of regret far away
Know, one day, it will be right - in every way...

V. K. Thomas

Dog And God

Hard, sharp, cut, gnaw, teeth.
Soft, warm, kiss, lick, jowl.
Mellow, liquid, discerning, knowing, eyes.
Silken, flowing at high speed, security antenna, ears.

Muscular, aerodynamic, heavy shouldered, slim waist frame.
Quadruple extension, surging, accelerating, legs.
High speed, whirring, pounding energy.
Padded, shock absorbing, gripping, thrusting paws.
Digging, scouring, clinging, holding, claws.

Miracle of movement - stop. Start. Go.
When we watch our hearts sing Ho - Hey - Ho.

Where have you come from? It's said you're from the wolf.
That twelve stone ancestor has done you proud - forsooth.
You're now the friend of man - no need to kill,
And sadly now, man's meddling can make you ill.

But in between the highs and lows of life,
You've become a star in human sight.
You give so much, when all you want is love.
You are mix of Eagle and the Dove.
I dedicate this to you and all the dogs I've loved.

T. S. Totten

Solitude

Soft blows the wind of Summer nights,
Soft to the touch of mind's
Surrounding thoughts of Innocence,
Converse with Tides that Bind.
And yes - a soul heart broken, amid the summer Haze,
And oh my Love with thoughts of Thee,
To the Summer night I gaze.
And treasured thoughts surround me, of warmth and
sweetness there,
Amidst the fields of emptiness my Spirit scents the air,
And yes my love the tears that fall, are aim'd from
Cupids bow,
And in my Heart there shall it be,
The Solitude I know.

I. C. Wells

A Game Of Chess

The fanfare has sounded, the banner unfurled
So rouse from your slumber and unconscious world.
Move into the sun and stand proud then
With kings and queens and lesser men
Ready your sword and lift up your shield,
To conquer or die on this glorious field.
So, arise gentle Queen and good Sir knight
And banish the darkness, to walk into the light
And herald the coming of the righteous and good,
To spill every drop of your enemy's blood.

Kevin Jones

Majestic Eagle

Great wings of power and of grace
Soars the Eagle above the earth,
The eyes forever darting at an alarming pace
Searches for the prey far below,
That the quickest hare nor the little mouse
Will escape this mighty birds so swift in flight.

Oh mighty Eagle what freedom you have
With wings outstretched and head held high,
Your travels take you so far so wide
You barely falter as you fly,
The thermal's carry you many miles aloft
And the skies are yours so go forth in pride.
Marilyn Anne Bos

The Last of the Seasons, Winter

The last of the seasons, Winter is here.
So soon, will come the end of another year.
The cold frosty days, and sometimes the snow,
There'll be ice on the ponds, as we all know.

The flowers all have died, and the gardens look bare,
There's not a leaf on the trees to be seen anywhere.
And with the dull wintry sky, and the cold chilly air,
There's a kind of stillness everywhere.

And so with the cold of the day, and the chill of the night,
The warmth of a fire is a sheer delight.
And so our thoughts are of the Summer and a nice warm sunny day,
But at this time, it seems so far away.

And so soon will come Christmas, and the New Year too,
A time to celebrate as we always do,
And then when it's all over,
We can be sure of one thing:
We can all look forward to the next season, Spring.
Margaret Platt

My Mind's Eye

Many religions say there is only one God,
So should it matter if I'm Catholic or Prod.
Should I not be free to live my life,
Without putting up with bigoted strife.
Should we not want a better life for all,
Is that not why Jesus took His fall.

Stop fighting over political borders,
Stop killing on someone else's orders.
Living as one with our futures together,
Banish this country's curse forever.
Together our children should live and play,
A better future will be theirs one day.

With the benefit of knowledge of past mistakes,
We should be willing to do whatever it takes.
For twenty five years we've had to take it,
A circle of destruction now we've a chance to break it.
Live in union with the spirit in the sky,
Looking at life through my mind's eye.
Paddy Douglas

A Mother's Reflections

You have to work you own lives out
So please be sure what you're about
Be always thoughtful always kind
And scandalous together please never mind
Help the helpless help the poor
What you can do is so much more

Keep your mind and body clean
A paragon of virtue you'll be seen
Walk in the light, keep out of the shade
The way you are is what you made
So keep heart pure, keep eyes bright
You'll always know what's wrong what's right

Keep God within your heart and soul
And only then your life is whole.
F. Shelvock

My Brother

This courageous man I knew so well
  So near to death, life had been hell
For five long years, aware of his fate
  Now eager to knock at that pearly gate.

Good Lord, He cried, I am ready to go.
  Call England he begged, they will know
The time of my death, that's what I mean.
  In his care worn face the pain could be seen.

His adoptive country of many years
  Was not his real home, down ran the tears
As he thought of England the land of his youth,
  But in Canada he had been happy that was the truth.

Dear wife, said he scatter my ashes
  under our son's apple tree.
Weep not, I will be with my boys at last
  remembering the joys of days long passed

In the spring when the blossom is on our tree
  Sit under, and know we are with you all three.
A. P. Holt

The Death Of Love

So long I dreamed of you,
So long I wanted you.
A few brief kisses,
A few stolen moments.
My heart weeps not for you nor me,
But for what could have been.

So now another phase has gone,
A new moon for a pale sky,
A long awaited love that came,
Passed on by with barely a song.
My heart cries out how can we let it be so,
But there is no other course.

So now another muse must come,
To stir my thoughts and make me cry,
When will love once again be mine,
Or am I destined merely to cry?

One last chorus for you my dear,
To sad heart nothing hurts more to hear,
Than the tragic phrase what could have been,
And shall be no more, no less, nor near.
Steven Adams

The Sun Is Throwing Shadows

Oh babe as you lay there so peaceful and still, I look at you and I take my fill. Isn't this summer day simply magic? The The truth of it is, I could watch you forever, oh babe you make me feel so together. Oh isn't this summer day simply magic? With the sweet fragrance blowing in the breeze, the birds singing their songs up in the trees. We lay here alone babe just you and me.

Even with the sun throwing shadows over your face, still your bright eyes shine. Yes even with the sun throwing shadows over your face, still I see the light in your eyes. You're glowing babe you look so fine, Oh I feel so glad that you are mine. As love shines from your eyes it's a wonderful place, as I watch the sun throwing shadows over your face.

Oh babe I wish this moment could last forever, just you and I here alone together. Isn't this summer day simply magic? You know you take my breath away, Oh how your beauty truly captivates me. Isn't this summer day simply magic? With the sweet fragrance blowing in the breeze, the birds singing their songs up in the trees, we lay here alone babe just you and me.

Even with the sun throwing shadows over your face, still your bright eyes shine, Yes even with the sun throwing shadows over your face, still I see the light in your eyes. You're glowing babe you look so fine. Oh I feel so glad that you are mine. As love shines from your eyes it's a wonderful place, as I watch the sun throwing shadows over your face.
Ray Bowden

A Woman's Lament

He says he really loves me
So how could he forget our anniversary
He say he really loves me
So why can't he remember I don't like peas
He say he really loves me
So why doesn't he listen when I tell him of my day
He says he really loves me
So why can't he help in the house sometimes
He says he really loves me
So why can't he find time to talk to me
He says he really loves me
So why do I feel so alone
He says he really loves me.
Really?

M. Marshall

Sweet Peas

Petals of gossamer flutter in the breeze,
So dainty, one's afraid to sneeze.
Making flowers, so very tender,
With long stems, green and slender.

They look like butterflies, on the wing,
Tendrils, like a baby's finger cling
Happily to its mother;
Cling to one another.

Almost in every shade they come,
Then, in the midday sun,
Or, in the evening hours,
These lovely fragile flowers,
Their fragrance are a flaunting,
Surely heaven smells like this; haunting.

Coyly, tiny pods peep out,
Whispering to those in doubt,
We will fade and disappear,
But bloom for you again, next year.

J. Purbrick

Together Forever

The journey seemed endless,
so cold and so dark
nothing was stirring
except, for the lark
her pillow was wet
from the tears that she cried,
part of her heart just went and died
all of her life she had known him
soul mates, good friends, and more
the phone call woke her to say
his mum found him dead on the floor
and now to his wake, she was going
part of her already dead
soon, she hoped she could join him
as she swiftly made plans in her head.

S. Baker-Moore

Home

In memory it returns to me, the house that once was home.
Snug and warm and safe from storm,
I never meant to roam away from those stout, secure stone walls
Where I never felt alone.
In dreams I hear the back door close and hear ghost voices speak.
Scents of cooking tease my nose, hearth's warmth caress my cheek.
'Round its flames they sit and talk, my parents and their friends.
Gone long ago, yet they still live on in memories that won't end.
Upstairs within my mind I go to wander through each room,
Then on into the attic too where eerie shadows loom.
How clear this part of my return;
Each detail so defined.
Heart stopping in its clarity, too real for peace of mind.
In old age now I keep going back on memory's kindly wings,
To the house where I was happy far away from worldly things.
Like a friendly shade I take my place in the fireside's ghostly zone,
Safe and loved as I was then in the house that once was home.

M. Sanders

Priorities In Retirement

I heard from Jill that Sarah was ill
So I wrote in my diary to call
There was washing to do, ironing too
So I didn't see Sarah at all.

Grandchildren needed sorting, one's started courting,
She brought him over for tea.
Church needed a clean; I felt terribly mean
For, poor Sarah I had yet to see.

There was the plumber to call for the leak in the hall
Knitting left half undone.
Dancing class Tuesday, walking on Wednesday,
But for Sarah it wasn't much fun.

Then whilst washing my frock I looked at the clock
And it pointed to quarter to four.
'I'll see Sarah to-night whilst it keeps light'
So I went and knocked at her door.

She looked pale and thin, but said, 'Come on in'.
And we chattered on topics galore.

I made her so glad and not at all sad.
Oh, I wished that I'd been there before.

Vera Lee

The Home Coming

Waiting patiently, warm glow of satisfaction expectantly,
Slippers warming by glowing embers, paper on the table,
tea brewing in the pot,
Door opens, excited greetings shut out the chill draught, door closes,
Oh glorious, wondrous, rapturous, joyous welcome.
The home coming.

Snuggling into cushions in favourite armchair, in loving cosiness,
Shoes removed, slippers warm on feet stretched out for comfort,
Paper read, tea savoured to the last exquisite drop,
Oh glorious, wondrous, rapturous, joyous welcome.
The home coming.

In the cosy harmony together, two hearts missing each other, join to share wonderful moments, peaceful, blissful
An understanding of comfort, wholeness, now completeness,
That knowing secret special smile of reassurance, of greater pleasure yet to come,
Oh glorious wondrous, rapturous, joyous welcome.
The home coming.

J. C. Tusel

Generation Gap

My teenage daughter comes in late at night,
skirt up to her buttocks, a shameless sight.
"Where have you been until this time?" I shout.
"You know where I've been Dad - I've been out."
"Do you think Mum and I are a couple of fools?
Whilst in this house you'll live by the rules."
A defiant look and a toss of her head;
runs up the stairs and off to her bed.
I think back to when I was a lad.
I had respect for my mum and dad.
If it was eleven and I was due at ten
And that only happened now and again,
I would look my Dad straight in the eye,
immediately telling him a plausible lie.
"Oh!" he would say, "that's alright my son,
it's just that, well, it worries your Mum."
Then I would go up to my room and into my bed.
Only then the defiance and the toss of my head.
You see my generation wouldn't dare to defy.
We showed our respect by telling a lie.

K. J. Callow

No Pain No Gain?

You see them in the gym
Sneaks, sweats, leotards
Trying to look thin
But sweat, diet and even a tear
Won't make the dimples
On your rear, disappear.

We sweat, slave and look forlorn
Our faces, brave but drawn
Yet can we lose an inch or two,
And keep on smiling, through and through
What of the dimples on my bum,
And all the creams I rub thereon.

Is it all in vain
I suffer this pain
With others in the gym
All feeling so grim
Weight we can't loose
Although if we choose
A "G & T" might do the trick
And make us all look like a stick.

B. Hobbs

Winter Poem

The children run outside to see the
snow on the ground.
With hats on their heads, scarves round
their necks, gloves over their hands
and a coat round the body.
When they walk on the snow, they make
footprints as they go.
the snow gently falling down, making
no sound.
Crunch, crunch as they walk going
to get some snow.
Children started to make a snowman
with the snow that was on the ground.
The magical snow that covers the
world starts to disappear.
Now the beautiful sparkling snow has
gone, it has been melted by the sun,
Now all that is left is mud, I hope
it will snow again.

Sasha Lianne Morse

The Eventide

When I walk in the room, once again
a happy smile lights up his face,
mistiness clears from his eyes,
as I sit in my usual place

Taking his wrinkled hand in mine
I say "Hello love, I'm back,"
"Oh! I've missed you darling" he says,
putting an arm, round my neck

Sitting, often in a world of his own,
dreaming of days gone by,
talking to loved ones - long passed on,
as back in time he will fly.

His poor bones creak, he winces, in pain,
then bravely puts on a smile,
cheerfully sits conducting a band,
he is back in command for a while.

Down's Syndrome born, he has given much love,
to all who his many hours share,
so, more than ever, in his EVENTIDE,
we give him our tender care

Roma MacNell

Two Edged Knife

He's all alone in deep regret,
Slumped on the ground and covered in sweat,
Not really believing what he's done,
It had all started out in harmless fun.

The knife he drove into someone called "a friend,"
The blow he gave was not pretend,
Looking over at the pool of blood,
Where they had landed with a thud,
He begins to realize his mistake,
And now it's his own life he will take.

Staring intently at the upright knife,
He falls upon it and ends his life.

Three words are said before he dies,
Though only heard in muffled cries,
"God Have Mercy!" he says in vain,
Now unable to take the pain.

His eyes close as he breathes his last breath,
As he thinks of "a friend" and his untimely death.

Luke Shotter

Recent Understanding

Jesus I love You with all my heart.
Singing your praises of how great Thou art,
Kneeling in front of Your crucified form.
Has now become an everyday norm,
You died on the cross so that I could see.
You died on that cross to set me free.
You died on the cross to save my soul.
To enter your kingdom is my ultimate goal.

Lucy O'Boyle

The Thrush Is an Endangered Species

I remember, hoar spangled lawn, diademed thrush,
singing the morning from a holly bush.
An anvil stone, a shattered snail,
hungry beak gleaning the last entrail.

Their spring delirium, flirting daring,
air spilling, rituals of pairing.
Their questing, the nesting
in gardens seclusion or wayside hedging.

Their friendly tune on a friendless day,
blowing the cobwebs of misery away.
Such carefree rapture, in vain they'd compete,
postman, milkman and boy in the street.

For theirs was a song of light and air,
soft summer rain, snowdrifts white glare.
Requiems they sang, on fields of the slain
and an Angelus for those who knew sunrise again.

Let me remember as the silence begins,
theirs was the voice of grace given wings!

W. H. Billington

"Count Your Blessings"

We see the sun, we see the moon, we often
sing our merry tunes.
Of joy, and hope, and peace within.
Then dance, and prance, and play our part,
to live our lives, with a glad heart.
But do we stop and think of those,
who'll never, ever do these things?
The blind, the lame, the deaf, the dumb.
Who've never seen the moon or sun,
or danced and pranced, as we have done.
Give them a thought along life's way.
Be kind - and hope that if you see,
someone less fortunate than thee-
you'll have the heart to stop and say-
God bless you Dear, on this fine day.

Kathleen L. Norris

Loneliness

Sunday always seems to be a very lonely time for me
Since all the family moved away, it is a long and dreary day.
I know that I should feel content with memories of the hours
I've spent bouncing babies on my knee, everybody here for tea.
I sit and think of days gone by, look around, and wonder why
my man, my partner, dear old Joe, got sick, and then he had to go.
It really saddens my old heart I never thought we'd have to part
The way we did, so soon I mean, for I had always had a dream
That we would always be together, no! That is foolish, it
could never have been so, I know, one day one of us would go.
The children know I do feel sad, when I sit and think of their dear Dad.
They have to lead their own sweet lives, now they are parents, husbands, wives.
"Tempus fugit" so they say, so I'll quietly pass the day
Then when it's time to go to sleep, I will not cry, nor will I weep.
I'll count my blessings on my own, then pray, that I won't be alone
Next Sunday, as it's meant to be, our wedding anniversary.
Mary Y. Holder

Seldom Saved

Sophisticated society salutes success.
Simpletons serving, sensational spectacular.
Sleeping soundly, silken sheets.
Sickly sweet shallow smiles.
Sorrowful surroundings, silent silhouette standing still.
Sadly swaying, so silver spare.
Shelter shattered.
Shaking, scared snoozing sometimes seeking solitude.
Sullen shoulders sharing scraps.
Sirloin steaks saute snacks.
Scarlet scoundrels searching stations.
Single starlets seeing spangles.
Sentence started seedy scenes.
Sinking slowly, sacrificed skins.
Sharon Cockett

Language Without Words

Observe expression gentle in a face,
    simple, honest straight forward grace.
Detect a raised brow above the eyes,
    fermented hatred ill-disguised.
Note a curl of lip in mealy-mouthed quoting of the Book,
    feel a raw red lie reflected in a look.
See a friendly smile in quiet calm,
    clasp a tendered hand, offered open palm.
Catch a glazed smirk and grasp a flabby grip,
    cold acknowledgement within a tight lip.
A creaseless brow of joy admired,
    a knowing sympathy of love inspired.
See irritation in the drumming of a finger,
    a furtive glance that hesitates to linger.
Perceive gaiety in a wave of recognition,
    real warmth devoid of inhibition.
Notice impatience in a foot beat,
    a glassy eyed suspicion when eyes meet.
Language never spoken, yet in transparent role,
    the action of the face and body gives away the soul.
D. W. Brown

A Place Of Rest

Beauty, tranquillity, a place without fear, a sunlit sky so blue and clear. The sweet smell of roses, the song of the birds, chirping and chattering in their own little words.
Peace reigns here and so I am told, there is much to remember both for young and old.
Tree plant and shrub intertwine as one, and high in the branches new life has begun.
A fountain does flow from flowering rockery, to a pond down below where ducklings swim free.
People come to sit and take in the view, a vision created for me and for you.
Could this be Eden you ask now of me, to some now it is, this cemetery.
A. S. Mckay

Forgotten Love

Hand in hand they walk on terraced paths.
Silvery shadows adorn their bent and crinkled brows,
which are flowing with the lines of olden views
of bygone pasts, mixed with unclaimed
passion of lost loves.

Their quest for solitude and comfort
broken but guided by their unrelenting
joy of family love and lingering memories
of grandchildren's kisses.

Their loneliness and despair
only matched by the strength gained from others,
in this older but non-exclusive club.

Society breeds them and now can
only reject and condemn them as a burden of age,
of time, of precious space.

These souls who bore us
who raised us, who loved us
and it is through them that
we can only come to understand, to survive
and not become them, who scorn.
L. G. Snell

The Visit

She sits in silent resignation,
Silver wisps frame the faded yellow parchment
Unseeing eyes above dark shadows.
The deformed arthritic fingers caress her crumpled skirt,
A fragile band of gold glistens in the autumn sunlight
Reflections of a bygone age.
A coloured woollen shawl draped in a mantle of dignity,
Her lips tremble in unspoken words
And her tired feet, clad in carpet slippers,
Move to and fro towards an unknown journey.
The smell of faded lavender hangs in the still air.
She nods farewell with a secret smile...
Maureen Withers

Nightfall

The brightness of the day does fade, slipping into twilight shade,
Silhouettes of mighty trees swaying in the gentle breeze,
Slowly silence stills the air, no other moment can compare.

Gently now the night creeps in, countless fathers peeping in
On little ones in slumber deep, all in fairyland to meet.
Peace prevails now day is done, the magic of the night is come.

A thousand stars adorn the sky like shining gems, so far, so high;
The captivating moon serene, casting shadows in between
Glimpses of enchanting scenes where darkness fails to intervene.

As the cool air turns to chill and winter's frost grips nature's wealth,
Wrapped in tender warm delight, I close my eyes and leave the night.
Marian Crossan

Untitled

Avalon our fine and favoured place
Shows a lovely green and pleasant face.
The weather is kind and moderate,
Come visit the famous abbey great
Glastonbury and the Holy thorn -
Flowers in Spring and at Christmas borne
Legends all the way from Palestine
Giving us a message so divine,
Bringing all pilgrims here together
Continually and year by year
Thousands of people from overseas
And many folk from our own counties
Christians meeting in the Western sun
All are drawn towards fair Avalon.
Margaret Joyce Smith

"Blitz Bandages"

Mr. Grandfather telling tales of cruel landmines.
Showering young pups with spittle and fright.
When the searchlight shines,
in the wailing night.

Fearful sounds that echoes the ack-ack
Choirs of air raid sirens cry with danger.
Cracking crack, crack,
die a stranger.

The sky alight with flares and flames.
Barbed wire scratches the beaches.
Heroes under a million names,
the jerries within their reaches.

Planes above like fighting fireworks in the sky.
The black-out shrouds drink and sin.
To defend the isle lives must die,
gunning for freedom, winning to win......

Steven P. Francis

Togetherness

Boots buckled, helmets down.
Shoulders taunt arms tucked in
Hugging tight there bikes to win.
The flags down, like beasts of prey,
They leapt forward
Battling out to find a place.
Smell of oil hung in the air.
Dust rose high to meet the sun.
Gears change, the bend they round.
Leaning over to the ground.
Hearts pounding in tune,
To the engine's sound.
Every nerve alive, keeping up the pace.
Flashing by an down the straight,
A mingled blur, ignoring fate.
Trying hard to win the race,
Bike was man, and man was bike
They rode as one so much alike...

M. Battye

Fall

Melancholy days of autumn shuffle by,
Shoulders stooped and collar turned up against the wind.
Children kick their way through windfalls of leaves -
Amber, red and gold - a myriad of colours.
Jack Frost leaves a reminder that winter's grip is tightening
As summer days retreat over distant horizons.
Street lamps glow red in the grey of early evening
As days grow ever shorter and night expands his realm.
Trees stripped bare, stark fingers reaching skywards,
Pleading for mercy from an unforgiving sky.

Katrina Cracknell

'Bessie' - My Old Banger

Check the battery, Check the oil,
Should the radiator boil?
Check the petrol, Check the tyres,
Don't forget to check the wires.
Check the steering if you must,
And whilst you're at it - check for rust.
Check the handbrake, Check the clutch -
It makes a noise I don't like much.
Check the crankshaft and the tank -
Hold on a while, I'll check my bank,
For I can see to meet your fees
I'll have to go down on my knees
And ask their Mr. Moneymaker
For funds to mend my old boneshaker.

P. M. Darwood

Now Journey's End

Stars out there they shine,
shine like eyes in a knowing sky,
a sky of blackness,
a sea of knowing,
like souls they see
and travel from a distant place,
a distant time,
where eternity burns and
opens the light to the wandering souls,
souls who see, see beauty
as their paths of light,
years ago began and now
find they are to them
as a beacon, for they meet
and explode in passion accrued
in that NOW JOURNEY'S END.

Larry Quinn

A Country Lane

Sunlight warm, on grass so green
Shows tiny rings where mushrooms have been
Here a daisy lifts its yellow eye
Seeking warmth and light from a pale blue sky

There a celandine shyly peeps
While near at hand a fledgling cheeps
Soon that fledgling will soon be flown
The hedgerow's grassy verges mown

Then comes Autumn, with berries and leaves of gold
This years story will soon be told
Next the Winter, with frost and snow
On and on, the seasons go

Now comes Christmas, carols, frost and rime
Then that old man, Father Time
The New Year starts then once again
Spring will be there, in that country lane.

Maria I. Scriven

Poison Apple

Don't touch the fruit of poison,
She will kill you with a kiss.
Don't enter the tunnel to happiness,
You will die from the journey to bliss.

Don't put your arms around her,
She will never let you go.
Don't let your glance rest on her,
She will tear your heart in two.

You can't make it stop,
And it's best if you don't try.
You can't free her of poison,
So leave and don't say goodbye.

Thea S. E. Ambury

Sleepwalkers

Unaccounted for,
She wept deep tears
But forgot that we create
Our own realities,
And that our lonely wandering
Must end in a self-imposed prison-house
Where sleepwalkers pace
Between angles of desire,
Never reaching
The inner fire of invention.

But there, in the dream forest,
Neither care nor sorrow
Enter her circle of motherhood.
And we siblings of another kind
Close critical paths to eternity
And tread another step
On the road of a thousand miles.

Peter Corbett

Mary And Fred

There was an old lady named Mary,
She thought that she looked like a fairy,
Her friends all said gee,
You look more like a bee,
You're far too fat for a fairy!
Now Mary had a friend called Fred,
He wore a trilby on his head,
One day when out walking,
To her he was talking,
When Mary went down on one knee.
"Please, please" to Fred she said,
"Will you marry me?"
"No chance!" said Fred,
His hand on his head,
I'd rather be dead than wed!
A. M. Rutter

The Sentence!

The Judge's hammer fell...
"Sentenced to death!"
A gasp of horror and surprise
Rang around the court room.
The startled Jury looked at the Judge-
"But the verdict is not guilty!"
"Yes", said the judge,
pointing at the jury,
"But you are all guilty
He is taking your place!"

The room fell silent.
The prisoner said nothing
- and was led away
And crucified!
Tony Ward

Hard To Get

In a classroom full of hopefuls
She stares beyond her destiny.
Past the delinquent and the desktops
Staring though distractions - right at me!

In a body so full of hormones
I challenge her thoughts to meet my threat.
Gazing through desire and temptations way
   ...I just play hard to get!

Attention will make her ego rise
And seduce my body naked.
Only avoiding contact from her eyes
Will keep her thoughts frustrated!

Insanity will make her blood boil
And make her dreams so hot yet wet.
But if that's what makes her want me more
   ...I'll just play hard to get!!
Laurence Mifsud

The Wallflower

When the music is slow and the lights are low
She sits and waits to be asked for a dance
In her plain blue gown she just looks down
And lads all pass by without a glance.

Supposing one stands and holds out his hands
And beckons her onto the floor
Will she hopefully rise with wide timid eyes
Or nervously glance towards the door.

She really doesn't care as she pats at her hair
When he asks the young lady in black
Who looks very nice, to partner him twice
Then takes her outside for fresh air.

Her eyes are now pained and smile very strained
As she picks up her bag with her shoes
Her throat fills with lumps as she changes her pumps
And without a backward glance she then goes.
B. Robinson

Cally

Soft as a whisper, quiet as a mouse, you wouldn't notice
   she was in the house.
Curled in a ball of soft and warm, the colour of earth tabby and fawn,
So proud she would sit and so patiently wait, for her dinner to
   be served on a China plate.
Chicken her favourite, cut up small, cooked to perfection nothing raw
A proper lady, full of class, even sipped her water from a glass.
Needed no pedigree to state her worth, she was high class
   right from birth.
Would not entertain any gentleman cat, she made that quiet
   clear, and that was that.
She would stare at them, huge eyes and a pout, "Come near
   me and I'll give you a clout."
She was a loner, rather stay home, did not care much for a
   neighbourhood roam.
Cats weren't her scene, in the garden she'd stay,
   the rabbit was more interesting for a bit of play.
One cold and sunny Winter's day, it was time for her to go away.
Teardrops fell, the house was still, the emptiness we all could feel.
Her little soul had flown away, but memories of her will always stay.
I will never forget you Cally dear, the feel of your fur, your
   little soft ear.
So pretty, soft, gentle, and meek, Cally my love, you were unique.
Valerie Hartley

Late Sacrifice

Serene and smiling peacefully,
She moves under the rays of the early morning sun.
In the Nunnery herb garden, her day has just begun.

She has no regrets,
She considers it no loss to have left the world behind.
She has permanent happiness now,
And peace of mind.

She reflects upon her past,
Her marriages, her affairs, her money, jewellery, modelling career
She is glad that there are no reminders here.

She looks down at her stout brogue shoes,
Her humble habit covering her swollen ankles,
Her lined and unmade face reflected in the garden pool,
Here, she'll never again be made to feel a fool.

She wonders though, if she's acceptable to God,
What's she offering HIM now?
Her much used body, her lost wealth,
She should 'have taken this step before,
Not left it 'till she was ninety four!
Ruth Owens

The Dream

The candle she lit each night whilst in bed.
She lit only in thoughts that were inside her head.
It shone on a face, a sweet memory of a Dad whom she loved.
Who was no longer there, but with Jesus above.
Sometimes as she slept she dreamt a sweet dream.
That her life was the same not in daylight what it seemed.
She was eight and had pigtails and a gap in her teeth.
But, she knew you still loved, your princess underneath.
Whatever her problems, no matter what went wrong.
All during her childhood, there you were big and strong.
The hours that you spent in your shed building toys.
Her Brother making Her play cricket like one of the boys.
When Her Boyfriend at 16 left Her feeling sad.
She ran home to tell Mum, but especially Dad.
When she fell in love and married, you walked her down the aisle.
She'd not in life since seen as proud a man's smile.
Then just when her life was the best it could seem.
Loving Husband 2 Sons, came the bad dream.
She thanks you now Dad for all the memories, you left behind,
When I close my eyes tight, there you are in My mind.
Susan Harris

The Stray

She turned up unexpected this cat so lean and poor,
She hissed and spat and spat and hissed
No one could get near.
Her weakened frame and frightened eyes
Did not betray the pain
So there she was and then she'd gone
not to be seen again
How wrong we were this creature lithe
returned and yes with joy
Did eat the food we laid before apparently happily.
She disappeared and once again we thought had gone
from whence she came
But Oh my word, lo and behold she turned up once again,
this time this cat appeared with glee
Not just her....plus family!!

Wendy R. Bird

Ugly Is Beautiful

Sitting on a chair in her bedroom.
She looked in the mirror and saw her reflection.
She thought to herself, oh no this can't be.
The person I'm seeing is certainly not me.
She combed her fair hair layer upon layer.
And piled it on top of her head.
She whispered a prayer to the God above.
And of course he would have heard.
She turned away hoping something would change.
And no doubt it probably would.
She looked in the mirror and saw her reflection.
And light just shone out of her sparkling eyes.
Then she thought this is it.
I must not tell little white lies.
I'm the most beautiful girl in the land.

Leanne Hume

Going Home

The old lady walked down the road alone
she felt happy for today she was going home,
lorries and cars rushed past her, polluting the air around
tins and bottles other people's rubbish lay on, the pulsing ground.
On and on she walked, a hundred miles it seemed
then it stood before her, her cottage thatched and beamed,
the garden welcomed her as she undid the gate
it's been such a lonely time, such a long long wait.
She sat upon her garden seat, the wood she fondly touched,
and gazed contently at the garden she loved so very much.
Her husband came up to her and tenderly did say,
"God bless you my dearest. I knew you would come today"
Arm in arm together they passed through the open door,
into eternity with God forever more.
A crowd gathered round her, what! was she doing there?
someone said,
"she's from the old folks home her cottage once stood here".
Her face was peaceful as in death she lay
a little old lady from a bygone age, on a busy motorway.

Millicent Hewitt

Magic Box

In a magical place my box lays,
Shaped like a heart,
This box is not made of oak or plastic,
It is made of something you may not have seen,
Sometimes it is as light as a feather,
Other times it as heavy as an oaken staff,
Red is the colour of my magic box,
White bars made of bone stop people stealing it,
It has been open since I was born,
It has all the love in the world in it,
I feel sad and selfish
When I close this box of love,
This box of love...
...is my heart.

Laura Morris

Ruby Memories

A single look in a crowded room and life was changed for me
she burst upon my senses like a crashing wave at sea.

Her hair was black as Ravens wing it tumbled shoulder long
it framed a face of beauty deep so delicate yet strong

My eyes of grey they locked with green my being filled with pain
that moment comes but once a life and never comes again.

Beneath the Castles ramparts high, the river Ness runs dark
'twas there that we did plight our troth and vowed to never part

We loved, we laughed and passions flamed as only lover's know
with pride we watched our children grow, we'd reaped what
  we did sow

It's 40 years since first we wed, and still I fill with pride
remembering how I wooed and won and she's still by my side

The Raven hair is silver now, those eyes a lighter hue
but love that crossed that far off room is still as strong and true.

J. Fitzpatrick

'Ma' Said I Would

I've been and done it, my 'Ma' said I would
She always knew what was best.
You believe in life you try your style
and never let sleeping dogs rest.

She'd a word for yes, and it was "I'll see,"
She never meant no harm.
She'd lump my bum upon her knee and
then she'd raise a storm.

Punishment! Was a hard felt word, she'd
cuss me raw and moan
"If I catch you round that pub again, I'll put
you in a home."

I went and did; "I was warned" I know!
What I did was pain and strife
I went to the pub, got drunk "I know"!
And got myself a wife

I know what you're thinking "I told you so"
I can hear it loud and strong.
With the drink, and the woman 'I love her so,'
Just how can a man go wrong!

Patricia Margaret Carr

The Sea Of Anger

The sea is crashing and thundering.
Shadows of blue, splashing, lapping up against the shore.
His long blue cloak hits the coast,
'Till evening when he is at bay.

Sometimes he becomes angry, smashing at the shore,
Climbing up the cliffs after people,
Whirling and spinning,
Glinting in the sun as he bobs up and down,
Ships and boats are rocked about in his anger,
Tossed to and fro, smashing at their hulls,
Frightening swimmers in his current,
Like a long arm,
Reaching out to drag people into this lair.

He makes patterns in his cloak,
As he whirls away, from the coast,
Only to come and hit it hard again,
Then he retreats,
Back out into his own world,
Soon he is silent,
He sleeps with a gentle rocking.

Philip Etherington

Tomorrow Will Be Just Like Today

She stared into space and fought back the tears
She had nothing to show for her fifty one years
Her hair was all matted her clothes were in rags
Her worldly possessions were in two plastic bags
She had no money and nowhere to stay
She knew that tomorrow would be just like today
Her thoughts wandered back many years ago
She was jilted by her lover his name was Joe
He left a note and walked out of her life
Just two weeks before she was to be his wife
Her heart was broken her life had been shattered
There was nothing to stay for, nothing that mattered
She put some clothes into a plastic sack
Walked out of the door and never looked back
What she is looking for she just doesn't know
Perhaps in her heart she is searching for Joe
"I'm closing up now" the bartender said
She rose from the chair and nodded her head
"Goodnight Lady" he called as he switched off the light
She gathered her bags and shuffled into the night

Norma Cousins

Mum

Mum is a woman who takes
She takes away the pain with a hug and a kiss
She takes away the loss, when your favourite toy you miss
She takes your hand to lead you safely across the road
She takes the time to teach you, the green cross code
She takes food from her plate for you to eat
She takes away the taste of medicine with a sweet
She takes away the fear of darkness, thunder, things unknown
She takes a house, and turns it into a home
She takes you in her arms, you tears to wipe away
She takes time to bake a cake to surprise you on your birthday
She takes all your problems on her shoulders to bear
She takes you through life with words of encouragement,
love and care
She takes all the ups and downs of teenage years and the strife
She would take on all comers and protect you with her life
She takes time to care, to listen, to mend and make things new
She took a tiny baby and turned it, into you
And most of all she took her heart, with love it overflows
For a mother's love is special, for it never goes.

Maureen Townsend

"The Phoenix"

A desolate wasteland, of ash and ember.
Seems hard to believe, such an unforgiving place,
Would herald the birth, of the magnificent phoenix.

From the black and the grey, rose the fire of the phoenix.
Beauty, captured both my breath and heart.
Spread your wings high, over me.
Entranced by your splendour, - I worship you, intoxicated by fire.
You reach skywards, voracity, setting the very clouds alight.

In my eyes, only the new flames are seen, ashen birthplace forgotten.

Amid the black, I lie below you, unnoticed.
I reach for your tail, red heat trapped, in my hand.
Even now, you fail to see, as you burn me.
I let your fire, encompass me, as you guide me upwards.

Still, I worship you.
From my ashes, wings of fire spread, into the sky.
Continue guiding me upwards, my heart is yours for eternity.
Fall below me, and I will rise above you.
Then, you will lie amid the black,
- Unnoticed.

Louise Ann Holmes

Rebel Thoughts

Why do men of power argue and fight all day,
Seeking to shape our lives in their particular way?
Why do the sages with intellect and reason
Seek to impose views they hold just for a season?
Why do holy churchmen urge all to be meek?
Is it to free us - or something sinister they seek?

Why does the school and the accent you utter
Determine your future in the boardroom or gutter?
Why are common thieves so harshly condemned
When "respectable" con-men only token time spend?

Why are police licensed to marshal us all?
Who are they protecting from taking a fall?
Why must the world pay homage and still bow low
To the few surrounded by guns wherever they go?

Why do we in mute humility still endure the yoke
Bestowed on us from birth by those illustrious folk?
WHY? shrieks logic from ten thousand years gone by?
Only a diminishing whisper weakly echoes a hollow why?

F. Rank

My Dreams

Thank you Lord for my sleep last night.
  Seeing my loved ones was a great delight.
  Taking me in your loving arms at last.
  Showing me faces I've lost in the past.
  Meadows and mountains bathed in the sun.
  Storm strew waste lands all wrapped up in one.
   Lights that shine from below or above.
   Showing me your passion of promise and love.
   Guiding my mind in this beautiful dream.

   Helping to show me that heavens for real.
   Rain lashing down or snow storms so white.
   Keeping the terror from out of my night.
   Scenery so lovely for my eyes to see.
   Oh Lord God in heaven you really love me.

D. M. Collins

Memories

When I was young I was happy and free
Secure and content that was me.
But age crept up and only memories remain
Of an oh so sweet childhood
Sheer pleasure no pain.
The smell of contentment
Filling each room
The feeling of love carved in each piece of wood.
The radio playing our favourite tune
The lovely aroma of Mum's sweet perfume.
Dad's familiar whistle when returning
From work, with our eager faces all red
and alert. I'm glad for such memories
and now that I'm grown up hope that I
can give out such pleasure and love.

G. Tooth

Mrs Roundabout

Round and round I go,
searching, waiting,
for what? I don't know.
Round and round, forever spinning,
entwined in a spider's web,
no hope of ever winning.
Round and round, the carousel cruises,
circles of my life, etch my soul,
leave bruises.
Round and round like Destiny's Wheel,
heart truly wishing, hopes rise, can I heal?
Round and round, earth orbits sun,
the heat, the passion,
it stops, have I won?
No, it slowly spins on.

D. B. MacFarlane

Images Of Time

Tick tock, tick tock, tick tocks.
Seconds, hours, weeks, years,
Pass me by in great haste.
Screeching alarms, magnificent grandfather clocks.
Minutes, days, months, decades,
Mundane extensions of timely waste.

History in the making, history in the past
A newly born child, a pensioner of old,
Lunatics living lives of hell.
Greed for the evil, starvation for the mass,
A vastness of wealth, a desert of despair
Men stagnating cocooned in a shell.

Purple patches, a corpse of white,
Angels of birth, angels of blight,
Enjoying moments, the real sublime,
Heavy blackness, a God of might,
Wrinkled with age, senile with fright,
The ghoulish demons of time.
Lawrence O'Neill

Love Me

Tangled, twisted, tired, tormented,
Searching, sorry, sad and longing,
The endless lonely nights, demented,
Disillusioned, doubting, dying.
Someone somewhere, hear my plea.
Someone somewhere, love me.

Perceive, pursue and penetrate
the melancholy mysteries of my mind.
Dispel the daunting darkness I relate,
Soothe my savage soul, be kind.
Someone somewhere, hear my plea.
Someone somewhere, love me.

Diminish and destroy this desolation,
drive away the darkness and despair.
Take away the tears of degradation,
Show me warmth and tenderness and care.
Someone somewhere, hear my plea.
Someone somewhere, love me.
Kate Crutcher

My Folly

Listen closely I will tell my story to you brother,
once from grace and power I fell for the beauty of another,
a Gipsy girl, a Gypsy girl stole my heart away -
her voice and laughter I can hear until this very day.

I lost my wealth, I lost my wife,
I lost my social standing,
I had no will to keep at bay her love
was so demanding

But her little mind was savage - my life is but a shred,
be careful all you vagabonds of who you take to bed.
E. Duff

Untitled

My need to bare my soul, to look beyond and
see the hurt below, to open all the doors that
make my prison, and show my self for what
I am, a woman.
I need the world to heed my cry for help,
To ask why life is sad and not for living,
To know my faults, and where I went astray.
Maybe to ask again another day.
Alone, in need of love, to feel the warmth
and see the sun, is all I ask, and so.
To age is seeing past today and living
yesterday tomorrow.
Vilma Peacock

My Little Pink Rose

Something wonderful is happening to me, week by week it's
   easier to see.
I can feel the movements, its every turn, soon I'll be a mother
   and have to learn.
Learn to change nappies, learn how to feed, but most of all
   learn how to succeed.
To bring my baby up, with happiness and love, and always be
   there whenever I should.
At the moment my baby is safe and secure. I think it's a girl,
   I'm almost sure.
Within my body my baby will stay, until that very special day.
When she will come into this world beautiful and new, I hope
   her life will never be blue.
Who is this baby we all can see? I wonder what her name can be?
Clare Louise is the name that I chose, she looks just like a little
   pink rose.
All curled up and so content, from heaven I think she must
   have been sent.
Eighteen years on, and she's all grown up. She's a lovely
   young woman just look.
Claire Louise was the name I chose, but to me she'll always
   be my little Pink Rose.
Mary Flynn

Drum Me Down (To The Devil On Broadway)

Drum me down to the devil on broadway
sear me deep with the heat
of the rhythm of the flame of the fire to beat me back
onto my feet
HEY!
Splash me rude as you master the making
of the stands I'm forced to take
and then high-hat to heaven 'gainst the gold time
mountains
as you ride my back to break

Roll me hold me slow me down
as my skin sweats up to fry
and then kick me to silence on the blood stained summit
'til you hear me tidal cry
PLAY!
and as you drum me down to the devil and to broadway
and wish me plunge my feet into stone
your cross playin' will rekindle all the embers in the
fire
of the burnin' I've made my home
SO!
Sally A. Hewitt

"The Photograph"

She called out to him, before the
sea took him to distant places,
Hey! Harry take this photo of me and the bay.
You'll be glad of looking at familiar faces.

She thought to herself when he's alone with no joy,
The friends and the noise slowly dying
He'd look at the picture and truly believe
it is still well worth trying.

Striving to keep normality, true love and all that,
Alive in your head and your heart
Whilst chaos, and meaningless slaughter prevailed.
This was precious, a hope, set apart.

A hope one day that when wars finally cease,
When rancour and hate gave way to lasting peace.
This family would be whole once again quite complete.
To live without fear and enjoy
victory, so wonderful, so sweet.

In memory of all who never returned from the wars
C. Stocks

The Evacuee

In the train station the platform is crowded,
Screaming comes from all around,
Children cry, panicking, desperately wishing to stay,
Everywhere is chaos.
I watch sadly as I climb onto the train,
My parents waving,
Tears pour out of my eyes - my heart beats fast,
I look at them once more,
Will I ever see them again,
Or will I return from the countryside?
My teacher says it will be nice there,
And I'll be happy
But I don't care, I want to stay
And live with my family everyday.
Horror seems to be everywhere.
Sadness, terror, fright; my feelings as the train pulls away,
Faster and faster and faster it goes,
I try to smash the window, wishing to get out
And cry and scream and loudly shout.
But it's too late; and now we're gone.
Sarah Couchman

Old Nog

On his pinnacle perch of pine, the bold
Scourge of the marshes, killer, cold,
Gleams silvery-grey in dawn's dim glow,
Baleful yellow eyes scan the fish below.

Old Nog, the heron, is no fool,
Quietly descends to the edge of the pool;
Endowed with wisdom of the ancient,
This hungry heron is ever-patient.

Patient until, poised pickaxe bill,
Flash of fish, lightning strike, the kill!
But not! The wriggling prey writhes free, in pain,
The heron instantly strikes again

Rashly: neck noosed in net, panic!
Entrapped by snare of man, satanic.
Flapping, thrashing, Old Nog flails free,
Seeks fancied safety in the nearest tree

Where the magpie mob, who milling there,
Grind Old Nog with a gritty stare
And raucous chatter, driving him away,
Feathers all a-tatter. He'll return another day!
Sydney Oates

Our Church

Our church means more than I can say, the people, the prayers once saved my day. years ago it helped me cope, it gave me all my strength and hope. now I think it's time to say, lets pull together to save the day. we need ideas to help raise money, some maybe hard some maybe funny. I have thought hard and long, and prayed for inspiration to come along. now through my door a pattern came, to knit two bears that look the same, though I don't claim to be a knitter (My best talent is a baby sitter). but now I mean to raffle my bears, hope you will buy tickets with none to spare. my second idea was to put a big jar, in the porch hall not too far, so you can put in all spare change, each Sunday as you pass in range. then I picked another idea from the bunch perhaps we could have a hot pot lunch- get outside people to spend money here, eating out for two sounds clear. now years ago when money was in need, we all got together with a lead. a pattern of our church we had, we each bought a brick and we were glad. we wrote our names on each brick we bought and watched it grow up out of nought. all ideas don't all make sense, better to try than sit on the fence. when all our troubles we do face, you never know what might take place. we will go on from strength to strength, build up our church with prayers at length. we'll live in hope and work together, whatever setbacks whatever weather, prayers can bring miracles here what I say, we are living proof, God knows the way.
Rita Fletcher

Not To-Day

Valentine's Day is no day to be parting
Saying good-bye with lips and hands and eyes;
Valentine's Day is a day to be starting,
To be meeting and seeking love and surprise.
Valentine's day is a day to be mating,
A day when winter begins to end its cold death;
Valentine's Day is no day for relating
Sad histories, breathing a last breath.
Valentine's Day is a day for beginning,
A day for lovers' looking forward to the sun,
Valentine's Day is no day to be sinning
By ending what was so sweetly begun!

Let us not weep for it's no day for weeping,
Nor for regrets for the "casual affair"
Started in friendliness, light smiles, but seeping
Into the flesh and the blood, unaware;
Let us remember a winter of snatches
Seized from the hum-drum of day-to-day ways.

We have not parted while the throat still catches
And mutters 'Damn Valentine's Days!'
Stephen Morse

New Age Christmas

Now that Rudolph's gone to rest
Santa has to do his best,
Though he's sad and melancholy
Pushing toys for girls and boys
In a supermarket trolley,
It squeaked and groaned as Santa toiled,
The poor old trolley was not oiled,
It swayed and strayed down every street
Bumped into everyone he'd meet,
When at last its work was done
Santa went to have his fun.
Christmas came without a hitch
Now poor old trolleys in a ditch,
Someone came on Christmas day
With a Sprig of Holly and card to say
Thank you dear supermarket trolley.
M. Porthouse

Happiness

I have mansions and yachts by the score
Said the man who had riches in store,
 And he sighed...

I have jewels and beautiful things
Said the star as she counted her rings,
 Then she cried...

I have power to command at my will
Said the Emperor ageing and ill,
 As he died....

Praise the Lord for my soul He has blessed
Said the maid with the babe at her breast,
 And she smiled...
Rosemary Williamson

Untitled

It will come, it will go,
Rush upon you, creep up slow,
It will come in a fit, it will go in a start,
Gently prick, then spear through your heart,
You cannot taste it, or touch it,
Yet it's it, the kiss of a loved one,
The ruffling of hair, all demonstrating,
Indelibly there, you'll not hear it or see it,
And yet you can, when you're given or offered it,
Be you woman or man, you'll take it to nurse,
As a matter of course,
Hoping you show,
Above all things,
You desire it to grow.
J. R. Foreman

The Cheat

The cheat is such a weak-livered man.
Runs around as much as he can.
He leads the ladies to believe
He's the love they have away dreamed.
It could be Mary, Jane or you, that he
would and could easily make a fool.
But when there's talk of wedding bells
he will run just like a bat out of Hell
But as he climbs up to bed, with
the woman that he "wed" the twinkle
in his eye. Still said "I'm not finished
yet!" "My pet!" "Not me!" "Not yet!"

J. A. Hayward

My Wish

Anything goes in this day and age,
Sensational news written on every page
Burglaries rife, and mobs causing strife
And those Macho people using the knife

People are so aggressive and selfish these days
Do what they want, and feel no disgrace
Blame other people for the mess they get in
These are the ones who kick up a din!

Others work hard and have no time to spare
Whilst the weak and the lonely just live in despair
If we carry on living and don't care a damn
This land that we live in will just be a sham.

So put on a smile and hold out a hand
We could all discover it's a beautiful land
With people - more sharing and friendly and true,
There could be more laughter the whole world through

Pat C. M. Mason

Mad March Days

Sad days, glad days, merry and mad days,
Rough winds with roaring cry
Fling fleeing clouds across seething sky.
Forest oaks sigh and groan,
Gnarled branches creak and groan.
Rag-rag rook and tattered crow
Toss and tumble, buffet and blow.
Still days, spring's gentle birth,
Soft mists rise from the warming earth.
Shadow -etched in pearly dawns,
Fallow does dream of summer fawns.
On wayside banks and grassy places
Shy primroses lift pale faces.
Over meadow and moorland a tide is creeping,
A flood of lambs, skipping and leaping,
Jumping for joy in the fleeting sun-
A sign perhaps, that winter's done.

Marie Roberts

Your Number's Up

Lengthening nights beckon the day,
Scarce now the crumbs laid out on the tray.
Against ember-days slumps the vulnerable figure,
Last in a line crippled rheumatoid vigour.
Comforts nor pleasures now patent this hold,
Age-allowance scent hangs in a diminishing fold.
Linoleum hall echoes to the splashing of bills,
Save the numbers on the mantel, along side the pills.

Care now not any save the stone,
Yet forsaking the vicar to exit alone.
Cherish the pictures all marching with zeal,
Venial fevered victims an inevitable seal.
Consciously scrambling for all, plus one,
Hedonistic masks the mayhem's begun.
Hush, quiet now descends upon the end of a terrace,
Except vermin cries, no, they will not perish.

P. Mulvaney

Untitled

A streaming convulsion of thoughts
Run wild to reveal the imagination.
There's a thirst for the knowledge
And understanding,
Of the passion, the desire,
Will this be an ongoing fire?

Tears of frustration
Roll down my face,
You don't need any weapons
Words alone will do.

In your eyes there's so much to be told.
Your life,
Your secrets
Can these ever be sold?

The deep meaningful stare
After the gentle kiss,
The tension almost seems evident
To my heart.
Is this love, the beginning
Just the start?

Sheenagh Rose Mulroy

Born 1900

And so faith walked with her to school
Rough roads, high hedges frowning as she passed
Confirmation - long golden tresses, then
Down the isle to meet her groom
Disproved by an absent father
The man his eye on an only child's benefits
Her father knew.

Winter Sunday nights to evening service
Wartime weather worrying for he who flew
Knowing not where or when
But gave him to God's care and cause home comforted
That the bomber's journey of right
Would be assisted, and return
To the welcoming flare path

Her own disasters bravely endured, not all cast on her shadowy God
Her tormentors pacified and defended
With ever a countenance for lesser souls to lean on.
Yet to pity her sad life may not be right, although
We, left behind in a never age where science outlaws God
Are we the losers now left behind without the "Everlasting Arms?"

J. Waddington

A Little Bit Of Heaven

We have a little bit of heaven
　right here on earth
It's an English country lane
Where wild flowers bloom, trees spread their branches
　and animals give birth
Dark days of the winter are very bleak
　with howling winds
Frost which sparkles, glitters on the spider's web
　so delicate as lace, and wonders here take place
Spring arrives with such splendour, new buds,
　exotic perfume of the May
All white it dominates the hedge-grow it illuminates the day
Hot the summer shines, radiant the honeysuckle climbs
Black, and white magpies flutter around
Magnificent autumn, brings the colours of
　flame red, and bronze
A carpet of leaves covers the ground
This fantastic beauty isn't a dream
The artist, the creator, just cannot be seen.

Violet Westney

Meniere's Disease: A Cry For A Cure

Can you imagine you are in a totally relaxed state of mind, riding your bike to work, happy with life, not a care in the world, but there is a thud from the side of your head as if someone is hitting you with a baseball bat.
Imagine you are in a state of panic, your head is spinning around and never stopping for long periods of time.
Imagine you are sick and feeling sick for most of the day, everyday, and you can't eat the food you wish for or the drink you wish for: A cry for Cure.
Imagine the humming sound in your ears, 24 hours a day, the sound in your ears of a baby screaming, hearing and feeling your heart beat in your ears.
Imagine the attacks of vertigo that are so severe that you have no control, you can't stop the baseball bat hitting you on the side of the head. You are feeling hot, sweating and waiting for the next attack to come: ear of no cure.
Imagine deafness, something taking over your life and destroying it to the full, Imagine all you want, for me it's reality, not imagination. Believe me (many don't).
   P. Falloon

Peace - What Peace?

When the Christmas choirs are singing
peace on earth - goodwill to men
when the Christmas bells are ringing
and the Christ child's born again -
all the people from the service
shake each other by the hand
do they mean what they are saying
peace must come to this our land?
Somewhere in the shadowy darkness
steals a youth - knife in his hand
Does he heed the Christmas message
Goodwill to men - peace to this land?
from the doorway of the tavern
drunken fools go on their way
what good thoughts have they of Christmas
but to sleep the hours away.
What's this peace on earth we pray for
will it ever come our way?
not until we think more clearly
What is meant by Christmas day.
   Mary L. Ward

Untitled

I dreamed I sat across from God
Right across the table, like I'm sitting with you now
He pulled himself up straight and sat still, very quiet, yet he wasnt' big
the way you'd think, but just about my size
and with his head held up so slightly he leaned back, and looked me in the eye
while I just chattered, talked about my aches and losses,
how I was happy but unhappy, jealous, needy, loving, sometimes grateful, sometimes bad,
I poured tea, I mopped up, I offered biscuits,
rambled on and on in that amorphous nervous way I do
He waited, listening, palms large and outstretched, like a perfect parent, dear, with eyes wide at attention
then reached out for his cap and said goodbye
Stood up, took my shoulders tight and kissed me
and then I think I said Don't Go, Please do not go, Come back! Come back! Come back!
Well now, he said, of course I'm coming back - you know, I live so close to here
So close to you
And as he banged the front door closed I woke
And with my heady secret rose to face the business of the breaking day.
   Rachel Frankel

The Quest

When men fought hard for maiden hand,
Rode and fought across the land,
Their love would be forever true,
And that is so for me and you.

We slay our dragons fight for life,
Battle against all past strife,
The fight for something tough and bold,
And with each book a story's told.

This young maiden and her man,
Walk to sunset hand in hand,
Their past behind their future bright,
Their happiness show they won the fight!

Every rose it has its thorn,
With each new growth another torn,
The battle for love is never done,
But we together are always one!
   S. Holloway

You Make Me Smile

You make me smile, and for a little while
Remind me of days gone by
Of days in the sun, with so much fun
No reasons to ask why
If my time were again, and you were then
Things would not be the same
I would have come to you, wanted to
And you'd have called the game
But my days are past, they couldn't last
For time will never wait
Your days are now, and we know somehow
We cannot alter fate
And if I'm true, I'd say to you
I'm happy as I am
With my children dear, my loved ones near
My very special man
But when I look at you, see the things you do
I still admire your style
But rightly I'll stay, content, just with the way
You, make me smile
   Teresa Leslie

Just Prior To Death

An overdose on pensive sadness, a breed of melancholy that kills,
Reluctantly addicted to a vial of bitter pills.
I have drained the cup of misery to the very last drop,
I have searched for the remedy that will make a bleeding heart stop.
Lost and bewildered, vulnerable to the end,
I take solace that Suicide be my only friend.
Death is the only sedative that will nullify my pain,
A heavenly shelter from stormy clouds of rain,
For Mother Nature's tears are coating me in rust,
Ashes to ashes, dust to dust.
   L. J. Lee

"My Friend"

I spend many hours,
Sending you flowers,
But the reason is not hard to find,
I try to pretend,
That we are just friends,
But I can't get you out of my mind,
I do things for you,
When you feel so blue,
And you think that I am just being kind,
But if you give in,
I am sure love will win,
And your picture can stay in my mind,
I spend many hours,
Looking at flowers,
But they just make me feel blue,
For when, I look at a daisy,
It just drives me crazy,
Because the flowers remind me of you.
   R. Scott

"Innocents"

Crying out in the darkness, uncertain of why.
Remembering the past and wondering why.
Thinking of his mother. Where is she now?
Picturing his home, burnt to the ground.

A single tear streaks his face
Falls into ashes beside blistered feet.
Stars in his head, drumming in his ears
Too innocent and young to understand his fears.

Just wishing it would go away
Just wishing for the end.
But there's one thing that he forgets
Who will love him then?

For his family have been wiped out
Their friends and village too
By a war he did not ask for
By a war that grew and grew.

Kept in the dark for so long now
The child asks himself why
Why is he alone now
Alone and left to die.

Lynne Russell

A Life Together

We were so young and in love when we wed.
Our hearts ruled our head
We didn't have much money
With love like ours, we were sure our future would be
  bright and sunny

The home we had was only a but and Ben.
To us it was perfect, our own private little den.
Creating a baby in our life, caused no strife
I desperately wanted to be a mother, like any other wife

Our love making was wonderful and my body receptive.
Frantically we made love, never using a contraceptive
Soon I was pregnant, we were over the moon.
Like fools we believed everything would be perfect no gloom

Sadly at four months I had a miscarriage
This was repeated three more times, putting a strain on our marriage
Still in love, I said the day we wed I will never rue
After six years we had a perfect son followed by another two

We now feel old and our hair is grey.
But I will still love you to my dying day
Despite the sorrows, quarrels, poverty, tears and fears
I have no regrets, we survived and have now been married
  forty golden years.

Marlene Forrest

Thoughts

Impinging on the subconscious
Relevant, strange, unreal, unwanted
Straddle our minds with unbecoming haste
Evoking responses in our ultimate actions
Driving, forcing, welcoming, invigorating
Patterned on our visages, scarred and lined
Jealousies, hatreds, kindly acts
All cocooned in the human span
Desires, hopes, unfulfilled wishes
Turbulent, dark, rushing round our heads
A cacophony of jumbled synapses
Evoking answers, pursuits and explanations
Commencing in our childish years
Conditioned by our cultural heritage
Striking out at perceived solutions
Rising ultimately only to demise
In fruitless inconsequence unexplained
Ere breath and life be taken
And our fate in death is sealed.

D. R. Linnecar

The Tramp

Swaying, Slouching
Relentless dripping of the rain
The grimy wetness of his brow
Face uplifted to the elements
Tinted blue eyes framed in untamed stubble
Flickering spots on ageing canvas.

Forgotten past, shrouded future
Living for the minute, the hour, the day.
Hands outstretched, touching isolation
Sidelong glances of fleeting pity
A mirror for our reflections
An unwritten book.

Margaret Staniford

While Yet There's Time

This world of ours by many conflicts torn,
Rehearsals for our final glimpse of hell,
Condemning those our sons as yet unborn,
For none shall live our epilogue to tell,
Lest swords of scarlet flame the heaven's climb.
Come with me walk with me while yet there's time.

B. M. Furber

THE RIPPLING STREAM

Whilst gazing into the rippling stream I saw the
reflection of the man of my dreams.
He looked so handsome there on the mound, and
bells were ringing with resonant sound.

He bowed to me with noble grace and said I
looked lovely in my dress of fine lace.

That suave gentleman was tall and dark, and
he broke into song like a warbling lark.

Then came the call of little lambs, they appeared
to be tempered by the song of that happy man.

Dew drops were glittering on the hills like diamonds
adorning the daffodils, and delightful to our ear
was the blackbirds' trill.

The beauty of that lovely man sent my mind drifting into
a trance, and butterflies all around us were starting to dance.

That fine gentleman is Robert Mills, and
we fell in love on those glittering hills.

Patricia Anne Handel

Red

Red is the sky on a shepherd's night
Red is the blood oozing from a shark bite
Red means danger
Send in a Ranger

Red is bright
Like a candlelight
Red is a rose
As bright as Rudolf's nose

Red is the warmth from a fire
Red is your face when you're a liar
Red is a bus that doesn't stop
Runs over a kid and all that you hear is pop

Red apples
Red paper
Star wish that comes a year later

Red is a Ferrari
That zooms right past
Don't you just wish
You could run that fast.

Neil Ritchie

Alone

On my own while she's away
receiving postcards along the way
different countries, different friends
penning letters to make amends
It started to hurt a month ago
Envy, jealously, start to creep in
As I want to put those cards in the bin
It's not fair I say to myself
Will I end up on the shelf?
Doubting to trust that it's good clean fun
I have heard before, the sarcastic pun
photos of strangers I've yet to see
start to burn up inside of me
A I now, imagine the worst,
I wonder if, I will still come first?
Peter R. Parker

Atrocities

Scattered tubs of boiling water contain
Remains,
Of Muslim father's war-torn daughter
Slaughtered.
It's sickness, sadness, hostile madness.
Witnesses,
Suppressed under threat of piercing blades
Afraid.
How can you halt an ethnic cleansing twisted
Torturer
Butcher a starving girl when it's his God given
Right?
Bosnia, Serbia, Croatia.
A tragedy of human nature.
Wayne Ingram

Sadness

Born in sin
Raised in Poverty
I had no home
I had no hope
I had no Fame
So I had to play the game of a beggar man.

My home was the park
There I stayed until dark
My food from the rich man's bin
My table was the lid
My chair was the grass
I did not care
For to survive, I had to play
"The part of a beggar man".

I often stop and think, Lord is this my lot
It is too much for me to bear
Must I keep wondering in fear
There must be another way,
Beside playing the beggar-man's game.
Veronica Campbell

First Sale Of The Day

Passing strangers watched through misty,
rain streaked glass.
Electronic chime squawks, the door swings open,
fresh hope enters.
An hesitant loiter, furtive glances at a
nearby bus shelter, cold attendance.
Practised ease, warmth, a colour of display,
a coax, flickers of interest.
Breath holding, a skip of heartbeats, price
and size considered, calculation.
Brief flush of anger - cools with
Steady movement towards the counter.
Relief smiles, electronic whirl of the till
Mirrors plastic compliments,
Mechanical farewells.
Hungry eyes return to misty rain streaked glass.
G. S. Moulds

Trees

T -rembling waving branches with
R -ustling dried brown leaves
E -scaping, flying, fluttering in the breeze
E -njoying their freedom as summer fades
S -eptember brings changes, autumn tints, golden shades.

T -hinking of orchards full of Trees
R -earing pretty blossoms, fruit with leaves
E -nglish apples, plums and pears grown to please
E -xported, delivered everywhere, here and overseas.
S -o ends the harvest of orchards full of Trees.

T -rees all dance and shake and sway
R -elease their fruit and leaves that way
E -nduring strong winds and showery rain
E -xperiencing perhaps a mother pain
S -uffering their loss, their branches bare
T -rees whispering sadness is felt in the air.
Stella Bush-Payne

John

The sharp wit, the callous remark,
Represent the man I loved,
They covered the pain and the bitterness
Of his lost mother's love

The silly laugh, the cheerful grin,
What did they hide?
Was it the suffering and sadness,
That were always those inside.

He found a woman he really liked
With her he found some joy
He found the world wasn't all bad
Like he thought when he was a boy

Just one short shot was all it took
To make his lifetime end,
The woman grieved with all her heart
And now his grave, she tends.
Michelle Armstrong

Blue Dawning

The sax sighs and cries
quicksilver of your smile
touches the hurt in my heart
negrito stirred to blue.

The horn breathes its understanding
gains its hold deep in gut wrenching
takes it way up, soul flight
blue sky flight.

Swans' necks outstretched
two daemons make their morning way
accelerating off lake's surface
night work done.

Muscles make their tension known
unconscious translations in dream time
images emerge out of foggy morning
waking to possibilities of this new day.
Robin Ladkin

Original Fashion

Chalice kouchie bong and chillum
Ram it and bun it five rizla
Lick it and stick it with sensemillia
You put it in it
Roll it cork it because this is Kyms hh-habit
Yes I am an addict
Bush doctors sell it
To make enough profit
But then again, let's legalize it
Kym shall advertise it because Kym recommends it.
Kym Adrian Carpenter

Lottery Blues

It's Saturday; - hurray - and lottery day
Put our pools aside, - no way
This for a roll - over
And millions is the pay

Mystic Meg, sits shrouded in mystery
Please put us out of our misery
Her words of wisdom and predictions
Just add more confusion with contradictions

Now the balls are set in motion
All our eyes glued to their rotation
Just time to offer a prayer - please make us rich
Now the balls begin to ditch

I've won ten pounds
I've won ten pounds
I've won ten pounds, — I chant
Vacant faces follow my reckless prance.

Now it's over we count the cost
But I say all is not lost
Though our prayers have gone astray
Next Saturday — is another millionaire's day.

R. C. Berry

Untitled

Lying here in a lazy dream
Pure as can be, silky and clean
I think of the land, the sea and the mountains
Life keeps running like a water fountain.

This place called Earth can be very scary
It's a cold world, rather weary
Don't treat life with contempt don't throw it away
It's the older ones that make the youth of today.

I blame religion for some of what is wrong
The fighting, the war and most of the bombs
It's mostly about greed and this thing called Money
That's what makes the whole thing funny

I gaze into space and hope it will go away
The pain and sorrow of everyday
The old, the poor and the very very weak
They all suffer from week to week.

Can you answer how the world begun
Did we come from monkeys and how far's the sun
Did the dinosaurs just fade and die
Is it evolution, is there a God in the sky?

Tony Charlton

The Pitwheel

The pitwheel stood foursquare against the sky,
Proud symbol of the power of the mine,
While at its feet communities so gay,
Depended on its strength from day to day,

Them grey faced men with water in their veins,
Who thought of people only with disdain,
Decided coal was finished as a power,
Not needed for the industries of tomorrow,

Now the mine is closed the pitwheel stands,
As ramparts of a bridge on reclaimed land,
And as new life is springing from the waste,
Around its edge communities decay,

Now once strong men stand idle on the bridge,
Despairing heads against the pitwheel spine,
And curse the folly of shortsighted men,
Who robbed them of the right to pay their way,

And now communities once gay,
Sit huddled in a no-man's-land of grey,
Their future hopes and dreams have turned to sand.
While new life springs afresh on reclaimed land.

Peter Waring

Beneath My Feet

I often think what's beneath my feet when walking
"Probably" insects talking
I walk the meadow along the path
Wondering what is under the grass
The grass is cushioned with each step I take
I think that's for the insects sake
I look down while walking slow
and saw a lady bird aglow
Then a daddy long legs, past
just to settle in my path
so I had to step right over
to avoid the beautiful pink clover
I wish I could just float across the path
so as not to disturb the meadow grass

Valerie Fitch

"The Newspaper"

Newspapers printed in black and white
Printed in colour they don't look right
Paper reporters give us up to date news
Journalists writing to give us their views

Page three models in topless poses
The garden section is all about roses
The second page is all about thugs
Dealing in murder theft and drugs

The racing pages are at the back
Look there's a horse called Jumping Jack
Look for a restaurant where we can eat
If I back a winner it will be my treat

The Daily Bugle full of quips
Will it end up wrapping fish and chips
Crossword puzzles full of clues
This is the end of the daily news

B. J. Sargeant

To Philip, My Father - Killed in Action

I, as a later lover, far removed
praise him that said "All these were lovely"
I say "He loved" now I love too.
Those that he loved do still remain
and are not faithless.
Not traitors they that could not pass death's door.
They changed and died no more than us;
Life's children - all rebirth of what has gone before.

You did not give your life in vain.
For we remember - we're aware
that country, conscience, pride
sent you to a slaughter
that has been our benefit.
All your loves are lovely still
and loved by us through you.

Lane Stokes

Bitter Woman

She stalks the streets,
Power growing ever dimmer,
As her lights begin blocking her reasoning,
Alas to me the seasons have stopped,
For the moment ever continues,
To once again feel that acidic embrace,
When the energy spiked.
Indulged by the toxicant screaming through my blood.
The stride grows shorter,
Gulf decreasing,
If that heart still pumped,
It would be the colour black,
Oh, but see that it does.
And I sense the spark,
For you are returning,
Battle no more,
For we are back.

Richard Hall

"My Sorry State"

Pot-holed roads.
Power-failed houses of the ill-fated.
Oozing sweat of the already drenched.
Tiring souls and evil minds
Resign to an optionless dictatorial supplication.

Corruption, oppression, depression, pollution and execution.
Endemically sweep in tandem.
The promises of rifle-stifled democracies
Are falsely often midwifed into termination.
Reducing us to an international caricature.

The favoured few flip-flop.
The illicit regime sets the clock aback.
Alien masters stand at akimbo
Masters that devirgined our ancestral past.
The past we remember with a mere mental orgasm.

Who dare question his animal boldness?
The 9 that did died on rope.
I'd rather give him a goat-like gaze
Or hang myself in protest
But the rope on my waist.

Vincent Oluonye Ogakwu

Touched By An Angels Wing

Amy touched my arm, "There goes crazy Sarah, talking to
 herself again."
"Poor things supposed to be a witch, she's completely round
 the bend."
I followed my friends gaze and saw an ancient, scruffy hag.
She was laughing and talking, just an old maid of rag.

As I observed "The witch," she turned and her violet eyes
 met mine.
I saw not a gargoyle, but noble features that were still fine.
I grew hot and embarrassed, but her face dissolved into a smile.
I couldn't, but was tempted to stay and talk to her for a while.

A week later I met her in the park, her manner so childlike,
 still laughing and talking,
She glowed with an inner light and I thought I heard tiny bells
 when she was walking.
"You know, don't you - about the spirit people? You can see
 them too?"
"Yes Sarah, I can see them - they're standing all around you."

It was a year later, right to the day, I grieved when I heard she
 had died.
I sat alone in the park, felt a shimmering presence, bowed my
 head and cried.
Something brushed my cheek, I heard Sarah's laughter and
 tiny bells ring.
I caught my breath. I knew I had been touched by an angels wing...

Linda Miller

Man Vs Earth

Man's greatest paradox is living on planet earth,
Pollution and destruction is not easy,
For greed and power,
Man will strive.

Love and peace is hard to find,
Who knows what man's purpose is,
His dreams are materialistic,
Life falls in his deepest spirit.

Technology is man's greatest achievement,
Evolving earth is plagued by man's inventions,
No sky untouched or deepest sea,
Traces of man are everywhere.

How long will man last,
Only time will tell,
Man is not immortal, that's one thing we know for sure,
Man's greatest paradox is living on planet earth.

Shaun A. Taylor

Island

Please don't stand too far away
Please don't stand too close
My remoteness is an unfortunate facade
That isn't there through choice

Do not judge me by my naivete
 my unshaven face
 my lack of grace

Look deep into my eyes
Are you afraid of what you see?
A soul that's seeking has lost its way
In a search for something
Which cannot be found

I destroyed myself a time ago
I now possess an iron heart
Like ice it wasn't always cold
Be warned you have been told

I sleep alone again tonight
I pen this my lonely friend
From this dark and hollow dungeon
A dream is my only escape

Peter Vincent Capaldi

Suicide

Suicide?
Please don't
For end your life you surely won't
'Tis only the body that you'll destroy
For the Spirit is the Real McCoy
Away the pills, Put down the knife
Don't shy away from physical life
Away the pen, Don't write goodbyes
Stop the tears and dry your eyes
The Temple of The Spirit is too high a price to pay
For whatever troubles you this day
There really is a purpose to your being on Earth
Which is why you achieved physical birth
Try to overcome the pain
For tomorrow will be sunny instead of rain

Rodney George Priest

Memory Lane

If you're feeling sad and low,
Please do not despair.
For down memory lane we'll go,
There's peace and pleasure there.

Your fears and worries pass away,
down that leafy glade.
There's sunshine down there every day,
Where promises are made.

Well sit and see the beauty there,
and share each others dreams.
Not a trouble or a care,
as the sunset and gleams.

So think and love with all your heart,
and very soon you'll be.
In the land of dreams sweetheart,
down memory lane with me.

J. W. Dunning

A Country Garden

In the garden of Senegal, called Casamance,
Papayas and mangoes grow in such abundance.
Down at the port - huge fish, prawns, piles of peanuts too.
Have you ever had rice with peanut butter stew?

Africans chattering in clothes so bright!
And mongooses playing in the dark night!
White egrets, proud sentinels are many,
And pelicans? Why, they're 'two a penny!'

Mavis Rodger

My Ellan Vannin My Isle Of Man

This island set in a silver sea
Place of beauty and tranquillity
A haven where souls can be refreshed
Where tired minds are needing rest
Somewhere to dream one's cares away
And there's always time for - another day,
Such lovely glens so fresh and green
Where water cascades into a stream
Born of nature- so we are taught
These precious things that can't be bought.
This little gem of rock and sand
Of streams and hills and marshy land
Where gulls and curlews take to flight
Surveying all this wondrous sight,
A place- one day where if God is willing
To down one's tools and wait his bidding
Oh! how my heart cries out for thee
My own "Dear Ellan Vannin"
With your green hills by the sea.
Margaret Butter Smith

Remedies

Pills, pills, pills, pills
Pills, pills, pills, pills
Pills, their the remedy for all
your ills take one if it only kills.
Hard to swallow this I know but
Easy if you're feeling low.
Had a pain the other day doctor
said it would go away.
Feeling dizzy sitting tight phenabarb will put it right.
Constipated, epileptic, epenutum's quite electric.
Can't you sleep dear here's the answer
500 grams of near disaster.
So here's the motto to the tale
Before you go a deathly pale.
Take ye heed of pink or white
You may end up blowing your kite.
The dawn chorus of the birds make
me think of Norway fjords.
Now we'll never know what's out there
Only one big bloody nightmare.
M. Hayton

Lingering Death

Through the darkness came the screams,
Piercing laughter, haunting dreams
Running quickly beating heart
Chasing me let me part away from demons, drunk with fear.
Blood soaked skins of boneless flesh
smear the pathway to my rest.

Gnarled hands and gripping claws strongly
pull aside the doors, open to the darkest
side of man's destruction, I must hide.

Blackened teeth, foul stench of breath heaving
bodies to their death. Upon the rocks of
Man's Desire, leading souls down to Hell's fire!

Overcome with shocking steel, coldly
struck yet feeling thrilled - to know that
pain is really there. Numbing senses no
longer aware. I close my eyes and no longer
see nor smell the taste of "Man's Liberty."
Maureen Hartley

Untitled

Glory's hand reached down inside of me
   picked out the worm that was asleep
Pushed with a great honourable rush
   all of the bone that had marrow unjust
Seconds pass waiting for the Stalwart heart,...
   nothing appears when separated apart
The glorious have tails of fear
   and with cowardice bravery is always near

So return to me my quaking limbs
   settled on body of gallant blood
Give me back the clipped wings
   underneath back of protecting love
Send me all weak things
   for I am and always have been
Harboured with great thoughts above
Wayne Colton

A Poetry Competition

A poetry competition! A poem I shall write
Perhaps I'll start it now or later on tonight
Oh, but what will I say and will it even rhyme
Every word thought out so I'll finish it on time
The first lines come so quick from then it gets quite hard
Rhyming isn't easy like on a birthday card
You have to think it out as to what you want to say

Concentrate, work hard, that will get you on your way
Once you've got the subject, the ideas begin to flow
Minds are good like that when they really get to go
People have this talent it's hidden well within
Everyone can write a poem, perhaps to even win
The winners or the losers, don't let it break your heart
In a poetry competition it's more the taking part
The feelings that are written are personal to you
Inside information in poems that shine through
Once you have it written you know the talents not lost
Now post it to the judges and keep your fingers crossed.
Theresa Dunton

Yugoslavia???

People dying, people crying,
People standing all around,
Soldiers fighting, soldiers killing,
Bodies lying on the ground.

Cities crumble, cities burning,
People's homes are gone,
In a country in shrouds of darkness,
Where once the sun had shone.

Beautiful mountains, beautiful trees,
overshadowed by fire,
Even people who are strangers here,
But who give their guns for hire.

Now it's time for the world to make a stand,
And help these people a while,
Stop the killing, stop the crying,
And make the people here smile.
Ken Norman

'Homeless'

Nowhere of my own to lay my head,
Nowhere private to make my bed,
In full view of scornful passers by,
Cardboard and newspapers to keep me dry,
My hands outstretched begging but my eyes looking down,
Grateful for a penny but not for a frown,
I sit in the rain with my hands open wide,
Muttering thanks and swallowing my pride,
Next time you pass and can't toss me a penny,
Spare me a smile, that don't cost any.
Vanessa Brown

The Sunset

The glory of the setting sun
Quite unsurpassed by anything
Has been admired by everyone
In Summer, Autumn, Winter, Spring.

From delicate gold and palest green
To yellow, orange, mauve and red,
Then great ripples of silver sheen
Behind soft pink clouds, like a coral bed.

Across the sky the beauty glows
Reflected in the village pond.
The river seems ablaze as it flows
As if by the wave of a fairies wand.

Then gather the clouds of night.
With the golds and reds behind them shining
Like huge wings spread in flight
And from behind, a silver lining.

So softly then it fades away
And clouds close in and night shades fall
As silently passes another day
And darkness envelopes all.

Marjorie Wright

Train Ride

The train is waiting on the track
people fill the luggage rack
excitement builds, the porter waves
the journey starts, we're on our way.

The Station Master gives the nod
the whistle blows, our thanks to God
it leaves on time, we start to go
his flag is up, it's tally ho.

Behind us now the station lies
we're on the road to paradise
it gives a strange, exciting feeling
back and forth the train is reeling.

The Guard comes by to check the fares
punch in hand he stops and stares
smiles and gives your ticket back
checks the bags upon the rack.

At last the journey's end is here
we have arrived we now can hear
the hooter blows, it gives a heave
the train has stopped, and we now leave.

Rosaleen Maguire

V. J. Day Remembered

The dream we had awaited reality became.
Peace for every nation and on our planet once again.
Gates of Eastern prisons were to us all unfurled.
The scenes that had been hidden
shocked the Western World.
Men struggled out to freedom
just living skin and bone.
Flesh lay sore and open for bugs to find a home.
Eyes deep sunken staring out,
emotions barely none.
Battered hearts out facing tho'
they knew their job was done.
Thank you men of courage who
suffered for mankind.
We hope that time has eased
your scars and given peace of mind.
At last the final curtain of
those years of toil and tears.
Our heroes could walk tall again
and loved ones have less fears.

Valerie Deacon

Even Bet

The Abyss inside my head left a void to the
Pain of the inner sanctity,
And unable to separate reality from visions,
The smile broadened,
Floating and alone Margaret first appeared.

O' lady from my minds creation stay awhile,
Admire my hair, take stock,
And try (If you can) explaining, the picture on the wall

The blame must lie with the card playing
Fool with the famous name,
Perpetual chance
The wheel of life
The wheel of fortune

Las Vegas will you beckon me?
Will the fat man ever buy a drink?

Richard Emsden

Aching Heart

Where am I going I ask you
Over the hills, into the clouds?
To the tranquil peace and quiet
To soothe my aching heart.

Where am I going I ask you
Back to the past ages ago?
To hear the bubbling brook
To soothe my aching heart.

Where am I going I ask you
Into the future to the grave?
No sunshine, no warmth, no love
To stop my aching heart.

Where will I go I ask you
To the present, to laughter and life!
To sunshine and warmth and love
To soothe my aching heart.

Ursula Atkins

Oh Glorious Sun

Oh glorious sun, when thou set tonight
Over bloodied field filled with limp corpses,
Do not, I beg, jeer at those who fought and died
So that others may live. Instead, I beg,
Light their way to the afterlife.

Oh glorious sun, as thou shinest bright today,
Do not, I beg, give way to tears of rain
Whilst we who do battle commit great
Slaughter and wonder why. Instead, I beg,
Shine bright today and let the people mourn.

Oh glorious sun, as thou rise up today,
Shine bright o'er copse and cottage and
River and wood, so the armies who fight
Today may take comfort from you. And, above
All, I beg, do not set for me this day.

M. A. Ford

Earwigs

Earwigs have the habit, according to "Old wives".
Of laying eggs in human ears, so that the species thrives.
To correct this misunderstanding and to allay all your fears.
Earwigs wouldn't like this, lest you're wet behind the ears.
They are nocturnal creatures i.e. they move about when dark.
And live among the fallen leaves and under rotting bark.
They're very caring creatures, the female a good Mum.
For when her young are born, protects them neath her "Tum".
The main mode of locomotion is walking, among other things.
For believe me when I tell you, they have two pairs of wings.
And as the moist they do prefer, and to really end your fears
When doing your ablutions, don't wash behind your ears.

P. R. Madle

I Want Some Of That

I want some of that, to sit all day and chat
Outside a French cafe in the shade
A french senior to look at me, and wistfully gaze
I want someone to write my name in the sky
Play rugby and score a try
I want to fly a plane, command a flight
Learn to surf and stay 'Upright'!
I want to throw caution to the winds to do all the sins
I want to see a sunset from the sea bed
See it lay on the water's surface above my head
I want to go shopping with endless money
And a gorgeous toy-boy to call me honey
I'd love to wear a pac-a-mac and Welly's into town
To sing outside a supermarket and earn me 'alf-a-crown
Just once I want to be first in the queue
Have a fairy-Godmother and three wishes that come true
The first I'd use to right the wrongs, to separate the wings and wongs
The second to make this world seem fair
And the third to make me look like Cher!
Sara Cox

Happiness

When we look back what do we see?
A glimpse of what was yesterday
Somebody's smile, a helping hand
A day so different to what we planned
We live our live's so carelessly
And often think what could have been
But before we know it the day has passed
With its joy or sorrow alas!
If we could live our lives once more
To live as we think best
Life's first lesson still would be
The search for happiness
Without it life can mean so little
We all find it in different ways
To great and small things it is there
To enjoy yourself and also share
So make the most of every day
And mankind will benefit
As you pass this way.
V. Cambridge

Paper Things - (Etcetera)

Paper hats and table mats,
Paper cloths and napkins.
It's all agreed, the paper you read,
Is great to wrap your chips in.

Ticker tapes and party plates,
Certificates and scrolls.
Paper clips and payments slips,
Towels and toilet rolls.

Paper lace, a paper chase,
Chains and party poppers,
Post-it notes and paper boats,
Notebooks and little jotters.

Paper bags and rolled-up fags,
Posters and paper stickers.
Paper pounds and paper rounds,
And pretty paper knickers.

Lighting tapers for blue touch papers,
Handkerchiefs and tissues.
tie-on tags and readers' mags,
Some half the price - back issues.
Ken Bruford

Memories

The winter of our lives draw near
  our memories we talk over,
Each child, born ever dear
The travels we took down trail and brook,
Always there, like a story in a book.
The golden days, the sad days.
How well we remember them.
Friends, some still with us
  from those early times.
We listened and gathered.
To hear church bells chime,
Our children married
  babies christened
How lovely our memories
  in the Winter of our lives,
K. Collins

Dad's Clanger

The day started out the best I've ever seen.
Our Kay looked divine and my mum looked like a queen
Everything was super smiling faces all around
But then came the reception 'twas then I hit the ground
My dad got up to make a speech and this is what he said
"Hey it's just dawned on me what it is I've just done
I've given away my daughter to your blooming ugly son
Well now I've just got this to say I'm not giving her away
She's my daughter still he said and will remain so until I'm dead".
My mum just gasped and pulled a face she really did feel out of place
She then gave Dad a mucky look but he just put two fingers up
Was he drunk or hurt inside because he'd given away the bride
My mum won't forgive him for what he's done
And I do feel sorry for my mum
I also feel sorry for our Kay it was meant to be her special day.
Melita Archer

Pace Of Life

It's a stressful time living in the nineties,
People are caught up in all sorts of anxieties.
Demands are increasing all the time.
Those without hope turn to crime.
The unemployed are in despair,
The office workers have no hair.
Teenage pregnancies are hardly rare,
Marriage breakups cultivate despair.
Even the young are in a mess,
At the age of five they suffer stress.
The worldly atmosphere is so thick with smoke,
Those caught up in it are bound to choke.
If things could improve so that people could cope,
Maybe then we could look to the future with hope.
Sonia Sweet

Awayday

Steady away, steady away,
out of the station and into the day.
Into the sunlight, through forest of wires,
sights of the city, of buses and cars.
Accelerate out, through the clicking of points,
the pull of the engine, the hiss of its joints.
Over the bridges you smirk at commuters,
hurrying back to desk, file and computers.
Out through the dirt, the grime and the grey.
Out through the factories and urban decay.
Out through the tunnels on tangles of tracks.
Out through the terraces, semi's and flats.
Out through the cuttings to flashes of green,
the gold of the corn, the sun on the leaves,
and you smile as you see the wind in the trees.
You flow with the vision and dream of the sea
and you know as you sip on your warm cup of tea,
what a thoroughly gorgeous day out this will be.
P. T. Fretwell

Untitled

On September the 12th 1994
our father passed away.
He left us all so suddenly
but in our hearts he'll stay.

A father of six children
and also a good friend,
for thirty years, a husband
together until the end.

In May 1993 the first grandchild
was born to be a boy,
for eighteen months a granddad
brought our father joy.

Our father was cremated
and his ashes laid to rest.
With just one thought that springs to mind
Our father was the best.

Samantha Brooker

A Symphony Of Love

I will play the melody if you will harmonise,
our emotions be the orchestra, ecstasy the prize.
Softly, slowly, starts this piece, my fingers caress the keys,
in this, a solo opening that whispers like a breeze.
For several bars the music flows, you start to harmonise.
Relaxed, inspired, a tune is born, a duet realised.
Orchestral backing enters now, the tempo is increased,
from slow, to just a medium pace, it seems will never cease.
The speed increases even more, the volume rises too.
The orchestra's ecstatic now, a crescendo to our tune.
Every note is clear and pure, every tone is true,
movement in perfect harmony is felt 'tween me and you.
Gently now, our tune slows down with the beauty of a dove,
for together we have just composed, a symphony of love.

V. T. S. Gower

Sharing

Along our lifetime journey,
Our different paths we tread.
This applies to all Nations,
Where the Human Race is spread.

Now in times of trouble.
Nations disagree.
Oh what a happy land.
This land of ours could be.

People come from far and wide,
And live in harmony side by side,
So let us try to keep Heaven on earth.
And remember sharing for what it's worth.

So in this our final struggle.
When all nations do unite.
All will find their peace on earth.
In sharing in this great land of ours.

Phyllis Cooke

Summer In Suffolk

Dewdrops hanging, like sparkling crystal tears
on wild rosebuds, that sweetly scent the air.
Rabbits play, forgetful of their fears,
and melodious song birds are everywhere.
Silken strands of spangled cobwebs float
like thistledown, upon a gentle breeze.
Stealthily hunts, the lone, but handsome Stoat,
among tussocks, hedgerows and roots of trees.
Contented cattle, on pasture land graze,
'midst Dandelion, Hemlock and Pheasant's Eye.
In solitude they peacefully laze,
serenely oblivious, as time slips by.
If I could stop the hands of time I'd stay,
In Suffolk forever, on a summer's day.

Violet Kingsbury

My Wonderful Day

She was born into this world in October last year
Our beautiful daughter was finally here
The waiting was over as we heard her first scream
With our tears of joy it was no longer a dream

Wrapped up in a blanket she was handed to me
Her face was so tiny that's all we could see
Her eyes slowly opened they were glacier blue
Still full with emotion to smile is all we could do

Back in the ward I held her so tight
Shielding her face from the golden sunlight
So peaceful she sleeps in her cot by my side
Tenderly I touch her just brimming with pride

This is our baby we'll love her for ever
Were a family now we'll always be together
Sitting on my bed I watched her for hours
This wonderful miracle is now all ours

The joy the laughter is still yet to come
I am so proud to be her mum
I'll protect her guide her and show her the way
This has been such a wonderful day.

Sarah Smith

A Personal Loss

How can they tell a part of you died
Or what is going on inside
Your mind and thoughts they are your own
How do they know when you are all alone

They do not know how you feel
Or what you do or say is for real
They say sorry, it will be all right
They do not know how you make it through the night

Times you do not want to carry on
Now that one of you is gone
No-one to talk to, no-one to share
No-one being there for me to care

But at the end of each lonely day
When the hurt will not go away
You close your eyes, open up your mind
And fond memories there you will find

Memories are alive and well
And in your heart will ever dwell
These thoughts with you will always be
Just close your eyes and you will see

Peter Howarth

"A Bouquet Of Dreams"

It doesn't matter what the season,
Or what ever the reason,
Come spring through to winter,
Flowers bring you laughter,
Even when your feeling sad and blue.

From little tiny seeds, they soon blossom,
They each have their own kingdom,
All different shapes and forms,
Come rain or sun, even storms,
These flowers melt the hearts of millions.

A beautiful, luxurious bouquet,
Like a colourful blanket,
They each have a wonderful aroma,
Christmas time, a spray of freesias,
For your loved one, a bunch of roses.

Amongst the greenery, feathery ferns,
Petals softly fragrant with pretty patterns,
Maybe for someone special, or just a celebration,
So say it with flowers, what ever the occasion,
Make someone smile today.

H. Philp

The Path

Like the rolling seas of time,
Or the lonely mountains, so grey, to climb,
Field after field, the grass, so green
Or the waters of the clear bubbling stream,
The solitary owl, at work during the night,
Or a plant feeding off the light,
Are proof that we all have seen,
The path where nature has been.

Like a cloud, overburdened with rain,
Or the sun, set to shine again and again,
And the waking sky, at the coming of dawn,
New rays of light, like colours drawn,
A second's flash of lightening, a ghostly flame,
Or the forceful wind of a hurricane,
Are proof that we all have seen,
The path where nature has been.

Peter Lapham

"Will It Just Be Darkness"

Do we lie along in our graves
or roam the universe like Indian braves.
Riding the stars is their choice
listening to Gods golden voice.
Are there tunnels of love or hate
or is there just one, heavens gate.
God will see us beyond the grave
All our souls, he wants to save.

Philip George Blockley

Ode to Gwen

Imagine Paris without its tower,
Or London with no Big Ben.
Well that's what it feels like now,
'Cause we haven't got our Gwen.

We didn't want to see you suffer,
We didn't want to see you go,
But what on earth, could we have done
You know we loved you so.

For as sure as night would follow day,
You were always there, come what may.
Winston Churchill is dead and gone,
Martin Luther too.
That sort of thing is for someone else,
But we never expected it of you.
At night, when we look in to the sky,
Perhaps one day we'll understand why?.
And as we gaze to the heavens afar,
We can clearly see, they've added a star.....

Stephen D. Colbourne

Pure Magic

Tell me where the mists pervading meadows go,
Or from where the trilling song-birds rise.
In the May-morn, dew-fresh grasses, daisies spring
And yellow wild flowers defy all lies
That the earth and magic are not one,
That all romantic dreams and love are nought.
I saw the magic and the mystery unfold at dawn
As golden beams of light the apple blossom caught,
Amongst the scent of blue-bells by the trees
And lacy willow-lady trailing by,
Beneath a blue, so deep, I can't explain,
The canopy around, we call the sky.

And in this wondrous wonderment, so it seems,
Such love as this transcends all realms of dreams.

Patricia Anne Thomas

Jealous Warriors

Battle weary, and ready to die
Only one reason, as to why
The field is full of bodies dead
Lacking strength, legs turning to lead
The last two warriors fight to the end,
But years ago they used to be friends,
Armies they built, and soldiers they trained
To fight each other, now only they remain,
A bitter row did boil and seethe,
How could one woman cause so much grief,
She gave her heart to more than one,
Now to the death they fight, in the setting sun
One more ounce, they hear each other plead,
One more ounce of strength is all they need,
But into each other's arms they fall
Now she has no one, no one at all

Kevin Fitzsimmons

A Soldier's Lament

Through the murky swamps we wade, looking for our foes.
Only mist circles round, the jungle now is without a sound.
Calm before the storm, with eyes dimmed with tears, I see
a big man fall, from where did the bullet fly.
Oh God I hope he never knew.
I shoot to kill my trembling hand grasps my deadly gun.
He had a name the man who died, a wife perhaps a son,
You stop yourself from thinking this and aim for another
fleeing shadow.

Familiar memories crowding back, haunt your banging head,
The village fair where I took my little boy, his eager step,
the coloured lights he pointed to with joy, his new blue suit
the coconuts we won,
Happy laughter and ice cream, the warmth of a summer sun.
A rifle range with pigeons falling one by one.
I have been sent to do my job, and do my job I must
but they are not clay pigeons, for there's blood in the
rotting dust.

B. Burgess

One

One glance. Confirming the care that is felt within.
One word. Saying all there is to say within its meaning.
One touch. Electric in its complexity, yet soothing in its simplicity.
One sigh. A message passed that could never be put into words.
One hug. To enable the warmth to pass between us, bringing calm to a troubled brow.
One kiss. Giving love and strength to carry us through another day.
One thought. Bringing love and understanding, health, strength and warmth.
One tear. Lightening the burden of our souls. Cleansing both of earthly troubles.
One look. That says "I Love You"...
One. As we are when we are at our closest.

Leonard R. Green

Today's World

Shoving and pushing, rushing around
People on feet, that don't touch the ground
How do we cope in this world of today
Who has the wisdom to show us the way
Commitment and marriage - a thing of
the past.
Just how long do we want this
to last?
Children today have no morals
to follow.
Their lives in the way are
awfully hollow.
Fatherless and motherless,
how do we know,
The feeling inside - so hard
to show.

G. Fletcher

A Lost Soul

The fortunes of a lost soul are bleak,
One day, each day all unique,
No one can say what the future holds,
Barred by beds in rows and rows.

This is not a service point,
Tidy beds are not just junk,
Live and life go hand in hand,
Don't preach, don't stand, don't lend a hand.

Warnings are with us day by day,
And foolish men decide to pray,
There is only one way, disbelief is today,
Be sure you know this every day

Spirits lost and spirits found,
Don't make a home from homeward bound,
Each precious person to be saved,
But count the cost of what is named.

There is only one true way to heaven,
The almighty has shown the way,
Believe it now and in the future,
Let all other spirits lie, in restless torment by and bye.

Kevin Rowan

Dead Man, Painted New

Stand in awe, honoured little soul,
Numbered little servant for angels cold,
All agents, a proxy, each with a role,
So discrete with compassion,
They need not accept your fables of rations,

You shall sit, no! shall beg,
That your humble soul may lick the dregs,
All for free, their gesture - your end,
Light your last cigarette for it too, soon must end.

Shine, now, little soul, radiate your gladness,
Take grip of your world stuffed with new madness,
Shine on, and for longer, with emotions a brew,
Happy cadet, confused spirit, it's true,

You will be here for always, this also is true,
Dead men turn blue,
Yet a pauper, still living can also turn blue,

Your controlled with such ease,
And it's frightening to see,
That a dead man painted new can look just like me,
Can look just like you, yet exist, not to be.

Martin McCluskey

Into The Land Of Dreams

When twilight falls
   on the dimmed olde walls
and the day has passed and gone
   as we sit and dream
in the fading gleam
   come memories one by one
voices known in the years long gone
   in fancy greets us still
but voices now which we long to hear
   the silence seems to pass
just when the day is over
   just when the lights are low
back to the heart returneth
   memories of long ago
far far away we wonder
   watching the twilight gleam
far far away in the world shadows gay
   into the land of dreams
      into the land of dreams
         into the land of dreams

G. M. M. Sullivan

The Sea

Slowly, slowly the sea comes in
over the bare feet in the sand.
It knows the way through the stones.
It washes away the sand castles
The children have made.
The children shout with glee,
for the sea has come in.
The mothers pick up their babies and run away.
Slowly, slowly the sea comes in.

Slowly, slowly the sea comes in.
Up the cliff it goes.
All the children follow the sea.
The mothers shout for their
Children, for they will fall.
The children don't come down
For the sea is their best friend,
Soon the tide comes in,
Mothers take their children away

Slowly, slowly the tide come in

Maxine Scholes

My Best Friend

You were there when I was born
on a sunny summer morn.
Watching me grow and make mistakes
yet all along your heart aches.

From childhood to a teen
I grew taller and lean
The trust you have in me would never fail
Through all the stories and the tales

Then I had children of my own
You watched the family how it's grown
Time goes by quick and fast
And all these years your love last.

All the words I write for you
Through all the things you watched me do.
Your love for me was always there
With plenty of understanding and care.

Though words cannot explain all I feel
I think of you when church bells peal
You are gone now, things are bad.
I am not sad, just glad, you were my dad.

Linda Nugent

Trees Of The Future

Oh tree you are so beautiful
Oh tree you are so tall
Oak, ash, cedar, poplar, elm
I love you one and all.

How I wish I were a tree
Swaying in the breeze, ever free
In wind and rain, all sorts of weather,
Nodding your heads and laughing together.

Dawn gentle breaks "Good Morning Birds"
Sweet chirrup, whistles are all to be heard
Then the bulldozer moved in with a crash and a bang
The tree's snapped and broken, no more the birds sang.

Oh wind blow my seedling to new meadows and vales,
Life must go on and must prevail
In the year 2020 what do I see
Look over there mother - is it a tree?

Kathleen M. Banks

Was It A Dream

There's a light shining,
oh so very bright,
like the moon shining,
in the still of the night.
Such peace and relaxation,
the atmosphere of recreation.
There's voices in the distance
leading to the light,
everything is beautiful, everything in sight
leading towards a path
smiles on peoples faces, I can hear the children's laugh
everyone here looks happy,
so peaceful and mild
I hear the words of encouragement
say 'I welcome you my child'
there is birds singing gracefully
there is golden fish in a stream
for these moments of contentment
WAS IT REAL.... WAS IT A DREAM
Lisa Marie Stott

Untitled

Already I find it's another weekend,
Oh God, I wish I had some money to spend.
But it doesn't matter I'll still be down in London,
For a few days of non-stop fun.
Every week I jump at the chance,
to spend all night just havin' a dance.
I've been doing this now for a whole decade,
And there's so many good memories that will never fade.
I love it so much, that, to lose my music,
Would make me feel so bloody sick.
Cos' the way I feel buzzin' on the dance floor,
I know I've just got to go back for more.
So now I've written down these rhymes,
I hope they remind you too of all those special times.
And of the feeling that are by far the best,
I know I feel as though I've been blessed.
for certain I'll never change my ways
While heading for some brighter days!
D. Hutchin

Two Worlds

"London streets are paved with gold"
Often I have heard that told
Harrods, The Tower, Trafalgar Square
Wealth and glamour everywhere
Flash cars - neon lights
Hustle and bustle - tourist sights.

But in the darkness of subways below
The pain of poverty starts to show
Old ragged clothes - a look forlorn
The people sad, their clothes are torn,
Two different worlds so close at hand
It tests the brain to understand.
Kerry Hinks

'Girl's Growing Up'

When at school - watch - bullies scare
Oft innocent crushes - yes - so rare

Biology explains - those monthly things
Not the boys - they could be kings

Later we're resigned - to our fate
Making us shy - and often late

But soon married - off shelf's shame
Will it last long - like Guinness fame

Suddenly I'm a pensioner - with loving guy
Pray we stay together - till we die.

Oh! Yes it's morbid - thinking thus
Cheers! I'm a multi granny - what's the fuss
P. M. McCarthy

Here I Am

Here are my eyes, open for all to see.
Offering you an insight of hope for all
eternity.

Here are my lips, poised for a kiss.
Offering you a taste, a chance not to
be missed.

Here are my arms, outstretched and open wide.
Offering you some comfort, all you have to do
is step inside.

Here is my heart, pounding and beating fast.
Offering you all my love, use it well and make
it last.

Here is my body, naked and cold.
Offering you such passion, let your power
take a hold.

Here is my future, held within your hands.
Offering me peace - from a man who understands.
Susan Kaye Bence

Autumn Winds North Lancashire

They came up from the Southwest,
off the Irish channel overland,
to the estuary, chasing the leaves,
seabirds swooping and screaming with the wind,
as it reaches a crescendo over the estuary,
chasing white horses off the waves.

Onward ever onward over the bay,
making a larger swell in the lone deep,
where seagulls ride majestic,
in their own right,
onward towards the land again,
now forever climbing,

Sweeping along the seeds,
off trees and plants,
till they rest,
sown for next year's growth,
and the winds fade going fast,
to the Yorkshire moors.
Peter Orr

Country Things

My joy is all of country things;
   Of wild-goose feather and owls' soft wings,
The cadence of lark-song, tinkling high,
   The first lilt of blackbirds as Winter slips by.

The trailing willow's narrow leaf,
   With green moss velvet underneath,
Apple-bloom petals of blushing pearl,
   The eager, rich green as new leaves unfurl.

The vital smell of new-ploughed earth,
   The green-flecked thorn, the cream May's birth,
Long silver arrows of swift Spring rain,
   Receptive earth, and new-sprung grain.

Ripe wheat, straight as marshalled army,
   Tasselled oats and bearded barley;
A burnished ripple ebbs and flows
   On seas of gold as the warm wind blows.

In country things my life began,
   Continues still, in blessed span.
God grant that at its end may be
   Some country thing to comfort me.
Margaret Mary Williams

Time To Care

Write a poem they said,
of what's going on in your head.
What is going on in my head?
A feeling of dread -
fear of a nuclear war,
or being hated by the man next door.
Sadness in the despair of the faces
of the people in different places.
Mothers, fathers starving with their babies
and the rich being full of excuses and maybes;
but no help comes to end their grief -
no help to bring a permanent relief.
And yet I know, people try to be good
and they really would help if only they could.
The solutions seems to be out of our hands
and each and everyone, deep down inside, understands
the answers lie with God in heaven above
and striving and giving and living a life of love.

No terrorist bombs or acts of war will help today
it's time to think of others and care and share and pray.

Lesley Nunn

Mill Cottage

Mill cottage stands just at the back
Of what was once a rail road track,
Gone are the people who once lived there
And no more the smell of grain in the air.

In the yard the hens are nowhere to be seen
And the grass in front, doesn't seem so green,
Some old stone steps up to the wash house led,
Well worn in the middle with all the tread.

Beyond the wash house stood the old mill
And but for fire, might be standing still,
Soldiers from the first world war were once housed there,
And later, the Milnathort agricultural shows and fair.

If a little nostalgic this may seem
One is, I suppose allowed to dream
Of days gone by, when I danced beneath the steeple,
Of Milnathort and its kindly people!

Margaret Meek

"The Traveller"

Gone are the days of hassle and rush,
Of the stress back home, it just got too much.
So I decided to travel, to escape overseas,
And I'm now on a beach, with swaying palm trees.

My body is relaxed, my mind is cleansed,
As I dig my hands in the sand I feel happy, content.
The sun feels just right, and the waves lap the beach,
And I think of family, friends, so far out of reach.

This land is so different, so busy, yet relaxed,
And you'll never feel lonely, or like an outcast.
Your life will have purpose, you'll have aims and a goal,
And you'll become a self achiever, your life will be whole.

Some natives are jealous of our way of life,
Of money and good fortune, well, in theory it's nice.
But I'm jealous of them and their simplistic ways,
It seems so far apart from my hectic days.

Yet my journey is not over, in fact just begun,
It will be many more months 'til my travelling's done.
You'll hear stories of this place away, so far,
And when you do, just shut your eyes, and think of me, and India.

Stuart Christie

My Friend's Gone

Sat down in front of the T.V. in the warm surroundings
of the ones you love.
Without a care in the world is there any reason why you should?
In the real world outside it all carries on.
Some soldier is killed by the terrorists bomb.
What do you care? What are your views?
Or is it just another item on the six o'clock news?
Well let me tell you now he was a friend of mine.
He won't feel the pain that's for the ones he's left behind.
To him just a job, although his mother never wanted him to go.
He wouldn't listen to her, why what did she know.
Well now it's too late, for her son won't be back.
As his face has been blown from front to back.
So tonight when you're sat in front of the T.V.
Remember that soldier whose life has gone.
And he won't be the last.
Until these cowards are done.

A. J. Milnes

After The Storm

The Oak Tree stood at the corner
Of the old church-yard not far
From the bus stop.
It stood as it had always stood
Watching generations come and go
Births. Marriages, Deaths.
Each year pulsating life brought blossoms in the Spring
Clusters of bridal flowers mid dancing leaves.
Birds nested in the high branches
Safe above the endless passing traffic.
People waiting impatiently at the bus stop
Found the presence of the old Oak lessened the tedium.
Man's life is short but there always the Oak tree stood
Strong. Solid. Unconcerned - Until one day......

People arriving at the bus stop found the great trunk
Stretched across the road, roots grotesquely twisted
Open to the sky. It lay where it had fallen -
Fallen gallantly opposing the rapacious wind
That had come rampaging through the night.
People at the bus stop had lost A FRIEND.

W. E. Leigh

Poem For Mothers' Day

Bonds of love between mother, and child
None put away or neatly filed.
A time to remember
When we grow old.
That a precious gift is not gold.
Or even one that you can hold.
But the gift of time.
Given with love.
So the lonely day ends.

I. Dunn

Just Talking

I'll never forget the day we met
Of the loves that have passed us by
We hadn't talked long before my worries grew strong
And my heart felt the pains of goodbye

I was ready for you but you hadn't a clue
Because my feelings I kept in the dark
I tried not to talk as we started to walk
At least we held hands in the park

I tried to feel free but you tortured me
As we sat on the seat by the path
You spoke of the past and the love that would last
Long after I'd forgotten your laugh

It started to rain as you boarded the train
And our eyes met for one final embrace
I loved you then and I'll love you again
But in another time and another place

C. Parker

Snow

As Heaven drops an instant veil,
On mountain high and lowly dale.
Oh! What shame that clumsy boot,
Treads virgin into prostitute.

Oh! Winter scene, all else forsaking,
Pure and white, a new creating.
All man's follies completely masking,
A new refrain to set hearts singing.

Oh! Mantle of snow, all else concealing,
A wondrous beauty now revealing.
Then goest now, your way to make,
Trailing freshness in your wake.

Then melts away the new found glory,
To leave exposed man's history.
A lesson for him, that he can too,
Cleanse his world and start anew.

Stan Johnson

"The Light Of The Dawn"

Has it now started the beginning of the end?
Of my existence, that I have no power to extend,
No longer to be embalmed in my warm dark place,
No power, no control, over what I may face.
Time passing by, my body now falling, falling
The darkness is fading, the light is now calling, calling.
Dropping down in the tunnel, struggling in vain
Pulling me down, against gravity I strain.
No longer can I hold back, the force is too strong,
I can't leave my world where I've slept for so long!
My strength is now waning the tunnel will win,
I'm fighting no longer my body gives in.
The light is pulling me, slowly but strong,
No longer the pulse of a heartbeat my song.
So long in this haven, warm, quiet and alone,
I hear voices calling, I hear a soft moan.
As panic and terror reflect on my brain
I cry out so loudly and yet feel no pain.
Loving hands reaching out to guide to the dawn
For this I've been waiting, today I am born.

Marie Foster

Homeless

Life is a dream, or do we dream
of how it should seem,
When we awaken and open our eyes
We see limbo and mournful sighs.

So much hope that laid ahead
Now gone and forgotten like the dead,
Why does life taunt us with such emotion
To give and to take with no proportion.

Your thoughts, your feelings, your energy
Look back at you now like an effigy
Of the love and care you had once given
Now used, abused and finally broken,
The spirit has gone, the ghost walks alone,
No love, no care and no home.

Noreen Almond

That's Life

How dreadful it seems to be caught in a stream
Of high sounding repartee and wit,
To be held thoughtless and wordless by a brainless
Vulgarian, with his tasteless and endless conceit,
To stand flushing and blushing while words go on rushing
From the hole in his dim-witted face,
His gaffing and laughing all patience surpassing,
With your friends rolling over the place
Oh! Why does the pun, the quintessence of fun
That would rock him right back on his heels.
Which would stay him and flay him and finally slay him,
Only come to your mind when he's gone?

I. Roberts

The Soldier

He'd tell you a tale if only he could
Of quarrels and battles and life at the front
Of caring and sharing a hole in the ground
While arrows and shells explode all around
He may face a brother, a father or friend
But now he's a soldier and facing his end
Gripping the weapon with which he must fight
"Oh" God will You tell me is the cause just and right
If I lay down my body, life and my soul
Will the world be much better for my blood on its soul
Will those who come after and walk where I lay
Know how I suffered and prayed on this day
My legs feel jelly, my eyes are not clear
"Oh" God in your wisdom forgive me my fear
The bugle has sounded the order relayed
And I must go forward to the hell that's man made
The darkness descends and cuts like a knife
While all around me the battle is rife
A man stands above me his face is so white
"Oh" God please forgive him for taking my life

K. Oliver

A T.V. Guide

As I sit down to watch T.V. horrific pictures shown to me
of distant lands I can't conceive, what I would do if it were me.
It's hard to know just how to feel, can't tell what's true, can't
tell what's real
Millions dying, many wars, children crying by the score.

Some people seem to take some pride in winning wars and
taking sides
how can you win when others die, when families break and
children cry.
When misery overshadows fast, and happiness seems a thing
of the past,
a thing we humans do the best is hate each other with a zest.

It's true that there will never be a time when we will all agree
How could the world have ever got to a stage where we've forgot
The very meaning of our existence, to love mankind with a
persistence
To help each other when we can, to get on with our fellow man.
To shower our children with all our love, to teach them of the
Lord above
To show them that what we do now
Could change the world, someday, somehow
We must start now, we cannot wait, or it may soon become
too late!

J. E. Shine

If Only They Knew (How Much It Hurts)

I'm grey and cute and swim like no other,
Of course I'm fat, I'm full of blubber
I'm just a seal.
I don't spend as much time on land as I ought to,
I'm far more superior when I'm in the water,
I'm just a seal.
Living life contentedly with a family to get fish for,
What more could any mammal truly wish for.
Yet there are some, who would like my skin,
My blubber, my flesh and other bits of things.
My one fear is being clubbed and left for dead
Something that humans don't have to dread,
I may not be human, I can't talk or walk,
But, I can feel.
If only they knew how much it hurts,
But they don't, they think......
I'm just a seal.

Shirley Thornycroft Kirk

The Prodigal Son

It's time to blend into the background
now the prodigal son's home again
they never listen to me
or my reasons
so I bear suffering
and pain
how can I be loved
when I am hidden by his shadow
perhaps they'd think more of me
if I was here today and gone tomorrow
would I be missed
if I were gone
I can only wonder
I need to absolve my thoughts
instead of turning them asunder
I've prayed so long for their love
which I know will set me free
longing for the words of comfort
son thou art ever with me.
J. L. Derbyshire

Summer Love

Summer love and heated passion;
Obsession, possession and so much more.
The moon, the stars, the wind and sea.
More precious than those, most precious to me.
You were my world, my life, my heart
But then you ripped it all apart.

The tears I cried, that pain inside.
Those wicked dreams I dreamt each night.
Of me and you embarrassed so tight.
I'd wake, then break.
When reality dawned, you were not there and so I mourned
All over again.

Then winter came,
the birds are singing and people are living,
and so am I
I do not cry
For you
No-more.
R. Hargreaves

Harvest Moon

You shine on a silent earth
O Goddess of the sky
Making the dew shine like a hoar frost,
You shine on the golden corn
their heads bent in silent homage
Turning them to silver.
The owl stares unblinking into your bright face
as if mesmerised by what he sees.
And man, when they see your fair beauty
O Lady of the night
Know the harvest is drawing to its end
and the Autumn Equinox will be upon us
J. R. Smith

Our Friends

Raindrops fall on the ground,
On the leaves, all around,
In the morning, misty and cold,
Find the animals scuttling back to the fold,
Back to their mothers dear,
Who keep them warm, and take away their fears,
Through the trees the sun it shines,
That melts the frost left behind,
Clouds pass by, one by one,
Past the Autumn-wintry sun,
In the cold and dead of night,
Find hunters spoiling for a fight,
To hurt the animals that we love,
One by one, but it's never enough,
On this note I will end,
But these animals are our friends.
Simone A. Blewer

Old Big Eyes

I think I'll sit at home today and stay here in my tree,
The sun is awfully bright and it's hard for me to see,
When the darkness comes around, my eyesight very good,
I fly around on silent wings when passing through the wood.

I listen hard to little sounds that might become my tea,
Maybe a mouse, perhaps a vole, I'll have to wait and see.
Mice are fat, I like them best and love to take them home,
And turn them into pellets that are made of fur and bone.

Now Winter's gone, Spring is here, a mate I'll find for me,
We'll make a nest together in the hole in that old tree.
My spouse has laid a lot of eggs, I think she's done too much,
I'll have to work all day and night to feed that little clutch.

I have to break their food in bits to put in their beaks,
But just as soon as I feed one, the next lets out a squeak.
So dream of all the lazy days I sat there on my branch,
Blinking at the sunlight, dozing in a trance.

Now this won't do, I have to go, and catch another mouse,
Perhaps I'll catch a bigger one and give it to my spouse.
Our little offspring soon will go, there isn't any room,
And I can do what owls do best, that's hooting at the moon.
John William Lane

Now

Now is magic in motion.
Now is a strange trick of light.
Now is the God that is living.
Now is the fullness of life.

Now is the one thing that's always.
Now is a moment in flight.
Then has to hide in the unseen,
Because Then becomes Now on sight.

Now is the surest of certainties,
Here is the feelings within,
It's a pearl on the string of eternity,
That shines when we dance and we sing.

Now is the place where our vision,
Lights a space between future and past.
It's the ever present eternal,
That continues beginning at last.

It's a pebble that's dropped in the river,
This very instant in time,
And the ripple that touches forever is now,
And I can tell by my heartbeat it's mine.
William F. Collison

Reflections

I'm sitting by the window looking at the view
Of a snow covered landscape with some children running through
I smile as a watch them play with snow so cold
I too remember such events before I grew so old
Many times I think of then and once upon a time
And most of all I think of her my late sweet Caroline

But we ourselves were children to in our own delightful way
From time to time when playing around this I'd hear her say
Now all I play are memories plenty they may be
Amid this game I play alone yet there she's still with me
Play on, live on till the final whistle blows
Where the victor holds no trophy no rematch this he knows

Being born and growing old is something all must do
and loosing someone as I did, a love I can't renew
But sitting here and looking still, one thought is in my mind
Besides the pain of loosing love life to me was kind
I'm bold and old, tonight is extra cold
And going to sleep, I know it's now
The Lord tonight will kiss my brow
Richard J. Bradley

Wedding Day

Oh how my love overflowed for you.
On that day, that was our wedding day
For there you stood, with flowers of peace and white
Oh veiled vision, oh beautiful sight

My raven haired beauty that now is mine
With a tear of joy, I view the world with pride sublime
So solemn the vows we swore
So beautiful the dress you wore.
Glad now I am, that our hearts eternally entwine

The photographers lens captures beautiful memories
Of a day of blue skies and cool breezes
With our love sealed, of the joy in our hearts of the deed
 we have done
Now we go on, not as two, but one.

A. P. Moreno

Fluffy Seal

Splashing in the icy cold waters catching salmon and trout,
Watching the whale spraying clear water from its big wide spout.
Running from its enemy, the one with the shiny gun,
One bang off that object and off the little seal will run.
Hiding behind the iceberg the little seal won't stir,
The human can't wait to get his hands on the little seal's fur.
Seeing the mountain of ice to climb he did try,
Thinking if the human catches him he will surely die.
With the human behind him climbing to the top,
It was all so very slippery but the seal couldn't dream to stop.
The human was going to make him into a little white purse,
And for all the killers in the world he knew that human was the worst.
The human had him in his clutches the seal's dreams of
 escape was gone,
In the back of the humans trailer from day to night they travelled on.
The next day he killed a penguin and the only thing to see was blood,
Now it was time for the seal to escape, he went running as fast
 as he could.
I will kill a seal yet the vicious and angry human said.
I'll kill from day to night till I've made sure every seal is DEAD.

Samantha McKendrey

Remembrance

Remembrance day is here again
we sold our poppies
in the rain,
from door to door
from shore to shore,
each year we try
to sell a few more.
We remember the fallen
who were so brave
to lay down their lives
that we might be saved.
Please wear your Poppy with pride
as each one represents
someone who died

Kathleen Titley

Whispers

Thrashing beating gurgling waves.
Frothy foamy sway and sway.
The air smells fresh,
The wind blows free.
I hear your whispers.
That you love me.

I turn around and you are gone.
The wind lifts up,
It blows so strong.
The sand beneath my feet is wet,
I still hear your whispers,
The first time we met.

Elizabeth Harries

Wedding Day

Oh how my love overflowed for you.
On that day, that was our wedding day
For there you stood, with flowers of peace and white
Oh veiled vision, oh beautiful sight

My raven haired beauty that now is mine
With a tear of joy, I view the world with pride sublime
So solemn the vows we swore
So beautiful the dress you wore.
Glad now I am, that our hearts eternally entwine

The photographers lens captures beautiful memories
Of a day of blue skies and cool breezes
With our love sealed, of the joy in our hearts of the deed
 we have done
Now we go on, not as two, but one.

A. P. Moreno

Christmas Time

The days become short, the nights they are long,
Now that winter is singing her song.

The trees are all bare, their leaves have all gone,
The birds look for food,
The robin sings strong.

Frosty fingers, frosty toes,
Eyes are all gleaming, I've got a cold nose.

Christmas bells ring out, the children all cheer,
For this is their favourite time of the year.

The tree stands tall, all pretty and bright,
Do not make a sound, Father Christmas comes tonight.

This is the time Jesus was born,
There in a stable, on a cold winters morn,
He brought love to the world, so cherish him,
Be nice to each other, and welcome him in.

Marilyn Todd

The Shepherd

Old shepherd dreary, frail and poor, in bleak mid-winter's chill.
So many hardships to endure, upon the barren hill.
Come spread, Jack Frost, thy coat of white across that cheerless hill.
Blow winter wind with all thy might, the shepherd toils there still.
No elegant words, proclaims no learning, steadfast as a rock.
For pastures new he has no yearning, watching o'er his flock.
Tempest fugit and anon winter sheds his sting.
Old father time still marches on, blithe promises of spring.
For every flow must have an ebb, days now are growing long.
Hoar thawing on the spider's web, the blackbird's joyous song.
New-born lambs glad shepherd sees, as to and fro they run.
Crocus sways in gentle breeze, as warmer grows the sun.
Flowers bursting into bloom, sweet petals now unfurled.
For from his mind is winter's gloom, all's right now with the world.
All nature surveyed from on high, a wondrous sight to see.
Contentment money cannot buy, oh happy man is he!

Tommy Barr

Free At Last

I wish I was a bird in the sky.
Just dancing in the wind the freedom to fly
The feeling of the wind within my wings
My mind thinking only thoughtful things,
the feeling of flying free at last,
forgetting all the pictures of the past.
As I'm flying up above, I look around
Everything seems so small on the ground,
I like the feeling of flying up here
for in the clouds I've nothing to fear
Up here there's no traffic or children to tease
Just peace and quite, space, to do as I please
for the sky is free there's nothing around
Just the wind blowing is the only sound.
Nothing can spoil this feeling I feel,
but soon enough I have to land where reality is real.

Amanda Webster

So Alone

She had no father or a mother.
Not a sister not a brother.
She walked through the cold and dirty street
Hoping someone kind to meet.
The buildings were shabby and dilapidated
Dirty, smelling and so outdated
She was hungry, thin and so alone
Dustbins covered with films of mould.
She had not eaten since God knows when
What a pitiful sight was this child of ten.
Her clothes were soiled through lack of washing
Her shoulders racked with fits of coughing
She'd never known a father's charm
A sister's laugh a mother's arms.
She had missed this through no fault of her own
What a wretched sight was this lonely soul.
God she prayed let someone love me.
I'll be so good, please believe me.
   All alone, so alone
Would no one give this child a home.
Sheila Hutton

Tomorrow I Will Be Happy

Lying in the dark,
Not a light in sight,
No candle flickering in the night.
A replay of memories running wild in my mind,
Looking for an answer that I just cannot find.

A lifestyle which is terribly mundane,
I believe that I am going insane.
I must break free form this awful prison
To find just what I have been missing.

Tomorrow I will be happy.
Nicola Pike

Piel Island

A tiny isle, set in the sapphire seas,
no trees
to stir in the freshening breeze,
but a quivering of soft grass
and drifts of harebells everywhere
save where the ragwort supersedes,
or brambles spread their thorny leads.

Inhabited by sheep, o'er grown with thorn,
forlorn,
the castle makes a silhouette at morn
built of great blocks of sandstone red,
now worn with age
and, crumbling, tumbles to the shore
washed by the sea forever more.
M. Edith Rose

They Can't Help It

Those little calves they used to suckle
Now in those crates their legs do buckle
Lost all dignity now known as veal
Just to provide an unneeded meal

Transported miles in some cramped death lorry
For their thirst and hunger I feel so sorry
No longer in fields or with its mother
Now sentenced to a short life in which it'll suffer

I wish we could go back in time
For everyone to have an idea like mine
To set them free, to let them go
To watch nature and let them grow

Is it so important they adorn your plate
Please think of them for their sake
Are you prepared to make a stand
If we all did, this would be banned.
M. Colella

Untitled

Oh children-children slumber sleep
No time for you or me to weep
When British man can snuff your smile
And shame our once Great Nation with his bile.

Nobody gives a damn these days
When another child is taken away
All hell is let loose at first
But soon forgotten, as is a thirst.

String them up, get rid of the flotsam
They've forfeited their life by being so loathsome
The evil these men do in anger
Let's rid our society of their canker.

Why should society want to forgive men
Who take the life of small children
Do gooders, ask us to forgive them
I say no forgiveness for the flotsam

Either string them up, or throw away the key
Let them rot in hell for eternity
No getting out in their lifetime
Let the garbage rot, for their hideous crime.
R. J. Dawson

The Garden Of Stone

The woman stood in the grave-yard all alone,
no one to hear her heart breaking in the garden of stone
Looking around with fear and despair,
searching for her son, who was here somewhere.

Like so many other's, her heart wouldn't heal
The damage done by a bullet of steel.
They say time heals, well they could be right
But I won't forget you son, although out of sight.

We didn't have the chance to say good-bye
When I got the letter, all I could do was cry and cry
I convinced myself it was a terrible mistake
That God would spare me from this heartache.

So I pray to the Lord above
Look after him, and give him my love.
P. A. Whatmore

My Special Angel

There is a heavenly quiet place
No one knows quite where
That is blessed with a special angel,
Now that you are there.

This special angel is now at peace,
From this hectic world we are from,
And I was blessed by God I know
To have this angel for my mum.

So please dear God look after my mum.
Now she's in your keeping,
Tell her I'm fine and doing alright,
Though part of my heart is still weeping.
Lorna Annis

"Time Goes By"

Time is essence so they say,
Time goes by in the usual way.
Time does not stand still on stop.
Time is our whole world, time for thought
Every second means so much.
To share our happiness, sadness and such.
Time to heal, time to pray.
Time goes by in the usual way.
Precious moments to give and take,
time we can never make.
Time is great so they say.
Time goes by in the usual way.
C. Hickman

Baptism Of Blood

The blood had dried upon the wall,
No one had heard her plaintive call,
The knife had cut her throat so wide,
Satan's child drank from the crimson tide.

Her shopping trip had gone so well,
For that God fearing Christian child,
A brand new top, a pair of shoes,
A fresh cut throat to end her views.

The killer, he has struck before,
He snatched the child from a front door,
He cut her stomach open wide,
To get that sweet meat found inside.

So be aware of Satan's child,
If God you fear he'll sniff you out,
He'll cut your throat for that sweet wine,
Baptism of blood, your hell, his love.

Mark Carson

Never Give Up

Never give up on your hopes and dreams
No matter how impossible sometimes it seems
Determination to do what you want to achieve
Will come true, if you only you will believe
The faint-hearted just sit, and let things pass them by
You will never get anywhere, if you do not try
Be strong in mind and heart and have a go
Something may come of it - you never know
Don't wait for luck to come your way
Do something for yourself each day
It will surprise you to find out that you
Can sometimes change the things that happen to you
When things go wrong that you have planned
And everything seems to get out of hand
That's when you have to be strong and try again
If you are going to achieve your aim.
If you never give up, sometimes, to you it may seem
You are trying to reach an impossible dream
But hopes and dreams, do come true
Sometimes though, it depends on you

Lilian Morlham

Dark Eyes

I open my eyes, yet no longer do I see.
No light, just dark, all black it is to me.
The colours of the world, the living I saw before.
The life within my eyes is not with me any more.
I see with my ears and picture with my brain.
After all their still intact, I'm blind but not insane.
My eyes sleep all day, I am told the time of night.
But I think they would awaken if promised of the sight.
Don't get me wrong my eyes are still here, it's the vision
that has gone.
It's really just like the night time, lasting a bit too long.
The sight I see inside of me is probably better than real.
But I'd like to be the judge of that, by chance my eyes will heal.
Disappearing of my light gave no warning and no goodbye.
My grief soon turned to pleasure, as I realize they still do cry.
So remember look at good, look at bad, look at old and new.
For I pray to God that one day, me, will never be you.

Nicola Temple

My Valentine

I love the smile that lights your face
Love the warmth
Of your embrace - I love the
Voice that says "I care" - love
Each little joy we share I love
Your way of being sweet
Of making my life so complete
Understanding, as you do
(I love you just because you're you.)

Janet Carter

Mam

My Mam was a strong lady
No if's, but's or maybe's
She worked hard from early morn
Running a Cafe to keep us warm

No help, no hand-outs, just sheer grit
We wondered how she managed it
She never moaned or got depressed
She made sure we were smartly dressed

In our teenage years she still coped
And would not stand for those who moped
"Life is for living" she would say
"Get out there and make your way"

Her strength of character she instilled in us
We grew to be people who did not fuss
Whatever life sent our way
We coped, like she did, we won the day

Now we care for our children and grandchildren too
It's the old pattern nothing new
Keep your faith in the Lord and do good where you can
Life is worth living when you stick to this plan

Olive Loft

My Fading Friend

Her face has changed.
No filled, blushing cheeks
no bright green eyes.
Narrow bones and sunken holes,
shining through, only hurt and sorrow.

"She's a tower of strength", everyone claims.
Inside she's dying like a decaying tree
Her leaves are no longer green, they've
gradually tinged over years of resentment.

No words can heal her pain,
no medicine has hindered her illness,
insecurity is her disease.
No admission of self-destruct,
starved of love and attention, she also starved herself.

The invisible guard that surrounds her feeble
body can't be broken.
Her self-denial kills her soul, yet
the love she shows others overwhelms us all.
"A tower of strength!" or
A crumbling wall?

Karen Loughridge

"Your"

Your lips, your hips, your eyes, your sighs.

Your hips. Lush wat'ring place in which
　my loving bird doth drink,
　and think
　his fill content.
　And yet his love is spent.

Your lips. Full-blossomed lips
　I hushed
　with a tender kiss;
　not having missed
　that smile....Hah! Who needs words.

Your eyes. Bright eyes, twinkle eyes,
　Laughing eyes.
　I see in them my love.

Your sighs. So satisfied that sigh.
　"You were good my love". (lady reads this line).
　"Yes, and so were you".

　"Yes, and so was I..."

Your lips, your hips, your eyes, your sighs.

Phillip S. Manning

Who Cares For The Carer?

Given a choice how life could be,
No fantasy riches in store for me.
Just an ounce of happiness, one small reason to smile,
A new heart, not one broken for too long a while.
A home not a house, a family at peace,
Time alone not just lonely, from torture release.
A chance to receive instead of donate,
Expressions of care, not part of my fate.
A face full of laughter, not eyes filled with tears,
A heart fuelled with hope, not cruel piercing fears.
People around me in whom I can trust.
Sincere fulfilled promises, now most bite the dust.
Support from a family not lost to lives to their own,
Willing to spare time now their children have grown.
Action given too freely, now no spark from this plug,
Cast aside without value this once priceless MUG.
A yearning so simple, yet a cliff face so sheer,
To forge treasured memories with those I hold dear.
An out of reach dream, a mountain too high,
Each day less worth living, who really cares why?

Sandie Choat

Cardboard City

They live in cardboard boxes, the people without homes,
No families, no place to go, the streets they often roam.
They flock the soup kitchens, their one meal of the day,
The food is good, the welcome's warm, there is no price to pay.

Some may choose to live like this because of foolish pride,
But most are here through circumstance, nobody on their side.
No fixed abode then there's no job, no job, no fixed abode,
It goes around in circles, a never-ending road.

Desperation often shows in this endless sea of faces,
Wrapped up in cardboard houses, they have no airs or graces.
We all walk by embarrassed, as they hold their hands out high,
We'd like to think they don't exist so quickly pass them by.

J. A. Lawreniuk

Holy Island

Holy Island is the place to be
Nine miles of land surrounded by sea
Once called Lindisfarne with its priory.
The settlement for St. Aidan and St. Cuthbert too
Who brought Christianity to me and you.
The Castle standing proudly on top of a hill
For you to visit at your will
The wildfowl, wading birds and flower-covered cottages
And after the trip take heed
There's always the Lindisfarne Mead.
Yes, Holy Island is the place to be.

Paul Ives

Black Lace

Trees now you've shed your lovely gown
of green, red, yellow, russet and brown.
How tall and splendid you stand with grace,
In your winter attire of fine black lace.

Last night the moon was smiling down,
and touched with silver your black lace gown,
and shone through the pattern woven there
making black lace of your branches bare.
This morning a thick frost adds to your charms
like thousands of jewels held in your arms
a fairyland wonder, a beauty so rare
caught by your black lace and captured there.

Soon comes the spring and your black lace will show
bright green buds, like emeralds aglow.
And, later, with splendour your beauty is seen,
in a wonderful dress of fresh cool green.

M. Wright

Drought End

A day of sun, and heavy showers, ended as
Night came in on clouds as black as soot
The three day old moon, upright bravely stood
Tears from heaven once more will fall,
The clouds are full as they are tall
Racing in answer to the many rain dancers call,
For farmers whose crops could fail,
As hose and sprinkler, silent fall, as stop, go's the call
T.V. and radio send out the ban, across the land.
We know how to desalinate the sea, we build the plant
So why can't we, an isle, beset by water, use the sea?
Rather than let pipes erode in disrepair, waste our reserves
Is the Divi more important, to those who have the shares

J. Beard

A Mother's Plea

I stir through the fog of sleepiness,
never quite there, just on the edge.
How does she know, this baby of mine.
I'm just on the verge, perched on the ledge
of deep sleep, to be pulled back again
and again. PLEASE sleep, please.

She wakes, she cries, she needs me.
How can she know I'm so tired.
She needs my touch, my love, my knee
to bounce her on, to reassure and calm.
My breast for food, my arms to comfort
again and again. PLEASE sleep, please.

Sylvia Doggett

Don't Despair

If you are being bullied at your school
never forget this golden rule
don't keep quiet or be struck dumb
tell your teacher, dad or mum.
Bullies are people who think they're cool
but behind their image they're just a fool.
They've no personality of their own
they pretend to be someone else, someone who's grown,
they rustle up a gang who think it's clever to fight,
but when they're alone, they're not so tough,
am I right?
Take no notice of bullies is what I advise
they live a life full of deceit and lies,
As you go through life you better yourself
bullies you'll notice are left on the shelf.
If you're being bullied, don't despair
think of your family and friends
Who love you and care.
Don't let them beat you, is what I say
and will come the time when you rule the day.

Michael Patrick Williams

Lottery Blues

I've tried the lottery, without success,
Now I'm in an awful mess,
I've begged, stolen and borrowed cash,
for one Almighty sinful bash.
'Cos eight million pounds is a lotto win,
it would help a lot with the mess I'm in.
I would give some to charity's strife.
And to my friends I've known all my life
the kids would laugh and think it's funny
I'd double all their pocket money.
A new car, a house in the sun,
pay all the bills, and have some fun
travel the world and see the sights,
not caring if it's day or night
but for now, I'll dream of whenever
I'll pay my pound, and win a tenner.

P. R. A. Somerville

My Son Rocky

I touched your face kissed your cheek,
My warm breath fell upon your face,
Your eyes stayed closed no smile, no frown,
No movement, no sigh, no heartbeat not a trace,

You lay upon a bed of roses with satin lace,
My world stopped turning I just couldn't see,
This young man, so young just so cold and still,
The only picture is a memory of you upon my knee,

You were so young, happy lad full of love and hope,
The you lied down to sleep so still so still,
No hope for your future, your love has not gone away,
My heart still cries out for you it always will

Six years have gone by but in my mind I do Keep,
The special memories of you that will always stay,
A love a special love from a mother to a son,
Just wait for me Rocky for my special day.
Y. Clee

Safari Smells

The man on the corner
Near Mr. Magoo
Has told both my parents he's starting a zoo.
While he named all the creatures he wanted to keep,
My mum screwed her nose up a bit like a sheep.
My dad said quite calmly
And what of the smell?
The man looked dumb-founded
The odour - yes well,
The rhino is house-trained
The lion's quite clean
And most of the penguins.....
They'll live in the stream.
So if by some off-chance there is a bouquet
Let's all hope the wind isn't blowing our way.
Kay Allum

A Dedication To Mary

Queen and dearest mother, now without reserve.
My whole self I give you with love that wills to serve.
Take my heart and bless it: eyes and ears and tongue
Keep in your possession: Shield from wilful wrong.
Since you are my mother I belong to you
as your child defend me, watch over all I do.
Give me eyes to seek you: ears to hear your voice
lips to praise you always and in God rejoice.
Through your heart I offer each act of the day
Bless each joy and sorrow my work and prayer and play
With each Mass unite it: Make it more worthwhile.
as I journey onwards passing many a mile.
Mary Laurence

My First Love

Love, I thought, was a wonderful thing
I once fell in love and what joy it did bring
Love came from a man so full of grace
But our love disappeared to outer space
Wonderful times together we shared
I ponder on memories when I know he cared
I wondered why love should suddenly die
Couldn't we give it just one more try?
But love was over, and I knew
Now I want someone faithful and true
I remember how I'd always maintain
The level of hurt and the level of pain
Through my distress, what did I find?
Love is amazing, yet love is so blind
Continuing life on a sturdy lane
Love can be tested once again
Decency has to be shown to me
Love, care and trust; a priority
I'll give love to one who will be
Someone God-given; someone special to me.
Miriam Scott

By the Window

I sit by my window and look out to sea,
My thoughts travel everywhere but without me.
For I'm wheelchair-bound and my limbs cannot move,

Sometimes I wonder if life will improve,
Then sleep overcomes me and soon I am free
I laugh as I dance and I shout out with glee
I'm running and jumping and fooling about,
Then all of a sudden I hear someone shout,
She's coming 'round now has it been a success
A voice close beside me is whispering yes

So never again will I be wheelchair-bound
And though life is good, there is one thing I've found
Never again will I drink and drive
I just want to say
Thank you for being alive
Marian Connolly

My Passion

My passion is as a spirited wind
My thoughts ebb and flow in the hemisphere of the sky
High and low I soar
On the altitudes of ecstasy and fear.

These thoughts I cannot tame
Like a tempest they race wild in my soul
Incarnating my innermost being
Confronting me, constantly taunting me
With episodes of exaltation and destruction.

If I could shake off this form, my captivity
I would take to the heavens and drift
Effortlessly from sky to sky, to embrace you
Carried in a tempest of desire.
C. Treadwell

The Big Five-O

I'm feeling kind of weary and my hair it just won't shine
My smile's full of sweetness, but the teeth they are not mine

My face is full of wrinkles and I know I've got crow's feet
I'll slap on loads of make-up but surely that's a cheat

I think I must need glasses, as I can't see very far
Maybe I'll get some contacts, and keep them in a jar

Now my body's not that bad though it's far from being slim
I s'pose I ought to do something to keep myself in trim

My feet, now they're a problem with bunions, corns and gout
I wasn't in the front line when beauty was handed out

My hips and bones are aching and my legs have varicose veins
Is it me, I wonder, or does everyone suffer these pains

I used to have a waistline, but I sat and watched it grow
Is this all life has to offer now I've reached the big five-O?
Sheila M. Hillen

My Four Friends

My first friend stands before me
My second to the right,
My third he stands behind me
Protecting through the night

To my left I have another
As sturdy as a keep -
Something like a Brother
Watching as I sleep.

I know they'll always be there
Every single day -
Helping to look after me
Despite what others say.

As long as they're still standing
Erect and fine, and tall -
I will always feel protected
By my friends - four stone, brick walls.
Paul Cooke

Sam's Day

My name is Sam, that is for sure
My owners aren't rich but they're not poor
She says put Sam's coat on when it is cold
To keep the peace he does as he's told
Close to our house are some playing fields
We go for a walk there before my main meals
Five days a week she catches the bus
But if they miss one they don't make a fuss
He goes for his paper and while he waits to pay
I rush back to tell her we're on our way
When we get home I go and eat
He has coffee and puts up his feet
He has to do housework, oh what a bore
When it is finished we can go out once more
Out on our walk there are friends to greet
Whether we're in the fields or just on the street
Now we go home he has plenty to do
I'll just have a doze till she comes back too.
V. D. Guidery

The Only Way

Standing at the cliff top I am looking out to sea
My once loving heart has been wrenched out of me
My hair is blowing wildly, tears are in my eyes
My body is but a shell for my life and soul have died.

The reason why I stand here is I don't know what to do
I can no longer bear the pain of living without you
There is no-one to see me save the wind who hears my cry
And if you were near me then you'd only pass me by

  O tell me why you left me
  I loved thee faithfully
  Now the waves are drawing nearer
  As I seek eternity
Karena J. Key

Down The Road

I sit alone my head in hands
My office cold and bleak
I've just been told my job is gone
And have to leave this week

Is this a dream I ask myself
This cannot just be so
For thirty years I've worked for them
And now I'm told to go

What have I done? Why must I go?
These answers I must know
I'm told my age is fifty now
And I'm too old and slow

With one last look back at the plant
I walked out through the gate
It was no comfort for to know
My age had sealed my fate
Mary Flanagan-Quirke

Natasha

Long hair, dark eyes,
My Love, My Life, My Pride.
Radiant beauty effervescent
Love, Life, Kindness ever present,
Arms to trust, hold trust within;
A face to Love, holds truth unseen.
Strong of mind, yet hope unerring,
Weak for me, yet caring, sharing.
Patient, knowing, understanding,
The question why; define God's blessing?
Nature's art, pure, breathtaking
If time stands still, I'm here waiting.
My soul you have, love's benefactor
My life I'd give to you Natasha.
Perfection's here, I've seen her face!
Love has a name, a resting place,
She has long hair, has dark eyes,
She is my Love, My Life, My Pride.
Tim Jordan

Days Gone By

When I was a Boy, we would play in the streets
My nan would give me 1p to go and buy sweets.
Or run on an errand, and a 1p you'll get,
We would play with a tin can, two sticks on a drain
Tin, can, Tommy we called that game.
we would play in the sunshine and even the rain,
We did not get colds, and we didn't complain.

Then came the days out, with buckets and spades,
A tram to Stepney station, and jump on a train,
To cockles and mussels, at Southend on Sea,
We would have a great day, my sister and me

Then came the cars, the lorries, and bikes
Things seem to alter, and change overnight,
The kids go in gangs now, and holler and shout,
And make bad noises very late at night
They don't seem to play now, like we used to do,
give me the old days
  I don't know about you.
J. T. Howard

Glance

The hurt would go on no more
The steal glinting in the almost dark
The knife clutters to the floor
Of guilt, no longer even a spark

A cry of pain a sigh of relief
Warm blood tracing paths over skin
Cold hard note, secrets buried beneath
The last decision, the only way to win

No seconds panic, no moments regret
Pain at what was, not what might be
This life's destiny already set
Scars so deep, yet not anyone can see

Pain so intense, consciousness waivers
Last glance, possessions of a life so futile
Give her this one thing, she asks no other favours
One object that remains brings a final smile

Her lonely grip on life so mercifully taken
Bitter sweet smell the aura of death
In her conclusions of life was not mistaken
Another's treasured memories is all that is left.
Fay Jenkinson

The Visit

Mo-jo pippin and tog are we,
Ian's mum we have come to see,
We race through the house we cause quite a stir
Up and down stairs with a flying of fur,

We go in a bedroom the curtains we wreck
She says it's a good thing it's only the net,
We go to another the paper we tear,
His Dad says you cats had better take care,

We hide in a cupboard, isn't this fun,
They can find two of us but not the third one,
We escape to the shed to find a mouse
But they yell at us 'get back to the house'

We hope they're enjoying their holiday,
When they come back they'll take us away,
Back to the boring old house that we know
Where they find the places we'd think to go,

But if we are good maybe one day
They'll let us come back 'no fear' they say
  We'll see,
  Well maybe.
Sylvia L. Brazier

When You Are Near

When you are near, my world seems ever brighter
My problems and my cares soon disappear
I feel a sense of overwhelming gladness
That brightens up my life, when you are near.

I dare not thing about the days without you
The emptiness that fills my heart with pain.
I need to feel the warmth of your caresses
To hear your voice, to know you're near again.

The miles that stretch so endlessly between us
Seem further still with every passing day
I treasure every moment spent together
And dread the hour that you must go away.

Yet though you stole my heart, my very being
I wonder as each second passes by
Can I endure this bitter sweet existence
When every breath I take becomes a sigh.

Yes, somehow I will carry on without you
And brush away each sad, escaping tear.
Then spend each lonely day in thoughts about you
Just longing for the time when you are near.
V. Browning

Battle Scarred

The black knight stands her lance poised there, a victor surely with no feeling.
No feeling for the soul within that shrinks away much pain to bear.
A pain that stabs the very heart until sweet death would hold so smart.

A glint of black her steed is strong, her very presence is so wrong.
From death's depths the white knight rises, stumbling forward, courage
building in her stance, as if awakening from a trance.

Weapons are not here enough; the power within of time and love must decide the fate of all.
The black knight now must shrink away as thoughts of endless years and memories come in to call.
The white knight can conquer all.

In those bleeding hands no power, nor wealth, nor worldly goods
Just love, respect and courage stood.
Battles are not ever glorious one person never just victorious.
But in a battle hell like this God played His special loving
role and though my wounds they bleed and weep
this is now the time to sleep.
To sleep and dream of what can be as God in
His wisdom joined you and me.
Yvonne Moffat

June In January (1996!)

The engines were warming to prepare for our flight,
Then, quite gently, we pulled away,
The terminal building was soon out of sight,
We were airborne - and off on our holiday.

The runway was drenched, the skies were so grey,
For weeks we'd had nothing but rain,
Of course, it was winter but we were now on our way,
To the blue skies and warmth of the sunshine in Spain.

The Captain updated us via the P.A.
As to our flight time, our height and our speed,
But his forecast was rain - for most of our stay,
And we thought - "oh no, that's just what we need."

In two and a half hours, we were down on the ground,
We'd had lunch and bought our duty frees,
But the forecast was right, for when we looked all around,
It was teaming with rain - and the wind lashed the trees!

June in January was what we were after,
It was not a great yearning to roam,
And since there's no doubt - the best tonic is laughter,
Why on earth didn't we all stay at home!
George V. Scott

The King Of The Jungle

He walks around,
The wind blowing on his fur
But he doesn't seem to care,
He is happy,
His mate a cub has had
And now he is a dad.

His cub runs 'round so lively,
He pounces
And he bounces,
He runs around wild
So cuddly and cute
Eating flies that are minute.

Whenever there's some danger
The father will roar like thunder
And the little cub will wonder
Why?

Now it is the evening,
They will all lie down
And the king of the Jungle will take off his crown.
Agatka Warsza

Billy's Cry

The graveyard was so silent. The church was grey and still,
The whole world was in mourning the day they buried Bill.
It was a dark and windy night the rain was pouring down,
As poor old Bill came running back from a good night down the town.
He was down a poorly lit street, soaked through to the bone,
When a car pulled out from the thick black mist knocking Billy down.
The car it didn't care to stop it drove into the night.
And that was when the much loved Bill began his long-life fight
A passer-by who saw him lying cold and white
fled quickly to a phone box to help him win the fight
Alas, it was so much in vain for there was nought to do.
As poor old Bill had passed away in loss are me and you.
and now it's come, his funeral day, everyone is sad
for ceremony's completed now for that brave and cheerful lad!
Bernadette Shaw

Management Thoughts

If one is part of a management team
The way to control or so it seems
Is by making objectives that one can meet
So your aims are clear and don't mean defeat
Training is an essential part
Also appraisals straight from the heart
Sincerity is a major event
If staff support is to be a hundred percent
The form of management where I seem to fall
Is human relations - concern for all
Do not ask how I cope with this
When dealing with people, it's hit and miss
One cannot manage a successful crew
Unless one gives a lot of you....
Hazel R. Churchyard

To Precious

From the day you are born, from the moment of birth,
There's a reason for being, a plan for this earth.
May be theirs a map, or certain path way,
May be it's a test, we live each passing day.
We grow old and we learn, good from bad,
Trying to be happy, even when times are sad.
Ability to progress, pass each learning stage,
Just like a book, when you turn a new page.
Think of others, show compassion, willingness to try,
Lend a helping hand, before it passes by.
The learning process never stops, don't let it slip away,
For it is far to precious, to miss one day.
Debi Cullen

Serious Thoughts Of A Reflective Mind

Staring through the window as the traffic passes by,
Thinking of the changes that I'm making to my life,
Fate takes a hold of the present,
But the cup that needs filling is the future,
No more drifting from day to day,
Purpose must be integral to everything,
But who speaks for spontaneity?
How will the knowledge be obtained to use it?
Problems are always easier to look for,
Sadness is always simpler to find,
Must this be the root of destiny,
just because it has ruled the past?
The stand must be made,
Turmoil but a memory,
Calm descends, awakening reality just in time,
to marvel at the wondrous dawn
that breaks on the new life that beckons.
Brian Edwards

John

The room breathes of you, pale face on white sheet,
Thin outstretched limbs, glazed eyes, prominent nose,
   A faint stirring of life -
   Then you were no more.

I looked for you in your favourite seat, glancing at your work bench -
I thought I saw you there. Walking down your garden path -
   I fancied I heard your step,
   But I knew you were no more.

I gazed at your works of art - those dear birds with delicate plumes,
Loving carvings of living wood, landscapes created by caring hands,
   Slivers of colour cut and blended -
   Yet I knew you were no more.

All around me are things that you made, each one a memory,
and in their own way
Pieces of your life smoothed with the plane 'till they glistened
and shone.
   Yes, I know you are there
   For they say, "This is John".
Anne Richardson

Children

They make you laugh, they make you cry.
They're sometimes naughty, good or shy.
They'll melt your heart with a single smile
For one of their cuddles, you'd walk a mile.
They like to argue and also fight
You're always wrong - they're always right
They play you up and drive you mad
If Mum says no - they ask their dad.
They run around all over the place
With sticky fingers and a dirty face
It seems to be, that all the day
You're forever putting their things away.
At the end of the day, when it's time for bed
Upstairs you carry the sleepy head
As they snuggle down sucking their thumb
They whisper the words "I love you Mum"
When you hear these words, it's all worthwhile
And with a great big tearful smile
You forget all the naughty things they do
And gently whisper "I love you too."
Dawn Harvey

Amongst Trees

- Move quietly amongst trees and it may come upon you.
- Then you will feel the true joy that life can bring.
- To share this with another is a double blessing,
- Because the power of love is often also there.
- And with this common sense of purpose,
- The peace of God is yours, as from a prayer.
David Osborne

Temple Of Desire

Nobody wants me for me that I am
They use and abuse me, they slaughter the lamb
I am a temple
A symbol of beauty
They make me a God
And tell me my duty
I live for their love and hope to receive it
And maybe one day someone will release it
I do what they ask and try all to please them
I put on my mask it that's what will tease them
And when they are done I go back to my bed
And think to myself I wish I was dead
I cannot cry although I am sad
I can't understand why, maybe I am mad
I don't know your name
I don't even care
I just know your aim
As I'm left here bare
Danny Barson

Shopping Precinct

Arriving at daybreak,
They spewed cement over the fields,
Smothering the long silver grasses,
Sealing off the stream,
Banishing the myriad burrowing scuttling leaping squeaking
cowering -
Inhabitants of the hedgerow.

Then came the fumes, the fast food,
The tyres, the traffic jams,
Greed and grabbit,
Hunger dozing in doorways,
Screeching roaring slamming crashing dashing stunning
deafening -
Magnificat of moneychangers.

But already I hear
Willowherb spearing up between pavements,
Dandelions disporting in car park corners,
Buddleias laughing on the tower blocks,
Wild things waking stirring breeding seeding buzzing humming loving -
And, at night, down silent streets,

A fox walks.
Jill Truman

Families And Friends

Families come in all shapes and forms
They always think they are the 'norm'
They criticise and often holler
Then sometimes they don't even bother

But friends are friends, you can choose them
You must cherish and never use them
Never ever take them for granted
Always, always make them feel wanted

Friendship's a love like any other
It must be nurtured and worked on forever
Because if you fail and don't even bother
You will loose it, it will never recover

With your friends you can laugh and cry
You can be on a low and then on a high
You confide in them, they confide in you
At the end of the day friendship shines through

Now think about it and think very hard
Does your family mean you have to be on guard
So think very carefully and tell me now
How many are friends and for how long?
Anne McPhee

Untitled

They say memories are a wonderful thing
They never fade away
But who wants to live with things of the past
When you can live from day to day

Thinking back on times gone by
That will never again return
Only leaves you feeling sad
And leaves your heart to yearn

So always look to the days ahead
of happiness and pleasure
Leave the memories for behind
and enjoy life at your leisure
There's plenty of time to turn back time
When days ahead are grey
Always live for the days ahead
and not for yesterday.

Jason Holt

Tragic Hands

In a voiceless body he drifts among heartless shadows,
they do not see or care or know.
How could they in a dying world?
A world lying, dying and blooded by a million murderous hands.
Now with nothing more to see and walk upon
no green no sparrows no song,
the regret is aplenty and deafening.
A man with no home, with no goodness is no longer a man
but there is tragedy in those eyes
which cannot see the harm.
Today still shines. Tomorrow will fall.
Fall into their tragic hands.

Adrian Green

Our Eyes Are The Windows

Our eyes are the windows to the world,
They are the key to the mood of the soul,
Look deep into those windows,
And you will see a person whole.
They reflect the inner feelings,
That are not seen upon first sight,
They do this from when you wake up,
To when you sleep at night.
Our ever changing feelings,
Are shown through our eyes,
They show the feelings that are true,
For our windows never lie.

Anna-Marie Smith

Spring At Last

When I walk in the garden, I hear the birds sing,
They're telling me all of those wonderful things,
They're picking up twigs and making their nests,
They're preparing for spring and doing their best.

The blackbird is hopping and listening for worms,
It puts up a fight just look at it squirm,
The fight's nearly ended, the bad deed is done,
It looks for another it needs more than one.

The bluetits are bobbing from branch to branch,
It looks like there're doing a mating dance,
Their little plump bodies so fat and so round,
I hope next doors cat is no-where around.

The feeder is swaying about in the breeze,
It's fixed to the shed, just in front of the trees,
The sparrows are queuing all in a line,
Enjoying themselves in the warm sunshine.

Gillian Castle

The Singing

When she was walking
there seemed no, reason
no, none at all
for breaking off.
In her vision
her skirt was grass
her bones were branches.
When she sings, he said
there is nothing but
the song; white shifting void
and notes from a hole in nothing.
Through the vertical grey-filmed rooms
she sprang, through living beams
where windows stills sat empty;
but in all ways he possessed her
desperate that she should live

In him alone, her voice alone.
Yet afterwards, holding life
like water in his hands
she still ran free and was forgotten.

Alyson Stoneman

Dreams

In my dreams I am a beauty and the world is at my feet,
Then I awake, and back to duty - many problems yet to beat.

In my dreams wild flowers are blooming, scented air and skies of blue.
When I wake, rain clouds are looming - never mind, a lot to do.

In my dreams fine food and wines appear as if by magic wand.
In reality it's leftovers, of which I'm not too fond.

In my dreams I stretch my hand out and you are always there -
When I awake I'm on my own again with no-one there to share.

So I think I'll turn my life around and send it frond to back -
In my sleep I'll slay my dragons till there's nothing I can't hack.

Then I'll wake and let the dreams come in, and I'll feel young again -
I'll only see the sunshine, even though there might be rain.

The kitchen floor beneath my feet becomes a field of flowers -
I'll skip through every minute, not struggle through the hours.

The leftovers are "a la carte", the water tastes like wine -
And, best of all, in daytime dreams, your hand is holding mine.

You think I'll dream my life away? Perhaps I will, my friend -
But if it smiles me through each day, could there be a better end?

Gillian Bolton

Our Home Cares The Gems

The Home Cares who befriend us, what a lovely lot they are,
Their job is far from easy, their clients under par.
Most people greet them with a smile others grumble, "Where have you been?"
They do their best, their time is full, how can people be so mean?

They clean up high, they clean down low, all the places we can't reach,
They cook, they mend, they shop, they write, the loo gets its squirt of bleach!

They are so kind and caring, I recall days when I've been tearful.
Then in she walks, her usual self, soon has me bright and cheerful.

Remember they are human, have their families and problems too,
They don't let it show, they carry on and be there just for you.

So please don't call them cleaners, their task is much more than that,
I ask you please, for our Home Cares, go on and raise your hat.

Joan A. Tebbutt

185

Journey Of Dreams

Look to your dreams and discover
The worlds a magnificent lover
Buy your fears, they are worthless, your tears though justified, are too
So go on your journey of life my friend, and make all your dreams come true.

Carry with you no burden, no pain to unleash at the end.
Enjoy your wondrous travels, with yourself, your one true friend
Take caution to those who approach you, for you've suffered enough to be fooled
Shed yourself of your misery, and with happiness you'll be well tooled.

For the only thing that can take you, to the destiny you dreamed of so far
Is the strength that you found, along the bumpy ground and the shiniest, luckiest star.
To walk though the valleys of wisdom, as you have and made it right through
There's only one more requirement friend, and that is belief in you.

Amanda Jayne Davis

A Farewell To The Moon

Farewell to the moon
The witch with midnight hair
Who wears stars upon her fingertips
And a gown of frosted air.
Farewell to the moon
For she must go away
No more will she wander
Along the milky way.

"Farewell to the moon!"
The constellations cry.
A silver meteor falls
Like a tear across the sky.
Farewell to the moon
The seer waves her magic wand, and from beneath the bonfire smoke
The covens cease their song.

Farewell to the moon
For the cats no longer stray, into the wild witch wood
For they all have gone away.
Farewell to the moon, All Hallows Eve is past
Her timeless reign is at its end, her spells have long been cast.

Andrea Selina Thomas

The Sea

With a great stupendous roar
The waves break on the sandy shore
White froth that sparkles in the sun
And pebbles shifting one by one
We swim and play when summers here
And never have a moments fear
But in the deep with changing face
The waves ascend and start to race
They rise and fall relentlessly
We cannot trust the moving sea
Many men have met their death
When water takes their every breath
And yet we love to stand and stare
At yachts and ships and men who dare
To pit their strength upon its waves
The lifeboats and the men it saves
The moon and tides and setting sun
Will change the sea when day is done
We listen and we watch with awe
The glistening sea with waves that soar

Edwina Fooks

Untitled

Oh what is it to be Loved? Truly loved....
The warmth of an embrace?
The look that passes between eyes?
Knowing what someone wants, before they want it?
Being loved, not taken for granted...
Knowing that you're special, even if your physique has changed,
The wrinkles, and time, have taken over,
The wisdom of the years has enhanced, and not ruined what was.
Does it matter? Why should it matter?
That kiss is not a cold peck, but a searing warmth of passion,
Without expecting more, then...
Taking you for what you are, not what you should be,
And the reasons why...
Not longing for what can never be.
Oh what is it to be loved? Truly loved...

Julie Thompson

Capital City

A cacophony of sound invades the ear drums
The very air is moving on its way
A million feet are pounding on the pavements
As this big city starts another day.

Vehicles relentless in their purpose
Speeding wheels on every busy street
Trains below the earth in dim lit tunnels
All creating stifling city heat.

Towering buildings blocking out the sunshine
Lights in office windows all day long
River boats and thunderous airborne traffic
Adding to the throbbing city song.

Shopping malls awash with drifting people
An undulating vibrant human tide
Citizens who have one thing in common
A patriotic sense of city pride.

For herein lies the heartbeat of a nation
Its people knowing well it can withstand
Every foe that threatens this great city
Symbolizing strength throughout the land.

Eleanor West

Nightfall

Unnoticed, unchallenged, the hours gradually pass away.
The twilight hours proclaim the passing of the day.
The curtain falls, life's drama gets a brief respite,
And the players disappear into the darkness of night.
To a world of fantasies and dreams, to a life reborn,
Yet so short-lived, curtailed by the approaching dawn.
Whilst human mortals, now deeply engrossed in sleep.
Nature's vagrants on safari, so stealthily so creep.
Whatever their antics, they can never be too forlorn,
Their mission is accomplished long before the morn.
The Moon sits placidly, ignoring each passing cloud,
Sometimes enveloped, as if dressed in an Astral shroud.
Twinkling stars, with their patterns, set the sky aglow,
Reflecting this Panorama to those on the Earth below.
Asleep. Those of life's assets, alas which we forsake.
Are returned with interest when we do at last awake.
And as we gaze at the heavens appearing so bright,
Do we ever spare a thought for the beauty of night?

Frederick William Westley

Our Mistake

The moon, its surface hardly touched by life.
The sun so dazzlingly bright.
Earth, polluted by its inhabitants, a disgrace to its fellow planets.
Lucky Earth, he has had the gift of life bestowed upon him.
But it has destroyed him,
Slowly the disease spreads across him,
Self-inflicted, yet unrecognised,
Soon all life, human or otherwise is no more.
Once the most envied of planets, soon the most pitied.

Amanda Brind

Devil Pulls Your Strings

Don't wrestle with my emotions, know how things are.
The tricks that you pull have gone just a bit too far.
If I forked out medals you'd be back of the queue.
Of a thousand miles long, they'd be none left for you.

You were my angel, but you have now lost your wings.
I smell a rat, it seems like the devil pulls your strings.
Come down from the mountain and go back to your cave.
Who do you think your talking to, I'm not your slave.

A stickler of deceit, a liar and a cheat.
What a tangle you're in this time, it's no mean feat.
You have worked my soft centre to the bitter end.
You are very close to sending me around the bend.

So hollow you would disintegrate at the touch.
What I think of you? quite frankly not very much.
Can you honestly look yourself in the mirror.
Honour and pride? or would it be ranging terror.
John Neal

Wallace

As the war cry rang out and the battle pipes played
The treacherous treasonous traitors were paid
With title and land
And gold in their hand
To betray our hero and laird

Let the spirit of Wallace kindle the fires
That glow in the hearts of the free
Through the loch and the glen
And the old but and ben
The voices whisper to me

The voices of Wallace and the men that he led
Cry from the dust where they bled
Scots will stay free
They'll ne'er bend the knee
To any oppressor they said
John Hunter

Way Up High In A Hot Air Balloon

The wind on my face, the view down below
The Time seems at a standstill thought the refreshing cool air
The movement of the smooth white clouds, the mist covers the fields
But up in the air I haven't one care, with the relaxing wind is hitting my face.

Over towns and fields the balloon glides, the thrill of way up high
the way the clouds shadow me, and make me feel so light
Floating up high with the freeness of the sky,
The thrill of floating over towns, fields and sea, way up high in the sky

The curve of the horizon, the sun setting on the sea,
Small sparkles of the street lamps glitter out at me, the view from way up high
The smell of the salt sea, the great green mass of forest trees
As I drift down slowly over the town and fields, floating down in the breeze

Waiting for the small gentle bump of touch down
The wind has now died, the sunset has arrived
While other watch and linger, an end of sheer beauty will arrive
So the bump that I am waiting for soon will arrive
Abigail Evans

To a Loving Daughter

To a loving daughter
The tears you shed were turned to pearls
By the prayers you said for me
Then taken as a bribe the gods
Extended life for me.

But when one day those pearls revert
To what they have to be
May they be tears of deep content
For the joy you gave to me.
Jim E. Brookshaw

Cutting The Lawn

Waking up early one bright Spring morn,
The sun was shining, I decided to cut the lawn.
Getting out the mower, from inside the shed,
Found I had to give it a clean, instead.
So then I got down, onto my hands, and knees,
To clean out, all the old grass and leaves.
Now the mower was, nice and clean,
I then decided, to cut the green.
When all of a sudden, something shot out in Front,
It was a large frog, which did make me Jump.
I saw it hop merrily, into the Glade,
Where it wouldn't come to any harm, from the mower Blade.
So after working hard most of the Day,
I then cleaned the mower, and put it away.
Dennis Calvert

Nature's Golden Glow

As I sit in the warm meadow's sunny glow,
The sun shining brightly so - I reflect on life's
Pleasures that I know nature's warm and marvels glow.
The tree's so majestic and tall - as old as no-one can know.
They are there as high as they can go.
Wide and green and billowing from bough to bough.
The butterfly he flies around and he glides
alone without a sound - so beautiful a creature
to behold blue and green and colours untold
Small ones and large ones as they unfold.
All nature's wonders to behold.
There for all to see.
There for you and for me.
God's bounty to behold.
Carol Howard

My Life

Another day dawns
The sun is shining bright
I've got no enthusiasm for the day ahead
Try as I might

People everywhere are rushing around
They're so lively and full
I sit back and look at myself
Why is my life so dull?

I give my all to people
I give them all I've got
But they just walk all over me
They leave me here to rot

Only I can change my failure of a life
It's all down to me
Where to start, I don't know
That is what I can't see

I could give in and end it all
I would, if I dare
If I did, the question is
Would anybody even care?
Billie Deans

Synopsis

Living is the hardest of all trades.
There is much to be afraid
Of in a life;
The twisted knife
Of anger in a soul
Can gash a jagged hole,
While played out here within an empty heart,
The saddest, self-deceiving part
Of one who thought he acted in a play
But never knew what he should do or say.
There's mortal danger lingers in the call
Give me your self,
Or give me naught at all.
Clement Murray

Ode To Winter

The Hedgerows are all tarnished brown.
The sun is on the wane.
And a blustery chilly winter wind,
Blows dead leaves down the lane.

The Hydrangea looking lonely now,
Once had blossoms big and lush;
And although they are all faded,
They are still clinging to the bush.

The Hollyhock near the garden wall,
Its leaves are turning grey;
And the cold and frosty morning mist,
Is moulding it away.

The Rosebush is all woe be gone,
It is withered and quite dead;
And the barren earth seems to mourn,
For those blooms of deepest red.

But all nature's beauty is not lost,
There is gold in the waning sun;
And silver sparkles in the late night frost,
Now that winter has begun.

Edith Garcia

"When"

We met in the Spring, when the world was new
The summer was magic, with skies so blue,
You had to go, the question was - when,
When will I see you again?

My heart it went with you, I cried and I cried,
The Fall came, then Winter, when everything died
Life held no purpose, when you didn't say when,
When I would see you again.

Spring came, and once more the world was new
Our love was rekindled, and oh so true
With so much happiness, and no more pain,
Now that I've seen you again.

Jean Hunter

Bridges

Silent communicators standing in solitude,
The stalwarts of the landscape,
Sometimes shielding troubled waters,
Stages to untangle muddled minds,
Stairways to stability when the time comes,
Offering new dimensions to a falling stone,
Seeking reflected images echoing at me,
Rippling into eternity.

Jane Bush

The Snow

As the gentle, soft snowflakes, fall
To the frosty clump off snow, below,
The snowballs are thrown,
It feels although the time has stopped.

The sun comes out, over the frosted sky,
The sun beats down over the snow,
As the snow turns to slush,
The sun has a special glow.

The frost hard and cold,
Lying on the window ledge,
Sitting by the roaring fire,
Everything frosted over, the cars, the trees, the hedges.

The sun is breaking,
The snow is gone,
The frost has disappeared,
And once again, our snow vanishes.

Adeline MacDonald

Summer Thoughts In Winter

The fog hangs low, the air is chilled on a bitter winter's morn.
The spruce is coated silver, and on its cones thin ice has formed,
The earth has hardened under foot, the berries laced in ice,
In leafless trees some hungry rooks seem fixed and loath to rise,
the countryside's in winter's grip, the first snowflakes begin to fall,
On ponds and pools the ice forms thick, the icy wind brings shivering squalls.

In the midst of frost and fog, I think of summer, May and June,
When butterflies are on the wing, and bats go hunting 'neath the moon,
When the swallows build beneath the eaves, and in the meadows they're making hay,
And trees unfold their new young leaves, and the cuckoo's heard through merry May.

But here I stand in frost and fog, and summer's but a dream,
The dreary winter marches on, the silent flakes fall clean,
Beneath the snow white carpet laid, all growth is dormant yet,
The wondrous view by Nature made, a silent scene is set,
But summertime will come again, with blossom, bud and leaf,
With winter's grip long gone past, I'll walk the untamed heath.

Finlay Shiner

I Only Hear Me

In a world that is silent, I cannot hear;
the sounds that come in through the door.
The birds in the trees, or the echoing breeze.
   I can't hear them any more.
   I can't hear them any more.

In a world that is silent, I cannot hear;
anything that is near.
My mum calling me, or the cat up the tree.
   I can't hear any of that.
   I can't hear any of that.

In a world that is silent, I cannot hear;
My world is clear.
With music I can't sing, or hear the church bells ring.
   I only hear me.
   I only hear me.

Helen Glover

Untitled

Today of all day's, a day of changes. The day that things were not the same anymore, the day that made you feel, as if nothing was real. If the clock was turn back what could you do, these are only thoughts. Thoughts that make you wonder and feel sad. It's a sad day for you, only you know how you feel. Cry if you must for that will release the pain in your heart. Don't forget that this day, of all day's was the happiest day. For someone who love you so much and who wish, she could be there for you. She is with you, you don't have to look for her anymore. She is within you. Please try not to feel sad, for she is free and happy. She will always be there for you in spirit. She will always watch over you, I am sure she wants you to be happy and not feel sad, because she has gone. She creates the path for you to lead your life, a wonderful life for you, so do not fall apart now. Don't let her teaching and guiding go to waste. The bound of a mother to her son is forever even if the chain is broken. Remember she has gone through another path, she is creating and waiting for when you will be part of her chain again. She hasn't really gone forever, she is waiting for her chain to be join again. This is your time to make a choice, only you can do that. I am your friend but one day I might not be here too. Things can't be forever, things have to change, so has to give the other things a chance to experience what we have. Be happy within yourself, only you can do that.

Clara Akpokomua

Untitled

Music to thine ears is like glory to thy throne;
The sounds are enthralling, tremendous, warrant applauding.
Who can compose such melodious compositions
To warrant the attentiveness and overwhelming
   memory - recording and repetitiveness,
Of the melodies one loves so much.

Man requires and upholds such godliness or
   worldliness appreciation;
To the music-makers whose brilliance inspires nations
Of people, to listen in awe of the sounds
   which cannot be explained
To the listener, but are recalled in the memory forever.
   Eileen Smyth

I'm Blessed

Curtains are drawn it is not yet dawn.
The snow flakes fall upon our garden wall.
The trees stand tall.
Soon our Robin red breast will appear.
It brings me so much cheer.
The cheeky grey squirrel is here.
It's always first to appear.
The blackbird with its orange break as just taken a peep to
See if nuts apple and bread have been put out.
The thrush, blackbirds, blue tits, magpies and the wood pigeons
Know there is food about.
I hear a cuckoo too, there is food for you!
The wild fox or rabbits must have eaten the carrot peel that I put out
I'm blessed to have such faithful friends, there is no doubt.
Thank you Lord now they have all been fed I am off to bed.
   Hilda France

Horror Of Trust

The night was calm and still.
The smell of peace lingered in the air.
Gentle was the touch upon my hair.
The hand of friendship and trust,
Changed to horrors of trust.

The night became tense and heavy.
The smell of lust hung in the air.
Rough was the touch upon my shoulders.
The hand of friendship and trust,
Threatened to horrors of trust.

The night became close and airless.
The smell of rape smothered the air.
Hurtful was the touch around my wrists.
The hand of friendship and trust,
Raged to horrors of trust.

The night became dark and cold.
The smell of betrayal clung in the air.
Weapon's was the touch to my body.
The hand of friendship and trust,
Tools to horrors of trust.
   Caroline

Lissadell

Oh, Lissadell, Oh Lissadell
The secret of your magic you will
   never tell
The Mystique of your walks
   through your leafy dells
The Haunting echoes of the children's yells
The sound of the lap at the water's edge
The splintering sunlight, peeking
   through the trees
Alighting the pathways, scented
   by the Breeze.
The magic is captured in the quiet and still
The wonder of all, your golden Daffodils
Their sprightly heads, their majestic dance
Touches the senses at just one glance
Oh Lissadell, and your Daffodils
Your secret magic haunts me still.
   Eileen McDonnell

The Flow

Transcending the page in the mind of change
The reader cruises the ink highway
With no horizon in range
Although very much alive, but at the same time, dead
The reader is no longer, because the shadows have fled the head

The poem is an engagement of the reader in the flow
But the poet who doesn't know it, sadly doesn't know
But the poet who does know it and therefore knows he knows
Is a poet who does know that it's a flow you can never know

In the end, there ain't no end
So let's begin where there ain't no beginning
Because the only thing, is nothing
Just the flow in endless spinning.
   John Gracey

Nightfall In The Vale Of Clywd

The westering sun has gilded fresh-cut corn,
The placid fields merge now with distant hills.
A whisper floats from rain-filled mountain rills
And brooding o'er the pass a mountain's drawn
In profile gaunt. Until another dawn
A darkened sky the velvet backcloth fills.
Such beauty is a cure for all men's ills
And smooths from furrowed brow cares yet unborn.

The daylight fades and frees the liquid night,
Thin tongues of mist lick at the valley's line.
From moon and scattered stars there falls a light
To flood this picture of a dream divine.
Dear God, did ever man view such a sight
And not believe the Artist's brush was Thine?
   John F. Allan

Time

Time within its raw state means nothing but everything,
The perceived concept in its entirety remains complex.
For some, it may destroy, for others - represent,
but for everyone, it alters.

Unchanging in form - yet changes all forms,
Continuous in existence - yet uncommencing.
Time, clearly a unique and solitary unit, we witness for a lifetime.

Never has such an 'untouchable' concept caused such poignant changes,
Uncomprehended by those who challenge its question of ontology.
Its unsatisfying, irretrievable form provides tiers of values,
'For time waits for no man'.
   Joanne Baker

It Only Hurts

It only hurts a little bit
The pain will dim in time,
My shattered dreams will mend and I'll forget
This broken heart of mine.
It only hurts when I'm alone,
Or when I think of you,
Or when I sometimes hold my pillow
The way I once held you.

I never said "I love you,"
I thought that you would know,
I should have known you needed words
To make the music flow.
If only I had shared my dreams
Before you went away,
"If" might have been the word
That might have made you stay.

But "if" is only make-believe
To mend this heart of mine
It only hurts a little bit
The pain will dim in time.
   Brenda Higham

Gloss

An ordinary woman dreaming of heights
The pages extolling the virtues of highlights
Of lotions and potions, gargantuan notions
Walking the catwalk, the glaring spotlights
"Slimming for sex!" but staying alone
Answering quizzes, "why he won't phone!"
Cooking like Della, a la mode on a plate
Balsamic vinegar, "make fennel look great!"
A large pad in London overlooking Hyde Park
Never lonely in bed (at least while it's dark)
Shopping at Fortnum's and oh Havey Nicks!
More than a job, she's leaving at six
The latest eyeshadow, the perfect lipstick
Herb drinks and fruit teas that make her feel sick
All this and more, the perfect ideal
But she's on the corner in Soho
Trying to earn her next meal.
Carey Wren

The Rag Doll

Christmas is over;
The old rag doll is slumped on a shelf.
She sits; a sad expression on her stitched face.
Left to gather dust.

She knows that, when the brand new Christmas toys break,
The little girl will play with her once more.
But she also knows that when Daddy has mended the new toys
She will be alone again; left to gather dust.
Catherine Bradley

The Wino

The winter nights are drawing in
The old man sits with a bottle of gin
His clothes are shabby, tattered and torn
No smile on his face he looks so forlorn.

The park bench, will be his bed for the night
People pass by, then go out of sight
I wonder what will become of him
When he's finished his bottle of gin

He'll sleep it off then wake again
Get a fresh supply and drink the same
Life as a wino must be tough
When you never know if you've had enough

I wonder why he's in this state
Alone and cold without a mate
There's lots more like him along the way
What can we do for them, we say

Perhaps one day he'll be taken in
To a home for old folk and won't need gin
They will give him a bed and food that's warm
And keep him happy and come to no harm.
Hilda Bussey

The Beast Within

He runs to the window and looks up at the sky
the night was coming soon it will be time.
Time for the moon to rise up high
time for the beast which would terrorize.
The demon seed that occupies his soul will be
released to take its toil.
The clock struck 12 the moon was high.
He runs to the door and locks himself inside.
He walks up to the table and picks up the cross
hoping the silver object would protect man from loss.
He clenches his fists and falls to the ground for it was
time for the beast to go out on the prowl.
So lock your windows and bolt your doors and hope
the beast will spare your souls
for if you live through the night the beast will return on
another moon rise.
Arun Sharma

The Time Traveller

Timeless time and time again,
The machine a tool to aeons tame,
He makes folding space a child's game,
As worlds collide and stars aflame.

He's seen the fall and rise of Rome,
On Jurassic shores the seas a-foam,
Read many a long gone sacred tome,
Forgotten where or when was home.

He's seen the future bleak and bright,
Armies old and modern fight,
Great empires fall as overnight,
Leonardo's first attempts at flight.

He's seen the start and end of man,
The secret of God's master plan,
As no one should in mortal span,
Unless bend the laws of physics can.

Timeless time and time again,
The machine a tool to aeons tame,
He makes folding space a child's game,
But can't his sanity reclaim.
David Geoffrey Addiman

Gemma
(Pantoum)

"She is my gem, I call her Gemma," thus spoke young mum Emma.
The midwife with care delivered the baby, the anxious father was there,
How could she say that the baby wasn't normal? The midwife was in dilemma
Eyes were slanted, the nose was flat, sparse was the little baby's hair.

The midwife with care delivered the baby, the anxious father was there,
Hands were broad, there was just one crease across her each little palm,
Eyes were slanted, the nose was flat, sparse was the little baby's hair,
The mouth was small, the tongue protruding but Emma was brave and calm.

Hands were broad, there was just one crease across her each little palm,
Down's syndrome - she was a mongol that's what people would say.
The mouth was small, the tongue protruding but Emma was brave and calm.
An extra chromosome - she would be therefore, slow to learn or play,

Down's syndrome - she was a mongol that's what people would say,
"I don't care how other babies look, Gemma for me is the best,"
An extra chromosome - she would be therefore, slow to learn or play,
Emma just smiled and held her baby close and tight to her chest.

"I don't care how other babies look, Gemma for me is the best,"
How could she say that the baby wasn't normal? The midwife was in dilemma
Emma just smiled and held her baby close and tight to her chest,
"She is my gem, I call her Gemma," thus spoke young mum Emma.
Amitav Ghosh

The Winter Mountains

The early morning mountain mist,
The low lingering valley frost.
The sky is darkened with unfallen snow,
And just a flurry of frozen snowflakes,
Search their way through the cold dark sky.
In this silent winter white wilderness,
The river flows sluggishly by,
And freezes as it cavorts,
over the frost bitten fragile stones.
The grass and plants,
At the river banks edges,
Are now an eerie shade of brown.
A slight breeze stirs the mountains,
No birds will sing in this unsociable region,
Such a bleak and unpleasant time.
Darren James Goodman

Silence

Listen! Hear what the silence has to say; the thoughts that
 emit from the leaves as they sway.
Words of wisdom drift on the breeze, solidness and peace
 emanate from the trees.
The slug oozes calm along with its slime, as nature oscillates
 from the plain to sublime.
Truth exuded like sap from a beech and peace, like its
 branches, is within our reach.
Spiders weave intrigue, webs immense; silken threads casting
 chaos to sense.
Listen! to the birds as they sing with mirth. Feel below the
 strength of the earth.
Energy passes along rays of the sun. Bees ever mindful to get
 their work done.
A scene no longer black and white but full of colours;
 nature's delight.
See the hues as they're never been, observe the abundance of
 colours called green.
Realize that it's not as you perceive, as in your inner self you
 believe.
It's all the same, but totally changed as concepts and ideals
 become rearranged.
The word from each leaf is very clear but only, when silent, its
 message you'll hear.
 Alison Tong

Untitled

How much we take for granted, I can see and also hear,
The joy of conversation, tender words of love, so dear.

The gentle purring of a cat always give me pleasure.
This is yet another sound which I enjoy and treasure.

No laughter, music, no singing birds, not a single sound.
How very lonely life must be, with silence all around.

Dear God I do appreciate all You have given to me,
May I use Your gifts as You would wish and so follow Thee.
 Barbara Chappell

The Forgotten Children

The Rumanian winter, a dark freezing cold night
The innocent forgotten street children are out of sight.

They are living in the sewers below our feet
Underground in the stench, pitch black, steaming heat.

Sleeping on pipes for warmth, squeezing into any space they
 can make their own
Sniffing glue to relieve hunger, block the reality of the living
 hell, now their home.

Filthy rags, scarred damaged skin, sad faces, heartbreaking
 beautiful eyes.
Sleeping strange hours, wandering the streets, scavenging, begging,
 while the darkness covers the skies.

Clang of the manhole cover echoing into the bowels of the earth,
Terrified, apprehensive, crawling down returning to their berth.

Can you imagine being so filthy no one wants to cuddle you?
Wary of strangers, malnourished, bereft of feeling, high on glue.

Suffer the little children have pity on them,
Neglected, no future, no luxury of growing old, living in their mayhem
 Dorothy Moran

My Intentions And My Cats

Out from the fridge the beef to slice
the fridge door closes.
No time to carve, feet run downstairs
'round the door two noses and faces that
 say it's theirs!
The pleading looks - they'll get their way
It's called persuasion or blackmail
Somehow you have a feeling
Sandwiches are off today
and thereby hangs a tail.
 Angela Moran

Untitled

The ghostly life I live,
the haunted mansions of my mind.
The spinning drops of liquid
fire, the incandescent ruminants
of laughter, the bolshevik remnants
of sleep. Each night I drift away
to the land of savoy waves.
To be sure of nothing, I lie
in naked rapture - lost forever
to gamble along wasted bedsides.
Never to know happiness, to vault
jugular veins of indifference
to long for so much - to achieve
nothing! To fall below depressing
scales. To slip down slopes of
utter vacuity. To taste the pits of life.
 Adrian Phillips

Children Singing

In the middle of the village
The grey-stone school has stood
For nigh two hundred years or so.
Heart of the neighbourhood.

And through those years, with voices
The dusty rafters rang
As children laughed and squabbled.
But above all, they sang.

Sang 'Clementine' and 'Richmond Hill,'
Sang 'Creatures great and Small.'
Sang all the songs that children sing,
And the walls absorbed them all.

The village school is closing now,
Converting to a home.
But it won't give up the singing
It has stored within its stone.

So when the dusk begins to fall,
Through the low wind murmuring
The people who are living there
Will still hear children sing.
 Jill Peck

Crisis In Africa - East Meets West

Awake my child to a brand new day
The ache in my heart will not go away;
For I know that I have nothing to give
And but for you, not the will to live.

For all around I see dead and dying
Starvation, hunger and children crying;
Unable to understand the reasons why
Their bellies are empty, their cup is dry.

Their tender years have known no other
Way of life like their Western brothers;
Who wake each day full of anticipation
A different race, a difference nation.

My child my heart breaks for I cannot feed
I am too weak for your simplest need;
But can only lay down by your side
And feel desperation I cannot hide.

For I see time slipping away
The help we need has not come today;
And without this there can be no tomorrow
Sleep in my arms child, escape from your sorrow.
 Beryl Wagner

The Message

No fish in the river, no life in the sea
The forests are bare, no birds in the trees
No love in the world, no peace on this earth
This poor world is crumbling, it's sentenced to death

What's the solution to all the pollution
What's the reason for all the conflict and hate
Are we blinded by greed for the power and the riches
That we won't see the danger before it's too late

Half the world is starving, while the other half's at war
While millions die from hunger, the same will die for power
Since time began it's been the same, as time goes on it will remain
No lessons learned, no wisdom gained.

The answer is we are all to blame
We must stop the world and change this game
And to have a future free of all despair
Let us love and care and share.

James Clarke

The Fighting Flame

Strike a match,
The flame will light,
To transform the candle,
Into life.

Gleaming glowing,
The flame gets fierce,
To stab the dark.
That it wants to pierce.

The flame pirouettes and twirls,
To turn the dark into light.
A tear rolls down its melting body,
Halfway through the long long night.

The candle flickers while it fights,
In an ocean of boiling wax.
The flame burns to the candle's base,
Leaving behind no traces of cracks.

People blow,
The flame goes out,
The flame burns no longer,
Now there's no-one about.

Christopher Young

The Disco

I went to the disco with Joan,
The first time I had been allowed to go alone.
We dressed ourselves up, both thought we looked great,
Promised Mum and Dad we wouldn't be late.
The lights were fantastic,
The music the best,
We danced all the time
Put our talents to the test.
When the time came to leave
The night was dark and cold
But as sixteen one must do as ones told.
So we ran all the way home
Scared of the dark.
At school tomorrow what a story we'll tell,
Of the disco, the music and of course the boys as well.

Jillian Smith

The Coast

Living at the coast as I
The beach, the sea, the wind, the sky
Seeing the waves, and the sand
Only part of this island
Seeing the ships that sail by,
The moon and stars that light the sky
Hearing the wind and stormy rain
Blowing sand around again,
Knowing the beach and coast are near
Makes me proud that I live here.

Andrew Brady
Bacton

Devotion

Words always fail me when I need to explain
The emotions that rise from your anxiety and pain
I hurt when you hurt and I'm blue when you're blue
Whatever you're feeling I'm feeling it too
You're never alone when you might think you are
I'm right there beside you. I'm never too far
You're my life and my world and I hope you can see
I'll never find anyone better than thee
Times have been hard. It's been quite a strain
Things start looking bright but we always get rain
We argue like hell yet I can see clear as day
I could never love anyone else in this way
I may not be worthy of a place in your heart
But I know mine would break if we ever should part
My heart is devoted solely to you
I've no means of escape so I'm begging of you
Look after it dearly, it's not made of wood
Although I would carve our names if I could
This leaves me with only one thing left to do
And that's simply to tell you that 'I love you'

Craig Nicholas Shorland

Hearts And Dreams Broken

The air is clear
The door inviting
Birds singing
Flowers blooming
We have come to stay
But ala's here is torment, heartbreak, and despair
The days grow longer
The time goes slowly
When will that door close behind us
Our dreams will be lifted
Oh' for that door to close behind us.

Janet Childs

For Marie "Home"

January is here again,
The cold begins to bite,
Our Summer seems light years away,
As we dream of some respite.

Your dream may be a far off land,
With sun drenched beach and golden sands,
The harsh truth of the dream behold,
You can't escape the icy cold.

You see, no matter who you are,
Your secret we all know,
If you could find a warmer place,
Then you would surely go.

Alas, I must confess my friend,
I often seek to roam,
But I never mind the weather,
Because the place for me is home.

George Thompson

My Blue Oasis

Your smile, the curves of your mouth turned up when you smile,
The curves of your body, the shape and fitness
Strongest moments enhance when you pull me towards you.
The smoothness and tenderness of each kiss.
The deepening of your mouth, tenderness and touch so strong.
To me this means my blue heaven awake me.
The sweetest burning feeling when I lay awake in your arms.
To feel you is to believe in you, and touch somewhere in your soul.
The stronger feel the stronger our souls will get.
You are my everlasting strength.
Your beauty is within you.
Your eyes say it all.
They lure the power, the excitement
And a heavenly body of bonding and togetherness.

Jackie Pusey

Little Rose

We waited to have you our little angel child,
The day that you were born our hearts just burst with pride
You were really perfect from your head to your tiny toes
A lovely little flower, and so we called you Rose

We watched you blossom through the years
Each day we loved you more
The baby years passed quickly
Then suddenly you were four.

Your birthday party over you asked, "can I go out to play"
How could we know a pervert waited to take our flower away
With broken hearts we waited the time was "oh" so long
Then the policemen came and told us our little love was gone

When we heard the awful news we just cried and cried
But our lives were really shattered when we heard
the horrific way you died.

He took our little rose bud threw her petals on the ground
Broke our hearts forever when he took our jewel from our crown
So parents guard your children for you never know the day
When an evil minded pervert
Will snatch your child away.

Annie T. Murphy

The Joys Of Life

Life as such unexpected joys as these,
The dappled sunshine through tall trees,
The drifting clouds across the sky,
Such lovely shapes as they pass by.

The babbling of a woodland stream,
And pink roses on a hedgerow green,
A skylark's song as he flies up high,
And patches of bluebells like a summer's sky.

The sparkling cadence of a waterfall,
And scent of honeysuckle on trellised walls,
A blackbird on a lilac bush,
And the evening song of a missel thrush.

The arch of a rainbow after rain,
And blissful ease after pain,
The hidden treasure in a tiny seed,
And kindness in another's deed.

The beautiful sunset at day's end,
And welcome sound of the voice of a friend,
How wonderful when we can say,
I found beauty, love and God today.

Edna Hay Helps

First Love - Spring '58

It crouched there - looking old and grim,
The chrome all tarnished, and grotty trim.
One lamp was askew, the other one pitted,
And none of the doors really fitted
On the old '39 big seven.

Her wings were battered, she was rather rusty,
Her tyres were worn, she did smell musty.
"She needs a good home and some tender care",
The mechanic said. But would I dare
Shell out for the old big seven?

The garage said I could have it for fifty,
(And in those days I had to be thrifty),
So stationed there looking weary and tired
And rather pathetic, and hardly desired,
Was the old '39 big seven.

I knew I'd be taking a bit of a gamble,
But made up my mind - without much preamble,
A thorough clean, and a good overhaul,
It really repaid me - twas fun - dash it all,
That faithful old Austin Big Seven!

Brian Fisher

"A Time Of Good Will"

Staring out my window at the glowing snowy scene,
The Christmas lights are shining bright and the land looks
    white and clean,
But I must say across the way is a city silhouette,
And in those streets poverty sweeps among young and old I bet.
There's always been poverty always been shame,
Always been pleasure always been pain,
There's always been suffering again and again,
We have to take action we have to set free,
All those people in misery,
Christmas means to me a turkey and a tree
With loved ones friends and memories all piling on the calories,
But to them Christmas is no different to any other time of year,
For when poverty is present it leaves no room for cheer,
So we have to take action we have to set free,
All those people in misery.

Elisha Jane Willett

Dreams Dying And Waking (Heart Attack)

I wonder while we dreamed our dreams,
the chores all done, the children sleeping.
Did our sweet Angel shed a tear,
to see the clouds toward us creeping.

Like 'Sleeping Beauty's own good fairy,
our Angel held the final blow.
Pain and Weakness, sad adjustment,
These walked with us, well to know.

Through kindly help, we can now see a light,
The paths we tread bring dreams again in sight.
Our Angel bans depression from the door,
Like others, we tread life's way once more.

Diana L. Towner

Winter Cometh

The leaves from trees are falling.
The branches bleak appear.
It is the new one dawning,
The ending of a year.

The sun sets on horizons cold.
The days are chill and damp.
We have the heating turned up high
And early light the lamp.

Tomorrow's world holds brighter things;
But, first, we'll have the snow.
In warmer climes the birds will sing
Wish we could also go!

Gillian Bush

A New Beginning

As snow and frost are receding now,
The birdsong seems to increase,
They welcome warmer, brighter days,
The cold sharp winds now cease.

Life has a new beginning and all is urgent now,
Time to make a home for young,
In burrow, earth and bow.

The blossom bursts between fresh leaves,
The plants push through the earth,
Once it was to hard to break,
But now it yields new birth.

Can we ever cease to marvel,
At nature's wonders here,
When our spirits are lifted at this time
With the blessings of spring's cheer.

Jennifer Smith

The Gift Of Music

Tell me, how does one describe
the beauty of a melody
to someone who can never hear
black and white notes in harmony?

The quick succession of a scale
along the keyboard's path ascending
or the journey from major to minor
weaving itself into themes unending.

Those who hear can tell apart
the clipping of the notes staccato
from the smoother dulcet tones
of notes played firmly 'ben legato'.

As if in a Pianoforte Concerto
with each movement our feelings can change
from pensive, andante to allegro
as one covers the keyboard's whole range.

As we reach the final cadenza
to that tune we wish would not end
we thank God for the brilliant composer
who left us so much, like a friend.

Joan Zambelli

Take Time

Take time to look behind the smile,
    that tells you all is well
The loneliness that it may hide,
    is very hard to tell
Take time to listen to the words,
    when they tell what might have been.
Take time to look into the eyes,
    and read the tale between

For a smile can hide the deepest heart ache
    with a longing to be heard.
    For a kind soul just to listen,
    and be concerned of every word.
    For smiling is a way of saying
    Please will you be a friend
    Then I'll be glad to listen to,
    your story without end.

Jill Wiseman

On The Farm

The coos that run around the braes,
That's whit the countryman says,
Thank ye ya sheep who gives up ye'r fleece,
The rope tha' ties tha' horse is lease,
The moose the lives beneath the floor boards,
Aye he has such sharp claws,
There's a snorting pig that lives in the pen,
From bull to horse,
From cock to hen,
The animals wake one by one,
An come to greet the morning sun.

Billy Renwick

Mother's Instinct

I walk around my local town and observe
The actions of others, some clean and fine
Whose life on paper is in an order they deserve
But reality is vast from those of whom divine

I observe mothers talking, engrossed in everyday matters
It overtakes the importance of what they have laboured for
Nine months and how many years the calendar clatters
A youngster strolls under a wheel, a life no more

Gone, all that effort and all that pain
A future generation cut down, a hero unsung
Words are not the only things cast in vain
So are lives, however young.

Barry Lee Walker

Sleep

Sleeping the sleep of the new born,
The babe of the soft rosy hue,
Sleeping, smiling, dreaming
Of her wonderful world so new.

Sleeping the sleep of the innocent
Relaxed and happy from play.
Sleeping as only a child can sleep.
To wake fresh to another new day.

Sleeping the sleep adolescent
With scares and worries and joy
Sleeping and fervently dreaming
May this life I have found never ploy.

Sleeping the sleep of a woman
With worldly trials in sight.
Sleeping, but not always soundly,
Through the long and oft weary night.

Sleeping the sleep of the aged.
When the cares of the world have flown.
Sleeping forever, that heavenly sleep.
When the Master's called her Home.

Dorothy Harkcom

The Tryst

Deep in the meadows by the chalk-born Avon
The ancient house lay lapped by crystal water.
The grey stone balustrades were hung with tumbling roses,
And ribbon lawns were shadow chased by fleeting clouds.
Around the roofs the scimitared swifts flew screaming in the sun,
And the mad cuckoo echoed to the rounded downs.

I still recall the beauty of that day,
And turning, hope to find you standing there again.
But no quiet footfall sounds along the paths,
Nor gentle laughter carries on the wind.
And yet, across the years our hands should touch
In loving recognition of this lovely place.

Clare Luckin

Cumulus

How many there are who look but fail to see
The beauty of the sky's amazing artistry.
Look up and see great lakes of sapphire blue
And shadowing the sun for a moment or two
Across the heavens unhurried and free.
Huge billows of myths and fantasy.

From whence have they come and where will they go
These mystical creatures, as white as snow.
Like ships a-sailing across the sky,
And chariots and horsemen riding by.
Fantastic shapes beyond the sculptor's skill,
Move quietly on, and never still.

Look up again and wonder at what you see,
And know the meaning of 'tranquillity'.
By unseen forces urging them along,
Great towers of silence stealing on
And on and on into infinity.

Christine Day

Meditation

I sit at night and meditate.
Some people sit and complicate.
Being pessimists all of the time.
Never stopping to draw the line.
Never rising above the confusion.
Never being part of an illusion.
Always seeing the darkness around them.
Always blind to the love that surrounds them.

Edna Hodgson

Blossoming Love

I am the rose of you my love
The apple on your tree,
And as the apple tree is the centre of the orchard
So you are the centre of me.
I want to clothe myself in your nudity
And lose myself in you,
Your fruit is sweet to my taste.

I am the rose of you my love
The lily of your valley,
And as a water-lily floats upon a pond
So you float within my heart,
You make my heart sing with a thousand voices
And with each of these voices, I whisper, I love you
I wish I could catch you in a jar ..... Like a butterfly!

I am the rose of you my love
The moonlight around your sun,
And as the moon shines in the still of the night
Silently, softly,
Petal by petal,
I open to you.

Christine Hammond

Worth Saving?

A lump of meat,
That's what they see.
Instead of a young horse,
At home by the sea.
The ferry to France from the harbour or bay,
Instead of a field and a net full of hay.
A fistful of cash that's all he is worth,
And soon his bones will be one with the earth.

He's really no bother, he's really no fuss.
We really should save him, really we must.
But he's only an animal, he's only a horse.
We'll have to leave him, show no remorse.

A lump of meat,
That's what they see.
Instead of a young horse,
Nature's mystery.
The journey with others, all of his kind.
A high pitch whinny. Human swine.
They know what is happening, really they do.
And their low pitch grumbles blame me and you.

Andrew Kirk

Space Race

Why don't you park sideways on?
That way you could fill three bays.
Instead only two have gone
For one car!

Do you imagine you're berthing a battleship?
Is it the "Ark Royal" you're aiming to place?
Don't you believe you can spare
Us a space?
Don't you care?

Perhaps you just like to feel the white line
Under your prop shaft, in neat equilibrium,
Balanced about an imaginary fulcrum,
As if on a tight-rope, tensioned and fine,
Existing, proving your power, telling the world:
"Here I am! Look at me, semi-divine,
You can't deny me, you are humdrum;
I have two bays
For one car -
My car!"

Alan L. Hersh

My Son!

Three pounds fourteen ounces of pure joy.
That was my one and only boy
Big blue eyes and blonde hair.
Oh how the passing people stared,
He was all I ever dreamt he'd be
My little man so much to me
I remember his face set all firm.
As he got his mouth round a wriggly worm
Then the first tooth did appear.
He took a chunk out of my left ear.
Sleepless nights with the colic,
At the time I thought diabolic,
For all this I would not swap at all
the nicest son, now big and tall,
He's grown good and grown well,
Someday he will have his own tale to tell,
Someday I hope he'll find a nice wife,
Then he may get what he gave my life,
Lots of pleasure, lots of pain.
But a wonderful son all the same.

Diana Cullingford

Missing You

What is it I've done so wrong
That makes you stay away so long
I miss you more and more each day
I love you more than I can say

Every day I sit alone
Hoping that you come back home
Wishing you had never left
Then realizing perhaps it's best

You tried so hard to be my friend
I let you down right to the end
I did not meant to cause you pain
My love for you drives me insane

Now you've gone I feel so lonely
I wish you could have loved me only
My heart is broken ripped in two
Because I've lost a friend like you

I've herd is said that time will heal
And talk away this pain I feel
I don't see how this can be true
Because I cant stop loving you.

Jamie D. McLellan

The River

The river runs cold with the breath of life
That startles the new born child to a cry,
In swirling eddies of fragile hopes,
Exhaling a soul with a silent sigh.

It sweeps along those who have loved and lost
In numbed arms of ice and tides of fear,
Leaving their pain to glint in the sun
And shatter on rocks like crystal tears.

We glance at reflections in its mirrors of light
In the dazzling calm of a surface emotion.
The undertow dredges the mud of deceit
In a cascade of pity and lies and distortion.

We flow in the wake of our current of dreams
That streams from the soul until eternal and dry,
Then surrendered to shallows of life's fluid time
In slumber's immersion we ebb and die.

Catherine Heenan

Time

What is time? That indefinable thing
that really is not there - and which we cannot see
for if we say, as many do, what is the time?
That moment has already gone, as it had never been.
For we ourselves are fleeting visitors - in Gods great scheme so vast
like specs of dust that float around, and only show that we are here
when lit fleetingly by sunlight shafts.
'Tis said, that if we try to fly - the infinite voids of space
to get to other worlds, and find another race,
we must perchance, traverse old time itself
to find perhaps ourselves.

Howard Wallace Gibbs

Who Will Take The Blame

Isn't it sad, what a shame
That our society is to blame,
People out there supplying ecstasy
Really totally baffles me.

Have they no shame or even a care.
Is it just that there's money out there.

To see so many young people die.
Leaving their friends and family to cry.

So to all the youngsters across the land.
Don't let death take you by the hand.

Averil Witherington

Angel On A Cliff-Top

Lift me up to those lofty crags
that only the sea birds can reach
Where no human foot ever did tread
and the wind-mastering birds make their downy bed.

Let me soar and on spotting a morsel
swoop down and gorge on my prey
Let me sit on the back of a dolphin
and listen to what he has to say.

Make me rear my young juvenile children
Help me to bring to the nest our food
Join me in looking all around the sky
watching my brothers glide two by two'd.

I am by the sea
high above your mortal ground
Man may rule down there over me
but here, not a sound, not a sound.

Ashley Rowell

Seasons

What is this teasing of softness in the air
That makes life trembled in anticipation?
Shyly, but with growing confidence
Spring's joyful delicacy and flare
For pristine loveliness is here.
No bashfulness as motors summer throws
A Joseph's coat before cur jaded eyes;
Colours urgently jockeying for position
And glorious perfumes, for who knows
How long this artistry will last
Till first a gradual and subtle shift
Begins within God's palette and the harvest
Like a ripe voluptuous woman
Flaunts herself, showing off her gift,
Before autumn fades, and creeps to hide
Beneath implacable winter cold.
Rain that chills the blood, and hail
Smarting, stinging 'gainst, arrogant and bold,
Till teasing softness tempts again.

Ann Jackman

The Penetrators

Beneath a soft, blanketed, virgin bed,
tentative tentacles furrowed,
through fungus, fossilized foliage,
into dark chasms of the primeval past
and tranquil fluids stirred.

Furious white horse warriors fought,
smashing, intrusive hollowed legs,
with thunderous, spluttering sprays
and the mist shrouded giant shuddered.

Huge pipes clattered and clanged,
red limbed roustabouts toiled,
on the mud-splattered, wind-swept drill floor,
and Mother Nature's, bilious, gushing gasp, was heard.

Howling hurricane screamed,
as black bursting clouds,
fanned the flame flattened flare
and wet suit workers fled for cover.

Prevailing winds abated, stormy seas calmed.
Guardians no more.
The great capped well was sealed.

John Fagan

The Traveller

I came early through the lanes
That far-off summer's day, treading softly
As a stranger should, when entering a place
That has existed long before he came
And will continue after he has gone.

Secure in timbered frame and weathered stone,
The village slept, its season - ordered life
A strength and shield against the world.
And, as I look the path up to the hills, it seemed
That Time, itself, was waiting there for me -
I, the only living thing, until the smallest sounds
Of early dawn began to stir the silence all around.

I lay, content to watch the pearl sky
Change to clearest blue, while strengthening sun
Spread out its warmth, like some great healing power.
Time stretched out and out; daylight lingered on
Beyond its span, and I, beyond my time, craving to belong.

At last, I went my single way, with laggard steps
Until, that most magical of sounds, the calling of an owl.
Gave strange companionship and reassurance that the
  solitary are never quite alone.

Audrey Ingram

This Is The Hand

This is the hand
that ate some bread,
that ate some cheese,
and made it sneeze.

This is the hand
that had a dog,
that made it bleed,
and had a lead.

This is the hand
that had a clock,
that rang a chime,
and spent a dime.

This is the hand
that squashed a chicken,
that had a rat,
and made it flat.

This the hand
that ate some bread, that had a dog,
that had a clock, that squashed a chicken,
this is the hand that never gets lost.

Charlotte Cross

Tears Of An Angel

I sit by my window time slowly goes by,
So I watch the tears as they fall from the sky,
From the eyes of an angel they flow evermore,
And I watch as they fall to the cold stone floor.

I remember the times I held you so tight,
God how I wish I could hold you tonight.

I sit and I stare at the thousands of lights,
That twinkle and glow on these cold winter nights,
But they're not as bright as the stars in your eyes,
So I look at the angel and I watch as he cries.

I sit and I listen to the howling breeze,
Sing a lullaby sweet as it blows through the trees,
It's calling your name but there is no reply,
So I watch as another tear falls from his eye.

I remember the times I held you so tight,
God how I wish I could hold you tonight.

I believe in angels for I know they are real,
And the tears they cry I know how they feel,
So I sit by my window each night we're apart,
As that angel is here, right here in my heart.

Ian Deal

This Window

This window has become my world, since paralysis was at me hurled.
Thank goodness folks have been so kind, it could be worse, I could be blind.
The milkman is the first one on his way, for him an early start each day.
The postman when he brings a letter, makes me feel a whole lot better.
Such a little lad delivers the paper, and all these break-ins, wish I felt safer.
School children quickly scurrying by, my school days, how they make me sigh.
The workers next, they're always hurried, whatever makes them look so worried.
Neighbours call as they go to shop, what would I like today - a chop?
It's on them now I must rely, without them all who would supply?
Behind the glass I feel the sun, if only my legs would let me run.
A girl goes by, call that a dress, she surely couldn't wear much less.
I feel quite sleepy, will have a nod, who's that waking me with a prod?
Oh, thank goodness, it's a friend, with some books she has to lend.
She tells me all the gossip, should she make some tea?
A suggestion with which I always will agree.
It's twilight now, I'm all alone, but then I have the telephone.
The lights are lit now in the streets, I see the lovers outside meet.
Oh how I envy them their youth, but really if I tell the truth.
My life's been good, I've had some fun, the battle to exist I've won.
And through the glass the world goes by, I'll watch it till it's time to die.

Beryl Caddy

Always

He will be with you always
That is all you need to know
His love will always be with you
Where ever you may go
While travelling on life's journeys
You may stumble or may fall
But the Lord will always walk with you
Just listen to his call
He comes with voice so quiet
He comes with words of peace
So men may live as brothers
And wars at last might cease
He'll come to call each one of you
People great and small
No one shall be forgotten
if they listen to his call
Remember if you follow him
He will be forever yours
The Lord will be for always
A name to be adored

Barbara C. Boon

Untitled

Alluring passion sets deep in the night
tempting to tantalise an unquenchable thirst.
Driving, devouring a burning desire
to touch, mould sensuously teasing,
manipulating the seething skin.
Mouth watering, craving to taste
The smooth pure creaminess so satisfying,
fulfilling the ravenous appetite.
Relishing the pleasure, overpowering ecstasies
fulfilling a lust so complete.

Intense passion silently controlled.
Delicately divine, a discovered intimacy
flaming bright, flickering tentatively in the
seductiveness of the enchanting moon light.
An inner-understanding that renders the night,
capturing wondrously the seeds of delight.
tenderly entwined, the love is blind.
The sun which shines through the light of the day,
Signifies our love as one that shall never fade away.

Jade E. Dutton

Wall In Time

Limestone, Sandstone, Gritstone or Granite
Technology by-pass, 6000 years span it
Bonds down the ages, none of them chemical
Spurn barriers laser, fences electrical
Man's skill and raw mineral,
dug from the soil.

Supported by buried, unseen foundations
Set on the earth by organic endeavour.
Lockstone and chockstone, binding the courses
Through stones linking the random faces
Bounded and capped by finishing topstones.
In dry stonewaller's jargon
The C-word's forbidden,
whisper it softly
CEMENT!!

Fred Robinson

When The Daffodils Bloom

Tears will turn to joy
Tears will disappear
Sorrow soon will be no more
Changes are in the air, joys will soon be here

The daffodils will bloom again
Its yellow flowers opening to welcome
The warm rays of the sun
Beauty will be all around
The yearning soul will be at rest.

No more tears, no more fears
daffodils bloom, wither and die
But my spirit will remain
tranquil and free
When the daffodils bloom again
it will be for me.

Cecilia G. Fraser

Star Maker

Would these dreams were darkness. Black.
Sweet slumber to thy grave;
Whence peace, a happy vigil keeps
O'er shadows, once enslaved.

Yet, freedom dares such sorcery
As this, unspoken name;
For life is yet the spell you weave -
My heart, the prize you claim.

Would love were this triumphant shore!
Loathe destiny - goodbye
Fond spirit. Fly, for thou art his;
One wish, so cometh I.

Donna Prime

In Praise Of Sparrows

Folk in high places with knowledge of such things
Talk of declining numbers of these tiny creatures with wings
But my garden and hedgerow - sadly so small
Is a hive of activity and haven for all

Twitchers know sparrows as little B.J.'s
Hardly worth noting on bird watching forays
But look very carefully at each tiny one
All different, marked beautifully, so perfectly done

Such gymnasts as they hang on the feeders and table
Devour peanuts, seeds and scraps as fast as they are able
They fight and they squabble fly up and fly down
No space in the bird bath when they are around

Oft there are 50 together on the garden lawn
Pecking and scratching - starting at dawn
The tits and finches gave up long ago
My garden belongs to the sparrows - and don't we all know

Such a noise, such a chatter, such a multitude of sound
A hedge full of twitterings as they all go to ground
The light of the day is fading so fast
The feeding for another day is over - at last.

Ann Englert

Tears After Dark

Small child so innocent, lost, sad and alone,
taken from security, only place she had known,
Mother immortal attendant upon God, she who'd cared,
small child suffering in silence, fearful and scared,
miserable dwelling, step mother solemn, callous and cold,
a chilling existence, for one five years old.
The coming of darkness, the door locked tight,
little child crying in the dead of the night,
neglected the child, once in her father's life,
forgotten the memory of his once adored wife,
locked in his own world unable to mourn,
no thoughts for the child, imprisoned till dawn.
No more white ribbons and silky soft locks,
discarded the teddies and the pretty pink frocks,
no more ice creams and sweet apple pies,
abandoned the outings in the Summer blue skies.
A sign, maybe hope, a mother's soft words,
longing for freedom, to fly with the birds.
To show her existence her name carved on bark,
small child so innocent, sheds tears after dark.

Colleen Hatherley

The Skinhead

Doctor Martins, tight jeans, funny looks from passers-by,
T-shirt, bomber jacket, earring, hair dyed,
Is he on drugs, does he sniff glue?
Do you shy away when he comes close to you?

You all have him sussed, you see them every day,
A thug, a thief, wasting life away.
He ignores the looks as he strides along,
They won't remember him when he's gone.

Through the hospital gates and still people stare.
What is a skinhead doing there?
'He must be there to see a friend'
Is the only reason that springs to their minds.

He doesn't care, he's used to it,
He just gets changed to do his bit,
In his nurse's uniform he enters the ward,
The smiles from the patients are his reward.

Be careful, through life, who you judge on sight,
You may be wrong, you may be right.
But if you're wrong, let me just say
He may just have to nurse you one day.

Andrew Shepherd

To A Pessimist

Death, and debt, and desolation,
Swallowing the entire nation.
Murder, rape and anguished screams.
Everywhere is sad, it seems.

The way you talk, all hope is gone.
I have to let you know you're wrong!
For every minus, there's a plus.
For each of them, there's one of us.

For every death, a child is born.
The darkest night precedes bright dawn.
For every loss, there will be gain
And sunshine always follows rain.

For every wrong, there is a right.
For every 'can't', there's always 'might'.
For every teardrop, there's a smile,
It has to make it all worthwhile.

When you are drowning in despair
There'll always be someone to care.
Yes, heartache touches everyone,
But, look! Beyond the clouds... a sun!

Clodagh Kendall

SLEEP
for those who have lost

Let sleep close your eyes till the new morn awakens.
Surrender all thoughts and the cares of today.
Forget all the heartaches that clouded your daydreams,
let the soft wings of peace waft your troubles away.

Dream perfect dreams of all that you yearn for;
climb magical, mystical paths to the moon.
Drift slowly away to an island of pleasure
with sun-kissed white sand by a purple lagoon.

Circle the stars on a rainbow of colour
then flutter away on a butterfly's wings
or walk leafy lanes hand-in-hand with a lover
to a crock full of gold while a nightingale sings.

Sleep, only sleep, will soften all sorrow
for loved ones you've lost guard each step of the way
and it's only in dreams can you hold them and keep them
till the angels of dawn steal them softly away.

Donis R. Muir
Gretna Green, 2 October 1988

Prelude To Spring

The Cuckoo sounds the alarm for Nature, awake and arise
Suddenly, spring has come with bewilderment and surprise.
Darkened shadows of a long chilled winter fades
As life inhales breath between tall green blades.

Delicate innocents of life are newly born,
As the Crocus peeps its head to colour the Dawn,
Spear-like petals appear from a long winter sleep
Piercing a sunlight ray to the buds from the deep.

Dancing spangles glitter across the river run,
Winking bright eyes, like gentle tears from the sun.
Clinquant crystal raindrops, reflecting like a star
And a tall proud yellow meadow, waving from afar.

Primular posies add pockets of charm in the clough,
While the blackbird and thrush nests in the brushwood rough.
The alerted fallow Deer, flee from the glade in a flurry
And their dapple bay fawns, from the thicket scurry.

With the pasture land and meadow turning a deeper green
Delightfully, the bluebells carpet the woodland scene.
The tender light and pastel shade that it will bring,
Mellow tones the warmer days of early Spring.

David J. L. Mallard

October Sunset

Going home along the lane wet from recent heavy rain
Suddenly, before our eyes, a miracle which filled the skies -
A blaze of colour surrounded the down, across the fields
 toward village and town.
Flame pink on orange, brightest red, soft rose, wild smoky
 grey, palest violet, deep blue.
Rich shining gold, silver so rare - was there a colour that was
 not there?
Black silhouette of bird on the wing, stark outline of poles and
 wires that sing.
Reflections in puddles grew quiet and still as shadows
 lengthened over the hill.
The colours all darkened and faded away and slowly the
 evening took over from day.

Ellen M. J. Day

The Thought Of Someone You Love Who's Going Away Forever

Will you find another love such as this,
Such as you've known,
Which has grown out of friendship and warmth,
Now forever gone. The last farewell,
Words unspoken, silence - but what is there to say,
 Does it matter anyway?
The final touch. The last caress,
Lingers on your fingertips. Sweet taste of lips,
She turns and walks slowly away,
 Does it matter anyway?
Gone forever. Now, a mere shadow in the distance,
Yet only moments ago she was everything,
Everything in life, your dreams. Now dreams of yesterday,
 Does it matter anyway?
Life is so short. Life is so cruel,
Yet beautiful when love is in your heart,
Now a loneliness fills this space,
Which was once filled with deep love,
Sadness and heartache. Tomorrow brings another day,
 Does it matter anyway?

George S. Johnstone

True Love

A story of love is beginning, in a chapter not
strange to relate, when as a boy; will turn
from a toy - meeting that girl, at the gate.
Oh what bliss, that first kiss. Walking and
talking together. Entering a kingdom of love.

A story of love has no ending, in a kingdom of
love you maintain, when each precious stone;
will add to a throne, outlasting the days of your reign.
Oh, what joy. Tied to a buoy. Sharing and
supporting each other. Still building that
kingdom of love.

Arthur S. Battey

Missing You

It's a long time since the day,
That Angels came and took you away.
And still, I don't know how we coped.
Even though we sat and moped.
It's strange that time has gone so fast,
It seems like yesterday that you past.
With your stunning look, and beautiful hair,
Why did you go?...
It's just not fair.
To leave behind a family so great.
But it was time to go, maybe fate?
You were the one who really cared,
Everything you had, you gladly shared.
We know you are still here in spirit and mind
So open your heart and you will find
The only thing we can send above
To you, we send 100% true love.

Donna Green

Brief Interlude

Exotic land for just one week
Strange culture quite bizarre
Oriental stunning location
Time passed like a falling star

Argued with an arrogant king
Chatted to a royal queen
A crown prince kissed my hand
How unrealistic was the scene

My accolade for all to see
A velvet night made for romance
With powerful and commanding voice
The king asked "shall we dance"

Two hundred people perhaps more
Cheered as alone I stood
One brief moment's happiness
A triumph for our drama group

It's back to basics, very sad
Who has burst my pretty balloon
Next season where to venture
Perhaps South Pacific or Brigadoon

Flora Cameron

Glamour

Down by the tired river,
Still charming in its lounging silky elegance
Like a naked drunken bride
Wrapped loosely in her transparent wedding veil,
His girl sleeps on a riverbank.

Her cheeks pale and wet with tears.
Mother's angel dress
Of dewdrops, cobweb, and diamonds
Cling roughly to her dirty stomach
Once again.

Glowing firelight curls of hair
Sweep the damp grass;
Small spiders stay there,
Secure in her state of desolation.

Elizabeth Page

Jo's Secret

I never was the child I wanted to be,
so now comes the time I feel nearly set free.
I am only human like everyone else,
so Jo come on and look after yourself.
I'm sick of self-punishment and sacrifice too,
look at yourself in that mirror, that's you,
What do you see, a person so sweet who's
kind, gentle and loving and nearly at peace.
Find your own identity and work it out
and that's what it's all about.
I who now has got to come first and think of number one
which is not too difficult, it can be done.
I am feeling happier and gaining confidence too
so come on Jo and just be you.

Jo Ellis

To You, My Son

One day, I gave you life my son and knew you would be strong.
So take the life I gave, and live it full and long.
For know I love you always, wherever you may roam
So far away across the sea, many miles from home.

If you should ever need me, of this you can be sure
I will always be here, until, I am "no more",
When I cannot touch your hand, I will always touch your heart,
Because, I think you know my son, of me you are a part.

June Lee

Snowdrops

Snowdrops growing in wild profusion,
Stepping near seems an intrusion
Into their idyllic scene
Wherein I can only dream.

February skies grey above,
White flowers as graceful as a dove.
How do they survive the rain
On stems unbroken by the strain.

Opal white and subtle green
First of the Spring to be seen.
Flower heads narrow and sleek
Opening wide when not asleep.

The inside of each pretty head
A tracery of delicate thread
Shyly hanging down unseen
Beautiful and serene.

Their short life cycle is soon through,
The joy they have given, pure and true.
Next year they will return again,
Snowdrops- Their pleasure will remain.

Glenda Richardson

The Race

In the ring waiting to go.
Standing there, adrenaline flow.
Look at the horses pacing out.
Owners and trainers standing about.

Time to mount. Let me on your back.
Steady, save yourself for the track.
To the start. Off with a surge.
Horse and rider, trying to merge.

Hooves are pounding, deafening noise.
The bends coming. Keep your poise.
Pulling ahead. We're going to lead.
Legs and hands, we're going to need.

A flick of the whip, a furlong to go.
Keep up the pace. I know. I know.
Salute to the crowd. Fist in the air.
We've won. We don't have a care.

People slapping my back, patting the horse.
Heart still thudding, calmer of course.
The winners enclosure, cheers so loud.
Sitting up here, feeling so proud.

Dee-Dee Lane

School My Way!

"I hate school it's boring! Make me work all day.
Sitting there in the classroom. Football, I want to play.
"Can't do these Maths Miss" she knows it, don't help!
I look across the table, I'll kick Craig- he'll yelp!

Yes, I've done it. Teacher's sent me out!
I'll skid up and down the corridors, when Mam shouts,
about the dirt. I'll pretend, "don't know, she's on about'!!!"
I'm bored now on my own, classroom window, covered!
hang on, if you 'tootie' down, a hole in the paper, I've discovered.

I think I'll make a face, at 'Ian', by the door,
I'm pressing my nose, up to the glass, and fall down on the floor.
I'm going for a wander, adventure time for me,
I find a cupboard. Cleaners I think, I wish I could see!
Where's the 'blinking' light switch. I'm getting bored already,
I just climb, on to the sink. I wish some-one, holding me steady...

I fell off and hurt my head. Still had a row as well,
My teacher doesn't like me. I know it, I can tell
I want to know that reason why? I do my work, love to read!
She tells me.... "I'm disruptive"; I think that's good..? I'm sure!
Very good indeed!....????

Ben T. Garvey

Stalked By A Killer

It was eating away at him, gnawing, like a dog would at a bone
spreading through his pulsating body with such silence and
the knowledge that it was there, lurking was not even known

It was growing, thriving, getting stronger every day now.

He awoke in hospital - having been diagnosed with a disease.

The treatment made him weak, they tried to cut out his disease
he can't walk, he can't lift things.

Progress was made, he slowly began to walk again

The man could not accept that this was happening to him
before he could walk, run, climb, teach, make things
now he does none

It was back lurking in the darkness once again, growing
it had defied the knife, this time it was here to stay

It crept upon him like a cat, stalking a bird
slowly but surely, it had a firm grip of him this time
no drugs or the knife would destroy it
it had struggled to survive, both of them had
But this time it would never let go.

*In Memory of Nicholas Bridgett, my godfather
who died on 19th July 1995 of cancer*

Joanne Mellor

Woodstock Nation

Perhaps, when dreams are infinitesimally,
Splintered into transparent ideals,
Naivety, unblinkered truth,
Or so one thought,
That flower strewn revolution;
Born of lysergies, mellotrons and outstretched hands
Joining fusion of a generation,
With clear sighted optimism!
And how seven years spanned
And cracked in the resolve,
Spewed forth dull shouts,
Hazy recollections and forgotten names:
That fired innocent emotions,
Spent in chaos and apathy
Policemen no longer smile,
Politicians reek and crawl,
And plastic coated cells
No longer painted walls!
We are optimistic generations,
In its death throes.

Henry J. King

"Fundamental Realization"
(The Dynamics Of A Feeling)

The universe's vast expansion pierces infinity,
Spiral rejuvenation refines the purest form,
The solitude screams like a sun,
Reaching out to the coldest one.
They are me

The universe apocalyptic interaction rages,
Chaos reigns in harmonious equilibrium,
Creation deriving synchronization to the absolute,
Intruding the silence, engulfing the essence.
They are.

The universal power evoking the changes,
A thread of consciousness expands to a cyclone of feeling,
Knowing all and I (are one).
They must be.
I must be.

But who am I!
But who am I?

Daniel Morgan

The Wind

If lifts and twirls the leaves around
Spinning them gracefully to the ground.
It rushes through the trees- and then,
All at once it comes again-

Flowers they blow from side to side-
With a rather stately glide-
Grass blows and it seems the blades-
Are just like soldiers on parade.

All at once a stillness falls,
Flowers stand very straight and tall,
With not a movement to be seen.
It's still - and very quiet again

Irene V. Carter

Reaching Out

A tear which glistens
Speaks a thousand words;
Frustration, anger, pain lie betrayed
Spilling forth as a fountain of truth
But go ignored.

Let's turn away, people say
As the knife slips further still
A drop of blood from a bleeding heart
Seeps, spreads, confronting, challenging
their clamped eyes.

Dreams, the only company;
Flickering, watery reflections of want, of need
Lend them your reality,
Offering a taste of treasure
So unfamiliar.

Touching fingertips dispel cracked despair,
As empathy reigns, so is the sweet smell of love secured.
The surrendering of your own,
A gift of life for another
Just in time.

Joanne Young

Athens

Rocky soil,
Sparsely clad,
With tufts of coarse grass.
Pine trees... (or are they olives?)
Sprout precariously
From the hillsides.
The hot sun beats down,
Relentlessly,
On white-washed houses.
The city becomes peaceful
During the hot siesta hours.
Then, with the sun appearing to move
Slowly to its evening abode,
The city awakes.
Hubbub returns, peace disappears
In the constant hum of traffic.
Voices are raised; street vendors peddle their wares;
Children laugh and chatter at the hotel's roof-top pool.
In the background ancient rocks and monuments
Stand guard over Athens.

Diane Hibberd

Promises

Lotions, potions, creams and gels,
some you swallow and some that smell of youth
Recaptured, for just an instant.
But who can hold back advancing years?
Why the manufacturers of course,
who tell us to apply each day times two,
or nightly sometimes is the thing to do.
Lotions, potions, creams and gels,
I wish them all very well.

Alison Bridgeman

Aboriginal Thought

The dream land dreams circle land.
Song lines tram their endless winding ways
through ancient wind blown memory.
Dark recesses deep and cool, shadow far fathoms from view.
The few try hard yet trying changes little,
How tiny and delicate this small shiny thought
That hides beneath our web entrapped in love and longing.

As seas of change rage beneath our cliffs,
It is late, perhaps too late for conscience to be felt.
A mist of grey has blocked the light.
Ending all chance of inner sight.

Deep song lines, chipping, clipping, clacking,
White striped mind men moved forward on our truth,
Silent in their advance,
We watch their silhouetted shoulders jerking in the sunset,
And all that is left is swirling dust

Christopher Richardson

The Way Of Life

In dreams or truth, people come and people go
Sometimes stay a lifetime
Only if one knows how to share the sunshine to warm you
The Moon to light the way, and the stars to show the way
when darkness falls
With just a few raindrops to take the thirst away, but remember
when the birds leave, and the sun forgets to shine, day turns to night,
The sky opens up to lightning, and thunder roars
Raindrops turn to torrential falls
Maybe, we have seen the hand
That sowed, but did not reap.

Joan Ester Maryan

Untitled

What's in the Mirror, the Sun and the Star
Some sort of prize let's hope it's a car
Keep checking the numbers and hoping to win
Who dares say that gambling's a sin
Back many horses and hope one comes first
If all yours are losers you'll never feel worse
So read all the tipsters who know how to win
Who dares say that gambling's a sin
Dealing the cards from out of a deck
Your hand looks so poor you think blimey, oh heck
You suddenly realise you might even win
Who dares say that gambling's a sin
You finally look to cross over the road
Your mind's just not on it, it carries a load
When the bus hits you, you know you can't win
I told you that gambling a sin

Barry D. Edwards

Reasons

People write poems for different reasons,
Some like writing about the changing seasons,
Others on nature their thoughts are bent,
Whilst to some their words are heaven sent.

Words may be thoughts of a simple mind,
Not always from the intelligentsia kind,
But meant to bring comfort, they can you know,
Leaving behind an inner glow.

We need to remember not all is lost,
When days are dark and heavy the cost,
Life is made up of highs and lows,
Take it from one who really knows.

The lows make the world look dull and grey,
And you feel somehow you have lost your way,
But remember that night is followed by dawn,
And a peaceful calm follows a raging storm.

So take heart in believing it's really true,
The tide will turn one day for you,
And when it does it will be so worthwhile,
Because along with your faith it's restored your smile.

Hazel Devonshire

An Inner Child Looks Out

The child who stands before me in questioning, her beauty
framed in soft white light.
Her arms reach out, tiny fingers beckon, a small hand slips into mine.

Her eyes plead, they seek answers. I have none.
They pierce into mine, exuding wells of uncertainty. They implore.
For a moment, we become one.

I cradle the child, now safe within my arms.
Her frail body, vulnerable and suspect, clings to the pain.

But she must let it go.

I kiss the soft cheek, smell the sweet fragrance of her hair,
caress the troubled brow.
For a moment, we become one.

The tears now run freely down her lovely face, in a paroxysm
of despair they fill the very fibres of her being.

Her body jolts in convulses, a mass of pulsating emotions,
uncontrolled, unaccepting.

Her petite frame, veiled in a cloak of darkness, is shackled to
the pain, unable to resist its forces, its power, its relentless pursuit.

The sobbing subsides, the pain insidiously quiet.
The torment that coursed through the tiny body is stilled.

She is free, at peace for a fleeting moment, but the eyes still
show the fear of entrapment. I hold her close, our souls unite.

We become one. We are one.

Barbara O'Grady

The Blooming Garden

I looked at our garden it was barren and bare.
So up to the garden centre to see what was there,
Some Fuchsias, Geraniums and packets of seed,
Compost containers and pots we will need.

I would like some nice plants for my baskets too,
Lobelia cascading in red, white and blue,
Even the leaves on some plants I am told
Are plain variegated silver and gold.

Having bought all the things that I could,
I think I spent much more than I should,
We packed all the shrubs and plants in the car,
To take them all home it's not very far.

At home in the meantime we laid down some turf
A beautiful lawn surrounded by Earth,
We planted the flowers and shrubs all around,
An abundance of colours coming out of the ground.

Jacqueline Mallinson

Soul Of A Dragon

I pray you bury me back in the land of my fathers
So that when I die I know I'll be coming home
And lay me in my grave with the flag of our great nation
To prevent my haunting spirit the want to stray and roam

I care not if I die from cold or starvation
As long as I am surrounded by the friends that I love
And all I ask of them is a little salvation
And lay me in the soil that I am so proud of

I vow to always love you, never shall I leave you
Your pure beauty a thousand women could not fulfil,
Yet if I choose to die in my love of dear old Ireland
Swear you'll bring me back to the world's greenest hills

On the night you cover me in dirt
Do not mourn or be full of sorrow,
But stand and watch my headstone,
Ignoring haunted cries
And the only thing you'll see
Is the soul of a dragon
Who has soaked himself in whisky
But is happy where he lies

Brett James Evans

Wisdom Of Sayings

All that glitters is not gold
So often true or so we're told.
It does not seem that we are able
To find the truth of that old fable.

Friends are like diamonds precious and rare
And when we are down a friend will be there.
To love one another is just what it seems,
Like the gold and the diamond it's not just in dreams.

He that hesitates is not always lost
For a hesitant man does what he loves most.
He makes his gold glitter as he feathers his nest
But with diamonds and friendship he's not at his best.

So let us take heed in the wisdom of sayings
Not follow greed of the man and his bayings.
Give kindness and love and a friendship that's true
And the diamond and gold will come back to you.

Edith M. Smith

Penestin

The little village
So long at rest
With Boulangerie and Tabac
Opening from 9 to 12
For Villagers and the like
Including rainsite campers
To do their morning shop.

The village clock rings out the hour
Eleven strokes in all
As we drink the first
petite café of the day
On our new regular bar crawl.

Then off to "Degusten, fruits der mer"
Our mussels of the day
Moules marinere
Eaten so delicately
With the first shell
Unlike our friends who suck away
And bounce the shells
Within the bowl.

Barbara Ann Bridgeman

David's Star

I saw a star high in the sky.
So bright, so bold, so very old.
A sparkle, glint, as the purest gold.
I saw a star worn, in David's style.
A race of people, heritage of old.
Waters parted, to make their way.
Across our world to have their say.
Freedom for peoples, we were shown.
Freedom can be ours, our very own.
A star of David in my hand
   Originating in a Jewish land.
A symbol to the world, of a given race.
   A people proud, never loud.
A people of peace, chosen by a Christ long gone.
The children of Israel, the world have roamed.
Teachings they brought, across our seas.
Children of Israel, you can be proud,
   As you settled, into your given crowd.
Stars up high in the sky,
   A star of David a symbol sowed

Harry Livesey

Red

Red reminds me of love when I hug my mum
Red reminds me of the sun going down after a
hot sunny day.
Red reminds me of fire when a fire breaks out and
kills people.
Robins singing in the morning
Red reminds me of roses growing from the ground.

Danny Bushell

When I Was Small

Wintertime when I was small
Snowy coats on pegs in the hall
Toasting bread on the open fire
Clothes hanging over a wooden drier
Robins hopping in the snow
Windows with a friendly glow
Red noses and rosy cheeks
Woolly socks on cold feet
We hadn't a fridge just a larder.
It made my mother's life a bit harder.
Friday night, sweets, comics and money
I really loved hot toast and honey
Whirling muffin the mule
I'd watch them sitting on my little stool
Fluffy puppy my father gave to me
The time I was stung by a big bee
I think a lot of my childhood years
The smiles, the laughter and the tears
I must say now I've done it all
The best times were when I was small.

Ann Dowding

Dawn

In the East, from the dark velvet sky of night,
slowly emerges a faint and iridescent light,
pearly grey as mist, and shadowy in form,
we behold the mystic aura of yet another dawn.

From deep kingfisher to violet, growing pale,
to farmer and to sailor, telling each his tale,
forecasting of the day that is to be,
the eastern light encroaches across the starlit panoply.

Gathering colour as it strengthens, on its way
to change the night into translucent day.
Traces of pink and gold now streak this shimmering scene,
deepening to a crimson, glowing sheen.

The night recedes, in other lands to dwell,
though the evening star still shines like a sentinel.
Suddenly, to rejoicing fanfare by the birds,
dawn breaks in majesty too beautiful for words.

And I am lost in wonder and enchantment, gazing
at the Master Artist's kaleidoscope amazing.
No human hand could paint this vision lyrical.
It's far beyond our spectrum, it's a miracle.

Eileen Lord

Down And Up

Slowly so slowly, I slid down this dark hole,
Slimy with mud and no place to go,
Can't get out at the top, where I chose to come in,
Out at the bottom, leads to nowhere, I can't dig,
A place of my making, though perhaps I've been here before,
Though this time it's deeper and narrower by far.

There must be a way, though with effort on my part,
Thinking of how, of just how to start,
I'll climb up the side, foot by foot, paw by paw,
Nine times out of ten, I'll fall back in the mud,
The nearer the top still not easy and yet,
Sun will shine bright, encouragement I'll get

If I just try hard enough, never give up,
I'll reach that horizon, I can't see at the top,
Persevering and determined, I'll make my own mark,
To dig each of my feet in, then each of my paw,
The point is I fell in, it was my own fault,
Will be my own efforts, to get out again.

David James Smith

A Jog At Dawn

I have heard the call of the sun and the sea.
(Sleep on, my dear, I'll turn the key.)
I must go where the tide runs free
To bathe in the rising sun.

Down the stair and out of the door,
Past the school and down to the shore.
Maker of all, I Thee adore
As I face the rising sun!

On virgin sand alone I stride,
Fresh as the air and free as the tide.
Chasing the wind with arms flung wide
I embrace the rising sun!

I thank the Lord, as I leave the bay
For the outstretched sand and the salt sea-spray
And the gift of life and another day
To exult in the risen sun!

John Thornton

Quantum

Serial killer stalks the cornfield
Slashing corrections to the rows that rise
And fall in digitalized wave functions
Collapsing as the crow's wings'
Constant ragged charcoal sweeps
Scan for particles scattering,
Seeking their ground state.
Some lie and are lost, ingested
Into flight, but the random buried
Interact with dark rotted chemical time
Also to soar and then, again,
Crest, or trough, wave before the spooling blades.

David Bell

School

School is a place where you're meant to learn
Six to eight weeks in a term
Maths, English, P.E. and Art
There's just one problem, you can't take part
Getting wrong is easy enough
But getting suspended is just too tough
All the teachers hate your guts
They think we're all bloody nuts
All we do is sit and listen
If we talk it's just like prison
Writing, reading, drawing maps
At least we don't need to wear caps
School is boring, but that ain't new
At least we've only got a few...
A few more years, and that is so
Now it seems so long ago.

Annamarie C. Lamb

Growing Old Gracefully

My Old Friend "Mu" is ninety today
So you can see she has come a long way
When first we met at a very young age
We looked and stared as if in a rage

But later on we made amends
And soon became the best of friends
We have spent Easter in Paris
And driven to Devon
Often leaving as early as seven (7 AM)
But now we can no longer roam.
For both of us live in a Nursing Home
Content and happy as we can be
With "Con" in the Country
and "Mu" by the Sea.

Connie Pleasance

The Old Ladies' Home

My heart is sad, as I see them there
Sitting in their upright chairs
What goes through their minds I wonder
Who can tell, if they really slumber

Once they were, like you and me
Bringing up their family
Now it seems, they are pushed aside
In this place left to abide

All heads are lifted expectantly
When a visitor comes, someone to see
Hoping to see a loved one there
With whom a memory they can share

The one who is lucky, is full of delight
A tear is quickly brushed out of sight
The memory is going, but with patience bear
One day, you might be sitting there.

Edna F. Tucker

What Symbolizes Love?

Is it a heart or is it an arrow
Or is it a noise made by a sparrow
Is it a rose or is it a flower
Or is it when you are high up in a tower
Is it a pair of lips
Or is it a kiss
All I know is when you go it's always you I miss.

Fiona Williams

Abused

A little boy, with a dirty face,
Sits staring at the floor,
Scars hidden below his tee-shirt,
He can't hurt him no more.
The neighbours hear his pleas to stop,
But don't know what to say,
Whilst slowly and methodically,
His life is beat away.
It used to be a father's slap,
Now, punches or a belt,
His cheeks betray, with tracks of tears,
The pain that he has felt.
A mother cruelly pushed away,
She's had the beatings too.
A young, old girl of twenty-six,
No idea of what to do.
She's tried to leave him many times,
Sick of violence and the lies.
Whence, once, before they loved
They now both just despise.

David George Thompson

The Decision

The skies were lightening, dawn was near.
She stumbled as she brushed a tear
The trees looked dark, forbidding as she blindly picked her way.
She couldn't face the future, she couldn't face today.
The nights events came crowding back, the disbelief, the fear.
They'd come for her, it was too late, she brushed away a tear.
The lake loomed up, so black, so still, like velvet soft and deep.
The mist was slowly lifting, as if from some long sleep.
The water looked inviting an end to all her sorrow.
She wouldn't have to face today, but what of them tomorrow.
He hadn't left a legacy, but memories so dear.
And four young lives to mould alone, she brushed another tear.
She had to go and face them, their grief would know no bounds.
Slowly, then one turned around startled by a sound.
A figure stood so silently, how long she didn't know.
She raised her eyes, I'm ready Dad, I'm ready now to go.
He took her hand, and led her back towards another day
Her mind was in turmoil with the words she had to say
She put her hand upon the gate, he suddenly felt near
She pushed it wide and took a breath and brushed away a tear.

Doreen Gray

Widows

Cretan widows, black swaddled,
sit in their doorways,
feet sun-warmed, face shadowed,
hands
buried in lacework or knitting;
minds
turned inwards, backwards
to blossom days, and nights
of warm whispering closeness.
Now branches are bare, each night
nothingness.
Nobody tells them
life must go on,
tries to involve them
in night school or aerobics.
Yet neighbours do not swerve off,
averting eyes for fear of reading pain.
The amputation is acknowledged, comprehended.

But I am not in Crete.

Jean Simister

The Colours Of Life

Like a ray from the sun
Shining through the black tunnel of despair
He burst into the darkness of my life
And led me forth into a glorious day.

Life was no longer an unattainable dream
Every minute of it was lived to the full
I grew, gaining strength from his reflected glory
Secure in the knowledge of his love.

Then all at once the world that was mine collapsed
He withdrew his words of love and flawless beauty
I was confused, for he had hidden his discontent
My world was empty, and I wept long, angry tears.

Now that my angry tears are gone
And the pain that ripped through my heart is numb
The sunshine has gone from my life
And the future has faded to grey.

Hannah Hinchliffe

A Child Is Born

Beyond the universe, lies a star,
Shining brightly far o far
Oh please Lord hear my prayer
I want to live again, it just ain't fair,

I came into this world, knowing nothing,
But deep inside, there's a lot of loving,
I just want to be happy, and be free,
Of all the badness and anxiety

I know there's hope, or I would be gone,
To the promised land, where I belong,
My life is not over, it's just begun.
Free me from depression Lord,
Let me have some fun.

I want to believe in myself again,
It ain't an easy task,
Free me from all the bad times in life,
And help me forget the past.

Gavin Lawrie

Elvis (My Idol)

When we have troubles, who do we turn to?
Our dear idol Elvis.
When we are down, who helps us? Elvis.

He's in our hearts, our souls, our minds,
Just put on his records, or his videos,
and we are calmed.

Helen Barrie

Past Wigan

Birds black against the cold sky
Shimmering like a migraine

A bird ballet thermal
A secret ritual
Of messages and formation

Dead yellow grass leaning wind-ways
Scratching a life
From the oily earth
Between the sleepers of the track

Flooded fields flat
With gleaming still water sky puddles
Animals like wooden toys
Graze on the upper slopes

Pylons stride mercilessly
Across the slow fields
And window eyed farms
Stand like fortresses
Alone against the sprawl of industry

Cari Sophia Hamblett

The Ghost Of Our Soul

Everyone sees her but nobody knows her.
She's always there, crouched in a corner.
Look away and she'll fade,
She has taken your problem now
And will sit somewhere else to sort it out.

She hugs her knees,
Rocking back and forth, sobbing softly to herself.
Taking everyone's problems from their deepest souls,
She sorts them out, crying over them,
Thinking them through.
And then hands them back organized but unharmed.
But never forget she won't always be there.
One day she'll leave you to sort it out for your self.

Catherine Hughes

The Gift Of A Mother

What is a mother?
She is a treasured gift
With a love, deep and true
She guides you through life's blues
Her unfailing strength
Keeps you from harm
With all the softness
Of her gentle grace and charm
A mother's encouragement
Comes with wisdom and smiles

You tell her of your hopes and dreams
Her understanding makes it so worthwhile
A mother is someone in our hearts
A mother is someone in our thoughts
A mother can never be forgotten
Because you love her so.
A mother in her own special way
Is loved and remembered in every way.

Ian Charles Thorogood

To Mother

There you rest amongst the swaying pines,
Snow-clad in their winter glory.
The sun's pale face barely above the trees,
And soft pure snow covering your grave.

You died when the winter's day was briefest,
When the sun's rays hardly left a mark.
You waited for us, your grieving daughters,
Then your life ebbed away in the evening's dark.

Rest there in peace, dear Mother, after lifelong toil,
Under ancient stars, and the clouds you loved.
Rest there forever, in Finland's sacred oil.
The flowers will follow, when the snows have thawed.

Anja Hassell

The Prayer

"Jesus, make my mummy well", his little daughter prayed,
"She doesn't read me stories and it's ages since we played.
She just lays there in that bed and it makes me very sad.
I know that I've been naughty but have I really been that bad?
I'll help her with the washing-up, I'll even make my bed!
For only you can help her, that's what my daddy said.
I wake up in the night and I hear my daddy cry,
And he says that if my mummy goes he knows that he will die.
So, Jesus, make her well again and help my daddy too,
So that we can take her out again to the park or to the zoo.
I know my mummy likes to 'cause we used to go a lot,
Especially in the summer when the day was very hot.
Please, Jesus, make her better and I promise I will be
The goodest and the bestest little girl you'll ever see."
He stood there at the doorway and watched her say her prayers,
And the tears ran down his face as he went back down the stairs.
His wife lay in a coma, as she had done from that day,
And memories came flooding back of words he'd had to say.
For how do you tell a little girl of four where Mummy's gone?
How do you start to tell her what a driver, drunk, had done!

Janice Steele

The Dragon And The Angel

In the dark misty caverns of my heart, a fiery dragon once
raped me of my very existence; she tore my emotions strip by
strip leaving only an empty vessel; with me the sailor lost at
sea, in the ocean of love.

For one thousand days I sailed without direction,
for one thousand nights I was adrift with troubled thoughts;
Alas! The most beautiful angel appeared, she banished the ghosts
that once haunted me; Nirvana was close and tranquillity near....
Or so I believed.

Just as her senses warmed me, the dragon lurched once more;
With vengeance on her side, she pierced the angel's
soul...The angel slept awhile. Once more sorrow encroached
my now diminutive piece of humanness; the evil spirit
initiated, I was led astray; the axe was ground, the door to
wrath unlocked.

Wave after wave my thoughts submerged, my reason
crowded, humane thoughts extinct; human feelings had
departed... The angel astir, a dolphin was born; we were on
the edge of the light, the sun was rising inside our existence;
Mother was giving birth to a new day,
our souls were now serene.

We could have swam the ocean alone, but faith assured we
swam as one. Together we learned to slay our dragons, to
find bliss within our beings. No longer was eminence considered a crime, no longer was passion something to conceal; the
axe was buried, and many doors unlocked.

Gearoid Grace

Returning Home

She felt the forest enclose her and knew she had to run,
she gasped as the cold air stabbed at throat throttling her
like a stranger's hand squeezing against her flesh,
the branches cracked and twigs snapped as her legs folded,
her hand grasped at the closest bark and her nails
clawed into the trees life mixing sap with tear.
The moon threw dawn its rays allowing her time to focus
her heart ceased to feel like it was fleeing its cage
   and offered a rhythm she recognized.
She looked back at the path she'd chosen and saw
the small imprints of a child shoe, like the impression
   made by a tiny foot clad in shiny patent shoes.
Her fear evaporated like morning dew
for she was safe with her memories,
pulling herself to her feet she faced her intended direction.
She strode out and through the lattice work of leaves spied
   the scarlet red she'd sought,
no natural bloom glowed this bright and then she was sure,
like cherry lips on an aged face this door shone clear,
and she could breathe,
for it was here that she would find the sanctity she desired, home.

Julie Rickard

Mother

She's always there to help me, in her quiet, unselfish way
She comes to mind my children, free of charge and every day.
She stands and does my ironing and runs round with the vac,
And never ever say's a word, when I say I'll be late back.
She gives a sympathetic ear, when I need to moan awhile
And when I've had a rotten day, it's good to see that smile.
What makes this mother special, some ones sure to ask in time
The thing that makes her special, is the fact that she's not mine.
I wasn't born her daughter, but a daughter I became
Mother-in-law and mother, to me their both the same.

Christine Stubbs

Loving Words

Darling hold me in your arms tonight
Squeeze me so tight, it always feels so right,
Together we are alight, never ever
Let me get out of your sight.
Spring time is getting near, you will always
Be my dear we'll go for long walks
In the Park, beside you I'll never be
In the dark, we'll look at the flowers
As they grow into full bloom, listen as
All the birds will be singing, the air is
So still and being with you is such a
Thrill, with your hair as soft as silk
Eyes that shine like diamonds, lips the
Colour of a ruby, and being with you
Keeps me from becoming all moody,
We'll listen to the gentle water flowing
And my love for you just keeps on growing

Duncan MacLean

Mosaic

What makes you think you're faced with
  Several choices,
You have no rules to follow,
  No Godlike voices.
I've seen it in your friends,
  See their faces,
I've seen it in their eyes,
  No friendly traces.

What makes you think it's easy,
  Never knowing,
I have no rules to follow,
  Just tensions growing.
I'm with new friends looking,
  To tomorrow,
It's still there in my heart,
  Full of sorrow.

John Stewart

Alarum

Alarms bells in the heaven sound.
Saint Christopher, you must be found;
Wake from your slumb'rous rest
On Bracknell's roads grave danger lurks,
So long as her Ford Escort works,
Now June has passed her test

How did we anger thee, O Lord,
That thou hast loosed Damocles' sword
On mortals sore oppressed?
Would prayer and piousness suffice,
Instead of human sacrifice,
Now June has passed her test

Heavenly Father, hear our plea.
Have mercy, we beseech of Thee,
Listen to our request.
We will be humble, and devout,
If Mike will take the engine out,
Now June has passed her test

Dereck Ripley

Yesterday's Silence

So tranquil by the water's edge. A burning sun
sent vibrant rays on nature's mirror
which, in light of landscapes
gave poetic justice whilst
amongst the trees children did play,
deep, deep golden treasures did swim
amongst binds of time.
Through such crystal rowing boats did steer at ease
slithering like fine brown monsters.
The arched delights of the bridge
sheltered us from the wavering heat.
I rest a while, with pity
focus on rustic decay outside these monumental arches.
A black sky sighs, waters shiver
with sympathy, our heritage is dying
amongst revolutionary aluminum, cheap plastic wrappers.
In yesterday's silence a breeze of sweetness
glided through ebony of oak,
Present water weeds die polluted
yesterday treasures do choke

Emma Daley

"Looking Back" (From Orkney To The Highlands)

I miss the rivers - tumbling, peat-brown,
  searching each stone on the way.

I miss the secret depths of the silent pools -
  times of reflection, of being still as life rushes on.

I miss the view through the filigree lace of waterfalls -
  dark recesses where drips move mountains.

Then in old age - majestic.
Too grand now for childhood dams and stepping-stones.
Sweeping selfishly on to meet the sea salt.

I miss the rivers, but now the endless sea.

Ishbel Borland

"Dancing Flames"

Picture a cosy fireside illuminating an instant glow
Search quietly for her secrets while flames dance fast and slow
Study each and every movement as smoke provides a screen
Enjoy her colours of warmth, the brightest you've ever seen.

View her dancing flames, study her heart down deep
Poker just the slightest to allow an extra peep
Imagine all the paths you see as her heart begins to light
Listen to her flames in sound with silence of the night.

Share secrets of these flames as they burn their colours bright
Topple on earthly life to keep them dancing through the night
A minds-eye filled with imagination, never letting go
Flames stretching high, coals shimmering low.

Exotic movements, dancing silence, elegantly quiet
Quickly changing her free style to a loud forceful riot
Gently, tearfully, dying down as in a silent sleep
Ending up totally exhausted, lying crumpled in a heap.

No more sights to view as she totally ends her day
No more warmth of colours, just a cold cindery grey
No more imagination as there's nothing left to see
No more dancing flames, just simple ashes to be raked free...

Anne Kerr

A Friend Unseen

Your coming was in silence,
  save your passage through the tree's.
You caressed me gently as you passed,
  you stirred the fallen leaves.

You took my sadness with you,
  as you hurried on your way.
Please call again I've need of you,
  so much more today.

David J. Strawbridge

Alone In A Crowd

When you're all alone in a crowd,
screaming in silence and silent out loud,
permanently longing to cry,
but your reservoir of tears has long since gone dry.

When you're aching and hurting inside,
with a pain in your heart, or a pain in your mind?
Hiking along Dead-end Lane,
the search for your sanity driving you insane.

When each thought is filled with self doubt,
reach to face them - no wait - turn around,
searching for your hidden strength,
seemingly destined to search till your end.

Remember your mind, though seemingly strong,
requires your heart to help it along,
recall how your heart, though apparently sore,
has ached and been broken so often before,
don't forget how some people have rallied for you,
think of these people - some old and some new,
Who've been there before and will be there again,
then call on these people - the ones you call "friends".

Brian Doig

Fathomless

Facing the horizon
on life's waterline,
my feet sinking
in the shifting silver sand.

I turn my face
into white spray that mists;
I taste the brine.
There's so little I know or understand.

Alan Butt

"The Fox"

Dark eyes peeping, ears pricked forward, nose up in the air.
Scents are shifting, swirling drifting, round him everywhere.
Carefully, a paw put forward testing muddy ground,
Senses tingling, body tense for any sudden sound.
Startled pheasants all a-flutter vanish through the trees
To hide away from teeth that chatter, dinner for his three.
Then suddenly it falls upon him, danger in the field.
Scents come drifting, floating downwind, hounds come running,
Baying, calling, kill him, kill him kill.
Red and white blur in a vision, don't wait, don't look, don't stare.
Lead them onward, outward wayward, through the copse
Across the common away from pups and lair.
Darting forward like an arrow, hounds upon his heels,
Heartbeat racing pulses throbbing lungs are bursting still
  he's running
Hounds are baying huntsman calling, kill him, kill him kill.

Coral Rose Wyles

The Village Bus

Ready for off, all fares aboard,
save one, a Miss Evadne Ford.
"I'll wait awhile, she's sure to come",
the driver said, more kind than some.

Hushed sounds of chatter filled the bus,
then cheers, she's here, oh what a fuss
as Miss Evadne sailed into view,
rosy-cheeked and hat askew.

Thank you driver, you're so kind,
I feared I would be left behind;
my clock had stopped, this made me late,
and then, my dog ran through the gate.

The driver smiled, clicked into gear,
"all in my day's work me dear,"
then on he drove up hill and down,
and dropped his ladies in the town.

Elaine Meakin

Sasha

I like to take my dog for walks,
Sasha is her name.
She is so friendly, she nearly talks,
Couldn't be more tame
She runs and jumps, and chases the ball,
She's always in a hurry.
But she always comes back when I call
I really needn't worry.
When she goes to sleep at night,
She flops down with a sigh.
If we turn on the kitchen light,
She opens up one eye

Danielle Mallabone

Seagulls

Sailing up
Sailing down,
   Sweeping seagulls onward bound
   Trailing trawlers for scraps afloat
   Who knows, what might be found.

Sailing up
Sailing down,
   Sweeping seagulls onward bound
   Fraught with fight for a morsel bite
   Endless noise of guttural sound.

Sailing up
Sailing down,
   Sweeping seagulls onward bound
   A relentless trek through natures search
   For survival, onward to another ground.

Ellie Gibson Reid

Tranquil Thoughts

Small exotic islands,
Set in an azure sea
Their mystery always beckoning,
To soul mates such as me,
I long to meet the people,
Their beauty is so rare,
To talk and share their life with them,
No others can compare,
As the evening sun is setting.
and peace descends on all.
There is no better place on earth,
That I can ere recall.

Elizabeth Casey

River Of Gold

River of golden light shinning brightly through the night.
Rushing ever forward the beams of gold keep coming and coming.

The river is two fold, running up and down, one of gold
and one of red, shinning bright through the night.

Look behind and what was gold has now turn red.
Look ahead it is red and look behind the gold is coming.
So much gold is cheers the soul.

Rolling fog, and dark, dark roads where no moon
or streets light shines.
They keep coming and shinning though out the night.

All through the night, up high, near the sky, yellow and
blue beams light the way for the golden river which stills
comes rushing on.

The golden beams are often alone no yellow or blue to help
the river flow.
But now matter what the flow goes on and on in every road and
every town through out the land. Each and every night. Each
and every month through each and every year.

Daphne C. Lynch

Each Sole, Soul-Felt Tear

Each sole, soul-felt tear
Runs down a cheek, soft water clear
Most unseen but if found
Stopped before they reach the ground.
Glinting lovely on their way,
But this their modesty betrays
The hope is with the ones who care
They have the strength to stop tears there.
The tears reach up into their soul
Often they fill an empty hole,
These ones who love will never cry
Like stars their dreams are in the sky
And whatever happens in their lives
Their dreams are up there in the skies.
But sobbing grievers don't lose hope,
These beloved carers on whom you dote
Would not rise high and lose their fear
Without each sole, soul-felt tear.

Christopher Brown

The Polar Bear

Sad feelings all around,
Rubbish has been dumped,
The polar bears home has been destroyed,
Polar bears surrounded by pollution.

Careless dustman, dropping their waste,
Crisp packets, bottles and paper bags,
Broken glass laying around,
Cutting animals to pieces.

Brooke Ritchie

A Terminal Case

His heart gave out, they said
Rosie smoothed the wrinkled dirty sheet across the bed
At least she'd had the money first
Rosie cursed
And he would never want her short of bread
So soft and warm, he'd said
Not like all the others
Has-been or would-be mothers with all mod-cons as lovers
Tell me, Rosie, look me in the eyes
Say you love me - no disguise
Love me naked as I am
With all my faults - I know you can
And not for all the rubbish I possess
Rosie felt the money tucked inside her dress
Money growing cold
She looked into his eyes and watched them growing old
She couldn't tell him no
And so she told him, yes
And he watched her in the moonlight
Begin to get undressed

Jean Watson

The Whales' Song

Come now and see the Sea,
rocking 'gainst the pebbled shore
where the tiny children play,
breaking against marbled rocks
in diamond-glistening spray.

Come now and hear the Sea,
hear the deep cacophony,
hear the thousand Whales' voices deep,
echoing in the watery caverns,
echoing in the watery keep.

Come now, dive into the Sea,
put your gentle hand in mine
and we will join the oceanic herd,
leave your clothes, heavy thoughts and words,
for all but singing is absurd.

Colwyn Griffiths

Pushkin's Salute To The Ocean

I take my fleeting throne on this
Ragged knuckle of royal rock,
In feeble tongue ensuing a sacrifice
Of mere words to Neptune's fluid kingdom.

So easily could I accept an embrace into
Her Emerald swelling bosom,
But I alas long to cling to the element of
My birth and for my ears to be caressed by her infinite song.

I am but an honoured guest before this wedding of the elements.
Bearing witness to the fusion of the constituents of life,
To reciprocate the bonds of my very existence.

Dominant mistress I am wary of your disposition, but forgive me,
For my apprehension is drawn from the deep well of mortal ignorance.
We meet again at our secret moon kissed rendezvous.
Once more I try to attain revelation from your rhythmic whisper.

Today you showed your anger, sculptor of continents,
Architect of the Earth.
In the frenzy of dance without form or reason,
I tasted your sovereignty and
Supped from your scented broiling cauldron.

Christopher Jeffcott

Sea Sense

Whispering into the hush of our serene and listening sea
Reveals the truth there's something much more gracious now than we
    Does our joy or sadness share an affinity
    In the salt of every tear?
    Can the needs that spill cries over
    Ever be new to an ancient ear?
    Tranquil magnificence tenders kindly
    To capture our escaping emotions
    Mirroring our Creator's love
    That spans horizons of global oceans.

Listening to the rush of our rolling troubled sea
Reveals the truth there's something much more knowing now than we
    Towering stubbornness obstructs our heeding
    The severe warnings in its tides
    Victims seek and worship a freedom
    That boasts it's healthy but ultimately dies!
    Waves roar home so positively
    They rest not on their wash to the fore
    Mirroring our Creator's Words (ever coming)
    To generations who reject God's promises (once more).

Graham Barger

Future

I look in wonder at your sleeping face
Resting now upon my breast
Is this for me this gift of love
My new born child, I have a son

Music laughter and a song
To see a rainbow bright and strong
Watching a child run and play
Listen to a bird sing at the break of day
Many more things I want for him

Lying cheating doing wrong
Killing, hating, warring all life long
So I can have and you have not
We have to stop now while we can
Let him live and love his fellow man

Lasting peace is my desire
Keep him safe away from harm
My gift to the world is this new
born man.

Anne Roche

Another Way To Dream

I walk alone, never by myself.
Reflections of a wife, my company, my wealth.
The stroll, betwixt mountain and vale.
Inspires endless affection, forever prevail.

A crystal clear stream, cascading its heart.
Conveying a message, Till Death Us Do Part.
Shimmering ripples, from a translucent sun.
Brings to minds, the love, the fun.

Flowers in the wild, with petals unfurl, enriching a smile.
Sensitive emotions, flow free for awhile.
As a dove in flight, looks for a niche.
The image is free, I've no leash.

The current of flow, ascending upwards, then down.
Falling amongst rocks, through meadow and town.
Into an ever-changing world, of nature, of life.
I've no need of worry, I have my wife.
Christopher Duke

The Tragedy Of Dido

Virgil's tragic Dido, how your mind must churn with hate,
Pierced with Cupid's arrow, tortured victim of cruel fate.
  The shore below is swarmed with men, your love is within view,
His heart so cold, it's chilling, your heart could break in two.
  You utter not one single word, yet you yearn for him to hear,
The desperate plea behind your lips. The ocean is your tear.
  Your bosoms heave with sorrow, to encase your swollen heart,
Within your soul, unmoving, sits the cherub's poisoned dart.
  Manic is your laughter, as it echoes through the air,
Your eyeballs blaze with anger, as your fingers tear your hair.
  Voices rage within your mind, It's not love you now desire,
The bitterness consumes you, like trees destroyed by fire.
  When your wailing became silent, and tears on your face did dry.
When the sobbing left your body, and no longer did you cry.
  Wind whistled round your lover's ship, and he heard upon its breath,
"Dido wails no more in life, but her cries are heard in death."
  As he turned his head towards the shore, the lover that he'd kissed,
Lay among fire of a funeral pyre, while smoke circled in the mist.
  Cold still his heart, he turned his head, to shun the sight he sees,
Yet, he'll never escape the guilt that Dido showers in the breeze.
Bonnie Birkin

The Whole World Cried

One bleak day, thunder crashed, and lightning lit the skies,
rain wept down, like bitter tears, the tears that left my eyes.
Grey clouds bathed the once clear sky, the sun was lost from view, the whole world cried, the end was near, as was my life with you.

Summer days have passed away, the laughs we knew are gone,
but in my heart a flame was burning, a flame for wife and son.
I begged you for another chance, a chance to change my life,
I could not live without you near, I love you, my dear wife.

I hugged you for the times we had, a kiss for days gone by,
but in my heart, I knew I'd lost, a teardrop kissed my eye.
You turned away, my heart cried out, I begged you stay with me,
I'd change my ways, I'd start anew, I'd change, just wait and see.

I touched your cheek with trembling hands, I wanted you to stay,
but you just pulled away from me, then turned and walked away.
I knew my chance for life had gone, you left and closed the door,
so what had I to live for? What would my life be for?

I stood alone, a weeping wreck, a man whose life has gone,
no more will I long to live, no will to greet each sun.
With aching heart I made a choice, a choice to end my life,
I cannot bear the thought of days, without my child and wife.
Colin Reeves

Firetime!

Afternoon leaving quietly, slipping beyond wooded hill
Quite still and bare as Winter calls her turn.
Clouds, stealing away westerly in crackling early evening air,
Tinted golden from setting sun as they follow her dimming rays
Before frost on freeze of easterly Siberian-blown breeze.
Firetime! Lighting set grate to radiate warmth,
Embracing home come school-child with chilled fingers and face.
Flames flirting flickering coals, hypnotizing, engulfing inky black,
Turning all into raging ruddy-orange hues of flaming heat
That meet tortoiseshell cat taking her place,
Reclining, curled, purring before warming hearth.
Curtains drawn against cold darkening world of winter night;
Bodies accustoming warming fire, eyes to artificial light.
So different our lives now from summer's sweltering scenes
Who would believe... was last summer real, or just a dream..
And who would have dreamt then of this firetime now?
Angela Jones

Memories

You are gone but not forgotten.
The memories are still here with me.

The good times, the bad times.
Are still here with me.

The friends we shared
Are still here too.

But you are not here to share them with me.

I feel you presence day after day.
I smell your scent every day.

I know you are here with me in spirit.
But life goes on, love.
It is time for you to let go.

Go now, my faithful love.
My life goes on.

Although I will find someone new.
No man on earth can take the place of you.
Patricia February

Jean

You left one day "showed no emotions
Probably because years of explosions
Your fiery temper went all calm
Then I heard the front door slam
I rush to catch you, you didn't stop
Then I felt my own heart stop
Dropped to my knees in so much pain
Surrounded by people in the pouring rain
Awake to nurses putting things on my chest
Saying not to worry were just doing tests
So I shut my eyes and started to think
It's not Jeans fault it's that awful drink
It's lost me Jeans love "nearly my life
I wish she was here by my side
Now I am sober and don't need to drink
My heart beats both ways
   For Jean and for life.
John Stewart

A Rose

A hand reached out to the beautiful bloom
Petals soft as worms' spun silk fragrant perfume
Artistry of sheer perfection nature's perfect rose
Inspires the poet in all of us words of verse any prose
Graced the world in all her splendour
Proud was she in all her prime
Pure sweet flower soon to wither
How short her earthly time
Radiant rose you gave such joy
Now death is at your door
I shed a silent tear and weep
Alas you are no more
Jeanne E. Quinn

To Philip, My Father - Killed in Action

I, as a later lover, far removed
praise him that said "All these were lovely"
I say "He loved" now I love too.
Those that he loved do still remain
and are not faithless.
Not traitors they that could not pass death's door.
They changed and died no more than us;
Life's children - all rebirth of what has gone before.

You did not give your life in vain.
For we remember - we're aware
that country, conscience, pride
sent you to a slaughter
that has been our benefit.
All your loves are lovely still
and loved by us through you.

Jane Stokes

Not Mine

He sleeps in my chair and he's dreaming
Of birds and of moles and of mice
He's known to be partial to squirrel
Though he knows I don't think that's too nice

I can't understand why I liked him
He was touchy and spiteful and mean
So I christened him with the name Tiger
As he was ginger and tabby and lean

I found out later, much later
That he was in charge of the pack
He was macho and tough and magnificent
And yes, he was next door's cat

He's sorted me out that's for certain
I can't get away from his charms
He's here on the dot every morning
Just waiting for these loving arms.

Jean King

The War Goes On

The sun so bright so warm but
polluted by this war,
Why can't they see past the hatred
and greed,
And see and feel the children so in need.
The young, and the old, frightened and scared
Bombs and gun's, God how they fear.
Foodless, homeless, family's lost
The young and the innocent they pay the cost.
Alone, sad, and weary how do they go on?
They just want to be free of the
torture, away from here
but what do they do? And
who really cares?
So they just sit back and
drown in there tears,
and the war it goes on.

Jane Dalton

Missed

It is hard to see through the veil
Of heartache and pain that is eroding my soul
His little face that lit my life
His great big smile that gave me life
I fear the tears that expose my face
For my little boy I miss so much.

Now that he is gone
All that are left are memories and so much time
I cannot shake him from the morning light and when
I close my eyes at night
And in my dark despair I grip my fists so so hard
For my little boy I miss so much.

Darryl Mundy

The Reward

Fireside crouched to strike the logs
Poker thrust arouses flame which casts
Shadow dancing 'gainst the whitened wall
Shows erect with guarded bayonet poised
Victorious advance across the stricken world
Ends forgotten in lonely hungers' misery
Raises glass which helps the mind to dream
Of hand with power to draw from thatch
The claymore, but too few survive
To strike a blow as justice fades
Once cheering populace ignores the needs
Establishments their hollow promises forget
Their pockets lining with unending zeal
While slumbering in beds throughout the realm
A generation uncaring and unlearned
Awaits unknown its part to play
In power mad trade enriching wars
Surviving to receive its own
Historical reward Betrayal.

John B. Cutting

Please, Mummy Mummy, Please

Mummy, Mummy why is it dark?
Please put the light on for me,
Please hug me close, and tell me that,
Your face I will soon see.

Mummy, Mummy I feel so cold,
I don't like being here,
Please hold my hand and take me away,
And tell me there's nothing to fear.

Mummy, Mummy why don't you answer?
Please won't you give me a cuddle?
I feel so frightened, small, and lost,
My mind is in a muddle.

Mummy, Mummy it's alright now,
Because Jesus holds my hand.
He's come to take my pain away,
He says you'll understand.

Mummy, Mummy I'm going to Heaven,
He says your pain will ease,
So Mummy, Mummy please don't cry,
Please, Mummy Mummy, please.

Christopher Rowlands

Moonlight Soliloquy

Ancient city, circumscribed by medieval walls,
Please, open up your four great walls to me!
In the blessed silence of your early moonlit hours,
Disclose you secrets of antiquity!
Your narrow cobbled streets, with antiquated houses,
And your minster, bathed in its flood-light glow;
The gargoyles, hidden from the eyes of busy trippers;
Secreted beauties, tourists never know!
Let me go beside your rivers; there to sit at ease.
Seeing mirrored, old buildings; ancient trees!

I shun your busy centre when crowds are milling past.
I may go to a concert or a play!
I delight in balmy nights, when grass is wet with dew,
And sun sinks low, at closing of the day:
Like a thousand fireflies, glow the hospitals's bright lights.
The University's fountains do gleam,
As diamonds, neath the lamp beams, while students stroll at will,
Past ducks and swans a-swimming in the stream.
New buildings blend with old, like grandmothers nestling babes.
Wondrous sights to see, in York; dear to me!

Barbara Saum

The Photograph

From a modest frame
Placed on a coffee table
My mother and my father
Gaze out at me through their small window as I look in at them.

She, young and solemn-eyed,
Slim-waisted, bodice high buttoned,
Wearing long white gloves
And a hat crowned with flowers, surprises me with her good looks.

He, in dark suit,
Wing collar and cravat;
Leans one elbow on a pillar;
One long-fingered hand drooping negligently,

And looks straight into my eyes.
Over the years I have learned his features;
High forehead, high cheekbones,
The long upper lip, the cleft chin, dark strong hair, brushed glossy,

Because we never met, except the once
When as a squalling baby,
I wetted his khaki suit,
Or so my mother told me.
   Gwen Matthews

Bitter From The Sweet

A heart so black,
pollutes the air.
He has no soul
Oh! What despair.

There is no gladness in his life.
Corruption is his game
though one can see through his thin guile
The shadow of the vain.

Loneliness was the life he choose
And now he does regret it.
He kills love with his eager plea,
a move that seems pathetic.

There is a kindness in his heart
A fact you can not delete.
Kindness that can only hurt
Turning bitter from the sweet.

Goodbye my fiend, or maybe friend,
Go find the road to your success.
You have lost your pathway, I've found mine
and like you, EVEN LESS.
   Elaine Chetwynd

DEE

Once upon a time; a memory of a hundred years ago
Perhaps it was yesterday? I wonder if time is relevant
So much can happen and yet so very much is lost in the
Void of time:
The tragedies: The happiness heavily topped with adrenalin
These are with us always.
I wonder, is it just a dream? Or is it all carefully planned
To fit into the insanity of it all?
To feel others' pain, to sense their wants, desires, greed and
Anger: A blessing or a curse?
To be able to run and jump into the wonderful world of
Make believe, for a time at least life can be what you want.
I wish I was a mountain that hadn't seen mankind, for surely
A mountain that has, has cried for a thousand
Years witnessing the suffering. And still she cries.
Then someone calls me a fool,
And I think to myself; how lucky it is to be a fool,
For a fool cannot think and thought is the pathway to truth
And beyond truth lies madness
   Dave Edwards

There'll Be Peace On Earth Some Day

There'll be Peace on Earth some day, there'll be
Peace on Our Mountains to stay. When those friends
and Loved ones so long said goodbye, shall come back
and see us again.

There'll be love and compassion some day. There'll
be Hope and laughter each day. When the things our
Creator, so long has promised, will be here some day
quite soon.

It was ever so long ago, and ever so far away, when
our peace was shattered by an enemy chatter, when he
told such a terrible lie but even so, our Heavenly
Father will soon wipe, all our tears away.

Oh my friends do you think this is true, dear friends
do you think this is good. Well do all that you can
now to make sure that you will be there, to experience,
true peace when it comes.

There'll be Peace on Earth some day, we'll have Peace
on Our Mountains to stay, for God our Creator so long
has promised, we'll have peace everlasting real soon.
   Adlin Watkis

Silence Of The Night

Once again tonight in thought
peace and tranquillity is sought
searching the answer that's right
somewhere in the Silence of the night.

Such a peaceful surround
where ideas are bound
plans in full flight
in the Silence of the night

Understand yourself and aim
mind with soul question the same
be noble and stand corrected
take life as fate elected.

Of life be a student
look listen and learn
whatever your plight
reflect in Silence of the night.

Time passes us by
thoughts expound with a sigh
sincerity in truth and insight
wondrous Silence of the night.
   Edward Lawrence Lane

Portrait Of Home

Crystal clear streams gently flow through your woods
Past tall gracious oaks, that for centuries have stood,
Bluebells carpet your forest floors,
Your beauty is etched in my heart.

A Blackbird is singing his haunting song,
It echo's all through the wood,
A Thrush and a Robin are now joining in,
Their music I hear in my heart.

Majestic cathedrals, statues and fountains
Theatre's and tea shops bustling with sound,
Cobblestone street's with picturesque houses,
Castles stand poised, over rolling green hills.

Lilacs and roses and blossoming hedgerows,
Quiet leafy lanes that twist out of sight,
Rivers that flow gently down to the sea,
I remember it all in the still of the night.

If only I'd known how much I would miss you,
My yearn to wander I know would have died,
My beautiful England, oh how I love you,
Locked in my homesick heart you'll lie.
   Jeanette Coats

Goodnight, God Bless

Close your eyes now, it's time go.
People you loved and lost are waiting to say hello.
I can see you're tired, this has got to be.
Your journey now, will be pain free.
The sun is shining, the sky is so blue.
It's as if heaven is opening just for you.

Your journey's begun now, I can tell by your face.
Gone is the pain
There's a smile in its place
As I kiss your cheek, and stroke your hair
Wondering why life's so unfair
But realizing I'm not the only one
To lose a very special mum
And when it's time for me to go
I know you'll be there to say hello.

Gina Holhmerr

Remember Her

As I passed the gate I saw her
she looked so lost and frail
A tear was rolling down her cheek,
her face, so swollen, and pale,
if only, I could touch her hand.
To see her smile, and blush.
But all I see is hurt, and pain.
In a place, so full of hush.
In time her hurt will fade, and die.
The memories, will always stay.
She'll never forget the love they had,
With a mother, wonderful, in every way
as you stood beside her grave
a brave young girl of eleven
just remember in your heart
your mum was gone to heaven.
the love you had was oh so good
she cared and dried your tears
always treasure what you had
for year and years and years

Evelyn Criddle

Divorce

In my head are secrets of my life.
Overwhelming passion I must hide.
Looking back on years gone by
What happened to me I did not try.
I was young vulnerable and naive,
How could so many people mislead.
The past is gone but still sad to me,
All went wrong but I suppose it had to be,
Looking now on a happier note.
I feel now I am able to cope.
My children are my life and love.
I am so sorry for the past above.
I did my best for them and me.
    Please forgive me.
    Love.
    Mummy.

Barbara Douglas

Eyes Of A Child

When does a child become a man?
Or does a man become a child,
through the eyes of a child.
Watching the world through child-like eyes,
violence, hate and love followed by uncomprehending scenes,
looking on but yet, understanding dawns,
through mine eyes, as a child.

Down to the deepest heart,
a fear and torn apart. To a night that fell,
the hated footsteps that walked towards
and roughly taken by the shadows claws.
To the tears upon the floor.
Through the eyes of a child.
Through mine eyes, as a child.
and still, The Shadows Call.......

Jason Berg

The Farm In The Fens

When we were children, we lived on a farm.
Over two fields to reach house and barn.
Deep in the fens, with no dwellings in sight.
But we as children thought it all right.

The winds blew so hard across the fens.
No trees to stop it. It ruffled the hens.
When it was warm we swam in the dyke.
We also fished, and caught some pike.

There were horses and pigs, and a very fierce bull.
We rode on the pigs, who were fat and full.
We teased the bull by climbing his gate.
The bull gave chase, and we scrambled back before too late.

My brother and I, we wrestled and boxed.
Mother was cross, and said girls do not box.
She wanted me to be sedate.
Not much hope, it was too late.

We had a little sister. Her clothes did not get torn.
She was very very good from the day that she was born.
Mother was delighted, because she kept so clean.
Our sister really was every Mother's dream.

Joan Francis

Wraith

You'd walk with me, you said
Over that parallel horizon of hope and mystery
When death's cool frame had seized my breath
And the film of love's warmth encased between us had gone

You'd wait for me, you said
Between that whispering invisible plain of night and day
Frantically forging our broken bonds
While they sifted my soul through the wastes of eternity

You'd come to me, you said
When my tortured cries stung your ears and pierced your soul
Your lullaby of love would soothe and lift
Until that moment when the reaper's dark cloak would bring you to me

Our love would live, you said
Knowing that I would breathe from your lips as you exhaled
And you would wear me like a second skin amid your innocence
As time intensified the longing and the need of two separated souls

And here I wait between the sheets of life and death
Bereft, as you meet the birds sweet song each successive dawn alone
Until that hour when we pass through time's cover as one
And our silent footprints retrace that first moment of earthly love

Anthea Diane Bailey

An Afternoon In Winter

We sat on a January afternoon.
Outside, the powdered snow came down,
Worried by a bitter wind.
We were warm, talking easily
Of old days, and wondering
Where all the time had gone.

One middle-aged, one elderly, together;
A mother and her troubled son.
Their husband and father died
Twenty-one years ago today.
We talked of how the young ones
Had all grown so quickly.

There had not been this closeness between us since
My childhood, and it made me sad
That I should bring you problems
Then and now, after all these years.
My fear was like that blizzard
Just outside the window.

I questioned, once again, life's meaning
And the reason for all its pain.

John Buckmaster

Dissipated Thoughts Of A Faded Bloom

It seemed to me, just strolling down the Ealing high,
Past gardens fronting semis with colourful display
...and then the common on the right,
Where youths, indulging cricket, think of love
For girls who wander giggling by
Hand in hand, that I had missed an early
Chapter in my life through discipline so hard.
And now, in middle age I have
Become obsessed with nature's oft compelling laws...
Ah! That I were young again!
And then the "The Baker's Arms", inviting any passer-by
Into its cool interior, glassware twinkling
In a gentle light, with beer on tap to cherish any thirst!
And waiting there, all warmth and rounded softness,
The buxom barmaid stands...ah me!
Such carnal thoughts, but nice and very natural.
And, on going in, her smile of greeting
Quite upsets my notion of drinking two cool soothing pints.
Oh no! A half will do. I could not stand the pace!
Silly greying man, go home and study stamp collecting.
   Edward Colson

Thief

You left this morning and took me with you.
Only I didn't go anywhere.
I'm still here, scrambling about
Trying to find some pieces to put back inside.
Each day you stole a small part of me
A fragment of pride here,
A chunk of self-esteem there.
Until one day I noticed that I was slowly vanishing,
And your suitcase was growing heavier.
Then you gathered me up in it,
Threw it carelessly over your shoulder and waved.
We should only keep what is ours.
You can have the records,
But can I have my heart back please?
I will have more use for it than you.
You can always collect another.
Meanwhile I will occupy the space
With bitterness, resentment and regret.
On second thoughts, keep it.
I don't think I'll be needing it again anyway.
   Joanne Alexander

Louth Our 'Market Town'

From North to South, East or West
Our small market town is one of the best.
Folk come from near and far
And find what friendly folk we are.
They love our markets twice a week,
and pick up bargains which they seek,
then stroll around our beauty spots,
remarking what a lovely lot we've got.
Our majestic church standing proudly in the sky,
is the envy of everyone's eye, can be seen for miles around,
No other like it can be found.
Our 'Hubbards Hills' we proudly own,
its landscape of beauty is shared by everyone.
There's a cafe standing on the hill,
all can enjoy a meal at their will.
Our little town has so much to offer,
nice shops, entertainment, good pubs and food.
First class schools and well staffed swimming pool.
To everyone I say, support your little town, help in every way.
Make future generations proud of it, as we all are today.
   Edna A. Nutt

Untitled

After 12 long years we still don't know why
our darling Michael had to die.
I put him to bed on that fateful night.
And when I checked he was sleeping so tight.
But then in just a very short time.
He belonged to the Lord, no more to be mine.
He died in his sleep, so sudden, so unfair.
We needed our Michael to love and to care.
He was taken from us at such a young age.
Our feelings, a mixture of sadness and rage.
Angry at God for what he had done.
To take from us our beloved son.
But as time goes by, we understand
That Michael was chosen for Gods special land.
We know there's a reason for all that God does.
Ever taking our son from us.
We're sure that he's happy in his home up above.
But we'll always long to give him and kiss and a hug.
   Carole Skerrett

Courage Is "Sean D"

Or is there a meaning?
Or is it just a man?
One single among many a mill.
Odds are off!
Odds aren't what's it about.
It's about leaders,
Leaders leading the blind.
Ones of black greed white fat,
Ones who know not of life.
As human as a baby's expression,
Eyes glancing in conversation of no words.
Hearth felt death awoke her,
A part of her died.
Died for being really alive.
Alive for something he could not see.
I dream of Africa.
No more! No more!
I now understand the real world!
   Gavin McGibney

Gone Away

I feel your presence within the house,
on touching the pillow I imagine my
hand stroking your hair.
Your light easy laughter echoes
around the lonely rooms.
A haunting piano melody hangs
over the silent hall.
Shadows come to darken the lawns.
I throw open the door,
To hear your voice tossed into the
air by the teasing wind.
Turning my eyes towards the sky,
I see your face dance between
the white clouds
And feel you close.
   Glenda Mary Anderson

Sunseekers

The sun is up and shining bright,
On the golden sands below,
And the sparkling sea that seems to invite,
All the worshippers that love it so,
Then the ceremony begins at last,
The half-dressed brotherhood begin to assemble,
The fat and the ugly stand aghast,
As they stare at the people they want to resemble;
The ritual begins by selecting a place,
And positioning themselves to pray to their god,
Then they lie down in order to face,
This entity in the sky they love to laud,
And when the sun goes down and they all return home,
They leave the beach like a cortege of drones.
   Derek Frew

Big Old Chub

As I crawled through the grass,
on my hands and knees,
I heard a splash 'neath some old willow trees,
Just a little closer I thought to myself.
That crafty old chub lies near the shelf,
I wonder if he's after a fly
or a big lump of cheese - let's have a try
As I poked the rod between some nettles.
My heart in my mouth, I hope the bait settles,
trembling with excitement I watched the rod top,
lowered the bait with a silent plop,
all of a sudden thump went the rod,
he felt like thunder did that big old chub.
The rod was bent over like never before,
off like a rocket and into some roots - I think I swore,
he's smashed me again just like before

Adrian Carvell

Waiting

I sat alone, waiting for you to call
Outside grew darker, the rain began to fall.
Thoughts of last night, flashed in my mind
The jokes, the laughter, compliments so kind.
The rumble of thunder, brought me around
Oh! please let me hear that ringing sound.
I stared at the telephone, wanting so much
Waiting and hoping that you'd get in touch.
The letter plate rattled, the room filled with light
Bang! Bang! On the door, oh what a fright.
Then there you were standing, soaked through to the skin
A smile on your face, raindrops on your chin.
No more am I waiting beside the phone
No more will I ever feel so alone.
There's a glow in the room now, fire so bright
Thunder and lightning, what a wonderful night.

Carrie Rutherford

Traffic Lights

They come it two's or sometimes four,
On busy roads there may be more,
Helping traffic along its way,
They change continuously every day,
Red to stop and green to go,
Forever altering to keep the flow,
Pedestrians 'press' and wait to cross,
The traffic lights know, that they're the boss,
When at red they start to beep,
People walking as if like sheep,
Engines revving, they can't wait,
Impatient drivers, running late,
Amber flashing, raring to go,
Little old lady walking slow,
See the frustration on their faces,
You'd think they'd lost their parking spaces,
A daily chose for a traffic light,
That's seen it all both day and night.

Carl A. Roberts

Bouquet Of Flowers

The seeds are planted row by row
Oh how lovely to see them grow
The passers by they stand and stare
It was worth all the time and care

Daffodils roses carnations too
A beautiful bouquet just for you
What a pleasure to give someone so kind
For a friend like you is hard to find

So plant those seeds again with care
Then once again we hope to share
A special bouquet for someone new
A mother a love or maybe you.

Frances Bailey

Life In An Elderly People's Home

When we get older, our hair turns grey
Often our bodies don't do as we say
Through the years, we've done our best
For our children, now flown the nest

So now the time has come to say
What does it matter, if our hair is grey
We will, knit and sew still doing our best
But most important, enjoying the rest

So younger ones, when working with us
Be understanding and don't make a fuss
Because in years to come, when we've had our day
You'll be the ones, with the heads of grey

Allison Stephens

Untitled

Whatever happened to England our green and pleasant land,
of unlocked doors and windows and many a helping hand.
Where people spoke to people from any a distant part,
with never a thought of fighting, just feelings from the heart.
There was laughter filling all the air with kids playing in the street.
A penny for a lolly was a very special treat.
Neighbours loved their neighbours they stood together well,
For many a pain and agony one never a friend would sell.
Now the fields are vanishing, England's beauty is going fast,
it's such a shame to see things go and end up in the past.
If only we could, just for a while, stop, and let things lay,
get rid of all the bad things that bother us in our day.
Start smiling in the morning at everyone at hand,
and back would come our England our green and pleasant land.

Benita Manners

Reflections

'Tis true the image you reflect good mirror on the wall
Of this old ageing face and frame, no trace of youth at all.
The wrinkles deep, beneath my eyes, you show them up so clear
And add another one or two for each succeeding year.

Those wisps of hair, once auburn red are now an Autumn grey
And the rosy cheeks-once full and round-they tend to fade away
My promised three score years and ten are fast becoming few
A short time left to reminisce - what else is there to do?

I sometimes dream of days gone by, when active, young and gay
In youthful bloom I knew no gloom; I lived from day to day.
No thoughts of age did worry me nor had I time to care
For morbid fears were new to me, I had a buoyant air.

The leaves, their wrinkles cannot hide when Autumn's at the door
Nor the old Oak tree with rutted bark almost to its inner core.
Why then should I with failing frame challenge the ebbing tide?
I must live with my years and nagging fears. I cannot turn aside.

Good luck to you who come behind like flotsam on a stream
Don't let life's trials worry you, take each one as a dream
And when you've reached the place where I am now just passing by
You trim your sails to the Winter gales and then prepare to die.

David Hamill

The Fire, The Shell Mr. Toomin And Nell

Standing, staring unseeing across the black wet earth
of the ploughed field.
Once warm, loved, filled with laughter always sunny, no more.
No more. The smoke, thick black choking, stopping the
life of the sleeping people. The flames red, hungry, licking
tasting, scorching, burning.
Now cold, empty, still except the slow creeping mist,
the chill moving ever nearer towards the blackened
shell of the old house.
The wind sighs and blows gently. The old man standing
staring unseeing, alone forgotten, turns and fades into
the mist - his dog behind him.

Eleanor Sadler

Untitled

Night is a time when many thoughts come creeping to the mind
Of other lands where happiness is very hard to find
Where children starve and parents weep
And old folks find they cannot sleep.
We think a lot and wonder why
These things have come to be.
For in his image God made man
And meant him to be free.
If every man knelt down to pray
And asked forgiveness every day
And lived to love and not to kill
And then obeyed the Father's will
This world of ours would once more be
A place of peace and liberty
Where children eat and play and see
Life as it is meant to be
So when these thoughts come creeping in
Do not bow down accepting sin
Lift up your head - be proud to face
The Father of the human race
   Frances Mary Burnett

On Being Deaf

No-one knows of the strain and stress
   Of not hearing all that is being said,
When two or three all talk at once,
   One begins to feel they are sadly missed out.

My hearing-aid is a blessing to me,
   Which has been part of me for fifty years.
Through those years, love and patience have always been given
   By the one who loves me, and to me is so dear.

In the spring I hear the black-birds love song.
   Along with the singing of the thrush,
It is my privilege to hear them - but
   To some with good hearing - it doesn't mean so much.

The laughter of children I love to hear,
   Along with their goals and squeals of delight
But when I say, Pardon - what did you say?
   They in their turn, look and wonder - why do you ask?

Lips-reading has helped me over the years
   But when I'm out shopping, and don't hear all that is said
One gets the looks of being "Just 'round the bend."
   I ask you - speak slowly, clearly and "Just be a Friend"
   Gwen Banbury

Le Femme Petite

Trusting in someone
Reverses the good intention
Now I'm numb dumb
Intrusion on an involuntary detention
One woman's touch word sight
Is the way I feel tonight

Impressing like we all try
Lessons in courtship's art
Two sides to every truth and lie
Wake up the heart
Occupying the space
The face the chase the embrace

Bitter to sweet
Admiration for another
Now we're almost complete
Forever is what we mean to each other
The rhythm flowing with its beat
Le femme petite.
   Earl Rumgay

If...

If you've never been to that land called Wales
Of mountains high, and deep dark vales
If you've never stood on that bleak slope
In the village that stood, and lost its hope
If you've never stood by those stones so white
In the stillness of the valley, in the bright sunlight
If you've never stood by that little church
And watched little sparrows on those gravestones perch
If you've never stood there in utter despair
As those children's hushed silence fills the air
If you've never felt that town touch your heart
And sensed on that hillside, of loved ones apart
If you've never been there, the folly of man
Then you've never stood, in that town, Aberfan.
   John K. Turner

Thanks!

Thanks, for the toxins in our oceans,
Of man's dumping his chemical potions,
Left sea life choking in our lotions.
Thanks, for the polluted sky,
Where carcinogen puts a tear in one's eye,
Even the feathered wings will no longer fly.
Thanks, for mother nature being raped dry,
The earth and the forests all must die,
While the perplexed politely ask why.
Thanks, for the hole in the ozone,
Or is it the new radioactive icon,
Still, advisory to keep all your clothes on.
Thanks, to the master race,
With its floating junk left out in space,
Another point to add to the disgrace.
Thanks, to the religious revelations,
Or has it all been lies throughout generations,
Causing the wars of our nations,
Leaving minds in critical fragmentations.
   Angus Jackson Hewitt McIntyre

Time

Time is life, the invisible culture
of each individual.
It creeps unseen in every corner of ourselves,
from birth to death.
We use it to work to play, worry and rest.
To be joyous and to jest.
In its worst state we use it to waste,
in its most elevated we use it to LOVE.
Time can be unutterably cruel, hasty, unjust.
But give it a chance, take time to explore,
Watch the creative conceptions time gives,
to everlasting contentment and tranquillity.
   Christine Dale

All Jazz In A Dream

I want the tune that surrenders me to unconditional bliss.
Of chords discordant with their rhythmic miss.
A piano that slow bebops and stops beginning a silence pure of affect.
Bassy deep bass revelling in its property fine allows alto and tenor sax to entwine.
Machine gun of drum feeling with sticks dispenses with clever electronic tricks.

A scintillating quintet of perfect sound
give me blues that diffuse and abound
into east coast, west coast, hard bop, hard core of the soft rock n' roll of all kind.
Big band sing sing of swing of old brass horns marching into pianos of ill repute, stride out into ragtime, glad time and sad time whispering through a bossa nova night
round midnight in Tunisia out of sight catching a bird in full flight.

Musicke, musak I need no crack.
Just jass my body and soul, and let old Jelly Roll
me into some sweet Savannahed scene
to insist an infinite encore of my dream.
   John French

The Dragon-Fly

Songs, and stories have been told,
Of butterflies, and moths covered in gold.
But, each summer means so much to me,
When the haunting flight of this monster I see.

It starts life a grub, down in the river.
Heading for safety, it learns how to slither.
Many body shells, it must leave, discard.
Until it produces its last glowing card.

Never lifting its body far from the ground,
Bushes and trees it just flies around.
Oh, has it landed, no, look it's there,
With gossamer wings beating the air.

This giant flyer, lifts its head to the sky,
A buzz hits the ear, as it starts to fly.
This beast, this beauty, with the silken sheen,
In its full glory, it has to be seen.

Its name belies it as it flies.
Its name belies it for soon it dies.
Its awesome shape set against the sky.
That dauntingly beautiful Dragon-Fly.

Jack Preston

March 12, 1995

Snowdrops sparkled bravely, weeks on end,
On grey-gloved days whose pall they were outfacing,
But even they were hard-pressed to pretend
That icy fingers were not all-embracing.

But suddenly, dark winter's in retreat.
The garden lounger speaks precocious pleasure,
As blazing sun, blue sky, forgotten heat,
Produce, this lovely day, brief hours to treasure.

Each sacrificial limb's all winter-white —
A pallid, flabby slab of pudgy, sallow
And waxen flesh which meets again the light,
Released from wraps which harbour tones of tallow.

I'm oven-ready, lotioned, set to start.
Great Cook Almighty's sun, the quick-grill fire,
Serves winter's pallor *flambéed, à la carte,*
Agog to glow and presently perspire.

Clinging winter's surely in retreat,
With frozen pipes and calling out the plumber:
Supine, perspiring in a searing heat,
I slide, self-basting, into dreams of summer.

John Slim

Shadows

Hate seemed like an illness - it only happened to other people.
Not me, oh no, well, until...
Until I met you and fell in love,
And sat and watched
As slowly
You ripped my heart to shreds,
And left - without a word.
No Good-bye. No sorry. Nothing...
My rage bred and festered
And like a creeping disease
Infected me.
Malignant choler and venomous spite
Transformed my once tender heart into rotting carrion.
I thrive on hate
And crave only one thing -
Revenge.
And believe me - I'll get it.
Someday.
Somehow.
Watch out!

Alison C. Jones

Felharmonic Orchestra

Various... (Stradivarius?) miaowing violins
Pad and creep about
Over rooves tiled with drilling drums
While thumbs in tambourines shake crumbs of hums
That fall about our toes
Past ogling oboes
That snigger as they watch the swell get bigger...

Various.. (stradivarius?) miaowing violins
Pad and creep and leap from hedges
Hung with cobwebs on the edges...
Gently dew dropped with tinkling drips and chimes
At times from tittering triangles...

Threatened by the gulping mouths of resonant
Double bases all at changing paces set
By the dominant magnetic baton whose prominent seal
Is met with the feel of each step and pause
Of the paws
Of the various (stradivarius?) miaowing violins.

Brenda G. Bradley

Good Humour

Never drag the 'Flag of Humour'
    through the dust of dirt or shame,
If you hear a horrid rumour,
    say, "the story's very lame".
If your fun would hurt another
    as you hold him up to scorn,
Say it not, of friend or brother,
    let thoughtfulness your words adorn.

Face the world with a holy boldness,
    lion-like in strength, yet kind,
Loving and true, shunning all coldness
    in everyone seeking the best to find.

Screw your courage up, face trials!
    work with zeal to 'get on top'
Frowning not at clocks or their dials
    saying, "the clock's too quick, can't it stop?"

Praying each moment for strength and ability,
    Guidance, faith, hope, and sympathy true,
Asking for cleansing from irritability,
    Follow on, good humour will belong to you!

Norah R. Simpson

What Are We Doing to the World

What are we doing to the world today
Nowhere's safe to live or play
The earth's polluted beyond repair.
Does anybody really care?
With Murders, Muggings and such like.
It's not even worth locking up your bike.
Gone are the days when children run free.
To play by a stream, or climb up a tree
The age of innocence has been taken away.
How can we let our children play?
Jealously guarding all that is ours.
Locked away in our Ivory Towers.
Greed is the name of an awful game
We leave people to suffer for this coveted fame
The world could be a better place if we could
put greed in its place. Out of sight out of mind
are the words to which we bind
Why is everybody in the world so blind
Can't they just take some time to be kind.

Janet Grant

Winter Scene

The children frolic in the snow,
Now that winter's here,
But older folk step carefully,
As falling they do fear.

The children shout and jump with joy,
Their eyes are all aglow,
Into balls they mould it,
As they gather up the snow,

In a garden, a snowman had been built,
And he was quite a size,
The little girl looked up at him,
With wonder in her eyes.

A pipe was stuck into his mouth,
A carrot for his nose,
Two small stones were used as eyes,
He really struck a pose.

The little girl will remember him,
For many years ahead,
Although the sun will melt him down,
And perhaps some tears be shed.
Joyce Crocker

Forbidden Fruit...

A hunger, a craving, till now suppressed,
Now out in the open, riding waves on a crest.
A whisper in the wind, a bird on the wing,
Frustrated feelings, emerge from within.
Finally a touch, that burns and scars,
Emotions that tear my world apart.
An alarm bell sounding in my brain,
Thunder clapping, torrential rain.
Misty thoughts, amongst muffled sounds.
Slipping down the avalanche of life,
Multi coloured contours, bright flashing lights.
A fleeting secret second, in the span of all time,
Forbidden forever, cannot be mine.
Ideas like demons, undress in my brain,
Longed for caresses, and you, whisper my name.
Like a tangle wood forest, in a web of desire,
A moment of lust, a soul set on fire.
In a world so forlorn, a precious love dawns,
Forbidden fruit, on sour vines,
Can only live safe, inside my mind...
Gwen McNamara

Addiction

It's that time in life when you feel so weak.
Nothing goes right, you're lost, alone feelings run deep,
The strength you had is running low,
You're tired, bored, but want no-one to know,
You run and hide so others don't see,
Searching your mind, what's wrong with me?
Looking around, trying to understand,
But you're giving up, you don't know if you can,
So you turn to something that helps you along,
The rough and rocky road of life seems to have gone,
But all of a sudden there's another hill to climb,
You can't face it, you're breaking,
Turning back to the same line,
Again and again you face the same fear,
Needing the same help, it feels good,
It's easy everything seems clear,
But then you wake up to find you've
Lost more than you've gained,
It's just a vicious circle and an addictive game.
Alison Cook

A Bolt Of Lightening Could Ruin Your Whole Day

A man sits on a hilltop
observing life go by.
The flowers, birds and trees
the movement of the sky.
A man sits on a hilltop
dreaming of a world to be.
Peace, love and compassion
What can be the key?
A man sits on a hilltop
considering his goal.
He's going to make life better
having just realized his role.
A man stands on a hilltop
understanding fills his head.
A bolt of lightening strikes him
he blinks and then he's dead.
Charmian Hembry

Childhood Memories

A small white-washed house, only one storey high
Ochil hills in the background reaching up to the sky
Daddy tending his animals, did he never tire?
Mummy in floral pinny, pancakes on the fire
Work to be done no time for sloth
New-baked scones on the table, wrapped up in a cloth
Oat-cakes and porridge, black pudding of course
Helping Dad in the stable while he groomed his big horse
Wood to be chopped, coal to be fetched, water to bring from the well
Blaeberry picking to make the sweet jam
Even now I can savour the smell
Across the moor to the farm, through the big five-barred gate
Milk warm from the cow, I can still taste it yet
A strong swing on the oak tree, hung there by our dad
When our chores were completed what fun we all had
Nothing is left now, all scattered and gone
Only sweet childhood memories winging thoughts back to home
Catherine Bridger

Castles In The Air

I'll climb the highest mountain and
  reach the highest peak
I might leave it till tomorrow or I may
  go sometime next week
I think I'll go deep sea diving or sail the
  world in a boat
I know you won't take me serious so I'll
  do it just for a joke
I think I'll swim the channel I know it's
  been done before
But it would be a real achievement
  now I'm 64
I'm going to do so many things you just
  wait and see
But for now I'll put the kettle on and
  make us a cup of tea
Catherine Chesters

Daniel Garwood

I guess this means goodbye
Our final act of sorrow.
But I will never forget you
As if it were tomorrow.

You were always such a clown
You brightened up my day.
With your cheeky cheerful grin
You were always bright and gay.

Now that God has found you
I'm sure you'll show him who's boss.
He's found a friend as well as an angel
And we are left with the loss.
Soo Castleton

Untitled

Now, summer snow adorns my hair
youth as long since flown
the journey, soon I travel
like the wind, my spirit blown

In the twilight of my years
my mind remembers much
the dawning of my childhood
my mothers gentle touch

The beauty of a sunrise
soft, sweet gentle rain
excitement of a seaside trip
on a locomotive train

These things I will remember
with fondness and with bliss
heaven, seems to whisper
death is but kiss

I see the light approaching
I see the peaceful dove
I leave my daughters, memories
I leave, my sweet, sweet love

G. Chambers

The Hunted Fox

They call this sport
Your very breath to extort
They think it's a game
To make you run again and again

There are those who say
You shall die today
If you perchance to find a hole
Think not it will save your soul.
Men with terriers and shovels
Will oust you from your hovel.

They think it's not a sin
To tear you limb from limb.
But the hunter kills at leisure
For meat that brings no pleasure.

E. A. Smith

Untitled

Inside my paper I found today,
your competition well what
can I say!
You said any style and in twenty
lines, impress some judges and
be paid in kind well this I wrote
In minutes few to show to you
just what can I do. I am very
shy and do this for fun
but feel I could do it for
the right someone. So have
a good read and pursue at
will. When all is said and
done we may have a deal.

M. D. Carr

Regrets

Why did I walk away from you
Without a backward glance
When all the time, my heart cried out
For just another chance
To tell you of my love for you
But now I sit and cry
I never will forget you
For in my heart you'll stay
Until the day we meet again
I'll sit and wonder why.
My love for you, could end this way
  Without a last goodbye.

B. Grant

For Our Dearest Dad

From the day that we were born
You show'd how much you care
By teaching us what's right and wrong
By always being there.

When we did wrong, you shouted Dad
When we did well, you praised
But, all the time you gave us love
Throughout our childhood days

We thank you, all; for everything
You've given throughout our life
For everything you've been to us
In everything we do.
And, in return, we've tried to show
That Dad, we all love you.

Kathryn Carr

Untitled

You always hurt the ones you love,
you said with a wry smile,
As you held me,
to soothe the sting of your slap,
and the wounds of your words.
And I nodded understandingly.
Wondering why,
If that was the case,
I'd never done the same
to You.

Pippa Dawn Slark

The Door Is Open

You can feel what you want,
You can see and believe,
It's all up to you,
You can go with the breeze;

You can struggle with the waves,
Or, just go with the flow,
It's all up to you,
There's nothing you don't know;

You can fly in the sky,
You can swim in the sea,
Be in touch with the earth,
Or, just talk to the trees;

You can walk hand in hand,
Or, roam on your own,
You can carry on walking,
Or, make you way home.

Lisa McGoff

By The Grave Stone

By the grave stone I do sit,
wondering why you had to die.
I look up in the sky,
to see the sun shining down,
upon the flowers in the ground.
I wonder to myself today,
why people had to go this way.
Rest in peace they
all must do.
Knowing one day,
it will be me and you.

E. Donnelly

Untitled

Look into my eyes
You always said they were
  like a book.
Open for all to read.
Look again for the pages are all
  now blank.
Just an emptiness, a void.

Will a tear ever well again in
  this empty cavern.
Will a twinkle dance and glow.
Will lively thoughts flicker
  back and forth.
Not even sorrow can be seen.

No feeling or thoughts emits,
  from these sockets.

Those dreams behind my eyes are gone.
They died with my child.
They are ashes mingled with his.
Scattered to the four winds.
Drifting in eternal darkness.

M. Bliss

"Armageddon Morn"

How fortunate you are
You earthmen now "DEAD"?
Deo grat, long ago, "Born"
You live not, in this violent,
Armageddon morn.

Thomas Maher

Child

To us all time is running
Yet to most it makes no change
So stuck up in our own worlds
Nobody seems to find it strange
That nowadays we think it normal
To see murder, pain and guilt
Don't realise until it is too late
Just what a future we've built
For our children so innocent
What chances to them do we give
All things go from bad to worse
No fit place for them to live
Yet we all still ignore the clock
Concentrate on having a good time
It may not be an offence
But what we do is still a crime.

Stuart Grant

Love Hunt

In your arms lies my happiness,
Yet I seek to be loved by you
  again and again,
Why "o" why is it hard for one,
  to show love or how to love,
Giving my heart and soul,
  just to be loved by you,
Realizing that I ask for too much.
Holding my hands as tight as I could,
Praying to God, and why so
  much heartache and pain.
Take me where there is no pain
Yet I still, say in your arms
  lies my happiness,
I treat you so kind and humane,
Yet you hurt me again and again.

Mohammed Ramzan

Time Passes

Time passes
witnessed by
the extending slender cream stem of
the slow unfolding
deep green
carefree leaves of
the wistful spider plant
dying gracefully
in a beam of stray winter sunshine
as white snowflakes
dance mischievously outside
the dusty window pane.

Penelope Lumley

Bereavement

The worst part of bereavement is
Within the dead of night...
When the dearly departed
Are there within your sight.
You see them breathe and smile
And walk,
So vital, real and true.....
And then you hear them
Start to talk,
And they're speaking just for you.
And for a while the happy times
Are back to stay it seems;
Until you waken up to find
That it was all
A dream.

Michael E. Ord

"The Psychiatric Patient"

She sits motionless and pale
Within a world of dreams,
Transparent skin and frail
As a broken butterfly.

At pictureless wall she stares,
Lone and infinitely lost
From sight and sound and cares
Of everyday existence.

Poor, gentle thing, the mind,
Easily pushed and jarred
Beyond the natural confines
Of cruel, relentless life.

Margaret Dowding

Looking Back

I never thought I'd see the day
With you beside me now,
Safe in this happy feeling
Tell me - when, where and how?
I've certainly known you long enough
To call you my best friend.
So when did love creep in
And friendship gradually end?
One day I guess you looked at me
In a very different light.
I looked back at you the same
And saw a pleasing sight.
I don't think it was difficult
To enjoy each other's time.
We grew in fondness steadily
And love was in its prime.
   Suddenly my heart is racing faster
   As I'm asked a question loudly,
   I smile, look at you and say 'I do
   With all my heart' so proudly.

Marion Tydeman

Summer Time

Oh roll on the summer,
With warm sunny days.
Let's lie on those sun beds,
Soaking up the sun's rays.

The cold frost and snow,
Chills you through to the bone,
Don't want to go out,
Wrap up warm and stay home.

The kids making snowmen,
Their faces aglow,
You hear them all laughing.
Playing out in the snow,

But you can't beat the summer,
When it's light until late.
Having meals alfresco,
Swatting wasps from your plate.

Slap on that sun block,
Of factor whatever.
Enjoy what you can,
Of our English weather.

Shirley Griffiths

Thank You, Mother Nature

Mother nature didn't bless me
With the skill to bear a child.
The need is great; painful
Yet I refuse to get wild
with anger and frustration
for she gave me so many gifts:
The windows in my face
An ability to feel the wind.
Priceless are those sights I see
My friends share their joy
With lengthy arms they look above
Pull faces at a living toy
Love they give, tears they dry
I do envy them, it's true
Still I ask the reason why
Not for me? Just fate.
Still I refuse to get angry
My heart finds a grateful note
Thank you, mother nature
For what I have, not what I have not.

Lewey Usher

The Purple Triangle

And they wore the purple triangle
With pride upon their breast
As they all stood together
Segregated from the rest

What evil crime did they commit
That gave cause for alarm
Refused the uniform and kit
Refused to hurt or harm

They had the choice to be set free
Just sign the dotted line
But that would seal their destiny
Cut off from the vine

Yes they wore the purple triangle
The symbol of the truth
They hope of paradise ahead
For this they gave their youth

With joyful faces they endured
The hatred pain and strife
Because they knew that they'd ensured
The promised crown of life

A. C. Kelly

Untitled

A dove on a quest
With a mind to settle
A people below, willing
To grasp the nettle
The powers that rule
Now with a chance
To lift and wave
The olive branch
A dove like peace
A fragile thing
Needs a gentle wind
Under its wing

W. G. Purse

Mummy Sends Her Love

I am awakened before the sunrise,
With my daughter at my side
And once again she asks me.
Why has Mummy died?
It brings tears to my eyes,
As I know, I should not lie.
So I tell her we'll meet Mummy.
When it is time for us to fly.
Mummy is now a star in heaven
Shining brightly way up above.
She is watching and waiting for us.
And showering us, with her love.
So rest now darling, and go to sleep
Mummy is safe in heaven above.
Close your eyes and do not weep.
For, Mummy sends her love.

Robert Steven Pike

Mums - Pride

I gave you life a long time ago,
With lots of love and pride,
For many of those years,
With doubts and fears,
Sometimes with tears

Then time went too quickly,
For you three to leave the nest,
Trusting you would do your best,
I had time then to have a rest,

You all did your best with pride,
Came through life's tests,
I've got three of the best,
Now your Mum can really rest,

In my old age your dad is not here,
All I see is his empty chair,
I've been put to the test,
I know you all do care,
God bless all your tomorrows,
Pray do what is always right
Ever more from your Mum and Dad.

V. M. Moore

The Abortion

With a telephone as his tool,
With distance as his glove,
With an anaesthetic smile,
He terminates our love.

I can feel it flowing through me,
As it kicks I hear its cry
As it whispers round my heartstrings
And pleads, begs, not to die.

With a click the call is over.
With a click is love denied.
And I sit alone, abandoned,
Filled with emptiness inside.

Martha Monday

Their Tomorrow

I watch my children growing
With joy I see them rise
To know their smiling faces
Brings tears to my eyes

But how I fear tomorrow
And what the future holds
Oh how can we protect them
And keep them in our folds

We teach them of life's values
In hope it's kept in mind
To see them through each day
As along life's road they wind

We cannot always keep them
Within our easy reach
So strive we must to make sure
They know why we preach.

Kathleen N. Merritt

The Widow

I sit alone and think of you
with crushing pain and grief,
so much we had, so much we did;
a lifetime seems too brief.

I still cannot believe my loss,
to think you left me first!
My life is empty, my existence poor,
only pity makes it worse.

The times we had, the things we did
are locked up in my mind,
I think of them I think of you
so good, so strong, so kind.

Now you're gone and greatly missed
by all you loved and knew.
They say time waits for no man,
not even one like you.

Mike Linley

Untitled

There is a little boy eyes so blue,
With a mop of golden hair too,
He is my little chocolate soldier,
And will be till he's much older,
Although he can be quite a lad,
He's never been really bad,
Even though he's only four years old,
And doesn't always do as he's told,
Mostly he gets his own way
But then he's only get to say
I love you Gran and hug me so tight
And we turn off the light and say
Nite Nite.

J. Bedford

Friendship

A friend is one to turn to,
When things are going wrong,
Someone to listen to your story,
And put you back on song.

A friend will always be on hand,
When troubles come your way,
Will help you make a stand,
To push aside that rainy day.

A friend will be by your side,
When all the rest have gone,
Help sort out your problems,
Make quite sure you carry on.

Friendship is a wonderful gift,
That cannot be bought or sold,
Do not turn away any friend,
They are worth their weight in gold.

H. C. Willmott

The Swirling Ice

The swirling flurries fall on glass,
wind that whips them up so fast,
like petals from a fading flower,
falling like an April shower.

Colder than an arctic breeze,
blown across a thousand seas,
clouded ice that falls so far,
without the warmth but like a star.

An endless stream so frozen falls,
the world below beckons, calls,
for just a second they seem to stay,
then in the warmth they fade away.

Reflected in the frozen light,
things begin to seem so white,
a covered cloak of ivory sand,
swirls like ice around the land.

Silence seems to follow the glow,
of the fresh and creamy snow,
mirrored in the liquid glass,
the white cover will not last.

C. Ayre

Others

In this beautiful world we live,
why has there got to be
grown ups and children suffering,
who never will be free.
each day they live a bonus
they always smile through
they don't hold a grudge,
or think I wish I were like you.
yet we who say we're normal,
are never satisfied,
we want what other people have
we have a greedy side.
we never think of others
who never will be free
from the wheel chairs that hold them
or the blind who cannot see.
so when your being greedy
and want more than you have,
just for a moment think of them
and for your freedom just be glad.

J. D. Jarome

My Dad...

His blue eyes always twinkled
With mischief and glee
When as a small child
I sat on his knee

He made learning fun
And my growing-up too
My dear darling Dad -
I do so miss you

He was always so good
To both stranger and friend
I always thought that his life
Would be without end

He was joyful and loving
And always happy to share
Now the chair in the corner
Seems so empty and bare

He cherished me greatly
So I shouldn't be sad
For his love still surrounds me -
My dear darling Dad

Sheila Clapham

Little Robin

Tell me little Robin,
Why don't you fly away,
What pleasure do you find here,
On this cold winter day.

Pretty little hopping in the snow
Your sad eyes say you're hungry.
Have you no where else to go.

Little bird so beautiful
Lonely as can be.
But stay here, I will promise
You will find a friend in me.

I'll protect you little Robin
Till summer time is due
For winter has no mercy
On little birds like you.

A. Shorten

Hope

Why, did God take your little one,
Who was so sweet and dear,

But you know.
He only takes the good ones,
And holds them close and near.

She got the call,
before us all
But some day we will meet
And be together constantly
Up by that golden seat.

I know your heart is breaking,
And you are feeling sad,
but think only of the good times,
and forget all of the bad,

She was a ray of sunshine,
Perhaps now, a guiding light,
For all of us to follow,
Through the dark and lonely night.

Shirley Austin

To The World From Alex

I know a lady
Who is having a baby
She is my mummy
It's in her tummy
My dad is happy as can be
He will put it on his knee
When I swim or ride my bike.
Baby can come too if it likes
I also hope it will be good
And eat up every bit of food
When the baby has been fed
It can sleep with me in bed
Now you know about my mother
I will be the baby's "Big Brother"

Mollie Nichol

The Girl

I look from my window,
what can I see,
A little girl, standing,
looking at me.

Her face is round,
Her eyes are small,
With brown curly hair,
She's not very tall.

She looks so young,
and tender there,
Peaceful and mild,
Without a care.

Richard Andrews

Found

I have found love
which there is no other sort

I have found love
which can't be sold or bought

I have found love
which is sincere and true

I have found love
which comes straight from you.

Mary Simpson

Soulmate

Where's the one that I might love,
who captures all my heart,
a gentle and a loving soul with
whom I'll never part.
As time goes by and we never meet,
I often wonder sadly,
why two souls are kept apart,
when they need each other badly.

I need to know just who you are,
and if you do exist,
I need to feel the passion of
your kiss upon my lips,
I need to feel the warmth of being
close to you and then,
another moment with you,
I have to have again.

H. A. Little

Who's Less Sane To Get The Cane?

My psychiatrist is crazy
  while I am lazy
This mad doctor's childish
while I am girlish
He is my non-sense
While I am his nuisance
So who is less sane
  to get the cane?

If Dr. Harrison Read is more insane
Than I am less sane,
or if he is more abnormal
then I am less normal.
Who's than less sane
To get the cane?

To be
Or not to be
is the question
Who is less sane
To get the cane?

Vivian Aston

Words From Spirit

In a world of peace
Where love and truth are law
In the light of God
We walk on a golden shore

We guide our mortal souls
Along that path of light
Until the doors of death
Becomes the doors of life

Eternal life there after
Our spirit meet our guides
Who on earth had helped us
And were forever by our sides

You to can help somebody
In life and when in spirit
by giving love and truth
And helping every minute

L. Baptist

A Cottage Fine

A cottage fine beside a stream
Where I can sit and idly dream
Pretty curtains at window pane
Sparkling in the summer rain
Flowers spread beneath window sill
Whose fragrances the air doth fill
Sunny bower at garden's end
Where I can see the colours blend
The winter brings its own delight
Snowdrops and crocus shining bright
No season spoils my lovely view
I see each scene with joy anew
Even when I'm fast asleep
The scenery I know will keep
As soon as I open up my eyes
I cast them around my lovely prize

Marion Pollitt

Enduring Love

Do you walk happy
  where as yet
  we cannot meet.

Do you look on us
  and wonder
  why we weep.
  Why:
  It's our love
  still felt for you
  we cannot reach

Sylvia Vann

Never Ending Love

It's so sad and unfair
When we lose someone we love
Although we still care
We should trust in God above
For He will look after
The person in our heart
So think of it as knowing
It's not the end, it's just the start
For they will be happy
Not in pain anymore
For us life goes on
Who knows what's in store
Believe me when I tell you
I know just how you feel
Coz it happened to me once
It isn't such a thrill
So remember when you're hurting
And you really need a friend
Just call and I'll come running
As life begins and never ends.

H. Fitzgerald

If I Can Help

If I can help, if I can care,
When I see you lying there
So peaceful in sleep you seem,
And yet I know it's all a dream.

Your illness makes it hard to bear,
And yet I know I'll always care,
The flowers all around you show
That you have been so great to know.

Your family and friends are sad,
Not everything can be so bad,
For knowing you, the way we do,
Can help us all when we feel blue.

Your memory will with us stay,
To help to get us through the day.

Phyllis Richardson

A Cautionary Tale

The cat was mauling the mouse
when tenderfoot came along:
champion of compromise.
"Naughty cat" he said,
"poor little mouse",
and he picked up the mouse
and the mouse,
harnessed in fear and rage,
bit him.
"Ouch" said tenderfoot,
"vile ingrate.
Here you are cat,
have it back."
And the cat said:
"He has seen the error of his ways".
And the mouse said:
"My instinct about him was right".
And tenderfoot rushed for a plaster
and recorded in the first-aid book:
"Mousebite".

Ursula E. K. Light

The Hungry Bird

I was lying in bed one frosty morning
When on the window a tap I heard
I turned to face the window,
And saw a little bird

He looked so cold and hungry
He's probably at a loss,
Where can he get his food,
It's such a hard baked frost.

I'll have to do my bit I thought
Whilst I lay in my bed
I'll not let birdie go hungry
He'll have a bit of bread.

I'll get him bread and water
And put it on the sill
Oh such a lovely feeling.
As birdie filled his bill.

I can't describe the feeling.
As birdie flew away,
But I'm so happy I did my bit
On that cold and frosty day

Peter Burton

Untitled

Will we look back from our journey
  When far beyond this place
And tell God our story
  Of how we lived the human race
Can we tell of how we loved
Or stopped a passer by
  Or how we wiped the tears away
When we heard a cry

Can we say we shared the cup
  When we saw their pain
Or did we leave them thereabouts
Crying in the rain

If we leave a little hope
  A glimmer to be seen
A spirit that's still burning
  A dream within a dream
Then to the sunlight far beyond
Our eyes that close in death
  A place in heaven all divine
We will find our rest
In thee

Valerie Cruz

Winter

A cold November day,
when all the trees are bare,
Their golden leaves lay on the ground.
And there's changes in the air.
You can still have fun,
So go for a run.
There are joggers everywhere,
but do not tarry for the winds,
do carry the sleet and snow.
On a cold November day.

Peggy Collins

Corn Dollies

As with the sea in a shell,
We hear in the ear
 Life.

The cycle of seasons
Caught in a web of wheat.

The stems revolving,
 convolving,
 involving.
Solving the mystery of eternity.

Lucie Wright

Joy In Living

There is always joy in living
When all is well with you each day
And the sun is bright and shining
As you travel on your way.

There is always joy in living
When good friends are ever near,
Sharing with you in the giving
Of their happiness year by year

There is always joy in living
When the skies are bright and blue
Overhead they are ever striving
To bring pleasure to us too.

There is always joy in living
When you listen to a band
As its merry notes are rising
When you are standing near at hand.

There is always joy in living
When there's a good deed you can do
To enjoy the pleasure of the giving,
Bringing happiness to you.

Tom Buchanan

Growing Older

When I look in the mirror
What do I see
I see the face of a woman
Could it be me.

My hair used to be brown
Now there are traces of grey
How it has altered
Through life's way

The wrinkles have come
The double chin too
There is no use me bothering
There is nothing I can do

The slimline body
That used to be there
I look at it now
It looks like a cosy armchair

Why should I worry
About what used to be
I look back in the mirror
And inside, I am still the same me.

J. McCoy

He Left Us A Year Ago

He left us a year ago
We really loved him so,
All our hearts were broken
No words have been spoken,
He left us a year ago.

Was abandonment a must
When I had such great trust?
My children need their Dad
Life has become so sad,
He left us a year ago.

For months I have tried in vain
Feeling pain from the strain,
Pathetic humble pleas
'Tis us not her he needs,
He left us a year ago.

Instead he yearns for a change
No husband here is strange,
My babes lose a father
Life is harder, because
He left us a year ago.

Katherine Brown

What Does Life Mean?

What does life mean?
We all seem so keen.
To get on too and from
Where we're going who knows?
Sometimes we're low
Then full of go.
Some people care
Some aren't fair
We have ups and downs
Sometimes ask like clowns
But get through with some help too
We haven't got a clue
Sometimes out of the blue
A lucky break
Or just a fake
But where does life end?
Have we got a friend?
Who knows where we go?
Friend or foe
Where does life go?

Lisa Mangan

The Squirrel

I sat out in the garden one day
Watching a squirrel at play
He jumped about from tree to tree
At first he didn't notice me
He pranced about, up and down
Throwing berries on the ground
Up and over the fence he went
Soon his energy was all spent

Into my flower basket he sat
Throwing everything out
Squealing and having fun
Dirt and flowers everywhere
All I could do was sit and stare

To watch him was delight
To move I'd give him a fright
I wish I'd got a camera that day
But he'd have probably run away
He made a bed in my flower basket
Curled up like a cat in a casket.

J. M. Drinkhill

My Biggest Mistake

The biggest mistake of my life
Was when I didn't tell you
That I loved you
I needed you to touch me
But the passion was gone
It used to be so much fun,
And wonderfully romantic
But now life has no meaning
without you beside me
Emptiness is my companion and
words cannot describe my pain.
I gave you my soul
and now you are gone
forever.

N. Dymond

The Beast

His fury is like a time bomb,
waiting to be unleashed.
With a rage as hard as diamonds
Enter....the beast.

Emotion can not be hidden,
nothing can survive.
With an unknown primeval passion,
the beast will come alive.

He'll enter into your heart.
He'll venture in your mind.
To dis-colour the coloured.
The pain he will find.

He'll accentuate the feeling.
He'll a mother the soul.
When the minds at its weakest.
He'll take control.

Zoe-Michelle Allen

Memories

I see the moon shining bright.
Upon the river out of sight.
Where no one can harm
its golden rays.
Upon my heart it will always stay.
Like a memory in a dream which
we can always keep.
It's just one little thing that
make's you glad, when you are ill,
or very sad.

N. J. Davis

The Village Green

I used to know a general store
up near the village green
we used to watch the cricket there
and have a nice ice cream

Now later in the summer
we had a lovely fair
and people came from near and far
with folks we knew were there

We always had a flower show
with vegetables as well
and some one on the fair ground
would always hit the bell

We had a pub across the road
it always done quite well
with different kinds of lunches
with home made soup they sell

The W.I. sold tea and cakes
with raffle tickets to sell
now when you see that fair there
just try and ring that bell

B. Salter

Restless Tide

Angry, grey and pounding,
Waves crash upon the shore.
White horses breaking all around,
You hear the Oceans roar,
Might and power held within,
To watch is such a feast,
Gale-force winds are howling,
No man can tame this beast,
Energy in restless tides,
While raging through a storm,
Clawing all within its path.
Whatever shape or form,
Fury of this vast great force,
A temper we should fear,
Deep inside a cold cold heart,
Its secrets bosomed dear.
So deep, so dark, mysterious,
One tries to understand,
Why doth this Mighty Ocean
Still try to take the land?

Pamela Simms

The Garden Of Eden

I see this beautiful garden
Unique and glances
One man and woman
At one with nature
Flowers, trees, ferns amidst
They hold hands

Up high a sky of heaven
Blue horizon of meaning depth
Wondrous, amazing, terrific
Abound with creation below
Carefully kept

The waterfall erupts and stirs
The birds sing out the gay
The flowers blossom and grow
Nature calls out for more

Tracy Charters

Untitled

You lie so still your body warm
The still of the night hears your call
You lie so still so free of pain
Please let me live just one more day
The times has come to go away
No more pain on this cold day

Sue Owen

Seasons Of The Forest

Summer comes to the forest.
Under a canopy of leaves
I laid me on a mossy bank.
The silence, save the sound of birds
Filled my whole being with a calm.

Autumn came to the forest.
Sadly the trees wept amber leaves,
Across the russet heath I found
Webs of silver, diamonds of dew,
Ruby berries and golden fern.

Winter came to the forest.
Through the tracery of bare branches
I beheld the first soft snow flakes
Descending on a frozen world,
And caught a glimpse of fairyland.

Spring came to the forest.
With pale primroses at my feet
I heard the message of Easter,
Bringing its promise of new life
Springing from the dark dead wood.

K. J. Stephens

Memories

I often walk through memory lane
Trying to trace my steps again.
Days of old
When I was a child
Dreams of gold on cotton clouds
Wild fantasies of what would be.

Showered with love pride and joy.
In the golden days gone by.
But as I wake, from fantasy.
I came down to reality.
Nothing will be the same.
As the golden days again.

Many a memory gone from mind
Happy years left behind.
Golden threads upon my head.
Wrinkled lines across my brow.
Different times I live in now.
Generation gap open wide.
Yet the power of love will survive.

H. P. Devine

Town And Country

Concrete mounds and walls of bricks
Town and Country do not mix
Glassy skyscrapers reach for the sky
Birds and animals lay down to die

Green fields and pastures melt away
Hotels and houses are here to stay
Wild horses will no longer roam
Rich men want their green home

The Eagle can no longer soar
The builders want more and more
Smoke and smog fill the air
The builders no longer care

No more fields left to till
The builders are never still
Trees and bushes are chopped down
The people must have their new town

The Rich mans range is no more
The price of houses soar and soar
Land was eaten like a Gannett
Man has ruined his Mother Planet

Raymond McPhee

Pain

It's taken me a long time,
To understand the pain.
It's taken me a long time,
To understand your game.

The way you treated me,
Teased and call my name.
It's just a way of saying,
I'm only playing a game.

A game with your heart strings,
To see if you care,
To see if you my sweet,
Will always be there.

You like to see me hurting,
You like to see my cry,
You like to see my face,
As you say goodbye.

These words you whisper,
At night when you're asleep,
With another angle you've
trapped in your keep.

Odele Stone

Just A Housewife

They say I'm just a Housewife.
To that I disagree.
I'm more than just a housewife
as I hope you will see.

I'm a doctor, nurse and mother,
I'm a diplomat and more,
because when there is a problem,
it's me that they yell for.

I wash and scrub the floors,
I mend a plug or fuse,
I wash the dishes
and even clean the loos.

I haven't time for a full-time job
because housework's never done.
I really think a housewife
should be classed as number one.

They say 'just a housewife'
how wrong can they be,
because if not for 'Just a housewife'
where would the family be?

Pat Laplain

A Lovely Man

A short story is what I require,
to read curled up by the fire.

Once upon a time it began,
there was a funny little man.

His hair grey, his eyes blue,
gnarled hands, wobbly legs too.

He wore a coat ragged and torn,
it was well and truly worn.

His shoes were old with holes,
nothing much left of the soles.

But his heart was in the right place,
and goodness shone from his face.

Everyone loved the little old man,
especially my dear old gran

For he was no other to say, I'm glad,
but my very lovely old grandad.

W. G. Lawson

Remembrance (1993)

To Whitehall in their thousands came,
  To march in mid November,
The men who once had won the wars,
  Their comrades to remember.

With medals shining on their chests
  And poppies worn with pride,
They stood in silence and recalled
  Their fellows who had died.

And while they stood in silence there
  How many were aware
That in Dubai that very week
  There'd been a massive fair.

Exhibited were tanks and planes
  And missiles guns and jets,
The traumas brought about by war
  One easily forgets.

These weapons of destruction will
  Make all arms dealers glad,
And also kill more men to mourn,
  My God, the World's gone mad.

B. W. Tyas Cooper

Peace

How wonderful it would be
To Live in Peace and Harmony
No more wars and no more fears
No more Killing and no tears
A soldier's life tough
Killing someone is bad enough
The tears I did shed
For my friends
Will this war ever end

Some were lucky some were not
The friends I lost at sea
I thank you Lord it wasn't me
The memories will linger
Some I won't forget
Lying on the battle grounds
With limbs torn apart
I hated leaving them
It was Breaking my heart
Jimmy and Johnny, Bob as well
Lord take them in Heaven
They have already been to hell

P. M. Wardle

An Evening In Paradise

A sea of blue, a trace of gold,
To intercept the sky,
No oarsmen there to steer our boats
As we went sailing by.
Only beauty met our eyes
As 'neath the clouds we went
And heard a thousand different sounds
Whilst there our tour was spent.
A thousand lamplights shone on us
Right through the night and day,
And all we met were birds and beasts
Who went upon their way.
A scene could never look so fine
As on that jewelled sea,
Which brought us closer there to God
Than one could ever be!

Sharon Howells

Young Boys' Endeavour

How we laboured in vain,
To hold back the Brook,
Swollen by the rain,
With stones and logs and
Lumps of sod
We fought against
Its downward plod,
A lake we sought to make,
But that was not to be his fate,
When with great anger and deride
He pushed our dam aside,
Then onward blew,
In rage and lather,
Unstoppable as time,
But we never knew,
That water will be master,
Of all, but few.

D. Williams

Death

Where do we go to when we die,
To that place up there on high.
With angels singing all around,
Of love that does forever abound,
Or down below where evil does grow,
Where Satan's followers all must go,
Buried by their sins, like a mire,
Amidst the agonies of hell's fire,
Or just to a church yard plot,
Where a body is laid and left to rot.

Robert P. Kay

Greetings To A Bigamist

It shouldn't be hard
To find the right card
For a friend getting wed
To that man called Fred

But he's not all he seems
With his endless daydreams
Of yachting away
To a Mediterranean bay

Then out it all came
Said he wasn't to blame
Had quite slipped his mind
Other wives they should find

So my friend didn't suffer
From wedding the bluffer
And the card which I chose
Had sympathy and prose!

Maureen Jones

My Love, My Life

Every nerve and every fibre,
Tingle with emotion,
The rushing blood in veins,
Pulsate in devotion.
Every beat and every breath,
Reach out with respiration,
Each yearning caress,
Brimming desperation.
Every touch and every feeling,
Longing for desire.
Flowing melting sensation
Burst with flames of fire
Every look and every glance,
Smoulders in embers
With gasping breath,
The racing mind surrenders
Every muscle and every limb,
Lay motionless together,
Retiring passion fading,
The memories last forever.

Michelle Atkinson

Time

Time on earth, and in space
Time to ponder and for grace
In some future begotten place
Comes forth our destiny,
A beam of light, from a distant star.
The comets wake is seen so far,
Life's bejewelled door is left ajar.
For us to enter.
As in the past, men's eyes are cast,
Upon horizons huge and vast
God give us strength that it my last
From here to eternity,
So let it be that man shall see
His inner kindly thoughts laid free
For all to cherish as time go`s by.

Robert Edward Wharton

The Car

Oh what a thing of beauty
this monster has become
it's taken toll of many lives
along its short, and colourful path
each year its looks get better
its lines are now more sleek,
it's going ever faster,
and costing more than we hath,
but should we become besotted,
or should we turn our heads,
or when it's time to go to work
leave the car and use our legs.

W. Nicholls

Make the Most of Each Day

You don't miss the water
Till the well runs dry,
This is a true saying,
And I know why.
For seventeen years for my dad
  I cared,
Many good times together we shared
But now he's gone, after downstairs
  he fell,
And I miss him so much
I want to tell,
When you love someone
Whatever the weather,
Make the most of each day
Because nothing, lasts forever.

Sheila Rider

Life

In his arms a child
the future.
In her arms a picture
the past.

In their hearts they are together
but past and future pull them apart.
In his arms a child hope.
In her arms a picture despair.

Laura Elizabeth Deacon

Inner Peace

We lived a life of luxury
Till that fateful day
The business and our money gone
Our home just snatched away

The worries that had come to us
Were ones we had not known
And with the passing of each day
Our bills had grown and grown

When at night we came to rest
Not knowing which way to turn
A feeling was growing inside of us
Of peace, that we did yearn

And as we walk our path of life
Our feelings we do not hide
For in our hearts we both knew
The Lord, stood by our side

We live our life through our church
A life we're sure was meant
For through our faith we have a life
Of peace, and content

D. N. Davies

All The Time In The World

What O'Clock? Said the guide.
  Tick tock
  way back.
  time out.

6 O'Clock. Said the guard.
  Tick tock.
  First half.
  Time gone.

12 O'Clock. Said the ghost.
  Tick tock
  Second half
  Time up.

What O'clock? Said the God.
Time chopped, said the cloud.
  Bang! No Extra time.
    Clock stopped...

Philip Holden

Father To Be

The times when life,
Though sometimes good,
Becomes to much to bear.

The years of tears,
And broken hearts,
Of which, I have had my share.

Then at last a wife,
Who gave to me,
The wondrous son of mine.
His look, his smile.
I know them well,
But will they stand,
The test of life.

But at least he will know,
The joy and hope,
That he has given to me,
When he has grown,
And shed some tears,
Then becomes a father to be.

Paul Baker

Am I Afraid?

It feels like a jealousy
  though it is not
It tears at me
  and steals my peace
Won't let me rest
  my soul does ache.

Yet with her
  I'm all at peace
Like an infant
  suckling Breast.
Totally safe
  Away from harm.

Then once again
  Fear takes its grip
And hunts my soul.

The only tranquillity
  When she is there
And all is night once more.

Peter S. Coode

Special Child

Angels said to the Lord above
This child needs a lot of love
He may not laugh, run or play
His thoughts may seem far away
In many ways he won't adapt
And he'll be known as handicapped
Let's be careful where's he sent
We want his life to be content
Please Lord find the parents who
Can do a special job for you.
They realise straight away
The leading role they're to play
But the child sent from above
Brings stronger faith
And stronger love.

S. M. Dudley

My Big Sister

I have a big sister
She has left home
And how I miss her
It's my sister
She has moved to a house
on her own and is all alone
How I miss her
And how I want her back.

Keith Bandy

Feeling Blue

Things that happen
Things that are said
They bring you down
You're left feeling blue.

You only want to be yourself
Quiet and peaceful
But the joke's always on you.

What do you do?
You keep feeling blue
You just can't win
Keep your feelings within
Yourself to yourself
But who understands?
Easy to laugh at
They don't understand.

Things that won't happen
Things you can't do
You're left feeling lonely
You're left feeling blue.

Paul Reade

Not Again

Repeat!
Television repeat?
No! History repeat,
Repeat! World at war,
Tanks, soldiers, guns,
Bang, gone,
Repeat! Bang, gone,
Not for long.
Showing again soon,
Near you,
Repeat!

J. Harrower

The Motorist's Lament

They sting him here
They sting him there
In point of fact
They sting him everywhere
Road tax - petrol - purchase too
Badgered by the man in blue
Parking fees - can't stop here
Enough to send him on the beer
Over fills the nation's coffers
Chased by all the blooming coppers
He'll go to heaven or to hell
Even ending in a cell
Villain of the piece he be
As any simpleton can see
Entered in the hall of fame
Percy-cution is his name
Not for us a revolution
Just constant percy-cution

Sidney Wilson

Complete

When alone, something's missing,
There's a gap in the atmosphere,
Your soul is divided,
Your heart is halved,
A feeling of emptiness.
Something needs to be with you,
But you're not quite sure what it is.
Then you realise.
That something is someone,
The someone in the picture,
The picture which makes you complete.

Nicola Pickard

Britain's Hero

Away from Britain's shore one day
There sailed a gallant crew,
Their staunch old ship was laden
With soldiers brave and true
They landed in the Middle East
Once more to fight the foe,
So England shall again be free,
For all to come and go.
Now when we have the Nazi's beat
And war comes to an end.
The boys will all come home again
To peace which they defend;

R. Thew

My Mind's Eye

In my mind's eye
There is yesterday, today,
and forever.
Yesterday has rested.
Painted into the mirror of our minds.
Today is like the wind.
Guided, yet unseen.
Forever, like the birds of the air -
Unspoilt by time.
In my mind's eye we are
Young and old,
Good and bad,
Friends and enemies.
We are our peace and
We are our anger.
In my mind's eye,
The day is enough -
Until tomorrow.

Sheila Newman

Let Us Live

We use to roam the country free
then white man he hunted me
he knew not the laws of our land
our tribes in their own little bands

Our territory he did invade
our buffalo and horses raid
to protect our homes we had to fight
against the white man in the night

Apache, Cheyenne all the same
persecuted time and again
to avenge our warriors brave
gave the white man an early grave

Our land was taken, destroyed
a reservation now our home
we're like animals in a zoo
we're not happy but what can we do

Let us live our life our way
give us our homeland back one day
to live like white man not for me
I just want to be set free

R. Collier

Pretending

I thought I saw a shadow move,
then pause a while to rest.
I thought I saw a crystal ball
concealed within a nest.
I thought I saw a rainbow form
beneath a darkened sky,
I thought I saw a falling leaf
pretending it could fly,
All this I saw, at least I thought,
beside a golden pool,
and I a scarlet butterfly
confined within a jewel.

B. Garner

Sea At Night

Lapping up the rocks.
The witness of anger
Eating away everything in sight
   in the dead of night

E. Birchmore

Halt The Sale Of Arms

There the rainbow another cries;
The sun prisms the tears of eyes
That, woeful, caste their gaze
While fat-cats idly laze.
There the torment in life's torrents
Where baleful eyes reflect like fonts
The losses that well up
To wash all from their cup.
Here is beauty as takes a bath
Two that care so at troubles laugh
And while wet, wash away
Their torments etched that day.

How can here beauty be
When Kwandas are there to see..?

Lloyd Carley-West

The Graveyard

Walking around the graveyard past
The spooky graves
Where someone is a sleeping in
The dark and haze
Like a little pebble under the dark
soft ground
People will be coming from far and
far around
Just to see their loved ones
Some people just like me come to
see the people who have past away
From the sorrowful and upsetting
For them who loved them most
Misery will be soon lost in a
land of joy and love

Victoria Robinson

The Child Within

The more you love the woman,
the sooner you'll find the girl,
the more you love the girl,
the sooner you'll know the woman.

The more you love the man,
the sooner you'll find the boy,
the more you love the boy,
the sooner you'll know the man.

The more you love yourself,
the sooner you'll find the child,
the more you love the child,
the sooner you'll know yourself.

Tom Beall

Top Quality Management

The ramps are bowed
The shutters bent
They're not even trimmed
We're not content
The housings are lethal
They slash your hands
The counters we just can't understand
The pistons we sometimes get to work
The chambers well that's down to luck
The strainers they are never right
So T.Q.M a load of tripe

E. S. Barrow

Autumn's Gold

Rich by far, the Autumn Gold
The setting sun throws its rays
And gentle river running smooth
As it goes its way

Crystal clear the water
From mountain tops so high
Bubbles look like diamonds
Leaves go floating by

Colours in the evening glow
Green and orange, soft brown
An earthy carpet of fallen leaves
Lies upon the ground

Oh wondrous are the colours
Such beauty here is told
Soften whispers of the rivers
Natures reward, is Autumn Gold

Shirley June Paul

The Blackbird's Song

I've lain awake with troubled mind
The nights they seem so long
But with the dawn comes hope again
Within the blackbird's song.

I do not like the way things are
I feel it ought to change
But something always holds me back
I'm safe within my range.

The world is full of good and bad
A mix of joy and sorrow
Sometimes today is not quite right
But there'll always be tomorrow.

One thing I know, I know for sure
E'en though life seems all wrong
No matter where I see the dawn
I'll hear the blackbird's song.

Wendy S. Hooper

Time Goes By

The days go by the weeks as well
The months they come and go
Time seems endless yet it's gone
I wonder why it's so
I remember yet the day we met
As though 'twas yesterday
'Tis forty years with many cheers
And lots of love I know
The families past alone at last
Our love has seen us through
Our love still strong well carry
On for many years I know

Peter Horslen

Lost Love

Yesterday has gone
Tomorrow is near
Life is too short
To worry my dear

The love you have lost
Is not far away
It's round the next bend.
To keep, hold and stay.

Don't cry on your pillow
At life that's gone by
But look to tomorrow
and see the blue sky.

Susan King

My Child

My heart was full of love for you
The minute you were born
Very pink and wrinkly too
so soft, cosy and warm.

The time flies by
I watch you grow
You've found your feet
and want to go.
I love the smile you give to all
the knowledge there
yet still so small.

It's off to school
I worry all day,
but soon your home
and out to play
more worry to come
that I know
but worth it all to be a mum.

P. Carter

Secret Lovers

Secret lovers
That's what we are
From one another
We'll never be far

We pass on the street
Without a second glance
The next time we meet
Is just by chance

Across the room
Our eyes may lock
Our hearts go boom
Our heads just mock

Secret lovers
That's all we can be
For no-one must know
About me and thee

L. M. Squires

My Raindrop Poem

Raindrops are wet
They drop on the Ground
I can catch the Rain in my Hands
And I can catch the Rain in my Mouth
And it is fun catching the rain
I Love the Rain

Poonam K. Chana

The Battle

As the battle began
The blood was shed
A light shone down
upon the dead.

The men fell from their horses
And their screams rang out
Was this still a good idea?
Everyone was in doubt.

As the battle carried on
More lives were shed
Evil was wining
and all seemed dead.

But out of the darkness
A light shone on
Good was saved
and evil was gone.

Rebecca Walker

The Sheepdog

As they approach
The bar door
He circles
Nipping at the rear,
Herding the three woman
Into a corner.
I'll get the drinks, he says
Stealthily avoiding the tables
On his way to the counter.
One escapes
To the Ladies.
Panicked
He arrives back.
When she returns
He moved her
Into the circle,
Penning them
With his talk.

Margaret O. Shea

Tranquillity And Turmoil

Harmonious with the expanse
The graceful submarine glides,
With knowledge of far worlds
Away from pernicious man.
Deep below the treacherous sea
Where the water is calm and serene,
The great blue whale sails
With elegance, peace, then alarm.
For as to the surface to breathe
The scope now scarlet in sight.
A long life to be - cut short
By sinister, sadistic man.

Penny Lodge

True Happiness

Look to the city,
that's not made with hands,
there will be people there,
as many as the golden sands,

It's a land of peace and love,
only from the father above,
one day we'll be there,
so try not to despair.
Shout hallelujah, Jesus
will be there.

People from every nation,
black, and white together,
giving God the glory,
forever and ever, and ever.

Mary Macfarlane

How I Escaped A Life Of Dissipation

"Now give it up!" The Doctor said
"This women, song and wine.
For if you don't you're surely dead
Before you're thirty-nine."
But my will-power was not strong,
My life I could not save.
And so with women, wine and song
I headed for the grave.
I did not meet of earth six feet
I found instead Salvation.
The credit is not mine to claim,
My saviour was Inflation.
The price of wine went up so much
To purchase it I could not.
Without the wine for courage Dutch,
A wooing go I would not.
So now I've toed the Doctor's line,
My life's no longer swinging.
I've lost the women and the wine,
And I don't feel much like singing.

D. G. Leaver

Nearness

The warmth of your touch
That shows how you care
The love in your eyes
Says you'll always be there.

The nearness we feel
When you touch my face
The kisses we share
When I'm in your embrace.

Your love has no ending
Your kindness sublime
I treasure your nearness
I'm so glad you're mine.

Your tenderness and love
Bring joy beyond measure
Our moments of closeness
Are secrets of treasure

Though the years have passed by
I just want you to know
My heart still skips a beat
And I do love you so.

Pat Whitmarsh

Forever February

A part of me went with you,
that night you said goodbye.
I guess I knew one day you'd leave,
though I still wonder why.

Forever I'll remember
the friend I found in you,
and think about the lover
I never really knew.

The love we shared together
left few ashes in your heart
but within me there's a fire
that now burns without a spark.

The feelings that you had for me
departed long ago.
The pain you branded me that night
is such you'll never know.

Our love it bloomed then faded
just like that single rose.
Although the rose is dead and gone
my love for you still grows.

Sarah Garrett

Whose Hands

Whose hands are these
  that cradled me,
  nourished me, and
  cleansed me.

Whose hands are these
  that took me to school,
  waved to me, and
  chastised me.

Whose hands are these
  that wiped away
  my tears of joy
  and sorrow.

Whose hands are these
  that prayed for me,
  counted the days for me
  and held my baby.

Whose hands are these?
  My Mother's.

Pamela McNamara

Grief

I swear animals cause us more grief
Than humans ever do.
When Orbit died, I felt as if a leaf
From my life's book had gone
With him to his heavenly place.
I wonder where their heaven is?
I only wish I could see his face
Looking down on me,
I'm sure he watches over us
And over Tilly B.

Nikki Martyn

What Is A Friend?

A friend is someone who,
tells of your faults to you.

A friend is someone who,
treats you fair,
stands up for you,
when you're not there.

A friend will tell you,
you are wrong,
they tell you why,
they keep you strong.

Fair-weather friends,
I've met them all
when things go well,
around you crawl.

If that's a friend
  God help us all.

J. M. Smith

My Spirit

My spirit...
  takes me away to places
  where only you can dream of
My spirit...
  sends petals soft as rain
  down upon my brow
My spirit...
  shines a light so white
  upon a very dark world
My spirit...
  is the water I need
  when I am thirsty
My spirit...
  is the air I need
  to breath... to survive

My body may die
  but my spirit lives on...
so here we are again my friends
for ever and ever
  Amen

Michelle Villagran

Winter

Icy path,
Starlings cries,
Unsure tread,
Grey skies,
Snow clad roves,
Bare trees,
Frozen pond,
Dead leaves,
Freezing wind,
Icy blow,
Sparkling frost,
Glistening snow,
Hot drink,
Frostbitten toe,
Merry fire,
Warm glow.

Lawrence Harold Palmer

Sussex

Sussex, Sussex land of joy!
Sussex, Sussex ship ahoy!

Where the Arun meets the sea,
And the Cuckmere Valley be.
Lighters love the Sussex coast,
Beachey Head's their warning post.
Far inland by Heathfield Town,
Full-ripe yellow corn hath grown,
Horses gallop through the lanes,
O'er the turf 'neath weather vanes.
Lasses sing in morning sun,
Maids for village buses run,
Chapel folk, or churchmen true
Ask the Lord what they're to do,
And thanksgiving offer they,
For a bumper crop of hay.
Of what scenery we'll tell
From Ticehurst Down to Arundel.

'Tis Sussex, Sussex good and true
It warms the heart like Irish stew
Sussex, Sussex, land of joy!
'Tis the best for thy employ.

Peter Buss

Golden Memories

In the warmth of the
summer sun,
The meadow pipit flies,
Swift on the wing.
Yonder, on the heath,
Rabbits scurry to and fro.

The flowing brook,
Its waters wind here and there
Fire lark ascends into
An azure blue zenith,
Its song trills down to earth

Softly the scent of new
Morn hay is on the summer breeze
The cry of the kestrel
Comes as it swoops down
From above, to seize a vole.

Martin S. Elsworthy

To Trust, To Lose

We were strangers,
Still we are;
But then, a bond was made.
Unsigned.
Yet,
With all the weight of generations,
I accepted it.
We did not touch save for observation.
We spoke but gently.
Why,
Your trust in me was true.
And in that lonely battle,
I joined.
Until
You called
"Don't go!"
As you vanished in my arms.

Thomas Jagoe

The Mystery Of Flannan Isle

Once on a dark night
The lighthouse light was shining bright.
After one minute it suddenly stopped.
The last drop of rain had quickly dropped.
Outside a ghostly figure appeared
  in the night,
to stop the light from shining bright.
The lighthouse men got carried away
and others remember that fearful day.

Peter Buckley

Magic Moment

The train was packed as usual
standing only all the way.
The longest thirty minutes
'til the highlight of the day.

I was off to view some paintings
by Impressionists - what bliss!
My very favourite artists
an occasion not to miss.

What a queue on my arrival
will I never get inside?
Then there it was before me
and I very nearly cried.

Auguste Renoir's 'Boating Party'
almost covering one wall
with vibrant colour - minute detail
gentle silence filled the hall.

As I drank in all its beauty
wondrous awe stole over me
because this lovely ancient painting
was still here for all to see.

Wendy Norman

The Carpet Children

I work at the loom
shuttles fly, do I toil
here till I die?
What about all the others
my sisters and brothers?
I protest then I am shot
forget me not.

Mavis Catlow

Breakdown

The mirror of the
Spirit cracked;
The image is distorted,
Fixed
In isolation, tightly wrapped;
No penetration of the
Sack
That stifles thought.

No life, no light, no warming sun,
A withered seed,
A man in need of sustenance
Yet cannot feed.

To hide away,
A hermit be, yet all around is
Industry;
See it, feel it, want a part.
But all is lost to
Soul binding dark.

Margaret Mawson Owens

North Atlantic

On the coast of Iceland,
South of Krisuvik,
Black sand marks the beach;
Old lava runs
Down to the cliffs,
And the sea.
Silver logs of driftwood
Lie tumbled among dark rock,
Stone courses of abandoned huts
Stand at the lava's edge;
Monuments to the lost
Way of life here.
The emerald sea breaks,
Sending its white foam
Sliding towards land,
As of old.

Roy Bizley

Untitled

lovers tiff
salt tears
call to arms
aphrodisiac

D. M. Henly

Memoriam

Figure upright, age deceptive,
Soldier's bearing, most impressive,
Eyes were bright, so decisive,
Life's for living, mind receptive.

Knew the hard times, not a whine,
Times of worry, gave no sign.
Grandma's passing, tears of brine,
Answer always, "I'm just fine."

So we grew up, strong and bold,
World our oyster, left the fold.
You grew older, fingers cold,
But heart was warm, molten gold.

When we left you, gone so long,
Though afar, the bonds were strong.
Looking back our thoughts belong
Yesteryear when we were young.

You've departed, separation,
Loss is bitter, sad extinction.
Since you left us revelation,
Learnt your secret - toleration.

Tony Channon

Whisper Of Agony

Softly you whisper,
Softly and low,
Softly you whisper,
A sweet hello.

Do you miss me?
As I miss you,
Do you miss me?
I hope you do.

Our days apart,
Are agony,
Our nights together
are - ecstasy.

Until we meet again,
I'll whisper sad adieu,
Until we meet again,
Because, I love you.

Teresa Spilsbury

The Inevitability Of Death

Death came in the guise of a woman
Soft sunlight snared in her hair
Eyes like the drift of moonbeams
Little feet bare

Come she whispered and beckoned
Smiling, strange eyes intent
See where the Phoenix wakens
Gladly I went

Slowly crumbles in ruins
The old loved word at my feet
Heartbreak, perhaps, to leave it
For her song sweet.

Now fades, is fading her music
No more the little feet dance
A grinning skeleton beckons
Still I advance.

Mary M. Biggart

Dawn Of Life

Life began at dawn,
soft golden rays spirited the silver
mist to rise,
below, timid reluctance to uncoil
awakened fragile beauty.

Sweet tenacious incense,
baptize to yield life all around
euphoria begun.

Heedful velvet silk withdrew,
stretched within a delicate vivid
heart rekindled.

Life begun, born the Crocus....
T. A. Peachey

Valentine's Song

If I could write a love song
So sweet and divine,
Would you open your heart
And tell me you're mine?
If I could promise you a life
Full of riches untold,
Would you stretch out your hand
For me to hold?
If I could offer you nothing
But my heart and my soul,
Would you stand by me
Till 'I'm frail and I'm old?
If I said that I'd told you
A little white lie,
Would you offer forgiveness
Or tell me goodbye?
If I told you I loved you
And that without you I'd die,
Would you be my one and only,
Would you be my Valentine?
Marvyn B. Candler

Fairy Rings

Do you believe in fairies
So small and slim and sleek
Who hide beneath the bushes
Then play while you're asleep.

They dance beneath the moonlight
Sing like the angels above
With elves and gnomes and dryads.
They fill this world with love

Their mother natures little helpers
To see them is so rare
They live deep in the forest
In the world in which we share.

So if you want to see a fairy
Be good and kind and fair
Then search among the flowers
And you might find them there.
Paul Holland

Rainbow's End

So many things make each day hard.
So often I complain.
Yet somehow, though I often fall.
I always rise again.
I set myself a goal to reach.
Maybe the rainbows end.
I find myself a shooting star.
And troubles I will mend.
I dream myself a dream each day,
I tend it with such care,
I pick up joy along the way.
And troubles are not there!
Tracey Oswell

Silent Dream

Wow!!!!
So many stars!!!
So much silence!!!

Whose footsteps are they?
Who is coming?
What are their names?

I am a sky of stars
        tonight
Crisp
  and
    cool

Alas,
  words are inane and unable.
Oh,
  my silent dream.
F. Fooladi

Michelle My Bell

I met a pretty girl.
So I sat beside her.
Then she went roar.
Like a lion tiger.

I said hello.
You've made a mistake there.
As my name is, slick rick.
Not flaky blakey until.
Oh golly gosh.
I was raising in hell when she said.
My name is Michelle the bell.
And there's a funny smell.
Wayne Cameron

Untitled

Laughter is a tonic
So have some every day
Every time you smile
It takes some stress away
If I was asked for a recipe
For the cake of love
I'd gather the ingredients
Form The Good Lord above
A half cup of sympathy
A half cup of kind
A half cup of wisdom
And as much patience as you can find
Mix it well together
And put it in your hearts
Then when ever you are asked for some
Share out in equal parts
J. H. Mardel

Ribbon Of Diamonds

Weaving through the valley
Shining as it goes
Like a ribbon of diamonds
The sparkling river flows.
Round a rocky out-crop
Past a bank of ferns
Like a ribbon of diamonds
The river twists and turns.
Tinkling over pebbles
On the river bed
Reflecting willow branches
Hanging overhead.
Underneath a stony bridge
By the wishing well
Past a patch of brambles
Growing in the dell.
Like a ribbon of diamonds
Sparkling in the sun
The river travels on its way
Its journey never done.
Nora Kathleen Cooper

Memories

The clock has moved on
Since those bright Summer days,
Where the corn stood,
So proud in fields all ablaze.

Windows were flung wide,
The warm air we did breath,
Life was worth living
Like prisoners just freed.

Each one had a smile
Young and old alike,
A cheeky wave from the paper boy
As he rode by on his bike.

But winter must come,
With Frost and Snow
To purify the earth,
So mother nature can grow.

So with memories of summer still new,
Close your eyes let memory stray,
Remember the warmth of every
Bright Summer's day.
K. Dale

The Dam

Dam sublime,
Should you cry?
Dam, so strong and dry.

Dam, please cry!
Dam, damn you
Foolish King.

Reign forever?
Who knows when
Cracks will appear.

Drench parched depths,
Soften and sigh
Then, tears of joy,
Peace at last.
Sue Passey

Queue

Waiting in line
Shifting weight
Foot to foot
Claim ground
Foot by foot

Queue for hours
Hours slip away
Away
As if time
Had time to waste

See nothing
Hear nothing
Say nothing

Row of strangers
Collectively alone
Sharing space
But not time -
By choice
Paul Quarry

A Mother's Lament

My daughter Joan is not at home,
so do not call again.
She will not speak to anyone,
especially to men.
She says that she's a different girl,
that she's no longer free.
And if you want a good night out,
she's recommending me.
J. Wilkinson

The Morrigan

Sleek and glossy, black and cruel
She pecks the eyes from erring fool
Feasts upon the beaten flesh
That battle, made a bloodied mess
Bides her time to claw away
The meat from off her gory prey
Her wicked beak will rip and tear
Mouth will gorge without a care
Wings will take her high to wheel
To seek another soul to steal
Can she love? I hear you say
Only once love came her way
Alas when the hound refused the maid
Returned she did to former shade
His fate with-in her claws was bound
And twice she tried to slay the hound
Where death lies, this lady soars
To catch the souls with-in her claws
And evil gleams deep in her eye
As she screams her battle cry

Lesley Stockley

The Storm

You came at night unseen,
Shaking my roots,
Tearing out my hair,
Destroying me, rough and chilling,
Cracking my limbs.

I tried to bend as in my youth,
You were relentless,
Splitting my spine,
I crashed to the ground.

No more to blossom,
To sway as in those gentle
breezes of my tender years.

Later humans came, and picked me up,
Gathering up my limbs,
Sawing through my body,
Cremating me on their fires.

Shelagh Mayson

The Night-Time Dreamer

Through the dead of night,
Shafts pale moonlight.

Dreams awake into your sight,
Gently putting wrong to right.

Dreaming of me standing there,
With no sticks or wheelchair.

Things you lost come back to play,
In your dreams at end of day.

Losing all your worries there,
Dreaming of your lover's care.

Lasting love from far away,
Haunt your dreams of yesterday.

Walking with your love in hand,
Over fields or through the sand.

Dreaming of the vows we said,
In the church that we wed.

I ask you not to pity me,
Let my dreams and sleeping be.

Wake me not till end of night,
To me reality is a fright.

Kieth R. Hirons

Spring Fresh

Snow has melted, the streams
run free, spring is here.
The sunshine breaks, the
sky becomes clear,
crystal blue, the air is fresh.
Time for fun and happiness.
So kick up your heels, and
go dance in those yellow
and green fields, then
lay back and watch the
butterflies dance in air.

Tarany Chapman

A Cornish Country Lane

Once there was a beauty spot
round about here,
walking down the country lane
no beauty could compare.
Flanked by hedges of wild flowers
of all distinctive hues,
overhead a rooflike bower
of branches from ye old Oak trees.
But walk this way today
its beauty is despoiled
by tin cans beds and rotting sacks
of rubbish, man has cast aside.
How can the eye be unaware
of beauties of the countryside,
is it that they just don't care
or thoughtless of another's pride.

Kathlees Smith

The Pearl Of The Water

The pearls of the water,
Rolling gently down,
The leaves point to earthwards,
As they bend and they twirl,
It catches the sunlight,
And ebbs away dark,
The swirling of colours,
The silvers and blues,
It's darkness no longer,
As the light, gives away hues,
A hand, gently catches it,
It's perfect, a sphere,
It gains some momentum,
It knows, it's been found,
The pearl of the water,
Falls gently to ground.

Patricia Westwood

The Lane

The lane enticed,
rivalled.
Its pelmets hung
with July fronds
and turned down counterpanes
of fettled hay,
drying posies.

Mottled tarmac,
heat-frost cracked,
creviced,
caught spores
and green texture took hold.
Humbly evolved,
softened
the professed unyielding crust.

And contrary to man's idea of road
the lane procured
its own

identity.

Ross Newton

At Last

At last my tiger came,
Quietly down the avenues of light
And shade.
Singing low, he sang
Through the waiting years.

Into my dark glade of fears,
Suddenly he sprang,
And made
The darkness of this troubled night
A flickering fantasy of flame.

Robin Menzies

Emotions

The pain and hurt so deep within
Rising up to the brim
Cascading down upon my cheeks
Tears! As I begin to weep.
Frustration anger surging forth
Emotions buried deep.
At last give rise to heal inside
A pathway from retreat.
Accepting things I cannot change
No matter how I try.
Remembering that love is there
Always by my side.
The seed of love within my heart
Radiates its warmth
Sending ripples out to reach
A balance which is sought.

A. Pardoe

White Sheets

White sheets show the stains,
reveal all the sin.
White sheets are for when you die,
there what they cover you in.

A faceless, emotionless person,
Lies within,
the crisp, white sheets
they cover you in.

No feelings, no face,
no tears of disgrace,
just crisp, white sheets
covering the sinner within.

Lynn M. Astley

The Longing

Come, sea,
Return me to my home in England.
I bear your salt on my breath,
Knowing I may face death.
I breathe you in,
You smell of the darkness within,
But I must find a way
To sail you.

Come, sea,
Help me steal past
The mangroves rooted in slime.
Let me see what lies
Beyond the bay, where the
Sky's edge meets the lip
Of your wave,
Let me see.

Come, sea,
Becalm me, my anxiety -
The sleepless wind and rain.
Let it be that
I sail you safely,
Past the burnt cliffs,
The great limestone monoliths,
Let it be.

Nilofar Hossain

Rape Seed

Screaming inside
Ready to explode
Pain clawing, grasping,
Searching for a way out.
Silent suffering.
The throbbing, the aching,
The colour of violence.
A physical explosion of emotion.
Sexual expression set free
At the expense of somebody else.
Who's prerogative?
Self torture.
Self burden.
Self blame.
Guilt;
On both sides.

Vikki Hayfield

Days Gone By...

I see you as my knight in armour;
Rescue me from the tortuous drama!
Whisk me off in shining car
to foreign lands, fields afar

We'll heal the wounds so deep within
I'm trembling now, so let's begin
to start again and build together,
cut old reins, release the tether

Gallop forth into the foray
Side by side to find the way
jumping every fence ahead
nothing will be left unsaid

Then in the sleepy twilight time
The world and you will all be mine
Troubles of the days gone by
Will disappear if we just try

To savour every living minute
Linger entwined within it
Feel the peace and joy unfold
(especially if my poem's sold!)

Linda Bolton

Golden Soldiers

Golden Soldiers marking time,
Regimental, straight of line.
Uniformed in green they wrap,
Crowned atop with golden cap,
Always in the same attire
From day of birth 'til they expire.
Gardens bask in Summer haze,
Shimmering with a golden blaze.
Towns and cities, soldiers there,
Golden soldiers everywhere!
On the woodland's leaf-strewn floor
Golden soldiers stalk once more,
See them marching to and fro
'Cross the fields, along hedgerow.
One golden soldiers guards the hill,
Proud, erect, a daffodil.

R. J. Pettitt

The Reluctant Thespian

"Punchinello!" "Punchinella!"
pit stomach-griping fear;
caking heat dripping
her young self;
Bible references to children
calling in a market place;
assuaging anger;
nauseous applause;
swirling ear-pounding effort;
"I can do THIS"

Nicola J. Metcalfe

Motivation

I have looked through a window,
Placed a door ajar.
But this step that I have taken,
Has not been a step too far.

I've searched for motivation
Deep within my mind.
Though I keep on looking,
It is still so hard to find.

I see people moving onwards,
With an inner will.
I see them through my window,
Which reflects me standing still.

Matthew Laffan

"Blood And Bones"

My equal lives in a stately hall,
 refined, scholastic, elite.
My equal lives in a cardboard box
 on London's well-heeled streets.
My equals are the fittest graced with
 favour and flair,
My equals rot in institutes
 confined by irons or chair.
My equals have a therapist to
 ease their mental strain,
My equals starve in Africa and char
 on dusty plain.
My equals are the infinite so
 different in shape and form,
My equals are the most bizarre
 my equals are the norm.

Ronald F. Dowles

Fate

The swirling depths of the Nile
reach out and touch my soul.
Another time, another place,
another creed, another race.

These are people I'll never meet
a culture that I'll never taste.
How I wish that death would come
and take me away post-haste.

There's many places I haven't seen
lots of towns where I've never been.
But now it's become too late
AIDS has decided my fate.

A long time ago, when I was young
before all of this had begun.
I was a good looking lad
always happy, hardly sad.

But sadness now is my bane
as I suffer from the pain.
They tell me, it's my own fault
but fate is something we cannot halt.

G. Lord

Latest Hymn

rainfall
pulled taught by thunder
unlocks the fragrant ground
spilling air into spring again

we have counted the
cloud-mounting hours
in silent congregation
your absence made passionate

reach past here quickly
between house, farm or tower
leave our flesh half wanting
as the startled earth

Stephen Baker

'Welfare State'

Millions crying poverty
queuing for their giro
showing their identity
and signing on in biro

Tried Employment training
Job club, N.V.Q's
Walked the local factory's
worn holes in my shoes

You made hide the figures
and tell the press it's fine
for every person you count
there is another nine

Tell us all get on our bikes
the country's doing great
there's no such thing as poverty
THIS AIN'T A WELFARE STATE....

Kevin McCarthy

Your Baby

So you want a child
Pink, sexual and calling
You mummy
The father?
Now that is a question
No
Just the sperm
Close enough I suppose
And if it weds and a lump
begins to show
What then?
Will you be satisfied?
And suppose later it asks
About Daddy
What will you say?
That you borrowed his seed
On indefinite loan
Or that Daddy was
A bastard who just
Did not want to know.

Martin J. P. Develin

Hope

Hope knows no law of common sense,
 Persists when even faith has gone;
Ignores the insurmountable
 And resolutely looks ahead,
Beyond the known and obvious;
 Despite adversity, it holds
The human spirit in its arms,
 To shield, to nurture and sustain.
Hope has no place for reasoning,
 The future that it has conceived
Is sacrosanct: If it should die
 There is a bleak memorial
Of nothingness - a void that dwells -
 Like silence after pealing bells.

W. K. Lane

My Carer

You wipe away the tears
of concern from my mind.

In the quiet hours of my
wanting, it is you, who
gives me dignity.

You are my strength
so that I may stand alone.

You are never distant from
the path I walk.

Will you often walk
beside me-
And be my friend...?

Peter Morriss

Eyes Of The Elderly

Eyes watch as you go by,
Read them!
Pleadingly they reach out
Acknowledge them!
Their reactions you will see
if you....
Heed them
Maralyn Flood

Beachy Head

Have you ever wondered why
People that just want to die
Come to Beachy Head to jump
Like a massive body dump

Devils chimney is the place
Where they just leap into space
And here time has been forgotten
Because they must feel very rotten

If only they were to think of others
All of man they are our brothers
Someone winches them to the top
When they decide to take the chop

This is a place to behold
Where nature does unfold
With a place of such beauty
Man should always do his duty

So when you visit Beachy Head
Don't always think of all the dead
Look around at this wondrous place
And all the splendour of its space
J. A. Marchant

The Joy Of Staying

I am waiting, shaking, sweating,
Pain deep inside
Thoughts running wild
I must not give in to doubts
Or failure will be mine

This moment I must hang, on
Go out there
Deep breath from inside
I can see no-one
But I feel someone there
I'm alone but proud
My chance has come
To remember my first time
Never to repeat
The joy of staying
Never giving in
My first solo
With my violin
B. Evans

Gambling On Us

In a cold and dirty room
On the outskirts of the town,
around a small old wooden table
they lay their money down,
and in the corner quietly smoking
a lady watches her man.
A bead of sweat runs down his face
as the dealer deals the hand.

Nervous looks with confident smiles
fear is hard to hide
twitching eyes trying to focus
on cards with one important side
for some the thrill begins to flow
while others have sinking hearts,
but bluff becomes part of the game
as the actors play their parts.
D. Triggle

Witches Paradise

It's Halloween, it's Halloween!
Over the roof tops
The Witch is seen,
High above on her broom,
Casting down sorrow and gloom.
So all you Christians, run and flee,
Or you'll end up just like me,
Under the Witch's evil spell,
Weird tales and stories I could tell!
The Cauldron,
The Fire,
The Witches' Brew,
Nasty spells they cast on you!
So take heed next Halloween,
Stay indoors, not to be seen!
As she circles in the sky
Let her pass your soul by,
Or you might come down to my level,
Worshipping Witches and the Devil!
J. Harris

The Letter

The distance is vast between us,
Over miles of land and sea
But naught can ever break the bond
That binds you close to me.

The sorrow of your going,
The joy of your return
The smiles, the hugs, the kisses
Once again for these I yearn.

Many, are the years gone by,
Many tears we shed at parting
But letters, going back and forth
Brought happiness and heartening.

You know I'll always miss you,
You know how much I care
For you my little sister
Are too close to me here, not there.
Winnie Milnes

The Nobody

I have no friends
Or letters to send,
I have no life
Or even a knife.

I have no mum
I'm not much fun,
Have no cosy coach
I'm such a grouch

Like I said I'm so moody
I'm never a little goody,
So go away
I'm having a boring day.
C. Huber

September Morn

Morning dew lies silent
On September morn
Red sun on the horizon
Breaking through at dawn
Crisp feeling in the air
Autumn on the way
Mighty sea sleeps peaceful
Knowing your special day
White cliffs wear a veil of mist
So pretty peeping through
Sands around are hushed
Their beauty can't compete with you
Not a whisper from the wind
On September morn
All around stand proud
Knowing you are September born
Katrina Epton

Too Late

If you have a message
Or a loving word to say
Don't wait and forget it
But say it right away

That tender word unspoken
That letter never sent
That forgotten message
Wealth of love unspent
For words heart's are breaking
For love words they wait
So today show you care
Speak; before it's too late

But rather than speak
Act upon that thought
Show love-kindness
You yourself once sought

And possibly you'll do
More than you contemplate
And save someone sanity
Before it is too late
N. W. Bracey

The Photograph

The photo lens a snapshot takes,
One seated in the studio, makes,
A photograph for those to see,
Who can admire such artistry.

By expert use of light and shade,
Someone so beautiful can be made,
From one who really is quite plain,
Gives new life, perspective gain.

Soft colours can enhance the grace,
Of lines upon an aging face,
Crowned by hair so shining bright,
Features stand out in the light.

Viewed at a distance takes away,
The strain of lines we see each day,
Makes one so grateful to be born,
With features God gave to be worn.

This masterpiece set in a frame,
Placed on a vantage space to claim,
Great pleasure from those who behold,
Makes one feel ever young, not old...
P. J. Benham

Untitled

Every line
 on every face
  betrays a problem
   trouble or
    loss.

A time
 of grief
  pain
   or pining

Everybody grows
 to bear
  the records
   of this theatre
    of learning.

The hurt
 felt deep
  in the soul
   is mapped
    on the parchment
     of the human face.
Kevin Smeaton

St. Peter's Church Greatworth

The parish church, standing
old and homely amidst
the wethers of the dead
and an ancient sycamore-
full set and broad with years,
that men may come to laud
and praise God's name in prayer.
The heart of the village, tis said,
echoing the silent thoughts
and hopes of its people,
and marking those great moments
when we are born,
when we are wed,
and when we die.

The parish church, standing
old and homely amidst
the centuries of the ages,
oft empty, but still loved,
a symbol of our faith
and God's eternal presence.

P. E. Coppen

The Death Of My Father

Life will never be the same,
our loss is heaven's gain,
we love you Dad with all our heart,
and in our thoughts we'll never part.

Malcolm Hurl

My Valentine

Saint Valentine is here once more,
Oh dear, what can I say?
Alone I sit, my heart is sore,
I miss you each new day.

How I remember first we met,
Red roses you sent me,
The scent I feel still lingers yet,
The card I plainly see.

What would I give to hold your hand,
Once more to feel you near,
Why - those who love can understand,
Just why I shed a tear,

Though now alone, this special day
Brings back the love we shared
A silent prayer once more I say,
Thank God, my love, you cared.

Nora Connolly

Colourful Katy

I hear the soft tread
Of someone, 'tis said
Dances through swirling mist.
'Tis Katy - in Amethyst.

Sunlight grows stronger,
No shadows linger.
Spring forth! Heavenly sight!
'Tis Katy - in White.

Gracefully soaring,
Twisting turning,
Chasing sunbeams mellow
'Tis Katy - in Yellow.

Nymphs and gnomes gaze in wonder.
Owls peer down and ponder.
Who is this dancing queen?
'Tis Katy - in Green.

Stars glitter: Moon dust gleams
As moonlight beams
Asleep and unknowing
On Katy, in silver glowing.

N. J. Smyth

To Touch The Sky

Upon the shore
of Autumn's misty veil,
and swallowed in the rushing
of a restless sea,
stands a poet
with a burning heart,
searching for a place to be.
And in his hands;
his broken spirit,
held like a wounded offering
to the stars.
And in his eyes;
the pain of learning,
as the fire of imagination
turns to cold reality.
And in his soul;
a loneliness,
which touches only those
who cannot find a way
to touch the sky.

Richard Galey

The Message Of The Woodpecker

Arising to the sound
of a woodpecker.
Tapping in the morning sun.
Calling me.
Get up.
Get up.
Get up.
There's a whole world to explore.
don't waste your life in bed.
Come on,
come on,
come on,
Put on your new red jumper.
Come outside
and seize the day.

Lisa Gray

Parent's View

Born of love,
Nurtured with pride -
Values develop,
Family to guide.

Success a feature,
Happiness the key -
Horizons broadened,
Trauma free.

Strength and fulfilment,
Independence, yet need -
Relationships prosper,
New direction agreed.

To watch and to wonder,
To know and to share -
The gift of a child -
Nothing compares.

Marion Horsfield

Together

Through life we walk,
our dreams are lost.
Through darkened tunnels,
at such great cost.
Mistakes are made,
through words in vain.

Great walls we build,
to hide our plight.
Break through these boundaries.
We can still find a right.

Philip David Jones

Little Tadpole

Hey, Little Tadpole make the change
Now's the time to rearrange,
Lose your tail but not your head
Grow some legs and hop instead.

Hey, Little Tadpole don't be shy,
It's your world so head up high.
Jump and leap from leaf to log
For now you are an adult frog.

Hey, Mr Frog see how you've grown,
Having Tadpoles of your own.
Teach your babies to be fond
Of life's great circles in the pond

M. J. Reynolds

"Dream Cottage"

Dream cottage hidden in my mind
Never quite coming into view
All my life have I dreamed about you
Are you real and just made for two
Secret glance will I ever find you
Or shattered dreams not for me are you
Make believe do you stay forever
Or one day will my dream come true
Yes we all have a dream within us
Perhaps one day we'll meet me and you
To live then happy ever after
In a home with enchanting view

Moreen Cunningham

Time (The Clock)

I am the master of your destiny,
My will cannot be questioned.
Quietly, unmercifully,
I ebb away,
Neither man, nor God,
Can question my finality.

How I love to taunt lesser mortals,
bringing forth wrinkles
and senility,
Where once there was
lustre and strength.

Yet, in my own way,
I bring about peace,
a quiet resignation
and restraint.

Yes, as I tick your life away,
neither heaven nor hell,
can bring about my end.

Leigh Organ

Wishful Thinking

To soar through the sky,
Like a bird that's in flight.
To have wings like a bat,
That floats in the night.
To have eyes like a cat,
Who can see in the dark,
To have a sweet voice.
And sing like a lark.
To leap like a deer,
And run like a hare,
To have each of these
You'll say isn't fair
But when you're a scarecrow,
And you've a cushion of hay,
You too would dream
About things of today

J. A. Erskine

Dad

Lean fingers catch
my eager grasp
hoisting me up
I balance
and walk on your feet
like water.

Cross and tired
you push me away.

Left alone
I stagger and stand
with sudden shame
at my delight
afraid
I bruised your hand.

Kate Clark

Winter Window

Harsh winter stirs
Must feed the birds
Clouds dim the light
Grass carpet white
Wind swirls the snow
Firelights glow
Sunshine on snow
In crystals show
Sparkle so bright
All coloured light
Still air serene
Ethereal scene

Tov Tovell

Gambling Shop USA

sitting brave barstool high
muscling down the springy arm
of a two-bit slot machine
eyes hunter-still straining
watching fruited wheels spin
whirling blurring no-can-win

wearing a string tie white shirt
faded jeans and cowboy boots
crowned with an eagle's feather
flying from a broad-brimmed dome
far from where the buffalo roam

hanging braids greyly shading
the carved red-skinned face
of a dying race
a tribe
the white men
around him christen

The noble
American
Indian

Robert Morris

November

Red and gold burnished beauty,
Mist-swirled moors so haughty.
On icy, nose-nip morning
The cloudy breath of yawning.

A Robin's crimson breast display.
Fallen leaves in disarray.
Biting winds that twist around.
Leaden skies and frozen ground.

Christmas anticipations rise.
Wonderment in children's eyes
At frosty patterned window pane.
November days are here again.

Susan M. Forrest

Baby Talk

Where do babies come from
Mummy do you know?
And what about the rainbow
Where do the colours go?
And where is Jesus really?
They say he's all around
But I have looked just every where
He's nowhere to be found
And what about the aeroplane
That draws pictures in the sky?
Why doesn't it fall down again
What really makes it fly?
And what about the spider
That's hiding in the bath
And when I get him out for you
Why don't you ever laugh
Mummy are you listening?
You must have heard of course
And when will tea be ready
I'm as hungry as a horse.

Linda Menhenitt

Sweet Boy

Sweet boy, I think of
Most of the time.
It drives my mum crazy
When I won't stop going
On about you.

I'm sure you have no idea
Of the high opinion I have of you,
Sweet boy, whom I hardly know.
I do not think you know me,
Though I want you to.

I can't make you know me,
And I can't make you care.
That is perhaps too much to ask,
So you'll have to stay in dreams,
Rather than reality.

I miss you when you're away,
And I worry for you too,
Although I must be stupid,
As I am unknown to you.
And probably always will be.

Kirsty Collier

By The Sea

To live by the sea a dream come true,
Lots of things that we could do.
Paddling in the freezing sea,
Running from a buzzy bee.
Sandy toes and sticky hands,
Rows of deck chairs on the sand.
Warm soft breeze upon my face,
Café windows full of lace.
Water stretching for miles and miles,
Pretty children with cheeky smiles.
Ice cream, teas, and hot dogs too
Model village, little zoo.
Rows of lovely smelling flowers
People walking round for hours.
Soaking up the summer sun
Before a lovely day is done.
Moon is full the sea is glistening
To the night time we are listening,
In the distance music plays
A perfect end to a perfect day.

M. Slaughter

Bedtime Prayer

Thank you Jesus for
my play,
for all the fun I've
had today.
Thank you Jesus for
Mum and Dad.
For all the food
and sweets I've had.
And to you dear Jesus
I will sing
Thank you for everything

K. M. White

Market Day

'Neath the churches watchful spire
Local traders gather there.
Each a stall they soon acquire
Upon which they will sell their ware.

Some have traversed many miles
Laden with assorted packs
Fresh fruit is marshalled into piles
And clothing neatly priced on racks.

Some early birds are soon embarking
The latest bargains they debate,
And village folk are heard remarking -
"There half-price over yonder mate!"

Townsfolk follow, keen and hasty
Viewing all the goods for sale,
Meat or fish and fruit most tasty
Cabbage, sprouts and curly kale

The time moves on, darkness falls.
And customers are on their way,
Tired traders close the stalls
But will return next market day!

D. G. Priestley

Love

Love comes love goes
Like the sweetness of the rose
like the rolling of the waves
we're in a love maze
always looking for the one,
who will be true
could that person be you.

Kathy Travers

Aspirations For Life

Crying comes so naturally,
Like dolphins swimming in the sea.
Sadness and I are so close,
It wraps around me like a cloak.
Loneliness shares my bed, my mind
We are truly two of a kind.
Isolation follows everywhere
Oh what an empty friend to share!
How often do I wish and pray,
At the end of every day,
That I could change my form, my style
Become another for a while,
Someone immune to what I feel.
Exciting, vibrant, whole and real.
Alas, I know I have to stay,
Being myself from day to day.
I cannot see that promised light,
Only darkness, eternal night,
So I keep on walking endlessly,
Waiting for my sun to rise for me.

Lorraine Elliot

Dial "G"

To pray to God is easy,
   Like a telephone call but free,
His line is always open,
   Try it out and see.
A twenty-four hour service,
   You know He's always there,
Tell Him all your problems,
   Let Him know you care.
Tell Him that you love Him,
   Thank Him for this day,
Tell Him He's terrific,
   This is how you pray.
Your Bible is your phone to God,
   Lift it up and look,
How can you accept His call,
   If your phone is off the hook.
He is a caring Father,
   Who hates to see you fall,
So do not wait till it's too late,
   Go now! And make that call.

William McKechnie

Time

Time alone does not stand still
Like a country lane it winds at will.
It goes along the country lane
Which has no end to close it in.

Time has no beginning, has no end,
But repeats itself again and again.
Nature uses it as a clock,
To breathe life, to take stock.

If only we could find the time
It's so elusive and never still.
It races on and never waits.
Unabashed, tho' brave, we never will.

Time is fast for man and mate
For human brings it will not wait,
Whilst they map out their lives
Time will never let man survive.

E. M. Bruce

Life

Life is a turbulent stream
like a beautiful dream
full of joy and sorrow
when you wake up tomorrow
happy with fresh hope
which makes one cope
with all problems and pain
thank the Lord again
for making this life
bearable and worthwhile.

K. R. Kadkol

A Touch Of Nature

I went into the woods one day
   just for a pleasant walk,
And what do you think I found there,
   that, all the trees could talk....

I said Hello to all of them - the
   daisy, the buttercup, the pink
And as I passed the large oak tree
   I'm sure I saw him wink.....

The flowers gave me a gentle nod
   the grass was all in song,
I heard the lovely echo long after
   I had gone...

One day I'm going back there
   to the birds all over head,
I didn't realize their presence
   until I found myself in bed....

Zena R. Parker

Wintertime Death

I'm saddened by the frost,
its icy grip,
draws the summer love,
from the flowers,
making them die.

It reminds me of you,
the way you,
crushed my love for you,
leaving me,
empty and cold,
leaving me,
a wintertime death.

Keith Bainbridge

Lost Love

My love for you was everything
It grew from day to day
A love so strong and endless
No one could take away
So when did you stop caring?
When did you start to lie?
why did you go and leave me?
Why didn't you say goodbye?
Now I lay here lonely
My hearts an empty shell
The pain that lives within it
No one will ever tell
How can I live without you?
How can I carry on?
How can I go on living?
My everything is gone?
I'd trade all my tomorrows
For one single yesterday
To hold you in my arms again
That is all I pray.

Kim L. Austin

The Temperamental Sun

The sun puts up to a test
It goes to sleep in the west
When the day is full and dreary
It seems to make us weary.

Up high it hides under a cloud
And maybe rain patters too loud
Sometimes it goes in and out
Enough to make us all pout

We grumble when it's overcast
Just thinking the sunshine
Is a thing of the past
Like times when clouds
Overtake its brilliance with
Electrical storms and vigilance
So when it rains of snows
And the strong wind blows
Let us not mind in the least
For the sun will rise
Again in the east.

P. I. Payton

Hope

For the power of pain,
is stronger than the love,
sing to your soul.
To free the heart and truth,
for it will give you the power
to never lose your pride
and to never give into the pain,
that is always there inside.

G. Davies

Life For Me

Life for me is work and play,
Life for me is a big way,
Life for me is a wonder,
Life for me is to ponder,
Life for me is a big light,
Life for me should always be bright,
Life for me is a muddle,
Life for me can be a puddle,
Life for me can be nice,
Life for me can turn to ice,
Life for me can be treated like lard,
Life for me can be hard,
Life for me can be God's Gift.
Life for me can be a drift.
Life for me can be a surprise,
Life for me can be a prize,
Life for me is a jar,
Life for me is so far,
Life for me is such a pleasure,
and life for me can be a treasure.

Priya Cheema

Soil Sister

Take me down, down to dust
Lie with me under moss,
Let the weeds twist about me
And the grasses braid my hair
Close to nature
Under stars
Soil sister.

L. Bull

To Peace, To See

One solitary rose
   Lays silent in blankets of snow.

One pink petal
   Lays quietly resting.

One garden
   The colours faded.

Two eyes
   The garden never seen.

To peace.
To see.
To suffer no more.
Free.
Forever.

Karen Stevens

The Seed Growing Secretly

Dormant in a live silo...
Knifing, gouging roots sprouting,
Gore shrouded in doomed flesh,
Now the vigil.
Drought quenched at an acidic oasis,
The coarse coal sickness as
The agony of the eruption tarries;
For a destruction can only
Self-destruct,
   A cell in the riot cell ran riot.

Nicklaus Thomas-Symonds

The Stream

Swiftly you slide like a sleepy snake
looking for a place to rest.
Over the rocks you slithery go,
making each a test.
Now up you awake,
moving from your crawl.
Slowly you pause and lift yourself
over the water fall!

Rachael Purvis

The Washing Machine

The washing machine
Is part of our life
Go out into the world
And ask any housewife

It is part of the house
That keeps your clothes clean
It keeps them so smart
That you are proud to be seen

Every mum knows
How important it is
And when it breaks down
How much it is missed

Remember these words
When things begin to go wrong
And you cannot find out
Where troubles coming from

That a washing machine
Is without any doubt
Something no family
Can be without

D. Mark Jackson

Face Facts

A face without any features
Is not a face at all
No eyes to see
No ears to hear
No lips to read
No face
No man
No life
No more

Samantha Leech

The Love I Have For My Child

The love I have for my child
Is more than I have ever known.
I sometimes feel that I
have been torn, apart
with emotion

The love I have for my child.
Took me by surprise,
Sometimes I can't believe
when I look into her eyes
That she is mine

The love I have for my child
grows stronger everyday.
She blooms like a flower,
and she is such a little ray,
of sunshine

The love I have for my child
Cannot be compared
but I know
that it will always be shared
by her loving father.

Sandra Bruce-Leggett

A Rose For My Valentine

All my love, I give you
is built into this Rose
Put it in some water
and see how my love grows.

Soon its buds will be bursting
my heart will do the same
I'm trying to say I love you
so figure out my name!

Shaun Fagan

Palladian Bath

A house at peace
Is a time release
Now decay is at cease
Walls glow in relief.

To ring again with sound of a coach
In royal crescent beyond reproach
Where even a ball game dare not poach
Dream on in regal approach.

R. T. S. Matthews

Gluttony

Worm your way inside me,
invade my every pore.
Infect me, dissect me
penetrate my core.
Satisfy this insistent lust,
abuse my aching flaw.
Taste my need, feed my greed,
then leave me craving more.

Sarah Wellband

Abstract Calmness

Unknown truths emerge
In willowy places
When aerialed life
Cannot be seen
Nor comforts;
Nor predictability.

Childhood games get
Carried on our back
For fun - uninhibited,
Our same spirit
Reflecting the openness -
Abstract calmness.

With camping stoves and tin mugs
We make do,
Even sleep well,
Until woken-up by song
And bright morning lights -
Reflecting gold from the dew.

Susan Crocker

Miaow

Mouse, mouse, not
In this house! See
A tail swishing. Eyes
Opened wide with
whiskers prickling - mouse hide!

D. R. Sharpe

Winter's Heron

Motionless he stood
In a frozen river of snow
Where to go now
In his search for food?

This elegant bird -
Grey, black and white,
In the bustle of life
Is a wondrous sight.

His graceful flight
And raucous cry
Are often seen and heard
At the end of night.

He is about more and more,
Especially now winter's here.
How lucky we are to have him
So far from any shore - the heron.

A. Colam Ainsworth

Untitled

Safe haven
    In my mother's arms
Tissue
    for my tears
Laughter
    for my triumphs
Comfort
    for my fears
Epitome
    Of everything
    I hear and do and see
Completeness
    and unselfishness
My mother's love for me.

Margaret A. Barclay

I Believe In You

The challenges you now confront,
In all you're going through,
Help me see the many ways,
That I believe in you.
It's hard for me to realize
The things you must face;
And though I try I can't completely
Step into your place.
But something in my knowledge
of the depth and soul of you
Gives to every real concern
an optimistic hue.
For when you must respond to life
with pure determination,
Your answer to the challenge
Is a source of inspiration
And though each day's uncertainty
The future oft obscures,
My hope for you is strong
And my belief in you endures

Mary Burns

The Exile

O! Ancient land
    I'll never tire,
of singing thy praises
    in rapturous fire!

Thy mountains so grand,
    thy valleys so dear.
None can withstand
    the love that is here.

Poets and minstrels
    have long sung thy praise,
for this land that I yearn for
    is my land, - is Wales!

Royston Lawrence

Chasing

The sun does shine brightly,
If you can visualize it's there.
Hold onto your thoughts,
Your aspirations, your cares.
For no matter what happens,
A path will lie ahead.
After the rain and storms,
Stop brewing in the air.
You'll see the clouds break,
And the sky become blue.
Birds flying freely,
At peace, to pastures new.
Not a care, not a tear,
No fear surrounding.
Take a breath, take your steps,
To a world, you belong in.

Sansel Ali

For My Sons

I know the hurt you feel inside
If only in me you could confide
To help you through your daily fears
Cushion the blow, shed your tears.

You're vulnerable, still young but old
To you these things I should have told
The rainbows you know they have no end
And people mostly are without a friend.

In fantasy land I see you withdraw
But life is real no secret door
No magic mountains to whisk you away
Each waking morning is a new day.

The truth is hard, cold and real
Our troubled lives already sealed
Fate is written, whatever it be
Still I would keep you safe with me.
Margaret J. Dalby

To A Loved One

If ever I am lonely
If ever I am blue
I think of all the good
times that I've loved
only you.

You are my one and only
no one else will do,
with all our faults and
failings our love keeps
shining through.

I hope you know how much
I care and appreciate
your love,
I will love you till the day
I die and join the Lord above.

If I should go before you do
A special place I'll keep for you
for in the end we will be
together, "Our love will be
ours forever and ever."
Sylvia M. Rook

The Unsown Seed, A Space, A Need

I long to feel you grow inside
I'd love to know you're there
I picture what you'll look like
The colour of your hair.

You'll be so very special
You'll mean the world to me
But where love yearns lies emptiness
Far deeper than the sea.

I hope one day you'll be there
I hope you'll give a sign
A burp, a kick, a cough maybe
And then I'll know you're mine.

I'll never give up hoping
I know one day you'll come
The greatest gift of all will be
To hear you call me mum.
Paula Wendy Walsh

Whispers

Upon this still high place above
My soul did move with whispered love
I saw the softness in your eyes
Through a window to the sky
For love did tremble from within
Could I be so certain then?
To touch your gentle soul again?
Sandy Parkinson

Ode To "Polly" My Cat!

Muddy paws, dirty claws,
Icy nose, chilly toes,
Tail twitchy, ears itchy,
Fur coat fluffy, - temper huffy!
Snowflakes falling, fireside calling,
Toilet finished, day diminished,
   Tummy flat, empty cat,
scratch door, do tiger roar!
"they" hear, - and appear,
Inside, food, - tasting good,
Clear plate, sit by grate,
Lick paws, tuck in claws,
Purr loudly, - doing proudly,
their house, - with no mouse,
caught that, clever cat,
that's me, - on "His" knee!
M. Luscombe

I Believe

i believe when i die
i won't know about it
until i hear my birthday
i believe in Luke Skywalker
mind set on target
like zen archer
you get there
no if's, and's, or but's about it
I'm wishing on a big, bright star
like Russel Grant
Patrick Moore, Carl Sagan
like the Highlander i scan
birth to infinity
knowing
every day the sun comes up
every day there is water
hopefully, a bridge o'er the water
Aye, i will lay me down.
E. Campbell

Doing Bird

For a second morning
I watch the birds migrating.
I wish I was one of them.
To be as free as a bird.
Leaving the Christmas rush
behind them.
Spending it somewhere
else, somewhere hot.

I keep promising
myself that I'll
go away one year.
The way things
stand at the moment
though it's just not
possible. I must stay,
do my time like everybody else.
One year,
one year I'll fly
away with them.
Tom Bramall

Tiger

A tiger prowls through the night.
Hunting prey, a scary sight.
Striped around a long, thin back.
Orange, yellow, gold, and black.
On the hunt, he's very sneaky,
Killing food, he's oh so sleaky.
Once he's fed it's down to sleep,
The jungle has a feel of peace.
By day they amble in the sun.
A sight we think is so much fun.
Beast of beauty, a joy to see.
In the jungle living free.
Kelly Simms

Paddy

The age gap was too wide to span
   I tried, but couldn't understand
When records roared of anarchy
   I didn't hear, I couldn't see

Hair dyed pink, boots sprayed blue
   How I hated each tattoo
Chains you flung upon the floor
   With studded jacket that you wore

In your jeans another tear
   How you made people stare.
A weekend gig, would you be home
   You had a tendency to roam

It was a crazy time I had
   Though you really wasn't bad
So now these memories I save
   For my punk lies in her grave
S. Wheelans

Dream Traveller

When I sit in my garden
I travel many miles
Through green woods and fields
Over wood gates and stiles

Down long leafy lanes
Up dappled green trees
Through bluebells and daffs
Heather buzzing with bees

Calm white beaches
Pounding blue waves
Reefs full of fishes
Rainbows and caves

Atop snow-capped mountains
By sprightly silver streams
My thoughts travel forever
Thank God I have dreams
Charles Roberts

Coming Home

I lift my eyes upon the scene
I squint and through the haze
The wind, she whispers in my mind
Remember! Childhood days

I do, I do, spoken in tears
Then right before my eyes
Angels five! With dirty faces
wee kids, when we were boys

Mysteriously! All was gone
The street returned to gloom
The wind, gave way to raindrops
But none! That I could see
I smiled, the sun was shining
One little boy was me!
C. R. Skelton

Silent World

Victims of a silent world
hold on in desperation,
hoping for a gentle sign
of merciful compassion.

A world of never-ending fear
stares back at them with hatred,
regarding hope with eyes of steel,
and tears, with loud contempt.

The world of broken unity,
where greed has overcome
the reality of life and living,
with heartless towers of stone.
Mary Bush

Without A Friend

Feeling sad and depressed
I sit here alone,
Wondering what was it I did
that was so wrong,
To deserve having no friends
with whom I'd have fun.
Everyone I know has got friends
I've got none.
What's wrong with me?
Please let me know.
If there's something I can change,
then God let it be so.
I'd love to have someone,
with secrets I'd share
If I needed a shoulder,
they'd always be there.
I have high hopes for that day
When I find my true friend,
Maybe then my sadness and loneliness
will come to an end.

Louise Sempey

The Queen And Me

This year's a special one for me
    I share it with the Queen,
It's difficult to realise
    The seventy years I've seen;
I wonder if she feels the same
    Remembering different years
Her wedding and coronation
    With the people's warm cheers.

My memories can't quite compare
    With Royal ones such as these,
But I am looking forward
    To events I've planned to please
And I do mean to celebrate
    In the best way that I can
Looking ahead, not always past
    Or even an "after ran".

Stella R. Long

Yesterday

Now that yesterday is gone
I must find a new horizon
Other stars to fix my eyes upon
Though my heart within cries on.

Now that yesterday is gone
The stream will flow on
Till it finds the sea
And a star shines through till it
ceases to be.

I am part of this mystery
which says, "Go on, Go on",
So I will rise and leave my sorrow
Seek and find some new tomorrow.

Though from the past I can always borrow,
Yesterday, Yesterday is gone.

S. Greenwood

"Guiding Light"

I am gone but I am here
I maybe far but I am near
I will be with you through each day
Until again you pass my way

When you are troubled I will appear
To help you overcome your fear
I will guide you through your life
So do not worry my dear wife

I maybe far but I am near
I am gone but I am here

A. G. Richardson

Alien World

Honeycombed vaults
Human bones decayed,
Lying their, age unknown,
From whence they came,
Centuries old and new,
Flights in space,
Dreams or reality,
Female intrusion,
Mutations produced,
Fantasy or fact,
On death answers unfolded.

Mary White

The Selfish Stolid

I love you my darling
I love you so much,
You can't imagine the feeling
I get when we touch,
So love me and leave me content,
My desire excused, all passion spent,
I know you don't love me
I think I know why,
You think I'm no good
There's no reason you should,
I know I'm a flirt
But that's all it is,
Please give me the chance
To show that I'm good,
If you don't care anymore
Then please let me know,
The thoughts in your head
Are beginning to show.

Ms. A. M. Taylor

"Valentine Lost"

A single rose, a single tear
I love you more each coming year
my love for you, it has no end
you were my lover and my friend

You had to leave an aching heart
a precious love too strong to part
and as on earth that love can't be
then heaven waits for you and me

I do know why you had to go
it broke my heart - I loved you so
my deepest love is always there
forever strong for you to share

I hope each day for your return
to know you care, that you too yearn
but wait I must, alone and true
so please remember I love you

Shirley Henn

Ode To An Astronaut

Am I going crazy?
I know I'm lonely and, well
I'm more than a million light years
away from humanity.
Up here a space
is a bore,
not like my childhood dreams
of stars and queer shapes,
but a huge, black, endless pit.
Soon I will see light,
wake up from my bed
and shut dawn's early rays
from my room.
But alas, this dream is real
and I shall never wake
to see civilization
or dawn's early light again.

Am I going crazy?

Linda Leahey

The Cat That Kisses You Better

I was in bed all sick and ill
I had a sort of sickening feel,
From my curtain came a light
A cat came out and gave me a fright.

It climbed on my chest
Its hair was a mess,
It licked my cheek
And made me feel meek.

In the morning I awoke
Felt like a brand new folk,
Remembered the cat
And that was that.

C. Huber

My Adventure

Wearing shorts and T-shirt too,
I decided to find something to do.
I packed my bag with sweets and pop,
Along with teddy balanced on top.

Ready for adventure off I set,
Interested to see how far I'd get.
Out in the yard, I wondered slowly -
Already I was feeling lonely.

I picked up teddy for a hug,
Then in the ground, a hole I dug.
I crouched inside and began to feel -
My idea of adventure wasn't ideal.

I ate some sweets and had a drink,
And saw my mummy, by the sink.
Picking up my things, I began to run
To my house! And to my mum!!

Rachel Harvey

Breakdown

Lightning strikes out
    I cling to the grass
The sea reaches up
    The thunder won't pass

Wind lashes out
    My minds in a whirl
The sea leaps again
    Then falls with a swirl

A flash lights the sky
    It won't leave me alone
The thunder cries out
    The wind starts to moan

The sky turns to black
    The rain starts to pour
The grass starts to break
    Then I am no more

Sue Drake

Butterflies At Bodlondeb Park

Butterfly of stained glass wings
Holds on a rim, droops and clings.
Emerald and black, zebra stripes
Fan-tailed, bat-bottomed
And dracula type.
Bird like, poppy-hued
And luminous blue.

Amazon memories hanging on Rose
Tranquil stream and dripping leaves
Of rubber plant and palm.
Marbled wing and furry headed
Dotted, regular like dominoes
Swiftly the swallow tail
Makes patterns
Against the emerald veil.

Ruth Goode

The Spider's Web

Upon a frosty Winter's morn.
I came across a spiders web.
The sun was o' so bright.
Woven secretly overnight.
With an open invite.

By moon the spider awaits his prey.
Invisible threads of the net.
Glistening in the mid-day sun.
The spiders lays in wait.
For the net to vibrate.

An unsuspected insect locked.
Dinner, lunch, an evening meal.
The spider keeps his larder stocked.
Stored away for a future meal.
As the day begins to chill.
So the spider lives to kill.
Pearl Jebb

In the Shadows of My Mirror

In the shadows of my mirror
I bleakly stare,
Who is this naggered person
Who is standing there?
I look deep beyond the mirror
way past reality,
and gently remind myself there
was once a child in me.
All of a sudden a small child
I can now see,
it all comes rushing back again
and I realise it's me.
I see myself in a sleepy meadow
beneath me, the soft grass I feel
I look around the other world
that looks and feels so real.
It feels so good to once again
See how it used to be,
And as I drift from the other world
that child I no longer see.
Kelly Roberts

A Widow's Thoughts

I often sit and wonder
How life might have been
If death had not divided us
Tis only thoughts,
That can't be seen
I look at older couples
It puts my heart on hold
For I shall never say those words
"When we grow old"
But life goes on with memories
Special thoughts for me
Will I grow old, I ask myself
Well that I cannot see.
Margaret Munro

Memories Of Heartbreak

He told his love with orchids
With brooch of silver spun;
He bought for her a gay parasol
To twirl against the sun.

Then in a summer meadow
with tender hands he wove,
A necklace of white daisies
A token of true love.

Of orchids brooch and parasol
Faint memories remain;
But etched upon her heart forever
a simple daisy chain.
John Clancey

Today Is Father's Day

I couldn't send you a card,
You're no longer here, and yet
I think of you every day
Since you left.
I miss you terribly,
Our arguments, our talks,
Your humour and jokes,
Your impatience and your tolerance
Of me, your daughter
Whom you loved, despite
My sharpness and lack of time
For you at times.
I wish now, I'd given you more.
I can't bring back time,
I only hope you know
How much I loved you
And miss you today,
This empty Father's Day.
Julie Caldwell

When You're An Artist

When you're an artist
   You're excused for being in love
When you're an artist
   You're forgiven for being mad
   it's called being eccentric
When you're an Artist
   You're given space and freedom
   to be you
When you're an Artist
   Everybody wants to find
   out how you work
When you're an Artist
   You're not worth anything till
   You're a dead artist!
Gordana Bjelic-Rados

Water runs over
Your cornfield chest
Like trilling flutes

Soaring skyward
In Memoriam of
Plague-free conjugation

Diluting reason into
Molecular fusion
And passionate fission

Amounting to flesh
As limp and spent as
Weary pilgrim's limbs

Their sexual Santiago
A gossamer relic of
Sisyphean pasts.
Jonathan A. W. Cartledge

Thank You

For coping in a world of men
When men can't cope.
For smiling through adversity
Not losing hope.
For listening into tiredness
Not wanting a reply.
For making me feel strong again
When I really wanted to cry.
For being there when I was alone
Staring into doubt.
For giving up your time for me
As I let my problems out.
You've made my long days short
And helped me through the stress,
May love hold you in its peace
Caressed by gentleness.!
Frank Glover

Farewell To A Mother

A hand reaches out for comfort
You take it and hold it tight
You squeeze it for reassurance
That everything will be alright

The response is overwhelming
You feel you want to cry
As you cling on to past memories
A tear comes to your eye

The hand begins to weaken
The finger slip apart
You know the end is nearing
You pray with all your heart

Inside your heart is aching
Your body goes all numb
A part of you is dying
When you say farewell to you mum.
Jennifer Day

Our Son Zeb

You grow so fast
You look so good
The way I knew
You always would
In you, young man
I put faith and trust
That you do your best
You know you must
You carry so much wisdom
And a power that's for sure
So use your gifts for the reason
They were given to you for
Your life will not be easy
It will make a man of you
Be of patience and understanding
And God will see you through
I'll do my best to guide you
To help you on your way
For life is just a journey
We travel every day.
Janet Browning

An Aquanliance

I like the way
you greet - me
each day
with a smile
a hello!
Then go on your way.
It helps to Banish
the cares of
the day.
Joan Gregory

The Clown

Bimbo the clown
Would make a frown
Disappear in a twinkle
When into the ring
He would spring
No one would have a wrinkle.
With his face
All covered in paste
He'd make the dullest day sunny
The children would laugh with glee
To see - Bimbo
He was so funny.
All the acts were very good
But it was clearly understood
Who was the favourite don't you know?
The fame of the clown
Was all over town
He was the hit of the show.
Dorothy J. Small

Words!

Words from my heart,
Words for a divine sweetheart.
Words which I know are true.
Words for my dearest, darling,
Beautiful Julie.
My words, simply, I love you!
Graham Mitchell

My Comfy Blanket

You're my comfy patch-work blanket
with colours bright and warm,

I wrap my arms around you to
shelter from life's storm,

I've picked off all your fluffy
bits so now you are thread-bare,

But I never meant to harm you
just meant to shelter there

Your patch-work has now faded
and your fluff has disappeared,

I'm feeling less protected and
often so afraid,

I'm afraid that I will loose you
or that you'll fray away,

So I wrap my arms around you and
hope that you will stay,

A silent tear escapes me when I
see your thread-bare state,

Cos you're such a comfy blanket
you're my extra special mate.
Ej Ward

I'll Be Here

How is it in this hi-tech life
With all at our control
There is no magic cure at hand
To ease a troubled soul
Nothing that is broken
Cannot be repaired
Even down to human parts
Most things can be spared
Yet with all this knowledge
Why is it deemed so hard
To reach deep within someone
And soothe their troubled heart
I can only sit and listen
To the hurt that you have there
And only let you know
I honestly do care
I wish that I could find a way
To erase your pain and tears
But I can only comfort you
And promise I'll be here
Eileen Riley

Seashore

As we walked down the deserted shore
We picked up fancy shells to see
The colours of the shivering sea,
The pearly pinks and greys
Of the swirling, twisting shapes.

The water raced and trickled
Around my sun kissed feet
We sat down in the wet sand
And the promise we did meet
The promise of the sunshine
The promise of romance
And in our passionate arms
The waves did dance.
Emma Jane Rugg

Stormy Seas

The stormy wind blows
wild across the sea.
clouds racing fast
as if at last set free.

High above the rocks
the waves dispense,
pounding hard against
the land's defense.

Lifting pebbles high.
crashing onto land.
Leaving only when the
tide recedes the sand.

At times the sea
doth lie in calm.
Beware its rages,
when, it holds no charm.
Beryl Smyter

North Yorkshire Moors In Winter

Snow falls and drifts
White on white
Freezing over all
Lone pheasant's plumage
Splashes colour
On dry stone wall.
Snow falls soft as
A lover's sigh
Trees are charcoal sketches
Against pale winter sky.
Christine Yeoman

"Peace"

Peace - mankind's eternal quest
When all men shall be free,
Is still beyond the furthest grasp
Still in the "Yet to Be".

In Pandora's sundered box
One Virtue only laid.
Hope still remained, yet fragile,
Too weak to move she stayed.

But Hope alone is not enough.
Man must catch the chimera
Of other Virtues yet still hid
Beyond the furthest star.

But man is ever wilful
With every vice endowed.
He kills and maims and tortures
Whilst he preaches Peace aloud.

Still Peace is for the future,
In imagination's mist,
With guns and bombs exploded;
When mankind does not exist.
David Rickman

My Field Of Primroses

Yellow is the primrose
which is small and petite
its face reminds me of the yellow sun
under which it dances and has fun.

In my field it is full of primroses
which sway gently in the wind,
This gives me the sense of freedom
This sense of care-free-ness.
This escape, to be free.

So when I want to be free
I come to my field where,
I can see, the primroses dancing
free, for me.
Allison Roberts

Togetherness

I place my arms around your neck,
whisper softly in your ear,
Words of love and tenderness,
the things you want to hear,
I gaze into your lovely eyes,
and gently stroke your hair,
Upon your lips I place a kiss,
to show how much I care,
We stroll together hand in hand,
through the paths of life,
Together we will always be,
as husband and as wife,
But if there is an hereafter,
in the heavens above,
A place with me I will reserve,
for my one and own true love.
Irene E. Fleetwood

The Realm Of Insanity

The realm of mad men
Where killings take place
Death to peace makers
The place to escape
No pain
Just confusion
No ruler
All equal
All crazy
Where fires blaze
Destroying
Sweet innocent minds
You know where
This place is
Inside everyone
What is it?
The realm of insanity
Gavin Stott

The Chair

A conduit for thoughtless rage
This harmless chair has been
It sought to gain no advantage
Did not try to run or scream
a martyr to a sorry cause
Regrets, piled on regrets
No logic thoughts nor learned pause
Just mindless emptiness
Casualty of the primal beast
Innocuous standing there
Is this an honest soul released
Or just another broken chair
Alan J. Rae

Life's Like That

Isn't it funny
When you need extra money,
And do a bit work on the side;
The Taxman will find you
And gently remind you
Pay up your dues — you can't hide.

It is energy-draining
When your spouse keeps complaining
Of the need for a break, in the sun;
And after explaining
Only five tours are remaining,
She decides she won't like any one.

But despite fickle weather,
Taking all things together,
We do always seem to survive;
So instead of just moaning,
We should be atoning,
And thanking the Lord we're alive.
Scott Armstrong

Who Are You - Mother

Where are you,
   When I need you most.
In other's eyes
   you're the perfect host.
I need a friend,
   you're not there.
With other people,
   you always care.
When I'm down,
   you're never around.
My life's a mess,
   you couldn't care less
Who are you?
   Mother.

Diane Jones

Introspection

What is my worth
what do I mean
is there anything that can
stop me drifting
what do I own?
What is my thing?
Can I pick up settle down
and stop dancing
am I impressive
or submissive
snub responsibility
and love nothing,
there comes a time
when it all has to change.
I reach out to scream but there is
no breath inside of me,
I open my salt stung eyes
but it seems to be too late
I fight on out of pride
and everything will stay the same.

Eugene Bruce

Come - Now Walk into My Arms

Come - now walk into my arms.
We have looked and longed
Have whispered and walked
So delicately as moving
In a field of spring flowers

Our hands have touched and laced
Our bodies moving
As through a mirror
Not quite touching
But with a closeness that
Evolves with ages

Our eyes have danced with
The others gazing
Glowing, smouldering
With the soft, gentle demanding
Looks of love,
Come - now walk into my arms
And complete the ecstasy.

Joanne Huntley

Just A Thought

At the end of certainty
We have doubt.
At the beginning of doubt
We have hope.
At the end of hope
We have faith.
At the beginning of faith
We have certainty.

Alan Davenport

A Country Walk

Across the hills and meadows
We happy wanderers go
To see all God's creations
and beauty to behold

From tallest tree to daisy small
On hill and meadow vast
The eye perceives a wondrous sight
Which nothing can surpass

Through kissing gates and over stile
We wend our happy way
Then come to fields of pasture green
Where sheep and cows both graze

With beauty all about us
Wild flower's at our feet
It's Mother nature at her best
With scent in air so sweet

Our country walk is ending
And as we backward gaze
To look upon that tranquil scene
And say may God be praised.

Douglas W. J. Pearce

Bee Kind

I saw a busy bee today, only it
wasn't busy any more,
it lay there soft and helpless
on the dusty, grimy floor.
People all around, not one could
spare a thought
to lift this little insect onto the
lifeline that is sought.
So I stopped a while and knelt down
to put it right up high,
high onto a sunflower, when refreshed
and feeling better off it did fly.
People are so engrossed in their
everyday lives
that lots of little bees never
reach their little hives,
So if you can help one please do.
All things have a right to live,
I think so don't you?

Carole Wakelin

Have No Fears

To find a friend,
Upon who you can rely,
Someone you can depend,
No fancy words or lies,
One you can trust,
This friend is a must.

Friendship is forever,
Two people together,
The truth from the start,
No broken hearts.

No lies to be told,
Only stories of gold,
The truth is best,
No need for a test.

Someone to believe in,
To wipe away the tears,
A shoulder to cry on,
Have no fears.

Gavin J. Docherty

Hooked On Hurt

Bullying tyrant husband
Treated as dirt
Must leave
But stay
I'm hooked on hurt.

Isabelle Wright

Strange Ideas

To me everything is strange
totally strange

People with strange ideas
strange dreams
strange realities

Being strange...
acting strange

This whole world is strange
even weird...

Learning to live with these ideas
these strange ideas
almost stupid ideas

How do they live with these
strange ideas.

Andrea C. MacDonald

Windmill In My Mind

Water's splashing under thee,
Tormented, sometimes by me,
Winds blowing, of rage,
Moving steadily, as it turns to go,
Grinding corn, for as we know
At least, with its power free,
Stillness, within our minds,
A spiritual wind,
In a desperate need for thee.

John Barry Robinson

Chimney's From Afar

I live to breathe the air I see,
Too late for me.
With distant eyes I view afar, the
chimney spew their vicious clouds,
Too late for me.
The silent clouds creep on the wind
I breathe the air.
Too late for me.
I have no choice I breathe to live.
Too late for me.
So now I lie, no more I breathe
Too late for me

Arthur John Cropper

Free Flight

I want to feel, I want to fly
to touch the stars up in the sky,
to feel the current flowing free
I want to be a bird you see,
To swoop and dive
to glide and flow
to see the things
these creatures know,
To take my food upon the wing
to sing the way the skylarks sing,
But heavy down to earth am I
I cannot rise, I cannot fly,
The only way that I will see
Is when my soul from earth is free.

Gillian Whetnall

Loss Of Freedom

Loss of freedom
   what does it mean,
locked behind bars
     so you cannot be seen.

Loss of freedom
   to roam the land,
to meet and shake
   a friendly hand.

Loss of freedom
   to see your family and friends,
who you may of hurt
   and only time will mend.

Loss of freedom
   to smell fresh air,
or to have a descent barber
   to cut your hair.

Loss of freedom
   for what you have done,
was it really worth it
   the crime you thought you'd won???

Adam Wickers

Memories

All to myself I think of you,
Think of you things we used to do,
Think of the things we used to say,
Thing of each happy yesterday.
Sometimes I weep, sometimes I smile
But I keep each old and golden while,
All to myself!

Ann Golding

To Mother

I wish I had been old enough
To know you in your youth.
I wish I had been wise enough
To learn from you the truth
About the future's turmoils
In all of life and living
To learn the art of taking
But mostly that of giving
I wish I had been old enough
To glean from you your wisdom
To accept from you your loyalty
With my wayward ways forgiven
Now that I am old enough
To appreciate your seeings
You are gone - but left behind
A better human being.

Franie Voller

Convergence In Gloucestershire

Distinguished in their ranks
the tall trees stand,
with firebreaks between
'mid chaos, planned.

And cottage sat above
calmly surveying
nature and man's checks
beneath it laying.

The sentinel sheep
at the side of the road
will not even move
with the horn as their goad
complacent in traffic
they graze at the verge
as nature and man
once more converge

James Wadeson

Untitled

It's over now
The time we knew would come is here
Just one last fling,
One last weekend
The final goodbye it has to end

  We loved
  We laughed
  We played the game
  We know the rules
   it has to end
  We met by chance
  and fell in love

Dawn Davies

For Eternity

I love to walk up a hillside
To breathe the pure fresh air
To stand and lose myself in thought
And throw out all my care

I love to sit beneath the sun
To bask in its warming rays
To close my eyes in ecstasy
And laze away the summer days

I love to stare up at the sky
To gaze at clouds of white
To wonder as the moon appears
And changes day to night

I love to feel the gentle wind
To feel it softly move my hair
To marvel when the wind blows strong
And every tree is stripped and bare

I love to be part of nature
To know that this is destiny
To believe it's always been this way
And will be for eternity.

Elizabeth Howarth

My Grandchild

I wait with bated breath
the child, I have yet to see
I wonder what it will take
to shape my destiny
A boy, a girl,
What do I care
The seeds already sown.
The love I give
The faith I share
A personality all its own

Florence Adam

Life Is Cruel

You mean so much
to all of us now.
You've been so brave
so take a bow.
You don't deserve
to be this ill.
I'll love you always
I promise I will.
I wish this cancer
wasn't true.
Or maybe just
that it wasn't you.
It makes me sad
when you're not so strong
Life is cruel
and can go wrong.

Jodie C. Morris

Unusually Late

Unusually late
To bed that night.
Then all her idle chatter
Continuing through this fog
Of half-sleep,
Answering "mmm" to the odd,
Well-timed question.

Then the sound of the front door key
And tittering,
And the she promptly fell asleep.

And next day, coffee after dinner,
She is dreamy and far away.
"That's the first one gone" she said.
"What do you mean?" he asks,
"She only went to a disco".

She gazed through the
Rising cigarette smoke
At something in the distance,
And said no more.

Jonathan Black

The Grains Of Sand

The grains of sand drift silently
   Through time and tides
And time and tides wait for no man
   Here on this earth.

Like the sand in an hourglass
   Turned up on end
We slide slowly through our life
   Until the final grain.

And then God upturns the glass
   For us to rise heavenwards
To everlasting life with Him
   Who gave His life for us.

Jane E. Bradbury

Drifting Away

As I wander back,
Through historic days,
Of all the things we lack,
I sit around and gaze.

Is this the day I might die,
I often wonder how and why?
Drifted away to another place,
Drifted away to join another race,
In God's arms I'll sit and cry,
In God's arms I'll rest and die.

Angela Bastiani

Childhood Dreams

As children we dream of the best
things in life
But as time goes by we begin
to find out
That nothing is ever quite what
it seems
And we start to lose all of
Our childhood dreams.

Maybe as adults we begin
to understand
That life sometimes deals us
a really cruel hand
The dreams they all slowly
fade away
As we wake each morning to face
another bad day.

With bills to be paid and
more work to be done
we wonder if dreams
can ever be won.

Caroline Wones

The Moon Gazer

Perhaps an unfamiliar observation
Three o'clock in the afternoon
Seeing the sunlight on the moon
I saw earth's shadow on it too

A vast empty planet, there, suspended
Some distance out in space
Cloud covering like lace
And its surface a mottled grey

I considered the marvellous precision
Of its orbit during each year
Transfixed I stare and stare
As steadily it moves position

Giving new and full moon seasons
Influencing the tides
Shown on calendars and guides
And silently lighting the night

Most marvellous of the wonders
Man on its surface trod
Footsteps observed by God
Who controls and once created all

John Remmington

Simple Truth

They fled
They cried
Many died.

They camped
Crop failed
Children ailed.

They froze
Some starved
Numbers halved.

One man
Autocrat
Saw to that.

Others tried
Kurd aid
Many saved.

...Yet on the hill
They're crying still

Enyd Muxworthy

The Old Old House

There was once a poor old house
That once was full of folk
But now is sad and sorry
And to me it spoke.

It said, "They have all fled,
And all my rooms are bare,
The front door locked and bolted,
And all the windows stare.

No smoke comes from my chimneys,
No roses grow up my wall,
Just ivy shrouds me
Like a green, shiny shawl.

No postman brings me letters
No name upon my gate
I used to be called the "Ivies"
But now I'm out of date.

Because there's no one here to care
The garden now is sparse and bare
I may be old and my wood all rotten,
I know I'll never be forgotten."

James Moore

Poetry

Poetry is,
Only an,
Expression of all,
That Mankind,
Reveres, and,
Yearns to describe.

Bill Kirkwood

The Leaf

The leaves have turned to orange,
they were once a shade of green,
They lived upon the tree so tall,
No better sight, I've seen.

But now the wind has caused them,
to flutter to the ground,
And as they drifted downwards,
they didn't make a sound.

It's nature's way of saying,
that winter's on its way,
No vivid green or orange bright,
just winter's solemn grey.

I know this change of colour,
it really has to be,
To give the tree a chance to rest,
'till its new leaf dances free.

D. Morris

"The Sounds Of Discontentment"

Once they were so happy
There was rainbows every day
Now he sits alone and drinks
She tut-tuts her life away

In a caravan in Bognor
They can talk without a sound
She dreams of Barbara Cartland kisses
He dreams of Common Ground

He cycles from the factory
With overtime on his breath
She's listening to the radio
And knitting herself to death

Lying in the king size
Her works her like a lathe
She thinks of England once again
And her disappearing faith

And the only sounds they make
As the night's chased by the day
Are the sounds of discontentment
As they cry their life's away.

Alan Baillie

A Steam Train

Clickety Clack goes the track
The train goes crack
The smoke is dirty
When it stops at the station.
The passengers can't see
because of the smoke.
The track goes smack
The train goes crack.
The passengers fall
off their seats.
The track is slack.
The train speeds up.
The track is broke,
but the driver brakes.
The passengers
and the train are safe.
They all go home.

Adnan Krzalic

The Fairground

Can you hear the music playing,
The whirring of the rides,
The shrill screams of laughter,
As the girls go down the slides?

Brightly the lights are shining,
Gaily - yellow, red and blue.
Oh let me go to the fairground,
Let me go with you.

The humming of the engines,
The singing of the song,
The shouting of the fair man,
The crashing of the gong.

Excitedly I run about -
I clap my hands with joy.
The man with his young lady,
The girl with her young boy.

I love the noisy fairground,
I love the greasy, sweet smell.
I know you love the fairground,
I know you do as well.

Brenda Drayton

Homeless

The ground is wet
The street is grey
A weary end to
A weary day

The light is on
The fire bright
To keep us warm on a cold, cold night

But what of those that are alone
They have no house to call a home

They live in boxes on the street
Begging pennies from those they meet

We close our eyes
Put the image away
We'll think of them another day.

Caron King

The Starving Children

We read it in the papers,
The starving children's plight
Their bellies fat and bloated
It surely isn't right.
If only we could stop and think
How much food they are short
Before we sit down for a meal
Without a second thought.

The feasts that lay before us
Will fill you to the hilt,
But I can't eat another bite
I'm already full with guilt.
If we only gave a little
To help them with their strife
You know you could be saving
A starving child's life.

Andrew Barnes

Untitled

War is an action
that appears to be greed
planted by men.
It will grow like a seed

The venomous poison
that's left behind

Will ne'r be forgotten
by folk of all kind

Jean Valerie Wixon

Unfinished Lament

My bones are old
The room is cold
My time is ebbing fast
But since I met you years ago
I knew our love would last

My body weak
I fear the night
Our children grown and gone
And when I feel the pain my love
I know it won't be long

As darkness comes
The pains begin
I reach for you in vain

I ask myself is this the end

Gerard Quirke

Winter

The wind it is a-howling
The rain is on the pane
Oh how lovely it's going to be
When spring is here again.

The snowdrops, they are beaming
The crocus flowers too
The nights they are a shortening
And trees are all anew.

Oh to have the summer sun
So warm upon ones arms
To wander down the leafy lanes
And share in all its charms.

Forget the cold of winter
The wind, the snow, the rain.
To once again have sunshine
To ease the troubled brain.

Fenn Jindra

Silence

I see
the pity in your eyes.
Your disappointment lies
in me.

I feel
the love that's in your touch.
Your gentle hands give much
to me.

I taste
the anger which is voiced.
Your bitter words are wrenched
from me.

I smell
the scent of hope and fear
growing with every tear...
from you and me.

Carla Faulkner

Himalayan Evening

Who has heard the bugle sound
The end of regimental day?
Who has smelt the evening smoke
Curling upward on its way?

Who has watched the eagle's flight
From mountain peak to dusty plain?
Who has breathed the upland air
That is sweeter than champagne?

Who, having dreamed of England
From such a place as this,
Has surrendered to the scents
And sounds of Himalayan bliss?

Gerald Wheatley

Untitled

Once
The light was bright
Brighter
Like snow
Like the summers of infancy

Once
The air was poignant
Painful
Like birth
Like gulps of starlight

Once
My mind was clear
Certain
Like love
Like...
Like only love

Helen E. Thompson

Love And Friendship

Today I meet
The girl I dream
From behind the mask
Herself is seen

This one new face
Behind the old
A ray of light
To save my soul

Her love is sold
Her heart is given
To one I hold
As dear as heaven

A friend she stays
My love forsaken
Or love she be
My heaven breaking

Wee Brother

My Friend Troy

When I get to heaven
 the first thing I will do.
Is search amongst the angels
 Until I have found you.
I miss your loving welcome
 that greeted me each day.
I want to come and find you
 So once again we'll play.
I loved your caring nature,
 How loyal you could be,
I'll never find another
 who could mean so much to me.
So when I get to heaven,
 When my time here's at its end,
I'm hoping you'll be waiting,
 My Troy, My dog, My friend.

Dee Ditchman

Allegory

At Sunset
The dark flowers shine,
Petals opening
For the drones,
Their pollen worthless.
Meanwhile,
The fruit flies multiply
By night,
To be eaten
By the rhythm of the day.
Sunrise,
And the fat cats
Race rats
To nightfall,
Becoming moths and butterflies.

Helen Green

Winter Scene

I see the distant, snow-capped hills,
The field and meadow, bleak,
As winter slowly ambles by.
His friend, the Spring, to seek.

Trees are dark and "sleeping".
Spidery fingers reaching high.
Devoid of rich and leafy coat.
Black filigree on sky.

The virgin snow begins to thaw,
Where daisies once have been.
Patterns of lace upon a field,
Striated white and green.

Nature's colour, much subdued.
Abundant shades of grey.
Pale watery sun that fails to keep,
The chill and frost at bay.

Days slowly pass, the snow returns,
Like icing on a cake.
God's precious gift of nature,
Leaving beauty in its wake.

Ann Timmins

A Sad Story

Are we alone?
The Earth is our only home,
So why do we neglect it?
We poison our beautiful rain forests,
It's a problem we know and admit.
So why don't we just join our hands,
And pray for love and peace.
To protect all life on planet Earth,
And to stop the unwanted decease.
The human race stands divided,
By war and pointless conflict.
How can we believe in a world,
That forces itself to submit.
I think about other life forms,
A million miles out in space.
Do they disagree like we do?,
And try to destroy their own race.
So I ask you again,
Are we alone?

Adrian Bach

The Sea

Purple blue green and white
The colours of the sea
Twisting twirling crashing swirling
Here in front of me
In the never ending battle
Of the shore against the sea

Men go down to the sea in boats
They earn a hard won living
To toil and strain in wind and rain
To fight to get there living

All in all we all enjoy
The pleasures of the sea
And the many things it gives us
Which we take for granted so easily

But there comes a day
In the not to distant future
If we don't give her respect
Her beauty does deserve
She won't be enjoyed by our children
In this ever shrinking world

James Carl Hughes

244

Belfast Soldier

The men patrol the city.
The city torn between,
fighting for republic or
fighting for the queen.

They patrol around the city
Streets, with weapon's in their
Hands, weapons which they
Cannot use against the rebel bands.

The government in parliament
Say "We've been in wars before"
But the British troop's upon
The streets say "This is
Murder now not war"

John Rall

And On Looking Into Mirrors

From brutal toes-foundation,
the cerebral armories marry
Greek Beauty with ugly jack-boots,
Ruinous nude truths
Insecure lines
creep over creating
wisdom, snakes and mostly
collapsing pillars of progress,

And on looking into mirrors
We pull demons of classical
description
from hiding.

Ian James Thompson

Old Folk In Spring

At the dawn of the day
The birds sing and pray
Spring is in the air
And no one has a care

As the change from old to new
Like the sky from grey to blue
Has brought a new life here
And tries to spread it fair

Our worries for a moment gone
While we burst out in song
We can now release the steam
As the trout jump in the stream

The evidence is clear
As we watch the painter smear
He is washing down our street.
To make it look so neat

Old folks emerge and say
Hibernation is far away
It is good to be alive
Where can we go to jive

Chris McCarthy

My Wish

To die with dignity,
that would be my wish,
pass to eternity,
in quiet dreaming bliss.
Drift through that open door,
where God awaits my soul,
to wake in pain no more,
my body cleansèd whole.
And when in time at last,
I meet all gone before,
their youth so quickly passed
yet aged are no more,
it's there I'll find a peace
a tranquil lasting calm,
to leave this life, this race,
as loved ones take my arm.

Edna Calderwood

Whose Garden?

Badger, as he digs the ground,
Surprises Mole, who turns around-
"Look out Badger! - where you trod-
This 'ere be my homely sod!"
"Sorry Littl'un", says he to Moley,
"I'll go dig another holey!"
Repentant Mole now begs his pardon-
After all - it's *Badger's* garden!!

Heather ScullyCaragh

The animals she loves
The birds she just adores
The insects they intrigue her
And anything out of doors
Will grab all her attention
And she will spend the day
"Over here, just look at this"
You'll often hear her say.
She'll wander through the forest
Or hike around the park
Inspecting all the wildlife
I'm sure she'd stay till dark
Soaking up the beauty
Of the planet at its best
Taking all that nature offers
You could put her to the test
She would answer all your questions
And help you understand
Why we the peoples of the Earth
Should be caretakers of our land.

Judith Gray

Obsession

An irrepressible mania
that overwhelms the thoughts.
Burrowing deep
within the mind,
an intensity unsought.

A compulsive burning passion
that plagues and haunts the soul.
Drains, consumes
devours,
far beyond control.

A single motivation, no
reasoning can curb.
Such deep irrational
stimulus,
must sanity disturb.

Barbara A. Baxter

Susan, My Love

You have the kindest face,
that I have ever seen,
your smile lights up a room,
like a million candles,
when you blush,
you outshine the prettiest rose,
your eyes sparkle,
like the brightest diamonds,
and to me your love,
is as valuable as any gold

I admit that my smilies
are all just cliches
but my feelings can be hurt,
so tread carefully with my heart,
it is easily broken,
but it is yours if you want it,
I do know what love is,
so give me a chance,
to give you shelter,
behind the walls of my heart.

James Ferri Smith

Snuffles

We have a hedgehog in our garden
Snuffles is his name
He snuffles up the garden path
Then snuffles back again.

He snuffles 'round the borders
And snuffles round the lawn
All around the veg. patch
He snuffles until dawn.

The other night I waited
For 'our' hedgehog once again
And sure enough 'our' Snuffles
Turned up, snuffling like a train.

Up the path, round the lawn
under the garden gate
I watched his every move
It had been worth the wait.

I kept quite still, he came close
In the dim light I could see
He seemed an inoffensive chap
"Do you like hedgehogs? Like me..."

Barry Harold Smith

Le Cimitère De Ma Mère

I walk alone amidst the stones
that harbour the decaying bones
of one's beloved lying there
in the Cimitère de ma Mère.

I know I look so very brave,
standing at my Mother's grave.
But, no-one knows how sad's my soul
as I remember the six-foot hole
by which the vicar said his prayer
in the Cimitère de ma Mère.

So many young, so many old
are lying there in the bitter cold;
Oh! I hope they know that I do care,
in the Cimitère de ma Mère.

So many days will yet re-dawn,
Just for us who ever mourn
our lost one, n'er returning
to salve our never-ending yearning
to join them, when we do but dare
in the Cimitère de ma Mère.

Jeanne Fillery-Handzic

Silent Moments

As the quiet of the night draws near
  So dark and silently still
I lie in the shadow of darkness
  My head with dreams to fill

Hushed by the sound of breezes,
  A glistening of a tear,
Memories filled with happiness,
  Few are filled with fear.

Thoughts of time passed on by
  Pictures of beauty make me cry,
  Now the dawn is almost here,
Time to let go of all the fear

My eyes grow weary,
It's time to sleep,
Out in the clouds I shall
rest my feet.

Tomorrow starts another day,
All the dreams will fade away,
That's the time I shall recall,
There's nothing to fear after all.

Doreen Smith

Tiger Tom

'Meow, meow', he's on the prowl.
That grey tiger cat,
So cool and so fat.
I stroke him gently.
His tail tosses up.
Then he claws at me with a scowl.

You seem so friendly Tiger Tom
As you leap to greet,
With your plaintive 'Meow',
Is it a game?
Are you wild? Are you tame?
Dear schizophrenic Tom.

It's true you're a stray,
You call day by day,
For mealtime you never come late.
If I stroke you once more,
Please don't claw as before,
And I'll wait on you at my gate.

Delia Laverty

Games

What happened to the games
that children used to play.
outside upon the pavement
on a hot and sunny day,
like hop-scotch and skipping
and acky one two three
there goes Peter, there goes Paul
tig, now you catch me.
It seems that children of today
only play computers.
Why don't they go but out play,
ride bikes with bells and hooters.
What happened to the games
that children used to play
outside upon the pavement,
they have all been washed away

Doreen Harrington

"The Whisper"

Come to me sweet whisper,
Tell me what I need to hear,
Come to me whisper,
Now that she is near.

Answer my heart sweet whisper,
Fill this empty void.
Answer me quickly whisper,
Before I am destroyed.

I need her love whisper,
To feel her soft embrace,
To steal a kiss, stroke her hair,
Run my hand against her face.

Don't fail me whisper.
Step inside her head.
Bring her gently to me whisper,
So that I may offer her my bed.

David Lewis

The Feast

"A simple meal," you said;
salad, cheese and bread,
a draught of wine.

To me it was a feast:
watching the shapely hands
arrange the food;
the exciting voice,
the keenness of your brain,
the mind alert, and ever kind,
a feast indeed.

Geraldine Squires

How Can They Say No?

Another day, fresh and young
Tales told, songs sung
New beginning, what's to come
Trees sway, bees hum
Curtains flicker, let in air
Giving life to whom is there
Maiden stirs, pristine bed
Harbouring a restless head
Shunning light, eyes shut
Rise to life, anything but
What of mates, dare not think
Classes looming, feelings sink
Oh! those tablets, calling still
Must take against her will
Held out so far, name is mud
Not wanted, far too good
Boyfriend straying, gone with crowd
Independence not allowed
So it's down the slippery slope
Another mug says "yes" to dope.

Doris Holland

Alzheimers

Total confusion
Surrounded by nameless faces
A forgotten past
A terrifying present
A pointless future.
Old friends,
Loving family,
And beautiful wife,
All strangers.

It should be a time for happiness
Memories, old and new
A time for family
A time for friends;
Instead, loneliness and confusion
Also a joy and pleasure
Coming to a close
In an unfamiliar world

Josh Harris

Nothing Is Forever

I stare at the window pane
Summer time is here again
I'm sitting in my class at school
I contemplate to leave you all
I study books I am here to learn
Not to worry it's my last term
Too much work for me today
I wish I didn't have to go away
Time is running out for me
Why does it have to be?
I know I've grown
I should have known
That nothing is forever

Claire Wallace

Who Cares?

A cardboard box is home for you
Subway hue of frozen blue
The stench of urine nothing new.
Being here is killing you
Who cares? Only the few
who've seen
and been there
alongside you.

Share a bottle,
drain it dry,
guaranteed sleep for two.

You watch the peoples tired faces
who go to work and step by you
and go to homes and nice warm places.

David Curtis

Summer Discovery

Laying in the morning mist
Sleeping in the humid night
A beautiful butterfly
Patchwork in colour
Flexes its wings
Whilst standing poised
On lavender.

Benn Raymond

Years Before Us

As the years lie before us,
Stretching out to ways unknown,
May they be paths of roses
With a fragrance all their own.
May your daily prayers be answered
And your friendships never fade,
And may you walk courageously
And never be afraid.
Yet if these wishes I express
Seem too good to be true,
Remember there is Christ above
Who always thinks of you.
So step out with a valiant heart
As you face your years ahead,
And trusting in the Almighty
We will be safely led.

Betty Morgan

A Monster Of A Summer

Flickering light,
  scares me at night,
especially when the
  Monster growls, through
the small open window.

Previously it was
Hot. Mothers soaked
in oil. Fathers in floppy
hats. Children excitable
splashing in their pools.

Again it growled.
Not so loud this time.
I think he's tired. Maybe
he will go to sleep

I can come out from
under the bed now.

Clare Cooke

Worlds Apart

Unicorns of freedom
spiritual in flight
a lazy dragon slumbers
against the moon of night

The beldam sits
all grin, snaggle-toothed
the gray-malkin wanders
all claws protrude

The loon lies
crippled in the maw
the jester continues laughter
with a riddle and more

Lemuria was all
but it seemed
a land caught in dreams
such beauty was graced

Castles in the clouds
fathomless things amend
an ambrosia for dessert
to serve a paragon way, life depends

Clive Ayton Bell

A Winter's Frost

A gust of wind gently blows the
soft white snow from the skeleton
twigs, and the snow lands as gently
as a mouse onto the dull ground
of the winter's wood.

A dull gloomy sky is in no rush
to move on inch while children
are having snowball fights their
feet step on crunchy snow.

A lake is nearly frozen but there
is a slight opening in one corner.

Julian Rose

Of A Time Past

Eyes.
So deep!
Dark, like limpid pools
Reflecting a turmoil of soul.
Revealing elusive thoughts
Of loving and caring -
Sadness and despair.
Anxiously seeking
Through ever-winding labyrinths
Of the lonely heart.
Thoughts of beauty, happiness -
Love and hope.
All seeing, yet blind.
Disappearing dreams.
Happiness foregone!
Sadly now,
Are shrouded with mists of time,
And alas,
Are but a memory!

Brendan McGrath

Torture

Ground looming, fear.
Skyline threatening,
Faster, faster, wind in hair.

Firm hands grasp, release,
Grasp again. Chain creaks. Sweat

Sweat drips. Please stop.
Firm hands push once more.
For God's sake

Stop. Turf edged concrete
Hastens towards Me!

Rising, rising, try to
Let go, hands will not Co-operate.
Rough hands, firm hands
Push all the more. Daddy
I'm frightened at last I cry,
Please stop, please I...
Slowing now, heart still races,
Tears stroke my face. Laughing,
Laughing lifts me from tortures toy,
Nervous wreck, little boy.

David J. Lane

Sleeping With The Stars

She's sleeping with the stars again
She's climbing high above the clouds.
Perched on ancient mother moon,
Bathed in mystic twinkling shrouds.
She's glowing in that purest light,
The magic that turns day to right.
I watch her sleep, caress her hair
And wish that I could follow there.
For little ones both young and free
Without the weights of age and time
Can travel through the velvet night
And play with endless silver light!

Christine Daniels

Aunty Jean

Aunty Jean the village queen
She bides at 10 Main Street
Her smile is braw
Tae ain an awe
And everyone she meets

She does her best
Tae help the rest
By makin tattie soup
If ye want a plate
Just open the gate
At number 10 Main St.

She goes tae kirk on Sunday
And you should hear her sing
The one and only Aunty Jean
Our Cumberland Village Queen

Jessie L. Gizzi

In The Dark

Lay in bed,
Spooky noises,
Statue still.
Stare at curtains,
Moving a little.
Sweating,
Creepy,
Creak thump.
Close eyes,
Heart pounding,
Shadows on wall,
Blood jerking,
Hot and tense,
That's it,
I run,
Turn light on.
Nothing there.

Emily Levine (Age 9)

Realization

Out of the night,
Scared by the dream.
Knocked to the earth
Ripped by the scream.
Taken beyond endurance.
Facing the truth.
One look in the mirror
At the fading of youth.
Closing the mind
Not wishing to see.
An old woman's profile
Just cannot be me.
But I am forced to acknowledge
As the images stick,
That beauty and youth
All fade too quick.
So what am I left with
Now youth is not there?
Why the strength and maturity
To realize I don't care.

Jan Alexander-King

Love Life, Love One Another

Our little time of love,
our little time of pain,
our destiny we don't no,
we have so little time.
Men fighting killing,
they don't know there own minds,
all different religions.
Of all different kinds
all fighting for different purposes
some of us in a straight line
but we all of one nature
one God through one time.

Jim Best

Untitled

Peace dwells in gardens
  sacred to the dead.
In fields of golden grain
  where poppies flame to red.
By opalescent pools
  where gleaming fishes swim,
In trees where birds build
  on each twisted limb.
Upon a shore, washed
  by a restless sea.
In contemplation of eternity.
'Tis also found in sandy wastes
  both vast and dry,
Beneath the turquoise
  vaulting of the sky.
Within all churches
  both the old and new.
But peace for me
  dwells only here, with you.

John Hume

Innocence

Children running, pitter patter
Running forward, hear them chatter
Laughter bubbling from inside
Excited eyes open wide
Arms outstretched to welcome life
They know nothing yet of strife
They know nothing yet of sorrow
Of worrying about tomorrow
Days for them are full of joy
Full of play, that special toy
Of Mother's love and Father's pride
That he's the one to be their guide
Children running, pitter patter
For now what does the future matter?

Gill Baulcombe

What Is It

It's very long
It's extremely strong
The squeeze is tremendously tight
It makes me shriek in delight
it's some height when you're
looking from a suspensions bridge
to a gorgeous gorge

Jacqueline Jordan

Yearning

The river is full and the mist
robs the hills of their tops.
  And you are away.

The river is frozen, and the
hilltops are white,
the sky is cold and vast,
and into it
  I call you home.

The river is still and chaste,
and dragonflies run the gauntlet
across its placid face.
  Then they are gone.

The river runs through time
and the hills are shading gold
and brown,
swallows dip and skew
  before they leave.

My tears drop to find their rest
in the seasons as they pass,
  And you are away.

Alex Laird

Sunday

She runs through the fields,
On a summers day,
Her hair is long and flowing,
She'd take your breath away,

A lovely red and white dress,
Hangs off her shoulders,
If a lover she should find,
He would be proud of her,

Six days a week,
Her life is dull,
Six moons until she's...
The sunday girl.

Jonathan Simms

I Knew It Wasn't True

A politician has stated
That he is going to die.
I knew it wasn't true
Do not some politicians lie?

Vincent Van Gogh woz 'ere
The brand new graffiti read.
I knew it wasn't true
Isn't Vincent Van Gogh dead?

I'm top of the world ma!
James Cagney did resound.
I knew it wasn't true
Wasn't he buried underground?

And now the sun has set
The darkness veils its glare.
I knew it wasn't true
For it is rising elsewhere.

John Sangers

The Yobbo's Creed

Sock it to em, baby,
Punch em in the gob,
Don't let the bastards grind yer down,
They gets paid, it's their job.
To hell wiv' law n'order,
What price a bit o' fun?
If boys in blue can't take the pace,
Then let 'em cut n'run.

A bit o' bobby bashin's
Fair game on Friday night,
A pint o' best'll stir yer up,
An' fill yer full o' fight.
So what's the use o' worryin'
Who cares what's gonna come?
A night in cells is reet enough,
But please - don't tell me mum...!

Derek Gregson

The Nature Of Things

To see the snowdrop blooming
or hear the blackbird's cry
makes me feel so alive
when life can seem so shy
the dreary days of winter
can make us long for spring
but take some time to notice
the wonders they can bring
my sight is sometimes blinded
by rain and lack of sun
but every day has its treasures
there's beauty in every one
miracles all around me
in nature's wondrous ways
the air is full of her magic
and I am full of her praise.

Deirdre Cahill

Wondering

I wonder if ever the rose.
Regrets the beauty it holds.
When being plucked, for the
folly of love.

Betty Dowle

A School Day

Playground full of children
Playing lots of games
Soon the bell will end their fun
and teachers shouts their names

At nine o'clock it rings quite clear
They all look at each other
Smiles from faces disappear
Sisters and their brothers

The classroom rings with chatter
As the children settle down
It's time to start their learning
When the teacher shows a frown

Soon arrives the end of day
With homework in their bags
They start to make their weary way
Home to their mum's and dad's

Bedtime comes around to quick
It is the end of day
It's time to go to bed now kids
that's what their parents say

Gordon S. Johnston

January

Awake, new year, new month
Past celebrations
new hopes, resolutions
Full of expectation
Grey days abound
Perhaps some snow
We never knew.

Comfort from cosy homes fires lit
Contentment is heaven sent
Oh! Blissful time
No gardening to be done
Just birds to feed
Each day they come
Singing as if to say, well done.

Jean Harris

Winter

Red skies in the evening
Over lakes and streams so cold,
The flame of summer magic
Is withering and old.

Birds are flying southward
Through a cool and mellow sky,
Over where few things are stirring
And where sleeping creatures lie.

The river ever flowing
Rears its weary head,
And settles down to slumber
On its warm and earthy bed.

Reeds standing on embankments
Whisper gently to the breeze,
That rattles round the bare limbs
On all the nearby trees.

So chilly are the evenings
And so short is the day,
For all who recognize it know
That winter's on its way.

Amy Walton

How Ordinary It Is To See

As the night folds like a wave
on the sea
It's apparent where they may be.
Transparent in light like wood
beneath its bark
An owl springs and traps a
mouse in the dark
In the night and in the day so
it is like a coin, two sides join
How ordinary it is to see a
girl and a boy called you and me.

Anthony Higginson

Untitled

It's raining.
Outside the world fills up.
Small puddles become ponds,
Ponds to lakes.
A grey blanket of cold,
Clear wetness.

A boat drifts,
Aimlessly,
Amongst the newly deserted houses.
A child standing alone on a roof,
Sees the boat,
Cries,
Shouts.

There is no reply.
The boat - an empty shell,
The child - a survivor,
Alone in a new, pure world.

Helen Chester

Dusty Road Son

The dusty road draws out,
Out of sight, not a car
To be heard, not a mortal
To be seen. Alone I stand
In this wasted expanse....
Shamelessly lost amongst
The desolate creatures.
With only an apple in my pocket,
And my four by four as company,
Making faces in the clouds;
Bringing back memories of
The laughable past that
I've left behind suffocating in
The bricks and smog of the city.
(Hoping that tomorrow brings
What I could not find yesterday.)
Until I break up my dreams,
Climb back in my machine,
Turn it around, and rapidly
Retreat... back to reality.

John A. Hall

Burns Eye View

What if we could see
Ourselves, as others see,
Would we be glad
Would we be sad,
Would we contented be,
With the reality,
Or would their perception
Bring forth dejection,
Would we wiser from this labour
Now seek to gain their favour,
For an author is related
To the image so created,
In accomplishing the task
Must we cast aside a masque,
Or continue with illusion,
You must draw your own conclusion.

Don MacDonald

Troubled Land

My life as a serving soldier
On the streets of the emerald isle.
Where death lurks round every corner.
But you just patrol with a smile.
Some greet with smiling faces.
And swords to say they care.
Others with hostile actions.
Who tell you, you shouldn't be there.
The murals and the slogans.
Tell you exactly were you stand.
In this beautiful but dangerous
Religiously divided land.

My tour will soon be over.
And I shall leave this land.
No longer walk in fear
With a rifle in my hand.
From the Creggan down to Derry.
From the Ardoyne to the Falls.
I've lived my tour of duty
Behind fortress walls.
Andrew W. Waller

Mother And Father

My, don't we take for granted
One's loving every day
Those kisses mother planted
Her worries as we'd play
Each loving smile, she gave us
Reached right up to her eyes
And also dad who loved us
No matter if we lied
Do none of us just realize
Fond love make's children good
A parent doesn't get a prize
'Though really they all should
How nice if they were always there
Each and every day
Remember them with loving care
When at your work or play
Iris E. Siddons

"One Moment In Time"

One moment in time
One glance, our world's would combined.
Feelings of warmth,
Feelings a glow,
I give to you my body and soul.
One moment in time
"I fell in love",
These are the words I give to you
My one and only my whole like through.
One moment in time
Looking back with a smile
These are my memories
I'd like to cherish for a while
Jaki Harris

A Little Ode To The Other Woman

Another me sits on my shoulder...
not like me she is much bolder.
When I am lazing in my bed
she tells me to get up instead.
She nags at me to do my chores
and forces me to go outdoors.
When I am in this cosy place
she forces me the world to face.
She forces me when I grimace
to show the world my happy face.
She really is an awful pain
but I hope she will remain
firmly fixed, for without her there
my world is sometimes hard to bear.
Anne Kendon

For Future Reference

The lease has expired
On the tranquil cocoon.
A forceful eviction
From the watery womb.

The journey embarked
A passage untold.
The circle of life
Regenerates the old.

A powerful new cry
Vibrates the air.
A weak final sigh
Inaudible, elsewhere.

With each fading day
Comes the red sun of dawn.
As yesterday dies
Tomorrow is born.

A new chapter begins
In the chronicle of earth.
Man's infinite story
Dependent on birth.
Barbara M. Flaherty

Lonely Country Girl

Beautiful lady stands alone
On a hilltop high
Underneath the changing patterns
Of a never ending sky...

Billowing wind across her face
Makes it all aglow
As she stares across the meadows
To the valley, far below.

Slowly she walks down the hill
To the welcoming riverside
Where sparkling waters roll along
Like a gentle incoming tide

Evening shadows begin to fall
As she makes her way back home
Nothing really to look forward to
Because she lives here all alone.

It's nice to be country girl
She thinks, as she lays in her bed.
Many things have come and gone
Others still lie ahead.
Frank King

Weird

I want to be catatonic
Not too supersonic,
Replenish my world
Mellowness unfurled
I want to be normal again.

I want to feel small and large
On a pretty barge,
I need everything
Eat a whole pumpkin
I want to feel normal again.

I want to seem mellon collie
As well as strangely jolly,
Have gold in all my socks
Control all the clocks,
I want to seem normal again.

I am a human being
Although I am not keen.
My mind is now sublime
What's happened to the time
I am normal again.
James Simpson

Odd Cups

O how I liked the odd cups
Odd plates and saucers too
When I sat down with Gran for tea
  Not any cup would do

I liked to choose my favourite
Though I changed from day to day
If they had all been just the same
This game I couldn't play

I liked to choose a pretty plate
On which to spread my toast
Though the one with yellow roses
Was the one I chose the most
So lay past all your tea sets
If I should on you call
And let me choose an odd cup
Like I did when I was small.
Gwendoline Smith

Mary Rose

Mary Rose
Now I see you
Your body, twisted, bent, and torn
From your graveyard
Of deep water
So at last, you are reborn.

Mary Rose
See the morning
Sunlight streams through broken skies
This is the freedom
You have been seeking
Mary, open wide your eyes.

Mary Rose
Though not a mother
Many of God's children did you hold
On that sad day
When you foundered
In the Solent, deep and cold.
Geoff Price

Age

The snow, white and pure
Lies undisturbed upon the ground.
It's half past three
The world's asleep
Nothing and no-one's around.
I watch it, marvel at it,
But then all too soon
The marks, the scars,
Betrayals and disappointments,
Aspirations dashed,
Ambition smashed,
Is this what Winter brings?
Elizabeth Ann Rees

Freedom

The best things in life are free
Nobody knows better than me
Can't afford fine clothes or food
Nature is my good mood
Seeing the birds in the trees
Enjoying the gentle cool breeze
The plop of a stone in a pool
Water so clean and so cool
Flowers growing in the spring
species of birds on the wing
Watching my cat chase and play
there purring for me everyday
Walking through grass without shoes
Freedoms the life I would choose.
Betty Price

Driving Force

In running away from myself
No solitude do I find.
Always there, haunting me,
darkest recesses of my mind.

Maybe a thousand reasons then,
but unto myself I cannot lie.
Maybe a thousand reasons then
to just break down and cry.

In eternal hope of one day finding,
on the crest of my life's tide,
this roller coaster of emotions;
through this mire may I glide.

Experience in my life has taught me
of myself, of my mistakes.
Still I've cried my thousand tears,
filled my thousand lakes.

Life's long road ahead may take me
on a steady, but wavering course.
Journeys ahead will be hazardous,
but at least I'm the driving force.

Anthony Clarke

Questions?

Who made the crow?
No beauty of form..
No soft soporific call
No beauty of colour
Like the collared dove
A blot upon the landscape
   Perhaps!

A thief to raid poultry runs
Or glean the stubble
After the corn is cut
And yet it is of the
Feathered tribe as
The peacock, the goldfinch
   The jay!

Why then the spider, the rat,
The bluebottle
Even the humble mouse?
Looking through crow eyes
At the world I would ask why man?
An endangered species?

Joan Lewington

Babies

Babies laying in their cots
Never seem to care a lot,
Gurgling, crying, tummy pain,
Baby's got the wind again,
In comes Mummy and picks baby up,
That's much better thanks a lot.
Rub my back and ease my pain,
Then you'll make me well again.
Lay me down and let me sleep.
In comes Daddy to have a peep.
Goodnight sweetheart, close your eyes,
Dream of angels in the sky.

Doreen Neale

Time Flies

Time, is by design
not intended to be held
you may glimpse but never catch it
it's quicksilver, self propelled

Fruit is better when it's fresh
but also comes in tins
Fruit Flies like bananas
while Time Flies like the wind

Angie Brain

My Light, My Life, My Love

I remember long ago,
My life was very sad.
My choice to wed so very young,
How things turned out so bad.

Then in my darkness, shone a light,
And as your face appeared.
I felt an intense ray of hope.
And life became more clear.

You led me from my darkness,
Out into the light.
You treat me with great kindness.
And taught me about life.

Our friendship grew to that of love,
Respect, trust and honesty.
Something perhaps I would not known,
If I had not met thee.

Jackie Osguthorpe

Ageing

Pains in the legs,
My joints all ache,
Arthritis has claimed me,
Which road shall I take?

Continue with teaching
And suffer my fate,
Or take early retirement
If it's not too late?

Each day is a struggle
The joy has now gone,
There's a sadness inside me
That's lasted too long.

Bryan Clark

Without You

The first time I went to meet you,
My heart missed a beat,
but the meeting never happened,
now my life feels incomplete,

You pass me and don't look,
I think you don't care,
I feel you avoid me,
and my life feels so bare.

When life moves on,
time quickly goes past,
too soon you are gone,
you walk by too last,

I want to talk to you,
but I'm too shy,
Is there nothing I can do,
as it often makes me cry.

Angela Brennan

The Golden Glade

O precious nymph,
My heart grieves for you.
You roam free; free
from the clutches of man.
And I can only peer
through a willow's tears,
as you bask in the light
of a fading sun.

Now the shadows fall,
and I turn away,
clinging to a fading dream,
eyes closed, whispering,
whispering farewell.

Andrew Turner

A Second Chance

As I see him standing close to me
My heart melts deep inside
I remember all the times I laughed
Forget the times I cried

He sees me and he smiles at me
A smile that's from the eyes
My senses reel, my heart leaps high
"A second chance" it cries.

I walk to where he's standing
And he asks me how things are
Trivial things like "how's the job?
Do you still have the car?"

Then as we talk, his face lights up
A smile of pure joy born
"This is she" he says to me
"The one I wed this morn."

Janette Craythorne

1996

As I walk along the sun shines on
Minute, moving mountains
Glistening cobbles hold their base
Eruptions cluster in the air
Trailing lengths despair
Withering in depths
Delicate marked drakes storm past
Rockets directed to follow paths
The wider world awaits!

Normality of a day whilst the
Pacific number 6 begins
Horror which we must bear
Destruct; damage; and devastation
All that we should hold in trust
Mistakes, devilish challenges to
Be rid of and overcome
Never, never let number 7 be begun!

Ann Lamb

The Painter

A hundred thousand
million hues,

Upon my palette for
me to choose,

And in this black and
stormy night,

With stroke of brush
put darkness to flight.

Geraint Ingram

Pure Desire

He comes to me.
Meeting his gaze, I know that
he is silently asking.
But what?
Does he by pure desire,
Will me into action.
Shadowing my movements
The asker does the taking
and we are resolved.

An innocence
that some would call naive,
Exits,
More beautiful than the forest
After the rains, tingling new life.
Deeper than the well
Arriving at the earth's core.
We are but two coins,
Without interruption,
Falling closer together, forever.

Julie Chalmers

All Alone

Old lady old man
me in my pram
how happy you both were,
but the happiness was not to last
you both made sure of that.
Old lady you knew what he was doing
you did not even help
even though you knew.
I stepped in your place
old lady you don't know
what I had to face,
the nightly sex he had with me
the sickness in my thought.
Old lady who was so scared
scared of him scared of yourself
scared of finding your own truth.
I stepped in for you so that
he would not kill you.
I am sorry for being born to live
a life with you.

Janet Grundy

Forever?

Forever is a myth
mankind needs to believe
Eternity is in his heart
Nurturing his dreams
Within he knows tomorrow
inevitable in its stride
Marching towards his grave
sealing his demise
So today rejoice
the present is for glee
Times ticking spells a word
that word is history

Colin Tasker

Lost Again

He stood there and stared, the
man by the car
I smiled weakly, he walked
away,
He stopped, turned round, my
heart gave a lurch, yes,
My childhood sweetheart was
back again
Then she walked by, he held
out his hand
She smiled, I cried,
He hadn't recognized me.

Georgina Elliott

GI Jed

See the demons of the winter of life
Like storm and hail and rain,
Demented they pound upon the windows
Throughout a night now so dark,
And with them so much strife
Oh, the eternal pain!
Yet he whose head rests peacefully
upon pillows,
Is unafraid of terrors so stark
For memories of the summer of life
That of yesteryears,
Like sun and colour and joy,
Defiantly hold back the tears
of the man no longer a boy,
Once a soldier, the smile of the man
upon the bed,
Is that of course of GI Jed.

Allan J. Rafferty

Defeat

Shoulders droop, head hung low,
Look at earth, what place to go.
Feet surge forward on the road.
Back is bent by heavy load.
Thoughts return of happy days
When one could die in so few ways.
Walking forward cannot stop
Another hill must reach the top.
To see a valley, or a plain
With devastation all again
Oh my God, Please pity me
A helpless, homeless, refugee.

James E. Cavie

The Lonely Circle

It's late at night
Lonely, so lonely
I write a letter
To get to know somebody
Lonely, so lonely
I carry the letter with me
I don't know what to do
Lonely, so lonely
The bin men have been
The letter has gone
Lonely, so lonely
What should I do now
Write another letter
Lonely, so lonely

Carolyn Robson

Lost Love

Endless days in midwinter's dusk
Lonely heart in rural thrust
Timeless mind o' where to roam
Forbidden thoughts cast out of stone
To wait for rays to flicker through
Where a beam surrounds the dew
Branches move so bare and forlorn
Can't hide away from time and morn
Despair it comes in waves so fierce
Ebbing inwards trying to pierce
This lonely being, this broken heart
This mind that so does want to start
To turn the corner and see the sun
And share her love all over again.

Joy Fairchild

Solitude And Loneliness

Solitude is a chosen pleasure,
Loneliness is hell.
To choose solitude is a treasure,
Loneliness is a cell.

When I'm happy, and friends
are around,
I'm busy and frenetic.

Then I seek solitude to
nurse my body.
To think and be myself.
For a while, I have chosen.

When I'm sad, and no one calls,
I feel the bitterness of loneliness;
Then desolation seeps into my heart;
who am I? What do I want?
someone please talk to me,
I'm lonely; I have not chosen.

Ann Collins

God's Nature

These mountain rills,
Like thrush's trills,
Tell stories old and true.
As foresters now hew.

The very heart of countryside.
Should this now be worldwide?
But let us now just spare a thought
and not now treat it just as sport.

The wisdom of the years is there
Let's not now make God tear His hair.
But save the beauty of the years
Lest one day we come in tears.

Gerald Buckland-Evers

Creation

Like a bee around a jam jar
Like a face on a balloon
Like a wheel upon a motor
Like a wrinkle on a prune.

Like the fondant on a chocolate
Like the words within a book
Like the icing on a cake
Like a meal for you I cook.

Like the charms upon a bracelet
Like the keys upon a chain
Like the scales upon a fish
Like the patter of the rain.

All these things were made to be
with God's creative hands
Six days he toiled to make the world
The deserts and the sands.

But on the seventh day he sat
And rested from his toil.
And gazed upon a world so fine
So regal and so royal.

Estelle Cohen

Horses

Horses are graceful,
elegant and kind,
beautiful and sweet
are they.

Jumping high,
up to the sky.
Galloping fast,
and stopping at last.

Emma Moir

Two Hearts

I want to say I love you
but the words are hard to find,
So I'll put pen to paper
and write what's on my mind.

The pen will write I love you
and you know this is true,
For I have a heart so full of love
and it all belongs to you.

Our love is like a golden chain
which binds two hearts together,
And if you ever break that chain
my heart would be broke forever.

They say that memories are golden
well maybe this is true,
But I never wanted memories
I want to be with you.

A smile may hide the heartache
a laugh may hide the tears,
But I will never forget you
never in a million years.

Matthew Carr

Valentine Love

We met on Valentines night.
It was love at first sight
and we danced all through the night,
I will never forget the
moment you held me in your arms.
It felt so wonderful to
have someone so loving
to love me at last.

Joan Ward

A Soulful Union

On the fragile and uncertain
journey of life,
chapters are written and
burdens conquered,
encounters are met and
acquaintances are no more
than superficial.

But what remains as the
journey continues,
is the priceless gift shared
by only a few,
as nothing exceeds the
everlasting friendship between two,
in a soulful union,
to purge the rue,
for constant is, my love for you.

Elias Achilleos

Gary Bennett Is Dead

Dead in your bed
it's not funny
so childish
feeling so good
on Sunday afternoon
with the telephone disconnected
and the smell of fish on your breath
dead in your bed
nothing in your head
no Jesus and Mary
just his dead feeling
only all this and nothing more
dead in your bed
who needs something or other
when you can play dead
no one to talk to
no time to get up
no one to tell you what to do
no one to play with you
dead in your bed.

Gary Bennett

Saint George's Day April 23rd

Let's all remember St. George's day
it's a day for us all to feel proud.
We should hold our heads high,
walk as tall as the sky,
and sing England's praises out loud.

Let's remember the people before us
who loved this dear land too.
A long line of faithful patriots
to king and country true.

The beauty of our countryside
is so gladdening to the eye
Many different greens,
many lovely scenes,
send our spirits soaring high.

Let's sing 'land of hope and glory'
it's a song to make us all proud.
Let's all unite,
and put up a fight,
to make England great again.

Joyce Grainger

Peace

If I could have one wish on Earth
it would be to have PEACE
because of the World's happenings
PEACE is what we need

I wish on Earth for no war
hunger or dying
people being badly treated
greedily, lonely or crying

Be happy for what you've got
some people are so poor
they've got no or little food
and no more

I wish for PEACE on Earth
happiness for everyone
because once you've got happiness
life is just a bit more fun

Emma Toms

The End Of Love?

Love is like the wind,
it grows stronger every day,
but then again, just like the wind,
it slowly fades away.

Love is everywhere,
it might just disappear,
and if it did - heaven only knows,
our hearts would fill with fear.

Fear of not knowing,
what would happen to the earth,
no good, no love, no peace of mind,
and even then, no new birth.

Our race would not survive,
it would vanish into space,
and never again be replenished,
our living would have no place.

So just before you think of hate,
think of what I said and you'll find,
that love is what we need you see,
we need it to make mankind!

Deborah Cottle

Only A Dream

I have a dad, who in my dreams,
   is very very kind
He picks me up and
   Swings me round and round
He has dark hair and
   eyes like ebony
and in my dreams, my Dad is always
   there with me.

He never pats my head
   and says well done!
   my little one.
It's in my dreams you see
   Oh! I wish that it was real
and my dad was here with me.

I'm grown up now
   but in my dreams? I see
If there hadn't been a war
If there hadn't been a gun
How wonderful it would be
   my dad would be with me.

Carole Fee

Daybreak

Into a maze of confusion
Into a depth so unreal
Under a blanket of illusion
Resting in solitude, still.

Whirl like a colourful circle
Dance like a fire-fly would
Ripples a soft song of mercy
And disappears deep in the wood.

Endlessness living like water
Flowing in streams of mirage
And whispering sighs of a daytime
Nature with sunlight is charged.

Happy in thought of a sunrise
And sleep in the cool of the eve
To once again rise in the morning
For in all this is belief.

Jeannette Anne Parker

The Path

The path that leads to nowhere
in the silent leafy glade,
the trees that hustle gently
in the tranquil evening shade.

The path that's gently winding
into a place unknown,
the trees all stand there wispy
all proud and overgrown.

The path that slowly takes you
to where you have never been,
into a World of colour
and to a nature you've not seen.

The path that's calm and peaceful
leads to silence you must share,
you realize without thinking
that you are honoured to be there.

The path that leads to nowhere
makes time for you pass slow,
you feel you are in heaven
so to nowhere you must go.

Elizabeth A. Edmonds

But I Loved Her

When Laura did a hand stand
In the playground, by the shed,
You could see her baggy knickers
With her skirt above her head.
They were navy-blue and woolly
The legs and waist elastic,
I'd never seen a pair before
And I thought they were fantastic!

Her hair was wild and curly
She had freckles on her nose,
And the way she smiled towards me
Well... It made me curl my toes.
Her legs were grazed and scabby
But I loved her nonetheless,
'Cos when she was the right way up
They were covered by her dress.

Janice Grainger

Bunny's View

My view, my view
East, West, North, South
My view, my view
War, Crime, unemployment
Poverty, looting, shooting,
Drug selling, housebreaking,
Drug taking, children dying
My view, my view who's
view, my view, Bunny's view

Ian Pinnock

Encounter!

He froze,
in predatory tracks,
this dark, impressive
male of cats!
His amber eyes
were staring; wide,
from attitudinal surprise,
caught, by a sudden shaft of light,
into his own rewarding night;
floodlighting
from the kitchen door,
where he, carousing, came before.

Now, on the frail dividing fence,
he crouched,
in hostile, mute defense.
We fixed each other, face to face,
yet neither would give pride of place,
then, arching up his angry back to hiss,
quite suddenly, he spat -
this most alarming male of cats!

Doris E. Hymas

The Same Routine

Where I walk, he walks,
In my footsteps, he treads,
At my pace, he paces,
What I speak he's said.

Where I go, he's gone,
In my sleep he's slept,
Where I kneel, he's knelt,
Where I weep, he's wept,
So who am I but a shadow,
A sheep of a forgotten flock,
A torch amongst London's lights,
A raft in between the Docks.

Where I eat, he's eaten,
With whom I speak, he's spoke,
When I write, he's written it,
When I am wet, he's soaked,
I am a book in a library,
A single fish amongst a shoal,
A solitary cross in a cemetery,
So who am I but a fool...?

Gael Lucas

Captured Moments

Have you waded ankle deep,
In a cool cool stream
Watched the silver sticklebacks
Or tried to catch bream.

Walked through fields barefoot
Catching angels in the air
Getting up at the crack of dawn
for mushrooms that aren't there

Have you seen a small leaf
Trapped in an eddying spring
Whirling in the circle
of the waters sting.

Your gaze rests for a moment
of fragments of delight.
The wonder lingers ever
in your memories sight.

June Maxwell

'Love Story'

Her egg,
My sperm,
Our son.
Loved.

Alan Welsford

All Alone

All alone at night,
I'm not quite sure,
If it's all right.
All alone on the moor,
I'm still not sure.
I think I'd better go.
Run like Billy O.

I asked for shelter at an inn,
She said "Come right in"
But when I saw her long, pale face,
I didn't really like that place.
Away I ran,
How fast I sped,
And then I found I was in bed,
With mother calling "Sleepy head!"

Breda McManus

Weed Killer

Nobody knows
I'm hiding under the loam,
Waiting for the power of
Moonlight.

The moon has come.
I see my victim.
I curl my roots around her.
Not touching,
Sucking the goodness from the soil.

I tighten my roots,
I suck the goodness from her,
Soon, I will duplicate,
Then I shall grow bigger
Than the humans.
Now, no-one is going to stop me.

John Yard

Heaven

Another time, another place,
I'll hold your hand,
I'll see your face,
We'll walk together on the sands
and in God's garden, holding hands,
We'll talk and laugh about the times
we spent together in our minds.
We'll have no hands or face you see,
Just two souls that are set free.

Jill Nash

War And Peace

There should never be wars.
If we love one another,
We would care for each other.
Love is the identifying mark.
Think about it, don't bark.

The weapons are lethal.
They should be banned.
Taken out of existence.
Destroyed forever.
Thrown in the river.

Wars are futile,
There is nothing to compare.
Only grief and degradation.
They interfere.
Some don't care.

The one who made us.
He will stop wars.
With his great war.
Then there will be peace,
And no more priests.

Beatrice Thompson

Time Seems Eternal

Time seems eternal.
If it should be some aeons on.
Upon Life's stage once more we tread.
How patiently I'll wait my cue.
How eagerly awaiting you,
Remembering still, that long ago.
A voice, a glance, a look so glad
  the meant to be,
Your lass, my lad.

Emily Walker

Robin Redbreast

I was there
  I was there
On that lonely hill
  At Calvary
You didn't see
  But I was there
I felt the prick
  The prick of thorns
I felt the thrust
  The thrust of spear
The drips of blood
  Yes I was there
On that lonely hill
  At Calvary

Denise Jordan

A Nightmare

I cry but there are no tears,
I smile, but there is no warmth,
I feel the pull of hidden fears,
Around me eyes peer,
In them nothing but hate.
Will there be rescue,
What is my fate?
In this dark and shadowy gloom,
Will I meet some impending doom?
Shaking and trembling like a leaf,
I shout but hear no sound,
And feel myself falling.
Deep into the ground,
Then, suddenly, I am wide awake,
A nightmare had, had me in its grasp,
It is just a dream, thank God I gasp.

Cyril J. Mawdsley

"Mr. Snow"

"Look what you have done"
I shouted at the sun,
"You've taken away Mr. Snow.
  Why did you have to come out."
  Tell me where did he go.
  My Mr.. Snow has gone.

I closed the gate.
So he couldn't escape.
He could never climbs over the wall.
  "Why did you have to come out"
  Tell me where did he go.
  My Mr. Snow has gone.

He's left his scarf and his hat.
If it snows he will be back.
I miss you Mr. Snow.
Why did you have to go.
  "Why did you have to come out"
  Tell me where, did he go.
  My Mister Snow has gone,
  I'm angry with Mr. Sun.

Brenda Mulchay

Animals Do Talk

Animals are dumb, they say
I hardly think that's true
They speak a language of their own
Not known to me or you

Eyes alone can say a lot
And very often do
Showing pain, anger, love and joy
And every bark, grunt, meow and moo
All mean something, if only we knew

They cannot speak like you or I
But understand they can
A blow, a harsh or kindly word
Affects them, just like man

So when next you meet an animal
Just look into its eyes
They are not dumb, as some believe
But very very wise.

Barbara M. Matthews

Love

I thought my life was ended
I had nothing to live for
Until you walked into my life
And opened up a door

You've made my life worth living
A life that's full of love
We seem so right together
Like a hand within a glove

So every minute's precious
Of the time we spend together
Like the diamond ring you gave me
You'll have my love forever

Gaynor Alison Morgan

Don't Cry

When I cry and someone sees me
I feel so shy,
When things go wrong
As they sometimes will,
I feel as if I am walking
up a hill,
And when I want to smile
I have to sigh,
To say to myself 'don't cry'
why did this have to happen
I ask why
Now I am fit and well
I hear a bell
it's time to go to school.

Cheryl Norgate

Parting

Hold me close for the last time,
Hold me close to you,
Make this the dearest memory,
To last my whole life through.

Feel the warmth of love flow,
Through veins that now are cold,
For yet we say goodbye love,
Our dreams will be untold.

Claim my lips, my whole, my soul,
Take my breath away,
Then turn and go without a word,
Lest I should beg you stay.

My life is all my yesterdays,
There are no tomorrows left,
If there's no you, there's nothing
I'm alone and I'm bereft.

Anne Jarvis

The Cosmic Memo

Distant starlight,
giver of our lives;
rises each morning,
falls each night.

Matter of fact,
is matter of self;
of ending beginnings,
on a much higher shelf.

David Paul Surman

The Brat Was Born

Mother, Mother
her lap grew fat
Mother, Mother
Don't have another brat
one girl two boys not fair
will you have time to comb
my hair
Mother, Mother
Please for my sake
Don't have another brat

James Andrew Briggs

The Shuffler

He shuffles along in wind and rain
He dare not rush.
He is in pain
He goes so slow, he cannot run
In years gone by he had his fun
The time has come,
He must go slow
He goes the speed
Old people go
He shuffles on at a certain pace
He's not at all
In the worldly race
The wind and rain is a bore
But he knows to well
He'll run no more.

Edward John Baker

Silver Things

Silver things and silver rings
have kept us apart,
we see each other now and then,
but nothing can go right for us
we have too much to loose,
and it's a very short fuse,
our feelings must be kept secret
away from you and me
and so we have our memories
that no one can destroy
and so the years go on
and we've done "nothing wrong"
just loved some one a little
more than we should,
and we knew it would do no good.

Catherine Daly

Lonely

I feel so lonely inside,
I need you to guide,
me through these horrible
times which I face,
we are so unkind as a
human race,
laughing at other people's
expense,
just thinking about it
makes me tense,
I just wish I could see the light,
through this terrible mess
that I face tonight.

Heather Trotman

"Peace"

Peace is basically: calmness and
harmony. Peace is a symbol of
calmness. Calmness is when quarrels
should surrender, and when only
happiness flows around us like music.
Never row, never fight, always have
a happy face. Smile splash smiles
around everyone like bubbles. Show
pride and confidence. Be proud,
but don't boast. Be polite, let
everyone around you feel
comfortable in Gods peace cushion
Never make other people feel unhappy,
and coax unhappy souls to join your
world of: Calmness and harmony.

Cain Smith

Living For The Moment

I wake
greeted by nature,
A smile
moments to capture.
A breath
whispers of worship,
A comfort
feelings of friendship.
Understand
freedom of giving,
Thank you
laughing and living.

Candida Grant

"Finlay"

Long and sleek he stalks the night,
Golden eyes with second sight,
In the garden bathed in sleep
All but mice and frogs that leap,
No - one heard the velvet paws
Crouched beside the sun house door,
No - one heard the last small squeak
Of the mouse that did not sleep.
One awake within the night
Heard the cat - flap door close tight,
Heard the paws upon the stairs,
Down the landing he who dares
Sleek and black, the witches' cat.
In the early light of dawn,
Looking down upon the lawn
There beside the sun house door,
Lies the mouse that lives no more
Victim of the sleepless night
And the cat with second sight.

Ann Thomson

Smells

Sweet smells, dirty smells,
Floating in the air,
From heavy scented woman,
And from unwashed hair.

Strong smells, lovely smells,
Petrol from a car,
Food from a restaurant,
And a strong cigar.

Sweet smells, perfumed smells,
From roses in a park,
And a warm tasty smell,
From a hot jam tart.

Strong smells, acid smells,
Orange and lemon zest,
But freshly mown grass,
Is the smell I like best.

Jane Smith

Snow in Winter

Breaking, crunching snow is trodden,
Footsteps in the snow
Parts untouched and looking perfect
Ultimately I must go

The wind howls, whipping
Bitterly cold, oh so very fast
Spinning snowflakes almost dancing
As they glide to cover paths
People trying to hurry
Slip, slide and even fall
What a mess they make
Skidding children halt a ball
Pretty pattern on the lawn
Cover grass and plants alike
Trees and bushes look forlorn
As children jump and shout

Children make snowballs
We look towards heaven
Wishing it to stay forever
Thanking God for His creation

Diana Cramp

My Prayer

Dear God, help us to be kind,
Give us a clean mind,
Give us clothes to wear,
And food that we may share.

Help us to recite,
Your name day and night,
Help us not tell lies,
Dear God up in the skies.

Help all the children,
Who are in need,
Look after them, care for them,
As you sow the seed.

Help us to follow,
The footsteps of great men,
You have jotted down,
In the scriptures with a pen.

Before I end the prayer,
There's something I have to say,
Give me the strength,
So I may follow the true way.

Jasvinder Kaur

Should Discipline Go?

We have removed all discipline,
From our homes and schools,
Our children cannot know we care,
When they break all the rules,
We must be responsible,
To teach them right from wrong,
A little smack won't hurt a child,
So they know they belong,
To parents, who care very much,
About the things they do,
Discipline is needed, so,
They know we love them too,
Hand in hand together,
Go discipline and love,
They fit quite snugly into life,
Like a hand inside a glove,
So let us curb the selfishness,
The violence, hatred, greed,
Then take responsibility,
For what we sow, we'll reap.

Janette Campbell

Scotland

You are in me,
And I am in thee,
From the smallest glen,
To the highest tree,
From the mountain top,
To the deepest loch,
Scotland,
You mean home to me.

Alan Bell

The Year Of The Ox

I'm not a rat as time will tell,
For rats are malicious beasts,
I've no desire to go to hell,
Consuming dark satanic feasts.

I'm an Ox outstanding,
Though slow to move
Yet still demanding
Your consummate love.

I am also a willing mate,
If wronged I will accept the blame,
To be an Ox is something great
Chronicled in books of fame.

Oh! I stand on stalwart rocks
And I am proud to be an Ox.

James Paterson

Cleo

I sit by the window,
For hours and hours I stare.
Longing and waiting,
For my time to escape.
The world outside
Looks so wide and wonderful.
Sun, rain and snow,
I know!
I'll plan my escape.
Tonight, yes tonight,
When my master comes home
I'll run,
Run like the wind.
I'll be free, free at last.
I sit by the window
Full of fish,
Warm and cosy.
I'll escape tomorrow
Yes, that's what I'll do,
I'll escape tomorrow.

Christine Haile

After The Rain

Sunrise filters in your stare
Foolish are the clouds that dare
To cover up the sparkle there.

Soon the lashes wet with tears
Reflect so many hidden fears
Marking lines along the years

But even they can find no place
Between the creases of your face
And drop with moist unseemly haste.

Sadness dulls those once bright curls
And shades upon your cheeks unfurl
Allowing gloom to prance and twirl.

Peep from behind your hooded lid
Let me see the things you've hid
So I can make a heartfelt bid.

I'll burnish every strand of hair
And catch the sunrise in your stare
To keep it always smiling there.

Jane Kendall-Bush

A Speck Of Dust

The world is just a speck of dust
floating in vast space.
There's galaxies in millions that
physicists can't trace.
The stars that twinkle brightly
in our velvet sky,
are countless suns and planets
where earth's destiny may lie.
For sometime in the future
mankind will travel on,
to seek a home, far distant,
'ere resources are quite gone.
Let's hope mankind has changed then,
and lost his warlike ways.
'Ere God in his great wisdom
May end our foolish days.

Joyce M. Baker

Soldier

I am a fiery storm,
Flashing thunder and light,
I'm an aggressive tiger,
Looking for a fight.

I am a stinging nettle,
Swaying to and fro,
I'm an electric guitar,
In the middle of a show.

I am a fire
Burning away,
But what you don't know is
I'm trying to say:
"I will risk my life for you,
Even though Hitler is trying
To kill me too".

I am a soldier.

Greg Jenkins

Questions To Answer

Strength and weakness,
Endure or submit?
Loyalty and deceit,
Enjoy or forfeit?
Questions and answers,
Doubt or belief?
Laughter and tears,
Happiness or grief?
Positive and negative,
Hope or despair?
Unite and disband,
Fair or unfair?
Lies and truth,
Black or white?
Judge and condemn,
Wrong or right?
Living and dying,
Together, apart?
You and me,
The head or the heart?

Isabel M. McNab

Drugs

DRUGS are Dangerous
DRUGS are bad
DRUGS make people very sad
So if you see some
Say NO! NO! NO!
Then shut your mouth
hold it right.
Because Leah DIED!
So that should give you one big
FRIGHT!

Jason Ryder

Eve Of Winter

Logs on the fire
Embers are aglow
Cosy fireside chat
Life going so slow

Candle flickers brightly
Shadows on wall
Cat snuggled closely
Next to my sole

Steam from the teacup
Cakes on the plate
Clock ticking loudly
It's getting late

Clear skies above
Leaves on the floor
Wind getting stronger
Creaks from the door

Smoke from the chimney
Rising up in the sky
It's a sure sign
That Winter is nigh.

Gary Walker

Soul Searching

Rivers of my feelings
Edging at my soul
Pulling me and pushing me
Seeing through my mould
Stripping me of skin and flesh
Left raw for all to see
No camouflage, no make up
Revealing the real me.
Take me as I am now
If your love is truly deep
Bathe me with your teardrops
If you feel the need to weep
Don't cover me with blankets
It will never hide my shame
But wrap your arms around me
And shield me from my pain.

Janet Patrice Owens

Of Days Of Love And Laughter

I think of you so often
During ordinary days
And feel myself transported
In memories eye,
To special days and moments
We were able to share
The happy laughing times
The sensual loving times
And in that sweet reflective mood
Of days of love and laughter
The ordinary day seems special
As I'm with you again.

Jean Ann Kitching

Erase, Eraser, Erasure!

Death to the teacher!
Death to his dross!
Death to his 'shut up'!
Cross! Cross! Cross!
Death to his temper
Death to his tools!
Death to his detentions!
Rules! Rules! Rules!
Death to his red pen!
Death to his scoring!
Death to his do it again!
Boring! Boring! Boring!

Gavin Hooper

Beyond the Embrace of Angels

Perhaps beyond here
Courage will break the fear,
But will it be too late
Am I beyond the embrace of angels,
Forever.

Jason Leonard

Leah Betts Died So Don't Take Your Name

I shall send it ringing
down the vaults of time,
woven in song,
joyous among
great pealing bells of rhyme,
echoing long into Eternity.

As four golden arrows
I shall wing it forth,
cleave Heaven's breast,
Southward and West
Eastward and to the North,
finding not rest
but Immortality.

I shall sear it deep
upon the mind of God
so He will ask
no further task
of me lest 'neath its rod
aught else should mask
that one Identity.

John Terry

Mute Witness

Covering my head
Doesn't help me to see
The error of my ways
What I know will happen
Hear the crowds
Cheering outside
But I can't see
Alone in my cell
I know they are out there
It's what they want
Eye for an eye
I'm there through it all
I know what's going to happen
I'm prepared
I am a mute witness
To my own death.

Janine Buckwell

The Arrival Of The Day

When is day "official"
does light indicate it's come,
do bells ringing on clocks
signify it for some.
Could it be when a baby
in darkness, opens its eyes
No, officially it's "official"
when birds lift their heads
to the skies,
and in their wisdom perceive
a new day being born
then sing their little hearts out
in reverence of the morn.
For morning needs no timepiece,
no-one could ever state
the "official" arrival of the day
because officially, we're late.

Catherine Campbell

The Dark Side Of Life

The hopes, the dreams,
    Disappear with the years,
The youth, the trust,
    Seen only through tears.

Enveloped in black,
    All cold and abandoned,
No light, no warmth,
    No tender distraction.

The hurt, the pain,
    The anger, the hate,
The pride, the prejudice,
    The living in vain.

The loneliness, the emptiness,
    The sadness, the strife,
The anguish of living,
    On the dark side of life.

Jacqui Holmes

Unborn

Mummy what did I do wrong?
Did you not want me all along?
If only you might think to pray
Then I might see the light of day

What is it mummy that you fear
I only want to feel you near,
Please mummy won't you let me live
Then all my love to you I'd give

Please oh please don't make me go
Don't you know I love you so,
Make the doctors go away
That I might stay another day

Mummy I can feel the pain
I beg you please to think again,
Let me live, let me see
Let me breathe, let me be.

Now I know, I'm fading fast
This little thought may be my last,
I hope some day, you can forgive
The fact, you didn't let me live

Elizabeth Dorrian

One Day

Why did you have to leave us?
Did you have to go?
Your life was just beginning
And how we loved you so.

We told you that you're needed
And how much we really care,
But as your life was fading
Our hearts began to tear.

We kept vigil by your bedside,
Leaving babies all at home.
Only once you sat and looked up
"Hello" was all you'd moan.

I couldn't sit and watch you
Pass over to the other side.
I waited for my sister
And the tears she couldn't hide.

I know not that you're waiting
One day I will be glad
When God will come and take me
I'll run to meet you, Dad.

Donna Prince

A Hopeless Situation

I see your face
dark and brooding
staring into space.

You're by the window
standing on the edge of time
watching the world go by.

The neon lights flashing
a light your face.
Your beauty strikes me
like a dagger,
deep in my heart.

I see the pain in your eyes,
as you watch
yet another human sacrifice,
and I long to stop
the bleeding in your heart.

But our troubles are a world a apart,
and for all the prayers I make,
your pain
I cannot forsake.

Helen Thompson

Two Edged Sword

Dagger sheathed, flesh is safe;
dagger thrust life force rushes hot.
Feel the pain, see the blood;
wound is mortal, wound is not.

Dagger sheathed, honour is sound;
dagger thrust, bloodless the wound.
Deep the breech, exquisite the pain;
wound is mortal reputation is doomed.

Joseph McCabe-Smith

Love

Love is a feeling
Coming from the heart
It sets the senses reeling
From the very start
A man becomes a giant
With his love returned
But bewildered and defiant
If his love is spurned.

Love is an emotion
Who knows from whence it came
With it comes devotion
And such feelings, quite insane
No logic can account for this
Reason plays no role
To greet a lover with a kiss
Is in our very soul!

John M. Evans

Untitled

Night listened to day
Day followed suit
The earth made its circuit
Stars studied their loot

The man roared at the heavens
In his pain and his rage
Who are you sculptures
To set me this stage

The joke is on you
For the beauty you planned
Your haste in our freedom
Is like the wind to the sand

A world filled with wonders
And life ever new
A land ruled by man
The error of you

Earl E. Verdant

Shadow's Armies

Woodlands and dark places
Cliff tops and Hills
Shadow's army without faces.

The armies of the night
Grey and black the silent
Uniformed vanguard

No sound of marching feet
Nor enemy to meet
Trees low and high, sigh.

Whilst the ghostly contingent,
Avoiding pale moonlight
Dark clouds hide away.

Evanescent, to flee when
Comes first light
Liken the shadows of my heart
In the passing of the night.

Emma Hood

Response

I said to her, I said
"Can I love you? If I
Stroke your cheek, will it
Be smooth until your smile?"

I said. I wish I'd said,
But ventured none of it.
We chatted, joked instead.
Then, with smiles, we parted.

He said to me she'd said,
As if that changed things,
"I'd hoped a chance
for him and me, but..."

"Well what was?" he said,
Wanting some response,
As she had mine, I hers
And again, I muttered "Nothing".

Daniel J. Radlett

Winter Sun

The winter sun
came from nowhere,
jagged as glass
in the snow,
cutting across the tracks
light deceiver
I shed my protective shell.

This is a false sun,
singing song's from long ago
walk on my dreams,
turn them into dust

I need you, you are welcome
even if discord is the price paid
for my deliverance.
The winter leaf reveals the truth
in the heart,
the heart reveals
the truth.

Joan Paul

A Dream Come True

I'm wishing, hoping, longing for
A time of peace for evermore.
A world of calm growing all around
No noisy wars, no, not a sound.
Where laughter reigns in all races
No more sadness on any faces.
Only happiness for me and you
This would be a 'dream come true'.

June Carr

Boulevard Of Broken Dreams

Pulled
by the flow
of deceit and damnation

Wallowing
in a quagmire
of rancour and regret

Drowning
in a cocktail
of melancholy and mistrust

Stranded
on the boulevard
of broken dreams

Elizabeth Norman

Re-Awakening

You asked me not to love you
but you left it far too late,
it wasn't meant to happen
now I'm victim to my fate,
tho' you cannot love me fully
doesn't alter how I feel,
how I long for things to alter
as my love for you is real.
When the centre of my being
died and left me so much sorrow,
I felt my life had ended
with no thoughts for tomorrow.
But suddenly it happened
without warning on my part,
a reason just for living
to be glad I lost my heart.
No demands upon your time
no wish to change your ways,
just treat me with affection
dear friend for all my days.

Ann Odger

Idyllic Childhood

Idyllic childhood, magic words,
But sadly, not for me.
My mother died, and I so young
Could hold no memory
Of how she spoke, of how she looked,
of her soft, sweet caress.
And one must wonder how a child
could cope with such distress.
Did she love me?
I don't know - no one seemed to care
But growing older, even now
I wish that she'd been there
To share my life - the ups and downs,
what friends we might have been.
Idyllic childhood, - not for me,
The heartache was no dream.

Joyce Sandford

Last Night

Maps of Africa
Are secret proof
Last night happened
It was no spoof

Across a pillow
One stray hair
The only sign that
You were here

A deep sigh
Before I rise
To wash away
Your smell - My prize

Jennifer de Sanchez

My Son

Now he is a big tall man
But once he was a boy
During his childhood years
He gave me so much joy;
His smiles and hugs upon my knee
The things that made him frown
Are memories that will ever stay
Although not written down.
Through his teens, like all of us,
He faltered once or twice
But he knew that I was there
To help him with advice.
As he changed from boy to man
I watched with heavy heart
For I knew the day would come
When we would have to part,
Now he has a goal in life
And I am justly proud
Because for me, his mum, my son
Will always stand out in the crowd.

Jennifer Shuttlewood

A Little Dream

I'd like to be a poet
but not the very best,
I'd like to write some poems
to give the boys some zest,

For if you are a poet
your job is never done,
for we can write some poems
if only just for fun,

Some of us do like them
the poems on the wall,
for some can take the crack
but others not at all,

Some people like a joke
even if it's clean,
some of us will laugh,
while others are to mean,

So if you write a poem
whether it bad or good,
only if it is a try
of which I think you should.

Buzzy V. Dance

"Another Chance"

And now another year has gone
Another decade too.
Thus giving us another chance
To prove what we can do.

What can we go
To right the wrongs
That we have heaped and piled
Upon the heads of innocents -
The unsuspecting child?

To those who lead and who advise,
It looks for guidance wise.
But who can lead or can advise
When wisdom is not wise?

For wisdom was the man who could
Look in a mirror clear,
And see himself as other saw
Not as himself would see.

So who can blame the child today,
If it should go astray?
It looks to us for guidance,
It's we who lead the way.

Bernie Warren

Thank You For Being You

I don't wish to make you feel old
But my feelings must be told.
To me you're like an older sister,
a friend I never had.
You help me when I need it
and for that, I'm very glad.

You're one in a million,
you have a heart of gold,
you're there if we need you.
When our problems you are told.
Don't change the way you are sue,
don't change the thing's you do,
for we love you, the way you are sue,
yes we truly do.

Janet Joiner

A Foggy Day

The fog's cold breath,
Brushes my face
Like a damp sleeve.
Everything is moist and clammy.
Sounds are muffled,
Bird song silent,
Traffic muted.

I feel insubstantial,
Wraith like.
A figure dimly standing
In a cotton wool landscape,
Seeking the way.

Jean M. Johnston

Into Dust

One love
broken into two
One dream
disappears from view.
It's you,
shedding your skin
changing again,
will I ever win?

Fading
just like the light
ebbing away
slipping from sight.
Falling
out of my life
Swept away
ashes of our love
your life with me fades
   into dust.
Turning once again into dust.

Ian Aldridge

Yet

Once the world was at my feet
Bright eyes big smile good health
But drink has no respect for these
It takes your greatest wealth.
You tell yourself that you're okay
And end up by believing
Tomorrow you will handle it
You only end up grieving.
I awaken from a drunken sleep
My Daughter sitting by.
Is that a Look of hate I see?
That look will haunt me till I die
I see the drunk lying in the gutter
Does the world owe her a debt?
I tell myself it won't happen to me
Or is that just a yet?

Anne Angus

'Monkey'

Mankind think monkey not so bright
(Brain as big as pea)
Monkey is not civilized
Should study man - and copy.
Mankind think monkey is 'fair game'
Put monkey in a zoo
Experiment and kill and maim
Send monkey to the moon.

Monkey think mankind is wrong
(Banana short of bunch)
What is word, this "civilised"?
Mankind likes so much.
Does it mean a right to kill?
To capture, hurt and cage?
If that true then monkey think
A blessing he's no brain!!!

Helen McCormick

Tragedy

Sirens and lights
Boys in blue
And ambulance crews

Names on a list
Loved ones
To miss

Searching for clues
Reporters scoop
Eyewitness interviews

Lawyers and insurers
Work out the cost
But no money can replace
The woman I've lost

James Medhurst

Mother's Love

A mother's love is strong and fair
Bonded like glue
She would do anything for you
A mother's love you can't compare

A mother's love will last forever
Be you apart or together
Be you a babe, so sweet and small
Or a man strong and tall
A mother's love will always be there
A mother's love you can't compare

Corraine Adamson

War

Guns shooting,
bombs booming,
it's all the same you see,
that man in all his wisdom be,
resorted to such behaviour.

Everything stinks,
that nobody thinks,
to speak to the other side,
so many people have died,
in these wars so needlessly.

People are shot,
it never stops,
until a barrier is dropped,
and someone wipes the blot,
away from the word love.

But this is too late,
for all the saints,
who are killed in the dreadful war,
that closed a door,
on how it used to be.

Gemma Mills

Laid Back In Thought

Gazing up at warm clear sky
Bluest blue 'cept sunlight's laughter
That's how it was before
That's how 'tis after the before
That's how 'twas before the after
Recharging souls and lingering hopes
of life to be
of life after the before
of life before the after
oh! sun-kissed days of lazy gazing.
Contemplating.

Eunice Kayley

Better Than She Can

The cradle holds the baby
Better than she can
'Cause now she's started shaking
And she needs to see her man.

The baby's safe in slumber
In the bed-sit on return
The sweat and pain are coming back
She needs to stop the burn.

She really needs another buzz,
Her baby's not enough
To rescue her just from herself
Her life was always tough.

Left by her parents as a child
Her head was full of pains
The only thing that she now trusts
Is that needle in her veins.

She said she loved her baby
But she didn't give a damn
The cradle holds the baby
Better than she can.

Alison Cogan

Heaven

Heaven is:
Being with you

Heaven is:
Being loved by you

Heaven is:
Being held by you

Heaven is:
Loving you

Heaven is:
Coming home to you

Heaven is:
You, homing my heart

Heaven is:
Hearing your sweet voice saying "I Love You"

Heaven is:
YOU

Andrew Rawlings

Untitled

I bow to a beautiful summer's morn.
A mother's smile, a child new born
I bow to nature's artistic hand
As she paint's her pictures
Across the land,
An autumn gold
A winter's grey
The glory of the
First spring day!

Anthony C. Givnan

Love On The Rocks

His heavy breath
Begins to stink
He hurls abuse
But does not think
His clouded eyes
With shots of red
Move aimlessly
Inside his head
A furrowed brow
Reveals his pain
As alcohol
Feeds from his brain
But deeper grows
The pain in me
Each time my dad
Comes home for tea.

Johanna M. MacDonald

Be A Winner

Don't accept that you're a failure,
Be prepared to have a go.
For then you are a trier,
And you have put up a show.

You can soon become downhearted,
When you seldom ever win.
But at least you are competing
And to lose is not a sin.

There's a joy in competition
That brings out the best in you.
But if you are a drop-out
Then what good does that do.

So whoever your opponents are
Just show you're not afraid.
Display your fighting spirit,
And the stuff of what you're made.

Gordon Barnett

Evergreen

Conifer's are evergreen,
be it winter, spring or summer,
to not be evergreen,
would mean for all to alter.

The loss of evergreen,
must and never ere be so,
this we must remember
for autumn settle, no.

If autumn ever settle,
and evergreen be lost,
a state of moribundity
would not come near to cost.

Cheryl Garlinge

A Peaceful Night

May the silver lights of evening
Be beaming down on you.
May they brighten up your home life.
Bringing good-luck and prosperity to.

Whenever there's a problem,
And no one's there to share,
Just look at the stars in the heavens
Because they really seem to care.

They twinkle and shine forever
And relieve your sudden plight
They relax and give you peace of mind.
Consequently a peaceful GOOD NIGHT:

Barbara Almond

My Lover, My Best Friend

You are my pot of shining gold
At my rainbow's end
You are my leader, giving strength
My lover, my best friend.

You are my four-leaved clover
Who brings me luck each day
You give me comfort, give me love
Take my pains away.

You are my twinkling, shooting star
Which brightens up my life
You help me be a winner
Through trouble and through strife.

You are my bird of paradise
That flies around my heart
To you I give all that I have
From you I'll never part.

You are my wisdom master
You teach me right from wrong
I know we'll be together
To each other we belong.

Helen Sutton

The Tracks

The path through life is varied,
As we tread our way with care
Guided by our inner selves
And with our loads to bear.

It isn't ever easy
To select the way that's best
The one that's lined with roses
May just be an added test,

But do not doubt the path you chose
Though it seems an uphill climb
You had a reason for the choice
That will be clear in time.

The next decision you will make
Will thus be better judged
And so we learn to recognize
The side tracks we have trudged.

So go ahead through all the doubts
And as you're heading home
Take courage in the knowledge that
We never walk alone.

Jill McPike

December

Men shiver
As cold winds blow,
Days are dull.
A chance of snow.

Fingers icy,
Gripping ones toes.
Frozen patterns
Painting windows.

Steamy breath,
Fogging the air.
Empty trees,
With branches bare.

Birds scavenge,
Searching the ground.
Hungry mouths,
Devour what's found.

At year's end,
We remember.
It's the month of,
December.

David Rossington

A Figure Of Speech

Hardly rotund,
but no less curvaceous -
a form that provokes
ideas salacious.

No end in sight -
beginnings are better!
Enveloping all.
But where is the letter?

Totally bowled.
The method's not cricket.
No chance of run out -
it's sticky, this wicket.

Bliss can be egg-shaped;
nesting's primordial.
This triangle's square.
The solution? Oh, Val!

David Clement

Forever

Forever
are diamonds
Forever
A prayer
Forever
a long time
for two people to care

Forever
A wedding ring
Forever
Bells chime
Forever and ever
You were to be mine

Forever
I remember
as I stare at your face
but the photograph
is fading
in its old silver case

Gail Thompson

"The Future"

Another bomb
Another shot
Innocent lives being lost
Starvation, despair, all around
Homeless in doorways
Some dead on the ground.
Money to gain
Land to steal
Power, the cause of mans greed.
What future for our old and young?
Our children's future being sold!
Our God given land, a mass of flame
No birds, no trees, no thing remains.
Our world destroyed
Our planet, lost
No one left to mourn our loss.

Gillian Hamilton

Untitled

I often sit alone at night
And then I wonder why
If there's a God in heaven above
He lets small children die
He watches rapist's muggers too
Evil their wicked crimes commit
While he up there just sits and sits
So when it's time for me to go
Up to heaven or hell below
I'll definitely be asking him
Why he lets so many sin

Gina Ince

A Winter Dream

When the winter nights are dreary
And the rain is pouring down
We sit here by the fireside
But we never wear a frown.

We just sit back and thank the Lord
For the lovely days gone by
For the beauty all around us
And the lovely summer sky.

The fire is glowing brightly
Outside the wind blows fast
But no matter what the weather
Our love will always last.

We never wish for great things
Each other we admire
All we wish is health and strength
for the day when we retire.

If all the people in this world
Could love like me and you
The sun would shine all winter
It would be summer all year through.

Grace Brown Ford

Reason Or Treason?

Why did reason abdicate
And Justice lose its cool?
To leave the world in such a state
Reason is a fool.

Why should violence have success?
For there should be no hope,
Victims always need redress
And criminals, the rope.

Please justice, do not hide away
The people need your power
Support us each and every day
And make the wicked cower

People God, you can't accept it
That the devil takes the prize
You cannot cry and crawl and sit
And listen to his lies

These days we seem to be resigned
To letting evil reign
Fervently, let's hope we find
The guts to rise again.

James Guest

My Mother

Now the dawn is breaking,
And I've lots of things to do,
I always find the time mum
To sit and think of you.

Your hair is like silver,
Your eyes are so blue,
Not a day goes by,
When I think of you,

I remember the days,
When I was a child,
I was never alone,
with you by my side.

So now I've grown up,
and years have past by.
I think of the memory's,
just between you and I.

Julie Taylor

Northern Winter

Damp, cold and bleak
Are the grey moors of winter.
Icy winds streak
Through valleys and woodland.

Raw, wild and blowing,
Cold heath and sparse heather.
No life and no growing
In the unfriendly earth.

Clouds grey and shrouding
Cast their shadows on valleys,
Where tense sheep are crowding,
Awaiting the storm.

Wild runs the stream
From the moor through the valley.
Lost seagulls scream,
Far from the sea.

Nights dark and long
Bring no warmth and no comfort.
The wind's shrill, sullen song
Deadens the soul.

John Gallagher

The Path Of Life

The path of life weaves onwards,
And forward we must go,
But where it's really leading,
None of us can know.

The path of life we travel,
And tread its twisting miles,
Its roughness and its smoothness,
And climb its many stiles.

The path of life is scattered,
With wishes, hopes, and schemes,
Some of them are granted,
While others only dreams.

The path of life one day will end,
Our unknown journey through,
That path that wound before us,
Behind us straight and true.

The path of life reveals at last,
Its course for us to see,
The way we've come, the way it was,
The way it had to be.

Avis Ciceri

My Children

I gaze 'round the room,
And cringe with despair.
I see nappies, books and,
Toys lying everywhere.

The dollies are lined,
Upon the settee.
The mess is disheartening,
Wouldn't you agree?

It takes me so long,
To tidy and clean.
I could dash round and do it,
But I don't feel that keen.

Then I look at the children,
My daughter watching T.V.
The twins lie there gazing,
In awe at me.

They are all so happy,
To watch me and play.
The room's not so bad,
I'll do it another day.

Julie Hart

Alpha

A new dawn breaks over my heart;
a genesis of thoughts unseen
by the naked I...

In the beginning
words made worlds;
essence of the unseen seen
to order chaos.

I see
a sunset,
scene-set
for players
with the unknown.

Jonathan Hayes

Tranquil

Sheep may safely graze
And corn may proudly stand
In this our blessed country
In this our rural land

Where horizon meets horizon
Over meadows and o'er hills
And the tranquil sound of silence
Your mind forever fills

The rugged seas surround us
Protect us from all harm
And the mountains and the lakes
Reflects to us their calm

Be thankful then for what we have
For the pleasant life we lead
And remember those less fortunate
Who have a greater need

David Godley

A Country Walk

Come for a walk with me
Across the meadow fair
Down the lane, across the style
Breathe in the country air,
Walk with me beside the stream
Beside the babbling brook
Hear the blackbird's tuneful song
And cawing of the rook,
See the busy bees at work
Amongst the sweet wild flowers
Come, oh come and walk with me
And while away the hours,
Feel the freshness of the breeze
The rays of golden sun
Enjoy the stillness and the calm
Until the day is done.

Dorothy Durrant

Just Dream

Time has passed.
And gone so fast.
Just like the world.
Will it ever last.

Just dream and dream,
You will never know,
What is in store.
Even if you snore

Wake up you will not
No any more even if
You are 104. Just be
Kind and smile a live for
A long while who knows
Just dream lovely.

Florence Clara Garner

This Is My Life

I'm ninety-one years old today
  And a tough old girl am I
But until the age of seven
  Each day 'twas thought I'd die.

When I reached that magic day
  I began to thrive.
I went to school, I went to work
  So glad to be alive.

My dad, he was a Lancashire lad,
  A gradely lad forbye.
With three girls to marry off
  Swore "No Irish need apply"

But in this life we must agree,
  That fate has her own plan
And Dad gave in most graciously
  When I wed my Irish man.

Now a widow of ninety one,
  I still enjoy a dram
My family swears that in nine years
  I'll get the royal telegram.

Dorice Houlton

Our World Today

We live by God whose path is clear
Although upon it, stones appear.
A rocky road sometimes it seems
That we have passed along the streams
Of daily life which keeps us living
With our neighbours, loving and giving.
This world of ours is in a mess,
I wonder where the happiness
Has gone, I do so often wonder
Who's responsible for this blunder,
Man, of course, who else but he
Who is so small, but who are we
To point or blame, or be the cause
Of such unhappiness. Do pause
And maybe stop to think
Before we put our pen to ink
To sign ourselves away to those
Whose wicked path is what they chose.
They do not like our way of life
And try to bring upon us - strife.

Evelyn Goldsmith

Soldier Of Nam

A rush to war
A boy so young,
Does he really know
Why he has come.

A man with stripes
Says shoot to kill,
How old must you be
For the blood to spill.

Give him a gun
To the front line he goes,
Will he come back
Nobody knows.

The jungle is quiet
There's a smell in the air,
Death is so close
He can sense this with fear.

A crackle for shots
Why must he die,
They said we would win
Was it a lie.

Henry Ilsley

The Beach

Soft, white sand
All through the land
The cliffs and sea look
Nice to me!
The pleasure of bathing
And people lazing
Litter swimming in the sea.

On the sea tide
The waves so strong and wide
Yellow, blue and green
The colours to be seen
The dirty sea all grey, not clean
Pollution on the tide
People come world-wide

Amy Connolly

A Non-Poem Poem

```
N o w      . A t
a y i      l e a
s t h      s t I
                .
i s a      h a v
p o e      e t r
m ! P      i e d

e r h      . ( A
a p s      n d f
i t i      a i l

s n o      e d .
v e l      ) O h
, b u      w e l
t I d      l , t
o u b      o o b
t i t      a d .
```

Alastair Marshall

My Baby

She was born in July
A treat for the eye
and boy, did I know
She had arrived
A more lovely child
could not be contrived

Her beauty, her grace,
the smile on her face
has given me pleasure
all through

And if you haven't guessed
who I think is the best
I will tell you, Caroline
it's you!

Jean D. Murphy

Life

Into this world,
A seed is sown.
Tiny fists slowly uncurled,
A child is known.

To grow and learn,
Be happy at play.
Soon to take your turn,
In the world of today.

When you have made your mark,
It is time to sit back.
Slowly to depart,
The long line of track.

For life is just a seed,
To be lived by everyone.
Full of want and need,
So easily undone.

Denise Staines

Confused

Now I have reached my middle years,
   A strange tale I can tell,
I used to have a Budgerigar,
   This I know so well,
His name was Billie this I know,
   Hello Billie Boy was his limit,
But now I am so confused,
   My Mother says I Didn't.

I used to have a Porcelain Doll,
   Dressed as a Royal Page Boy,
Was not allowed to play with this,
   Told this was not a toy,
It was so beautiful I recall,
   But hold on just a minute,
Again I am so confused,
   My Mother says I didn't.

Have I had two separate lives,
   Of this I'm not amused,
Will I ever know the answer,
   Oh I'm so confused.

Eileen M. Stone

Untitled

When Jesus was born
he was born to save
But then he was
Put on a cross
Just like a slave
Some people were sad
and other were glad
that Jesus was put
on the cross.
But now those days
have gone
and Jesus lives on!

Liz Jones

Then Tear Fell

The fiery copper tear
Hangs against a lifeless green
In a pigeon grey ocean.

As it sways
I wait with baited breath
To see it rise Phoenix-like
From the ashes of its home.

A triumphant, glorious warmth
Will wash over me in a
Violent wave,
And I will be uplifted.

Then,
The Tear Fell.

Paul Kerr

The House Spider

The house spider's here,
He's come in from the cold,
He run's over my carpets,
He's really quite bold.
He run's like a race-horse
Away from my gaze,
Then stop's by the fireplace,
He's having a laze.
My hand goes to touch him,
So off he does go,
Away round the corner
And out through the door.
I really won't harm him,
I think he's alright,
But still he' goes off
And away in the night.

Ruth Burns

The Joker

Head in hands and spirits down
The Joker, silent, wore a frown
Life was hard and full of pain
Thoughts were clouds and tears rain.

Be a hero?
   Act the clown?
Run away?
   Or stay and drown
In this world of dark confusion
Happiness a lost illusion.

Looking up he saw her smile
Uncertain as a little child
Felt a stirring in his heart...
Now, at last, their dream could start.

The storm was over - calm the sea
Love had come to set him free
Gone the clouds, and gone the pain
Love made the Joker smile again.

Rosemary Rea

A Deep Loss

It's an injustice to hate
A harder one to show love
Friendship is all I wanted
A struggle is all I got
Opposition coming from both sides
Ongoing weaknesses materialize

A heated debate
Home truths come out
And I shut the door
In tears, on the floor
Bottling the rain
Imprisoned by pain
A sense of loss
A deep loss...

How many times
How many lives
To feel this hurt
To feel this pain
A loss...
A deep loss.

Dean Francis Meazza

Lovers

Moonbeams shining down from
a dark blue star kissed sky

Bathing lovers with arms
entwined as they slowly
wander by

Beads of dew sparkling on
an emerald carpet of grass

Reflect the moons aura
like a mirror of glass

A night made for lovers
for stealing a kiss

A night for enhancing
lovers bliss

Be they young lovers
or lovers of old

The warmth of true love
will never grow cold

June Bown

Sound Is Everywhere

Listen with your ear,
A sound you may hear,
A squeak of a mouse,
A creak of a house,
The tweet of a bird,
I'm sure I heard.

Listen with your ear,
A sound you may hear,
A twang of a guitar,
The chatter in a bar,
The roar of a car,
Outside and afar

Listen with your ear,
A sound you may hear,
The rain on a window,
And the tune on a piano,
Ticking of the clocks,
The sea against the rocks.
Sound is everywhere

Choices

They said we had choices
But oh what a decision
The hardest we ever had to make
To terminate the pregnancy or not

With our thought all muddled
We made our choice
We didn't even see our little son
His body went for medical research

It has taken years to come to terms
With the decision we'd taken
The wrong one in my opinion now
Hard to live with that decision

It would have been easier
To give birth and let him
Take him chances of life
Our little Down's syndrome son.

Patricia Francis

The Clown

As the time passes
across the clown's face
his expressions change
with revolving hands.
As dead he stands,
no distraction is too great
to divert his eyes
from the steady watching...
...watching the world change
for the better, or for the worst!
No-one will understand
his blank expression.
There's a twinkle in his eye,
or is it a tear?

Paul Davidson

Whisper

A whisper
A fleeting
Intangible air
Of music
So muted
And dancing
Fair hair
A breeze
In the trees
And a fluttering
Touch
And somehow
You know
She is loved
Very much

Vicky Bryceland

To Yvonne Denise

Chameleon is her day wear,
Her night wear, and her life,
You know that I am talking
About my DEAR WIFE.

But that is not the end of it,
Her talents do extend,
Not only to a baker, but
Mother, nurse and friend.

She has so many facets,
They cannot be confined,
Two words of just one syllable,
That would not be too kind.

She's given me a son and heir,
To continue the family line,
How can I write just what I feel
About this wife of mine.

Only that I love her,
Admitting that I care,
For her to be my Valentine,
My love, my life, my prayer.

Nigel Lloyd Maltby

My Woman's Charms

Her angled nose.
Her kissable toes.
Her sexy lips.
Her perfect hips.
Her eyes that shine.
Her legs so fine.
Her happy grin.
Her bubbly chin.
Her eye brows lovely arch.
Her beauty born of March.
Her cheeks so sweet.
Her smooth sculptured feet.
Her chiselled fingers.
Her laugh that lingers.
Her shiny hair curls.
Her teeth of pearls.
Her creamy arms.
Her woman's charms.

J. P. K. Hoare

The Last Time I Saw Him

The last time I saw him,
he was laid out to rest.
No colour in his face,
his clothes were his best.

He was old and fragile,
he'd died in his bed.
No smile on his face,
his cheeks were not red.

He was wrapped in a shroud,
just his head to be seen.
They'd made him look young,
if you know what I mean.

They'd filled out his face,
and coloured his hair.
Why he had to die,
it didn't seem fair.

It was six months ago,
and I still see him clearly.
No smile on his face,
but I still love him dearly.

P. Grogan

He's Siamese

He is no ordinary cat,
He has a pedigree,
Of Thai ancestors he is born,
Pure aristocracy.

His features are distinguished,
With eyes of sapphire-blue
Like Asiatic jewels that
Bewitch and dazzle you.
His tapered face, so beautiful
Wears a mask of brown, and he
Has velvet paws and pointed ears
That match, quite perfectly.

His limbs are long and elegant,
His fur is sleek and pale,
He wears an air of arrogance
And a kink in his brown tail.

Loved by Kings this special breed,
Respect him if you please,
He is no ordinary cat,
He is Siamese.

Yvonne Hall

Holding Hands

Darling hold my hands.
Guide my footsteps
which falter on the
path so steep.

My Autumn nears.
As a leaf falls then
so shall I when my years
having gone their span.

As our hands unite
our wedding bands touch.
Symbols of our love.
Untarnished with time.

My end has come.
My soul departed.
God will comfort
you and wipe your tears.

Eventually,
and for eternity,
we will again
hold hands.

D. C. Hyde

Solitude

Mountains, trees and streams
Give me life long dreams
To be free from city dirt
Observe the animals in habitat flirt
Flowers lay a carpet down
Our friends the birds fly around
Birds carry out their chores
Must be millions even more
Grass fresh and green
Giving off a heavenly sheen
Nature's gift to man is bright
Giving him warm sunlight
Forces day or night
Humbling, even man to fright
Air around us fresh and clean
Substituted by no machine
Those who tarry in the city
  deserving of our pity.

Knox Johnston

The Journey

B-A-1-4-3
From L-H-R
To D-E-L
In a 7-4-7

Peter Ramsay

The Seasonal Cycle

Winter trees, hunch, raped and bare
From cruel winds without a care
Broken branches stripped and bald
Once proud oaks, groped and mauled
The icy tempests break once more
To reinforce their biased law
The hailstones beat a rhythmic sound
Hammered down into the ground
The banshee winds, their mighty roar
Eating in right to the core
Frightening wails from unseen blades
Swiftly cuts during nightly raids
Every year is just the same
The winter comes to kill and maim

Matthew Bawden

Lest We Forget

Lest we forget
Forget the messages of old
Old memories of the past
Past lessons often told
Told with a hint of pride
Pride though tinged with tears
Tears of what's been lost
Lost and gained over the years

Years have gone by since then
Then what is it that we've seen
Seen changes brought by time
Time changes even me

So you and I all must
Must try and remember why
Why on this Armistice Day
All those people had to die

They died to earn us peace
Liberty, their aim
Which ought to be our right
Else they'd have died in vain

Mairianna MacDonald

Seasons

Spring is a time of awakening,
for every living thing,
Birds, bees and flowers,
and even fairy rings.

Delicate little snowdrops
pushing through the snow,
their tiny heads drooping,
like bells, sway to and fro.

Next comes the golden daffodils,
in pretty gowns of gold,
with aprons green surrounding,
they stand so firm and bold.

From then on there's profusion,
of colours bright and gay,
till Summer fades to Autumn,
then, Winter's on its way.

Until again come Springtime,
once more their heads they peep,
up through the earth they struggle,
the cycle is complete.

Sandra McKinnon

Re-Encounters

In the shrubbery you searched
for a ball,
you with your child
you who were once my child.

In the dim light
your image seemed to change
till it became as mine
when there I searched with you.

The wheel completes its turn;
the next I may not see
nor yet hear the laughter
when your grown child with his

Seeks for that same elusive toy.

Louise Rogers

Goodbye Pretty Boy

Fly free little darlin',
fly free,
You have been my friend many a
long day in dark winter
or in summer in the garden,
When no one else was there
this fleeting life to share,
you liked to watched the trees
waving in the breeze
and the wild birds searching
for their food, I like to think
you've joined them and happy with
their brood, and hear you
chirping cheerfully
Pretty Boy, Pretty Boy

Mona Jackson

Confused?

Cyclone yellow belly
flea ridden noise,
upside down peanut butter
noisy silent voice.

Backwards, skywards
inside out lemon tree,
free style cricket bat
green and orange bumble bee.

Criss-cross mishaps
chest of drawers, pine,
baby bottle castor oil
and bubble gum wine.

Cheese slice filtered tips
blacked out mirror too,
multi-coloured black and white
long sleeved shoe.

Dry water flip-flops
Forward in reverse,
Macaroni splish splash
End of poem verse.

Mike Giles

The Big Man

With pride we watch him leave the
field for the last time,
this man who is our hero.
He wears our colours and brings
honour to our land,
he who is also our god.
We worship at the shrine of
this son of Scotland,
he is captain of us all!

Shona Meiklejohn

Sitting By My Window

Sitting by my window
Feeling so alone
Watching children playing
People going home
Sitting by my window
Remembering times gone by
We used to be so happy
My husband Ron and I
But then one day
He had a fall
And broke his hip you see
He never did recover
And come back home to me
So I'm sitting by my window
Watching children play
I know I'll see my Ron again
Somehow, somewhere, someday.

S. Austin

Love Lost

You hurt me - you
Feel pain - you know
Momentary - cutting
Eternally - aching
Promises - broken
Dreams - mocked
Hopes - murdered
You showed me real life
Not grateful - you know
Was better off without it
My feet used to dance
You hurt me - you.

Paul Liddiard

In Vino Veritas

Come brother of death expected
Feast me in your waters golden sip
Of sweet forgetting,
Poured in the bowl of dreams,
Blunt the teeth of day begetting
Warm cowl for nights threat,
Of dark visions fret
That spoil the plot to play
Our favoured way to keep.

Blur the sharpening sword
Of wheels that fortune favours
In the world,
And run our ruin into warm,
Our blistering fears make safe
With opiate storm,
Woo us into tombs of restless sleep.

Michael Faulkner

Everyday Things Forgotten

Full stops, commas,
Exclamation marks.
The colon and the semi
Just leave me in the dark.
Question marks
And Hyphens
The old apostrophe.
The cabbage in the basket
Looks more and more like me.

Adverbs, nouns,
Adjectives, proper nouns
And verbs
Make me look even dimmer
And leave me lost for words.
The green and crinkly cabbage
Sits in the basket gracefully
and I'm not sure who's the greenest.
The old Savoy or me.

A. Harrison

"Changes"

Oceans return as rain,
Everything comes back again,
Time changes what we see,
But life is as it has to be,
Materials we throw away,
Come to life another day,
Sparkling laughing eyes,
Turn to dark and screaming cries,
The energy,
Man fails to understand,
Yelling us this earth is,
Our precious living hand.

W. E. Mead

Our Lord

Every insect that falls
Every rose that blooms
Are accounted for.
Every person in pain
Or those who are lost,
His hand will hold.
Every smile or frown
Every word or prayer,
are heard.
Every orphan or queen
Every adult or child,
are in his eyes.
Every beast plant or bird
Every planet, lake or shore
Are close to Him.
Everyone who departs
Will know Him.

P. Rusbridge

Why?

Why is it I can't see the sun
  Even though the day's begun
Do you think he's hiding there
  Like me when I'm behind my chair.

Maybe he's a sleepy head
  Doesn't want to leave his bed
The clouds are fluffy soft and new
  Upon his bed of deepest blue.

He must be warm and cosy there
  Beneath his blanket unaware
That I await to see him shine
  So I can tell the day is fine.

D. E. Batty

Missed

I miss you lots,
even though I knew you not,
never here, but you were there.
We were waiting to care,
meant to be it was not,
help we could not,
beyond aid doomed to die,
you will never be forgotten.

Stephen Ali

At The Meeting Of The Four Winds

Blizzarding;
Dry and rattling,
Jumbled and jagged;
Mounding and mountainous,
Heaped up and composting;
Cacophonous and confusing
cooling fast.
Avalanche in the spent words,
at the meeting of the four winds.

Sid Twyning

Mississippi Mud Pie

Russian rhythms at 12 am
Even Auld Lang's Syne
It wasn't this hot in 1800
When Edward came to dine

He came to open the first dam
Lizzie opened the last
We danced away beneath their gaze
Another Xmas past

Ant, me mate, with his Nicholson hat
Shining in a brand new role
Head Chef and proprietor
At the Elan Valley Hotel

Had he lost the acting bug
Or was this just another part
Did he argue with his partners
Was this business or was it art?

We paid our way in chocolate pie
And did the guests no harm
Our first kiss of '96
Was wildly Welsh and warm.
Paul Bonel

Minerva's Trap

A single strand of silk,
Entwined into a snare.
Where lies a predator
Calm, awaiting there.

A slight movement poses,
Tension on the thread.
A rush to get the victim
A bite, but not quite dead.

Then wrapped in parcel fashion,
And placed in larder store.
Repairs are made speedily,
More captures to ensure.

Eight legs of skilful craft,
Work hard and rarely rest.
Eight eyes of constant survey,
Make chances seldom missed.

The spangled web of jewels,
Catch the morning light.
The unseen web of evening,
Hold the 'dead' of night.
Liz Gould

24 Hours

Brilliant day
Cascading sun
Sensuous feelings
As warmth comes

Setting sun
Colours build
Picture framing
Valleys and fields

Fire red
Skies ablaze
Melting colours
In awe I gaze

Velvet sky
Pearl moon
Silver haze
On every dune

Probing light
Gently surrounds
Sunrise again
Over villages and towns
Paul Willis

Never Reality

There never seems to be
enough hours in the day,
and we never seem to see
clearly, the right way.

We seem to be lost
in a world that doesn't care,
and we can't count the cost
of a friend who would be there.

There isn't any rainbow
with a pot of gold at the end.
Life isn't like a show
with applause just round the bend.

Life never seems to go right,
never how it should be.
We dream a good life each night
but next morning, it's never reality.
Maria Arnott

His Mother Sea

Her grey silk dress, high necked,
Edged with Brussels lace,
Swirls and turns,
Sweeping the ground.
Never still,
It rounds on all in its path.

He stands, deep in its folds,
Hand in hers,
Soft yet strong,
Learning to swim.
She holds him, moulds him
And inexorably drowns him.
Norma Rhys-Davies

Nothing

Our life
Ebbs and flows,
No-one knows
Who created it.
Some form of God,
Maybe,
But is there Heaven
And Eternity?
Or is it all
In the mind
And in the end
We'll find,
For sure,
NOTHING!?
Raymond Paul Kirby

Memories Of Love

I sit alone in my room,
Dreaming of how it used to be.
Seeing your face once more,
Retracing all the memories.

I lie awake for hours,
Remembering your lips against mine,
The soft touch of your hands.
If only I could turn back time.

Another day, another week.
Everything is all the same.
Me, a pen and paper,
Continuously scribbling your name.

You said we'd always be together,
So why did we fall apart?
You said that you loved me,
And then you broke my heart.
Sarah Jasper

Girl In A Yellow Dress

She scrambles over rocks
Down to the pebble beach
Where she dreams away the hours
Plays her secret games.

A Tamarisk lined haven
Of kingfishers and pools
Guarded by a lonely Egret
Fishing silently.

High above this Eden
Sit coffee drinking tourists,
Transported back to childhood
By the scene below.

The girl in the yellow dress
Completely unaware of
The presence of strangers
Watching her,

Pulls off her shoes
And steps into the sea
Then skips along the water's edge
Splashing diamonds.
Winifred E. Moreland

The Country Side

How I love to amble
Down the country lanes,
Where mother nature reigns
In glorious splendour.

Further, beyond, lies
The open meadow, a luscious green,
Buttercups and daisies can be seen,
In complete abundance.

Close by I hear
Bees buzzing from flower to flower,
Hour after hour,
In unexplainable frenzy.

High on the hilltop, I gaze below.
Smoke curling skywards.
Old man river, a steady flow
In his maturity.

Here I long to stay,
To dream, to work, to play,
And live my life away
In pure tranquillity.
Phyllis Lancett

To My Little Dog 'Mickie'

Just walking along
Down that tree lined Street.
Can't get my breathe,
Aching old feet.
I suppose it really stops
  the mess on the floor.
But you do one there, and stop
  for one more.
But I still love you,
You daft old hound.
Saves me being lonely
And getting chair-bound.
So long as the weather is
  quite sunny and fine,
I'll walk you forever
  you old dog of mine!
Kitty D. Phillips

Danaid

Am I among the Danaids,
Does not my bridegroom live?
Why must I then, in Tartarus,
Fill breached casks with a sieve?
R. Ingrid Clapham

End Of The War

The six years' war it could be said
Caused much sorrow, doubt and dread,
Families were torn apart
Many left with broken heart,
Bombs were dropped on innocents
Curses reigned on those who sent.

In '45 the conflict o'er
The enemy beaten to the floor,
The bells were rung
For we had own,
Peace forever was forecast
But we wonder will it last?

H. G. Irvine

Do I?

Do I make you feel happy?
Do I make you feel sad?
Do I make you feel calm?
Do I make you feel mad?
Do I brighten your evenings?
Do I cheer up your day?
Do I make you feel wanted?
Do I push you away?
Do I banish the bad times?
Do I then bring the good?
Do I help with your problems?
Do I do what I should?
Do I say the right thing?
Do I act the right way?
Do I care what you think?
Do I care what you say?
Do I sit here in sorrow?
Do I sit here and cry?
Do I wish I'd been different?
 Well, do I?

M. C. Haslam

Ireland My Ireland

Rolling fields of green,
dividing walls of stone,
this land of heavenly beauty,
will always be my spiritual home.

I loved you as a boy,
I love you more as a man,
I return to see you when ever I can.

Where the people are so friendly,
Dancers on the green,
where the music and the crack
is the best you've heard and seen.

As I sit here in the twilight,
Listening to the evening tones,
I think of Ireland my Ireland
You'll always be my home

Michael O'Rourke

Red Rose And Black Veil

Red rose and black veil
disguise the pain, was love so stale
red brick and black slate,
you sold the home, now it's too late
red sky and black day
pick up your life and turn away.

He's gone away
to climb the stairway hall,
he's gone away
through the gates so tall
he's gone away
where no shadows fall

Love died today,
your love died today.

Tom Bagge

Closure

Wrap the day tightly
Close the blind
The clock has run down
Mice are out
Rock the day slowly
Drop the lid
Quickly the morrow
As a flash
The tortoise still sleeps
Spring awaits.

Marian Acres

Special Place

In this special place of my own
Deep within my very soul
I think of days that's come and gone
And often of the very young
Because in their innocence
I can see
A cause worthwhile
That's worth a smile

I feel happy
I feel sad
Just to know
That I'm not that bad
I maybe wrong
That's for sure
And in this song
I ask for more
A precious thing
That only a child
Can bring

H. Quilt

I Don't Like Coming To Town

People rushing, children
crying mums shouting, people
frowning.

Winds as cold as ice,
mum says would you like
a nice cup of tea, and a
slice of cake in Woolworth's.

Oh no my hat it's blown away
with the winds.
Smell the burgers, as I
splish splash, through the puddles.

Oh what a morning I know
I'm moaning and groaning
But it so boring.

Whoops I've dropped my glove,
Now you see why I don't
Like coming to town.

Nicola Ray

Space

Going into space,
at a really fast pace.
I crash on a moonbase,
not a good landing, with a red face.
Going to tie my lace.
When to my amazement
I see a case in front of my face.
On the ground,
the case is found.
Henry gets out,
everywhere are booms and zooms.
Me and Henry go to my room
Only we think we are doomed.
On the moon we see an alien.

Nice he is!

Peter Spencer

Space

Going into space,
at a really fast pace.
I crash on a moonbase,
not a good landing, with a red face.
Going to tie my lace.
When to my amazement
I see a case in front of my face.
On the ground,
the case is found.
Henry gets out,
everywhere are booms and zooms.
Me and Henry go to my room
Only we think we are doomed.
On the moon we see an alien.

Nice he is!

Peter Spencer

Despot

Ego is a thousand voices
crying
Look at me, look at me.

Pay attention to me now.
This is a song without an end.

If the do not bend, I will break.

In that darkness
rubbish blows;
Here is a crack behind
the eyes.
Trees are snapping,
Bullets popping
in the wind of this regime.

Stagnation brings its own reward.
Change is coming
change is coming
If you did not bend
then break.

Ros Hoggard

Loving You

Believe in yourself. Have natural
confidence - that's the way.
Don't upset yourself, you are who
and what you are. If you weren't
you would be someone else.
Time is precious.
Don't waste it.
Don't let anyone *or* anything
get you down.
Get a life, once and forever
And
Live a life.
Your life.

Lisa Coffey

Caring

In this age we need more
Caring,
Loving thoughts and more
sharing.

This would make life worth
living, instead of taking we
will be giving.

Giving love to one another
as a sister and a brother
let us love
one another,

I'll be your sister
will you be my
brother?

B. M. Fuller

Unrighteous Lords

Unrighteous Lords of mortal men
Contrive a plan to war again
And gather where the fodder run
To place inside their hands a gun

Unrighteous Lords of mortal men
Will cause the blood to spill again
Committing some excessive sin
To raise the sound of war within

Unrighteous Lords of mortal men
Will march us down that road again
Towards the conflict pain and grief
Into a hell beyond belief

Unrighteous Lords of mortal men
Will promise peace but in the end
Will trick the masses with a lie
And cause the innocent to die

Unrighteous Lords of mortal men
Will from their pinnacles descend
To usher millions into strife
And cause a massive loss of life

William Richardson

Ancient Awakening

I stand before my past
Clothed in my defences
I stand before my Love
With naked, open senses
Freed at last

With truth he clothes me
Wraps me round
Our beings merge
Without a sound
Our old worlds fade away

His eyes tell me, silently
How deep is his emotion
I sink within, dissolve my skin
Their gaze my sweetest potion
And then his kiss...

Memory stirs, deep within
I've known my Love before
A buried trigger, set to trip
As he stands at my heart's door
And enters again

A. J. Taylor

Promote Hope.....

Rise and be determined
Champion the right
Construct your hopes in confidence
Battle through the fight.

Secure your place and prosper
Build castles in the air
Trust your intuition
Draw upon your flair.

Reach above the riot
Faith you must apply
Presume and you will conquer
Accept and you will fly.

Work to win each day is yours
Success will be your thrill
Eventually you'll realise
Your dreams you can fulfil.

Rise and be determined
Set it like a book
The chance is there so take it
Good luck my friend, good luck.

Paul Hardy

Rendezvous

Date arranged
  and imminent guest
'twas meant to be.

Ponderous wait
  anticipate meet
'twill surely be.

Day arrives
  infants cry
twin sons are he.

Patricia Crane

Child Of Darkness

Child of darkness
Can't you see the light?
Are you blinded
By ignorance?
Your own view
Of what's right?

Child of darkness
Don't forsake
The one
Who gave his life
For you.
Jesus is his name - he loves you!

Child of darkness
Turn from your
Old ways
To the one
Who can set you free
And be with you, always.

Roger Hampton

Ladder

Mortality. We see this when,
By chance we see a tree,
Remind me of my coming doom,
And your great longevity.

The tree is a ladder of life,
Its branches hold many secrets,
Many things has it seen,
But never does it speak.

Proud, majestic,
Feared by all cats,
The trap that leads,
To the men in yellow helmets.

The wind will come,
Turn the leaves brown,
What a lovely sight,
Not for the tree.

It stands bare, embarrassed,
Its limbs exposed,
Oh dear,
Then we forget 'til next year.

Paul Bamford

Daybreak

Stay forever, Autumn,
Burning ball of fiery peach,
Silhouetting leafy veins,
Of bare limbed Ash and Beech,
Seen through eyes half open,
Fighting light in dewy day,
Meeting morning's misty mouth,
To kiss the night away,
Stretching breath to boundaries,
Unattained by any phrase,
There's eloquence in silence,
At the dawn of autumn days.

Colin J. Cairns

Exile

Driven from home,
By a force within.
Longing for more,
But gaining less.
Caught in a race,
With others unknown.
Striving for recognition,
Gaining anonymity.
No identity here,
Just numbers.

Strange how,
That you long to be,
Back up in that
Once forsaken place.
Where faces smile,
And the air is pure.
Where your heart lies,
And in dreams you go.
A place you once.
Called home.

Philip Reid

Forever

Two lives thrown together
by fate,
love's fire rekindled
too late?
Youth's bloom is gone,
not yet.
Passions are roused
to forget
don't look back
it's wrong.
hear sweet music
bird song,
once more we're young
last glance
hold now and love
love 'till death

J. Capper

Graduation

Graduation I have at last achieved
But who should be aggrieved
My parents, my husband, who
Tickets alas I only have two
An extra one I could procure
By no means secure
Unless there was a cancellation
Then there could be jubilation
With this problem I've been met
I feel as though caught in a net
What to do I do not know
They all should see the show
Hurrah someone called to cancel
At this I really did marvel
Now everyone could see
What this meant to me

E. Chambers

The Chase

The smell of death is in the air,
Bittersweet to some, others not,
See a deer running to save his life.
Hounds catch scent.
Barking, panting the hounds run,
Desperate for the taste of blood.
The chase is on.
Thirsty, exhausted,
Twice shot,
Half drowned,
Shot again.
Oh the thrill of the chase

Sarah MacMillan

The Sea

Bright and sparkling
Blue and green
Move to and fro
Majestic queen

Wild and raging
Calm and still
Deep and silent
Like distant hill

Alive and rolling
Horses white
Kissed by sun
At morning light

Patrick McFadden

Epitaph

We were born of this world
But we paid it no heed
It told us of destruction
But our minds were on greed

It warned us with tear's
That were once ice and snow
Followed by a rain
With an eerie toxic glow

The children tried to warn us
Our lives would have no worth
If we carried on it would be
The death of mother earth

Alas we didn't listen
And used our world as a whore
From our self-indulgence
Our species is no more

A. Scott Robertson

Invitation To Manhood

I don't know how to tell you son,
But the time is almost here.
When you have to become an adult,
And face the biggest fear.
It's hard to take the responsibility,
Of finally being a man,
But I know you will handle it,
Like only we know you can.
It's time to forget your childhood,
And search deep amongst your soul,
To try to find the ultimate work.
Before you end up on the dole.
I'll be right behind you, son,
Cos, I've already been there,
And I'll understand your faults,
I'm full of love and care.
You've got to make the effort,
For that, you're on your own,
But whatever you choose to do,
You'll never be alone.

Ron Wood

Starlings At Bread

Packing thrashed at
As if it were a live thing.
Tiny pincers, tweezers tear
In a dive on, all-in frenzy.
Black-draped executioners
See this wan piece
As one to be killed and eaten.
Singly, obsessively.
Beaks grab and drag
This flat mass
In greedy lumbering.
Ignorant that more will come,
This is the last slice of life.

Tanya Parker

The Baby Elephant

I am a baby elephant
Born to circus life
I've been on my first train ride
With my father and his wife

I've just come into town now
Along the frightening roads we trail;
But I'm not all that worried
Because I'm holding mummy's tail

I've been all decorated
For the trip from place to place
I'm wearing a jewelled head-dress
With tassels hanging by my face

I will soon be warm and cosy
Snuggled on my bed of straw
I'm very near the Big Top
So I can hear the people roar

I'm too young for the circus ring
Where my Mum and Dad perform
But one day I'll be out there
And take them all by storm

Rebecca Hardiman

First Day At School

The bell has gone
And we are late,
There's pushing and shoving
To get through the gate.

The hall is quiet,
The classrooms are not.
But something feels strange,
Now, what have I forgot?

Something is missing,
There's something not done.
Oh crumbs, can you believe it?
I've forgotten my son!!

Now where have I left him,
I'm sure he was dressed,
His underwear was waiting,
And his trousers were pressed.

He couldn't wait to get here,
And he seemed so keen,
Now, slowly, I'm awakening,
What a relief, it's just a dream......

Sandra Bird

'Like That Last Sip'

We work and do the best we can
But nothing satisfies,
And much goes on without regard
Then through it all, time flies.
You look back to when you were born
And realize, time's getting short,
Very much is left to do
But help is hard to court.
But one must be humble, then to ask
For some it's very hard,
As this goes hard against the grain
In the independence yard.
But pride is hurt before a fall
As help's there for the asking,
If one would only wait a-while
Then it would be less tasking.
The trouble is, you know my friends
Once, you did all, without thinking,
But now your ability has gone
Like that last sip you was drinking.

Robert Philip Mead

O' Come, Come Away

O come to the seaside,
and hear the wild waves,
on the dark rocks we'll stand,
while the storm wildly raves,
and we'll watch the white sea-gulls
through tempest and spray,
while the mighty ocean
rages fierce and loud
O' come, come away".

J. E. Clarke

Life

Today is as usual - quiet, peaceful
   but
This has not always been so.
   How come?
First, youth
   Joyful, happy fun times, games
Yes, games of love
   games of work
   until
Steady, very steady, middle age,
then, chaos.
   Parents ill,
   Parents die
Feelings of sadness,
Feelings of distress,
Feelings of depression
   but
Life goes on.
Spring of the Spirit comes, so
Today is as usual: quiet, peaceful.

Sylvia Jackson

People Of England

We the English people
born of a mighty land
seem to sleep, while others strive
yet underneath were much alive.

We sleep with one eye open
keeping a watchful eye
for the many that turn to
us for help.
Readily given, we seldom deny.

God in Heaven, guide us
Almighty God, who sees
Please guide us thro' the
darkest hours.
When we can't miss the
wood for the trees.

In our days of strife
We may say a prayer
as the Almighty God
is everywhere.

R. C. Ellis

My First Kiss

   His lips touched mine
and mine touched his.
I walked away going red
instead of staying
I went to the park all
I saw was his face
I lay my head down
on the pillow dreaming
of that one first kiss
and hoping it would all
happen again

Toni Donovan

Be Us Human

Be us not strong.
Be us not Brave.
Be us not weak.
To carry on.

Be us in time.
Be us in mind.
Be us in peace.
To carry on.

Be us to be free.
Be us to help.
Be us to please.
To carry on.

Be us as one.
Be us to have fun.
Be us to love everyone.
To carry on.

Be us to pray.
Be us to stay.
Be us in this world.
To carry on.

Peter E. Southwood

New Dawn

High on a mountain
At the end of the night
Life begins stirring
And the ground is pure white

How loud the silence
Sweet scents fill the air.
'Tis a reason for living
And a reason to care

Out on the horizon
There's a magical glow
And broad shafts of light
Light the valley below

The morning dew glistens
Then a beautiful scene
As the white covered landscape
Starts to melt and turn green

As the golden ball rises
Its rays soft and warm
I await new surprises
And behold the new dawn

Paul Simpson

Who'd Be A Spinster?

I'm tired of being a WALLFLOWER
at the BALL of LIFE
I'm tired of being a SPINSTER
I want to be a WIFE...

With all those lovely MEN about
there MUST be one for ME
how I would love and care for HIM
if HE would come to ME...

I'd let HIM get my breakfast
I'd let HIM get my tea
I'd let HIM have ALL MY OWN WAY
if HE would come to ME...

I wouldn't ask for very much
just FURS and JEWELS and GOLD
I'd want a HOUSE and CAR and YACHT
and HIM to HAVE and HOLD...

HE won't think I'm more than FORTY
if HE doesn't see
my PENSION BOOK or CRUTCHES
or my SUPPLEMENTARY...

Kathleen Tomlinson

Born To Die

Child abuse is growing,
At a horrifying rate.
A home that's once contented,
Turns so slowly into hate.

An infant needs its parents,
On their loving they depend.
A beating they can do without,
This crime they can't defend.

Scalded, kicked, and battered,
And their family life is spurned.
The broken ribs, the bruising face,
The flesh that's cruelly burned.

A baby made to suffer,
Undernourished, under-fed.
A four year old dejected,
As the horrors fill her head.

A sickening illusion,
Which will make you want to cry.
To hear an infant sobbing, saying,
'Daddy, let me die'.

Ley Mitchell

Tales From The Rails

Booking clerk smiles sweetly
Asks me what I'd like
I'd like to go to Wakefield
I'd like to go tonight

I'd like to have an Apex
I don't want song and dance
The booking clerk smiles sweetly
"Book it in advance"

Well then I'd like a Railcard
"You'll need proof of age"
I say "You just bugger off"
And stamp me feet in rage

Is it that I'm difficult
Is it that I'm loud
Is it that I'm Northern
Or stand out in a crowd

We're all damn rude in Wakefield
Call us hard as nails
We're good at being difficult
To staff down on the Rails

Samantha Lakehal

Crying In The Courtroom

You were crying in the courtroom.
As they led me to the stand.
You knew soon I would meet my doom.
But still, couldn't hold my hand.
Then the jury found me guilty
Of a crime I didn't do.
When the judge gave his decision
I turned around and looked at you.
You were crying in the courtroom
Because you knew I told the truth.
But the jury found me guilty.
I'm innocent but have no proof.
The judge said I took a life
Which I must pay for with my own.
But you know I'll go to heaven
And stand where no man stands alone.

Tommy Downing

Affair of the Heart

To know you is to love you,
And to love you is a pleasure,
To walk along life's road with you
Is something I will treasure
Everyday together, sometimes apart.
I know it will always be,
An affair of the heart.

Moira Coventry

Untitled

Hours turn to years
  and to God's very sleep,
But oh! For the hours
  our hearts' troubles keep.
We limp through our days
  as sinners and saints,
Yet my friends we pass by
  never this way again.
I may fear Heaven's judgement
  if I'm not by thee,
But your laughter my friends
  is all the Heaven I need,
So I ask only love
  with a prayer for you all,
And a song sung well
  as to soft earth I fall.

Steven Unsworth

Apples Galore

Apples galore
As heavy a crop
That I have seen before
Apples here and apples there
Some lay routine so beware
But strange to say
On the orchard in front of me
Not one apple do I see
the geese there
Gobble them up
Gobble them as they drop
And very soon
They have eaten the lot.
So apples there may be
In many places around
But not one apple
Near me is to be found.
But if you want sweet apples
You might have to buy
Whatever you do, buy British, or try.

D. Robertson

Take My Heart

Please take my heart with you
as a knight with his charger,
Keep it safe next to yours
entwined like two roses
the thorns for protection
against all others.

Please take my heart with you
as a bird soars the sky
for I do not need it
when you are not with me
my love for you fills the space
of where it should go.

Please take my heart with you
as a flower needs water
my memories fill the void
of the emptiness you leave me
for I wait for the day
that you return my heart to me.

Karen Dallas

Love Me Forever

These words that I write
are for your eyes alone
Give me your love forever
for I will give you all
that I hold.
All my todays and tomorrows
belong to you alone.
I will love you forever
this man that you are
you are my North, South
my East and my West
Put a hat on the sun
give me shades for my eyes
You have made me sparkle
I light up when I
see your beautiful eyes
Give me all your love forever.
Not for just a day
but for all eternity.

Kathleen Scarborough

My Feet

My feet are a pain,
All they do all day long is
itch itch itch!
It gets on my nerves
I'm at school and I have to
take off my shoes,
It's embarrassing,
Do your feet do the same?

Rebecca Easthope

Growing Old

Memories of early years
are easy to recall,
yet things that happened yesterday,
I forget them all.
Am I growing old?

People oft times question me
about the previous day,
"Do you remember what you did?"
My reply to them is, "Nay".
Am I really growing old?

I now look back
and count the years,
three score plus twelve in number,
It's then I realise my fears,
I am growing older.

If this is so
then let it be,
I have no cause to grumble,
my memories are dear to me,
now that I am older.

T. K. Frogson

"A Chair By The Window"

He sits and watches every move
At the windows his feet on the ledge
You know he's angry you can tell
You've seen that look
And you become aware
He's been waiting for me awhile
A look of hate
No need to conceal
He needs someone I know it's me
To bear the brunt of his misery
But trees grow tall just like me
I say the words, and I fight back
For years of torment and fear
He's confused he's lost for words
He says I'm your father
And I say go to hell

Margaret N. Hainie

Fifty Years On

The years roll by
And you and I,
Dear sweetheart are together.
We've been through life
Love, hate and strife
In every clime and weather.

We've friends and foes
The good Lord knows
Who'd like to see us sunder.
Both black and white
Some wrong, some right
Would like to steal our thunder.

Love's true sweet song
Lasts just as long
As hearts beat without bother.
Frank thoughts and smiles
And naughty wiles
Endear us to each other.

John E. S. De Graft-Hayford

Too Late

Too late to say I love you
And to show how much I care,
so much I want to tell you
but you're no longer there.

Now that your chair is empty
It's too late to hold your hand,
Why God took you so quickly
I will never understand.

Too late to say I'm sorry
For the times I made you blue,
My sister, friend, and mother,
I'm just lonely without you.

I want your arms around me
It's too late to kiss your face,
There are people all around me
But my world's an empty place.

But I must try to remember
For you it's not too late,
there are loved ones waiting for you
just inside heaven's gate.

N. G. England

The Peaceful Ending

Sitting in his garden
an old man in the sun.
Thinking of his life time
all the things he's done.
Waving two great wars
they quickly passed him by.
Thinking of his dear wife
why'd she have to die?
Quite a few times lately
he's been missing her.
The pictures in his mind
of the love that they had shared.
And thanking God sincerely
for the good times they had had,
make the old man lonely
he's feeling very sad.
So looking at the daisies
the buzzing of the flies,
give the back ground music
as the old man quietly dies.

D. J. Byerley

The Friend with the Quiet Eyes

Friends with the quiet eyes
And the warm steady hands
It is the strength I prize
your heart that understands
when sorrow's clouds unfolds
my day I feel the force
of you the rock that holds
my faith to its high course
I face the troubled years
With confidence because
your words can still my flaws.
Your smile can mend life's flows
Be near, comfort me
Till the last sunlight dies
Lend me serenity
Friend with the quiet eyes.

R. E. Butler

An Ode To The Stylist

Snip snip snip
And the constant drone
The dryer breathing life
Into the hair that's lying prone
Laughter in the background
A sneeze and then a groan
Spring is in the air again
Where is wide-toothed comb
The curls begin to spring to life
My head now feels at home
I forget about the cold I have
No longer shall I moan
A visit to the salon
brings relief from one's despair
The stylist blows the blues away
Not a worry nor a care
Spring is not just on the outside
It's also in my hair.

Philomena McCrudden

A Wish

I want to be a child again
And sit on my father's knee
I want to feel all the love
My mother gave to me.
I don't like this grown-up world
There's too much pain and sorrow
I'd like to close my eyes
And forget about tomorrow
Oh if, I could play in the garden
To feel the sun upon my face
Just run away forever
For my heart's an empty place
When I was, but a little girl
All that mattered to me
Was to grow up so quickly
A woman I wanted to be
Now I have my wish
I want to go back through time
Back to someone who really loved me
That special father of mine.

Lynda Riding

A Comet?

It came hurtling on towards us,
a blinding flash of light.
Its heart a raging fire,
its tail a glorious sight.

We gazed upon its wonder
and watched its splendid flight.
One journey in our lifetime
to lift the sullen night.

But,
in the blink of an eye
it had passed by.....

C. H. MacTaggart

270

Sweet Child....

The wings of an angel
appeared from above,
To take our sweet darling
we so dearly love.

A life that's so precious
just drifted away,
Our hearts left with sadness
once sunny, now grey.

Our sweet child in heaven
forever now sleeps,
An innocent soul
now the angels shall keep.
Maureen L. Lewis

Life

Life! You are within me
and I know not how you came,
but whilst you dwell within me
then I will play your game.

But life! You are so fickle
in so may different ways,
in some you stay a lifetime
but in others only days.

I have still to meet your brother
but it's a meeting to delay,
so pray O life, please stay with me
if only for today.

Life! You've been a good companion
and when your mystery lies unfurled,
I hope that we may meet again
in a far far better world.
K. Ashmore

Ireland's Cease-Fire, Broken

The cease-fire has ended,
And hearts are filled with fear
Families of the victims,
Have shed a tear.
Police patrol the streets,
And carry heavy loaded guns,
The IRA have started again,
Planting many, many bombs.
They know that they should stop,
But they just won't,
Many people will be killed soon,
If they don't.
I wish that the cease-fire,
Would start once again,
This would save many families,
From suffering and pain.
Rosemary McGuigan

Memory Of Life

Many years did pass on,
And before I knew it,
My life had gone.

All those years of sadness and love,
Finally I floated up to heaven
As light as a dove.

When I got there,
Before my eyes
I saw my love
My pride and joy.

He had past on years before me,
But when I saw him there,
My spirit filled with glee.
Rebecca Vesti-Nielsen

Melonie

With hair black and silken
And eyes just for me
It was love at first sight
When I met Melonie
She welcomed me home
At the end of each day
And listened intently
To what I would say
For ten years it lasted
In truth I can say
That my heart it was broken
When she passed away
The deep understanding
That grew through the years
Left fond memories later
To soften the tears
She's still in my heart
And the feeling's so strong
That I often forget
My alsatian has gone
Michael C. Eames

Billy And Milly

Billy I think is rather bold
And does not do as he is told.
Milly his sister is also there,
They really are a lovely pair

I wonder now if you know who,
I'll do my best to give a clue
A beard is to be seen on Billy
But this is never seen on Milly.

They're not fussy what they eat
And never ever miss a treat.
Grass and ivy from the wall,
They never fail to eat it all.

Have you guessed who these two are?
If let free they'll go afar.
Climb they do and climb they will,
These two rascals from up-hill.

Now after all these clues from me
You must know now who they can be.
Both have black and hairy coats,
They've got to be two special goats!
D. I. Balfour

Last Flight

Once we were young
and burned the sky
but little thought to die.
Now we are old
how dampened the fires,
how bitter now the cold.
The days grow shorter
and the memory too.
The fight is fainter
and the victories few.
My eye lacks lustre
but my heart beats fast
I go to meet The Master
in whose image we are cast.
Shall I see my fellow fliers?
Shall I laugh again on high?
Or will it be those fearful fires
when airmen lit the sky?
D. W. A. Stones

"As the Season Go By"

As the seasons go by
and another one beckons,
Thoughts of you
will not be forgotten,
As I lie here and think
how it could have been,
Now sadly I know for sure
that by me it won't be seen.
For all the mistakes I made
that caused nothing but sadness,
Although it may be too late
all I ask is for your forgiveness.
No matter what I do or where I go
we will meet again,
Don't know when but only where,
it will surely be in heaven.
J. Mistry

For Mick

For giving me hope,
Amidst all this pain.
For showing me love,
And all I could gain.

For showing me life,
When death was at hand.
For giving me joy,
And squeezing my hand.

For telling me I could live,
Without sorrow or pain.
For giving me all I could have,
When I'd taken the rein.

For taking me by the shoulder,
With firm belief;
That joy could be mine,
When over the grief.
C. L. Harris

Friendship

It was so nice to see your faces,
After an elapse of time.
How happiness can be captured
Through company shared divine.
I love to hear your laughter
From your impish faces so warm.
It made me feel so tender
Towards your welcome embrace.
You have never changed towards me
No matter how we have changed.
Let's hope the future still instills
That friendship which is so warm.
D. E. Pryke

The Sea

I have a love of the sea
A feeling that is free
To look out as far as the eye can see
How refreshing it is to me.

When stormy clouds arrive
The sea becomes alive
The endless windy days
The crashing pounding waves

Suddenly the quiet calm
This is part of its other charm
The gentle copping of the waves
Heralding in some balmy days

This special feeling for the sea
Comes from deep within for me
I know that I will always care
To view that wide expanse out there.
C. Sanders

My Pain

How happy the day when you were born
Although you suffered ills,
And you were taken away from me
To show the surgeon's skills.

The surgeon he used all his skill
But all to no avail,
You closed your eyes and slipped away
Your body it did fail.

Today my tears still flow for you
My heart feels empty still,
I long to hold you in my arms
But know I never will.

They say that time will ease the pain
But not the memory,
And if there is an after life
Together we will be.
    My Son
Mark Roberts

Reunited

I beheld you,
and I held you.
And I kissed you.
And caressed you.
Reunited
lovers, we;
as I held you,
and you held me.
Then as our bodies
there entwined,
you pledged your love;
I pledged mine.
We held each other,
kissed, caressed:
Love's full splendour
there expressed.
But then dawn broke
upon the scene,
and I cried to find
'twas but a dream!
Stephen Gunner

The Road

The road, an asphalt jungle
A way from place to place
Where cars end up a bundle.
The drivers set the pace.

When roads first made were sandy
For use by horse and man,
And bikes and carts were handy
And only few trains ran.

The car was then constructed
And commenced to use the road.
The years of life deducted
The driver on he rode.

His eyes were closed to danger.
The day the car was made.
The horse returned to manger.
His gravestone partly laid.

To bring this story to an end-
A driver's life is cheap.
He only needs a hill or bend
To end it in a heap.
W. H. Howarth

Celestial Neighbour

One orb of light fantastic
A silver glow of mystery
This opalescent feldspar
Turning future into history

Its dark secrets running deeper
Than any of its seas
It draws us to its brilliance
Bathing within its beauty

The hub of all that's living
Silent clouds pass by its light
Casting shadows on the landscape
A solar sentry of the night

Never sleeping in tranquillity
Breathing life into the oceans
Through liquid variation
Controlling our emotions
A crystal clear enigma
A satellite of inspiration
Illuminating all our lives
With hope and aspiration.
Leonard Halliwell

Whiteout

Down came the snowflakes
All through the night
Covering the ground
With a blanket of white
Starving the birds
They scavenge for food
Searching for morsels
To feed their young brood
It hangs from the roof
Like some fancy cake
Icing it thicker
With every flake
Each one unique
They fly to the earth
Then disappear
In a lemming like death
Down came the snowflakes
And were gone overnight
Baring the earth
Letting in Light
Lindsay Brockie

Affair Of The Heart

To lie beside you is just a dream
For our love can never be
One who's married and settled down
Has not me to play around
So into space I sit and stare
Knowing that I never dare
Live a life with whom I love
Gone is the dream that I once loved.
Annisse Hudsmith

Significant Other(s)

You are my first thought
in the morning,
my last one at night;

The rhyme to my reason,
the cause to my fight.

I've met you a hundred times over
yet never known your name,
I've walked away from commitment
and let fate take the blame;

So tonight I dream
of a love divine;

The future was ours
the past is mine.
Tony Chiswell

Providence

He lay - awaiting
Cold earth to his breast
The smell of Death
Upon his breath
Almost fainting
Oh! Lord, my prayer to hear
At thy behest
To keep away my fear.

The battle waged
He hugged the hollow
Muddy staged
Screams and groans rent aloud
Sorrow - Tomorrow?
Whistling down with a thud
It almost buried me
But not a sound...
'Twas a dud you see
A shell sent by HE.
D. R. Rowe

Bearing A Child

Sixteen that's all I was,
A child, bearing a child.
Immaturity was the cause,
A child, bearing a child.

Now I have a healthy son,
A child, raising a child.
And have realized it's not all fun,
A child, raising a child.

Live your life to the full,
A child, being a child.
Maturity is the only tool,
A child, being a child.

Now nineteen, a lot has changed,
A child, no longer a child.
A life totally rearranged,
A child, no longer a child.
Roseanne Connelly

Christmas

Carol singing at the door,
Holly hanging by the score,
Red are our noses in the cold,
Inside mince pies one hot to hold,
See the presents round the tree,
Tightly wrapped so I can't see,
Making lots of things to eat,
A big fat turkey what a treat,
Santa's coming what big feet.
Delma Round

The Glistening Pearl

It runs unheeding
Across the cheek so soft.
A lip quivers and moans
The glistening pearl
Moves slowly or quickly.
Maybe joined by others
In the light of a lamp
Or maybe on a sunlit day.
It trips down out of sight
The eyelash moves
So quietly and yet
By its very movement
It releases this pearl.
Maybe a sob arises
Then all is quiet
Sleep comes at last
And that is the end of
The glistening pearl.
Margaret Pearce

Yesterday And Today

They said "you will be old one day,"
I knew that they were wrong.
How could I with the sun so bright,
And the world so full of song.
But now it seems they were so right
My skin is wrinkled my hair is white.
I wondered why they made a fuss
Now I can't even run for the bus.
It's true what they said about time and tide
My old bones creak, there's a pain in my side.
Still I suppose I should not complain
I think I could do it all again.
B. Wilson

If It Were Me...

I discovered just the other day, a fact that now will change the way,
I look at life and make my plans, as now I find the grains of sand,
are shifting through at rapid rates, I have to see that things are straight.
Oh what decisions I must make, before the sands have sealed my fate.
Do I stay and live in my homeland, or go and join my family clan?
Here in England I can see, the snow and robins in the tree.
My childhood friends are here and more, my career plans, an open door,
to wealth success and new found glamour, it was to this that I did clamber.
But now I know I'll never see the prized success that was for me.
And so I think that I must travel to distant lands as plans unravel.
To palm trees, sun, and long white beaches, to family bonds within my reaches.
And in the time that I have left I'll write some more, I'll pass the test.
I'll show the world that in the end I found in me a special friend.
The glamour and success I sought, was at a price most dearly bought.
But if just one of my great schemes is left behind to make dreams
come alive and live for me, while my spirits wanders free,
then it will all have been worthwhile and I can exit with a smile.
To know that in the afterlife my work will lessen someone's strife,
is something I must now ensure, before great powers close my door.
And so to work, there's not much time, to assure that final rest's sublime.
Lynn Santer

The Summer Storm

The summer storm has ended
I lay here with a burning heart.
My body aches from wanting thee
My eyes are weak from flowing waters
My love is in a far-away land
My hand is reaching out to God.
God give me strength I pray that soon
the summer storm will return once again.
A storm like this should never end.
But life goes on they say.
Dear God, Sweet God, I pray that
soon the summer storm will return once again.
Sylvia Brooks

Through The Eyes Of A Child

Now that 1996 is here
I hope that all children
Can live without fear
That none will be hungry, sick or sad
Used, abused or treated bad
The world should be such a lovely place
For all the children, regardless of race
I wish that all hatred and fighting would cease
So the whole wide world could live in peace
With plenty of love and food for all
Whether crippled, ugly, tall or small
I may only be twelve and not very bright
I also am blind, that is my plight
But despite this I can clearly see
What a beautiful planet the earth could be.
R. Heller

Smoking

A dried up leaf wrapped in paper,
I know you will not agree,
To you it may sound disgusting,
It sure sounds like heaven to me,

Two tipped weights at eleven years old,
That's how it all started for me,
Three years later at least ten a day,
It began so innocently,

Numerous times I've given it up,
But always I light up again,
Through pressures of modern day living,
Or cause someone's being a pain.

I know to continue could speed my demise,
Still young in my grave I would drop,
Despite all the dangers and financial cost,
To be honest I don't want to stop.
Terry Gowers

Because I Have You

What would I do, if I did not have you?
    How would I exist?
How would I feel without someone to love me
    Like I know you do

I would feel like an empty shell
Lying alone on an empty beach
With just the sound of the waves
Crashing against the rocks to keep me company

But I do not have to imagine this feeling
    Because I have you.
Poet Brathwaite

A Poem For Life At Midnight

The greatest pain of all, is in my heart tonight,
I know I will not sleep, but they will sleep tight.
As I write this poem, just to keep me sane,
I look threw the window, is he caressing her again?

What have I done to deserve this?
I gave all my love to her.
Now she loves in front of me,
I receive undescribable torture.

But it is better to have loved,
Than not to have loved at all.
These words of wisdom often spoken,
They could not of left what I'm going through.

There should be a cure for unrequited love,
A strong medicine prescribed.
Something to soothe the incredible pain,
Could it be suicide??
R.A.M.

The Comforts Of Madness

I sit by a window where the sun shines through,
I knew not why.
I glance up and see a ghostly face reflected in the pane,
Everything looks as it should be.
But somehow within myself I am not me, and yet I am.
So confusing be muddled.
My head is a ball of tangled wool, but if I put
my hand in my hair I can unravel the twine and
pull it out, bit by bit, and still I sit, oh so still, not moving,
The sharpness of the needle reminds me of something, but
I cannot recall exactly what it could be, now let me see,
Dissect the past, it will come to me.
Little boxes locked with a key in the pigeonholes of my mind
keep them locked and everything will be fine.
I like the fluffy clouds in my head, but it cannot last,
can't stay forever in this comfortable shell,
must claw my way back, make myself well.
I sit by a window, a reflection I see, and through
the comforts of madness I realise that the reflection is me.
Laura Smith

Missing You

On still, dark nights, when owls call,
I hear your voice.
When no moon shines, when stars are bright,
I see your eyes.
When the day is bright and the sky is blue,
I see your smile.
One true friend, even when you're not near,
I think of you.

Sandra Philpott

Passing Time

When first I broke the surface the land was young and new,
I knew little of the world, men were very few.
As years went by I grew to be a mighty Oak,
And covered surrounding land with my beautiful leafy cloak.
Through the years my limbs have been many different things,
In summer I have been shade, in winter sheltered kings.
My twigs have given warmth, my branches weapons of war.
I have seen flooded land and rain that would not pour,
Maids have swung from garlands wrapped round my mighty girth.
Pigs have fed by generations from my young dropped on the earth.
Green clad men have hidden among my thickening bough,
Thundering animals now replace the man pushed plough.
Were once swallows flew up in the sky,
Great big shiny metal things dart about on high.
I have seen such wondrous sights since I was planted here,
Fought elements and man, shred an amber tear.
I stand alone now were once my peers surrounded me,
Time has not been too cruel, man now lets me be.
Although many years have passed, I stand another dawn,
I may be old and ragged now, but still recall when I was an Acorn.

Lesley Ann Wilson

A Poem For My Mum, From Her Daughter, Who Was Sexually Abused

I am not blaming you so get it out of your head,
I just think of him when I'm in bed.

I haven't got over it yet, though I put on a brave face,
Because if I don't, I feel out of place

I love you Mum, I'm sure you know,
But I'm not silly, you too feel low

I never thanked you, for being on my side
Because if you weren't I would have died

Thank you Mum, for all your love and support
I needed you and you were there just as I thought

One day, you may find this poem as I couldn't give
Because I didn't want to let you down but I'll live

Thanks again Mum, I love you and appreciate what you have done
Maybe if I get a chance I'll thank you properly, Mum.

Maxine Ward

Strawberry Girl

Strawberry girl, I know I never said goodbye,
I just never said hello,
You the precious butterfly, my love I never showed.

Thinking, not a day goes by, the reflections of what I've been.
Little hands of China doll, the angel I've never seen.

I can't make tomorrow, say it today
Heartache for you to know me, the missing, it never goes away.

I need to feel you close, I wipe away the tears,
I'm sorry for the missing and bitter wasted years.

Days have passed, the years so fast, birthdays have come and gone,
Your candles I've never seen you blow,
Your eyes like stars they shone.

My strawberry girl, your love is where your heart is,
And you have got it all, you're looked upon and cherished,
My angel you won't fall.

Richard M. Noonan

Images of You

I piece together images of you, to dreams and thoughts.
I hope we shared
I have much space and time to kill
A year in time of our life passes on quickly as time itself
Our fleeting dreams are already gone to somewhere distant
deep in our minds
Memories are so precious, they're all we have to recall, to
laugh and cry.
It's then we wonder doesn't time fly!
They say that time can heal but you're in my thoughts forever
until the day will come.
When again we can be as one.
But until that day I'll continue to pray
So in my thoughts that's where you'll stay.

L. Pilfold

Peace And Harmony

If I could wish a wish or two,
I know what I would wish for you,
I know what I would wish for me,
A life of peace and harmony,
No death or destruction on this land,
And all mankind standing hand in hand,
A place where hatred stood no ground,
And only love would be abound,
So hear my wish and you will see,
My wish starts here with you and me.

Kerry Bacon

Crying Into The Night

From the depths of my soul
I hear a voice crying,
Crying into the night.
Or, is it just my imagination
Playing tricks in my mind?
Were you really there
Or, was it just a dream?
I had those funny feelings
When you were here before;
When you used to touch me and hold me.
But, when I turn to look
As ever, you're no longer there.
My tear stained pillow
Is a reminder that
The voice crying,
Crying into the night is mine.
Just mine.

Kim Biggins

Prisoner

Locked in a cell for many a year.
I have no sadness nor shed no tears.
I've grown so cold with these walls of stone.
I once had, if I can just recall, a place quite
different, a place called home.
I remember it was once happy warm and good,
but all I wanted was a knife and blood.
I have a window, or should I say three bars
in a hole, it's as sad a thing as my very own soul.
A man's life what a waste, if only I hadn't angered in haste.
The days I bear, the nights I loath, the darkness seems
to stay much longer, if only I didn't in a moment of rage,
grabbed that knife and went and stabbed her.
I should of listened - listened to her,
She only stayed out with a tearful friend.
And me in my jealousy caused her end.
And now I shall lay down my tired head,
and wait for judgement, which will come the moment I'm dead.

M. Murphy

Summer Memories

It's a beautiful summer's day.
I gaze out of my window and what do I see
An ocean blue sky, cotton white clouds and a sun
Which shines through my window penetrating a
warm feeling against my skin,
I hear voices of children playing in the street
As I gaze further on I see an ice cream van approaching.
I look back to see the expressions on the children's faces.
Expressions of excitement expressions of joy.
Whilst opening my window I feel a light breeze.
I have a warm feeling in my heart as I exhale
slowly, and visualize myself down there.
I'm eating that ice cream, I am playing in the street
To me, summer is the best time of the year
hence the fact that summer brings happiness
warmth and golden childhood memories to us all
Sandra Smith

Silent Flight

My eye sight, is not so good,
I flitter from barn, to wood,
And make a high pitched sound,
Several feet, off the ground.

I sleep upside down, all day,
Thousands of us, wend our way,
We don't come out in sunlight,
Come into our own at night.

Over towns, and country side,
On leathery wings, we gently glide,
Always searching, for food,
Our eating manners, are so crude.

We are supposed, to get in your hair,
Half the time, we are not there,
People are not afraid, of cats,
But they are petrified, of small fruit bats.
Robert Thompson

The Shelter Of Your Arms

In the shelter of your arms
I find the only peace this world has to offer,
And in the very presence of you
I know my only joy, my only strength.
Just to hear you speak my name,
Just to feel your hand in mine,
Is the sweetest gift that God could give.
I am complete - I could never want for more
As long as you are near,
As long as you are mine.
I find more love in the touch of your hands
Than in a thousand lips,
I see more beauty in the message of your eyes
Than in a thousand sunsets.
What we have, what we share, is beyond all words.
If this is but a dream
Forever let me sleep,
Forever let me stay
In the shelter of your arms.
Katrina Relf

Down But Not Out

Don't think that I am lonely as I walk along my beat,
I am really quite happy with all the friends I meet
A penny here or maybe two from people who think just like you,
Can keep me in a cafe for an hour or even two,
Don't think that I'm ungrateful for that would not be true

To tell the truth I'm sorry for people just like you,
Who work all week to keep off the street and end up feeling blue,
For when you add up the bills there's not much left for you,
Yes sometimes I feel sorry for the likes of you,
So don't think that I am lonely because I'm not like you,
I have my wine to kill my time and even cigarettes too
And if you chance to pass my way I'll have a few pence from you today.
Ronald Harkness

The Promised Land

Walking through the countryside on a warm and sunny day.
I felt the need to pause a while and then I bowed my head to pray.
I could see a glorious vision, as I beheld that rich green land.
Of a dream where man would never fight, but take hold his
  brother's hand.
And lead him to a new world, for this has been our Saviour's plan
To make us see that we must love and pray with our fellow man.
For life has much to offer us, we must be glad in what we see.
There's beauty in Gods country, in every flower and every tree.
For as he works his miracles, we should rejoice for all our worth.
For there's a greater Kingdom, when we leave this life on earth.
But we must learn the lessons and promise every day,
to spread his word, to follow him, for we must pave the way.
To show others of his power, we're all messengers you see,
and we must not forsake him, because he has set us free.
He died for us upon a cross, his suffering, the agony of pain.
They spread his arms, nailed feet and hands, let his death not
  be in vain.
For on that day of Judgement, we'll have to take the stand,
and those who've earned the privilege, will sit at God's right hand.
They'll be the one's who learned so well, as all good spirits should,
that our lives are but a footpath, which always leads us back to God.
Moira Oldham

Hello, Confusion

Hello, confusion, it's me again
I don't know what to do
I can't seem to work it out
so I've come to talk to you.
I hear this and I hear that
till doubt slipped in my brain
there are clouds where the sun once shone
and I think it could be rain.
Only you, confusion, can sort it out
and put my mind at rest
I need to swap doubt for trust
we know it's for the best
so, please, confusion, throw me out
you don't need me as a friend
confusion and doubt will get on fine
but, doubt and I, must end.
So once again the sun can shine
and the rain, it will dry
I'll have trust on my side
thanks, confusion and goodbye
Yvonne Smith

A Little Girl's Dream

I am a little fairy, they call me Snowy White,
I dance on the toadstools all through the night,
I skip through the flowers, I fly through the trees,
I often have to land on the water lily leaves.

I talk to my Froggy friend, he answers with a croak,
I sometimes think he is a funny little bloke,
I talk to all the ducklings, they are so soft and shy,
They tell me that their mother can fly up in the sky.

And when the great big moon appears, it makes me look so white,
Perhaps that's how I got my name, while dancing through the night,
And when I wave my magic wand and all come out to see,
I'm sure that all my friends agree, I dance so Magically.

I fly across the sparkling stream, to meet my friend the owl,
He sometimes says "How do you do" then gives me such a scowl,
He sits alone the whole night through, I wonder what he thinks,
While all the other fairies are having such high jinks.

But when the moon begins to fade, and night turns into day,
I quietly close my silky wings and gently fly away,
I fade away right out of sight, into my mushroom home,
But I'll be back another night, dancing the hours away.
Vivian A. Smith

Evensong

My soul is young, though my body old,
I creak and ache and I'm always cold
With an active mind - which is sometimes sluggish,
When words I try to convey often come out as rubbish.
Deep down I'm still the young girl I was years ago
When I was pretty and full of go.
I feel the same feelings,
The hurt and the pain,
So please don't act as if I'm not sane.
A bright cheery word, or a smile will do
To help me see my long day through.
A posy of flowers to brighten my day,
As I travel along life's pathway.
So don't stand and stare or hurry by.
A smile, a wave or just say Hi!

Marie Aldridge

Friends

I remember the first time, I saw your smile,
I could have run a bloody mile!
On that warm August morn,
All hope would have been forlorn.
Your presence filled me with intrigue,
But I knew, you were out of my league.
Nothing I could say, would realise my dream,
because the first time I saw you, I was only sixteen.
Many times since, our paths have crossed,
and in all of them, my words were lost.
I just wanted to say, to ask or to touch,
but when it came to confidence, I didn't have much.
The past was then, now the present is here,
And it fills me with joy, just to have you near.
There's not a quality in you, I wouldn't defend,
And I feel so lucky,
    to call you my friend.

D. Carmicheal

The Alcoholic's Wife

My husband's an alcoholic
I can't stop him, God knows I've tried.
Once he drinks he wicked potions
His moods are like Jekyll and Hyde.

He loves me, hates me, loves me, hates me,
Punches me, pulls my hair.
In the morning he says he sorry;
Tells me he loves me, says he cares.

Someone, somewhere must hear me
Inside I feel I'm dying
Day in, day out, my life consists
I'm shouting fighting crying.

If ever a crime I committed
And must make a sacrifice
I've done my time, I've paid my fine
This marriage of hell has been the price.

Mandy Bishop

Bitter Sweet Memories Of Mum

As I gaze deeply into the mixed grey sky
I ask myself why?
Why did my mum have to die?
Week after week, month after month I cry only
to be traumatised with the same old echo -
"We did try."
That's a lie.
Those doctors they are so sly.
They simply failed to diagnose inflammation of the bronchi.
So in a grand coffin we put her to lie.
Her skin was so pallor as though smothered with dye.
Homeward bound well-wishers hovered just to pry.
Once again, I ask myself why?
Why? Why? Why?

Opal Vanessa Prince

The Thoughts Of An Old Man

I often wish that I were dead
I can't get this out of my head.

Life is such a bore
I feel I just can't take anymore.

Since the loss of my dearest one
I just exist without purpose, aim or fun.

I should be thankful that I exist
these sinful thoughts I must resist.

Please forgive my misguided mind
I must carry on with the daily grind.

If only I could find companionship and love
I would be so grateful to the one above.

Let's hope that I will see sense
in all the daily events.

Try hard to mix with people I have been told
So taking heed I must be bold.

Who knows, one day I might strike lucky
before they cart me off on a buggy.

J. R. Thomas

My Mother

When I was a baby (I don't remember)
I bet you held me warm and tender
You rocked me gently to and fro
And never ever let me go.

When I grew into a tot
You'd dress my knees if they got cut
You'd look into my tearful eyes
And whisper to me not to cry.

As I got older and into my teens
I shared with you my every dream
You taught me how to make them true
For that Mum I'll always love you.

Remember when I got quite sick
You stuck by me and made me fit
I could clearly see the pain in your eyes
But you tried not to let me see you cry

I guess that what I want to say
Is that I'll love you till my dying day
In my eyes you are the best
You've definitely passed every test.

Lucy Dowd

Memories Of The Heart

To find a love that's oh so true,
I close my eyes and think of you.
Of days gone but never past,
for the love you gave will always last.

When I was weak you made me strong,
the wisdom you gave will be lifelong.
I think of you each and everyday,
as I go along life's busy highway.

Remembering things we used to do
so little time I had with you.
I'll never forget your wonderful face,
in my heart for you there's a special place.

You always were so honest and true,
no one on earth could replace you.
There's so many things I'd like to say,
and I know I shall when we meet again one day

As I open my eyes I see your face,
on a photo I keep in a special place.
Everyone will know of the love I have,
the respect and admiration for my wonderful Dad.

C. M. Sadd

Remember Me

I am the wind which travels the sky,
I am the innocent who wonders why.

I am the stars which glitter the night,
I am the lover who holds you tight.

I am the gun held in your hand,
I am the bullet that killed the man.

I am the babe deep in your womb,
I am the man who wanders the moon.

I am the light at the dawn of time,
I am yours and you are mine.
Mike Brown

Lonely, Yet Not Alone

The birthday party is in full swing,
I am surrounded by loved ones as I go in.
Yet I feel so lonely as I join in the fun
And I open my presents, one by one.
For my loneliness can never end
(Though around me I have many a friend)
As my heart still aches for the man who died,
The man who is no longer by my side.
It is thirteen years since he passed away
Yet it seems like only yesterday.
But one of these days we'll meet again
In a mystic place, where there will be no pain.
Then my loneliness will be gone forever
On that day my spirit from this earth I sever.
Stella Frusher

"The Tramp"

I am rich, but have no money
I am rich, but have no home,
I have all I need for comfort, for I have
the world to roam,
See the blossom burst with spring,
Watch the swallows on the wing, I've everything,

See the golden dawn arise,
See the colours in the sky, change before my
very eyes, I've everything,

Silver sunbeams in the sky
Watch those birds, they're riding high,
Like they know what I have seen, I've everything,

Angels coming from above, sing to me a word
of love, oh what pleasures I have seen,
I've everything,

Thank you God for what I've seen,
Thank you God for what I've been,
Thank you Lord, I'm very rich indeed.
Patrick

This Child Of Mine

When you came into the world
I cried with joy
At last my own baby boy
I no longer feel sad or broken in two
Life seems worth living at last for you
You gave me courage
You gave me strength
The meaning of life makes much more sense
There are no more doubts they are all gone
For you I must be strong
I must get on with living everyday
For you my child it's the only way
And while you are sleeping I look down at you
My own fair Angel
My wish has come true
Marcia Mcgriele

Drowned By Love

God help me, somewhere in the sea of longing
I am drowning, yearning, wishing waiting
I am sinking further, further, falling deeper and deeper
He draws me into another world
Another world safe and warm where only we belong
He raises his arm, places it around my trembling waist and rescues me
Beneath his body I can feel his passion crushing me
Until I lose my heart somewhere near to paradise
Waves of emotion swelling, pounding with each beat of his heart
my heart of our heart
We are one and then he walks away and I am deserted
On the beach of reality, brokenhearted, I realise I love him.
Lindsey Elvidge

Faith

When winds of sadness and all grief
Howl their way, to test belief,
It's always known, oh trust can fade,
Hope disappears, cold heart be made.
The hurting pain, we cannot see,
Sadness, sorrow, grief, all three.
Tear-filled eyes, a silent prayer,
To the One we know is always there.
Who listens, and knows that precious you,
Who never leaves, His words so true.
Who pours strength in, and holds you high,
Who softly takes those winds on by,
Who gently tells you, and will heal,
Who knows every moment how we feel.
We know, and in our heart can't hide,
We know our faith cannot be tried.
The comfort, inner warming glow,
We thank You Lord, because You know.
To let us fall, You never would,
Thank you Lord, Your Grace, so good.
Linda Hayes

Mother, Mother

Mother, Mother, of love so pure,
How the world doth envy thee,
Thou who's light doth shine the way,
To lesser mortals, every day.

A God-like angel strong and true,
To serve and care, thy destiny,
Through life thou art a mighty rock,
A shepherd attending to her flock.

Thou givest all in every way,
And in return expect no gain,
Shed tears of joy, for the smallest gift,
For the thought of love, surrounding it,

Mother, Mother, the chosen one,
Thou givest all in sacrifice,
And those who feel they must compete,
In doing so, admit defeat!
W. T. Shenton

My Love For You

Within my heart, my tears are there
How much more of this pain, can I bear?
The love I have for you, is beyond measure,
Come to me darling, for togetherness is treasure,
I have always loved you, from the depths of my heart,

Be mine alone, never more to part,
I know you love me, it shows in your eyes
The sadness we feel, when we say our good-byes,
In your arms I feel the entire world is ours
The nearness of you, are like scented flowers,
The love that you show me, will stay forever
Please don't let us part not now, no never.
Pamela Mann

Sorrow Too Late

I never knew how much you cared,
how much I meant to you. The seed
of love that glimmered shyly, so
deep within your heart.

How long it must have hurt you dear,
to sense my blind indifference. My wall
of silence, cold and hard as you waited
in the wings, for romance.

So now I understand, the looks you gave,
the spoken words, the gestures that you made.
The times you must have tried so hard,
to speak the words you felt.

And now I know the truth you hid, as I read
your dying word, and weep with sorrow too
late to speak. How you lived in hope I would
see the light, of the love you held for me.

So, as I wait in silence, is lonely memory
of you, unwilling bride to life's cruel fate.
To know that love so close, was lost within my grasp,
and suffer the pain of sorrow, too late.

Laurence Winston Perry

The Visitor

He arrived at the door, nose bleeding, ears torn.
How could I ignore a look so forlorn?
After dining on milk and cheese
Naturally I thought he would take his leave.
This was clearly not his intention or perhaps he thought!
Necessity, was after all, the mother of invention
Necessity was just the right word,
Any thought of leaving would be absurd.

He made himself known to the rest of the family
And settled by the fire quite calmly.
T.C. we called him and all kinds of names,
He treated our efforts with sheer disdain.
Then for a year we called him cat.
He clearly wasn't taken with that.
Then one day we tried another, ginger it was
because of his colour.
So ginger it was and ginger it stayed and ginger
He was for the rest of his days

Ginger's no longer with us though we are pleased to have
known him. He left as he came, all of sudden.

Marilyn Wilson

Realization

Artificial light filters through a fevered brain
How can the ceiling represent mortality?
A panoply arranged of thought inane
Portrayed by angular patterns of nostalgia.

Why does the finger of light
Epitomize the summer times of life?
Whilst shadow reminiscent of the night
Dominate the picture overall.

One is but lazily aware
Of voices kind, but far away
Nothing however halts the stare
Of doleful eyes reflected by the light.

Does that plastic encapsulate it all?
The realization that life has gone
The clumsy effort to recall
Lost in swirling mists.

Overnight, eternity becomes the focal point
Previous joys inconsequential
Pain in every calcified joint
Will God's presence lift this web of doom?

Russell W. Doyle

Joyride

Freaky Evans cut classes at quarter to two
Hot-wired a Porsche at ten past
Snorted coke with a chaser of acetate glue
Gave himself and the engine a blast.
Twin exhausts billowed thunder to quicken his blood
Death was a sleek, silver squeal
With two hundred horsepower under the hood
And twelve-year-old hands at the wheel.

Pre-nursery school toddlers were crossing the lane
The Porsche slashed them skyward like chaff.
They fell sprawled, smeared in scarlet, keening and maimed
Because Freaky "just wanted a laugh."
Shattered limbs, doll-like corpses cut off at the neck
Whey-faced paramedics struck dumb
Freaky walked free from the blood-spattered wreck
Bemoaning a lightly bruised thumb.

He's parentless, pitiless, too young to goal
What use prattle of sparing the rod?
If you're burning for justice and right to prevail
Don't ask Freaky Evans. Ask God.

Roger Jones

Commuted Sentence

Boxed, beaming heads - passing!
Hot tarred space - must be first!
Sad pedlar of power;
Laughed, teasing the hearse.

Brewed, lipstick love - echoes!
Drained-glass thirst - can't escape her!
Blocked, winded and shopped;
Caught by the chaser.

No license to thrills, just
A ticket to ride
Stark platform chills, then
Nowhere to hide.

Richard Dunne

Far Away Lands

Cold with the polar bear in his polar icy chair.
Hot in the desert all sand all rocks.
Rainforests all trees animals and rain.
Jungles full of lions and tigers
The jaguar waits on a branch for another victim to come.
The indians wait for fish to eat while others eat and eat.
On the beaches far away the waves sway and sway
By the river, boats just sail away.
By the shops people queueing and saying
hey we've waited all day.

Toni McCartan

"Slaughter Of The Innocent"

A Tribute to Hans Ruesch

Nobody hears this dog's cries, entering the gates of hell,
His vocal chords severed, immobilized.
Two steel rods rammed into the orbits of his eyes.
Clamps that crush his eardrums, squash his tongue against
  the palate.
Burnt, gassed, irradiated, shot. Scrambled intestines, crushed
  tissues.
Scared, scarred, scalded. A small life is crippled.
Rats and mice have few friends among men.

Are the secrets of health to be found in their tortured bodies?
The naked empress, science, is a lie that is killing us.
Grant - hungry charlatans work the devil's miracles
  (Ten thousand little monsters) while giants with feet of clay
Enjoy cigars and brandy, yachts and aeroplanes.
Operation successful, patient dead.

Sheila Edwards

Afterwards

Glistening rippled body in sunshine's lance
Hot afternoons ecstasy frenziedly filled
Tremulous is yesterdays troubled will
Forgiven all in horizontal shadow's trance.

If there is at this moment a glimmer
Of times' backward beckoning rush
It is in the body language of hush
Lanterned by freshly moonscape shimmer.

For if there is a personal Genesis
The salvation surely is only to reckon
That the world's illusory movement seconds
Stop in the timelessness between breaths.

So time runs back to personal Genesis
The colourful lovemaking puts time on hold
And terminal offal flesh gangrenous and cold
Awakes to tricks of Muses' caress

Can the remembrance of painless light
In the languid attic's wicked secret
Slake blind December drought of regret
With noontides tremulous dancing wight?

P. G. Hayward

On Hearing Her Play The Crumhorn

O fortuitous antique shop
hoarder of forgotten obscurities.
O fortunate wife, blower of duck decoys.
O unfortunate husband
hearer of defunct wind-capped instruments
O forlorn neighbours,
feelers of antediluvian vibrations.
O demented children
crazed dreary by concentric bore holes.
O unhappy bank manager
on sudden arrival of large overdraft.
O dark, mothy cupboard, holder of a
J. Luckbaum original; Prague 1551

Sue Higginson

It's Warm Out

Once upon a time there was a very funny man,
His name was Mick, he came from the bank of the bann.
He said "I always try as hard as I possibly can."
But people made up stories so he bought a petrol can.

There is always someone to emulate the town crier,
They enhance the truth because their lives are drier.
They wallow about in self pity, lost in the mire.
So Mick thought f*** this, doused them down and set them on fire.

When the fire engine came to see what had caused all the fuss,
Mick duly coughed and caught the no. 10 bus.
He left without a backward glance and began to cuss.
An old lady bumped into him, Mick just looked.

J. P. MacMurphy

The Tramp

His hair is white his face is old
His clothes are grey with dust
He has no care for wealth or gold
He has the wanderlust

Through open fields and country trails
He passes by each hedge and brook
And when each day begins to pale
He finds a place to rest and cook

The cold and damp of each new day
Kept out by old torn clothing
Food caught from traps along the way
For modern living a total loathing

His only friend the wayside track
Will lead him on and on
'Til even that one friend will lack
His presence when he's gone.

Timothy M. Clegg

My Happiness

I'm all alone tonight, just thinking of you
I know it isn't right but what else can I do
You're always on my mind, you're there wherever I go
You are my life, my love, my darling, I love you so
I have no way with words, I never could express
The way I feel about you, you're simply my happiness

Patricia Todd

My Boy

There he stands all alone struggling to find a place called home
His mind is filled with deep despair
With strangers all around him, everywhere
Searching to find someone who will truly care
In time he'll grow into a man, and do with life the best he can,
But for now he'll bide his time this bright but shy boy of mine

A life at home is all he craves, family love is what he needs
He has to bare the problems we've got
And believe me, there are an awful lot
He's been pushed from pillar to post
Taken from me and his sisters both
This bright, but shy boy of mine

He is living in a land of fear
Not knowing where to turn and who'd be there
To love and to hold him and wipe away those tears
He had it all once and now it's lost
At to what price and at what cost

K. V. Hogwood

Rust

The rusted figured of a man sighs,
His mind infected with corrosive monotony.
Strands of frustration creep into him
Gently itching at his mind,
a constant reminder of his guilt.
He can no longer hide
Behind his bleached innocence.

The shiny metallic body before him lies loaded with intent,
Blow it all away and shatter the fallacy.

The heavily balanced trigger
Forced backwards.
The echo repeats,
Bouncing off these four walls
Again and again.

Within this destitute cavity,
He no longer hears the monotonous chimes
of his guilt polluted conscience.
He no longer feels the knots of anxiety urging him to lie.
He no longer fears the capacity of his own madness.
He has ceased to exist.

Karen Silverlock

Lonely Man

The stars that shine and twinkle
High in the dark night sky
Are like the tears that silently fall
From his weary eyes

Eyes are the windows to the soul
I heard somebody say..
His eyes, show many sorrows
That he's met along the way.

To the outside world, he laughs, he plays
But others don't see the damage
The loneliness he feels inside,
The doubt that he can manage

But I see his pain and feel it too
And I long to hold him close
To give him all the love I have
The very thing he needs the most...love!

Michelle Claydon

The Musician

He sits before them all alone,
His fingers gently touch the keys,
A hush falls at the first sweet tone;
Then a rustle as from trees.
Now from the hills in roll on roll,
Surges the mighty thunder;
It fills the air and stirs each soul
To awe and fear and wonder.
A lark in tones of rapturous glee,
Welcomes the sun to earth again.
He sings with throbbing melody
In scorn of fear and human pain.
His notes quiver and die away,
A few soft chords and all is done.
There comes a hush as at break of day
Before the rising of the sun.
He stands up then to face them all
The vision fades and earthly things
Return once more and then the hall
With loud applauding wonder sings.
Sheila Nankivell

Hair

Every hair is a lock
Every strand is a shock
From brown to Grey only
Age will show the shade of change, it may
It may because of varied hues
It may for bleach we ever use
All this stops the natural way
To colour grey without dismay
Pauline Will

The Tramp

His boots were once someone else's,
His clothes were tattered and torn.
The most striking thing in his whole get up
Was his funny old hat (Tricorn).

As he trudged along, with a shuffling gait,
Unaware of the bustling crowds,
He seemed to be in a world of his own,
With twinkling eyes, his hair windblown
And his trousers tied with string.

I looked once again at his weather beaten face
And saw such serenity and calm,
That I felt so ashamed
Of the way I complained
Of things that meant nothing at all.

So, I said to myself,
"Here's a man of great wealth
With nothing in cash or kind,
But the very best thing the world cannot give:
Wonderful peace of mind."
Mary Gardiner

A Little Orphan

A lonely girl sits by a stream,
Her eyes are sad as she sits and dreams,
She dreams of friends and pets and toys
Of games with other girls and boys.

Her mind wanders to a distant land
There's people dancing hand in hand,
She dances with her Mam and Dad
It's the happiest time she's ever had,

She has brothers and sisters and lots of friends
Dogs and cats and pigs and hens,
They go to the seaside and have such fun
With lemonade, ice cream and sticky buns,

That little girl then comes to life
There's none of these things in her life,
She's an orphan and always alone,
Please take this little girl, into your home
Sandra Thirkettle

Nightrider

No-one knows who he is, but they know
    Him by sight, his bike is big and black,
And makes an almighty roar
    The nightrider is known by all.

He helps people who are lost in the night,
    And gives directions to lonely truck drivers,
No-one ever sees his face as it is covered
    By his full-face black helmet.

Many people tried to run him off the road
    But the nightrider always won,
But then one night someone tried again
    They were well behind him!

Then out of the night came a dog
    The nightrider swerved to the side,
And before he could get back straight
    A truck came from the black.

There were bits of bike all over the ground
    And a body lay still,
Now on that lonely road you can still hear the roar
    Of the ghost of the Nightrider!!
K. Hammond

Is It True?

Is it true the smog of London
Hides the sky of blue my dove?
Tell me true. Is the grass there any greener
Than the grass in our backyard,
And are there rows of trees a-growing wild my love?

When night falls and you lie awake
What can you hear my sweet:
The leaves rustling, stirred gently by a soft summer breeze;
The crickets chirp, a barn owl's call?
Or the raucous clamour from the street.

Is it true there are parks a-plenty there
Where folks dare not walk at night:
Streets that stretch for miles and miles
Where the air is stale and no-one smiles?
And no-one cares whether you live or die.

Is it true the lights of London turn the night to day
To light the lonely traveller on his ways?
Do the buildings loom like giants
Do they hide the stars from view?
Then there's nought left to say my dear; I do not envy you.
C. A. Moggach

Untitled

Dear Freedom,
Hi, I'm sorry I haven't written in ages,
Had an essay to do, pages and pages.
A graph for Maths, learning for Latin,
A nightshirt for needlework made out of satin.

There's a couple of things I would like to say,
Like, how is your family, have you had a nice day?
But I haven't got time, dentist at three,
Life's full of hassle I wish I was free!

Life must go on and so must I,
But oh when I look at the birds in the sky,
Soaring and gliding, happy, carefree,
I think to myself I wish it was me!

I long for the summer's warm, hot days,
No science homework, no Shakespeare plays.
A large cool cocktail by the pool,
I'm only dreaming, what a fool!

I mustn't complain that I am not free,
After all there are worse off than me.
I am happy with family and friends,
But halfway 'round the world people's lives come to a miserable end!
Laura Cromer

A Whisper Away

I'm here, just a breath, a whisper away
Here at the start and close of your day,
Don't be afraid, don't fret nor grieve
I'm not far away I tell you - believe.

I'm in the wind stirring, a sigh through the trees
In foam crested waves even far out to sea,
Here in the heavens when you gaze at the stars
I may seem to you lost but I'm not very far,

You love and you loved me and for me you pray
I'm peaceful and happy and not far away
So let the tears flow then banish your sorrow,
It seems years to you, but I'll see you tomorrow.
Wendy A. Cudd

The Snowdrop Is Dying Now

The snowdrop is dying now,
He's taken his final bow.
He's gone all brown and dry,
The flower came to die.

The crown of thorns is still there.
Put by people who did not care.
"Crucify Him" we heard them call,
"Crucify Him on that cross so tall."

Jesus died in the place of a thief,
He disciples were overcome by grief.
"Forgive them" we heard him say,
"For I must rise on the third day."

Mary went to the tomb on the third day,
To her horror the stone had rolled away.
Two angels sat where her Lord had been,
Jesus was nowhere to be seen.

Mary turned away to cry
"Why, O why, did my Lord have to die!"
He had to die for mankind's strife,
and win for us Eternal Life
Rebecca Russell

A Son

What is a son, the boy, the man?
He's part of the pattern of God's Holy Plan.
Born to a Mother with a heart full of Love,
Given with pride from the Lord up above,
To hold and to cherish a child in her arms,
Protected, warm and safe from all worldly harm,
Slowly to grow to a boy full of fun,
Filling your heart with such pride in this son,
Who gives you his love with no thought of reward,
Filling each day with his laughter and charm,
Mischievous and naughty he sometimes can be,
But always he loves you, of this you can see,
Then the day comes along and you look with new eyes,
To see he has grown from a boy to a man,
Loving you still in his own special way,
His actions will tell you what he will not say,
And the love and the pride that within you will know,
That the boy and the man will still love you so.
V. Reid

Hard Times

I think so often we do not love enough,
her ourselves go; draw back, and stay the hand.
Throw all into the game, and risk our hearts
be brave, and take no thoughts for consequence.
What is it holds us back? The fear that it
will hurt too much to love,
then lose, feel real heartbreak,
yet that would totally enhance,
give shallow soul a stage
to act like Angels in a worldly dance.
R. A. Gardner

The Callers

Listen, we call you here from the woods,
   Here at the break of day.
Will you not come to the lonely call,
   Answer, and come to stay?

When the diamond drops of the morning dew
   Hang in the violet's heart,
we call again, as we called before
   Why are you loth to start?

We call yet again in the heat of noon
   From the bluebell-studded glade;
Come leave the cares of the mortal world
   And rest in the scented shade.

Often we called in the still of the night
   Through the tangled web of sleep,
When the far, far jewels of the distant stars
   Shine in the infinite deep.

Who are the callers, here in the wood,
   Morning and noon and night?
Who but the ghosts of the vanished years
   In their swift relentless flight.
D. Sherwin

Love After Dark

It's 9 o'clock and, finally, the children are in bed
Her "mummy" role is put on hold, other thoughts, go through her head
She tidies up the house a bit and packs the toys away
Then pours herself a nice long drink, she's had a busy day
She puts her favourite records on the music's soft and slow
Excitement starts to build inside, there isn't long to go
She hears his car pull up outside, he's here - her dream come true!
She hasn't felt like this for years, she's sure he feels it too
She opens the door silently and welcomes him inside
They both embrace so lovingly, their feelings cannot hide
They share each others warmth and touch, their cares all fade away
The love they make is magical, perfection all the way
Again time passes hurriedly, morning's here so fast
Reluctantly he has to leave - if only night could last!
Their goodbyes are made tenderly and all too soon he's gone
Uncertain when they'll meet again she hopes it won't be long
She breathes a sigh as, wearily, she lets the daylight in
The children will be waking soon, another day is to begin
As if on cue they both arise, they've had nice dreams they claim
No sandman's help for me, she mused, my own dream-maker came!
Kathryn Cook

Remembering Eveline

They said she had no quality of life
   her limbs were still, refusing to obey
the message from her brain. Her constant strife
   to make her body work, for this she'd pray.
But through the wearying months in vain she'd try
   to gain her independence, feed herself, persist,
but still for every action on others she'd rely
   for washing, eating, drinking, helpless to resist.

Was her life thus a useless entity,
   her being just a drain on social care?
Or was there something she could give society,
   something infinitely precious, just by being there?
Oh yes! I see her now, her happy face aglow
   with laughter and a merry quip, a wink.
An inner beauty with every smile, she'd show
   appreciation if one held a cup for her to drink.

Now she has gone where earthly ills are shed
   there is a void, a light extinguished there
Where once she lay immobile in her bed
   and we were privileged her life to share.
E. E. Martin

Lost Love

The Weeping Willow hangs her head
Her broken heart in two,
She looks so lonely standing there
Like me, when I lost you.

The Forget-me-nots are mocking me
Their tiny flowers look sad,
They seem to me to be calling out
"Remember the love you had"

The gentle rain cries silent tears
Upon each nodding bloom,
It echoes how my tears did fall,
During those days of gloom.

But old loves, just like flowers
Eventually fade and die
And hope springs from the darkest depths
Like seedlings reach for the sky.

Mary Meredith

The Light

The light at the end of the tunnel
Helps those depressed or sad
The light at the end of the tunnel
Makes our problems seem less bad
The light at the end of the tunnel
Helps the less brave be bold
The light at the end of the tunnel
Is hope for the young or the old
The light at the end of the tunnel
Helps to guide our way
The light at the end of the tunnel
Is the beginning of a new day
So if this light you fail to find
Dig deep and search your heart and mind
For the light at the end of the tunnel
Is beyond somewhere out there
If you search hard you'll find this light
And someone who really does care.

Samantha Jane Wood

The Lion

The sun glows across the open plain,
heeding the lion hunt for its game,
the lion it's still, tempting its prey
this relentless pattern he repeats everyday.

By the light he lies with his pride,
waiting for dusk, his time he does bide.
As once again darkness falls,
He moves for the scent of the tiger horse.

The quarry is tentative, as it feeds,
the lion attacks for want of his needs.
Gliding silently across the plain,
his prey's defences spoil his game.

M. Goodman

A Special Friend

He was a fireman, strong and tall, how my heart would flutter
when he'd call.
Hair as black as coal, could he see my very soul.
Brown eyes that shone so bright, they seemed to sparkle in the night.
Angry words he never uttered. Loving words he often muttered.
Lazy days in the sun, we always had a lot of fun.
Romantic evenings by the sea, he really cared for me.
Red roses by the score, the florist, was fed up delivering to my door.
Writing love letters in the sand, offering a wedding band,
for my hand.
He thought the world of me, it was plain, for all to see.
Then, one terrible night, the angels, brought a shining light,
they took him away from me, but, I'll always treasure, his memory.

Lyn Pickering

Winter Mist

She sits hunched and low in the straight backed chair,
Her head drooped forward perhaps lost in sleep,
The thin pink skin shines through the wispy hair,
Wrinkled stockings around her ankles creep.
Gnarled hands in her lap, they lie very still
With loose band of gold worn thin through the years.
She stirs, looking up and I think she will
Speak with me about her hopes and her fears
Of death, or perhaps much worse, living on.
But no, the old lined face and red rimmed eyes
Look blankly about. It's as though she's gone
From me. She becomes restless and then sighs
Till she settles with a look so sublime
I know she's passed into the mists of time.

Marjorie Haddon

The Passing

She was cold to the touch. I knew she was gone.
Her eyes dull and lifeless where once they had shone.
I should feel grateful - we've had twelve happy years
But it's no consolation and can't halt the tears.
It was instant attraction the moment we met.
We were soon as close as a couple can get.
She'd had a hard time - much sorrow and pain
To obliterate this was my primary aim.
It took time to break down the barriers around her
Gain her trust and respect, and with love to surround her.
We became constant companions, best friends and bed-mates.
Always true to each other through joys and heartaches.

I didn't know the pain would be this hard for me to bear.
In the mornings I still reach for her - in vain - for she's not there.
I have my memories of her - they will not be denied
The many wonderful years I've had with my dog close by my side.

Mary Andersen

A Daughter's Eternal Shame

My mother died five years ago
Her death was quick it was not slow
I had no chance to bid farewell
Nor thanks and love for her to tell

I last saw her lying still and cold
My chance to kiss, my arms enfold
I told her then of how I felt
As by her side I wept and knelt

The many things she had done for me
And all the love I could not see
For at the time she seemed unjust
But now - in her - I'd put my trust

I long now for the phone to ring
And down the line her voice to bring
And hear her say - just one more time
'It's Mum here' - that would be sublime!

I wish for all these things and more
My mum I ignored - like a selfish bore
For lack of gratitude I take the blame
It will stay forever - my eternal shame

Margaret Hartley

Life Line

A little bird high in my apple tree
he sang to me, Oh how he sang to me.
With fluffed out breast and warbling throat,
so sweet and clear, each and every note.

Birds must know sadness and still they sing,
lift up their hearts to what each new day brings.

My life was empty but he gave me hope,
no longer do I sit around - content just to mope.
I now have a purpose for carrying on,
each day a new day of laughter and song,
and all because he sang to me,
Oh! how he sang to me.

Patricia-Ann Peacock

Our Navigator

"He's the best we've had" the Captain said,
Hearing this, I turned my head,
"Can't find my pen, it was here before"
That man must be our navigator.

In him we trust, our lives depend,
His longs and lats he has to send,
Left and right, round and around,
His charts and maps are upside down.

"I think we're lost" was all he said'
I bit my lip until it bled'
We're on an island, let me check,
The craft is not a total wreck.

We've been here now for many years,
He won't give up, he perseveres,
Two of us left out of twenty-four,
That's me and our navigator.

Ten years on now I'm all alone,
Will he ever get me home,
I don't think so, you see he's dead,
"He's the best we've had" the Captain said.
A. Davis

Confronting The Inevitable

Jack saw the enemy approach,
Heard the cannon roar.
Was this now to be the end
So many battles won before.

He saw his friend fall at his side,
Held his dying hand.
Felt his death grip, saw his eyes,
Then left him lying in the sand.

The firing was much nearer now,
He thought of John and Ann and Beth.
They did not know and could not see.
How near their father was to death.

How far away the green of home,
The welcome of his mat.
The smell of supper on the stove,
The purring of the cat.

It was to protect his way of life
He stood and fought so hard.
But now he would lose it just the same.
As fate dealt out her final card.
Marian Jackson

Rainbow's End

Today I saw a Leprechaun
He was sitting on a wall
I didn't speak or wave to him
Scared that he might fall

He looked so colourful all dressed in green
A dashing little fellow
A little purse around his waist - and he wore a scarf of yellow
He began to dance, while humming a tune
Clapping his hands in the air

Till all the 'Little People' came - he had such a flair
'Be jeepers - Be gorrah' one and all
"Good evening - how do you do"
I have a little message - I have to pass it on to you

They say that at the 'Rainbow's End' there is a pot of gold
This is just a fairy tale - a tale that humans are told
But it's true - it's not a tale, it really does exist

It's way up high above the Rainbow - hidden in the mist
So remember people - listen well - keep it close to your heart
The pot of gold is not at the 'Rainbow's End' - it's at the
  Rainbow's Start!
Marilyn A. Ruse

The Poet

A sharp shiver of the October air runs down his back
He stands over the creaking floorboards of the old cottage he teeters
Stokes the fire and back he wobbles to his cushioned throne.
The old soldier looks out of his window and over the moors,
For a moment he watches the snow settle.
He casts his mind back over the years,
He recalls the harsh winter of '39.
His first of many others in a trench
"And for what", he thinks out loud
Glancing towards his medals on the wall.
He remembers the fighting, the bombs,
The screaming men and boys
As they awaited death at arm's reach......
The poet reaches for his pad,
For he now has his next poem.
Martin Ryan

The Tearaway

A tearaway, is what he is,
He really loves his bike, a whiz!
Scrambling up, then down, he twists and turns.
On undulating ground, it burns.
This vehicle's his challenge.
Never will beat him.
He's always in control
Of its every whim.
If he comes off, he'll rant and rave,
This machine he makes his slave,
His temper flares and sparks his fuse,
He's determined not to lose.
He's its master, rev's up faster,
Never fearing near disaster,
Boring is what some may say,
I think, exciting is his way.
His fortitude and daring,
I'm happy to be sharing,
Prejudiced is what I am,
'Cos I love him, he's my man.
Muriel Edna Owen

He

Revolution. Turns he over a card.
  He plays Fate's game.

Destruction. Turns he blind an eye.
  He will not see.

Rape. Turns he deaf an ear.
  He will not hear.

Anarchy. Turns he over his control.
  He takes no part.

Blasphemy. Turns he away to Eternity.
  He washes his hands.

Death. Turns he to After-life.
  He meets you there.

Questions. Turns he to answer. But.
  Only the dead understand.
Paul Akridge

"His Special Friend"

His fur is soft, his nose is warm,
  His eyes are bright and clear,
He sleeps so snug on bed or rug,
  And wishes she were here.

He waits so still, his eyes closed tight,
  And sleeps all day until it's night,
He longs to hear that sound once more,
  Of her key placed in the door.

And then he'll see her once again,
  The one he's missed for so long,
She's been away for such a while
  The one he loves - his special friend.
J. C. Giles

'Our Milkman'

Our milk is delivered by a milkman called Mick
He never lets us down and does his round quick
Sometimes you'll hear him, the other morning it was three
But every morning without fail, we've milk for our tea

His job is a job most people would hate
He never knows what's lurking behind your gate
I'd say that Mick puts his ass on the line
As his ass nearly 'Got it' the day he walked into mine!!

I apologize Mr. Milkman for your 'Run-in' last week
But really my 'Dog' wanted to play hide 'n' seek
I'm sure he must of gave you an awful fright
But really his bark is worse than his bite.

So cheers for delivering our milk once again
My 'Dog' has been ordered to stay in his den
I hope you've no more 'Run-in's and you're over your fear
As from now on I promise, the coast will be clear.
Marie Scott

Lion In A Cage

I saw a Lion in a cage,
He didn't roar, he didn't rage,
But couched in stately symmetry,
And robed in tawny majesty
He turned on me his topaz eyes
Serene and deep, and cool and wise,
And it seemed they held all mysteries
And lantern'd all philosophies.
Samuel Harry Bates

My Brother

Oh my dear brother he is so bold,
he never does what he is told,
if Mum says, "Have manners and sit on the chair,"
He'll, right away, jump up in the air.

If he goes to the shop he'd bring me along.
But when half way down, he'd do something wrong
Like steal my comb or pull my hair,
And I'd usually end up running home.

The way he dresses is something rare,
with red Doc Martin's and a ring in his ear,
Mum bought him new shoes and here's what he said;
"Hope you kept the receipt or are they paid?"

He may crack a joke with Mum or me,
Then leave us laughing and in stitches we'd be,
but what can I do, he's the only one I've got,
Down deep in my heart I love him a lot.
Karen Friel

The Widower

The old man pauses in the park
He looks up to the sky
He fills his pipe and strikes his match
Then asks the question - Why?
Why do I have to be alone
With people smiling all around
Why do I feel so all alone
And then he looks down at the ground
He looks at every flower
And knows their names by heart
Because he is a gardener
So he can play the part
But outside of the park gates
When he's walking slowly home
His pipe goes out, his shoulders stoop
He knows he is alone
Well over fifty years ago
He took a lovely bride
They lived, they loved, they had three sons
And just last week, she died.
J. Taylor

The Alcoholic

He shuffles along a lonely road,
his bed under his arm, with nowhere to go,
his eyes red, his mind is blurry,
he stumbles and falls, and cries like a child.
People go past, what do they care?
With lives of their own
And someone to share,
but that lonely old man, without a friend,
just lies there and whimpers
It must be the end.
Somewhere inside that muddled mind,
a flicker, a memory of a time
When he laughed and sang, and played and romped, with a little girl,
But where has she gone?
Life was empty, he needed a friend.
With no one to turn to, but just one thing,
with shaking hands he holds it tight,
to find a corner for the night.
The world goes by, what do we care,
About the little old man just lying there.
E. Gibbons

The Journey Of A Lifetime

Small and restricted in the womb
He felt the need to be free
The tunnel stretches before him
And he is pushed towards the light he sees

As he arrives he is helpless
But he grows stronger with the years
Soon he finds love and happiness
Along with many fears and tears

He soon has children of his own
He watches over them as best he can
Until the time that they have grown
And the years have made him weak again

The children have now left home
And his wife grows as weak as him
He knows he faces now the tomb
But the light is still quite dim

The tomb restricts and he feels small
But the tunnel stretches before him
This is how he began it all
And again he finds his freedom.
Kerry Jones

Love?

God gave the gift of love to man
He didn't teach him how,
To cope with all it did entail,
Learning came with the pace of a snail.
But when He found the joy of love
Could change his lonely life.
He used his skills in many ways
To find himself a wife.

He then found coping harder still.
With troubled mind and heart,
He tried to understand his spouse,
But couldn't even start.
He'd think he had the answer,
And joyously resound.
To alter ways and love her true.
But suddenly it all turned round

God gave the gift of love to man.
He wished he'd take it back.
It would make life much easier
If he could give his wife and sack.
B. L. Jones

Ode To Frankie

"Have you touched the cloak of God's Great Kingdom?"
"Have you seen the splendour, that only Angels see?"
"Is that why you sit in silence, unable to utter a word to me?"
"Days into months, months into years, we've learned how to tackle our stresses and fears."
"From childhood into Manhood we've watched you grow, and where do you drift to we'll never know?"
"What do you dream of, what do you see?"
"Do you hold photographic memories, of your Dad and Me?"
"No chance of romance?"
"No bands of Gold?"
"No gift of a Grandchild for us to hold?"
"But such things are trivial in life's domain,
we've seen more sunshine than dark day of rain."
"We love you Son and always will, and hope the World you live in is peaceful tranquil and still."

Robert Cole

My Sense Of God

Have you heard the thunder of the sea?
Have you heard the rustle of the leaves on a tree?
Then you have heard God.

Have you glimpsed the smile on a baby's face?
Have you seen a cobweb that's finer than lace?
Then you have seen God.

Have you felt the tender touch of a mother's love?
Have you stroked the feathers on the back of a dove?
Then you have felt God.

Have you smelt the perfumer of the rose?
Have you tasted food when hunger goes?
Then you had a taste of God.

Have you been touched by healing hands?
Be they a woman's or a man's.
Then you have been touched by God.

Kathleen McManus

Tree Feelings

Oh! I have just hit the ground, it's a good job I am small and round.
Have rolled quite away, so now I will have to stay.
Will sleep for awhile, dream of what I may be.
Nestling in my little bed, leaves lie around me, they are dark, brown and red.
Many days when it's nice and warm, my roots are growing from dusk till dawn.
I could not see much at all, just can not see over a wall.
Creatures came and looked at me, said (lovely little tree).
Winter times are very cold, icy winds blow, scattered all over me is snow.
Welcoming in the spring, hearing the song birds sing.
Over the years I am standing tall, I can now see over that wall.
Crocuses are at my base, snow drops too, look beautiful covered in dew
My leaves are bursting into bloom, for birds as well there's plenty of room.
My bark is sturdy, branches reaching to the sky, I know I am a tree,
I thank God on high, for making me.

J. Hagger

Fred The Bassett Hound

Everyone loves Fred the hound, a big soft lump who's close to the ground,
His ears are huge and drag in the dirt and when he's excited he's inclined to squirt.
He looks at you with doleful eyes and runs like he clappers when a female he spies.
His legs are stumpy, his body plump and he takes offence when called a chump.
The gardens a mess, he's ruined the lawn, he's a true tricolour - black, brown and fawn.
He flops on the furniture, sleeps on the bed, you can't help but love him because he's our Fred.

J. Chisholm

Problems

When the problems of today,
Have been forgotten and gone away,
We can look back and think,
What was it that caused our hopes to sink,

When the stresses of tomorrow,
No longer cause us pain and sorrow,
We can look to ourselves inwardly,
Then surely we will start to see,
That all the stress and all the pain,
Was meant to be for us to gain,
The strength and light of immortality,
That lies within both you and me,

When we can learn to accept,
That man should have really wept,
When he decided that he, amongst all things,
Would be above the destruction that he brings,
He was given the right for man to last,
But he lost this way back in his past,
He lost his soul and his heart,
He had lost them both right from the start.

S. Ford

The Awakening

The darkness that covered my life and my soul
has gone and the light shines through.
The weight of my world is lighter now,
My eyes see clear and new.
Night holds no fear of what the morning will bring.
And the day isn't a load on my mind.
And I looked and I searched, till I realized.
I'd thrown away what I was trying to find.
It was there all the time in front of my eyes
I was blind and I couldn't see.
So full of myself and no one else, surrounded by only me,
I knocked and a door was opened,
The door that I closed myself.
I sought to find what I'd left behind.
Right there on the shelf.
Simple things of love and peace.
They can't be bought for gold.
A sheep got lost, but love tracked it down,
And returned it to the fold.
I was asleep and dead to all the world.

Laurence McKee

My Trip To Wig-On

I must tell you about something that
Happened on the bus today
There was an old man
With an ill-fitting toupee

There was such a commotion
He caused such a fuss
When he sneezed
And sent it flying down the bus

One old lady went hysterical
She thought it was a gerbil
They tried everything to calm her down
From Barley sugar, to something herbal

She tried hitting it with her brolly
Which I thought quite funny
I really think my bus fare
Was well worth the money

The poor old Gentleman apologised
To the lady for her scare
And when he finally left the bus
His poor old head was bare.

Sarah Stubbs

The Swing

The swing beneath the apple tree
hangs empty and still.
Its ropes could bear no more a child's weight
and are beset with damp and rot
but it matters not
for the child has gone
departed long ago
from this loved spot.
The grass that grew beneath the tree
has seeded fresh.
For once it had been trodden bare
and always there would seem to be
a paler patch
where little feet
had swept and scratched
along the ground.
High in the branches of that gnarled old tree
I hear the echoes sound
echoes of laughter and childish glee
from the child who was you and a part of me...

Ruth Kennedy

Elizabeth The Second

Many long years we've served under kings
Great kings have reigned in our time,
They've served us well as we have them
Now England has a Queen in her prime.

England's young Queen served us well
As a princess so fair in her teens,
Has risen to be our sovereign lady
Elizabeth the Second, England's Queen.

With royal greetings she received us
Her subjects loyal and true,
To serve her in her time of reign
Elizabeth, our best respects to you.

To all who live within her realm
In England's great empire,
To serve them both in years to come
Both Elizabeth and her sire.

From the golden throne she's crowned
And her royal standard is cast,
She's proclaimed Elizabeth the Second
England's Queen until last.

Merlin Parrington

The Pictures Within

Cracked and shattered picture frames
Hang from crooked hooks on the wall
The tattered state of the picture within
Brings back the memories of it all

Cracked and shattered pictures frames
Just waiting to fall apart
The sadness of the pictures within
Produce the mirror image of my heart

Memories of the precious times
That I was once proud to put out on show
But now those pictures are tattered and torn
Something tells me now it's time to let go

Memories are such a powerful thing
And sometimes they can hold you down
As the pictures finally fall from their hooks
I see my memories just crash to the ground

With broken glass across the floor
I begin to put things back together
Cracked and shattered picture frames can soon be replaced
But my memories will be in this state forever

Martin Tranter

Life

As we walk, down the pathway, of life,
Hand in hand, husband and wife,
Seen lot's of happiness, joy, sorrow and pain.
Walked, with our children, down this, same leafy lane
boys, who have, grown up to be men,
They walk now, with their children, hand in hand.
Down life's long lane,
Seen season's come and go.
Leaves turn, red, brown, yellow, and gold.
With many shades of green.
Life's, like a picture book,
to turn page, by page, each day
But what I like the best
sit back, and take a rest.

D. Sharp

Soul Of My Father

Rain falls on autumn leaves that gently
glide through rays of sunshine, flowing
streams sparkle reflecting light that
awakes you and I. The sounds of birds
singing that morning has arrived and
darkness is but a dream that is
scattered in drops of tears which fall
on the earth to enrich souls of a new
journey that awaits us all.

Peter Head

Me Granddad's Prize Shallots

On either side the garden lie,
Great rows of spuds that caught the eye,
And oft you'd hear me granddad cry
'Just look at my shallots'.

Tomatoes ripened, neighbours whispered
You'll never find a lettuce crisper
Me gran complained that when he kissed her
He shouted "that's shallot".

He took 'em to the village show
And said, "that's how shallots should grow
But how it's done you'll never know
'The secret of shallots'.

His secret he would never tell
And probably it's just as well
'Cos none could ever stand the smell
Of granddad's prize shallots.

And now me granddad's dead and gone,
His secret he did not pass on,
He never told a single one,
Just how he grew shallots.

Kerry Kinch

The Last Puff

Is this to be my last cigarette?
Good job I bought twenty,
Didn't want to give up just yet,
Made sure that I had plenty.

Dreading the time when there are none,
But then, I'll feel healthy and good,
"Talk to your friends on the phone,"
Or "raid your fridge for the food."

But then when the deed has been done,
You feel so fidgety and broody,
And when you think it's your last one,
You become exceptionally moody.

Don't the medics know that it's hard,
It's not as easy as they say,
Told my loved ones, "Be on your guard,"
Or else there'll be hell to pay.

Sue Butcher

Going Home

Going home I am going home
gonna stop myself from roam cause I am going home

Well I packed all my bags ain't got nothing to lose
going home to the place that JAH choose
gonna find me a dance late night blues
gonna find a girl and take her for twos

Moving back to inner city where there is less iniquity
man it's hard to find a friend with some honesty
in a town like this one specially

Going home I am going home
gonna stop myself from roam cause I am going home

So now I am here I went on a detour
but it's all over now and that's for sure
right here is where I am staying so baby what you saying

Gonna check out my good friend Jonny Brown
gonna go uptown and settle down
gonna work in this town and earn some pound and
I went to school I didn't play the clown

I am going home I am going home
gonna stop myself from roam cause I am going home
T. C. Fears

Why

The summer air ably found its way though the green and golden reeds,
The smell of the farmers' fields were carried in the warm air,
And the smell of the rape seeds,
Reeked out of the fields as if they were an oil or gas,
The rain which had fallen in the past days was bubbling
as if it were a boiling kettle,
A lady bird flew by as proud as anything could be and landed on a nettle,
A lady was walking with a straw hat on with a stick and golden hair,
And she sighed and said, "What's happened, who cares?"
In days to come this wonderful secret place was to be destroyed,
Tractors would come a-digging as if they were big toys,
Yet for this place no one would fight,
fight for this beautiful sight,
Then she fought and fought for the place and air,
She really did, yes really cared,
She saved the place and all was well,
A secret place for no one to tell.
Karen Jane Waite

Purely Divine

Lend me your heart, just for a while
Give me the flash of your beguiling smile
Lend me your time, let's make it ours
Just offer me love that never sours.

Hold onto your dreams lest they pass you by
Give me your spirit and watch my heart fly.
Share with me your secrets, let them be mine
Show me a love that's purely divine.

Share with me tenderness, lasting and true
Keep showing me reasons why I keep loving you,
Step into my arms and capture my heart
And stay with me darling, never to part.

I'll give you my heart, my love and my life
My secrets are yours, now we are husband and wife,
My thoughts are of you, my time is yours
You've captured my heart with feelings unforced.

Meanwhile we'll hold onto our dreams, lest they pass us by
We'll share in one spirit, and watch our hearts fly
My secrets are yours, what's yours is now mine
Cos we've found a love that's purely divine!
Sue Butler

Winter Moon

The coal fire burns in the heart,
From it flames leap bright and high,
Casting pictures round the room,
And outside the snow shines,
From the light of the winter moon.
Looking out of the window, you can see
The flowers beginning to grow.
Their buds will soon burst,
Into colourful bloom.
Then the snow will melt and thaw,
No longer to shine
From the light of the winter moon.
Ronald Findlay

Autumn

Autumn colours bright and beautiful
Golden leaves fall light and wonderful

Carpeting the path as I walk along
Filling my heart with happy song

They crackle and crunch beneath my feet
Along the sidewalk of the street

Making me want to dance and sing
About the magic and wonder that Autumn doth bring

Crimson berries adorn bush and tree
Making a glorious sight to see

Bobbing and dancing on heavy laden trees
Gleaming like jewels in the Autumn breeze

Foretelling that winter will be long and cold
Warning the animals to prepare in tenfold.
Millicent Boal

Early Morning

Mist-like a milky gossamer veil
Hanging across the ground and over the dale
Ghost-like figures of trees dressed in mystic finery
Standing straight and proud, a living history.

Not a sound can be heard
Not a sign of animal or bird
Early morning in the forest is quiet and still
Except the constant tapping of the rill.

An awesome vision seen by few
Until the rays of the sun break through
Then as if by magic the shroud is lifted
Colours emerge as the light is sifted.

Dew glistening like sprinkled diamond beads
On bushes, grasses, cobwebs and trees
With an unseen conductor birds begin their song
Encouraging the new day along.
Marilyn A. Hounsome

A Radio

Alas, my life is oh so sad,
Here I sit, not inclined to move,
People make me really mad,
Just switch me on, and I will prove
My huge capacity to soothe.

My enemy the T.V. set
Seems always to be blaring,
While here neglected, I would bet
That you have just stopped caring,
I feel so helpless, stranded, staring.

In times gone by, there was only me,
The centre of attraction, I seemed to be,
Plays and drama, music and news,
Even people singing the blues,
Switch me on and then you'll see
How sweet I am, in comforting thee.
M. Woodcock

S-Word Play

Silver steel flashes in the sun
Glittering arcs dance to a deadly tune
Life or death is held in perfect balance
By the razor sharp musical perfume.

All eyes watch the circling rivals
Engaged in a subconscious battle trance
Fluid motion attacks turned back by deadly ripostes
Both of equal skill, same defiant stance.

Time waits patiently as the fighters forge on
Creating a breath taking display
Each man a legend in the making
Unparalleled speed, the princes of the day.

Limbs soon tire as the sun sets
A break is decided to give each a rest
The outcome then settled in words not swords
No need for a life to be put to the test.
Neil Gould

Seven Pairs Of Eyes

Seven pairs of eyes,
Gleaming bright,
Staring intensely,
The small king lies helplessly in a rotten cot,
No crying,
No mewing,
Just the smell of incense,
And the hot breath which roams the musty air,
The animals murmuring and breathing,
The hot air being sprayed onto the baby king Jesus,
Lying helplessly in his straw and makeshift cot.
Thomas F. Morgan

Bedsit

I lifted the lids of my eyes yesterday
Glazed by too many Sunday nights
Surrounded by thoughts of the darkest ones
Enveloped by the grimmest sights
As I walked towards the cupboards then
I tripped on Thursday's dreams
The mist that was three weeks ago
Does the dusting as it cleans
Give me the strength to smoke this day
Into the past with all my hopes
The wallpaper looks sick of where it's been
The bedspread coughs and chokes
I swore to myself I would sell my soul
For a chance to escape his hell
How long is a day and when is next week
Don't ask me I cannot tell
Blacked out is where I'll be one day
To surf the dusty skies
I see this place is what pumps my heart
And the lids close on my eyes
Robert Hughes

Glad For Sleep

Glad to touch your about, where I'm within
Glad of your advancing, so now I'll be given
Glad for you're coming down, so smother and take
Glad of your return, to nightly snug out my wake
   All-surrendered, wide open at pleasure of sleep
Glad in this shimmering, till morning I'll keep.

Glad for this sapping, so soon the man you take
Glad that you'll have mine, render me all your sake
Glad of your ensemble, the lulling strings and their swooping aroma
Glad I'm the one to regain into this surest dark-coma
   When gaping I am gilled with a wonder that's all of sleep
Glad for this inkling, till the morrow she'll keep.
Nick J. Boocock

Untitled

Boom Boom Boom
God what's that,
Boom Boom Boom,
It's the neighbours from hell.

What shall I do,
I switch on the light,
Look at the time,
It's almost light 3 o'clock in the morning
Damn, it's the neighbours from hell.

The music so loud
please God make them go,
Head under pillows quilt on top,
please o please make them stop,
It's the neighbours from hell.

I feel so ill,
Head pounding stomach churning
It's all so draining
But wait, what this quiet at last
Back to sleep for me
Those neighbours from hell.
Leeanne Shires

Bill Hicks R.I.P.

Don't sing me words of hearts and flowers
Give me verses to crack the ivory towers.
Teen-age angst I just don't need
I want your words to cry and bleed.
Don't rap me a rap of political stances
Rhyme me a rhyme of drug-induced trances,
Your folk-sing pose just isn't art
Don't tease my soul, RIP out my heart.
I spit on your lyrics of technical wit
Yet worship the sonnet that stinks of the pit,
I need you to suffer. To sweat and to choke
Then to kick-out screamings at this musical joke.
Your thoughts are like bullets from a toy-gun
Instead of like lasers from a dying sun,
So cry for the child brought up on this crap
There is no remission from mediocrity tat!
For Keith and for Miles for Kurt for Sid
For Jimi for Janis view a coffin lid
You spend your eternity in a deep dark hole
While plucking the strings of my deep dark soul.
P. M. Roche

Healing Waters

Healing waters from the heart of the motherland,
Give life to a sea of barren desert sands.
Valleys hills mountains and plains,
A paradise of colour in the forests of rain.

Springs from wells within,
Form rivers of nourishment for your kingdom and kin.
Seeds absorb you germinate and grow,
Into mighty trees and soft perfumed flowers,
In the lush grasslands below.

Gentle yet strong are you,
From the raging rapids and breath taking waterfalls
To the fresh morning dew.

Healing waters quench the thirst,
In man's drought of harmony,
Concerning the last and the first.
And to labourers of an entangled vine,
May they see healing waters.
Pure source of the wine.
Peter A. Jones

Heart Ache

My heart is like an empty hole, I have nothing left to
give. In time I may learn to love again, but for now
I am learning to cope with this new terror that I have found.
It lurked in the shadows of the heart, waiting to pounce
on the unsuspecting person. This terror that I am, experiencing
is called heart ache.
The love that I found I thought I would keep, but as
usual I have lost what is most dear. Every time I
love someone I lose her, and every time it gets harder to lover again.
I wish I could find someone special that loves me and I love them.
I do not want anymore distress in my life. I have lode
my fare share. Let someone else get the bad luck instead of me.
I have so much to write but where to begin. So many
unhappy thoughts trying to break out. all I wish to
do now is sit drink, and smoke and then leave this world
to the one I knew before.

Reece Bigwood

A Message In A Bottle

A man was walking along the beach,
Getting a breath of fresh air.
His eyes caught the gleam of a bottle,
At this he began to stare.
With sea water he filled the bottle,
Right up to the very brim.
Replaced the cork, cast it in the sea,
Oh so very far from him,
Now look, the sea is in the bottle,
The bottle is in the sea.
So, if I be in the Lord Jesus,
Then Jesus shall be in me.

Bill Going

Cri De Coeur

"A garden is a lovesome thing,
God wot!..."
The poet said.
It's not.

The thistles prick, the nettles sting,
My hands drip red;
The 'lovesome' roses claw my arms
And rip my dress;
They con me with perfidious charms.
I look a mess.

There's been no rain for weeks and weeks.
(The weeds look fine).
The watering can's developed leaks.
The garden line
Marks where I sowed the carrot seeds;
No germination!
(I wonder what that poet reads for relaxation?)
I've had my fill of gardening, God wot.
"A garden is a lovesome thing..." what rot!

E. M. Perry

Childhood

Skipping in the street
Games of hide and seek
Conkers from trees
Scabs on both knees
Marbles for swaps
Penny sweets in the shops
As children we knew how to play
Not like the vandals, called youth of today
Machines are needed to excite their brains
Not sitting in a box, playing at trains
Imagination took us far away
We didn't have computers or walkmans to play
But we knew the joy of making a den
Cowboys and Indians, ambush at ten
Children today, lose the magic we knew
Once past 5, they need a V.D.U.

Sue Harper

The Shirt

It lays upon the bedroom floor
Gets kicked about for days
If it goes into the basket
He will get lots of praise

It's chucked into the basket
With all the dirty stuff
Then in comes mum to sort it
She really does get tough

It's thrown down stairs with all the whites
And in the drum it goes
Will it be ready for tonight
Well only heaven knows

Around the drum the washing goes
The washer does work hard
A tangled mess, it's nearly time
To hang it in the yard

Upon the line the washing blows
It really has come white
With a little ironing
It will look just right

Terry Mayfield

"Graceland"

There was a lot of talk in town that this young performer was
gonna get far. He was groomed from an early age to be a star.

His first recording was in 1954, and all the airwaves were
jammed with requests for more. He married his teenage
princess witnessed by hundreds of admiring guests.

He was soon known all over the world as the king by millions
of fans who worshipped him, puttin' other rockers like Bill
Haley and the Comets in the shade. It wasn't long before the
legend was made

And as a result of his overnight fame he was never out of the
news. He always performed on stage with his customary white
outfit guitar and blue suede shoes.

At his shows the majority of the girls used to end up screaming,
spending most of their lives constantly dreaming.

His manager Colonel Parker was overwhelmed by all his
success, and with shrewd handling his prized asset would
always impress.

He moved to a home called Graceland in Memphis Tennessee
in a beautiful mansion in the country. Elvis soon made his
fortune with millions of record sales, but sadly was soon to go
off the rails.

With many reports of drug abuse and sleeping pills, his
sadness the pressure would reveal. And his tragic death was
a shock, at the young age of only forty-four, and was
shrouded in mystery and suspicion all the more.

Otis Blackwell who wanted to put the record straight and right
all the wrongs, in an autobiography called "These Are My Songs".

Vicas L. Bailey

Winter Trees

Trees, standing bare of leaves,
gently cry, crystal tears that visibly
grow longer and fall to the ground from
the morning rain. The wind blows their
branches to and fro, and in the winter days
of silence, all nature stands alone in
mother earth's time of sleep and death,
trees await the time of spring buds,
alone they stand, only a host of crows
cawing above, mixed in with screaming
immigrant seagulls, twirl 'round in the
sky above, whilst man sits by his fire
with his dog, tucked away from winter's cold.
The trees face winter's cruel
elements and sadly await a better day.

Laurence Wood

Creation

Life is one long contradiction
Full of purpose undisclosed
Freedom valued by restriction
Love revealed and hate exposed
Light by darkness complimented
Happiness by grief enhanced
Villainy with force presented
Virtue's cause the more advanced
Pain increases joy or pleasure
Black by white is emphasized
Poverty is riches measure
Bad is good when analyzed
Peace retained when strife engendered
Weakness lends support to strength
All is gained by all surrendered
Reason yields to truth at length.

Maurice W. Howard

"If I Were Blind"

If I were blind, my world would be,
Full of darkness and misery?
My family and friends would just be voices,
My life would change, fewer choices.
My hopes and dreams that I once had.
Will have disappeared, I would be sad.
Colours I could no longer see,
Only memories to help me.
If I didn't have those I wouldn't cope,
I'd have nothing to see, I'd lose all hope.
But lucky for me, I am able to see,
And was able to write this verse of poetry.

Neil Kelly

The Wind Of Love

With a heart and soul we are born to love,
From those who bore us we receive much love.
Loved and yet we take it for granted.
I search for love.
Other people, Love has found.
I need love, I want to be loved.
But I cannot find Love and Love can't find me.
Love is like the wind, I can't see it:
The effects of it, I can see.
Bringing smiles to faces and songs to the heart.
Even the wind blows around me,
Blowing my hair and causing a shiver,
As I shiver, so my heart grows cooler.
I follow Love, yet I can't catch Love,
Or, do I run so fast that Love can't catch me?
I need to be loved, I want Love.
Nobody can tell me where to find love.
So alone I search for the love that will not find me.
I call to the wind to bring me Love.
The wind does not answer me.

Mandi J. Lochead

Dunnhill

Poor little Dunnhill, our puppy dog
He looks awful funny, when he goes for a jog
With a little tiny head, and a lions mane
Crooked back legs and his tail's the same

By the fire he lies, on his back, like a sheep
With his mouth wide open, although he's asleep
He's an amorous dog, he likes to be kissed,
when he's hungry, he'll bring you his dish

He yowls and cries when you put him out
He thinks he is human, of that there's no doubt
In fact he's quite clever he'll go to the shop
With his bag and note and off he'll trot

He's a lovely little dog, all golden like honey
And I wouldn't change him for love nor money
He's misshapen, and backward and floppy eared too
But we all love him, and so would you.

Margaret Jean Yates

Migrating Words

When sorrows press, I cannot turn away
from shapes and sounds of words
for like migrating birds,
their measured flight, their studied cries
impress
a form upon the anguished gape
of feeling rioting inside
the deathly cold they've left behind.

Some say that words
are helpless to express
the weight of grief in men,
its dark unutterableness,

and yet I think of birds
migrating to a warmer land
in search of light and nourishment.
Do not fail me, words,
don't abnegate all grief and pain
but, like migrating birds, return
this spring and build
your fertile nests again.

Margaret A. Valk

Perfect Creation

Why does the sea change its form
From raging waves as in a storm
To smoothly calm and serene
When hardly a ripple is seen?
Why do some birds at times
Fly south to warmer climes
But some remain, in many ways
To cheer us up on darker days?
Why do some flowers of different hue
Bloom, then fade when each is due?
Why do leaves wither, but not all
For some remain green and do not fall?
Why does planet earth remain in place
Whilst many stars do change and race?
God's plans for mankind are always good
Although not always understood.

C. J. Partington

Life

Is this how it's going to be?
From now on for you and me.
We used to be so full of life,
Now it's full of trouble and strife.

Our time together was full of fun,
But then we had only just begun.
False attitudes, things to impress,
And look at us now, we're one big mess!

Mortgages, bills, loans and debts,
Life is one long list of regrets.
Nothing to be proud of, no feeling good,
Things never turn out the way they should.

No spare cash, working just to survive,
No wonder it's hard to keep our love alive.
No more good times, only bad,
What happened to the nice times we once had?

But we mustn't give up, we must plod on,
And one day our troubles will have gone.
Once again it will be like it used to be,
Only good, happy times for you and me.

Tracy McFall

Alone

The night is grey, I'm far away
from human beings, and where animals stray,
The days are short, the night's so long,
Being alone is not for anyone.

Please hold me close and for so long,
Because now you're here and then you're gone,

I prey thee Lord if I shall fall,
Promise me You will keep my soul.

If I see the light, I will follow,
No more breaths, no time to swallow.
I see the flashers of my life, no more
Sorrow, no more strife.
It's now the time to say good-bye,
Please my darling, don't you cry.

Terri Midgley

Freedom

I wonder what it is like to be free
Free as a bird, as the sky, as the sea
It must be wonderful to be able to go
To just suit yourself, just go with the flow

Freedom is many things to many men
Freedom for me is release from my pen
To do the things I want for me!
To be myself alone, just me!

Death is freedom, by why wait 'til then
Life is for living when freedom's a yen
Freedom's for anyone willing to be
Take courage to reach for it
Shake your own tree!

So let freedom come in
Let go of the past
Take your life back!
Live in freedom at last.

Leonora Ball

Friends

Friends are there when you need shoulder cry on
Friends are there to give you a helping hand
Friends are there to look out for each other
and also to laugh and cry together.

Some friends are there went things are good.
Some friends are there just to annoy you
Some friends are there just to split up good friendship
but some friends are there to see you through the good and
bad times.

There also those who laugh and chat with you but behind your back
the drive a stake through your heart.
There are some who will lead you up the garden path.
There are some who will give you the push in life and help
you climb the ladder.
There are some also will help you at first, but instead step all
over you before they give you a hand.

Lorraine Adams

The Dead Mill

Yeah though I walk a factory floor, I fear no ill
For this grease sodden floor, was once a prime mill
Stood in this room were, ten or more weavers
Beside five labourers, all busy as beavers

Opening a door to a silence so deadly
Previously full of machines, which sang a medley
Once contained wool, noil, yarn and weft
Cats who lived here free, now nothing left

No noise, no spools, no cloth, no hooter for tea
What's left is sadness, cobwebs, rats and me
Over lookers, spinners, warpers too, all gone away
Now here come the bulldozers, to flatten this display.

J. R. Nash

Seasons

The first rose of summer
Fresh picked strawberries and cream
A field of waving golden corn
Sunshine sparkling on a stream
Autumn leaves falling from the trees
Red and yellow and gold
They lay like a carpet at our feet
Alas they will soon turn to mould
Winter then is thrust upon us
Wind and rain and snow
Hurrying home to toast by the fire
Warming hands and feet in the glow
The new awakening that is Spring
Soft breezes and gentle rain
Buds just waiting to burst with colour
The world is reborn once again.

J. Allen

Thoughts

I listen to the lonely rain
Forever falling, plinking, plonking.
Reflecting on life - again.
How amazing at how many days, passing -
Feeling it's time to write - again!!

It was dawn, light creeping
Turns the square 'round my curtains
Into a room.
Grey, lazy light of late October,
Days getting shorter, me shrivelling.

Yesterday the seagulls landed -
Visitors at last!
I've always wanted to live in the woods
Friend to all creatures that hide from the rest.
Childish dreams. Fantasy world!

P. Hogg

Untitled

So close! Not even a whisper away. A vibration only. A few
moments' fragrance. Yet so strong, so very real. Like the
sweetest oranges, yet more like flowers' scent. If oranges
were flowers this is how they would smell. I cannot touch, nor
feel, nor hear, nor taste; yet this vibration fills me
some times for long, lovely moments; others for but a micro-
second of time. It is not his ghost, nor a memory - even these
are too tangible.
I can only believe that the essence of his love remains. That
the very nature of this man lingers to touch me in rare, quiet
moments with the gift of purest fragrance.
I know then with blissful certainly that he has not left me.
That his spirit waits for mine somewhere near. And I am content.

Valerie Durham

School Holidays

The holidays have just begun,
Four kids at home, that should be fun.
They'll be yelling and screaming all day long,
No rest for me, it's like an everlasting unmelodious song.
When will they learn to behave like children should?
In the old days when I was a kid everyone would,
We played peacefully together without a sound,
Apart from when we played with Barney, my beloved hound,
But that was then and this is now.
Why did those days have to change?

A week to go, I'm going mad,
This is the worst holiday I've ever had.
What happened to my husband? Where could he be?
The kids are sending me delirious can't you see,
What these kids are doing to me?

My husband is back, he'll be able to hack it,
Just call me Moses and stick me in a strait-jacket.
Send me to a mental home, see if I care,
At least it will be quiet and peaceful there.

Kelly-Marie Wood

Some Tea For A Tramp?

I answered the tramp who knocked on the door.
From behind me the priest said: "Give them no more".
A shiver went down my spine as I saw him there;
Cold and hungry and lost and all alone, but I had to say "No".

A staggered BUT was all he said,
When the Men of God turned him away.
"Sorry" said I, closing the door quickly:
just to hide my deistic embarrassment,
and turned to see my rectors embarrassed smile.

A hollow CLOMP, CLOMP of boots
followed him down the stairs.
He turned by the lavish primrose bush,
turned up his collar, looked towards the rain,
and wandered on, still cold and hungry.

Then the rector, the Man of God,
made his way back to his cocoa and video,
Whilst I recalled Christ's Gospel:
"Lord, when did we see you hungry or naked?"
And I felt a deep sense of loss,
for Christ had visited us, and left us.

Michael Feeley

Egryn, North Wales

Washing the pebbles, talking through the leaves,
Fresh from the mountain top, rushing down to the sea;
Heather and gorse vie with fern for a refreshing drink,
Time matters not as the river runs free.

In the distance a sheepdog obeys a whistled command;
Sheep, startled, on their spindly legs move down the fern-clad hill.
The hum of a tractor in the farmyard below,
While the mountain stream bubbles and rushes at will.

Wind swirling, buzzard soaring, high up above;
Storm clouds gather in a sky moody blue;
Night falls o'er the mountain, all seems so still,
But the river still dances and rushes on through.

Filling ditches and gullies, mountain pools and lakes,
Black clouds let fall their life-giving rain;
Drops racing and dancing as they fall ever downward,
Down from the mountain top to the plain.

Water washing pebbles, talking through the leaves,
Nature rules supreme in her glorious magical way;
Time matters not as season follows season,
And the river runs free each and every day.

Wendy J. Wearing

Remembering Those Who Have Gone

I went there that summer's day, to another era far away,
Forgotten lives and dusty streets, where antecedents went to meet.
I saw them there in my mind's eye, I saw their tears, I watched them
cry at poverty and hopelessness, their lives a most demanding test.
The mossy walls, the blackened doors, I compared to barren moors,
The windows cracked, the turrets bent, their lives could not be
  decadent.
The railway arches tell their tales, they hear the moans, the cries,
  the wails.
The steam has gone from ancient trains, but smoke has left its
  soot remains.
I saw the children at their play, long ragged clothes were in their way.
A baby balanced on the hip of mothers, stooped and down of lip.
In me, there's part of them that smiles, along the road of life's long
  miles,
I feel them deep within my bones, I feel their laughter, hear their
  groans.
I hope they know that their long fight brought brighter days and safer
  nights.
And so I salute all those who struggled, and lived their lives amid
  the rubble.

Patricia Dobinson

The Rustling Of The Bag

Ducks and drakes, cobs and pens
Forage in the ebbing tide.
Green and black, brown and white,
Waddle and slip and slide.
The ripples in the water
Break the silence in the air,
Until we bring their scraps of bread
To show them that we care.
They call to one another
And gather to form a line,
Then swim to where their breakfast is
Served at half past nine.
Some feed from the hand
And some peck from the ground,
They squabble and jostle
But there's plenty to go round.
With all the crumbs devoured,
Their tummies all a-sag
And wait for tomorrow's break of silence
- The rustling of the bag.

Susan E. Small

Aberfan 21st October 1966

A tragic day this for Aberfan
for 'twas today the mountain ram,
without sound or warning it moved down the hill
it moved down the hill till it covered the school.
It covered the school and the children were lost
the dear little ones that were treasured the most,
but from this tragic moment true courage was shown
even by those who'd lost one of their own.
For they dug and they scraped all the time without rest
and they prayed that at least one young life would be blessed
But no! All their labour was given it vain
for they found it the rubble no life did remain.
The village is silent with the children away
and oh how they long for the voices so gay,
There's many a moment a teardrop is shorn
but with "Him" all about you new hope is reborn.

William Watson

Untitled

My sorrow in abatement lays
For the swans lasting beauty,
My worries futile remain
As long as my heart is,
My heartache exists not
Whilst the ocean frequents the shores.
Thou are the swan,
Thou are my heart,
Thou are the ocean,
Thou are my life and I adore thee.

Sophie Barrow

Gentle

Let not your energy be negative
Forever tense in all you say and do
Release all tension, just relax and live
And be the person, that you are, just you!

Keep all your anger, always in control
For others can detect if you are tense
Far better if there's peace within your soul
And serenity for everyone to sense.

Make calm your vocal intonation, so
Anxiety is kept within its bounds
Let positive vibrations rise to flow
And really try to make just tranquil sounds!

Be gentle in the movements you perform
And graceful when you have to move around
Yet always keep your constitution warm
And make but only unobtrusive sound.

Nicholas Winn

The End Result

At last the race is over, there's not long now to wait,
For the result that seemed unthinkable, way back at the starting gate,
From there the course seemed easy, a push-over of a ride,
With no thought for the unexpected that loomed on the other side,
The flag went up, the hurdles were cleared, all was going well,
Till an uphill stretch took a heavy toll, and the pace began to tell,
Suddenly, the partnership started drifting off the rail,
And though they battled gamely on, it was odds-on they would fail,
'Broken-down', the word was spread, as they turned the final bend,
Their claim to fame and future hopes brought sadly to an end,
So now the race is over and the numbers are in the frame,
The favourite lost, the bet went down, but gambling is the game,
Life's a lot like that sometimes, depends which course we choose,
And only Fate and Lady Luck knows what we'll gain - or lose.

C. A. Holdaway

Life

One walks through the tunnel of life, wondering what is before them,
For some the tunnel ends quickly, for others their life is unknown,
One walks through the tunnel of life watching the world go by,
As if we were fish in a bowl, thinking of how we can change
  this place we call home,

Of all of the things in this world, how much do we understand?
Do we know what effects Nuclear tests will have 100 years from now?

What about all of the children, dying all around?
Will we always just look and turn away, hoping to be lost in a crowd?
What about the animals? The elephants and their tusks?
Will ivory always be a trade and a cause for such a loss?

We walk through the tunnel of life, blinkered to the world around us,
Not noticing other people's troubles just deep in thought of our own,

Will the wars ever end where people will make amends?
Will there be a time when crime is never again?
Are people going to be safe walking on their own?
Or will things never change, until this world is not our home?

Kerry Eley

Betrayal

Did he ever love me I ask myself,
for I shall love him with all my wealth.
He hurt me more than any other guy,
but even so without his love I wish to die.
He used to make me happy but now I just pull through,
I pray for him to love me but it never will come true,
as he cares more about his pride than who he wants by his side.
If things were different maybe he would be here,
but then again I also fear,
that he is happy with his new love,
I mustn't be jealous but must rise above.
Forever I shall love you and wait for your love,
whenever it arrives through letter, message or dove,
then I shall be happy forever here on earth,
for knowing life without you will always be a curse.
Farewell for now as I must part,
and wherever you go so shall my heart.

B. Evans

Elsa

We planted a rose of peace today,
for our dear Elsa, who passed away.

I think of her, from time to time,
that four legged pal, and friend of mine.

I held her close, and said goodbye,
but she just stared up, at the sky.

"Elsa", has gone now, what can we do,
it's up to the Lord, to take care of you.

So in His home, I know you will be,
having a good time, perhaps thinking of me.

Well goodbye our dear friend, we will miss you, you know,
we're all so sorry, that you had to go.....

A. L. Sutton

But You Will Wake

Sleep on oh Lord of childhood,
For now you sleep and dream,
And know no fear
Harmless beasts surround you
And mary's love us hear.

Oh sleep my Lord, and do not wake
I cannot bear that you should know
The pain, the loss, the bitter ending
On the cross
Your future heritage.

But blessed son of God you know
And you will wake, to lose men's gifts,
And cattles low,
And wonder.

and serve you earthly span
To ponder, on mans apathy,
And shed your tears of blood
My Lord
for all men's sake.

Margaret Swann

Their Cause

The bugles sound their farewell shrill
For men at Flanders, that lay so still
Their cause to die, to end all wars
Their sons in the morrow would need no swords

They gave their all, this cause to gain
Using their bodies, as if for grain
The harvest of which, must surely reap
The joys of everlasting peace

If this true, their cause to die
No longer should we weep and cry
Place no poppies upon their graves
In return for the life they gave

For surely they could never forgive
Taking away their right to live
What of their sons if victory is gained
Can we be certain it won't happen again

So England we're asking, do not forget
Or give us reason our cause to regret
We fight not for glory, only for peace
Remember that England, of our sons whom you teach

C. V. Willingham

Dion's War

I'm sorry, Dion Stephenson, you died for a dollar sign;
For safe-home politicians, rattling pockets, swilling wine.
No longer do we die for dreams, dreams are almost dead,
We die for something somebody never really said!

We die for earthly icons, for power and for gold,
We know the ones possessing power, prosper and grow old.
Did you die for your country, Dion? Is that what you thought?
No, you knew, but you said that was why you fought -
that was why you fought.
  You had to have a reason, all of you did -
   Dion, Davy, Sam and Bill; Fred and Wayne and Jed -
   Fred and Wayne and Jed.

Echoes in the playground, hear your childhood's call;
Blood upon the desert, silent witness to your fall.
Your family's so proud of you - forgive their loyal hearts,
The gods condemn the country, that tears her sons apart.

I'm sorry Dion Stephenson, you died for a dollar sign;
For safe-home politicians, rattling pockets, swilling wine.
I'm sorry Dion Stephenson, young son of mine -
  young son of mine!

S. Thomson

No More

For him no sun
For him no smiles,
For him no wandering gentle hours

The day as gone when we did wander
Hand in hand through fields and streets
or ride our bikes down leafy lanes
no care about the Summer rains

Or play with jigsaws on the mat
with roaring fire and cups of tea
And Sunday paper at page three

Or scour the hills for daffodils
and bilberries nestling in the leaves
or plain and shape and sand with care
The piece of wood, a dollies chair

Or listen as he played the organ
Now crescendo, now diminuendo
The day as gone when I did sit
So proudly there on Daddies knee.

Sheila Yvonne Jones

Contemplation

I looked through my window, thought, what a dull day,
For everything was so damp, dismal and grey,
The sky, why it seemed to reach down to the floor,
And I was not tempted to open the door.
The temperature was low, oh yes, it was cold,
Everywhere was gloomy - not one trace of gold.
The sun had departed, quite hid by the cloud,
I have to admit it, my spirits were bowed.

I turned and looked inward and thought what a fool
To shiver and grieve because outside it's cool.
I turned to my room, then smiled with great pleasure.
Looked and enjoyed everyone of my treasures.
Coal and pine logs on the hearth all a-glowing,
What does it matter if outside it's snowing.
My armchair is there, pulled right up to the heat,
I'm short of nothing, I have plenty to eat.
The 'Telly' is there to turn on or turn off,
I'm perfectly well, I've not even a cough,
I have a good book - it's quite near to my hand,
Its pages may float me to some sunny land.

Winifred M. Bossen

The Boot Sale

Come stay the night at sixty six
For boot sale day, will show your tricks
Just pack your car the night before,
And line it up outside the door.

Fill it high with this and that
But watch they don't snatch Gordon's hat;
A jig saw here, a lamp shade there,
They're buying fast without a care:

Can you believe they'd be so active,
That empty box is so attractive!
They pick it up look inside,
I'm so confused I want to hide,

A petrol can a football game
To look or buy it's all the same
It's fun to wander through the rows,
But watch your goods be on you toes!

They pass along so busy browsing,
Licking ices picking, choosing,
Strolling, touching, nearly buying
Moving on, to leave you sighing!

K. Gahan

Tongue Of The Vitriol

Her life is so ugly yet she never despairs
For it's her life and she's use to the mire
What a pitiful life no concept of care

Nourishment drawn from tragedies of helpless victims
A caustic tongue forwarding pearls of wisdom deduced from
her doomed treadmill existence

Perhaps her mother delivered the same sharp sarcasm
Trampling feelings with neither conscience or thought
Using bitter speech to such deadly effect without dignity
Wearing her talent for abuse as if it were a badge of honour
Yet only dishonour shines from her ever dimming star
The line between the two so easily misconstrued

Pity the Vitriol so embellished in loathing and hate
Her tongue is not only her stigma but also her fate

Leanda Chappell

A Message To Summer

Oh! come sweet lady, come to me with all thy charm and grace
For I long to feel thy presence and yearn to see thy face.

Winter was so cruel to me and quite indifferent - Spring,
Oh! Summer, if thou wilt be kind thy praises I shall ring.

Bring thy fair family everyone - the grass - the trees - the flowers,
And we shall wander hand-in-hand along the sun-kissed hours.

And I shall hear thy radiant voice in every bird that sings,
So with the skylark arise my heart on joyful wings.

Then I'll linger by the sea, my happy heart and I,
And even when the night clouds fall, my roof shall be thy sky.

And so enchanted I shall be that all my cares shall cease,
For the music of thy silence fill my soul with peace.

K. F. Laird

The Nail

The nail was a sharp invention,
For holding joints and wood in tension.
Long or short, fat or thin,
The nail can be used to hold, a host of things.

But oh, what trouble a nail can bring,
When across the room you hear it Ping!
Just one more tap should drive it home,
Then off the nail decides to roam.

Bending over and twisting about,
A pair of pincers, now, you will need,
To pull that nail with any speed.
Head buried well below the grain,
That nail has now become a pain.

A nasty hole left in the wood,
This does not look so very good.
A mug of tea will put things right,
As you hide that piece of wood from sight.

H. Parker

Canary Wharf, February 1996

Destruction, pain and sorrow, each is there
For eyes to see near London's ancient docks.
Is this the bomb that peace endeavours mocks
And wrecks the hope of tranquil days so fair?

Can we rise up above the terror dire?
Must seventeen months of beauteous calm be torn
To shreds by one short moment's rage reborn?
Will we return to matching fire with fire?

It must not be, it cannot finish thus.
Each party must be calm, reflective, cool,
The nations throw their anguish in the pool
Of love and patience prized by all of us.

So seventeen months will grow to forty-seven,
And the millennium shine as bright as heaven.

Ruth A. Binns

Oh!

Oh Manatee, Oh Manatee you big lovable oaf,
For being so gentle you get my vote.
Suffering so much because of us,
You harm no-one and are herbivorous.
Horrific cuts on your back are man-made,
By speeding boats with their propeller blades.
Oh Whale, Oh Whale either toothed or baleen,
The Blue the largest mammal this world has seen
Killed for your whalebone and your oil,
To fight for you I will remain so loyal.
Oh Dolphin, Oh Dolphin, I love you the best,
You are so friendly, approachable and full of zest.
With your beak like snout and cheeky grin,
Perhaps you are trying to tell us something.
Polluted, trapped in nets or hunted to die in pain.
Will you be around for our future children?
Oh Manatee, Oh Whale, Oh Dolphin be forgiving,
And pray that this earth you will continue to live in.
From the heart this is a tearful plea,
That you continue to swim in our rivers and seas.
Susan King

Orphaned By Battle

Distant drums, battle cries
Flashes in the sky, soldiers die,
Orphaned by battle,
Tears subside from little girl's eyes,
Your daddy was a hero when he died.
Little girl wiped tears from her eyes
And spoke, my daddy was a hero
Before he went to war,
Now he won't hug me anymore.
A. Lewis

Let's Make The World A Friendlier Place

A friendly act, will put a smile on their face
For anyone that you do it
No matter their colour or race
Be brave and never quit.
Always find the time
Excuses will never be in favour
Be the first in line
And never, never quaver.
A good deed is a wonderful thing
We should all try our best
It will make people's hearts sing
Not thinking of ourselves, but the rest.
Why cannot we all be friendly
Never be full of hate or lust
It would soon become trendy
Much better to have trust.
Come, let's try it out today
Don't wait until tomorrow
Be helpful and mean what you say
Bring gladness, not sorrow.
J. D. Groundsell

Heartaches

I told my girl that we must part,
For a while to fight a war,
That she'll be forever in my heart,
Each day I'll love her more.

I left her standing on the quay,
she said I love you dear,
As I boarded ship I turned to wave,
In her eye there was a tear,.
We did our job and won the war,
Then straight back we started,
My heart missed a beat, as we dropped anchor, for,
she was there on the quay where we parted.

That night we walked beneath the moon,
The air echoed with our laughter
Tomorrow we'll be bride and groom,
And live happily ever after.
S. Hodge

Daydreams

Out of nothingness they rise, these dreams
  flimsy and fair,
Frail as gossamer, fragile, seeking touch
  in an atmosphere.
Dreams of daytime, in a mind to be spun
  with tender care
As romantic, beauteous, floating, vapoury
  castles in the air.

I see the sun! I see the moon! and revel
  in their beams.
My senses find contentment in the flowers,
  forest and streams.
But what my heart desires, I cannot reach —
  it really seems
My heart's desires are imprisoned in a castle
  of daydreams.
Margaret Starck

Together Again

The wrinkled old man, sat watching it snow
Fluffy white flakes, flutter to the earth below
There's a conifer in the corner near the shed
With a crown of white, like the old man's head
He watches the snow as it melts away
Like the days, when he used to play

Soft and gentle pure and white
Like the girl who became his wife
The lights of the street make everything shine
Just like his love, that wife divine
Onto the lawn struts a tiny Robin
The thought of his love one starts him sobbin'

Less and less do the flakes descend
Gently the storm draws to an end
The rays of the sun from on high
Makes the dawn steal across the sky
Gone is the night gone is the snow
To the grave he'll gladly go
G. B. Walmsley

My Heart

As I have grown older, I weep a bitter tear
For my childhood dreams, which were made to disappear
All my life I've born the scars,
that the abused person bears.
When the abusers someone related, the rest of your life
seems deflated
You push loved ones away, even though you want them to stay.
Now, I have reached the ripe old age of 40,
and what my abuser did still haunts me.
The pain is not as deep, at least now I can sleep.
I hope this person is sorry for what they did,
to me, when I was such a small kid.
Kathleen Byrom

Cry of the Eagle

Spreading its wings,
flying above the rooftops
in such a majestic manner.
What a sight!

I watch as it swoops
gracefully downwards
into a steep dive,
its talons grip an unsuspecting prey.

It rises once again,
a careful last glance at the city
before it sways and flies away,
never to return.

I turn and head for home.
But as I listen I hear
the gentle flapping of its huge wings,
and the cry of the eagle.
Ryan Leahey

Bible Garden

A Bible garden of herbs and trees
Flowers and fruits and seeds;
All these good things with the birds and the bees
Were there all the time with the words and the deeds
The garlic from Israel, coriander and sage
The fig tree, the mulberry and grapes
the poppy and lily and page after page
of wisdom to say life's a stage
For loving and giving; and life is for living,
For the young, the middle life and old age.
Praise to the Lord, Accept all these things
There are some things we just cannot change.
The Bible is full of wonderful words
It's not easy to understand.
Sit quiet and still and read it again
And pray for this beautiful world that God made;
His son Jesus Christ who died on the cross.
Sit quiet and ask for his love and his pardon
Just think of these things; of the herbs and the flowers
of a wonderful Bible garden.

I. Simpson

Meon Seasons

Autumn comes to Meon
Fish breeding on the "Reds,"
Coloured leaves a constant flow
From tall trees overhead.
Rushes that were lush and green
Now brown, limp and dank.
Lay swaying in the rivers run and tangled near the bank.

The river now is rising
Swamped with winters rain.
Meadows now turned into lakes till springtime then they'll drain.

Brent Geese now find their haven in Meadows wet and green.
The frosty sun sinks early reflecting wintry sheen.

Suddenly, the river starts to change the scene.
Water meadows clearing
Quickly they are clean.
Young rushes quickly growing, birds begin to sing,
Coots nesting in the rushes, winter turns to spring.

The river now is thriving
Young fish they flash and dart.
Once more on peaceful Meon another season starts.

Stan Lewis

Feelings

The Shower of Rain, after Weeks of Drought,
Finding a Key, when You have been locked out,
An open Coal Fire, when it's bitter cold,
Your Grandchildren's touch, when growing Old.

To see a Truss of Tomatoes, that was once a Seed,
A freshly dug Garden, without a Weed,
The Smell and Taste, of Oven Baked Bread,
To return from Holidays, to Your very own Bed.

The Wonderful Scent of New Mown Hay,
A comfortable Armchair, at the end of the Day,
The Taste of Welsh Rarebit, spread on Toast,
The elation, when your Horse, is First past the Post.

The Tang of the Tar, when Workmen repair a Road,
After Shopping, getting rid of the Load,
Having good Friends when advice You seek,
The pleasure of drawing a Pension each week.

When you reach the Milestone in your Life,
Fifty Years Together as Man and Wife,
With a Wonderful Family, well able to smile,
Because the feeling you get is, that life's been worthwhile.

L. J. Jeffries

The Mantel Shelf

This old mantel shelf, once erect and so proud
fine colour was lively, quite bright, even loud,
lovingly cared for, touch tender, worked light
polish and duster, made this a fine sight,
alas those days passed, all glory now gone
time took its toll, decayed to the bone.

Left in neglected, through darkness and cold
all cracked and worn, timbers so old,
four marks on the top, where ornaments stood
covered in dust, diminished nice wood,
shallow trail of a beetle, remains of a fly
gave credence to life, that lingered awhile.

Only memories are left, of a fine work of art
what life it has seen, some joy made its mark,
laughter and tears, sadness and strife
tenderness, concern, throughout a long life,
Oh look at you now, too frail to stand tall
this once proud mantel, will crumble and fall.

Laurence Peter Wray

Yesterday's Thoughts, Today's Dream

I long to stroll the sandy beach
Finding your hand, whenever I reach,
Watching the tide which comes and goes
Filtering sand, through the toes,
Feeling sea breeze on the face
Blowing hair out of place,
Climbing rocks side by side
Discovering pools, where fishes hide,
Hearing the gulls as they cry,
Catching fish, then flying high,
That, which was an idyllic scene,
In reality, a perchance to dream.

P. Fisk

The Echo Of My Past

Sunlight on my pillow,
Filtering through the willow tree,
Scattering dreams that were long forgotten,
But which now come back to haunt me.

Sunshine dances before me,
Flickering on the wall,
I woke up and thought you still loved me,
But that was just a memory,
That was all.

Time has left you behind me,
How I wish I could find love that will last,
But I guess until then,
I will keep on dreaming of you,
The echo of my past.

Paul James Hurrell

The First Refuge

I can afford a green carpet; a roof
filtered with stars, pretending to be aloof;
so rest on my shoulder, weep your sad tears,
grievous, my broad bosom drains your nightmare fears,
still saturate with yesterday's great deluge.
I am your home, and I am your refuge.
An arm protects a face from staring eyes
that pry, and lips that tell their infamous lies.
I know! I know what weeping is. I wept
through all the years that nature's embryo slept
beneath my leaking roof, dripping conscience.
My dreams are older than night's lorn suspense.
— Ne'er ending night.—
       The day is overdue.
Cry on my shoulder, child, only the stars view.

Richard Slinn

The International Society of Poets

45c Joseph Wilson Estate • Millstrood Road • Whitstable • Kent CT5 3PS • TEL: 01227 773111

Dear Poet:

Congratulations on being published in this fine anthology! We believe you deserve special recognition for your poetic accomplishments, so we have enclosed a News Release Form which you can -- and should -- send to your local newspapers to announce the publication of your poetry.

If you have never seen a form like this before, don't worry. It's standard, and any newspaper editor will recognise it.

All you need do is:

* Fill out the parts that apply to you personally (your name and address, poem title, etc.).

* Make copies of the completed form.

* Send a copy to each of your local newspapers and to any other publications that might be interested.

* If you have a suitable photograph of yourself on hand, include it, but it is not essential.

* Write News Release on the outside of the envelope so it goes to an editor's desk without delay.

Chances are good that some of the newspapers will publish the release and perhaps even do a longer story. Many newspapers are eager for news about local people with unusual talents and achievements -- like you. You will be helping the newspaper by letting them know!

Again, congratulations, and good luck with your poetry in the future!

Sincerely,

Howard Ely

Howard Ely
Managing Editor

P.S. If a paper publishes the news about you, would you do me the favour of sending us a copy of the article? I and the staff at The International Society of Poets take a great interest in our poets, and we would enjoy seeing it.

The International Society of Poets

45c Joseph Wilson Estate • Millstrood Road • Whitstable • Kent CT5 3PS • TEL: 01227 773111

For Immediate Release				Contact: (Your Name)
						Phone: (Your Telephone Number)

Local News Interest
Local Poet Published in National Anthology

(Name) _____

(address) _____

(phone) _____ has just had original poetry published in (book title)

_____, a treasury of today's poetry compiled

by The International Society of Poets. The poem is entitled _____,

and the main subject is _____.

The International Society of Poets seeks to discover and encourage poets like

(name) _____ by sponsoring competitions that

are open to the public and by publishing poems in widely distributed hardback volumes.

(Name) _____ has been writing for

(amount of time) _____ and (his/her) favourite subjects and ideas are

(your subjects and ideas) _____.

Poets interested in publication may send one original poem, any subject or style 20 lines or less, to The International Society of Poets, Dept. 9311, FREEPOST LON 2229, WHITSTABLE, Kent, CT5 3BR. Please be sure to include your name and address with your poem.

All poems received are also entered in The International Society of Poets' International Open Amateur Poetry Competition, which awards over £16,000 in prizes annually.

Fear Not

Fear not my friend, the trials of life,
Fear not the horror of war,
Fear not the aches and pains of health,
Fear not what lies behind the door.

Fear not the poverty that strikes us all,
Fear not the views of others,
Fear not the dark and tragic times,
Fear not the death of our mothers.

Fear not what's round the corner,
Fear not fear, for fear's sake,
Fear not living your life as it comes,
Fear only regret at your wake.
  Teresa Toal

Racism

Black, white mixed together always
fight. Wherever you go you see racist
attacks. Something you see whites
beating up blacks, or sometimes you
see blacks bashing up the whites.

  You just can't help the way
  you look.
  It is the person high up in
  the sky who gave you birth
  and your colour.

Black and white people are
friends, but while walking
down the street together
others get jealous and
try to break your friendship up.

  To survive in the world you have
  to communicate with everyone whether
  the person is different from
  you. Because it doesn't matter if you're
BLACK OR WHITE
  Nazia Tahid

April

I do not trust you toothy April
First you smile your primrose smile
Offer green buds to beguile,
Then your teeth snap shut and bite
With frosty chuckles of delight.
Your true love winter reappears
Turning April showers to crocodile tears
In regret for the sun so soon stillborn.
Bringing again the skin slicing morn.
Putting back the weather clock
Making spring a sham, a mock
Give May her cue and hope she brings
Sensuous summer on call in the wings.
For the world's a stage
The weather's acting too
And of April playing Christmas
I take a poor view.
  T. G. Jenkins

To My Child

I have carried you loved you nursed you
  fed and clothed you
And now you're leaving
I have kept you warm safe and protected
  enriched you with my love
But still you're leaving
I have watched you learn fed your
emotions expanded your mind
And still you're leaving
I love you adore you cherish you
  admire you,
take my blessing and go.
  W. McHugh

These Foreign Lands

Marching to their front line trenches.
Failing not to see.
Haunting graves large and hollow, excavated
from the ground for all to follow.
Whistles blow and Over the Top, wave after wave
and still they never stopped.
Machine-guns traversed these foreign lands,
perilous pathways and front lines too.
Death and destruction walked and in hand,
incessant bombardments and large mines too.
Young men cried and fell with pain,
help at hand was to no avail.
  Kurt Clegg

The Bird

A bird that hums a tune, upon the horizon
far from noon, sits so far in a tree
spreading happiness into a world so free,
sends the joy and warmth of spring
sing little bird sing please sing,
Sing for our world now the wars are at cease
sing out your tune of freedom and peace,
Through the blossoming trees that look a picture
in the breeze, for the heavens above
that send down all their love.
Thanks to this bird for the happiness it brings
open up your heart spread out your wings,
fly little bird fly proud with glory
spread your tune sing out your story,
bringing the smiles bringing the laughter
bringing at last the happy ever after.
Sweetness is your thoughts
sweet thoughts hide in your mind,
sharing all your passions
with our world, with all mankind.
  Karen Baker

Our Tribute

A little flower stands all alone.
Far away in a graveyard in Rome.
But in our hearts it's ever so near.
A small tribute behind a silent tear

God had His reasons but we wonder why
So many young men had to die.
For their country they did their best.
So why? Had they, to be laid to rest.

Maybe now we will have peace of mind
With that flower we left behind
We gave a mother's love to her son.
After all the war was already won.
  P. Porter

Reflections Of Youth

When I was a young girl, summer days I recall.
Family and friends came to call.
Over the fields to play ball.
Rounders, cricket, tennis anything at all.

Running each other across the fields.
"Shoes and socks" snapping at heels.
Full of wild flowers.
Fields full of colour and fragrance.
A field where memories are made.
Family and friends in harmony.

Now my mother has passed on.
The fields also gone.
Some family and friends too.
Where flowers once grew,
Stand houses in full view.

In the small dark hours.
I project my thoughts,
Back to the fields,
Where my mother and I once talked.
  I. D. M. Hale

'At Last It's Christmas Day'

On waking at the crack of dawn, there isn't much to say,
except "Today's a special time, at last it's Christmas Day!!"
At breakfast one just cannot wait, to dress and go outside,
To breathe that fresh and sparkling air, to feel a glow inside.

And yet it's cold and wet out there, the wind chill cuts one through,
with ice, and snow just drifting down, I expect you'll feel it too!
Yet move again indoors to find, a roaring radiant fire,
red rosy cheeks, a fireside lamp, too early yet to tire.

With decorations round the room, and Christmas cards galore,
the beauty of the Christmas tree, and presents on the floor.
There's holly and there's mistletoe, I think I'll steal a kiss,
then in comes Mum, my favourite girl, a chance I cannot miss.

Not long to go to dinner now, I bet there'll be a spread,
remember last year, what a feast, much more than daily bread.
Turkey, sausage meat and sprouts, a feast before your eyes,
with Christmas pud, and brandy sauce, and gorgeous mincemeat pies.

To while away the afternoon, whatever shall we play?
Wherever is that Scrabble board?, we used it yesterday!
"Is anyone out there," call's Mum," that's ready for their tea?
I've got some ham, and strawberry jam. No thank's Mum, none for me!"

Tony A. Jay

Night-Crossing (For Siobhan, With Bone Cancer)

I wake to find myself
exactly half way
between last night and
touching you.

I can tell by this uneasiness.
By the way these feverfews have come to harm,
how the thin velvet
of their dusted wings
weakens and folds beneath a litany of false alarms,
that are exactly halfway
between burning down and coming true.

This is the season of falling satellites, the internal bleeding
of unwritten poems, forest-fires for no reason,
and I am waiting for news of all of these, and cannot sleep
until you put your arms around me like a bay
and I tide in and out of you, until we run aground
and have nothing left to say.

you are listing, now, unsure

if it is my hand in yours or yours in mine

if your pulling away will leave my falling behind.

Michael O'Reilly

England

There is no place like England, no, not any place on earth,
It is a land of kings and queens, and the land of my own birth,
This tiny island nation, this kingdom, and this realm,
Though men may rule this nation, 'tis God's hand at the helm,
The trooping of the colours, the union Jack on high,
On Remembrance Day and poppies, you'll find a misty eye,
Who has not quoted Shakespeare, is one who has not read
And one who knows not Churchill, is one who has never led,
Who has not heard of London, her wonders to be told,
She is mentioned in many stories, by youngsters and the old,
The children run and skip and smile, as they walk on sacred land,
Let us nourish and encourage them, our future is in their hands.
I could speak for hours of this my native land,
A country of such heritage is not built on sinking sand,
We are a part of Europe when all is done and said,
But first last and always. I'm English, born and bred,
And when I come to die, bury me deep in England's heart,
To become one with my nation's land, and never more to part.

James F. Woodard

"Life"

Hold the hand - touch the skin of
  every wondrous living thing
A baby's head - a loved one's face
These precious moments you'll never replace
This exquisite touch which means so much
Is timeless and tenderly given
Its memories lay with remembered dreams
Kept in the garden of heaven
"Life" stands still for you at such times
Savour the glory while it is thine
Breathe the sweet air "life's" fragrance creates
Its taste lasts forever - its love never hates
These treasures of "life" locked in your heart
Lovingly cherished - never to part
Take each days "life" while you can
Tomorrow's fate is not known by man!

Vera E. Grant

Palace Of Pain

Tears role down like falling rain
Every day in the Palace of Pain.

Emotions flirt with the good and bad
Either way it can end up sad.

Things can work but not like before
No one knows not quite for sure.

And then the pain comes back again
And all the work goes down the drain.

And in this place no fun is stirred
It's only the pain that is heard.

Rising above the thoughts of today
And giving time to so much dismay.

In the palace of life's long pain
You always see all of the stain.

That has reached out from torn deceit
Manufactured by all those you meet.

Martin Booth

If

If you knew how much I loved you
Every hour of each day
If your eyes could read the love in mine
Your heart would never stray.

If the moon could tell its secrets
It would tell you how I pray
Each night beside your window
While asleep in bed you lay.

If I knew that you would love me
As the years had passed us by
I'd close my eyes and say to God
I'm ready now to die

Richard Ian James

Time

What am I to you?
Enemy or friend?
Do you say please hurry
or can you please slow down.

Moving along I won't be still
so enjoy me as you will.
A smile, a kiss, a touch or word
all makes for a better world.

Yes to you I can be kind
if you just take a little time.
Time to listen, time to look,
a smile, a word, a friendly look.

Don't take me for granted.
Because I move so fast.
And when you say if only.
Alas! You might find your time has pat.

Rosemary McIlhatton

The Road To Nowhere

It seems we have walked this road before
Ever seeing in our mind
A promise of that which lies ahead
Of dreams shared and near at hand
If it were real
On this road to nowhere

Many times, all peoples have walked this road
Its varied turns and twists
Following the fate of those gone before
And never quite realizing
'Twas journeys end
On the road to nowhere

Always; this road which never ends
Beckoning to lead us on
At the end of time will still be there
To hold us in its thrall
HOPE, it's called
The road to nowhere
  William F. Park

Life

Imaginations and thoughts mean so much.
Even though we cannot touch.
The thought that life could not be again.
Would make life seem so in vain.

When two minds meet and bodies too.
The magic starts, and you twine as one.
Then life lifts away past pains.
And makes life go on again.

The webs we weave are sometimes hard to bear.
But life goes on if we're prepared to share.
A loving glance, a little smile.
A heart that's shared is well worthwhile.
  G. Hadley

"Looking Out Of My Window"

Looking out of my window things are looking grey,
even though I do not like it here I know I have to stay.

The world is changing every day the sun is
getting brighter, people do not understand the
damage they are creating.

I once know the world was round and then
we found these holes. We know there are
causes and what to do I'm just glad there are so few.

CFC gases and fuels and things we can keep
under control, bio-degradable boxes and tubes
carrier bags please try to re-use.

Looking out of my window things are looking
better, another day will stay just keep
my hands together and pray.
  Shelley Louise Lloyd

Melancholic

A dull, dreary and dismal grey day, with little that I care to do,
Even my panoramic window, shows precious little to view.
An occasional flock of small birds wheel by,
Momentarily fleeting, they sweep through the sky.

Solitudinous feelings beset me with fear,
As the rain slough and spatters, and leaves the mood drear.
A flit past my window, first starling, then chough;
Then monotonous greyness, that's heavy and tough.

A dread clap of thunder, a reverberant crack,
My heart pleads for sunshine, my soul feels so black.
Such dark sombre feelings, I beg for release;
Bring me sunshine, pure light, my heart's ease.
  P. T. De Artin

Forever

What does the word forever mean,
Eternity, till death us do part,
Till the end of the world,
And on and on beyond time.

What does it mean for me,
Probably till the day I die,
But much more than that with regard to you,
If you think of it this way.

Like being on a train with an everlasting engine,
with no stations and no destinations,
No way of stopping, no way of getting off,
or even wanting to get off.

I'll still be with you after the physical me has gone
Haunt you in the nicest possible way,
Be with you until the end of time, and then some!
I'll seek you out in another life after this.

To spend forever with you is all I want,
To part never from you is all I want,
To live together us two is all I want,
So that is what forever means, In simple terms just you and me.
  Thomas Robert West

The Train

To travel on a train is fun
Especially when you're small
Cause when the train stops suddenly
You haven't far to fall.

You shake and you wobble about
And hold onto the strap
And sometimes lose your balance
And fall on someone's lap.

You have to be so careful
Don't play on the track
Or you could be in trouble
In hospital on your back.

It could be worse or fatal
So don't you ever dare
Because there are people who love you
And people who really care.

So please listen to what we're saying
Don't go near the trains
Unless to enjoy a journey
Have sense, and use your brains.
  Sheila Ashman

The Senile One

I reside in a room in an old people's home
Equipped with bed, robes, sideboard and sink
It's the kind of place from which I may never roam
No matter what I may consider or think.

Each morn I am awakened by a member of staff
Come to help me to wash and to dress
Deep down inside of me I have to laugh
As they struggle with this human mess.

I'm led to my breakfast and encouraged to eat
I'm offered beverages, coffee and tea
I view other residents each sat upon a seat
With table manners oft repellant to me.

I shuffle along I no longer walk well
I stumble, shout, threaten to faint
I don't want to be moved from my room or should I say cell
Where warm and secure I can study wall paint.

The aim of the staff of this salubrious place
Is to keep all things quiet as can be
So they put us to bed nights at considerable pace
Whilst adding things at required to our tea.
  B. Lattimore

The Lord's Unfailing Love

God's love is like a river, both flowing deep and wide
Entering our thoughts and dreams, there always to abide.
Pouring out its ministry in message to impart
His special gifts of grace and love, He stores in every Heart.
Preparing for the darkness that lies just up ahead.
When we'll recall we have the key when we, by Him, are led
To open the door to Light and life in His redeeming love
Received from Father, Son, Holy Ghost, in newness from above.
Amazing New redeeming Love, that sets our hearts on fire.
To set our sights on prayer and praise, will be His one desire.
Then men throughout the world shall bow in humble adoration.
From high ranking man, to prisoner, no matter what their station
Will be called forth as sons of God, to serve their heavenly Father.
It will be a royal following to saved souls, He is about to gather.
So be prepared to heed His word, and listen for His call.
Thank Him with true repentant love, for you He gave His all.

Rose Morris

Tribute To The Woodland Fern

Frilly fronds of restful green
enhancing every woodland scene,
gently waving in the breeze
soughing through the old oak trees.

Intricate patterns of embroidered lace
arching out with poise and grace;
what lesson is there we can learn
from the cool and everlasting fern?

When summer fades and frost draws nigh
the bright fresh leaves turn brown and die;
but down among the oak tree's roots,
warm and strong are the fern's new shoots.

Awaiting the call of spring's warm light,
faith in nature's strength and might;
the promise made on His authority
the faithful shall have immortality.

R. H. Allan

Innocents In Turmoil

Their wide dark eyes,
empty of emotion.

Their unclean faces,
showing their despair.

Their voices once filled with joy and laughter
can only just be heard.

Their tiny hearts where love lies deeply inside
bears slowly.

Their once strong bodies which ran and played
now weak and feeble from illness and starvation.

Their homes, neighbourhoods and places so familiar
are long since forgotten for the here and now.

Their only hope in these troubled times
is peace and understanding from the adults in the worlds
nations.

Michelle Rowley

Ode To The Thrush

Celestial being, angel in disguise.
Ethereal spirit, master of the skies
Riding on winds,
By thermals swept on high.
What heavenly view
Is seen by you
As above the earth you fly?

Mercurial songster, chorister supreme.
Melodiously you sing your well worn theme.
Repetitive but never clear and shrill.
The summer long
Your echoed song
Fills valley, wood and hill.

Peter D. Purbrick

Rebecca 'Lost Childhood'

To suffer in silence, tiny heart born
    emotions so raw, body so worn
Not knowing tomorrow just where
    she would be
but praying each night
    'sweet Jesus love me'.
She knew upon waking her dreams
    were no more
footsteps and terror, his hand on
    the door
Tiny hands clenched, heart rigid
    with fear
the call of her mother she tried to
    hear
But silence remains and the tears
    start to flow
they trickle so softly, pure flakes of snow
The ghost of her mother plays
    tricks with her mind
"Come with me Rebecca, the snow we will find".

S. Laity

To Sail the Seas

To sail the seas, to be at ease.
Do never fear, the roughest seas.
To trust in God, has He trust thee.
For has He guideth us through the seas.
For danger ahead, we must stand by
To be prepared to live or die,
For those who die, the Lord shall rest
And we there names shall not forget

J. A. Richardson

Salvador

Pigmented surreal images in bleached white canvas,
Elephants reflecting swans, the great masturbator,
Desert landscapes, political abater,
Distorted watches, egg - headed men,
Who could perceive his genius then?
Raphaelesque head explodes,
The invisible bust of Voltaire,
The disturbing conviction of a waking nightmare,
Le visage de la guerre perpetuates,
Galas image accelerates.
Geopoliticus child watching the birth of a new man,
Crowded spectacle of the battle of Tetuan.
Lincoln meets Gala, Beethoven becomes the ink of cuttlefish and squid,
As Mae West curtained face once did.
The man of Figueras, the image he brought,
Of people with clouds in their heads — il est mort.

Tony Boden

Nature's Gift

Beauty born from reality
Echoes from far off lands could be heard
Landscapes with hidden treasurers
Trees casting shadows on the ground.

Flowers gave colour as if to say
Life could be so romantic
Streams glistening, from rays of sunshine
    through the trees
Clouds just rolling by giving warnings

Wild life enjoying such freedom
Wild flowers looking majestically
The wild rose protected in all its glory
Such colours could only be seen

Thunder lighting gave vibrations
Danger brought sunshine anew, protecting
    Natures wonders reaching unknown lands
    to the depth of the sea.

J. S. Mitchell

Perhaps

The circle divides and becomes two.
Each part is unequal.
Each part becomes an enigma of the mind!
But what of the missing part?
Perhaps—Time exists, and it's hiding in the corner.
Love is a circle without closing, but does it?
An imagination like the stones is what we all should be!
Perhaps? There again—Forget the pain.
Why should the pain of birth stop there?!
To hear the singing robins, and to watch the blackbirds drink—
Perhaps—Just an illusion—Perhaps?
Who knows—Perhaps! Then it becomes the entity of divine, and utter realism.
Realism—There's a thought!
To be able to concentrate- without the destruction of membranes.
Who knows the spatial difference between now and then?
The oneness of marriage shouldn't be put into one person?
Or should it?
Perhaps.
Martin James Holleran

The Dog's Winter Memories

The frost is hard as nighttime falls
each house it has a fire alight
a voice from out a doorway calls
a dog which has gone out of sight

The dog looks through the gate and sees
himself so young and long ago
over fields and under trees
he ran in sun and winter snow

Now he walks with awkward pace
his aching legs are tired and slow
no longer through the woods to race
on nimble feet and eyes aglow

He shivers in the winter chill
his coat is sparse his body cold
and turns to trudge the frosty hill
which was in summer bathed in gold

With joy at last he reaches home
and at the door with much delight
decides he will no longer roam
'neath moon and stars in cold of night
G. Bagley

Remorse

I saw no flowers in Normandy.
Felt no sun upon my face.
I heard not the familiar buzzing bee.
No did I see a laden tree.
Summer was out of sight.
Rain and wind swept over plains.
'Twas winter dark and drab.
But it was not that I stood around.
  So still.
Winter winds and rain can meet.
They will go and spring will come
I stood alone upon a spot.
In the corner of some unknown plot.
Roughly dug with just a cross.
A grave a British loss.

Who can say that he is not forgotten
None but those alive to day.
I passed along the wind still in my face
Winter still in my heart
Rain still swept the normandy plain
On! On! To further gain.
E. V. Walkden

Ships That Pass In The Night

Our journey through life's a voyage,
Each has their own course to steer.

Sometimes we travel in convoy
Others we plough on alone.

Sometimes the going is easy
Sometimes it's stormy and rough.

When through the darkness a light gleams,
Do we ponder the future?

Will our paths parallel forever,
Or will they diverge again?

Perhaps we'll lay up together,
Or might we only remain...

Two ships that pass in the night.
Robin P. Turk

Beauty Of Life

R is for being rewarded in life,
E is for the energy I now have,
N is for newness of happiness,
E is for the endeavouring to be happy,
W is for the wonders of the world,
E is for enjoying things in life,
D is for the dawning of the renewed beauty of life.

I is for inspire to live life to the full,
N is for the newness of the wonder of things.

H is for having a happy feeling,
A is for applying for freedom,
P is for people around me,
P is for popularity of life,
I is for innocent of things in life,
N is for knowing the newness of things,
E is for eagerness to be happy,
S is for soluted of what is to come,
S is for solidness to be alive in life.
Sharon Wandless

The White Clad Maiden

I watched the white clad maiden
Drifting through the trees
She walked so quietly, smoothly
In the early morning breeze.

Sun rising over distant hills
The light becoming strong
I looked again where she had been
And the maiden now was gone.

Who the lassy was, I do not know
As I did not know then
But I'll climb the hill the morn's morn
And watch for her again.
Roderick MacLean

Untitled

At night, one dreams
All else apart,
The brightest of hopes
They seldom depart.

Then morning breaks out,
Reality appears,
One can't live on dreams,
A return of one's tears,

But, forward one goes,
A brave face to the world,
One step at a time
One standard unfurled.

Hope springs eternal,
Our tomorrows are past,
The future uncertain
But, God's love will last.
Ursula A. Blain

Old People's Home

The slops they call lunch are spooned as you hunch
Down low in your chair all alone
Then wheeled in your damp dress
Having wiped up the mess
You are parked to sit with others on your own
And as you stare in the air they begin to drag
At the hairs that dare to defy the plastic comb

Your appearance now neat and levered down in your seat
They are happy once there is no disarray
Left unable to rise you gaze out at the skies
As the clock counts out the minute of the day
Yet they are all unaware of your feelings of despair
That are hidden by the "Thank you's" that you say

But you know they don't care about you
As they swear and laugh in groups
And cackle like crones
So in this desolate place you are left there
To face the tragedy that this is now your home.

Sue Williams

'Beautiful Night'

I've waited so long, for this night,
Don't worry my love, whether it's wrong or right,
The way we feel, how can it be wrong,
Oh let us make love, all night long.

Take me higher and higher, right to the top,
Love me all night long, please don't you stop,
Take me to the point, at which my head starts to roll,
Take me to the point, at which I lose all control.

I never thought, that it could be like this,
Warm is your body, and sweet is your kiss,
Lying so close, I feel your heart beat,
I feel so content, I feel so complete.

There's no going back, what's done is done,
Lying here together, we are as one,
Now that we both, have had our fill,
We lie together, oh so still.

I rest my head, on your soft breast,
It's so warm and snug, in our love nest,
I'll always remember, this beautiful night,
Sleep tight my love, until the morning light.

Peter R. Williams

Our Mary

'Twas in the year of '89
A century ago,
A little baby girl was born
In Springburn, near Glasgow.

Now this wee girl, with kith and kin
To Ulster's shores did come,
Years later she was married,
And soon became a mum.

With boys and girls this girl was blest,
She did have quite a few,
She had so many children
She didn't know what to do,

Now this "wee girl" is a mother,
A grandma, even great,
And all her kin are loved by her,
In her world there's no hate.

Today it is her birthday,
She's one hundred years and three
And so this ode is sent to say
"Happy birthday," our Mary.

Colin Ross

From The Heart

Don't walk in front of me.
Don't walk behind me.
Just walk next to me.
Just walk beside me.

When I need a shoulder to cry on,
Don't turn away.
Just be there and listen,
To what I have to say.

When there are times of joy,
Don't leave me on my own.
Without you there beside me.
I am all alone.

My life is incomplete,
Without you there beside me.
No-one can compete,
Against the love I have for you inside me.

Soroya Bachu

As Night Closes In

It's the end of another perfect day,
I sit and recall as light fades away,
The flowers I've planted with new found pride,
Much pleasure they will give, a colourful tide,
Even the lawn looks splendidly green,
The mowing has created a beautiful scene,
The hedges are standing like soldiers on guard,
Surrounding the garden with formal regard,
Patio tubs spill over with colours galore,
Their fragrance drifts past the kitchen door,
I sit and ponder with glass in hand,
How much pleasure it gives from working my land,
When evening arrives and the light fades away,
Yes it is my idea of a perfect day,
Maybe it could go on forever and more,
This kind of a peace we try to restore.

Trevor Reeve

My Daughters

Now I am old and my brow is furrowed
I thank good fortune for time I have borrowed,
For the past twenty years, in spite of ill health,
Have taught me a lot about life and myself.

I've travelled abroad and met women and men.
I've loved and I've laughed and cried now and then.
But through all the adventure it can't be denied
I've kept a devotion deep down inside.

There's been moments of silence, it has to be said,
When sometimes a tear has sadly been shed,
And thoughts from the past have haunted my head.

Now I am here confined to my quarters,
Hidden away in life's quiet backwaters,
I still think of you, my lovely dear daughters.

Terence Jacob

Topsy-Turvy Winter

Spiralling, twisting, flirting,
pirouetting like ballerinas in mid-leap.
The snowflakes fall to earth
To lie so softly,
As if the world turned upside-down
And billowing fields of summer cloud
Enfold the land.

Chaotic skies, heaped into furrows
of heavy grey,
Like winter ploughlands waiting
for the sun,
Release their chilly tears
on all below,
Transforming dismal earth
With dazzling snow.

Alice Ruddy

Birth Of A Millennium

As we tumble and stumble to its birth,
Do we rush forward as we do on earth.
Or with held breath step quietly on tiptoe.
Two thousand years have passed,
Since when Jesus gave us a chance.
Before we take this step should we not cast a backward glance,
To the many wars won and lost,
Millions of lives sacrificed, at what cost.
With the loss of life the shedding of the tears,
Is this to be our future in the coming years.
Knowing our weakness of the past,
Can we have a future that will last.
From these lessons of the past have we learnt,
Or are there still more answers yet to learn.
Have all the sacrifices been made at last,
Shall we now have peace that will really last.
Let our tears of the future be of happiness and joy.
And the world a place for everyone to enjoy.
Has mankind yet reached the age,
Where we can begin to turn the page.

E. S. Mayne

Work

I write... in this time of slackness at work.
Days have been going by very quickly recently
Due to the lack of small orders from builders merchants
That usually account for most of the hassles
That I usually have to sort out,
But as it had been so cold recently
Builders have been staying at home with feet up on their dogs,
Reading the Sun and drinking beer.

Spencer Jay Mudie

Words And Deeds

What is it, that we want to say?
Do we mean it, in that way?
We regret sometimes a word so harsh,
Can't take it back, or pay with cash
Compassion we must learn to use,
Have no intention to set a fuse,
Understand ways that are not like ours,
Stop making so much fuss
About those who are not quite like us,
Must not need praise for deeds we do,
Just don't use words that we may rue.
Abide by these simple rules, that's all
From grace we then would never fall
Togetherness gives comfort and pleasure
In our work and in our leisure
Use our words and do our deeds
But only those, we know, will please.

E. Cook

Heaven

I wonder what it's like up there in heaven
Do the angels really live there and wear wings
I wonder if there's lovely music playing and everybody sits around and sings.
Do the doggies and the baa lambs and the birdies and not forgetting pussy cats as well, chase each other around the garden of Eden,
Stopping only when they hear the dinner bell.
I wonder if there's lots and lots of sweeties, that you can eat and never ever feel sick, and lots of tasty looking lollies you can lick and lick and lick.
I wonder if God really has a beard, I wonder if He really is quite old,
I wonder if everything is pretty, made of silver and of gold.
I wonder if I'll see my Grannie, and friends who were young when they went.
Will we all live up there together, all in one big tent?
I guess I'll have just have to be patient and wait till He calls out for me,
I just hope that I will be ready and not sat there eating my tea.

K. V. Bonney

To My Conscience

We have three hours, my lover, and I,
Do not begrudge us this.
She is married, and so am I,
Life is not all we would wish.
We meet right here in our secret place
By the side of this cool, clear, lake,
We need this time to be alone
Three hours is all we can take.
Making love to each other - we touch and caress
And so many kisses we steal,
The world beyond is a fantasy,
Only here is it real.
We kiss again, I smother her lips,
Taste myself on her beautiful face.
Hurry, my love, it is time to go
And she leaves me alone in this place.
Back to our families - our passion on hold,
Where our lives are so dreary and flat,
For I am a woman, and so is she,
And nothing we do can change that.

E. Leslie

Thank You

It's a quarter past three, there's just silence and me,
Dim lights and the thoughts in my head,
Thoughts of the past which travel so fast,
And you, without whom I'd be dead.

Although at the time it felt like a crime,
To be stopped on the point of decision,
But now looking back and facing the facts,
I owe you my life and my vision.

I'd just had enough, my life was too rough,
The future was nowhere in sight,
Now rescued and living by your caring and giving,
How can I thank you for giving me light.

This is the beginning my head is still spinning,
And things are still bleak round the corner,
But I'll do what you said, it's stuck in my head,
So you won't have to be the chief mourner.

I can't thank you enough for being so tough,
Yet so gentle and drying my tears,
I can never repay you but whatever you go through,
When you need me I'll always be here.

A. T. Giddings

The Pennine Way

You never did do it.
Did you? Walk the Pennine Way?
You were always, going to walk the Pennine Way.
You never did do it did you?

To walk through nature's wind and rain:
To tread, the rocky Pennine Way,
To feel the gentle summer rain, the morning sun.
To breathe again the clear fresh air, the Pennine Way.

You never did hear the curlew's call
The skylark sweeping through the air.
The dancing grasses, shaking, trembling in the breeze
The purple heather on the moor, bracken turning autumn brown.

Walking in the evening light
Closing in the expansive countryside, and sky,
Become mysterious, filled with nature's sounds, from dawn of man.

You never did do it, did you?
Walk the Pennine Way.
Only! in your mind.

Mary Greenway Strong

"When The World Was Young"

Long ago in the mists of time, the formless earth from the void
did climb, the new born land was bubbling slime, in the days
when the world was young.
The dust-strewn sun was red as blood, the molten rocks
cooled by the flood, and Saurian reptiles crawled from the
mud, in the days when the world was young.
The ravaged cosmos writhed in birth, the hills took height and
depth and girth and strange huge creatures roamed the earth,
in the days when the world was young.
From dust rose man, unfettered free, his God's the earth the air
the sea, Christ had not yet died on calvary, in the days when
the world was young.
For peace Christ made his sacrifice, but homo-sapiens men all
wise, hath spawned the bomb, most foul device, since the
days when the world was young.
A blinding flash, a muted scream, incandescent rocks and steam
And civilization's again the dream, it was when the world was young.

Robert James Watson

Fear

The boy is tired, his eyes bloodshot red,
Despite all this he can't go to bed,
Bed is not for him, it means terror and fear,
As shadows of laughing clowns start to appear.

Darkness and solitude is not his friend,
He is in a haunted tunnel that can never end,
Life is constant danger in his dreams,
Such a desperate struggle, **STOP** he screams.
He pleas for help but is never heard,
His tormentor laughs as he drowns out each word,
Tonight he has to fight tiredness, stay awake,
He needs a friend for his sanity is at stake.

However his eyes are heavy and start to close,
Where will this child travel to? No-one knows,
He bolts the door, kneels to say his prayers,
That this night no-one will climb the stairs.

For you poor, lost child I shed a tear,
You are never alone, I am near,
So call me and I will watch you sleep,
I cannot bear to see you weep.

Patrick McGrath

Memories

As I sit in slumberous state,
Dependent on a whim of fate.
My thoughts fly freely through the air,
Journeying I know not where.

Over France the Pyrenees,
To Italy and Sicily
Then Malta looms across the bay.
What memories of childhood days!

Nostalgia has me in its thrall -
I float above the isle so small
So deeply scarred from days of war -
Remembered scenes, are they no more?

The sea, the sky are oh! so blue,
The silhouette still there, it's true,
The buildings, they don't seem the same
As when I, in my childhood came.

This sparkling Isle no longer seems
To be the Malta of my dreams.
So I float upon my way
To dream again another day.

B. Pease

All Mod Cons!

A young couple went to view a house
Deep in the countryside
An old countryman offered to show them 'round
As he opened the front door wide
"This 'ere be the parlour,
An' the scullery's there" he said
"An' yer goes up tha' there stair case
When yer wants ter go ter bed".
The garden was looking lovely
with roses and sunflowers tall
But at the end a ramshackle shed
Was perched against the wall.
"Oh, tha' there be the privy"
He said, opening the door,
Inside was just a plank of wood
With a bucket on the floor.
"There's no lock on the door" the young girl cried
"Now me gel, don't 'e be starting ter fret,
Tha' bucket's been there nigh on thirty years,
And nobody's pinched it yet".

M. Betteridge

When???

Chris O'Donnell, John Alford, Brad Pitt,
They all sit in front of me and stare.
Together the image of my ideal man,
Although that is within my grasp,
Forever out of reach.
Fantasy is good and helps me to carry on.
Another month gone and I'm still waiting.
Every morning happy cheerful faces but never any more.
How deep is your love? Take That sing for the first time,
I wish I knew,
I think to myself,
So much I've never been able to give,
So much I hold inside waiting for the "right person"
One day soon it will be your chance,
Is all I hear from everyone I ask.
But when, when is it my go?
So much to give but no-one willing to take,
One day, one day!!

Lindsey Greaves

The Heart Of A Violin

Oh, violin I hear your strings of sorrow,
Don't break your heart oh, violin,
Play, play, play me a melody of happiness,
I want to hear you laugh and sing.

Oh, violin I hear your strings crying,
Yet you sound like angels serenading the moon,
Have your strings been wounded like mine,
Or, is there something you cannot play.

Oh, violin of love let me caress your heart,
I hear you strings throwing fragrant flowers,
Petals floating with coloured sounds,
You carry me through rainbows.

Oh, violin do I feel the vibration of your heart,
Or are your strings crying again,
Don't cry oh violin, dance 'dance' dance with your strings,
Play, play, play me a melody of rainbow love.

Oh, violin do I hear strings of joy and delight,
Oh, happy violin play, play, play to me,
Laugh sing dance with me,
Fly me, with you on rainbow clouds.

Rosina Drury

The Precious Gift

You're now here little one, arrived, you are born,
Dear innocent new soul, lovely child of life's morn,
So small and so helpless, so new and so pure,
A unique living treasure from the Almighty's vast store.

Conceived in love, your priceless gifts to exist,
Unplanned surprise you, fruit of passion's sweet tryst,
Precious dust of the universe, immortal spirits, your essence,
Magically formed, grace this world with your presence.

Be content being you, seek tranquillity don't stint,
Absorb life's rules quickly, suppress wayward instincts,
Enjoy being educated, for knowledge is hard won,
Strive to love learning, for learning's never done.

And listen to your parents, learn from them well,
Ingest their selfless guidance, love, respect their guardian shell,
Love is loyal, it's insistent, the power that binds us all,
Stalwart bastion during stressful times, be sure you heed its call.

Malcolm P. Dick

Curious Paradox

It is my great and personal loss
Dear friends of first awakening
That you cannot share this walk
This feast of life with me
For I have gathered around me like black ice

The fragments of lost love
And from them forged a wall or tower
That grips the flesh - fruit of my heart
Like dead-men's fingers.
I have become stone.

Blackest night in the noon of life
Tumbling into some other orbit
Cold as the moon.
But what curious paradox.
In my hopelessness I have found hope

In my faithlessness I have found faith
For your words have kept me warm
Your love has fed me
And I have hidden it.
Like miser's gold on a stormy night.

Paul Jennings

Depths Of Peace

Reveal an inner secret
Dare not I.
Darkest thoughts wander about
forming a black evil sphere.
Demons and devils contribute to
hatred, bitterness and anger.
Peace is within a pure soul,
A soul free of mortal sin
Does such a soul exist?
Inner tranquillity is found in the
depths of ourselves.
Love and happiness fulfils
our hollow empty souls.
Let light shine through into this darkness.
Raise your spirit, warm your heart, forgive all.
Shun not the evil, as we have all sinned.

Sandra Campbell

"Gracious Lady"

Gentle, kindly, gracious lady,
constant in our darkest days:
stands serene when sorrow sears,
source of ever-flowing grace.
Sweetest smiles bless little children,
quiet words to heal distress;
sweetly gathers flowers proffered,
warms our hearts through tenderness.
Never was nor e'er shall come
Such a well - loved "Nation's Mum."

A. J. Pawsey

Bring Back Those Days

Running through meadows with hints of green
Daisies, cowslips lay down near a stream
Brambles are full of blackberries ripe.
Trees are all sizes, colours so bright.
Dog roses and lady smocks look delicately made
Under tall hedges lay cows in the shade
Checked tablecloths laid for a Sunday treat
Straw hats and caps protect us from heat
Moorhens and swans glide on the still waters
Parents go for walks with their sons and daughters.

Whatever happened to our family days out
Everything was ruined by some lousy clout
Learning was there always to enjoy
Instead it's computers or electronic toy
Our wildlife was destroyed by humankind
Foxes and badgers seem always to hide
Innocent children are frightened to play
This is the price we are having to pay
so let's start trusting and loving once more
Instead of turning nature into a war.

A. Redhead

Kingfisher

Kingfisher perched motionless
Dagger poised in hunched concentration.
Stabs the air - jerks
Points, stabs again.

Still - shadows sombre
In underworld stillness:
Gloom of their stillness:
And caverns dim and vast disturb his eye.

Small particles of light
Perfect - as each forming eye,
Uniting, hold - and mirror back
The world of bird, and branch, and sky.

Now light striking light
Liquid blue brilliant sparks of light
Bounce from light -
Fuse - in stillness.

Martin Stubberfield

'Soulmates'

Sleek, - as a well groomed jungle cat,
Curved as the graceful swan,
Perfumed; - heady, like the lotus flower -
So is my lovely one.
Mood changes:
Teeth bared to bite -
Claws poised to rip,
Eyes glowing; body arched, awaiting,
Sweet animal scents as passions rise,
My love and I, are mating.
Tender is she as love's lust dies,
Fulfilled; - free from passion's rigour,
Would time forever but stand still -
For you and I, - "Sweet Tiger"!

Alfred Johnson

Love Me

Cover me in autumn colours.
Cover me in love.
Cover me in what you will,
But not in cupboard love.

I'll live with you in autumn colours,
I'll love you all the while.
I'll live with you in what you will.
But not in cupboard love.

I'll walk with you in the autumn garden;
I'll love you all the time.
From beginning to end of a rainbow.
My love will always be thine.

L. Penney

My Spring Day Walk

As the blowing wind blows the leaves on the trees.
Cool air refreshing breeze.
I like to hear the birds singing.
And the church bells loudly ringing.
The soft chirping that the baby birds do.
I like the big bird's voices too.
As the ducks swim on the lake.
Bluebells you can gently pick and take.
And finally it is time to go home.
It is not nice without the birds, alone.

Kimberley Ellen Stothard

My Miracle

The veil has now been cast aside,
crystal-clear vision, eyes open wide.
A world restored to former glory,
verdant pastures, flaunting flora.
Overwhelmed by contrasts of my yesterdays,
clusters of colour, now spectacular displays.
Visual explosions assail reluctant eyes,
bombarded without mercy, tears and surprise.
Shattering the dream, shutters snap down
controlling intensity, easing a frown.
Dazzling sunshine confined to shade
flashing reflections instantly fade.
Beguiled by a daisy, simple, demure,
unworldly unheeded, chaste and pure.
Trampled beneath feet, no momentary fame,
consistently blooming again yet again.

Sheelagh E. Evans

Life

Laughter is sin
crying is poison
but only in time will these things
pass throughout my life.

When I grow old laughter will be
the drug of happiness
and crying will be the same
but more deadly with age.

As I travel through time seeing
wars in the news everyday, every year
nobody would be able to stop this.

People will die throughout my life
those that I have loved so much
but as I grow older everyday I will
get closer and closer to them and one day
my time will come when I will rest in peace.

Lesley-Ann Ross

Rooks

Seven thirty they began to gather
crowding the telegraph wires both near and far. Pairs
side by side. Some preferred tree-tops rather
than sagging wires. All ready for their shares
of grain that would be scattered in due course.
Regular as clockwork came the woman,
Her nightgown flapping in the wind, the source
the birds waited. As a sign or an omen,
two doves alighted next, timed by the clock.
The rooks regroup, face windward, feather sleek
they still await a signal. All the flock
will move together. No single bird will seek
to oust his fellow at the daily feast;

Then comes a swirl of wings a pall on grass;
They move as one the greatest and the least
A miracle of nature come to pass.

We think of NATURE as apart from us-
Does making of the bomb supply our plus?

M. Swords

Rooks

Seven thirty they began to gather
crowding the telegraph wires both near and far. Pairs
side by side. Some preferred tree-tops rather
than sagging wires. All ready for their shares
of grain that would be scattered in due course.
Regular as clockwork came the woman,
Her nightgown flapping in the wind, the source
the birds waited. As a sign or an omen,
two doves alighted next, timed by the clock.
The rooks regroup, face windward, feather sleek
they still await a signal. All the flock
will move together. No single bird will seek
to oust his fellow at the daily feast;

Then comes a swirl of wings a pall on grass;
They move as one the greatest and the least
A miracle of nature come to pass.

We think of NATURE as apart from us-
Does making of the bomb supply our plus?

M. Swords

A Prisoner

I am a prisoner - a prisoner in my body, though I have committed no crime
I feel bitter, frustrated, useless, but intelligent and whole in my mind
There's so much I want to do and so much I have to say
The difficulties in my life words alone cannot convey
Most people take for granted the simple, every day tasks they have to do
I'm a observer of life, I need a carer with me to see each day through
My limitations are endless, even a simple trip into town
I can't use the buses, Dial-a-Ride and booked - oh, it gets me down
Now local government are thinking of charging for services -
those that we don't pay for yet
The fact that our families/spouses pay taxes they seem to forget
I am angry at the expense to which all disability leads
I am tired of fighting for basic rights and needs
Still, believe it or not, there are plenty worse off than me
At least I am able to speak, hear, think and see
And when someone meets me in the street, I smile and say I'm fine
Even though I am a prisoner who has committed no crime!

Vicky Giles

I Believe

I do believe that God above
created you for me to love
He picked you out from all the rest
because, He knew I'd love you best
I have a heart so warm and true
and now I give my heart to you
take care of it as I have done
because now you've two and I have none
if I go to heaven and you're not there
I'll paint your name on the golden stair
if you don't arrive by judgement day
then I'll know you've gone the other way
I'll give the angels back their wings
their golden harps and everything
my darling just to prove what I would do
I'd even go to hell for you.

Michael John Evers

Night

The crescent moon swings low in winter skies,
Cradled in blackened branches, stripped of leaves.
Upon her lap, the evening star, she lies,
The velvet cloaks of night embrace the trees,

The spangled velvet clark holds close around.
Owls, weary, hooting, glide in silent flight,
Familiar themes of other creatures sound,
The fox will stalk the rabbit as her right.

The rising sun glows in the eastern sky,
Birds find their voices, Robin, Lark and Jay.
As fingers of light creep slowly 'cross on high,
Withdrawing the drapes of night, to welcome day.

Peggy Fountain

"Steven"

Steven my grandson is my pride and joy.
A happy, fun loving, bright little boy.
Bright red hair eyes of green.
He looks a picture when first seen.
When he's in trouble he sits with a frown
Then he gets up and jumps up and down.
He handcuffed his dog Hamish to a chair
Hamish just sat with a mournful stare.
I don't know how often his mother has said
"Any more nonsense and you're off to bed"
Steven says, "sorry" and promises to be good.
Then he forgets and starts being rude.
So off to bed, Steven must go.
His face seems to lose, all of its glow.
The blinds are pulled down, when it's still light
Steven is having another early night
If I didn't have Steven what would I do.
I wouldn't change him, who would? Would you?

Elizabeth Tees

October 10, 1995

Aren't I a very fortunate man
able to walk. Wherever I can
having passed three score plus ten and more
I count my blessings by the score
and I have many many friends
and sing in choir's great amens

Oh this beautiful October day
this indian summer October is May
the jolly old sun warm on my back
My heart of joy, what do I lack?
Suddenly I burst into song
This world of ours, cannot be wrong.

Oh these beautiful October tints
Even ripples in the river sing
then suddenly I realize
that I have more, than any king.

David W. Davies

A Friend

There he sleeps upon my bed
A yawn and stretch as he raised his head
It's time to get up is what I say
And still no movement to my dismay
I go down stairs to make the tea
And as I turn he's there with me
My day's busy, his is not
I open the door and out he trots
The morning is bright, crisp and cold
The leaves on the trees are not brown but gold
I closed the door when there was a knock
It's buster back home from his morning walk
He spoke as he entered to get some attention
You're a handsome cat and full of devotion
Be a good boy, I won't be long
Another day has just begun.

Jenny Levey

Baby Boy

I saw a new born child today,
A tiny baby boy, the sweet young mother
smiled at him all radiant with joy,
The tiny form was beautiful, and wonderfully
placed - a perfect living thing, fresh from
the Great Creator's hand. And as I watched
I prayed that he would use this little life.
To work his purposes amid the pain of
human strife, Each child creates his
destiny who knows what it may bring?
Oh may those tiny hands be used to do
some splendid thing!

Alice M. Reynolds

The Lone Cowboy

Now this is a poem to be my own, about a life by me idolized,
About a man who travels alone, save for his horse and a gun
    at each side,
A Cowboy he is just one of a crowd, no more than others by
    nature endowed.
But in that life of the Great Wide Range, he typifies all and to
    nothing is strange,
He may be tall with an easy stride, or perhaps he's small but
    he can ride,
A cheery face bronzed by wind and sun, the usual clothes
    with an extra gun,
The Rambling Kid his name might be but what's in a name
    where names are free,
'Tis just the part in life he portrays, what he does and what he says,
He and his horse they wander far, between them a bond no
    man could break,
At night a camp by a creek 'neath the stars, living his life but
    gambling with fate,
Then when the round-up time comes along, he's there amidst
    the cowboy throng,
Roping, throwing and fixing his brand, he's young - yet he's a
    top-hand man,
No ranch can ever keep him long, the Wanderlust hold on him
    is strong,
O'er the Prairie with his horse he goes, like the tumbleweed
    when a strong wind blows,
Too many he may be an ornery cuss, to others he may be a
    dog-gone sight wuss,
But I know to me he will always be, a Lone Cowboy and an
    ace-high hombre.

Irene Steel

The Symbol

For years the tree had stood there,
    a testament to life,
No gale nor drought could staunch its will
    to grow towards the light.
Through the gentle rains of springtime
    and the summer's golden days
Its green and leafy mantle reached to
    catch the sun's warm rays.
Through autumn gales and winter cold
    it stood there, proud and tall,
A child of Mother nature and a symbol for us all.

As winter's snows retreated and springtime came around
The woodland tracts awakened to a loud
    and threatening sound
And metal jaws devoured their prey,
    from dawn until the end of day.
No longer does that proud tree stand,
    a child of Mother nature's hand,
Its fall by man was deftly planned —
    a symbol of our ravaged land.

Jane Scott

Memories

We said our last farewell,
A year ago today.
There's sadness still within my heart,
But time heals, so they say.
Your happy smile, your teasing ways,
Each one brings back a memory,
Of lovely times, that we both shared,
I treasure each one dearly.
But now I have to start again,
My life to build anew.
It will be quite hard work I know
Because I'll miss you so.
But I shall try so very hard,
To make life good again.
Enjoying beauty all around.
The love of family and friends.
As times goes by, I know I will,
learn to smile again,
But I shall treasure your memory
And be a little sad - till then.

Constance Barton

The Switch

I saw him by the lorry
A switch was in his hand
He used it on the cattle
But they did not understand

He beat the beasts right smartly
They had to mount the wood
But round and round they milled and turned
And they never understood

Just dumb they are we say
But numb is not there pain
And if that man himself could see
He'd never use that switch again.

Joan Dunkley

Dad (James Arthur Railton)

My Dad had a smile for all to see,
A special warmth, when in sadness or in glee.
Blue eyes and sun-tanned all year round.
A pleasant, calm chap everyone found.

Never an argument or temper you saw,
He was so proud of Alan, David, Joan, Ann and Mo;
He'd work in the fields, and see to his stock,
The hours went by, he'd never notice the clock.

Nancy worked in the house, and the kitchen all day,
Dad still in the fields harvesting the hay,
Working the months to the time of the year,
When holidays were planned for the family to go away.

Scotland he loved, his tartan was "Black Watch".
The bagpipes, the Glens, and "Nessie" in the loch.
Annual holidays were spent in Dundee and Inverness,
Camping or Caravanning these times were the best.

His dogs Flossy and Glen were Dad's favourite pets.
Jinxy the ginger cat, the cockerels that pecked,
Geese were not his choice, they were angry at play.
Pitt House and Snods Edge...Let's call it a day.

Ann Willis

Feeling The Colours

An amazing azure sky drapes its silky blueness over
A pure and snow white rabbit in a deep green sea of clover

A blazing burning sun projects its flaming finger down
through the choking smoking cloud above a grey and fuming town.

A smooth and cream skinned finger feels its silky path across
A soft white face of innocence, drowned in deep ethos.

A screwed up scarlet face throws its fiery anger out
towards the crouching purple child with his rainbow wrapped about.

Jennifer Moore

Baby

I turn my diary to another page
A red circle ringed around a date
The sorrow and pain turn into rage
Voices in my head saying it was fate

Looking out my window, a beautiful day
Tears sting my eyes, fall to my cheek
You should be here now, I hear myself say
Too little they said, your body so weak

Would your hair have been blonde, your eyes blue?
I wanted to hold you close to my heart
But God wanted a Baby, and so he chose you
Miscarriage again, it's torn me apart

So now this month you should be born
I'll try to be brave, and be strong
Tomorrow's another day, breaking dawn
Birds will chirp for you a lullaby song

Barrie-Jaine Bright

My Last Crusade

A thousand years in the time of our Lord,
a shield, a horse and a worn-out sword,
fighting for a place of holy soil,
three long years of blood and toil.

A baking sun on barren earth,
our campaign, the church of birth,
the choice of the king, this war to start,
so stand by your men, brave lion-heart.

When the Saracens call their battle cry,
hoards of men are sure to die,
yet we march on for our king,
a story of home, aloud we sing.

We ride for a town called Bethlehem,
never seen before, never will again,
and if it be my final rest,
then by God, I'll fight my best.

For my sins, I have slain,
and for my crest, I will again,
for England breeds the finest stock,
and to its banner, we shall flock.

David Towers-Clark

Heartache

"You only saw the face not the heart"
A saying I long pondered, now we are apart
No I am not beautiful with special style
Julia has charisma and must beguile
My heart still aches that is so very true
I thought I had found my other half in you
Now Julia is all you really desire.
She certainly sets your loving heart afire
I have tried to console myself from the start
You saw only my plain ordinary face
Not my truly faithful loving heart

Irene Wenstrom

Now

Today is sweet, breathe it all in.
A moment now enjoyed is worth
a day that may never begin.
Inhale the air, how sweet, how pure.
The power of life! A tool to endure

Friends departed, loved ones gone.
The blackbird still appears and sings a song.
Tomorrow is an age away,
true it is another day!
The time warp works, it's very odd.
Tomorrow now? Can this be God!

Life goes on, it goes away.
Sometime for all! No other day.
Today is sweet, take it all in.
A day now enjoyed is worth
a moment that may never begin.

David A. Stow

The Wonderment Of A Child

The child sits staring up into space
A look of wonderment on his face.
The magnitude so hard to comprehend
Is taken for granted by most grown men.
But the innocent child sees glory abound
And magic in everything can be found.
To him space is a wondrous sight
And one day when he's older he dreams that he might
Take a trip to the stars and see their beauty first hand
Or on a distant planet land
But for now he's content to stare into space
With that look of wonderment still on his face.

Anne E. Buckley

Mahatma Ghandi

Gentle in manner, concerned with right,
A little man of awesome might;
Neatly attired in simple fashion,
Filled with kindness and compassion,
Ghandi must have been a joy to know-
His strength infected others so.

Deep lines of humour adorned his face,
As, with such dignity and grace,
He laboured long to free a nation,
Seeking not such adoration;
For though his light shone all around,
His feet were firmly on the ground.

And millions mourned him as their friend,
When Ghandi's life came to an end.
Carole Tovell

Challenger R. I. P.

Lost in the night, adrift with the stars.
A hero's welcome should of been ours.
Brave are the warriors who strive for the free.
Morbid fears, we couldn't see.
Erased from time with no more sound
An endless silence heaven bound.
Gerardine O'Sullivan

So Many Beautiful Things

Amid the pale blue atrocities,
A life spills over the edge.
A vertigo of Hell dismisses itself.
(Flames flicker out in the eyes of a girl who...)
A scream explodes the night
In a kaleidoscope of dissonance.
I cannot close my eyes.
A kind of voyeurism;
I can sit and watch,
Witness so many beautiful things.

A fleeting glimpse of Heaven
As a life spills over the hands
Of a lover.
A cry echoes and pulses in the aftermath.
(I close my eyes and see a girl who...)

Once I saw two people amongst the waves of a large, dark ocean,
And oh! The beauty of it all as they held each other down!
I try to recapture the scene,
But see only the eyes of a girl who....
(I once saw the demise of a girl who...)
Donna Enticknap

My Life's Wish

My life has been full of love and happiness,
A life of toil, struggles, but with a tenderness,
Of the joys one can remember since childhood days,
Of a being-togetherness, in so many ways.

I have led a full life, with not a regret,
Looking back over the years, never to forget
The Sunday walks we had, through leafy lanes,
Laughing and holding hands, and watching the old steam-trains.

Memories such as these fill my heart with great joy,
Knowing that I have been happy, since I was a boy.
I shall never fear eternal slumber, when it comes to me.
I shall be strong in my weakness, my soul to set free.

My love shall remain in my dear wife's heart,
Only with her will my life's love impart.
My children, I wish to be as happy as we have been,
To live a full life that is happy, blissful and clean.

And I pray to the Lord he will join us again
In the heavens above, where He doth sit and reign,
Keeping watch on those dear, we have left behind,
And giving them tenderness, that they deserve to find.
Dennis James Cannings

"The Job Club"

"You've signed on" now, for near 12 month,
A "Job Club", may be the answer,
It, just might help, it 'Dun't Cost 'Owt',
Go on! Be a "chancer!"

I took his advice, and went along,
All ready, now to sample,
'Flip charts', talks and videos,
With letters - 'for example',

Teens and twenties, gathered there,
Looking with enjoyment,
At sad, tired, 50 odd year olds
Searching for employment,

But 'Proper Jobs', were very scarce,
and "Few and Far" between,
"Tha'll not find 'owt', but rubbish 'ere,
No matter "weer tha's been".

I stuck it out, for o'er a month.
But left when sick and tired,
I'll not go back, no matter what,
I'd sooner be expired!!
Harry Baron

Alderney

Alderney and what it means to me,
A jewel of an island in the Channel sea,
With friendly people, a close community,
Where folks are not scared and children can roam free,
With cobbled streets, it's really quaint,
Artists love to come and paint,
The beaches full of golden sand,
The breathtaking views from my homeland,
A small island that's not oversized,
With unspoilt beauty and not too commercialised,
It really is a tranquil place,
Far removed from the so called rat race,
A gem of an island surrounded by blue sea,
Alderney, the place where I love to be.
Julie Main

Blood, Sweat An' Tears

Here's tae the men, fae the East an' the West
A grand bunch o lads, aye the Vera Best
But yon tory crew put us tae the test
Noo thir's hardly a wife, hingin oot a Pit Vest

Aye ah mind o' the days, when pits wir abundant
Noo thir is but a few, with lads aw redundant
But Arthur an' Mick an' thair lads knew
That the seams lay thick, nae need fir the broo

Wi oor blood sweat an' tears, we howkit the coal
An' you crew they peyed us, wi years on the dole
But nae shame tae us lads, we've nothing tae hide
Jist anither raw deal tae tak in oor stride

But bear it in mind lads, tho' we ta'en the sting
Tae the sons o' oor sons, folk'll hear them sing
Come awa noo lads, yir aw aff the dole
Aye thirs plenty wark, at yir grandfaither's coal
Andrew Lamb

Streets Of London

Come buy my sweet lavender,
A ghostly call from a by-gone age,
Places and people have to change,
We ask but why!
Horse-drawn cabs, with the rustle of skirts,
No such thing as high finance with something called perks.
Are we in a better age,
Is time moving too fast,
Could this be another phase,
Time will slow down, so that we can all adjust.
With this new hi-tec computer age
It's got to be a must.
Jean E. Gadeke

A Warming Wonder

The first days of summer arrive so unexpectedly.
A glimpse of sun, shining through a withering flower -
Soft cloud. Nature timidly appears, blooming into
Glory. Tender blades of grass look succulently more
Greener. A gentle breeze whisps among the activity.

As the warm weather turns mildly heated, people
Begin to relax. They turn from a pale pink to a
Tender golden brown. Children can be seen,
Without a worry, careless, playing with many of
Their friends, enjoying the warming primrose sun.

Days sneakily progress, becoming more of a
Sweltering kind. Things change, making people
Irritable. Brows are mopped and places of
Shade are packed full like unharvested fields
Of corn.

Before it is noticed, the wanted or unwanted
Summer days disappear. All nature is changed,
Having been touched by a miracle. Again, a flower -
Soft cloud appears. It hides the sun from view.

Anita Hardcastle

The Sad Story Of The Muscle Man

He walks down the beach all muscle and tan,
A girl by his side, and a towel in his hand.
But heckled he was by the boys round the pier
They said we only want divers around here.

"I can do that", burst our hero, so proud.
"Then why don't you do it", said a voice from the crowd
"I will" cried our hero, "I've seen how it's done"
And without any delay he started to run

Off of the beach, and on to the pier.
He called to the people to move and stand clear,
And off of the pier our big hero flew
As swift as an arrow, and into the blue.

Yes into the blue, like a hot knife through butter
Then swam like a brick, and he coughed and he spluttered
There's a part in this story I neglected to tell
Although he looked good, he couldn't swim well.

Towards the sea bed our hero went down
The law of the sea says if you can't swim you'll drown
There's a moral to this tale, don't end up like him
Before you go diving learn how to swim.

Christopher Manchip

This White Man's Burden

At the window I can see the hills, and the red brick of the old
cotton mills; I see pylons march across the land, towards new
horizons, regular as stitches, sewn by a surgeon's hand, in a
wound, of a man, in a war, who at least may have known what
it was he fought for

The past is present always, at the cemetery in Dukinfield
So much like Tyne Cot, Passchendaele, where death alone
forced men to yield, men who were never to see their prime,
cut down like corn before their time

And me? Early 30 something, still craving and yet hating praise
Wondering what it takes to be a hero in this world nowadays,
a sometimes desperate man, whose life never quite went to
plan; cautious... Hesitating, waiting always waiting, for a time,
when I strike with the speed, of a serpent, and justify my
existence, in an insanely moment

This white man's burden: the blood on the hands of his forebears;
The childhood guilt of keeping eyes open during Remem-
brance Day prayers, and the emotional baggage of his
country's hand-me-downs, that he has no choice but to wear,
despite others' gibes and frowns

I wonder whether I'm missing something, when I look at all my
friends. Can there be heroism in mortgages, and babies, visits
to IKEA at weekends? With my wife I am much happier than I
have a right to be. But if I can be a father, will our child be
proud of me?

John Spiller

Your Love

Like a warm glow from a winter's fire,
A gentle kiss of loving desire,
A rainbow after the storm dies down,
A flag of truce on battled ground,
A snowdrop's beauty on a snowy day,
Your love reaches out this way.

Like a bird singing in the trees,
A sound of humming from the bees,
A gentle flowing of a stream,
A warm glow from a sunbeam,
A sight of bluebells in May,
Your love reaches out this way.

Like a smiling baby in mother's arms,
A soft sweet voice that calms,
A first word spoken by a child,
A first step taken as parents smiled,
A memory of happy days at play,
Your love reaches out this way.

Graham F. Blissett

What Is A Daughter

A daughter means a loving voice and gentle touch.
A daughter is someone you love so very much.
Someone who is always in my thoughts.
A mother thinks of the love she has brought.

A daughter is someone you share,
Also someone who is so full of care.
A daughter is someone who shares laughter and sorrow.
Someone you are pleased to see on the morrow.

A daughter is someone who is full of love
A daughter is someone you are always proud of.
A daughter is someone who shares a mother's love.
A daughter is a daughter so fondly thought of.

A daughter is a daughter.
Also a friend.
As she travels through life.
From beginning to end.

Beryl Shipman

Waltham Windmill

There's a windmill at the top of our street,
A beautiful sight a real treat,
The five sails whirling up in the air,
Makes old and young visitors stand and stare,
Going closer for an extra look and to explore,
You'll find crafts, antiques, ice cream tea shop and much more,
There's gardening, tools, herbs, plants, and how to store,
Beehives, how the honey is made, many workers that's for sure,
There's car boot sales with nick knacks, gifts galore,
A ride on miniature railway for youngsters who ask for more,
It's a lovely day out with a variety of thrills
Even buying real flour crushed by big flat wheels in the Mills
Back up the street time to stand in awe and wonder
At those big sails going round in the sky over yonder.

Colleen Pearson

Invitations

  Come dance with me - said the man of straw
a barn dance played - as they took the floor.
  Come dance with me - said the man of steel
the rafters rang - to the sound of a reel.
  Come dance with me - said the man of clay
strains of a waltz - the band began to play.
  Come dance with me - said the man of stone
they trod a stately measure - to a solitary trombone.
  Come dance with me - said the man of sand
a soft shoe shuffle - with a Dixie Jazz band.
  Come dance with me - said the man of tin
they whirled the hours away - to a gipsy violin.
  Come dance with me - said the man of snow
with a melting glance - the lady stopped the show

Doreen Beverley Stephenson

"The Mourning Stars"

"Away in a manger, no crib for a bed..."
A cute little baby rested his head
On the side of his buggy, fast asleep:
The shoppers around him shuffled their feet
As they sang with the Salvation Army Band,
And clasped their donations in generous hands.
The roof of the precinct was shaped as a dome,
And reflective glass sparkled, and twinkled, and shone,
Like the stained-glass windows of a beautiful church.
A thin 'soap-box' preacher cried - "God is here ... search!"
This was the season of loving and giving -
The people were full of the pure joy of living:
Their crescendo of thankfulness rose as one song,
And exploded on high with .... A BOMB!!
Mayhem and carnage raged through the night
But the cowardly bombers were safe, out of sight!.....
"The stars in the bright sky looked down where he lay" -
At the shattered, small victim of mental decay -
   And they wept as the baby died.
    Joan True

A British Ruin

Now ghostly seems the ruin on the hill
A crumbling tower and soft decaying walls,
Whose shadow on the cowering landscape falls
An atmosphere so strange and sadly still.
Of life it seems the scene has had its fill,
Fast visions in an empty hall
Left only to the wind to sing and call
Is now succumbing fast to nature's will
An edifice of mortar stone and wood
Is left to stand, a sorry silent face,
The times are gone that once perhaps were good
Oblivious to times relentless race,
That once was bathed, was washed by life's sweet flood
Now is old and tired and lacking grace.
   David Stephen Marshall

Nan's Brooch

Nan gave me a brooch when I was sixteen,
a cameo, cinnamon with cream silhouette,
its concave back, like a shell,
filled with echoes of zeppelins and kisses.

A girl who was not yet Nan
had worn the brooch, pinned to her blouse
by a lover not yet Grandad,
waltzing around war-time dance halls.

I wore the brooch like an amulet
to the cabbalistic discotheques.
I pinned it to my wedding dress
then put it away from tiny prying fingers.

I found it in a box today,
peeled away the layers of tissue
until Nan's brooch lay in my hand.
The spicy glow had faded to white.
   Gill Smith

To Be One

It's time to dance the fire of life,
to enter into the rain,
to feel a child's own worries,
for some to escape the pain,
for some to realize meaning,
for those who do not know, who surely must be dreaming,
as from this little view of the game,
I know why, feel no worries, no pain,
to nothing shall I be blind,
experiencing with awareness the waking mind,
the realization of things unknown,
confusion is so clearly shown.
   Simon Marks

The Snow

Snow, a great white show
a blanket of ivory shining bright
sunshine revealing diamonds glimmering, glitter shimmering
snow so cold to touch and hold,
turns to water so fresh and pure.

Clouds all grey, bleak on this day
Cushions enfolding more feathery flakes
they fall lightly gliding drifting
whether breeze or not.

Trees all white clasping cotton wool on branches
One small breeze the disperse of shreds
to carpet the floor of the outdoor beds.
Bright is our light no bulb to bare, enlightening,
to see it feels you're in a stare.

People pink faced and full of glare
footprints leaving their place on the ground
animal or human, whatever found, signs of life.
Another day fades away, darkness falls
one white sceneries, instead of black
   Diana Neill

Untitled

Of all the things I've ever done
To be at the birth of my daughter's son
Will be a time I'll never forget
To hold him close all warm and wet

The going was tough we laughed and cried
But I was so glad I was by her side.
To see a new life right from the start
Is something I'll always hold close in my heart
A day I know I'll never forget
The day my grandson and I first met.
   Pat Kirtland

Band Of Gold

My wedding ring was sparkling bright,
Tipped back and forth, it caught the light.
As bright and shiny as our dream,
A never-ending love, it seemed.

But year by year the brightness dulled.
And hopeful dreams were unfulfilled.
How sad that love turned out that way
When we thought love was here to stay.

And now my finger is quite bare -
My ring no longer circling there,
That cherished, simple band of gold
Tarnished by the lies he told.

Does his new wife admire the band
On the finger of her hand?
Divorce is painful, cruel and sad,
Omits to mention love we had.

Has he forgotten all the past -
Forgotten love we thought would last?
Perhaps one day I'll love once more,
Be happy, as I was before.
   C. A. Read

Byrness 1993

Twenty years have come and gone
times have changed and now moved on
chainsaws few and far between
we fell trees now with big machines
cutting and restocking can still be seen
to keep the worlds environment green
Our managers know the problems here
and strive to save the ozone layer
planting moor that had no use
to grow the world some sitka spruce
spruce trees, willow and mountain ash
to save our precious ozone gas
   H. Tait

A-Hopping We Will Go

Their hands were willing
To earn a few shillings
In the morning mist heavy dew.
Gypsies, town folk, country all
Picking away till evening fall
Shire horses I hasten to say
Pulling the drays of hops, picked that day.
Cold tea green fingers, cheese and bread.
That was the menu, it had to be said.
The measure man, who blew his whistle
Stern his voice, "No leaves, no thistles",
And all for just a shilling a bushel.
Evening came the bonfire bright,
Singing and dancing, stars there that night.
Pay day came, for them heaven sent.
Now hopping is all over.
The money now is spent,
They only went a hopping,
To pay the ruddy rent.

Sybil Grace

If

If I bought a lottery ticket
Though I doubt I ever would
And if I won the jackpot
Which, of course, I never should
I'd buy up every dictionary
In Britain and the USA
Send a copy to all scriptwriters
And this is what I'd say
Scan the pages and you'll surely see
More pleasant alternatives for ess, itch, eye, tee.

L. A. Graves

"My Gift To You"

I have a Gift for you today, My Dear,
To cherish every day throughout the year.
Its value? Priceless. Beyond all worldly ken.
It cannot be bought or sold, but then
To own this Gift one must be richer by far
Than any Merchant or fabulous 'Prince of Alcazar'.

How came I by such a rare Gift as this?
By having known two years of such bliss
From which has grown the most precious gem of all.
Bidding the brightest of stars to fall.
Making my Love and Faith in you so deep,
That, so for ever, shall it keep.

My Darling, as we start this New Year of Love,
We have another Gift sent to us from above.
So that in the future, wonderful years,
We may never know the loneliness of tears.
There will always be one to soothe the pain
Until we are all three, together again.

Mary Durant Taylor

In The Bath

Your breath rises, mingled with steam,
To cast a fog across the distant horizon
Of the mirror. You sink down and dream
Of expanses of ocean-bathed in the heat of the sun,
Which flows like honey, or of a sheltered harbour
Where the tide-lapped ships sway in the darkness,
As you lay at anchor
Marooned in a sea of forgetfulness.

Cup your hand to your ear,
Concentrate and hear
The roar of the storm-stirred sea
Flowing through the blood in your veins.
You could almost be free
Of every care,
But the stilted song of distant trains
Drifts in on the air
To shatter your silence.

Nicola Barnes

Fill It Full Lord

When it's grey we need to keep our spirits up,
To believe we've a half-full not half-empty cup;
To mentally picture pretty wild flowers growing
Or the scent of summer grass just after a mowing!

We need thoughts that put a smile on our face,
Of a good time we've had or a beautiful place;
To stretch out our arms and give a big hug
To all that is hopeful, to kindness and love.

We actually need to turn to the One
Who will do as indeed He has always done,
When it's grey and we cry "Please help me Lord"
Has into our cup such a blessing poured!

P. M. Warren

Poetry Is Great

I have not been fired but I am retired, with lots of
time to spare, in weather like this it's nice to sit
in a cosy chair, trying to write a poem or two just
hoping to please both me and you, it's really hard I
have to say trying to write good words each day,
but some folks overcome this tasks and really reach
their goal at last, it must be great to reach such
fame then in bright lights you will see your name poet
Laureate the aim, but a poet is all I hope to be and the
Laureate bit well I just can't see, but I'll keep on trying
and that's for sure until it's time to close that door
the door to writing that's what I mean but even then I'll
still be keen to write some more, and even then,
I will try my hand again.

W. Passfield

A Matter Of Time

What is past, now and tomorrow,
Time is just too hard to follow,
Going forwards, never back,
Along this endless, linear track,
When will tomorrow be today,
What is tomorrow anyway,
How long will time in this form last,
Will we be lost within our past,
Is time doomed to repeat itself,
Will we have time to grain great wealth,
Did time begin at a place finite,
To make the change from day to night,
Or was it constantly arranged,
For time must exist, for things to change.

Thomas Elliott

Ceremony

Gowns to be made, flowers to arrange for the alter
Time has come yet again, to wed another daughter

The wedding bands were set, the day was forthcoming
The bride and groom were happy and very unassuming

A practice run, to get everything fixed in their head
Prompted by the vicar, remembering the words to be said

Selecting the right songs that everyone could sing
Choosing music and hymns, hoping they've done the right thing

Wedding rings were purchased, then adjusted to fit
The best man was selected for his charm and for his wit

Cars were at the ready, the reception was out of their hands
At the alter like a nervous statue, the bridegroom stands

Music plays, everyone turns their head to see
Enter the bride, looking as pretty as she could be

Gold rings were exchanged, they finished with a kiss
Best wishes were given, for many years of wedded bliss

Joined in marriage, they said the words they had to say
It's a son-in-law gained and another daughter given away

Roy Hunter

Friendship

You'll never know what friendship means
'Til things have all gone awry
And then you'll find the stalwarts
For they are standing by
With gentle words of comfort
And loving hands to hold
You learned that there is something
That's worth far more than gold
a whispered word of courage
An arm to share the load
A shoulder just to cry on
and just to say a word
They all add up to friendship
There is no better word
Tom E. Clark

To A Brother

Though gone from this earth are thee
Thy memories still live in the heart of man
Famous works of the Bards ye ken
Now sang and recited by women and men.

Still they dress smart shirt and ties
And yearly meet with tears in their eyes
Raising their glasses to a loyal friend
It's early morning before the end.

Thy picture, it hangs upon the wall
Yearly greetings verses for all
YER bust on the mantle it is sat
Brothers then, Aye Brothers now
The world over still. For Awe that
AND Awe that...
Ruth McIntyre

Ode To Spring

"Now maiden spring has come at last.
Through the meadow she has passed.
Painting each leaf, opening each flower
Scattering gold coins in the primrose bower.

Soft green hedges, white with May
Look down on fields, with lambs at play
And from a copse, the cuckoo's call,
Lifts our hearts with hope for all.

Gone is winter's snow and sleet.
Now, green shoots of oats and wheat.
Soon to turn to waving gold,
splashed with red of poppies bold.

Children play out, light and free.
So much to do, so much to see.
All nature seems to stretch and wake.
And gives to all, who care to take.
B. G. Metcalfe

For Mary-Jane Hanlon (My Grandmother)

Warmth, Cuddles, Smoke and Perfume,
Through the eyes of a child, all else is immune.
Kisses and Tickles race on to the night,
Till the laughter dies, and silent is the room.
Peace, safeness and feeling secure,
Brings back to my mind, all thoughts of you dear.
Whispers, giggles, and secrets shared,
Till the sounds of dawn, come creeping up the stairs.

Singing, dancing and rolling around,
To the pains of illness, and lying down.
No longer a child,
but like the bird on the wing,
Sits back to watch everything.
To days in the sun,
To days in the rain,
To loving, crying, living and dying.
From her novel "A Prayer for Mary-Jane"
Karin Benson

Snowdrops

Clustered like glistening teardrops peeping
through fresh white snow, ever searching for
the sunlight to help them to stretch and to grow.
When the wind stirs their petals ice cold
maidens dance to and fro.
Offering forth life's future comings and the
end of winter's snow.
Once the winds and snows are over and their
time to flower is done, gently offering for
your perusal snowdrops in their beauty
snowdrops pure and shy.
M. W. Adams

Mystery

You keep a secret, the mystery of ages
Though probed, questioned and explored
You keep the truth within
You are intrigue, akin to ancient mages
Though intimately known
You'll ever be a wonder
You give enough to excite the mind
But never know for sure
You give to each his own idea
And for each a different lure
I'm thinking now if you could talk
What a tale you'd have to tell
Of the passing of millennia
As you slowly tired and fell
Our ignorance of the needs you have
Has led to your decline
For our neglect of nature's ways
You are a potent sign
Our ignorance is your revenge
For our neglect of you Stonehenge
A. J. Wilson

To Laughter

To laugh, and laugh aloud, be unafraid,
Though men should stare, and women turn and frown,
Though they should nudge, their pleasing looks should fade,
Yet with your pleasure, their displeasure drown.
Forget them all, they have not heard the words
Which caused the ripple in you to arise
And wind its way with speed of winging birds
From brain to lips, from whence it caused surprise.
Throw back your head and let the laughter ring,
They are too slow that have not seen the move;
Go, stab the silence with a happy sting,
For such a mood bears roots of purest love.
Laugh while you may, who knows, perchance tomorrow,
The tears you laugh today you'll weep in sorrow.
Rosamund Browne

That Special Moment

Those wonderful words "I love you", from your lips, did flow.
Those wonderful words "I love you", were all, I wanted, to know.
I knew my prayers were answered, the day you told me this.
I held my hands, about your face, and I thanked you, with a kiss.
"I love you too, my darling", I replied in ecstasy.
I felt the warmth of love, that flowed, between, both you, and me.
I felt my body tremble, from-the-excitement, in my heart.
I thought of all the hours, that-we'd-spent, in vain, apart.
I wish that you confronted me, the minute that you knew.
Because - I've, gone around in circles, not knowing what to do.
This feeling that's so mutual, is burning like a fire.
This feeling, that's so strong inside, has left us, with desire.
Nothing in this universe, can kill the love we own.
Never, has a love this strong, ever-before, been known.
We kissed each other tenderly, and held each other tight.
The comfort, that we felt from this, definitely felt, so right.
This special moment in our lives, will always be, a treasure.
The moment, for the first time, we both felt, so much, pleasure.
Thank you for confronting me, in this beautiful way.
You've left a very happy, person, standing in dismay.
Linda George

Just A Little While

What lovely days we had in that past time;
Those fleeting moments, snatched, when you loved me.
Although I must say I was past my prime;
Our love was there for all the world to see.

But we both knew the spell could never last;
That outside pressures would be brought to bear
Upon our sacred secret. That is past.
Our time has gone, but I will always care.

I loved you more than you could ever know;
As I look back I brush away a tear,
My happiness depended on you so;
But it has gone, and so have you I fear.

When I look back I will recall and smile,
That you were mine for just a little while.

H. R. Miller

The Ruby

We caught our breaths, for diamonds seemed alight
"This" we cried "is brightness of the bright"
And brightness here means richest of the rich
Apparently, to foolish man's delight.
'Tis in this carbon splendour so arrayed
That witless man his treasure has displayed'
And in the shape of things that are to be
Sees us proudly march in grand parade,
But balm there's none for those in mis'ry bred
For e'en the wand that struck their spark is sped,
And in the breach 'tis dolour deep in tears,
That sad some aching heart in anguish bled.

But diamonds? They have yielded- strongly pressed
To a ruby which surmounts a velvet breast.

Ron Taplin

A Mothers Pain

Sunflowers standing tall, wilting,
This lonely mother crumples weeping
A lost youth, a tattered life
Who's to say, in this world, what's right?

Children suffering, holding on to their keys
Coming home alone to watch their T.V.
Mother's out working, she's not at hand
As her children grow up in this violent land

Haunted live's seeks solace
In drug filled clubs for fun
Tragedy strikes, in lives of hardship
And this family are mourning one

She weeps at the endless horror
Alone at the graveside she stands
As she whispers GOODBYE to a loved one
All the guilt, she will feel first hand

GROWING UP IN THIS VIOLENT LAND..........

T. W. Whelan

Paradise

Lying on a beach of fame, admiring all the pretty dames,
this is where I want to be, until the day my finality.
The sun beats down goes through my brain, it reaches parts
that keep me sane the sea in front the waves ride high,
give me a board I'll ride that tide.
A dame walks by I flick an eye, she cutely smiles says hi! mate,
I raise my body from off the ground, politely ask, Do you mind?
She takes the bottle and fills her hands, then slowly rubs my body
down, my body tingles as she feels, could this be my dream female?
And now she's finished her little job, I wish she'd ask the
same of me, she wipes her hands on my short trunks WOW!
Could this be a sign?
Listen love I have to go, my husband would be oh so cross,
but if you'd like we'll meet one night at that club called PARADISE.

Steven Daynes

This Is Justice

This is the cocky criminal
This is the old lady he attacked, hospitalized in intensive care
This is the courtroom and the hearing a year after the attack
This is the old lady, finally out of hospital, terrified
This is the criminal's lawyer saying it was his first offence
This is the lenient judge's decision - two hours community service
This is the cocky criminal, strutting out of court
This is the old lady, tormented by him and petrified
This is the smug criminal doing his community service
This is the old lady fearful of opening her front door.

This is the cocky criminal committing another crime
This is another old lady in intensive care
This is the courtroom and the hearing
This is the criminal's lawyer saying it was only his second offence
This is the lenient judge
This is the harsher sentence - six hours community service
This is the relieved and smug cocky criminal
This the terrified old lady
This is the law
This is justice?

R. J. G. Bakewell

That Empty Space (My Dad)

I write lest I forget this new intruding space
This hole that has appeared, that makes my heart lose pace
Oh the emptiness within
The hopelessness, the helplessness that isn't cause by sin
Can't you feel it? Don't you understand?
Where is he that I so loved that I may hold his hand?
People go about their day, they feel no hurt or pain
My spirit rebels that they don't share, my loss of love unfeigned
At home he is there in everything I see
The garden shed, the winding path, the little apple tree
The vegetable patch has gone, and the old dump too
There's only grass to cut now, not a lot to do.
I fancy I see through the greenhouse glass
Him dressed in gardening clothes and hat, but no, they're just
  dreams alas.

No more "hello chic how are you today?"
He went before I knew, and I never had a chance to say...
I love you.
My prop of forty years, dependable and loving
Has gone the way of all the world, and I never saw it coming
But as long as my day upon this earth shall be
My heart will always be sad
Because no one, nowhere, could ever take the place of my dear Dad.

A. Newitt

Where Is Love?

Oh where is love? my soul has searched for years.
This greatest attribute escapes my heart.
I have but searched to find there's only tears
Of sadness, woe and fears that ne'er depart.

Oh where is love that man can feel secure?
To escape the malediction and the pain
Of hatred with his whip that has no cure
For man's release from tears that fall as rain.

Oh where is love that's picture as a steed?
That I may ride to empires long unknown
Where peace would rule as king and take the lead
And I would bathe my thoughts in tender tone.

Oh where is love? gone as a vanquished foe
To pastures new, I cannot go my way
To tend the gentle plants of love that grow
And blossom at the dawning of the day.

Oh where is love? my desperation grows
As ivy on a long forgotten wall.
For I shall search until my quarry shows,
Then love shall charge my heartbeat when I call.

Philip C. Gilbert

The Amateur Dramatic

What is it called, what can it be.
This feeling seated deep inside of me
The urge is great, and so compelling
The words I'll speak, instead of yelling

With all my heart, I will deliver
A torrent of words, strong as a river
To make my point, I'll state with pride
All my emotions, here, inside.

These boards I'll tread, my heart a flutter
Words are perfect, I'll not mutter
The robes I'll wear, and with furrowed brow
The nerves I'll climb, I know not how

Ornately clad in robes so fine
Centre stage, and spotlight mine
No words slurred, nor erratic
You see I am, the amateur dramatic

R. Pilbeam

My Dream World

As I lay awake at night
Thinking how to set the world to right,
One half struggles to make ends meet.
   (At least they have shoes on their feet.)
The other half struggles just to survive
   (They wish they had a 'nine to five')
In my dream world: No wars or starvation
But who will come to our salvation
And make us in our world as one,
Brothers and sisters under the sun.

Patricia A. Scicluna

Unfinished Words

When I finally lay down to sleep
Think of me but do not weep
For I am the sunshine, the wind, the rain
I am happy, I feel no pain.
I am the trees gently blowing,
I am the grass that keeps on growing,
I am the moon, the stars the sky,
My life is over, but don't ask me why.
I am the morning, the night, the day
I'll always be here, come what may
If you feel you need me, you have things to say
Just close your eyes then wish a way.
Now I am at peace but still all around you
I'm beginning my new life in the sky up above
I'm flying high and I send you my love.

Michelle Taylor

Six Times Ten

In thirty three, when I was born,
Things were really hard.

In forty three, when I was ten,
we were having a world war then.

In fifty three, I'm now a man,
at war in Korea's most desolate land.

In sixty three, prepare for war,
to the jungles green of Borneo.

In seventy three, much nearer home,
I fight the IRA's bullet and bomb.

In eighty three, I've reached the half ton,
from where did all this boredom come.

At ninety three, I've now retired,
Freedom, freedom at last,

But why the sense of loss,
something was lost along the way.

Or was it just forgot.

J. G. Murray

The Heart Of A Rose

The petals of a rose are sheer delight
Their softness and beauty radiates light
The perfume an enchanting smell
Who put it there how can we tell

The colour of a rose a virginal white
Like a shining star in the night
Then there's a rose deep and red
Lovers delight in it - it is said.

In an English garden you will find the rose
Its magic it brings wherever it grows
Like a benediction from above
In the heart of a rose you'll find love.

D. M. Stell

'Words'

I've used my words all up, there aren't any left,
they've danced along the page
a dance of wordless death.
I've no more on my paper and no more in my pen
I'll never ever write, a single word again.
I've picked them out of magazines
and put them where they should have been.
The lines have gone, the page is blank.
And in a wordless pond I've sank!
I've looked all over everywhere,
there isn't a word around to spare.
They're all gone, all been written about,
pinched and seen, now full of doubt.
They've disappeared like they didn't exist.
I wonder, will they all be missed?
They've all been spoken, all been sung.
They've been used up one by one.
We have no words now to write or rhyme
Will they all come back in time?

Margaret R. Blight

Wind Farm

Skyline dotted with flashing lights
They're on their way to spoil our sights
A scar which takes time to heal
Nobody cares how we feel
The great intruders will dominate
And spur along our sudden hate
The countryside I love to keep
Hope it won't affect the sheep
Scattered there for all to see
Vulnerable; like you and me
They would not listen to our cry
So we can only watch and sigh
I wonder if in years to come
Someone will say, what have they done?
The scarring of our land's no fun
Gamebirds, wildfowl to name but two
Are sure not what to do
The future looks bleak for our little friends
Will they think of making amends!

Maeve Walker

Morning Mail

Great Aunt Marje was sick in bed, so Aaron and Nicole thought,
They would send her a Card to cheer her up
And tell her about their new little pup
His name is Worcester as in Sauce this pup their Mum had bought.
The Card they drew had a bed and a dog, a bird and squiggles
   and things
Great Aunt Marje was lying there
With turned up toes and frizzy hair
And the children drew flowers, a heart and a kiss and one or
   two fancy rings.
We hope this poem will make them smile - specially written for them.
We hope their aunt will soon be well
And ring on the phone, her tale to tell
And the world will turn round again and again for them.

Marjorie M. Ainsworth

The Hunt

I knew that my legs couldn't take any more,
they were aching, numb and very sore.

I could see that the hounds would gain,
I cried out but it was in vain.

The snow was hitting my face,
I tried to quicken my pace.

I knew there was only one hope,
to go to my den at the base of the slope.

I ploughed down the slope and into the den,
I could hear the shouts of the hunting men.

Then I heard the loud bark of a hound,
it was a most terrifying sound.

There was a clink as a spade hit a stone,
then I felt scared I was all on my own.

I was digging as fast as I could,
but I knew that it was no good.

The terriers entered the den,
I could hear from above me the laughter of men.

I breathed a heavy sigh,
I knew then that here I must die.

Kate Harris

Loneliness

Turning my head I see dampened imprints in the smooth sand
They stop just as I stop, shifting sands are stretching out before me
The silent shore, peaceful in its seclusion.
My gaze lingers on the horizon where the sea and the sky fuse.
My brain seems to whirl for an instant, whilst in my ears the
sea sings a melody
Of mystery and tranquillity, salty sea air tastes tangy upon my lips,
Breezes gently play around my face as I walk the forlorn shore.
Stooping, I pick up a shell, brittle, lumpy, gritty, to my touch
Turning and turning in my hand vacant thoughts invade
as I scrutinise,
One side rough and course the other smooth as silk.
Suddenly blue sky, blue sea, rough, silken, shell, dampened imprints
Fade into nothingness.
No gentle breeze playing around my face, only the gathering
gloom of the clouds
Invading the solitude of my physical being,
My lonely room enveloping.

Norah Darbyshire

Hospital Life

Pain among the ward was clear,
Nurses to and fro so dear.
Doctors in their coats so white.
Peace, as day turns to night.
Hospital life is so rewarding
When patients are well to whom you have
been boarding.
Sister in her placid way,
Assures smooth running day to day.
Who are you to choose your bed
Or even say that your neighbour is dead
With screens around you, you await
That dreaded operation date.
And then that feeling when you awake
A drink. No not that mistake,
A prayer would not go a loss
After all, him up there, he is your boss.
And finally comes the day you are leaving.
Happy with your life, still breathing.
Thanking the staff for a pleasant stay.
Hurry up, let's get away.

Alan G. Sadler

The Quiz Of Time

Some say that time is measured. Some say time starts and ends.
They say we see its passing through all the moods and trends.
Through seasons in their splendour. From cradle to the grave.
Through seconds on a watch face. Once lost cannot be saved.
In every living creature. In every single cell.
Time's story leaves its traces for those who live to tell.
And once the tellers are no more time ceases to exist,
to all who have awareness to recognize all this.
But time itself is like a sea in which things grow and die.
An ocean where all things reside, divide and multiply.
The universe is but a ball in the endlessness of space,
where countless other universes all have their own place.
If space itself is infinite then time must also be,
where atoms, man and galaxies must find their destiny.
If time itself is always still the future and the past,
would have no real meaning. The first would be the last.
Perhaps the spirit holds the key which solves this riddled rhyme.
No clue in this dimension can solve the quiz of time.

Stephen Randle

Friends

Friends are people who know when you're down,
They say they can tell by the darkness of frown.
Your friends pull you up and help end your sorrow,
By telling you that there's always tomorrow.

When daylight comes after a sadness filled night,
You phone your friends and say "you were right"
They know when you're happy, they know when you're sad,
They will always care but tell you you're mad.

These friends I mention are always there,
But just remember you also must care.
For friendship is a two way street,
So call them now and tell them they're sweet.

Margaret Guntrip

Tuned In

Two little poodles can be such fun,
They lie on their back saying 'tickle my tum',
The box of toys is not enough, they want me to play
Lets have a scruff, four front paws and teeth?
Now that's enough -
Who need a clock with these two little friends,
With expressive eyes, and a paw that says please,
The times are set in a natural frieze,
Each his own way of making known
When he's hungry or wants a bone,
I'm the pack leader that picks up the vibes,
It's walkies time or time for dinner,
When you've kept dogs for so many years,
You get to know the different needs,
To understand the varying barks,
One says stranger, one says friend,
Or an returning, from the shops,
They say 'Hello', 'got the chops'
The companionship, the joy, the pleasure,
I'll keep a dog for ever and ever.

Margaret Kinshott

Untitled

The fish in the sea seem strange to me
    they have such peculiar habits
Swimming around without feet on the ground
    no tail like a dog or a rabbit
They seem strange to me the fish in the sea
    they shelter from rain in the ocean
Good Lord on high I am wondering why
    such a strange and peculiar notion
Unlike a bird not a sound to be heard
    no sign of fur or a feather
How do they get by without land sun and sky
    I suppose they think they are clever.

Robert S. Pateman (Margate)

Life

The wounds of love never die,
They grow old with time itself,
If meaning is lost, no reason, no point,
To endless days and silent nights,
In your own time you must search,
For the love that will fill your heart,
If you can hear what I dare not say,
Then you will find in me,
The love I have found in you
In our shared silence,
There is no need to shout.

J. M. Gibson

The Humble Bluebell

For poetic joy, take the humble bluebell
They grow in profusion in woodland and dell
Alone or in clumps, or a wild woodland bed
Give scent to the breeze, all our senses are fed.

With colour the eye is instinctively caught
The blue and the green, delicately wrought
A glimpse of the sun then invading the scene
The all around vision, so calm and serene.

The sound of the breeze worked its way through the wood
Rippling the plants, every one where it stood
The various colours are there all displayed
Dancing away in the peaceful wood glade.

We write now in praise of the humble bluebell
Which grows in profusion in woodland and dell
We write of its merits, its beauty and power
We long for the peace of its idyllic bower.

The touch and the feel of this natural flower
the scent and appeal will enhance the hour
the eye gladdened soul will remember so well
The day that we first saw the humble bluebell.

F. J. Skillington

Friendship

Acquaintances are made each year,
They come, they go, they disappear.
But friendship grows within your heart,
And of your life, becomes a part.

A friend is one who knows your ways,
Sees your faults, or sings your praise.
Understands the things you do,
Stands beside you all life through.

From school days, to a life full grown,
A pal that you can call your own.
I have a friend such as this,
And when we meet we reminisce.

Of all the things we used to do,
At school, and all the folk we knew.
The years have flown, but we're the same,
Friends forever we'll remain.

P. R. Howe

A Christmas Message

The carol singers are on there way
There lanterns shining bright
There voices ring out loud and clear
Upon this holy night

The church bells ring out in harmony
There message very clear
To join with them to wish you well
Great happiness and cheer

As we pray for peace throughout the world
Out heart's reach out to them
With hope and joy and peace on earth
And goodwill to mankind

M. Fardell

Ode To Unwelcome Guests

It feels like they've been here forever, how long isn't easy to tell.
They claim they arrived from Australia but I think they came here from hell.
The cats all left home for a fortnight, the fleas on the dog did the same,
The washing machine thinks it's having a fit, but maybe it's me that's to blame.

I should have known just what would happen, my house would not be my own,
Instead I said "Treat the place just like it's yours, please make yourself feel at home."
I wonder if their house has multiple showers, and loo rolls that never run out.
I wonder if their house resembles a bomb site. I'll hopefully never find out.

They've changed my routines as a matter of course, and didn't have any say.
they make me feel awkward and sometimes as if it's me that gets in the way.
But soon they'll be gone leaving me all alone, doors won't be locked anymore, and if in the future they ever return, I'll refuse to open the door.

R. Norris

Untitled

Flowers are a treasure of the earth a joy to behold
They cheer the sick and comfort the old
Bring messages of love with their beauty
And carry out with grace their duty.
By giving flowers loving care they will
reward you with their beauty fair
whatever the message whatever the rhyme
flowers will say it till the end of time.

V. Windridge

To My Children On Mother's Day

As I read once more, the cards
They brought on Mother's Day,
I'm filled with overwhelming love,
Much more than words can say.
My thoughts drift back into the past,
Remembering the pleasures,
The laughter and the tears we shared,
Those days I hold like treasures.
With a love that's deep as any ocean,
And the pride I have in them
For being, 'just themselves',
Each one a precious gem.

And so, God's special blessing
Could not be any other,
Than the day each child was born to me,
And I became their Mother.

Margaret Doran

Early Morning Riser

It's six o'clock in the morning,
there's a new day dawning.
Am I late for work I ponder,
as for my clothes I look in wonder.
Then upon me it dawns,
it's only Sunday morn.
So back into bed I climb,
to get up there's plenty of time.
The bedding is all in a heap,
but it won't take me long to drift off back into sleep.
i'm already feeling quite dozy,
this bed's so warm and cosy.
I feel so tired and worn,
already I start to yawn.
Just another forty-wink's I think,
my eyes already starting to blink,
as back into sleep I do sink.

P. N. Dawson

Thought

The ideas that come from within, fuel the hungry emotions
    that follow these winds.
"Where does it stop?", pleads the lonely inside,
before being engulfed by similar heart wrenching cries.
I'm not sure anymore, all the world appears grey.
Everything's messed up, with people too frightened to say.
Wars ravage many countries, whilst famine and drought do the rest.
Religion so varied, everyone reckoning on their version being best.
The people are divided, between the masses and the 'right'!
With a few in the middle cloaked in their materialistic delights.
"Who am I?" - "What have I got?"
I hear myself whisper, my body rocking softly in time to my sobbing.
My head buried deep with my arms completing the cocoon
    that comforts me so.
Like this I stay sat whilst the tides ebb and flow.
Waiting for the light that'll raise my spirit up out of this hole.
Suddenly a thought! A way springs to mind.
The butterfly emerges, its wings proud and wide.
The metamorph now stretches, manoeuvring for the breeze.
Waiting for the moment that will bring the right currents.
"I can't wait", my soul joyfully shouts,
as I catch the wind, enabling flight.

Simon Henstock

Where Are We Going

Violence, graffiti, drugs and sex.
There's too much of it now, whatever next.
Where are we going, this world is a state
can it be helped or is it too late

Rent boys, pollution, guns on the street
bent coppers patrolling the beat
drugs in the prisons, no discipline there,
The world is a mess, does anyone care.

Kids murdering kids, think they're the boss
Mother's a junkie but no great loss
Innocent elephant suddenly shot
Ivory's taken then left to rot.

Aids is here, how did that come about
It will kill more without a doubt
Oh my God what have we done
There's so much hate
Save this world before it's too late.

L. Collier

Untitled

She speaks from the top of her head
There lies the froth, the inconsequential clown
Yet she speaks from the top of her head
Never from deep, deep down
Oft time past comes to haunt her,
Invited the small ghost?
She does not exorcise him,
But makes herself a host,
Looks for him in her wandering
And finds herself almost
Seeking the small sweet pain of him,
But pain it is, and so
She puts on a festive gown
And speaks from the top of her head
Never from deep, deep down

Nora Cairns

Poem Of Age

The old will never love the same again,
Through all the wars, and, aching pain.
The children have all grown up, and now gone away.
To live their lives the best they can, and not to go astray.
But Mother's do hope, and pray the world won't be to them
be unkind.
So all at home, can find some peace of mind.
For one day for sure, they will get old.
And, say the same as I have told.

Thomas C. Rush (Easter House)

Imagination

My love is imagination only few know how to use,
there is no limit to its scope and nothing to refuse.
My mind is full of thoughts, that never can come true.
For if they came within my reach, I'd surely not pursue
sometimes a dream, or just a wish whichever way it goes
none of these we'd have as truth, as everybody knows.
It's just another world to me, endless times it seems
music sometimes sets the scene, as words turn into dreams.
Things that can't be said aloud, keep pleasure, in my head.
It doesn't matter where you are if words are never said
shadows turn to forms at will in corners of each room
images of something past may occupy the gloom.
Those ghosts arrive if prompted from images of mind
not nightmares uncontrollable but of a gentle kind.
It's nice to know at any time that door is always there
escaping from reality into a time so "Rare"

Valerie Canning

Honest

Sincerity is the commonest con;
    There is ever likely to be;
Practised by the majority;
    By us on you and me;

When someone starts to with 'Honestly';
    With wide and open eyes;
You can bet your granny's knickers;
    They'll tell you a pack of lies:

"Trust me", is a signal
    Should make alarm bells ring
Who needs to qualify trusting
    If it's honesty they bring

Here's another quite often used;
    'You're not going to believe me but';
They're really saying 'Believe me';
    If you do then TUT TUT, TUT TUT, TUT TUT

F. H. Smart

Footprints In The Snow

It is said that beneath some countries,
There is an essence of the worst of them.
Fast sealed with in the rock,
Since last it strove to do its master's will.
To rend and rip defile and spoil,
The goodly things of human toil.
So deep it be, that many know not of it.
Yet it is not stilled,
But it does move continuously,
Screaming and frothing,
Dashing itself against the stone,
Retching with hate.
And it wants - oh it wants,
To walk the earth once more,
Clothe its people in the thrilling garb of war,
To sow the fields again with wire and mine,
To stride the land
And fire, destruction, agony, death and grief,
These shall be its footprints in the snow.

Malcolm E. D. Bradley

Your Prayers

Each night you pray, your prayers are heard,
They carry to Heaven on the wings of a bird,
The words that you speak turn to silvery thread,
As each one is taken from the thoughts of your head,
The thread gleams and glistens as it flies with the dove,
Upward and onward through all eternal love,
Till the prayers land before the feet of their quest,
And Angels of Mercy tinkle out your request,
Then colour meets sound in a rainbow of light,
And your prayers once again take up the flight,
But this time descend back to where they belong,
In a dancing display of a magic silent song.

C. S. Owen-Smith

A Special Someone

When I need someone to share my thoughts
There is a heart that understands
When I seek the warmth of a comforting touch
There are welcome outstretched hands
When I need someone close to me
Someone who will really care
Your heart and your hands reach out in love
And I'm happy to know you are there
Someone with a smile so warm
And a heart so kind and good
That words are not always needed
For so much is understood
I need someone very special
To depend on come what may
And because you are that someone
You bring loving thoughts my way
How wonderful it is to know
There is someone always there
Who really wants to listen
And to understand and care.
Margaret Ford

"End Of The Season"

One is never prepared for death, the most definite thing about life,
There are those who would welcome release from their pain,
There are those who would live all their life, once again,
But never let anyone say, that when death calls to them,
They won't pray, to stave off the last, and cling on to the past,
One is never prepared for death

One is never prepared for the end, though it comes not as foe, but as friend.
There are people who fear, when the end's drawing near,
And those whose past sins, they'll defend.
But when someone you love has to leave, and although they will tell you
"Don't grieve", there is emptiness there, that is simple despair
And you have to let go, and just leave.

One must just trust that God finds a way,
To give help to the ones that remain,
But when you are bereft, of someone, who has left,
You are never prepared for their death.

You were never prepared quite for this,
"Though I'm sure that you gave a last kiss,
One final "Goodbye", as he drew, a last breath,
But you weren't quite prepared for his death.
Wendy Vickers-James

Is This Love?

Strange, how this feeling evades me,
then seizes my heart in a flash.
Odd, how I long to be taken,
yet cry when there's no turning back.

Strange, how your face is so gentle,
then passionate almost in rage.
Odd, how I cherish the comfort,
yet feel like I'm trapped in your cage.

Strange, how your eyes look so empty,
Then dance with a flickering flame.
Odd, how the fire can burn me,
yet draws me closer again.

Strange, how I long to hold you,
then turn away in despair.
Odd, how I feel you beside me,
yet turning I find no-one there.

Strange, how I feel like laughing,
then tears begin to flow.
Odd, how I'm sure what I'm feeling,
yet truthfully I'll never know.
Paul Loughrey

The Tough Assignment

This is a tough assignment.
There are times when I wish I hadn't taken it on.
It's been tempting to cop-out.
It would be nice to be back home.
Everything comfortable, safe and secure.
But I agreed to take it on.
I was told it would be tough.
Real tough.
If I copped out now it wouldn't look so good.
It wouldn't look good on my report card.
I've got help here anyhow.
Maybe I'll get a C
Perhaps a B if I work real hard.
The title of the assignment?
LIFE.
Michael L. Taylor

Differences

People are different in every way
There are white people and black people too.
Some live with parents but some live in foster homes.
Many people have blonde hair but some have brown.
People speak different languages.
English, German, French even Spanish.
Some people are tall, thin, fat or small
Lots of people are kind, happy, funny and even generous.
There are people who are rich, but there are
also people who are poor and that live on the streets.
Some people wear glasses or are blind and maybe deaf.
Some people have terrible diseases that can kill them.
Yes! were all different in many ways
And I'm glad to be my own different self.
Sonia Platts

A Mother's Love

I watch our darling boys, as they sleep in their beds
their eyelids flickering as dreams fill their heads.
Two beautiful boys so perfect in every way,
growing up so fast with each passing day.

I look back with wonder, to the time of their births,
these precious gifts of life, brought forth on this earth.
Their adorable little faces with enormous dark eyes,
so peaceful and contented in their cots they lie.

I'll treasure each moment of the precious times we share,
the loving hugs and kisses and beautiful smiles they wear.
The love deep inside too endless to measure,
the love of a Mother is forever.
D. C. Taylor

Promise.

A world spins round, dissolving fire,
Then melts in hot and surging seas
Where pungent fumes breathe their desire
For calmer skies, for gentle breeze.

In bubbling pools the life chain forms,
Nor dreams of future so remote,
Enwrapped within these primal storms
As warmth within a winter coat.

So many million years must pass
Before the creature that is Man
Will populate the Earth en masse,
And try to mould it to his plan.

If long ago the single cell
A second's prophesy could know,
Would they have fought for life so well,
Or sunk in boiling undertow?

They lived the onset of a dream
Envisaged in a Cosmic Mind;
Our damaged planet's sunset gleam
Could yet give Dawn to humankind.
Pamela Harvey

Definitely Perhaps

I shall hide; yes, I will hide away, behind myself:
Then, peeping out, through narrowed eyes
　I may have time -
To consider a decision - or not.
　My alabaster front will charm; and mostly
Deceive.
　But, in the space where I shall write;
There will be deep colours
And love of several kinds;
And, perhaps a meeting of Minds
H. J. Tagg

What Beast Is Man?

What beast is man? That can disregard another's feelings.
Then looks for inner truths and deeper meanings.

What beast is man? Who treads on others.
Then shows such tenderness, the kind between lovers.

What beast is man? Creating glimpses of true magic.
Yet whose own future appears increasingly tragic.

What beast is man? Hunting another species to extinction.
Then saving another with heartfelt conviction.

What beast is man? Whose own responsibility he so often denies.
Waiting for absolution from a 'father' in the skies.

What beast is man? To flatten forests and fill skies with pollution.
Racing to become the full stop of evolution.

Every beast kills for survival and the feast.
Only one kills for fun, man the enigmatic beast.
Paul S. Howroyd

Hide And Seek

What is it like when something is put away?
Then it cannot be found at the end of the day.
At first you say, "I put it there"
But as time goes by, you pull out your hair.
I've looked there, it's not in the drawer.
But it's surprising what you store.
If you know where it is tell me please
You're sure someone hasn't hidden it just to tease.
The family sit there, saying, "We don't know."
In such a temper I just want to go.
Drawers, cupboards, everything I've had out.
Even stood there and gave a shout.
I will have to give up and watch T.V.
The picture I cannot really see.
Time has passed, I'm ready for bed.
All the goodnights have been said.
Just about to go to sleep.
Oh yes, downstairs I creep.
I can remember where I put it away
So now it's found at the end of the day
P. Watson

Leaves

Leaves, that break upon the bough
Then finally dressed,
Hide the scampering squirrel
And the robin's nest.
A world of green, of every hue,
Clothing the countryside anew.
Leaves, that shimmer the summer long,
Rocked by the breeze they sing their song.
And softly to a gentle hush,
They pause to hear the mistle thrush.
Leaves, that change with autumn's call,
To reds and browns then softly fall.
And silently as curled they lie,
They drift away. And slowly die.
Leaves, forgotten the beauty that they gave,
As children rustle on their grave.
They feel no pain, and shed no tear,
Another generation of leaves
Will come next year.
S. A. Snelling

Untitled

This great earth, so beautiful and old.
Then greedy man came, and took the gold.
They bled it dry but did not care.
Me first, me last, they thought was fair.

Some people, stopped, to sit and think.
If we don't change, we will sink.
If we gave, more, and took less.
Perhaps we could sort out this awful mess.

Other people did not agree
They took an axe, and chopped down tree
Maybe one day, they will wonder.
What have we done, over yonder

Then and only then, we must strive
To work with nature, and survive
One day, maybe, we'll have peace
No more wars, they will cease

It's a lovely earth, a beautiful sight
Lets make sure we keep it right
Everyone should play their part
Now is the time, lets make a start
R. E. J. Stokes

Yet To Be

A feeling starts from deep within.
Then climbs and grows from her to him.
A mouth alive to touch and taste.
Devours a kiss with lasting haste.
A mind which bears the scars of life.
Binds the flesh with emotions rife,
A kiss the way to sensual delight,
Perfect love on a perfect night.
Yet to be:
Peter Whale

Sitting In The Park

Time well spent - sitting in the park
Their so much to see.
The birds singing their sweet song
The tree's so tall nearly reaching the sky.
On the ground grass so green.
The flowers bed's full of bloom.
Sweet smells all around.
Colours Red, White, Blue and Green everywhere to be seen.
The children playing on the swings
The sounds of laughter fills the air with joy.
The old lady sitting on bench having forty winks.
A gentleman reading the times
Time to unwind, time to enjoy.
Watching the world go by.
Just sitting in the park.
Maryann Hurley

Sadness

We all moan of aches and pain
Then find others worse off in strain,
Children born of dreadful disease and limbs gone
Where is God, what has gone wrong

They sometimes don't make an age for future to come
crippled for life is for some
Life is good when you have your health
Money makes no difference with your wealth
So when you feel sad and think of others
　that's not too bad
Other countries no home, food, all family gone
Lots of tears, no love or future, it's all wrong
I cry each day for them all
Wish the world could live in peace
And God to hear their sad call
Families should not be apart
Live in peace, it is a start
The world would be a happier place
If we helped to love any kind of race
Edna Louisa Bareham

Temperance Building

High in the gravel of society
The yawning Master gave his words,
And it was with burgundy glee
His error was seen,
No more nightmares
From flea bitten rodents
The war was over,
The dogs are gone
Not a single wolf,
Our eyes of anguish conquer the rules,
Go home peaceful
And take away your diamond
For I love you no more,
He crawled away alive, a reflex kick
They thought he would never return.
R. I. Standring

Poppy

The battle is over,
The war has just begun,
The smell of death still lingers on.
Ten thousand men all die in a day,
Yet a single man can only pray.
But through these fields of death ridden power
Stands a small but proud single red flower.
Mark W. Hancock

When You Are Young

You are young with a decision to make
The world and its ways are piece of cake
Sometimes things are rough
And you feel you've had enough
You find a world you never knew
And with courage you struggle through

You have feeling you can't compare
There is work and friendship everywhere
Always someone in whom to confide
And try to do your best with pride
You look at yourself and smile
And say I'll travel mile by mile

As through life and over the years
Things go wrong and you shed tears
But come what may
Look forward to a new day
You see life in changing mood
Frustration, fears and solitude
Lilian M. Williams

A Moment Of Time

Take the time to help preserve the beauty of the planet earth,
The wondrous things that are about that make us want to sing and shout,
Let them be heard above the noise of modern man's gigantic toys,
The cities crammed with high-rise towers,
Stop now and then to smell the flowers,
The tiny snowdrop pushes through,
Spring is on the way it's true,
The trees with leaves waiting to be born and birds that sing at crack of dawn,

The little lambs that run and skip,
Marvel at the joy of it,

Have you seen a setting sun,
The clear bright shining of the moon,
Twinkling stars and pale blue skies where our lovely planet lies,
Our seas are wondrous places too with many creatures swimming through,
Just spare a thought as on we sail to really want to save the whale,
The summer comes to make us smile and then it's Autumn for a while,
Winter starts and snowflakes fall,
Just stop and think about it all,
Take the time as you pass by,
Our planet surely cannot die.
F. V. Young

I Didn't Do It

I went to court one day,
They accused me of stealing,
I didn't do it.

I watched the T.V.
I was on Crime watch U.K.,
I didn't do it.

I was in an identity parade,
The person pointed me out,
I didn't do it.

They put me under arrest,
They chucked me in jail,
I didn't do it.

My cell mate fell down the stairs,
They accused me of doing it,
I didn't do it.

They sentenced me to death,
They gave me the electric chair,
I admit it, I done it (but who's gonna know).
Royston Newell

The End And A Beginning

Raging winds, lashing rain.
The weather's motions are like my pain.
No one knows my inmost feelings.
My heart, my mind, they both are reeling

My life is empty, the rooms are bare,
And I pretend I do not care.
My children gone, my wife is free.
For she no longer cares for me.

The pain will ease, my heart will slow.
But memories, they will not go.
I'll try to smile and be a man.
But truly, I don't know if I can.

Should I go, or should I stay,
Can I face another day.
Yes soon the weather will be fair.
And the warming sun will touch my hair

Bad times will fade and I will smile,
Yes, it may take a little while,
For life is short, and precious too.
So, wife, I'll take it, without you.
Mary Palmer

Good Morning Mrs Murphy

"Good mornin' Mrs Murphy - and 'ow are you today?
The weather now is overcast - the skies are very grey,
It's also rather muggy, I've an 'eadache coming on,
But if I'm not mistaken, there's some rain that won't be long.

I saw old Mr Markham as 'e was walking down the lane,
'E's gawn and 'urt his leg again - 'e's in a lot of pain.
'E said his veg had all dried up - now isn't that a shame?
But mark my words, before too long, I think we'll have some rain.

Was that your Sid I saw last night? - I couldn't be too sure,
Before I'd 'ad a chance to speak, 'e'd gawn and shut the door!

This 'eat, you know, it gets folks down and makes you feel dead beat,
I don't know 'ow you find it, but it swells up all me feet!
But not to worry, won't be long, before we 'ave some thunder.
And then you know before quite soon, 'when will it stop?' we'll wonder!

Now look at that, what did I say, it's starting up .... you'll see,
I'd best get in before it pours - now where's me front door key?

I'll have to knock my Sid up - I 'ope 'e's not in bed,
Working nights these last few weeks, 'e's sleeping days instead...

Well, I'll be off then Mrs M, I've really got to run,
Cheerio, take care - what's that you say, 'ere comes the currant bun?!"
Teresa M. Pigney

Euthanasia - A Baby's Plea

Jesus' plan is to let the strong live,
The weak are lent to be loved for a while,
I was born with a purpose, don't know what it is,
But I'm happy if my 'being' made you smile.

My body is frail but my soul is intact,
So listen, listen please, to my plea,
Medication is fine for restoring good health,
But let nature set MY soul free.

Then ask my mother if my birth meant regret
I know she has thought it worthwhile,
For amidst all her sadness and sorrow she'll say,
"I am happy, just his 'being' made me smile".

"But God wants him back, of this I've no doubt,
His purpose is greater than mine".
And she knows that if love for a moment brings joy,
Then a moment's more precious than time.

Linda Lancaster

Elastic Band

I'm afraid it's getting out of hand
The way you treat me.
I am an elastic band.

I do my job. I do it well.
When you bundle up mail
You cast me away.
You don't pick me up,
So there I stay.

I can be used 50 times and more.
You use me once and throw me on the floor.
You think I'm not useful any more.

So, postal staff, please recycle me.
You do it with paper, to save a tree.
I'm as elastic band. Why not me?

Nancy Sharp

'Secret Lovers'

Secret lovers that's what we are,
The way we look at each other it shows by far,
When we're all alone, your tender touch,
As we feel each others bodies
The passion of love and lust, is oh so much,
The way we caress,
The way we join and become one,
Two lovers making love, until the morning sun,
So much pleasure and joy we bring,
But being so deceitful to our partners,
Is this a sin? Is this a sin?
As I run my fingers, all over your naked skin,
But now the hour has come for us to part,
As we kiss goodbye and finally depart,
Still we both know deep in our hearts,
That that time will come near,
When we will be together again, despite the fear.

R. McNally

My Perfect Lady

I can feel the days starting to shine,
The warm feeling of wanting you to be mine.
I can smell her body where she touched,
A beautiful face I want so much.
A smile that could light the darkest heart,
I felt that stirring jump at the start.
With hands so soft, her gentle touch
Her wanting eyes, a needing much.
I want to protect a heart that wants me,
I want the want of you want me.
My perfect lady

Kelly Oliver

A Happy Crowd

A happy crowd is who they are
The visitors come from near and far;
Preparation has been the name of the game
And decoration shall remain tame.

The months spent waiting have all gone
Where they've all waited patiently for so long;
Emotions run erratic from deep inside
They show the costumes they've had to hide.

Summer flowers lend aromas and beauty once more
The birds sing so sweetly, like never before,
The children will attend for this special day
And Holy Reverence helps them on their way.

Life is so perfect, everything is just right
While everyone sings as the families unite;
Two people who will never be lonely
Have now pledged their lives to matrimony.

Pauline Bamforth

Hypothetical Justification

Suicide of love
the ultimate desire of admiration
a sanctimonious sacrifice
frail in the light of retrospection.
A heretical weakness
adulterous guilt
endless unforgiving guilt of betrayal
not social or moral - ironically.
A personal self-betrayal
eating away inside
silent toothless mastication
sucking me to death.
So hypothetically stupid
dying a death for mental chastity
absolution of natural physical frailties, a sacrifice
justified and laudable by the sheer weight of its unworthiness.
The glorification of ultimate vanity
hypothetical suicide
mental pills and razor blades already used (and forgotten)
no turning back, now hypothetically dead.

Patrick Purser

Man Kind

Man wants what man can't get.
The two wars, we won't forget.
A bow-legged cow, cannot walk.
Yet with enthusiasms our scientists talk.

That old woman, let's have her purse!
Now you live your life with a curse.
Saddam Hussein in all his might.
So Kuwait we'll help them fight.

Other places, the civil wars.
But they don't supply us with our stores.
So helping them a waste of time.
So isn't that a bigger crime.

A wrong so mild,
To kill our wild.
The animals, they don't see.
The animals, they have no plea.

All this done by us.
And only now, we make a fuss.
Still, not much done.
Most just live under our dying sun.

B. D. Doherty Jr.

Memories

My love has gone, but memories linger on
The touch, the feel, the thoughts of yesteryear
How can we forget the good times and the bad,
How can we forget the love that we have had
No, not now, not ever it's always in my mind,
The friendship, joy, and happiness true lovers always find.
And then the day of parting, when one of us are gone
Will the memories leave us, or will they linger on.
Yes my love, remembering is all we have to share,
The walks, the talks, the life we lead, we never can compare
with anyone, or anything the future holds in store, for now
we're only one, there will be two no more.

Vivien Walker

Cartoons

The labyrinths of the city crawl on into the night,
The tunnelled gloom is weary in the shaded, shallow light
Of street lamps, curtained windows and the rushing traffic's glare.
The broken bones of crushed cartoons are dying, laughing there.

The channelled blood of fairy tales dries and cracks in
  children's minds,
A sea of foam floods and flows across the gulf that no one finds.
The licking flames and charred remains of hidden stores of
  broken bones
Are crushed beneath the shadowed forms and restless tombs
  of blackened stones.

The mazes of your memory's dreams are now lost in yesterday,
The coloured lights don't call now and your eyes just see the grey.
The silver sun, with silent tongue, has crossed the sky and
  swiftly gone
And stalked by night, with tired sight, you close your eyes
  and day is done.

The labyrinths of the passing years rush headlong into space.
The days don't change and the nights, so strange, are lost
  without a trace,
In memory's curtained vision where shadowed time won't care
And the broken bones of crushed cartoons are still dying,
  laughing there.

Norman Wilson

Life

The rivers flow,
The trees they grow,
The sun shines all day long.
But as for him,
And me and you,
We know we've got a job to do.
Some get famous and very rich,
Especially on the football pitch.
Most have jobs and can survive,
But even with a 9 till 5,
Still some workers and their friends,
Work all hours that God sends.
Some give up and lose their face,
Living in this human race.
But I don't care, we are alright,
Me, my kids and my wife.
And hopefully in years to come,
Nobody will drop the bomb.
Then we all can live in our own way,
Until our last peaceful day.

K. Paterson

April Weather

The flying clouds from East to West.
The sun gaily peeps' ore their crest.
An earthly odour fills the air
Raindrops come pattering here or there.
The sun disappears with lightening speed
Then it's raining, raining with all April greed
The sun reappears as strong as before
The heavy rains cease to pour.
Again the ploughman diddles to and fro
Tilling the earth for all God's gifts to grow.

L. N. Warren

A Summer Sunset

A bugle, soft, in the distance
The sunset call is sounded
And at this sign of eventide
Our country's flag is grounded.

Colours in the sky, of red
A sight that never palls
Silence; not quite, a background sound
Of summer song bird calls.

The clearing up of garden tools
Nightly stored by tidy folk;
And wafting in the evening air
The smell of bonfire smoke.

Stars appear above our heads
Sun almost gone. Too soon?
This will shortly be replaced
With a silvery, glinting moon.

And in between there will be sounds
These do not entirely cease
But after a summer sunset
There is a time for peace.

W. J. R. Baggs

My Walk

As I walk o'er the hill and gaze to the sky,
The sun warms my face the breeze flutters by,
And my mind wanders to the days gone by.

When the scramble of little feet raced upon
  the ground underneath,
Where a little boy kicked a ball with joy
And another ran on in another ploy.

To the dreamer behind who explored and enjoyed,
Creeping about the foe to be found.
To the shouts and the glee when they reached the trees,
Shoes and socks off as they dipped their feet
in right up to their knees.
In the cool, gurgling burn flowing down through the trees.

The sun shineth down but time has not stood still
As I start to return to our home down the hill,
In my heart I don't walk alone, as the
memory is warm of a hand in my own.

Karen Mackay

My Jigsaw

My jigsaw puzzle, 1,000 pieces almost complete,
I soon find out I am facing defeat,
The last one piece is just not there,
I feel frustration, disaster, despair.

Patience and determination have brought me this far,
My puzzle of life is not going to par,
Nothing else can fill this gap, nothing can compare.
My complicated picture, has me pulling out my hair.

My life is sometimes difficult, not always pleasant and nice,
I know just where, to find the piece I need,
but, you see it has a large price.
Emotions run high, and I hit a low, I no longer know which
way to go.

My age is a fact that I cannot hide,
I will not give up whilst it is on my side,
The length of my battle cannot be told,
Until I have my piece, my child to hold.

S. J. Hurley

"A Spring Garden"

A garden of flowers is a beauty untold
The trees that are leafing begin to unfold
The daffodils raise their heads up high
Like trumpets of gold pointing up to the sky

The dawn awakes to welcome the spring
The birds in the treetops start to sing
The rising sun comes into view
Casting rays of every hue
"Spring" comes in on this first morn
In her gowns of green adorn

Patricia Parker

The Stream

The stream of love flows through the Town
The town beside the sea

The stream it is a lovely colour brown
made brown by twigs and leafs

The stream it reaches for four miles or more
It bends and weaves beneath the trees
It makes the way towards the sea

The stream it seems to tell me things as it whispers and hisses
over rocks and stones

The stream it never seems to stop
Even when the sun shines bright drying up everything in sight

Without the stream life would seem to end for me

You see I am the tree that stands besides the stream
and it gives life to me and makes me grow very tall for all to admire
as they stroll along the seashore.

A. E. Studd

School

As I stepped out of school,
the teacher said, "You fool!
Pick up that litter you know the rule."

"But Sir," I said, "I'm not in school anymore,
The bell has just rung and you know the score."

The teacher said "Don't talk to me in that way young lad,
Pick it up anyway or I'll get mad."

I picked it up and put it in the bin
and out of my pocket jumped my pet frog, Tim.
I looked at the teacher with a innocent grin,
He said, "ok, ok, ok, you win."

I put Tim in my pocket and said, "Thanks."
The teacher said, "ok, but no more pranks!"

Laura A. Smith

Untitled

As you look out from your window tell me what do you see
the steep rugged cliffs across the bay or
the surging swell of the sea.
Do you see all the beauty around you listen to all of the sounds
of the waves crashing in and the gulls shrill cry
or do you look up in wonder at the beauty of the sky
do you take in the view of the
cliff top with its colours of brown and green
the gold of the dunes far down below what a staggering scene
with the blue of the sea and white horses
that crash onward toward the shore
do you tell yourself that you are blessed could you ask for more
the clouds in the sky are drifting way, way out of sight
the sun is setting in the west and soon the only light
will come from the moon and stars above a truly lovely sight
peace and quiet soon will reign and
throughout the hours of night we will sleep awhile
and when we wake at the crack of dawn
we will give thanks for another day and the beautiful start
of the morn.

M. Brooks

Corruption

A child without a father, like a house without a roof
The storm gathers, infiltration begins
Build your own f***ing roof
They proclaim in anger

Sorrow they say can only bring on self-inflicted grief
Stand on your two feet
They proclaim in anger

Murmurs on individualism festers
The iroko tree grows older
Lost cause, they scream

The division widens
Crazy policies emerges
Religion a key player

Confusion erupts
A time bomb waiting to explode

Next generation arrives eager to participate
Consumed with power, greedy enough to act on impulse

The iroko tree, too old to see
"Watch out," echoes the wind.
A child without a father is like a house without a roof.

Yinka Adeyemi

The Old Age Traveller

Looking out from my window, I stare at the sky
The stars are shining brightly, I often wonder why
Night after night, they emerge without fail
On a sea of black velvet, they seem to sail

My thoughts start to wander, of films I have seen
All my childhood heroes, good and bad I've been
Fighting enemies, in far off lands
Spacemen amongst the stars, pirates on the sands

The battles fiercely fought, and evil laid to rest
Throughout those early years, my bravery stood the test
The outcome never changed, and always remained the same
Me forever shining through, in my made up game

I think to myself, of children everywhere
Will they be fighting baddies, among the stars out there
I close both my eyes, and rest on the bed
A smile comes to my face, as I lay my weary head

Robert O'Connor

Spirit Welcomes You

When you depart the world of pain
The spirit door is open wide.
You may be reluctant to pass through
But there's peace and love on this side.

You pass from earth's dark shadows, to where
The sun shines bright, the grass is green.
The flowers bloom, this surely is
A paradise you've never seen.

On the earth plane loved ones grieve
If only they could see
How wonderful, how peaceful here
This surely is the place to be.

The world is full of suffering
So throw off your cloak of fear.
Just take my hand and follow me
Happiness awaits you here.

Don't be afraid, your friends are here.
Just take that step and then,
You'll see you pets, for they're here too
You'll never feel that pain again.

Shirley Hawkins

My Son

The infant smile lights up your face,
The sparkling eyes so blue,
My mind goes back to bygone days
When there was just us two.

Your school days brought us loads of fun,
The occasional heartaches too,
But I was always there for you
To give my love, so true.

The years passed by so quickly,
And as I watched you grow,
I realised the bond we shared
Would someday have to go.

At seventeen you went away
To serve your Sovereign Queen,
And like your Dad before you
Around the world you've been.

Every picture tells a story,
And as I glance at yours,
I wonder where it all went wrong,
And why we are friends no more.

Margaret George

Battle's End

The sounds of thunder - are in my head
The sound of gun fire - it's what I dread
Shell shocked men - with battle scars
How I hate these Bloody wars.

The sun is up - but can't be seen
Hidden from view - by a thick smoke screen
Days they are no longer bright
Battles have made them - eternal night

Men once stood - like fields of wheat
Now lay massacred at my feet
The smell of fear - mixed in with death
I watch those men steal one last breath

As we prepared - for our last stand
Come forth the enemy - white flag in hand
No more blood - to wash the field
Officers and men - both wish to yield

It's a victory - but have we won
As they lay down their sword and gun
I've seen no cowards here today
I'm alive - thank God I pray.

Michael Schofield

Lost Love

The sightless eyes from old portraits stare,
The rockers still on the old black chair,
Years of neglect without repair,
Now there's no one there.

No footsteps now from the empty hall,
The great clocks bells no longer call,
No children's laughter without care,
Now there's no one there.

Up the uninviting stair
Into the bedroom cold now bare,
Where a new born first breathed air
Now there's no one there.

The walls and ceiling drab and damp,
I remember the lovely bedside lamp,
The wedded bliss of that first year.
Now there's no one there.

Away from here back into the light,
Away from the feeling of endless night,
Just look back, don't feel despair
Remember when someone loved was there.

Winifred Nichols

Friendship Memories

The sun has finally set upon this structure, calm and still;
the sound of comradeship and laughter, friendliness and joy is muted.
Such strength and succour once bestowed upon those who,
in kind affection will share with others all their deepest feelings,
is dissipated and no longer convoluted.
Shed not a tear for this bond, forged from the alchemy of
differing moods, now broken.
Remember instead, the intricacies of mortal thought
transformed through speech, to help and comfort all;
that each will derive encouragement and lasting peace from
this small token of their love and gratitude, exchanged in
convivial surroundings small. Farewell then, but surely not
goodbye, for how could we divide in such a way?

Instead, let us cheerfully, and in light-hearted frame of mind
depart, and with determination, walk our separate paths until
that certain day when we shall meet again, and richly converse, mind to mind and heart to heart.

A. R. Woodward

Thoughts Written Between Patients

Sometimes in the quiet moments
The soul is shaped;
Sometimes in the cacophony
The soul is destroyed.

Now good,
Is good enough,
Need is greed,
And right only comes in paper dollars.

Time was:
When children created a future
not a liability.
Time was:
When growing old
was inevitable but not feared.

Time was, when the collective soul
had vitality and conscience.
Now all is changed, changed utterly;
Not for beauty or grace,
But the graven images of a new idolatry.

Kieran D. O'Malley

Ode To A Sparrow

Shall we come out, this cold frosty morn?
The sky is so pretty and welcomes the dawn.
We're huddled up tight, secure in our hedge
will there be food on the window ledge?
The sunlight's inviting, let's try and see
what others are stirring
in the silver birch tree.
Blue tits and robins, how pretty they are
the blackbird is chirping and the wren
is not far.
The sun is now shining
Though weak but inviting
but oh that north wind, it's really is biting
We'll brave the cold weather
and look forward to spring
meanwhile we'll just forage.
And maybe we'll sing.

Valerie Knight

My Nanna

My Nanna had the nicest smile in the world,
  The sound of her knitting needles clicking,
The sound of her watch ticking,
  When she went away, my life died a little,
I cried a lot.
  I miss her so much,
She had the very softest touch,
  Every night I pray that she will appear,
The next day,
  But I know that cannot happen,
My wish will never come true.

Victoria Fish

The Birds In Winter

The clouds are white,
The sky is blue,
The trees are bare,
Then I see you.

You're flighty, you're chirpy,
You always sound happy,
But what you're hiding is,
Feeling hungry.

The nut box is full,
Also the net,
There's a big fat ball,
So there's plenty for all.

But what do I see,
Fighting amongst thee,
When there's plenty to have,
Each one of you wants it all.

Pecking and shoving,
And pushing too,
But I suppose it's a thing you have to do
It's a case of survival for all of you.

Linda Passmore

The Choice

Then Torquemada donned the dreaded cap.
The sentence you shall have is death,
But first a long slow torture is your fate,
And may our God have pity on your soul.
Dragged mercilessly to dungeon deep and dank,
The prisoner, bleeding, broken, slumps against his chains.
Hot irons, all glowing red and pincers meant to loosen nails,
Make no inroads into his staunch resolve.
He will not yield and satisfy their lust with baleful cry.
Half dead he hangs his head, accepts the pain but makes no sound.
The jailer, hooded, he dare not show his face,
Takes pity on this wreck, that lately was a man.
I'll give thee choice of how thou means to die,
With axe, to sever head or on yon thicket pyre, thy flesh to burn.
Still proud, with eyes yet bright
The prisoner whispers: I will choose the fire.
Aghast, the jailer asks why such a choice of lingering death.
The prisoner thus replies:
Better a hot stake than a cold chop.

J. Kerrigan

Successful Failure

A hopeless flop: was never top of any form.
The pattern from the very day that he was born.

Came school day sports, they cast their lots for Billy's side,
but balls or scrums, were fingers thumbs? The others cried.

With Dad to fish, so long his wish, the scene was set,
thought prey all hooked, so nearly cooked, it slipped the net.

The same with girls, straight and with curls, both bold and shy.
They knew his past: things couldn't last, so didn't try.

Then letter came in formal name to be installed
as Private Brown, to serve the crown - so he was told.

Too soon the war showed all its gore: the battle raged.
his buddy gave a piercing shout, and Billy dragged.

Him gently from the blazing fire - shells all around,
(please God, don't let my pal be dead) to safer ground

away from guns and blood and flame. Then utter void.
But later from their stretched beds — joy unallayed.

So home once more, his wounds of war so soon to heal.
A brilliant medal; toast of the town; could it be real?

Along came girls then, big and small; forgot the past.
The pick of the pebbles from the beach were his at last.

May Cowan

Smitten

Such a delight when a smile lights up her face.
The one I adore, has measure and more,
of natural beauty, of charm and of grace.
But real beauty is presented, to me the beholder,
in her eyes, which sometimes express
the feelings that move her.
And what makes the parts exceed the whole
and what makes me forever love her,
is the presence of a gentle soul.

Robin Nicholas Skinn

Seasons Of Love

Spring - First I saw her came the taste
The self control against the haste
Awaiting for the time the place
To be with her for love so chaste
Summer - Wrapped in the warmth of her touch
Awoke the feelings missed so much
Musing content grew as such
"Life's so good" Oh for her touch
Autumn - now serpents like a cancer grow
a feeling hidden deep below
For one so near not long ago
She strikes my heart with dreaded blow

Winter - seasons of love I'd climb the hill
Baiting springtime, summer thrill
Then cruelly cast to autumn's chill
I'm dying inside winters kill

L. G. Bate

The Harbour

The sea was rough.
The seagulls wild.
The waves danced high and low.
The little boats at anchor, were rocking to and fro.

I thought about the fishermen
Out there in waters deep,
Their lives at risk, to bring home the fish,
For you, and me, to eat.

The stars went out.
The moon went down.
The sun began to rise.
The daylight brought a calmness,
To sea, and ships, and line.

The fishermen were home at last.
With such a catch so fine.
They came ashore to rest and sleep,
For just a little while.

V. Morris

Harvest Time

The golden corn is cut and stacked
The rosy apples cleaned and packed
The trees are standing stripped and bare
Their fruits were gathered in with care
For now we know it's harvest time
And soon the bells will ring and chime
They tell the people far and near
The harvest festival is here
Then farmers each with sweating brow
Will send up prayers, and each will vow
  that when the autumn chills have gone
    the winters flown, and spring has come
Once more it's time, the seeds to sow
And once more nature clothes the trees
In blossoms plenty for the bees
Yes, when it's harvest time we sing
Our voices rise and like bells ring
Until they gently fade away
Then we give thanks, and to God pray.

V. Biddle

The Uncertainties

The sun rays of the morn
The rocks in the sea
Angry waves reached the shore
Seagulls flying high gracefully

Waves receding
Human eyes scan the shore
Thunder and lightning showing destruction around
Changing life's reflections and unbelievable sounds.

Riding the waves - memories drawn in the rays
Sun breaking through, changing the breakwater's routine.
Soon all was calm, the days life begins
Smiles brought direction, stirring all around

All people gazing upwards to the sky
Proving the wonders with sun rays of the dawn.
Reflections and shadows fade away
Awaiting the dawn of the forthcoming day.
 J. S. Mitchell

The Visit

The morning was in shadow
The robe of grey clothing the sky
 Reflected the darkness of my mind.

Suddenly, 'as tho' tired of gloom,
 The sun came flashing through
Tossing rainbows and shapes of light
 Across walls of white
Stayed awhile and was gone.

All became as before,
 The show was over; the curtain down
But in myself,
 Darkness no more.
 D. M. Newton

Black Friday

It was August fifteenth nineteen fifty two
 The river Torridge boiled.
Around midday the sky turned black,
 And all the street lights failed.
Only sounds of horror and groans of pain
 Could be heard above the
  torrential rain.

Ninety tons of water
 Fell on that fateful day
Bound for the beautiful Valley below
 Boulders were bouncing down,
  Some were ten tons in weight
 What chance did people have,

The break of day bought silence
 The horror there for me
Houses, streets and people
 Were swept into the see.....
 Margaret J. Broomhall

To Parkside

Rays of sunlight ripple through
The quivering shade of dancing yew
And as each sunbeam settles down
It touches cowslip's golden gown.
The ash tree bends as though to hide
Fresh blades of grass that grow beside.
Soft white daisies raise their head
And stretch to face the sun instead
For sunlight stirs them from their sleep.
A sleep that nighttime holds so deep.
And as their petals each unfold
Release a secret never told.
This world of beauty and of sun
Will close its eyes and soon be gone.
For fields of bliss cannot complete
With high finance and deals complete.
 Linda Ann Burns

Out Of Town

When that old sun shines brightly down,
The place to be is out of town.
In lush meadows where wild flowers grow
By meandering rivers which gently flow
'Tween ancient willows that sigh and creak,
And swans stab the water with orange beak.
Silver skirted ripples dance in ordered lines,
Tortured vapour trails scratch the azure skies.
Dragonflies skim the water with gossamer wings.
A kingfisher dives, a blackbird sweetly sings.
Then a-wander through woodland on yonder hill.
The silence seems to make time stand still.
Woodbine clasps the trees in close embrace
The sun dapples the ground with delicate lace.
A startled pigeon flaps, the robin has no fear,
This stranger poses no threat to wildlife here.
Suddenly with joy my soul to heaven soars,
Gratitude for such beauty from my heart pours.
This is why, when that old sun shines down,
The place to be is out of town.
 Stella Rosemary Ward

Vintage Love

The springtime of my life is far behind me,
The petals fall from summer's last red rose,
But in my autumn days I've found a treasure
Could this be lasting love, do you suppose?

New wine is sold in bottles bright and shining
The bottles round the old are thick with dust.
But when you taste, the wine is sweeter, stronger
The wiser, ageing heart is worth your trust.

I cannot run up hills the way I used to
Nor can I dance or sing the whole night long,
But take me in your arms and say you love me
And all my being bursts forth into song.
 Miriam Galway

Timeless Nature

See the burning red of the setting sun,
The panoramic scene before our eyes;
The soft changing light when the day is done,
What mighty hand does paint the carmine skies?
How relentlessly runs the wide river,
Rippling over the ancient stepping stones;
Florescent fish flash, their tails a-quiver
Darting with such vigour and changing tones.
The sound of the sea, and the crashing waves
Comes to a crescendo against the shore;
The unceasing way that night follows day
And all life carries on just as before.
No use to wonder the why and the how,
But enjoy the day that's here and now.
 E. Pinniger

This Tree Of Life

A lonely tree by the lake
The weight of fallen leaves will take
And takes them slowly to the shore
And so to die and shine no more
Where branches bare reflect no light
On darkened waters on darkened night
Where seasons do so await the tree
And sunlight make's a change for thee
Where spreading buds that once were bare
A hint of new life now is there
As leaves and branches start to spread
Reflection now on watery bed
This tree now alive with sound
Branches comfort new life found
This tree of character integrity honour
This tree of wisdom and age
Its history taking centre stage.
 Sheila Nixon

Our World

I look at the world and what do I see,
The pain, the fear, the animosity,
Where is the peace I long for so,
Why does it evade me, I just don't know,
How can some get fat, while others just lie,
So weak with hunger and waiting to die,
There are those on the street who live in there rags,
Their worldly possessions are carried in bags,
The rich look down on them with scorn,
So high and mighty "to the manor born,"
There'd be plenty of food if we'd only all share.
Plenty of love if we'd only all care,
Then there are some with bills to meet,
Children to feed - put shoes on their feet,
As God looks down on us from above,
He showers us all with equal love,
If we all did the same - that includes me.
What a healthier, happier world it would be,
Let's all do our best in a way that we can,
And end this suffering made by man.

E. J. Brumby

The Storm In My Mind

How my head aches, those sad tearful memories from the past.
The pain is heavy like the deep black thunder clouds
That line the sky when a storm brews and is about to break.
But the storm in my mind is not about to burst, it is more like a
whirlwind, small at the bottom where life is at its beginning
and growing to the sun, where its width eclipses the sun and
blocks the warmth that could lighten up my heart.

In the shadow of this eclipse my heart sinks
and its beat pounds against the cage which encloses it and
tightens its grip with every breath that the experience of life
gives to me.

And what has life given to me?
Scars, deep emotional scars,
scars so deep that they have dug my grave for me already
for which I have no need of, as I wish to be cremated.
A grave needs to be tendered, loved and cared for,
something I missed out on in life
and would not understand the meaning of it in my afterlife.
Life I have not enjoyed,
the living can inflict so much pain on others knowingly or
otherwise and in death their memories keep that pain alive.

A. Ambridge

War

War, War is stupid I say, what's there to fight for anyway.
The greedy people who just want more, let all the unfortunates
go fight in their war.
They sit in the office in great big armchairs, and tell the great
stories of those men who dare, of whom they are talking, they
don't even care.
Fame, fame is their one big aim, who were those men and what
were their names?
War and Fame, it's all the same, it's such a bloody stupid game.

R. M. Fagan

A Dream Come True

My special - dream is for a new abode,
I don't wish for diamonds, rubies or gold,
Just a sweet humble home in which to live
With those I adore,
To me in life who could ask for
anything more.

Somewhere to cherish those that I love,
with thanks to our dear Lord
in Heaven above,
A place to provide friends with a
Homely - chat,
My door will always be open with
a welcome - mat.

Denise Frost

Untitled

Soul, arrives,
pre-agendered...
Finds...

'Life'
more interested
by far
in 'this' and 'there,'
than guessing
Soul's intent

Ergo
DISINTEGRATION.

M. S. Barley

Once In A Life Time

September, was the month we met.
  The night was warm,
    I'll never forget.

His big blue eyes, were shining bright,
  His dazzling smile, was sheer delight.

He walked me home, held me tight,
  Kissed my lips, oh! What a night.

As time went by, we fell in love,
  No-one could thrill me, like he could.

Precious moments, nights of bliss,
  The loving memory, of his kiss.

Alas, our love could never be,
  The Lord had other plans, you see.

Now my life ahead, I just can't face,
  As no-one else, could take his place.

September, was the month we met.
  And, the month he died.
    I'll never forget.

Margaret O. Bryant

Last Farewell

They told me heaven was up above me, but now I wonder why
The night I flew alone up there, I found a hell up on the sky.
A hell where death and horror walked hand in hand with life.
Where the souls of gallant airmen were trampled in the strife.
Where Jack and Jim and Harry and all my gallant crew
Died in the fight for freedom, and in my heart there grew
A bitterness so frightening that I alone could tell
That they were wrong who told me that down below was hell.
My friends are now departed, somewhere to a heaven sublime
A land of smiles and sunshine where you live again, not die.
I know that I shall meet them, for I only know too well
That tonight in the hours of darkness I have a rendezvous with hell.

S. P. Davies

To The Christ Of Today Yesterday And Forever Amen

Awake sweet dawn to the Christ of today
The miracles and wonders when you pass our way.
Oh Lord of the heavens Lord of the earth
Praise to your life being born on this earth.

Born for a purpose your life to be
One of torture for all to see.
You came to save to show the way,
Oh God of our hearts be with us today.

Forgiveness is thine, Lord, so sweet to embrace
Lord of wonders grand us thy grace.
The will of Thy Father thou camest to do,
Son of righteousness it all came from You.

Kings of this earth, emperors galore,
Oh God our Saviour how many more
Parliament Senates counsels too
Given to unrighteousness by the few.

Swamped by their sins which is nothing new,
government's falling, prophesied by You.

G. A. Ogden

A Shaman's Quest

Quick silvered sip, in blood does flow,
the nature of our karmic law.

Not understood by natural science,
transcendental thoughts in spoken silence.

In waves of space, in Brahman's face,
a vital heat in flow.
A psychic link in shaman's drink,
of cosmic H_2O.

With grasping hands we follow through
till meet we face to face,
expanding minds, contracting times,
encapsulate space times race.

A being's life, a planet's death, a finite time is this,
to leap ahead with Billows Breath, too late a chance to miss.

And take with us the memory of a place we may construct.
A world full of shamanic dreams, that time cannot disrupt.

Through Black Holes vast, take from our past,
a life flux ever flowing.
A Mystic Breed, a Crystal Seed,
the great ones are now sowing.

Luke Holgate

A Mother's Christmas Prayer

A brand new baby starts to cry,
The mother holds it close.
Oh, my darling your nose is so sweet,
Just like the bud of a rose.
She kissed it on its tiny hand,
And sang a lullaby. .
She smoothed its brow and tiny cheek.
Then she began to sigh.
Oh! If I were a healthy lass,
I'd manage very well,
I wouldn't need find you a home.
I'd beg borrow and sell.
She gave it a smile and closed her eyes
No other words were said.
The angels looked down where the baby lay.
And gently shook their heads.
A beautiful light shone from on high.
That wonderful Xmas morn.
The mother entered heaven,
Along with the child she had born.

M. Fiddes

Memories

As we walked hand in hand beside the lake.
The mist was sleeping on the distant hills.
No other creature seemed to be awake.
"Oh", but then we heard the birds with their sweet trill.
Lake Winderemere has many moods.
Over the years we have grown to know them well.
She changes like the trees around which winter doth denude.
In summer time when sailing, ships glide softly o'er the waves.
And little children paddle by the water's edge
While some run through the trees pretending they are Indian braves
Dashing hither and thither behind each bush and hedge.
The scenes are very English so very much a part
Of Britain's glorious heritage I hold close to my heart.
At night time when the darkness falls upon the lovely lake.
The birds have long since gone to rest our homeward trek we make.
And now we have reached the cottage
with the roses round the door.
Our cup overflows with happiness and love.
We know the Man we have to thank.
Is the Lord God up above.

Marjorie Robinson

A Peaceful End

He was released on Sunday morning,
The pain he suffered died peacefully
With a soul being finally set free.

The pain he suffered was alive.
His anguish was shown through his expressions
And his face told his story.

His face was so thin, his strength so weak.
Each bone pierced his skin like a spike.
A monster reduced him to this.

The monster had raged inside him
Destroying his will to live.
Too powerful to be controlled.
On Sunday morning his soul was released.
A body, once so full of pain, left as a shell.
His face lay expressionless, his story told.

Dedicated to my Grandfather, William George Swinnerton (1929-1996)

Louise Kennedy

The Sailors' Grave

O'er the oceans to far off lands
the merchant ship did sail
her cargo hatches filled with steel
and paper by the bale

A week from port a storm arose
the heavens roared with thunder
a sea tore o'er the lower bridge
a lifeboat smashed asunder

It carried on for days and days
until it reached gale force
a roll tore the wheel from the helmsman's hands
and took her off the course

The dreaded words abandon ship
came from the weary master
for him he knew the end had come
and prayed it would come faster

No lifeboats, rafts were to be found
no life here could he save
for all on board the ship that day
would find the sailors' grave

A. E. Rendell

Going To Work

I struggled in this morning to get to Cudham Hall
The lanes were like an ice rink but the hill was worst of all.

I slipped and slid my boots wouldn't grip the ground beneath my feet
All of a sudden there I was sitting on my trouser seat.

I got up and continued to walk gingerly along the lane
Then would you believe it, there I was sitting on the ground again.

I thought to myself I must be mad, completely out my tree
When I started to climb the hill a car came straight at me.

The bumper was coming closer to me, I froze and held my breath
The driver turned the steering wheel and the car slid to the left.

I got out my inhaler and took a puff or two
And realized I was two thirds there, so I had to see my journey through

I got up to Cudham Lane a big sigh passed my lips
I could now walk normally as my boots they did not slip.

I strolled along quite casually, thinking I must be a silly jerk
As this horrendous journey wasn't for pleasure, I was only going to work.

Sheila Brooks

The Guiding Light

Buffeted by the elements
    The lonely sentinel, standing high
        Throughout the day, a landmark
            Stretching into the sky.
As darkness falls, a beam of light
    Will sweep across the sea
        Warning any boats around
            That it's not the place to be.
Too many rocks around the shore
    Too many lives at stake
        The lifesaving light of the lighthouse
            Ensures there's no mistakes.
As the gulls continue to circle and wheel
    Overhead in the deep blue sky
        And the ships that pass in the dead of night
            Know they're safely sailing by.

W. Carlin

The Death Of Summer

And now the summer has been gone,
The land has gone to sleep,
Days shorten, darkness falls,
Shadows start to creep.

Winds moan through leafless trees,
That stand like skeletons against
A lowering sky: Snowfalls cold against my face,
Desolation, I walk beside a leaden sea,
Coloured grey instead of green,
Fog swirls in wreathes around me,
No substance for me to hold,
Just nothingness wherever I look,
How I wish it could be eternal spring,
And winter a forgotten thing.

E. M. McGuinness

Wildness

Hark! I hear the wild pounding of a distant drum.
I love the wild surge of the sea,
The frenzied wild dancer Flamenco beating
And eyes of a gypsy Lee.
A wild passionate nature appeals to me.
All nature is wild,
The animal world and wind and the rain
Sweeping through a tree.
The mountain peak and craggy wild moor
That runs so free.
'Tis a beauty to see an antelope glide
For shelter to seek,
A pussy cat in a contented heap.
All these things make me want to leap.
What an aspect of life is a wildness to keep.

Margaret Malindine

Caring For Mentally Ill

My mam lies so very ill in bed
Depending on us to be watered and fed.
Some of us come, some of us don't,
They find excuses or just won't.

A mother like ours is a very special gift,
When as ill as she is needs no family rift.
She needs everyone round to love and care,
As mothers like her are very rare.

When we were small she watched over us,
We should return this love without any fuss.
Some should not act, as she does not exist,
As when she's gone she'll be sorely missed.

For then she'll have gone through the pearly gate,
She'll be God's angel, so it will be too late.

L. J. Moreland

I Was There

I was there when Judas gave the signal to betray:
The kiss of treachery which led to crucifixion day;
I was there when jesting Pilate "washed his hands of Him",
Declaring, in his judgement, he could "find no fault in Him"
There when troubled Peter his dear Master thrice denied,
There upon the fateful day our Lord and Saviour died;
Looking on at Calvary I saw Him nailed to tree,
O! Why did I not realize that He was there for me?
Yes, I was there, for I am Judas, Peter, Pilate too,
Betraying Him, denying Him, the steadfast and the true;
Still heard, in my imagining, the mocking shouts and jeers,
And one loud cry of anguish that has echoed through the years.
My guilt no less - as, to remind me, Easter never fails -
Than had I laid the cruel thorns, or driven in the nails;
So I, though far removed in time, the guilt and shame must share,
For I am part of all mankind, and all mankind was there.

Stanley Mitchell

Normans cross

Out of the dark yet into the dark
The journey with no end
A brief moment, life held in the light
Then into eternity out of sight

Round and round the vehicles go
In a never ending headlight gleam
Roaring, fuming, a dark growling flow
Cars leaping ahead as salmon upstream
Big bulky lorries powering the pace
Spurred to beat in life's race

Mud flaps spitting clouds of spray
Blinding water crashes against the glass
Red eyes show with weakened ray
As people jockeying to pass

Out of the dark yet into the dark
The journey with an end
But for a moment life held in the light
Then into dark and eternal night

Richard Keller

Ode To Stoke

Could you see the potter throw,
the fiery ovens as they glow.
could you smell the gas and coke
see the clouds of endless smoke.

Could you see the terraced streets
old back yards with smoke-stained sheets
Mines within the depths of hell
where old king coal used to dwell

Could you see the blackened sky
hear the sound of children cry.
To people then, this was no joke
to people now a better stoke.

R. F. Bayliss

Images

Shadows of darkness descend on the light.
The sun almost set brings the start of the night.

Getting so tired I'm starting to yawn, I may even
sleep past first light of dawn. Settled in bed
I drift into sleep, into the world where
memories we keep. Floating through corridors
of places and years, passing through chambers
of heartache and tears.
    Going on deeper to
essence itself memories thought lost crash from
the shelf. Familiar faces of present and past,
Images you treasure slip from your grasp.
Out of the corners come hopes and your fears,
Sat upright and cold while the images clear.

Michael Keszeg

Dark Days

There comes a time in everyone's life when death knocks at their door
The grief you feel is hard to bear and that's what tears are for
"If only", is a common thought and guilt can be there too
But life is a mystic puzzle and there's nothing you can do
You'll often lie in bed at night and ask the dear Lord why
Why did he have to break your heart and let your loved one die

When the black clouds start to disperse and the sun comes shining through
Remember that through those dark days that God remained with you
So now the sun is shining and things start to look clear
The worst of it is over so wipe away that tear
To lose someone you love so much is something hard to bear
But one thing that can comfort you is to know your friends are always there.

Sharon Tomlinson

"Heartache"

I am cold, so cold,
   The icy fingers of despair
Have entwined my heart
   For you have gone, and love has gone
The burning fires of love
   That once warmed my heart
Are quenched by my tears
   And filled me with fears
The once joyous days and soft warm nights
   Were filled with rapture and delight
Each morn, with the sun, a new day begun,
   We would plan it with pleasure
Each moment to treasure
   Now days are so long
      Where has love gone?

E. Hawkridge

Twilight And The Fox

Along the lane the horsemen come
the hounds bay out for your princely blood.
A cry goes up the prey's been seen,
away now fox and flee the scene,
up the hill towards the old oak tree,
find sanctuary under its ancient spread,
to rest and mourn for your family dead.
Be quick young Lord away from this oaken tall,
for the dogs now howl out your own death call,
away down to yonder barn and in the warm hay,
dream safe of a better more peaceful day.
But too late to rest for the pack already comes,
to seek out and take your own royal blood,
quick back to the wood 'tis your own clan's land,
where none shall take you for his master's hands.
Crash on through the bracken run into the dark,
the pack they have lost you in rage they now bark,
and as the sunlight falls away across the land,
let us think of the day when we may walk with
each other man and nature together hand in hand.

Peter Routledge

Do You Know

Do you know how much I love you
Do you know how much I care
Do you know how much I miss you
When I know that you're not there.

Do you know how much it hurts me
Do you know how hard I've tried
To make everything seem more worthwhile
When you're not by my side

Do you know how much I hate it
Do you know how bad it seems
That I can only be with you
When you are in my dreams

Do you know how much I love you
You mean the world to me
I wish that I could be with you
For all eternity

Tina Pruden

The Troubled Mind

If one could understand, the troubles of the mind,
The highs, the lows, the peace you seek to find.
The muddled thoughts, the helplessness, the tears that blur the yes,
The friends that try to help and say, "you have really got to try".

The face you try to hide behind, the smile you try to keep,
Comfort from others, in desperation seek.
The hand of God is there, stretched our for you to take,
Reach out, take hold, and with faith, he will ease the ache.

These trials are sent, to make us understand,
That we can come through anything, with God to hold our hand.
If through these trials, a better person we become,
Then as the cloud lift, and we emerge, then we know that we have won.

With thanks to God, for everything, my trials, and troubles too,
I hope, that one day, there words from him to me, may someday comfort you.

R. H. Bond

Morning Farewell

No time for dalliance - I must fly!
The hard world waits for me;
the hard and implacable world and I
have a battle to fight, you see.
So there's no time for love any more,
no time for love today;
but why I must answer this call to war
I really cannot say.

Oh, why must I loosen the velvet tie
of your soft clinging arms and lips?
And why must I say "Goodbye! Goodbye!"
and weep on your finger-tips?
Oh, I can but say, my darling one,
that custom and duty drive;
but oh, how I long for the day to be done
and then we can come alive............

Tom Shailer

"The Rose"

As the pollen was scattered, and the seed was planted,
the growth of a new life, left me enchanted.
The uncurling of the petals, progressed very slowly,
the beauty it posses, is almost heavenly and holy.
Like rolled red velvet, it stands there so still,
appearing so innocent and reluctant to kill.
Deep beyond the beauty, exists a protective life,
Thorns more lethal, than the slashing of a sharp knife.
Throughout its entire existence, the charmer's on constant guard,
gentle to the touch, but with the power to be hard.
And as the passing of time, pursues its rapid course,
The diminishing youthfulness, begins to use its force.
Like the gracefulness of age, that shrivels the skin away,
The death of the once known beauty, draws nearer every day.
As the colours fade discreetly, the dullness creeps in,
and the wilting of the flower, starts to begin.
A crisp, brown stem is left, striking a bended pose,
To remind me of the previous occupant, the beauty of "The Rose"

Michelle Fabo

My Precious Gift

I watch and wonder at it all
The grass so green, the trees so tall,
No greater gift God gave to me
But these two eyes for me to see
There flies a bird, his wings spread wide
Upon the breeze he takes a ride,
The spiders web, so pretty a sight,
With dew drops glistening like stars in the night,
The river rushing, gurgling past,
A rainbow, flower, a shadow cast,
These are the things He gave to me
And my two eyes for these to see.

Patricia A. Mitchell

When Man In His Agony Is Struck Dumb

When man in his agony is struck dumb
the gods gave me a tongue to tell:
thus Goethe.

Then, poet, come with us to Auschwitz...

Take the second turning on the right,
follow the so-called 'Heavenly Way'
to that building there...

Open...

Enter...

Then....

on behalf of dumb struck man
say your vocational piece..

Proceed...
We are listening...

What? You too struck dumb?

Victor Jones

A Child Dream

The castle on the hilltop and the unicorn running free
The fairy and the leprechaun, both sitting in the tree
Watching over the children and the little games they play
While love and laughter echoes throughout the hills so gay

The lion and the dinosaur rolling around and around
While the sun plays hide and seek with many of the clouds
The tooth fairy has done her work and off to bed she goes
While poor old little Rudolph tries to warm his big red nose.

The child sleeping softly surrounded by her toys
Would not be woken by one little noise
The gun shots outside her window, seem to fade away
As her paradise is in dreamland where troubles float away.

Lorraine Marshall

'Essentials'

Food, clothing and shelter
The essentials we need to survive
Food, clothing and shelter
Essentials that dominate our lives.

Pounds and pence, dollars and cents
Cash in the bank to thrive
Pounds and pence, dollars and cents
Essentials we need to survive.

The sun, the moon and the earth
Air, the stars and the sea
Eternally taken for granted
The essentials to life that are free

The computer, the video, the tele.
We touch, we hear and we see
But blind and deaf we are becoming
To the essentials for life that are free

Robert John Ganderson

Winter

The sky is dark, and cloudy now.
The flowers have all died
And wind doth blow, and chill the earth
And squirrels run and hide

The trees have shed, there glowing glory
They stand so straight and bare,
No more to wave there leaves, and beckon
To call you over there

The snow doth fall, a sheet
As white as it can be
And mother nature, will spread her gown
In all her majesty.

E. Foster

Higher Ground

"Free At Last" I heard the old man cry, as the mist rolled through the glen,
"There's more to come" He said "much more than this,"
"Listen hard
you'll hear it in the wind".
100 years the dragon roamed this land, till Modred's spirit set us free,
Courage and valour laid the beast to rest, leaving a better place for you and me.

There is a castle on the "Higher Ground", it's such a special place to be,
One day I'll be King there, and you can be my Queen, don't disbelieve it is my destiny.
Soft music plays and magic fills the air, you see I've been there once before,
Take my hand and I will lead you there, for only I can show you the door.

There is a chamber with a large oak bed, covered in feathers and in fur,
A night of passion, or just to rest your head, the choice as ever will be there.
There is a castle on the "Higher Ground" where a warm mist blows in from the sea.
One day I'll be King there, and you can be my Queen, don't disbelieve it is my destiny.

E. D. Jones

Untitled

A Dedication to Margaret, 12 June 1996

For angels crying, villains laughing,
the donkey that is mute
pictures displaying, sounds that disturb,
maybe they suit.

On a high, down to earth,
could be on the curve,
running free, digging deep
maybe it's just a nerve.

Holding hands, isolated,
drifting in between.
A smile of love, a love to smile
what if it's just a screen.

Passions burning, angered rage,
a compound of just two.
Love is all, all is not love
perhaps even for the few.

For dimensions, parameters,
a complex definition.
Don't seek - accept,
it's that simple word, emotion.

G. F. S. Jones

Nursery Work

Our busy time is drawing near,
The customers will soon be here,
Come end of April, beginning of May,
We will have had a hectic day,
Answering questions, selling plants,
Mums, dads, kids and aunts,
They all pour in and spend their money,
It's not a bad life, but not all honey,
Fuchsias, Geraniums and Heather go,
Although it seems incredibly slow,
It can be pleasant on a bright sunny day,
Especially if it's all going our way.
Greenhouses are filled to the hilt,
Dad, with his hose pipe is stopping the wilt.
Martin sifting and mixing the peat,
Walking about on his tired little feet,
Keeping everywhere looking spick and span,
Serving the customers whenever he can,
This all goes on till the end of June,
We all think that it can't come too soon.

B. M. Langley

Springtime In The Orchards

Down in the orchard where the fruit trees grow,
The first signs of life as green leaves begin to show
Apple trees with blossoms of pale pink and white
Branches swaying in the wind, what a pretty sight.

Tufts of young grass so very soft to touch
These early days of spring are worth so very much
Young fledglings dancing through the rows of trees
Showing of their skills as bloom scatters in the breeze.

No matter what the time of day or throughout the year
This picture reminds me of a story that I once did hear.
'Twas of Johnny Appleblossom who lived up in the sky
For it's him who paints the sunsets just for you and I.

When the fruit has set and gives forth its yields
You can see autumn coming in way across the fields
The frost in the mornings, the coolness of the nights
The sunsets in the evenings, the birds upon their flights.

In the cold of the winter, trees standing stripped and bare
Silhouettes on the landscape, where once they'd stood so fair
The sleep of Mother until this time next year
When she awakens in the springtime with her gifts so dear.
A. Limbrick

A New Day

The thunder roared, the sky was lit,
The earth was gently shaken,
Then it died and all was still,
That's when the morn did waken.

The dew it shone upon the ground,
It does that every day.
Just like diamonds, sparkling bright,
But the sun steals them away.

The flowers yawn and open wide
To catch the warmth of noon,
They scent the air and splash their hues,
But often die too soon.

When evening comes, all closes down
The scent and the flowers wane.
The sky grows dim, the wind may rise,
And then it starts to rain.

The night is quiet and very dark,
So sleep is what we do.
We have our dreams and then we wake,
To meet the morning dew.
W. Jones

The Evil Drug Pushers

On the streets every day
The drug pushers wait in silence for their prey.
They are ready to perform their tricks
To sell their victims an expensive fix.

Their victims are slowly taken in
By those beasts that are riddled with sin.
The drug pushers may be a her or a him,
Either way they are driving their victims to a future that's grim.

The patter they give to the vulnerable young
To obtain money for drugs - and their lives just begun.
To hell with the victims the evil drug pushers must think;
We have made enough money for our cigs, gamble and drink!

They have wicked thoughts along with the life they lead,
To blow young people's minds to satisfy their greed.

Drugs pushers are the scum of the earth
So you youngsters out there - from them keep a wide berth.

When I was young I had plenty of fun.
I didn't need drugs - and so I took none!
Please say "NO" to drugs, if you want to survive.
Enjoy yourselves without drugs - and stay alive!
Lillie Janet Cobb

"The Four Seasons"

Spring comes in - with such delight
The earth awakens - to its sight
Shrubs and seedlings - are aware
Of the magic in the air
Then comes summer - following on
With the sun shining brightly - all day long
Then - as summer fades away
Autumn takes its place - in full array
Wondrous colours everywhere
Before winter takes over
Making everything look bare
Snowflakes - falling gently down
On our little sleepy town
Christmas time - will soon be here
What a lovely way to end the year!
Mary Eileen Evans

The Mist

In the middle of nowhere,
The dull, thick mist surrounds me.
It's like a black sheet,
Coming closer and closer and closer.
I try to crawl underneath it,
But it stops me.
I'm trapped in the mist,
And no one can save me.
But suddenly, unexpectedly,
I see a tiny light shining through the side.
It breaks through,
And I'm finally free.
Laura Chilton

Caution

Careful now! we hold in our hands,
The delicate bloom, so fragile and fair,
Easily crushed by the slightest force,
We don't appreciate, or feel remorse
For so great a gift, but do we care!
When trampled on, forever lost,
Too late to discover, at our great cost,
　So many decades, before we regain
　　the flower!
　　　delicate, enveloping, free,
　　　　treasure it deeply —
　　　　　Democracy.
V. Miele

The Fox Hunt

He senses it on the mist
The echoes intensify
Panic, refuge
Swishing, swirling, slipping, squirming

The image is clearer
Blood red their colours
Unfamiliar territory
Dashing, darting, diving, driving

The danger is immanent
Their wailing unbearable
Gaining ground
Writhing, reeling, rushing, resenting

The earth is thunderous
The confusion despairing
Suppressed, enclosed
Exhausting, enduring, exhaling, expiring

His fur torn to slithers
Blood red his colour
Victorious climax
Corrupted, ceremonious, chaotic, carnage
Lorna Mayne

My Winter Creature Comforts

The hedgehog flattens himself to crawl under
the garden gate,
He fell in the garden pond getting a drink,
I saved him before it was too late.
His antics make me laugh,
As he comes wobbling down the garden path.
The Robin comes to visit us every year
it gives me such pleasure when his red breast appears.
The blue tits and yellow hammers
feed off the seeds of the lilac tree
The sparrow hawk dives down from the sky
Gives us the once-over with his beady eye,
The blackbirds stay here all of the year
The starlings send the cats fleeing with a peck on the ear
best of all come the frogs to spawn in the pond
with their croaking song
So happy that spring is here and winter has gone.
E. B. Calder

This Is The Day

This is the day you have dreamt about, a new chapter in your life
The day that you'll walk down the aisle, and start out as man and wife

The sun is shining brightly, the church bells start to ring
And as you start this perfect day, your heart begins to sing

And as you tread life's rocky path, and go from day to day
You'll have each other's loving care, to help you on your way

You'll both share new horizons, and make your future plans
Let's hope your life together, on firm foundation stands

May you always prosper, as you start out anew,
And learn from one another, in everything you do.

And so I bring to you this wish, to send you on your way
May Good Luck be with you, on this your wedding day.
Yvonne Dines

Untitled

How hard I cried that day,
The day God took her away.
I loved her, and praised her,
But still he took her away.
He took her away that day,
Perhaps it was for the best,
Because she was so depressed,
And now she can rest forever.
But I loved her so, I know she had to go.
It was for the best, so I am told,
But she was never too old.
There she lies in her grave,
She'll never be back with us, I am afraid.
So until we meet again in heaven,
It's goodbye, because there will be no other,
Like you, my dear Mother.
J. G. Merritt

Light Of Inspiration

Shafts of light stream gently through,
The effortless, natural mosaic of cloud,
And falls delicately upon distant hills,
Hills which have stood majestically;
Watching over us since,
Time began.
The impressive, yet natural panorama,
Sends us a divine message.
A message that claims life is a natural process,
One that exists in stages,
Through which we all develop,
And when we reach the summit,
We too can stand majestically,
And watchful over our loved ones who remain,
Like the hills which have stood,
Since time began.
Sarah-Louise Clegg

Axe

The axe descends and in its place a celebration
The bride adorned and the congregation.
The axe descends and in its place the ringing
Of joyous laughter, of heavenly choirs singing.

The axe descends and with each fall of golden tress
The anger and tears, the drunken cold caress.
The axe descends and with each summoning to hell
Ends life - and echoed in the wedding chimes, the funeral bell.
K. L. Cromwell

Letting Go

Another life was soon to draw last breath.
The cruel compulsory act of human existence
But this time the breath was of my flesh and blood
And I vehemently rejected, all logicality, and acceptance

I stood in silence (almost hunched) viewing the figure lying below me,
- motionless and grey,
Surviving only through a maze of plastics tubes.
The cold white walls that mistily surrounded us,
Seemingly added substance - to the artificial reality - of my view.

Realisation was forcing me to let this being go,
Her time had come.
I turned and nodded agreement, the switch was authorized off...
She breathed no more.
I touched her hand - No response - just a draining of her warmth.

I took the bag of clothes, that were pushed into my arms
And holding them, I turned, and walked away,
I looked at the looming reflection in the automatic doors,
A solitary reflection. A confirmation of the loss I had just known,
A click, a swish, the hospital doors slid open - I shuffled through
And without a backward glance - I left my mother behind - and
 carried on alone.
P. W. Milton

Champions On Ice!!

The feel of sheer ice under their feet,
The competitors skating around.
The spectators sitting on their seats,
The funky music sounds.

Triple toe loops and axles.
The sequence is very familiar,
All the crowd are laughing and cheering.
The marking - cards are similar.

The twirls and spins are fantastic.
The real atmosphere is created,
There have been no falls, so far...
The judges are elated.

The gruelling routine is nearly finished,
The music comes to a stop.
A tremendous applause is given,
The American couple are on top.
Sarah Clarke

Winter Warrior

Snow falling to the floor
The cruel wind knocking on my door
But I will never let him in
I'm a mere mortal he's sure to win
The wind is wise, clever and old
He'll tie me in a chain of cold
He controls the snow the frost and all
At his old knees I'll never fall
Although the wind cannot be seen
I know he's there and that he's mean
He's out to get me I don't know why
If he gets me I'll surely die
Because I can not take the cold
Just like the wind I'm very old
Steven Prior

334

London

I love to go to London, the City alive is she,
The bustle of the people shopping in Regent Street you see.
Pigeons in Trafalgar Square resting on Nelson's Column.
Guards at Buckingham Palace looking rather solemn.
The changing of the guards is a sight to see.
So is Eros statue in Piccadilly.
Artists on the pavements painting people's portraits in quick time.
On the hour, you hear Big Ben chime.
Theatres in the West End with their splendid plays like
Phantom of the
Opera and Miss Saigon, with lots to see, the days not long.
Sights to see in London there are heaps it's the City that never sleeps.
E. C. Facchini

December Shoreline

Verse sand, is damp and crumbling
the colour seems to fade.
Before my weary eyes, the cold cry of
winter is surrounding my bones.
Leaving me thoughts of summer, yes I can manage a smile.
Waves and dancing foam spray, to every
breaking roar. The dissolute colour of grey,
of the cruel sea is everywhere I look.
The turning point of a December morning
cocoon the bay. Arise with fear into
the hearts of petty mortals who hear the mermaid, sing.
A ship can be seen as far out on the horizon. Coming into the December shoreline.
Peter K. Ward

Winter Woes

Resembling Mammon world of warmth come boots and patent toes
The clicking, clacking, oft skipping sounds of mortals free of woe
Smug, contented and well fed, they spy not another's plight
Nor ponder how stone pavement felt throughout bitter cold night

They know not of gut wrenching pangs as hunger sears through frame
Nor of the humbling of one's self, degradation and the shame
A beggar's foodless torment seldom cause largesse to spill
As profound experts expound their views on ways to cure this ill

The platitudes come mouthed by those who claim we're in the wrong
To seek the street with asphalt chill amidst the hurrying throng
But do they know that parents can and will expel offspring
For seeking explanations to some acts against their will?

Can I not seek a hearth, a roof, a meal, a well warmed bed?
Or are these gifts for those who strove and maimed to get ahead?
For 'mongst the human race are beings who plunder by the hour
Destroying basic creeds and yet, their lives have not turned sour

So with my ebbing strength I stalk, the busy streets the crowds
For those who will proffer their coins to make up welcome pound
And ponder on the fate of many who sometimes cannot win
'Cause critics seethe and loud decry our way of life as sin
S. C. Young

The Tree

It stands in the garden tall and straight
The branches bend over, but it takes the weight
The birds the squirrels take shelter from rain
When wind and lightning strikes it groans with pain
She stands with all her might
To stand tall again to challenge the fight
When winter comes with gales and snow
Leaving the branches bare
She stands alone with her forlorn stare
Will it last and will spring come
To bring back her foliage evergreen with the sun
I have stood tall again with all my might
To once again challenge the fight
Terence Nicklin

Christmas Day

Although 'tis early Christmas morn,
The children awake long before dawn,
What will this magic day hold in store?
Could that be Santa at the door?
No, they saw him late last night.
Hope today will be alright!
Off to church the family go,
Pity there isn't any snow.
Home again, time for dinner,
Bet the 'pud' will be a winner!
First a sherry for Mum and Dad
When dinner's over they will be glad
For opening presents time is here
And still time for more 'good cheer'
Singing carols in the firelight glow,
My how quickly time does go.
Now it's time to go to bed,
And so to rest their weary head.
But first they kneel and pray,
To thank 'All three' for a lovely day.
Dora May Smallridge

Eating With Charcoal Girl

Hot meat and bones, stimulant to the bowl
the charcoal girl would help herself,
picked the most tender,
the tongue refused the sinews,
her lips stung by peppered knowledge.

How long has she been here
could I bring back the time,
there are recalled times
when she has laughed with me
across many a chilled wine glass of poetry
and warm salmon flesh meals
in the restaurant of memory.

The breakfast-room overlooked the sea,
my charcoal girl had crumbled bread
scented with tea and lemon
eaten gently with the waters of my mouth.

Later in the morning she and I
walk in fur-coats down to the sea,
when the breaking waves subdued the shingles
we hungered.
J. W. Giles

Crystal II

A great yellow moon hangs in the sky
The black earth below is slim and bleak
A door comes to light, etched sharply in both.

So you can walk to the moon...?
A lamp shows the way.
The moon takes on the shades.
A ceiling and door coolly welcome, sub-lining the way.
A clinical workshop spans the globe, holding it firm.

A delicious pink Dorad sits aloft;
A firm black mussel waits below;
Two lights show the way...
All this in the moon.

Two roving eyes watch through the moon...
Or are they men with torches coming for me?

The tension's too great, a divider in the brain.
A great hand steals from the moon,
The pink, black, to grey.

Yellow rises again, against the black earth.
Peace in each hand, stroking the brain.....
Peace and near sleep.
Mike Watts

The Sealord

For as the nights gave lust to darkly feats, and from
the ceaseless crest a power of a bite, at gun and ready
a doubtless Scot cradled in a metal cabby blew the breath
of humanity over his icy fingers lending warmth to memory
where in a million moments past he spied verdant dales
of a summer's day; and to his ear a sweet sonata of brilliant
innocence born into youth, lost to mischief. Beith tonight is
a hostage to my heart! But war is the signature to peace and
due honour. For my country I brandish the instrument of not
a considered killer, but the tool that will trigger off a
justice bound to truth. Is it now I hear bashing against this
ship an irony of despair or a missile with a mission to murder?
Before the night could close out all hope, the resplendent Orb
cracked through the firmament casting fingers of light upon
the waters of war. As darts to a target, the enmity a flight took
their maleficent intents upon the metal trojan, pelleting,
sparking, spitting bits of death at the ship; the Scot took refuge
in the mastery of faith and trounced the rising sun! Today we
were victors; and tomorrow the will of the winning shall go out
with the tide. Liberate Pro Multis!

Keith M. Wallace

No Hope!

Just two years old a baby still, but the pain,
The cancer, a bitter pill.
Who knows when it all began
The treatment, who can even understand? The pain.
The sweetness in those loving, trusting eyes — although
The pain. Then others pain when a baby dies.
The tiny coffin, a long walk uphill but, the pain of doing
What has to be — standing stiffly, silent, in the rain.
Even clouds cry at such a thing,
Do angels really stand and sing?? But, the baby no
Longer has the pain — who knows just what is best?
As baby put there now to rest — the pain lives on
In others, a bitter pill, — walk slowly down, leaving
A child upon the hill... life does go on, we have to cope.
But can never really know, — the pain, - of a child,
Who had no hope!

A. G. Robertson

Catwalk Salmon

I know a woman who tried to dress a salmon - she heard
   that's what you do.
She nearly got the trousers on but could not find
   the shoe.
The overcoat was far too big-it fell right off the
   shoulders
The eyes were replaced with radishes - the sockets made
   good holders.
There is a moral to this tale - it's meant to warm
   all food
Beware of women who get food home, that think
   nude food is rude!

Marlene Winters

The Statue

Cold as stone, alone I stand,
The birds my only company.
In this great expanse of humanity,
I pose for all to see.
But no one seems to care for me,
My stone has long turned green.
It's not a pretty sight at all,
People just abuse me.
I used to look so splendid,
But that was so long ago.
Where did all the good times go?
Who took away my splendour?
It's worse at night, it's when they come,
Come with spray cans at the ready.
Then without a care they start to spray,
Destroying me even further.
But they will not always be here,
I will - won't I?

Neil Kelly

Midnight Glory

In midnight glory,
The Black Unicorn stalks my soul
His mane,
A miasma of lost hope,
Unfurls the tortured cries
Then snaps suddenly back to silence

A dark gleam,
Flashes, sparks from ebon light within
Corrupted,
His being mocks all our dreaming
Malignant shining now, as purest light
Altered, he moves as deepest evil

All beauty still,
His grace, his power fill my heart
He strikes,
And even as he damns me
I pity
The wisdom in his captured eyes

Lorraine Phipps

How?

It's strange this sight we see by light,
That rests upon the sands.
This pyramid shape that's built so high,
And only made of sand.
It puzzles me the age of this,
For how they got so high
Without the tools we have this day,
It makes me wonder how?
My only guess has got to be,
They came from outer space
And left this strange amazing thing,
To have us wonder how?

M. Bryceland

"Brownie, My Friend"

Every morning at first light
The birds arrive, they've spent the night
Huddled in some bush or tree
Awaiting human sounds and me
Dressed in my dressing-gown and hat,
Checking first for next door's cat.
The coast is clear so out I go
Calling "Brownie," seeds I sow
Across the path and shake the tin,
Cold feet stamping, what a din!
The frozen water I replace
It's glistening pattern looks like lace.
Above me in the Malus Tree
Sits Brownie, Mrs Blackbird she
Looks down at me as if to say
"I'm coming now, out o' the way."
I stand and watch her for a while
Chatting, "Good girl", then I smile,
Thinking what eccentricity,
Talking to birds for all to see!

Leonie Jeffrey

Southport Exhibition

Look to the Sky Birds, champions of daring,
The "Arrows" parade their glorious wings,
Spectacular motions of courage and decision,
Men and their flying machines.

Swooping the sky with perfect formation,
Taunting the speed of low flying cloud,
Commanding the beam of vivid elation,
Thrilling spectators eyes.

An exhibition of splendid excitement,
Entertainment of the highest esteem,
A moment of wonder, suspended animation,
The "Red Arrows" and their flying machines.

C. Abson

Modusvivendi

The eyes behind the windows stare explosive situations flare
The all night vigil when the troubles began,
incurred the wrath and the laws of man
Everyone was in limbo when the deeds were done
The eyes were glistening not a tear was shed
on the streets of Ireland they were burying their dead.
The pipes and drums rolled on, in an interlude of despair,
going back to another year.

As eyes behind the windows stare.
The wind of change is everywhere;
The Irish in there eloquence, are talking about their sufferance,
with ministers on both sides of the water
talk about chaos and disorder; when the troubles cease to be,
hopefully they will agree, and respond with a democracy,
The Irish eyes are smiling and light up at last,
the troubles seem a thing of the past,
and let all sides live in harmony
explosions and killing if they do begin
and living in harmony seems a sin;
Those eyes behind the windows stare the wind of change is
everywhere.

Robert E. Nott

After The Air Raid

We had sat in the shelter for most of the night
The "all clear" sounded - we were alright.
Then, just as we were getting out,
'Mam' (who was quiet) began to shout!
"Stand still our Margaret" and "stay right there"
Gently she took a beetle, from out of my hair.
I screamed - ran in - took off all my clothes
But put them back on - because I was froze.
I couldn't sleep; tried with all my might.
So, mam, held me close to her the rest of the night.
From then on I vowed I never would
Go in there without my pixie hood.

Margaret Schofield

Spring Bank Holiday

There was no wind,
The air was full of sound of cuckoos
And the rain came in straight lines.
Then the hail,
White ice on the dog's black coat.
Ahead the lane curved sharply -
A well known track to girl and dog.
The corner turned, they stop.
No rain, no hail, a hint of sun,
And she stands
Surprised by blossom in the village gardens.

R. Willett

The Longest Day

Little boy lost on a summer's night
The air is warm, the sky yet light,
Troubled hearts search anxiously round
Where, oh where, is he to be found?
Could be have trudged so far to the fair?
But he'd know that one needs money there.
Neighbours, friends have searched in vain,
I'll use the telephone again,
Call the police, it's the only way
They'll find my little boy astray.

How long have we waited? The time is flying.
Somewhere he wanders, forlorn and crying.
He is so small, a baby still,
Surely he wouldn't go down the hill
Or, dreadful thought, maybe a car
Stopped, then carried him off afar.
I stand at the gate, so helplessly,
Then - but it can't be - under the tree,
A dear, tightly-wrapped bundle, fast asleep,
And now, at last, I dare to weep.

Sylvia Ayers

Faith And Trust

Have faith and trust, I guess I must,
That's just the way we're meant,
For it was God that made this world
and with it faith He sent.
If only I could understand why life is full of hate.
These things are sent to try us, so they say,
They call it fate.
I've had my share I do declare,
And now I want some peace,
For time is young, there's more to come,
Maybe one day will cease,
Roll on that day, that's all I say,
But still I guess I must,
With all my might, I'll hold on tight,
To faith and trust.

Patricia Hunt

Winter Blues

The summer sun is laid to rest.
The colourful trees are past their best.
That cold, depressing time of year
Approaches, once again, I fear.

Days are short, the nights are long.
We all sleep heavily, what is wrong?
Bring me sunshine, bring me Spring,
I yearn to hear the birds all sing.

The skies are either black or grey,
I shan't be going out today.
I'll sit beside a warm log fire
And dream of sun - my heart's desire!

Everlasting fog and rain.
Another day indoors again.
So, come out sunshine, make me smile
And then I'll know that life's worthwhile!

Marie J. Hawkins

Rites Of Passage

Rites of passage
That's what they call it.
It will strengthen you,
They say it will give you
Character.

The first part was easy.
The quickening flame,
The purifying fire
Burning off the dead wood
Consuming the old self, leaving
A new more vital soul to rise from the flames like the phoenix.

But the wind changed course
And the glowing ember spluttered and died
And the rites of passage
Are the cold dank ashes of the cinders
Suffocating
Spitting dust into my mouth
Foul tasting
Of desolate landscape with the cremated ruins of a new life.

Stephanie Comis

Lottery Dreams

Would it be too great a task,
That my dreams become reality;
We could indulge ourselves and bask,
Wanting for nothing would be normality;
Enjoying pleasures normally reserved,
For worthier folk than working class;
We would prove we are deserved,
Doing our best to help the mass;
Those in genuine need who have suffered,
Spreading our good fortune if this comes to pass;
Helping the sick and poor and dottery,
Would it be too much to ask -
That our numbers win the lottery.

J. B. Bentley

One More Week

Just one more week.
That's all it took;
And the sun, shone.
Brilliant, vibrant, and the earth found hope,
Life escaped from winter's evil grasp
And the land could cope.

But you couldn't.
You couldn't wait that week.
You couldn't see the signs,
An optimistic view? That life can be sustained,
Can hibernate for cold, lonely months
And be reborn, again and again and again!
Hopes eternal spring; was dying.

So, you said goodbye,
But every autumn I! Recall,
With painful, depressing memories
Of another winter's past,
Who never saw the sunlight,
We could not hold on.
Your eternal hope of spring, has gone.

Nichola Bland

Wayne

Some people may think
that you have no brain
but I can see, through all the pain
that you are the most intelligent boy
who has to suffer and seldom cry.
You are autistic and unable to speak
and you also are an epileptic.

Your smile is so bright
But empty inside, and yet there
is something that catches my eye
you are with me for a second
that's all you can give. It's enough
for me. It gives me reason to live
But remember you have parents
who care and no matter what
happens. We will always be there.

So thank you Wayne
for opening my eyes
to children like you
for showing the light

Kathleen McKeon

Some Kind Of Despair

Oh barren land of so much suppose
　that yet is turned to grief,
Where waters flow and raindrops fall,
　to shield man's disbelief.

Amidst the misty, saddened night
　an echo comes to call,
To bid the world a fair good night,
　to gently stay its fall.

But still within attempts to soothe
　there dwells a restless heart.
Brought down by effort in this life
　of duty's heavy part.

For none can sit and muse a while,
　or risk to duck the race.
'Left standing' then becomes the plight;
　brings frowns from human pace.

So run man must, despite his pain,
　alone but for that grace,
That gives amazing visions glow,
　beyond earth, to heavens base.

Mary McCormack

The Pig

It really seems a bit unfair
That pig should always look so bare;
While cats have fur and dogs have hair,
　A pig...is bare.

You must admit a pig's not pretty;
We gaze at him with shame or pity;
At his expense we're rude or witty,
　It seems...a pity.

He simply does not care a fig
For sentiments of prune or prig;
His just to grovel, grunt and dig;
　The pig's no prig.

With nose a-twitch and eyes agog,
Disdainfully we murmur, "Hog";
We much prefer a cat or dog.
　Alas....poor hog.

Yet gourmands rapturously talk
Of bacon, gammon rashers, pork;
And elevate with knife and fork;
　Poor pig...now pork.

W. Barnett

The Merry-Go-Round

Time is just an utter illusion
That offers a limit to confusion.
No! Rather it seems an intrusion
To the spirit, for the mind - a delusion.

Thus we exist in Time
And before, and beyond the sublime,
Into an emptiness without any space
Filled with the Divine Grace.

So we fumble in matter - it's Real,
Yet as individuals we're immaterial.
Sight, smell, touch, taste and sound,
Senses on a merry-go-round.

Inward search, an outward map,
Time and space are just a trap.
A hidden smile that knows that Truth,
The body a universe - it is The Route.

Tashmin Kassam Khamis

An Introduction to a Diary

I wish my writings to be such
That man can neither rue, nor praise too much.
So pen to paper I will put
and pray by judgement not by luck
That what is written, will be read
As thoughts within my simple head.
My writings I want you ne'er to mock
If that's your wish, then read them not.

S. M. Belfield

Little One

Open wide your eyes on day so bright with light,
Terrified by exaggerated sound,
That makes the bird like heart to pound within the tiny breast,
Unaware of all the mystery's to come,
Of joy and laugher, love that others have to give,
Blow breeze and sun shine bright upon his face,
It is his first, the day of birth,
He gasped and screamed as he was dragged into the world,
Then crooned with pleasure as they stroked the wrinkled skin,
That separated them from him,
Like a tiny hairless mouse, frightened, with a curious willingness to trust,
They envy him the world unseen through eyes still closed,
They begrudge him every feeling yet to feel,
But one and that is the sorrow of things undone,
Enfolded in their loving arms,
They welcome him, their little one, to life.

L. Bedford

My True Love And I

I lost my true love on that morn
That morn so cold and damp,
He spoke as if his heart was torn
His face shone in the lamp.
His face it was so sweet and firm
His eyes so crystal blue,
But as my true love passed away
I knew what I must do.

He asked me not to cry for him
He asked me never to mourn,
But how I miss my true love dear
My love to him was sworn.
So try to understand my love
My feelings deep inside,
And try to understand my love
Just why I chose to die.

P. M. Holland

How Sad This World!

How sad this world!
That men make mockery of God's creation,
To pander to the selfish whims of wealthy few -
Who could gaze at lifeless eyes or dull coat
Lacking life gloss? Who could wear the life skin
Of another being - partner on our planet?
Animals hunted for vanity,
Pollution soiling our seas.
Even the very air we breathe, laden with
Poison, choking the last life out of our world.
And yet, in spite of all the omens,
All the signs and portents of a passing age,
Still the destruction races forward,
Ominous, odorous, onerous, unabated
In its relentless, frightening inevitability:
Statistical figures chill me to the marrow,
How helpless, how vulnerable I feel,
An aching, empty feeling for an aching empty world?

Pamela Bassett

Kelly's Ghost

On cobbled streets in pouring rain
Tap tap tap hear that refrain
It is the sound of young Gene Kelly
Whose legs I think were made of jelly

But now his ghost is ever ready
To dance once more with lovely Debbie
Forty four years have gone since then
They'll be singing in the rain again

Retained on film for all to see
We'll ne'er forget his jollity
Dance with Angels in the sky
Stars and stripes forever fly.

D. S. Margerum

My Feelings

The worried feeling
That makes me feel sad,
The guilty feeling,
That makes me feel bad.

The lonely feeling
That makes me feel out of place,
The cheerful feeling
That makes my heart full of grace.

All these special feelings of mine,
The ones that are good
The ones that makes my heart shine.

All these bad feelings of mine,
The jealousy,
The hatred,
The ones that do not shine.

These good feelings make me feel better inside,
And make the good side of me feel heavy.

Nadine Brown

"What You Mean to Me"

I know I've said before
That "I love you" and have tried to
Tell you how much you mean to me -
But I wonder if you really
Know how strong and sincere
My emotions are, and how deeply touched
I am by your feelings.

You are such a tender and special person;
And you make me feel "special" just by
the ways you talk with me, and listen with me,
And share with me the warmth of your touch
And the desires of your heart.

I want to give so much in return...
For I do love you,
And I just wanted to let you know...
How nice it feels inside
When my smile is showing
And my heart is full
And my thoughts are all for you.

Ronald V. Lodge

Freedom

Freedom is a thing most dear,
That I would place on record here
My thoughts about this simple word,
That means so much to those who've heard
How some suppress this sacred way
Of life in other lands each day.
God grant that we may always be
Free to serve and follow thee.
Free to work and free to play
Free to live our lives each day.
Free to love and free to care
Free to pray to Him up there.
Free to laugh and free to cry
Free to help the passers-by.
Free to write and free to print.
Free to speak the words we think,
So long as words and deeds are kind
And loving thoughts are in our mind.
Then we'll know in this our age
That freedom is our heritage.

T. R. Pickering

Inside Out

Life seems full of empty spaces, yet
swimming with oceans of faceless faces

I wonder sometimes how long I will last
empty of energy to deal with my past

Is it natural for someone who people see as young
to feel that their life hasn't even begun?

Try as I might, I can't climb my ladder
so I find myself sinking lower, feeling sadder

Surely there's something, just waiting for me
to relieve all the pain and set me free

And so if I asked you, would you know the secret?
Or is it hidden inside where you want to keep it?

Self-pity and sadness is all that I have,
I can't find a reason why I should feel glad

My clock is still ticking, but I don't know for how long
Would I really mind if it stopped, would that be so wrong?

I go on with my life, struggling with each new day,
and all I can do is hope and pray, that one day I'll find
what I'm looking for,

and finally be able to open the door.

Samantha Stephens

Forbidden Love

My dearest love if you but knew
That I am dumb and cannot speak
Of all the feelings in my heart
So secret lie and hidden deep.

If I could just once say to you
I love you dear with all my heart
Would you not run a million miles
To distance us .... and break my heart?

So dumb I'll stay and from afar
I'll gaze upon your face so dear
And kiss the air should you pass by
Just to feel your presence near.

And this my love will always be
My secret to eternity
And only I and the Lord above
Will know about my secret love.

Pam Esgate

Mam

Mother plodding along the shore
Swollen ankles sandal sore,
Bearing beach ball, shrimp net, picnic lunch,
Wincing at the shingles crunch.
Hung with discarded shirts she comes
Binoculars bumping on her bum,
With towels and camera, flask of tea,
Enjoying her holiday by the sea.
Scanning the sandy sunlit vistas
For a spot of shade to rest her blisters,
While way ahead in the shimmering haze
Dad and the kids are stretched out to laze
Calling to "Hurry", "Come on", "Make haste",
As the trundles her bundles across the waste.
Then in twilight back to the caravan
Trudges weary good old 'mam.'
And to enquiries "Oh yes", she'll say
"Yes! We've had a lovely day."

E. A. Groves

Goathland Nr Whitby

Heavy laden air, clouds of weight
    suspended in eternity.
Beauty - grandeur daring not to breathe
Hate - sadness animosity whelm up
    inside me.
    Afraid -
Once I could laugh and sing a
    tuneful song -
No more - I sit in frenzied state
    Contemplate - where is the joy?
    Gone -
What is there - here in me?
    Afraid -
This awesome majesty
    Frightens me -

Mary Mason

Love Lingers On

As I walked through the sand remembering your hand in mine
Taking my pain and the tears that I cried all alone inside,
dry in my eyes.
I held you so tight recalled how that night above whispered
it's love, touching a flame inside showing me how love
could be mine for awhile,
You gave me a warmth in my heart, a love dredging the depths
of my soul.
Now that these moments are gone my love lingers on for you
Watching the shore and hoping one day you'll return to my side,
Love never died.
So will the pain ever leave will I always grieve for you
Recall your love, knowing the taste of your warm lips on mine
Watching the tide rolling in,
Yes you gave me a warmth in my heart, a love dredging
the depths of my soul.

M. Jennings

No Hope I Hold Too Small

I can peel back darkness, gather stars in my hand
Tell of heaven's truth here on earthly sand
I can stop time for an instant, cause the moon to shine
All this I could do, and more, if only you were mine

The universe but a tiny speck
Compared to the thoughts I hold
The sale-of-the century, small
For on your smile I'm sold

The wind and waves are quiet
To the volume of my sighs
I telescope from sea, to see
That beauty in your eyes

No flowers at your hand outshine
The light I see in your face
I can take the "time" from time
To land and share your space

I've seen the four corners of the earth
But find I return and fall
For the grace and sweetness that you show
No hope I hold too small

Leslie Payne

Untitled

White roses climbed a Cornish wall.
    That evening in July.
They hung above valerian
    As pink as cherry-pie.

At intervals along the way
    A purple foxglove stood.
As if to guard all forms of life
    As any soldier should.

The air was warm despite the breeze
    at seven O' the clock.
The weather man was right it seems
    he, whom we love to mock!

He promised us a glorious day
    now 'bonus' hours too.
For as I looked t'wards Mullion isle
    Both sea and sky were blue.

A wooden 'finger' just ahead
    "Coast path" it did proclaim
So on I strode, "why not" - I thought,
    For was that not my name?

Frances Coast

The Ever Open Door

We knew it was never far away
that awful, fateful, sad old day.
Granddad was to be no more.
he took the ever open door.
The door to a world free from pain,
We cried and cried but all in vain.
We could not stop the journey he took,
and on his face was a peaceful look.
A look we'd missed for quiet some time,
a look that said "Everything's fine."
We didn't cry because he was free
We were all crying Me! Me! Me!
We would miss his ever loving face,
in our lives he'd left a big space,
A space that no one else could fill
never could, and never will.
We're left with Memories good and bad,
and for quite some time we'll all be sad.
Then one day we'll take the same door,
and the sad empty space will be filled once more.

N. E. Williams

A Rose

Winter is here. With a covering of snow
Summer has gone
   A long time ago
Yet "standing" so proud against
   The cold wind "is a rose".
"A rose" standing there, in the
   cold winter air
"Like a blush" on the cheek of
   A maiden so fair
"So fair" so pink "in repose"
   Is a rose
   Mrs. Evelyn Collingwood

Sunday Evening

Echoes across the dell, of the bells,
Tell of Sunday eventide, and of
Church goers and hymns, and such like things.
I pause by the way a short while, and
In my mind's eye I can see the folk
Quietly walking along the carpeted aisle.
The Altar, covered with flowers, and
The Altar's candles flickering.
The choir, half hidden behind the pulpit and
By the shadows thrown off the chancel roof.
The pious figure of the priest
As he kneels reverently at the Altar.
The service is about to begin, and as the
Sound of the bells fades into the evening dusk,
I walk on, wondering which will be chosen this evening
As their first hymn, and think to myself of the words,
And softly sing, "Now the day is over", and
I silently thank God for this time;
This quiet and peaceful Sunday evening.
   T. W. Cotterell

Springtime In Glenmoriston

I watched in awe as Winter in her dying throes
Succumbed to the warmth that melts the last of Winter's snow.
As flowers peep and birds begin to sing
I look around and suddenly it's Spring.

The warming sun, the melting snow
Water cascading to the loch below
Rainbow colours across the hills
Mingle with primrose and daffodils.

I stood enthralled, amazed and dumb
To witness such beauty Spring has brought forth.
I look for more, and there and then
Resplendent in his glory stood the Monarch of the Glen.
   Sonny Cheetham

Mobile On The Mobile

I'm just standing here alone,
Talking on the telephone,
I don't care if it's wet or dry,
I've got a phone to call you by.

I'm just standing here alone,
Talking on the telephone,
You might think I'm talking to myself,
But I'm switched on with no nuts off the shelf.

I'm just standing here alone,
Talking on the telephone,
Call my number and I'll speak to you,
It's me and you just us two,

I'm just standing here alone,
Talking on the telephone,
Stuck or the loo,
I can still talk to you.

I'm just standing here alone,
Talking on the telephone,
Call me here, call me there,
Call me everywhere.
   Seumas Neil Ferguson

A Lost Child

So painful was my life when I was very small
Taken away from a mother who didn't care at all
Sent to a children's home then fostered suddenly
Lost in a bewildered world that doesn't care for me

Sadly I look back at the things that aught to be
Now I really know they where never meant for me
Taken from my brothers and my sisters too
I wonder in this world what am I gonna do

Our lives are so precious loving and true
Forgive me dear God if I feel I don't love you
I try so hard with all of my heart
To forgive my sins and make a fresh start.

Heavenly Jesus so perfect and kind
Take all of this hatred out of my mind
Help me to try and to start anew
Then maybe one day my dreams will come true
   A. T. Bedi

"A Prayer"

I said a prayer for you today, and asked the Lord, if He would
Take you gently by the hand, and lead you to the Promised Land.
There'll be no fears or grief, or pain,
For in God's House you will remain.
As I kneel beside my bed in prayer, I feel your presence very near,
I hear your voice, you whisper low.
"At last, it's time for me to go.
I'm going forth, into the sun.
From now, my life has just begun.
I lived on Earth, and stood the test, and now,
God's brought me Home to rest.
So, if you look into the sky, you'll see a star,
So bright and rare, and you will know that I am there.
For I will be your Guiding Light, your Guardian Angel through the night, I will be with you all the while,
So please don't weep, but softly smile.
I'm here to open up the door,
Whene'er you reach this Heavenly Shore.
At last, I'm free from all the pain,
God Bless you, 'til we meet again."
   Valerie McCann

Alone In A Crowd

He was ordinary, just a tramp shuffling heavily out of the
   shade into sunlight
Tired feet reluctant to obey, amidst calls of jeering children.
He almost understood the sealed within dread of small minds
Fighting the fear passed on by mothers' struggles.
God gave him strength to stand and glare at those who chose
   to gather close,
His mind in turmoil as they closed in upon him,
To run, challenge, or hide his eyes denying them their so
   called pleasure.
Small hands begin to pull at his, drawing on his non-resisting
   strength
As earth slowly fades from sight.
In unreal slowness, he meets with dust.

The love that bound him in life struggles to leave him in death,
Love's sweet song in hushed - crushed by death's hand, that
   touched,
As he qualifies to pass from darkness into light,
The stillness tense, all living blood had chilled
As Heaven and earth in closer contact knit,
The sound of silence pounding now as hearts are stirred with
   feelings mixed,
A thought, which seems as if from nowhere sprung
Embedded deep within hearts so young, will lie there still, and
   grow as they.
As a veil of sadness shrouds the sun, he is once more, alone
   in a crowd,
In the shadows.
   Yvonne Hill

On Safari

While on Safari Lou and his friend
Stopped the Jeep just around the bend
They both decided to take a stroll
Across the plains to the water hole
While walking they heard a fierce lion's roar
But Lou didn't panic he knew the score
He put on his running shoes with a grinning smile
Though he knew the Jeep was back at least half a mile
But you can't outrun the lion said his friend
He's sure to pounce before you reach the bend
But I don't need to outrun the lion said Lou
I only need to outrun you.

S. Richardson

Song To My Sons

Put away your surf board.
Take off that cocky grin
Were going to squash you into shoes.
And touch you all about sin

Put away your sun block
Take off your loose quick drys.
You're going to have to wear a suit
And conform under grey over cast sky's.

Put away your county things
Cut off your prized dread locks
For you'll be singing geordie songs
Beside the Tyne side docks.

Put away your drum kit
Take off your bass guitar
For what you are about to learn
Is different by far

Put away your cane tree like
Take with you your sun-brown face
Bring along your warm glad heart
To know a love you can't replace.

Mary Joyce

The Cycle Of Life

Those ashen sons of ashen wives,
Take in their hands those rusty knives,
And so destroy more ashen lives,
And on the blood their power thrives,
All under the misty sun.

They tidy up their honey hives,
Their profit gains, they maximize.
And up the ladder, so they rise,
All under the misty sun.

Their icy heart, it shatters fine,
And from it flows a sparkling wine,
Grown on the peoples, blood soaked vine,
All under the misty sun.

They grow so tall, and then they run,
Their power grows, they are the hun,
Their trigger finger, opens wide,
And now their ashes burn inside
And no glimpse of the misty sun.

Sean Hanson

Childhood

Tiny feet they pattered on the cobbled
streets of the Aberdare valley.
 Up the mountains down the dales,
round the pit-heads through the alleys.
 Play at soldiers shoot and duck,
goody baddie who's in luck.
 Play at leap-frog hop and jump,
miss a step get a bump.
 Rolling marbles in the playground,
teacher saying, home for tea.
 Time goes by so fast so soon we
are in the age of man on moon.

Michael L. Laycock

Waiting For The Bus

He stood at the bus stop, sturdy,
straight and very still; his
unruly straw-coloured hair lifted
upwards from the crown; every bit
of two and a half years old, impish,
unflinching in his gaze, splendid
in the brightly coloured clothes
of today's children.

Suddenly, there burst from him
a child's uninhibited, unselfconscious
chuckle - a cascade of sound sparkling
and joyful; his face mirrored his happiness.

He did not reveal the secret of his joy
but, for a moment, the world had seemed
transformed by the laughter of a child.

Margaret Willoughby

"Free To Be"

Let go of your dreams and you're lost
Take charge it may seem, you're the boss
Don't live in sorrow, there's no room for pain
A person is blind when he's up in his brain.
It comes from the heart, not the soul, not the mind.
It's there from the start, it's been there all the time.
Free to lose, free to gain, free to still remain the same.
Free to run, free to be, free to live my life as me.
To give up hope is to give up fighting
To keep on trying is a bolt of lightning
Take a deep breath and search for a clue
What you see, is what's really true.
Go ahead and look inside
What's in there is what you hide
The power withheld is just to decide
Who you are and why you try
Free to capture the spirit inside
Free to run with the wild
Free to live with faith or without
That's what living is all about.

Lee Paris

To A Tree

You look so masterful and strong
Surveying all below.
What secrets lie within your wooden heart?
What have you seen - what have you heard
Have you been standing long?
I wonder if some tale you could impart.

I've heard you talking to the breeze
I've seen your branches sway
I've watched your green leaves rippling with mirth
Won't you even whisper to me
All the things you say
And let me be the judge of all your worth.

How many lovers carve their names
When summer breezes blow
What bird's nest free within your leafy gown?
I wish that I could hear your tales
But now - I'll never know!
I'm sorry tree, I've come to cut you down.

Anne Rosewell

The Perfect Rest

Lives my soul in a human frame
Striving for peace on this miraculous plane,
Looking for God in my hour of need,
Yet ever conscious of Satan's greed.
Tossed here and there by all who dare
Resist its claim and conscious power.
Soars high and low with fleeting breath,
'Twill come some day the perfect rest.

Marie Pinnington

At Sea

Alone on a balcony
Sunshine searing my chest
I listen to the sea
As the ship sails through
Each spouting swell.

Watching the cutting edge
As she ploughs through blue water
Seeking the horizon
Nothing passes through my mind....

Sun glints on waves
Revealing creases in the sea
Shadows allow qualities of light
Chasing one another to darkness
From white foam pillows to a peacock blue

Dolphins play off the coast of Portugal.
Carry on...
Confront yourself...
Realize - there are no horizons at Sea.

Paul Lucas

Record Run

Remembering the Silver Jubilees run from St. Pancras to Kettering carrying the Duke and Duchess of Gloucester to their honeymoon on 6th November 1935.

Sat on the fence, book and pen in my hand,
Suddenly England is a wonderland.
Carrying the royals on their honeymoon to Yorks,
Now to see something of all the talks.
Patiently looking down the line,
It seemed a long time when you are only nine.
Someone had said it would pass very fast,
Make sure see enough 'cause it has to last.
A white puff of smoke from the chimney stack,
Hurtling along all silver and black.
Into the climax of a record run,
Thank goodness the rain had made way for the sun.
I watch in amazement, wonder and awe,
At 5552, Silver Jubilee of the L.M.S.R.

A. B. Webster

Lily - (Portrait Of A Dead Grandmother)

Her petals purest white,
Striking yet not bold,
But gentle, soothing, calm,
A pleasure to behold,
Such deep and lasting beauty,
Seemingly from within,
Promising as striped bud,
And shapely in her prime.

As time erodes edges,
Petals droop and blur,
Still purity remains
And silently she fades
Into eternity.

Margaret Galbraith

Sonnet: Oh Noble Tree

What is more noble than an aged tree
Stretching its gnarled and twisted limbs up high
Into a cold and bleak December sky,
Its strength exposed for all the world to see
A stalwart skeleton of dignity.
Steadfast it stands through sunshine, rain and snow,
Watching the generations come and go.
Remote, unmoved by man's inconstancy
Head held aloof in solemn majesty.

Oh Noble Tree, would I could be like thee
And stand up ever proudly, rain or shine.
Would I had roots that went as deep as thine
That I could weather storms and never shake,
For like a sapling do I bend and break.

J. D. Winchester

Biafra? Vietnam? Ireland? Bosnia? Anywhere?

I open my eyes and what do I see
Such hunger, pain and misery
I shut my eyes and then open them wide
Then turn to look at the boy on his side

Lying there injured in a pool of blood
Watching, whilst it mingles in with the mud
I watch whilst he stares, his expression blank
No one is bothering, he's a lower rank

Why waste time on the weak and less able
After all, he hasn't a label
There will soon be one less mouth to feed
Pluck him out like all the other weeds

Save the food, don't give him any
Soon he'll be dead and still there are many
Thousands to feed, they hunger for food
Distended bellies and bones showing through

The heartfelt people doing their best
To feed the hungry, lay the dead to rest
How can a country allow this to happen
Or are we just guinea-pigs used as a weapon?

Patricia Nolan

Holidays? "Oh No"...

Choosing your holiday is a chore, where shall we go, this year? You suggest a cruise, no Egypt maybe? Hubby, "Here we go again. Why not just stay here!"
You look at pictures, "oh, that's nice, you read, and it's for singles, That's done it, turn the page, "oh yes, Barbados that's for me" (to the price)...'Enthusiasm dwindles'!
Good old Majorca, Magaluf or Greece...I whittled it down, to a choice of three? Maybe Butlins, for Peace!
Ask the kids,..."America! Disney world we pick"
"Them Yanks think their something "(Jealous)" Butlins, I think we'll! stick"!
"What about Euro Disney. What's wrong with the French"?
"Not enough, the Francs per pound, all garlic, I hate the stench"
Ibiza seems a favourite now. "Are we decided then?"
"Yes, err.. Wait, bay or town?" here we go again!
Sitting quiet, keeping out. Hubby starts to dream.
"A single holiday, yes just me. No nagging wife. No screams!"
Odds on now, it's Turkey. Union is in reach....
Then eldest daughter, pipes up with, "not much of a beach!!"
You'll arrive home from your hols, refreshed. Kids, ready for school
You've been away, for ten days, Thoroughly enjoyed..
Blackpool!

Lisa M. Garvey

Do You Know?

Like a budded flower I'd like to unfurl,
Stretching out my tentacled fingers: Air fresh
Face raised towards the power rays of the Sun
Sighing in the gentle breeze that reflects Soul.
No dust or dirt or polluted micro dots
That lie invisible to the naked eye,
Man-made fibres environmentally free.
What? The question: Where? The scene it might have been.
I see, I feel, but everything un-real,
A dapper pose of ripe repose all missing.
I link hands with Brethren from ev'ry Climb,
Language is a barrier we can't surmount
Yet faces; eyes; shoulders that droop in despair,
Show most of the picture of those who would care.
Bureaucratic 'clap-trap' drones on like a Bee:
Faceless ones, Powers of Industry, stand aloof.
Progress? Useless if we cannot stand and stare,
So wrapped up in a Medieval chain-mail.
Space, more space, where wind and sleet and torrents pour
The valued value of things from long ago.

Maureéne Matthews

An Ode To Sailor Jim

Whatever you love beside seas,
Stop and think Jimmy with an ease,
If you sail at storm and dark skies,
Sing it out, it will be more wise.

Sail with precision the storm away,
Plain sailing is at lucid day,
Mystic is; God chooses his saints,
Marco Polo never had faints.

Turn trembling fear into your glory,
Read with open heart good story,
And do your work and choose your mate,
From now on, go after your fate.

Always do enjoy your duty,
And be patient with the beauty,
And keep low your voice and tender,
Be resolute alike splendour.

Milan Trubarac

Change

The tree that faces winters rife, bare and
stark and stripped of life,
Had shed its leaves all on the ground like
falling snow without a sound,
Spring arrives, leaves born anew dripping in
the fallen dew,
Tiny shoots on tree of old, surviving seasons
oh so cold,
Pruned and nurtured throughout the year, summer
buds and blossoms appear,
Opening out with scent so sweet, petals falling
at my feet,
Autumn winds, leaves golden brown - a sorry
sight their falling down,
In two weeks time our tree we love holds
nothing but a lonely dove,
Seasons come and seasons go, scatter seeds
that later grow,
The cycle starts again for sure and
winter's back with us once more.

Linda Jane Garraway

Looking Towards The East

I am looking towards the East, to find some real peace.
My body has just ceased with the pollution of sin.
I need the Lord to rekindle my soul,
and set me free from this spiritual disease.
Oh how I need to find myself, before I derail in the
pitfalls of hell.
Oh hell please spare my soul, because my God, I
want heaven in me.
So let there be peace inside of me.
That's why I need to pray to the East.

Chris Michanicou

I Wonder What's on the Telly

I wonder what's on the telly tonight,
That film that I saw today was alright.
It seems pretty quiet now, next door's gone away,
They told me new people were coming today.
The nurse came this morning, she seems quite nice,
She made me some dinner, I think it was rice.
It could have been roast, no I'm sure it was rice,
Anyway, whatever it was, it was nice.
Don't feel so warm now, in fact I'm quite cold,
You notice these things more when you get old.
I'll turn up the fire and make some tea,
Yes get something warm inside of me.
Tomorrow I think, I might go for a walk,
Perhaps I'll meet Bert, we can stop for a talk.
I'm feeling quite tired now, think I'll retire,
Oh mustn't forget to turn out the fire.
These stairs seem to get longer each night,
Still once I'm in bed I'll be alright.
I wonder what's on the telly tomorrow.

P. Saxon

I Am Watching My Life Pass By

I AM...
Standing in there all alone,
Apart from the howls and cries of the crowd,
The stamping of angry beasts,
Not a comforting sound.

I AM WATCHING....
Men and women, pushing and shoving,
A pitiful attempt to get to the front,
Cold fear over takes me,
I am trapped, no way out,

I AM WATCHING MY...
Final stand, I feel a pain,
A slashing cut, again, again,
I turned to his angry face,
I'm going to die in this lonely place.

I AM WATCHING MY LIFE PASS BY.

Marc David Gales

Ode To Stuart Sutcliffe

Thunder exploding, applause through the night,
Standing and looking and beating just right.
The brush in the hand, the bass of the soul,
Meeting looks with that girl, bang! Stu's got a goal.
Shaded eyes from the stage, meet unknown faces,
Mersey blood mixed in shaded places.
The beat grows monotonous, taking a pill,
The storm rages on, but is worsening still.
The fabulous five fall by one, to fab four
With brush clenched in hand Sutcliffe falls to the floor,
The red on the canvas, the blood in his head
The thunder exploded, Stuart was dead.
Yet although the guitarist and painter is gone,
His beat, in the soul of the Beatles lives on.

Melanie Spence (age 15)

Visions In Clouds

High above white steeds of the skies
Stables unknown far beyond abides
Riderless rein, the hidden hand
Eager to race o'er distant land.

Wind in pursuit, unwilling relent
Onward ever onward, till passion spent
Iconic portraits appear in view
Castles, Angels, yet visions anew.

Dale, meadow, steeple and stream
Images above these, their mists seen
Journeys endless till their demise
Lost forever white steeds of the skies.

H. Taylor

An Innocent Man

A love horseman rode into town
Spurs on his boots leathers of brown
for many years he served his time
An innocent man he committed no crime
A murder on a hillside many years ago
The death of a woman he didn't know
He saw a man running from the scene
Tall and rugged, dirty and mean
A pretty young woman had lost her life
Battered and bruised, stabbed by a knife
Innocence was proven now he's a free man
He'll take his revenge the best way he can
He's here for justice to claim an old debt
A duel on a hillside tonight at sunset
Ten paces forward then turn and draw
He now has the man he's been searching for
Glory was his he could now leave town
He'd done what he came for, brought the
man down.

H. Finneran

The Legend

Singing in the rain
splashing in the puddles
Twirling his umbrella
blowing out some bubbles.

His silken voice while singing
the smile on his face
he sang the bells are ringing
and danced with style and grace

Gene Kelly was this legend's name
whose dancing was a treat
his charm and smile brought him fame
and so did his dancing feet.

He's gone away, up to the sky
to watch the angels prancing
This legend we bow and say goodbye
and hope he keeps on dancing.

He sung in rain, got soaking wet
danced a scene, we won't forget
He'll be remembered, as the fella
who danced the streets with as umbrella.

Mary Roberts

Life's Epitaph

If we had the will to understand
that heaven and hell is life's command
when we leave, through death's dark door
do we start again, as we did before?
Should we leave our life, with this our thought
to inherit what, we left before.

In God's great wisdom, we shall find
only what we left behind
all of life is nature's test
is life immortal with the rest?
If this theory does work out
life's great tragedies are in doubt.

If we all made this our cue
we'd all know now, just what to do
waste not a thought, of life's great fear
as life goes by, and death draws near
see to it now, then close your eyes
we could all return to paradise

P. Pepper

The Enemy

The scream arises unbidden from the core of my being,
Not gently arousing, but wrenching me tainted from my sleep.
The tentacles of pain wrap around my body,
Slithering and sliding inwards, to parts of me so deep.

The invasion continues relentless in its pursuit
Of becoming my new owner, my very essence to keep.
Each slight movement drains the fight from me
And leaves my body jagged, scarred, in a heap.

My strength is eaten from me by this monster called pain
Uninvited, the evil invades me, breaking me as it seeps.
Through the haze I ask myself, When? Where will this end?
In capitulation and lamentation the tears fall and I weep.

But like a candle in a wind, my spirit flutters with a will.
Now I will fight. An inner strength hesitantly, begins to creep.
Then quickly through nook and cranny the life flow surges,
Battling evil so devoted to harvest my body and reap.

I won't be undone; captured like a wounded animal and ensnared.
With each breath I must conquer, trust in myself arises with a leap.
This hideous pain I must bear, but with courage and strength.
Now I lower my head peacefully and await trustingly for sleep.

Diane E. Mahood

"Garden Life"

Our garden friends, are such a treat.
   Striking colours from head to feet.
Their calling sounds, "Hark" "tweet, tweet, tweet."
   Our robins found the garden seat
Blackbirds, thrushes, just a few this time
   A bird table with goodies they may find.
With lots of treats, even bacon rind.
   That's from the man inside, ain't he kind?
Our garden pond with water lashing.
   Sparrows abundant, always splashing,
Wait a moment, something came crashing
   Maybe a heron, with colours flashing
Hanging nut feeders, blue tits galore
   Down below, a squirrel we saw
Please don't break, or take no more
   Whilst he chewed them, from his claw
Our little piece of ground is free
   For all to wander around like me.
It's such a peaceful place to be.
   Now don't you wish, you lived with me.

T. Hall

Quarter To Nine

Not come too soon,
Nor missed with fear,
Autumn comes but once a year,
And with it comes,
A bright red glow,
That passes before the glistening snow.

Not the beginning,
Nor the end,
Not the middle,
But just autumn,
That passes by unnoticed, silent,
So much so forgotten.

Quarter to nine,
Not half past six,
This is the time to pick up sticks,
To heal old wounds,
Begin to pray,
Not worry about another day.

Amelia Weller

Lottery Dream

   Twenty two! - Ten! - Three!
Nope - it isn't me
Put the pen away, live to work another day
next week, perhaps, we might find
Those golden numbers or be back behind
The counter? The desk? The machine? The pram?
And carry on having bread and jam
We've got another week to plan and scheme
What would happen if we won that dream
Some to family, some to friends,
Some to charity
No more having to borrow and lend
We'll send some to the dog's home
The cat's home too
We'll even send some to Edinburgh Zoo!
Whoops - get down from the cloud
Getting carried away
Must go and collect my weekly pay.

Heather Cowan

No More

No more do I smell the new mown hay,
No more do I see the early morning dew.
No more do my feet tread carpets of green,
No butterflies flit among the flowers and trees.
No more can I walk down leafy lanes,
No more can I be among the few.
No more can I lay in solitude and dream,
No earthly creature can now be seen.
No more are any of these loving things,
No more - but only grey concrete, noise and fighting.

Dorothy Bartley-Berry

Eve Versus Lillith

Why wasn't Lillith treated like a queen?
Not made of man, but different, a separate entity.

Eve was a weakling under Adam's thumb.
Lillith wanted her way the only way it's done.

Lillith stood up for her right's, she did, when Evie said okay,
I'll be your servant, Adam.' And Lillith said 'No way.'

Lillith always had to argue when she knew he wasn't right,
But Adam's in-built arrogance hid the real truth from his sight.

Eve never questioned, she accepted what he said,
But Lillith she asked 'Why?' when the snake said what he said.

Lillith is forgotten by historians, you see
But Lillith is forgotten by historians, you see
But she lives on in all of us and fights for liberty.

Why wasn't Lillith treated like a queen?
She would bow to no man but demanded to be seen.

Jenny Rogers

Eve, The Plant Of Life

The Garden of Eden rose from its sleep of tranquil peace.
Night had slipped back to the heavens to give way to the
Innocent dawn
which is older than yesterday, younger than tomorrow.

Birds were singing to their little ones,
Butterflies opened their wings of softness silk
Peacocks roamed freely looking for their true love
To complete their existence of life.

Christ's soul was in the lily's heart waiting to be conceived.
Roses' essence captured the air.
Eve sat with long hair shining against the water of Eternity,
The colour of no importance.
Looking at the serpent curled neatly around the tree of Destiny.

'Taste the fruit of red lust. Be dazzled by the jewels of rubies
That beckon to your call' He said.

She thought, 'I need to have free-will, my own identity.'
The apple mingled with her blood like wine.
The serpent shed his skin. God cried.
And the sky rained tears of dismay.

Barbara Posner

Patchwork Puss

Brightest white and rusty orange, brown and black and grey,
My patchwork puss, alert by night, bathed in the sun by day,
Playful in her watchfulness - never missed a trick,
Soaking up those memories of days so full of bliss.

When in the eve the sun went down - so dignified was she,
Fast asleep upon my lap - so neatly curled up tight,
With tiny pink nose softly buried in paws of snowy white,
Caress her fur and remember her purr - a sound not from her youth,
Still nervous now as she was then - my little patchwork puss.

The most timid, most gentle feline, stretched out upon the drive,
In house and garden 'keeping guard' - green eyes still so alive,
And each new morning so pleased was she - she'd mew with such delight,
And be sure to regard each one of us and show no sign of fright.

Sleek and soft - eternally perfect,
She meant the world to me,
When on that day she slipped away, so calm - with dignity,

If times were ever sad, and she doubted my love at all,
Just remind her of dreams and perfect days when I was there to catch her fall,
For now it's me who is left alone with just her memory,
I can't forget, I won't forget the day I set her free.

Caroline E. Hughes

Untitled

Like a Butterfly emerging from its cocoon
my soul began unfolding.
The years of pain were ending
the darkness crept away.
The sounds of tears throughout the years
soon turned to tears of joy.
Why am I still weeping.
I'm weeping away my past.
My arms embrace the future
I feel I am home at last.

Anna King

"Copy Cat"

I had a conversation,
  Not long ago with Mum
I told her about my abusers,
  I named them one by one.
I told her of my torment,
  I told her of my shame.
She stopped me in my tracks right then,
  She said I was to blame.
Was that my Mother talking?
  I really felt so hurt.
Although I was only twelve
  she said I was a flirt.
Without even thinking,
  the words just blurted out
I've been told on good authority
  of which I have no doubt.

"Children only cop what they
  see others do"
So tell me my dear Mother
  where does that leave you.

Janice Leisk

The Journey

I slowly stroll over sandy shores
Not a person I see, I'm here all alone
The sea calls out to me, with waves crashing down
The only company I've got, is the wind whirling round
I stop and stare, out over the horizon
The aura of the ocean, constantly rising
The colours combine, and make an amazing sight
Telling me to continue, with my plight
I carry on down the beach, and come to a big rock
A solitary seabird, sits silently on top
Its beady stare, digs deep to my soul
Trying to digest, even things I don't know
The sea shrinks back, the sun slides down
Now I'm left standing, with nothing but sand
But my journey will continue on into the night
Hoping that one day, I will see the light.

Helen Jeacock

Inheritance

A little man...insignificant
No talent his...save that of love
With quiet steps he walked this earth
Not many knew his hidden worth

He did not boast of worldly things
Possessions few...no hidden wealth
And yet...he held with-in his hands
A way of life...so simply planned

Old friends around...some children, too
Enough to eat...something to do
To watch the things of nature grow
The birds and bees...the seeds we sow

I live my life...as once he did
A new awareness fills my mind
I only want to the things he had
A precious will he left...MY DAD.

Joan MacDonald

A Time To Be

Golden beaches, clear blue sea,
No-one here, but the birds and me,
Early morning, break of day,
Utter perfection in every way,
I dream my dreams or laze awhile,
I think nice thoughts to make me smile,
I take a stroll along the sand.
I feel the breeze caress my hands.
I hear a noise and turn around,
And see a dog towards me bound,
He's on his own, he wants to play,
Please be my friend, he seems to say,
We run into the surging tide,
Enjoying freedom, side by side.
Both tired out, we wade ashore,
Revelling in this day, so pure.
Time marches on the sun is high,
It's time for me to say goodbye.
Tomorrow I'll return once more,
For this is paradise - I'm sure.

Irene Hoare

Looking Back

As I wandered through the lane
My head was dreaming once again
I stayed awhile, and looked around
And suddenly, I saw the mound.

The flowers and plants still growing wild
The fresh perfume was just the same
I still remembered as a child
The daisy chains and simple things
Where toadstools grew and fairy rings

The stream has gone, the well is dry
It makes me feel I want to cry.
Time marches on, but I remember
How it was that last September
Fifty years have passed since then
We had such fun, when I was ten.

Joan O'Reilly

My Dreams

My dreams are full and free,
my dreams I hope will become a reality.
My dreams are to sing and to dance,
my dreams are to create a new art.
My dreams are to be in a kind community,
no dangerous heartaches, no needed apologies.
I want to live in a golden globe,
and have a beautiful home.
I want honesty and love,
and let it shine above.
My dreams are not just for me,
but to be shared amongst the
good people who are in need.
My dreams are full and free,
my dreams I hope will become a reality.

Amy Burnell

Companion

Sense of time, and boundaries hold
No thought of single keeping.
For kindred lives the faith of years
Is felt in honour sleeping.
In shifting times of doubt and fear
A thought is sacred treasure,
And tempting distance parts no soul,
With understanding measure.
consider past, and future joys,
To bring a thought together,
In union to a certain end,
A woven, binding tether.
Two minds in one, an instant breath
Of recognition waking,
For present lives, a friendship grows,
From thoughts, heartfelt in making.

Anthony S. Hyland

Suddenly There's You

You hide behind the corner and spring out to shout Boo...
Lurking out of sight you tumble from within and suddenly
    there's you.
Your life is separate; I wander thro' my own but all at once
    you're standing there.
To remind me we're still as one... you appear as from thin air:
(My son lives far away, in another place and time)
But often hurtling out to shout Boo and suddenly there's you.

Jackie Callow

Cry Not Child

No swing shall you sit upon, no horse shall you ride
No laughter for you, newborn child.
No gleeful laughter, no face of pride
No stories at bedtime, no bike shall you ride.
No restful slumber at night shall there be
No playhouse, no tears when you fall from a tree.

You are born in despair, your mother is there.
She will desperately love you, but do they really care?
When your belly is swollen, your eyes red and sore
Crying for hope and a chance to survive.
What will they give for a chance of a life,
Born only to famine, decay and distrust,
No food can you grow from lands barren with dust.
Weep not dear child, shed not your tear
Let your silence of suffering deafen their ears.

Anita Vesti-Nielsen

Colours And Code

Youth carries no experiences
No guilt, no worries, no thoughts,
Not because youth is uncaring
But they're all at the beginning,
Learning the colours and code of life.

Time within itself creates situations,
Which in turn creates moments,
Which blends along with patterns
And folds itself up into memories
Leaving us with pages of colours and code to retrace.

I remember the days of my youth,
As youth carries no colours and code to retrace,
And maybe, that's why youth understand so little
When others of past youth share their experiences,
To say - walk a mile in my shoes'

Now that I've learnt the colours and code,
It seems so strange to learn also,
That those colours has inner shades
The shades, that leave us in between,
A brighter shade of pale.

Augustus Beresford

Our Mum

Dearest one of childhood years,
No care could last beyond a day
For always were you there
To wipe away the tears.

The summer's day hath taken on a winter's chill,
The birds have hushed their song
The sun that gave us warmth alas! Has gone.

Dear Mother of our birth
Where, **oh** where have you gone?
Without your love we cannot carry on.

They say: 'it is with God you now belong'
Your pain and sickness far away
For in heaven you now will be.

We pray; You'll look upon and guide us
With your splendid love
As life we journey on.

Irene Isabell Brown

O My Beautiful Canada

O My beautiful Canada I'm coming home
No more to ramble no more to roam
It's been so long since I've been gone
O my beautiful Canada I'm coming home

I've missed your prairies your cities too
I've missed your forests your lakes so blue
I've missed the Rockies so high and wide
How I've missed my blue Canadian skies

O my beautiful Canada I'm coming home
No more to ramble no more to roam
It's been O so long since I've been gone
O my beautiful Canada I'm coming home

O my beautiful Canada I've missed you so
I've missed your sunshine I've missed your snow
I've missed your summers I've missed your rain
O God grant me I will see you again

O my beautiful Canada I'm coming home
God grant me speed across the foam
No more to ramble no more to roam
O my beautiful Canada I'm coming home
   Joe Ennis

Shadow Of Life

The shadows of life pass, over us all.
No life is better than no life at all.

Untried for our convictions,
On earth, sorrowful, bashed and bated.

I think about people and not myself,
Huh! Mad on this world
Yes! Correct
Jumped off the top shelf.

Shadows of hate, life and fear
elevated events the next year,
Trust not this life,
'cause it's just a shadow,
hate life and fear.

Earth wind and fire, that's life
as in nature.
Killing, plundering, maiming,
that's the shadow of life
God bless our world.
   John Francis Davidson

A Man's Game

If soccer's a game for which you rave,
Needless to say you'll become rich,
Then you'll learn of professional foul,
Elbow and face and knee-up tackle 'fun'.

Rugby's a game some folk crave.
Naturally you must learn of hitch.
Also ken eye gouge, stamping, growl,
Then, ear bite and clothes line done.

In the world of golf some are slave.
Offers fresh air and sandy ditch.
No physical height's needed to vowel.
And funds are essential, no pun.

Longing for outdoor expression brave
Some to athletics training, which
Orders each day, not too much howl,
Cash healthy, inoffensive, wait for gun.

In cricket I admit yearning grave
Exertion on very controlled pitch.
The game love by Kipling, to bowl
Yes, 'make a man of you, my son'.
   Gordon A. Wright

Phantom

Nameless you remain, my only child, a face I can only imagine,
my body a temple, a silken cocoon, your chosen home,
my nipples seeped milk, prepared for you to suckle,
I basked in a jacuzzi of fluffy exquisite emotion,
you made it possible for me, to feel like a natural woman,
like no man, could

I felt you breath, turn your position, a slight shudder,
did you hear my heart a-flutter, maybe you curled and hid,
you were life in me, or just a desperate bid,

Father time whisked you far away, years have passed, at last,
yet, your still with me today, not just in the past,
thank you, for letting me experience, true love,
maybe I'll meet you, if they'll have me above,
so father time, I'm depending on you

To cherish, teach and share with my child, even when their strife,
let them snuggle safely to sleep, as though in my womb,
let them laugh aloud and play, in their new life,
never to shed a mournfully tear, on my silly tomb,
dear Lord, I know that love is never truly free,
but why a phantom pregnancy?
   David Teakel

In The Shadow Of She

I lay beneath the canopy of night
My window is the eye whereby
A leaf, in dalliance before the wind of chance,
Brushes, like conscience, upon the pane contrite
Rain droplets, upon the seeds of sadness, sigh
What purpose tears, if not for mood to enhance.

Soon, drifts a cloud across a silvery sphere
One such, now moves upon the senses of my mind
Emotion now comes gently and replete,
To take the place of sleep, which hovers near
There is a feeling for her to whom I've been unkind
Sentiment was betrayed by words tempered in heat
Remorse: In the shadow of one so dear.

Now, a fragrance fills my reverie
The moisture from both sadness and regret
Then upon each cheek, leave traces to declare
No matter: There is no one here to see.
My pulse quickens: I feel her close; and yet —
Soon, there is that realm 'twixt waking and sleep
I drift onward into the shadow of she.
   Brian G. Tuckey

January's Over

So starts the year, dark, biding, dismal days,
No single song birds cheer,
In hard gleaned meagre warmth
Life's things lie slumbering here.

Freezing ice cold beauty forms hard in icicles,
To dam up all the guttering
And white perfection, petrified to smother,
Giving an impression, pure misconception,
That all is still beneath this cover.

But under this blanket's cluttering,
A glimmer Micawberistic,
Springtime's slender schemes, relentlessly striving optimistic
No loud intention spluttering.
Silently forging upwards, a new season's tender dreams.

Ah, but I have seen their dance, the love-sick, mad, March hares,
With lifetimes' new exuberance leaping, bounding, frolicking
Unaware, their ritual following, a-boxing and a-rollicking,
Filled with joy which sets my sad heart humming,
Spring is near and Summer's coming!
   Ann Luxford

Stolen Love

I'll burn a candle to you
My love of past years gone,
As we remember our heartfelt love
As only we would, together
Lost in love, high to the sky
Music and swirls of dancing.
To feel again your hand in mine
Your soft touch to my hair,
Your warm embrace showing how you care.
Sweet kisses caressing my face
My lips succumb to pleasure,
For here and now, this time is ours,
Tomorrow, lost forever.

Gloria Jackson

Peace

I sit all alone, motionless, still,
My mind is racing, against my own will,
I sit outside, on this hill, fresh air,
Watching thick smoke from that Chimney, over there,
But still it's quiet, almost tranquil,
The Jet powered Plane roars over my hill,
Looking across the valley all pasture green,
The new pipeline, disturbed, grey stream,
But still I sit here, amongst all the flowers,
Looking around myself of Chocolate and Crisp Wrappers,
Is this what we want,
Is this what we want to see,
It all seems so senseless, stupid to me,
It's time to look and see what we've done,
It's time to do something and stop this destruction,
We all want to sit on this green mound,
To relish the peace and quiet of which we are bound.

Christopher J. York

River Bank

There is a river running gently by, whispering softly you cannot catch me so don't try, it never stops and never yields flowing through Valleys and on pass fields.

The sun reflects a sudden light, a beautiful coloured king-fisher is in flight, he dives into the river to catch a fish then returns to the bank with a tasty dish.

Trees they cast shadows where the sun is peeping through, the flowers amongst the grass so green is a carpet just for you.

Movements and noises on the ground, little creatures are busy scurrying around.

The birds in the tree's are in full song, the sun is hot and the day is long.

Walk by a river on a summers day, everything's free so you don't have to pay.

Carole Pierce

Nine From Ten

"Write a poem", they invite - I'd like to have a go.
My mind is good, I have the words what more is there to know?
yet it's a mine field writing is, with grammar and all that
or me and mine of mine and I? My confidence? It's flat!
And then there are the tenses and the past participle
the commas and the colons, be they semi or just whole.
My talent, I believe, has fled, my writing's past its prime
but I remember long ago, a school girl at the time,
I had to write an essay with the title "Country Life"
so I took on the mantle of a buxom farmer's wife.
I described the work so hard and pleasures that were few
but managed to convey the peace of true contentment too.
Nine out of ten was my reward plus "please write on, you've flair"
but I left school and went to work - the words they stopped right there.
One half a century has passed and I regret, my friend,
I let her down, the caring one, who gave me nine from ten.

Doreen Oldbury

My Brother

We played away in the scorching sun
My brother and I strayed down to the burn
To the banks of the burn I got to close
Keeping my balance was uppermost

Down the banks of the burn I stumbled and fell
Straight into the dark muddy water from hell
My five short years passed before my eyes
Just murky darkness between my cries

Up and down in the burn I bobbed
My flailing arms reaching out for God
All of a sudden I was on dry land
My brother and I hand in hand

On this dry land my five years grew
A lucky escape if only I knew
Luck my have helped replied my mother
But the hand of God was the hand of your brother

Colin Henderson

"Ecstasy"

In this wide and wondrous world,
My body grew, my mind unfurled,
And yet my life is on the line,
To end my life before my time.

Ecstasy of life is taken,
My thoughts were great, if not mistaken,
Before I sank in abyss deep,
A tablet sent me off to sleep.

Life is hanging by a thread,
Lying here, so warm in bed,
My will to live will find a way,
To live again another day.

And when at last I do recover,
My life on earth to re-discover,
I promise I will never be,
A worry to myself or thee.

Brian F. G. Mortimer

The Allotment

The time is nigh on midnight and the lane is dark and bare, but I must go to the allotment to see what goes on there. I creep along so quietly, to the hedge beside the gate, for here I shall be out of sight while I sit and wait. Suddenly the clouds roll back and the moon peeps from the skies, now what I see at the allotment I cannot believe my eyes, for cabbage is dancing with cauliflower, turnip is waltzing with swede, and all the little Brussels sprouts are playing with the weeds, the carrots look like soldiers as they hold themselves so tall, standing in a long straight line backs against the wall.
Suddenly there is music and the band begins to play. It's potato and the spudlets I think I heard them say. Lettuce and tomato do the highland fling, while shy little turnip begins to start to sing, now here come the joggers feeling fit and keen, let me take another look, why it's the runner beans. Suddenly the cock crows and with it comes the dawn. Feeling rather sleepy now, I try to hide a yawn. Then at once I realise with the rising sun, the vegetables at the allotment are no longer having fun.

Barbara Josephine Blyth

Lottery Fever

Getting excited when Saturday comes
Mums sitting down doing her sums
Lottery fever in our house again
Let's choose the numbers between one and ten
You never know who will be lucky tonight
It could be you with fingers crossed tight
Mystic Meg looks into her ball
"It will be a bus driver who is very tall"
"That rules us out" mum does shout
"Your father can't drive and I'm too stout"
"Oh well, there's always next week"
"You're right you know I'm a lottery freak."

Diane Sperring

Stars

Stars they shine so clear and bright.
Like tiny jewels in the sky at night.
Twinkling in the dark above.
As I see a shooting star, I wish for peace
 and love.

Jayne Bardsley

Evening

Swallows are flying low,
Mosquitoes dance,
A late bumble bee drones past,
Seeking shelter, from this gloaming sky.

Children play upon swings and round-a-bouts,
Shadows dance, with the last rays of light,
All the lands aglow,
From the peach tinted sky, and through the trees, a lake,
Upon which a water lily gloats.
A fisher-person casts their line, spending but a few moments,
To catch the last fish, before supper-time!

The wind rises,
A passing badger snuffles the scent of evening roses,
Such exclusive is this fresh air,
Distant cries, of a mother's call, brings children from their
World of play,
To warmed beds, to sleep, then dream, of another day!

The ball of fire sinks into a grey mist,
Good night folks, and God bless!

Clive A. Baldwin

Plassey

I dream of Plassey
My memory, like wood smoke, wafting
towards the mill.
Carried on the river from
upstream, down. Where
wandered men, waist deep in water,
cast treacherous flies at fickle fish.

While an old fisherman, his legs
too unreliable to brave the stony falls,
tells a polite listener of record fish
caught, almost
of nights in Jack Welsh's and mornings too.
Smoky lies and pints of creamy porter

And long necked brothers of the
children of lir.
All power, white and grace,
float with effortless majesty.
Then erupt with a whosh-slap, step and fly
A yard from the water or soar
in the sky over Plassey.

Eddie Clancy

Eternal Love

Flowers a reef to symbol grief
Mixed emotion clutching devotion
Complacency gone with memories strong
Remembering the good as we should
Does honesty gain through surging pain?
With things to forget or even regret
Like words not spoken by hearts now broken
Or did we draw near relaxing fear
To the one we mourn, or did we scorn
True love in wealth of giving of self
With time to spend so at the end
We are content that our life was spent
Making them aware with our loving care
That our love was true all their life through
Not perfect but real, enough to seal
Love so sure until deaths door
Closes for either with one survivor
Holding the rest to survive the test
Of love so real to carry and heal
Love for living and never dying.

Charmian Cox

A Child View Of Dying

Dying is a cruel and unwanted subject.
It is black and gloomy.
It's dark, no light may shine.
It's slow and sad
Boring and unwanting.
Peace, calm, and tears.
Headaches and curtain shut,
Black and blue or white with grief.
WHY?

Gabrielle Louise Potter

Heat Wave

Hot sultry night,
Midges out of sight,
Waiting for sleep,
Curtains still keep
Heat in the room
Adding to gloom

Windows open,
Curtains flap,
Old dogs yap,
Tired eyes widen.

Hot sultry night,
Buzzing and bite,
Restless and cross,
In vain we toss,
Car alarm shrills,
Old magpie drills.

Sleep comes with dawn,
Frantic and worn,
Soon shrieks a train, up roars a plane.
What a bad plight! Hot sultry night.

Hilary Jackson

'Lovers Passion'

Soft, silent shadows eclipsed by the night,
Memories fading that once were so bright.
Innocent childhood they now have defaced,
Arms reaching out for a loving embrace.
Ripples of passion like stones in a stream,
Seeking the answer to love's endless dream.
Slowly, but surely, they settle their dues,
Love's sweetest seduction, so tender and true.
Confessing their love, a bond of the heart,
Nothing, nobody, can tear them apart.
The darkness is fading, as light shines through,
The silence is broken, they're one now, not two.
Passionate sighs, as arrows of pleasure
Strike deep in the senses, a moment to treasure.
Now silence takes over, movement is trapped,
Sleep hovers around, in his arms she is wrapped.
Dreams now surround them, how peaceful they lie,
Will the day ever come when their passion will die?

Charlene Jenkins

Growing Old

Look at the old, gnarled decaying oak,
Look at her now, would one ever think
A bright new leaf once fluttered on each bough?
Would one think the birds once sought shelter from the sun,
That in her rich foliage built their nests,
And from the old oak once begun?

Alas, look at her now, desolate with barely a leaf,
The agony of ageing is quite beyond belief.
The others seem to shun her, she stands just slightly apart,
They think because she's old she doesn't have a heart
But that's not true, and the woodland creatures
 can surely tell them so,
For when they need shelter from the storm,
 it's to the old, gnarled oak they go.

Jennifer Allen

Shadows

In the murky mist of a twilight torn by shadows
memories and thoughts my only companions;
the inky canopy of tree tops
echo the darkling chambers of my mind.
My feet, by habit, following the well known trail
as ribbons of vapour swirl slowly, and unwind.

Grey upon grey and ghostly tree bark,
solitude like balm to the wounded soul;
a slight breeze momentarily releasing dry leaves
to softly patter as the feet that are not there
and then revert to silence, waiting, watching,
a stillness to be broken if you dare.

And, as softly as it came, the mist is lifting
a muted glow depicts the way to go,
solid forms replace the faded images
and, in the distance, replacing quiet, - sound
and at my side, as I go forward
not one but *two* shadows on the ground.
   Brenda Heath

Glitter In The Gravy

September onwards is the start,
Making Christmas cards which must be smart.
Robins, butterflies and flowers,
How I spend the happy hours.
Photos of the balcony and sea
Is there really time for tea?
Each one must be different is what I say
This goes on day after day.
Meals must be quick,
And dust piles thick.
No time to spare for another thing.
Not to dance or even sing.
We all get slimmer by the day,
And food is missed, we hear them say
"When she eventually decides to cook
It doesn't deserve a second look.
For when it's dished up before our eyes
What is this? Do we spy...
I think it is, no, it can not be,
oh yes, it really is Glitter In The Gravy"
   Brenda Elvery (Folkestone)

My Valentine

I love the smile that lights your face
Love the warmth
Of your embrace - I love the
Voice that says "I care" - love
Each little joy we share I love
Your way of being sweet
Of making my life so complete
Understanding, as you do
    (I love you just because you're you.)
   Janet Carter

Reincarnation

When he came back, he came back as a cougar
Lithe and lissome, strong and agile.
Tawny blond with a dark anger
Flexing feet and indefinite smile
Soft sweet paws and terror claws
A face to adore. But when he swore
No folklore could save the victim's limbs he tore.

Once a cuddly cub, with golden curls
Now summer brown with amber swirls
Puma concolor, handsome and wise
Clever at climbing, swift in the trees.
Great muscular thighs and purring sighs
Dragging three times his body weight, was just a breeze
His eternal spirit, this mountain lion
Will never reside in the kingdom of Zion.
   Diana L. Poliak

Tears On An Empty River

Be with me until dawn, please don't leave me all alone
love me from the heart not the stone

Yesterday was just a dream, time a precious moment in
your eyes, alone your tears an empty river flowing back
to the sea, found yourself on the outside looking in
nobody loved you like I did.

We were lovers for a day saw our future melt away
into sunlight summer days being together was
all our care. The sands of time stood still.
For us our parting was a desert waiting to bloom
farewell my love until we meet again.
   Jim Adams

Love In Your Heart

Love is tender and cherish, as we will always be cared,
Love is kindness and thoughtful as we shared,
Love is filled with joy and pride,
Love is takes our hands together and walk side by side
Love you always feel the warmth no shiver or cold,
Love in our heart to have and to hold,
Love has reached your heart and here it lies.
Love is a beautiful feeling no one can describe
Love that gloom like a flower will grow,
Love is filled with happiness like streams that flow.
Love you always be loved, and to talk, laugh and play.
Love grows more and more day by day.
Love you always be treasured and happy memories too,
Love never says goodbye it will always be with you,
Love never grows old and or may we fear.
Love as we share our moments together year by year,
Love means so much for us to say I love you with all my heart today,
Love is forever and it will always be that way.
   Ann Shipley

"The Gift Of Love"

Love is for giving, love is for sharing,
Love is a beautiful, wonderful feeling.
Love is so tender, so warm and so caring,
Yet powerful and strong.
Love is enduring.
With love in our hearts we would be richer by far,
With love we could end all this hurt, pain and war.
With love we could spread much happiness,
With love we could overcome sorrow and sadness.
So let us try harder to give and to share,
Our Love for each other and show that we care.
Love is a feeling off deep tenderness,
Love is a gift we all each possess.
   Jean Ashworth

Widows

The widows' bungalows stand side by side,
neatly curtained and fair weather gardened.
Along with plants survived from Mother's Day
and random sowing spared by errant cats
roses that marked an anniversary
brought from the old place.

Linen lines
hold solitary washing to the wind.

Neighbours chat in village shops, and call
to one another over fencing wire
bright reassurances and weather talk,
but comes the dusk,
doors locked and curtains drawn,
the evening telly ends another day,
familiar photographs for company.

And night on night how many hands are stretched
from those single beds, in a half sleep,
to find and hold a hand no longer there?
   Joan A. Bidwell

The Mortal

Gone is the smile so bright
Lost is the joyful voice of happiness and love
Like the darkness of the night
The Quieting of the dove
That is not life eternal
It is the life of a mere mortal

The meek, mild and virile and strong
In this land of love, hate wrong
We live survive and die like fallen petals
As we are mere mortals

Gone are the cowards also the brave
Off this land they fought to save
This was the love of mere mortals.

George Little

"If Only"

The sun shines perceptibly redder, as it ebbs over the hills.
Losing the yellow hue it once bore.
Lovers narrow their eyes against its fading rays.
Their outlines silhouetted, starkly, against the crimson ball.
Yet another night creeps slowly in, heralding the end of
another lonely day.
Vanishing with it all the paroxysm of fear.
It's now eight o'clock and the door is locked.
Shut in solitude with my thoughts.
The mists of my mind casting its ghosts.
Spectres of what's been and of things still to pass.
Nightmares of yesterday's worries.
Of how to overcome the trials of the new day.
Then these visions turn to dreams.
The kind that begin, "If Only."
The biggest being "IF Only" I was with you.
"If Only", we were those lovers whose bodies the sun silhouettes.
My only comfort at these times is the thought it will soon be over.
Behind us, pushed to the far recesses of memory.
I long for this day with all my being.
Once again the sun to shine on my life instead of dying at the
day's close.

Gerard Steven James

Untitled

She sat at the window watching the street,
Listening for the sound of silent feet.
The pale sun shining on her withered frame,
Waiting for the caller who never came.
She has a friend she's never seen,
Chatted to neighbours who have never been.
Laughed with people she's never met,
While crying behind a curtain of net.
Looking with eyes that are now so dim,
At a world that's passed her by.

Bruce Townsend

Fear: Shadows In The Forest

As she travels further into the mist,
Looking around to catch a glimpse of her stalker.
Maybe it's not there and it's all in her head.
Either way, it fills her with dread.

Trees looming over, suffocating her happy thoughts.
Branches sway vigorously as if to warn her.
She carries on into the dark, dense wood,
She tries to imagine a happy place;
Oh if only she could.

The fear sets in as she begins to run.
Her heart beats fast, as she runs into the unknown.
The trees glare at her as she passes.
The shadows welcome her into their arms.
She is their victim now, there's no way out.
For soon she will be a shadow in the forest no doubt.

If only she had listened to the trees way back,
she would not be in our world so black.

Heidi L. Tinsley

Night Thoughts

Night time.
Long, dark hours.
In tunnels running from daylight's last to first.
Silence.

Not quite.
Voices echo like footsteps, moving closer.
In my mind, from my past.

Ever closer and ever louder.
Right and wrong and why and how and...
Sympathy and accusation.
Wishes and regrets.
Wishing for now, for the future, for the past...
I wish.

Regretting now, my past, that yet to come...
Sorry.

Apologies to shadows long past, that cannot hear...
That would not hear, and will not rest....
And leave me in silence
in these long, dark hours of
night time.

Garry Steven Jamieson

Come, Walk With Me

Trees, birds, and hedgerows,
little meadows, stiles to climb, and paths
to follow through,
a gentle hill, to amble up, and see the distant view.
A sunny day, in early May,
bluebells in the wood, sunshine filtering through the trees,
cast shadows on the ground
so beautiful this sea of blue amid the dappled green,
while twinkling little white star flowers
compliment the scene.
Cooing doves up in the trees,
chattering of the jay,
breaks the silence of the woods as I go on my way.
The beauty of this spring time walk
brings so much joy and pleasure,
a precious gift, from God to man,
with memories to treasure.

Elsie Lambourne

Children

Little heads that peep around the doorway
Little eyes that shine so very bright
Little hands that tug your hair and stroke your cheeks
Little arms that hold you oh! So tight
Little bodies that wriggle when they're tickled
Little legs so strong you can't believe
Little feet with toes that curl with pleasure
Little packages of mischief, wonder and adventure
Little bundles of love and childish wisdom
Little people with so much to learn, so much to teach.

Barbara Wallace

Sheer Bliss

Lend me your sweetness dear summer,
Let me borrow your lovely blue sky,
Minus the wind and the showers,
Let your sun shine for hours and hours,
Let me borrow your smile for awhile.

Let me swim in your seas of the morning,
Never let me get out of my depth,
The occasional cloud like an awning,
Gives me just that gentle wee warning,
Perhaps tomorrow could be a bit wet.

So open your arms balmy evening,
Drench me with warmth that will last,
A red sky as my crown,
As your sun's going down,
Makes my winter a thing of the past.

Joseph Simpson

Flow Gently Sweet River

Flow gently sweet river, flow gently along,
List! While I praise thee in verse and in song,
Your sons and your daughters have brought thee fame,
Surpassing all others in Catherine Cookson, by name.

Upon your broad water, majestic boats sail,
Both large and small, down the ship ways, without fail,
Tyneside's sons have produced the best, their skills can procure,
Employment for all of them, their futures ensured.

But times, they are changing, as change they will,
There is no demand now, for their toil and their skill,
The yards they are empty, the steel works are stilled,
Hungry bairns bellies are crying to be filled.

But we have always been, a resilient folk,
Hard times ahead, although it's no joke,
Will be met head on, and we will change our ways,
Until providence provides us with happier days.

But like a beacon, shining through the mist
The first lady of Jarrow, illuminates the stage,
With her love, and her talent, for we Geordie folk,
We shall be ever faithful, and never revoke.

Fred O. James

Love Is...

Being there in body and mind.
Like walking in front as well as behind.

> When you feel afraid.

Chasing away doubts as they come along.
Agreeing with you even if you are wrong.

> When you feel unsure.

Having time to listen each day.
Making sure that you hear what they say.

> Just having time.

It does not really need a rhyme to describe it.
Nor does it need writing down.

But this is the way that I know how to tell you.

> That love keeps the world going round.

Clarice Scott

Home For The Harvest

I had come home for the harvest
Like the Prodigal Son, I had returned
And no one knew of my passing.
Birth and Death were as one to me.
Intimacy was ever present and assured
On the bleak, Ulster hillside
Overlooking the glen

I was the last stranger in Ireland
And I was forced to hold my tongue
And listen to the endless questions
I could not, would not, answer.

In life I had become the sleeping tiger
In death I had avoided the pain.

Eric A. Caldwell

West Country Villages

West Country villages with quaint sounding names
like Norton St. Philip and Berwick St. James,
Hinton Blewett and Newton St. Loe,
Lulsgate Bottom - where else did I go?
Peasedown St. John and Bishop Sutton,
Guerney Slade, and a place called Clutton.
I loved all the names wherever I went
from Stow-on-the-Wold down to East Brent,
Which name appealed most?
that's very hard to tell,
perhaps Leigh upon Mendip
or Nempnett Thrubwell.

David Luton

My Life

It's like I'm on a journey,
Like I'm sitting on a train,
Looking out a window,
At sorrow, anger and pain,

People all around me,
Struggling every day,
Looking for something easy,
To take the hurt away,

They resort to drugs and fighting,
Evil works and crime,
As I watch and wait for Jesus,
And the going on of time.

He's coming again my Saviour,
Someday very soon,
He's coming to conquer evil,
And fight away the gloom,
He's going to win all hearts,
Of all men of all kinds,
He is King of Kings and the King of all times

Belinda J. Howells

Ode To Anorexia

Dieting is an Art.
Like everything else, I do it well.

Stand sobbing like a cool fool
in lace-up f***-me boots and
leather trousers against the insistent humming of
monotonous microwave
Frozen from the inside out with impotence.

Pounding punch-bag
seeing fictitious enemies' faces in its supple sag.
My own face.
Arch and limby on a stool in the corner of the next room
Hiding/waiting to be found
because the kitchen where I must go
swarms with sticky bodies.

They are potential witnesses to my Shame.

Deed done final break for freedom
Tinned fish old lettuce urgent crisp bread
stashed apologetically in plastic
and run, run into final test
Wall of fish and chips stench

Emily Spiers

Anaesthesia

I remember the year suffering stopped
like a slow ache in a limb taken care of by pills
and I knew then that though one was cured
one was also bereft of the pain
that was caused by a positive grief

Now one lives on vicarious feelings
other people's achievements, bereavements and joys
with time passing over all
half-forgotten, passionate things that one did,
when it mattered so much to be wanted,
forsaken, discovered or hurt.

Esther Gravett-Pollicino

Nighttime

The day ends when the sun goes down, the night comes back,
all the light disappears. Darkness looms all around not
to hear a twinkling sound.
Up above in the skies the stars sparkle brightly.
Scattered about here and there brightening up which before
was bare the dark night sky in all its light, a colourful and
peaceful sight until the morning comes back around the sun
shine to be found, now until tonight, some light to see before
the darkness returns to me. The Peaceful nighttime ends.
This gives its life something to be,
to show the darkness all to me,
also what's in life for the world to see.

Brian Day

Snow Showers

Snow showers falling once again
Lightning striking with no sign of rain,
Wind blowing with its icy breath
So cold- so frozen just like death
A few cars slithering around
On skating rink suppose to be ground
Looks like mist way up a head
Fog swirling causing dread
But no it's the snow showers filling the air
So fast- so thick as if no time to spare
All through the night falling quickly
Covering trees and bushes thickly
For magical scenes to be seen by all
When dawn awakes by birds' shrill call
Carpets of white snow laid far and wide.
Trees bedecked standing full of pride.
Glistening flakes sparkle like diamonds
Everywhere, even on lakes and ponds.
Mother nature has been dancing again
Waving a wand during her endless reign

Hilary Brattan

A Picture Of Nature The Changing Scenes Of Life

I look out of my windows each lovely day at the changing
    scenes of life
The peace and the quiet of nature away from our world of strife.
I see the sun as it rises, bringing warmth beneath its ray
And I hear wildlife around me as they start another day.
I watch these birds and small creatures, some come to me to be fed.
And I watch as the trees fill their branches with leaves as they
    come back from the dead.
I look at the flowers in my garden some grown from a tiny seed,
I see them blossom and flourish, so little in life they need.
A little rain from Heaven, the sun to warm the soil
Is all they ask from God above, they do not fret or toil.
I watch the bees and butterflies with all their colours bright,
As they flit around the garden or on the flowers alight.
I see the gentle raindrops and dew upon the grass,
The lovely cloud formations as across the sky they pass.
There is the silent river, flowing peacefully on its way,
Rippling over its stoney bed on its journey day by day.
I love to watch the snowflakes pure white as they can be,
Remembering our risen Lord and what He did for me.
Each day I thank the Lord above for these lovely things so rare,
And I thank Him for my seeing eyes that I these gifts might share.

Anne Prudence Sawyer

Mary

Petal soft woman
    My life beautify
And I shall love you till I die
    Fragrant as a flower
Whose nectar I ply
    Graceful and delicate as a pretty butterfly.

Honey sweet woman
    You know it's no lie
I shall love you till I die
    Soft as feather down
In the wind blown
    Warm and welcome as a sunny summer sky

Words cannot express
    As hard as I try
How I shall love you till I die

Should death take me early and deal its cruel blow
    My ghost shall follow where'er you go
When in the dead of night you hear a deep sigh
    'Tis my spirit impatient till your time is nigh

Ian Anderson

Your Step On The Stair

I wait each night for your step on the stair, I
lie there thinking that I have heard you,
and watch the bedroom door.
I wait for an age,
the truth dawns that it is only my
imagination, playing its tricks again,
and I weep,
weep because the world is a cold place,
without you,
I muse on happier times,
then, when I am lost in my thoughts,
there it is again,
your step on the stair.

John Anderson

Why?

Why did You come Lord Jesus, to this world so full of strife
Leaving the Realm of Glory, for a very different life.
You left the worship of the Angels, for the hate and curse of men,
And became the little baby, who was born in bethlehem.

Was it for the Wise men You came to test their skill
And knowledge of the Scriptures Your coming did fulfil
Did you come to teach us the way we ought to live
How to be compassionate, show mercy and forgive?

You brought comfort to the needy, You raised people from the grave,
You instilled an air of confidence that made the coward brave.
You even showed the Elements were under Your command
Revealing Your Authority as God, disguised as Man.

Were these the only reasons why You came so long ago
And put on Human frailty?...You wanted Men to know
That they could be forgiven for the sins that they had done
And thus be reconciled to God by faith in His dear Son.

Daphne Kelly

Alone

The loneliness of solitude
Leaves a saddened man no choice
He has to bear the brunt of silence
Or hear the sound of his own voice

The tension of your own mind
Tightens like a vice around the throat
And the ghosts of your imagination
Just laugh and continually gloat

As the walls begin to close in
And your heart just wants to cry
All consciousness is fading
You let your soul curl up and die

Will you let this force defeat you
Or fight it right to the bitter end
Because you are better off alive and lonely
Than dead and cold without a friend

Dean Franklin

A Change Of Use

Stark abbey, hidden midst the trees, rough track from highway
to it leads, Grey stone walls, an atmosphere to sense, its past;
a place of reverence. Conversion now to Nursing home, hides
not its sombre aspect
Yet enter and the once bare floors no longer are so abject.
Huge corridors branch off to cells, where learned monks
    found solace,
With furnishings for patients needs, but far from princely palace,
Heating, lighting, wardrobe, bed, lonely window chair,
to gaze out to a world now lost, the heart beats in despair.
Personal trinkets on display, flowers fresh from friends,
Nurses answer ring of bell, to inmates wants attends.
If long dead monk make ghostly haunt, Old Abbey do not fear,
Approval is most certain, we adapted their idea.

John W. Smith

A Mouse Called Fred

I am a mouse,
My name is Fred,
Please do not laugh,
It must be said.
For I am not your average mouse,
Seen tiptoeing round your house.

I am a mouse,
My name is Fred,
A mighty army I once led,
A fed my 'men' on cheese and bread,
They liked their 'general' it has to be said.

I fought our campaigns with ruthless precision,
My 'men' obeyed my every decision,
We swam across a sea of milk,
Fought our enemy then bedded on silk.

I am a mouse,
My name is Fred,
My 'army' once so many
Now, I live in solitude,
My 'army' there ain't any!

Barbara Helen Dance

That's Life

We struggle as were born not
knowing what to do, we fight
to be heard as we grow.
Fate can be cruel, it can really
bring us down, the solution isn't
always to be found. What is the
answer to be at peace within,
are there angels guarding over us.
Who really knows and who really
cares. But when there's faith
there's love. You read about the
misery there is about the world.
You wonder how folk suffer every day.
Some give up the ghost of living. The
pain's too hard to bear, at least there is
some music when at last they're there.
But when you see flowers blooming,
and hear birds sing merrily. You look
into a babe's sweet face, then things
are right you see.

Iris Smith

Who Am I?

Sometimes in the silence Your voice I hear, I cannot see You
  but I know You are near,
And as I listen and try to understand I ask "who am I?", in this world
  You planned.
I have shared Your joy along the Palmstrewed Road, "I have
  struggled and fallen as You carried Your load
I have stood and wept on Calvary's hill, but Your words have
  comforted "I am with you still"

What have I done to deserve such love, for me You left Your
  Father above
For me You lived and loved and died, for me You rose precious
  crucified!

Show me the way You would have me go, be it through joy or
  sorrow I cannot know
Show me the need in another's face, no matter the time, no
  matter the place
Let Your love to be there, let it flow through me, give me Your
  eyes that I might see;
Give me Your lips that I may tell of Your wondrous love that I
  know so well.

No need any more to ask who am I? You loved me so much
You were ready to die
So take me and use me Lord wherever You will
I rest in Your promise "I am with you still"

Brenda Tabor

The Mind Of Man

The mind of man has one intention,
"KILL THE GOD of intervention -
Make him bleed, accuse and blame,
Deity can bear the shame".

Ego first, corruption, lies
(Though empty heart and lifeless eyes
Besiege the deepest part inside)
Oh, man can run...But can he hide?

"TO HAVE, TO HATE, TO HURT, TO HOLD,
NEVER break the godless mould,
Point the finger, fight the pain"
And still the clouds of sorrow reign.

When the fear and nightmares breed
"PUSH OUT GOD - deny the need"
Yet in the darkest, weakest hour
to realize that human power
is not enough, "Admit `defeat'"
Find the wounded hands...head...feet...
The mind of man screwed tight with tension
Cries to God for intervention.

Emma L. McPhail

Parenthood

The joy you feel after giving birth.
Just feelings you can't explain,
you feel your life is secure and complete,
you forget about all that pain.

But as your child grows day by day
the reality of security soon fades away,
as they venture out into the world you
pray they won't go astray.

But in this world there's so much
wrong, you hold out your hand,
and hope your child will always hold on.

Joanna Marsh

Family Tree

Mum, when you left and you were gone
It was like the birds had lost their song,
Slowly life took a new direction
And settled on its own vocation.
The years rolled by with their ups and downs
But we always knew you were around.
Now we have the wind of change
Something that will never be the same,
So, darling Mum, we want to say
We'll love and miss you more each day
But always you will be to me
The roots beneath our beloved family tree.

Jeanette Clay

The Countryside

I look across the fields each morning
just as the sun starts its dawning
it begins to climb high up in the sky.
The birds wake up and start to fly
they look for food to keep them strong.
Then they all sing together, what a beautiful throng.
Some birds have young ones in the nest.
They fly all day, they do their best.
To keep them fed, to keep them warm.
Also to protect them from any harm.
I turn my head, look to the ground
there are lots of wild flowers all around.
Different colours some dark, some bright,
they turn their heads towards the sun's light.
For warmth and protection from a very cold night.
They know to survive they will have to fight.
I look at the water in a stream close by.
With its reflection of a clear blue sky.
I close my eyes, and listen to the sound.
Of the countryside, where only peace can be found.

John McKenzie

I Looked Up to the Sky Tonight

I looked up at the sky tonight, to see your star shining bright,
It's two years now since we dressed you in white,
It's two years since we said good night,
God only knows why they came for you,
Those beautiful little angels dressed in pink and blue,
By now you will be walking, you will certainly be talking,
We never got a chance to say goodbye,
But God must have had a reason why? He took you up to the sky,
It must have been to spread your love,
And fly with the angels up above,
To help them spread the meaning of love,
To know that you are looking on, gives us strength to carry on,
Josh please, for Nana, help keep me strong, to help your Mummy
Carry on, maybe you could ring a bell,
Just to let her know you're doing well,
You have your wings to spread your love,
God rest your wee soul, you're an angel of love,
Eileen Smith

Autumn Term 2995

The traffic jams are back in Ballards Lane;
It's quieter at Brent Cross, the voices pitched
At least an octave lower; while in the parks
The swings and roundabouts and "areas of children's play"
Are still and silent.

Now at Moss hall the new Year-Ones,
With brash new pencil-case and glowing ruler,
Give little thought to what's to come,
And just as summer's end from its beginning
Seemed so distant, eternity will pass before year two.

Not so for those Year-Ones
That now have reached their three score plus;
For them last year was yesterday
And tomorrow is as good as done.
They only ask to fill each passing minute,
Have time to savour it before it's gone.

But time accelerates,
And while they know they can't go back,
They wish it wasn't going quite so fast.
Jeffrey Segal

The Wedding Band

Sitting still twisting and twirling my wedding band.
It was given with such deep love and passion.
Worn with pride promising wonderful dreams.
Oh how it gleamed upon my hand.

Sitting still, ten years on, twisting and twirling my wedding band.
Now worn with time, just like the love given with it.
Sadness and confusion look deep into my face.
My little girl's words echo around my head and rest heavy
upon my heart.
Mummy, Mummy if Daddy's love was so very strong, why oh why
didn't it last for very long?
I embrace her and give no reply
I sit twisting and twirling my wedding hand wit tears upon my face.
Geraldine Dunleavy

Bird Of Peace

In a sceptre of light there hovers a bird,
Its song is the wind, its flight unheard.
Wings glide on light, it makes no sound
As it falls from the sky and touches the ground.

The white dove of peace gently lands amongst men
Who fight in their war, a war with no end.

Lay down all your weapons and look to the light,
As the white dove of freedom continues its flight,
Into the souls of so many young men
With hate in their hearts, and a thirst for revenge.

Its wings touch lips that now utter no sound
As lifeless young bodies fall and cover the ground.

Its song is the wind, its flight unheard
In a sceptre of light, glides a single white bird.
Colleen Harley

The Accident

There is a cloud over my concentration.
It's my health, my back pain.
It troubles me more than I can say.
People are concerned at first, but then quickly loose interest
as your recovery is not imminent.
There is a darkness over my future, an unhappiness exuding
from within.
Lack of performance is automatic, the natural result of things.
I feel worthless, undervalued.
My manager stopped asking my opinion long ago- after the
many conversations about -
How are you doing? When will you be better? - My brain isn't sick!
It's a downward spiral, the less he values me the less I value myself.
Why me? Why did I have to have an accident?
My failing physical health is failing my state of mind.
I'm usually so resilient, why not now?
Too many problematic issues in my life to deal with.
My body is tired - and so is my mind.
I want to give in - I want to give up.
But still something inside - says keep going.
But for how long?
Anne-Marie Price

The Importance Of Sadness

I've gathered my thoughts in the madness of time.
I've ran through the field of the life that is mine.
I've climbed every bow to the roofs of tall trees.
I've played in the dirt on my child like knees.

In life I have sailed like ship to the shore
Problems and heartaches my shoulders have bore,
As I looked through the windows of my troubled mind,
The cogs of my sadness began to grind.

Real peoples sadness is what sits in their chest
No love to hold, kiss or caress.
Alone and cold in the damp streets of time
No bows of trees through which they could climb.

Mine is the sadness of guilt and greed
Mine is the sadness that no man should need
Love, peace and passion, is the sadness to trust
This is the sadness which all men should lust.

Wake for the day to know you're alive
Through time, through tress, through dirt you must strive,
For sadness is something you need no less.
If every man is to know true happiness.
Hadrian Cooper

Wasted Education (I Have Not Learned)

I thought a taste would be enough; I did.
It seems I have not learned.
After just one taste I wanted more,
Dear Lord, I have yearned.

Your voice ran through me; I felt it
Coursing down my skin.
How I prayed that you'd let me
Bid you enter in.

Your hand touched softly; I was
Pulled towards you.
My body torn apart as
I felt me want to.

You are the primal source; and
When at last we kissed,
I nearly cried with longing
In all the years we'd missed.

You stepped back and left; I see
Still I have not learned.
For all that you have taught me,
I have not yet learned.
Alison Linklater Watson

Dusk On The Veld

As the land begins to breathe again,
Its daily suffocation at an end,
The clouds unsettled by the coming darkness
Start their movement across an inflamed sky,
Ever quick to escape the unseen danger.
On the horizon come dark shapes then,
Mirror image of the cloud forms,
A wall of movement pounding the earthliness,
Away from the glistening flank and gleaming eye
Belonging to the predatory hunter.

The parched earth cracked beneath the rushing herd,
Its barren surface crying out for rain,
Needs these few short hours of replenishment,
Before the sun resumes its daily battery.
Thanking God for the passing of the hordes,
And for the chance to live and breathe again,
In the distance, danger is receding,
The night has clothed this prey in anonymity.

Jane Horsey

True Love At Last

Dear husband mine you will never know,
just how much I love you so,
our life together it would seem,
so very happy, like a dream,
thank you dear for the love you give,
I'll do my best as long as we live,
together we'll tread softly
hand in hand,
the happiest couple in this land,
so many years you have given me,
at last my troubled life you set free.

Jean Mary Chappell

The Colour Of Purple

The colour of purple wild and strong
It must be a banner among the throng
Purple colour in a flag flying tall
A patriotic emblem loved by all

School colours, purple blazers, ties and caps,
Are clothing many of these college chaps
Chic purple dresses are worn by the girls
Pink and cream complexions beneath the curls

We see the colours in a rainbow nigh
A beautiful arch high across the sky
Black and purple clouds bringing rain and storm
Now we wait for the sun to come in warm

The colour of purple worn for sorrow
But hoping for a brighter tomorrow
such grand splendours in many a circle
Would represent the colour of purple.

Audrey J. Veltom

Night

I wait for dusk to descend,
It is my favourite time,
A calm and peaceful time
Of stillness, a coolness, a time to breathe
Peace, tranquillity, to let
My mind wander.
To relax the hassle of the day,
Let it all drift away.
A time to let fancy take to flight
From dusk to darkness.
Night, like a velvety cloak
Reaches out to caress me,
hugs and holds me in its realm.
I drift in space aloof from others,
The trees gently whisper all around,
And stars suspended, clear and bright,
Decorate the peaceful night.
And I defy the light of day
To come and take it all away.

Elizabeth Ann Condron

The Dream Machine

He wants a Harley Davidson
it's been his childhood dream
he hasn't got a reason, just
'What a truly great machine'!
He says he wouldn't use it,
just look at it with pride,
so what's the point of paying
for a bike he'll never ride?
He thinks I'm really stupid,
he'd be on it like a shot,
with his helmet, gloves and leathers
(yes, he'd have to have the lot).
He'd be off along the waterfront
with Brando and James Dean,
then round the racing circuit
with his old mate Barry Sheen.
His hair is flecked with silver
though still black in every dream,
and you'd think perhaps he's snoozing,
but he's on his dream machine.

Dee Johnson

My Love

Laughing and talking together we sit,
Just friendly and cosy discussing life's
Puzzle, and the pieces that don't seem to fit.
Then suddenly you gaze into my eyes, and
My head goes all funny as I try to disguise
This feeling inside me, which I do understand,
Your lips brush by cheek, you're holding my hand.

I want to say I love you, because
I know that I do, but the words,
They don't seem to fall into place.
Maybe it's because I'm frightened,
Frightened, that you'll disappear and
Leave without any trace!

I'm crying now I reach out,
Oh! My love - but I can't touch your face!

Joan D. Harvey

To Live

The air is thick with smoke and fire
It travels is upwards higher and higher,
The sky and sun can no longer be seen
How can these soldiers be so mean.

The snow is falling thick and fast
All around our country is overcast
So many people sobbing and crying
So many people pitifully dying.

Our country once so beautiful green
How could those soldiers be so mean
We have the right to live and thrive
We have the right, we want to survive.

Could someone, somewhere help us out
Don't just whisper lets hear you shout
Help us stop this hatred and awful killing
Please let us live if four God is willing.

Carol Ray

My School

That big place with iron gates,
is where I play football with my mates,
that big place with books and pens,
is where my work rarely gets ten out of ten,
that big place with the dreaded test sheets,
is where the canteen serves its mystery meats,
that big place with the register the teacher does call,
is where we have assemblies in the hall,
that big place where the teachers rule,
is where I go to school!!!

Belly

The River

I wish I was you, river
It would be fun to go to the sea.
I wish I could be you, swan,
Diving down to get bread.
I wish I could be you, duck,
Always going, "Quack! Quack! Quack!"

I wish rubbish from people's homes
Would go to the dumps.
I wish I was you, waterfall,
Falling down, going Splash! Splash!
I wish I was you, frog,
Always going, "Croak!" Leap!" Croak!" Leap!
I wish the river would flow through my garden
Every day and night.
I wish I was you, grebe,
Popping up here and there.
I wish I was you, kingfisher,
A flashing colour of blue and orange.
I wish I was you, dragonfly,
Flying above the river.

Benjamin Jewkes

September

September, the most beautiful month of the year,
It warms my heart the moment it's here.
All the beauty that I can see, on every leaf of every tree.
Autumn with its special glow.
The hazy sun, the earth below.

It makes me want to dance all day,
To laugh and blow my cares away,
Nature has worked all Summer long, to bring
this special month along, the flowers, the fruits
the beautiful colour, and human beings should
love one another.

Bathe in the gentleness that surrounds them,
be so grateful love has found them.

Perhaps it's the month that I will die,
and quietly wave my life, goodbye.

Janet Fulham

Untitled

By candlelight I seek the might of courage dwelt below, my voice
it speaks in hollow shrieks beside your rampant glow, I take your
hand with golden band and ask you to be mine, you laugh
away so hard and gay consumed by flowing wine, what could
I gain from a man so vain and no riches for to hold, I walk
alone chilled to the bone by this woman heart so cold, retreat
must I from a shattered lie completely blown aside, I know one
day I'll break away from the place I chose to hide.

James McCaig

"Women"

Never absent never late whenever we date
Knock at your door with gifts galore.
Passion, love, you to hold bringing jewels and gold
To mend our tiffs and riffs offer in galaxy of gifts,
Compassion, kindness, loving care, undying love I swear
With bouquets of flowers in sunshine and in showers.

Despite all, total rejection.

Always late, drunk and unable to stand I'm treated grand
Gamble house-keeping money as I call you my honey,
Always swearing, always shirking, never never working, as
With my mates really Pally, and with women enjoy to Dally
Forget all birthdays, special occasions, go alone on vacations
I'm cruel, callous, couldn't-care-less, yet you kiss and caress

Despite all, total and undying love.

Duncan Robson

Untitled

As I sit here in the park
It is a lovely spot
With roses for remembrance
And blue for get-me-knots.

There's pelegonians and geraniums
And dear little lady smock
And towering high above them
The giant holly hock.

Blue lubelia and white allison
Make a border neat
With one or two begonias
Put in for a treat.

There's clematus climbing up the wall
And blue delphiniums standing tall
But what is that, what can I smell
They've got the scented stock as well

There're flowers of every colour
And plants for you to see
So if you'd like to look and smell
Why don't you sit with me.

Joan M. Dover

Untitled

Crack, snort - call it what you will,
It gives some people their 'sweet' thrill,
You're on a high, and then a low,
Oh God, how far will you go?

What will you do? Where will it lead?
Does it really fill your needs?
Can you honestly tell me that
It doesn't bother you - that crack?

I pray at night that you will learn,
The value of the life you yearn,
I also hope that one day you,
Will have the strength to pull us through.

I know it's hard to leave it all,
And that your days will rise and fall,
but I know God will help us both,
If only we'd utter his loving oath.

Remember please that I am here,
A shoulder to lean on, an honest ear,
I'll give advice, the best I can,
I'll stand by you 'cause you're my man.

Annora Halferty

Golden Anniversary

Do you remember fifty years ago?
It doesn't seem so long.
You were young and beautiful
And I was young and strong,
I picked you for my sweetheart
I chose you for my wife.

I promised to love you dearly,
And I've loved you all my life,
Now your gold hair has turned to grey,
Your back is bending low
But I will always love you dear,
I'll always be your beau.
My eyesight is not too good now dear.
I guess yours is just the same,
It's not so good as on that day,
The day you took my name.
But as long as we can see each other,
I thank the Lord above
For giving us all those happy years
Those happy years of love.

James Archibald

Love's Gift

Love is a precious emotion,
It cannot cost much just to give.
A smile, or kind word to the lonely
A little, to help someone live.
In a world where hurt is increasing
Take time to show neighbourly care.
Remember God's love then and share it,
It means something just being there.
Who can know a hearts pain in the darkness?
We all need compassion today.
People immersed, far too busy
Can never find time, just to stay.
A moment taken out of a lifetime,
To reach out and take some ones hand.
For only a heart that's been broken,
Is a heart, that can understand.
So if you will stop for a moment
And pray, for an increase of love.
And spread it abroad in good measure,
Then you will find rewards, up above.
   Janet Parry

"Wishful Abduction From A Marriage"

Darkness;
It always begins in the night,
   As does everything;
A dark, secluded silence surrounds;
Even the bathroom is out of bounds.

There a whirring, a humming;
Here a flickering, shadowy wisp of life;
It moved, it groaned, it stirred;
Never mind, it was the wife.

Then, as is usual, I am returned;
Not conscious of sleeping,
   I feel absurd.

Darkness;
It always ends in the night,
   As does everything;
Am I free?
No, damn it, the wife is
   still a fright!
   David J. M. Samson

The Waves

A big hand pushes the waves.
It is the north wind's hand.
When he is sad the waves go gently on.
When he is happy the waves are swiftly moving
When he is angry the waves are rough.
The little north wind thinks it's a game.
So he blows the sea gently, till night,
but the little north wind is the breeze, for the summer.
So he gets pulled down it into the sea.
   Gina Wallace

Winter

I like the feel of winter
it sends chills up and down my spine,
the piercing winds and driving rain
that makes a walk a challenging strain,
testing our bodies not to complain
So refreshing to clear our minds
of all the cumbersome junk we find.
The cold creeps through
finding cracks we never knew,
but when a nip is in the air
and the sun shines down with a watery stare,
far off vistas unfold
and the countryside looks so barren and cold
I feel the intensity of LIFE.
   Jennifer Precious

Reflection

Thinking of you whenever I can
is what gets me through the day.
I miss you more than ever—
more than words can say.

Our lives have been separate for many years,
and through those times I've shed many tears.
These thoughts are very special—
as you can simply see
the reason they're so special
they're just for you - from me.

Please keep these words with you
as a reminder of the times we have shared
and remember—
it's the words of a loving heart
that really, really cared.
   Elizabeth J. Hunnaball

What's It All About

Are you like me so full of doubt why are we here what's it about
Is there a God or mastermind who plots the moves of all mankind
Or are we aimless and alone an accident or rolling stone
If there is a God on high why does He hide why is He shy
Some people say believe He's true we should have faith
without a clue
To some He never did exist they call these people atheist
Another group they hedge their bets
They're called agnostic clever gets
Both good and bad they try to please
I think that I am one of these
Our final group who think they're right
Believe in God they've seen the light
I hope the light they've seen is true
If they are wrong it's God help you
The atheist before you shout here's something to think about
Those of you who've seen the light will one day know if you are right
But the atheist as time will show if he is right he'll never know
   Doug Sharkey

Wishes For The World

'Twas the night before Christmas and all was still
Is that Santa's sleigh coming down the hill
The children in bed awaiting the dawn
They'll open their presents with the coming of morn

If only all cares the people could shed
If fighting could cease, the world have peace
No youngsters in doorways to sleep in the cold
No stories of violence newspapers unfold

God has given us all that we need
So much has been spoilt by hate and greed
Man makes his own hell on life's pathway
But God's light will always brighten his way

So shine on the light of the Bethlehem star
So carry on Santa keep travelling far
So sleep on you children in beds safe and warm
With faith in these things we can weather all storms
Good thoughts and love come shining through
Remember that God will always love you
   Chris Freeman

The Alotted Span

In years, the allotted span of men
Is said to be three score and ten;
But who scan count the pleasure
And who the kindness measure
That you have given in your life
To your sister and your wife;
And who knows the many others
Be they brothers - fathers - mothers?

Life is measured not in years
But by its joys - its hopes and fears
By service which to others rendered
In later days is oft remembered.
So may today and all your days
Be filled with happiness and praise
To God, the giver of all good
And whose wondrous name is Love.
Eunice Dance

Roses

A little baby newly born
Is like a rose, without a thorn.
Complexion, like petals of a lovely rose,
Tiny fingers, tiny toes.

From taking in the very first breath
Right up until the time of death
Prickly thorns begin to grow
The more of life they get to know.
Whatever made the miracle of birth
Created roses on this earth.

When bleak winter turns to spring,
And little birds begin to sing,
The rose bush comes to leaf and bud,
Having survived the cold winter flood.

In the warmth of summer air
Their perfect beauty with us they share.
A rose without a single thorn
Is the way we all are born.
If only we could then arrange
That living life this would not change.
Gillian S. Roberts

What Is Love

What is love oh what is love
is it gifts and birds like doves
I feel so lonely on my own
Listening to conversations like
a telephone.

Just standing there being used
like an old toothpaste tube
I can't help it where does it come from
if I had it, it has surely gone.
Emma Rock

Enigma

It's with you from the day you're born
  It has no shape, it has no form.
To every one it's theirs alone
  There is no other there is no clone
It never leaves you all through life
  And with you always, day and night.
How does it know, the time to go.
  And leave its earthly form below,
Will it look back upon the scene.
  And ponder to, what might have been.
Or will it fly on into space,
  Be lost forever, without trace
Or will it as its earthly form.
  Return to dust, to be reborn.
But as like time, that comes and goes.
  from where and to, well, no one knows.
Claude (John) O'Donnell Ryan

What Makes You Tick Quentin James?

What is that makes you happy, wappy, happy?
Is it the trees that blow in the wind,
Or the cars that pollute the sky,
Or the people with their brainless jobs,
That keeps you going, keeps you going.

Is it the rush of trains up to Waterloo,
Or the kids coming home from the polluted school,
What is it that makes you happy, wappy, happy?
What is it that makes or fakes,
The true belief of what is is.

How do I know, when I know what I want,
How do I know what's going on,
When will I find the answer and know it,
Am I fool in a land filled with plenty,
Am I a fool to be one of the many.

What is it that makes you happy, wappy, happy?
Can I see the truth of my life,
When will I find the truth, will it hurt,
When will I feel I am there in myself,
What makes you tick Quentin James?
James Howard

Life's Worth

An entry in the lottery
Is it a mockery?
Or a lack of the jackpot on the pools,
Can make you lose your cool,
For most of us learning in life's school

After all, those with more than they need,
Not needing to fight to succeed,
Swim in the pool of plenty
But lack in life's needs,
Love, security, sense of identity.

So, if struggling to make ends meet,
Means getting weary on your feet,
Think - is the grass really greener,
Or is it better?
To stay as you are,
Though you think you may need,
Is it a necessity?
Or is it just greed?
Ian Bromidge

In Defence of Pride

The man who standeth broad and proud, with wisdom in his eye
Is he who holdeth in his grasp the ocean, earth and sky
To conquer science, art and law, and feebleness and fear
Should be to what all men aspire, what manhood does inhere

The man who lives with only words shall wield intelligence
But when confronts him angry foe, words yield him no defence
In match of wit no match has he, in letters none compete
But in life's bloody match of strength, his surely is defeat.

What of he of slighter heart who seeks in life no harm?
His lot shall be a fireside, no stimulus, just calm
Until the day when at his home does malice come to call
Afraid and unprepared and without hope shall he fall

The man who seeks to torture men, by force to take their toil
And spends his life in readiness with bludgeon, scorning foil
For him comes life of misery, for he is truly poor
For strength shall overcome him, or shall sanction of the law

But he with body strong and proud, who feels his knowledge grow
Shall be prepared in mind and soul that all who see him know
The vigour, vim and effort that did make him once perspire.
So mock not the man who standeth proud, for in his heart is fire.
Andrew J. Wilshaw

Insincerity

I have somewhere a certain
Insincerity inside
The futile fault which does affect
A falsely fashioned pride.

The folly of the fool
Is fully foolishness uncouth.
It devalues the delight of love
And at last traduces truth.

Such ill-fated nature
Those innocents to destroy;
The poor fool's fortune it ever is
Top weep without woe, to jest without joy.
Greg Coyle

A Nurse's Prophesy

"The invention of the pill.
Is a disaster" said old Nurse Hill.
"One thing for sure
With this contraception
It's the end of adoption.
Women will think they are free
But you wait and see!
It's the beginning of corruption
That will cause an eruption
Where mankind by and large
Might well suffer the wrath of the Lord.
New diseases will emerge.
And cross infection will be a scourge.
Cancer will take its toll
In young women, as opposed to the old.
Rape and fornication will be rife
Dejecting forever many an innocent life
By the end of the century
Remember my prophesy
And ye will stop laughing at me"!
Bernadette Kennedy

Life And Death

Lingering around inside a womb
Into the world we will arrive soon,
For the first few years we will not know
Exactly how it feels to grow,
All so strange in surroundings new
Never quite knowing what to say and do,
Decisions one day will have to be made
Destiny foundations will have to be laid,
Enduring all life's high and lows
Awaiting the path that has been chose,
Till we reach the end of life's biblical cord
Heaven receives us and we are back with our Lord.
Brian Edwards

Ye Of Yonder

Come ye, O' my darling
Into my waiting, but yet....
Still loving arms.
Time, yes, oh great time
Spans the waiting years
Yet elapsed but not eluded us
Reminiscent - oh memory!
Precious - the lingering and shared moments -
Flooding the mind.
Streaming and flowing are tears,
Down the cheeks.

O' ye my darling,
Still yonder - so a far
But sweet, yes oh sweet, and great ....
Desires, ecstasy and pains are moment -
Yet to be explored.
Gentle bodies soothing touches -
Passion, curves and strength, all blending
In the divine's gift - love.
Chandanee Jagmohan

Broken Friendship

Within us all there is a crystal ball
Into which we gaze with sparkling eyes
Of expectation, perhaps to sadly realise
There may not be a future there at all.

When a friendship buried in the ashes of the past,
Like a Phoenix resurrects itself at last,
It sharpens memories, dulled by time's relentless course
Which slash our consciences and stab us with remorse.

The Paradise of meeting you again,
Tumbled to Purgatory at your unresponsive face,
Then down to Hades at your calculated cool disdain,
Am I a leper to be banished in disgrace?

Though I try to make amends and compensate,
It seems nothing that I do will expiate
The loss of four decades or more,
So there will never be a welcome at your door.

Life's breezes have blown away the years,
Our wounds still wince with the salt of bitter tears
And having seen your cascading chestnut tresses turned to grey,
I know time does NOT heal, no matter what they say.
John Martin

"The Old Shepherds Hut"

I packed a bag and walked that day
Into a wood not far away,
And there amid the bluebell haze
Chose to spend my holidays,
My sunshade was the big oak tree
Where I sat for hours just lazily,
My fire was the twigs I found
Tinder dry about the ground,
My dinner was a rabbit stew
With carrots onions and dumplings too,
No crowded beaches where seagulls cry
Or busy streets where cars rush by,
But just the quietest spot I know
Where the scented Summer breezes blow,
Where the moonbeams along the woodland trail
Dance to the song of the nightingale,
Not my choice hotels by the sea
But that old shepherds hut by the sycamore tree
Geoff Clacy

The Leopard's Spots

Brown spots hidden so well
in the bushes down a well
the spots of the leopard are so swell.

They are not black they
are not brown they are kind
of in the middle so don't feel down.

The camouflaged spots hide so well
lurking in the grassland you can't tell
now beware and don't dwell
the leopards around and
he's not very well.
Chris Dick

Shattered

To try and explain my heart ache
is something I cannot do
For a true friend I thought I had
On the day when I met you

You won me over with your sweet way
And promised me love was here to stay
The tears in my heart are but a pool
The day I learnt you took me for a fool

To stay with You dear Lord I must
For You dear Lord can I only trust
Peace in my heart will be mine when I lay
Over the green hill far away.
Hazel Rowe

Feelings

So many feelings you just can't express,
Inside you're such a mess.
Loving, needing, wanting more,
Inside of you your heart is sore.

Why can't we be glad, instead we feel so sad.
When it's very late at night,
You can be overcome with fear and fright,
But morning comes, and with it another day,
You'll feel better, yes, you never know, you may.

Missing people you once loved and adored,
No once about it, you love them even more,
Without their love we feel so poor.
Spirits are there, this I'm sure.

The thought of this is what keeps me sane.
I know they won't come back again,
But wishing they could help in some other vein.

I wish I didn't feel so strong.
No, to have no love inside is wrong.
This wanting, needing, yearning, just has to be.
I can't be anyone else but me.

Elaine Murphy

Vauxhall Inn

I've been this pub's landlady for 26 years
In that time there's been laughter and tears
We moved in the pub without too much fuss
April '69 seemed a good time for us

We scrubbed, polished to get the pub clean
The local soon realized we were both keen
We built up the trade and did very well
Had really good holidays and life seemed swell

Life went sour in '87
My husband died, oh where was heaven?
The pub trade now was on the decline
What shall I do?, I must decide.

I decided to stay, on advice from all
Family, friends were always on call
For all the hours you work in this trade
It is only worthwhile for the friends you have made.

I'm glad I stayed, this has been my life
I'm engaged to Calvin, I will soon be his wife
With pressures from Bosses it is now hard to stay
Perhaps it is now time to call it a day

Diane C. Turberfield

Not To Be Born Today

I'm glad I'm not born today
In a world that is selfish and mean.
I'm glad I've no future in this cruel world,
Where hatred and crime seem to pay.

I'm glad I won't have any part
In a world torn by man's lust for power.
Where greed reigns supreme, and peace just a dream,
And the gun and the knife is forever.

I'm glad I won't have to weep
When violence leaps from the page -
Of a daily news - headlines abuse -
Child victim of torture and rape.

I'm glad I won't have to ask why
When an overdosed body is found.
Was it Speed - Ecstasy - done deliberately,
Did everyone turn a blind eye?

I'm glad I'm not born today
I'd long for the peace that I knew.
The love and trust that used to be, people united in harmony.
I'm glad I was born Yesterday.

Ivy Atherton

Finding Hatred Or Comfort?

Hark at the moon!
In two different worlds
Firstly the chilly, eerie scene
A biting frost, the painful surge o'er mystery and evil.
Werewolf images, not really keen
Rapid cloud clothing reality -
A death, related shrill
Summoning and calling, thus beckoning its next victim
But it's warm, welcoming to some
Its beauty showered amid the stars
Of Southern Cross and deepest woe.
Can this alive, romantic scene,
be called subdued?
It's fantasy, answers, longer they grow
Truthfully it's all the same
Can the fright vanish from mood
And build acceptance for what I now know?

Deborah Johnston

Ode To My Daughter

The blossom that blooms
In this the garden of my life
How softly you sleep.
Your face like a precious pearl
Encompassed in the shell of my arms.

And as the night like ivy creeps
Softly shadowing the day's memories
Your joy still lingers.
Blocks lay scattered, and big ted rests
While you dream your kaleidoscope of pleasure.

So as I lay you down to sleep
And caress your tiny brow
I wonder,
Are you flying through the clouds?
Or dancing among the stars?

Jennifer Ralston

The Memories That I Hold

No one can steal away the memories that I hold,
In the labyrinths of my mind, engraved into my soul.
Always embedded, deep within, never cast aside,
Strolling through my thoughts, my feelings I can't hide.
Every moment, spent with you, is a moment spent in bliss,
Do you remember, the first time, you sealed it with a kiss?
I was shaking like a leaf, my body and yours were one,
You were the one that took control, to you I did succumb.
A kiss that seemed to last all summer,
then set with the autumn fall.
What went wrong, I messed it up,
the winter took it all.
Now you're gone, I'm on my own, my life was once complete.
But the memories in my mind, I kept, no one can delete.
So now I send a message to you, take note and listen well,
Thank you for the precious times, and in your life,
I wish you well...

Damian Potter

Restless Spirit

She comes back to me through the mists of time
in fond remembrance how I loved her
she held out her arms to me and called to me
to come with her to her eternal sleeping plain
where no time passes
where names have no meaning
where once you stop
there is no moving forward nor backward
how fresh the pain of her loss
etched upon the very flesh of my heart
yet she comes back to me.

How the tears flow over rose red cheeks
amid the sadness of her soft blue eyes
my memories of her are but unwritten events
yet engraved upon my very life.

Gina Charles

A Jigsaw Made In Heaven

The 13th May, 1994, the day my heart was broken
In so many tiny pieces, when sorrowful words were spoken
One piece each for those I love, before me to depart
A jigsaw made in heaven, to rebuild my heart
Please do not forget me, or how you called my name
Catherine and of course man, it will always be the same
The brightest stars in heaven, to light up all the sky
Are my Dad and my two children, and I still wonder why
Piece by piece my heart will mend, until it is complete
Until the day my life must end, the day that we all meet.

Catherine Lambton

The Thoughts Of Saddam Hussein 1996

I think I'll go into Kuwait once more,
   I'll raise hell and it will make the Yanks sore.
If I am successful I will go on;
   Arabia will fall to this Megadon!

We have chemical weapons, fire and will,
   Let's have a bit of rape, pillage and kill.
The Western World is spiritually dead,
   If Allah wills we'll take over instead.

Mind you I've heard their policies changed,
   They've started to speak as though they're deranged!
They reckon a nuclear bomb on Baghdad
   Will stop the deeds of this fellow-me-lad.

I can't see it happening; they've too much to lose;
   And yet, I know, they could if they choose!
My people all dead, and what's worse me too;
   Oh Allah please guide me to see it through.

I don't think I'll risk it; I might retire;
   I'd just hate to see my life expire.
I'll get rid of the weapons, blow up the mines,
   Just relax and play with my concubines!

Dennis G. Stephens

Autistic Child

Mind's eye staring, unseen, unseeing, tethered.
In body free, but imprisoned spirit pinioned, unreceptive.
Puzzling those who seek to see, but see not,
nor understand his need for order, ritual,
to make sense of his isolating lot.

Obsession masks pulsating panic, stems the flow of fear.
Awareness - none of danger lurking near.
Striving to comprehend life's verbal maelstrom.
Who dares to change routine, he muses,
in one stride crystal clear, the next confuses.

Behind the mask, in solitary, life sentenced,
aloof but pleading for parole,
Vain scanning the muddied waters of his mind,
to loose the fetters on his shackled soul
and render him whole.

Harry Mulford

Angle Tarn

Cowled, like priests, in anoraks;
In awe of sky stricken wild
With the breath of gods
While beneath the deluge of all
Heaven's tears, the scenery slurs
Hopelessly across a landscape
Smudged in water-colours as the
Palette of the storm is overturned.
The weather mixing violence
In the cauldron of the tarn;
Water writhing in a myriad of
Tiny agonies to baptize the wrath
That sends us stumbling drunk with
Pain - hiding our faces from the wind,
As if guilty of some blasphemy.

Derek J. Pluck

Painful Contemplation

He came in a dream, or a thought, or a sigh,
In a moment of silence flowing through my mind's eye.
His name wasn't mentioned, or it was, I don't know
Just a feeling of warmth and a bright golden glow.

He reached out his hand and my eyes gazed upon
Lands barren and scorched, ruled by fear and the gun.
Men dead in the streets, women too shocked to cry
While toddlers hid, shaking, as the bullets flew by.
My mind was in turmoil and I felt so ashamed
As screams pierced my soul from the tortured and maimed.
I begged and I pleaded, "Take me back if you can"
My thoughts turned to Britain, but it started again.
A boy of thirteen sleeping rough and abused,
A girl in her teens who'd been beaten and used,
"Oh help me" I screamed, "I can't take anymore"
"Do we live in a world were we hurt people so?"
That look in his eyes full of sorrow and pain
Seemed to burn through my heart, I bowed down in shame.

Elaine Farnworth

A Cafe In Newcastle, Near A Bus Station

Sunbeams through lace, shines.
In a cafe in town,
as people come to sit, to eat,
and talk of things they do today, and look
through windows, at the sky
so blue and neat.

A funny day, first snow,
then sun, will it snow again,
I'll have a pie and cup of tea.
Did you see the telly,
I liked it very much that show.
I'll sit here if I can and
watch for my bus, through this window pane.

"My husband's on three days, is yours,
no, thank God, he's still on five,
mines on the dole, said one, and we've just had
our electric bill.
All this as sunbeams shine through lace
that hangs down a cafe window sill.

John Robert Hauser

My Life Is So Sad

My life is so sad it didn't start off all bad, where did I go wrong
In childhood days to church I did pray in God I put my trust
At sixteen I had wings on my feet dreams of a love I'd meet
Married so young love so strong life was worth living three
wonderful children I'd been given my life went on something
went wrong. I'm so sad does it mean I've been bad God
brought us together.

Then he took him from me it was cancer you see each day I
did pray to God to save him please don't take him from me for
life was worth living for the love we would give him we fought
this battle together till one night it just happened, God he
forsook me you see. Oh God most high I look to the sky You
can be with Your Son, You took my husband from me and our
children three, can't You see what You've done to me.

My world all in tatters if only I knew what was the matter,
where had I gone wrong my life is so sad was I really that bad,
I'm looking for my love just like a dove giving peace to all
mankind, my faith has grown weak. Oh God give me rest can't
You see I did my best. You can't give him back to me please
have a heart for me if this is the game I must play

Guide me I pray to the man I once new, so patient kind and true
A dear friend for life and I, a dear wife
Please don't leave so sad forgive me if I've been bad whatever
went wrong let me be strong to live and love once again.

Jane Dewey

My Choice

If I should die - don't cry for me
I'm where I want to be - free - from pain
Don't bring me back
I can't be again what I once was -
Whole - and well
Don't shout my name and tell
Me I must stay
When all I want is to drift away
Into this quiet and peaceful sleep
Yet you
Tell me what I must do
Fight for life -
And through my pain and strife
I hear your voice
And my choice
Is gone
Come back you plead
I love you -
And so I do
Because I love you too.

Brenda Raynes

The Big Win

I feel lucky, oh so much
I'm sure I've got the Midas touch
An estimated forty million, for the winner tomorrow
It's a cert, I'll never have to borrow.

Instead it will be spend, spend, spend
With loads of treats for family and friends.
The fall of six ping pong balls... all so round
Will be my numbers, and the forty million pounds.

A millionairess of the lucky lot
Congratulations with champagne from Camelot
The road to riches, makes me feel flash.
I'll need a good advisor, to sort out my cash.

One pound stake paid, and go with the flow
The time has come, for the weekly draw
Six numbers pulled, they look fine
Only thing is..... they don't match mine.

Joanne Crownshaw

A Moment In Thought

I stood by my window,
I'm not quite sure of my
Thoughts, feelings of sadness,
Took over my heart.

My thoughts were on you dear friend
you've lost your lover your friend.
Your troubled heart knows he's at peace.
I hear your cry, why, why, why?

I cry aloud, I pour out my heart
to the world. My heart is troubled
because of you. I am gentle and humble
in heart. I pray your pain goes away.

Your heart weak with sorrow, your
eyes see no tomorrow.
With a smile and thought I know in
my heart you will smile tomorrow.

Brenda Cameron

The Ocean

On summer days when the sun is high
I'm dressed in blue and diamonds fly
As I dance and sparkle, look so gay
But I change my mood on a winter's day
Then my dress in gloomy grey
As I toss and turn like a restless night
Spitting and foaming, heaving with might
Sobbing and screaming, compassion for none
Who venture near till my wrath is done.

Dorothy Parfitt

Keep It Burning For Rab

Flickering candle in the gloom
Illuminates a darkened room.
A dip of ink, the scratch of quill,
Penning words that haunt us still,
Igniting fires within man's breast
To fight for those who were oppressed.
Even those who could not read
Railed against a tyrant's creed!

Like Robert Burns, with scathing ire
Would I, the common man inspire.
Respect and honour ground to dust,
Replaced by envy, greed and lust.
Senseless wars and deprivation
Wrecking each and every nation,
Hatred, finding fertile soil
Where nothing else will grow at all!

Those melting orbs, beset by flies,
Stomachs swollen thrice their size.
Such pain and suffering of mankind
Our eyes can see. But we are blind!

Christine Grady

Mummy

Close your eyes Darling, and rest your weary head,
I'll sing you a lullaby, as you lay in your bed,
The words say "I Love You," as I hold you tight,
That tender kiss, your eyes so bright,
The thought of you leaving, I feel I could cry,
As long as there are memories, I will never say goodbye,
So sleep well my darling, as dusk turns to night,
I'm here close beside you, until God turns out the light.

Elizabeth Spencer Smith

'Atomic War'

The feathers of the birds,
lay thick and tarred,
the ruins of our castles,
lay burnt and charred,
the green, green grasses,
lay dead like weeds,
the great pine trees
all fallen down,
the atomic bomb,
has done all this,
how I wished that it had missed,
bodies now litter the countryside,
The tears I've cried,
I will not hide,
I breathe in once more,
for my final breath,
again the thick air enters my chest.
I lay myself down preparing for death,
because I my friend,
am the only one left...

Diane Louise Fryers

Akin

It was his bag.
Inside was his life; Hippocrates' life.
The profession had been passed on but
the instruments were no longer played.

I opened it.
Inside lay the necks of two black swans. Dead.
Life did not throb through their bodies;
their diseased heart and lungs had failed.

The silver shone.
An upside down cup and saucer. Metal.
It touched me as it had touched many when
pressed cold against their ailing bodies.

I remember:
'Daddy, daddy tell me if I'm breathing.'
The swans echo with my own heart beat;
we are connected to each other.

Elizabeth Smith

The Gift

If I were not me, would you be you.
If you were not here, what would I do.
You're a person to talk to, in the darkest hour.
A person of love. A person of power.
You're someone to care for, and hold real tight.
Someone who'll love, and treat me right.
Sent to earth, for me to love,
A gift from God, from the heavens above.
The love I have, will never say goodbye.
It'll live with me, until I die.
So no matter what, you do or say.
No matter if, you go or stay.
Remember this my darling do,
Throughout my life,
I'll always love you.
Donna Maria Christie

"If Only"

If only I could span the ocean that lies between our love
If only you could say "You Love Me" like I think you should.
If only lips could meet, I'd shout to Heaven above
If only God would send the answer by his pure and peaceful dove
If only you could come to me and be my very own
and share our love forever just with me alone
If only God would see the sadness of my heart
He would never, ever have come between us, and we would never part.
If only! These two small words that have condemned me
in my cell and sent my Holy Spirit to rot in Satan's Hell.
If only you could or would come to me I'd worship at your feet
And life for me, and I hope for you, would forever be complete.
Arthur Eric Holmes

The Cardboarders

The streets are paved in gold, they say.
If only I could pick a little every day,
I would give away my cardboard sheet.
  To the first guy I'd meet.

The streets that are paved with gold
Are leaving the cardboarders very cold.
The tramp all day- longing for warmth,
But meeting only coldness and wrath.

They streets that are paved with gold
Are deserted now, left only for the bold.
The cardboard camaraderie lives on,
  Waiting, hoping for a home.
Dante Bertorelli

Beyond Death

"Are you there? Your face is hidden in the coldness.
If only I could feel again the gentle patter of your heart
Such boldness, such life was locked in the warmth of your face,
Where has it gone? Has it really ended? Your life was to embrace.

Ah my sweet, if only again your eye would glisten with pride,
You held such elegance such passion was yours you are alive,
Just hidden, obscured by this rock, this mountain of stone,
You still breathe and move within, yes; I feel you, I alone.

You have not left me; you still clutch strongly to my heart,
You have not gone, your warmth is here we are not apart.
I see you clear, though I cannot clearly see with my eye;
You are seen with my soul, with my inner eye.

Do not weep my love, I see your warm tears through the stone,
I see your soul now; your life our love, it is clear, hidden yet shown
And yes, at last you have come; you surround me. I know now what you meant;
Our spirits will live on past the coldness, forever locked away safely by this monument."
Abigail E. Blaker

"If-Only"

If I won the lottery, here's what I would do,
I'd buy the biggest rocking horse
To make my dream come true.
Ever since a tiny lot, it's been my one desire
And if I won the lottery,
I'd buy myself a flyer.

I've reached the age of seventy four,
Without my rocking horse,
It's still my wish to own one,
For my grand kids now, of course
I'd stand it in my hall, taking pride of place.
To see the children on it, would put a
Smile upon my face.
J. Francis

Untitled

This is the era of high technology
If I laugh, I make no apology
If only "They" could see
Those "Mighty powers that be"
As they struggle to win the arms race
They are making the world an unhappy place

There were men once proud
Who would shout aloud
But now no more, their hearts are sore
No pride, no job, no future bright
No sweet delight, just endless night

While our masters pull the strings
We see and hear of terrible things
Ethiopia, Biafra whole races dying
While they do their wheeling, dealing, and lying

Come the day, and come it will
When the piper demands payment of his bill
Persecution prejudice, ignorance, greed
A hefty bill to be paid indeed.
Agnes McCaig

To Fit My Hobbies In

Cleaning, cleaning, scrubbing, wiping,
I'd rather sit and do some typing.
Cooking, peeling, roasting, frying,
It smells delicious,
But so frustrating.
Please pass the easel, paints and brushes,
I'd rather create a vase of thrushes,
I sit and see all sorts of colour,
To fill the paper fuller and fuller,
This part looks right,
That part looks wrong,
I swap and change till it gets done.
The shape, the texture, light and shadow,
Come through the picture of frustration.
The time, the place, the weather too,
All add up to what to do.
Jayne B. Kelly

From One Dimension

When my end has finally come
I would love to see with a different sight
This planet getting small and smaller,
While I'm ascending higher and higher.
Above the cloudy sky I'll go,
How far how high I'll never know?
I will not die I'll pass away
I'll go where there's no night nor day
And from dimension to dimension,
Only stopping when I reach that station.
I would like to write my memories here
To read to those I love so dear
And say farewell to my every friend.
My epitaph will say in the end
Here lies my body and not my soul
Then my soul will go on to the spirit world.
Dalsie Mullings

First Day At School

I don't like to get up in the morning
I'd rather just stay in bed
But I had to get up this morning
'Cause of something my mother said

"Now Johnny, come on my wee darling"
"The weather is just really fine"
"I'll give you a hand to get ready"
"While you're washing, your shoes I'll shine.

So there and then I got up
My wee heart filled with dread
As I stood there, in my wee jama suit,
Sadly, I looked round at my bed

I got washed, and then had my breakfast
I thought that I would play it cool
You're wondering why all the bother and fuss?
I was starting my first day at school.

Helen Stainsby

No Regrets

Had I but guessed the path we took so many many years ago
I'd ne'er have had the heart to tread the road that led before.

The storm clouds still were drifting then, with taste of war and
  unsure days.
And shadowed years just meant for joy - but somehow failed
  to change our ways.

For we were young - were straight of limb - took hardships
  lightly in our stride.
We learned to only want the things that we could have - the
  rest we'd hide.

We wanted just to be quite free of urban grime - of clash - of din,
And gloried in the rush of winds that cleansed our minds of
  petty ills.

That was fifty years ago - the bairns we had have gone away,
But never fail to have that love of the steps we took to pave
  their way.

And they have kin themselves who love to feel the dew on
  young bare feet -
To taste the freshness of the hills - to sense the balmy days of
  peace.

Frances Alder

The Mind Of A Dress Aged Three

I am a dress and I am green and blue
I would like to go to school
To see what the children get up to
I sit in a chair and have a good stare

I laugh and I scream
When I am going to play on the green
The rain comes down
When I am going to town

Then I have a look around
And I see the clowns
I go into a shop
And get a shock
When I am hit by a sock
Which is blue and green like me

Then I go home for my tea and watch the TV
At the end of the day I count up to nine
And I am hung on the line to dry
I am still blue and green aged three

Gean Hunt

"The Parting"

Beside the lake, my heart bled
In fear not knowing what lay ahead,
The future was a grey everyday thing
Hovering like a bird on the wing
Of time, my love was gone out of life,
And I was left his lonely despairing wife.

Jean Banks

"The Ultimate"

I would like to journey through the galaxy
I would love to touch a star
No human being on earth I believe
Has ever done that so far

Floating about the heavens
Way out of telescopic reach
Travelling over exotic places
The Bahamas, the enchanting Bondi-beach

Without the aids of technology
I doubt if I would show fear
I would close my eyes, put my hands together
Knowing that God was near

Going through the stratosphere
Thrilled at seeing untold delights
I could bring back a wealth of stories
A sort of heavenly Arabian nights

Getting back on Terra Firma
Definitely feeling far above par
I would have achieved "The Ultimate"
Because I had touched a star.

David Robert Screen

My Kind Of World

If I could change the world today.
I would change it in many ways.
I would make the rich, not filled with greed,
I would make the poor not be in need.
The lame and sick walk through a door.
Where there would be pain no more.
Drink, drugs, no abuse.
No wicked, people, they're no use.
No war, no crime people would not dare
Happy not sad, people who care.
Children playing in the street.
No broken glass at their feet.
No crazy drivers, at their wheels.
Killing, maiming, family crying on their knees.
No earth quakes, or disasters of any kind.
In my world the sun would always shine,
I wish I could change the world.

Janet Elizabeth Isherwood

Untitled

Sitting alone, with time to reflect
How life had been, without much regret
Often I wonder, what would have become
If I had said no. When no would have done
No lovely babies, with skin so divine
No lovely kisses, no husband to find
No excitement, no thrills, a lonely old life
Thank God I said yes, I have been a wife

Joan Andrews

Necrosis

Through this drunken slumber
I watch her dry and dead
she's been that way for a week or so
and now my courage is full

Back to the bar my mind does go
where the bottle upon the table said
"Drink me till you can drink no more"
so I obliged like anyone would

The Demons spoke, they laughed at me
"were beauty in death a better thing?"
I gave them my heart, for them to decide
"Do it boy, do it", was their solemn reply

I kiss her lips, blue and cold
No seep of breath, no chest did heave
The tides of love flow through my veins
"Were beauty in death a better thing?"

Craig J. Smith

Exile

What visions of my homeland rise before me,
   I see Old Cheviot towering in his pride,
Deep woods of birch and pine are bending o'er me,
   I smell the heather on dark Simonside.
By Tyne and Tweed my footsteps go a-roaming,
   I see o'er high Peel Fell the evening star,
I pass grey towers in the Autumn gloaming.
   I watch the sunrise from the Carter Bar.

Fair is old England fair and full of glory,
   But fairest far of all that land to me,
That Borderland, far famed in song and story,
   Between the wild hills and the Northern Sea,
May dreams of thee still hover round the pillow,
   of a lone exile on a foreign strand,
For though I sojourn far across the billow,
   My heart is ever in Northumberland.
     Elisabeth Sisterson

For My Son

The first time that I met you
I was struck by the profound knowledge
And the infinite wisdom within you.
Although you were only seconds old
Time had left its tracks
A thousand times on your face.
The peace emanating from you
Spoke of a myriad of lives
Already gone before.
So tiny and yet so immense
In your quiet acceptance of a new beginning.
I watch as the days march by
Taking with them your memories
And leaving a void
To be filled with new experiences.
And I come to realize that it is you
Who has taught me
The most important lesson of all
—There is nothing to fear, there is no end.
     Amanda Aldridge

The Birds

In that peculiar moment that's neither day nor night,
I walked beside the ferry burn in fastly fading light.
The winter sun had barely set, the rain had cleared away,
The sky an artist's masterpiece in shades of pink and grey.

The town across the river looked like some strange foreign place
Its church towers and its monuments took on a misty grace
I stood and watched that silent world and I was lost for words
I heard a whispering ruffling sound, and then I saw the birds

Hundreds of them swooped and swirled and met and swept away
Like some magician's handkerchief they'd turn and swirl and sway
They kept time to a music beat that only they could hear.
One last circassian circle and lo' the sky was clear.

I turned my steps and called the dog and made my way back home
A thousand years of birds, and clouds have come and gone
Did I see a sort of miracle, a living hymn of praise
That left me with an inner peace that stayed with me for days.
     Frances McGuffie

True Sight

Instead of sunshine,
I see a dark satanic gloom.
Instead of flowers,
Shadows brighten my room.
Even what my lover appears as.
Is an answer I do not bear.
But, although I know not my child's looks,
For her I know I honestly care.
So, even though I am blind,
And darkness shields my light,
I have still love within me,
And love is my true sight.
     Hayley Hunt

A Walk Besides The River

As I stroll beside the riverbank
I unite with the beautiful natures.
The bees traffic around glowing buttercups
like miniature aeroplanes.
Feather like ferns brush against my ankles
As the sun shines on the trees costumes
of glistening leaves.
I gaze at the light blue sapphire sky
and the soft candyfloss clouds.
as the river lies like a green rippled sheet.
Shadows reflect dancing in the water
Ancient rusty chains hang down the
riverbanks, like orange snakes.
Swans flutter their wings
like pale elegant ballet dancers
A perfume of daffodils lingers in the air
Giving such a warm inviting atmosphere.
So lucky we are to have these pleasures
oh how I love to be here!
     Josie Devitt

Reverie

No longer nimble, now facing the truth,
I still try to capture the days of my youth.
Guide book and compass, fell boots and pack,
I'd make for the topmost peak on the map.
Hills all around me with Scafell in view,
Bowfell and Gable and Helvellyn too.
Up in the mountains and traversing high,
Ending the last pitch to reach for the sky.

Days full of promise, climbs full of thrills,
That's where I long to be, back home in the hills.

Carefree and happy away from the town,
I'd roam through the valleys from dawn till sundown.
By flowing stream I would stroll on my way,
And would welcome the freshness of each new day.
Lakes all around me enhancing the view,
Thirlmere and Derwent and Ullswater too.
Pikes over Langdale, the Lion and the Lamb,
And smiling on Coniston, the Grand Old Man.

Days full of promise, climbs full of thrills,
That's where I long to be, back home in the hills.
     Bernard Miller

Not My Friend

I received some exciting news today when I was all alone.
I thought I'd share it with Carole
But instead got the answer phone.

Perhaps I'll ring my friend Ollie
I'm sure she'll be at home.
But the voice at the other end said,
"Leave your message after the tone."

Then I rang Anita, she'll be having a nice hot toddy.
The voice at the other end was Anita's
But it wasn't attached to her body!

Well, I could ring Piera, she's always in at this time.
I didn't get the answer phone
But I did get an engaged line.

I know, I could try Sylvia
But maybe she'll be asleep.
Sure enough the answer phone said,
"Leave your message after the beep,"

Now answer phones provide a service for many
But sometimes when I need a friend,
I feel I haven't got any?
     Jennifer Batson

'In A Cell'

In a cell in a cell
I always say
I find myself in dark everyday
I ask the law to let me out
Just to explain what it's all about
Whilst time is passing, so slowly, I am so lonely
Forgive me my love if I have done wrong
For I shall not see you again

Christine Lavinia Terry

The Other Side Of Life

It's nice to sit alone in this warm and cosy home
I think of all the people in the cold
Like the starving mass of aged, and the young and lonely teens
No matter who they are, they have no hold.

As I sit here tonight thinking of other people's woes
I hear the key turning in the door.
I have finished all the cleaning, cooking, washing, dusting gleaming.
Now I walk home lonely, like all those others, who are poor.

Back home in my cold room, I still think of that big house.
I clean there almost every night.
I sit here by myself, lonely, cold and hungry.
There must be something that I'm not doing right.

But no, I'm not complaining, cos I earn an honest bob.
The world is full of people who haven't got a job.
Compared, my life is easy, to some of them I meet.
So if you see the lonely, begging in the street
Don't shake your head and walk by, you could be next, you know
The world is such a lonely place, when you have no place to go.

Hilda Smith

Was He Allowed!

I told you I was going out,
I told you yesterday.
Why don't you listen before you shout,
and listen to what I say.
I'm going to the round about
to watch the cars go by,
and if you do have any doubt,
I assure you it's no lie.
So mummy can I go out,
I promise I'll be good,
and never to play the silly lout
who plays chicken in the road.
I'll be back to you at tea time.
I'll be home to you by five.
To wash my hands of all the grime
as soon as I arrive.
I'll have my tea straight after,
and then I'll sit and read,
I'll wait until it's eight o'clock,
and then I'll go to bed.

Jean Lloyd-Williams

As Time Goes On

As time goes on and the years roll by,
I sit, I think and I wonder why,
everyone ages and there's nothing that lasts,
everything dies once its lifespan has passed.
Isn't sad to think once long ago
of a world full of people with none that we'd know?
now they're all gone making room for anew,
today's world is for people like me and like you.
Isn't it sad to think for us is the same?
Death in time's hands will they remember our name?
The people of tomorrow let us hope they shall find
a world unlike the present that is loving and kind.
And so for us in today's world let's hope it will be,
Fulfilling of happiness for you and for me,
before time takes its toll and death takes us away,
let's make most of our lives and live for today.

Juliet Ann Driscoll

To My Granddad On His Death

Because I cannot see you this day,
I shall remember the days before.

The day you taught me the "two little dicky birds" trick,
The days you showed me your collection of drawings,
The days I ate picked plums from your garden,
The days I wrote "thank you" letters to you,
And the days I had you in my mind.
And as I remember those days my tears wet the very paper I write on,

Now in heaven you are Granddad,
Once again reunited with Granny,
Walking together again down heavens gold roads,
And you once again can run and leap like a boy across the heavens
With Granny at your side.

Not only can you run and walk together, but with Jesus.
Down here on earth we mourn for you.
But we shall see you again soon in heaven,
And walk down heaven's gold roads with you and Jesus.

Jason Fleitz

Seeing You

Gazing through eyelids, eyes tightly closed.
I see your visual form, no imagination needed,
I really know you after all this time.
No need to ask anything,
you appear in my mind,
I read your thoughts, nothing left to say.
You feel it too, a kind of mutual sense.
We are really in tune but do not play together,
knowing the frustration of uncomposed melody.
I dream you up in my mind,
feeling your uncommunicated thoughts,
recording mentally the unwritten sheet.
We need to play, be instrumental with our tune,
as music must be and be heard.

Julie Allison

Hurting

All I have left are memories and a broken heart
I really believed in you, but I am torn apart
You overcame your drug addiction for nearly a year
But shattered my illusions and brought back, the fear

Why did you throw it all away?
Heroin has overcome you and for this you will pay
You had become so wise, I was so proud of you
Seemed to see the world with a different view

I put you on a pedestal because I saw what you'd achieved
I couldn't be more hurt but it is yourself you have deceived
My nightmare has returned and I am finding it hard to cope
During the past year Steve you gave me such hope

I know now that you have had your first taste
You will always be addicted to Poppy seed waste
I have no more fight, no more to give
It is all in your hands if you want to live.

Eve Thirlaway

I'll Be...

If you're cold I'll be your blanket
If you're hot I'll be your breeze
If you're thirsty I'll be the water
When you're tense I'll try to ease
I'll be the hand if you need to hold one
I'll be the shoulder to catch your tears
I'll always listen if you need to talk some
Of joy and pain throughout the years
I'll be a shelter from hurt and anguish
To make you smile I'll be a clown
I'll reach my arms far out to hold you
To pick you up if you are down
With someone special deep down you know it
You're someone special - I hope you see
That as a friend I'd do this for you
And that your friend I'll always be

Cain Leathem

The Journey

With pounding heart though light of step,
I reach the chosen place,
I look around, my throat is dry,
I cannot see your face.

The room is filled with strangers,
Looking just as I must look,
An aged prince enters the room,
In his hands he holds a book.

He passes through them gently,
Touching each with loving hands,
He whispers words of comfort,
Though they be from many lands.

Each passes through a doorway,
In the brilliance of the sun,
They lift their arms in greeting,
Love surrounds them, every one.

The light is on my face now,
As I enter through the door,
I knew you'd come to meet me,
I'm not frightened anymore.

Alexandra Burness Bothwell Mills

Dream Catcher

Some years ago I had an odd dream
   I often wonder what did it mean?
I was in a dark place I think a tepee a silver haired native
handed a baby to me
   This is Kuyai I give him into your care
A swarthy child with thick dark hair
The wise old native said when Kuyai's full grown he'll be a
leader of men
   I took the child my dream faded and then
I saw the name Kuyai etched into a sheer rock face of stone
   Yet I stood on a hillside quite alone
Many times I've tried to write Kuyai's story
   Certain he fought many battles the pain and the glory.
Kuyai remembered well the stories of old
   As round the camp fire his grandfather told
Of many brave warriors now gone to their rest
   But the stories Kuyai loved the best
Where the mystical legends of the catcher of dreams
   Who spirit bestows on a sleeper in star dusted moon beams
Sweet slumber throughout the night
Nightmares are held till dispersed in dawns early light.

Barbara Stockham

This Lovely World

As I look back on days gone by
I often stop and think a while
If only my loved ones had lived today
And enjoyed some pleasures along the way

They worked so hard from morn until night
It was their only pleasure as money was tight
I often drop a silent tear
Of ones I loved and wish were here

They deserved so much good times came late
But they never grumbled with their fate
So considerate kind and grateful
Give a helping hand while they were able

But in their day it was a quieter place
Such lovely fresh air to blow on your face
No pollution or noise from planes up above
Or travelling so fast and not see the country we love

Our loved ones enjoyed the stars and moon
To help them to see and get around
God loves us all, you and me
He made this lovely world you see

Gracie Lawson

A Cry For Freedom

How do I tell you, I want a life
I no longer consider myself "The wife"
I don't want to hurt you, please believe that's true
I will be thinking of you in all that I do

It's so sad when a love affair ends
It's true what they say, broken hearts mend
Or at least you learn to live with your loss
Eventually you stop counting the cost

Somewhere through the years I've lost who I am
You're making me helpless, like a lost little lamb.
I'm not allowed my opinion, or to say what I think
I've got to break free, or I will be turning to drink.

What happened to me I've faded away
Diminished being me, bit by bit, day by day
I was first known as a daughter, then a wife and mother
Don't you realize I feel I've been smothered.

So I will have my life back, if you don't mind
Stop taking responsibility for you or your kind
I will live my own life and do as I like
If you don't like it, feel free, take a hike!

Angela Monk

Cruel Beauty

Beauty, why entice me so much?
I nearly kill myself with the desire,
To relish the thought of your merciless touch.

And is your spirit such
As to render hurt by lighting a fire
Beauty, why entice me so much?

To know, that in my heart I feel your clutch,
An inferno that does not tire,
To relish the thought of your merciless touch.

That one so cruel could be a crutch,
To tortured senses upon a pyre,
Beauty, why entice me so much,
To relish the thought of your merciless touch?

John H. Clinton

Over The Years

Looking back over the years,
Hurtful times, lonely times, happy times too.
Times when you were so down you didn't
know what to do,
Gaining friends, losing friends
In and out of love,
they said they really loved you but then gave
you the shove,
sometimes you're mad and sometimes you're glad,
because over the years things are good and bad.

Gemma de Quincey

"The Shiny Penny"

My memories of Christmas were of such happy days,
I didn't have a stocking, I had a pillow case.
'Twas filled with goodies, what a thrill,
Excitement through me ran, to find outside my pillow case a
   dolly and a pram.
Inside the pillow case however, and at the very bottom
Was a brand new shiny penny tied up with silky cotton.
Each year an apple and an orange and chocolate figures too,
And then there was the sugar pig- I'm telling you, it's true.
I'd keep the penny in my coat with all its brightens shone,
Until the day that come around, my shiny penny gone.
My shiny penny was no more, 'twas brown and rather dull.
So I wrapped it in some paper and tied it with some wool
I kept it there for ages, until one day I found
My friend she hadn't got one, so I gave it her all bound.
That penny made her happy, and I never shed a tear
For there would be another one, all shiny, the very next year.

Ivy Pursglove

"A View Of A World"

I wake up once more and see the sunrise,
I look back at my life that as gone by,
a time when I was young and full of strength,
when I had family and friends,
to love and to care for.
But now I'm here all alone,
no one in this world for me to love,
in a world of hatred and destruction,
where love is no more,
I wait for time to pass me by,
when I'll be free from this world,
a world destroyed by pain and fear.

Graham Miller

My Husband

From a wild and lonely hillside I searched the starry skies
I knew my love I'd find you underneath that same dark sky
Our paths they weaved and crossed many times across the years
But destiny was to play her part the time was not yet right

Across the oceans we did travel our paths in life not smooth
There were many tears and heartaches to be had along the way
From the heart of the country to London City
Our paths they weaved and crossed
Then came the day we finally met in a high rise office block

United at last in this lonely world two peas in a pod are we
No parting again our love is sealed through time and all eternity
As together life's journey we make

Caroline Hearn

Basic Ingredient's "Faith And Love"

For many years I have trod this earth
I have done a lot of living.
Many pleasures I have received.
But the greatest one is giving.

Lend a hand to those in need
They don't mind if you're old and grey.
Just visit them and talk awhile
It helps pass their lonely day.

Your children may now be grown up
Some many miles from home,
But love can reach across the miles,
When you talk on the telephone.

Never let age rule your life,
Just keep busy when you can,
After weeks of studying, I'm proud to say.
I have passed my first aid exam.

So a word to those who get depressed.
At the passing of the years.
Just you ask God into your life,
And he will banish all your fears.

Jean Monteith

Sleepless Night

Are you awake or really asleep?
I hate this distance that pride makes us keep
It would only take a word from either one
But instead, we both long for morning to come.
Please make a movement or give me a sign,
Let your body move closer to mine
I know how you're feeling, I feel the same
The anger, the hurt, the terrible pain.
Emotions in turmoil, there's really no need
We could say "sorry" and end this with speed.
At last you move and I pretend to sleep
I hope you don't notice the tears on my cheek
Your arms come around me, our anger diminishes
A long loving cuddle and the argument finishes.

Debbie J. Boone

Retirement Is Fab!

At last the time of my retirement is here,
I had no need to await it with such fear!
It's just been wonderful for me so far
My life has changed so much - I could even become a star!
To retirement fellowship meetings each month I go,
Also attend their dinners, outings and the odd show,
Became permanent organist at a church nearby,
Took on a piano pupil whose progress I would not deny
Is due to my efforts as his teacher
I could not be more successful had I been a preacher.
Swimming, water aerobics, walking are among my fitness regime
Sewing, music, knitting, gardening, writing on which
    I'm also rather keen
There's more time for all those jobs around the house
And places to visit with my now retired spouse
This we accomplished in the first year of our retirement-
Jetting off twice to South Africa and Germany in one year, my visit
    to Australia was also an acquirement.
However, this year we have stayed at home for many reasons,
But abroad we will go soon to experience the seasons.
We're off to Germany as surprise guests at the birthday party
    of a friend
A visit which we no doubt will enjoy to no end -
Yes - RETIREMENT IS FAB!

Bertha Lakey

ALBINONI 1671-1750

Strange that singularity becomes a praiseworthy state.
I had always thought that to be alone
Was a state to be avoided at all costs
Lest thoughts and feelings best ignored claimed stronger hold.

Vivaldi, that lone priest of Venice, shunned isolation
And going against the tenets of his calling,
Joined in the melee of the city state
Where revellers abused the night and crumpled silken sheets
with heady lust.
Steps and balconies would take centre place
As bedecked girls, lately virgins, caroused the night,
Oblivious of recriminations to come.

Surely Tommaso could not have thought such scenes to be
debauched.
He knew the ins and outs of life and all the murky alleyways
Of music and musicians.
Yet concerto grosso? Solo concerto?
The music of life will have its way and cannot stay -
It moves on and like the dog
Will have its day.

David McKenna

Once

ONCE
I found myself embraced by shimmering shadows
and unclouded evenings
I pondered on their shapes and fancied that a smile might distort
them into pictures of merriment

ONCE
I yearned greatly for the dawn, when the rain
would glance my cheek and drench the earth
And leaves of flowers be soaked up by the soil
and drown before me

ONCE
I watched and waited for you to lift me
from my prison of weary misty daydreams
As I fumbled through my blindness and disillusion
with midnights starry beltane descending faster

NOW
I think of you, close to me with the sun's
weary mane searching through your hair
And springtime in my heart, will be the sunlight
in my growing, reflecting your image in my eyes

John Montgomery Bateman

Living Near A Wood

As I contemplate the trees,
I find myself drawn more to thee.
As thoughts pass through my troubled mind,
I find myself start to unwind.

A wood is home to many creatures,
Which makes it a delightful feature,
and gives me many hours of pleasure,
To fill my life in times of leisure.

The sweetness of the birds' 'Dawn Chorus',
An orchestra played solely for us,
Never fails to lift my spirits,
And all life's cares elope 'long with it.

The squirrels antics, so amusing,
Leaping, flying, daily storing.
Summer's sun will soon be gone,
Another year rolling on.

Now I'm in my golden years,
Woodland pleasures erodes my fears.
From buds in May till late November,
Young fires aflame to passing embers.
Audrey Donoghue

Tears, In Dreams.

With daylight gone, in darkness here,
I dream my dreams of you, my dear,
Dreams of your fragrance unsurpassed,
Dreams of your beauty yet unmatched.
Dreams of the day our eyes first met,
Our love was first revealed,
Dreams of the secret we both kept,
So sad, and so concealed.
Dreams of those days we laughed and talked,
Together, hand in hand,
Dreams of the time when first we walked,
Along those moonlit sands.
And dreams about that day we feared,
That time when we would part,
These secret dreams I hold, my dear,
Eternal in my heart.
And now inside God's heavenly gates,
With one who loves you too,
So young to leave me, now I wait,
And cry my tears, in dreams of you.
James C. Crawford

"Rose Street Breeze"

In Edinburgh in sunny January
I looked and saw people the same age as myself...

I saw three crusties in their uniforms
with a dog and a little child behind.
I saw a boy play soul on his harmonica,
sublimely while he stomped his feet without conviction.
I saw four lads as tall as me
playing electric guitars and supping tomato soup.
I saw a beautiful girl in a black suit
holding a hand as she looked at a menu in a window.

Slowly towards me
And pushed on wheels through this dance
came a twelve year old boy
With his short blonde hair and still blue eyes
his hands lay gently at his lap.

I had never seen anyone look so content.

As a breeze picks up some paper and some dust
I drink down the cold light of the sun.
The future screams with possibilities
While my senses slowly grind to a halt
David Liddell

Forgiveness

Why do I feel so sad?
I don't think I was really bad,
Yes, I could have maybe done it better,
But how many can live life to the letter?
My parents now both dead and gone,
Sometimes I hurt almost to the bone.
I did not bother much while they were here,
In loneliness they must have shed a tear.
How sad that we can only know,
The guilt and sadness that makes us low,
When it is too late to do a thing,
The time is past, the bells do ring.
It's not so much the empty chair,
Or the feeling they are no longer there,
It is the guilt of my lack of caring,
Not inquiring how they were faring,
After all the love that they had shown,
Even after into an adult I had grown,
In an attempt to help repay,
I'll do as I was taught, and pray.
Grace M. Ritch

Different

Why do people stop and stare?
I don't mean to be different
I didn't make myself the way I am
It's nobody's fault I'm like this.
I didn't want to look like this.
I didn't want to sound funny
I just wanted to be like everyone else
At least have a friend of my own.
The problem with me is horrible you'll see
I have something mentally wrong with me,
I wish I was as well as everyone else,
But I'm not and never will be.
Carla Stott

Why?

Why did you have me if you cannot love me?
I didn't ask to be born,
I'm only a baby, quickly contented,
Why do you leave me forlorn?

Why did you have me if you cannot love me?
Your love is all I desire,
I just want some cuddles, some kisses, some loving,
It isn't much I require.

Why did you have me if you cannot love me?
You leave me alone while I cry,
It's either that, or you beat me, bite me, abuse me.
Perhaps it is best that I die

Why did you have me if you cannot love me?
I'm your child - a fact you deny,
I could grow up to love you, respect you, adore you,
Instead I must just say - "Goodbye".
Jean L. May

Virtual Reality

The other day I found myself alone in a cold dark place,
I could see this figure all dressed in black,
 but couldn't see its face
Time was ticking, I could hear the sound,
 though there wasn't any clock.
And then I felt a key in a door, but I didn't see the lock.

For through the door is not a room, but a table with no chairs,
And a staircase with no up or down, that hasn't any stairs.
And water falls upon me, it's from the tap of life,
And the first cuts not the deepest, but it isn't with a knife.

Where the colour black is not, it's light, and white is never found,
And shapes are always circular but never really round.
If I was sure this was a dream my future may be set,
But am I safe in trusting this, to a world I've never met.
Emil Haye

Secret Agent

I thought my life was boring, but when I dream at night.
I could be a secret agent and might just have to fight.
The last time I was sleeping, I got shot right in my chest,
But I expected this that night, and made an iron vest.
I put two spoons in my pockets, and a tray stuck up my front.
I climbed into my Bond Bug and then began the hunt.
BANG! A shot was fired, it bounced right off the tray,
Then like a mouse into a hole, I just slipped away.
The Black Bond Bug was nippy, I drove right through a store,
Weaving through the people, more scared than I was before.
I drove to a home in the country, although I never cried.
I crouched down in a corner, still even more petrified.
The bad men right behind me, I waited for them to arrive,
I heard their car and a knock on the window it was 7.05.
It was 7.05 in the morning, I woke up a still as a stone,
Snug and warm in my bed, laying all alone.

Carol Kavanagh

Untitled

Between you and me,
I can't remember how things used to be,
I've always heard the guns,
And the screams,
But I wished it was all in my dreams.

Between you and me,
The bodies and the fires I never used to see,
I always saw the birds,
And the clouds in the sky,
And the peaceful blue waves of the sea.

Between you and I,
I never saw my parents cry,
I only saw the tears of laughter,
And the tears of joy,
These things always made me give a happy sigh.

Between you and I
Today I can see all the people cry
I can see all the bodies and fires
And the blood curdling screams
Maybe now it's my turn to die.

Esther F. Burrell

Untitled

The noose is tightening on my neck
I can feel the cry of despair,
tighter and tighter it is choking me
un yet I feel no pain nor care.
Locked inside my head alarm bells
the noise seems so great,
un yet I feel no hurt, nor yells
the blood goes whooshing, like a river
in and about the ear canals.
The blood vessels pop
yet now I seem to be plain,
not me anymore
just is - empty my shell
I won't look back, my life is ended
gone no return, forgotten no more.

Anne Small

First Love

I - ten at the time.
Home from school in the donkey and trap.
He - one hour old.
Still damp from his brave struggle into the world
After his lonely sabbatical in there all alone
- no one to talk to.
Mother-proud-tired - happy.
He having his first picnic on Mother's left breast.
Old Nurse Ryan - the midwife - still busy.
Then sadness - it would be years before he and I could play
get up to mischief together.

David MacSweeney

You Came To Me In A Dream

You came to me in a dream last night
   I awoke and started to cry
Oh! How have we got everything
   Except the gift to fly.
The dream was brief but I saw your face
   And tried to touch your hand
If I had wings I know right now I'd be
   Coming in to land.

Perhaps dreams are a way of God giving us wings
   And letting our souls go free
But bodily shapes we had to take or
   How would you know it was me
You came to me in a dream last night
   And it helped me to see more clear
Why God gave us an earthly form
   and exactly why we are here

For it's with our bodies as well as our hearts
   That we learn to give our love.
What I longed for most you see
Was for your arms to reach out and cuddle me.

Joanne Field

The Observe

I watch
I am on the perimeter
I am unnoticed, I am not involved
They are involved they are noticed.

I watched I am unnoticed
Each states a point
There is the occasional interruption.
I do not speak.
I am not involved.

I watch I do not speak.
They shout. They shout loudly
I am noticed
I am not involved.

I watch I am involved
They strike out to hurt I speak out
I am involved they watch.

I watch, I am the perimeter
I am present I am noticed, but I am not involved.
They are involved
They are noticed.

Carol Lesle Lane-Cilmeri

Fertilizer Fred

They call me fertilizer Fred
I am farm labourer like my bed
Down on the farm I love by heart
Nye ten o'clock before I start
Field to plough I'm none the wiser
More my line is fertilizer
Corn a-ripe, combine ready
Don't say to that get up Neddy
No one there with a stick or gun
Watching and waiting for the rabbits to run
Bales in store for winter feed
Stored in a bin this little seed
Winter to come, to the plough
Ain't no leaf, upon the bough
Rain and wind, pain and stitches
Fertilizer in the ditches
Down the river, gently flows
Reservoir, and stomach goes
Spring she comes, farmers in the red
Down at the local, I'm fertilizer Fred

James Deeks

Golden Fruit

Even though we spent miles and months apart,
I always truly believed in my heart
One day we would be together
And our relationship would last forever.

The distance tested our bond
The time tested our love,
But we always looked beyond
And maintained our faith in the Lord above.

I long to be with you
When our hours apart will be few,
To hold you in my arms close to my heart
When no distance or time will keep us apart.

Your patience and support kept my hope alive
And it enabled me to reach my goal.
Without you I would not survive
Because my life would have no soul.

My love for you should be easy to see
Indeed, you mean the world to me.
Our time together is something to cherish
A unique fruit that will ripen but not perish.
Jay McClellan Jenkins

Anguish

Oh stop, please stop, you cannot see
How much your pain's bombarding me
The sickness swirls around inside
Nauseous, draining, spreading wide

The void is vast, I feel how black
The energy as it feels its track
Around the world to seek me out
It's pain and anger one long shout

Don't suck me out, I could not see
How there could be a you and me
The path ahead revealed its way
There was no more that I could say

This onslaught is too much to bear
I need a pause to help repair
My shrunk and shrivelled, drained out soul
I strain to climb out of this hole

My honesty you always sought
My promise I gave without a thought
For this pain-filled power you could assert
My ice cold knife, your searing hurt
Angela Priddle

"I've Been Here Before..."

I don't like this room, it's too dark and dusty,
I look to my right, I smell something musky,
I cannot believe it, the woman in red,
Why is she here? I thought she was dead,
She beckons to me and points to a door,
Somehow I think, I've been here before......
My head starts to spin as she blows out a candle,
Walks to the door and then turns the handle,
I try not to move but my feet lead me there,
Through an archway and then down a stair,
Another archway comes into sight,
Where birds can be seen high in their flight,
I stand on a ledge, don't care if I fall,
'Cause now I've got wings and no arms at all,
I then discover, I cannot speak.
I try to communicate by using my beak,
I leave the ledge and start to fly
Dive through the clouds and soar through the sky
What a feeling! What a sensation!
I know what this is, it's reincarnation..........
Jacqui Gillies

Fill-Up

Three meals a day, sometimes four,
How come? Boys always ask for more?,
They drink all liquids down to the dregs,
I really do believe they have hollow legs!,

Please may we have more for our tummies?,
Little boys like 'Oliver' don't have mummys!,
Each day, us mums have tried very hard to think,
What more can I make to fill them to the brink?,

Breakfast, lunch, dinner, supper, think that's it?,
Not on your life, they are a bottomless pit!,
Two days cooking cakes, pies in a big batch,
All consumed quickly, I lose the battle, no fair match!,

The above is a fact, it is very well known,
It doesn't stop, even when they are full grown,
Times are very rare when you can fill a man's tum!,
Not many men would swop to become a wife or mum,

Hear one male here say, "That's what women are for,"
They'll find out just how backsides can get very sore!!
Dee Sellars

Audience Participation

The darkness finds me
hot-eyed and hurting,
screaming my hate silently
at the black-cloaked stage below.
The atrocities before my eyes
delivered with velvet sweet tongued lies
by cold hard men whose alibis
bear us false witness,
we the hungry jury.
I bay for blood,
slaver at the kill
and thrill at the redemption of the slanderous hero.
Then just as my blood begins to boil
the curtains fall and I'm left
blinking and confused.
I fumble - must regain my place.
Stumble back to sanity's cold embrace.
Wipe the webs of wonder from my face
and don again society's well worn mask
of bored indifference.
Jean E. N. Walton

The Frozen Fountain

Neptune in bronze sat high upon his throne,
His sparkling trident resting on hoared stone,
His mouth that spat the fountain now bound tight,
By ribbons cast by Winter's steely might,
And waters which beneath pale sun's flowed free,
Now fell a beard of silver to his knee,
While at his feet two marble dolphins white,
Leaped from their icy sea to greet the night.
Barbara Barlow

Untitled

I'm writing this poem straight from the heart
Hoping the young ones will all play a part
In making this world a much better place
Where we can all go at a steadier pace
Amongst kind peoples who one's troubles will share
And all those in need will know someone's there
It's not asking much just a little each day
To help some unfortunate soul on their way
Respect and good manners come very cheap
Use them a lot and see what you reap
I use them myself and the harvest's sublime
Mind you I think it took me a very long time
But now I have made it I feel very glad
When I hear people saying I'm the best friend they had.
But I'm an old gal now and I've done my best
Please take over you young ones and give us old ones a rest
Irene Dutton

Ghosts

Dreams turned to dust - companions lost in smoke
Hope merged with fear - a confused brain.
Standing alone with eyes forever searching
I look to Heaven - then I am lost again.

There was a time when life was for the taking
When laughter filled our lives and love was free,
We had so much - we never knew the darkness
I took it all - the world belonged to me.

You and the others lifted me above you
Now you are ghosts I stumble on in pain
You said to me, 'When I am gone - go forward.
No looking back' I face the world again.
Walking with care I journey without falling
Hope is ahead, I cherish my relief.
Can it be true? Live for each day they tell me
Lord I believe - help throw my unbelief.

Elizabeth R. O'Malley

A Dahlia Too Late

A robin flashes his flame red breast,
 his slimy mess sliding down granite onto, Edward,
A "dearly beloved husband", at rest.

Mourners huddle close on ankle chilling earth,
 united in grief, and sorrow.

Fluorescent striped men wait a respectful distance away
wondering how much tax has gone from this week's pay.

Imitation grass is doing its best, to camouflage the
hole for the one who's at rest

One unaware, of quarrels, excuses,
 trivial really, in retrospect

As tears are dried with shredding tissue
Mother has ceased to be the issue.

Joan Cirino

Psychopath

Incarcerated in this room, six foot by ten
his mind deep in thought, knowing he'll never taste freedom again

They called him a viscous animal and have put him in this cage
hoping he will become placid and mellow with the coming of old age

They labelled him a sadist with no regards for fellow man
the doctors called him a psychopath and other words he
 didn't understand

He can't explain to them the way his mind becomes a mist
and his heart begins to pump and swell
like the time he killed the taxi driver and the young girl

They try to get into this mind but they never will
for only he understands the excitement of the kill

To him it's like other people making love
or a child getting a special treat
part of him is happy knowing
He will never again be allowed to stalk the street

Jack Palmer

Our Father The Teacher

A brave courageous fight against a cruel illness
His love for us outshone any fears
he may have felt.
He protected us through out.
Being with him and helping him was
a pleasure we all miss.
His sense of humour patience and
witty remarks: gave us strength.
The slow painful steps to sleep
were taken with utmost dignity.
A well respected and very much
loved Father.
He lives on through us

Carol Poulter

My Best Friend

The softness of his touch reaches my soul,
His gaze searches the depths of my thoughts
And senses the love flowing forth.
His deep-throated song soothes away
All the stresses of the day.

He wears his fur so well; black suit, white tie,
White gloves, a mustachio of white whiskers,
The perfect gentleman.

Fastidious beyond reproach he reclines upon my knee.
He smells of sweet grass, clean air,
And all the goodness of healthy outdoor activity.

White whiskers twitching in the dreams of sleep,
Paws pouncing on prey in slumbers deep.
At a sound he awakens, alert and keen,
Something startled him, what had his mind just seen?
Imaginary mice, or birds perhaps,
Water running from fanciful taps,
Licking his lips, with a stretch and a yawn,
He settles down for a new cat-day to dawn.

Christine Welland

Thomas

Thomas my cat was tabby and black
His eyes were as green as grass
His face was daft
He slept in a draught
And on what a size he was
Both fat and chubby, tubby and round
His little tum near touched the ground
He followed me here, he followed me there
He simply followed me everywhere
He never did bite, nor did he scratch
He never did have a frightening match
And now my story is over
Alas my heart is sore
I left him back in Cyprus
Poor Thomas is no more

Denise Felstead

Times They Be'Ard

Tell me, tell me, tell me the trick
How to pay gas water and electric?
Some folks can manage and stay alive
but how do they do it and still survive?

I tried robbing Peter, to pay Paul
But I still have to pay Peter back after all
It's the same one week to the next
How do others manage I really am vexed.

I tried cutting down on food and booze
Also on fruit machines cause I always lose
But still I'm in the same old boat
Hard up and unhappy and barely afloat

I need a rich fellow with money galore
but knowing my luck he'd be an awful bore
Ugly and old and probably what's more
a dirty old man - I think I'll stay poor!

Jeannette A. Catterall

Running Scared

Danger approaches.
Her eyes are wide,
Jaw tense, every muscle tightens.
She runs.
Runs away from the attack,
She's trapped,
Trapped in a prison of fencing.
There is no escape, she stops and turns,
Ears pricked, rotating, listening.
Her muscles slowly relax, she checks again,
Slowly she drops her head and grazes,
The danger has passed, and is forgotten.

Anita Friskney

A Brother-In-Law Died

I wasn't allowed to my brother-in-laws funeral
His daughter was very bitter.
On his wishes he saw me before he died,
When she arrived, I had to bide, outside,
Never Mind you can all come to mine
And have a bloody good time.

No forgiving minutes as the man was dying
Past present moments hung in crying
I did not, I don't believe in lying
Truth can't hurt, get your own back darling
When I'm dead, come to mine
And have a bloody good time

Iris Williams

A Single Parent Treasure

He's my best friend
He's my fun
He's my future
He is my son
And when I'm down and life's a pain
My love for Ben is still the same
He is the day
And also night
He is my strength
The dark and light
And when the future seems so grim
I always stop and think of him
For Ben to me is everything
My love my hope the winter and spring
And if by fate my life should end
I leave behind a son and friend.

John Evers

The Tramp

Do not look and gaze at him when he passes by
he's just a person just like you the world has left
to die, he's just some one that needed care,
but no one heard his plight. He has
no home he doesn't care he wants to stay from
sight. He just needs someone's friendship to
help him on his way. A warm bed for to
sleep on instead of bales of hay, a meal
a drink to warm him, a shelter from the storm.
Some clothes and woolly blankets to keep his
body warm. Next time you see him walking
or resting on a seat, just look at him with
pity and see his sore cold feet. Then give
a smile a helping hand to guide him on his
way, and give a kind word in his ear
then you'll have made his day.

Josephine Blackford

She

Her face is so snowy, her eyes are like pearls,
Her shiny blonde hair falls soft with curls,

Her face is alight with innocence and trust,
To cherish and love her, I know that I must,

I watch her while she sleeps, so relaxed, so deep,
Her body is still, she's not making a peep,

She smells so sweet her skin is so new,
She's a new life that's starting, as fresh as the dew,

My need to hold her close, brings an ache to my heart,
She's mine for a lifetime, that bond you won't part,

She's grown from a seed, like a flower in the ground,
All that she asks is that I'm always around,

As she enters the room my heart swells with pride,
It's my hand she reaches when she needs a guide,

I'll love her forever through glad times and strife,
She's my new baby girl and I gave her life

Amanda Mooney

Aging With Dignity And Grace

The lines on her face are grouted within
Her hearing faint and eyes are dim
The wispy grey hair thinning with time
And the creaking bones all out of line
The struggle to stand or take a step
The effort involved is a secret kept
To proud to utter of aches or pains
So independent, help refused in vain

Happily confused, given dignity and grace
We communicate by the look on her face
Her expressions understood by each and all
Verbally repeating each beckoned call

A name for each, perhaps not right
Who cares what you're called, she is so polite
Her little world seems so ideal
Why be in our world it is far to real.

Ann Tarbuek

Animal Testing

Alone and dying in a small cage she lies,
Her fur is all shrivelled from testing hair dyes,
Where the dyes were too strong her skin is red raw,
She is covered in ulcers from paw to paw.

Around her eyes broken blisters weep,
From where into her eyes mascara did seep,
Her nose is bleeding, her pads are cracked,
All so your cosmetics purse is tightly packed.
So next time your out on the town,
And your looking stunning in your gown,
Dark satin and a touch of lace,
Remember the blood smeared over your face.

Mascara, foundation all make you look nice,
But some little animal has to pay a great price,
Make-up not tested on animals buy,
Or alone in a small cage she will suffer and die.

Emma Fauré

A Lonely Soul

A silver-haired lady that I hardly know
her body is fragile her movements are slow
She's full of illness her life's been unfair
Does anyone love her does anyone care?
She knows many tales, stories untold
Things from the past the ways of old
she was once beautiful and filled with grace
Now her looks have been taken by lines on her face
She had ambitions she's seen them through
Built the foundations for me and for you
she lived through the war and helped win the fight
A mother by day, a worker by night
She raised a family, her children have grown
They've all gone away now she's left on her own
She sits lonely and weak in a chair
Does anyone love her?
Does anyone care?

Helen Finneran-Dinsdale

In Her Absence

Despondency dwells in the stain on the armchair.
Heavy curtains hang in grim resignation,
Speared by hooks - talons of gold.
Sunlight stabs the flirtatious dust,
Which dances and swirls in a room filled with loss.
The mug drained of coffee,
With lipstick-stained rim.
And the ticking clock which doesn't stop like the heart.
Faded photos of loves which left long ago,
Meaningless in the eyes of another.
The tiny thread that preserved them,
Has turned to dust, their identities lost forever.
Thick mouldy air stains the walls like nicotine.
And though everything is as it was when death called,
Nothing is quite the same.

Joanne Daniels

Justice

It's not fair! It's not fair! He almost shouted.
He was being blamed, it wasn't all his fault.
He remembered back to that night-
They jumped out onto the old man
They had scared him actually scared him,
Stole his money, kicked him and punched him,
All for a laugh, for fun!

When the police came everyone scattered,
He had been caught and charged.
"Murder" they said.
He didn't kill the old man by himself
"Guilty" said the jury,
"Death" said the judge, "I'll make an example of you".

Walking to the death chamber he cried,
He was strapped into position in the electric chair.
The priest gave him final absolution for his sins,
The black hood was placed over his head,
Everyone left the chamber.
He was executed in the name of justice!

Catherine McPherson

Albert

To my Husband he was a Father
He was a Grandad to my Sons
To me, the Dad, I never had
And a friend to everyone.

He was a happy cheerful man
Hardly thinking to complain
But he did have strife, within his life
That gave him sorrow and gave him pain.

He was well known for his thoughtfulness
Never missing a time or a date
He would write things down, so when time around
He knew that he wouldn't be late.

He loved the life that was given to him
It was full - he remembered it well
The stories he told were exciting and bold
While others were to sad to tell.

He could always ease your sorrow,
He would charm away the hurt
He will be remembered for a long, long time
Our Dad, your Grandad, ALBERT.

Diane Howard

An Englishman In France

"Esque vous avez un kilo de poires?"
    He said with a tentative grin:
The vendor madam, with a beard like a man,
    Was silent, she just looked at him.

She toured a ca mari: "Un anglais" she snarled
    Her lips curled again and again:
"Attendez..." she said, and his visage went red,
    "Pourtant I shall servez demain."

My wife silly cow, thinks I can't speak the lingo
    Because I'm not served straight away,
But I'll get my own back, on that silly old vache:
    Je demandez again - "si'l vous plait."

"Le homme est aveugle, he can't see the fruit,"
    The madame said airing her views,
The Englishman's wife, with a grin like a knife:
    Said "sortez"... you've just been refused!"

"Non non" he replied, as he went to her side,
    "My standard of French is too good:
I'll parle a grade lower, and speak a bit slower,
    Pourtant I shall be understood."

Harrydan Howard

For King The Country

I hear the sound of music
hear the beat of drums,
and hear the prayers of a fighting man
as closer the battle comes.

I see the fear in his eyes
this man by trade a baker,
but I know he will do his best
for his country, he won't forsake her.

The baker's been given another trade
to face that awesome task,
lay down his life for his King.
for a baker it's a lot to ask.

To make a baker kill a man
and make him hate his foe,
is something that comes to him
when a thousand miles from home.

At the end of the battle win or lose
the baker would know by the dead,
never to make war no more
but live forever baking bread.

David Biggs

Go And Reap

Do not be deceived, for God you cannot mock
He sent His Son upon the earth as shepherd of the flock
Listen to the voice of Jesus, for man reap what he sows
So be not weary of doing good, your Heavenly Father knows
Take the opportunity, of doing good to all
Especially God's children when on you they call
And when it's time to harvest whatever you have sown
You'll be singing with the angels around God's heavenly throne

Brenda Ottley

Butterfly Wings

Time began, and with its dawning
    he was there, within or was it without.
Aeons of time and he passed by,
    I could not see except with doubt.
Some would say it is sheer illusion,
    yet I know him not as a dreamer's dream.
Ageless, matchless, formed and formless,
    he flows with the unflowing, spilling stream.
Had I but silken stars where I have eyes,
    the molten shafts of love's first light
might then have been more clearly seen.
    The silent glow of his burning lamp,
glimmering, shimmering, now ne'er to die,
    takes my hand in gentle persuasion
to lead me where I've yet to fly.
    If I should stumble or fall in my flight
I will no more but softly sigh.
    I will mount once more on butterfly wings
to reach my soul's desire.

Jean French

Simply The Best

How would I describe my man? I'd smile and then I'd say
he makes my life so happy, he's the highlight of my day
all though there's times he makes me mad, a there have been a few,
It never stops the way I feel my love for him is true
We've built this temple of our love
it took so many years it represents the things we share
the love, the hurt, the tears
We've shared a lot of all these things they, helped to
make us stronger
when other marriages have failed ours has laster longer.
we've learned to love we've learned to lose we've had our
share of sadness,
there have been times when we both thought to carry on
would be madness
But we came through when others failed I think we stood the test
My theory is this man I love
Simply is the best

Jane Cope

Mummy

My mummy is an Angel, my daddy told me so,
he said that Jesus called one day and Mummy had to go.
She went away to heaven, to do the books and things,
ordering from Angel stores, harps and pairs of wings.

Now Mummy has a funny house, its door is made of stone,
we often go to visit her, but Mummy's never home.
Daddy says this is because my Mummy's out on call,
but I can't make myself believe, that she is there at all.

There are lots of funny houses, from which there's not a sound,
and all have little doors of stone, leading underground.
If every door that's in here holds a mum or dad,
then Jesus up in heaven, makes a lot of children sad.

Each day I ask my daddy, "When is Mummy coming back"?
and each day my daddy says to me, "When she gets the sack,"
She's been gone a long time now, and Daddy's getting old,
I often hear him cry at night, when the bed is cold.

Trying to help my daddy is always lots of fun,
and he introduces me to friends, saying, "Here comes little Mum."
But you know...pretending is really not the same,
I wish my mum would get the sack, and then come home again.
John Price

Our Dad

Our Dad he was a gardening man
He loved his tools and his watering can
He'd sow his seeds and watch them grow
He knew all about gardening he needed to know

Our Dad he was a soldier true
He fought in France in World War Two
We have his medals side by side
And we look at them with great pride

Our Dad he liked a bet on the horses
He'd study form at all the courses
His favourite horse he told our Mum
Was the one and only great 'Red Rum'

Our Dad he loved the open air
He used to walk his dog named Clare
Sometimes he'd catch a rabbit or two
We really loved his rabbit stew

Our Dad he was 'Simply The Best'
And now that he is laid to rest
In our hearts he'll always stay
Loved and remembered everyday
Jackie Kingham

White Man Says, "Walk With Me"

Thickly encased in senseless smoke,
He is perched chameleon like
On concrete ground.
He listens to me woo his culture from its birth place.
And his scarred earth breaths a final crackle
As I embrace, envelop it and adopt it,
But I drown out, he cannot hear, its dying sounds.
His maker, Old man Coyote didn't howl
When his armies of red men
Ripped windows in each other's faces,
Opening each other's skin
To let their eyes see.
But now he cries long and loud
Into the ears of his people,
Who are unable to hear through
The growth of skin over their lobes
That creeps across their faces
From the seeds we planted there
When we asked them to come
Walk our world with us.
Hannah Daw

Christmas Eve

Father Christmas crept up the stairs.
He heard the children saying their prayers.
Gave a big grin, then put his sack down.
All of a sudden his face wore a frown.

"Dear Lord" said the children, "we know you are kind.
We don't want any presents, we hope you won't mind.
Give them to the poor and the needy" they said.
"We're grateful to have a nice home and a bed.

Take care of our Mamma and Poppa as well.
We know Santa's coming we just heard his bell.
We love you Lord Jesus, please hear us we pray.
And keep us all safe to enjoy Christmas day.
Brenda Ewart

Peter, The Fisherman

As Peter fished beside the sea
He heard Christ say "Come follow me".
He left his friends, he left his nets
And hoped he would have no regrets.

While in a boat one stormy night
Christ walked on waves, and gave them a fright.
Peter boldly said "Can I walk to you?"
But lost his faith when the strong winds blew.
He cried in despair "O Lord, save me,"
A hand stretched out and held him firmly.

In the garden Jesus went to pray
The soldiers came to take Him away.
Peter took his sword and with no fear
He cut right off the servant's ear.
To defend his Lord had been his aim
But Jesus said it was wrong to maim.

He warmed his hands by the glowing fire
To stay by Jesus was his desire.
Three times when asked if the Lord he knew,
Denied it, and wept bitterly when the cock crew.
Cynthia Joy Dixon

Winter's Visit

Winter has been hiding in Autumn's shadow, waiting for her to go,
he has his cold winds ready, together with the snow,
that will make everything around us completely covered in white,
glistening and shimmering, lighting up the night.

Winter has been instructed to make us appreciate-
the beauty of flowers, trees and sunshine,
for which we patiently have to wait.

But winter allows us some compensations, like log fires glowing warm,
the cosiness of shelter, to protect us from the storm.
And for all, he will reward us by leaving us a legacy,
for when he leaves us he will beckon Spring,
to come with her beauty for you and me.
Ivy Sparkes

The Lord's Prayer

The Lord God who reigns above.
He comes with joy, and peace and love.
Everlasting.

Lord our Father this we pray
Our love for You will ever stay.
Rich with hope and deepening faith
Dearest Saviour,
Supreme.

Praise we sing to You our Lord.
Reaching out with one accord.
Always knowing You are there
You are with us everywhere.
Eternal love to us You give.
Rich in blessings that we may live forever.
Gillian Carey

Headlines

Have you seen the news today?
Have you seen the news?
Another child murdered, another lost along the way.
They change so quickly, grow so fast
The age of innocence does not last.

Have you seen the news this week?
Have you seen the news?
All of it depressing, the outlook is so bleak.
The world is filled with so much hate
Where twisted minds decide our fate.

Did you see the news last year?
Did you see the news?
Pensioners robbed and beaten, others live in fear.
They fought for us in two world wars
But now sit alone behind closed doors.

Will you see the news tomorrow?
Will you see the news?
Wars are fought, people starve, their eyes are full of sorrow.
Can we help to ease their pain
And give them a reason to live again?

Caroline Bower

Time

What is time, and why?
Have we time to think, and time to wonder,
Time that comes, time that goes,
But where from, and where to, who on this earth knows.
Time of the universe, time of the earth,
Time of space, time of the human race, time of people and place,
We all have time to live, we all have time to die,
A split second, is time enough for life to pass us by,
We each have time to love, laugh, be happy, be sad and to cry,
Some wish there time away, and never think of another day,
We each have time to sigh, and time to say goodbye,
Some think of the future, some think of the past,
And yet, wonder, if it will ever last,
We all have time to fulfil, I wonder if we ever will,
We know that there is a past, but is there a future?
Who can say, who can tell, will there be another day,
Some have no time to give or share, some have no time to even care,
But I often sit here in my chair, and wonder, what would happen,
If time ever stood still.

Allan Young

Small Black Cat

Oh small creature of this earth, so black and sleek like velvet
Life was so near and yet so far, all gone in one short moment
The daylight gone for a short time, and night is once more with us
The fear of dark is not of you, and yet your life has ended
I cry for you oh small black cat, although I never knew you
How could those torch like eyes of yours, misjudge those wheels before you
The light went out forever that night so unexpected
You next life comes with painless grasp, all life is so important.

Margaret Howell

A Poet's Soul

Thoughts found on an alternative wave
Have fought the conscious to enslave.
Felt the pull of dream pursuits
And scorned the need for flesh-like roots,
Have isolated self from friend and foe
And taught to run, go, go!
Learned to deny yet also to accept
That those who have cried, have not wept.

Life that feeds on another plain
Has known the friendliness of pain,
Tasted many passions however crude
And seen the visions of solitude,
Has learned to love the invisible scar
And anchored deep while travelled far,
Learned to welcome both chime and toll
Such the plain of a poet's soul.

Bronwyn Lewis

Wonder

Winter's icy breath numbs fingers -
Hardened frost in furrow lingers.
Dartmoor broods as chill winds blow
Through dips and gulleys patched with snow.
Gaunt, ghostly limbs of wind rocked trees,
Silhouettes on hill top frieze,
Defy the elements.
Then through the gloom emerges, cold and white,
Leviathan of space to cheer our blinkered sight -
The pulse of life, serene, untouched by man
Unquestioning monarch of the solar plan,
Declares its presence.

Is it possible that such a tiny sphere
Rolling like a coin in space,
Has power and strength to warm and cheer
And fire the blood of all life here
In cosmic's earthly place?
That power can change the world of grey
To sun-kissed buds, young lambs at play -
Continuing life in nature's race.

Angela Atkin

War

Shattered buildings stand gaunt to the sky
Like accusing fingers point heaven high
Men women and children gasping for air
Horror filled eyes full of despair

Bloated bodies stare at the sun
They no longer care and cannot run
From all the suffering stench and disease
That brought mankind down to its knees

Loved ones lay beneath rubble and mud
Moaning and screaming covered with blood
Homes are destroyed there's nowhere to live
People around have no help to give

What was the cause of all this despair
Such is the question that hangs in the air
Just greedy governments who disagree
Over countries that only want to be free

The quarrels start then war begins
Who is to answer for all these sins
Who is to say that war is right
And comfort the orphans and widows through the dark night

P. Thompson

Watching

Stand by the side of a busy street and watch the crowds go by,
each face tells a story to the discerning eye.

A smiling face, a thoughtful face, a face that's full of woe,
a young face, a wizened face, a face that's nowhere to go.

A boy who's lost his mother, his face all wet with tears,
an old man wanders slowly by thinking of yesteryears.

A father hot and bothered as he pushes through the crush,
a motorist looks on hopefully, waiting for a push.

Tired eyes, angry eyes, eyes that are full of pain,
eyes that search the leaden skies, waiting for the rain.

The strong, the feeble, young and old, all throng this crowded street, each person hurries homeward bound to escape the sweaty heat.

The boys, the girls, the lovers who wander hand in hand,
going about their business, all swell this milling band.

So stand and watch the crowded street and try to understand,
the story behind each pair of eyes, and pity their tired feet.

A. C. Dalton

Mind's Eye In The Night

Kidnapped in the darkness,
my house left for dead.
I saw my neighbours come.
My home became transparent as I watched
them take what they could find,
Smiling, laughing, animals in a zoo.
A carnival on the move.
Knocked to the ground by a strike to the head,
I felt nothing.
Seeing my world deteriorating,
I was nobody.
Dead and despised they took me away,
Victim to my own bestial thoughts,
my own callous mind.
An uncontrollable realism was emerging,
flourishing against my will.
I wanted to live how my other half was living,
Asleep, and at rest,
in the comfort of my bed.

Rachel Ellen Goodman

A Year's Gone By

A year's gone by, it's still the same,
My heart it breaks, to hear your name
Recalling all the times we shared
And all the time I thought you cared

It's not the sex that I miss most
It's not the kissing too,
It's snuggling up on the settee
Just being close to you.

I long to see you in the park,
I long to hold your hand
All those future plans we made
Like drifting grains of sand.

Life's not the same without you,
You've left an empty space
A space which only you can fill,
The tears run down my face.

You'll never know how much you hurt me
You'll never know how much I've cried,
A year ago you left me
A year ago, inside, I died.

R. Chapman

The Richest Treasure Of All

The one thing I bestow upon you is
my everlasting love for you
The one thing I only possess

No gold do I bring no ruby can I give.
But remember just this one word.
That you will keep locked away in your
heart it is a treasure worth more than
only jewel I could ever bring it is my
greatest love of you

A. W. Hart

The Heart Of A Poet

In comes a daydream in my mind's eye,
my heart feels the joy of happiness,
wherever love comes to stay today,
feeling all the words come to the poet,
his heart reveals a new experience,
all around our world hearts will beat
to seek the heart of a poet,
he starts his daily routine on a walk,
to stand in public places like a artist,
revealing his glorious dreams into words,
he knows about everyone in the street,
to start his ideas flowing like a stream,
he is a man with be gone like the west wind,
to be a poet it is only beginning to happen.
And so goes the heart of a clever poet.

Richard Chapman

My Psalm

Oh my Lord You've changed
My heart and life
You gave Your only son
As Your Holy sacrifice.

I'm Your servant do what you will
Because oh my Lord
I will fear no ill

Your glory is known throughout the land
For us to show love and compassion
For our fellow man

There's nothing to compare to the beauty of Your face
And when you reach out Your arms
Which are full of hope, love and grace.

Nick Conolly

Parents

I know of two people that are close to my heart,
my feelings for them will never depart,
they brought me up knowing what's right and what's wrong,
with the passing of time, my feelings grow strong.

I know they'll be there if I need them,
to comfort or give me advice,
to put my life into perspective,
is a thing that they're sure to devise.

Nothing compares to this couple,
they helped me grow honest and true,
to take my life as I find it,
is what I am going to do.

You should know to whom I'm referring,
that's the reason why I feel so glad,
to walk throughout all my life knowing,
that I love my mum and my dad.

Martin Booth

Despair

With hope and thought that wisdom taught
Might guide me through life's journey fraught
Then to end or to forever abort
This terminal thought I am nothing

At worthless and useless I am second to none
Battles for success never fought or won
So in my mind I remain this no one
With this terminal thought I am nothing

Surely I must be someone of worth
Weren't all men equal at their birth
My only answer is to add some mirth
To this terminal thought I am nothing

Paul Richard Gardner

The Hurricane Of 1987

I travelled o'er the Sussex Downs through villages and even towns
My eyes surveyed the awesome sight of trees lying dead, both left and right,
Like battle stories historians tell, the dead lay silent where they fell,
Trees that were so big and stout lay flattened useless all about,
Devastation of the woods where once majestic trees had stood,
Thousands of trees did fall in Sussex alone I do recall,
Once homes for birds and animals too, oxygen providers for me and you,
The Stein, Patcham and Chanctonbury Ring each a victim of this frightening thing,
Slates off roofs and houses down both in the country and in the town,
A wind so powerful that its wake made Earth tremble and people quake,
An act of GOD or maybe more, a certain warning we can't ignore,
Such chaos there for all to see, yet only GOD can make a tree.

Ronald John Buzzle

Why!

In days gone by
My dad and I
Walked woods, and leafy lanes

We gazed in awe
At birds that soar
Or smelly pigs, and horses manes

Our Sunday walk
Gave chance to talk
Of hopes, and dreams, and happenings to come

We didn't know
Life's tragic blow
Cut short our own children's future fun

Your quick demise
Brought darkened skies
Took years to realise extent of harm

My children too
Missed out on you
No walks, no baby pigs on farm
No granddad

S. D. Hallam

The Shopper

A feeling of dread has descended,
My cupboards are bare, yet again,
It's time to embark on the shopping,
Just the though of it is such a strain.

I try to establish a trolley,
And one without devious mind,
One grabs me and takes me to 'diary',
Where milk, or all things, I can't find!

At last I can head for the checkout,
My trolley I start to unload,
The cashier is merrily 'beeping',
Until there's a faulty bar-code!

While I am bagging my shopping,
Another fear enters my head,
Bad weather is forecast for tuesday,
I've forgotten the 10 leaves of bread!

To conclude, I'd like a kind fairy,
Who'd live in my cupboard for free,
And replenish my stock as it leaves me,
As reward, I'd invite her for tea.

F. Hammond-Kaines

Memories

We went for a walk with my mother,
My brother, my sister and me,
We strolled over the fields, and down shady lane,
And men were coal picking on the pit tips,
Hard dusty work, and the pickings were thin.
We turned to go home, and heard a voice,
Singing a lovely old song, and a little further we could see,

A young man resting on the stamp of a tree,
And by his side, a bag of coal,
Tied up and ready, for him to take home,
When you come to the end of a perfect
Day, and you sit all alone with your thoughts
The words faded away as we went home,
The words had a meaning of their own -
My father was killed down Morewoods pit,
In the year nineteen seventeen,
And in the pram, sat his little son
The child he had never seen,
Memories like this don't fade away
I'll remember it always, that rather sad day

M. Hemsley

Lament To Aids

What have I done that I have to pay?
Must I suffer so much, and die this way?
I wanted to show how much I cared;
But in showing my love, my life is not spared.

I thought that being faithful and true to one;
My life would be happy and full of fun.
But fate was cruel, from a one night stand;
It dealt me Aids from its wicked black hand.

Even though this stand was two years ago;
I should have thought first, I caused this woe!
If only I'd sense and used a french letter;
I'm sorry my love; I should have known better.

So if you don't want to end up like me,
Just think before sex, it's the way to be;
If only I could have used my head,
I wouldn't be dying, I'd be living instead.

M. Kennedy

She Said!

I know all about poor Mrs. Smith,
Mrs. Brown told me....
Her husband ran off with another man,
But I'm sworn to secrecy.
Well, what about Mrs. Phillips?
I really shouldn't say,
But did you know she slept with Pete,
When her husband was away.
Carol, now there's a one,
She's pregnant so I heard.
But don't you go saying I told you.
It's our secret... Mum's the word.
Anyway dear, it's lovely to see you,
Biscuit with your tea?
You look down in the dumps love,
In need of some sympathy.
Now then, what's your problem?
I promise I won't breathe a word,
I'm not like some of the women round here.
Who repeat everything they've heard. She said.

Lisa Polya

The Confused Teenager

I'm too old to act daft when I'm with my friends,
I'm too young to stay until parties end,
I'm too old to sulk or have a mild tantrum,
I'm too young to go out and have a bit of fun,
I'm too old to rely on everyone else,
I'm too young to be allowed to look after myself,
　But one thing I just don't get,
is I'm too old one minute then too young the next!

Rebecca Redfern-Mason

He's Not A Drunk

He sips on a beer in the bar room,
His eyes don't sparkle no more.
The life that he loved has no meaning -
He just stares at the bar room floor.
His world is where he is sitting
With a glass that is cupped in his hand,
Sipping as if there's no tomorrow
With his problems only he understands.
People watch him and nudge each other,
Why you can even read their minds:
"He's a drunk", that's what they are thinking
People can be so unkind!
People don't care when they don't suffer,
They are not really in touch,
It's easy to criticize another
When you haven't suffered enough.
He's not a drunk 'cause he's drinking,
He's not a drunk 'cause he's there
He's just drowning his sorrows -
'Cause he's got no one who really cares.

Julian Alan Snaize

Untitled

Time - like the winged beat of butterflies wings
moves fast,
don't waste it.

Words, like the breath of life
once used
cannot be taken back.

Love uses time and words
and stays forever
unless time squanders love
and words destroy it.

But love, when true and deep
can encompass all that time may send
and words can repair and revive the joy
committing the sadness and despair of loss
to experience.

The beauty then of love
can be in the eye of the beholder
for the heart - although unseen
beats fast
like butterflies' wings.
Patricia Allen

The Fairy Ring

Did you ever see a fairy ring upon the
mountain high, with all the little folk
a-singing as flames rise to the sky. From
midnight to the morning you can hear them
sing and dance and if you want to tag along
come on for now your chance. They're a wonder
of this world the like you've never seen, all
dressed in little costumes of mostly emerald
green. Upon a toad-stool sitting so grand
is the Queen of the little people. The fairy
Queen of all the land and by her sides are
fairies at hand. As the hours go by the
night deepens, magic is shown when
ones are sleeping some magic lost and
some magic found and even some fairies
act the clown. As morning comes with a
heavy flow there are only ashes left
to show you can hear a whisper in
the wind saying this is the fairy ring.
Peter McAnulty

The Anagram of Life

Life is a broken glass sitting in a cupboard,
Life is a tear cascading to the floor,
Life is a letter that's never been written,
Life is a spec of dirt in the old man's pore.
Life is an experiment still sitting in a test tube,
Life is a doll with a sewn on smile,
Life is a painting that is fading in the attic,
We were born to die said the creator of it all.
Karen Elizabeth Warbey

Memories

Memories are part of our life locked in our minds yes good or bad.
Memories bring back the sad days but also the days we were glad
Memories are something we all retain within our very own world
Memories will visit us often seemingly when things seem to
    be in a whirl
Memories can recall the best of things for making the bad seem good.
Memories you know you can never change or wouldn't if you could
Memories of people and friends who perhaps are gone for evermore
Memories such as these we keep for they've only passed
    through a special door
Memories are a possession you keep sometimes under lock and key
Memories that you yourself alone disturb when no one else may see
Memories are of time gone by fleeting as time often may seem
Memories are the one thing which can make reality seem only a dream
Memories are kept by everyone yes everyone in the world
    don't you know
Memories are many in a lifetime keep them don't ever let them go.
Robert Tate

The Owl

In the middle of a cornfield,
moonlight bathes an old oak tree,
high up in the leafy branches,
sits an owl so patiently.

Far below the corn is stirring,
something moving stealthily,
an ear of corn bends over slightly,
a mouse appears so timidly.

The owl detects the meagre movement,
spreads his wings and dives with grace,
not a sound is made whilst travelling,
down he falls with talons braced.

The mouse feels cool air wash around him,
tries to flee but is to late,
darkness wraps its cloak about him,
hesitation seals his fate.

As owl takes off from corn now trampled,
light breaks slowly from the east,
lands upon his perch on oak tree,
then begins his lifeless feast...
T. P. Acock

The Truth

The past enters the future
missing the present -
The Truth, traverses through to reach
nowhere, like the wishes of a poor child

Born together, human bodies disguised
as The Truth but, become non-existent
like the clouds in the sky
with subtle waves of death

Each human body and its pain blends with
many others with an unknown influence
but the Truth ventures to escape
from this cynical physicism

How far one can go without a thought
of hope carrying tempestuous wishes
away from the egoist self
awaiting - Eternal Peace

On a corolla, a dew drop hopes for the
first sun-ray a golden ray strikes the dew
It scintillates like a diamond
But, dew can never be diamond
Kumar Ashok

My Llan

When I walk around my Llan. I'm also looking for a plan.
Meadow St., perhaps meadow vein,
Railway St. is just the same.
Partridge Rd. is a name by then Jones has an equal claim to fame.
For Cae-Flein St. I've searched in vain, but then my Welsh
    was never very good
Some say it means a mill or wood.
As I walk up Walpole hill to bathe in the sunlight and stand still,
The Rugby Club they say is a must but then I only want to
    catch a bus.
Commercial Road is for shopping but then I rarely feel like stopping.
The High St. is the place to be
The Top Hotel, well, it's not for me.
In the central they say the beer is free but they charged me
    one pound forty three!
Someone said "go down the 'Stute" but that's for the more acute
The Con Club tote is very good,
I think I'll take a walk down the wood.
The royal oak is not far down
But then it is a little out of town.
No, I know the place I'd rather be.
It's in the park by the old oak tree.
When I die I'll make this prayer, that my old bones are buried there.
Ron Selway

Happenings

My legs start shaking, my body goes cold. It's moving towards me slowly but bold. Footsteps behind me there all around, I try to shout help but can't make a sound, they grab me and suddenly everything's clear, drained from my body there's no longer fear. I rise upwards my mind goes blank, I no longer have feelings my consciousness sank.

I open my eyes to bright lights and beings, poking me, observing me, they have no feelings. As a different species they want to know more, my functions my thoughts deep inside to the core, I scream with pain as they play with my life, they smirk and chatter as they trifle. They no longer need me. They've discovered why, humans thoughts are amazing till they die, as even themselves don't know what's going on in their head, or why sometimes they feel low and tears are shed. I'm back home now everything's all right, but I feel changed and can see a new light. My heart sinks despite everything I've learned, my mind goes crazy, my insides feel burnt, I'm going to leave this world for good, I'd stay here if only I could. I climb the rail and let myself drop, I no longer exist, I'm nothing yet I rise to the top.

B. Evans

Tormented Mind!

His soul and spirit are exhausting and no one knows the way to help?
May the good Lord be with you Dan, and may your sleep
to filled with sweet dreams and most of all the calmness
be peace itself and the quietness of silence and the
solitude of safety.

Whilst your eyes are closed tight and your mind
in a drift and your body so vulnerable lying there still.
May your dreams be in flight of a beauty and sweetness
you look for or maybe a dream to conquer the dark
things and the battle be ended.

Because the strength you have needed and the
courage displayed is for no man to fault and no man
to say, you have given your best and carry on so. For
this journey in darkness is only a test.
Fear of sleep!

Larraine Simpson

Norma Jean

Born into a world full of passion and desire,
matriarchal links of fears and schizophrenia.
Patriarchal links will remain unknown,
by the environment in which she lived, sadly she was overthrown.

Taken from one home to another
far away from her natural mother.

Loved and adored by many men,
admired and envied by many women.

White House links were a mystery,
and began to strengthen in 1960.

Schizophrenia was setting in,
barbiturates were crammed within,
was it suicide, or was it murder?
It's a terrible tragedy, we never heard her......

Sally Ward

Docklands Diary

A few years ago in our docklands 'twas!
Many a man who lent a hand.
The liners they came in with glee,
Plenty of work for shipwrights to be.
The sailors they would come ashore,
All in the pubs! Still room for more.
How happy then our little town,
It seemed then that no-one wore a frown.
Up swung the bridges! A banana boat through,
I think blue star line has one due,
The docks have gone now, and time has passed,
An airport is built now, watch Dash 7 fly past.
It's all in our history and change is a must.
The glory of Docklands, forever we trust!

Pat Bredee

Children

The joy they bring out ways the loss, of more
   material things.
I'd never trade my children for necklaces
   and rings.
I'd hate to be without them, although at
   times I think
their little temper tantrums, could drive
   me to drink!
But when they come and cuddle me, they
   cheer me up no end.
So I soon forget the day before, when I
   nearly went round the bend.
Their little jokes and sayings, really make
   you want to smile.
Their tricks with rubber spiders, make you
   want to run a mile.
But all in all, the love they give, means
   a whole lot more,
than whether or not, you have got that
   trendy new front door!

Tracy Woodcraft

Spring

Golden sunlight streaming through the window
Marks the newborn day.
The birdsong and the cool refreshing breeze
Inspires new life to take its hold
On land relinquished but of late
From nature's grip of frost and snow.

New wood replacing the dead wood of old:
Strong overcoming weak.
Seen only are the sprouting bulbs,
Not dying trees that once were grand
And now no more than twisted boughs
Which ne'er again shall see blue skies.

For so many years those titans strove
To stay alive:
Battled with gale and tempest strong
To give cool shade on summer days.
And what reward for noble toils?
To be ignored for daffodils!

Kathleen Larkin

Music

Listen to the music
Listen loud and clear
Although it may be song you don't want to hear
Let the music touch your spirit
Let it find the love inside you
Let it grow and become true
Give it to others
Let them find the love inside
As you did too.

Sarah Massey

Advancing Years

My face is wrinkled, legs are bent
Many a day is gone and spent
Yet inside I still feel young and fair
With lots of love to give and share

I sit on the benches in the parks
Watching the youngsters up to their larks
They laugh and shout and are very gay
I remember my youth as if yesterday

When my grandchildren come to tea
They like to hear stories of the younger me
The fashions, the times and about the War
Photograph albums, what I remember and sew

We have crumpets, toast and cake
These are the things I still like to make
I can manage the gardening, I knit and sow
I may be doddery and old, but still a person, you know.

Marion Bicknell

Flanders' Fields

In Flanders' fields where the poppies grow.
Many feet marched to battle a long time ago.
They fought a war, land gained and lost,
Not comprehending the terrible cost.
Seventy-eight years on from the end of the war
Yet in that time we've seen lots more
Of wasted lives, sacrificed in vain,
Marching to battle, never seen again.
We see the wounds in people and land,
Hoping then we'll all understand
Why it happened, for what they fought
And this is why we should give a thought
For the rows of graves all around,
The plaques for the bodies claimed by the ground.
For there, in Flanders' fields, where the poppies grow,
Where feet marched to battle a long time ago
Lie the memories of the 'Great War'
The likes of such never seen before.
The men, the boys defending what's right
Going to battle, to join the fight.
Kedra Goodall

Welsh Love Spoons

A sycamore branch, a carpenter's skill
Love of life, pinch of God's will
A chip perhaps from Cupid's bow
Or Ancient yew in September blow.

Daffodils for Gran at retirement time
Single rose for a true Valentine
Hearts of oak for a loving wife
Many such spoons portray natural life.

Lovelorn sailor whittling a special spoon
Proposal of marriage under silvery moon
Little Welsh lady dons hat and shawl
Carved leaves captures Autumn fall.

Live in a palace or a tiny house
Be a princess or a country mouse.
Discover Welsh treasure near castle of old
Unique love spoons a sight to behold.
Raymond H. Povey

Gone

Those country walks, Sunday afternoon
Love's road ran its course but ended too soon
Long lazy strolls on a sun bleached shore
Endless sand castles that are no more.
Cease, the flowers and candle lit dinners
That's yesterday, and for the beginners
Cease, the full moon, glistening over the sea
Gone are the days when it was "Just you and me".
The old photograph still staring at me
Are they so heartless, can they nor see?
The charr'd orange fire burns, into the night
No more love struggles, there's no one to fight.
The thoughts come back at the end of the evening
It's all over now, just love lies bleeding.
Philip Robert Wright

Untitled

In London town I roam
Lost and far from home
Rows of houses and towering places
Smog and fog and strange faces.

Cars and Lorries in long files
Stretching for a hundred miles
People rushing bustling around
Almost knocking me to the ground.

How I yearn for the green grass of home
With valleys and mountains to freely roam
With cosy houses and happy places
With helping hands and kind faces.
Rhoda Fletcher

Ecstasy?

A life,
lived to the full, on the edge.
Every moment savoured, precious - lived.

Ecstasy?
'An exalted state', the dictionary defines.

A death,
terrifying, painful - pointless.
No more precious moments to savour.

The definition is false - a deceiver.
Ecstasy?
'Waste of a life.'
Rita Darby

Bircham Riversed Sunset

Looking out of my window high and across the fields to where
    you are lovely bright pink lily grey blue sky
Amazement and wonder as I stand graze
At your far setting sun how beautiful you are
Beautiful Bircham Riverbed Sunset
In wonder I stare never seen such beauty only you so fair
Towards the twistening narrowing roads I roam toward your
setting sun
In cold winter's afternoon I hear you cry lovely riverbed sunset
Beside the holy hedge I spy flutter of wings as I pass by
Across the fields I ride on a early winter's night
In the furrows across the sunset for all to see I gallop
Towards your sails Bircham Mill I ride.
In early evening listening to the wind driving your sails as I
gallop by
Faster faster no further now I roam
As you lovely pink lilac grey blue sky has gone
    Gone disappeared for a while only to return next evening
Katherine Hatham

Feelings

Love me forever,
love me true,
love me and hold me so.
You never seem to understand,
that I'll always love you more.

If you do all of these things,
my heart will simply glow.
And when it does,
I'll make sure that you will know.

You see my world can never be perfect,
without you here with me.
My heart will collapse without your love,
and I'll suffer for eternity.
All you need to do is,
love me forever,
love me true,
love me and hold me so,
and I'll always be here with you.
Mary Davidson

Snake

You slimy snake, I've heard them say.
Look how he stares, bewitching his prey.
Shedding skin, disgusting,
Squeezing life out of his victim.

But don't they stare,
Confronting others as in a dare,
And don't they throw their skin away,
In bits and pieces, I must say,
And don't they squeeze the life from others,
To get on top and sod their brothers.

So tell me, tell me, tell me do,
Who is the snake, is it me or you?
It's my name, I was made this way,
Human snakes, excuses,
No way!
Susan J. MacDonald

The Signs Of Time

I bring you the sign - knowledge is mine
In your solar system - last for the requiem
My rainbow is disappearing - my signs are appearing
Deep from my heart - you are tearing apart

I bring you the sign so you can be fine
Flood and drought - still you have doubt
Changed in the seasons you don't seem to respond
Killing the atmosphere to make me suffer

I bring you the sign to save all living kinds
In your cornfields I have placed my rings
I melted your ices, tightened your vices
Burning everything on site - a hole in my side

I have given you the sign before you put end in time
I will not tolerate you must co-operate
I am the nature I am life and future
The destruction you bring a new world will sing

The sign of time from the one that shines
My signs are clear, it is to be feared
I will not receive those who deceive
I will bring new creation with more appreciation

J. M. Noël-Céphise

Sweet Little Angel

Sweet little angel, you make life bright
lift up our hearts, keep us in light
From the smile on your face to the tip of your wing
you bring beauty from heaven to make the earth sing

Magnificent love, sweet smile, such grace
dreams can't imagine such a precious place
Your kiss, your touch, the light in your eyes
bring love to life if the earth gently cries

Give us strength to have faith, hope and charity
show us the peace in vision and majesty
Join our hands, walk with us always
one sweet caress brightens the darkest of days

Touch our hearts, let our lives be content
angels turn the tide of bitter lament
Love burns so bright it lights the night skies
waking pleasure within like an eternal sunrise

Thank you for helping us with things that are seen
from your celestial life in the infinite unseen
Come and be with us making all things bright
enter our hearts so we may be in the light

Tim Carter

Invisible Wings

Sometimes, for no apparent reason
    Life is good.
On these sweet occasions, I peer into the mirror,
An Angel peers back, radiating heavenly glow.

She's not just content with what she's got
She loves herself for what she is,
    different, special, unique, alive.
Her faults are perfections, an artist's gently brushed signature
    on a painting of exquisite beauty.

She sees these perfections in others and loves them for what
    they are, each different person shining their own light.
Shimmering stars lighting a heaven on earth.

As if she is seeing the world through sky tinted, crystalline glasses
    She notices how wonderful this world is,
the trees, the earth, the soil, the air,
the houses, the road signs, the factories, the lights.

Every sound she hears is God's sweet music
I can live, I can breathe and, on occasions,
I could take of, beating invisible wings.

I thank the angel that lives within, and the spirit above.

Sarah Palmer

Our House It's Home

This is a house of great repute.
Lots of activity comes from here.

There's a son so active in sporting activities,
never still it's much his head doesn't spin,
with sparks flying from his chin.

There's a daughter, comes back and forth,
for she is at college you see,
in the dance world is she,
the theatre type you know.

Myself well, that's a different story,
Sketches and Paintings and Poetry too.
Very different from my two offsprings.
As you can see.

We all come together every now and then,
have a chuckle, a laugh and finally a big grin,
as we talk of our activities and where we have been.

Sometimes we laugh, sometimes we cry,
but the main thing Lord we are happy because we are a family.

Valerie Groom

The Accident

A dog wandered in the crowded street.
Lost by his master, who had turned to greet
A neighbour, and pass the time of day.
While the dog unnoticed slipped away.
Now on his own havoc began.
First he walked, then he ran.
Crossed the road, crash and bang
Went the car, bus and van.
Children spotted him go by
Nose to ground, tail held high.
The chase was on, he must be caught
then the owner would be sought.
But the master closed his door
The wretched animal lived there no more.
Unaware of his plight, he who'd had a nasty fright
Ran for home, but was turned away
Making yet another stray.

R. Cocker

Glimmer of Winter

I looked above the pale sky
Little birds were flying by
The snow was gently floating down
So bright like diamonds on a gown
Trees so still, like they were sleeping
Children playing, hiding and peeping
Around the garden they did run
Laughing, giggling and having fun
The light was slowly fading fast
Alas the day had nearly past.
Tomorrow comes and then we wake
Another day begins to break.
The rain was pouring down so fast
So sad, so cold it should not last
Daylight fading, darkness looms
Lights go out in all the rooms.

Lynne Ridge

The Daisies

Take time to look at the daisies
Like stars in a carpet of green
In the rush of life you pass them by
A beautiful sight unseen.

Take time to look at the daisies
They are a sign of spring
Of hope that springs eternal in the breast of everything
This tiny flower again and again appears every year for our pleasure.
In the bustle of life we pass them by we have no time for leisure
But take time to look at the daisies a minute is all it will take
Your heart will be lighter, your future seems brighter
You'll be glad you've taken the break.

M. J. Barron

The Mighty Seas

The waves menacingly towered and crashed, like snow-capped mountains. Lashing the deck, and leaving the scuppers like frothy champagne fountains. The briny unmercifully battered the hull, the timbers warped, the sails were full, the yardarms heaved and creaked. "The wind it blew" growled and shrieked. The crew scurried through rigging, across decks, "brave and bold", hands and face blue, bodies cold! Hair and ears salty, lips cracked, eyes stinging red, best be alive than dead!

Alas the mighty swell didn't abate, and the bosun yelled to the mate Rocks ahead on the port bow, "Abandon ship, and save yourself now!" The ship was blown to her grief, and torn apart on the black reef. The cold swirling water swamped the wreck, crew jumped from the tilting deck. Only the guardian of the deep, will know the fate of the boson and the mate.

The lifeboats were lowered, rafts afloat, as the crew escapes the stricken boat. The once fine ship was holed stem to stern, timber cracked, wires parted "and this was the sea just getting started!", booms swayed, ropes untwined, the wind blew, howled and whined, yardarms gave way and slipped, sodden canvas was all ripped, masts fell one by one. The proud vessel's power had all but gone, she was now just a shell, and would be joining her crew....in a watery cold dark hell.

She finally eased from the bank, and nosed her way as she sank, toward the kingdom and king they would meet, crew and ship, 'now part of Neptune's fleet'!!.
Michael William Campbell Henny

Perfection

I saw you again today
looking beautiful as always
nothing can described the way I feel
sometimes happy, sometimes sad
but I'm lost without a cause

When I hear your name my heart beats faster
I feel like exploding, my emotions care
going hay wire
Please God, another night, another time
another place

Why does it have to be me, led like a
lamb to the slaughter
trust me to look into your eyes
oh those eyes, those deep dark eyes
go ahead discover me

You look so lonely standing there
all, alone in this world with no one
to acknowledge you
come with me, I'll keep you warm
for you are my perfection!
Michelle Yardley

Nightmares

Stumble upstairs worn out and weary
Look back on the day, God it was dreary
Sink into sleep, the nightmares begin
Hugh menacing figures all black as sin
Pursuing unceasingly - too tired to care
Bright scarlet flashes entwined in their hair
Running and running over plains dark and drear
Figures cowering and screaming, oh why am I here
I try to wake up but to no great avail
But hope beats more strongly as I seem to prevail
A heavenly blue light appears 'fore my eyes
And a soft golden glow - is this paradise?
I feel I am worthy that I can be saved
From the frights and uncertainties my mind is enslaved
Wake up with a start look around with relief
Perhaps life's not too bad and not too much grief
To go on with routine and just do one's best
I am in this world along with the rest
There must be a future of hope and release
Turn over and go back to sleep now at peace
S. Sweetenham

Together

Gentle sweet sparrow lay in my arms
Let me caress you with my peaceful charm
let's fly with the wind, on clods that knows no storm
and reach for the place that know no harm
with the gaiety of butterflies spreading it decorated wings
our laughter will identify with the same sweet theme
And once in a while we will swim to the bottom of the ocean
relax peacefully with the community
and find that place where our difference share a sameness
peacefully, respectfully at one.
J. M. J. Matreaux

Hopeful Or Hopeless

Faith and trust, love and lust,
Living and giving, fear and forgiving,
Hope and despair, they are all there.
Is there no one to share, the dreams I have,
To see the fields and feel the grass,
to fly in the sky, before I die.
I must not give in, the strength to win,
I must hold on tight, to keep the insight on the miracle of life.
To overcome the strife, to throw away this cluttered mind,
to help the heal the sorrow of Mankind.
If only one can pass on hope,
to cut away the binding rope,
To throw our arms up in the air,
to shout out loud how much we care.
If only I can pass on love, this world and the next will be above
The little narrow minded souls, who keeps us down, because
they know that life will never be the same.
And some still want to play the game.
If only I can rise above and show my love, then there is HOPE for all of us.
Kate Bevan

Tribute To Time

The older I get the move I realise,
    Life is too good to waste,
Good times and bad should be noted,
    Always to your advance in knowledge and wisdom.

The more I blink the more memories seem to fade,
    But the ones I remember I will never regret,
The playfulness as a child,
    The prize on an adult,
The peace and happiness as I grow old.

The wisdom I have been given
    From parents, grandparents and friends,
Is a priceless gift of a valuable sort,

    It would be wasted if not passed on,
To the zealous but unwise youth of today.
T. Rhodes

'Hopefools'

Unemployment's a name, causing Heartbreak and Pain
Makes all type of workers face invisible strain
Creates misery and strife through all walks of life
Cuts deep into families like a sharp knife
The Mortgage is smaller now but too far to go
How about the next payment? I'm afraid I don't know
Your house will be safe, suited men have confirmed
Employment prospects better now so don't be concerned
In a month or two we'll have covered the debt
Sleeping better at night, credit easier to get
Re-training courses are good, keeping Dole figures low
Obtaining new skills, still nowhere to go
Things are getting better, Government Ministers stress
But 'Feet on the Floor' people know we're in a mess
The workload is less for Electronic Devices
No toilet breaks needed, no lateness, no crisis
Computers, the Robots and power that they need
May also run short and not supersede
So the Mechanical Workers and Human Androids
Will have no work to do and become Unemployed
Mick E. Baker

To The Love Who Will Never Be Mine!

As I sit here, and the candle is flickering
like the sound of a humming bee,
my thoughts wander back, but all I can hear
is the flickering of a Humming Bee,
I try to place my thoughts and keep them all in tow,
but the flickering distracts me so!

My love has left yet once again,
but my thoughts are still distracting me so,
why do I let my thoughts tow, with my emotions so?
Is it because my love has left me so?

My hopes and dreams are yet so far away,
but my heart tells me that the ocean is not too deep,
and the sun is not too far away.

So why are my dreams yet so far,
when all I have to do is leave my emotions with the
sound of the humming bee.

Sandra Marsden

Oh Little One

Oh little one, run and play, while you can.
Long may your innocence and laughter fill my head up again,
Oh little one, run and play, while you can.

Oh little one, you love all that you can,
As long as you love anybody you'll be everybody's friend,
Oh little one, you love all, that you can.

For little one, you'll soon be gone,
And then you'll notice all the bad things going on.
So little one, you have your fun,
For soon you will be older,
Maybe you'll become a soldier,
Playing games that make us colder, little one.

Oh little one, stay as young as you can,
May your sweet ignorance and love fill my head up again,
Oh little one, stay as young as you can.

So take your time, little one, take your time,
And I just hope and pray, you will stay as you are today,
So take your time, little one, take your time.

R. Berritta

Peace Of Mind

Why don't you sit awhile, and still your mind,
Let go all those problems, so that you can unwind,
Favourite music for some, is one way to start,
Especially if it penetrates, deep within your heart,
For others poetry, may fill that need,
Relieving that tension, that may truly lead,
To heartfelt peace, deep within your being,
Compassion and love, you'll soon be freeing,
Pleasant thoughts of happiness, in days that have past,
Return to the conscious mind, from deep within they'd been cast,
Childhood memories that were happy, and free from sorrow,
So start today, do not leave, to the morrow.

A. L. Toon

Winter

Pretty snowflakes rushing past
Lifted by the howling winds
Swirling twirling dancing madly
Lying deep like glistening sand

Snowmen, sledges, frozen hands
Just watch the children playing
Laughing crying screaming shouting
Oh happy wonderland

Huddled in the frozen bushes
Beady eyes alert
Robin Redbreast looks for some kind soul
To feed him bread of life

But all he sees are pretty snowflakes
Swirling, twirling, dancing madly past.

P. M. Garner

The Four Seasons Of Life

When we are born, it is the Spring of life,
Like new leaves on the trees, and flowers are rife,
The gentle hum of the bees, birds sing their songs,
Carefree days, no thoughts of rights or wrongs.

Come the Summer of life, we are growing up to be,
Who knows what or where we will be
We play and learn, and enjoy our life,
But sometimes find, there can be trouble and strife.

The years of Autumn, bring to mind, we are Older, Wiser, more Kind,
Remembering our younger days, going through each different phase,
Now, we find there can be Laughter and Tears,
As we face up to our Adult years.

It is Winter now and time to see, how our life turned out to be,
Has it been Bad? Has it been Good? We cannot change now,
We did what we could, to do the right things,
But somehow the Seasons passed by on wings.

Margaret Brocklesby

The Photograph

Reminiscence stirs when this, your image, calls
Like muffled fanfare for a ghost returned
To attic souvenirs; its shade enthrals:
Dust filtered Sun illumines past still yearned.
Soft as snowflakes in ethereal dance,
That gently thrill upon the slightest touch,
Your memories within me still entrance
Emotions that have always meant so much.

Days, long with happiness and future's hope,
Fulfilling by the challenges achieved,
Still echo now their friendship's laughter:
As if they would to present time elope.
Here they intertwine,
        within my psyche weaved:
A precious pulse,
    to warm me,
        ever after.

Wilfred Gaunt

Memories

Memories are precious things,
Like jewels in a crown,
Some you remember with smile.
Others with a frown.
These memories belong to you,
And no one else can know.
The joy and sadness that they bring.
For over many years, you'll find they always cling.
So don't try to forget them,
They'll help you through the years,
Not only with the laughter,
But also with the tears.

C. J. Maunders

Deserted Wife

My mind turns and turns, my thoughts dart and run
Like a terrified child lost in the crowd.
Why has he done this - taken the light and the sun,
Leaving me whisp'ring his name out aloud?

His past was my past, and our present a plateau serene,
Our future a prospect warming my hopes and my heart,
Now it seems that past decades never have been,
The future's a blank, in which he'll play no part.

How can two lives, intertwined close for so long,
Be rent by one's whim to go free?
How can two voices, long joined in one song,
Suddenly seem pitched right off key?

I will silence my voice with its out-of-tune note,
Hide my thoughts and my hurt and my pain,
Let him sing the new song which someone else wrote,
Whilst I pray for our music to start up again.

Marian Cull

Darkness

Oh darkness, darkness fills the streets,
Like a big black curtain covering our eyes for sleep.
With shadows to match,
It makes a horror film scene,
With tall black trees
In long black gardens,
It isn't the perfect place to be.
All alone people walk the streets
No laughter like in the daytime,
When the sun makes us smile.
Even flowers go to sleep,
Waiting for the morning's rise,
When they can bloom and stretch free.
Oh darkness, darkness is everywhere,
The streets look so bare,
No cars roar up and down,
No birds whistle their perfect tune.
Only bats flutter at night,
And the stars twinkle,
And the moon shines its very little reflected light.
Kimberley Johnson

My Disability

Being disabled is a bitch,
Life's so hard it's like an itch,
You know the type the one you can't scratch,
You have to put up with,
But it drives you mad.

Sometimes there's a problem there,
Especially when people stand and stare,
Or talk to you as though you have no brain,
But their the ones that are insane,
But these things I can put up with though.

But I tell you what upsets me the most,
The thought of my disability getting worse,
And wondering what my future holds,
Please O Lord listen to my prayer,
And make my disability disappear.
Sean Ward

Loneliness

Loneliness pervades your soul.
Life's outward semblance lies constantly,
Smiling fixedly on the world outside
Showing to the unseeing multitude none of its reality.

The door that seals the outside from the home
Is never as unyielding as soul's loneliness -
It opens often at bell's command,
While the shutters and bars of loneliness tighten their stranglehold.

Polite nonentities hide the cavern
That sometimes friendship bridges,
Simulating normality of love and fellowship
Banned by loneliness from the soul's dwelling.

Crying silently, smothering, whimpering so none should know.
Desperate to appear as others appear - together, soul-mated.
Shrinking with time, love blossomless,
The invading stone overwhelming.
Sadie Dray

(Sweet) Valentine

Take my hand,
Lead the way,
Through fields of green,
At break of day,
Where bluebells and buttercups bloom,
Trees flourish and streams gently flow,
And beauty; like love, doth grow,
Walk with me,
Come steal my heart,
Be mine,
My Sweet Valentine.
Tracey Wiggins

Delusion

Close the door softly, tread light when you leave
Lest my heart hear you and cruelly grieve.
The fire burning bright would seek only to die
Expire in your breath, should you whisper goodbye.
Cold grows the cinder with its bright flame fled
Cold grows the hearth with its fire spent and dead
Ashes and dreams mourn in gossamer grey
One careless breath blows them swiftly away.
Cold grows the heart when its dreams are all gone
Cold grows the spirit when hope there is none
One tiny dream is a magical thing
One tiny hope is a cold winter's spring.
Close the door softly, tread light when you leave
Let me pretend, let my heart make believe
Close the door softly, breathe not a word
Leave me the firelight — dreams undisturbed.
L. Duncan

Yesterday's Dream

I dare not love,
Lest love depart.
I loved but once,
I gave my heart.
Now he is gone.
And I'm alone
Those happy years
That haunt my dreams.
Now happiness evades it seems.
I smile, but in my heart the tears.
How will I fill the lonely years.
I'll talk to God,
I know he's there.
Who else will listen to my prayer.
Oh! God help me to carry on,
When all my friends their roads have gone
I won't be bitter.
I won't be sad.
I'll just thank God
For what I had.
M. Rowney

Young At Heart

Planted in a row so strait
just inside the garden gate
next the carrots, and the beans
pray behold the winter greens
came the summer's awful drought
dried the garden plants right out
can't use hose, and butt's gone dry
save all water got to try.
Now comes winter veg is scarce
greens are brought into the house
strip off outer leaves so tough
here's another well have enough
Pull the blooming things apart.
You'll find the cabbage is young at heart.
Margaret Vinal-Burnett

Abydos

Black eyes watching, land of the Khem
Khem as mud, Khem as raven
Eyes can see to the very heart, the very depth of your soul
Amidst the bile and putridness you call love
I know what it is you are
And it is not as you think
You are no better than I for all your civilisation,
For all your wealth and compassion
Time after time you stare at the carcass
Trying to feel for the life that once was.
Fool, you cannot get life from bones, only the blood,
And that has long since gone,
Sunk like the rest into the sand
Or torn apart by the savage jaws of the wind.
Go home to your comforts and to your own time
For that is where the answer lies.
In life never in death.
Kitty McCormick

To An Artist

You lose yourself in your paints and oils,
Leaving behind the world's cares and toils,
Wandering among life's lovely things,
With a flick of your brush, like magic springs,
The house on the hill by a tumbling stream,
Where the willow weep and the gnarled oaks lean,
Under a dappled summer sky,
To entrance the heart and please the eye,
Butterflies dancing on gossamer wings,
Over the flowers as a blackbird sings
Down in the garden in the still and hush,
These are the pictures that drip from your brush,
Black on the skyline, like etchings they stand,
Pines in the dusk from the painter's hand,
Dresses of satin and silk and lace,
The character seen in a careworn face,
All are set down on your canvas there,
Portraits and scenes on life's thoroughfare,
There's little difference 'twixt you and me,
For I paint my picture with words you see.

Ruby A. Houghton

Metamorphosis

Silence,
Like no man could disturb.
Two contrasts, available to one's eyes

It's the grass with a blanket of white,
The multicoloured sun,
The jean blue sky.

Abandoned flags, In corners no more.
A perfect oak.

Its treasures far and wide
Birds playing games,
Around the pale goal posts.

Rejected shoes homeless at dawn.
The plague of frost,
On the tennis courts, fields and cars.

The grand pavilion, Inviting new wood,
But not frost.

Suddenly, silence attacked,
Bright young boys attack,

Silence falls, silence defeated
Metamorphosis

William Sparks

Beginning And End

Naked we come into this world if we are wanted or not
Later we are washed weighed clothed and fed then we are
    placed in a cot
We go to our schools learn all the rules we are supposed to obey
We all carry on not knowing why, not even sure of the way

Most of us work earning our keep whether we want to or not
Some have no need because they are rich others just don't
    give a jot

We who are left to live out our days grow weaker and slower
    some get so grey
We still carry on not knowing why and still not sure of the way
All this life we spent on this earth we have just had a lend
Surely a force though we don't know the source is guiding
    our lives to the end
And what we call our souls will find other schools
With rules we all will obey then we'll still carry on knowing just why
And being quite sure of the way

And if after death there's a heaven with angels and trumpets galore
We'll all be happy to be there and greet these who've gone on
before a price

A. L. Price

The Steam Express 1946

The steam express has signed its name.
Indelibly etched upon my brain.
In coal and ash and steam and dust.
I went too near as others must.
I gripped grass stubble with all my might
As the steam express burst through the night.
Oh holy smoke, oh holy hell,
Oh holy flaming macker-el.

Thomas A. Liddell

Autumn

"Oh for Autumn"
Leaves lifting and hurling in the air.
Trees winding with strong gusts of winds
Leaving all the trees looking weary and bare.

The golden hue of tranquil scenes
bearing fruits and berries
Providing food for the birds
On their long journeys far away to warmer parts.
For those who are hibernating in woodland parts.

Soon it will be desolate and bare
With beaches becoming barren,
Only the sounds of the crashing of waves and howling winds.
Birds upon the rocks looking for food
The seals barking and looking for their mothers
to provide them with their rich milk.
So they too can be strong.
To be ready for the harsh winter
Now Autumn ends.

Lilian Haycock

A Feathered Friend

There in the silver and chrome
Lay a lifeless and friendless body
Of snowy white feathers, claws clinched
Straight as an arrow
That will not fly to freedom any more.
Head slides side to side
Picked out of the silver and chrome
Hole dug deep a place for her to sleep
Encircled in flowers
Rest in peace snowy.
The sun shines the birds sing
The day is new when your mind thinks of many things
Of cowslip and heather, and country walks.
The sheep lambing the cows for milking.
The chatter of the farmers as they talk
The clucking hens the snorting pigs horses nay the dogs bark
The chickens hatching, the linnet, and lark
The wheat and chaff blowing in the wind
All these things on a summer day we thank you Lord as we pray.

B. J. Arnott

How Many Ways

How do I love Thee,
Let me count the ways.
With my hands, closed together
When I pray.
With my lips as I speak
Your words.
With my eyes as I see the beauty,
of the world you have given to me.
With my feet, to follow your footsteps
up the path of peace.
With the heart, as it opens fully
to receive your love.
With my mind, seeking to find Thee.
With my body, willing to come to Thee.
With my soul, the love cannot be
counted in numbers,
For I will give my all.

P. Cornish

Untitled

All my love is all I have to give to you.
It's now or never
For us to see that this lie we live will not last
forever.
Let me go
let us go
go back to where we were.
To the love we had
my love is all I have to give to you.
Patricia Wyatt

Do We

Do we? Do we remember them - I think not.
Keen, fresh-faced, eager young blades; innocent wide-eyed country boys
More at home with a plough than a sword. Do we remember or do we forget? I can't begin to understand what it must have been like...
I wasn't born. I can't remember... You must remember! Please do and don't forget.

These young bloods and wide boys - brothers, lovers, sons, husbands. Gone one day, some never to return. What of them now - do we remember
I think not. A blurred photograph, a distant memory, of what? For what? For honour - I think not. For duty - whose duty?
For God did not decide or want that man would fight with man for want of whatever reason powers that be decide or not, what will be will be.

Whatever became of the eager young blades, the wide-eyed boys from the country lanes?
They died my dear friend, they died in their hundreds... And thousands... And millions... For what you may ask, what possible reason? No reason on earth can give us the answer.
The grim stark reality of human endurance that makes us go on.
War my dear friend is a blight on our landscape and we shall grow old. But not them the departed. Do we remember them - Do we?
Wilma Cairns

Resolute Urgency

Find a truth for which you can live and die
It's not possible, there are too many lies.

Hold bitterness, suffer nothingness
Anxiety knocks at your door
Humanity leads to rejection.

Declare the death of God
You only declare the death of yourself
And hold dreams, shattered pieces of troubled sleep.

Abandon your convictions
They are lost and no one knows where forgotten hopes go
Insecurity impregnated in your soul
Dread breathes and sighs
No escape for the recognised
Holding hate and pride
Kill the desire.
Sarah Burton

Flirting

I love the thrill of flirting.
It gives me such a fuzz.
Furtive looks through lowered lashes.
A glance that last much longer than it should,
My body tingles with pleasure from head to toe
Eyes that keep meeting across a smoky bar.
Who will be bold and look the longest.
The briefest of touch as you pass by.
My breathing becomes harder and faster.
Tiny beads sweet begin to build.
My skin takes in a rosy of glow.
In the end you go your separate way.
And to someone else I will turn my gaze.
Suzanne Monk

Mother And Son

We're alone in the house, my son and I,
Just counting the days as they pass us by.
We haven't much money to spend on ourselves,
There's enough to buy food to put on the shelves.

Being single and a parent is pretty hard work,
But having my son around has been quite a perk.
He's so full of mischief and plenty of fun,
He's the man of the house, he's my No. 1

He's going to school and his teachers all say,
There's one thing for certain, he brightens your day.
Sometimes when he does things to make me quite mad,
He says that he's sorry for being so bad.

He knows when I'm tired, to leave me alone,
Because I'll just get ratty and constantly moan.
He knows that I love him with all of my heart.
And I'll never let anyone tear us apart.
J. Beaupierre

Magical Place

As I walked a woodland path, winding and twisting
its contours existing
I passed by leaves of brown and gold
some were young leaves others old
a cuckoo's song, distance and far
a tall oak tree almost touching a star
this path controlled me, its age and history
I could not leave, I had to follow,
I had to believe
and then I came to this magical place
a meadow covered in daisies,
like white satin lace
an occasional buttercup placed here and there
can you imagine? I want you to share
this magical place
W. F. Shuter

To Andrea

Return to me my treasured friend,
I've missed you so, these many years -
For you alone my mind can tend,
Can dissipate the woe, the tears.

Do you recall the happy days
We spent in blissful harmony,
Delighting as we did always,
In one another's company?

Those transient, indelible
Sweet times, have not since been surpassed -
Indeed, my life - just bearable -
Has been unhappy to the last.

Thus, Andrea - please do return,
Transform my features - dark and stern -
To those of brighter attitude.
Stephen Ryan

My Eyes

How wealthy I have just become
I've just found out I own the sun
I own the stars that shine at night
The moon is mine with its pale light
The hills and valleys that I see
These also all belong to me
I own the rivers running deep
The wind and seas are mine to keep
No matter what in nature see
Through my eyes belong to me
We don't need money in the bank
It surely must be God we thank
Who gave us eyes that we might see
How beautiful the world can be
Our sights worth more than all the gold
The biggest vault on earth could hold.
F. Kenrick

More Questions Than Answers?

Why are we here? Where will we go?
Just two of answers I'd like to know?
God and the devil, one? many? a few?
Oh how I long to know what's true
What's down to choice, to chance or fate?
Who's to be poor or famous or great?
Is there a Heaven above us, a Hell below?
Does anyone, anywhere know?
So many facts, so many fables
Choose the right ones, if you're able
Do we live once or twice, again and again?
Is there life after death, or is death the end?
Can anyone tell me, what's wrong and what's right?
Do ghoulies and ghosties come out in the night?
Chinamen, Arabs, Catholics and Jews
Protestants, Sikhs, who believes truth?
We live and learn, or so they say
Existing 'til our 'Judgement Day'
So learn your lessons, learn them well
And then my friend, well, who can tell?

Lynne Storey

Untitled

As I watch the flight of the winter birds
I seems as though they mock my words
They speak to me in such a quiet voice
It seems as though I have no other choice
Than to have a girl like you so fine
Hoping someday that you would be mine

Kirk Harris

On My Own

Feeling cowardly, emotional and uptight,
Keeping it in, not able to speak a single word,
Thinking, debating, staying up half the night,
Is it him, is it me, or is he getting bored.
Over possessive, jealous and so headstrong,
There are bad points, can I think of any good,
Putting up with this sheer nursery for oh so long,
These are points which were obviously overlooked.
Every quarrel and disagreement, bad feelings are spread,
Feel guilt and anger for letting the fuse ignite,
Turned backs and thick atmosphere laying in bed,
There won't be any lovemaking tonight.
What should I do, ignore or come on strong,
I don't want to lose him, but yet to raise a point,
He is just as bad, by letting it prolong,
Both as stubborn, an effort that is joint.
I have to learn to control this nature of mine,
Or he will raise anger and leave me all alone,
And just a short while, a period of time,
He will be gone and I'll be ON MY OWN!

N. Cohen

Winter Joys

In the sombre days of winter
Just as the new year starts
When days are short and nights are long
Now is the time to look around
And see the wonders of nature
The tips of slowly awakening flowers
Which bring us signs of spring
The beauty of the leafless trees
Adorned on a frosty morning
And sticky buds, held tight and fast.
To withstand the icy blast
Soon to release their priceless treasure
Unfolding leaves, in countless measure
The red gold of a winter sunset,
Once seen, in memory, never to forget.
Jasmin shows its golden face
Amongst spiders webs of finest lace
All this, and more, is there for all to see
In nature's wondrous finery
Soon, the days extend, spring comes again at winter's end.

I. M. Owen

To A Liverpool Dock Road Carthorse

No more will your hooves strike sparks from cobbled streets
Journeying from northern docks to Wapping station
The Pennine Mills have closed, and with it your
carted burden of bales of cotton from the American South

    Your sacking - shouldered carter no longer brings you to rest
    At the sound of the "One O'Clock Gun", when the bucket for water
    Is unhooked and the nose-bag put in place
    What little reward for so much toil, but this has
    Always been your fate

You escaped when dock-aimed incendiaries set your stable alight
Some of your friends did not, brave creatures for whom no
memorial exists for their death in war.
My time has nearly gone, so when I am no more will I hear the ring
Of your hooves again and the rattle of burnished harness.
Will I see your nostrils steaming in the cold, as once
I did in my youth now long gone.

Robert J. Harry

"Who Cares"

I'm in a residential home,
I've all I need, even a phone,
My bills are paid, my meals are cooked,
But one important thing is overlooked,
I wasn't asked, I was simply told,
"Don't make a fuss, just be bold."

I have to laugh when I think back
Talk about I'm alright jack,
We still have our respect and pride,
It's just unfortunate our partners died,
We was once young just like you
We had our hopes, our love lives too,
We had our troubles, and our strife,
But we had a happy life.

So please don't smirk, and act so cold,
Because like me you will soon be old.

Pat Biscoe

Fergie's Secret

Fergie's got a secret
It's not one you'd imagine,
Nor a skeleton in a cupboard,
Though she's had a few.
It's not affairs with baldheaded men,
Not even one called Len.
It may come as no surprise,
When you realize, it's not one to compromise,
The fact of Fergie's secret is,
She's got no cash to pay her debt...
... On the other hand she may have a secret stash,
What's the bet!

Janet Wilding

I Fell You Slipping Slowly Away

I feel you slipping slowly away.
It's worse at night than it is in the day.

Some times you look with an unholy stare
Slumped in a chair without a care.

What will you do when the love's all gone.
Look to the bottle to tell you what's wrong.

I am so strong and you are so weak.
But without your love the future looks bleak.

You're sometimes the most charming man alive.
2 or 3 drinks the romance takes a dive.

If only I could tell you how I feel.
Give up the drink and make this thing real.

There are times when I cringe at what you do
but at the end of the day my love's for you.

I feel you slipping slowly away
to the bottom of a glass and the end of the day.

Moira Clelland

The Pottery Class

The pottery class the pottery class
It's very refined and not at all crass
We sit around the table and look at the clay
What on earth can we make for someone today

Some plant pots for Mum, a fruit bowl for Gran
A tall skinny vase a little flat flan
What wonderful things we set out to do
But oh I'm afraid, the mistakes we go through

The clay is too dry, the clay is too wet
It's nobody's fault the result that we get
The teacher is helpful he's really quite gallant
And it isn't his fault if we haven't got talent

Yet some pupils shine with the pots that they make
And some, well they try so please give us a break
But not in the pots though they may turn out funny
We make them for love and not for the money

So just before you scoff or groan
Do come and try to make pots of your own
You might even like it, it's really a gas
When you join a night school Pottery class
  Olive Headen

The Best Times

The best time is the early hours
   Just after dawn creeps up
When treetops catch the sun's first rays
   and birds - at puddles sup.

The best time is when ones you love
   are laughing in the house
And babies sleep, with happy grins
   and bubbles at the mouth.

The best times are when friends are near
   Just at your time of need
And times of giving bring the joy
   That kill the times of greed

And times like when your first is born
   and to the world you run
And show your pride for all to see
   Like you are the only one.

A best time is when you can say
   that life is just a ball.
But best times would be twice as good
   If they were seen by all
  W. Sallis

Continuity

Explore with me the quiet land.
Let Celt and Saxon take your hand.
Let Vikings make their bloody stand
And Kings ride by your side.

Retreat to Cedd's enduring hall
Across the Romans' warlike wall
And hear the Gospel's early call -
The chant of thousand years.

Then touch the ancient mason's mark,
The cut of adze, the beam stained dark
By pious torch of pitch and bark -
And feel the pulsing tide.

Where'er you walk, on land or shore,
Another walked that way before,
Another built the passage door
Through which your steps resound...

The common bonds that weld a land
And weave its future strand by strand
Relentless, like the running sand
Of time, will hold you bound.
  Robert Hallmann

Shopping

Friday today - Hooray! Hooray!
It's supermarket shopping day
I'm busy shopping with my trolley
I have my pocket full of lolly
I'm looking at the shelves to see
If there is something nice for tea
I think that we'll have chips and fish
It always is a tasty dish
Or perhaps we'll have a chicken roast
It is the one they like the most
Into the trolley goes the food
To feed my ever hungry brood
I think that I had better stop
I can't get any more on top
So now I queue to reach the till
To pay my ever-rising bill
Then home to sit with my feet up
And drink tea from my special cup
To have five minutes on my own
Before my family come home
  Sheila Mary Williams

Nancy

Now when I married Nancy's son
It was just like a new life had begun.
So different was this village life
But I had to learn, I was Alan's wife.
She took me under her wing at the start
I'll never forget the day we had to part.
I remember how we would sit and chat
She even adopted our ginger cat.
She introduced me to the game of 'Bingo'
And also explained the new foreign lingo
What do they mean when they say 'it's nesh?'
'It's cold, lass,' she's say, 'you know, goosey flesh.'
A port manta I'd never heard of before
'It's a suitcase' I found out and learnt more and more
I often think of Nancy in a peaceful land
And remember she cried as Alan took my hand.
  Lillian Askew

Albert Einstein Quote:
"The Best Psychiatrist For Any Man Is..."

Albert Einstein, physicist of aplomb,
It was his reluctant mission
To save the world with the devil's bomb;
Explosive atomic fission.
But he used to say,
In a wistful way,
"To relieve a mental condition,
Abandon all hate;
Shack up with a mate,
With her wiles and her intuition."
  Michael D. Maher

Creepy Crawly

There is a spider on my wall,
It was fine until it crawl
up the wall to the ceiling
It gave me such a creepy feeling.

It stopped awhile and looked around.
It made me wonder, what it had found.
It then began to retrace its track.
The shiver's were still going down my back!

If it comes down a little further,
I could commit an awful murder,
but if I hit that spider flat
I'd have a mark where it went splat!

So I'll let it walk, up and down my wall
and try to pretend it's not there at all!!
  Susan Ann Higgs

The Devil In My Mind

In nature's arms my spirit breathes
Its soothing honey-sigh,
And feels the warm and loving touch
Of Heaven's golden eye.

From distant mount or endless sea
Crawl clouds of demons-grey
Dark shadows slide across the mind
And drain soul's light away.

Through living flesh and bloody veins
Soaks black and inky fears,
Then dreams are lost in weary bones,
Hopes drown in their own tears.

'Please dear God send forth a spear
Of searing bright blue light,
To pierce this heart of Hell's black mist
And split it with your might!

'With silver shafts of sparkling light
Make darkness slip behind
And save me from the crushing grip
Of the Devil in my mind.'

Paul Lyons

The Whip An Peerie

For Christmas, Wee Lyndsey, I gave whip an peerie
"It's lovely aunt Nance, Yeve made me fair cheery."
"But whit is for? am whit doe sit dae?"
Ye'll have tae bide here, an show me the way.

Her mammy, ma sister, an me, baith did oor stuff,
Whippin yon peerie, till baith oot oh puff.
Lyndsey was laughin, an dancin aroon,
I'll whip that wee peerie awe roon the toon.

Sic a grand time wae a simple wee thing,
Brung back ma youth, memories o' spring,
Lang simmer evenings, wains in the street,
Bright coloured peeries, rhuematic, free feet.

Bairns we had little, we cared even less,
Faither at war, the world in a mess.
The wee whip an peerie, it took me back hame,
Ah wis there standing, a lassie again.
Moosey broom hair, daft gigglin grin,
Wishin ma mam!! could still shout me in.
But life must go on, toys laid aside.
Yet!! Still in that child world, I'd happily bide.

Nancy Craig Blaikie

Fostering (What's It All About)

It's caring when no one else can
 It's feeling when some find it hard
It's also taking the good with the bad
 that's what it's all about

It's understanding others
 when things in they're lives go wrong
And helping them get through it
 to make them grow strong

It's taking in the children
 when they have no where else to go
And watch their smiling faces
 when they return home.

It's sharing all that you've strived for
 your family, and your home
Your life, patients and understanding
 but most of all your love

It's hard to imagine not doing this
 and dread the day, when it ends
Out lives will be so empty
 with no children to tuck into bed.

J. E. Hill

Love Poem

There's no other man to replace him
It's not a passing phase or whim
This handsome, kind, sensitive man
No one can love him like I can
A love so strong it brings tear to my eye
I couldn't forget him, I wouldn't try
So many memories so many thoughts
Such real feelings, a hero of sorts
My first true love as long as I remember
That lasted from January to December
I can feel his arms giving me a hug
His touching my hair and giving it a tug
Him wiping my eyes and drying my tears
Listening to my hopes dreams and fears
I'm so lucky to have this love
That fits like a handmade glove
To have known this man, I am glad
To have loved this man, my grandad

Natalie Lloyd

Next Door's Cat

I've always hated next door's cat
It's far too ugly and much too fat
Green eyes squinting and a look so smug
Like a shiny smiling back-door rug
He looks at me with an evil smirk
As I pass his gate, on the way to work

A "Know it all" look across his face
As he goes through life at his own pace
Much too fat to walk too far
The catflap's too small so the door's ajar
Oh to find a way to bring him down
Knock from his head that feline crown

A huge Alsatian I thought to buy
My family begged for reasons why
This strange behaviour is not quite you
Your love of dogs is something new!
I never told them it's not really that
It's just I hate next door's cat

Keith Ashwood

Feelings Of An Owner True

The gale it wakes me blowing loud and long
It's cold and white, with more white to come
But as those eyes look leading at me
It's time to get ready for my daily routine
As I took responsibility for this extra life
He needs me for food, play and warmth on a night
So on goes a coat thick and warm,
Scarf, a hat, and wellies well worn.
We set off out into the cold gales and snow
But he doesn't mind where it is we go.
We have the ball to be thrown and brought back
As we walk along the old dirt track
His love's unconditional with a loyalty that's rare,
The time is very precious that we both share
He lifts my day without needing a cause
This best friend of mine with cold nose and four paws.

P. Hodgson

To View

With staring eyes so tired forlorn.
It seems they have been watching from the day they were born,
Pictures of terror, trouble and strife.
Is this the real view of everyday life?
Pornography, greed, and illicit sex
Does all this make their life complex?
Politicians, breweries, banks, and building societies
 advertising their wares,
All these things occupy their soulful stares.
With ageing sight I just look on,
Where have our poor healthy fresh air activities gone?

Tom Tombs

"Imagination"

My sister laid a coat upon the bedroom floor.
It turned into a sailing ship, heading for a distant shore.
We kept our tiny feet wrapped up inside the coat,
Trying to keep our feet dry, fighting! To stay afloat
We used our hands as oars to guide 'our ship' along.
We sailed around 'our world' we were young and strong!
Singing songs of Islands far across 'our sea,'
No storm in sight? The weather bright so carefree!
"Trouble! Ahead! Mind the bed!" "Don't you mean the rocks?"
"Get your feet out of the water! Don't you see the Sharks?"
Our mother called from a distant shore,
"What are you doing?! With my coat on the floor?!"
"It's not a coat! It's a boat!" "Oh no, it's not! It's a ship!"
Mother calls louder, "Is that a rip?!"
My sister says, "I think, it's time to head for shore?"
'Our ship' becomes a coat again, 'our sea,' the bedroom floor.
Wendy Ann Allcock

Spring Reappeared

One very cold spring morning
It was snowing hard outside
The snow drops were starting to peep through
But that morning they wanted to hide.

The milkman had to be careful
As the footpaths were covered with snow
Winter had returned that morning
So traffic would have to go slow

The ground was so hard and frozen
Birds were desperately looking for food.
The children were allowed to stay at home
But were told they had to be good.

People set off for work early
It might snow all day it was feared
By mid-day the sun started shining
Quite suddenly spring reappeared.
Moira Emslie

Looking Back On Love

I remember the day we met,
It was just like yesterday,
The sun was shining and flowers blooming,
Our hearts were full of love,
The sun seems to shine so bright above.
I'm sure it's because of our love,
We are at peace with ourselves we are not blue
Everything is alive, and colourful too.
It's true what people say, we change from day to day
So we will stay together for the rest of our life,
The flowers will die, but they will bloom again,
For our love will never end,
So spring will be here again,
There will be fresh buds,
With many more young loves
Combine the two for you know it's true,
To look back and you'll never be blue.
E. Nash

Sunrise

Today I saw the sunrise it was a heavenly sight.
It slowly rose above the clouds shaking off the night
So many different coloured rays suddenly appeared.
Heralding a new day, dawn had disappeared
A gentle breeze is blowing filling all the air,
Promising a lovely day, with sunshine everywhere.

Now the birds are singing, the flowers raise their heads
They greet the morning gladly arising from their beds
I look again at the sunrise, it's now taken hold,
High in a sky of blue the colour a lovely gold.
To stand and watch this happen, quietly before my eyes
Alone and in wonder I look toward the skies.

May I never take these things for granted, they are
  gifts in life, from above.
Gifts that we should treasure gifts for us to love.
Sheila M. Birch

A Changing World

Through my eyes as a little girl,
it seemed to be a great big world,
Lots of space to run and play,
the sea the sand the lovely day.

Fields full of grass, trees and flowers,
it was easy to while away the hours,
but look what they have done,
taken away all that fun.

The fumes from cars pollute our air,
the trees are no longer there,
the fields are now a motor way,
why don't they stop,
leave a space for children,
or is it they just don't care.

They fill the sea with oil and pollution.
I just cannot see a solution
Oh how I wish I was a child again,
to play in puddles not acid rain.
Karen Harrison

Do We Care?

When you are bored with the housework, the Hoover goes away
It doesn't really matter and the works still there today
When there is nothing on the T.V. you can just switch off the set
You can choose when to go to bed, no! it's still too early yet

Yet when it comes to illness, especially of the mind
No one really understands and often are unkind
All of us are guilty although some will say "Not Me"
Of making fun of others just because of what we see

Have you ever tried to put yourself, in the place of someone who
Is not quite so fortunate as me or maybe you
It is easy to be complacent only ever considering I
When your life is running smoothly, you don't even have to try

Yet we should still consider others in every walk of life
Those with illness, handicaps, poverty or any kind of strife
If we all cared for each other just a little more each day
Maybe some of the sickness in our society would gradually
fade away

We boast about teaching our children
The values for living today
Perhaps it is up to the next generation
To find where "caring" got lost on the way
Sara Angell

Journey's End

Deep in your heart you know where to go,
it may not be easy, you're all on your own,
your focus, your vision must stay in sight,
repeat to yourself "I know I am right".

In moments of weakness it's hard to refrain,
from wandering away from the path you have lain,
temptation beckons to an easier route,
where the paths are smooth and free of the truth.

But don't be fooled and led astray,
by those who'll say there's a better way,
for the alternative routes you've already explored,
in your mind you've been down those roads before.

It's a steep climb up and only one way,
no stopping, no U-turns and no give-way,
and if a block in your road appears,
take the diversion but return without fear.

If you're carrying a heavy load,
don't be afraid, take the safest road,
it may take you longer but be patient, my friend,
for you will reach your Journey's End.
Karen Fleming

The Purpose Of Life

Always remember the Purpose of Life,
It may not be easy when we struggle and strive,
We may have so little,
Yet others a lot,
But we should be thankful for what we have got.
It is not a matter of money and wealth;
Far more important are people and health.
The Poor and the Needy, thankful are they,
Although all they have is to wake up each day.
Throughout our Life Span we live and we learn,
Love and Respect are things we have to earn,
Material things boost the Ego, it's true,
But no better person will these things make you,
The Sun and The Sea, a purpose have they;
Without them we would not be here today.
Our purpose in Life may not yet be clear,
We certainly have one,
That's why we are here!

Wendy Head

Man's Future

Another day, another night
Is this man's future
Wrong or right.
Man cuts down trees for the timber and the land,
    leaves emptiness were forests used to stand.
Man over populates with sons and daughters,
    spreads around chemicals pollutes the waters.
Man goes through life wanting money and fees,
    kills of animals puts waste in the seas.
Another day, another night
Is this man's future
It's not looking bright.

T. Codd

A Child's Prayer

This poor little lass knelt beside her small bed
Is there no one to hear the soft words that were said
Her Mother of beauty has long passed away
Leaving a little mite with a father who drinks every day
Through eyes full of sadness her hopeful heart brings
Dreams of chocolates some toys plus those cuddly things
Chapped hands clasped, praying to God up above
To deliver to her just a portion of love
Surely there's someone who will answer her prayer
Or have the words been lost in space somewhere
Keep praying little angel your reward comes at the end
When all others have deserted you God will be your friend.

Sheila Walker

Mother Earth

She sleeps all winter in the cold
Keeping the trees and plants in the mould
The earth is a blanket to all the trees
Helping their growth, helping them breathe
The little snowdrops are first to appear
Then comes the crocus all so fair
Daffodils follow in all their glory
What a lovely beginning to nature's story
The buds bursts open in the spring
On trees on hedgerows everywhere
Flowers in gardens so gay in parks
In fields and meadows green
The earth wakes up to nature again
As winter has flown for spring to appear
April comes along with soft showers
Helping to nourish the trees and flowers
Birds singing making their nests
Bees and butterflies flitting by
It's a lovely time when spring is here
The earth's awake to nature again

N. Tomlinson

In The Country

The countryside is the place to be
It is where I was born and bred you see
With cows and sheep and farms to see
And lots of other animals running free
The farmer walking with his dog
On land that he owns and ploughs and sows
Then he watches all the seedlings grow
And he knocks the weeds out with a hoe
The pond in the yard is large and round
We see lots of fish swimming around
The horse stands drinking on this hot day
He has just come back from turning hay
The cows are walking into the shed
They will be milked before going to bed
Hens are clucking round the yard
Telling us that their eggs are laid
Then into the coop they all go
To sit on perch and wait for another day
So if you like animals be like me
Go into the country and see them run free

Walter G. Smith

Retirement

When you retire, life should be fun,
it is silly to think your day has come.
Get out and follow your pursuits,
have a good time, perhaps research your roots.
To sit in front of the box is a waste of time,
to waste what is left of your life is a terrible crime.
Make good use of what you have left,
help the weak who's lives are in a mess.
Hospitals, day centres always want help, and are in need,
why not go along, maybe to teach some one to read?.
Have a good time while helping yourself,
prolong your life, get off that shelf.
Live your life to the full,
it doesn't matter if you act the fool.
Have a good time, live for today,
you do just that, you are bound to enjoy the rest of your stay.
I KNOW I AM.

A. G. Snow

Tomorrow

Never leave 'til tomorrow what you can do today.
Isn't that something we've heard others say?
"Postpone it today" we might remark.
Perhaps the excuse is it's getting rather dark.
"Another day will be just as good"—
only to wish we had gone whilst we could
reality stepping in as sure as fate
unexpectedly it became far too late.
Unable to show that we really did care
opportunity now lost to make repair.
Plainly given one last chance,
simply wasted, just no backward glance
worthwhile doing what we can today
since tomorrow may not always go our way.

B. Hover

Truth

Do you think that a child could believe that a star
is only a spark in repose,
has man ever made anything to compare with
a beautiful flower like a rose,
is the moon up above just a candle of love
do the gates of heaven ever close.

Is the lightning that splits the storm laden night
acclaimed by the clouds in applause,
do the stars that shine down from the heaven's above
number more than the sands on the shores,
or is truth the surprise - lighting up some ones eyes
be they his - be they mine - be they yours.

B. M. Furber

A Squirrel Surprise

A little poem to amuse you
it is really true.
About albert a grey squirrel
something he did do.

He was being transported by car
on a busy motor way.
In his cage nice and snug
he was on this particular night
after journeying during the day.

Some how this night from his cage
he got free.
Owners unknowing continued
journey Happily.

Our driver on his head
not a profusion of hair.
Albert squirrel decided on his head
he would reside their.

Our driver a lover of animals
stayed very calm
a laugh now as a, memory know one harmed.

Victoria Joan Theedam

Winter Wonderland

I saw a little snowflake land on my window sill
It looked so very perfect, so small white and still
Soon others came to join it, it really was a sight
Slowly, gently falling in the middle of the night.

In morning there's another world, so clean, so bright and new
Surprising what a covering of clean white snow will do.
In this silent world of white you cannot hear the sound
Of peoples heavy footfalls as they trudge around the town.

Soon children in bright boots and coats
Bring sledges out to play on slopes.
Make snowmen big and snowmen small
Loads of fun for one and all.

Shouts of gladness, squeals of glee
Bring memories of a younger me.
Then evening comes, the quiet spreads
As children are tucked up in their beds.
The snow will melt into the ground
It slips away before your eyes and never makes a sound.
Seasons will come and Seasons will go
Still nothing is like the winter snow.

May Monaghan

Dear Pain

Dear Pain, Why are you with me again today?
  Is my body your abode to stay?
  O cruel instrument, why take you my rest?
  Who invited you? Thou unwelcome guest?

Dear Man, I work a work, a job to do,
  One of which is to afflict a few.
  Cruel instrument, that I may be.
  The reason, I've not been given to see.

Dear God, I will come before you now to pray.
  Must I drink this cup again today?
  Pain says he's not able to see,
  Why this affliction, on me, must be.

Dear Called One, My beloved Son on earth did wrest,
  Upon you is not such great a test.
  But it's necessary, at times, to hold you down
  As you'd chase other pursuits and lose your crown.

My promises must suffice for you.
  As another day I see you through.
  Stay close to me for I'm always there.
  I'll put no more upon you than you can bear.

R. Padgham

My Mother's Cottage

I have a cottage that faces the sun,
It belongs to my mother, but now she
has gone and left me on my own. The
cottage belongs to me I wish she was
Still here to enjoy it with me. There's
her armchair by the window just where
she left it; I sit there and think of her
and wonder if she is thinking of me.
My friend is coming to the cottage
today, I hope she will stay for the day.
She is a pretty women in her own way
Here she is at the door. Do you know we
have been friends a very long time.
Hello! come in! Shall I come to your
house then you can come to mine so we
can be together one more time, so I
shall say goodbye my friend till we meet again

D. Anderson

Hope

Awakening to a winters day,
It appears most dreary in every way.
You pull the curtains open wide,
Only to see grey clouds outside.
Small children with their mums going to school,
Wishing, and wishing it wasn't so cool.
Then walking to the patio door,
Across a warm carpeted floor,
The smell of coffee on the go,
Gives the body a satisfying glow.
Oh look there's a robin over there,
Two tiny blue tits in the air,
Bulbs bursting through the ground.
Nature is such a wonderful thing,
Winter is gradually becoming spring.

P. Reda

Untitled

The fierce monster from the deep,
is dark dark down in your sleep,
when you close your eyes and see this vicious beast,
with sharp thrashing teeth and gnarling nails,
as it is an abominable animal.

It steals your sleep then it gives a great leap,
you wake up and call down to your parents,
your parents say it was a nightmare,
but it was a very big scare,
now go to sleep,
go to sleep forget about the monster from the deep but I can't
but I can't, the monster from the deep has stolen my sleep.

Patsy Hughes

My Heavenly Dream

A beautiful sound came close to my ear, the sweet voice of
Jesus is what I did hear. He bid me come and took my hand
together we walked, in that heavenly land. Through beautiful
valleys we did stroll, a perfect peace restored my soul.
Animals came to greet Him for all of them are His pets and
even all the flowers bowed their little heads. A beautiful
fragrance filled the air and then I saw all my loved ones,
waiting there. My heart felt so light and wanted to sing no
greater joy have I ever, felt within.
Then Jesus said; my daughter! Time hasn't yet come for you
to stay, go help the sick and weak to pray. For I am with you
through your difficult task and if you need guidance you have
only to ask.
Lo, I am with you always and always will till the end of the
world. I'll be with you still. I thanked my Lord Jesus and went
down on my knee my God, my God I shall always serve Thee.
And when I awoke I thanked God for my dreams for all the
beauty that I have seen the peace, the joy I did obtain but
most of all, I saw my loved ones again.

L. G. Sharp

The Mountain Lions

On the vast tracks of the lands of Idaho
Is the key to the hunters where the cougars go
The hounds are used to trace their scent
It was up in the trees the cougars went.

The hunter would hear the loud bark of the hounds
We knew then that a cougar was found
They have keen sight and hearing, with sharp teeth and claws
They have a slender body with long legs and chubby paws

They sharpen their claws until razor edged on a tree
They are retracted into sheaths when there's no need
Their sightings in the wild are so rare
Their ability to attack may sometimes flare

They like to eat duck from the pond, this precious meat
   they are so fond
They have a rest in their sanctuary place, far away
   from the human race.
Rose Bell

Warrior Of Spirits

Your finesse of relating, sharing
Is smooth as silk gliding on warm air
Yet strong as a weathered oak, bearing
Roots holding rich mountain soil
You have stood by me

Through turbulent turmoil
My heart has been warmed
By strength you've endured toil
When our union has wept, forlorn
And you have stayed, not recoiled
Showing true devotion you've formed

Thank you for being my side
Remaining constant as the sea
For my soul to confide
Allowing my spirit to be
As love rushes forth like spring tide
From your tender charm to me
Lisa M. Minton

January

Steel clad the fields lie
In armour bright.
Gaunt trees lean against the sky
Their lances stripped of summer's green.
Testy winter tenants screech and keen
Crow black their feathers fly
In the stingy whining wind.
Seared reeds white rimmed and dry
Crack in the frozen stream
It's summer melody now a dream
In the deep winter's sleep.
Tom Gurney

"The Curse Of Marriage" - Once Bitten! -

The second time around
Is just as it's the first
Because you're so in love again
Your wounds have all been nursed

You fall in love again
As time and time before
It takes a little longer
To know when you are sure

So when you take that step
The one you know is right
Remember on the second time
The first is out of sight

The second time around
Is just as it's the first
Each moment is a memory
For now that you've been cursed.
G. M. Clark

Trapped

Does this body belong to me,
Is it what I want it to be,
It looks o.k. that's what they all think,
But they can move as quick as a wink.

I remember the times when I walked far,
But now it's slow, and only to a car,
On wheels I manage to see the world,
I love my craft with pieces curled.

I also help others like me,
With advice on their disability,
So why O why don't I feel fulfilled,
Is it because that it was willed.

I know we have to like our lot,
But there are thousands like me who do not,
So trapped I'm sure is what they say,
The same as me, all we can do is pray.
Theresa Law

What Is Christmas?

   Do you ask yourself this?
Is it the thoughts of presents, or a Mistletoe kiss?
Is it the turkey with all its trimmings, or singing Christmas hymns?
Could it be the Christmas tree, or the three wise kings?
Maybe it's the shepherds in the field seeing the blinding light.
This came from Gabriel, the angel, in the dead of night.
What is Christmas?
   Will it ever be the same again?
The birth of Jesus Christ, good will and peace to men.
Today it's lost its glory, commercialised through and through.
No longer does the birth come first, to me and all of you.
Who did this wicked thing? Who can be put to blame?
Everyone that lives on Earth must now admit their shame.
What can we do to right the wrong, to clear up this awful mess?
On Christmas Eve to church we'll go and all our sins confess.
What is Christmas?
   It's the time for rejoicing and praising.
To celebrate the Holy Birth and our souls that he is saving.
Susan D. Gutteridge

A Scorpio Behind The Mask

There's a mystery that deepens when you look into her eyes,
Is it power, desire or jealousy or simply a disguise.
Her soul is full of passion and her feelings flow like water,
She's emotional with fixed ideas and doesn't want to alter.

She's cautious and perceptive and a very loyal mate,
Successful, spicy, sexy and her lucky number's eight.
Though you'll often see her dressed in black or possibly maroon,
It doesn't mean she's hard as iron or always full of gloom.

A snake that's cute and devious but peaceful like a dove,
Though beware the ruthless eagle when there isn't any love...
Attraction can be fatal if you can't keep up the pace,
With her it's all or nothing or you haven't got a case.
Louise M. Moore

What Is A Tear?

What is a tear?
Is it loneliness?
Wanting of a fond caress,
We shed our tears,
When our thoughts are distressed,
Unhappiness shown with tears on our cheeks,
Distraught we may suppress our sorrow,
But the tears will fall,
The tears of sadness.

Tears of happiness,
May fall to our cheeks,
Laughter of joy, that we may recall,
Jokes we may hear, incidents befall,
The cold as we hurry, on through the wind,
Illness, loneliness, injustice, or fear,
All of these feelings encased in a tear
Patricia Austin

January Blues

Why does death creep into my thoughts,
Is it only the January blues?
At this time in my life mortality looms,
Is it only the January Blues?

The fragility of life
Seems to flutter and taunt,
Or is it only
The January blues?

Another year on,
Another year older,
Another year gone,
Another year ahead.

And what am I going to do?
And what am I going to change?
And how will I mark its passing?
And loose the January Blues.

Shirley Jane Allan

Who Cares

Who cares, when we are born,
into this world of pain and scorn,
The suffering on this earth renown,
Through ancient times, till life declines,
Who cares - when sadness rules our lives,
Until the day we all must die,
We pray that God will help us on our way,
And give us strength on our final day.
To leave this world of great despair,
And be in peace, with never a care.
Who cares - God alone can help us now,
We strive to help our family born,
Sadly, often encounter only scorn,
Who cares - God cares.
To give us strength to leave this world,
of discontent, for everlasting eternity sent.

E. J. Cranfield

Love is

Love
is a flightless bird
that sang once within me,
but went unheard by you
too blind to see.

Love
goes on - unloved,
drowned in the noise of silence
that is you unmoved,
uncaring in my presence.

Love
is a game you play
as a child without shame
spinning me like a top, in hands of clay,
running to then from me
far and far away.

A. Taylor

The Child That I Am

There is so much inside, her heart is full of give
Inside herself she cries, she thrives in life to live
A life full of happiness to learn to love you all
Her love is full of bless, her heart is never full
Her eyes they search for you, her smiles brighten by the day
Her feelings are so true she loves you in every way
Her mind is always preying, waiting for the day
To carry out her feelings, hoping we will never go away
Her hands are waiting patiently to grasp us with her care
To hold you so lovingly, for the love she wants to share
Her legs there waiting to get strong, her body's just asleep
So one day close to you herself she wants to creep.

R. Rowe

A Whiter Shade Of Black

What is depression?
Is it linked to recession, or is it the distinct impression you're in for a one hour session?

Is it associated with stress?
Or you couldn't care less, is your life in a mess, or do you just have to confess?

Do you just stand and stare?
With your nose in the air, can a friend help repair, or is it all just despair?

If it's not all this-
What else is amiss, would a rose and a kiss, return everything to bliss?

If the answer is no-
Why is that so, if you're not really mad, then why are you still sad?

So what is this feeling?
That has your head reeling, if it's not all the above, then could it be love?

This cannot be likely-
It's not in your psyche, or in your stars in Pisces, it's quite simply caused by MID LIFE CRISIS.

Mary Crawford Brown

Embers

And if this Love, burning in the hearth of Life
is fed with foreign fuel
and left smouldering like a cancerous slate
amongst the glowing embers, it will die.
Who left it there?
He will not say, or own that he was wrong.
The apple will not burn with spitting willow
or slaty shale,
It dies in blackened ash.
If only he would say, 'I put it there.
I took another fuel when fires were low.
I choked the faithful embers
and they nearly died'.
He could not see that he was wrong,
he would not say what made him put it there.
Before it is too late, rebuild the hearth;
Breathe warm love on ash
and see a spark rekindle.
Not blazing logs of passion, like fires new,
but warm and gentle comfort, lasting through.

Margaret Thirlwell

The Visitor

A stranger came to visit us
Just the other day
He arrived here uninvited
And I think he means to stay
He hasn't shown himself to us
His face remains unseen
And though he's keeping out of sight
I can see just where he's been
He's very inconsiderate
And very impolite
He seems to sleep all through the day
And keeps us awake all night
He's no respect for property
I think he's very rude
And you should see the mess he makes
When he's looking for some food
Four tiny feet have invaded
Our once, neat little house
Have you guessed who the stranger is?
Yes, that's right! "He's a mouse"

Margaret McNeish

"Tempest"

Pitter patter on the window pane
In goes the sun, down comes the rain,
The streets are wet and slippery too
The grass in the morning, wet with dew.

The rain runs down the side of the wall
Flowing so fast like a waterfall,
But in my bed I'm cosy and warm
Though outside rages a thunder storm.

Lightening strikes and thunder cracks
Down come people's chimney stacks,
The sky turns blue, the rain it ceases
And we are left to pick up the pieces.

L. M. Turner

Him

Even though I'm far away.
In my mind you'll always stay.
And when I'm lost and all alone.
I think of you and of returning home.
A dream I've had for so long now,
a reality, maybe, who knows, somehow.
But resentment will linger until he's gone,
so I hope and pray he'll leave some day.
But he's still there. I know I phoned,
words failed me as he slurred hello.
You work so hard from dawn till late,
while he stays drunk and vegetates.
No more abuse or marks that show,
a replacement for Dad, I don't think so.
The days are long the nights so cold,
a cardboard box to call my home.
Some part with money, some moan, some groan,
you've brought it upon yourself, but what do they know.
I love you Mum, I feel you know,
but as for him, please tell him, go.

Philip Reid

Long Distance Love (A Sonnet To Simon)

Though parted by miles and physical things,
In my mind I can hold you and love you again.
Your loving words in my ears still ring,
I remember your absence and then comes the pain.
Time goes so slowly when we are apart,
Every day passes like a year.
Your love keeps me strong as it grows in my heart,
Physically parted yet in spirit you're here.
I think of us two whilst alone in my bed,
Remembering each kiss and each loving embrace.
Even though you're away, you're here in my head,
Alone in the darkness I can picture your face.
  No distance can part us, our love is so strong,
  No time can uncouple us, no matter how long.

Sarah Jane Bell

Love and Marriage

Fate decreed that we should meet, be mutually attracted.
In my dreams I'd set the scene, now it was enacted.
Is this for real and will it last? Oh! God please say it will.
I only know, I love him so, will he my dreams fulfil?
Tall, dark and handsome is he, with eyes of full of love.
Surely the one you chose for me, will be my turtle dove.

As a sequel to this little tale, is the fact we are still wed.
For some fifty years or so, a happy life we've led.
Our children now have fled the nest, are living on their own.
They seem to be as happy as we, long may it go on.
For life is very different today, with marriage no longer a must.
Children are often abandoned when liaisons bite the dust.
They then become undisciplined, which has a bad effect,
But it is their way of coping, for they often feel bereft.

Oh! Why can't life be simple, as in the days of yore?
When family life was paramount, need I say anymore?

M. Pescodd

Innocence

What place do we have in the journey of time? What innocence is left in our world filled with crime? What leaders do we have to guide and inspire? Where can we hide from the circle of fire that surrounds our very existence?

Innocence is lost when a babes' eyes are opened to a world filled with hate and death and destruction. The bleakness that surrounds us, upon our anger does it feed, who can heal the wound from where the world bleeds?

If love could be stronger than the hate which consumes us there may be hope for the unborn, the innocent.

Until then we must struggle with a conscience laden with weight, heavy with our anger, suffocating from hate. Where can we find words that comfort and soothe, how do we console the embittered youth with whom our future is resting? What lessons do we teach?

How do we learn love from the adult out of reach? "The meek shall inherit the earth", so it's said, how do we teach meekness when no books we have read? When we have not learnt from the mistakes of the leaders proclaimed great. What examples do we give of compassion and love that are not cancelled out by anger? The iron fist in a velvet glove.

Nadine Tanya Hill

A Puff of Smoke

As I look back over the years
into my eyes there comes the tears
when I think of all the folk
who are not here because they smoked.

The first behind the shed with friends
that was the day to make amends.
A couple of puff that's all it took
we'll curse the day we got hooked.

At first it's only one or two
but slowly it becomes quite a few,
the weed that once made us sick
is now the one that gives us a kick.

We don't realise that it's no joke
to walk around in a cloud of smoke
and it's now become quite a drag
to be totally dependent on a fag.

But saddest of all in later years
when children ask, their eyes in tears,
Why didn't Mummy stay to watch us grow,
Smoking's bad for you didn't she know?

T. P. Jenkins

We Have But One World

We have but one world to love and to cherish.
In return it grows all we need to live and flourish.
But what do we do to this wonderful world of yours.
We pollute it with rubbish and fumes from our cars.

The world provides us with all we need for free.
From fruit on the trees to fish in the sea.
Yet man is so greedy and thinks he needs more.
but do you really need it just think, are you sure?

We have wars to take from others not content with our lot.
If they don't give it willingly then they get shot.
The bombs that we drop pollute up our air.
Think of our children do you think that is fair?

We chop down our forest and soon there will be none.
And without our forests our oxygen's all gone.
Then how will man or beast possibly survive.
The world will be barren with nothing alive.

We kill our creatures some species are gone.
If we keep up this killing pretty soon there will be none.
So stop all this killing pollution and such.
Look after our one world is this asking to much?

Rita Hough

Marking Her Time

For ten years I've watched her,
in this room I have seen her every move,
from her dancing at parties,
to her crying when her fella moved.

At Christmas I've seen her happy
and dressing the Christmas tree,
to all alone when John had gone
with just the Queen and me.

I mark the passage of her life
for every second counts!
Each step nearer to her hopes and fears.
Every second I count.

I lie in wait, upon the mantle,
She cannot escape me.
For I am prisoner, to my counting,
and she is a prisoner of me.
   Jane Holloway

The Hunted

I'm hunted by dogs and men riding horses,
I'm given a start so they say,
Then someone blows a bugle and the rich folk start to play,
Two dozen dogs led by one man,
Someone shouts Tally-Ho catch the fox if you can,
Black-booted men with coats coloured red, Thundering hoofs
   hunt the fox till it's dead,
Even small children covered in mud want to be smeared with
   their first fox's blood,
The hunter, the hunted it's one and the same,
To me it's my life to man it's a game,
After the kill they laugh whoop and gloat,
They've a fresh piece of fur to add to a coat...
   C. E. Lally

Where Is God

Where is God in this world of violence and pain
In this cruel dark planet, where men fight to gain
Where is God in a child's tears, that mingle with the dust
When love turns to hate, and there is no one to trust
Where is God in this world, of famine and arid lands
When the hungry and impoverished stretch out empty hands
Where is God when the sun beats down, and the rain is no more
When the skies turn black, with the ravages of war
Is there a God out there, compassion does he lack
Does he look just once, then turn his back

He is in the moon and stars, that shine throughout the night
He is in the sun that warms, and gives us the light
He is in a mother's caress, upon a baby's face
He is in a helping hand, given to people of different race
He is in a look of adoration, shown to a lover
He is in the love and devotion one has for another
He is in a sparkling river a mountain top of white
He is in a colourful rainbow, the sun shining through the rain
Yes, God is all around us, his promise is ours to claim
   Margaret-Jean Wright

A Childhood Dream

Oh to wander through the woods again
In sunny dell or pouring rain
To hear the birds their merry notes to sing
The blackbird and the thrush on wayward wing
And see the rabbits scurry to their hidden lair
The sound of rustling trees are everywhere
Where meadows bore their primrose so fair
And buttercups and daises everywhere
This was my childhood long ago
In springtime or in advent snow
This was my childhood that I loved so much
When everything was beautiful to touch
The smell of spring and singing brook
And all wild creatures in their hidden nook
This was my dream of long ago
And only I and mine will ever know.
   B. E. James

War Torn

War torn, guns a-blazing,
In this city a hell is raising,
They are angry and breathing fire,
Every day a funeral pyre.
Some-one dies, what a waste,
In the mind the blood you taste.
It's not fair what happens here,
Everyday they shed a tear.
All the suffering and all the pain,
Seeing life wasted down a drain.
They are innocent victims of a war,
Another death, add to the score.
Why can't they fight with words,
Instead of being ignorant nerds.
Violence is their only way,
They say they are religious, they say they pray.
Thou shalt not kill is one of the sins,
Well, that one they threw in the bins
Will there be and end to this war,
I suppose there will, it's happened before.
   Michael John Loe

My Happy War

I had to leave London when the bombs were coming down
I was put on a train with my gas mask and sent to Crawley town
London was huge and grey and Crawley was little and green
And I thought Crawley was the loveliest place that I had ever seen

We waited for what seemed ages in the Railway Hotel yard
Some of the children were crying and found it very hard
But I can still smell the blackberries and feel the warmth of the sun
And hear the bees and the birds in the trees and was glad that
I had come

There were fields and farms and forests and rabbits and
squirrels galore
I was in my element and couldn't ask for more
We found a swarm of bees one day and followed them to their hive
And during the war in Crawley I was the happiest girl alive

But now I am old and Crawley is huge - A concrete jungle no less
And the fields and the farms and the forests have gone
   Is this what is called progress?
   P. W. Leigh

Brother

I wanted the world to stop today.
I wanted to scream, and shout
"How dare anyone laugh and lark about
when I've lost my big brother today".
But I know, deep down, that I'm being unfair.
And I know that Alan, who's sitting up there,
where the sky is azure and the sun is gold,
Would say "Come on Tracy, now I'll never grow old."
You must live your life as it's meant to be,
Just remember the good times,
and remember me."
   T. Clarke

Melody In Moonlight

ALONE
I walked in the shadows of moonlight
The breeze soft as the wings of dove
Through nights trees it whispered a melody
Played on harps from above.

ALONE
Golden moon hung a great disc of beauty
Tracing silver crosses of magic in grass
Streaming the river in cascades o' music
As over the bridges trespass to pass:

ALONE
In blue moonlight the spirit wanders
Gathers her grey sea-sounds in light
Charms that will hold me tightly ever
With you - the deep spell rose velvet of night.
   Stella Browning

Edinburgh

Oh! Edinburgh, how I loved you
In the good old days
When lads and lasses roamed through
Your alleys and your ways

Down the High Street we would wander
Passing barries, buckie-wives and brokers
Then the Canongate we would saunter
Laughing with eccentric jokers

Through Holyrood Palace gates we'd go
To climb Arthur Seat for a view
Then we'd stand in awe at the sight below
Oh! Edinburgh there's none such as you

The castle still stands upon the rock
But it must look down in sorrow
As modern buildings seem to mock
And more to come to-morrow

But Edinburgh! I still love you
And you must march with time
But leave me with my good old view
And memories that are mine

Nell Ferguson Riordan

Always There

I'm there where the rippling waters flow,
In the hush of softly falling snow,
The dew of the wild rose, on the thorn,
The cry of a babe, just newly born.

I'm there in a field of waving grain,
In raging storms, and gentle rain,
In winds that bite, in scented breeze,
In tiny flowers, and tallest trees.

I'm there in the darkness of the night,
When the moon is high, and stars are bright,
When early birds sing in the sky,
As dark is o'er, and morn is nigh.

I'm there where the traffic never stops,
In quiet vales, on mountain tops,
In winter's ice, and autumn's fall,
The warmth of summer, spring's recall.

I'm there if you want me, to be found,
I'm here if you need me, look around,
I'm land, I'm sea, each breath of air,
For I am love, I'm always there.

Sarah H. Blackwell

The Tug Of Love

No mental peace can I find,
It really does disturb my mind.
There is one long battle after another,
To keep my children, I am their Mother.
The battle one must face in divorce,
Scar one very deep of course.
The children in the middle of the battle,
Pushed around like herded cattle.
He wants them for his own,
To leave me lost and all alone.
But I must always fight on,
For a Mothers love is Oh so strong.
He loves them as much as me,
A Mother to them he could never be.
In divorce the family is no longer one,
And children put in the middle become.
First pulled this way and then that,
We fight over them like dog and cat.
All they really want is love and security,
What will happen when they reach maturity.

A. Dimmock

Bathroom

The happiest man in the world
In the happiest house in the world
Eats the happiest meal on the happiest
Sunday dull morning, crooning over the happiest
Beautifully arranged plates with the nicest ever
   Knife and
Fork and a little grumbling spoon -
Looking, smiling, at a nobody-knows-who friend
In the happiest manner he knows in the world
Says he, "I'm the happiest man in the world
That knows he's the happiest an' everybody should
   know this, since I'm the happiest man
In the happiest world in the happiest time in the
   happiest history ever, ever, ever"
And the cat yawns beside him, yawns, yawns, yawns
Till the night finally breaks up open, gulping down
The world, the house, the tablecloth with small
Sauce-stains on it, and leaves him but tormented
   before the
Bathroom mirror.

Ken Oishi

Deadly Weapon

Why was the gun invented? A lethal, deadly machine
In the hands of tyrants, murderous, evil and mean
A single bullet obliterates man from the earth, he exists no more
And opens torturous avenues, creating all out War

Countries divided use it, as a political power struggle game
With violent oppression, they mutilate, cripple, disfigure and maim
No thought for the terrified victim, what images transpire in his mind
As he breathes his last breathe, leaving his bereaving family behind

How do they live with their conscience? How do they sleep at night?
Do their victims haunt them and continually emerge into sight?
Or are their some savage and ruthless, with blood-curdling
   thoughts on their mind?
No pity, remorse or compassion, no guilt ridden thoughts for mankind

If only the gun hadn't been invented,
countless more humans would still be here
And peace and harmony would abound, as opposed to
foreboding fear.

Pauline Thompson

Nightmare

I'm running, running, running faster,
I must get away or there'll be disaster,
I'm getting nowhere, I'm standing still,
I'll get away, I will, I will.

The waters swirling and churning
I'm frightened, my stomachs turning
The waters all murky, horrible and brown
I'm falling, falling, I shall drown.

My hands are clammy, my face all wet.
My body trembling and covered in sweat
My life flashes by me, I'm dead
Oh no I'm not, I'm alive, I'm in bed.

M. Simms

Money

Will someone tell me where I've gone wrong,
I'm finding it hard to get along
I work all week to earn my pay,
But it comes and goes within the same day.

Does anyone have the same trouble as me.
I handle accounts but not a penny do I see.
Kids need some shoes or even some clothes.
With little money this a problem does pose.

I dream of the day I'll have something to spend,
Maybe have some left over or even to lend,
Still I have my health and a roof over my head,
For those two things only there's a lot to be said

Wilma Cockerill

Autumn Leisure

One would expect to see, the splendour of a tree
In spring, in March, but come along and ramble
Through the bracken and the bramble,
Behold the beauty, of the Autumn Larch.

Sunlight streaming through, golden dappled pine,
A woodland waterfall, shimmering, cascading down
As autumn magic turns the larch,
From green to gold, and shades of brown.

A startled pheasant from its perch
With rat-a-rat of beating wings
Thrills the passer by
Fills the heart with sounds of things—

Sounds of things forgotten
In the city's toil and scramble
Lucky those, with time to amble,
Through the bracken and the bramble.

Friendly ramblers, who with knowledge
Let their footsteps guide
Sharing natures beauty
Of the autumn countryside.

M. F. Barney

The Power Of God

We face our troubles daily
In bed each night we pray
Dear God please give us courage
To face the coming day

Like wanderers in the desert
No lamps to light our way
Our souls cry out in anguish
Dear God please with us stay

We had our share of good times
We thought they'd never end
And then the storm clouds up above
Upon us did descend.

We cried Dear God please help us
We did not ask in vain
Your helping hand sustained us
We lived to fight again

And when our lives are over
And our bodies laid to rest
We ask Dear God 'Please take our souls
We tried to do our best.'

H. Waller

Canada 85

I fasten now my seat belt for to Canada I do fly
In a Wardair DC10 we travel very high
With my pockets full of dollars and my bank balance in the red
To the Delta Chelsea Inn where it cost me forty pounds, the bed
To record all the wonders of Niagara I did photograph a lot
Then we travel up the Skylon Tower to the very top
We dined in the revolving restaurant it really made my day
We viewed the Spanish aero car, the floral clock then went
   on our way
To see Saint Marie of the Huron's mission we went another day
The church and all the mission were rebuilt the seventeenth
   century way
We followed in Pope John Paul's footsteps to the Martyr's Shrine
And throughout the day the lovely sun did shine
My last trip out was from Lock 42 on the Trent-Severn waterway
We travel on the "Lady Belle" boat on a hot and sunny day
We passed through Swift's Rapid Lock a drop of forty five feet
To the big chute the marine railway an engineering feat
But all too soon my holiday in Canada came swiftly to its end
And I did have to say farewell to my cousin Edith and her friends
From Toronto airport we left at half pass ten at night
We met the sunrise above the clouds it was a glorious sight

H. Skinn

Remembrance

God bless those that fought for us,
In battles long ago.
May we ever grateful be,
They died, to make us free.

In two World wars, their courage was shown.
Most did not choose to go.
Many returned disabled.
Did we, enough caring, show?

Today we see so many wars.
How futile they all seem!
Will peace, ever be, a reality?
Fighting never seen.

On this remembrance day, we pray,
For peace throughout the world,
And wear our poppies, lest we forget.
The terrible price. They paid.

Dear Father. May there never be,
World-wide war today.
Which touches, "Oh" so many lives.
The young. With their life. Have to pay.

Pamela Theobalds Bailey

The Crazy Daisy

The crazy daisy lies alone
In its bed of earth and stone
Impregnated only by drops of rain
The crazy daisy has gone insane
It waves its petals madly
As other daisies look on sadly
The poor daisy has lost its head
The hope it stays out of their bed.

The crazy daisy dreams of flying
It's so sick and tired of just lying
The crazy daisy wants to sing
Waiting for what only death can bring
The crazy daisy rocks hard and fast
Hoping today's winds will be its last
It grins and hopes as a child comes round
And with a kick sends it from the ground
The crazy daisy starts to fly
Into the world you enter when you die
The crazy daisy has gone home
The crazy daisy is no longer alone.

Stuart Allen

My Anguish

I sometimes feel that I'm all alone
In a world so cruel, it ignores my pain.
There's nowhere to hide from a future unknown
Or the life that I'm now forced to sustain.

I'm not in control; my body's not mine,
Some crafty alien has invaded my space,
Stealing my independence; now that's a crime
But I'm the one with the sentence to face.

No-one can help me; that's why I despair
And panic and fear for what lies ahead.
It's so strange, unreal and oh, so unfair
And happening to someone else instead?

"Why me... Why me?" I want to scream
And lash out at anyone; someone to blame
For the crushing effect on my self-esteem
And a quite inexplicable feeling of shame.

How I yearn to go back to my life before,
When it seems to me now that I had no woes,
Blissfully unaware of what lay in store,
Of how precious is health and how quickly it goes.

S. Miller

"To The Glory Of God"

In Bethlehem town where Christ was born
In a stable scattered with husks of corn,
They've raised a Church, where the stable stood,
With marble walls and gilded wood,
The Christ to glorify.

Yet, on the day Christ came to earth,
The glory was in the Saviour's birth,
The stable mean was filled with joy,
The arrival on earth of a Baby Boy
His Father to glorify.

The angels sang, the shepherds adored,
And Kings from afar came to worship their Lord.
God's Word was fulfilled, the Messiah came
To save our souls from sin and shame
His mercy to glorify.

Man's glory is shown in a Church of some worth
Which will stand for many a long year on earth,
But to God's Son, only, is glory shown
When men give their souls to Christ to own,
His name to glorify.

B. Morton

Memories

The flower may have faded but the seed of love still grows
In a secret place deep in our hearts that nobody else knows
You may have gone in person but your spirit is still here
Giving us fond memories now and every year
Your smile is in the sunshine your tears in the rain
We watch you on video dear daughter - time and time again
Your laughter is in the wind your sadness in the cloud
You were a wonderful daughter of whom we were so proud
You always had a smile for people everywhere
Even though a life of pain was the cross you had to bear
So each time a flower opens we see your smiling face
Photographs and memories that cannot be replaced
And we hear your whispers in the rustling of the leaves
Saying we must keep smiling, telling us not to grieve
It's hard not to darling daughter - you were the apple of our eye
We only hope that God's taken you to that special place
   up in the sky
So we try to keep on going until in heaven we meet again
Telling ourselves sweet memories will take away the pain
So until that day when we will knock on heaven's door
We will hold you deep in our hearts now and forevermore
Dedicated to our daughter Mandy

J. M. Harwood

The Traveller

He didn't care much for work,
In a planned out suburban town,
With their well kept lawns and terraces,
With gas lamps from the sea to the downs.

So he left on a Tuesday morning,
While the sun was in the sky,
And he headed for the open country,
Not quite knowing the reason why.

So he walked along the dusty lane,
Singing with all his might,
He'd left the order of the cities,
And he knew what he'd done was right.

But an hour or so behind him
A sports car was racing along.
Soon it would catch up with the traveller
And end his merry song.

Now, in the hush and darkened evening,
While the birds fly overhead,
Several well dressed orderly people,
Stand around the traveller, who's dead

M. M. Arbon

The Story Of The Willow Pattern

Long, long ago in a far off land,
In a land where the beautiful green willows stand,
A young Chinese boy's love for a girl was so true.
The shy Chinese maiden, she loved him so too.
For they had both been forbidden, you see,
To meet on the bridge by the green willow tree
He knew that she loved him but what could he do?
For her family loathed him and his family too.
A wooden bridge divided his tribe from hers,
over the river where the blue water stirs.
They both went to the bridge one morn to draw water,
and he loved her so deeply, the enemy's daughter.
They vowed that their love would always be true.
Then they jumped into the water, so deep and so blue,
just then two little love birds flew up into the air
Their love was so sweet, their love song they share,
The two tribes called a truce and now while China sleeps
The blue water still stirs and the green willow still weeps.

E. M. Stevens

Visiting Time

Like a silent shadow I entered the room.
In a corner my father sat upright in a chair.
A sickly smell of rose-petal perfume
And disinfectant hung heavily in the warm air.

Our false smiles failed and fell silently away.
Cards, flowers and pictures stared awkwardly from the sill.
Under the bed a cardboard bottle lay,
A pool of piss on the floor rested peacefully still.

By his side the liquid of life grimly hung,
Like the sucking leech of a quack, as if to be bled
And cured. Withering petals sadly clung
Lifelessly to their stalk, then fell, soft stains of blood-red.

Desperately I searched for the right words to say;
They too fell silent. Instead I gazed through the window,
To stare at the sunny September day,
At the dying leaves and the people far below.

I hated them, but why should they have to care
For a man whom they did not, and would not, ever know?
How lonely is a grief one cannot share;
Angry and ashamed of my weakness I turned to go.

Peter Charles Anthony

Pregnant Pause

It's a wonderful thing I hear people say
I'm pregnant you see, I suppose it's okay
The only thing is, I think you'll agree
Is a gaze in the mirror, "Oh Lord is that me?"

My belly's all swollen, it looks like a ball
Tears streams down my face, I'm wider than tall
There's tuna with custard for something to chew
And heartburn and sickness to name but a few

The moment arrives and I stay very calm
It's my husband that panics to raise the alarm
We head for the hospital, packed ready to go
Then on to delivery I waddle off slow

The pain is so bad, "Oh please knock me out"
"Is anyone listening?" I constantly shout
But one more good push for my bundle of joy
"Congrats Dad and Mum, you've just had a boy"

There's no preparation for the pain and the fears
And holding your son, your face covered with tears
It's a beautiful moment, couldn't wish any more
For here in my arms the son I'll always adore

Lesley Carter

Military Cemetery, Taiping, Malaya

The men beneath the crosses lie in serried rows,
Impervious to sun or monsoon rain,
Not thinking of the men who were their foes,
Not knowing that their deaths were all in vain.

These men that fought to keep an Empire fair,
And died so many, many miles from England's shore,
They never thought that people would not care,
That mention of their fate would only bore.

And so they lie and wait the Judgment Day,
When they can say with pride, "We did not run,
As British men we turned not from the fray,
And tho' the battle lost, the war was won.

And all we ask of those, who ever live in peace,
To sometimes think, and sometimes kneel and pray
For the forgotten few, and remember without cease,
That for your Tomorrow, we gave our Today".

F. O. Green

Ode To A Parkinson's Disease Sufferer

Kelly Timpson-Prior
Is a lady we admire
Though unable to keep still
Because she was so ill
Her mood was always cheery
Though the road was long and dreary
She always kept her spirits high

Kelly's husband Albert gave support
With every deed and thought
For her he gave his best
It was his lifetime's test
And on the day she died
Poor Albert sobbed and cried
There was only one beloved Kelly

She'd want us to go on
Despite the fact she's gone
And so this story ends
Its message it transcends
Of devotion love and struggle to the end

Robert H. Mears

I Am, I Will Be

I am the rook upon the chessboard,
I move sideways, though never forwards.
I am the hands upon a clock-face
Going round, but going no place.
I am the wheel upon a car,
I go round, but don't go far.
I am the raindrops on the glass,
Running down, but nowhere, fast.
I am the morning sun; I rise each day,
But every night, I fade away.

I will be the tree that reaches to the sky,
The clouds that float by, up so high,
The newborn foal that fights to stand,
The child that takes life's out-stretched hand,
The river that rushes to the sea -
These things will one day, all be me.

Karen C. Gocher

Dream Diamonds

I will gather diamonds twinkling on the sea.
I'll make a necklace rare for all
the world to see.

But they disappear so quickly
before there on my twine.
So that lovely necklace never
will be mine.

While ere the sun is shining
The diamonds gather there.
I know I cannot own them
there they for all to share.

M. Calton

A Loving Afternoon

We're meeting at one, my heart's beating fast
I'm sitting here waiting and it's already five past
I know you'll be there, you're just running late
But I just long to see you, it's so hard to wait
You pull along side my car, your smile says it all
I'm with you in moments and feel ten feet tall
We share a sweet kiss and then break away
Say 'where shall we go! We've got the rest of the day
We head for the coast, but stop for a drink
Shall we have a quick snack, what do you think?
We have a drink and a meal and play the machine
We hold hands and laugh, it's like living a dream
We get back in the car, kiss, there's no fuss
We touch as you drive, it seems natural to us
We park by the sea and walk on the beach
We're together, no secret, not at arm's reach
We stroll back to the car, where we laugh and we kiss
At this moment, life's perfect, it's heaven, it's bliss

Ronnie Lee

Steph

Steph get up I hear Mum shout
I'm not, I'm not, I lay and pout
I'm tired and I want to stay
Just one more tick and I'll be o.k.

The bathroom is free
Come and get your cup of tea
I'm not going to beg
Steph show a leg

Your hair's alright, give that mirror a rest
Get off to school you are a pest
Your dinner money is on the shelf
Get that eyeshadow off or else

I know we'd rather not attend.
Miss really isn't her best friend.
My girl, Steph, is no one's fool,
But oh! this last year at school.

J. Cox

The Lottery

I have the money in my pocket
I'm out the door just like a rocket,
I'm running late, I'm through the gate,
I'm down the road, they just won't wait.

"Get out the way" people hear me say,
"Is he mad" I hear them say,
I'm almost there, I hope there's time,
This time it's mine, it's mine, it's mine

The kids are waiting, so the wife,
This ticket could really change our life,
I have it now it's in my hand,
I'm not greedy, just a few grand,

Just six little numbers, that's all I need,
Or five and one, to quench my greed,
We watch the screen, it's not to be,
Oh, how we love the lottery

J. R. Thorogood

Memories

Memories I treasure, locked in my heart.
I mean to keep evermore,
Of all my treasures one stands apart,
Saved from the dear days of yours.
I hear a voice so sweet and low,
The voice in the old village choir,
It sings to me of long ago,
The voice in the old village choir,
In dreams I drift through a twilight haze,
Back again to my childhood days
To hear again when lights are low,
That voice in the old village choir.

F. C. Turner

Six Years Old

Six years old,
I'm scared of death,
Six years old,
I hold my breath.

Six years old,
With six year old's fears,
No one listens to my cries,
They fall on deaf ears.

I'm six years old,
Death comes stalking,
The room is cold,
Parents talking.

Raging father hits my head,
'You little brat, you will wish you were dead'
Six years old am I,

God damn you Mother and you Dad,
Why was I born of life so sad.

Forty six years old am I,
Come on Death, I spit in your eye.

Kevin Archbold

Untitled

Sail on the tide and take me home,
I'm tired and will no longer roam.
My heart is left in one small place
Where there is one familiar face.

A smile that I have seen before
And honest eyes that I adore;
That fell in watchful gaze at night
When absence kept me from their sight.

I know I will feel rested when
I'm home with those I love again.
Now, emptied out with pain and fear,
I know that I should not be here.

A dream I held once in my hand
Has now become a barren land.
A passing whim I once held dear
Took little time to disappear.

Hope, I have long believed in you,
Restore my faith and get me through.
Lift me from the ocean floor
And bear me to that distant shore.

Maia Bishenden

Untitled

I'm the out of work builder I love to work and create,
I'm out looking for work early mornings
There's always a man by my gate.

He asked me to come to his office
He's from the D.H.S.S. is Mr. Brown,
maybe he's got nothing better to do to me he's just a clown

He said you're out early every morning
And most times you're out all day, well I was just trying to
explain but he just wanted to stop my pay.

So when you go out looking for work keep looking to your back
Because Mr. Brown is watching you I wish he'd get the sack

I'd watch him every morning, I'd watch, him every day
I'd even give him a job so I could sack him and stop his pay

To see my baby in the bath all the bubbles just watch her laugh
Red wet hair down her back
She kicks her legs for the water to smack

The joys of watching children grow who are we what do we know
So innocent is a child who sings her nursery song and smiles

The joy to my life that she brings but I'm not supposed to
know of all these things.

M. Whitehouse

Grandma's Love

A Grandma's love is for life no matter what you do.
I'm here to answer every call, I'm here for all of you.
There's no one different from the rest, I love you all the same.
I love you when you read to me, or when we play a game.

I love you when you're quiet, and when you're playing loud.
When you say you love me too, of that I'm really proud.
Then it's time to go for shopping, or play down in the park.
Your laughter still excites me, be still my ageing heart.

I'll wait here by the window until you visit me.
We can go into the garden and play under the tree.
We can have a picnic on the lawn, until it's time to go.
Tomorrow is another day, 'till then, I'll miss you so.

I write this poem just for you, my flesh, my blood, my soul.
To tell you that you are my world, without you I am old.
And when the time has come for me to spread my wings and fly
At least you'll know that love has found the way for you and I...

I. Beecham

Special

With a child-like giggle she exclaimed an extraordinary request,
"If the wind takes my wig away will you bring it back?"
Theatre seats were ours for a few special hours as we drooled
In admiration of an incredibly handsome leading man.

"Oooh!" She cried with excitement when the telephone rang
one night, "It's a man and he wants to talk to you!"
That Saturday evening she helped me dress to impress
on my first date,
"You'll knock him dead!" as I went off to meet my new beau.

With utmost efficiency she arranged the interview for me,
Primed and coached by her, I was given my first job.
Evening was the time for explaining and complaining about my
new post.
Words of assurance, she encouraged and told me I was
capable of anything.

"Pass me the bowl darling" she urged as yet again she was unwell.
"I feel a lot better now, thanks a lot"
The chemotherapy always had that effect, she'd retch and
fight for control
A tired smile and a joke would shrug it off.

With a kindly smile she spoke to me an extraordinary request,
"When the cancer takes me, will you take care of your Dad?"
A few special hours were ours to say goodbye to our special lady,
My friend, my advisor, my number one fan - my mum.

Susan K. Farrow

The Dividing Door

When I was young, at party-time we had a favourite game.
I'll try to fill you in on it, for I can't recall the name,
A room was shown to be prepared with hurdles in a row.
We'd be admitted one by one to bravely, 'have a go'.

But first we'd be blind folded and carefully led inside
To step around these obstacles, or a forfeit be supplied!
We weren't to know as we came in, the path would be made clear.
All we could hear was laughter as each child tried to steer,
The laughter built to climax as blindfold no more bound,
Now victim shared the secret, as peace of mind was found.
Each one was so courageous, entering singly in the dark,
But there were hands to guide you, and this, of course - a lark!

In course of time the queue reduced, friends fast would disappear.
We wished they'd come back to explain, and take away our fear!
We really could not join them without going through that door,
Yet happily knew they were alright, how could we doubt it more?

So when you find your folk and friends have crossed that
great divide,
Remember, keep your chin up, there's nought to fear inside!

Lola Perks-Hartnell

Writing A Poem

What can I write for this contest
I'll try quite hard and do my best
I sit all night and try to think
It's enough to drive you to drink

All the people from which poems stream
Creation so great, written out in reams
With Wordsworth, Keats and Byron too
I cannot compete, what shall I do

Open the bookcase and have a look
I might be inspired by some great book
Wait a moment, I have an idea
Better write it down before it disappears

I don't know if I can make this rhyme
I'd better have a think and take my time
Now the ideas start to flow
See it come alive, row by row

Now the Twenty lines are in sight
Still so much left to write
With the due date for posting pending
I really must think of an ending

F. Stanton

Watching

Life during wartime through a misted lens
I'm feeling this distance and lack of compassion
For those on the screen.

The images are only images
Human emotions flatlined and burned away

Maybe it's the distance
And I'd react somehow if there things happened right here right now.

I'd start kicking and screaming
Burning with righteous fire.

Or perhaps

I've entered this state, this place called emotional neutralization
I've found safe harbour behind borderlines of medical excuses
I can justify, hide away, with every psychological nuance explained.

So I go on
Please, let me go on
Watching life during wartime
Letting compassion slip away.

Vernon A. Leigh

"The Lord Is My Master"

The Lord is my master, I shall not want
I'll lie down at his feet
In kennels or home he'll feedeth me
Or shelter clean and neat!

My doggie soul he'll restore again
And me to walk doth make
And on my lead in faithfulness
The road of love I'll take

Altho' I walk in death's dark vale
Yet will I fear none ill
For thou art with me, with my lead
And collar round me still

My doggie bowl he doth fill
In presence of my foes
My head he doth give a pat
And my heart glows and glows.

Goodness and mercy all my life
Shall surely follow me
And in God's Heaven for little dogs
There'll be a place for me to be!

Minette Angus

A Stranger Called

Who's that out there?
I'll go and see,
A stranger tapping on the door.
I opened wide,
He walked right in,
Without a word, or by your leave.
He wandered through the rooms,
Until the kitchen he did spy.
Then stood aside, while I,
The back door opened wide.
Without a word he went outside,
Such rudeness should be quite absurd,
If he were not a chicken bird.
He did not fly, just scratched around,
For food which lay upon the ground.
So tame, a pet must be,
In fact he's taken over me.
I bought some corn, and spread the word,
But no one seemed to know the bird.

Norman Wharry

A Treat

There was a treat in store tonight, so my dad had told me
If you eat all your tea, do your jobs, then you will see
So six o'clock came and off we went, a kiss for Mum
She had too much to do so she couldn't come
Down the Lane, through the woods and over the gate
I held Dad's hand, we didn't want to be late
Keep quiet now or they will all run away
And I knew, we are going to watch baby rabbits at play
We crept up the hill just to the top
There, there, there I could see them hop
Some were sat up and some were laid down
Some were grey, some were fawn and brown
Their ears were pricked up and looked pink in the sun
That's when I thought, I wish Mum could have come
These are memories of how I felt that lovely summer night
The warmth, the happiness, the baby rabbits, oh what a wonderful sight

Marion Slater

Life Without Water

Life without water would be very sad.
If you didn't waste it everyone will be glad.
Animals need water as well as us.
If we didn't have canals,
We'd have to catch a car or a bus.
Creatures, plants and the garden turf,
all need water which we have got on earth.
Life without water would be very hard,
Your throat would be as dry as card.
If I never wrote a poem which would,
Never, never rhyme,
This poem would be very much like
  SLIME!

Tammy Withers

Christmas Questions

Santa, has he been or passed me by?
If the latter please tell me why?
But if he came what did he give?
Does he know just where I live?

Down the stairs as quick as light
Lost sleep, throughout the night
Check the stocking it looks full!
I'm glad today, there is no school

Packaging ripped, shred and torn
Earlier pleasures lie forlorn
A gun, ball, and bus and radio set
What other goodies, did I get

What's that sound that I hear?
Will Santa Claus at last appear?
Ah! It's only Mum and Dad that are there!
And I don't suppose they really care!

E. G. Borwick

Giving

Only love can change the world
If you care you can change anything
Give the love that's needed, show people you care
How can we watch a starving child cry
See its body ache for food and not care
Whatever the colour of their skin
Your heart aches to see such pain
Why do some seem to have it all and some have nothing
Life being a child's most precious gift
We will help you and I
It only takes a little from you and a little from me
I cry for your right to live
And I pray for rain to given your barren land life
We will help the children
What price life no one can say
Sometimes caring isn't enough
But little children of pain we will work together
We will help you grow strong
Underneath we are all the same
So we will give, so you can live

Sue Moody

A Fact Of Life

Life could be so good
If it were to be all that it should.
Why can't others see
That their little be a lot to me.

If I could do things others can do
I would feel on of the chosen few.
There is an old saying, "little thing mean a lot",
People ignore it, people who should not.

To live a normal life, for just one week,
To do things without effort, would be a relief.
Things that should come naturally, are effort for me
I hate being disabled, but I am, it's a fact,
And it's always to be.

Margaret Baker

Headlines

He walked along aimlessly scuffing his shoes.
If he had a choice, who knows what he would choose.
He picked up a fag-end and struck up a match,
he didn't seem to care what diseases he'd catch.
He wandered around going on his weary way,
in his own private world with nothing to say.
His clothes were shabby and by no means clean.
you could tell that around the dustbins he'd been.
It came as a surprise only a month after that,
when I went to the newsagents for my paper and chat.
I took the paper and I avidly read
the front page headlines, "Millionaire is dead".
They showed a photo of the millionaire
and he looked familiar with his vacant stare.
It suddenly dawned on me that I knew this bloke.
He was the shabby man who we all thought was broke.
I finished reading the story and then I cried,
for he wandered the streets when his wife tragically died.

R. Telford

Granddad Died

When my granddad died
I was so sad, I cried all night
it was so bad.
All my friends were nice to me,
but I felt so sick I couldn't breathe.
All my cousins standing there,
at the altar with a glare.
I thought to myself standing there,
my granny alone, nobody to care;
but I know that when I pray I'll have
Granddad both night and day.

Lydia Doolan

My Father

Today I heard, my father died,
I wasn't sad, and I never cried

I feel quite guilty, cos I know I should
but as my father, he was never cry good
The memories are bad, and still hurt like hell,
And the beating's I remember so very well.
So please understand, if I don't mourn.
Or feel all alone, lost and forlorn.

He never earned no love from me,
and in a sense, I'm now quite free.
I've learned to trust, and feel no pain.
So his great loss, was my real gain.

To have a daughter, who loved him so,
is a privilege, he'll never know.

Rita Monk

The Unseen

I the unseen, I the unheard,
In my world of safety I live undisturbed.
You the mother, your face unknown,
Your voices an echo, in you, my home.
And when you smile, when you cry,
I know it too, but not understand why.

I wait eternally, I wait until
My soul inflames and I becomes real.
I want to leave, want to stay.
In the confusion my world given way.
I feel the panic, want to scream
Now sliding downwards to where I've not been.

Feeling pain, feeling fear.
Voices seem louder but still so unclear.
I try to retreat, but now it's too late,
My head is trapped and there's no escape.
I close my eyes, my body heaves.
Goodbye safe world that nobody sees.

Paula Wright

"Flo Handy"

I hope you enjoyed your last place to stay,
I tried to make you comfortable in every way,
You as a resident, me as a carer we were well paired,
I'll always remember the times we shared,
I wish I could hear you sing just once more
No one knows what we have in store,
But I'm glad we had the time together,
Honesty Flo you were a treasure
I'll always miss you more than you'll know
I've got your plant and together we'll grow
A cup and saucer I shall proudly show
This belonged to my 'old pal Flo.'

Susan Hollins

The Sea

Let the sun shine blue and bright
In the paths of the liquid light
Shining like grapes in the beam
Rippling like a world of dreams
Beauty shining over there,
A presence in the summer glare.

Roaring through the azure waves
Pearly-white foam in the lave.
Leaping waves ready to pour
Like rainbows lightening up the shore,
Gushing waves cascade the rocks
Like unfurled flags streaming the locks

They say the sea is like a child,
Torrently and ever wild
The roaring seas going fast
Erupting! Howling! Like a blast
The mighty seas with smothered sighs
Tired and tangled, but never dies.

Mary Myles

'A Promise Of Absent Help'

Please, do not leave me alone, again,
it would only sustain the curse, contained,
within my spirit, which you once befriended,
but now, from you, it must be defended.
Why did you do this?
Stay, with me, and I will take care of you,
I plead,
I would defend you with my heart,
Provided from you I never part,
just to hear the sound of your voice, again,
compassion hidden in its tone,
Without you I would kill.
Have a crisis I need you to, leaven
only then, could I attain my heaven.
In bloom, is my peril's mute legacy,
Its soft height, teasing the sky,
I will always think of you, even when alone.
I need you, to mend me.

H. K. Grimwood

"Oh Dear"

It's raining today, I think I'll stay in
I will sit by the fire and get a video in.

Now what shall I get, "Gone with the wind", or "Wuthering Heights:
Or maybe a murder - "Strangled with her Tights".

I know, I'll clean out the cupboards, or maybe the drawers
Polish the furniture or mop the floors
No, on second thought I'll take a nap, because there's\
   Nothing on telly
And my fingers have started to tap.

I can't make my mind up, I'm really in doubt
Oh, put your coat on and go on out.

D. Wesson

Tree

If I were an oak tree big and tall
I would stand up straight looking over all
With outstretched arms, head held high
I'd nearly reach up to the sky
The birds would nest among my leaves
A whistling and singing
Along with the breeze.
On a sunny day in a sleepy glade
Where the dew is glistening in the shade.
The bluebells swaying to and fro
Jingling their bells sweet and low.
The green grass with its glossy sheen
A lovely sight to be seen
A rabbit scurries to its burrow
The farmer with his fields a-furrow
All these things and more I see
Because I am a tall oak tree.

O. Warner

Changing World

I sat beside the waterfront looking out to sea
I thought of the world we live in and how it used to be
No more football in the street a sign of times gone by
Now it's muggers in the park who leave you there to die
Where are the great industries that gave us all a job
Now they train you for the pole and class you as a yob
They used to house the homeless from the rain sleet and snow
But now their sleeping in the streets and no one wants to know
No more community spirit where life was so much fun
Now they prefer a life of crime and steal from everyone
A politician used to have honour and panache
This sleeky lot that we have now prefer to take the cash
When I was young a knees-up was classed a real good night
But now it's drugs and ecstasy surely that can't be right
The world we know I regret to say will have to change and how
Because if it stays the way it is I'll go quietly now

C. Gilliland

Christmas On A Scottish Isle

At 4:00 a.m. I rose and said farewell, so fond,
I wish we could have stayed there, if I'd waved a magic wand,
But you and I both know, for one week, that we must part,
I don't think you'll ever know, the pain deep in my heart.

Waiting at the bus stop, on an early winter's morn,
I thought I'd never see the coming of the dawn,
It was a cold and it was bleak, and my thoughts returned to you,
What would the New Year bring for my love and I, so new.

The coach took me to London, and then to board the plane,
I had to ring my Vivienne to stop from going insane,
As I flew up north to Scotland, I sat back in my seat,
It was hurting me to visualize, how long before we'd meet.

With many miles between us, I felt so sad and lost,
At Glasgow's lonely airport, I tried to count the cost,
I know I must see mother, and I was duty bound,
But what of Viv, my Guardian Angel, the new love I have found.

At last on board the ferry I looked off the starboard bow,
I saw the Island's lights, twinkling for me now,
I knew I'd done the right thing, and I think you will agree,
A week a year for Mother,, is not too much for me.

T. J. Shearing

Dole Doldrums

I lost my job in the coal and went to sign on the dole.
I was told to wait my turn and given a book of rules to learn.
After playing the waiting game I finally got to state my claim.
I was given a wad of forms to fill in, in which I admitted I lived in sin. When I handed them to the clerk, she looked at me with a smirk. I see you have only worked a year, I'm sorry we cannot see you here. Go along to Westfield house, don't forget to take your spouse. Off along to the social I went to beg of them to pay my rent. I was given more forms to fill out, in which they asked if I had gout. Special needs allowance they said, well I do get pains in my head. Go along to queue number nine, there they told me it was after time. Come back here tomorrow at ten, your claim will be dealt with then. By this time my patience had worn thin, I put the bloody window in. I was up before the judge the next day, who asked me what I had to say. Well sir I'm here today in this court because
of my claim for income support, and if I have to pay a fine I will have to go and do my time. The judge replied you no good slob, why don't you get a job. Six months in Armley jail, if I gave you less my duty I would fail. We have a compassionate welfare state, if you are prepared to wait.

B. Spencer-Moore

Pursuit

And since nothing is left to drink,
I'll drink myself
Had you ever imagine that things
will go so, My darling?
Me either.

And still wonder, love
were you ever mine?
Me neither.

But is it because you were afraid
the feeling of belonging
or, sharing?

Please if you know the answers
write them in a paper,
throw it in the ocean
WITHOUT a bottle,
I want to be sure that I'll never find out.

      My only and everlasting passion.

And since nothing is left to smoke. I'll smoke my self
I can see you in the smoke... Thin as always.

Kostas Nektarios Attia

407

First Day At School

He gets up early he's so young and shy
I really hope he doesn't cry
Breakfast is eaten with hardly a word
It is so quiet it's really absurd
Eight forty five he's dressed and he's ready
Quickly a kiss and cuddle for teddy
Out of the door we're now in the street
The neighbours all think he looks sweet
Into the schoolyard he walks with pride
Feeling, so brave with Mum by his side
Now he's gone, what no tears oh dread!
I think I'm gonna cry instead.
  B. Marley

My Perfect World

I want to create a world where all religions unite
I'd banish all hate and racism and bond all black and white,
I'd take all orphaned children and wrap them in a blanket
I'd give them each a family and the starving would sit at a banquet.

There'd be no cause for peace talks 'cause I'd put an end to war
I'd cure all illness and disease and A.I.D.s would be no more,
I'd open the door to my home and invite all the homeless in
violence would be unheard of and I'd take away all the sin.

I'd stop all the pollution the sea would be bright blue
I'd banish all nuclear weapons and everyone's love would be true,
There'd be no such thing as abortion and no such thing as greed
I'd take all the third world in my arms and individually feed.

The weather would always be warm and harvest would always
grow ripe everyone would have a job and animals would have rights,
This worlds seems so unrealistic it may seem a little bit odd
but there is such a place (and I'll meet you there!)
  In the kingdom of God
  Kelly Colledge

Trees

Summer gone; winter won't be long
I walk the lanes and woods
So free, underneath the great oak tree
The carpet of leaves I tread at night
So beautiful and bright in the autumn light
Big trees so high they reach the sky
Why do you spread your leaves so high
And how do others grow? No one would ever know
If you could speak to me alone
Of bygone days, so long ago
Men fought beneath your brows
And died of honour, I've been told
You kept poor people from the cold
With burning wood, so red and bright
You kept me safe throughout the night
You brighten up their homes with light
When the axeman comes along
To cut you down without a song
You won't be dead for long
With windows, doors, stairways strong, you will live forever on
  J. G. Jones

Reflections Of A Lost Love

Standing by the water's edge, beneath a clear blue sky
I saw my own reflection, and felt the need to cry
I saw in that reflection, a world of love gone by
I saw only hunger, and children willing to die.
I saw a world being destroyed, by prejudice and greed
People being brutally killed, for the sake of colour or creed
On all the children's faces, I saw only hurt and pain
Giving all they had to survive, without one little complaint.
I saw the pain and torment, of children going by
The question on their faces, asking me why?
I heard a voice behind me, but did not turn to see
The voice of God had spoken, and he had chosen me!
  Mary Ferguson

When I Went to Confession

When I went to confession in Kentucky
I told the father that I said something mucky.
He peeped at me when he drew the little curtain
but the light was so dark and poor,
he came round and opened the door.
There he gave me such a look that I've seen once before,
and that was on an ugly, stuffed wild boar.
Now I was shaking at the knees and
also finding it difficult to breath,
when he barked and said, "Would you kindly repeat that again!"
Well, I looked down upon my lap,
and the water was running down from my wee tap.
I thought, am I the only one who tells the truth?
That's when I put on my poor mouth,
but I mumbled up the courage to say it again.
So he handed me a paper and said,
"Would you write it in pen?"
It was then that I ran and
I've never seen that church. Amen.
  Peter Dragoonis

Love

Why does love hurt so much
I thought I would feel ease not pain.
Love should be honest and just
I don't think I can trust again

I answer the phone no one there
you are afraid each time it rings
our friends say we are the perfect pair
can't you feel the heartache this brings

Be a man I know you lied
If you no longer love me tell me so
I look in your eyes the light has died
So hard as it is, I must let you go.

You take my hand say you are sorry
I suddenly feel so alone and sad
You say I don't realize the pain and worry
I stop you there how dare you make me feel bad

I looked at the face I loved so much
I search for the look of love in your eyes
I prayed for the feel of your touch.
What greater loss than a love that dies
  E. Hemmings

Yellow Ribbons

My son has gone to war, gone to the desert war.
I think of him and pray for him, but I can do no more.
Where is that little boy who I used to hold so tight
When he needed me, for I made him see they were shadows in the night.

My son has gone to war, gone to the desert war.
So far from home and so alone. What has that madman done?.
Life goes on the same but they don't see the pain,
I don't feel brave I'm so afraid we'll never be the same.

My son has gone to war, who knows where it will end?.
Time ticks by, our hopes die. Fond messages we send.
I'm very proud of him. But then that's nothing new.
He'll be so brave, the world he'll save. That job for me and you.

My son has gone to war. He wears the 'Desert Rat.'
He'll be the proudest soldier there, you can be sure of that.
Yellow ribbons tied at home, our love for all to see.
And all I ask of his mighty task is, "God keep him safe for me."

My son has gone tow war, and in that hostile land
The sky is black, the sun is cold, there's danger in the sand.
But in this land of ours, life burst with flowers grown.
They may grow tall, but best of all, my son is coming home.
  Linda Farrow

Homeless

It's very dark and very cold,
I stumble on along the road,
A glimpse of light I spy ahead,
I envy those tucked up in bed.

My roof is now the sky above,
The dog beside me gives me love.
Why am I out here all alone,
With just my dog to call my own?

'Twas not like this a year ago,
I'm now all hate and full of woe,
I had a family and a home,
But never ceased to fight and moan.

It was so hard when I was there,
"Tidy your room and wash your hair",
I now have freedom, I'm the boss,
I often think, "well it's their loss".

But being honest, as I should
I'd love to go home if I could.
I've really, really, really tried,
I just can't do it, too much pride.

Sylvia Russell

I Loved You Harry

I had a little hamster called Harry
I use to think he was as happy as Larry
Until one day his eyes were all starry
I could have cried my poor little Harry

We went to the vet Harry and I
I prayed to God "Please don't let him die
if you take him I swear I'll cry
Oh please, please God don't let him die."

The vet told me "Your hamster will be fine
just give some cheese and a little red wine"
Three days later Harry was fine
until he fell and broke his spine

In the end God took him away
but that's the price I'll have to pay
for letting him out of his cage that day
I thought he loved me but he went away

Lyn McQueen

True Worth

While I was searching among some old forms, I came on a folded sheet. I opened and showed it to Jacob, as he sat alert at my feet. "This is your pedigree", I said to him. Your registered family tree. "Very aristocratic, old chap. The canine nobility!"

He sniffed at the paper and looked at me, not knowing what to do. "A lot of names are written in red. That means they're champions, too. Your great-great-great grandad was Roundtable Cognac, an American champion, and great-great grandpa Roundtable Brandy Sniff was his champion son.

Several more were winners, and that's only Father's line." "Well, Jacob," I said, the sire's all right. Let's see if the dam is as fine. It says your mother's great grandad was Piccoli Peacock's Pride, while great grandma on her mother's side was Wharfholm Lizzlan White Bride.

Several other relations have earned rosettes in the ring.
It seems to me, old fellow, that you rank the same as a king!
No wonder you trot along proudly, with your poodle nose in the air!
There are very few humans around you who can claim a breeding so rare."

I know full well as I say this that it's not the star of the show
Who makes the best friend and companion when it comes to the test, you know.
The breeding's not important. Just two things count in the end.
They are the life-long trust and devotion that make a dog our best friend.

E. J. Earley

'After Goodbye'

Why do I see your beloved image
In these things passing?
Eye in another's eye,
Limb in another limb,
A sudden shape remembering
Stirring a sadness that blurs the eye.

I see your strong body
With its rhythmic muscular moving,
In a swaying branch.
Or I hear your voice, and start,
The shout not my name
But another's calling.
Laughing in my sighing.

The flashing holding of eyes
I look for in these,
But they cannot show me -
Just mocking
In their coming and going.

Philip Meninsky

Mother's Love

I love you for who you are and for what I am when I'm with you
I love you not for what you've done for me but for what you've meant to me
I love you because you've done more than anyone could have done
To make me good and more than any fate could do to make me happy
That you're my mother my friend my life
You've done it without a touch without a sign
You've done it by being my mother my soulmate my life and most of all my love perhaps that's what a mother means after all
mental illness may take your mind your body your life
But only friends and love and God can take one's soul

Lynn Cook

Sunday By The Shore

Along the shore I do adore to feel the sea air clear
I love to mingle, toes on shingle, the seagulls' call to hear
In Winter's chill a certain thrill, the sands are free and bare
I'm all alone by sea of foam, it's here I have no care.

It's Sunday morn' and I am torn to stay or go to Church
I hear the bells, early Service tells to leave my walk and search
for other sources of God's courses and find a different calm
I do this gladly, leave sea sadly, but know this does no harm.

Today is rest, I'm put to test to leave the Coastline, how!
To join the throng with their song, but cleansed I feel right now
I leave the sea and I agree to come here every Sunday
To help me work, my life not shirk and work hard come the Monday.

Lucy-May Bloxham

The Visit

Mo-jo pippin and tog are we,
Ian's mum we have come to see,
We race through the house we cause quite a stir
Up and down stairs with a flying of fur,

We go in a bedroom the curtains we wreck
She says it's a good thing it's only the net,
We go to another the paper we tear,
His Dad says you cats had better take care,

We hide in a cupboard, isn't this fun,
They can find two of us but not the third one,
We escape to the shed to find a mouse
But they yell at us 'get back to the house'

We hope they're enjoying their holiday,
When they come back they'll take us away,
Back to the boring old house that we know
Where they find the places we'd think to go,

But if we are good maybe one day
They'll let us come back 'no fear' they say
  We'll see,
  Well maybe.

Sylvia L. Brazier

Stay With Me

Don't leave me now, Just stay a while.
I need you here, I need your smile,
to see your face brings so much pleasure,
You're one of the things I'll always treasure.

I feel lost and lonely without you near,
but safe and secure when you are here,
Just hold my hand and stay a while,
till dawn breaks through on your golden smile.

When dawn breaks and I have passed,
the silence of the mourn will last,
Remember though my body's gone,
My spirit always will live on.

So if you're lonely or you're glum,
Just look at that picture of your mum,
Always remember the love that we shared,
And never let it be compared.

Tracy Kay Clifton

Trapped Thoughts

A poem is a word picture
I would dearly love to paint
But words do not come readily
My poems can be quaint!
So many themes I've tried to start
But none resemble any art!
I can think of countless things
Lacking the power to give them wings
Though thoughts are deep I can't impart
Their impact left within my heart
These feelings stay in my own mind
For sadly, words I cannot find
If I could only find a way
To spill thoughts out to light of day
I'd give folk the joy to see
What 'word pictures' can do for me

Vera Prentis

Stay With Me

Don't leave me now, Just stay a while.
I need you here, I need your smile,
to see your face brings so much pleasure,
You're one of the things I'll always treasure.

I feel lost and lonely without you near,
but safe and secure when you are here,
Just hold my hand and stay a while,
till dawn breaks through on your golden smile.

When dawn breaks and I have passed,
the silence of the mourn will last,
Remember though my body's gone,
My spirit always will live on.

So if you're lonely or you're glum,
Just look at that picture of your mum,
Always remember the love that we shared,
And never let it be compared.

Tracy Kay Clifton

Where Is My God?

I stare at the stars with a frown on my face
I need someone here who'll plead my case
My body is aching
My bones show right through
I can't lift my head
But that's nothing new.

Where is my God?
The one that I love
Where is my God?
My help from above.

The camp is so crowded
There's a smell of death
I gasp all of a sudden
My final breath.

Kerri-Anne Clark

Where Is My God?

I stare at the stars with a frown on my face
I need someone here who'll plead my case
My body is aching
My bones show right through
I can't lift my head
But that's nothing new.

Where is my God?
The one that I love
Where is my God?
My help from above.

The camp is so crowded
There's a smell of death
I gasp all of a sudden
My final breath.

Kerri-Anne Clark

The Disabled Able Gardener

The breath of spring is in my home, forever and a day,
I plant a seed and watch it grow, a miracle, nature's way,
And soon it blossoms with rich green leaves, a truly lovely sight.
Gentle flowers that follow, to give me pure delight.

I surround myself with Flora, sweet-smelling rainbow hues,
My pleasure lies within my home I forget my aches and "screws".
For tho' I cannot go outside, I'm happy with my lot.
My plants I treat with tender care in each and every pot.

God's nature is a precious gift, some people take for granted
But the joy and pleasure that is mine is the miracle that I've planted
For I look around and there I see, my riches and my treasure,
I nourish them and flourish them; my reward? Heart-warming pleasure.

I know I cannot walk around and neither can I roam,
But I've done the next best thing and placed my garden in my home.
Pretty plants are everywhere, what more do I need to say.
Yes! There's a breath of spring in every room
    FOREVER AND A DAY.

Raymond Jones
Churchdown, Glos.

Come Home For Tea

I sat there waiting for you to come home for tea,
I looked out the window but I couldn't see,
You were already an hour late,
I went and stood by the gate,
Every child that went by I thought was you,
But there wasn't many only a few.

Where had you gone why didn't you come home,
You were out there left all alone.

I knew if you didn't come home I'd die,
I would go crazy break down and cry.
How long does all this have to go on,
What really happened what went wrong,
Please come home don't do this to me,
Just come home for your tea.

Mary-Ann Adams

As I Kneel At My Father' Footstool

As I kneel at my Father' footstool,
I look up to His Eyes and say,
Thank you my beloved Father
For helping me along life's way.
I will always treasure His friendship.
That's so helpful, loving and kind.
Because we know, as through life we go
Love is not always so easy to find.
So thank you my loving Father
For all the help I receive.
And I will always try to show others I know,
You are a very true Friend indeed.

Winnie C. Mapletoft

410

Never

Many a time I have visited Never;
A never place of a never time
Where church bells never chime.
I sit upon a Never hill
And watch the sky, so calm, so still.
As far away as Never may seem,
I visit Never in every dream.
The land of Never is always near,
Yet the land of Never us never here.

I sit beside a Never lake
And watch the ripples it never fakes.
I listen to the church bells peals
And wonder what secrets it never reveals.
The birds that never squawk or scream
Have flown away from my Never dream.
Though Never may never be,
Soon Never will visit me.

Jayne M. Rothwell

The Cave

On the rocky sea front,
Along the jagged cliffs,
Hidden in a crevice,
In between the mist.

Its presence so inviting,
With an eerie tint,
Craving for its maybe treasures,
In this cave of flint.

Hidden so intently,
Away from prying eyes,
The contents of this damp, dark cave,
Remains but a surprise.

But if one day a stranger,
The secret they unfold,
Inside for there are treasures,
And wonders to behold.

Kerry Maskell

My Valentine

I bet you never realized
A handsome chap like me
Had fallen rather heavily
In love with you, you see,
Each time I caught a glimpse of you
My heart just missed a beat,
And if you looked and smiled at me
It made my day complete,
A doctor couldn't heal the pain
I've suffered every day
If, one, I never saw you
Or two you went away,
So darling end this misery
And the anguish that I hate,
Find out it's me who loves you
And let us "Make a date".

Norman Mew

Melancholic

A dull, dreary and dismal grey day, with little that I care to do,
Even my panoramic window, shows precious little to view.
An occasional flock of small birds wheel by,
Momentarily fleeting, they sweep through the sky.

Solitudinous feelings beset me with fear,
As the rain slough and spatters, and leaves the mood drear.
A flit past my window, first starling, then chough;
Then monotonous greyness, that's heavy and tough.

A dread clap of thunder, a reverberant crack,
My heart pleads for sunshine, my soul feels so black.
Such dark sombre feelings, I beg for release;
Bring me sunshine, pure light, my heart's ease.

P. T. De Artin

Fate

Of all the strange multitudes of the mind
I have a special kinship with fate.

It's an oasis in my desert nation
A magic that fills the existential void
That regulates the rhythm of my life.

In fate I discover
The mystery in my being
The misery in my living
And the tyranny of living without being.

Fate is a unique vehicle of flight
For the citizens of grief to ride
In their search for a dream
In a world robbed of life-sustaining dreams.

In fate I find a faithful companion
A companion that neither fails nor frails
In the face of evil power and arrogant technology.

Fate is a religion of peace and eternity
The architect of the Real World Order.

Hassan Abdi Keynan

Beyond The Skin

I wandered here, there and far and wide
I often used the colour of my skin to take
Refuge and hide.
But then I realized and fortunately found
That when in a country where colours
Many did abound
Beyond the colour, pigment or what of
The skin.
There lies a frail human being deep within
Scratch my surface will I not bleed
When I am thirsty will I not need, water
I welcome the time when I return to the
Place on earth
Where people are judged on merit not
What they are worth
And colour is looked on as something
Of little value
A place where everyone smiles whatever
Hue.

William E. Farrell

The Cruel Face Of War

Only a child, yet all alone.
Copes on her own, day to day.
One day begins, while the other ends.
There's no meaning of time, for this
vulnerable one.

In her short lifetime, she has known
Love, unlike her "neighbour",
Who has always known hate.
They aren't abused, at least not by a human.

That little girl, hobbles about,
She tries to balance on her two wooden sticks.
Learning again to walk has been hard.
As the reality of war hits home.

Both have lost a family,
One by the soldiers, the other by 'friends',
as religion unites, it also divides.
And the cruel face of war, once again in
life shows.

Roberta Binnie

The Devil's Visit

The devil came to Ireland for he had just been told
That in this land of beauty there were buried pots of gold
He stood and looked around him, and marvelled at the scene
He thought "This must be heaven, this land of emerald green"

But he was here to find the gold and wouldn't be denied
So he just started digging, "It must here" he cried
Just then a voice called out his name "Satan, you be gone"
And there beside the hole he'd dug, stood an Irish Leprechaun.

"How dare you dig up our dear land because you think there's gold
Our treasures aren't buried, they are right here to behold
Have you not seen the shamrocks grow, or viewed our lakes so blue
Have you not seen the Antrim coast, or sampled Irish stew?"

"Come on now Satan, on your bike, you've been here long enough
I suppose because you live in hell you think you're rather tough
But I don't care if you are strong and stubborn as a mule.
I know a man to match you, his name is Finn Mc Cool

That was enough for Satan, he left without the gold
And to this day he hasn't dared to stray far from his fold.
But should you see a man with horns digging at a well
Just be like that Leprechaun and send him back to hell.

J. D. Mant Smith

An Ode To My Dad

The best if the only one I've had,
I searched and searched for the perfect card,
but for someone so special, it proved to be hard,
I wanted to express exactly how I felt,
to tell you, you're loved beyond any doubt.

When I was little, you were my world,
then as I grew up, my life unfurled,
I trod many paths, some wrong, some right,
but with in my corner, I wasn't alone in a fight.
I wanted to thank you, for unconditional love,
and for having you as a Dad, I thank heavens above.

I just want everyone on the planet to see.
how much I love you and what you mean to me.
want them all to understand,
you were always there to hold my hand,
I want them to believe my point of view,
that the world would be a better place, if we all had
A DAD LIKE YOU.

L. M. Squires

Sweet Thoughts Of You

I looked into those loving eyes
I saw a sadness of time gone by.
Eyes of sorrow, love and cheer,
Growing soft beneath my stare.
Eyes forever watching, waiting, misting, through anticipation,
Gone are those thoughts of wild desire
Where bodies embarrassed and love transpired:
I looked at the nose so strong and proud.
Its nostrils slightly flared,
What was he thinking? Why was he waiting,
The stillness filled the air.
Breathing slowly as in a trance despondency appeared:
I see the mouth, the teeth, the smile,
A hidden expression lay pensive for a while
The lips of passion that I once knew
Were gently curved and still,
The teeth were lovely white and even.
The tongue just gently wet the lips, how I wish for those to kiss.
Thoughts of memories gone by, drifting endlessly in time:

P. S. Sibbert

"On Tenement Square"

HOPE
He had a goal once,
just to see tomorrow.
Laugh, and you're handsomer;
he kept his eyebrows furrowed.

HOPE ABANDONED
Eighty years of living.
First east end, then west,
then back east;
and never moving an inch.

STOICISM
The old nutter lit up a fag
and blew smoke in the spam:
revealing his superior intellect.
Then they waited for him to speak.

DEATH
Cashed Giros, raised Knives
They stripped his bones clean.
Reporters asked "Why?"
Neighbours saw nothing.

James Stuart

In Spirit

Last night,
I told you that I loved you
And needed you, so much
That I didn't think I could live
If anything ever happened to you.
You told me not to worry, that whatever happened
You would always be with me,
Looking after me
In spirit.

This morning,
I had just eaten breakfast
When I recalled this conversation.
A realisation
filled me with so much fear that
I was violently sick,
And afterwards I sat there
Breathless, heart thudding, so frightened,
Because what do you do
If you don't believe
In spirits?

Maria Warren

Isolation

When you were poorly mam you would often say I.
I hope this doesn't happen to you one day
now one knows what it's like to be
disabled part of your life
to rely on others to help you cope
to be on your own with no hope
loosing your independence and feeling down.
No one to help you get around
staying in bed to get some ease
watching the telly to try and please
day after day in the house you would stay
crying your tears in your own private way
gone to disablement that stood in your way
Jesus took you with Him to stay.

L. Race

'A Dream'

If I were God the world I would save,
I'd teach the people how to behave
Rivers wouldn't be polluted, no more lives would be lost,
The world wouldn't be mistreated, no matter what the cost.
There would be no more persecution,
No more racism or sexism at all
Everyone would be treated as equals,
No matter how big or small.
If I ran the country,
These things I would list
Poverty and homelessness,
Simply wouldn't exist,
The royal mint would print the money with extra speed,
So the starving I may feed.
For every disease there would be a cure
So people needn't suffer premature death anymore.
The world would be perfect, and as you can see
That the control of this world should be given to me.

Sarah Symons

Turning Back The Time

I wish that I could turn back time
To start all over again
To share the love that we once had
Instead of being so lonely as I am

I miss your smile, the touch of your hand
The scent of your perfume
The kiss of your lips
God, how I miss all this

Just to reach out and touch you
To embrace you in my arms
To pull you closer to me
To smell your heavenly charms
To run my fingers through your hair
And touch your tender skin
Oh God, how I miss all this
If only I could turn back time and
My love
I would throw away the key.
Harry Hartland Leach

My Great Escape

When the apparition first came to my bed
My heart, it raced and then stood still -
I feared that I, too, was dead.

Her lips were blue and her eyes, they bled;
I begged her to leave with all my will -
When the apparition first came to my bed.

Teasing me playfully, on fear she was fed;
She beckoned me with an uneasy chill;
I feared that I, too, was dead.

To the hades below I would surely be led,
"Come hence," she spewed in an unearthly shrill -
When the apparition first came to my bed.

Frozen with fear, ghostly thoughts spun my head -
Her putrid breath filled my lungs until;
I feared that I, too, was dead.

As fast as she came, she turned and fled
My drapes blew aloft and then hung still -
When the apparition first came to my bed;
I feared that I, too, was dead.
Hartley Taylor

Lissadell

Oh, Lissadell, Oh Lissadell
The secret of your magic you will
never tell
The Mystique of your walks
through your leafy dells
The Haunting echoes of the children's yells
The sound of the lap at the water's edge
The splintering sunlight, peeking
through the trees
Alighting the pathways, scented
by the Breeze.
The magic is captured in the quiet and still
The wonder of all, your golden Daffodils
Their sprightly heads, their majestic dance
Touches the senses at just one glance
Oh Lissadell, and your Daffodils
Your secret magic haunts me still.
Eileen McDonnell

Untitled

"What are you doing"? he asked as she caressed his face and hands
"I'm making memories to last as long as I can"!
"Why do you this"? he questioned again
"I fear I will lose you and I shall never love again"
"Be not so foolish, your words cut like a knife"
He took her in his arms and gently kissed and walked out of her life
Carol Keightley

My Poem

At 23, I had a child.
At 25, another.
I tried my very best to be
a first class wife and mother.

The 'wife' bit didn't last too long,
but the mothering carried on.
I cared for, guided, loved a lot,
spare time, I just had none.

I've tried the 'wifey' bit again,
this time it's very good.
The girls and him get on real well,
as I always hoped they would.

And now, it seems I'm 55,
the years have really flown.
But, joy of joys, I now have time
to do things on my own.

Three friends and I are off abroad,
to laugh and have some fun,
We'll send a post card home, of course,
Just part of a job well done.
Maureen Tomkinson

Realist Or Fatalist?

Can't quite decide just what I am,
I take each day as it comes.
The future always looks quite dim,
And yet I enjoy its anticipation.

Am I a realist or simply a dreamer?
If I'm a realist I'd accept things as they are,
And I do - to a very large extent, but
There is always in my actions and thoughts, a doubt.
Whatever will be, will be!

Am I then a fatalist?
If everything is predetermined, where is my future?
Where indeed is the future for all of us in such a life?
If a birth, or before, our span on earth is all mapped out,
The environment, education, family care and love, mean nought.

But that can't be true either.
Whatever will be, I conclude, will be what we make it.
But can I conclude? I am not God!
W. A. Cameron

What To Say

What to say to one who cries within your arms, frightened of death.
What to say to one you love whose body stills and fails to move,
for fear of pain.
What can you say to ease despair, to someone who's just lying there
Too tired to fight, to carry on, how will you feel when she is gone.
You feel so helpless, desperate despair for the one you love
who's lying there.
She turns her face, eyes water and shine, where has she gone,
that love of mine.
Please fight on, you want to say, but slowly she just drifts away.
Fight on, fight on, you want to say, but should you take her peace away.
Although it hurts, just let her rest, it's you that now must stand
the test of empty days and lonely nights, no more laughter,
no more fights
And there were fights, so many up and downs, life wasn't quiet
with her around.
She'd have her say, she'd have voice, of that you never had a choice
But still you loved her, through and through, a love returned, for
she loved you.
Through thick and thin you stuck it out, of that you never had a doubt.
The hurt will fade, but never dwindle, a word, a though, will just
rekindle a memory of something shared, and she'll come back,
because you cared so very, very much.
Try not to think of death and pain, but her still with us once again.
She'll never go, she'll always be, that special love, to you, and me.
M. Sears

Drugs Attract Mugs

I watched the leaves fall and saw the sun rise
You saw the good side but I heard the cries
Why did she do it why I don't know
She said she had to try it had to have ago
Okay so she tried it but it didn't end there
Her life was in tatters but she didn't seem to care
The money it cost her built up over time
She couldn't afford it so she turned to crime
How could this happen to someone so nice
Once wasn't enough some have to try twice
It's hard to stop it after a while
But who wants to stop, drugs are in style
Those who are users those who deal drugs
In my eyes are labelled, labelled as mugs
   Tammie Kirk

Weary Me

When I grow weary and tired,
I close my eyes and imagine
a small cottage, in the English countryside;
Where I could go and rest and hide.

Plain and simple would it be,
nothing fancy, not for me.
With open fire and cosy chair,
I would while away the hours there,
letting my thoughts just wander free.

Where time could pass as slowly as it wished,
and I could read of things, I'd missed,
whilst amid the turmoil in which were forced to live.

A dream, a longing 'tis but true, but that is what I'd
like to do, to get away, but for a while.
From dull routine, and those that treat me like a machine.

Think of that cottage, with and chair, and wish to myself,
that I was there.
With scented roses round the door, perhaps I could
abide for evermore.
   A. Gray

The Tree

Without the tree we wouldn't live
on earth for very long,
never hear the chirp and trill
of birds in morning song.
Miss the blossom in the spring,
no more summer green.
The rustic gold of autumn.
Stark winters never seen
The rain would never fall at all
Oh, why can't those fools see
That they're committing suicide
When they kill the tree.
   Lorraine Calland

A Day In Spring

Shell fire cascades on that country path where a
   springtime ago two lovers had laughed,
And old mother nature gazed and sighed as all
   around her men fought and died
No peace now in that once quiet glade, just the
   dreadful roar of the fusillade
The scene all around no artist would draw, as
   this pleasant land lay plunged in war
No green fields, no sign of the bird, just men
   all around muttering an angry word
And before this day was over many a man would die
   and many an unborn child would ask the reason why
And many a man tormented as he lay in bed at night
   with the memories of this battle and way he had to fight
And history books would tell of how this battle was won,
   and braggarts would boast how they slaughtered in the sun
But all this in the future when skies are not so grey
   At the moment man must fight as has always been the way
   Brian Rysdale

Emptiness

No one will ever know the pain I feel
I wish it were a dream but I know it's for real
For I am so very sure
That I can feel you moving no more
For months I've carried you inside
Filled with such happiness and pride
I wanted you so very much
Longed to hold you feel your tender touch
One day I felt so much pain what could I do
I guess then I realized I was losing you
I close my eyes something was very wrong
When I awoke I knew you were gone
People were kind they'd say time will heal
But they will never know how I really feel
I often wonder were you a girl or boy
You would have filled my life with such joy
There are others who have suffered like this
But every day it's you I miss
And in my life wherever I go whatever I do
I'll never stop loving you
   Marion Evans

Life's Paths

When the miracle of life breaks into this world,
an untold journey begins to unfold,
Paths are chosen, some not easily made,
as we experience life's mysteries and unknown fates,
One may lead to happiness and wealth
with run filled days brimming with health,
Some filled with darkness and sometimes dread,
as we search for the shinning light ahead,
Innocent faces of children done wrong
show a million expressions of people long gone,
And as the hands of time passes by,
The grief and pain slowly die,
When there is no hope, life finds a way,
to guide you through another day,
But now a shimmering light appears,
to a path untrodden until today,
The days seems brighter now, despite the rain,
the feeling of emptiness, has left with the pain,
this shimmering path, that leads the way,
may bring joy and happiness to the end of my days.
   Catherine Martin

All To Stop A Heart

Come into my room, wire up my heart
"It's time" one says, then let's make a start.
Babbling priest he can see my leg's shaking
Fear! Not in the end but all in the taking

Door opens near me I find myself screaming
To die with dignity now has no meaning.
Small from my seat, I struggle now weakly
Kind voice in my ear, listen, breathe deeply.

Strap me in, blind my sight,
lock the door, everything done right.
It's so dark now, quiet and lonely
"What you can't see won't hurt you." If only.

Hissing beneath me, terror inside
Darkness surrounds, but nowhere to hide.
Please make it quick! Please make it now!
Deserving of "Why?" under serving of "How!"

What's that smell? Aniseed!
Childhood sweets and hearts that bleed,
can't breathe now, just can't breathe,
your justice served, my time to leave.
   C. Doyle

Ode On Time

Time! What changes you create,
Your lows tick past problems, jealousy, hate.
Minutes full of sadness, drifting by so fast,
No need for the present, swallowing the past.

Yet, what of the future that lies a breath away?
Will you pause to ponder, or steel another day?
Another year, children growing, will into their prime
There is no answer, you are endless, here forever - time!

Jean Power

Legends

The music roars out; the people shout, they clap and sing but if only they knew the tragedy of this concert that brings several of the people they see that day would play their very lives away.

Hendrix, Joplin are the people they did shout. Hendrix the man with fingers of steel made his guitar rock and reel.

Joplin sang through blues like only she would choose. Time itself would tell of the hell Joplin had when Hendrix fell.

The people say she loved him this day but who are we to really say what happened.

At Woodstock on that, their last big play. And now they have passed away, people say, "Who is Hendrix and Joplin", this day legends.

Terence Wall

A Christmas Tree's Lament

For years I have longed for this day
For the tree cutters to come and take us away.
To be placed in a Garden Centre in the ground
Waiting for people to come and look around.
I dream of being dressed in tinsel and coloured lights
That twinkle and shine in the dark nights.
A fairy at my top or maybe a star
Like the one that shone long ago from afar.
Children dancing around as they receive presents from me
With carols and laughter full of glee,
But day by day passed
I am left standing there.
My branches are green
But oh! so bare.
My dreams are shattered
It is now too late.
To be thrown on a bonfire is now my fate
Why does nobody want to buy me?
This sad disillusioned Christmas Tree.

W. Pain

Slick

Lick my thoughts and you will see
Through crystal clear what is me,
Study it, distrustful friend,
there thoughts you will never end.
You created them subtly,
you found my brain with a key,
dark, rusty and old it is
bluntly stabbing dizziness.
Look in it and see your face
On my mind with splendid grace,
under your skin, evil drips,
into the crystal and rips.
You don't know it's your doing
black acid which keeps dripping,
affecting my life; they sing!
Their songs of navy, they sing!
Vibrations give tears to lose.
You keep on licking there thoughts
Truth would render you distraught
Because nowhere are they clear, but black with stupid love, dear.

Richard Cramp

The Performer

An actor on a stage
I stand and create my lines
Like many before me
But this stage is mine
A self creation
My lines never before spoken
In the context I speak them
My costume, I wear
To express my social beliefs
This is not a look
Created by another's eye
These emotions are not superficial
Being created by my life that went before
As this heart does not beat
For another's script
I stand on the stage of life
Surrounded but alone
Playing my part in man's existence
Pondering will I get it right
For this is no rehearsal.

J. Ettles

I Saw A Blind Man Tonight

I saw a blind man tonight,
coming towards me along the pavement.
Tap, tap, tapping his white stick,
tracing the gutter.
His eyelids closed,
flicker slightly,
the only movement
in his creased-up face.
I turned and watched
as he disappeared
into the crowd
waiting to see
the Christmas lights switched on.

J. D. Chisholm

Refracted Light

Refracted light,
An optical illusion causing confusion inside my head.

Reflected sight,
A mirror image that will not diminish beside my bed.

Isn't it strange I can still visualize
Your pose, your posture, your perfume,
But your voice, I can't remember your voice,
Its tone, its texture, its tenderness.
Perhaps my drinking has washed it from the chalk board of my mind.

Refracted light,
An optical illusion causing confusion and why?

Reflected sight
A spectre absurd mouthing one word, goodbye

Gary J. Cox

The Artist

He stands at his easel, so deep in thought
   Unaware of the world around
   Transfixed and quite spell bound
   Oblivious of every sound

Ah! His eyes light up - the subject he sought
   Has materialized in his minds eye.
   Across the canvas his brushes fly
   And he breathes a contented sigh.
He works very fast, blending colours with skill
   Drawing a line here and there,
   Sometimes pausing to stare,
   Then leaving so me canvas bare.
The daylight is fading - his hands at last still
   But now he no longer feels blue
   For his picture's complete and on view.
   He has captured the likeness so true

E. J. Sharman

At The End - A New Beginning

Awake one day, once more a young and healthy man,
With wife, child and grandchild weeping,
A preachers words paying tribute to your life.
The words fade, and heavenly music surrounds you,
But one voice still penetrates the music,
The innocent grandchild, "Goodnight Granddad."
The words linger, until the curtains draw to a close.
Old friends long gone, begin to emerge
As your body is consumed by the flames,
Your soul escapes, free into the light.
A last glance back to the church,
Where wife, child and grandchild are smiling,
"Sleep now, God bless... Granddad."

Duncan Hartley

Untitled

I wander along in a dream of dreams,
I'm in the woods, sun streaking in beams,
A squirrel running up into the tree,
Woodpecker sounding, I cannot see,
The thrush in a wonderful sounding song,
Sparrows flitting about all day long,
The lake is twinkling through the trees,
A faint distant buzzing of the bees,
I'm now by the lake, I see a sailing boat,
Fisherman in view throwing his float,
I stand as still as still as I can,
A water not moved and then it ran,
I wander along by the side of the lake,
Looking for wild flowers, I love to paint,
My favourite foxgloves, pink and white,
I capture their beauty in the light.

Mary Lane

A Shaft Of Light

Sleeping in a clouded room
Time recognizing all dust,
All four walls no longer waiting.
An open window shatters all silence
Essence of green reaching in;
Handful of rain that filled the ocean
Suddenly violating all wood.

Alone in a forest
Filled with love and mercy,
Cascade of leaves upon your soul.
Glory welcomes the air;
Soft whispers in the wind.
In the distance a smiling face
A child with opens arms.
with taken into the life
Awaken to all elements of sound.

Sleeping in a clouded room
Alive with realization.
Waiting for a shaft of light
To break the day before it's past.

Julie Wills

Circle Of Life

No one wants you when you're old
And the heating's turned up because you're cold
They talk about putting you in a home
But all you want is to be left alone
You sit all day in your old worn chair
It's not you have time to sit and stare
The long ago memories come flooding back
But it's short term ones that you now lack -
Life is a circle from start to finish
And now your ears and eyes diminish
You children take over - it's their right
To repay the debt of the sleepless nights
You had when they were finding their feet -
The friends they brought home who you'd rather not meet -
Yes life is a circle from beginning to end -
It's in their home now - your life is to spend.

Pauline Ash

The Dentist

Following a night of raging toothache the morning finally came,
In a crowded anxious waiting room the receptionist called my name,
"Please come in" the dentist said to me with a kindly smile,
And asked me to lay back in the chair "Hold your mouth open wide for a while."

Although he was very gentle as he inspected my troublesome tooth,
I knew it was no use pretending and would have to face the truth,
"I'm afraid it will have to come out" the said, trying not to look glum,
And before I knew anything about it the injected my tender gum,

All I felt was a kind of numbness in the area that had caused the pain,
Then he asked me to wait a few minutes till he looked in my mouth again,
"Please open once more", said the dentist, as I shrank down in the chair,
And with a yank of his wrist my molar was no longer there.

You can have this as a souvenir he said I finally walked to the door,
I thanked him very kindly as the pain in my mouth was no more.

The moral of this story is to regularly give your teeth a brush,
And always have a check up, even if you need a push.

M. J. Baron

Untitled

In dreams I go back
To a village near Oban
To Benderloch's shores
Which are sunlight with gold
To Tralee's green pasture
Surrounded by beauty
To the land of my fathers a joy to behold
As I sit by my fire
In the still of the evening
My thoughts linger back
To the days that have gone
I feel nostalgic my sad heart is yearning
The urge is to get up and move on
Back to the land of sweet-happy childhood
of laughter and glee
I see the old homestead
I hear the dear voices
I see in the distance the old Rowan tree

MacBean

In Memory Gwen Harwood

What is love? 'Tis now hereafter:
Vanished mirth, vanished laughter,
memory of happy greetings -
recurring never.

Yet for the future, joyous greetings
of minds together, without sound,
from printed page; or in the air,
no livelier if she were there
speaking her verse, her silent voice,
technically vocal, offering choice
to read or hear her art, wherever
books and tapes survive, forever.

Thomas Riddell

The World's Best

Mother means a lot of things
But no one can beat the pleasure she brings
Over the years I've caused some flak
But now I wish I could take it all back
To me there'll never be anyone as good
And this I want to be understood
From now on Mum I promise to be good
And repay you your care and love
There's been times we've argued and fell out
But I still loved you of that there's no doubt
Compared to God I think you're better
That's why we sent you this with my letter
To me there'll never be another
Half as special as my mother

Warren Brain

A Resting Place

A desolate Church, gaping.
Dark sombre sentinel yews,
Brooding, ageless - absorbing
Autumn's child winds, while
Secret blood-shot eyes watch over
Lichen-covered limestone flags.

A spiny speckled ball, camouflaged,
Nestled in yellows - citrus, jaundiced,
Piled-up sepia browns, soggy beige.

A yawning hole captures a wayward gust.

A sensuous rolling motion to darkness.
A cold cadaverous cobwebbed womb -
Cradling.

For one, come spring, a Resurrection.
James Counihan

Where Is God?

Separated from my father, my uncle, my brother,
Alone in my bunk waiting for my mother.
She's been gone so long, I don't know where she went,
Maybe to showers where the others were sent.

Why are we here? I don't really know
What did we do to be treated so low?
Where are you God? So many are dead,
I shiver in my sleep, huddled in my bed.

Who will I hug when I'm feeling unwell
Please God, tell me, who will I tell.
How can I survive this life of horror
Without my mother, or no one to bother.

I pray to you each night in my bed,
And I know that you listen to all that I've said,
I know that you're with me I know that you're here,
So see me through this, my God so dear.
Gillian Doig

The Seasons

How many times have I wondered why
As I look up to the sky
Why it looks so grey and unappealing
On this winter's day, a miserable feeling

As night does fall it seems so black
The moon and stars the heavens do lack
As winter time passes into spring
Daffodils will bloom, what joy they bring

Now summer does not seem so far away
The sun comes up at break of day
Its gentle rays upon my brow
Does warm my inner soul right now

As the summer days go quickly by
Soon into autumn we shall fly
Some of God's creatures will hibernate
To shelter from the winter's fate

It helps to dream of things to come
New hope, and better ways for some
So take heed my friend, do not be sad
As seasons come and go, not all are bad.
Marjorie Harris

The First Snow

I opened the curtains and oh what a sight!
The view from my window was brilliant white.
The rooftops, the hedges, the church and the tree were
all painted over as white as could be with snowflakes.
They had come in the night, they had not made a sound.
Yet millions and millions lay all around.
Alas, I discovered this scene couldn't last.
For the sunshine was melting these snowflakes so fast.
I looked again later, that very same day, but the view
from my window was dismal and grey.
Constance Clough

Unquestioning Love

What shall I do for you
Which no-one else may do?
I shall love you with a love that's true,
That asks no question when a question's due,
That seeks no answer when the answer's plain,
But welcomes you with open arms
When you are pleased to come again.
Mary Bailey

Thoughts Of The Night

Looking through my window.
On a cold and frosty night.
The streets so still.
The lights so bright.
Not a soul to be seen.
Not a friend in sight.
Everything seems peaceful.
Sudden memories come to mind.
Many of laughter, many of tears.
The odd regret.
Through the passing years.

Tomorrow is my future.
What it holds I do not know.
As I look to the sky.
For an answer.
I'm suddenly wishing on a star.
Denise Hemingway

Is This Love?

Is this pain in my heart called love,
　the pain that never goes away,
　the pain that I know is here to stay.

Are the tears I shed for you called love,
　the tears that trickle down my face,
　the ones that stain the pillow case.

Are the memories we shared called love,
　the ones in a park on a winters night,
　the ones where you would hold me tight.

Is this love or is it a game?
Is this love or is it insane?
Louise Buckley

These Old Eyes

Now these old eyes no longer see
The world is very different to me.
I have the time to hear the birds,
The wondrous sounds I rarely heard,
To feel the breeze upon my face
And the texture of this cloth of lace.
The scent of flowers, plants and trees,
I never really noticed these.
The world is very different to me
Now these old eyes no longer see.
Shirley Lambert

Winter!

Outside the wind roars loud and harsh,
the snow falls crisp and white,
you pond is frozen hard as starch,
Jack Frost takes a sharp bite,
silvery drops fall from the larch,
grey rain clouds dull the light,
the land no longer dry and parched,
blue skies no longer bright,
the heather's branches now so sparse,
with leaves rolled up so tight,
its purple flowers in the marsh,
bedecked in moss and blight,
but time 'twill surely onwards march,
to beat the winter's might.
John J. Bradley

Youth

Fresh and new the blossom springs,
Crisp beauty on a pane white petal,
Noble sweet and tall as kings,
Silver jewel drop shiny as metal,

Grip of roots, a steel like jaw,
Life, strengthened as the sun glows brighter,
Fragile quiver as clouds pour,
Humid hard rain, flower draws tighter,

Evening comes with orange glow,
Head petals pull the crown head forward.
Enter dark night, leaves hang low,
Drooping dead bud falling flower land.

Cold white glow springs upon frost,
A frozen seed pod caught hard and fast,
Autumn leaves fall, trees are tossed,
Fresh new beauty will never last.

Kristina Holt

No Goodbyes

I was a child, I should not see
You were my dad, you must love me
Stood on the stairs, as you walk away
The words in my head, I could not say.

In my mind, I scream don't go
On my face no expression I show
Your saddened face, and guilty eyes
A life I face, with no goodbyes.

No birthday card no photo frame
Without my dad life's not the same
What did I do to make him go
All my life, I'll never know.

In my memories I'm still on the stairs
But life goes on, and no one cares
I can't forget those, sad sad eyes
And no one hears my silent cries.

Yasmin Cummins

War

Crying faces, cold and bloodstained,
grieving mothers, look helpless and forever pained,
another country's fate is being framed
just another part of the military game.

Young soldiers full of fear,
praying they shall last another year,
pictures of loved ones they hold near,
no reason for this conflict to them seems clear.

Red traces of gunfire light up the night,
caught on camera to the media's delight,
revealing to us only one side of the fight,
How can they be sure what is right?

Politicians and their contradictory talk,
attend a battlefield for a vote winning walk,
for without them this battle would never have been,
death on this scale never would have been seen.

John Gallagher

St. Mary De Castro, Leicester - Meditation

Slenderly striking at the night,
high above each chestnut-shaded grave,
high above the arches and the nave,
Romanesque in gentle yellow light,
loudly ringing out the practice hour,
trembling waves from pinnacled gothic tower,
bounding back from blank commercial walls,
above the grim demented caterwauls
of this long lost and lonely day;
and will we ever find the better way?

St. Mary's, wiser than the wisest sage,
Proclaims a deeper and a quieter age.

Charles Lamont

Rush Hour

Rush, rush, heave and shout,
hundreds of people dashing about,
backwards and forwards, trying to get in,
and making such a terrible din,
who would have thought there was such a rout?

Trains pausing briefly to let the crowds in.
If you are lucky you keep a whole skin.
Strap-hanger's fingers numb with the strain;
A short pause at stations, and off once again.
Who could have dreamt such a maddening thing.

Hardly a pause each morning and night,
the speed of the trains keeps one in a fright.
The noise of it all make one quite dour,
this senseless haste of the City's rush hour.
And who would have thought they would pack in so tight?

G. D. Sharp

My Childhood

I shall always remember my childhood
  When we lit our fires, with stick and coal
Where everyone in our house had to play a roll
  Mum did the cooking, Dad worked down the mine
Of children we were seven
  And our house used to shine
Not only with cleanliness, but the happiness that was inside
  With Mum our door, was always open
To neighbours, tramps, and friends, no one was denied
  We lived in a valley in South Wales
And we made up our own game
  None of us had television
But oh how Mum could tell us tales
  Far better than any book I've read
And all this before we went to bed
  I miss my Mum and Dad
And all the things we had
  Things that money couldn't buy
And now that I've grown old
  I thought this story should be told

Lily Dawes

Seeds Of Love

When God made you, he said to himself,
I'll make someone special, and you'll fall in love
I'll make the road rocky and I'll make it steep
with a river where your love can run deep,
I'll give you love and I'll give you pain
along with the sunshine, you'll have the rain
through the hardest frost a flower can grow
and it this seed of love that I will save.

Shavon Sykes

I Wonder

When my spirit goes into the blue yonder
Towards Heaven - I wonder
Will God reveal, or still conceal
The mystery of the Universe for real
Those who claim their souls have taken flight
Tell of tunnels, peace and light
Of meeting their loved ones for a fleeting spell
Funny - nobody ever glimpses Hell
Strange, no mention of dogs, cats, pets
Even it these fleeting moments nobody gets
To see past monsters of human breeds
Maybe none repented of their evil deeds
And do you think those billions gone
Can see on Earth what's going on
What frustrations are they feeling
Watching us killing, maiming, stealing
Do they see God shed a tear
For us poor mortals living hear
I wonder...

Brian Cross

The Memorial For Peace

Build to us a monument...
   Recovering God's intention to place upon a statement;
The commemorative peace-day in action,
   And blown up our hopes that devastation's in retraction.

Name us a statue, so we can believe in,
   And call to in times of trouble;
To take away bad memories that we could re-live in
   All that we wanted, but not turn them to rubble.

Find us a place, where we can dwell among men,
   And live together without shame;
Make us a world, we won't need to defend,
   Then war would become a word, and the sword be slain.

Given us leadership, in the hands we will follow,
   And our faith shall be strengthened there on,
In the depths once depraved is now just a hollow,
   Then from his guides knowledge we can depend upon.

On the grounds of our firm foundation,
   We hail, "Peace!," to the flag we fly freely,
On the topmost there stands its commemoration,
   And salute the Memorial for Peace, we hold so dearly
   Paul S. Gordon

Untitled

My mind has been cast adrift
Like a ship on a rolling sea.
Thoughts of you gently lift
The loneliness within me

I can see your face in the sky
In the clouds and the light of the day
I can hear your voice as you cry
And watch you leave as the clouds blow away.

Now the sun is dimming and going down
Its brightness is that of your eyes
The thought of you leaving me, makes me frown
And I have always hated goodbyes.

In draws the night like a veil over the sky
As it covers you up with its cloak
There isn't a gap within which I can spy
No more beauty within which I can soak

So farewell my love and keep you well
Till one more I can hold you near
Don't fret for me as I go through this hell
And shed one more lonely tear.
   Laurence Russell

Ryan Giggs

3 o'clock the tensions rising
Atmosphere's wild, not surprising
The REDS walk out, fearless and proud
To face the loyal OLD TRAFFORD crowd
GIGGs takes his place on the left wing
Dodging them like a pendulum's swing
Passing to players with rhythm and skill
Sweating and swerving with ease until
The balls passed onto his Reebok boot and
With a blast of energy from his golden foot
The ball swerves into the net
They're in the lead but it's not over yet
The number '11' shirt strikes once more
The crowd goes ecstatic
Throats get sore
HE SPRINTS
HE DODGES
The goal is so near
He crosses to another with his own will
And they've won thanks to those curls of great skill
   Charlene Neill

Ben The Bassett

Ben is a Bassett, black white and brown
big feet, short legs, big ears dangling down.
A sorrowful look to get his own way
and go out for walkies six times a day.

He likes to play ball when he goes to the park,
he likes to chase cats, off they go with one bark
He climbs on the bed when your trying to sleep
he'll pinch knickers and socks, and he likes "sheep".

He just wants to play, just wants to have fun,
but they don't understand and off they all run.
He watches you eat, but knows he must wait
to have the left-overs put on his plate.

He jumps on the couch when no one is looking
when you're out of the room, cleaning or cooking.
He puts mud on the carpet and fur on the chairs
he scratches the doors and the car's full of hairs.

He'll sit down beside you waiting for a gap
and climbs up upon you, five stone on your lap.
He won't come when you call him, he won't do as he's told,
but that's been the bassett, more precious than gold.
   L. S. Davies

Enchanted Dreams

Glittering dreams, with musical streams,
And rainbows that fill every sky,
Unicorns prancing, and fairy folk dancing,
To a breeze which is merely a sigh.

Mountains of pink, up to clouds soft as mink,
Silver linings through pure cotton wool,
Waterfalls cascading, butterflies masquerading,
As fishes swim by in their schools.

Webs made of lace, with pure nectar to taste,
Queen bees offering homemade treasure,
With clean fresh air, for all nature to share,
To enjoy it, and taste, it with pleasure.

Bluebells are ringing, with birds softly singing,
To the tune of meandering streams,
Where warm flower beds, are swaying their heads,
And life has been filled with sweet dreams.

Do not let me awaken, from this dream I have taken,
Let me stay here and watch the sun rise,
Pray hear me this day for it's here I must stay,
For this dream is where my heart lies.
   Suzanne Smithdale

The Theatre Of Life

And if life were but a theatre,
in the grand universal scheme of things,
a mere playhouse where we act either
the part of villains or the part of saints.

Today, I am playing a nasty role,
I'm detained at her majesty's pleasure,
perhaps to learn true freedom of the soul,
before my next dramatic adventure.

Tomorrow, I may play a pleasant part,
may enjoy a millionaire's paradise,
perhaps to learn money can't buy a heart,
before my next theatrical franchise.

New people enter our lives every day,
old friends are making their final exits,
leaving this planet for a better play,
according to a just scale of merits.

And if life were but a theatre,
I must speak with its divine director,
I want more fun, more joy, more laughter,
a better part, I'm only an actor.
   Rozarya Dyka-Gerard

All Growed Up

Why do I feel so useless
Now the kids have grown,
I feel such an emptiness
That I have ever known.
No more bath time fun and games
As a family, we took part,
No more cries, "Don't want to,"
Bless their little hearts.
How I wish I could go back
To when the kids were small,
The mess, the noise, confusion,
I wouldn't mind at all!
What happened to my baby girls
And my little son?
They grew up, that's what they did,
And I love them, every one.

Gladys Carre

The Re-Union

I flew in through the golden gate
A beautiful kingdom to await
The angels smiled and held my hand
Here they said is the Promised Land!

In the distance my loved ones stood
Their arms outstretched it felt so good
To see their faces lit with light
As they came towards me in their flight

There was Mother, Father and little James
And Auntie Peggy and Granny Haynes
Uncle Tom and Cousin Nell
Here they were alive and well!

We have waited so long for you they said
We've watched over you and now you're dead
But your second life has now begun
In God's wondrous Kingdom beyond the sun!

There is no sorrow here they cried
And Love can be your only guide
Peace and caring is our food
He's chosen us - He's chosen you.

Barbara Potter

Christmas Eve

It's Christmas eve and time for bed
I try to remember the list that I said
A racing car, teddy, play soldiers, a bike
I hope I get all the things that I like
A cup of coco and some custard creams
And off to sleep and have sweet dreams
Then Santa will visit on his sleigh
And leave all the presents for Christmas day.

Andrew T. Blackmore

"Baby Goodbye"

Your tiny hands reach out and touch my finger
As I place my shaking hand on your baby brow.
I look at you and for a moment I still linger
And treasure each moment that they will allow

There were moments when I thought I could not do it,
My heart is breaking and the pain so hard to take
But here standing beside me, are your mum and dad to be.
And I must let you go, for all our sakes.

So baby please forgive me, when you're older.
Because I'm only doing this for you.
I will fold my empty arms and cry on someone's shoulder
Because there will be nothing left, for me, of you.

May God take care of you my little one
May each day for you be filled with joy
I hope with all my heart you will be happy
Goodbye my life, my love, my baby boy.

Grace Wozencroft

Without You

The birds still sing, the sun still shines,
The rain still wets the ground.
I listen for your sweet voice,
But cannot hear a sound.

I feel you all around me,
I know you're somewhere near,
I listen for your footsteps
But nothing do I hear.

I sleep in your pythons
I cuddle your soft toy,
At night I cry with sadness
There's no more tears of joy.

I know you had to leave me,
This hurt's pure selfishness.
But nothing in this world my child
Could fill this emptiness.

Lynn Tinkler

Untitled

My childhood days,
were not to be,
The pain and suffering
no one could see,
But inside lies a child crying endlessly.
I was only a child of three
when you took my innocence away from me.
I've grown up now
Look close and see
The pain and turmoil will always be
I've looked for a long time
for the child hidden inside
and now I finally found her
It's time she was set free,
remember she was not to blame,
she played no part,
she didn't agree,
For if you remember
she was only a child of three

Karen Ann Adkins

Dawn

From black and white an orange glow,
within her mist all were still.
Timeless beauty, cool, sooth, warm,
singing sweet harmony they rise,
sleep soft under soothing skies,
the gentle wake to grace,
from safety bold to us.
So the smile adds warmth,
full her flow she leads my heart,
now this land has thunder.
Till dark skies hint,
a yawn to meet my slumber.

Michael Sinclair

Springtime

All hail, to a beautiful springtime,
With lambs all skipping around.
The trees all bursting into bloom,
To shower their petals on the ground.

There's sunshine in the bright blue sky,
And birds, their songs are singing.
Happiness is all around,
To us such joys are bringing.

The lighter evenings, to enjoy,
With picnics in the park,
Making us feel happy,
As merry, as a lark!

E. A. Blissett

420

Forbidden Fruit

He longed for the taste of her bittersweet lips
Her full rounded breasts and slender white hips
Those sensual warm juices that bounced on her tongue
The ultimate moment that says they've begun

Her hand that caresses and searches with greed
The arch of her back impatient with need
Kisses that devour their very being
The flash of her eyes all-knowing and seeing

To fight it is futile it's gone much too far
Their bodies entwined leaves a permanent scar
The memories that linger and stay in their heads
The bite from the apple the soiled crumpled bed
Kevin Parker

Roses In December

Beneath the winter winds pale petals bow,
  A few late roses bravely sway
Amongst the shrivelled leaves : so see we now
  June flower live on beyond their day.

December's icy tears upon them fall,
  No longer summer's soothing dew,
Snow with cold kisses lays a wintry pall
  To cover where the green grass grew.

Of summer flowers these are the phantoms fair,
  Sweet ghosts of roses past and dead,
Leaving a fleeting fragrance on the air
  After the petals soft are shed.

Thoughts of happier days we call to mind
  When life's long winter season closes:
So mem'ries of some brighter flowers we find
  In these last pale December roses.
Sonia Cardwell

My Love Is True

Now you are mine for all to see
this light will burn inside of me
this fire you started with our first kiss
bring back to me all I had missed.
My life in ruins, my heart still cold
from all the lies that others told.
Now in my heart, this fire's aglow
and day by day my love will flow
just like the rivers to the sea;
my endless love is just for thee.
So when you're lonely and feeling blue
Remember this, My love is true.
John Wray

Untitled

The earth is warming every day,
Each evening grows much brighter,
Spring is pushing winter out,
My steps are getting lighter,
I took no heed in days of yore,
Just thought, it lasts forever,
The changing seasons, meant new clothes
But never, ever, leather.
Now alas I've run the course,
I can't believe, I'll ever,
See spring again, tread the grass
Explore once more, with my bus pass:
Peggy Cummins

Horror Of Trust

The night was calm and still.
The smell of peace lingered in the air.
Gentle was the touch upon my hair.
The hand of friendship and trust,
Changed to horrors of trust.

The night became tense and heavy.
The smell of lust hung in the air.
Rough was the touch upon my shoulders.
The hand of friendship and trust,
Threatened to horrors of trust.

The night became close and airless.
The smell of rape smothered the air.
Hurtful was the touch around my wrists.
The hand of friendship and trust,
Raged to horrors of trust.

The night became dark and cold.
The smell of betrayal clung in the air.
Weapon's was the touch to my body.
The hand of friendship and trust,
Tools to horrors of trust.
Caroline

River Dee

On nature's address colourful and free
She sparkled so brightly to say the least
On the brightly lit shores on the river Dee.

Rhapsody brought peace teaching me to see
What wasn't before: Now became a feast
On nature's address colourful and free.

Shining golden hills brought me to my knee
As they shone profusely: So butter kissed
On the brightly lit shores on the river Dee.

Water rich and clear: Were I a flea
I could fly with her; so pleasantly pleased
On nature's address colourful and free.

Sweet scented trees, were trying hard to be
Pillars of this scene, from south to its east
On the brightly lit shores on the river Dee.

On this perfect day on a joyful spree
I lay down to rest having found the key
On nature's address so colourful and free
On the brightly lit shores, on the river Dee.
George Livingston Shand

Emotions Of Old Age

Pride in many things that I have done
Regret for the prizes never won
Pleasure from each lovely sunny day
Dread of winter's chill, so cold and grey
Sadness for the years I've left behind
Heartache for my loved ones who are gone
Fear for the failing of the mind
Pain from a body old and worn
Gratitude that I have sailed this far
Through all the troubled waters of this life
Thankful that my faith has stayed secure
In spite of all the struggles and strife
Anxious as I face the lonely night
Relief with the dawning of the day
Swift as the early birds in flight
Is how my time on earth has slipped away
If only I could feel again once more
The joy of youth and life expectancy
I would not mind so much to face that door
That leads me to unknown eternity.
Elizabeth Sallows

The Midnight Hour

When night falls; the ghosts appear
They scare people from a story of Shakespeare
Nobody can see them, only hear
People will only hide and peer.

Ghosts never die; they keep on pleading
They threaten the living on hollow-evening
Ghosts are never really dead
They hardly ever leave their bed

The midnight society join hands
They pass through their fingertips, deadly plans
The ghosts always appear
They never ever disappear

The midnight hour draws on
The night of the living dead isn't gone
The legends of the past meet at the graveyard
While people are scared and stay out of the backyard

The houses are threatened,
The hallways are darkened
The ghostly noises are still there
Nobody can make them disappear.

Antony Smith

To A Childhood, Sad Farewell

When I was a child I grew as a child in love with Nature and Man.
I wandered aimlessly to and fro from school with abandoned bliss.
Through fairies' countryside I roamed in meadows
    awash with flowers galore and colours beyond belief.
Birds on the wing the insects chased through skies of purest blue,
Also in awe and affection so, I viewed the mighty pylon of the ESB.

Through streams of gold I played my games as well as in the
    dusty lanes.
The hedgerows emblazoned with their wares so great
    filled my hunger with strawberries and raspberries wild.
I dreamed, I dreamed, I dreamed, for the world it was alive.

Alas, grown up I have, in love with Nature but not with Man;
    and times
    they are but changed, so bad the God His wrath has brought to bear.
I wander still in aimless spree, but through the jungles of
    concrete grey,
Whose "plants" with evil glee the human flesh destroy.

The streams of gold now sewage-filled deny me of my games,
Haystacks replaced by concrete stacks where humans dare to dwell
    with ugliness a prince would sure bemoan.
I cannot fill my hungry self for poison lurks around,
On roads of the past I dare not play as hedgehogs squashed do show,
I do not dream, I do not dream, for the world it is but dead.

Klaus Armstrong-Braun

Miracles Of Love

When first you see the tiny child,
Your heart just swells with pride,
This little being, meek and mild,
That's lying at your side.

But time flies by so very fast,
There's school and work and friends,
You worry that your time is past,
And you have reached the end.

The joy you've known throughout the years,
Is lost when she leaves home,
Remember, and smile through your tears,
You'll never be alone.

The wedding and reception passed,
And they moved in nearby,
My joy abounded, when at last,
Their news - Oh Me - Oh My.

The months dragged slowly, most unfair,
There's two of them, by jove,
They're beautiful with golden hair,
These Miracles of Love.

Yvonne Parker

Keeper Of The Dragon's Gold

In caverns deep,
In caverns cold,
I am Keeper of the Dragon's Gold,
Have you come to seek,
Have you come to stare,
Come closer my little friends
If you dare.

When the light of day shines no more,
The caverns quake, as the Dragon roars,
His wings sound like thunder,
As he soars through the skies,
His fiery breath touched the,
Fear in our eyes.

So if you have come to seek his Gold,
Listen to the words that I have told,
Brave of heart though you maybe,
The Dragon's kiss will be the last you see.

Lewis Martin

The Night He Left Me

As I watch him, my only love, go
away. All my life I dreaded, this would
happen one day. The night drew near
and all was dark. I was all alone
with my thoughts. My bed was empty and cold,
without the heat of your body.
All the night I cried with no-one
to calm me. I looked beyond my
window and saw a rose. I felt the
same way! I had blossomed then grown
thorns, that's why my true love went away.

Joshua Griffith

Shadows

Lately I have not quite felt the same,
Lately I feel that I might as well be insane,
It's just this feeling inside that tells me all is not right,
As I try to settle down I can't rest easily at night,
A shadow creeps along my wall as night drifts by,
This disfigured shape disturbs me as I lie,
It moves along the ceiling and across the floor,
And it doesn't disappear as I let the light in through my door,
It suddenly dawned on me as I looked at the figure closely,
And staring right back with glowing eyes was me,
I couldn't get it into my head what was going on,
I didn't want to wait 'til the morning when the sun shone,
And at last I knew what I had done,
But when the end is here it will have only just begun.

Spencer Pugh

The Mouse

I sat beside the garden shed,
The day was very warm,
Mum said, that likely later on,
She thought there'd be a storm.
I watched a beetle in the grass
Its back did gleam and glisten,
And then I heard a funny noise,
Which made me stop and listen.
It sounded like a scuffling
A rustle, muffle, shuffling,
It seemed to be inside the shed
What could it be? I thought with dread,
Then through a crack beside the door
I'll solved the mystery for sure,
I saw a tiny little mouse,
Using my shed to make his house,
I watched awhile, then came the storm
So I left him snuggled up and warm.

Louisa Harwood

Message To An Angel

I look to the stars to see your face.
in my mind there are memories time can't erase.
I look to our child and see you there.
I hear your voice almost everywhere.
I go for a walk and as the leaves they fall.
I look around and hear you call.
As a breeze goes by I feel your touch.
The one I really miss so much.
I long to hold you once again
And feel your love, not all this pain.
Carol Elliott

The Naked Truth

Tumbling freefall in a black hole,
Feeling no pain yet hopelessly empty,
Sought is a light at a stage of the journey,
To alter the passage of darkness.

Devoid of control, no spirit to guide,
All drive and ambition consumed,
The forces of fate and prophets of doom,
Throw further tests unto the fray.

Yet for those of the torch or the ray of the sun,
No comprehension of the turmoil around them,
The pond on the surface, calm and serene,
Cover for great depth, an illusion.

Confidence, vision, replaced soon by doubt,
A puzzle, a problem, presented,
Longer elapsing, patience eroding,
A scream for outside intervention.

Solitude standing, the gathering throng,
Concerned but not near understanding,
Through time revealed, the wheat from the chaff,
Providing the light in the tunnel.
Stephen Easingwood

Coma———(An Amulet)

Do you dream of the war my love, do you dream once more of the war?
The war that took you away from me
Away from me to a far off land
A far off land so strange and cruel
Strange and cruel with killing fields
Killing fields that claimed innocent young lives
Innocent young lives wasted in a man-made hell
A man-made hell that stole your mind
Stole your mind and left you without sleeping
The sleeping of one who is now close to death
Now close to death my love, as you sleep, do you dream?
Do you dream of the war my love, do you dream once more of the war?
Ken Shaw

Always You

When autumn leaves wither and fall
from the sea,
When cold winter winds change
the warm summer breeze,
When the dark silent night
covers the daylight...
THERE WILL ALWAYS BE YOU.
When things don't seem to be
going right in a troubled world so
full of strife,
When the roses in the garden,
their beauty have lost,
for heavy lies the silver frost.
When dreams are broken by reality
I shall not mind or care,
for you will always be there.
When I see the stars and morning dew
I count every blessing...
There will always be you.
V. Askey

Marilyn Monroe

Norma Jeane is a Hollywood dream
she so sensitive and insecure
found in a aeroplane factory

A father she had
but does not know
He left long ago

A mother, who wanted to be a movie star
but ended up in a mental home

pushed from foster home to foster home
but she made it on her own

Curly blonde hair, sexy blue eyes
rose bud lips, a lovely smile

A perfect cute body
and sexy clothes

In front of the camera
She came alive
cooperative, eager and bright

A movie star was she
singing and acting in her sexy voice
as beautiful as can be
Valerie Ryan

Hill Of Hope

Mountains crags, gorges and cliffs,
days, minutes, hours and years.
In this modern world of despair,
riddled with pain and fear,
which are the greater to climb?

Oh, for childlike naivety, to permeate
all our days. That incessant cry
of hope, that is childhood and
youthful innocence, should never
be torn away.

Experience is man's greatest enemy.
For it destroys our blinkered perception
and renders impossible complete absolute,
wonder and joy for the world we
inhabited, in our pre-fallen state of
perfection. Despair is not the
answer for us, for man is not
forsaken totally, we must all
climb and reach the summit
of our glorious hill of hope.
Mark Mailer

Love Me My Love

Love me my love
Love me now, or I will be gone
To feel your touch upon my face
To hear your voice
Love me my love

Love me my love
Love me now, while I am near
To walk the fields
To feel the air upon our face
Love me my love

Love me my love
Love me now, walk hand in hand
Unaware of things around
To be as one, just you and I alone
Love me my love

Love me my love
Love me now, while we can see
A shining star and see the moon
The heaven above, and feel God's love
Love me my love.
E. Satur

Untitled

If I should die
Let it be tonight
For today has been the perfect day
the sight of you at the end of the aisle
Filled my eyes and stole my heart away

If I should die
let it be tonight
No more joy could a person withstand
The planning, the preparations of the months past
Ended today with you in my hands

If I should die
Let it not be sad
For I have loved you like no other
To have been blessed with the touch of your smile today
and to have known you as a lover

But if I should live
let it be with you
I have no words to describe
The feeling of knowing you are part of my life
For today you have become my bride

Bill Clayton

Myself

I live within myself you see,
a world that's just unique to me.
My fantasies I do believe are
caught within this web I weave.

This world in which I choose to live
I'm sure has nothing much to give
But one things very plain to see,
it expects nothing back from me.

Hayley Iachetta

Dust To Dust

Follow the path up the hillside, in Spain.
To the broken-down farm,
Where the wind plays her games.
The salt-laden wind, no longer barred,
By the cracked sun-bleached door,
That lies on the floor, and the stars
Winking down the moon's bright beam
Spotlights the swirling brown dust of gossamer veils,
In a gay exultant dance of lust,
Reclaims the land, that once was lost.

Jean Williams

Farewell

Eight hours of rest, work and pleasure
So this is thought to be the measure
How true this is in certain cases, but not of that in our work place
As for tomorrow who can say
Our yesterdays are here to stay
To absent friends of whom I was so fond, they now rest in the land beyond.
Part of the team I say with pride
Their loss, my sorrow I cannot hide.
The sun has gone the leaves are falling, the weather's bleak the grass stopped growing
Summer's gone winter's calling
Tomorrow comes without knowing
The joys of life are there for the taking love and happiness is in the making.
When sadness rears its ugly head
Remember all the joys instead
To see your youth your smiling faces, your friendship and your fond embraces
Life patterns like the seasons
Many changes many reasons
My admiration shall always remain. I sincerely hope we will meet again
You're all good friends that I shall miss
I wish you all a life of Bliss

Ivor Williams

Chance

I'm singing to you about the game of chance.
If you lose it makes you sad but when
You win you want to dance.

Beware of the jollier at the top of the pack,
he's there he's waiting, ready to attack

When the ace is around, be firm, stand your ground,
If you don't he will wear you right down.

The king of spades can hurt you like a knife
he is cunning and cruel; he can take away your life.

The king of diamonds is full of greed and lust,
he will leave you broken-hearted; after he has stolen
your trust and ground is into dust.

The king of hearts is the one that you need
he will love you completely and take away the pain
when he is around the pack is in order it won't
  be played again.

Chance if you lose it makes you sad,
Chance when you win, you sing and dance
  This is the game of chance.

Catherine Fahy

Seasons Of Life

My dear Lord as I close my eyes
Something stirs in my heart and begins to rise
A feeling of love and peace within
As my thoughts of what I have seem begin
The gentle smile of someone kind
Lingering on through the mists in my mind
Amidst wisps of colours entwined to be
At one with the Earth, Sky and Sea
Of the pure opening up of Spring
Like life itself it does surely sing
To catching the warmth of a summer's day
On a breeze we float along life's way
Through to Autumn and its powerful glow
As along its path we gently flow
Then to Winters so crisp and white
Giving frosty patterns through the light
So gentle all these things can be
As they touch our hearts and make us see
So my Lord I will close my eyes
And thank You for this wondrous prize

Catherine P. Nimmo

"The Open Sea"

Across the vast and open sea someone somewhere is calling me
A friend, a loved one, a voice unheard of, it cannot be
Perhaps it's ship in the storm trying to get free
Or the wind making noises far out at sea.

You stand on the seashore straining your eyes hearing the noises
  passing you by
Some noises you make out, some you cannot comply
You look and you listen then with a sigh
The night has grown darker no stars in the sky

Next day at daybreak you're up and you're out
The seashore is calling the tides turned around
What is it that calls me to the vast open space
Where the waters are fierce and the noises are great.

Summer nights when you're standing something twinkles so bright
A star on the skyline or a plane, in flight
Your mind is so large, as vast as the sea
Unlike the sea it cannot get free.

The sea is just one thing that nature provides
The Lord he has giveth he does not take sides
Nature is proof the Lord does not hide
It's the wrongs that you do He cannot abide.

Samuel McKay Birrell

Untitled

My dearest love if you could know,
How would you do I love you so
Each long and lovely day I miss
Your sunny presence and your kiss
Your wisdom and your shoulder strong
to prop me up, when things go wrong
and yet I feel, I think, I know,
that you are there, where e'er I go
To keep me safe on journeys long
tell me there is still a song
for singing, in my world believe,
though I am lost, a lot is Celi
a little babe with eyes of I love,
who looks at me, and I see you.
Elizabeth D. Rogers

The Sea Of Night

At night I float along the beach with waves of foam
to search the sky and no-one sees me land upon the
rich and darkened sand,
A skin that stretches far away and covers creatures
from the sea, the blanket changes dry then wet and
moon appears, a bright spun net,
That catches glimpses of those things roaming free
whilst you and me sleep away the voodoo hours of midnight.

Ears that hear the silence deafening more as
dynamite exploding, gradually scaling the crash -
swept rocks, deteriorating through the ages,
Ancient accidents of nature's present, past and
destination,
And still I roll along those waves that seek to
change the dawn of day,
Continually avoiding the decay by breaking on the
barren shore and watching who could ask for more.
V. Leigh

Sorrow

Are you passing through some sorrow
is your pillow wet with tears
There is only one that can help you
He will banish all your fears.

Do you wonder why you suffer
and if God does understand yes.
He knows your future pathway
all your life is in His hands.

All God's testings have a purpose
someday you will see the light
all He asks is that you trust Him
walk by faith and not by sight.

Do not fear when doubts surround you
just remember He is near
He will never, never leave you
He will always, always hear.
Simon Oakley

Injustice

Who took all my dreams
My most desire fantasies
Who took everything I ever wanted
The creator not the thief
And when all I ever wanted was theirs
It was moulded together
And then with grave injustice, it was given to another.
Brendan Ashton

The Statue Of Liberty

Proudly she stands outlined against the sky
The statue of Liberty with her head held high
Her light shines out across the sea
And brightly beams for all to see

The immigrants reach out for help
Tired and weary, and sad,
Their fears are soon forgotten
When they see the promised land

She welcomes those from many nations
Giving hope to generations
To live in freedom with all mankind
And face the future with a grateful mind

As her sons return from foreign fields
Homeward bound once more
They'll sing "God Bless America"
When they see the light on shore
Isabel McMillan

The Black Rose

The black rose that grows,
In only the dark lonely places,
The colour of your petals
Are as black as my soul.
It holds the key to unknown places
With many different faces.

The light that shines on other roses.
Always seems to miss you out.
Just like the people that I want, to care about me
They always just seems to walk on past.
If only they would stop and realize
What I want to say to them.
I am sure they would understand.

I can't help it if, I'm just like the black rose,
We just want to be loved.
Isobel Edment

"Beautiful Sadness"

She was beautiful sadness
Wrapped up in mystery
Amid vale - glen and mist
On a wet June day
On a Trent bus way.

Green fields and hills swept by
Quiet winding ways looked
But never brought smile
for even one mile.

Dressed in black - yes
But bright red nail
Half dead and alive
About age thirty-five.

I left her at the turn of the road
Still wondering why
She didn't cry with such a heavy load.

Saw her off in the rain
Never again do to speak
Or see her again
But I thought for a week.
Mildred T. Kendrew

Friendship

Who'd really think after all this time.
That we would still be together.
They do say opposites attract.
They couldn't have judged any better.

10 years it is since we first met.
And in that time we'll never forget.
The ups and downs that we've both had.
Me being a lassie and you being a lad.

Through all the laughs, tears and pain
We've been through the seasons, the sun and rain,
And now you say you're going away,
Our love will last for another day

Out of sight, out of mind,
That want the say
That won't be the case
Once you've gone away.

Tomorrow is another day,
I'd like to think when your far away.
That now and again you'll think of me.
We go together like 1, 2, 3.

W. Richards

Controlled Frustration

I'm sitting here
No words can I find
To express the confusion,
That's controlling my mind

A day of panic!
The one that's still,
A day of enchantment
With aims I fulfil
A day where forceful things
Like jealousy take charge
a day when ambitions seem distant
Although the wish is large
A day of boredom
But also of rest
Damn it! Someone tell me
What wind of day's best!

I'm sitting here
No words can I find
To express the confusion
That's controlling my mind

Sarah Buckley

Untitled

It was a morning when everyone should feel grand,
Everybody happy, strike up the band.
As I walked I wished that it were really so,
But life has changed, as we all know.
Rapes and murders reported every day,
No property safe from the Aerosol spray.
Instead of singing as I strolled along,
It set me wondering what's gone wrong?
Drug pushers earning untold wealth,
By ruining other people's health.
Muggers robbing the old and weak,
And the rest of us too afraid to speak.
Old people as their end draws near,
Living behind locked doors in a state of fear.
Is there no one to lead us to change our ways,
And life be as it was in the good old days.
We've recently celebrated the birth of a baby boy,
Who came down to earth and brought great joy.
He changed the world in days of yore,
Come again dear "Lord" and do it once more.

David Anderson

Think Before You Leave Home

To all young people before leaving home
Think before you leave
Think about tomorrow
Tomorrow where you will be

Among strangers, no friends no warm beds
No clean sheets no hot meals no sweet dreams
No one to help you if you feel lonely
No loving arms to hug you to make you feel homely

Think before you leave
Think about tomorrow think where you will be

On the streets on park benches sleeping
In rough and not eating enough
Is that where you want to be among the rough

Think before you leave
Think about tomorrow where will you be
Think before you leave home

Eddie Ross

Untitled

I am told to be assertive, to create my own space,
That this is the way forward for the whole human race.
But I am having difficulty, I fear I am quite meek,
When I should be saying 'No' I am always very weak.

My employment is stressful, I lead a large team,
When a member is scolded I feel guilty and mean,
I'm accused by my colleagues of being soft and too kind,
In a similar position a harsher punishment they'd find.

At home it's no different, my family demand,
Child minding, dog-walking, I have it in hand.
I wish, Oh I wish, for a weekend of rest,
But cannot say 'No', I give of my best.

My neighbour is elderly, refuse I cannot,
To assist with the ironing, the shopping, the lot.
My friend she has problems she wants to discuss,
I just can't refuse it would cause such a fuss.

Is assertion the answer in a world hurt by crime?
Is it really so bad to give of my time?
I've no wealth to offer but my heart I can share,
I am not truly weak, it's just that I care.

Christine Isherwood

Life

We're born from the fetus to the egg,
Then we grow into women, or men.
We age, and begin to learn
We get jobs, and then we earn.
We marry and have children of our own,
They get jobs and leave the home.
They live their lives and have children too,
Then soon there is no place for you.
You see life is so precious it is dear,
We worry we have pain, we also have
Fear.
Hold on to every minute,
Make it last,
Because life is like a train moving
Fast.
One second you're here,
The next you're not,
Make the most of life,
It's all you've got.

Andrea Michael

Untitled

When tension gets too high
Mind strains until it's taut
There's creatures in the night
And monsters in your thoughts

Guilt, hurt, you feel the pain
Smashing, thrashing out in vain
No-one's there to help you through
Alone you cry, it's up to you

I'll tell you friend from where they come
From jealousy, anger, guilt and rage
Can't turn your back, they still remain
You're trapped with hell inside your cage

There's just one thing before the night
As you pray for sun and cry for light
Demons hide throughout the day
But they're still here, they're here to stay

You can't lose demons, they won't go away
And they're not so hard to find
But if you're strong, you'll cast away
These demons of the mind.

Gillian A. Young

Boat Of Wishes

If I could find a desert,
I'd fill it with my tears,
I'd build a boat of wishes,
And sail from all my fears.

My crew will all be promises,
The ringing all my dreams,
The rudder made from memories,
My hopes in all the beams.

I'd sail from all this loneliness
And all my troubles too, and,
When I find peace of mind
I'll sail on back to you.

Pamela Kempton

"Arbeit Macht Frei"

No-one helped the Jew though
they all knew what went on
inside those gates of hell.
The death knell sounded loud
and clear, they lived in fear
and believed the sign "Arbeit Macht Frei"
They went in droves; no questions
asked, the facts were masked
behind lies.
Stripped naked of humanity and pride
caught in the tide of war, and
no-one saw.

Vivienne Young

Have Faith

I have little money or worldly wealth
But my troubles they are few
My most precious treasure on the world
Is the love I have for you

I'm contented with the modest things
But what I'd like to do
Is to buy a little home
That's good enough for you

Where by the fire we can sit
And contented be
Like little love birds on a nest
Just keep your faith in me

I'll make a vow to you my dear
Come blizzards, snow or vain
I'll buy that house, all furnished out
When spring comes round again.

George Empson

Old Soldiers

The sound of the battle has long gone by.
But those who live on still have to cry.
Tears for their comrades who row lie at rest.
Each soldier a memory only he knows best.

The whine of the bullet, an exploding grenade.
A chance of safety behind the blockade.
Where once there was danger, death and screams.
The battlefields now quiet, so full of dreams.

For the men who fought hard and battled their fear
The memories live on with each passing year.
Our fallen heroes we should never forget
Now and forever we shall be in their debt.

Keith O'Toole

Not Long Now

Holy men have been heard to say
What God gives, he takes away
But what God knows is beyond their ken
Too much for minds of mortal men
For as the light of life grows dimmer
And earthly senses but a glimmer
How can the Holies comprehend
"God doesn't give he only Lends".

W. McGougan

My Children

My children, when you were born
You gave quality and meaning, to my life
Your love meant everything to me
You were my source of joy and hope for the future
You inspired me and made me dare to be who I am
You made my life a warm and happy place to be.

And now my children, our lives will take a different path
You will learn people don't always say what they mean
For the road is never straight, and never as it seems
As you start your own adventures in life
Remember these words and realise all your dreams.

May you fly with the eagle and learn to be free
May you swim with the dolphins as they flee captivity
May you ride a wild pony, see the beauty through their eyes
May you hunt with the tiger and learn to survive
May you sing with the skylark, let there music caress your ears
And, may you walk in God's footsteps for the rest of your years.

Maureen Gentry-Evans

After The Earthquake

First to rush to the City Gate
Was the drunken ragged poacher,
Who had laid his whole life to waste.
Swallowing the town's tone of reproach,
Swallowing my watchman's words of hate,
And unsurprised, I stood aside,
Yet heard him loudly state:
"The poor fool and drunkard
Was a rich masquerade.
Oh, I drank always, always I drank,
But always slowly - I was never drunk.
Mine was never a dream-shop fate.
Tell them to bring their travelling clothes:
Open the City Gate!"

Martin Kelsey

A Winter's Tale

A thousand ice cubes
   drape the trees,
Windows - kept in Purdah,
Toes - half dead
crunch thro' the rime,
muffled and unsure,
Icy bed of purity
waiting to be sullied.

Gentle ammunition,
Winter clamps us all.

Joan Plant

Our Beautiful World

Our beautiful world
Where innocence was born,
Once was so treasured,
Is now tattered and torn.

Our beautiful world,
Where children could play.
Those days of safety
Are now so far away.

Our beautiful world
With her mystical skies
The wonder inside
Has gone, hate fills our eyes.

Our beautiful world
With such radiant sun,
We only feel safe
With our hands 'round a gun.

Our beautiful world
She still plays the same tune,
It's our dance that's changed
To the ballad of doom.

Jennifer Emery

Love

Who can describe this thing so great
Which dwells within one's heart?
Who can explain the loveliness
More beautiful than art?
Who can describe the inner warmth,
To match the sun above?
Who can explain the power
Or experience of love?

John Millar Kent

Teacher

A teacher is multi-coloured
Summertime
In a class-room
A precipitation of moods
A mask nobody can see
A blind date hiding without sight.

Mark Grainger

Loss

Oh, how my heart is aching,
The pain too harsh to tell,
My nightmare is of waking,
As each day's a living hell.

It's said that time will heal,
I pray to God it's true,
My life just seems unreal,
Like a curse that touches few.

Perhaps the sun will shine again,
And maybe I'll grow strong,
Until then my tears, like rain,
Keep falling, hard and long.

Christina Derrien

The Visionary

I sit here,
I sit there,
I sit all the time
And I seem to stare,
I'm in the sitting room
  With no stair,
I have no legs
So I go nowhere.
Also I cannot see
  I am blind,
I am not concerned
Sadness is hard to find,
My vigorous brain is my sight,
I have no grey skies,
Everything is bright.
My insight
Gives me a wider vision.
All I feel for normal life,
Is just derision.

D. G. Field

Lilac Time

I strolled amongst the lilac trees
Upon me came a gentle breeze
The fragrance was so divine
I stopped to admire the delicate blooms
Of bluely move and perfect white
The flowers swayed gently to and fro
Like a whisper saying do not go
I lingered longer than I should
To watch the bees and hear the birds
Nature is a wonderful thing
A prize which one does no have to win
A gift for everyone to see
And cherish for eternity

E. Teiwel

Untitled

Should I take them?
I don't really know,
I think I will leave them,
"Oh dear no",
My box of memories.
Lies there on the floor
I have just five minutes.
Before I walk out of the door
School photos, kids' drawings.
Of days gone by.
My old box of treasures
Brings a tear to my eye
"Hurry up dear"
That's the voice of my spouse
The van has arrived
And we are moving house.

Beryl Bowers

When The Night Is Gone

Sleep my darling sleep.
Within images of light.
Sparkling all around you.
And disappearing into the night.

Sleep my darling sleep.
Dream of far and distant lands.
Where children laugh and play.
And walk on golden sands.

Sleep my darling sleep.
Dream of me my love.
Watch me drift down.
From the stars above.

Sleep my darling sleep.
And when you wake at dawn.
I'll be there to hold your hand.
When the night is gone.

Iain Wilson

Untitled

What a strangeness it is
when you wake up in
the night and you
near something spooky
creeping about.

What a strangeness it is
when you switch
on the light in the
night and everything
is so very bright.

What a strangeness it is
when a bright light shines
on a dark figure who
blends in with the
darkness of the night

Matthew Brown

Death

Panacea of all my pain
come to me
with promise to rest,
remoulder of this terrible reign
come to me
cease this beating breast.

Redresser of all that's wrong
quell this fire
which burns so weak,
singer of time's oldest song
quell this fire
let the darkness speak.

Harbinger of all withered harvest
embrace me now
with hold so tight,
nuzzler of the eternal nest
embrace me now
let life take flight.

William Quinn

One Heaven Away

My Mother,
  meant the world to me,
She was perfect, in every way.
Her golden heart stopped beating,
And then she went away, Mum
was tired and weary so I know
it's for the best, free to go to
Heaven to have her peaceful rest,
there are things we never said Mum
But there will come a day, when
we can talk for ever, in are own
special way.

Leslee McMahon

"Winter Beauty"

From outside, the winter wind
Is blowing cold and sharp,
Whistling softly through the trees
Like music from a harp,
Clouds move swiftly in the sky
On their journey never ending,
Trees just shake and let them pass
Their branches bare and bending,
Glistening front upon the ground
Reflects that rays of sun,
Pictures that have never changed
Since time that man begun,
These sights are of real beauty
And all of them are free,
To rich, to poor, and middle class,
It's there for all to see.

R. Maben

Biographies of Poets

ACHILLEOS, ELIAS
[b.] September 13, 1967, London; [p.] Theophilos Achilleos, Androulla Achilleos; [oth. writ.] Several unpublished poems.; [a.] Enfield, Middlesex,

ADAMS, JIM
[b.] June 16, 1958, Paisley; [p.] Thomas and Dorothy Adams; [ed.] Johnstone High School Glasgow College Building, Printing; [occ.] Glazier; [memb.] Renfrew and District Astronomical Society, Old Ranfurly Golf Club, Member of Paisley Abbey; [hon.] City and Guild of London in Glass and Glazing, English 'O Grade; [oth. writ.] School and Church Prizes, one of my songs (Where Eagles Fly) being sung by (Gaberlunzie) Scottish Folk Duo.; [pers.] 'Seek Ye after truth. In your journey. Through life' is my idea of correctness.; [a.] Johnstone, Renfrewshire, PA5 0DJ

ADAMS, LORRAINE
[pen.] The Medusa; [b.] February 8, 1962, Ipswich; [p.] Mr. and Mrs. Ruby Adams; [ed.] Writing School Comprehensive Course; [occ.] Child Minder; [oth. writ.] Everything is going to be alright bullies has been published yet.; [pers.] I was very surprised and happy after receiving the letter stating that I have made it to the semi-final I never thought that my poem would make it. Thanks for considering my poem.; [a.] Hackney, London, N.I.

ADAMS, STEVEN
[pen.] Steven Adams; [b.] January 20, 1973, Liverpool; [p.] Maureen, Ted Adams; [ed.] Knowsley Higherside Comprehensive, Sheffield Hallam University, Liverpool John Moores University; [occ.] Optoelectronic Specialist; [memb.] Alphaworld Cyber Community; [hon.] HND BSC Hons Optoelectronics/Optical Sciences; [oth. writ.] Short stories rejected by all the best publishers! Possibly some Science Journal.; [pers.] I only write as a Poultice on my soul. If someone likes my poetry I am happy for them!; [a.] Liverpool, Merseyside, L34 4AE

ADAMSON, LORRAINE
[b.] August 7, 1951, Merton, London; [p.] Patricia Black and Dennis Black; [m.] Derrick John Adamson, September 1969; [ch.] Four sons - Steven Adamson, Ian Adamson, Mark Adamson, Paul Adamson; [ed.] Fortescue Comprehensive Adult Education Centre; [occ.] Special Needs Support Worker; [hon.] B.S.L. (British Sign Language); [oth. writ.] Currently writing my autobiography - children's stories poem published in hospital newsletter. Son has two poems published in poetry now, expressions in verse.; [pers.] Through verse we can express our innermost feelings, inspiration is all around us. I am greatly inspired by the courageous and happy children despite their many disabilities, that I work with.; [a.] Manchester, Lancashire, M40 1HJ

ADDIMAN, DAVID
[pen.] D. G. Addiman; [b.] November 12, 1966, London; [p.] Geoffrey Addiman, Rita Addiman; [ed.] Hedley Walter School, Brentwood; [occ.] Security Officer, Property Protection Guarding; [pers.] I normally write poetry about events in my personal life (usually with a comic twist). So it gives me great pleasure to bring my more serious work to a wider audience.; [a.] Brentwood, Essex, CM14 5JJ

ALDRIDGE, IAN
[b.] June 25, 1969, Birmingham; [p.] Barry Aldridge, Brenda Aldridge; [ed.] Hodge Hill Secondary School; [occ.] Foil Blocker, Oak Die Stamping C degrees; [memb.] Great Britain Tae Kwon Do Association; [pers.] I feel poetry is an important form of communication and I try to achieve this is in my writing. I hope anyone who reads my work can understand and gain as much from it as I have from writing poetry.; [a.] Birmingham, Warwickshire, B35 6DT

ALDRIDGE, JEAN MARGARET
[pen.] Jean Margaret Aldridge; [b.] July 7, 1931, London; [p.] Florence and Hubert Aldridge (Deceased); [ch.] Fostered, 8 teenagers; [ed.] Secondary Modern; [occ.] Enquiry Officer Wiltshire Constabulary; [oth. writ.] Started writing a historical mystery called Raging Torrents. Several letters published in local paper, written several other poems.; [pers.] My poems come from places, I visit when writing Nessy, I had just visited Lochness while on Holiday. Other poems are I taught up on events that have happened and I love the old poets like Wordsworth.; [a.] Bradford on Avon, Wiltshire, BA15 2ND

ALEXANDER, GEORGE HAROLD
[b.] February 24, 1899, Laxey, Isle of Man; [p.] Mr. and Mrs. G. Neely; [m.] Bessie, March 26, 1932; [ch.] Elsa; [ed.] Douglas High School, Isle of Man; [occ.] Civil Servant - Ordinance Survey (Retired 1960) after an Army career; [hon.] Army long service medal. Named on Lonan (I.O.M.) church wall. Plaque as a survivor of active service in the 1st World War (Royal Engineers); [oth. writ.] My father started writing poetry when he was in his fifties, discovering an interest which he enjoyed throughout his thirty three years of retirement. He wrote three full volumes of poetry 1) On topics which took his fancy and portrayed his whimsical sense of humour 2) About his beloved Isle of Man and 3) Spiritual matters during his lifetime, he had only one poem published in a local paper - the only one he submitted; [pers.] When my father left school in his early teens. He joined the army. He saw action in the Dublin rebellion, Ypres during the 1st World War, was part of the peace keeping force in Shanghai. And on the home front during the 2nd World War.; [a.] Christchurch, Dorset, BH23 4PJ

ALEXANDER, JAN KING
[b.] October 11, 1942, Guildford, Surrey; [p.] Gladys King, Gordon Christian James Alexander; [m.] Divorced; [ch.] Lucy, Giles Claire; [ed.] Rydon County Girls School, Chelsea College Art, Camden Technician College, Northbrook College; [occ.] Student doing two year and stage management; [memb.] T.A.T. (Tell a Tale), Theatre Company (Lighting, sound, and performance in community; [hon.] GCE 8 O-levels incl English Lit and Language, Math, History, Art, GCE A-Level Art, B.S.A. Foundation Art Course, C.S.S. C.S.G.W. and Modular in social work; [oth. writ.] Book of poetry, title soul-provider gone for publishing. (Observations on a woman's life); [pers.] I feel we all have poetry in our soul our lives reflect that poetry in all its varied shades of dark and light; [a.] Worthing, Sussex, BN11 2DS

ALEXANDER, JOANNE
[b.] June 8, 1967, Essex; [p.] Frederick Bines, Doreen Bines; [ch.] Madison Eloise; [pers.] Each day is a struggle, a circus of dreams and disappointments. My only reality is my wonderful daughter.; [a.] Canvey Island, Essex, S58 0HQ

ALI, SANSEL
[b.] April 18, 1962, London; [p.] Ismail Ali, Cemaliye Ali; [ch.] Miss Nisan Ali; [ed.] North London College Holloway; [occ.] Sales Assistant; [oth. writ.] A book of poems and a novel, awaiting offers for publication. Three songs written and released on vinyl, (records) to public.; [pers.] I strive to reflect my words, as a source of inspiration, to motivate and capture, the creative imagination.; [a.] London, N16 5RE

ALLAN, KENNETH MARK
[b.] July 31, 1953, Burnley; [p.] Edward, Minnie Allan; [m.] Ann Allan (Poole), April 28, 1973; [ch.] David, Simon, Claire,; [ed.] Went to local schools and I did not take any exams, but now I go to night school at Burnley University to in further my Education in English; [occ.] Production Operative, I am the second youngster of five children; [hon.] Fame certificate the high level. And I got a poem published in people friend magazine where I won a prize for the poem Thoughts of You.; [oth. writ.] Short story which I have completed one call A Tall From Becket Farm and several poems; [pers.] I have always been interested in stories and special in poetry and hope I have a future in writing romantic and dream like poetry.; [a.] Burnley, Lancs, BB11 2LH

ALLAN, SHIRLEY JANE
[pen.] Shirley Allan; [b.] November 12, 1960, Scotland; [p.] Jean Allan, George Allan; [ch.] Greg Andrew Allan; [ed.] Royal Scottish Academy of Music and Drama Moray House College of Education; [occ.] Visiting Teacher of Drama of Primary Schools; [oth. writ.] After the phone call - poem published in poetry now publication heart and soul.; [pers.] I am interested in all art forms and particularly like the poetry of Roger McGough and Sylvia Plath.; [a.] Inverkeithing, Fife, KY11 1AR

ALLEN, JOHN MICHAEL
[pen.] "Nemo Three"; [b.] March 22, 1925, Clacton-on-Sea, Essex; [p.] Kathleen and Frank Allen; [m.] Audrey Elizabeth Graham Allen, February 4, 1945; [ch.] Rosemarie Palmer; [ed.] Technical College, North East Essex; [occ.] Retired Caterer; [memb.] Fellow of the Cookery and Food Association, Member of Hotel and Catering Institute Management Assoc., etc.; [oth. writ.] Occasional articles on Catering and Cookery Subjects.; [a.] Saundersfoot, Pembs, SA69 9EJ

ALLISON, JULIE
[b.] January 14, 1965, Chesterfield; [p.] John Allison and June Allison; [ed.] William Rhodes Secondary School, Chesterfield College; [occ.] Mature Student (Computers); [memb.] New Life Church (Chesterfield), Chesterfield Community Centre; [hon.] City and Guilds 726 Computing Personal Survival Swimming, Bronze, Silver. Duke of Edinburgh Bronze Award.; [oth. writ.] Poems published in three previous anthologies, church magazines.; [pers.] Be a vessel to take from the divine to the sublime, always promoting good and spurning evil.; [a.] Chesterfield, Derbyshire, S41 8NU

ALMOND, DAVID JOHN
[b.] October 23, 1946, Blackburn; [m.] Christina; [ch.] Paul and Mark; [occ.] Calligraphy Tutor; [memb.] East Lancs Calligraphers Guild; [hon.] Open University of the North West Diploma in Calligraphy and Fine Arts.; [pers.] Poetry has developed as an offshoot of Calligraphy allowing originality in composition as well as script and design.; [a.] Darwen, Lancs, BB3 3JM

ALSTON, FRED
[b.] April 5, 1909, Radcliffe, Lancs; [ed.] Bury Grammar School Scholarship 1921-25; [occ.] Retired Established Civil Servant; [memb.] Life Member Lancashire Authors Association; [hon.] Being born and still alive; [oth. writ.] Books, articles etc and poems in standard English and dialect.; [pers.] Many published in Lancashire authors journal - the record, and with BBC Contract personally on air on local radio. Subjects - very varied, principally nature, philosophy and human nature.; [a.] Bury, Lancs, BL9 6LR

AMBRIDGE, ANN
[pen.] Ann Ambridge; [b.] April 27, 1965, Luton; [ed.] Manshead Upper Coddington Beds; [occ.] Shop Assistant; [oth. writ.] Objects In The Mirror published in an anthology called connecting poetry now.; [pers.] I have suffered from depression for the past 5 yrs. The poem describes my inner thoughts at the start of my illness and was my 1st poem. I dedicate this poem to all depression suffers.; [a.] Spaulding, Lincs, PE11 1LH

ANDERSON, LUCY
[pen.] Lucy Anderson; [b.] February 24, 1969, Northampton; [p.] David Anderson, Christine Anderson; [ed.] Chichele Girls Comprehensive School, Rushden; [occ.] Studying - Counseling Studies; [memb.] Nene Valley Writers Group; [oth. writ.] Plenty of poems in my briefcase; [pers.] To be truly honest with oneself is to truly know oneself to ignore what we find - pleasure or pain - is to limit oneself. It is natural to express my observations of life through poetry. If anyone should be moved by it - it is all the more rewarding.; [a.] Rushden, Northants, NN10 9HQ

ANDERSON, ROBERT
[pen.] Bob Anderson; [b.] March 10, 1949, Forfar; [p.] Robert and Margaret Anderson; [ch.] Tracy Elizabeth; [ed.] Forfar Academy; [occ.] Forklift Driver; [memb.] Canmore Bowling Club, Forfar Bridge Club; [oth. writ.] The Expert, Night Time Caller, Business Mans Vacation; [pers.] There is no honour in coming second last if you cheat to achieve it.; [a.] Forfar, Angus, DD8 2BN

ANDREWS, MRS. JOAN
[b.] February 25, 1916, Slough; [p.] Mr. and Mrs. Reymond and Fanny Whitelaw; [m.] Phillip Saunder, 1940, Alfred Willdew, 1975, Ronald Andrews, 1983; [ch.] Six; [ed.] Boarding School St. Mary's College Hampton Hill; [occ.] O.A.P.; [oth. writ.] One poem published in woman not the one submitted to you; [a.] Chelmsford, Essex, CM1 6FB

ARCHER, LINDA JOYCE
[pen.] L. J. Archer; [b.] October 27, 1952, London, England; [p.] Mr. Reginald, Mrs. Doreen Maynard; [m.] Mr. John David Archer, December 23, 1988 2nd; [ch.] Georgina, Chistopher, Catherine, Michael; [ed.] Comprehensive School Member; [occ.] Housewife, Mother, Care Assistant to son; [memb.] The Child Growth Foundation; [hon.] Fund raiser for the above charity.; [oth. writ.] 1 other poem published, 3 just been excepted the last 2 weeks, 1st poem in the 1996 British Poetry Review, 2nd Family Pets, 3rd Funny Strange-Situations, 4th Summer Review, 1996. All by Rivacre Ltd. Cheshire England.; [pers.] I write for both adults and children, I believe my writing to be a gift. My greatest influence is life itself. I love, I feel, so therefore I am.; [a.] Hornchurch, Essex, RM12 5PB

ARNOLD, MAUREEN B.
[pen.] Maureen B. Arnold; [b.] July 19, 1939, Edmonton; [p.] Mr. and Mrs. Goodrich; [m.] Brian S. Arnold, March 5, 1960; [ch.] Tracy and Ryan; [ed.] Secondary Modern; [occ.] Housewife; [memb.] Eastern Enfield Royal British Legion; [hon.] None as I have never entered anything before.; [oth. writ.] Poems and articles for Eastern Enfield Royal British Legion Bl. Monthly Magazine.; [pers.] I write as a hobby for myself, my family and friends about everyday life and current affairs.; [a.] Enfield, Middlesex, EN3 6DH

ARNOTT, MRS. BEATRICE J.
[pen.] Lady Bea; [b.] October 3, 1940, Salford; [p.] Deceased; [m.] Mr. C. M. Arnott, December 23, 1981; [ed.] Mossley Rd Sec School, Ashton-u-Lyne Manchester; [occ.] Housewife; [memb.] Penlan Poets Society; [hon.] Won $20 for short story in woman's mag.

ARNOTT, LINDA
[pen.] Linda Nugent; [b.] August 26, 1963, Cheshire; [p.] Terence Nugent - Margaret Ollier; [m.] Divorced; [ch.] James, Malek, Samira; [ed.] Middlewich County Secondary School; [occ.] Housewife; [pers.] I enjoy writing and hope other people will too. Also in future I would like to write my own book of poems.; [a.] Withington, Manchester, M20 4TD

ASHAYE, ANTHONY O.
[pen.] Poetic Heart; [b.] February 7, 1970, London; [p.] Josiah and Rachael Ashaye; [m.] Sally M. Ashaye, April 8, 1995; [ed.] Birkbeck College, University of London, BSC Hons - Financial Economics Second Class Upper; [occ.] Local Government Employee; [memb.] Green Pastures Christian Ministries; [hon.] Financial Economics; [oth. writ.] Article for local church newsletter and several other poems.; [pers.] I try to show that the greatest gift of a human being lies within. Tapping into it can bring uncomprehendable success. Inspired by the book of Proverbs and the Psalms in the Bible.; [a.] Grays, Essex, RM16 6PS

ASKEW, LILLIAN
[b.] November 6, 1953, Wigan; [p.] Maria and John Price; [m.] Alan Askew, January 13, 1973; [ch.] Jacqueline Askew; [ed.] St. Mary's, Leyland, Lancs; [occ.] Owner Hairdresser; [hon.] Q.D.M. in hairdressing; [oth. writ.] Many poems on relatives friends, neighbours and customers but Nancy will be the first I have ever entered.; [pers.] I like to write about people I know, mainly humorous poems to give enjoyment without naming names.; [a.] Preston, Lancs, PR3 0TA

ASKEY, GLYN D.
[b.] May 5, 1959, Birmingham; [p.] Dennis Askey, Margaret Askey; [ed.] Easingwold School, Business College; [hon.] L.A.M.D.A., Cert Drama Business Admin., N.V.A.R.S.A. Business Admin. Cert. Achievement; [oth. writ.] A number of poems and plays; [pers.] I believe that if you have a talent for writing you should use this gift, so that people can enjoy your work which brings satisfaction to oneself.; [a.] York, Yorkshire, YO6 2BN

ASKEY, VIOLET
[pen.] Vi Askey; [b.] June 4, 1919, Acton W3; [p.] Rose and Bert Streams; [m.] Charles Askey, June 4, 1938; [ch.] Daughter - Yvonne; [ed.] South Acton Girls School; [occ.] Retired; [hon.] Swimming and Life Saving Certificates, 1st Certificate for Garden, a letter from the queen on behalf of writing to her for the children of Ruislip Gardens School for her Majesty's Jubilee June 1977; [oth. writ.] I am hoping before I leave this world to one day maybe get a small poem book printed for my two wonderful grandchildren "Sally Jane" and Stephen.; [pers.] I write many poems all of which are true to life past and present harmonious and sad something of which I and many others feel and see at times.; [a.] Ruislip, Middlesex, HA4 6PG

ASTON, VIVIAN
[pen.] Poupee; [b.] August 14, 1939, Paris; [p.] Max and Ela Aston; [ed.] Brussels Montreal Canada, England, Royal Academy of Music McGill University, Trinity College of Music; [occ.] Music and poetry; [memb.] Royal Academy of Music Club, a friend of the British Federations of Festivals for music, dance and speak.; [hon.] Prize for piano at music festivals and prizes for poetry at festivals and a medal for essay at a festival.; [oth. writ.] Written poems for festivals.; [pers.] I had people in my life who did music but had misery so I decided to write and it became a hobby.; [a.] London, NW2

ATKINS, URSULA
[b.] July 18, 1936, Hamburg; [p.] Otto and Margarethe Kaeding; [m.] Frederick R. S. Atkins, August 8, 1970 in Canterbury; [ch.] Jennie Atkins and Martina Atkins; [ed.] Elementary School, Hamburg and Austria, Commercial School, Hamburg; [occ.] Housewife; [oth. writ.] "Fraulein Tomm-Tomm" (Childhood memories during and after the Second World War in Germany and Austria) published in Spring 1997 by Book Guild Ltd.; [a.] Sittingbourne, Kent, ME10 2QL

ATKINSON, HEATHER
[b.] March 17, 1942, Uxbridge, Middlesex; [p.] Margaret Stuart; [m.] Walter, September 25, 1965; [ch.] Graeme; [ed.] Rupert Road Sec. Modern Arts and Crafts College Liverpool; [occ.] Housewife; [hon.] Hairdressing Diplomas; [pers.] I am a gardener and dreamer, dog lover and a lover of beauty and of mother earth itself. I see beauty in all these, and I am inspired to write it down, I hope that through my poetry others stop to see, feel and smell the beauty that is surrounding us all; [a.] Ashton-in-Makerfield, Gtr Mcr, WN4 8QZ

ATTIA, KOSTAS NEKTARIOS
[b.] August 20, 1976, Athens, Greece; [p.] Eneim-Antonios Attia, Evanthia-Stavroula Andreadou-Attia; [ed.] Lancaster University; [occ.] Student; [memb.] Lancaster University, Hellenic Society; [oth. writ.] Stories published in high school newspaper; [pers.] I try to reflect my inner feelings in my writing. I have been influenced by pessimist poets. I'd like to dedicate this piece of work to Mariza, Dimitris and to the memory of my grandfather Konstantinos; [a.] Lancaster, Lancashire, LA1 4YL

ATTWOOD, RUTH
[b.] June 1, 1927, Watford; [p.] Rev. and Mrs. A.L. Baxter; [m.] Dennis Robert Attwood, October 23, 1954; [ch.] 2 Sons, Three Daughters; [ed.] Normal for the 30's didn't make grammar school; [occ.] Retired; [memb.] Local Church and Appropriate Activities. Coffee morning quizzes in my middle age assisting teachers in local junior school by encouraging pupils with basic skills. Knitting reading etc.; [hon.] My only claim to fame was winning a bar of chocolate for a school essay competition at the age of 12 years. Plus sunday school prizes for attendance. Bible exams; [oth. writ.] Poems some spiritual some light hearted, for a birthday, anniversary, amusing incidents or something for the grandchildren.; [pers.] The only daughter (middle child) of a mission hall pastor who later became ordained. My early memories are of rambles, sunday school outings and cycling.; [a.] Watford, Herts, WD2 7HE

AUSTIN, ELIZABETH ANN
[pen.] Ann Austin; [b.] November 25, 1947, Cheadle, Staffs; [p.] Cyril Perry Wright, Elsie Wright; [m.] Thomas Austin, November 20, 1982; [ch.] Craig David; [ed.] Mackenzie Secondary, Cheadle Staffs, Cauldon College, Stoke-on-Trent; [occ.] Nursery Nurse in Special Education, Abbey Hill School; [memb.] Stoke-on-Trent Disabled Anglers Club; [hon.] N.N.E.B. E.D.Y., UEI Typewriting; [oth. writ.] Several poems none sent for publication other than this; [pers.] I write from the heart to ease the heart, of my fellow man.; [a.] Werrington S-O-T, Staffs, ST9 0DY

AUSTIN, SANDRA
[b.] November 29, 1955, Birmingham; [p.] William and Muriel Garbett; [m.] Trevor, July 31, 1976; [ch.] Tracey, Lee, Matthew; [ed.] Kingshurst High School for Girls; [occ.] Health Care Assistant for Elderly Care; [pers.] I usually write poetry for family and friends. This is the first time I have entered a competition and I'm thrilled to get this far.

AVERY, ROBERT
[pen.] Bob; [b.] June 16, 1956, Biddulph; [p.] Eric and Phyllis; [ed.] Knypersley Hall Boys School; [occ.] Unemployed due to Spinal Muscular Dystrophy; [memb.] Friends of the Royal Marines Museum, Muscular Dystrophy Group; [hon.] Certificate for doing a 10,000 foot tandem parachute jump.; [oth. writ.] Poems for the Local Parish Church Magazine Sports Parachutist. Muscular Dystrophy Magazine. (Search); [pers.] I try to write about the important things in life, past, present and futuristic thoughts, romantic, funny things with a meaning.; [a.] Biddulph, Staffs, ST8 6LF

AYESH, ALADDIN
[pen.] Aladdin 1986, Aladdin Ayesh since 1990; [b.] May 31, 1972; [p.] Sa'ad Ayesh, Sabah Al-Batrokh; [ed.] Msc. Essex University, Ph.D. Liverpool, John Moores University.; [occ.] Research Student; [memb.] The Poetry Society, P.E.N. English Centre, B.A.S.C.A, G.I.S.C., Lancashire Authors Association, Royal Musical Association; [oth. writ.] Many poems in several magazines, songs under composition.; [pers.] Simplism is my school while symbolism, structuralism and surrealism are my influences. I believe art is the mirror by which humans see themselves undressed.; [a.] Liverpool, Merseyside, L6 5AL

BACON, KERRY
[b.] November 4, 1967, Pembury; [p.] Ita and Tony Shaer; [m.] Mark Bacon, November 15, 1987; [ch.] Lee and Kaylee; [ed.] St. Patricks (Junior) Sacred Heart of Mary (Senior); [occ.] Carer; [memb.] Shields (Great Ormand Street Hospital, Charity); [oth. writ.] Written other poems which I have shared with family and friends.; [pers.] I feel that our world needs saving from possible destruction, maybe people like me through poetry, can get those who have the power to save our world, "Please Listen To Our Message".; [a.] South Hornchurch, Essex, RM13 7BX

BAILEY, ANTHEA
[pen.] Arabella Tay; [b.] March 22, 1952, Durham; [p.] Joseph/Gertrude Bishop; [m.] Divorced 1989; [ch.] Jarrod, David J.; [ed.] Washington Grammar, University of Sunderland; [occ.] Marketing and PR Consultant/Lecturer; [memb.] ABSA (Assoc. of Business Sponsorship of the Arts). Inst. Marketing MENSA; [hon.] B.A. (Hons) Fine Arts/M.B.A.; [oth. writ.] PR Journalist/Newspaper Articles Highlighting the Arts.; [pers.] The most treasured key that one can own is merely a smile.; [a.] Newcastle-upon-Tyne, NE1 5PG

BAKER, CHARLES
[occ.] Reading history at the London Guildhall University; [a.] Camden Town, London

BAKER, COLIN PHILIP
[b.] May 2, 1932, Tickhill, Yorkshire; [p.] Doris May Gowler, Albert Edward Baker; [pers.] I write poetry in the hope that people may read and then in some quiet moment reflect upon the memory, and say - "Aha! That is true."; [a.] Gosberton, Spalding, Lincs, PE11 4NP

BAKER, JOANNE
[b.] December 15, 1975, Lewisham; [p.] John and Irene Baker; [ed.] Orpington College; [occ.] Administration Assistant for the Ministry of Defence; [memb.] Bromley Network Radio; [oth. writ.] Previous publication in regional anthology.; [pers.] I endeavor to explain the unexplainable in my work. To pursue subjects with deep meaning and powerful emotions.; [a.] Bromley, Kent, BR1 4PG

BAKER, KAREN
[b.] July 5, 1978, Bath (R.U.H.) [p.] Don and Margaret Baker; [ed.] I attended the college of Frome for 2 years then exchanged to Whitstone Community in Shepton, left full time Ed at 16 with 3 GCSES in English, Maths and Geography.; [occ.] I have been employed for the last year and 1/2 working as a Retail Assistant at a successful superstore (J Sainsburys).; [oth. writ.] I have been writing poems for the last 2 years. This is the first competition I have entered a poem into and I feel proud with the achievement.; [pers.] I express all my emotions and feelings in my poetry. I like to think my poetry can uplift each individual that reads it. I believe that poetry can release everyone's dreams into reality.; [a.] Frome, Somerset, BA11 5AD

BAKER, MICK
[b.] December 28, 1937, Nuneaton; [p.] Edna, Stafford; [m.] Jacky; [ch.] 1 boy and 1 girl; [ed.] Secondary Modern College Education, Motor Vehicle Studies; [occ.] Motor Vehicle Lecturer College of F.E.; [memb.] I. Eng. (Industrial Eng), M.I.M.I. Member Motor Industry, AMIRTE Institute of Road Transport Engineer, LAE Licenciate Automotive Eng.; [hon.] Cert Ed. Certificate of Education; [oth. writ.] Poems used for friends, workplace. Local newspaper etc.

BAKER, WARREN
[b.] July 2, 1948, Ohio, USA; [p.] Owen and Dorothy Baker; [m.] Sandra Middleburgh; [ch.] Michelle; [ed.] West Holmes High School; [occ.] Security Officer; [a.] Stevenage, Herts, SG2 9PJ

BALDWIN, CLIVE A.
[b.] June, 29, 1958, East Bourne; [occ.] (Hospital) Operating Department Assistant (Senior); [memb.] St. John Ambulance - County of Sussex; [oth. writ.] The 1996 British Poetry Review; [pers.] I take my influence from a local poet, aged 96, I too would like to publish my own works, under one cover, but complemented with my own photographs!; [a.] Polegate, East Sussex, BN26 6JH

BALL, BARBARA ANNE
[pen.] Leonora Bell; [b.] August 5, 1939, West Bromwich; [p.] Joseph Caswell and Doris Maude Caswell; [m.] Michael Ball, October 1, 1960; [ch.] Inga Louise; [ed.] West Brom. Sec. Tech. School; [occ.] Sec./P.A. to Chartered Surveyor; [memb.] Cats Protection League; [hon.] Prize for Scripture 1952, highest grade GCE 'O' level, English Language 1955 Commendation; [oth. writ.] Poetry for school magazine also short stories for same 1950's. First poem published in 1994.; [pers.] My poetry helps me to express a completely different side of my personality. I am very inspired by nature. I strive to make my poetry personal to me, or to the person I compose for.; [a.] Dudley, W. Mids, DY1 2SY

BAMFORD, PAUL
[pen.] Paul Scott; [b.] February 15, 1973, Chesterfield; [p.] Arthur Bamford, Nora Bamford; [ed.] Netherthorpe School Staveley, Chesterfield College of Technology and Arts, Sheffield Hallam University (School of Cultural Studies); [occ.] Student on 3rd years of a degree course; [memb.] Several film and media societies. Laserdisc Clubs Film and TV Modellers Club for Advanced Modelling and Sculpting; [hon.] 8 GCSE's C and above 3 A Levs D and above, Hnd Art and Design (specialized in photography), BA Hons History of Art Design and Film.; [oth. writ.] Several articles for drone magazine, screenplays and short stories (unpublished) - illustrations for various small press publications.; [pers.] My experience of the world fuels my work - I just write what I feel when I look around me.; [a.] Chesterfield, Derbyshire, S43 3BA

BANDY, KEITH
[b.] May 10, 1980, Northampton; [p.] Avril Bandy, Robert Bandy; [ed.] Duston Upper School GCSE 1996; [oth. writ.] Currently writing a "Star Trek" story; [pers.] I was inspired to write this poem when my sister bought her own house.; [a.] Northampton, Northants, NN5 6UZ

BANKS, JEAN
[pen.] Jean Kidd Banks; [b.] February 14, 1925, Stone; [p.] James Kidd, Alice Jane Whittingham; [m.] (Late) Reginald Loynton Banks, July 19, 1947; [ch.] Gary Loynton Banks; [ed.] Granville Secondary School and other varied primary and Junior Schools. 3 days lectures (Weg Wood College) night school courses.; [occ.] Retired - Keen Gardener Artist - Verse Recitals - Writing; [memb.] Townswomen's Guild, T.G. Choir, St. John's United Reform Church.; [hon.] Vocal voice training studying with the late (Hylda Roberts) piano tuition for five years. Stage performances many and varied both musical and dramatic; [oth. writ.] Many poems unpublished - one poem published local paper. 2 in local poetry magazine.; [pers.] I greatly admire the lyrical poets. Wordsworth etc., also modern poets: - John Betjeman, especially "Christmas" I seek to explain my innermost thoughts and memories.; [a.] Stone, Staffs, ST15 8HU

BARCLAY, MARGARET
[b.] November 8, 1958, Lancaster; [p.] Fallen Gilfillan and Ann Gilfillan; [ch.] David, Alec, Kate, Heather, Thomas, Robert, Rachel; [ed.] Queen Elizabeth Grammar, Kirkby Lonsdale Lancaster, Morecambe Cof F.E.; [occ.] Housewife, Mother, Carer for Disabled Parents; [oth. writ.] Poetry written from childhood first publication in school magazine 1972.; [pers.] My mother, the subject of this poem, tells me she feels that all attributed to her should also apply to myself since taking on the care of her with terminal cancer and my father after his stroke.; [a.] Morecambe, Lancs, LA3 1BL

BARLEY, MARGE
[b.] August 28, 1929, Canada; [p.] Kath and Sydney Thorpe; [m.] June 1951; [ch.] Ellis Mary - John Fredrick; [ed.] In New Zealand confused; [occ.] Painting Tutor; [memb.] The Local Library that's the best I can do; [hon.] I wish; [oth. writ.] Autobiography poems - short stories written after a badly broken arm limited my freedom of movement for painting.; [pers.] I trust my inner voice.; [a.] Auckland, New Zealand

BARLOW, THELMA
[pen.] Thelma Barlow; [b.] July 31, 1934, Abbasia, Egypt; [p.] Leonard Fountain, Eva Fountain; [m.] Christopher Barlow, September 2, 1967; [ed.] St. Joseph's Convent Stafford, NE Essex Technical College, Colchester; [occ.] Retired; [memb.] Friends of the Minories, Colchester; [oth. writ.] Two small books of poetry "Doubts" and "Times" published by me. "No Going Back" published in The Cream of Eastern England published by Anchor Books.; [pers.] I write mainly from personal experience. My favourite poet is Thomas Hardy.; [a.] Colchester, Essex, CO1 1UN

BARNETT, GORDON
[b.] October 13, 1932, Hull; [ed.] Naval Training School; [occ.] Retired; [oth. writ.] Poems printed in: Obs seen on T.V. Barrel Of Laughs and in Gentlemen Of Television.; [pers.] I was raised in Dr. Bamados Homes, and life has been quite a struggle. I currently gain great pleasure and inspiration from helping the elderly folk in the community where I live. I've had several poems published in my church magazine. My motto 'Never Say Die'.; [a.] Sheffield, S. Yorks, S2 3GZ

BARROW, GILLIAN
[pen.] Sophie Barrow; [b.] May 22, 1976, Cheshire; [m.] George Barrow, September 11, 1995; [occ.] Advertising PA., Charterhouse Advertising.; [memb.] Institute of Legal Executives, Chartered Institute of Marketing.; [oth. writ.] Portfolio consists mainly of copy writing. Also factual debates, poetry, short stories (and long stories!).; [pers.] Writing should enrich the reader - not pamper the authors ego.; [a.] Sale, Cheshire, M33 4UG

BARSON, DANNY
[b.] July 15, 1966, Mansfield; [p.] Howard and Jacqueline; [ed.] Garibaldi Comprehensive; [occ.] Carpet Sales Adviser; [oth. writ.] Poetry now book of gay verse (1995 anthology) love is (1995 poetry now). Anthology.; [pers.] Many people are able to write poetry but seldom do, which is a shame. We all need to communicate and with me, poetry is an easy vehicle to climb.; [a.] Nottingham, NG1 3PW

BASSETT, PAMELA
[b.] May 19, 1937, Hastings, Sussex; [p.] Ronald Procter, Nora Procter; [m.] Roy Noel Bassett, December 14, 1963; [ch.] John Bassett; [ed.] Sacred Heart College, Hastings, Maria Assumpta Teacher Training College, Kensington, London; [occ.] Teacher (Primary) and Artist Yardley Primary Chingford; [memb.] Paws Club (Wildlife, Conservation and Art) Cats Protection League, Asthma Society; [oth. writ.] Poems and Articles in Local and National Magazines, poem in Anthology (on being over 50)!; [pers.] My writings are usually mainly influenced by my love and care for animals and world conservation. I work for charities that protect wild animals and pets, and am particularly interested in the care of big cats. I also love writing humorous poetry for fun.; [a.] Chingford, L.B. Waltham Forest, 7PF

BATES, ERNEST DENNIS
[b.] March 1, 1919, London; [p.] Will and Rosina Bates; [m.] Joyce Bates (Nee King), July 16, 1949; [ch.] Graham and Gordon; [occ.] Retired; [hon.] 1939-'45 Star, Burma Star, Defence medal, war medal 1939-'45; [oth. writ.] For Britannia and Castle Newsletter, Suffolk Regt. O.C.A.; [pers.] Known Warriors Unknown Graves is a memorial to my army friend George Blake 5827015 The Suffolk Regt. killed on Patrol at Imphal 12 April 1944 and sadly has no known grave, is commemorated by name on Rangoon Memorial Burma.; [a.] Harrow, Middlesex, HA3 5JY

BATHGATE, TRACY S.
[b.] March 10, 1983, Maidstone; [p.] Janet William; [ed.] Buckhaven High School; [occ.] Student; [a.] Kennoway, Fife, KY8 5LJ

BATSON, JENNIFER
[b.] August 16, 1944, Leicester; [m.] Eric Batson, October 20, 1962; [ch.] Christopher Dean; [occ.] Renovating, extending and furnishing our 300 yrs. old cottage; [oth. writ.] Presently writing a book, giving a humorous, sometimes sad, slant on my own everyday experiences.; [pers.] I have been writing for only 18 months. This is my first poem entered for a competition and accepted for publication I hope this will inspire others to take up the challenge.; [a.] Leicester, Leicestershire, LE2 2FL

BAWDEN, MATTHEW
[pen.] Matthew Banden; [b.] September 1, 1970, Bristol; [p.] Lesley Wilkinson and Jon Bawden; [m.] Louise Reilly; [ed.] Armthorpe Comprehensive South Yorks; [occ.] Electrician; [oth. writ.] Personal collection of my own ramblings.; [pers.] Keep on shining, this "ain't" no dress rehearsal. I am honored to be influenced by the lyrics of Pink Floyd.; [a.] Onchan, Isle of Man, IM3 4HS

BEDI, AGNES THERESA
[b.] January 26, 1939, Scotland; [pen.] Trish; [p.] Deceased; [m.] Deceased, September 23, 1961; [ch.] 2 daughters, 1 son; [ed.] Government schooling; [occ.] Housewife; [oth. writ.] Occasional song writing wrote one novel but did not send off for publication as it was personal.; [pers.] I am rather a quiet person I like reading, doing crosswords, watching soaps, but devout most of my time and energy to my children since the loss of my beloved husband.; [a.] Wolverhampton, West Mids, WV1 2AW

BELGIN, OLIVIA NOREEN MARGAR
[b.] October 3, 1931, Killanne, Co. Wexford, Eire; [p.] Frederick and Florence Crabb; [m.] Alan Belgin, June 8, 1963; [ch.] 1 Son (Kevin); [ed.] St. Annes School, Leaving Certificate; [occ.] Machine Operative, (childrens nanny before I married); [pers.] Inspired by the love of nature and all things beautiful, this poem was written on the spur of the moment after spending all day working in our garden.; [a.] Forest Hill, London, SE23 1RH

BELL, ALAN
[b.] June 20, 1960, Galashiels; [p.] Stewart Bell and Kathleen Bell; [m.] Hazel, June 17, 1983; [ch.] Nicola Jane and Amanda Louise; [pers.] Dedicated in memory of David Thomas Bell.; [a.] Galashiels, Scottish Borders, TD1 2HZ

BELL, CLIVE AYTON
[b.] February 20, 1971, St. Helier Hos., Carshalton, Surrey; [p.] Stuart and Jennifer Bell; [ed.] Art and Crafts, English Language, English Literature, History, Integrated Science, Technical Graphics, Mathematics - All CSE's; [occ.] Warehouse/Assembler; [memb.] Runrig Fan Club, Scotland Enigmas - The Journal of Strange Phenomena Investigations, Scotland; [oth. writ.] I've had several poems published on a religious and other themes i.e. crime and romance.; [pers.] To my ancestors who fought in the battles for independence, like many others, fighting for honour with Wallace and Bruce, fighting for Scotland's right for freedom and peace.; [a.] Sutton, Surrey, SM1 4HT

BELL, ROSEMARY
[pen.] Bello La Figlia; [b.] August 25, 1946; [p.] Mr. and Mrs. T. Galer; [m.] John Patrick, June 21, 1969; [ch.] Colin Stephen, Ian Charles; [ed.] Housewife/mother; [pers.] I picked you a rose from our garden today. I would love to pick you one every day. There aren't enough roses I want to give you the best and most precious are only a few. I counted each petal on that rose for you. It had twenty three petals with a lovely perfume. It was the most precious bloom I had picked for you.; [a.] Newtownards, Down. BT22 1AU

BELL, SARAH JANE
[b.] November 18, 1976. Enfield; [p.] Colin George and Valerie Ann Bell; [m.] Simon Peter Holme, July 27, 1996; [ed.] Comberton Village College, Bassing Bourn Village College, The Kings School (sixth form), Anglia Polytechnic University; [occ.] Typesetter for Harlequin Music going to A.P.U. in Sept. 96; [oth. writ.] One poem published whilst at school. Articles for school magazines. Several short stories although none have been published as yet. And numerous unpublished poems.; [pers.] I believe that life is a series of swings and round about what goes around comes around. Therefore it is important that we treat others as we would expect them to treat us for, what we give out now will, eventually return to us.; [a.] Cambridge, Cambridgeshire, CB3 7ET

BENNETT, REBECCA
[pen.] Becky Bennett; [b.] December 3, 1981, Truro; [p.] Mr. and Mrs. Statham; [ed.] Coquet High School, Comprehensive Amble, Morpeth Northumerland; [occ.] Student; [hon.] Swimming and Ballet; [oth. writ.] Currently short stories, unpublished.; [pers.] I live with my Mum and Stepdad I'm the youngest of 5 children, I have 2 brother and 2 step-sisters. I love my pets, reading, writing, family and friends. I'm just a normal teenager.; [a.] Warkworth, Morpeth, Northumberland, NE65 0UL

BEST, JAMES HENRY
[pen.] Jim; [b.] March 23, 1950, Reading, Berkshire; [p.] Pheobe and Jim Best; [m.] Margaret Best, July 27, 1968; [ch.] Four Sons; [ed.] Very little; [occ.] Landscape gardener; [pers.] In life I live for the moment and in this moment I live to love my nature, the God with in me. If by my poem I can touch the minds of others, not to inflict pain and kill. All of us want to live, peace; [a.] Haslemere, Surrey, GU27 1NA

BETTY, HOVER
[b.] November 30, 1928, Dartford; [p.] Herbert Fidge, Winifred Fidge; [m.] Divorced; [ch.] Anne, Shirley, Keith, Alan; [ed.] South Central Secondary School, Ashford (Wartime, Inc. Evacuation) Age 53 Gained Grade "A". O'Level Ashford Tech. (English Lang); [occ.] Retirement, Active (Time for playing scrabble)/Embroidery; [memb.] Local over 60's, Club, Ashford Dog Training Club, Trophy Steward and Helper, Member of R.A.F.A., Member of Small Entertainment Group, Mother and Toddler Group Voluntary Helper, P/T Choir Member at Local Church; [hon.] Lifetime Awards: 4 Children and 6 Grandchildren!; [oth. writ.] Several poems published in local parish magazine; [pers.] Tend to take the philosophical view in most things. Biographical books interest me the most. Interesting to note how others cope with difficulties in life.; [a.] Ashford, Kent, TN23, 5UU

BIGGS, DAVID
[b.] May 7, 1936, Shropshire; [occ.] Design Modeller; [oth. writ.] Poems; [pers.] I am influenced by John Keats.; [a.] Stoke-on-Trent, Staffs, ST6 5SS

BINGLE, DOROTHY CLAIRE
[pen.] Claire Bingle; [b.] February 13, 1938, Cardiff; [p.] Susie Parker; [m.] Divorced, December 20, 1958; [ch.] 4-1 daughter, 3 sons, 3 grandchildren; [ed.] Blogg's College Cardiff; [occ.] Bridal Buyer; [oth. writ.] Love Alone Survives and Endures entered in this comp.; [pers.] First attempt always wanted to write. Always desire to succeed. Hope it comes true. Would like to write a novel.

BIRCH, HAZEL MARION
[b.] April 20, 1925, Coventry; [p.] Hamilton and Dorothea Lindsay; [m.] Leonard Walter Birch, August 21, 1946; [ch.] Leigh, Denise and Lynn; [ed.] Stoke Park Sec. School Coventry (and due to Evacuation in 1939) Leamington High School for Girls; [occ.] Retired and widowed (1994) (I'm also an artist

- have painted numerous oil paintings); [oth. writ.] 9 poems published in various anthologies by Arrival Press, Peterborough, since 1993.; [pers.] From my school days, I've always enjoyed teaching poems, and find my deepest thoughts are better expressed in poetry rather than prose.; [a.] Bingham, Notts, NG13 8SY

BIRCH, SHEILA
[pen.] Sheila Margaret; [b.] January 19, 1936, Birmingham; [p.] Charles Veasey, Violet Veasey; [m.] Divorced; [ch.] Tracey Jane, Brian Bernard; [ed.] COE Schools in Kidderminster and Stourbridge Worcs; [occ.] Retired; [oth. writ.] Have written other poems nothing published yet.; [pers.] After working for so long doing shifts in a carpet factory, found after retiring couldn't sleep so, I lay awake for hours, this started me writing poetry to help me relax. I have never done anything like it before; [a.] Kidderminster, Worcs, DY10 2YG

BIRD, MISS WENDY ROBINA
[b.] November 9, 1943, Wisbech; [p.] Harold William Bird Father (Deceased August 7, 1982) and mother-Joan Evelyn Bird - age 77 yrs. (b. May 24, 1918); [ed.] Wisbech High School and Isle of Ely College of further education; [occ.] Own business part-time secretarial service. Also full time secretary credit controller to branch of builders merchants; [memb.] R.S.P.B., St. John Ambulance; [hon.] Qualified Industrial First Aider; [oth. writ.] Poem and short story; [pers.] I enjoy creative work and have displayed my work at craft fairs. I consider poetry an extension of my creative work as it can reflect all moods.; [a.] Wisbech, Cambs, PE13 2RY

BISS, MISS KATIE SARAH
[b.] July 5 1984, Hounslow; [p.] Paul Biss, Gaynor Biss; [ed.] Longford Community School, Bedfont Middx; [occ.] Pupil; [memb.] Bedfont United Football Club for Girls; [oth. writ.] School Magazines, Local Paper; [pers.] I love to write about cats, after losing my beloved cat, Fred, my poems are based on personal observations.; [a.] Feltham, Middx, TW14 0DB

BISS, MR. E. L.
[pen.] Edward Biss; [b.] 1912, East Stour, Gillingham Dorset

BIZLEY, ROY
[b.] June 22, 1930, Swindon; [p.] Mr. and Mrs. A. H. Bizley; [m.] Patricia Mary Bizley, February 1957; [ch.] Stephen John Bizley; [ed.] Elementary and Secondary, Schools, Swindon, Swindon School of Art, Slade School of Fine Art, University College, London; [occ.] Painter, Printmaker, Maker of Artists Books; [memb.] Printmakers Council; [hon.] 1958 Shared 1st prize for Painting, Perth Open Art Competition, Western Australia, 1959 Awarded Painting Prize by Victorian Artists Society, Melbourne, Australia; [oth. writ.] Poetry, Artists Books; [pers.] Although Painting, Printmaking, and Artists Books are my main concern. I have been writing poetry since I was in my teens.; [a.] Leicester, Leicestershire, LE2 2BL

BLACK, JONATHAN
[b.] October 1952, Portlaoise; [m.] Elizabeth, August 1977; [ch.] Ruth, Emmet, Lizzie, Karina; [occ.] Factory Electrician; [hon.] B.S.A. Writers, C. Day-Lewis; [oth. writ.] Poems published B.S.A. Awards, Family Blessing, Read National T.V.; [pers.] With a preference for rhyme, I explore personal relationship, especially our relationship with nature, emphasizing our place in history and our perceptions of life, death and the passage of time.; [a.] Atny, Kildare

BLAIKIE, NANCY CRAIG
[b.] April 30, 1933, Falkirk; [p.] Mathew and Mary Craig; [m.] Stuart Blaikie, September 21, 1956; [ed.] Comprehensive; [occ.] Just retired, Sold Cycles; [oth. writ.] Been writing poetry and childrens stories for forty years never tried to have them published.; [pers.] Live and let live.; [a.] Bo'ness, West Lothian, EH51 9JB

BLAKEMORE, ARTHUR THOMAS
[pen.] Arthur Thomas Blakemore; [b.] February 17, 1939, London; [p.] Mother, Father (Deceased); [m.] Lyn Blakemore, August 22, 1984; [ch.] Four; [ed.] Secondary Modern School New Cross, London; [occ.] Electrical Surveyor, Inspector; [oth. writ.] Several poems, not put forward for publication until now.; [pers.] Having spent a great number of years of my life either working as an engineer or my earlier days in the merchant service, much of my writing is in many ways connected with the places I have visited and the people both rich and poor I have lived with.; [a.] Leeds, W. Yorks, LS26 0BU

BLAKER, ABIGAIL E.
[b.] December 14, 1976, Sheffield; [p.] Stephen and Joy Blaker; [ed.] Thomas Rotherham College of Further Education; [oth. writ.] One poem published in "Carousel", a "Poetry Now" Edition; [pers.] "To look at life and not passed it is short sighted".; [a.] Rotherham, S. Yorkshire, S65 4BE

BLEWER, MISS SIMONE
[b.] September 5, 1968, Birmingham; [p.] Ray Blewer and Teresa Blewer; [m.] Ed (Divorced), July 27, 1990; [ch.] Ashley James (5), Adele Kerry (3); [ed.] Archbishop Mastersons R. C. School; [occ.] Mother; [oth. writ.] I have quite a few unpublished poems, I also enjoy writing short stories as a pass time.; [pers.] In my writing I aim to show the good and bad in people. I also have in my poems. The purpose of love, and loving and to realize the love you have is special, but we don't know that until we lose it.; [a.] Aberystwyth, Dyfed, SY24 5BQ

BLIGHT, MARGARET ROSE
[pen.] Rose Tremarden; [b.] July 27, 1936, St. Austell; [p.] Reg and Hilda Walkey; [m.] Dennis Blight, February 5, 1953; [ch.] Evelynn and Gillian (both M); [ed.] West Hill, secondary school, St. Austell Cornwall; [occ.] At home looking after my very ill husband.; [memb.] W.I. Carclage, Con. Club, Writers Circle, Sequence Dance Clubs (3) Speaker for W.I. and other groups on 5 subjects. I had my own Radio Cornwall series on 'Herbs' and also Poetry and S. Stevies Libraries.; [hon.] W.I. Cert. in Embroidery, Quilting, and Judges (Crafts) Awards: Flower Arranging, Crafts Gen. Painting. Cooking Wine, but never writing?; [oth. writ.] 1981 'Poems of Cornwall' under pen name sold as presents all over Gt. Britain and Worldwide. My poetry pub. in local mag. and 'E.C.C. Press' for whom I wrote a series of regular articles poems. 400 unpublished.; [pers.] I hope my poems reflect the beautiful county that I live in, some are humorous, a lot about my fathers life (now 92) and local events, in fact something for everyone. Life is a paper to be read.; [a.] St. Austell, Cornwall, PL25 4LL

BLOXHAM, MRS. LUCY-MAY
[pen.] Lucy-May Bloxham; [b.] October 12, 1938, Midlands; [p.] Lucy and James Stokes; [m.] Richard, March 23, 1969; [ch.] One grown-up son; [ed.] Midlands Grammar School. Later Secretarial College. Also education in Dentistry.; [occ.] Retired Legal Secretary and Estate Agency Business; [oth. writ.] Various clubs and magazines have published my poems, also newspapers; [pers.] Enjoy working with poetry my poems likened to William blake, which gave me much encouragement. Always work and 'hope' is a good motto!; [a.] St. Austell, Cornwall

BLYTH, BARBARA J.
[b.] May 1, 1947, Hastings; [p.] Peter R. J. Josephine Smith; [m.] Andy Blyth, October 11, 1985; [ch.] Tom, Robert, Lisa; [ed.] Convent School Bedford, St Andrews School Bedford, Bonbeach High School, Carrum, Victoria Australia; [occ.] House Wife; [memb.] Multiple Sclerosis Society; [oth. writ.] Poems and childrens stories in rhyme, a diary about the day to day life of a multiple sclerosis sufferer. At this moment in time ll writings have been for my own pleasure.; [pers.] I while away many a happy hour expanding my collection of writings. I greatly admire the late composer schubert and how he was able to put many poems to beautiful music.; [a.] Penzance, Cornwall, TR19 6DW

BOLTON, JOHN M. L.
[pen.] Georgiana Aurora-Barrington; [b.] August 25, 1978, Worcester; [p.] David Bolton, Jacky Bolton; [ed.] Stourport-on-Severn High School, Birmingham University; [occ.] A level student; [pers.] All of my writing tends to have a moral, at times quasi-religious under-tone, most often about people all either deserving or getting a second chance, but rarely the two together.; [a.] Stourport-on-Severn, Worcestershire, DY13 0NP

BOND, DORIS R.
[b.] January 21, 1935, Godalming, Surrey; [p.] Both Deceased; [m.] Husband Keith, July 1956; [ch.] 1 son and 2 daughters; [ed.] Sec. Modern at Old Woking Surrey; [occ.] Retired; [oth. writ.] Some poems published in Firm's Monthly Mag. (J. Player and Son) before retirement as cashier for 20 yrs; [a.] Nottingham, Nott'shire, U, NG8 5PQ

BONEL, PAUL
[pen.] Danny Zorn; [b.] January 6, 1947, London; [p.] Rene and Marion Bonel; [m.] Felicity Bonel, August 6, 1977; [ch.] Rachel and Finn; [ed.] Archbishop Temple, Rose Bruford College of Speech and Drama, University of East London; [occ.] Training Development Officer; [memb.] The Poetry Society; [oth. writ.] "Burglars" BBC schools radio drama. "Playing For Real," "Good Practice In Playwork" non fiction books. Occasional poems and articles in magazines.; [pers.] The children of today are the citizens of tomorrow - if we care for them, they will care for others.; [a.] London, SE9 4SN

BOOCOCK, NICK
[pen.] Nick Boocock; [b.] March 1, 1976, Dewsbury; [p.] David Boocock, Sandra Boocock; [ed.] Rodney School, High Pavement 6th form College University of Sheffield; [occ.] Social Science undergraduate, University of Sheffield; [oth. writ.] Editorship of College magazine. I have written many poems since early 1995 - they're just waiting to be discovered, that's all!; [pers.] Favorite poets include romantics (particularly coleridge), donne and the alternating sensuality and brutality of D. H. Lawrence. I try to illustrate the struggle between material and self-decadence in my generation through my poetry.; [a.] Whatton, Nottinghamshire, NG13 9EL

BORWICK, GEORGE EDWARD
[b.] December 7, 1941, Kirkwall, Orkney; [p.] George and Betsy Borwick; [m.] Jamesina Louis Borwick, March 20, 1964; [ch.] James, William, Susan, Edward; [ed.] Educated at the Kirkwall Grammar School, Kirkwall, Orkney; [occ.] Police Constable, A.E.A.C.; [memb.] Amateur Artist Association, Volunteer Collector for the Blind School, Edinburgh, Volunteer Collector for the Romanian Children; [a.] Thurso, Caithness, KW14 8NN

BOWN, JUNE E.
[b.] August 24, 1937, Nottingham; [p.] Henry Hayes, Catherine Hayes; [m.] John Bown (Deceased 1980), December 15, 1956; [ch.] John, Beverly, Valerie, Sonya and Matthew; [ed.] Sycamore Sec. School for Girls Nottingham; [occ.] Work for Agricultural Firm; [memb.] Cub Scout Leader 10 years, School Swimming Instructor for primary children for 22 years; [hon.] Won Scholarship to Nottingham Art College; [oth. writ.] 2 poems published in local newspapers, write poems for family and friends for birthdays etc.; [pers.] Usually write poems purely for my own pleasure. To see one come together gives me a big 'buzz'; [a.] Dunham on Trent, Notts, NG22 0UB

BRACEY, DENISE
[b.] October 14, 1954, Lowestoft; [p] Margaret and Colin Maxwell; [m.] Divorced; [ch.] Richard, Jon and Kathryn; [ed.] Kirkley High School Lowestoft, Suffolk; [occ.] Agency Nurse; [oth. writ.] Several poems not published or offered for publishing yet this is my first attempt to have anything published; [pers.] I feel that with all the ups and downs of my life, I have endeavored to become a better person and like what and who I am.; [a.] Tilney, St. Lawrence, Norfolk, PE34 4QQ

BRADLEY, MRS. PATRICIA MARGAR
[pen.] Margaret Bradley; [b.] December 15, 1935, Devizes; [p.] Charles and Edith Hampton; [m.] Henry, March 16, 1957; [ch.] One daughter - Lynn; [ed.] Grammar School - Devizes; [occ.] Retired; [memb.] Poetry now, Arrival Press, Parish of St. James; [hon.] In piano, ballet, English language; [oth. writ.] In editions of poetry now also a personal diary of verse covering events from 1963 when my daughter was born, for my own enjoyment; [pers.] My poetry is the search for perfection - never attained - forever a challenge.; [a.] Devizes, Wiltshire, SN10 5AZ

BRADY, ART
[pen.] William Quill; [b.] December 9, 1959, Middlesbrough; [p.] Frank Brady, Norma Brady; [m.] Susan Brady, June 2, 1980; [ch.] Charlene, Ryan; [ed.] Fleetham Jnr, Stainsby Secondary; [occ.] Poet - song writer event organizer for the poets gallery; [memb.] Erimus Quoit and Rifle Club; [oth. writ.] Poems published in local and Scottish press also local poetry magazine also awaiting publication of two books 1996, titles The Good Seeds Guide, Songs and Prayers For Religious Affairs.; [pers.] I feel it is important that children should be encouraged to read and write poetry, a lot more, how can the children of today encourage the children of tomorrow if they are not.; [a.] Middlesbrough, Cleveland, TS1 4RF

BRADY, PAUL
[b.] August 7, 1955, Derby; [p.] Vincent Brady, Marie Brady; [ch.] Toni Louise, Hayon, Mark Anthony; [ed.] Sturgess Comprehensive; [occ.] Full time Dad single parent; [pers.] Take life as it comes; [a.] Derby, Desbyshire, DE22 3WD

BRAIN, ANGIE
[b.] May 6, 1961, Oldham; [p.] Ronald James Brain, Valerie Brain; [ed.] Grange Comprehensive, Oldham Art School, Rochdale College of Art; [occ.] Graphic Artist, West Pennine Health Promotion Unit; [memb.] Former Vice Chair Person of The Union of the Friends of Kranj; [hon.] NWRAC, 1985 British Council, Bursary to Edvard Kardelja University, Ljubljana; [oth. writ.] Other poems published: 'Paintbox' poetry now Northwest 1994, 'Homesick' winning through 1995; [pers.] I hope my poems raise a question, a glass, an eyebrow or a smile. Poetry is to be shared and I'm grateful to Angie and Zana, the friends who taught me to share.; [a.] Oldham, Lancashire, OL9 6LP

BRAIN, WARREN
[pen.] Woz; [b.] May 11, 1973, Sheffield; [p.] Linda and Reg; [ed.] Comprehensive School; [occ.] In prison; [memb.] BAWLA; [oth. writ.] 'Dad' Getting by Old Stone Face (Armley); [a.] Rotherham, S. Yorks, S66 0LT

BRATTAN, HILARY
[b.] February 26, 1938, Kingston-upon-Hull; [p.] George and Jessica Souter; [m.] George Brattan, July 15, 1961; [ch.] Michael - John - Jill and Stephen; [ed.] St Mary's School Wilton St - Hull; [occ.] 22 years at Bird's Eye - Walls - Factory - Hull; [oth. writ.] 10 poems in local paper 4 in works magazine 6 published in books in the past five years; [pers.] Have been writing poems since the age of nine on any subject - Usually write a poem within half an hour. I have a nine year old granddaughter getting her poems into print. My sister Joan Thompson is alike to me and getting a poem published in this book.; [Tn.] Kingston-upon-Hull; [a.] Yorkshire, HU9 4DX

BREDEE, PAT
[b.] October 23, 1935, East Ham; [p.] Doris, George Lewis; [m.] Harry Bredee, March 26, 1960; [ch.] Twin sons 2 girls; [ed.] Secondary Modern Vicarage Lane E6; [occ.] Housewife; [oth. writ.] Will be writing others. Suffer with chronic psoriasis. In hospital quite often. Also colonic cancer 5 years ago.; [pers.] I was so pleased I read I had been chosen for semi finalist award I will purchase book near future; [a.] London, North Woolwich, E16 2NL

BRIND, AMANDA
[pen.] Chris Knight; [b.] March 31, 1976, Rush Green; [p.] Graham Hall/Margaret Hall; [m.] Kevin Brind, October 14, 1995; [ed.] Bromfords Secondary Sch., Southend Enterprise Business College; [occ.] Group Administration Controller; [memb.] English Heritage; [hon.] Business Studies Diploma; [oth. writ.] Poetry now anthology 1994, poetry now anthology 1996; [pers.] Poetry - to express ones view without inhibition, prejudice, morality...or sometimes even sanity.; [a.] Wickford, Essex, SS11 8QE

BROAD, ERIC
[b.] September 19, 1920, Ilford; [p.] William Broad, Frances Broad; [m.] June Broad, August 4, 1951; [ch.] Margaret, John; [ed.] Coopers Company's School, Peterborough College; [occ.] Retired; [memb.] W.E.A. (Eastern Region) Braintree Recorded Music Association; [oth. writ.] Memoirs, short stories, verses, letters to the press.; [pers.] Most of my written works are echoes of the past and reflections on our yester years.; [a.] Witham, Essex, CM8 3RP

BROOKS, DEREK FREDERICK
[b.] June 16, 1934, Nottingham; [p.] Frederick J. Brooks and Anne Alice Eite; [m.] Sylvia Eleanor Nee Morley, August 6, 1970; [ch.] Martin Frederick and Colin Anthony; [ed.] Claremont Sec. Mod., Notthingham College of Education; [occ.] Retired Teacher - Religious Studies; [memb.] Berean Forwarding Movement Open Bible Trust, Local Bowls Club; [hon.] B. Ed. (Hons.); [oth. writ.] Parish magazine articles and poetry.; [pers.] Practising Christian, I try to reflect the concert and love a God for mankind through the hard Jesus Christ in my reflections.; [a.] Nottingham, Notts, NG3 6DA

BROOKS, SYLVIA
[b.] April 3, 1940, London; [p.] Deceased; [m.] Raymond Brooks, March 11, 1961; [ch.] Three sons and four grandchildren; [ed.] Grammer School R/C; [occ.] Housewife; [oth. writ.] So other poems written one read on Radio 2.; [pers.] I am a emotional woman a writing poetry is very fulfilling; [a.] London, Snaresbooke, E18 2VA

BROWN, CHRISTOPHER EVAN
[b.] October 8, 1977, Canberra, Australia; [p.] Pamela Brown, Desmond Brown; [ed.] The Greenhill School Tenby; [memb.] Rock Band, Jazz Band, School, Regional and Area Orchestras; [pers.] My poem in this book is dedicated to a friend Julia who died of cancer. Like most of my poetry, it tries to find acceptable answers to the unexplained parts of life. My thoughts on paper, positive or bleak, help me to more fully understand the world and I am very pleased if anybody else finds anything lasting or helpful in my poetry.; [a.] Tenby, Pembrokeshire, SA70 8JH

BROWN, DENIS W.
[b.] June 29, 1929, Plymouth, Devon; [p.] William and Doris Brown; [m.] Lilian M. Brown, August 9, 1957; [ch.] Martyn D. Brown; [ed.] Plymouth Art Collect; [occ.] Retired Company Director; [memb.] The Society of Amateur Artists; [oth. writ.] Limited number of poems published; [pers.] Interested in the relationship between painting and poetry in abstract mood reflections.; [a.] Richmond, North Yorks, DL10 4BP

BROWN, IAIN ROBERT
[pen.] I R Brown (Impressionist); [b.] October 30, 1975, Paisley, Scotland; [p.] Margaret and Thomas Brown; [ed.] Girvan Primary, Girvan Academy, Ayr College; [occ.] Studying a degree in Computer Science; [hon.] Interior Design Diploma Mensa Certificate of Merit Award for Technical Subjects (Girvan Academy); [oth. writ.] Several poems, one play and two novels. Also two short stories. All at present unpublished, most in 2nd Draft Form.; [pers.] I try to reflect the feels and aspirations of mankind in my work. I try to create images that are a realistic fantasy, I do this in both my writing and painting.; [a.] Girvan, Ayrshire, KA26 9AT

BROWN, MRS. IRENE ISABELL
[b.] January 3, 1942, Ireland; [p.] Mary and William (Both Deceased); [m.] Kenneth, August 18, 1962; [ch.] Elaine Paul and Alan; [ed.] Technical College; [occ.] Care-Worker for the elderly; [pers.] This present poem was composed for my very dear Mother The "Exiled" one below for my dear Father. A poem printed in the book of — "New Poetry" 1981 called - "Exiled".; [a.] St. Neots, Cambs, PE19 1PW

BROWN, MIKE
[pen.] Lyric, Lust and Jade Draven; [b.] October 30, 1976, Wiltshire; [p.] Trevor and Mary Brown; [occ.] Landscape Gardener; [memb.] Count Dracula Fan Club, New York, Anne Rice - Vampire Lestat Fan Club, New Orleans; [oth. writ.] Immortal Beloved, Dawn Rise, also various songs, also a book entitled

Ravens Kiss; [pers.] Thank you Mandy live life to the full be yourself don't change, thanks to Anne Rice long live Lestat.; [a.] York, North Yorkshire, YO2 4PS

BROWN, NADINE
[pen.] Nadine Flowers; [b.] September 5, 1983, Pendelton; [p.] Pamela Brown, Neil Ashcroft; [ed.] St. Georges Primary School Atherton Deanery High School Wigan; [hon.] As my primary school I won many English awards, I won an award for best diary of events.; [oth. writ.] I have had articles published in Church magazines and local newspapers. Many reflecting issues of every day life. Also many children's stories.; [pers.] I have always loved writing poems and stories. My influences and inspirations come from my life, my Mum, Mrs. Jones and Mr. Twist, from St. Georges Primary School, Atherton, my head teachers has wrote and said many good things about my work including 'I have rarely seen such a talented young writer as Nadine.'; [a.] Pemberton, Wigan, Lancashire, WN5 9NE

BROWN, RALPH FREEMAN
[pen.] ARE, EFF, BEE; [b.] August 27, 1912, Welford, Northants; [p.] Joseph and Mary Brown; [m.] Muriel Vyvyan Brown (Deceased), September 20, 1939; [ch.] Gerald and Graham Brown; [ed.] Welford C and E School, Market Harborough Grammar School; [occ.] Retired Master Baker; [memb.] Council Member of the National Association of Master Bakers, until Retirement 1983; [hon.] Prize Winner in many Bakery Exhibitions; [oth. writ.] Only poetry.; [pers.] Vegetarian, Political Animal; [a.] Grantham, Lincs, NG32 2LE

BROWN, SHIRLEY
[b.] April 27, 1952, Belfast, Northern Ireland; [p.] Rachel and David Douglas; [m.] Divorced; [ch.] Micheal, Glyn, Kerry, Vicci, Billy; [ed.] Secondary Education - Part-time College for O-Level English; [occ.] Disabled House, Person Writer and Poet; [pers.] The wheelchair gives a different spectrum to life the disadvantages could make me cry until I remember the advantages. Forget about always having a seat to sit on but I can now flirt and get away with it. Laugh at others reactions while I study them. Life is too short to cry.; [a.] Hemel Hempstead, Herts, HP2 4PE

BROWN, VANESSA
[b.] March 26, 1972, Carshalton, Surrey; [p.] Paulette and Peter Brown; [m.] Michael Byrne; [ed.] Carshalton High for Girls; [occ.] Training to be Veterinary Nurse; [oth. writ.] A poem in another anthology in U.S.A. on the Threshold of a Dream; [pers.] My poetry reflects the victims in life.; [a.] Carshalton, Surrey, SM5 2RN

BROWNING, JANET
[b.] March 8, 1958, Battersea; [p.] Rosa Browning, Thomas Browning; [ch.] Zeb Robinson; [ed.] Breezehill Secondary Girls School, Wellingborough; [occ.] Cook; [pers.] I write from lives experiences of which I have had my share.; [a.] Wellingborough, Northants, NN8 2PB

BRUTHWELL, DOMINIC
[pen.] Dominic Bruthwell; [b.] December 12, 1967, Leighton Buzzard; [p.] Ron and Joy Bruthwell; [m.] Melanie Parr, Engaged in 1995; [ch.] (One son) Four months Kai Brutwell; [ed.] 10 level 5 CSE's Vandyke Upper School; [occ.] Studying to become Hypnotherapist; [oth. writ.] 'Mysterious Wings," published in "Central Words" anthology 1994. 'Mourning Mother' - published in "Central Words" 1996; [pers.] If we deny ourselves of natural suffering, always opting for pleasure and comfort, we deny ourselves of the victory of overcoming I wish my life to be a victory.; [a.] Leighton Buzzard, Beds, LU7 8PZ

BRYAN, CATHERINE
[b.] January 20, 1937, West Pelton, Co. Durham; [p.] George Bryan - Emma Scott Bryan; [ed.] West Pelton County Council School; [occ.] Retired Civil Servant; [pers.] To the memory of my dear grandparents, James and Ruth Jacques.; [a.] Swansea, West Glamorgan, SA6 7PP

BUCKLAND, E. R.
[b.] July 28, 1927, Newbury; [p.] R. W. and E. M. Buckland; [m.] Stella Buckland, April 16, 1949; [ch.] Michael, Alan, Mandy and Brett; [ed.] Secondary; [occ.] Retired, Hobby Pyrography; [pers.] I have not tried to have any of my poems published. This has come as a pleasant surprise. The bible has been a great influence for me.; [a.] Lambourn, Berkshire, RG17 8XZ

BUCKLAND-EVERS, G.
[b.] May 15, 1939, Gloucester; [p.] James, Edwards Harold B-E, Phyllis Steer; [m.] Dinah Eirys Buckland-Evers, July 7, 1970; [ch.] Ffion; [ed.] Birrenhead Institute 953-1958; [occ.] Retired; [memb.] R.S.P.B.; [hon.] Vice-Captain Old Instonians R.U.F.C. 1989/60 - Captain Oxton Tennis Club 2nd Team 1960; [oth. writ.] Other poems published by anchor press; [pers.] Also wrote — "Moments of Inspiration"; [a.] Ewloe, Deeside, Clwyd, CH5 3BJ

BUCKLEY, LOUISE
[b.] January 28, 1977, Chesterfield; [p.] Hazel Filsell and Ronald Buckley; [ed.] Highfields School, Chesterfield College; [occ.] Personal Assistant at Derbyshire Probation Service; [pers.] This poem is dedicated to my family for making my life what it is today, that you, I love you all. Richard Crowder my future husband, Vicky Buckley my sister, Hazel and John Filsell my mum and step dad, and my dad and nannan.; [a.] Matlock, Derbyshire, DE4 3TA

BUCKLEY, PETER MARTIN
[b.] July 28, 1985, Leicester; [p.] Mary and Hubert Buckley; [ed.] Peter attends Bishop Ellis R.C. Primary school in Leicester, he also has had treatment in Hungary at the Peto Institute also he attends B.I.R.D. in chester for brain injured and rehabilitation and development; [hon.] Certificates of achievements for his poetry work given to him by Bishop Ellis the school he attends.; [pers.] Peter Buckley age 10 Suffers from cerebral palsy. He attends Bishop Ellis School in Leicester. Peter has been many times over to the Peto Institute in Hungary. He has many certificates of achievements for his poetry; [a.] Leicester, LE4 9HP

BUCKNELL, BETTY H.
[b.] April 7, 1914, Newton Abbot; [p.] Joseph Coleman - Alice Coleman; [m.] Frank Bucknell L.R.I.B.A., July 16, 1938; [ch.] Wendy Julyan B. Th. Tim Bucknell, NCA; [ed.] Cumberland House Paignton Barnstaple Grammar; [memb.] Have exhibited paintings with the South West Art Society; [pers.] Memory of a very happy childhood and the love of flowers; [a.] Truro, Cornwall, TR2 4HZ

BUCKWELL, JANINE
[b.] July 29, 1975, Eastbourne; [p.] Christine Buckwell, Roy Buckwell; [ed.] Ratton Senior School, Eastbourne College of Arts and Technology, Brighton College of Arts and Technology; [occ.] Photographer for a band called Dreams Fear; [hon.] BTEC First Diploma in Design, BTEC National Diploma in Design (Photography).; [oth. writ.] Nothing published; [pers.] I try to reflect my inner thoughts, feelings and fantasies in my poetry. I am influenced and fascinated by a the "Poems and Ballads" of A.C. Swinburne and the music of Cradle of Filth.; [a.] Eastbourne, East Sussex, BN22 9PH

BURGESS, BARBARA ELIZABETH
[b.] November 19, 1946, Salford, Lancs; [p.] Albert McDiarmid, Megan McDiarmid; [m.] Harold Burgess, September 3, 1976; [ch.] Deborah, Lee, Faye, 2 step ch. Kevin, David; [ed.] Winton Secondary School for Girls; [occ.] Housewife; [oth. writ.] I have written other poems over a duration of years, which reflect my life's experiences. This is the first poem I have ever entered in competition; [pers.] Whenever anything in life touches my heart sometimes personal, or what maybe happening in the world, I write the words that flow in to my head.; [a.] Manchester, Lancs, M27 0HA

BURGESS, MICHAEL P.
[b.] March 30, 1968, Ramsey Tyrrells Cottage; [p.] Peter Burgess, Sheila M. Burgess; [occ.] Manager of Community Care Services; [oth. writ.] Poems include 1) Love 2) I'll Forgive 3) Lifes A Gift 4) How And Why; [a.] Ingatestone, Essex, CM4 9RZ

BURNETT, MISS FRANCES MARY
[b.] January 1, 1928, Plymouth, Devon; [p.] Frank and Beatrice Burnett; [ed.] Stoke Damerel High School for Girls, Plymouth Emergency High School, Plymouth Devon; [occ.] Retired State Registered Nurse; [memb.] Currently Deacon Victoria St Baptist Church Gosport, Hants; [hon.] London School Certificate, State Registration Nursing Certificate; [oth. writ.] Numerous poems for church magazine. Hymns used as solos in Church; [pers.] My life is guided by my Christian beliefs which I try to reflect in my poetry and hymns I like classical music and well written books; [a.] Gosport, Hants, PO12 4UD

BURNETT, VICTORIA
[b.] May 3, 1950, Nottingham; [m.] June 1, 1974; [ch.] Four; [ed.] Guild Hall School of Music and Drama; [occ.] Wife and full-time Mother; [memb.] Imperial Society of Teachers of Dancing Equity; [hon.] Dancing Teachers Certificate I.S.T.D. Guild Hall Performers Award; [oth. writ.] "Time"; [pers.] To strive to realize my full potential and to encourage my children to do the same.; [a.] Christchurch, Dorset, BH23 4DZ

BURNS, MRS. M.
[pen.] Mary; [b.] January 2, 1945, Scunthorpe, England; [p.] Mum (Mrs. E. H. Betts); [m.] Deceased October 95, February 29, 1964; [ch.] Ian 27, Kaye 31; [ed.] Secondary; [occ.] Machinist; [pers.] Written from the heart for my beloved husband, before his illness.; [a.] Scunthorpe, North Lincolnshire, DN17 1SE

BURRELL, MRS. ESTHER F.
[pen.] Esther F. Burrell; [b.] June 24, 1974, Kings Lynn; [p.] Yvonne Sturman, Fred Sturman; [m.] Mr. Steve Burrell, December 3, 1994; [ch.] Expecting at the moment; [ed.] Flitcham Voluntary Aided Primary School, Flitcham Norfolk, Springwood, High School Kings Lynn Norfolk; [occ.] Hygiene Operator, Safeways Superstores; [oth. writ.] First writings. (First of many!!); [pers.] I like to make people understand how other people including children feel in war situations around the world. Make them realize how families are affected.; [a.] Fakenham, Norfolk, NR21 9RT

BURROUGHS, PATRICIA LORRAINE
[b.] April 9, 1942, Abersychan; [p.] Mr. and Mrs. J. Williams Latter (Deceased); [m.] Mr. R. Burroughs, November 6, 1958; [ch.] Lyndon, Mandy, Christian; [ed.] Secondary Modern British School Abersychan, Pontypool Gwent; [occ.] Royal Ordinance (retired 2 yrs)

BURTON, MR. PETER
[pen.] Mr. Barry Just; [p.] Mr. and Mrs. E. Burton; [ed.] Tipton Grammar School, further Education Dudley Technical College; [occ.] Patrol/Audit Inspector; [memb.] Social Clubs, Severn Valley Railway, Hobby Club; [oth. writ.] Some not published; [pers.] I like to effect truth in life, but whenever possible I like to do it in a humorous way.; [a.] Tipton, West Mids, DY4 0TM

BURTON-PYE, SHEILA J.
[b.] July 26, 1941, Norfolk; [p.] David and Margery; [m.] Keith C. Burton-Pye, July 19, 1969; [ed.] Secondary Modern School; [occ.] Housewife, gardener, ex merchandiser; [hon.] Speech, art, and needle work at school. I am one of six sisters, the 3rd, and I have one brother who is the youngest, and it is an Honour to be part of a large family.; [oth. writ.] Many more poems, - over 30. Also children's stories and tributes. People ask me to write poems for their friends and loved ones all have been done for my own pleasure and theirs (so far).; [pers.] I feel very deeply about things, most of my poems are true experiences, of my own and people close to me, I feel the need to write about things that make me happy and sad. Life is a mixture of so many things, and so, is rich in words, even for amateurs.; [a.] North Walsham, Norfolk, NR28 0HL

BUSHELL, DANNY
[b.] August 23, 1988, Birmingham; [p.] Dawn and Graham; [ed.] St. Annes Roman Catholic Primary School; [occ.] Class 5 at Primary School; [pers.] Not just a poet what a centre forward. Sisters Hayley and Sam, and Brother David.; [a.] Birmingham, B37 7LX

CAIN, LEATHEM
[b.] June 17, 1969, Glasgow; [p.] William Leathem, Sheila Rutter; [ed.] Simon Digby Comprehensive, Solihull Sixth Form College, Royal Air Force Technical Training School; [occ.] Manager and Staff Training Supervisor of Workout World Fitness Stores; [memb.] Member of the Institute of Optimism Nutrition Qualified Personal Fitness Instructor; [oth. writ.] Poem entitled 'Time To See' in earlier Anthology. Articles for several specialist fitness magazines including Nutritional and Training Information.; [pers.] I'd like to think that the love that we can all feel within us can one day overcome the preduduces we should not feel around us. I'd like to thank those few very special people who have shared that love with me.; [a.] Birmingham, West Mids, B37 6DU

CAIRNS, WILMA
[pen.] Rae Chalmers; [b.] October 16, 1055, Kirkcaldy, Fife; [p.] William Cairns, Flora Cairns (Dec'd); [ed.] Brae Head Secondary, St. Andrews University; [occ.] Due to graduate June 1996 - B.D. (Hons); [memb.] Church Elder - Buckhaven Parish Church. Support the work of 'International Association Cancer Research (IACR) St. Andrews.; [oth. writ.] Many other poems as yet unpublished. I also enjoy writing short stories and hope one day to see some of those published.; [pers.] The world is a beautiful place. If only we would learn to live alongside one another in love and peace then the potential for good would be enormous.; [a.] Buckhaven, Fife, KY8 1HD

CALDER, EILEEN BERYL
[pen.] Eb Calder, Tiny; [b.] September 13, 1937, Hatton Cross, Middx; [p.] Nancy Roberts and William Roberts; [m.] Terence Calder, March 31, 1956; [ch.] Steven, Mark, Paul and Matthew; [ed.] Stanwell Secondary Modern Girls School; [occ.] Housewife; [memb.] A member of Staines Congregation of Jehovah's Witnesses; [oth. writ.] Two poems published by Anchor Books.; [pers.] I have been greatly influenced by God creation and everyday life.; [a.] Stanwell, Staines, Middlessex, TW19 7QQ

CALDWELL, ERIC
[b.] March 24, 1953, Limavady, NI; [m.] Ann Marie Caldwell, July 22, 1994; [ch.] Eric, Fiona (previous marriage); [ed.] Lumavady Technical Colleges; [occ.] Custody Officer, Inner Courts Service; [memb.] Practising Freemason; [oth. writ.] Nothing published.; [pers.] I try, through my poetry, to get peoples to look at themselves, and to come to terms with whatever demons they need to exercise. Influences seam us heavy/ Ted Hughes.; [a.] Enfield, Middlesex, EN3 4UH

CAMBRIDGE, VERA
[b.] October 31, 1917, Isle Worth, Middx; [p.] Mr. and Mrs. Chadwick; [m.] Cambridge, Francis Jack, June 6, 1936; [ch.] 1; [ed.] Elementary R.C. School, Isleworth Middx, Saint Mary's; [occ.] Retired; [oth. writ.] Poems for a hobby; [pers.] Delighted of my accomplishment.; [a.] Hanworth, Middx, TW13 6PE

CAMERON, WAYNE
[pen.] W.A. Cameron; [b.] March 25, 1972, Nottingham; [p.] Jenifer Cameron; [ed.] Elliott Durham Comp, Westbury Special Manvers Pierpoint, South Notts College; [occ.] Part time, student, unemployed; [memb.] International MacIntosh Society, but would like to join Ramblers Association for Pedestrians and Environment; [hon.] A.R.B. in life skills and distinction in R.S.A. typing endeavour award for hiring at school holidays; [oth. writ.] Started script writing for comedy but failed. Wrote two books but failed, but now writing scripted dramas.; [pers.] I use my writing as a weapon against hypocrisy fascism in people. I see to make down to earth, writing, a fight for me.; [a.] Nottingham, Notts, NG3 3DL

CAMPBELL, CATHERINE
[b.] July 16, 1956; [p.] James P. and Joanna Campbell; [ch.] Son, Stepson; [ed.] St. Augustines Secondary Glasgow; [pers.] "There are depths we sink in, which are uplifting."

CAMPBELL, E.
[pen.] Bebe Campbell-Vemon; [b.] May 6, 1945, Coatbridge; [p.] Frank and Jessie Campbell; [m.] Divorced; [ch.] Anthony Gavin and Andrew Clark; [ed.] Jordanhill College Dip Social Work Royal Scottish Academy of Music Drama (Tech), (CQSW), Coatbridge College 35 NCPA subjects, Glasgow Royal Inf. Scottish Nursing Prelims,; [occ.] Poet (disabled), (Brain disorder) not working. Ex-voluntary Soup Run, Worker.; [memb.] Glasgow (Samye Ling Project) Anti-Racist Alliance, Glasgow, Samey Ling Homeless Project Glasgow; [hon.] See education and other writing. Higher English Grade A. Auchemuckty Silver Cup Story Telling 1992, 3rd Prize story telling 1994 (T.M.A.), Chorus Cup Singing (Scottish Traditional Music and Song Assoc.) 1994.; [oth. writ.] Published social work today. 1st May Poetry Prize Scotia Bar Anthology. Finalist (Semi) Sunday Times Fourth Bridge Centenary Comp. Published Fife Leader. Airdrie Coatbridge Advertiser Fife Advertiser Arran Banner Gartnerhill Writers Anthology.; [pers.] There will be on answer, let me be.; [a.] Lamlash Arran Island, Scotland, KA27 8ND

CAPALDI, PETER VINCENT
[b.] September 16, 1956, London; [ed.] Passmores Comprehensive School Harlow Essex, Ware College of Further Education Ware Herts; [occ.] Technician; [memb.] Harlow Running Club, Harlow Sports Centre; [hon.] Cadburys National Writing Competition for Schools 1964-66; [oth. writ.] Another Excess (Mag), O2 Margerine (Mag), Electric Whelk (Mag), Earth Works (Anthology); [pers.] To make someone laugh, to make another cry, to touch upon your soul, that which I have seen with my eyes; [a.] Harlow, Essex, CM19 4SQ

CAREY, DOROTHY
[b.] Carndonagh; [p.] Robert and Henderson; [m.] Lexie Carey; [ch.] Garry Carey and Sharon Carey; [ed.] Malin Head Primary, Carndonagh Community; [occ.] Running small business and housewife; [pers.] I strive to capture in verse the life experiences of myself and my fellowman, each steeped in diversity yet bonded in humanity.; [a.] Carndonagh, Donegal

CAREY, MRS. GILLIAN
[b.] October 31, 1937, Old Bradwell; [p.] Merridith Cross, Rosa Cross; [m.] Michael Carey, June 23, 1962; [ch.] Julie, Jacqui; [occ.] Housewife; [memb.] Resting from music makes of Milton Operatic Society; [hon.] Certificate awards for solo singing, Oratorio and Opera; [oth. writ.] Poems in local magazine; [pers.] Give thanks for every new day, be content and you will be truely blessed; [a.] Milton Keynes, Bucks, MK13 9AD

CARMAN, JOHN
[b.] August 4, 1949, Glasgow; [p.] Johnston Jean; [m.] Julie Ann Carman, July 10, 1971; [ch.] Shawn James Carman, Lisa Jane Carman; [ed.] Riddery School, Denniston School both in Glasgow, Peterborough Tech College for Music; [occ.] Setter, setting machines to be operated; [memb.] Active Member of St. John Ambulance; [hon.] Grade three in music; [oth. writ.] Several poems printed in local paper, three published in paper back, money made from books went to charity; [pers.] To me poetry is a way of life its so relaxing and fulfilling in writing knowing it gives pleasure to others, my all time poet, Robert Burns; [a.] Peterborough, PE4 7XZ

CARMICHAEL, JAN P.
[pen.] Jan Mossman; [b.] September 27, 1941, Etonwick Nr Eton., now Berkshire; [p.] Squad Leader Don Mossman (D. 1955), Mrs. Joan Mossman; [m.] Divorced 1982; [ed.] 1946-1958 11 schools (forces child), last school Slough High School Berkshire, up to GCE Standard. RSAI Word Processing 1992.; [occ.] Unemployed due to Myalgic Encephalomyelitis ('89) Prev. Buyer-House Builders.; [memb.] Pax Christ MCC Southampton. Action for me.; [oth. writ.] 1995 I complained and typed my 1st booklet of poetry and reflections of the countryside and some of God's creatures who gave life, laughter and fun to "Raindrops and Roses". 'A Rose' was one of two 'Raindrop' that were my first attempts at writing in 1983.; [pers.] After I 'came out' mid '83 I started writing poetry. It was like a cork bursting from a champagne bottle. My faith and being 'true to myself' are important to me and is often reflected in my writing. Although being dyslexic, suddenly being able to give pleasure was and is a delight especially after a close friend told me I had talent which is all God given.; [a.] Southampton, Hampshire, SO15 2YE

CARPENTER, JOHN
[b.] March 1, 1941, Newcastle-upon-Tyne; [p.] John and Annie Louisa Carpenter; [m.] Yvonne Margaret Carpenter, July 20, 1985; [ch.] Patricia, Stephen, Laura, Anna, Liese; [ed.] Whickham View Second-

ary Modern Newcastle-upon-Tyne; [occ.] Disabled; [memb.] Newcastle-upon-Tyne writers circle M.E.A., House the Church of Jesus Christ of Latter Day Saints; [oth. writ.] (Proverbs (Gem-thoughts) (Song Lyrics (Hymn-Lyrics) Three children's novels. Third one almost complete. As yet, unpublished but hopeful and confident of eventual success, particularly with 3rd book 11-18 age grow; [pers.] 'Life is but a school. And all it's people are pupils: and yet, paradoxically, all are teachers, by virtue of example".. (it's not a play! Sorry Shakespeare) but life is a serious business we all do effect eternity. (Inspiring thoughts); [a.] Newcastle-upon-Tyne, Northumberland, NE12 8LF.

CARR, JOHN
[pen.] John Harrison; [b.] May 14, 1941, Nottingham; [p.] Lancelot Harrison and Vera Harrison; [m.] Frances Carr (Nee Russell), September 18, 1980; [ch.] Gary, Robert, Amanda, Jacqueline; [ed.] Abingdon (John Roysse's) School, Berkshire; [occ.] Document Courier; [oth. writ.] Various, including short pantomimes, dialogue, prose and poems of which one entitled "The Tree" sent to the Green Party and to The Woodland Trust in Grantham, Lincolnshire.; [pers.] I believe "Life is now". If we worry too much about the future we can't enjoy the present therefore we have no past. The present shapes the future and creates the past.; [a.] Chorley, Lancs, PR7 1UD

CARTER, MRS. JANET
[pen.] 'Jan'; [b.] January 6, 1941, London; [p.] Mr. and Mrs. Nabain; [m.] Mr. Royalfred Carter, December 26, 1959; [ch.] Sylvia Burton (nee Carter), Daryl Carter; [ed.] Greenwich Park Secondary School, London SE10; [occ.] TEF/L teacher; [memb.] Angling clubs, Book clubs; [hon.] R.S.A. English, French, Maths TEF/L Certificate; [oth. writ.] Children's, Newspaper, Women's Magazines, "Voices on the Wind" (The International Society of Poets); [pers.] Tima nd tide waits for no man, so I furthered my career when I was a grandma. I love having six grandchildren.; [a.] St. Leonards-on-Sea, East Sussex, TN38 0NN

CARTER, LESLEY JAYNE
[b.] May 8, 1969, Stourport; [p.] Roger Harrison and Christine Harrison; [m.] Jonathan Carter, September 3, 1994; [ed.] Stourport High School, Kidderminster College of further education; [occ.] Personal Secretary; [memb.] Figarama Fitness Gym, Anthony Nolan Bone Marrow Donor; [oth. writ.] I have written several poems for fun, but this is the first competition I have entered. I have since entered Royal British Legion Competition in Aid of Remembrance.; [pers.] My family and friends have inspired many of my poems which have in turn reflected, everyday living.; [a.] Kidderminster, Worcs, DY11 6NU

CARTER, LINDA
[pen.] Linda Shakespeare; [b.] December 13, 1957, Middlesbrough; [p.] Alec and June Shakespeare; [m.] (To be) Alan Smith, September 23, 1996; [ch.] Angela, Michelle and Stephanie; [ed.] Southlands Secondary Modern School; [occ.] Sales Consultant for American Designer Liz Claiborne, Binns, Middlesbrough; [oth. writ.] Personal collection of poems written for family and friends. Also shown in employers monthly staff newsletter; [pers.] You only have one chance at life, use your time spent on this earth by appreciating what you have, as your time is precious and your life is limited. Nothing as valuable will ever come again.; [a.] Middlesbrough, Cleveland, TS6 9JN

CARTER, TIM
[b.] June 14, 1957, London; [p.] Eric, Irene; [ed.] Masters degree in Business Administration from Aston Business School.; [occ.] Commercial Manager; [oth. writ.] Currently writing a book on creativity in business.; [pers.] Writing is a wonderful interlude from life's more hectic side. I believe it is one of the many ways in which light can shine into the world.

CARTER, VICKI DANIELLE
[b.] November 19, 1981, Worksop; [p.] Denise Carter; [m.] Tony Carter, not married; [ch.] No children; [ed.] At School Valley Comprehensive; [a.] Worksop, Nottingham, S81 0HF

CASTLETON, SOO
[b.] April 16, 1953, Kent; [p.] George Henry and Lucy Mona; [m.] Tony, March 28, 1981; [ch.] Jane, Laura and Casey-Soo; [ed.] Secondary School; [occ.] "Skilled" Housewife; [oth. writ.] Written several poems for particular occasions, both happy and sad ones.; [pers.] I get so much joy and satisfaction from putting my feelings on paper in the form of a poem. They will be a lovely reminder for my grandaughter in years to come of her Nan.; [a.] Barnehurst, Kent, DA7 6PU

CHAMBERLAIN, MRS. ALMA
[b.] Over 21, Derby; [p.] Deceased; [m.] Philip Chamberlain, December 8, 1955; [ch.] One female; [ed.] Grammar School Parkfield Cedors, Derby; [occ.] Housewife; [hon.] Silver award for twenty one years as treasurer for the "Mental Health" research society (raising funds for research) re-mental illness; [a.] Rearsby, Leicesters, LE7 4ZA

CHAPMAN, TARAMY
[b.] February 23, 1969, Canvey Island; [p.] Ken and Carol Chapman; [ed.] CSE's English, French, Gardening Office Practice; [occ.] Self Employed Punch Pattern Operator/Designer; [pers.] Life is no full and challenging, fear always steps in the way. Like a black bird shutting out the sun light. On a clear and most beautiful day.; [a.] Southend, Essex, SS2 6XJ

CHARLESWORTH, RICHARD JAMES
[pen.] Charlie James; [b.] March 15, 1952, Cheltenham; [p.] Malcom and Gwendolyn; [m.] Sally Christine, September 21, 1974; [ch.] Bethany Jane and Oliver James; [ed.] Arle Secondary Modern, Gloucestershire College of Art and Technology (Gloscat), Open University undergraduate; [occ.] Project engineer; [memb.] Gloucester Angling Club, Cheltenham and District Clay Club, British Association for Shooting and Conservation (BASC); [oth. writ.] Several poems published by arrival press; [pers.] Favorite poets include: John Masefield, Charles Kingsley and W. H. Davies. Some of Shakespeare's Sonnets. "Treat the Earth well....it was not given to us by our parents....it was lent to us by our children."; [a.] Tewkesbury, Glos, GL20 5HF

CHEEMA, PRIYA
[pen.] Gurminder; [b.] February 1, 1985, Perivale; [p.] Amardeep Cheema, Devinderpal S. Cheema, Brother: Jose; [ed.] Ravenor School; [occ.] Student; [hon.] English Literature; [oth. writ.] Letter Competitions; [pers.] My poems are reflecting my own life and others.; [a.] Southall, Middx, UB1 2HS

CHETWYND, ELAINE
[b.] November 16, 1965, Atherstone; [p.] Terrance and Doreen Chetwynd; [m.] Maurice Clark (partner); [ed.] North Warwickshire College, Wolverhampton University; [occ.] Mental Health Support Worker for Friendship Housing; [memb.] Student of the Institute of Welfare Officers; [hon.] BA (Hons) Humanities - English Literature and Contemporary Cultural Studies.; [oth. writ.] Other poems include: 'Aquarius Dawns', 'Heart So Raw', 'Roses and Blisters'.; [pers.] As someone who has just started waiting my own poems I am very pleased to have one of my poems published. I believe that a positive mental attitude helps me through life which is channelled into my written work.; [a.] Nuneaton, Warwicks, CV10 0RF

CHILDS, AMY F.
[pen.] Nature Lover; [b.] January 10, 1915, Loders, Dorset; [p.] Anne and Harry Bowditch; [m.] Arthur Childs, November 12, 1933; [ch.] Two girls one boy; [ed.] Dorset Village Schools Beaminster Hooke Puncknowle Witten Cheney; [occ.] Pensioner; [oth. writ.] Poems in local magazines. 1 poem in Dr Banardo's, 'Childhood Memories'; [pers.] I was brought up on Dorset Farms worked on farms all my life.; [a.] Beaminster, Dorset, DT8 3EZ

CHILDS, JANET
[pen.] Jan; [b.] August 21, 1935, Kettering; [p.] Mr. and Mrs. Rose Hebbes; [m.] Victor Childs, May 21, 1955; [ch.] Christopher, Josephine, Jennifer, David; [ed.] Secondary Modern School, Park Street Wellingborough Northants; [occ.] Retired; [memb.] Wellingborough Ladies Bowls Club, Tresham College Tap Dancing; [hon.] Bowls Ladies Pairs Outdoor Cup 1989, Bowls Ladies Triples Outdoor Cup 1995; [oth. writ.] Verses for bowling dinners when I was Bowls Ladies Captain and President; [pers.] My poem is about a true life experience.; [a.] Northampton, Northants, NN6 9DE

CHISHOLM, JUNE D.
[b.] June 13, 1925, Birmingham; [ch.] Jeremy and Claire; [ed.] Left school at fourteen. Took 'O' and 'A' levels in my forties at Sutton Coldfield College of Education, then to Bordesley College of Education in B'ham. Taught in a B'ham primary school for fifteen years. I specialized in art and science.; [occ.] Retired I write, paint, garden and care for my dogs.; [pers.] When teaching I encouraged children to write poetry stimulating them into connecting the visual arts to the written word. I could survive a desert island existance supply of pencils and paper.; [a.] Boston, Lincs, PE22 4JS

CHISWELL, TONY
[b.] October 3, 1970, Greenwich; [p.] Percy and Rita Chiswell; [ed.] Bexley Heath Secondary Modern; [occ.] Financial Advisor; [memb.] Surfers Against Sewage; [oth. writ.] This is the first time I have ever attempted to have any of my work published.; [pers.] I have always loved both poetry and music, one of my main influences has been 'Wendy Cope'. I believe life and love are very precious - never take either for granted.; [a.] Bexley Heath, Kent, DA7 5NB

CHRISTIAN, TRACY
[b.] March 7, 1969, Paignton, Devon; [p.] Ann Denny and Allan Moores; [m.] James Fernley (Partner); [ch.] Benjamin William; [ed.] Priory Grammar School, Shrewsbury, Shropshire, Wolverhampton University; [occ.] Registered Psychiatric Nurse; [oth. writ.] This is my first!; [pers.] I write poetry for fun and as a way of telling my family how much I love them.; [a.] Shrewsbury, Shropshire, SY3 6AB

CHRISTIE, DONNA-MARIA
[pen.] Donna; [b.] September 6, 1976, W Midlands; [p.] Leonora Christie; [ed.] The Royal Wolverhampton School, Joseph Chamberlain, sixth form college; [occ.] Sales Assistant, Student; [hon.] 8 GCSE's and a credit by the English Speaking Board (E.S.B.); [pers.] My inspiration to write poems comes from all around me, but most of my inspiration comes from the most important person in my life, my Mom. As a dyslexic I have to work twice as hard to achieve my goal, so to gain approval from such a high status is the best reward I could ever receive.; [a.] Halesowen, W Midlands, B63 2PR

CHRYSTAL, CHRISTINA A. MOGGACH
[pen.] C. A. Moggach; [b.] October 5, 1932, Huntly; [p.] Ernest and Mary Smith; [m.] William Chrystal, September 15, 1956; [ch.] Thomas, William, Joshua; [ed.] Gordon Secondary School Huntly Aberdeenshire Scotland; [occ.] Housewife; [memb.] The Parish Church, Church of Scotland Huntly Aberdeenshire; [oth. writ.] One poem published in the poetry institute of the British Isles in 1995; [pers.] The school that I went to was my inspiration that gave my love of poetry. I love all kinds of poetry.; [a.] Huntly, Aberdeen, AB51 5RG

CHURCHYARD, HAZEL
[b.] December 6, 1947, Feltwell, Norfolk; [p.] Barry; [ch.] Faye and Jeff; [occ.] Care Manager; [pers.] My writing reflects my inner thoughts, these expressions relieve day to day pressures!; [a.] Rainham, Essex, RM13 7AR

CICERI, AVIS MARIA
[b.] February 10, 1935, London; [p.] Edith (Nee Godly) and William Collins; [m.] James Ciceri, June 6, 1981; [ch.] One Stepson - Alan; [ed.] Nothing special, Secondary Modern School; [occ.] Retired Accounts Dept. Supervisor; [oth. writ.] Several poems published in a variety of poetry books. I also write children's stories as a hobby.; [pers.] Through the words of my poems, I try to express my deeper thoughts and feelings about life.; [a.] Saint Albans, Herts, AL2 3NF

CIRINO, JOAN
[pen.] Joan Cirino; [b.] April 21, 1948, Accrington; [p.] Agnes Dunn, William Mercer; [m.] Antonio Cirino; [ch.] Maria, Luisa, Christina, Raffaele, Marcella; [ed.] Secondary Education; [occ.] Housewife; [oth. writ.] One poem about Alzheimers disease - plus one humerus poem - both published in local books.; [pers.] My poems are of every day life from my own experience's and from being privileged to care for some older people in the past, some not so old, very brave people in spite of illness, when I was a care assistant and a community cater.; [a.] Accrington, Lancashire, BB5 6HR

CLAPHAM, SHEILA
[pen.] Sheila; [b.] November 10, 1942, London; [p.] Charles and Ethel Nicholls; [m.] Richard Clapham, June 3, 1967; [ch.] Peter Charles and Julia Carol; [ed.] Ruckholt Manor Sec. Mod.; [occ.] Partner - Driving School; [memb.] Botley Players (Amateur Dramatics) folded 1995 after 39 years. Kingston Bagpuize Amateur Dramatics; [hon.] Silver cup - Best Actress - Four Shires Festival 1985 - Amateur Dramatics; [oth. writ.] Poems galore.; [pers.] I need coffee to wake me in the morning and thereafter my fluffy dog slippers keep my feet warm.; [a.] Oxford, Oxon, OX2 9JU

CLARK, BRYAN M.
[b.] June 6, 1937, Dorchester; [p.] Ronald Clark, Christine Clark; [m.] Valerie Adams, January 1, 1959; [ch.] Linda Joy, Nicholas James, David John; [ed.] Dorchester Grammar School Weymouth College of Further Education; [occ.] Teacher, Damers First School, Dorchester; [memb.] Dorchester Swimming Club, British Judo Association; [hon.] Cert in Education, Diploma from Academy of Children's writers, ASA Teacher's Certificate, Swam British Channel as member of Relay team in August 1984; [oth. writ.] Several short stories for children (unpublished); [pers.] A keen mimic, especially of old Hollywood stars.; [a.] Dorchester, Dorset, DT1 1LW

CLARKE, ANTHONY
[b.] May 10, 1968, Manchester; [p.] Jean Clarke, Brian Clarke; [ed.] St. Damians R.C. High School, University College of Salford; [occ.] Chef, R.M.C.H.; [hon.] Trainee Chief of the Year, Y.T.S. 1985; [oth. writ.] Several poems written but as yet untitled or published; [pers.] To come to terms with my hidden fears and desires through my poetry in order to become a better person; [a.] Manchester, Gt. Manchester, M43 6HJ

CLARKE, JAMES
[b.] January 22, 1939, Bellshill; [p.] Mathew and Jane; [m.] Catherine, October 31, 1964; [ch.] Raymond, Brian and Lorraine; [ed.] Ordinary; [occ.] Retired Engineer; [oth. writ.] Local magazines, but mainly for personal pleasure.; [pers.] I hope I can through my poetry express my feelings about anything I feel strongly opposed to, or anything that I love.; [a.] Eastkilbride, Strathclyde, S74 4ED

CLARKE, MARGARET ROSE
[pen.] Margaret Rose Stewart; [b.] May 9, 1942, Londonderry; [p.] Margaret Stewart; [m.] Robert John Clarke, September 1, 1962; [ch.] Janet, Allison, Gaenor, Joanne; [ed.] Culmore Primary School, Londonderry Technical College; [occ.] Housewife; [memb.] Local Community Environmental Group; [oth. writ.] Few poems published by U.K. publishers; [pers.] I draw my inspiration to write poems mainly from personal or family life experiences or events, whether funny or strange, happy or sad.; [a.] Londonderry, Northern Ireland, BT48 8JW

CLARKE, MISS SARAH
[b.] June 16, 1981, Chelmsford; [p.] Robert and Rita Clarke; [ed.] Honywood Coggeshall, Essex; [occ.] Still at school, studying for G.C.S.E.'s; [oth. writ.] Three previous poems published these are La Plage, Fatal Attraction, A Seal's Peril; [pers.] My poems paint pictures in my mind of life itself.; [a.] Colchester, Essex, CO5 9JX

CLARKE, SARAH
[b.] March 19, 1976, Edwinstowe; [p.] Ann Clarke and Richard Clarke; [m.] Justin Flame; [ed.] Rufford Comp. School (Edwinstowe) and West Notts College (Mansfield); [occ.] Student in Art and Design; [oth. writ.] I have wrote many poems but never had one published.; [pers.] I adore writing poems and I only write what I feel and by what I may of been influenced from the time. My influences are my surroundings, family and the world situations.; [a.] Mansfield, Notts, MA21 9PL

CLEAR, JUNE
[b.] June 6, 1941, Bognor; [p.] Fred, Edith; [m.] Malcolm, August 3, 1957; [ch.] Tony, Sylvia, Peter, Heather, Allison, Yvonne, Phillip and Julie; [ed.] Birdham and Chichester Lancastrian School; [occ.] Housewife, Care Assistant; [oth. writ.] I would like to dedicate my poem to my darling mum who died on March 25th 1996 age 89 years.; [pers.] I love both reading and writing poetry my favorites being. Patience strong. Pam Ayres; [a.] Angmering, West Sussex, BN16 4LW

CLEGG, SARAH-LOUISE
[b.] November 8, 1973, Whitehaven, Cumbria; [p.] Philip Garth Clegg, Brenda Clegg; [ed.] Aberdeen University; [occ.] Student of Sociology; [memb.] Bon Accord Spiritualist Church, National Trust for Scotland; [oth. writ.] First publication, white poetry for pleasure and enjoyment.; [pers.] Poetry. for me is a release from daily routine. My influence is from our environment and those with whom we share the world, I try to express the beauty of the natural world in my poetry.; [a.] Westhill, Aberdeenshire, AB32 GR4

CLEGG, TIMOTHY M.
[pen.] Gopher, Pirate; [b.] February 21, 1950, Ormskirk; [p.] James Blanco Clegg, Mary Clegg; [m.] Divorced; [ch.] Selina, Russell, Victoria; [ed.] Repton School, Biralinh Gad College; [occ.] Legal Administrator and Independent Sales Consultant; [memb.] Institute of Direction Artist Gliding Association Chamber of Commerce; [hon.] Numerous Marketing and Legal Certificates in Recognition of Skills and Training.; [oth. writ.] Numerous poetry in all subject and all mood types. All rhyming poetry no blank verse.; [pers.] Deeply reflective of serious and humorous occasions and ability to compose instant poetry to suit.; [a.] Exeter, Devon, EX4 5DP

CLEMENTS, WILLIAM EDWARD
[b.] January 23, 1927, Battersea; [p.] Lillian and Alfred Clements; [m.] Freda Rosina Clements; [ch.] Six; [ed.] No. 1 Grammar School, Morden, Surrey; [occ.] Retired; [pers.] I have written several poems but this is my first attempt at publication.; [a.] Grays, Essex, RM17 5SJ

CLEVETT, MRS. MARILYN
[pen.] Marilyn Clevett; [b.] May 3, 1972, Sutton; [p.] Alan and Barbara; [m.] Mr. Paul Clevett, April 24, 1993; [ed.] Ewell High School, JHP Training, Surrey Training; [occ.] Lunchline Assistant and part time Sales Assistant in an off-license; [memb.] The King's Church, Epson; [oth. writ.] A few poems for anthologies with Triumph Have, Peterborough. "The Listener", Mixed Blessings, "Take Time", Expressions of Faith, "There Are No Answering Machines in Heaven", Christian poets.; [pers.] Thanks to my husband Paul, but above all to my Lord and Saviour, Jesus; [a.] Epson, Surrey, KT19 8SW

COGAN, ALISON
[b.] February 25, 1966, Andover; [p.] William John Page, Shirley Page; [m.] Divorced; [ch.] Lee and Dean; [ed.] Winton School, Cricklade College (Andover); [occ.] Deputy Warden for Elderly Sheltered Housing; [memb.] I-S-A (International Songwriters Association); [oth. writ.] I have been writing poetry since the age of sixteen and have much unseen, unpublished material; [a.] Andover, Hampshire, SP10 4BD

COLES, GILBERT RONALD EDWIN
[b.] October 19, 1937, Saint Austell, Cornwall; [p.] Cyril Albert Norman and Edna Honor; [m.] Mary, November 19, 1960; [ch.] Susan Anne, Mary Angela, Andrew Gilbert John; [ed.] Comprehensive, Shorthand Typist in the Royal Army Service Corps.; [occ.] Senior Meat Hygiene Inspector with Ministry of Agriculture, Fisheries and Food; [memb.] Saint Mary's

Church Choir, Royal Society of Health, St. Johns Ambulance, Royal Institute of Public Health and Gygiene, the Association of Meat Inspectors Several Local Choral Societies; [hon.] Medal for Blood Donations; [oth. writ.] None printed - only within my family circle for special occasions, i.e. Birthdays, Weddings, and occasionally at social functions for friends and neighbors.; [pers.] I like to think that my poems bring joy and comfort to others, particularly if they are undergoing ill health or stressful times, and that they Aid recovery., [a.] Bideford, North Devon, EX39 3NL

COLSON, EDWARD
[b.] August 30, 1936, Calcutta; [p.] Edward Barron Colson, Georgina Beatrice Colson (Both Deceased); [m.] Patricia Colson, August 29, 1987; [ch.] Edward James Colson, Georgina France; [ed.] Prep. School (Holme Grange) Public School (Victoria College, Jersey), R.M.A. Sandhurst, Ex-Army Officer (The Royal Northumberland Fusiliers); [occ.] Nominal Company Secretary, although unemployed; [oth. writ.] To date, over the last two years, I have written 60 poems and some articles and short stories totalling some 21,000 words. As yet, none are published, although 2 are due to be through entering competitions (one thro' the I.S.P.); [pers.] My poetry is wide ranging initially the two world wars formed the main subjects, but I have learned to spread my ideas further out to try to capture life in as many forms as I can. I try hard to keep an open mind!; [a.] Earl Shilton, Leicestershire, LE9 7FY

CONNOLLY, NORA
[b.] June 21, 1911, Louth, Lincs; [p.] Mr. and Mrs. Basil Bratley; [m.] Frank Johnson (former marriage), October 1936; [ch.] Shirley Carol, Patricia Jane, Johnson - now married; [ed.] Louth Pupil-Teacher Centre - King Ed: Di Girl's Grammar School, Louth Lincs.; [occ.] Retired - 84 year old infant teacher.; [memb.] Originally - Louth Playgoers Society now - Member Legbourne forget-me-not Club.; [oth. writ.] Poems published in local W.I. Magazine. Essays for age concern competitions - came 2nd.; [pers.] Having had such a loving family - now career for by-two daughters four grandchildren - loved by three great-Grandchildren.; [a.] Legbourne, Lincs, LN11 8LX

CONNOR, BRIAN HARVEY
[b.] March 12, 1915, Maidstone; [p.] Ada and Frances R. Connor; [m.] Kitty D. V. Connor (Nee Snaith), June 25, 1939; [ed.] Christs Hospital Horsham, Jesus College Cambridge; [oth. writ.] Further poems. But longer than requested.; [a.] Impington, Cambs, CBN 4Y6

CONOLLY, NICHOLAS
[pen.] Nick; [b.] January 5, 1958, Bognor Regis; [p.] Stella, Renee; [m.] Michaela Conolly, March 2, 1996; [ch.] Two - James and Gemma; [ed.] Bognor Regis Comprehensive; [occ.] Retired Naval Chief Petty Officer; [memb.] Salvation Army Welcome Sergeant at an Alcohol and Drug Treatment Center; [hon.] City and Guilds of London Institute, 707/1 707/2 717/1 Distinction Hotel Management (Catering); [oth. writ.] Words, Love, Wisdom, Oh What A Friend; [pers.] Life is so sacred, that we don't realise until it's too late. But with love and compassion lives can be turned round to live full and joyous.; [a.] Shaftesbury, Dorset, SP7 8NA

COOKE, PAUL
[b.] March 11, 1963, Guildford; [p.] E. Esther Morrisson; [ed.] Glen Eyre Comprehensive, Southampton; [occ.] Barristers Clerk; [memb.] Institute of Barristers Clerks Competitors Companion; [oth. writ.] "In the Glint of an Eye" amateur film, writer, characterization, screenplay. Articles for local newspaper. Film Reviews. Several attempts at songwriting.; [pers.] Life is too short and opportunities too few, if you've got it, go for it, but be yourself.; [a.] Southampton, Hampshire

COOKE, PHYLLIS
[b.] April 19, 1910, Savile Park; [p.] William and Winifred Haigh; [m.] George Michael, January 10, 1937; [ch.] Michael and Gillian; [ed.] Church School, Halifax Yorkshire; [occ.] Housewife; [oth. writ.] Poems published in WI Magazine and local magazine.; [pers.] Dedicated to my daughter Gillian.; [a.] Brent, London

COOPER, BRIAN WILLIAM TYAS
[pen.] B. W. Tyas Cooper; [b.] April 23, 1923, Bolton; [m.] Frances; [ch.] 2 sons; [ed.] Rugby School and Oriel College, Oxford; [occ.] Retired; [hon.] J.P., MA, FCA; [oth. writ.] Several poems published in Bolton Evening News (Poet's Corner). 3 printed booklets of poems produced for friends - 1) A year in the Life of a Golf Club (1984), 2) Of Golf and Other Things (1986), 3) From Bad to Verse (1994); [a.] Bolton, Lancashire, BL1 5BQ

COOPER, NORA KATHLEEN
[b.] August 14, 1934, Glossop, Derbyshire; [p.] Edgar Hallam, Ellen Hallam; [m.] George Ernest Cooper, July 11, 1953; [ch.] Norman, Leslie, Derek, Joy, Diane, Roger; [ed.] West End School, Glossop, Derbyshire; [occ.] Farmer's Wife; [oth. writ.] Several poems published.; [pers.] I just hope some one gets pleasure from reading what I have written.; [a.] New Mills, Derbyshire, SK12 4QN

COUCHMAN, SARAH
[b.] November 28, 1983, Croydon, Surrey; [p.] Linda Couchman, Christopher Couchman; [ed.] Warlingham Secondary School; [occ.] I am in my first year at Secondary School.; [hon.] Too young for any yet.; [oth. writ.] I have only just started writing poetry. I am hoping to have more poems published.; [pers.] I hope to create an atmosphere in my poems.; [a.] Sanderstead, Surrey, CR2 0EN

COUNIHAN, JAMES
[b.] December 14, 1933, Kilrush, Co. Clare, Ireland; [ed.] C.B.S. Kilrush, Cranfield Inst. Tech., City University, London; [occ.] Retired (early); [hon.] M. Sc. Aero Eng., PL.D Industrial Aero Dynamics; [oth. writ.] Novel completed 'To Balance The Scales.' Seeking publisher!; [pers.] Still regard words worth, shelley and keats as the best.; [a.] Tenby, Dyfed, SA70 7BU

COUSINS, NORMA
[b.] December 5, 1936, Bournemouth; [p.] Ellen and Charles McDowell; [m.] Ray Cousins, October 20, 1956; [ch.] Stephen Raymond, David John, Michael Frank; [ed.] Boscombe Secondary; [occ.] Housewife; [memb.] Harrow Angling Society; [pers.] I enjoy poetry of all topics. However, this is the first poem I have composed; [a.] Park Royal, London, NW10 7EN

COX, GARY J.
[b.] August 8, 1955, Bristol; [p.] John and Barbara Cox; [m.] Eileen Cox, September 5, 1986; [ch.] Katie Hanora; [ed.] Filton Secondary School Filton, Bristol/Brunel Technical College, Bristol; [occ.] Emergency Lightning and Fire Alarm Engineer; [oth. writ.] 5 published poems with poetry now and active press. "Postscript Poem" printed by the pimps of the alphabet press. Lyrics for the forthcoming T.M.G.C. Disc "Orleans is Burning"; [Tn.] Bristol; [a.] BS16 4EP

CRAMP, DIANA HELEN
[b.] February 20, 1940, Brighton; [p.] Mabel and Walter Jarvis; [m.] James Thomas Cramp, September 16, 1961; [ch.] Nicola, Martin, Christopher, Anne-Marie; [ed.] Secondary Education English, Shorthand, Typing, Book-Keeping course (Night school); [occ.] Housewife, (Formally Book-Keeper); [memb.] Was Brownie, Guide, Sea Ranger of S.R.S Shoreham dmiralty recognized Crew. Was Bos'un, signalman of crew, also was a Guider; [hon.] Awarded certificate for art passed with honours for typing first aid certificates; [oth. writ.] Not sent for publishing; [pers.] I was leader of Southwick, British Red Cross Team (Brighton Area First Aid Competition). The team came first, and subsequently, I was chosen to attend a reception at St. James's palace, and met Princess Alexandra in June 1954.; [a.] Southwick, Sussex, BN42 4TN

CRANE, PATRICIA
[b.] September 16, 1955, Halifax, W. Yorks; [p.] William Drury, Linda Drury; [m.] Peter Crane, July 1, 1974; [ch.] Terence, David, Belinda, Peter and Louise; [ed.] College N.E. London Middlesex University; [occ.] Student Midwife; [memb.] Drew School of Dancing (Manor Park) Royal College of Midwives (London); [oth. writ.] A book for my son Peter poems published in local press; [pers.] My heart is the writer I am merely the scribe. My love is the thinker I merely abide.; [Tn.] Waltham Abbey; [a.] Essex, EN9 1QG

CRAWFORD, JAMES CUNNINGHAM
[b.] July 26, 1947, Douglas; [p.] Margaret Crawford and Alec Crawford; [m.] Single; [ch.] Wendy Margaret Crawford; [ed.] Douglas Junior Secondary (Lanarkshire); [occ.] Demolition Specialist; [pers.] This is my first attempt to have any of my work published, and has therefore strengthened my confidence.; [a.] Larkhall, Lanarkshire, ML9 1QB

CRITCHLEY, ADAM
[b.] October 10, 1973, Raf Wegberg, Germany; [p.] Barry, Christine Critchley; [ed.] Parklands High School Chorley; [occ.] Semi-Professional Footballer; [pers.] To my brother Mark. Your resilience and humour in the face of suffering and pain is a constant inspiration to me.; [a.] Chorley, Lancashire, PR7 2QJ

CROSSAN, MARIAN
[b.] May 21, 1949, Swinton, Nr. Manchester; [p.] Ernest Ringer and Leah Ringer; [ed.] Woodlands County, Secondary School for Girls, Basildon, Essex; [occ.] Technical Manager (Pensions) Leading Insurance Company.; [pers.] I try to create an atmosphere, a scene in the reader's mind, through which they can experience the feelings I have when I write the poem.; [a.] Pitsea, Essex, SS13 1RJ

CRUTCHER, MRS. KATE
[b.] September 7, 1949, Sherston; [p.] Dorothy and William Hadland; [m.] David, September 15, 1979; [ch.] Colin, Donna, Helen, Peter; [ed.] Malmesbury Comprehensive School; [occ.] Child Minder; [hon.] Butlins Talent Competition 1976; [oth. writ.] None published.; [pers.] I write about personal struggles in life - also about the funnier things that make life worthwhile.; [a.] Malmesbury, Wilts, SN16 0LX

CUDD, WENDY ANN
[b.] October 28, 1941, West Byfleet, Surrey; [occ.] Full-time home career, used to work in children's homes and boarding school as house mother and house mistress.; [oth. writ.] Have always maintained an interest in reading poetry but only started to write this decade - on all subjects and styles sometimes drawing on my own experiences of life for material.; [pers.] Have lived most of my life in Strood and Rochester, Kent but have worked in live-in situations based away from my midway home. During the a 70's spent several years working and travelling in Australia. Apart from poetry, other great pastimes are gardening and pets.; [a.] Rochester, Kent, ME1 2PR

CULL, MARIAN
[b.] November 7, 1934, Preston, Lancs; [m.] Michael Cull, March 31, 1992; [ch.] One son, three daughters, one stepson, three stepdaughters; [ed.] Convent of the Holy Child Jesus, Preston (Grammar School); [occ.] Retired; [oth. writ.] This is first attempt, apart from poems published in school magazines during teens.; [pers.] Most poems evoke my own memories of situations or places.; [a.] Coventry, Warks, CV5 6AS

CULLEN, MARGARET
[pen.] Margaret Cullen; [b.] June 20, 1930, Blackpool; [m.] Geoffrey; [ch.] 1 girl - Ansela; [occ.] Scientific Palmist; [hon.] 2 Certificates for singing when very young. Also when young, 2 Caroll Lewis Discoverers. Blackpool, Lanc's; [oth. writ.] Poems; [pers.] Like to bring nature to people.; [a.] Brighton, Sussex, BN2 3DD

CULLINGFORD, DIANA
[pen.] Diana Cullingford; [b.] February 11, 1954, London; [p.] Margeret Phillips; [m.] Divorced, July 4, 1970; [ch.] Michael; [ed.] Mountford Manor Junior, and Walcot Secondary; [occ.] H/wife; [oth. writ.] Have written many poems. This is the first time that I have ever entered a competition.; [pers.] My (Junior School) Teacher Mr. Wainwright did say many years ago I should make the effort. He seemed to think I had a flair for writing. Seems he was right.

CUNNINGHAM, JAMES FERGUSON
[b.] April 17, 1913, London; [p.] James Ferguson Cunningham, Emily Pleasance Cunningham; [m.] Sally Cunningham (Deceased), May 22, 1937; [ch.] Carole Ann Cunningham; [ed.] West Silvertown - London; [occ.] Retired Aircraft Engineer; [memb.] B.A.C. Association; [pers.] I began to write poetry after my beloved wife, Sally, died in 1967. I found that expressing my feelings in this way helped me to cope with the grief and in this I was greatly encouraged by my daughter, Carole Cunningham-Jones.; [a.] Addlestone, Surrey, KT15 2JF

CUNNINGHAM, MOREEN
[b.] 1942; [p.] Mary and Michael McLoughlin; [m.] Thomas Cunningham, 1965; [ch.] Six children, 3 girls and 3 boys; [occ.] First job with a French Textile Company named Dormeuil Frere in London's West End, I have a part-time job three morning at a local nursing home; [pers.] I have been writing for myself on and off since 1986 when I attended a creative writing class at the local College of Arts in Sutton, Surrey. This was something I have always wanted to do but never seemed to have the time. I was quite ill in 1991 and believe I only survived because my husband was so wonderful, he gave me something and someone to live for. The doctors told Tom I would not be able to do many things I had enjoyed before mt illness and not to expect too much of me but here I am, recovered, writing again and performing once more, with the Woking based Karen Clarke Theatre Company. Tom and I also love to visit the theatre as often as we can. However, I do have one small dream, I have always thought it would be wonderful to be a proof-reader for a well known publisher and althought I am not familiar with what that might involve it is something I would love to try.

CURRAN, MARGARET FRANCES
[b.] October 30, 1927, Durham; [p.] John W. Ord and Elizabeth E. Ord; [m.] Neville Curran, September 3, 1949; [ch.] Pamela, Gilliana, Julia, M.E.; [ed.] Secondary; [occ.] Retired; [oth. writ.] Tributes to friends and family.; [pers.] I'd like to think I brought a little peace beauty and tranquility into peoples lives.; [a.] Kingston upon Thames, Surrey, KT2 6RA

CURTIS, DAVID
[b.] March 20, 1967, Portsmouth; [ed.] Comprehensive; [occ.] Hospital Porter; [oth. writ.] Unpublished poems and short stories; [pers.] I always write about the things that move me in the hope it may help others to see that life happens to everybody. My influences and role. Models are the people around me.; [a.] Gosport, Hants

CUTTING, J. B.
[pen.] John Bernard; [b.] October 23, 1927, Coventry; [p.] Deceased; [m.] Carole, March 16, 1959; [ch.] Adrian John and Jeremy Bernard; [ed.] Not yet completed; [occ.] Design and Methods Consultant; [memb.] Freeman's Guild, Bradfield Cricket Club, North Walsham Rugby Club; [hon.] Freedom of Coventry 1950; [oth. writ.] 1.) Industrial Essay (Through One Door With One Aim), 2.) Thirty Years After (Polish Radio 1975), 3.) Technical Booklet. Other poems.; [pers.] Life is a learning experience; [a.] North Walsham, Norfolk, NR28 9DJ

CZUBA, DAVID
[b.] March 6, 1961, High Wycombe; [p.] Stanislaw and Olive Czuba; [ed.] 5 degrees BA: English/ Creative writing graduate diplomas in Education and Instructional Technology, Post-grad diploma in PR and Honors Diploma in Broadcasting.; [occ.] Unemployed; [memb.] Leicester Dramatic Society, Little Theatre, Leicester since 1991; [oth. writ.] Presently, working on "Dorset Street", a two act play. Of course, other poems on the occasional short story.; [pers.] Inner aloneness allows the heart to speak with the might of the pen. The mind simply interprets the passion.; [a.] Leicester, Leicestershire, LE3 7FE

DALE, KATHLEEN
[pen.] Kath Dale; [b.] September 14, 1920, Cheshire; [p.] Deceased; [m.] Deceased, April 5, 1941; [ch.] Wendy Jones, Peter Dale; [ed.] Retired S.E.N.; [occ.] Retired; [hon.] State Enrolled Nurse; [oth. writ.] One poem accepted for the hospital magazine where I trained.; [pers.] My poems are simple and helped by events in life in general; [a.] Rhosybol-Amlwell, Gwynedd, LL68 9PT

DALTON, ARTHUR CHARLES
[b.] September 29, 1919, Cleethorpes; [p.] John Henry Dalton, Ethel Dalton; [m.] Constance Dalton (Frith), June 8, 1940; [ch.] Colin, Graham, Simon; [ed.] Elliston St. Elementary School Cleethorpes, Lincs; [occ.] Retired Inspector, Trade Joiner Construction Ind.; [memb.] Local Conservative of Sequence Dance Clubs in the Scunthorpe Area; [hon.] Pass English Literature Adult Education, City and Guilds Construction Passes Pre 39-45 War; [oth. writ.] Several short stories 1 adventure novel (none yet accepted) 5 poems (not yet submitted); [pers.] I enjoy writing poems and stories. This has been more for my own satisfaction, watching other person's faces, attitudes, sometimes gives an inspiration to write. As shown in my submitted poem.; [a.] Doncaster, S. Yorkshire, DN1 2LD

DANCE, BARBARA H.
[b.] April 14, 1951, Sutton Colfield, England; [p.] Stan and Joan Jones (Sister Jennifer); [m.] Phillip, April 6, 1985; [ch.] Simon, James, Catherine-Jayne; [ed.] Parkfield Comprehensive. Later Qualifying as a State. Enrolled Nurse at New Cross. Enrolled Nurse at the New Royal and New Cross, Hospitals Wton; [occ.] Housewife (also trained nurse); [oth. writ.] Only poetry ever done before was awarded a prize for excellency in poetry (at school), other poems written, but never submitted, used for family, delight and amusement only.; [pers.] My dearest wish is to give a different and amusing edge to poetry, so in doing so I give pleasure to those reading it, and in particular to children.; [a.] Nr. Stratford-on-Avon, Warwickshire, CV35 9PJ

DANCE, MISS EUNICE
[pen.] Eunice Dance; [b.] June 13, 1911, Reading; [p.] Mr. Sydney Christopher and Mrs. Eunice, Eva, Agnes Dance; [ed.] Grovelands Comprehensive School, W. Reading; [occ.] Retired Nurse Housekeeper; [oth. writ.] A number of short poems and one longer work.; [pers.] My writings usually have a family background. Looking back with gratitude and inspiration for the future.; [a.] Reading, Berkshire, RG1 6HT

DARBY, RITA
[b.] October 1, 1944, Ilford; [p.] Frank and Marg Chandler; [m.] Mike Darby, July 3, 1965; [ch.] Amanda and Matthew; [ed.] Ilford County High, Essex University; [occ.] English Teacher, Chelmsford County High for Girls; [hon.] BA (Hons) Psycholinguistics PGCE (Cambridge); [pers.] I write on subjects that have been important and of significance in my life. This poem I dedicate to Joe.; [a.] Rayne, Essex, CM7 5BT

DARBYSHIRE, NORAH
[pen.] Estelle Thomas (Novels Only); [b.] July 27, 1929, Wigan; [p.] Thomas Roberts, Esther Roberts; [m.] Harry Darbyshire, February 23, 1949; [ch.] Glyn and Pamela; [ed.] Westhoughton Parochial and Westhoughton High, Left School at 14 went to Work in a Manufacturing Chemist in W'Houghton; [occ.] Retired; [memb.] Bolton Evening News Club, Left the M.G. at the age of 23 to have my first child, Pamela. Four years later my son, Glyn was born. Did several part time jobs. While the children were small. I worked at the Metal Box Company in the Drawing Office Print Room for 17 years making the blue prints from the Draughtsmen. When I was made redundant in 1981. I began to write.; [oth. writ.] I have written 2 novels my agent is Canadian My first novel was accepted for publication by Amar Publishing Manchester but went out of business at the beginning of the recession.; [pers.] I have four granddaughter and one grandson, Thomas aged 6 my eldest granddaughter Claire is 19. My favorite authors are, Emile Zola, Honori-Balza, Harry Gole a present day author.; [a.] Westhoughton, Lancs, BL5 2HN

DAVENPORT, PAULINE
[pen.] Paula Dee; [b.] September 4, 1960, Shrewsbury; [p.] Anita and Bryan Davenport; [ch.] Matthew aged 41/2 yrs; [ed.] 8 C.S.E. grade 1 and 2 passes, at, Charlton Comprehensive, Wellington, Telford, Shropshire; [occ.] Single Mom, and Part-time Sales Assistant; [oth. writ.] Various other poems, none published yet!; [pers.] I find when I'm re reflecting, on life, I release my feelings in a poem, I find it very relaxing, the written word has more impact, than the spoken word; [a.] Telford, Shropshire, TF1 3NS

DAVIDSON, MR. JOHN FRANCIS
[pen.] Scotty; [b.] April 26, 1942, Aberdeen; [p.] Mrs. W. C. Geddes; [m.] Doreen Chalmers, October 26, 1974; [ch.] Stepson - Gary; [ed.] No higher; [memb.] Meca Bingo; [hon.] Saved 2 boys life's from a carbon monoxide calle in England 1973; [oth. writ.] Doreen Tattered Chair, Just All Alone, Picture On The Wall, My Heart Is On The Fire, Just As You Are; [a.] Clydebank, G81 1JN

DAVIDSON, MARY
[b.] May 14, 1982, Blackburn; [p.] Mr. and Mrs. R. K. Ware; [ed.] Student of Beardwood High School; [memb.] Drama Club, (Red-Brick House Singing Club, Art Club; [hon.] Swimming Awards, Dancing Trophies and Certificates, Chosen to Represent A Review Book Panel Inc.: Debates at B/Burn and Cutheroe Library Lifesaving; [oth. writ.] Poem Published in 'Write And Shine,' and several poems published in Lancashire Evening Telegraph.; [a.] Blackburn, Lancashire, BB1 8JA

DAVIES, DAVID WILLIAM
[pen.] Dai Blaina; [b.] January 24, 1920, Resolven; [p.] Thomas James Davies and Elizabeth Mary Davies; [m.] Doreen Mary Jones, January 17, 1947; [ch.] four sons; [ed.] Council School Resolven and evening classes; [occ.] Retired N.C.B. Deputy Overman, Resolven Royal British Legion; [memb.] Neath Constitutional Club, Cor Meibion De Cymill since 1982; [hon.] Letter from queen for civil defence, Certificate from the Royal British Legion for sixteen years as sick visitor, County Committee; [oth. writ.] Several poems published in church magazines and choir news sheet; [pers.] When I retired in 1980 I said I would be never bored. I do not call my work poetry; my education being limited, I call all my work "playing with words".; [a.] Neath, Glamorgan, SA11 4BG

DAVIES, DENNIS N.
[b.] February 20, 1937, West Bromwich; [p.] Edith and William Edward Davies; [m.] Marie Therese; [ch.] Jason Darren (son) and Michelle (daughter-in-law) and grand daughter Emma; [occ.] Having worked for the last 30 years at GKN Sankey in Telford as a Production worker, served with the British Army in Egypt and Tripoli 1955-57 as a driver in the RASC attached 35 FLD AMB; [oth. writ.] Took to writing poetry in 1994, when William pet dog and good companion for 15 years died, Willie was a Tibetan terrier got so upset to put feeling on paper and wrote a poem called Goodbye Friend published by Anchor Books Title Anchor Lines; [pers.] Friends and neighbors reading poems urged Dennis to enter a contest run by the International Poets Society, became excited when learned they were going to Published poem Inner Peace.

DAVIES, DENNIS N.
[b.] February 20, 1937, West Bromwich; [p.] Edith and Edward Davies; [m.] Marie Therese; [ch.] Jason Darren (son) and Michelle (daughter-in-law) and grand daughter Emma; [occ.] Having worked for the last 30 years at GKN Sankey in Telford as a Production worker; [oth. writ.] Took to writing poetry in 1994, when William pet dog and good companion for 15 years died, Willie a Tibetan Terrier got so upset to put feeling on paper and wrote a poem called Goodbye Friend published by Anchor Books Title Anchor Lines.; [pers.] Friends and neighbors reading poems urged Dennis to enter a contest run by the International Poets Society, became excited when leaned was going to Published poems Inner Peace.

DAVIS, ALAN
[b.] June 9, 1940, Windsor; [p.] Eileen and Thomas Davis; [m.] Janice Mary Davis, May 14, 1988; [ed.] Secondary Modern; [occ.] Local Government Officer, with Emergency Planning; [memb.] Emergency Planning Society, National Association of Retired Police Officers formerly Superintendent with Thames Valley Police; [oth. writ.] NIL; [pers.] My wife is my inspiration; [a.] Sonning Common, Oxon, RG4 9TS

DAVIS, DOREEN
[pen.] Doreen Davis; [b.] July 12, 1925, London; [p.] Elizabeth, Frank Norris; [m.] Harry, February 28, 1947; [ch.] Three; [ed.] Little Ilford High School 10 Level - B (Taken at Night School English Grammar); [occ.] Retired; [memb.] Help the aged Newhaven Women's Institute; [hon.] See Education Above; [oth. writ.] Many short stories sold to magazines. WI Poetry (Just to be read at special party).; [pers.] "Acceptance"; [a.] Peacehaven, Sussex, BN10 7RB

DAVIS, HOWARD STANLEY ERLE
[b.] May 21, 1930, Wolverhampton; [p.] Albert Edward Davis, Eileen Emily Davis; [m.] Ursula Mary Davis (Nee Foster), July 4, 1953; [ch.] Christopher Philip - Mary Elizabeth; [ed.] Brewood Grammar School; [occ.] Retired; [oth. writ.] My other interest is writing lyrics and putting them to my music.; [pers.] Never look back; [a.] Bewdley, Worcs, DY12 1AG

DAW, HANNAH CLAUDIA
[b.] August 28, 1975, Maidstone; [p.] Robert and Janet Daw; [ed.] Maidstone Grammar School, 1993 Norwich University: studying English and American Literature. At the moment studying American Literature at the University of Eugene, Oregon. This includes studying creative writing under Robert Long (Poet) and producing a dissertation on Native American Literature.; [oth. writ.] A poem entitled: Me "Half Cracked" published in `Expo' (a collection of New Writing from Norwich.); [a.] Maidstone, Kent, ME17 4NJ

DAWES, LILY
[pen.] Lily Dawes; [b.] May 29, 1929, Wales; [m.] 1950; [ch.] Two; [occ.] Housewife; [hon.] Some poems published; [oth. writ.] Poems; [a.] Senghenyo, Glam S. Wales, CF8 2HW

DAWSON, MR. PHILLIP N.
[pen.] Phil D.; [b.] August 25, 1959, Stone-on-Trent; [p.] John and Sylvia Dawson; [m.] Jacqueline Elizabeth, August 25, 1989; [ch.] Philip, Bernadette, Tina, Louise, Wayne, Daz; [ed.] Berry Hill High; [occ.] Ceramic Placer; [oth. writ.] 10 other poems published in separate anthologies, best known of these being, C.S.A., published in Heebie-Jeebies vow to Jacqueline, pub: in obsessions Christmas time, pub: in writer words; [pers.] My family and the fears and dreams of everyday life are all contributing factors to the majority of my writing.; [a.] Stoke-on-Trent, Staffs, ST3 6OF

DE GABRIELLE, MR. PATRICK THOMAS C
[pen.] 'De Artin'; [b.] August 29, 1946, Doncaster, Yorkshire; [p.] Joseph and Mary de Gabrielle; [m.] Meg de Gabrielle, March 14, 1969; [ch.] Maria, Sharon, Sharna, Charis, Lara, Michelle; [ed.] Negligble, Worked from the age of fourteen. Presently completing an a level English literature course at North Devon College, Barnstaple, N. Devon; [occ.] Became disabled October 1994, after a series of back injuries, was a multi-tradesman; [hon.] None yet, but I live in hope. I have been invited to continue onto a literary degree course, on the strength of my present work.; [oth. writ.] Since September of 1995 I have written seventeen other poems, and am now writing at least one a week. Some are memories of life as a child, others are more contemporary and inspirational.; [pers.] One of my greatest influences is without doubt Thomas Hardy, my driving force when writing, is to share lifes moments, of joy or pain in a universal style that can be identified and made personal to the reader.; [a.] Wrafton, N. Devon, EX33 2DS

DERBYSHIRE, J. L.
[b.] April, 12, Liverpool; [ed.] Archbishop Blanch (of E. High School, Accreditation (Continuing Education) courses at Liverpool University; [occ.] Civil Servant, Health 8 Safety Executive (HSE); [memb.] Dead Good Poets, Alternative Identity Theatre Company; [oth. writ.] Several poems read art on local radio stations, play last in thoughts of paradise to be performed at the Unity Theatre Liverpool in June; [a.] Liverpool, Merseyside, L8 9UU

DERX, HENRY CHARLES
[pen.] Harry Derx; [b.] September 21, 1921, London; [p.] Henry Derx, Emily Derx; [m.] Doris Audrey Langdale, September 1947; [ch.] Beryl, Peter, Stephen, Linda; [ed.] Atkinson Road Junior Technical School, Newcastle upon Tyne; [occ.] Semi Retired; [oth. writ.] Various poems published in other anthologies; [pers.] I find creative work very satisfying; [a.] Hatfield, Herts, AL9 7NB

DEWEY, MRS. JANE
[b.] June 8, 1961, Patridge Green, Sussex; [p.] Mr. and Mrs. Carter; [m.] I am a widow, February 10, 1979; [ch.] 3; [ed.] Art CSE - O Level, English CSE - O Level, Math CSE, Biology ER; [occ.] At home looking after my 3 children. Since I lost my husband from terminal cancer going back to college Sept to do G.M.VQ in; [memb.] Health and Social Care working with the terminals ill. I am helping St. Barnabas in fund raising events, to fill my spare time. We have set a fishing Memorial Trophy in my husband's name, event for fishing takes place every year. I want to be able to help cancer research and Hospices who give so much help and time to people like my husband.; [oth. writ.] I have been writing poetry since my husband died. I have sent in to you two other poems Love Divine and Living On The Edge Of A Dream. March and April entry's. Awaiting to hear from you on these.; [pers.] Poetry has helped me to express the two years of suffering. My husband had a very rare cancer. I nursed him by myself, with the guidance from St. Barnabas Hospice Durrington. I also have three young children we have been through a lot. I have also gone back to painting and friends and family are impressed with my work. I also aim to carry on looking after terminal ill patience.; [a.] Durrington, West Sussex, BN13 2SP

DIANE, BELL
[pen.] Diane John; [b.] March 2, 1940, London; [p.] David and Pricilla John; [ch.] Angela - Tony; [ed.] Coleridge Road Secondary School for girls; [occ.] Retired Lollipop Lady; [a.] Sheffield, Yorkshire, SI3 8HA

DICK, MALCOLM PATTERSON
[b.] November 24, 1950, Glasgow; [p.] Margaret and James Dick (Deceased); [m.] Val, May 17, 1974; [ch.] One Boy and Two Girls; [ed.] Glenwood and John St. Secondary Schools - Jordanhill College (Strathclyde University - Youth and Community Work; [occ.] Unemployed; [oth. writ.] Several poems published in the recent Glasgow and Strathclyde poetry anthology (publications).; [pers.] I strive to write poetry which has a spiritual uplifting aspect. It seems to me that the higher nature of people needs to be regularly nourished with words which provide them with hope and comfort - even humour.; [a.] Glasgow, G31 2PR

DITCHMAN, DENISE ANN
[pen.] Dee Ditchman; [b.] January 17, 1959, London; [p.] William Ditchman, Sylvia Ditchman; [ed.] Mandeville Comprehensive School Edmonton, London N9; [occ.] Supervisor Manufacturing Plant (Ford Motor Co); [hon.] Education - O' levels various awards for company; [oth. writ.] Several poems published (mostly when I was around 15/16 years of age.) Book title - 'Poems Immortal.'; [pers.] I find emotions flow much easier from my pen. The words I write are not words I could speak.; [a.] Edmonton, London, Middx, N9 0EF

DIXON, C. J.
[b.] April 16, 1930, Nr Edinburgh; [p.] Vernon Triggs and Ethel Triggs; [m.] John Dixon, November 13, 1976; [ch.] (Previous marriage) Pauline Wheeler and Professor Peter Wheeler; [occ.] Supply now a teacher. (Retired 1994), full time teaching for 42 years. (20 years at last school, St. Nicholas, Old Harlow Essex); [memb.] Soloist at churches in area, for many years and also have spoken at my women's meetings (Church). (Played organ at chapel also for many years.); [oth. writ.] Composed an Easter hymn for Anglia Television competition, music and lyrics (recommended).; [pers.] Have only started writing poems since I retired.; [a.] Harlow, Essex, CM18 6AG

DOBSON, GEORGE WALTER
[pen.] George Montgomery; [b.] September 20, 1927, Darlington; [p.] George Walter and Lavinia Dobson; [m.] Jean Mary, (2nd marriage, previous spouse died of cancer September 25, 1994), December 29, 1995; [ch.] Two stepchildren; [ed.] Elementary and Technical College and Private School for Shorthand; [occ.] Retired Accountant - semi senior; [memb.] English Heritage, also won 'National' award for 'Recruiting' the most members of English Heritage out of over 200 English Heritage Properties; [hon.] Poems accepted and printed in local newspapers - also "English Heritage" magazines. Won a literary first prize through local newspapers Junior School Competition; [oth. writ.] Over 170 each everyone demands to be read - they vary from happy-go-lucky. Sad and serious comment on the state of our 20th century world - other qualify as light verse.; [pers.] A poems an artistic expression of mind. Relaxing to read, and so help you unwind. It can be inspired by a beautiful scene. An unusual happening. Or events that have been. It's a collection of symbols written in rhyme. For all to enjoy whatever the time 'tis hoped what is said. Will strike up a chord. And awaken memories. Your mind has long stored. It's aim to enlighten. Bring joy from it's verse. Reflecting on things. Real and diverse. Saying what is felt - when truly inspired can only be helpful. Tho' not always admired.; [a.] York, N. Yorks, Y03 9UL

DOCHERTY, MRS. ELIZABETH
[b.] September 21, 1935, Port Glasgow; [m.] Widow (George), November 11, 1958; [ch.] Six; [occ.] Housewife; [hon.] 12 poems. Published by triumph house. One by anchor books

DOCHERTY, MARGARET
[pen.] Quentin Ray; [occ.] Artist Painting in oils; [hon.] Some years ago had my picture taken by the local paper - beside a painting that was highly praised; [a.] Motherwell, Lanarkshire, ML1 1YR

DOIG, GILLIAN
[b.] June 26, 1980, Forfar, Scotland; [p.] Richard Doig, June Doig; [ed.] Wellbrae Primary School, Forfar Academy; [occ.] Pupil at Forfar Academy; [memb.] Forfar Youth Dramatic Society; [hon.] Merit certificates for first, second and third year at the Academy. Burns certificate for Recitation; [oth. writ.] An article published in a teenage magazine, (fast forward); [pers.] I wrote the poem "Where Is God" at school, as we were discussing genocide and were asked to submit a poem.; [a.] Forfar, Angus, DD8 3JN

DONOVAN, ANGELA
[b.] November 22, 1964, Scotland; [m.] David Hallsworth; [occ.] Currently Studying Information Technology; [memb.] Northampton Theatre and Northampton Jazz Club; [pers.] I believe that poetry is the art of self-expression. As a poet I get my greatest inspiration from my own personal metamorphosis.; [a.] Northampton, Northamptonshire, NN5 6PP

DOOLAN, LYDIA
[pen.] Jackie Casey, Gemma Gill; [b.] November 25, 1983, Galway; [p.] Breege and Colin Doolan; [ed.] Primary School; [hon.] All-Ireland Champion for Handball and Community games; [pers.] I wrote this because my grandad died, and I wrote my feelings on a page because that's how I deal with deaths and other things that depresses me.; [a.] Roscommon, Roscommon

DOUGLAS, BARBARA
[pen.] Ah-Oon (Tepid); [b.] June 30, 1938, Withington, Manchester; [p.] William Ford, Lilly Warren; [ch.] Two born in Kuala Lumpur/Malaysia; [pers.] I wish to dedicate this poem to my two pretty Eurasian daughters. Lay Toh (Pretty leaf) and Lay Heoh (Pretty peach); [a.] Worthing, West Sussex, BN11 2DQ

DOUGLAS, PADDY
[b.] September 23, 1969, Ballymoney; [p.] Margaret and Patsy Douglas; [ed.] Our Lady of Lourdes High School, Ballymoney; [occ.] Self-employed, Tattoo Artist: Own Studio; [oth. writ.] "So Hard To Find Peace of Mind": A poem published by Arrival Press in a compilation called "First Time Out".; [pers.] We do not inherit the earth from our ancestors, we borrow it from our children. (Quote from Native American Writing.); [a.] Ballymoney, Antrim, BT53 6PT

DOWD, MISS LUCY JAYNE
[pen.] Lucy Jayne Dowd; [b.] May 27, 1975, London; [p.] William Dowd, Anne Dowd; [m.] Gary John Down (partner); [ch.] Billy John Down; [ed.] Holy Family College; [occ.] Housewife; [hon.] 1st prize in singing competition and 2nd in the finals 1992; [oth. writ.] Nothing published, I do write alot of poems although this is the first one I have ever sent off; [pers.] I strive to reflect my very own personal feelings into the poems I write as shown in the poem I dedicated to my mum following a very serious illness seven years ago. (I am overjoyed to have my special poem published); [a.] Epping, Essex, CM16 5AL

DOWDING, ANN
[pen.] Ann Dowding; [b.] May 13, 1941, Maidenhian, Berkshires; [p.] William and Elizabeth Kennedy; [m.] Windowed, husband Charles, 2nd Marriage 1971; [ch.] David and Shirley; [ed.] Magdalene Rd Primary, SW.18, Swafford Rd SW.18, Upper Yooting; [occ.] Part time Secretary; [oth. writ.] Nothing published but quit lots of poems on notebooks and in my head.; [pers.] Started writing poetry when I was 10, was discouraged by my father who thought I day dreamed too much, started writing poetry for friends since my husband died, work to sudden inspiration; [a.] Brixton, London, 5DT

DOWDING, MARGARET DOROTHY
[b.] July 24, 1928, Weymouth, Dorset; [p.] William and Oliver Palmer; [m.] Albert Dowding (2nd Marriage), April 8, 1979; [ch.] Christine, Miriam, William and Faith (the latter Twins); [ed.] Secondary - Technical College; [occ.] Secretary - Receptionist General Factotum - Veterinary Surgeons.; [memb.] 15 yrs. Bath Literary Society (Secretary 3 yrs.) - 30 yrs. Amateur Theatrical Groups, Solo Singer. 42 yrs. with the Vet, employing the pleasure and care of animals.; [oth. writ.] Over the years, Anthologies, Local Paper, Magazine items, Parish Magazine.; [pers.] My writing is simply a spontaneous reaction to some event or emotion, which I feel can relate to other people. I come from a seafaring family where events be quite dramatic.; [a.] Saltford, Bristol, Bath and North East Somerset, BS18 3JE

DOWN, GEOFFREY PAUL WILEY
[pen.] Paul Wiley; [b.] February 15, 1937, Burgess Hill, Sussex; [p.] Harold and Ethel Down; [m.] Rhoda Down, August 18, 1965; [ch.] Helen Down, Martin Down; [ed.] Brighton, Hove and Sussex Grammar School; [occ.] Retired School Master; [pers.] Died March 28, 1996; [a.] Bexhill, Sussex, TN39 3QE

DOYLE, GEORGE
[pen.] Charles Duffy; [b.] March 31, 1941, Liverpool; [p.] Edward Doyle, Kathleen Doyle; [m.] Divorced, March 27, 1979; [ed.] Liverpool Collegiate; [occ.] Dry Stone Dyker; [oth. writ.] Adult novel series children's stories articles for local newspaper several poems published anthologies.; [pers.] I like writing. I fill can assist, amuse or motivate others then that is an added bonus.; [a.] Co. Balvicar, Isle of Seil, Argyll, PA34 4TE

DRAGOONIS, PETER
[b.] November 9, 1927, Glasgow; [p.] Pauline and Joseph; [m.] Margaret Hughes, January 30, 1994; [ch.] Linda, Peter, Brian and Alison; [ed.] Sacred Heart, Bridgeton Glasgow, SE; [occ.] Retired, Painter and Poet; [oth. Writ.] The Time And The Pain

DRAKE, JACQUELINE
[b.] June 29, 1962, Newton Abbot; [p.] Edward Peter Bearn Dermer (Deceased), Melinda Dermer; [m.] David Edward Drake, October 4, 1994; [ch.] Lucy Ann Honeywill and Shane Anthony Honeywill - from a previous marriage; [ed.] Coombeshead Comprehensive; [occ.] Cashier; [memb.] Neighborhood Watch, Co-ordinator for Helston Close; [oth. writ.] I have written other poems, and stories for my two children, none of which have been published. This poem is my first publication.; [pers.] I write on a personal level, from the heart, whenever the inspiration takes me.; [a.] Paignton, Devon, TQ3 3SQ

DREWETT, DAVID
[b.] November 22, 1945, Chatham; [p.] Harry and Gladys Drewett; [m.] Rita Drewett, May 16, 1970; [ch.] Jason age 21; [ed.] Secondary Modern; [occ.] Licence Trade Consultant; [memb.] Society of Life; [hon.] Just to be alive; [oth. writ.] Entries in charity magazines; [pers.] To share my innermost thoughts through my poetry, makes me feel I have a million friendly eyes and ears.; [a.] Tenterden, Kent, TN30 6DQ

DRURY, ROSINAN
[pen.] As a child my father called me Tiger; [b.] Older Generation Paddington, London; [p.] Herbert Dixon, Rosaneha Dixon; [m.] Norman Drury, April; [ch.] Carole Ann, Christopher Nonan Francis; [ed.] St Edwards Convent, Maryledone - London; [occ.] Housewife - come gardener general home comforter; [memb.] Garden Centre Club; [hon.] Poem runner up in the RSPE/BBC Radio Bedfordshire Countryside Campaign Competition. Judges extremely impressed with entry, awarded book on drawing birds, Won videos Ect. for phone in Comp's from BBC Radio Beds; [oth. writ.] A poem published in local paper - poems read out over radio, Bedfordshire. I have

written true short stories from my own experiences - these I've just filed; [pers.] I have a great sense of all things having feelings - and respond to me, even the trees and flowers, I know God gave me the gift of poetry to ease the - heart that broke so many times - when suffering came.; [a.] Dunstable, Bedfordshire, LU5 4SU

DUNNING, JAMES WELSH
[b.] May 27, 1928, Scotland; [m.] Mona, November 22, 1947; [ch.] 1 girl, 3 boys; [ed.] Left school 14; [occ.] Retired; [oth. writ.] Many, many more, My Prayer, A Visit Home, Winter, Ireland, Mona To Name A Few; [pers.] My poem was written to my wife on our 48th wedding anv., so I'd like it to be to Mona this has been the first chance for me to get one in print never tried before. I like burns.; [a.] Ferrybridge, York, WF11 8NV

DURRANT, MRS. DOROTHY JOY
[pen.] Dorothy Durrant; [b.] July 4, 1936, Rotting, Dean; [p.] Frances and Leonard Geall; [m.] James William Durrant, March 11, 1961; [ch.] Geoffrey, Gregory, Rachel, Christopher; [ed.] Holy Cross Parochial School, then - Greggs Secretarial College; [occ.] Housewife; [memb.] Baptist Church; [oth. writ.] "Two Wonderful Words", "A Winters Day", "New Years Resolution", "No Chocolate" all published by Anchor Books; [pers.] God is so good and has given us so much to enjoy - poetry is one way of expressing my thankfulness to Him and to give pleasure to others.; [a.] Eastbourne, E. Sussex, BN23 8HP

DUTTON, IRENE
[b.] December 24, 1913, Painthorpe, Kilburn; [p.] Bert Kilburn, Alice Maud; [m.] Ernest Dutton, May 3, 1934; [ch.] 1 boy and 1 girl; [ed.] Elementary School; [occ.] O.A.P. but I do a lot of voluntary work; [hon.] Community Service award from Rotary Club 1993; [oth. writ.] Had poem and recipe published in church magazine and poem in bingo news; [pers.] Mostly about friends and asking people to help and be kind and respect others, I have written some in Broad Yorkshire.; [a.] Wakefield, W. Yorks, WF2 7ST

DUTTON, REBECCA
[b.] April 13, 1964, Chester; [p.] Bernard and Kathleen Dutton; [ed.] Christleton High School, Chester I.M. Marsh P.E. College Liverpool; [occ.] P.E. Teacher, South Wirral High School - Wirral; [oth. writ.] Personal bereavement poems - written in memory of the diseased or through their eyes.; [pers.] I write numerous poetry based on my life and the experiences I've had but feeling loss through bereavement touched my rawest nerves.; [a.] Chester, Cheshire, CW6 9TA

DYKA-GERARD, ROZARYA
[b.] May 30, 1947, Alfeld Leine, Germany; [p.] Waclaw Dyka, Maria Dyka (Polish); [m.] John Watt (Scottish), December 27, 1968; [ed.] Dinamt (Belgium) Institut Notre Dame, Champion (Belgium) Ecole Normale Moyenne (Catholic Convent School) Equiv. of Teachers Training College for Sciences-Geography; [occ.] Owner of Marriage and Friendship Bureau; [memb.] Writers' Group in Stuartfield, Scotland, A.B.E. Scotland (Adult Basic Education), Inner Peace Movement (IPM), Writers Group in Peterhead, Scotland, M.E. Arts Club; [oth. writ.] Several poems published in 2 local writers' group booklets and 1 local prison magazine; [pers.] I always write rhyming verses not free verses. As rhymes come naturally to me. All of poets are written in stanzas. I love metaphysical poetry concerned with the problems of the nature of the universe and man's place in life. I am influenced by French poetry.; [a.] Peterhead, Aberdeenshire, AB42 4UJ

EARLEY, E. J.
[b.] February 13, 1938, Nottinghamshire; [p.] Deceased; [ed.] Sydenham County Grammar School for girls; [occ.] Retired Civil Servant; [memb.] By Fleet Ladies Bowls Club; [oth. writ.] Nothing published yet, but I live in hope!; [pers.] I hope my work will go some way towards encouraging people to give animals the respect they deserve within our society.; [a.] Woking, Surrey, GU22 8TW

EDGE, EMMA
[b.] January 10, 1977, Isle of Man; [ed.] Ballasalla Primary. Castle Rushen High School. Attending Nene College, Northampton in September 1996; [occ.] A level student (English Lang, English Lit, General Student); [memb.] Mount Murrey Health Club, Isle of Man Karate Federation; [hon.] 9 G.C.S.E.'s Stages 2,3,4,5 in S.A.I.L. (Standard attainment in literature); [a.] Ballasalla, Isle of Man, IM9 2DD

EDWARDS, JESSIE
[b.] July 6, 1917, Wakefield; [p.] Arthur and Lily Arran; [m.] Frank Edwards (Deceased), July 23, 1949; [ch.] Avril and Catherine; [ed.] Thornes House Girls, Secondary School Wakefield; [occ.] Housewife; [memb.] St. Helen's Church of England Sandal Magna, Wakefield; [hon.] Matriculation Certificate, (Northern Universities) Several Musical Examinations; [oth. writ.] Many poems, stories, pantomimes and plays for Church productions.; [pers.] Church pianist and organist to 1992, my poems seems to come to me with no conscious thought. Most are sad, serious or nostalgic, with a few humorous ones here and there to show I have a funny side to me/somewhere.; [a.] Wakefield, West Yorkshire, WF1 5BJ

ELLIOT, LORRAINE
[b.] February 25, 1967, Greenwich, London; [p.] Robert Elliot, Bridget Teresa Couch; [ed.] Currently studying at Greenwich University for BA Hons in Humanities due to qualify in June '98; [occ.] Student; [oth. writ.] Have written several poems, all for personal pleasure. Currently working on my own personal Anthology.; [pers.] My poetry is mostly written from personal experiences. I hope that reading my work will enable people to relate to personal circumstances that occur in life, any my poetry may offer some form solace.; [a.] Greenwich, London, SE12 7ND

ELLIOTT, CAROL
[b.] March 16, 1969, Little Thorpe Hospital; [p.] Mary and Harry Stevenson; [m.] David Elliott; [ed.] Yohden Hall, Comprehensive Horden and Blackhall, Co. Durham; [occ.] Packer-Crisp Factory; [memb.] G.M.B. Union; [oth. writ.] Just my own personal writings not yet published; [pers.] Dedicated to Aunty Brenda and Uncle Robert, worlds apart yet always remembered. I like to think my poems reflect on life and feelings that sometimes can't be shown.; [a.] Seaham, Durham

ELLIOTT, MRS. IVY M.
[b.] December 5, 1924, Birmingham; [m.] Widow, December 8, 1944; [pers.] Attempts Writing Panto's and plays down the years I have to smile I've made it!; [a.] Kinmel Bay-Rhyl, Clwyd, LL18 5LR

ELLIS, JOSEPHINE
[pen.] Jo Ellis; [b.] May 19, 1944, Scarborough; [m.] Richard Ellis, October 24, 1964; [ch.] Three; [ed.] Secondary School; [occ.] Housewife; [oth. writ.] Couple of poems published 1st book "Jo's Secret" The Poetry New Book of Traditional verse December (1995) 2nd poem "My Black Hole" out in the spring 1996 book called "Mystical Wondering's" (out any time now).; [pers.] I strive to reflect my inner feelings in my poetry resulting from a very bad childhood. And I am proud of the results I am getting now. It has not been an easy road to travel. But feel now this is the most wonderful achievement I could have ever made.; [a.] York, Yorkshire, YO3 9DS

EMPSON, GEORGE W.
[b.] February 23, 1921, Maske, Cleveland; [p.] Deceased; [m.] Joan, 1946; [ch.] Georgie, Kathleen, Pauline, Lorna, Raymond, Sharron; [occ.] Retired; [hon.] Six naval war campaign medals; [oth. writ.] I volunteered for the navy, for the second world war, I served six years. Convoy duty and invasions of North Africa, Sicily, Italy, Yugoslavia, Sth. France.; [pers.] I wrote the poem for my loving wife, Joan; [a.] Doncaster, S. Yorkshire, DN2 6QG

EMSDEN, RICHARD
[pen.] Trickey Windrupp; [b.] December 30, 1944, Suffolk; [p.] Dorothy and Benjamin Emsden; [m.] Margaret Emsden, April 1, 1967; [ch.] Mark William and Jonathan Charles; [ed.] Hadleigh High, Cambridge University, "Indalo" - School of Higher Education; [occ.] Sales Manager, Southern Counties; [memb.] Hadleigh Operatic, Dramatic Society, Grosvenor Clubs, Globe Industrials Clubs, Rabbi Burns Apprelition Society, (Yorkshire District); [hon.] Computer Programming (with Honours), Computer Programming (Degree), Diploma at "Stock Management" (Merit); [oth. writ.] Various poems published in a variety of magazines. i.e. People Friend, Golfing Monthly; [pers.] I endeavour to bring an element of humour and light-heartedness in my writings in the hope that it will bring a smile to the face of the reader. I owe my talent to my very best friend - Ian Fleming.; [a.] Ipswich, Suffolk, IP7 7BG

ENNIS, JOSEPH JOHN
[pen.] Joe Ennis; [b.] February 14, 1945, Liverpool; [p.] Jimmy Ennis, Ellen Ennis; [m.] Susan Ennis (Divorced), January 18, 1975; [ch.] Claire Suzanne, Joseph James, James George, Louise, Cheryl; [ed.] Our Lady of Mount Carmel Comprehensive School; [occ.] Home Carer; [hon.] At 17 I entered and successfully passed the Fairbridge Farming Training Course, Sponsterred by the Canadian government with view to emigrate Canada 1962. Liverpool; [oth. writ.] Have written many poems but have not submitted them for publication; [pers.] I'd like to dedicate my writings and poetry to the inspiration behind them, a Miss Thelma Bates.; [a.] Liverpool, Merseyside

ESGATE, PAMELA
[b.] January 10, 1928, Bombay, India; [p.] Arthur and Dorothy Benfold; [m.] William Esgate, June 18, 1949; [ed.] Presentation Convent Kodai Kanal South India, Cathedral Bombay India; [occ.] Retired Civil Servant; [memb.] Local Church Choir, Worple Art Group, Wimbledon, Exhibiting three times a year; [hon.] Highly Commended in a Nationwide Art Competition Held in Bath.; [oth. writ.] Several poems published in India. Recent poem published by Triumph House in book entitled, "Expressions of Faith", title of poem "Our Gift"; [pers.] I try to reflect the gifts that God has given me through my poetry and art.; [a.] Worcester Park, Surrey, KT4 7AE

ETHERINGTON, PHILIP J.
[b.] September 3, 1978, Chelmsford, Essex; [p.] Catherine and Edward Etherington; [ed.] Great Baddow High School; [occ.] A-Level Student (History and Computer Studies); [oth. writ.] None writes stories for my own pleasure; [pers.] I am influenced by the works of J. R. R. Tolkien, Terry Brooks and Robert Louis Stevenson.; [a.] Chelmsford, Essex, CM2 8NY

EVANS, BRETT JAMES
[b.] December 28, 1972, St. Asaph, Clwyd; [p.] Geraint Evans, Joan Evans; [ed.] Ysgol Emrys AP Iwan, Abergele, Clwyd; [occ.] Unemployed; [hon.] Self Read Psychologist, Bar Room Philosopher, A-Level Unnecessary Sarcasm; [oth. writ.] This short poem will be my first publication, though I do hope to have other work, someday, noticed I.E. other poems and short stories.; [pers.] Although most of my work reflects the darker side of human essential in accepting this outlook.; [a.] Abergele, Clwyd, LL22 7HW

EVANS, MAUREEN GENTRY
[pen.] Maureen Gentry Evans; [b.] May 11, 1947, Woking, Surrey; [p.] Joseph and Catherine Gentry Evans; [m.] Victor Jasso Evans, May 1, 1987; [ch.] Mark, Caroline, David Rosinski; [ed.] Marist Convent at West Byfleet, Surrey Rowley Bristow Hospital Pyrford, West Byfleet, Surrey; [occ.] Writing Ceramics; [memb.] Poetry Now - Woodston, Peterborough; [oth. writ.] Poem "Winds Of Change", published in a little gnome poem. Poetry Now: Central 1996 Regional Anthologies.; [pers.] My dearest wish is for my little gnome poems, about the environment, homelessness, elderly and American Indian, to be read by our young, to see through the eyes of my little gnomes adventures, what we are doing to this planet as our future is in there hands.; [a.] Luton, Bedfordshire, LU4 9DY

EVANS, SHEELAGH
[b.] March 30, 1929, Liverpool; [p.] Thomas and Elsie Byrne; [m.] Arthur Evans, July 4, 1960; [ch.] Christine, Kathleen, Julie, Glyn, Caroline; [ed.] Won a scholarship in 1940 to Queen Mary High School, Liverpool. Left at sixteen after attaining school certificate in all subjects.; [occ.] Retirement; [oth. writ.] Various poems published by "Arrival Press" and "Anchor Books" during past three years; [pers.] A blank sheet of paper, a pen, the opportunity to express unique paragraphs or verse attributed only to the writer. Twenty six letters are the building blocks for our vocabulary, a face I find fascinating.; [a.] Winsford, Cheshire, CW7 2EE

EWART, BRENDA PATRICIA
[b.] October 14, 1949, Oxford, England; [p.] Eric Pettit, Patricia Pettit; [m.] Alan Spencer Ewart, July 6, 1989; [ch.] Kelvin Stock, Derren Stock; [ed.] Parkside Grammar School for Girls Cambridge.; [occ.] Disabled housewife.; [memb.] Osteoporosis Society, National Diabetic Association, Cambridge Disabled Access Group; [oth. writ.] 'The Cross To Bear', to be found in a book called 'Inspirations From Eastern England'.; [pers.] Since I have become disabled I have found my outlook on life and people has changed. There is more to life than material things. I find poetry very relaxing.; [a.] Sawston, Cambridge, CB2 4TB

FABO, MICHELLE OLIVIA
[b.] March 10, 1978, Birmingham; [ed.] Cardinal Wiseman R.C. School and Sutton Coldfield College of Further Education, Broadway School of Dancing, Central School of Music.; [memb.] Alexander Stadium Pulse Point Gym. Other pastime include, songwriting and travelling and socializing.; [hon.] Fourteen GCSE's, including English language and literature, and city and guilds in mathematics. Three awards won for modern dancing. Two awards won for gymnastics.; [oth. writ.] This is my first publication but I still seek publicity and recognition.; [pers.] "Love, and you will be loved! Hate, and you will be hated!"; [a.] Birmingham, West Midlands, B6 6AD

FAHY, CATHERINE MAY
[pen.] Risa Ges; [b.] Olwen and Michael Fahy; [ch.] Liza Marie; [ed.] Markeaton Girls Sec. School; [occ.] Artist/Fabric Designer; [hon.] GCE 3rd art and design ceramics a star, GCE English B., Certificate of Merit, Paint a Wildlife Subject 1994; [oth. writ.] Many songs and poems also thoughts for quiet moments.; [pers.] Look forward to each new day.

FAIRCHILD, JOYCE MARGARET
[pen.] Joy Fairchild; [b.] April 13, 1941, Surrey; [p.] Florence and Thomas Willis; [m.] Brian John Fairchild, July 30, 1960; [ch.] Four, two sons, two daughters; [ed.] Chigwell Village Primary, Kingswood Secondary Modern Chigwell; [occ.] Health Care Support Care of the Elderly (Nurse); [memb.] Poetry Now Magazine; [hon.] B-Tech N.V.Q., Care of the Elderly, Anglia Polytechnic; [oth. writ.] "Forgotten", Medicinal Verse, "Tears of Pain", Mightier than the Sword; [pers.] My inspiration comes through lifes experiences and travel.; [a.] Chelmsford, Essex, CM3 6LZ

FARROW, SUSAN
[b.] May 5, 1965, Nottingham; [p.] Josephine Gooch (Deceased), David Gooch; [m.] Antony Farrow, May 7, 1988; [ch.] Samuel Antony, Adam David Peter; [ed.] Christ The King R.C. School, Arnold, Nottingham; [occ.] B.T. Operator; [pers.] I write from the heart so that others can feel the joy and sorrows of life with me.; [a.] Trowell, Nottinghamshire, NG9 3RE

FAULDS, ANDREW THOMAS
[pen.] Kargroth; [b.] May 11, 1977, Dumfries; [p.] Stuart Faulds and Eileen McDonald; [ed.] Dreghorn Primary, Greenwood Academy, Kilmarnock College; [occ.] Student; [hon.] 2 certificates of Distinction in Religious Education; [pers.] All my life I have been fascinated by "Undeath". In my poems I try to bring out the averice and need for immortality and power in others. It is my ardent wish to let my readers look into their own secret heart and take their secret desires.; [a.] Irvine, N. Ayrshire, KA11 4DD

FAULKNER, MICHAEL
[pen.] Michael Faulkner; [b.] July 27, 1956, Seaham Harbour; [p.] Abbigail and Ronald Faulkner; [ed.] Ushaw College, Durham: Philosophy - Theology, R.N.M.H R.M.N; [occ.] Manager in Residential Care; [memb.] Poets Society, Latin Mass Society; [oth. writ.] Published in six anthologies over past year. Two pieces published in competition, Surrey Country Council; [pers.] My work seeks to show the truth which lies at the heart of experience, the vision of God in creation.; [a.] Sutton, Surrey, SM2 5JN

FEELEY, MICHAEL
[b.] August 19, 1967, Glenmavis; [p.] John and Philomena; [m.] Gillian Urquhart; [ed.] St. Andrew's And St. Margaret's (Airdrie). Roehead Mirfield. Mission Institute of London. Lime Grove School of Building; [occ.] HGV 1 Driver; [memb.] President: The Official Michael Feeley Fan Club; [hon.] To Follow; [oth. writ.] Numerous poems first novel in progress: Insured only.; [pers.] Just one smile makes life worthwhile. Be ever happy.; [a.] Airdrie, Lanarkshire, ML6 0HG

FILLERY-HANDZIC, JEANNE
[pen.] Jeanne Fillery-Handzic; [b.] January 13, 1933; [p.] Deceased: Mr. and Mrs. R. R. Fillery; [m.] Mr. Ibrahim Handzic: Divorced and Widowed., September 4, 1964; [ed.] Selhurst Grammar School, Selhurst, Croydon, Surrey. Portch's Secretarial College, Park Lane, Croydon, Surrey.; [occ.] Retired but until retirement Jan. 1993 I was a Legal Proofreader in the city.; [memb.] Founder of "The Maria Callas International Club" - founded by me: September 16, 1990 - Patron and Hon. Members: Luciano Pavarotti and Mme. Jackie Callas (Maria Callas' sister). Member of: The Bronte Society, The Dartmoor Preservation Society, The (UK) Wagner Society, The (Hugarian) Wagner Society, The Berlioz Society, The Beethoven Society, The British-Hungarian Society, The British-Hungarian Fellowship, The Pro-Motor Society, The Pavarotti Society, The Puccini Society. Founder of "The Central and Eastern European Society" - but this is currently somewhat "dormant" - future uncertain.; [hon.] I was "nominated" in the Bavarian press in about 1978 as: "Jeanne d'Arc II" - a "play on words" on my own name and for my work for their King Ludwig II of Bavaria and my defence of his reputation.; [oth. writ.] Dozens of "Letters to Editors" various newspapers. Various short articles in magazines. Reviews written in my own International Club's Magazines. Many things published in various forms in Bavaria (in German) in connection with my 25-year research into the life and death of King Ludwig II of Bavaria, also my own entry in the Bavarian Archives on King Ludwig II in Munich.; [pers.] I endeavour to improve and co-ordinate business, political and personal relationships between the "new" Eastern European countries and the "West". I also promote opera, specifically Maria Callas, I work for orphaned children in Europe. I am a great romantic, classical music, languages, Eastern Europe.; [a.] CR0 8AH

FINCH, MARIA TERESA
[b.] August 13, 1963, Warley, W. Mids; [p.] Mr. and Mrs. J. D. Cooper; [m.] Mr. Clive Finch, May 4, 1985; [ch.] Sarah-Marie, Danielle and Elizabeth; [ed.] Secondary School - Bristnal Hall High School and Bournville College of Further Education; [occ.] Wife/mother/part time student; [pers.] Appreciate all you have while you still have it, but most of all be happy and believe in yourself!; [a.] Sloak, B'Ham, W. Mids, B29 6QE

FINDLAY, RONALD MCCALLUM
[b.] March 4, 1961, Aberdeen; [p.] James Findlay, Jean Findlay; [m.] Catherine, August 6, 1990; [ch.] Shirley-Anne, Charles, and William; [ed.] Banff Academy; [occ.] Unemployed; [memb.] British Legion; [hon.] U.N. Medal Cyprus Unicef Medal; [a.] Rosyth, Fife, KY11 2JZ

FIRTH, ANNA
[b.] February 3, 1983, York; [p.] Geoffrey Firth, Vivien Firth; [ed.] Easingwold County Primary School, Burnopfield Primary School, Whickham Comprehensive School; [occ.] Pupil at Whickham Comprehensive; [pers.] My aim is to encourage and challenge people to think more about other people and happenings in the world through poetry. I also want to help them realize that they can make a difference to change this world into a better place.; [a.] Burnopfield, Newcastle-upon-Tyne, NE16 6JF

FISHER, BRIAN
[b.] April 24, 1936, Northampton; [p.] Benjamin and Kitty Fisher; [m.] Rose Fisher, September 19, 1964; [ch.] 3 girls - Wendy, Anne, Ruth; [ed.] Northampton Boys Grammar School 1947-1952 School of Life - still learning; [occ.] Self-employed, Decorator; [memb.] Automobile Association Local Church (and singers) Northants Cricket ICI Decorators Network; [hon.] GCE 0 Level Distinction; [oth. writ.] Poems for family occasions, local church parties. Poem broadcast on local radio. Contribs to readers digest (unsuccessful so far!). any random or sundry jottings!; [pers.] Happy to contribute any thoughtful, amusing or witty observations that make life more interesting.; [a.] Northampton, Northants, NN3 3EY

FITZROY, JOSEPH "TEX"
[pen.] Tex; [b.] February 9, 1954, Dominica W.I.; [p.] Edith Jermaine; [m.] Xanthe Joseph; [ch.] Lisa, Donna, Hasani; [ed.] Self-Educated in Life University; [occ.] Singer, Songwriter, Musician; [memb.] A.S.C.A.P., Music Licensing Agency; [oth. writ.] Wrote article for Forward magazine, dealing with reggae music in the U.S.A.; [pers.] I wish for mankind and womankind to enjoy nature to the fullest and to remember God is watching us all, always.; [a.] Queen, N.Y., U.S.A., 11434

FLEMING, JUNE MARY
[b.] June 28, 1938, Consett Co., Durham; [p.] Hannah and Barron Griffith Williams; [m.] Rev. William Hillis Fleming, August 25, 1965; [ch.] James Alexander, Martha Elizabeth; [ed.] Annfield Plain Sec. Mod. Consett Grammar, Shotley Bridge Gen. Hosp. Dudley Rd, Maternity Hosp. B'Ham, Forest Gate Maternity Hosp. Londoney; [occ.] Housewife and Duties Associated with being a Minister's wife; [oth. writ.] None published; [pers.] Some deeply felt feelings and thoughts are difficult to express. Eg appreciation of beauties of nature and complexities of human nature coping with living. My poems seem to be an attempt to put these thoughts into words, to help and inspire others. I think the greatest poet is the Psalmist David.; [a.] Liverpool, Merseyside, L17 2AH

FOLEY, PATRICK JOHN
[pen.] Patrick J. Foley; [b.] November 4, 1959, Carrick-on-Suir, Co. Tipperary, Eire; [p.] Eileen and Willie Foley, Father (Deceased last July); [m.] Eileen also deceased last June, April 3, 1984; [ch.] One daughter Lorraine age 9 1/2 I would like to dedicate the poem in the book to the memory of my life Eileen (Nee Hallissey) who died tragically of a brain hemorage on 13/6/95; [occ.] Laboratory Technician with Avonmore Foods, PLC, Miloko Branch, Carrick-on-Suir, Co Tipp.; [memb.] Local Athletic Club with a good interest in all sports mainly field games; [oth. writ.] Several poems published in work magazine the Milky Way and in local newspapers; [pers.] Only that I attribute any poetry writing flair I possess to my father Willie Foley R.J.P. who spent lots of time through out this life writing songs and poetry.; [Tn.] Carrick-on-Suir; [a.] Tipperary, Eire

FOLEY, PAUL
[b.] March 29, 1969, Stepney

FOLLY, JOSEPHINE
[b.] June 5, 1936, Ireland; [p.] Irish; [m.] Frank, February 24, 1984; [ed.] Convent School Orphanage, no Particular Education; [occ.] Housewife; [oth. writ.] The arrival of the plover in late winter early spring I heard the sound of rustle bells the sound so familiar the jingle of the plover they have just arrived as if to celebrate of spring.; [pers.] A spur of the moment decision to put pen to paper.; [a.] Ireland

FOOKS, EDWINA MARGARET
[b.] August 19, 1930, Bournemouth; [p.] Ivy Manning and Edward Ricketts; [m.] Roger John Fooks, February 16, 1952; [ch.] Terri Lynnette Campbell-Smith and Russell Julian Fooks; [ed.] Stourfield School; [occ.] Retired; [memb.] Ex Telegraphist; [hon.] Best Actress; [pers.] My inspiration comes from the beauty and wonder all around us and everyday happenings; [a.] Bournemouth, Dorset, BH10 6JD

FOREMAN, ALAN ALBERT
[b.] August 9, 1948, Maidstone; [p.] Albert Foreman, Edith Foreman; [m.] Fiona Mary Foreman, September 28, 1967; [ch.] Lara Christina, Estelle Marie; [ed.] Old Borough Manor Comprehensive Kent Horticultural College; [occ.] Landscape Contractor and Designer; [memb.] Ex-Serviceman's Angling Society, Whitbread Fremlin Sea Angling Club.; [hon.] National Certificates in Horticulture Management Landscape and Design.; [oth. writ.] Poems published in magazines. I write mainly war associated poems and light hearted (Amusing).; [pers.] My interests are anything to do with 2nd and 1st World War and associated writings. Art, painting in watercolor. Design of landscape areas mainly private gardens. Angling. Local history, local natural areas and conservation Horticultural Judge Produce.; [a.] Maidstone, Kent, ME16 0QB

FORSYTH, HELEN
[pen.] Belly; [b.] April 27, 1982, High Wycombe; [p.] Jill Berry - Bill Forsyth; [ed.] Wycombe High School; [occ.] Student; [pers.] Dedicated to a lovely Grampy and a thoughtful papanan.; [a.] High Wycombe, Bucks:, HP12 3PA

FOSTER, DANNY GORDON
[b.] October 10, 1942, Southwell; [p.] Ernest Foster, Annie Foster; [ed.] Manor Sec., Modern, Northampton College City and Guild 147/151 in Catering; [occ.] Head Chef, Belvedere Hotel Torquay; [memb.] N.A.F.A.S., National Association of Flower Arranging, Society, Member of Chesterfield Choral Society (Sing Tenner); [hon.] 92.4 Pass with Hon Brgad Mailing and Flour Confectionaries; [oth. writ.] Write songs composed a balard, have written a variety of poems on all topics of life; [pers.] I love life, and the beauty of our world, and try to put into words what I see and feel so others can benefit.; [a.] Chesterfield, Derbys, SL0 4SW

FOSTER, MRS. KATHLEEN
[b.] August 25, 1908, Bexhill; [p.] William Rober Lye and Goodden Lye; [m.] Edwards John Foster, August 1949; [ed.] St Josephs Convent Bexhall on Sea, Ryefore Hall Ladies College, Ryefore Glouster Shire; [occ.] Retired; [oth. writ.] Non published several have been written this is the first entry; [a.] Wisbech, Cambs, PE13 2QW

FOSTER, SYBIL GRACE
[pen.] Sybil Grace; [b.] March 26, 1934, Portsmouth; [p.] George Grace White; [m.] Reginald Foster, March 29, 1962; [ch.] Four; [ed.] Porstmouth Benificial Primary, Buriton Primary, Petersfield Secondary; [occ.] School care taker. Titchfield Primary until April 30, 1996; [pers.] I have always worked. Retiring this year at 62. I still have ambitions what I set my mind to I like to achieve. I would like to write a books of the HOP Fields including the war as a child in old Portsmouth.; [a.] Lee on Solent, Hampshire, PO13 8JP

FOULSHAM, NICOLAS JOHN
[b.] May 11, 1963, Langley, Slough, Berkshire; [p.] Sheila and Ronald Foulsham; [ed.] Marish School Langley, Langley Secondary, Langley Berks; [memb.] The Young Vic Theatre Company in 1983. The Cockpit Theatre Company in 1982; [oth. writ.] Before his death in the summer of 1994. He wrote many poems which brought to light his stark and truthful observations on life, which sadly were never published.; [pers.] I have given permission for my son Nicks. Poem it be published, they say the good die young, and in this case it was so very true, he was so special with such a loving heart, everybody loved him because he cared, about everyone and everything.; [a.] Langley, Slough, Berkshire, SL3 7QZ

FOULSHAM, TERRY
[b.] March 13, 1967, Langley, Slough; [p.] Ronald Foulsham, Sheila Foulsham; [m.] Sarah Jane Price, (Engaged) December 29, 1993; [ed.] Langley Grammar, Thames Valley University; [occ.] Architectural Technician Working in Maidenhead, Berkshire; [hon.] Building Technology O.N.C.; [oth. writ] Variety of poems about love, life, joy and pain which have never left the pages of my notebook, until now.; [pers.] My published poem 'technicolor death' is dedicated to my late brother Nick, who is much loved and much missed. "See the truth, speak from the heart and keep smiling."; [a.] Langley, Slough, Berks, SL3 7RH

FOWLER, ANNE-MARIE
[pen.] Anne-Marie Fowler; [b.] June 15, 1981, Leeds; [p.] John M. Fowler and Dawn A. Fowler; [ed.] Currently studying several GCSE courses, Brigsham Comprehensive (High) School, Allerton Bywater; [occ.] Secondary school pupil doing GCSE courses; [oth. writ.] Various stories - not published (as yet). Working at moment on full length sci-fi novel. As well as other poems and short stories.; [pers.] As a young writer I believe I have the potential to expand my abilities in to a full writing career. Given an opportunity. My enjoyment of writing I hope is reflected in this piece of work.; [a.] Leeds, West Yorkshire, LS25 7NQ

FOZZARD, TERENCE BRENDAN
[pen.] James Thomas; [b.] October 12, 1936, Queensbury, Yorkshire; [p.] Evelyn and Joseph Fozzard; [m.] Patricia, October 22, 1960; [ch.] Dawn Elizabeth, Rachel Teresa; [ed.] St. Joseph's, Halifax Yorkshire; [occ.] Joiner, Site Controller, Sindlesham School; [oth. writ.] Personal and humorous poems for friends and relations, and special occasion's; [pers.] Family man with three lovely grandchildren. A devout catholic, love of life, both in nature and human kind, are at the heart of my faith.; [a.] Wokingham, Berkshire, RG41 5DL

FRANCIS, STEVEN
[pen.] Steven Francis; [b.] August 23, 1971, Burry Port; [p.] David Francis, Susan Francis; [ed.] Stradey Comprehensive; [occ.] Writer/Playwright/Poet; [memb.] Joining The Llanely Writers Circle Soon; [oth. writ.] Four poems published in a local poetry magazine.; [pers.] I live to write, other occupations have no meaning to me. My influences include Coleridge, Ginsberg and Dylan Thomas. I write for my own pleasure, but if at the same time it pleases others, I am grateful! When I write, I create!; [a.] Burry Port, Dyfed, SA16 0AA

FRANKLIN, DEAN
[pen.] Frankie; [b.] January 6, 1969, Harpenden, Herts; [p.] Eddie and Frances Franklin; [m.] Tracey Franklin, September 1, 1990; [ch.] Nil; [ed.] Wheathampstead Secondary Wheathampstead Herts, Royal Naval College of Maritime Communication (HMS Mercury) Petersfield, Hants; [occ.] Police Officer, Slough Berks; [hon.] Maintain Certificate of Communications (HMS Mercury Sept 86); [pers.] I hope others enjoy reading my work at much as I enjoyed writing it.; [a.] Windsor, Berks, SL4 5LW

FREDA, SHELVOCK
[b.] May 29, 1910, Aldersiloi; [p.] Dora and Frederver Bailey; [m.] W. Shelvock, April 29, 1952; [ch.] Five; [ed.] Ordinary; [occ.] Retired; [oth. writ.] Daybreak our 2 little girls daughters St. Jude the house that James built my Birthday 29th May; [pers.] I started writing at the age of 10 and was awarded at School for daybreak my last poem was at the age of so. I am now 86.; [a.] Leicester, Leics

FREEMAN, PATRICIA M.
[b.] May 29, 1940, Northampton; [p.] Dorothy/Alfred Riley; [m.] Donald P. Freeman, June 5, 1965; [ch.] Tracy, Paul, Mark Freeman; [ed.] Secondary Education; [occ.] Housewife; [memb.] Duston Camera Club, Northampton, Morman Family Centre. Northampton; [hon.] Photographic Awards; [oth. writ.] Our family tree, published in poetry now, 1996 anthology book.; [pers.] The idea for the poem came, while I was researching my family tree, and I dedicated it to my parents.; [a.] Daventry, Northants, NN11 4AD

FRENCH, JEAN
[pen.] Jane Champion; [b.] Westminster; [p.] Laura Atkinson, James Alkinson (Adopted Parents); [m.] William French (Deceased); [occ.] Psychotherapist; [memb.] Mensa Shirley Park G.C. I.T.A.A.; [hon.] Destination in Gordon Blue cooking, dancing awards.; [oth. writ.] Gardening articles for Popular Gardener. Poetry is a talent developed only this year, after it was painted out to me that I had talent in this direction.; [pers.] My aim is to inspire people to reach beyond any limiting belief, about self and life.; [a.] Bechenham, Kent, BR3 3AB

FRENCH, JOHN
[b.] January 4, 1941, Gorleston; [p.] Alfred French, Ada French (Deceased); [m.] Christine Mary French, April 19, 1969; [ch.] Charlotte Rebecca, Joseph John Michael; [ed.] Gt. Yarmouth Grammar School, Gt. Yarmouth College of Art and Design; [occ.] Ice cream Salesman; [oth. writ.] 2 poems published in anthologies to raise funds for children's charities.; [pers.] Strong interest in song lyrics, music criticisms, record reviews and beat poetry.; [a.] Gorleston on Sea, Gt. Yarmouth, Norfolk, NR31 6DJ

FRIEL, KAREN
[b.] November 15, 1982, Donegal; [p.] Mary and Patrick; [ed.] St. Marys Cashel National School and now first year student in Loreto College, Milford, Co Donegal; [occ.] Student; [memb.] Youth Club, get involved in Community games - Pioneer Association

FROST, MRS. DENISE
[pen.] Denny; [b.] July 24, 1949, Doncaster; [p.] Mr. and Mrs. John and Lily-Hale; [m.] Mr. Michael Frost, August 13; [ch.] Andrew, Cheryl, Garry; [ed.] Secondary School, Wilby Carr High School, Cantley, Doncaster; [occ.] Work for (Age - Concern) Doncaster; [hon.] Just receive 4 poetry magazines, annually, rhyme, arrival, received, but keep striving with my poetry; [oth. writ.] Educated - Secondary Modern - School won writing - competition at School named Poet of Hyde - Park - 10 years ago had slim - volumes Published my Poems; [pers.] Enjoy Helena Steiner Rice several poems published in verse seperate anthologies, I write to please a varied audience, on light, hearted rhyming - verse - poetry, very proud of my efforts; [a.] Doncaster, Yorkshire, DN4 5DX

FRUSHER, STELLA
[b.] June 17, 1935, Sandwich, Kent; [p.] Frank Brett, Violet Brett; [m.] Geoffrey Frusher (Deceased), February 8, 1958; [ch.] Lynn Frusher, Jane Frusher; [ed.] Dove Grammar School for Girls; [occ.] Retired; [pers.] My poems are motivated by my own personal experience and feelings.; [a.] Folkestone, Kent, CT20 2HW

FRYERS, DIANE LOUISE
[pen.] Diane Fryers; [b.] September 8, 1970, Crawley; [p.] George and Grace Patterson; [m.] Peter Fryers, December 18, 1993; [ch.] Lois Ann and Josie Marguerite; [ed.] Thomas Bennett Community College; [occ.] Computer Operator for Information, Management and Technology - Crawley NHS; [oth. writ.] Several poems published in books with triumph house and forward press.; [pers.] My writing expresses my hopes, dreams feelings and my life. I'm supported by a wonderful husband and two beautiful daughters.; [a.] Crawley, W. Sussex, RH11 8UT

FULLER, BETTY MAY
[pen.] May Dean; [b.] December 29, 1933, England; [p.] John Shea (Died 1972), Lily Dean (Died 1982); [m.] Leslie James Fuller, July 14, 1977; [ch.] My son died June 13, 1986, age 23 from previous marriage; [ed.] Church School, and back to school age 50, Comprehensive School O'Level Art and Crafts; [occ.] Retired; [memb.] Readers Union Group of Book Clubs, Society of Amateur Artists, Tuesday Friendship Lunchen Club; [hon.] I have had painting in Walsall Gallery, and in London Westminster Gallery; [oth. writ.] Started writing poems after the death of my son to relieve my feeling. This is my first contest.; [pers.] I have many hoppies cross stitch, carving, gardener, scratch board, and artists, married 26 years previous husband died 1976, age 47.; [a.] Walsall, S. Staffordshire, WS3 1AH

FURBER, BRIAN
[b.] August 16, 1923, Much Wenlock; [p.] Frank and Caroline Furber; [m.] Mary Elizabeth Furber, July 30, 1949; [ch.] Susan Jean, Malcolm Colin, Helen Denise and Linda Lucetta; [ed.] Church Preen C of E - and Burwarton C of E; [occ.] Retired; [oth. writ.] Two war poems (not published); [pers.] I have always been interested in poetry and also in wildlife. I am a home lover and family man. I also love my country.; [a.] Shrewsbury, Shropshire, SY3 5BY

GALEY, RICHARD
[b.] May 23, 1967, Norwich; [p.] Sheila Hawes, Fred Hawes; [ed.] Wymondham High; [occ.] Window Cleaner; [memb.] Guild of International Songwriters and Composers; [pers.] I view life as an opportunity to explore. Learn and share. My influences include the lyrical landscapes of singer/songwriters such as Marc Bolan and Nick Drake, and the poems of William Blake and James Fenton.; [a.] Wymondham, Norfolk, NR18 9NB

GANDERSON, ROBERT-JOHN
[b.] July 7, 1944, Newbury, Berks; [p.] John and Noreen Ganderson; [ed.] Collegiate (independent) school, Winchmore Hill, London N21; [occ.] Unemployed; [memb.] Fellowship of the Institute of Sales and Marketing Management (1993); [hon.] Diploma in Salesmanship Awarded by the National School of Salesmanship Manchester: Licentiateship for Sales and Marketing Awarded by the City and Guilds of London Institute. 1st Dan Black Belt for Judo (1968).; [oth. writ.] Black belt and beyond an article published in the magazine traditional karate 1991. Various articles and letters published in local and national publications over the past 10 years.; [pers.] Great enjoyment from poetry since my school days when it was taught in my school as a separate subject. Favourite poet. Alfred Lord Tenyson.; [a.] Enfield, Middlesex, EN1 3EH

GARCIA, EDITH
[b.] June 30, 1925, Denton, Lancs; [p.] Fred Barlow, Edith Barlow; [m.] Leonard Garcia (Deceased), August 4, 1970; [ch.] Denton St. Lawrence Cof E. Manchester Consevatoire of Music and Drama; [ed.] Retired; [hon.] Diploma of Merit Musical Theory. Certificate of Merit Solo Singing and Voice Production; [oth. writ.] Numerous, but never submitted for publication; [pers.] The observance of nature, in all its aspects, provides the food for the writer's expression.; [a.] Blackpool, Lancs, FY4 1HE

GARDNER, CHRIS
[b.] November 29, 1946, Fleckney; [p.] David Briggs, Doris Vera Briggs; [m.] Keith William Gardner, July 10, 1965; [ch.] Two children, three grandchildren; [ed.] Hanbury Secondary Modern School, Church Langton, Leicestershire; [occ.] Housewife; [memb.] Of three Triumph Motor Car Clubs; [oth. writ.] Three poems published in books during the last six months, three more have now been accepted. Also write for local magazine and car club magazine.; [pers.] To be at peace with yourself and enjoy all life has to offer to express in my writing feelings of many personal experiences.; [a.] Fleckney, Leicester, LE8 0BU

GARDNER, PAUL RICHARD
[b.] May 1, 1959, Gillingham, Kent; [p.] Robert Gardner, Patricia Gardner; [m.] Sarah Beby, July 25, 1987; [ch.] James Robert, Lauren Emma; [ed.] Howard School Gillingham; [occ.] Telecoms Engineer; [pers.] My poetry reflects life.; [a.] Gillingham, Kent, ME7 2QT

GARLINGE, CHERYL ANNE
[b.] January 27, 1974, Whitstable; [p.] Valerie Garlinge, Louis Garlinge; [ed.] Sir William Nottidge School Whitstable, Anglia Polytechnic University; [occ.] Geography Teacher Baylis Court School - Slough; [hon.] Earth Science; [a.] Whitstable, Kent, CT5 2AF

GARNER, FLORENCE CLARA
[pen.] Dancing Poet; [b.] August 4, 1915, Cambridgeshire; [p.] Dead; [m.] Dead, 1936; [ch.] Five; [ed.] High - Grammar; [occ.] Retired; [memb.] Science, dancing poetry, acting, honest charity brought up 5 children helping sewing; [hon.] Royal Proclamation today 3/3/96.

GARNER, PATRICIA M.
[b.] July 7, 1941, Leicester; [p.] Elizabeth and George Inskip; [m.] Derek Roy Garner, March 17, 1962; [ch.] (Three) Geoffrey, Kathryn, Joanne; [occ.] Housewife; [pers.] I live in the hope, that one day the world will be one big happy family; [a.] Rothley, Leicestershire, LE7 7PX

GAROFALL, ELIZABETH WISE
[b.] September 24, 1907, Plumpstead; [p.] John and Elizabeth Doswell; [m.] John Garofall, July 1, 1939; [ch.] Two sons (both with honours degrees); [ed.] Grammar School, Teacher's Training College, Diploma English at King's College London; [occ.] Retired (widow) Deputy Headmistress; [hon.] Distinction/English, 1st prize (all London) for Essay on League of Nations. 3 years exhibition roan grammar school for best scholar of the year; [oth. writ.] VF or Fun Humorous verses on birthday cards; [a.] Eaton Bray, Beds, LU6 2DJ

GARRETT, PATRICK JOSEPH
[pen.] Pat Garrett; [b.] March 12, 1946, Perth, Scotland; [p.] Peter Garrett, Marie Garrett; [m.] Patrick Garrett, August 22, 1970; [ch.] Mark (Deceased), John, Joseph; [ed.] Bishop Wolstan High School; [occ.] Warehousing; [memb.] Leicestershire Microlight Aircraft Club; [hon.] 96824 B.G.A. Pilot; [oth. writ.] Works magazine, M.C.N. Cruse Chronicle; [pers.] Life is what happens to our dreams. I try to "fix" time by writing. Poem in memory of Mark Anthony.; [a.] Rugby, Warwickshire:, CV22 7LN

GATEHOUSE, DEREK
[b.] March 18, 1944, Gillingham, Dorset; [p.] Ron and Alice Gatehouse; [m.] Julie Gatehouse (Separated), March 25, 1967; [ch.] Helen, John, Claire; [ed.] Gillingham Primary, Gillingham Secondary

Modern left at 15 to be a Jockey, grew too big.; [occ.] Police constable in Portishead.; [memb.] Flydresser's Guild Avon and Somerset Police Cycling Club; [oth. writ.] One poem published, title 'A Worthy Opponent' in a book called poet's Angle. All poems were written about Angling by anglers in conjunction with poetry now magazine. I've written lots, but they've not seen the light of day.; [pers.] I am a country man, not found of large towns, I enjoy the company of my family, reading, writing, fishing, horse riding, cycling and anything done outdoors. Most of the poems I have written would reflect the above.; [a.] Portishead, North Somerset, BS20 9JP

GAUNT, PHILIP
[b.] September 30, 1976; [p.] Christine Benton and Gordon Gaunt; [ed.] New College, Pontefract; [occ.] Office Junior; [pers.] To be a successful writer takes time, self confidence and a lucky break.; [a.] Normanton, West Yorks, WF6 2JX

GEAROID, GRACE
[b.] February 10, 1971, Dublin, Ireland; [ed.] Scoil Tosagain and St. Kevins both in the Crumlin area of Dublin; [occ.] Unemployed; [oth. writ.] None published, never sent my writings to any publisher. I also write lyrics, short stories and music.; [pers.] Through my writings I am a communicator. I am happy being the middle man between circumstance and text. My greatest influence is life itself. My writings do not reflect life but merely one man's observations of it.; [a.] Swords, Co. Dublin

GEDDES, YONA ELISE
[b.] November 24, 1918, Alton, Hants; [p.] Ralph, Rhoda Hinkins; [m.] Deceased, 1st 1938, 2nd 1960; [ch.] Rhoda, Diana, Vincent, Frances; [ed.] Tutored at home until the age of eight by grandfather then church schools till the age of fourteen; [occ.] Retired, teacher taught art-craft, pottery, to mentally handicapped; [oth. writ.] Short stories as hobby as a child none published; [pers.] I feel my background is my spur. Mother, Romany, and Father, Pioneer Photographer, Artist, Illustrator and many other talents, a very liberal upbringing for the time.; [a.] Prevensey Bay, E. Sussex, BN24 6RX

GEORGE, MRS. LINDA
[b.] February 17, 1951, Gower, S. Wales; [p.] Robert William Phillips, Anna Phillips; [m.] John Ernest George, September 28, 1974; [ch.] Gaynor George, Anna George, Helen George; [ed.] Mynyddbach Comprehensive School for girls in Swansea, South Wales; [occ.] Secretary; [oth. writ.] I only discovered my talent since August, 1995. I have written 30 poems to date and the very first one I entered in a competition is to be published.; [pers.] I only started writing poetry in August, 1995, when a very special person, whom I love deeply entered my life. Thank you Stuart for inspiring me to write. I would like to say that I believe the best things in life are free. I would also like to say that no matter how many knocks you get in life, have faith to go on.; [a.] Swansea, W. Glam, SA6 7NZ

GEORGE, MARGARET
[b.] April 17, 1943, Worcestershire; [p.] Victor Davies, Gladys Davies; [m.] David Edmund George, June 25, 1966; [ch.] Richard David George; [ed.] Local Secondary Modern (Head Girl), Goley College (Commerce), Banking College; [occ.] Housewife; [memb.] Local Church; [oth. writ.] Am at present a student with 'The Writers Bureau' and although I have submitted some of my work to magazines and newspapers, to date have had nothing published.; [pers.] My main interest is writing about personal experiences.; [a.] Stourbridge, West Mids, DY8 5PY

GIBBONS, CHRISTOPHER DAVID
[b.] December 23, 1955, Liverpool; [p.] James (Deceased), Alice; [m.] Lesley, September 24, 1977; [ch.] Philip (17), Tracy (16); [ed.] St. Aloysious Sec. Mod. Huyton Liverpool; [occ.] Retired (Ambulance Man); [pers.] I have always believed in my schools motto "Nil Sine Labore" Nothing Without Work!; [a.] Liverpool, Merseyside, L36 8BW

GIBBS, HOWARD WALLACE
[pen.] Howard Gibbs; [b.] March 27, 1928, Maidenhead; [p.] Deceased; [m.] Shirley Ann Gibbs, September 2, 1957; [ch.] One; [ed.] Normal, What Was Then Elementary Schools, The Further Education Slough Tec for Institute of Work Study, Institute of Office Managers, Institute of Works Managers; [occ.] Retired; [memb.] A.S.P.R.O.M. (Ass for Presentation of Roman Mosaics), A.R.A. (Ass Roman Arch), Institute of Works Managers; [oth. writ.] Short Story's, (Novel) Unpublished, I also write protest poetry, mostly I rail against low moral standards and crime and against the EU; [pers.] Another Archeanlogist ..... Historian Roman Period Dousing; [a.] Aldbourne, Wilts, SN8 2DF

GIBSON, DAVID CHARLES
[b.] September 4, 1958, B'ham; [p.] Father Ireland, Mother B'ham; [m.] Sheila Joan Gibson, September 1, 1984; [ch.] Three Daughters; [ed.] Normal Secondary School no exams taken; [occ.] Care Assistant Devon Social Services; [memb.] Prisoner Abroad which helps English people who are in prisons abroad; [pers.] For the rights and dignity of all people in care whatever there age or culture, religion: including those who are in prison abroad; [a.] Plymouth, Devon, PL7 3JU

GILES, MIKE
[b.] May 13, 1972, Bradford; [p.] Barry Giles, Sheila Giles; [ed.] Salts Grammar; [occ.] Assistant Supervisor at Computer Cable Firm-Service Power; [hon.] English Literature; [pers.] If I could change the human race for the better in so few words, believe me - I would.

GILES, ROBERT
[b.] February 4, 1944, Dartmouth; [p.] Florence Christina Ellen; [m.] Kathleen Hodgson (Partner); [ch.] Beverly Jane, Amanda Jane, Paul; [ed.] Churston Ferrers Grammer School, National Extention College; [occ.] Writer, Retired: Royal Navy/HM Prison Service; [hon.] English Literature; [oth. writ.] Several articles to magazines. Completed novel 'Out of a Dark Continent', yet to be published - still searching for a publisher!; [pers.] I am a committed royalist, British and longing to see our society return to the proud values of a war-time Britain 50 years hence - a dreamer!; [a.] Featherstone, Staffordshire, WV10 7TD

GILES, VICKY YVONNE
[b.] July 24, 1954, Islington, London; [p.] Yvonne and James Reynolds; [m.] Michael Robert Giles, March 26, 1988; [ch.] (Son) Sorren Mills; [ed.] Infant, Junior, and Secondary Dola, Zambia Secondary at Florence Treloar, Alton Hants, Hereward Collage F.E. Coventry; [occ.] Running my home by speaking to my personal carer; [memb.] Art group at Audley's Resource Centre, Basingstoke; [hon.] O.N.D. in Business Study's; [oth. writ.] 5 poem's published in local news paper. A collection of 60 poem's (from the age of 16 onwards).; [pers.] I find poetry a way of releasing my emotions. I suffer from Freidreich's Ataxia, a slowly progressive disease. Began using a wheelchair at 15. My poem expressing frustrations felt through disability.; [a.] Basingstoke, Hampshire, RG22 4EN

GILLEN, MARGARET J. J.
[pen.] Margaret J. J. Gillen; [b.] October 26, 1971, Edmonton; [p.] Jo Peplow, Violet Peplow; [m.] Darren John Gillen, August 15, 1992; [ed.] Salisbury Comprehensive School; [occ.] Manageress/Insurance Blokers Autosure Insurance Ltd.; [pers.] Poetry reflects the way I feel and experiences I have encountered. May my poems bring depth and understanding to our own emotions.; [a.] Edmonton, London, N9 8NX

GILLETT, MALCOLM PAUL
[b.] May 3, 1967, Bridjend, S. Wales; [pers.] Through my personal experience I would like to state a fact that there are innocent people sent to prison my only message to others is don't give up hope and forgive those who make false testimony against you.

GILLINGS, REGINALD
[pen.] Gil Lings; [b.] April 5, 1914, Gt. Yarmouth; [ed.] Council School, Sheringham Norfolk; [occ.] Retired

GIORDANO, MISS DOLORES
[pen.] Zippy; [b.] February 15, 1939, Edinburgh; [occ.] Housewife; [oth. writ.] None at the moment but I intend to start writing seriously. I was clever at school but was put into factory work as my parents were very poor.; [pers.] I had the same chance to have a poem published about 20 years ago. But I did not have the finance to follow it up then. I am now age 57. (A big more secure); [a.] Edinburgh, Midlothian, EH8 9SX

GLENDINNING, ALAN
[pen.] Alfie Calder; [b.] July 30, 1957, Glasgow, Scotland; [p.] Robert and Christina Glendinning; [m.] Single; [ed.] Newbury, Dorchester (England); [occ.] Electronic Technician Aberdeen College; [memb.] International Songwriters Association Limerick City, Ireland; [a.] Aberdeen, Grampian, AB2 2UN

GLENN, KEITH
[b.] October 21, 1946, Belper; [p.] George Glenn, Irene Glenn; [m.] Margaret Mary Glenn, January 1, 1966; [ch.] Paul, Kevin, Steven, Joanne Marie; [ed.] Allestree Woodlands Secondary Modern; [occ.] Painter decorator; [oth. writ.] Other poems unpublished stories; [a.] Derby, Derbyshire, DE22 2RR

GLOVER, FRANCIS JOSEPH DAVID
[pen.] Frank Glover; [b.] February 16, 1954, Litherland; [p.] Frank Glover, Julia Glover; [m.] Linda Glover, May 14, 1977; [ch.] Stephen Paul Glover; [ed.] St. Bedes R.C. Secondary School Ormskirk, Lancs; [occ.] Sales and Marketing Director; [memb.] Institute of Directors; [oth. writ.] Unpublished poetry; [pers.] Greatly influenced by my father, and poems such as Blake, Chesterton, Nici, I write from inspiration.; [a.] Hatfield, Herefordshire, HR6 0SQ

GODDARD, PAUL
[b.] August 7, 1963, Hull; [p.] Herbert and Brenda Goddard; [occ.] Hospital Theatre Technician - Hull Royal Infirmary; [memb.] North Cave/Blackburns Bowling Clubs; [hon.] Computer, Literacy; [oth. writ.] Limerick Published in a book; [pers.] In my writing, I am to bring out people's sense of humour; [a.] Hull, E. Yorks, HU5 3NS

GOING, WILLIAM HENRY
[pen.] Bill Going; [b.] March 27, 1939, Rochford; [ed.] Rochford Secondary School; [occ.] Manual Labourer; [oth. writ.] A child of God, New and Old Wine Skins, A Glance at Heaven, Don't Let Go - published by Triumph House.; [pers.] My father was born in Limerack Ireland and since I became a Christian God has develop within me my gift of poetry. Word seem to flow into my mind and I just write them down.; [a.] Rochford, Essex, SS4 1HJ

GOLIGHTLY, JOHN
[b.] November 26, 1963, South Shields; [p.] Irene and Edwin Golightly; [m.] Clare Golightly, May 7, 1994; [ch.] Ragan, Shanelle, Ebony, all girls; [ed.] Chuder Ede Comprehensive; [occ.] Train driver at Newcastle Central Stn; [oth. writ.] Just personal poems and stories for own satisfaction; [pers.] I'm to laid-back to be philosophical, I just enjoy reading what my right hand and pen create in ink.; [a.] South Shields, Tyne and Wear, NE34, 9AS

GOODE, BARBARA IRENE
[b.] August 14, 1924, Bournemouth; [p.] Alex and Margaret Dowding; [m.] Geoffrey Goode, June 10, 1990 (Second); [ch.] Three; [ed.] Council Schooling 5-14 yrs.; [occ.] Retired, Housewife; [oth. writ.] Several poems in various books. 1 compilation of own poems. 1 articles on self publishing. 2 in books by International Society of Poets. 1 in book for Poetry Guild.; [pers.] I solve my problems by writing about them in verse. It is a very deep sincere way of writing, otherwise it would be worthless.; [a.] Oakington, Cambridge, CB4 5BE

GORDON, PAUL SAMUEL
[b.] June 18, 1957, Aberdeen; [p.] Harry Gordon, Christian Gordon or MacDonald; [ch.] Five; [ed.] Willowpark - Infant School, Fernielea - Primary School Summerhill Academy, Aberdeen Technical College; [occ.] House Father; [oth. writ.] Two manuscripts - titled 'The Mysteries Uni-verse' and the resurrection mysteries - unpublished. Work, in Woman's Mag. and Versity Mag.; [pers.] To capture the visions, translate them into verse, and change my world accordingly.; [a.] Aberdeen, AB2 6HH

GOUGH, CLAIRE ALISON
[pen.] Claire Alison; [b.] April 13, 1977, Walsall; [p.] Kenneth Gough, Julie Gough; [ed.] Brownhills Community School, Chester College of Higher Education; [occ.] Student; [pers.] The world of imagination contains far more peace and love. That world will last forever, I wish our world could.; [a.] Brownhills, West Mid's, WS8 7DW

GOULD, LIZ
[b.] July 22, 1958, Paulton; [p.] Elizabeth Florence Ruddick, Cecil Bertram Ruddick; [m.] Raymond Gould, November 15, 1975; [ch.] Emmajayne Gould; [ed.] Norton Hill Comprehensive; [occ.] Animal Welfare and House Person; [oth. writ.] One Rain Drop, published in 'West Country Poets Today 94', Soul Searching, In 'Remember the Time' Pretty Frocks and Scabby Knees, in poetry in motion.; [pers.] Simple words clearly defined enable poetry to be easily understood and more so enjoyed; [a.] Camerton, Avon-Bath, BA3 1PR

GOWER, VICTOR T. S.
[b.] February 4, 1949, Salisbury Wilts; [m.] Divorced; [ch.] Catherine Gower; [ed.] Highbury Ave. Sec. Mod. Salisbury; [occ.] Self-employed; [oth. writ.] A Fireman's Nightmare, One Woman Man, True Friendship, The Morning After the Night Before, Feelings, Confession of Love, True Friendship, Brown Paper Parcel, A Lovers Last Lament etc.; [pers.] I did not realize that I could write poetry until I became the victim of divorce. My poems tell how I developed a platonic friendship with a lady who saved me from myself and helped me recover from the agony of the past. I dedicated this poem and my thanks to her.; [a.] Salisbury, Wiltshire, SP2 9EJ

GRANT, DAPHNE JOAN
[pen.] Julia Summers; [b.] October 20, 1933, London; [p.] Elsie Stowe; [m.] Peter Grant, 1952 Carindington; [ch.] One son Robert; [ed.] Literary Extension Course with Mrs. Brenchly Ma Cam 1961/2 influenced by Sigfried Sasoon's work and Dylan Thomas; [occ.] Housewife; [oth. writ.] Occasional poem published in magazines; [pers.] I write when something is crying out to be written.; [a.] Southampton, Hants, SO16 8EH

GRANT, FRANCIS J.
[b.] June 23, 1944, Plymouth; [p.] Francis J. Grant (F), Winifred R. Grant (M); [m.] Sandy, 1976; [ch.] Victoria, Paul and David; [ed.] Sec. Mod. Portsmouth, Durham University, Newscastle-upon-Tyne Poly; [occ.] Writer, Antiquarian Bookshop Proprietor; [memb.] B.A.S.W. (British Assoc. Social Work), N.A.I.R.C. (National Assoc. Independent Resources For Children); [hon.] C.Q.S.W. (Social worker), C.Y.E.C.W. (Youth leader), Cert. counselling skills; [oth. writ.] "The Silent Victim", A Fractional Viewpoint of the Issues Surrounding Child Sexual Abuse, 1992, "Thoughts and Feelings", 30 Years of Poetry Writing 1996; [pers.] Mountaineer, pacifist, lover of nature/mountains. Influences by John Ruskin's works. I like to express the feelings thoughts in my poetry.; [a.] Carlisle, Cumbria, CA2 4LT

GRANT, PATRICK
[b.] February 29, 1936, Waterford; [p.] John, Eileen (Deceased); [m.] Philomena (Deceased), October 9, 1965; [ch.] Three (two boys-one girl); [ed.] Primary/secondary; [occ.] Shop-keeper; [memb.] P.T.T.A. Ass.; [hon.] Harmony Group award with my two sisters Anne and Helen, Best comedy award in local "Tops of the Town"; [oth. writ.] "My Friend" (poem), "Her Winning Smile" (poem), "Simply My Friend" (poem), Getting On" (poem), "Easter Time" (poem), etc.; [pers.] I am very interested in live theatre, love to write poetry. I adjudicate talent competitions and variety choir, love singing and meeting people. Reading poems by other writers.; [a.] Waterford

GRAY, JUDITH A.
[b.] June 7, 1958, Lincoln; [p.] Aileen and Malcolm Elvidge; [ch.] Gemma L. Gray; [ed.] Robert Pattinson School, North Hykeham, Lincs North Lincs College, Inter Business and Admin. College; [occ.] Managing Part Charity Clothing Agency Voluntary Work with Oxfan; [oth. writ.] Selection poems written for my own personal reasons.; [pers.] Poetry for me is a way of bringing the inside out. You could say I'm a "Secret Scribbler" let out of the closet.

GREAVES, SHIRLEY ANNE
[b.] June 14, 1950, Stamford; [p.] Stanley Rickett/Joan Rickett; [m.] Anthony Charles Greaves, September 11, 1992; [occ.] Computerized Accounts Clerk; [oth. writ.] A host of poems I have never offered for publication these have only been read by family and close friends; [pers.] I write when something stirs my imagination or when I am deeply moved by a personal experience.; [a.] Stamford, Lincolnshire, PE9 1LL

GREEN, ADRIAN
[pen.] Sheldare Barton III; [b.] October 1, 1969, Bristol; [p.] Barry Green, Ruth Green; [occ.] Eternal Dreamer!; [oth. writ.] As yet, only 'Tragic Hands' submitted for publication but completed works include: Your Dying Tear, Photographs and Memories, Sounds of the Forest, By the Light of the Flame, Cold Rain Cold World.; [pers.] Writing gives me most pleasure and satisfaction when I use the subject of nature. If I have an aim, it is to raise awareness of the beauty of the natural world. Let the dream live!; [a.] Bristol, Avon

GREEN, F. O.
[b.] January 12, 1920, Whyteleafe; [p.] John and Dora Green; [m.] Amy, June 24, 1950; [ed.] Warlingham Council School and Life; [occ.] Retired; [memb.] Gresham Crolf Club, Hythe Club for Snooker, Hythe Conservative Club; [pers.] Travels with his wife to distant lands hoping to find a reason for life.; [a.] Sandgate, Kent, CT20 3RS

GREGORY, MRS. JOAN R. M.
[pen.] Joan; [b.] November 11, 1933, West Coventry; [m.] Died, 1960; [ed.] Enough to get by Sec. Mod.; [occ.] Retired, widow, housewife; [hon.] Daily mail 3 times, 1 big win 19 yrs. ago with spurs; [oth. writ.] One get me a prize of E31160 9 years ago. I wrote a story about the famous Dick Whittinghams, cat. In 2 different years. That is! The title is a Child's Greeting.; [pers.] Very fair " I love the way you greet me, each-day. Your smile Hello! and gaily dance away. It helps to Banish the cares of my day.".; [a.] Harrigay, London, 4RX

GREGSON, DEREK
[pen.] D. G. Kreed; [b.] September 3, 1941, Gt. Harwood; [p.] Robert and Clara Gregson; [m.] Madeline Gregson, August 10, 1963; [ch.] Deborah, Carl, Michael and Joanne; [ed.] Secondary Modern Education at Local Schools, Engineering Training at Higher Education College; [occ.] P/T Handyman at Goonig Run Home for Elderly; [memb.] Institute of Advanced Motorists; [oth. writ.] Letters and poems published in local and national newspapers. Number of poems (for children), currently under consideration elsewhere.; [pers.] I am retired police sergeant and a keen observer of life - which I try to reflect in my writings which are aimed principally at the younger reader.; [a.] Accrington, Lancs, BB5 1BZ

GRIERSON, HELEN MARGARET
[b.] November 21, 1945, Dundee, Scotland; [p.] James and Margaret Greig (Deceased father); [m.] Brian, September 29, 1973; [ch.] One - Joy; [ed.] Rockwell Secondary School Dundee, Pre-Nursing College Dundee; [occ.] Nurse at a local Hospital (night duty); [hon.] Registered General Nurse, Registered Mental Nurse.; [oth. writ.] Another two poems unpublished as yet.; [pers.] In the quiet moments during the small hours of my night shift I compose poetry in my head. The peace is my inspiration.; [a.] Carnoustie, Angus, DD7 7AJ

GRIMES, KATHERINE LATHAM
[b.] June 6, 1951, Stowhall; [m.] July 5, 1975; [ch.] 4; [ed.] Downhamm. KT Girls School, Downhamm. KT Norfolk, Norcat College, Tennyson Ave Kings Lynn, Norfolk; [occ.] Housewife; [hon.] G.S.E. double Science pass for Nursing College Course Red Cross certificates, Pone Course in Norwich studying feet passed; [oth. writ.] Poem published in paper back and two other poems published. Two lines of my writing on ITN News at 10 television London, to end on a finer note and upon my return on my white hunter; [pers.] I have been influenced by the area where I live. Story Lydia (short story) written a long time ago.; [a.] Bircham Newton, Kings Lynn, Norfolk, PE31 6RD

GROGAN, PAUL
[b.] July 11, 1956, Shipley; [p.] William and Elizabeth; [m.] Jacqueline Holdsworth, October 2, 1976; [ch.] 7 children: Michelle, Vicky, Daniel, Rebecca, Racheal, Martin, Luke.; [ed.] Woodend Secondary; [occ.] Hand Presser; [pers.] I try to capture my emotions on paper and pass them on to you.; [a.] Shipley, W. Yorks, BD18 1HQ

GUTTERIDGE, SUSAN DENISE
[b.] April 20, 1958, Coventry; [p.] Raymond and Iris Gutteridge; [ed.] Stoke Park Grammar School, Coventry Henley College Coventry; [oth. writ.] "Floss the Fairy" (in process of being published by Avon books) a children's story book.; [pers.] I hope that my inspirational thoughts will influence anyone who reads them to be inspired themselves.; [a.] Christchurch, Dorset, BH23 4NT

HAINIE, MARGARET
[pen.] Margaret Hainie; [b.] December 25, 1940, Hamilton, Scotland; [p.] Bridget Wemyss; [m.] James Hainie, October 3, 1959; [ch.] Delia Cathie Pamela Ian; [ed.] St Mary's Hamilton; [occ.] J Sainsbury PLC; [memb.] Hamilton Public Library; [pers.] Putting these words onto paper made me feel satisfied and put at ease because it reflects a past now to get on with the future.; [a.] Hamilton, Lanarkshire, ML3 8BY

HALE, MRS. IRENE
[pen.] Dorothy Meachem; [b.] September 6, 1950, Bilston; [p.] Mr. and Mrs. George and Irene Meachem; [m.] Mr. Roger Hale, July 25, 1970; [ch.] Tree and five grandchildren; [ed.] Secondary Modern Higher Education; [occ.] Manageress of a Small Residential, Care Home, Residential/Daycare for Adults with Learning Disabilities; [memb.] Grand Theatre Wolverhampton, "Friends of the Grand"; [oth. writ.] I have only wrote two other poems. They were published in the starcraft magazine.; [pers.] I try to reflect my life experiences through my poems.; [a.] Bilston, West Midlands, WV14 6DG

HALL, JOHN ALEXANDER
[pen.] John A. Hall; [b.] January 27, 1979, Welwyn Garden City, Hertfordshire; [p.] Michael J. Hall, A. Elizabeth Hall; [ed.] Welwyn St. Mary's JMI (84-90), Monks Walk Secondary School, Knightfield, Welwyn Garden City (90-95). Currently a block release student, with C.I.T.B. Sponsorship, to study Heavy Plant Mechanical Engineering; [occ.] Trainee Engineer with Miskins plant and tool hire, Welwyn Garden City; [memb.] International Youth Hostels Association. Baldock CB Radio Group; [hon.] Nine GCSE passes; [oth. writ.] Various other poems written, but nothing previously published!; [pers.] I hope my poetry reflects my love of cars and driving. I would like to publish a book of "vehicle" poems to raise enough cash to purchase my first car. (Being only seventeen I suppose time is on my side.); [a.] Welwyn Village, Herts, AL6 9DW

HALL, TREVOR
[b.] December 3, 1948, Whitchurch (Salop); [p.] Ron Hall, Jean Hall; [m.] Marjorie Hall, April 12, 1988; [ch.] Tracy, Ann; [ed.] Wem., C. of E. Shropshire; [occ.] Retired Health Worker; [memb.] H. M. Forces on Completion appointed 2nd Lieutenant Cheshire Army Cadet Force, Detachment Commander Malpas Cheshire, Malpas Bowling and Institute; [hon.] Carpenter; [pers.] My aim: Is to see what I write and to write what I see.; [a.] Sutton, S. Wirral, L66 1HJ

HALLIWELL, LEONARD
[pen.] Michel Stewart; [b.] November 22, 1950, Manchester; [p.] Leonard (Died October 25, 1990), Mavis; [m.] Divorced from Sharon Halliwell, August 17, 1974/April 7, 1993; [ch.] Lance, Jennifer, Victoria, Glen; [ed.] Old Trafford Sec. School for Boys, left school with no qualifications. Self qualified in my personal university of life. You just never give up; [occ.] House person. The children live with me.; [memb.] No literary society, apart from Padgate Library, Fearnhead.; [hon.] General Service Medal with Clasp. Bessbrook Mill, Glenan (Whitecross), and Crossmaglen 1975-76 and Manchester Corn Exchange 1977, a 100% profit and great relief; [oth. writ.] Various poems inspired by Michel Nostradamus, Al Stewart, Christina Rossetti and Captain Charles Hamilton Sorley. I have composed poems for Charles and Christina in tribute to their sufferings and dedication.; [pers.] Individual talent can be suppressed by ones own inability to realize what knowledge lies within. Look far beyond your own horizons if you really want to find the truth. This life is just a proving ground.; [a.] Warrington, Cheshire, WA2 0BS

HALLS, MICHELLE E.
[b.] August 29, 1967, Dorking; [p.] Mr. T. R. Halls, Mrs. V. A. Halls; [ch.] Three; [ed.] Howard of Effingham Secondary School, Guildford College of Technology; [occ.] Housewife; [oth. writ.] I have written over 120 poems but had no other poems published.; [pers.] Poetry is a favorite past-time to me by way of relaxation. I feel influenced by everyday life and events.; [a.] Dorking, Surrey, RH5 4DF

HAMBLETT, CARI SOPHIA
[b.] June 6, 1946, Amersham Bucks; [occ.] Filmmaker, Artist and Writer; [pers.] My concerns are with man's relationship to his surroundings and ability to achieve harmony with natural as well as industrial environment.

HARDIE, CATHERINE
[b.] May 29, 1942, Leicestershire; [m.] Bill; [ch.] Andrew, Terrence; [oth. writ.] I have been to a creative writing class for three years. My poems have appeared in the yearly journal. Also one was published in the Mind Magazine.; [pers.] I wrote my first poem after my Mother died. The adoption of my oldest son in 1959, because I wasn't married. Had a long term effect on me. I never told anyone for years, as I thought I'd done something so bad, it had to be kept a secret. The dark days of the fifties or over, though the legacy lingers on! I made a bit of a mess on the form provided, so I hope this will do.

HARMAN SUSAN
[b.] Harrogate; [m.] Ian Harman; [ch.] Jayne, Paul and David; [ed.] Secondary Modern; [occ.] Housewife; [memb.] Harrogate Writer's Circle; [hon.] Two shorts stories in our local paper competition. I also won a prize as a child for a poem and a Child's Writing Competition; [oth. writ.] I'm in the process of writing a novel, I've also been writing short stories for children in the hope to get them published; [pers.] I do live into today and I let tomorrow take care of itself I try very hard not to judge other people. And I let my children get on with there own lives.; [a.] Harrogate, N. Yorkshire, HG1 4NB

HARPER, MRS. LYN
[b.] December 20, 1930, Birmingham; [p.] John and Violet Hurley; [m.] Dennis Harper; [ed.] Lea Village Comprehensive; [occ.] Retired; [memb.] Age Concern Stourbridge; [oth. writ.] Monthly poems for age concern published in their own magazine; [pers.] Feel much pleasure, in bringing pleasure to others. Interested in non fiction; [a.] Stourbridge, W. Mids, DY8 1EY

HARRIS, BRIAN
[pen.] "Avalon, Capricorn, and Pendragon"; [b.] December 30, 1933, Neath, W. Glam; [p.] Martin Bernard and Ethel May (Nee Singleton); [m.] Joan Mary (Nee Parry), August 16, 1955; [ch.] Jonathan David, Roxane Elizabeth and Philip James Singleton Harris; [ed.] Neath Grammar School (Scholarship Entry 1945); [occ.] Retired Company Director (p.t.o.); [memb.] Formerly FCIS, FCCS, FSCA, FBIM, FIIM, FIWM, FI of D.; [hon.] Certificate of Merit and awarded the Africa General Service Medal with Clasp for active service in the R.A.F. in Egypt, the Sudan and Kenya 1952 - 4. (A rare award to the R.A.F. not given since 1956 and only once before in Somaliland (1920)).; [oth. writ.] Collected Poems - "To All Our Yesterdays" (ISBN 0 9527058 0 X), numerous anthologies and contributions to house-magazines etc. The collected poems were compiled in aid of a Registered Medical Charity. "A Threnody for South Africa", "At Rorke's Drift, Natal, South Africa", "From Talana Hill To Bergendal", A Path of Life", "A Gentle Love", "To Mary on Mother's Day", "In Memory of General Gordon", At Anchor in Table Bay", "Greetings to the Queen Mother", Sunset in San Francisco", "To Mary", "The Colosseum, Rome", "To a Beloved Father", "A Prayer for Her Majesty's 70th Birthday".; [pers.] I am very concerned about the way in which our World's environment is being irrevocably destroyed. I am appalled by the decline in standards of human health and hygiene, particularly how in our own country where Tuberculosis has returned.; [a.] Stoke on Trent, Staffs, ST1 4RB

HARRIS, RONALD ANTHONY
[pen.] Tony Harris; [b.] October 15, 1944, Middlesbrough; [m.] Eileen Harris, March 27, 1966; [ch.] Peter Harris, Chris Harris; [ed.] Sec. Mod. (1956-1959), B.A. Open University (1986), B.Ed. Sunderland Univ. (1991); [occ.] Previous, Mechanical, Writer, Driving Instructor, Teacher or Emotionally Disturbed Children; [pers.] Lost Light is my first poem. It was written while I was suffering from severe depression. It is an expression of that illness.; [a.] Middlesbrough, TS8 9XN

HARRIS, V.
[pen.] Valerie Annette; [b.] August 10, 1941, Birmingham; [p.] Elenor and Bertram Hawkins; [ch.] One; [ed.] Secondary Modern Bournville College, Matthew Boulton College, Hairdressing Teacher, R.S.A. Counselor; [occ.] Care Officer for The Elderly and Learning Disability; [memb.] Victim Support; [hon.] R.S.A. Certificate for Concealing, Heart of Gold Award for Saving Work, Golden Heart Award, Care Work; [oth. writ.] Writing for children of family, Critical, Incidents of Actual Covers I have dealt with: I want to reflect the goodness of people in my writings.

HARRISON, ROBERT
[pen.] Bob Harrison; [b.] January 2, 1943, Stockport; [p.] Robert/Ethel (Deceased); [m.] Ann Doreen Harrison, November 16, 1963; [ch.] Karen Julie and Sarah Jane; [ed.] Christ Church Primary School Stockprot, St Michaels Sec Modern School; [occ.] Security Officer Expolice Force, 15 years in Cheshire Constabulary; [oth. writ.] Have written a number of poems (mostly childrens or of a religious nature). I was inspired by reading "Rupert Bear" books belonging to a friend as a small boy.; [pers.] "I am an idealist and would love to live in a world of peace, where no one went hungry, and all things possible to all men". As a contestant on a TV Quiz Show "Spellbound" 1995 was able to narrate a verse of a poem giving me an audience of thousands.; [a.] Stockport, Cheshire, SK4 1NA

HART, ANDREW WILLIAM
[b.] August 26, 1950, Sheffield; [p.] Arnold William Hart, Winifred Hart; [m.] Nile; [ed.] Secondary Modern Went to York Tec Collage from 73 to 76 to study English and History; [occ.] Night Porter in large Hotel in York; [oth. writ.] Eveing Tide Published and made into a song in the early 70s went to Washvill to be written and is now in Valts in Washington USA; [pers.] I like to think I'm a poet of the heart and I enjoy writing love poems which I make of as I go along these poems of mine I think enlighten the soul as the soul thrives on love and romance; [a.] York, W. Yorkshire, YO2 2TP

HART, KEVIN JAMES
[b.] January 30, 1956, Christchurch, New Zealand; [p.] Morel and Kathleen; [m.] Monica (Nee Kelly), December 10, 1983; [ch.] Aine Kathleen; [ed.] Aranui High School; [occ.] Waiter/Restaurant worker; [oth. writ.] Song recorded for Red Cross Charity Album; [pers.] If you wake up you may as well get up if you get up you may as well do something.; [a.] Celbridge, Kildare, Eire

HARTLEY, MRS. MAUREEN
[pen.] Maureen Hartley; [b.] August 8, 1953, Halifax; [p.] Jack Halstead and Jean Maude Barbara Halstead; [m.] Ian Hartley May 17, 1975; [ch.] Christopher Ian Hartley (1 child); [ed.] Warley Road Junior School and Haugh Secondary Modern; [occ.] Senior Clerk at Halifax Building Society (Head office); [memb.] Ovenden Rugby League Football Club. I'm an avid supporter of first my husband and secondly my son Christopher and can be heard across the Pennings every well-end. Hence the sore throat on Mondays; [hon.] None - I live in hope! Apart from my CSE's for Commerce, English, History and DOM Science; [oth. writ.] Several poems, scribbled or neatly, written and kept in my cookery binder! Alas none published till now. Maybe I should change the recipes, it might bring me some luck.; [pers.] I wish to pay tribute to the late Frank Turnbull and Donald Osbourne who taught English to me at Haugh Shaw School and gave me an enjoyable insight and taste for the written word (Wordsworth being my favorite).; [a.] Halifax, W. Yorkshire, HX3 6JQ

HARTNELL, MRS. G. LOLA
[pen.] Lola Perks-Hartnell; [b.] Wolverhampton; [p.] Robert and Kate Perks; [m.] Thomas Hartnell (Died Jan 81), August 15, 1964; [ch.] Barry aged 26; [ed.] Wolverhampton Municipal Grammar School (now Member of former Pupils Assn.); [occ.] Retired (Music Teacher at what was Bilston Girls High School); [memb.] South Staff Operatic Scy., A.R.P. (Associate of Retired Persons over 50), Wolverhampton Friendship Centre, The Scy. of Amateur Artists; [hon.] Several poems published in local magazines and in a few anthologies.; [oth. writ.] I have written children's stories, but not done much yet about getting them published.; [pers.] As I run a healing - help small prayer group, a number of my poems are written with this in mind, to try to help folk with life, in other words - religious poems. (I also love to cheer up people with humorous poems); [a.] Wolverhampton, W. Mids, WV6 8SU

HARVEY, A. R. ERNEST
[pen.] Roland Harvey; [b.] April 20, 1922, London; [p.] Ernest C., and Florence M. Harvey; [m.] Daisy May Harvey, February 26, 1944; [ch.] Caryl E., and Karin A.; [ed.] Dame Alice Owen's School, Islington; [occ.] Retired Display Designer and Artist; [memb.] Royal Naval Association; [oth. writ.] Only one other poem "My Boss" has been published. I am new to writing by I have many short stories, poems and two novels ready for submission, widowed only 3 weeks ago. (11/3/96); [pers.] I can write Philosophically only about subjects I feel strongly. Homelessness, hypocrisy in the establishment, injustice, I have a wealth of creative past times. Art, music, woodcarving, etc.; [a.] Burnham-on-Crouch, Essex, CM0 8SY

HARVEY, JAMES ERNEST
[b.] December 13, 1920, Wimbledon, Surrey; [p.] Amy Andrews, Adopted by Harvey family in London; [m.] Married Three Times, 1943/1954/1969 (3rd wife died June 1995); [ch.] Two daughters of 1st wife - Gail and Helen; [ed.] Elementary Schools to age at 14 then private part-time studies to University Entrance Level, also Teacher Training; [occ.] Private Music Teacher and Church Organist; [memb.] Guild of Church Musicians, London College of Music Society; [hon.] Music Qualifications: LTCL, LLCM(TD), ALCM; [oth. writ.] Various poems published in anthologies and local newspapers during recent years.; [pers.] Vivid memories of the "Battle of Britain" as seen from a heavy anti-aircraft gun-site in Kent while in many successful actions.; [a.] Sleaford, Lincs, NG34 8IU

HARVEY, PAMELA
[b.] London, (Borough of Enfield); [ed.] Edmonton County Grammar School; [occ.] Writer; [memb.] Enfield Writers' Workshop, Tai Chi Club, 'New Renaissance' Poet's Society.; [hon.] 'A' level Oral French, 'O' level (Dist.) English Lit., French, German. Certificate (Enfield Short Story Comp.); [oth. writ.] 'Poetry', 'Quiet Lines' (Anthologies of my poems published by Stylus Press, Wymondham, Norfolk.) 3 small Sci-fi poems in 'The People's Poetry', 'Romantic Heir'. Articles on social history, also on Celtic subjects in 4 magazines, including 'Celtic Connections', and 'Keltria' (USA). Also Haiku in 'Time Haiku', 'Azami'.; [pers.] We need a more caring, less materialist society. A deeper understanding of life. A sense of our place in the Eternal Cosmos. Awareness of personal value. I have been influenced by history, by scientific enquiry, and by Romantic poetry.; [a.] Edmonton, Enfield, London, 9HX

HARWOOD, JANET MAUREEN
[b.] August 22, 1942, Hitchen; [p.] Edgar and Alice Driver; [m.] Michael Phillip, September 9, 1972; [ch.] Scott and Mandy; [ed.] Secondary Modern; [occ.] House Wife; [pers.] I have lived in Norfolk all my life. Devoted my time to look after my live sick children my son is a diabetic my lovely daughter was very ill from the age of 5 she went blind when she was 15 she was so prove and always had a smile and gave lots of pleasure to other people Mandy died on 25th March 1995 age 18. Because she was such a wonderful person it inspired me to write the poem in her memory; [a.] Gorleston-on-Sea, Norfolk, NR31 8BU

HASSELL, ANJA
[b.] February 19, 1931, Ahtari, Finland; [p.] Elvi and Risto Rantakangas; [m.] Peter Hassell, December 15, 1971; [ed.] Grammar School for Girls in Kouvola, Finland. Some Open University Courses.; [occ.] Housewife; [memb.] Dartmouth Poetry Club, Member of the Labour Party, Member of the Finish Church Guild, Members of the South Hams Weaving Group, Member of R.S.P.B.; [oth. writ.] Poems and articles published in local booklets.; [a.] Dartmouth, Devon, TQ6 9NU

HASWELL, FIONA
[pen.] Fiona Swann; [b.] March 23, 1979, Little Thorp Hospital; [p.] Gloria Haswell; [ed.] Hetton Comprehensive, Shiney Row Sixth Form College; [occ.] A level student; [memb.] Durham County Archers Assoc.; [hon.] A* in English and seven further G.C.S.E.'s. Prefect and Librarian, Wear Award for Recycling.; [oth. writ.] Play performed by a local group.; [pers.] I'd like to dedicate this poem to my mother who gave up 25 years of unhappiness for myself and my sister. To all those seeking happiness, things will get better.; [a.] Hetton-le-Hole, Tyne and Wear, DH5 9AH

HATHERLEY, COLLEEN
[b.] Cheltenham; [m.] Thomas Hatherley; [ch.] Gareth Kevin, Damian John; [ed.] Longlevens Comprehensive, Gloucester; [pers.] Tears after dark, recounts the memories of my lost childhood.; [a.] Truro, Cornwall, TR2 4BN

HAUSER, JOHN ROBERT
[pen.] J. R. Hauser; [b.] September 29, 1942, Stoke-on-Trent; [p.] John (Deceased), Anne; [m.] Jean Hauser, June 7, 1982; [ch.] Mark, Julia, Mandy, Alison, Paula; [ed.] Heron Cross Secondary Modern School, Heron Cross Fenton Stoke-on-Trent Staffs; [occ.] Unemployed; [memb.] Staffordshire UFO Group (Memb), Potteries Organization for Paranormal Investigation (Memb), Chairman, Bucknall New Road Residents Association, Hanley Stoke-on-Trent, 5 years Officer Estate Management Board; [hon.] Certificates in Housing Management "Tenants Participation", "Newsletter and Publicity", "Crime and its Causes", "Capitol Works" etc. Nine in all.; [oth. writ.] 'I'm Glad We Met', 'The Prisoner', 'The Troubles', 'Dream of Aquarius', 'Song for Christmas', and other poems have been published in various magazines.; [pers.] If my work, poems etc, can change peoples awareness of the world, cause a shift in consciousness a little, then I'm a happy man. I have been influenced by Blake and Lord Byron, I also like Lord Tennyson's work.; [a.] Hanley, Staffordshire, ST1 2BA

HAWKINS, PAULA-ANNE
[b.] May 14, 1964, London; [ed.] La Sante Union Convent Highgate-London; [occ.] Air Stewardess/Instructor United Airlines; [memb.] Royal Academy, Clipped Wings; [oth. writ.] Poetry published in various anthologies; [pers.] Everything I write, I write from the heart. The goods, bads, highs and lows - total polarity. I'm thankful for all my diversity. It's created a kaleidoscope of concepts and impressions - within me. As the song goes..."It's a Wonderful Life"; [a.] London:, SW3 5TJ

HAY, SHARON
[b.] February 22, 1970, Glasgow; [ed.] Lamlash Primary, Cranhill Secondary, Glasgow College of Commerce; [memb.] International Guild of Songwriters; [oth. writ.] Lots of other songs and poems, but never have tried to get them published.; [pers.] Whatever is for you, will never go by you.; [a.] Glengormley Newtown Abbey, Co. Antrim, BT36 6DY

HAYES, JONATHAN
[pen.] Jonathan Hayes; [b.] August 25, 1965, Stockport; [p.] Mr. William and Dorothy Hayes; [m.] Samantha Beckett (Fiancee); [ed.] St. Mary's Comprehensive School Grimsby; [occ.] Rank Xerox, Specialist; [oth. writ.] One poem 'The Supervisor' for modern management (BI-Monthly), two for Rank Xerox 'Document Matters.' (Monthly).; [pers.] I give thanks to God for inspiration, that there is a voice in poetry that can speak to everyone.; [a.] Grimsby, South Humberside, DN37 9QQ

HAYNES, BARBARA
[b.] July 27, 1931, Pewsey, Wilts; [ed.] Secondary School - Guildford Teacher Training; [occ.] Retired; [hon.] Teacher's Certificate Art (Merit); [pers.] My love for poetry began at school and has remained with me through the years. I have always been grateful for the early introduction to Wordsworth, Tennyson, Browning, etc.; [a.] London, E3 4LQ

HAYWARD, FREDERICK GEORGE
[b.] November 15, 1924, Brighton; [p.] Lilian and William Hayward MM; [m.] Doris Eileen Hayward, NE Coates, August 7, 1954; [ch.] Frederick George Hayward Jr.; [ed.] Coombe Road and Moulscoomb Elementary School; [memb.] Committee Member of Brighton Trades and Labour Club; [oth. writ.] Have written many poems, on numerous subjects, such as "My Brighton", my thanks to the National Trust, and numerous other titles, none of which I have ever submitted for publication.; [pers.] Forth son of six to Lilian and William Hayward-MM served in the Royal Naval Home Fleet and Pacific Fleet, World War II, proud wearer of the "Atlantic Star, Burma Star, and Pacific Clasp."; [a.] Brighton, East Sussex, BN2 4RR

HAYWARD, JACQUELINE GOERGINA
[pen.] Jackie; [b.] February 5, 1942, London; [p.] Harold Lake and Lilian Lake; [m.] Was married long time ago; [ch.] Alison Louise May, Nicholas John May; [ed.] Essendine Secondary Modern, Maida Vale London W9. No Certificates passed for Art College, also Training Hairdresser, Medicine Sec. (Jack of all trades); [occ.] Housewife; [hon.] City and Guilds for Hairdressing in the 1960. Was told would pass English Exams; [oth. writ.] Many not published on seen.; [pers.] I write from experience of things in real life and emotional anger. It could be funny on it could be sad.; [a.] Sudbury, Suffolk, CO10 0LA

HAYWARD, PAUL
[b.] June 1, 1952, London; [pers.] I also like. Freelance Artist and Etcher. Slide Guitar. "5 Billion Humanoids but only one mind". Timeless Transcendence. Sacred Ecstasy (Tantraics). To dance with compassion as partner.; [a.] Edgware, Middx, HA8

HEAD, GEORGE JACK
[pen.] Jaques Hedeni; [b.] September 22, 1913, Southwark; [p.] D.; [m.] Annie Laurie, March 25, 1939; [ch.] Four, 1 daughter, 3 sons; [ed.] Passed various exams; [occ.] A retired old, gentleman, as granted by the College of Arms'; [hon.] Armorial Bearings Granted by Sir Conn Cole, the Garter King of Arms, I am president of the Stoughton and Westborough Royal British Legion. Northway Guildford.; [oth. writ.] A few more poems that relate to the proper ways of life, good things.; [pers.] I try to put my feelings into my works by using my poems or lyrics to say to my readers this is the good way; [a.] Guildford, Surrey, GU2 6RY

HEAD, PETER
[pen.] Buck Peters; [b.] February 9, 1960, Middlesbrough; [p.] Thomas Raymond Head - Margaret Head; [ed.] Boynton Comprehensive School, General Education; [occ.] Gardener-co-worker; [hon.] City I guilds in horticulture.; [pers.] I work in a environment which is concerned with a non-chemical approach to soil and health. Which I believe in and which reflects in my poetry.; [a.] Middlesbrough, Cleveland, TS8 9DY

HEENAN, CATHERINE
[b.] September 21, 1976, Caerphilly; [p.] Patrick and Eileen Heenan; [ed.] Heolddu Comprehensive School, Cardiff University; [occ.] Student; [memb.] National Union of Students; [hon.] Current Studying BA Honours Degree in English Literate.; [oth. writ.] Poem published in Poetry Institute of the British Isle Anthology 'Island Moods and Reflections!' Co-Editor of Local History book 'Bargoed Bygones!'; [pers.] Good poems raise a smile, raise a tear or touch the heart. Good poems are creations of life.; [a.] Brithdir, Gwent, NP2 6JF

HEIBNER, ERROL
[pen.] John; [b.] June 13, 1945, Cape Town; [p.] Albert and Nellie Heibner; [ed.] Nautical Naval School Parkstone, Poole, Dorset; [occ.] Inmate, H. M. Prison Coldingley; [memb.] The Penman Club, Pall Mall Leigh-on-Sea, Essex; [oth. writ.] Collection of several hundred poems prose, philosophy written over 21 years of an injustice and my conviction which I continue to contest and asset my 'Innocence' of the crime of which I was convinced!; [pers.] All my poems were composed within H. M. Maximum security prisons of which a substantial amount developed as a result of time spent in tray isolation. They erase my condition, circumstance, reflect my pains, passions through relationship what they represent with those I fear affection for.; [a.] Bisley, Surrey, GU24 9EX

HELPS, EDNA HAY
[b.] January 1, 1911, Leicester; [m.] Deceased 1970, April 11, 1933; [ed.] Very little brought up in a foster home and my foster mother was often ill and we I had no were very poor. Oftenning shoes to wear to school; [oth. writ.] Several other poems published; [pers.] I strive to reflect the Beauty of nature that is the Creators gift to us all.; [a.] Leicester, LE4 2JZ

HEMINGWAY, DENISE
[b.] December 17, 1961, Barnsley; [p.] Ernest and Nellie Hemingway; [ed.] Broadway Comprehensive, Broadway, Barnsley South Yorkshire; [memb.] P.D. Society, Parkinson's Disease Society; [oth. writ.] Published book "Time For Memories". Dorrance Publishers Pittsburgh, U.S.A.; [pers.] I've always loved writing. My favourite subject at school, was English. And my ambition was to be a Published author, of which I am now proud to be.; [a.] Barnsley, S. Yorkshire, S70 3JG

HEMMINGS, EVE
[pen.] Eve Rumney; [b.] August 30, 1932, Cumbria; [p.] Dorothy-Wesley Rumney; [m.] T. Hemmings, February 12, 1955; [ch.] 4 Children-Peter, Carole, Craig, Patrick, 5 Grandchildren; [ed.] Village School, Nursery Nurse "Royal Cross School for the Deaf Preston; [occ.] Company Director; [memb.] Book Club Charity Organizations; [oth. writ.] Now Accepted; [pers.] I have been influenced by the love and compassion I felt in my 5 years as a volunteer teacher at a school for behavior problem children. The parents gave me the courage to write; [a.] St. Brelade, Jersey, LE3 8FE

HEMMINGS, EVE
[pen.] Eve Rumney; [b.] August 30, 1932, Cumbria; [p.] Dorothy-Wesley Rumney; [m.] T. Hemmings, February 12, 1955; [ch.] Peter, Carole, Craig, Patrick; [ed.] Cleator School, trained at Royal Cross School for deaf children as nursery nurse; [occ.] Retired; [memb.] Book Club; [oth. writ.] None published yet; [pers.] Started to write poetry after witnessing the tolerance of parents of behavior problem children I was teaching. Their love and devotion was an inspiration; [a.] St. Brelade, Jersey, JE3 8FE

HENDERSON, COLIN
[pen.] Colin Henderson; [b.] October 26, 1962, Edinburgh; [p.] Jack and Sheila Henderson; [m.] Irene Henderson, June 27, 1987; [ch.] Daniel, Kayleigh; [ed.] Forrester High School, Edinburgh; [occ.] Civil Servant (Ministry of Defence Dog Handler); [pers.] My writing, reflects the events of my past, the good times, the bad times, the sad times.; [a.] South Queensferry, West Lothian, EH30 9RU

HENHAM, MRS. MARGARET
[b.] April 21, 1922; [ch.] 3 boys, 9 grandchildren, 2 great-grandchildren; [hon.] Bronze and silver medals, The Poetry Society's exams in verse speaking; [oth. writ.] Many poems the age of 16. (Unpublished).; [pers.] My poems are very simply an expression of personal feeling at the time of writing, often written for a specific person.

HENSTOCK, GEORGE AUBREY
[b.] November 24, 1924, Newark, Notts; [p.] Ted Henstock, Laura Henstock; [m.] Divorced; [ch.] Paul, Avril; [ed.] Stanislaid Comprehensive Boston, Lincs Wainfleet Methodist, Wainflect Lincs., Spring Grove Polytechnic Isle Worth Middx; [occ.] Retired, Ex B.T. District Catering Manager; [memb.] Hotel Catering and Institutional Management Association, Cookery and Foods Association, Normandy Veterans Association, A.R.P. Over Fifty, Army Catering Corp Assn., Active Life.; [hon.] City and Guilds 1st Class for Bread and Flour Confectionery; [pers.] "There is no greater love than that of a mother for her child and those words of wisdom she speaks in it's memory filed."; [a.] Beddington, Surrey, CR0 4PH

HEPPEL, PATRICIA ELIZABETH
[pen.] Pat Heppel; [b.] February 24, 1930, Plymouth; [p.] George and Daisy Shobbrook; [m.] Roy Heppel, April 26, 1953; [ch.] Timothy, Susan and Linda; [ed.] Plymouth High School for Girls Street, Elmhurst Grammar School. College of Further Education Plymouth, College of St Mark and St. John; [occ.] Retired Primary School Teacher; [memb.] Chairwoman Salisbury Road, Baptist Church Women's League. Member of Plymouth "MENCAP" Daughter Susan Spashc/Mentally handicapped; [hon.] Teacher's Training Cert. (University of Exeter); [oth. writ.] 16 poems published in various anthologies. 3 Narioity plays for Juniors.; [pers.] I write about "the sleeping stones" in my life, my family, the beauty around me and God's goodness to us all.; [a.] Plymouth, Devon, PL9 8H

HERD, DOROTHY M. E.
[b.] September 24, 1900, Allahabad UP, India; [p.] Evelyn and Harriett Paxton; [m.] Cyril Charles Herd (Deceased), October 3, 1927; [ed.] High School Mussoorie India; [occ.] Retired Pensioner Widow Living in 'Kings Haven' Rest - Home - Southsea, Cosham, Hants; [memb.] Past Civil Service Club Cosham - Flora L-Club Whist Club, Highbury Thursday - Club Scrabble - Club; [hon.] Four for Floral Arrangements; [oth. writ.] Written a biography not yet published.; [a.] Southsea, Hants, PO4 0QP

HERSH, ALAN LAURENCE
[b.] October 26, 1934, London; [p.] Harry Hersh, Hettie Hersh; [m.] Ann Louise Cohen, July 18, 1962; [ch.] Ruth, Deborah, David (Deceased), Rachel; [ed.] Raine's Grammar, University of London, UCL, Birkbeck College, Institute of Education; [occ.] Senior Lecturer in French, Brunel University; [memb.] Fellow, Institute of Linguists, Association for French Language Studies, Association of Directors of University Language Centres (DULC), Union Des Professors De Langues Etrangeres Des Grandes Ecoles, European Association of Linguists and Language Teachers, National Trust; [hon.] Modern Languages Prize 1951, 1952, ESU Exchange Grant to USA 1962-63, Fulbright Travel Grant to USA 1962-63; [oth. writ.] Some poems published in University magazine (Brunel), some unpublished poems, Conference Papers, Chapters in Academic publications on Language Teaching (AFLS-CILT), etc.; [pers.] I believe in humour as an antidote to anger (at unfairness or injustice). I prefer individuals to administrations human devices (especially in professional and teaching contexts). I hate the "Rat Race"!; [a.] Harrow, Middlesex, HA3 0LL

HEWITT, MILLICENT
[b.] Norfolk; [p.] Richard Browning and Dorothy May Sayer's; [m.] Michael Charles Hewitt; [ch.] Jacqueline Anne and Carole Marie; [ed.] Terrington St. Clement Secondary School, King's Lynn Technical College; [occ.] Housewife; [memb.] Women's Institute; [oth. writ.] 2 other poems published in East Anglia Anthology. Several poems published in St. Mary's Church Lakenheath Magazine.; [pers.] I write most of my poems for the residents of Lakenheath Christian Home and read them at the Sunday evening service they, and my family, have given me every encouragement.; [a.] Lakenheath, Suffolk, IP27 9DA

HEWLETT, MRS. MARION
[b.] November 11, 1943, Smithfield; [p.] Irene Henry Griffiths; [m.] Mr. John Hewlett, February 19, 1994; [ed.] Ravensworth Secondary School Mottingham; [occ.] Housewife; [pers.] I believe that writing poetry comes from insight you get with experience of life through suffering also there is not enough religious poetry about today for my liking.; [a.] Mottingham, London, Kent, SE9 4LD

HICKFORD, PAULINE ANNE
[b.] March 7, 1966, Hitchin, Herts; [p.] Robert Headland and Brenda Headland; [m.] Andrew John Hickford, December 21, 1985; [ch.] Grant, Matthew and Hannah; [ed.] Collenswood Senior School; [occ.] Housewife; [pers.] I wish to dedicate this poem to my husband, my children and my parents, with all my love always; [a.] Stevenage, Herts, SG2 8HY

HIGGINS, FIONA
[pen.] Fiona Higgins; [b.] November 1, 1951, Brechin; [p.] William and Ann Higgins; [ch.] Pauline 19 years; [ed.] Buckmaven High School, Northern College, Dundee Campus; [occ.] Social Work; [oth. writ.] Various poems published in anthologies; [pers.] My writing reflects my belief in the love of God and the hope of peace and love for all. I write what I feel.; [a.] Perth, Perth and Kinross, PH2 6BL

HIGGINS, MARTIN
[b.] July 15, 1966, Dunlarvan, Ireland; [p.] Michael Higgins, Anne Baker; [ed.] St. Augustines College; [occ.] L.G.V. Driver; [oth. writ.] Various poems, short passages; [pers.] Influences Seamus Heaney, Leonard Cohen; [a.] Bristol, Avon, BS12 7QG

HIGGS, SUSAN ANN
[b.] May 11, 1952, Northallerton; [p.] Joyce and William Dobson; [m.] David George Higgs, August 7, 1971; [ch.] Louisa Marie; [ed.] Ripon Secondary Modern Sch., Northallerton School of Nursing; [occ.] Electric Shop Proprietor; [oth. writ.] Poem published in "Poetry Now" Yorkshire Edition 1995.; [pers.] My poetry is written instantly reflecting and recording whatever I feel and see at the time.; [a.] Thirsk, N. Yorks, YO7 1SB

HIGNETT, STEPHANIE CHRISTINE
[b.] January 3, 1975, Liverpool; [p.] Josie and Steve Hignett; [ed.] Saint John Bosco (8 G.C.SE's) 4 A-Levels Gov and Pol. English, Sociology and Psychology.; [occ.] Student, B.A. combined degree, Soc. and Psy.; [memb.] British Psychological Society, Liverpool Football Club; [oth. writ.] Many other unpublished works.; [pers.] Strive to be yourself, and all shall become clear. Thomas Hardy talks of fate, but you have the ability as a human being, to change, reinvention is the key to the disaster of what you do not want to become.; [a.] Liverpool, Merseyside, L45 3SW

HILL, JANET ELAINE
[b.] March 16, 1953, Aberbargoed, South Wales; [m.] Graham Barry Hill, November 13, 1971; [ch.] Two daughter's; [ed.] Very little, as I moved around quite a lot.; [occ.] House wife also foster cearer; [oth. writ.] This is the first.; [pers.] Happily married with two grown up daughters. And one grandson. Have fostered for nine years and have looked after twenty children to date. And find it rewarding and fulfilling. And hope to continue for many year's ahead.; [a.] Aberbargoed, Bargoed, Mid-Glam, CF81 9BT

HILTON, LINDA
[pen.] Linda Hilton; [b.] October 29, 1952, Clapham; [p.] George Hilton, Violet Hilton; [m.] Future husband Ray Sibley, Divorced. To be married in summer 96; [ch.] Robert, Mark and Tracy Davison; [ed.] Sutton Common County, Secondary Girls School; [occ.] Creche Supervisor at Banstead Sports Centre, Tadworth; [memb.] Banstead Sports Centre; [hon.] Diploma in Child Care; [oth. writ.] Several poems written only for pleasure.; [pers.] Having had many near death experiences, I now value my life and wish to put my feelings into words. Encouraged by my Mum who died of cancer, with her spirit behind me my boundaries have no limits.; [a.] Tadworth, Surrey, KT20 5LD

HILTON, PHILIP
[pen.] Pip Hilton; [b.] August 8, 1946, Kingston upon Hull; [p.] Charles Henry and Florence Mary (Both Deceased); [m.] Divorced, June 4, 1968; [ch.] Philip Peter and Jeremy John Hilton; [ed.] Elizabetha Hall Comprehensive School Hull; [occ.] Ex fisherman and airframe fitter but I am now disabled but trying to make it as a published writer; [memb.] Elite Racing Club; [hon.] Swimming, 1st, 2nd, 3rd and mile, certificates, silver service, stearing ticket and Merchant Navy - C.P.R.; [oth. writ.] Short story published for school magazine; [pers.] Arctic corsair was the last conventional trawler I sailed in out of Hull. I Have penned three novels-unpublished and over a dozen short stories. To keep my hand in the writing game I wrote to Lord Tebbit - columnist for the sun - for over a year, each week, giving my own-on year bike awards!; [a.] Hull, E. Yorkshire, HU3 2LU

HIRONS, KEITH RICHARD
[pen.] Layne Woodway; [b.] October 2, 1946, Coventry; [p.] William Hirons, Kathleen Hirons; [m.] Divorced; [ch.] Wendy, Judy; [occ.] Voluntary Worker; [memb.] Local Committee's, Deaf Club, Sports Club, Coventry Dragons; [oth. writ.] Several poems published in local news papers, magazines. Also in other anthologies; [pers.] I write what I see and feel at that time. I try to be accurate yet instill humour or a twist in the poems tail; [a.] Coventry, West Midlands, CV2 2LW

HOARE, IRENE
[b.] December 23, 1954, Redditch; [p.] Albert and Lillian Marshall; [m.] Frederick Hoare, July 23, 1976; [ch.] Debbie Hoare; [ed.] Walkwood High; [occ.] Sales Staff Supervisor; [hon.] English Language, English Literature; [oth. writ.] Two poems published by Arrival Press and Anchor Books. Special poems written for friends and family.; [a.] Redditch, Worcs, B98 7TY

HODGKINS, KERRY ANN
[b.] June 15, 1985, Worcester; [p.] Mr. George and Mrs. Evelyn Hodgkins; [memb.] Member of Mr. Vales Poetry and Drama Group, Driotwich member of Gemini Dance Centre; [hon.] Won gold medal at Worcs Festival for poetry prose and drama, dance awards from competitions all over Britain, Distinction Award from Lamda Exams; [oth. writ.] Stories at school reading which I enjoy a lot. Poems from Distinguished Poets.; [pers.] I would really like to fulfill my ambition to write more poems and prose to visit other countries and study their poetry and stories as well as recite them and go to university; [a.] Redditch, Worcs, B98 0AY

HOLDER, MARY
[pen.] Yvette Redding; [b.] October 8, 1937, London; [m.] David Holder, December 1, 1979; [ch.] Veronica Lee; [ed.] Wycombe High School; [occ.] Housewife; [hon.] English Literature, English Language; [oth. writ.] Poems and short stories, none published to date; [pers.] I endeavour through observation, to reflect in my work, the frailties and emotions of everyday human life. My other works include poems for/about children. Wild life, and fantasy.; [a.] Reading, Berkshire, RG4 7LZ

HOLLERAN, MARTIN JAMES
[pen.] Martin James Holleran; [b.] October 20, 1950, London, England; [p.] James 'Barney' Holleran, Joan Holleran; [m.] Mary Bolland, May 22, 1982; [occ.] Telecommunications Engineer; [memb.] Great Britain-China Centre; [hon.] Being published. Higher Certificate in Computer Technology. Diploma in Stage Management from London Academy of Music and Dramatic Art.; [pers.] I have been influenced by all manner of thoughts, people and places, in understanding life. A special 'Thank You' must therefore go to all my family, drama teachers: Rodney Archer and Powell Jones, and to a special friend I never met-but saw once. Jimi Hendrix.; [a.] High Wycombe, Bucks, HP13 7EY

HOLLEY, CEEJAY
[pen.] CeeJay Baker-Holley; [b.] 1923, Southampton; [m.] George, 1949; [ed.] Elementary; [occ.] Retired; [oth. writ.] Unpublished; [a.] Southampton, Hampshire, SO15 8LN

HOLLOWAY, RONALD H.
[b.] September 10, 1920, Poplar; [m.] Joan Holloway; [oth. writ.] 1st prize and certificate for a Christmas poem. Poem read on local radio. Poems and ditties wrote on local newsletters.; [pers.] Ronald passed away 25-12-'96. He wrote many poems which (I his wife has) he loved life and wrote about things around him, places he had been to etc. His life interrupted by the war which he spent in the raf. He had managerial jobs, and eventually had his own small business. Please use his own name when printing his poetry.; [a.] Norwich, Norfolk, NR2 4QT

HOMER, KENNETH
[b.] September 9, 1950, Bebington; [p.] Kenneth and Hettie; [m.] Glynis Catherine, April 21, 1995; [ch.] Lucie (19), (Step-children) Paul (20), Laura (11), Emma (18); [ed.] Grange Secondary Modern Ellesmere Port; [occ.] Instructor/Support Worker, People with Learning Disabilities; [memb.] Former Lions Club Member, Former Guild of Master Craftsmen; [hon.] City and Guilds Woodwork/Machining; [oth. writ.] Assorted prose and poems (unpublished).; [pers.] Encouraged by Glynis (wife) to portray my inner feelings in writings I reflect mainly on personal reflections.; [a.] Tarvin, Cheshire, CH3 8EF

HOPKINS, JAMES THOMAS
[b.] October 19, 1946, Merthyr, Tydfil; [p.] Oswald Hopkins, Violet Mary Hopkins; [m.] Eira Hopkins (Jones), February 1, 1975; [ch.] Lee James and Kerry Ian; [ed.] Gellifaelog Boys School, Merthyr Tydfil; [occ.] Unemployed; [oth. writ.] A variety of poems and two short stories unpublished; [pers.] The two biggest influences on my writing are Apathy and the Hypocrisy of Mankind. I feel Philosophical on a full stomach.; [a.] Merthyr Tydfil, Mid-Glam, CF47 9UY

HOPWOOD, BARBARA
[b.] November 9, 1948, Staffordshire; [ch.] Sam and David; [ed.] Belvedere School, Liverpool; [memb.] British Tennis Umpires Assoc., L.T.A., Bramhall Paric Tennis Club; [oth. writ.] Articles for the Lancashire Magazine; [pers.] I feel very fortunate that I have found a way to express emotions that I would otherwise find difficult to deal with, or even admit to one of my hopes is that people not as fortunate can identify with my words and take comfort, courage or simply pleasure from them.; [a.] Stockport, Cheshire, SK2 5AJ

HORSEY, JANE
[b.] January 31, 1965, Bristol; [ed.] Bristol and Plymouth; [occ.] Reflexology Student; [oth. writ.] "Dusk on the Veld" is my first attempt at poetry writing, and first published piece.; [pers.] "A day during which we have laughed is a day that has not been wasted" Regina Barreca.; [a.] Bristol, Bristol, BS6 7TZ

HORSLEN, PETER
[b.] October 11, 1929, London; [m.] Joan Margaret Horslen, July 2, 1953; [ch.] Two girls, three boys; [ed.] Elementary, The war desrufert my education; [occ.] Retired; [oth. writ.] 6 other poems; [pers.] As I am left handed I was made to write with my right hand, as a result I would not write, I look up writing quite late in life; [a.] Bunny, Nottinghamshire, NG11 6QJ

HOWARD, BARRY
[b.] September 30, 1945, London; [p.] George and Olive; [ed.] Comprehensive; [occ.] Aquarist; [memb.] Greenpeace; [oth. writ.] Several poems, short stories and articles have been included in a mixture of books, magazines and trade-journals; [pers.] A late starter, creative writing is a new venture for me. I find poetry to be a particularly stimulating medium of communication.; [a.] Carshalton, Surrey, SM5 1JA

HOWARD, DIANE
[b.] November 15, 1942, Portsmouth; [p.] Joy Ansell and Tom Ansell; [m.] Cliff Howard, March 31, 1962; [ch.] Andrew Francis and Julian Robert; [ed.] Cranbourne Secondary Modern Windsor Grammar School S.E. Berks. Coll. of Further Ed.; [occ.] Administrator; [hon.] Area Finalist - Daily Mirror Mrs. Britain Award 1971; [oth. writ.] Poems published in other anthologies short plays have been staged in the past for local church youth group; [pers.] I would like to think that my poems cover any occasion and suit every emotion. My inspiration comes from everyday life and the people I meet I listen to conversations, and many of my titles and poetic content comes from them.; [a.] Blackwell, Berkshire, RE12 2QD

HOWARD, JAMES
[b.] November 26, 1968, London; [p.] Wilmer Howard and Sylvia Howard; [ed.] Wimbledon College, North East Surrey College of Technology.; [occ.] Cruiseship Photographer in the Caribbean; [hon.] Runner-up in short story competition Oct. 1995; [oth. writ.] Novel: 'Oh Bugger!' Play: 'Friday 14th', numerous short stories and poems. Cartoon strip: ' The Adventures of Private Investigator Wilbur Wildebeest'.; [pers.] I feel the importance of being happy is my ultimate goal. 'Life's Too Short'. How many times have you heard that? We've all only got one life so let's make the most of it.; [a.] London, SW20 9BG

HOWARTH, ELIZABETH
[b.] January 31, 1938, Preston; [p.] George and Lilian Simmons; [m.] Peter Noel Howarth, March 15, 1957; [ch.] Lynne, Peter, Michelle; [occ.] Hospice Housekeeper; [pers.] I write a lot of personal poems for my family and staff at the hospice.; [a.] Preston, Lancs, PR1 9NN

HOWARTH, PETER
[b.] April 21, 1943, Colne; [p.] Robert and Hazel Howarth; [m.] Pauline Howarth, April 21, 1967; [ch.] One daughter; [ed.] Highfield Secondary Modern Blackpool Technical College; [occ.] Carpenter; [hon.] Diploma Clinical Sciences, Diploma Clinical Nutrition; [oth. writ.] I have at present written about 200 poems both humorous and serious.; [pers.] I write purely for pleasure of myself and others I have written poems on specific subject for various people.; [a.] Nelson, Lancs, BB9 8SD

HOWE, PEARL RUBY
[pen.] Peggy Howe; [b.] April 10, 1929, Totton, Hants; [p.] Adopted by Percy and Nellie Summerlin; [m.] Bob Howe, February 25, 1950; [ch.] One daughter, three grandsons: Trudy, Andrew, Barry, Peter; [ed.] Langley St. and Surrey St. School Luton Beds; [occ.] Retired; [memb.] Committee Member League of Friends Glan Clwyd Hospital, Treasurer for 10 yrs, Guild, Hospital Charity Work and Shop, Ran my own over 60's club.; [hon.] They tell me my reward will be in heaven!; [oth. writ.] Numerous poems, short story. Life story from birth to 21; [pers.] Poems published in magazines. I am an ordinary person with a love of life and people. The simple things of life interest me, hence my poems. I have a sense of humour, church goer, always ready to lend a helping hand.; [a.] St. Asaph, Denbighshire, LL17 0BL

HOWELLS, BELINDA J.
[b.] February 8, 1967, Pontypridd; [p.] Marilyn and Glyn Chappell; [ed.] Local Comprehensive School and Local Technical College; [occ.] Accounts Clerk; [hon.] Secretarial Diplomas; [oth. writ.] Although I have written several other poems. This is the first time I have ever entered a competition.; [pers.] As a Christian I feel God has inspired me to write poetry.; [a.] Pontypridd, Mid Glamorgan

HOWROYD, PAUL S.
[pen.] Paul S. Howroyd; [b.] September 24, 1972, London; [p.] Pamela and Geoffrey Howroyd; [ed.] University of East London the Green Church of England School; [occ.] I am currently studying for a degree in psychology.; [memb.] Choi Kwang Do - Martial Art International; [oth. writ.] This is my first poem to be published. I have, however written many other poems which I hope to be published when I have a greater amount to hopefully have a book entirely of my own work.; [pers.] I don't believe poetry can change the world, but it would be nice to think it might make people think before they act. After all, what we do today shapes what is our tomorrow.; [a.] London, N17 6TP

HUGHES, ELIZABETH MARGARETTA
[pen.] Elizabeth Hughes; [b.] June 18, 1947, Valley, Gwynedd; [p.] Hugh and Mary Williams; [m.] Robert Hughes, November 2, 1968; [ch.] Two daughters, one son; [ed.] Llandudno Welsh Primary School, Holyhead County Secondary School; [occ.] Housewife; [oth. writ.] Other poems published called, "Hope" "Blessed" and "God's Kingdom"; [pers.] I am a born again Christian and I love flowers, the countryside and anything to do with nature my favorite passtime is writing poetry one of my favourite poets being Henry Wordsworth Longfellow.; [a.] Holyhead, Gwynedd, LL65 2RR

HUGHES, JAMES CARL
[b.] December 31, 1952, Whitehaven; [p.] Kathleen Jackie Hughes; [ed.] St. Beghs Secondary Modern Workington College Whitehaven College; [occ.] Maintenance Technician; [memb.] Whitehaven Bottle Club West Cumbria Vintage Club; [hon.] City and Guilds of London with credits, Computer Data Certificate, Computer Programming 5 CSES; [oth. writ.] Poem published in anthology out of the dark called Whitehavens Memories; [pers.] As a pupil at school I was put off poetry by a series of bad teachers who said my poems were not any good but as a adult I enjoy writing and reading poetry.; [a.] Whitehaven, Cumbria, CA28 6BP

HUNT, GEAN
[b.] August 24, 1938, Hutton Magna; [p.] George Thomas Hodgson, Edith Anne Hodgson; [m.] James Hunt, September 17, 1994; [ch.] Paul, Conrad, Debora, Fiona; [ed.] Whitecliffe and Barnard Castle; [occ.] Retired Nanny; [memb.] Womens Institute, Barnard Castle Playing Fields Association, Barnard Castle Cricket Club, Hutton Magna Choir; [oth. writ.] Article Printed in Lancaster University Student Magazine; [pers.] It gives me great pleasure to make children happy. I like to make my own cooking recipes up, also to crochet my own designs, and listening to classical music.; [a.] Richmond, N. Yorks

HUNT, HAYLEY
[b.] January 13, 1981, Liverpool; [p.] Debra Hunt and Stuart Hunt; [ed.] Currently attending Holy Family High School, Thornton, Liverpool; [memb.] Mensa, Interact - Charity and Social Youth Group; [hon.] Attained IQ of 176 which placed me in the top 1% of the population according to a Mensa supervised IQ test. Attained two awards for class achievement in Holy Family High School.; [oth. writ.] Poem published in the local newspaper regarding war in Rwanda.; [pers.] I like to write poetry regarding issues of importance often ignored by society.; [a.] Crosby, Merseyside, L23 6UZ

HUNTLEY, JOANNE
[b.] Yorkshire; [oth. writ.] Varied and interesting working life - but long!; [pers.] I love sculpturing. This my first poem seemed to come out of nowhere. It makes me feel warm and evokes thoughts and precious, delicious memories.; [a.] York

HURLEY, MRS. MARY ANN
[b.] October 31, 1930, Ballina, Eire; [p.] Deceased; [m.] Deceased, 22 years Army Service, April 17, 1954; [ch.] Teresa and John, British Army School; [ed.] John Duke of York, Royal Military School Dover; [occ.] Community Care Worker; [a.] Ballina, Mayo

HYDON, MR. DON H.
[pen.] Don H. Hydon; [b.] December 12, 1933, Burham, Kent; [p.] Kimberley C. Hydon, Hilda G. Hydon; [m.] Madeline Isabel Hydon, January 24, 1953; [ch.] Kim Shirley, Susan Annette, Stephen Neville; [ed.] Maidstone Technical School and College; [occ.] Recently retired. Computer Systems Design and Administration; [memb.] Former Member of 'the Institution of Computer Sciences', Tudor Park Golf Club; [oth. writ.] Co-author of a series of articles in the Computer Management Magazine. (Late 1960's) A host of 'Funny' poems based on my experiences with my granddaughter, and several others which depict the pleasures of myself and my wife. I have never thought to seek publication until now.; [pers.] I loved poetry in my school days but did not rekindle my interest until the birth of my eldest granddaughter. I love writing rhyme which makes the children laugh - because laughter is a great part of life.; [a.] Snodland, Kent, ME6 5PS

HYLAND, ANTHONY
[pen.] Anthony Hyland; [b.] March 27, 1965, London; [ed.] Alleyns School, London (1978-79 Eastern Junior High, Conn. USA); [occ.] Theatre producer, director, agent; [memb.] MENSA, Directors Guild of Great Britain, British Actors Equity, Player's Theatre, Equity S.M. Committee; [oth. writ.] Play/film Scripts, Ongoing Over The Last 15 Years.; [pers.] Greek and Egyptian Classicist. Any influence on my writing stems from these Era's, in particular aeschylus, homer and aristophanes.; [a.] Streatham, London, SW16 2XN

IBOLO, MARIA
[b.] February 20, 1978, Nigeria; [p.] Mr. and Mrs. A. C. Atiomo; [ed.] Maryland Primary School Lagos and Maryland Secondary School Lagos; [occ.] Just completed 'O' levels in Nigeria and awaiting University Placement.; [hon.] 3rd Prize for excellence by the National Committee on the World Decade for Cultural Development in 1984.; [oth. writ.] "Incomparable Love", "Still In Control", "Arranged Pains", "I Remain Rustic by Choice"; [a.] Lagos, Nigeria

INGRAM, WAYNE
[b.] January 18, 1971, Bournemouth; [p.] Christine Ash, Melvyn Ash; [ed.] Ringwood School, Roehampton Institute, University of Surrey; [occ.] Aspiring poet; [hon.] 2:1 Honours English and Theatre; [oth. writ.] I have many more poems written on toilet rolls, envelopes and sweet wrappers. They are all simply dying to meet the masses. A publisher would be nice! Give me a call. 01425-479314.; [pers.] Atrocities: Read it, shout it, scream it aloud!! Let everyone everywhere hear its horrific imagery and factual content. Now, go next door and confront your neighbor with my poem, and then ask them one question: If God himself instructed you to kill your fellow man, would you do it?; [a.] Ringwood, Hampshire, BH24 1AX

IRVINE, JOANNA
[b.] October 31, 1973, Ormskirk, Lancs; [p.] David and Marie Irvine.; [ed.] Comber High School Northern Ireland. Also Numerous Primary Schools around Co. Down.; [occ.] Royal Navy Stores Accountant; [oth. writ.] A few short poems for magazines as a teenager.; [pers.] Leonard Cohen and Dorothy Parker amongst some Shakespeare sonnets influence most of my works, trying to reflect the more darker sides of peoples emotions.; [a.] Comber, Co. Down, BT23 5QE

ISWERWOOD, JANET ELIZABETH
[b.] November 21, 1952, Widnes, Cheshire; [p.] James Ann Violet Brookes (Deceased); [m.] John (Deceased) Now engaged to George Minorton; [ch.] Four; [ed.] Secondary Modern school Fairfield; [occ.] Part time Domestic Worker, full time mother; [oth. writ.] Local newspaper, church magazine, many to poetry now; [pers.] I have only been writing for 3 months and have been successful for my first poems to be published as a new writer I hope to have my own book one day. I write all types of poetry which I hope will be an inspiration to others I suddenly found my lift in poetry; [a.] Widnes, Cheshire, WA8 3LU

JACKSON, MARK
[b.] October 16, 1959, Swansea; [p.] Darrel Jackson, Norma Jackson; [ch.] Nathan and Ainsley; [ed.] Pontardawe Comprehensive School; [occ.] Book Binder, Reploy Limited; [memb.] INCD Golf Club; [oth. writ.] Poems printed in works magazines and on Christmas Cards; [pers.] I take great pleasure in writing poems and wish to dedicate this to my mother who was a great influence to me; [a.] Swansea, West Glam, SA6 5HE

JACKSON, MRS. GLORIA
[pen.] G. H. J.; [b.] September 1, 1949, Enfield; [m.] Graham, July 2, 1976; [ch.] Steven, Angela, Sandra; [ed.] Chingford County High School; [occ.] Retired Office Service Manager for Financial Institution; [oth. writ.] Poems published in local press anthologies.; [pers.] Since being diagnosed with M. S. (Multiple Sclerosis) (having taken early retirement due to ill health), writing poetry is therapeutic to giving me a positive attitude to manage my condition.; [a.] Peterborough, Cambs, PE2 8RY

JACKSON, NANCY
[pen.] Louise Hammett; [b.] October 20, 1928, Broughtom, Hampshire; [p.] Mr. Bertie William Hammett, Mrs. Margaret Hammett (Nee) John; [m.] Kenneth E. Jackson, June 18, 1949; [ch.] Pauline, Richard, Phillip, Alan; [ed.] Elementary Wreccelesham St. Peters, C of G. Farnham Sj Strong Artist Leanings, which were not recognized in those days very good at Essays; [occ.] Retired Housewife S of T Toy mankind writing poetry short stories; [memb.] Aldershot Underwood, Bowling Club - AE Writing Class. AE - Painting and Drawing Class Sculpture. Musci; [hon.] Poem printed in Voices of Surrey. Five Bowling Trophies last season; [oth. writ.] Short Stories none printed yet; [pers.] Inner knowingness and contentment, that comes only with age and trusting the Universe, only then can we be in Harmony with ourselves. And those around us. Then we have played our part.; [a.] Farnham, Surrey, GV9 8LR

JAGMOHAN, CHANDANEE
[b.] April 14, 1965, Edinburgh, Guyana; [p.] Donald Rampersaud - Seeta Rampersaud; [m.] Dhanesh Jagmohan, December 3, 1994; [ch.] Tovash D. Jagmohan; [ed.] Educated in Guyana; [hon.] High School; [pers.] We all need the Divine's Gift: Love.; [a.] Thornton Heath, Surrey, CR7 8JE

JAMES, WENDY
[pen.] 'Melody Jaymes'; [b.] October 15, 1947, Manchester; [p.] Rose and Derek Williams; [m.] Bob James, February 13, 1987; [ed.] Actors Church Union Boarding School UK Northfields Girls 2 'A' Lev. 6 'O' Level GCE's; [occ.] Co. Director (Own Co.); [oth. writ.] Novel - (unpublished) children's book of poems sev. published odes (comedic).; [pers.] Prefer to do personalized odes/poems to order want to share the joys of the english language with less literature with less literature people.; [a.] London, W2 6QT

JENKINS, LEONARD WILFRED
[pen.] L. W. Jenkins; [b.] September 15, 1941, S. Wales; [p.] Margaret Mary Jenkins, Edward Leonard Jenkins; [m.] Mary Jenkins, March 18, 1994; [ch.] Mark, Stephen, Ian, Mary-Jayne; [ed.] Marksbury Rd. Sec. Mod. Bristol, Gloucester Government College; [occ.] Disabled, formerly Instrument Mechanic.; [memb.] Formerly Hutton Drama Club, Q.E.H. Players (drama) Scout Master, Amateur Football Manager; [hon.] City and Guild London Inst.; [oth. writ.] Several poems and songs as yet not published.; [pers.] My poetry reflects my own personal feelings. I hope that others will be touched by them.; [a.] Bristol, Bristol, BS5 8NG

JENNINGS, PAUL
[pen.] Paul Jennings; [b.] June 12, 1965, New Mills; [ed.] Cheadle Hulme County High, MacClesfield College; [occ.] Locksmith; [memb.] The Revolutionary Army of the Mabinogion, The Peter and Gordon Appreciation Society; [oth. writ.] A poem published by anchor books and a novel and complete book of poems as yet unpublished.; [pers.] Honour God, love life. My influences are Dylan Thomas, William Shakespeare and C.S. Lewis.; [a.] Stockport, Cheshire, SK3 0NN

JOBEY, KAREN
[b.] January 14, 1959, Salford; [p.] Francis Jobey, Mary Jobey; [ch.] Nathan, Lee, Robert; [ed.] Pendleton High School, Salford University; [occ.] Officer in Charge, Salford Social Services; [pers.] My first published words dedicated to a very special person.; [a.] Salford, Greater Manchester, M38 9XL

JOHN, MARTIN
[b.] 1923, Calcutta; [ed.] St. Xaviers College Calcutta, Kettering Grammar School; [occ.] Retired Accountant; [memb.] R.A.F. Association, Stirling Aircraft Association, Age Concern, Parkinsons Disease Society, PROBUS and Pensioners' Societies; [hon.] Various medals, certificates and cash prizes in poetry competitions.; [oth. writ.] Short stories, contributions to and illustrations for books on service life. Poems published in a number of Anthologies and the press. magazine articles etc.; [pers.] Having served in the R.A.F. from 1942 to 1947, on a theme of "Lest we Forget", many of my writings are reminders of the sacrifice, suffering and heroism of the British people during the war. I am anti EC as I feel that the dictatorship we overthrew has been replaced fifty years later by Brussels.; [a.] Kettering, Northants, NN15 6HF

JOHNSON, KEITH
[b.] February 20, 1932, Bath; [ch.] Mark, Lucy, Damian; [occ.] Company Director; [ed.] Minimal, due to overcrowded classrooms, with war evacuees, and dyslexia handicap.; [memb.] As original virgin soldier at 18 gained invaluable experience of international horror giving me a perspective on what life was really about. I was awarded the G.S.C. medal that I have not proudly worn.; [hon.] I founded a community in 1952 being one of the first to recognize the need to actively protect the environment.; [oth. writ.] Much written and published in the Bath Chronicle encouraging people to recognize a new age was coming.; [pers.] Leaving school at 14 years of age at the bottom of the class focused my intelligence. What little ego I had I abandoned in favour of the will of the Gods. This enabled my gifts to flourish and to become a millionaire without losing my naivete, and my love of the arts. I admit this in the hope that others will take heart.

JOHNSON, KIMBERLEY
[b.] June 10, 1981, Doncaster; [p.] Raymond Johnson, Gillian Johnson; [ed.] Ridgewood Comprehensive School; [oth. writ.] The Four Sorrows, in Natural Words. My Street, in Yorkshire Voices.; [pers.] I give thanks to all my family, you know who your are. Special thanks to Mum, Dad, Mark and my best friend Emma Wainwright.; [a.] Doncaster, South Yorkshire, DN5 8RD

JOHNSON, MR. STAN
[b.] June 3, 1921, Merseyside; [p.] Deceased; [m.] Deceased, March 22, 1941; [ch.] 1 son; [ed.] Elementary; [occ.] Retired; [memb.] Pensioners Social Club; [hon.] War Service Medal R.A.F. 1946; [oth. writ.] As a school boy won League of Nations Essay Competition 1933. All schools from liverpool and Merseyside. Organized by the League of Nations Union 1933; [pers.] Nature our best guide.; [a.] Moreton-Wirral, Merseyside, L46 6AW

JOHNSTON, DEBORAH
[b.] March 26, 1979, Enniskillen; [p.] James Johnston (Jimmy), Jacqueline Johnston (Deceased); [ed.] Irvinestown Primary School, Enniskillen Collegiate Grammar School, Fermanagh College (At present); [occ.] Student - studying BTEC National Diploma in Leisure Studies; [memb.] Irvinestown Tennis Club, Lough Erne Yacht Club, College Hockey Club, Britannia Music Club; [hon.] English Literature - Grade

A at GCSE Level English - Grade A at GCSE Level, Duke of Edinburgh award (Bronze) Squash Leaders award; [pers.] "Go to the open ground and wish, for you are not alone on a day like this." I love Charles Dickens work and especially the Bronte sisters, who have inspired me greatly.; [a.] Irvinestown, Fermanagh, BT94 1RN

JOINER, JANET MAY
[b.] July 13, 1960, Birmingham; [m.] P. W. Joiner, April 26, 1985; [ch.] 1 girl age 6 - 1 boy age 9 months; [ed.] Basic grade, 4 English grade, 4 Elementary Math's; [occ.] Mother Housewife; [oth. writ.] None sent for publication as I don't know were to sent them, would like to make income from published poems, I have one called "Homeless Plight".; [pers.] Write poems from life events and events during the day, week or whenever something catch's my thoughts, or an occasion.; [a.] W. Mids, B69 3NB

JONES, ANGELA
[pen.] Lizzie Chambers; [b.] October 21, 1948, Cilybebyll; [p.] Jack and Peggy Jones; [m.] Divorced; [ch.] Julie Margaret, Linzi-Ann, and Gareth Bryan (James); [ed.] Pontardawe Sec. Mod., and College of further education; [occ.] Solicitors Secretary; [oth. writ.] Unpublished works; [pers.] My writings reflect my moods at those moments; [a.] Crickhowell, Powys, NP8 1HD

JONES, DIANE
[b.] September 6, 1969, Manchester; [m.] Andrew G. Morrison, Common-Law 9 years; [ch.] Dean Darren, Rebecca Marion; [ed.] Greenhall High, Gorebridge; [occ.] Mother and P/T General Assistant; [memb.] Bridge St., Christian Centre Parent and Toddler Group Musselburgh; [oth. writ.] None printed so far.; [pers.] My poetry is from the heart, and I try to show my feelings in them.; [a.] Prestonpans, East Lothian, EH32 9AN

JONES, EIRWEN ANN
[pen.] Eirwen Ann Jones; [b.] January 6, 1933, Raymney Bridge; [p.] William Powell, Maud Powell; [m.] Glynceiriog Parry Jones (Deceased), September 19, 1966; [ch.] Elizabeth; [ed.] Princetown Elementary Rhymney Grammar School; [occ.] Retired Care - Assistant; [oth. writ.] Five other poems published by Trinity House Peterborough; [pers.] Poetry has always been my delight.; [a.] Aberdare, Mid Glam, CF44 6HD

JONES, JANET ROBERTSON
[b.] January 3, 1939, Musselborough, Scotland; [p.] David and Margaret Hill; [m.] Mr. Leslie Gordon Jones, October 1, 1960; [ch.] Two Daughters, One Son, Five Grand-children; [ed.] Stockport High School for Girls, Six O'Levels, (same as Joan Bakewen); [occ.] Writing for Pleasure from Home; [memb.] I have been on the Parish Council at Poynton for 5 years. And Management Committee C.A.B. Wilmslow, Cheshire; [hon.] General Finance and Pensions Exams Passed during my Financial Career; [oth. writ.] Two local anthologies I have offered all my work recently to Minerva press to be published in book form under the heading "Reflections" ISBN 186106 0300.; [pers.] I feel deeply about family life and other personal issues God is very much in my life always, and as such he is reflected in much of my work included in "Reflections."; [a.] Stockport, Cheshire, SK12 1XL

JONES, JEANNETTE
[pen.] Jenny Jones; [b.] January 24, 1960, Devon; [p.] Mr. K. D. and Mrs. R. F. Hill; [m.] Phillip William Jones, October 7, 1988; [ch.] Justin and Jayde ages 16 and 14; [ed.] Ilfracombe Comprehensive Wirral Met College; [occ.] Care Assistant; [memb.] British Horse Society; [pers.] I use poetry to express my innermost emotions and worries of the world today. This leaves me free to concentrate on my mad but happy family.; [a.] Wallasey, Merseyside, L44 9DH

JONES, JOHN HEITH
[pen.] Dawn Riddler/Paul Buxton; [b.] September 6, 1960, Bangor; [p.] John Ifor Jones, Rougna Jones; [ed.] University College of North Wales, Bangor, Ysgol John Bright, Grand, and Cardiff College; [occ.] Researcher and Composer; [memb.] Various Drama Groups and an Animal Rights Supporter; [hon.] B.A., Music, Economics and Psychology, Post Graduate Certificate in Media Studies; [oth. writ.] Many letters published in various newspapers as well as articles or broadcasting. Author of six plays and the folk opera 'Chronicle'.; [pers.] I am greatly interested in the works of Byrd, Larkin and Coleridge. Life is full of thwarted ambitions, let's write about them so we may learn.; [a.] Rain Hill, Merseyside, WA9 5DR

JONES, KERRY
[b.] February 2, 1978, South Africa; [p.] Cynthia Jones; [ed.] Adams School Wem till year 3, Left school at is due to financial difficulties.; [occ.] Market Stall Assistant; [oth. writ.] One published in South African newspaper, several poems written but none submitted for publishing.; [pers.] My poems mostly show how we are all striving for perfection but seldom succeed, they also show that our lives are a spiral, when we complete this life we move up.; [a.] Birmingham, West Mid, B23 5LN

JONES, MADSHALL
[b.] December 15, 1936, Treforest; [p.] Deceased; [m.] Patricia, December 26, 1958; [ch.] Mandy, Marshy, Ryan; [ed.] Central Secondary, Modern School, Treforest Nr. Pontypridd, Glamorgan; [occ.] Postman; [a.] Caerphilly, Glamorgan, CF83 1RP

JONES, MAUREEN
[pen.] De Boinneau; [b.] November 8, 1954, Shrewsbury; [p.] Joyce and Wilfred Jones; [ed.] Phoenix Comprehensive and Walker Technical College, Shropshire; [occ.] Property Administrator for Foreign Royal Family; [oth. writ.] A book of poems (entitled "At The Third Stroke"), short stories and currently working on first novel.; [pers.] If but one person is inspired by my contribution to literature then what other reward could compare? For my own inspiration I return again and again to Beryl Markham and Rumer Godden.; [a.] London, SWIV 3PE

JONES, MR. PETER A.
[pen.] Longhair; [b.] August 4, 1967, Bath; [p.] Marie Elizabeth and Alan Howard; [occ.] Book Keeper; [oth. writ.] Mitakuyae Oyasin and the Fish Return to Water (not yet published); [pers.] Seekers of truth the patient and still. Yield arms of war, for the power of the quill.; [a.] Bournemouth, Dorset, BH9 2JB

JONES, MRS. ANNA MARIE
[pen.] A. M. Jones; [b.] January 24, 1961, Knighton, Powys; [p.] Edward Morris, Jessie Morris (Both Farmers); [m.] John Jones, August 18, 1979; [ed.] John Beddoes, Presteigne, Powys and Hereford College of Art, Hereford; [occ.] Farming partner, (Breconshire); [pers.] Born and bred on a Radnorshire Hill farm, I am a great admirer of R. S. Thomas. Both literature and rural life must endure, to lose either would be an infinite tragedy.; [a.] Builth Wells, Powys, LD2 3LH

JONES, PHILIP D.
[b.] March 21, 1975, Swansea; [p.] Terry and Helen; [ed.] Penyrheol Comprehensive; [a.] Swansea, W. Glam

JONES, SHEILA
[b.] October 16, 1934, Stafford; [p.] George and Ada Starley; [m.] Robert Vaughan Jones, December 19, 1953; [ch.] John, Glyn, Robert, Alexander; [ed.] Riverway, Secondary Girls, School, Stafford; [occ.] Housewife; [memb.] Kennel Club Registration for Dog Showing; [oth. writ.] The House on Laurel corner. The move, short stories several poems.; [pers.] I wrote this poem after the death of my father so that I could come to terms with my loss and realize the value of the memories I still have.; [a.] Coven, Wolverhampton, Staffs, WV9 5AA

JORDAN, TIM
[b.] January 9, 1973, Sutton, Coldfield; [p.] Derek Jordan, Christine Jordan; [m.] Natasha, August 31, 1996; [occ.] Conductor, British Rail; [memb.] Independent Martial Arts Society, Stag Owners Club; [hon.] Dune of Edinburgh Bronze and Silver Awards; [oth. writ.] First submitted writing; [pers.] If you take the time to look you'll see the beauty in everything.; [a.] Tamworth, Staffs, B77 4MB

JUDD, JEAN MAXWELL
[pen.] Jean Maxwell Judd; [b.] April 20, 1920, Hawick; [p.] Florence Hope and Thomas Maxwell Hope; [m.] Judd Sianey Thomas, February 10, 1945; [ch.] 3 boys - Norman, Rodney, Geoffrey; [ed.] Hawick High School Borders Region; [occ.] Housewife (Retired); [memb.] NB "This poem is dedicated to the memory of my dear friend Silvie."; [oth. writ.] "A Comrade" published in Contemporary Verse 1992 Arrival Press Peterborough.; [pers.] Jean Judd has brought her family up in Essex and has retired back to her poets in the border town of Hawick, spending part of her spare time writing short poems, and to lend a sympathetic ear to ease the hart and pain and tries to reflect this in her writing.; [a.] Hawick, Scotland, TA9 0DN

JUDE, PHILLIP D.
[b.] May 17, 1938, City of Westminster; [p.] Eva Jude, Daniel Jude; [m.] Deceased, July 7, 1962; [ch.] Phillip Jude, Angela Jude; [ed.] Sec. Enfield College, City of Guilds for Engineering, Physical Training Instructor HMS; [occ.] Unemployed; [hon.] City of Guilds; [oth. writ.] Many more poems I'm writer but never tried to have them published before this time.; [pers.] In the reality of my perception, I am free and in my freedom, in my enlightenment.; [a.] London, Middx, 6BL

KADKOL, K. R.
[pen.] K. R. Kadkol; [b.] January 21, 1937, Rajmandry, India; [p.] R. K. Kadkol and Mrs. T. Kadkol; [m.] Margaret Kadkol, April 2, 1966; [ch.] Malcolm Kadkol (28 years); [ed.] Secondary School Leaving Certificate - 8 subjects including Science, Mathematics and additional English; [occ.] Administrative Police (Civil Staff); [oth. writ.] I have been influenced by Thomas Hardy and William Shakespeare.; [pers.] Be a good listener. Treat others kindly with consideration and respect.; [a.] Twickenham, Middlesex, TW2 6PA

KAVANAGH, CAROL
[b.] December 23, 1955, Wolverhampton; [p.] Jack and Doreen Jeavons; [m.] Divorced; [ch.] Jack and Katy; [ed.] Parkfield Comprehensive, East Warwickshire Art College; [occ.] House Mother Voluntary Worker; [pers.] My words come from my heart and I reflect life as I see it at the time of my writing; [a.] Newquay, Cornwall, TR7 3HF

KAYLEY, MRS. EUNICE
[b.] June 14, 1959; [p.] Mr. Frederick James England and Mrs. Paulina Maria England; [m.] Mr. Tony Roy Kayley, July 14, 1980; [ch.] 3 (My youngest is 16 years old so now I have a little time to myself for thought before the stereo is turned on; [ed.] Regents Park Secondary School, Southampton Technical College; [occ.] Registered career; [memb.] Memberships to do with work, nothing literary; [oth. writ.] Past articles published in local magazines; [pers.] Trudging puddled pavements in the rain or the long lazy drive, radio'd accompliment, warm, relaxed. Gathering thoughts the loveliness of life I snatch my influence in a moment from everything and the breeze inspiration, for me, lies within 'even' the nearest crumb on a carpet.; [a.] Southampton, Hampshire, SO16 4FW

KEACH, DEBBIE J.
[b.] May 27, 1965, Nuneaton; [p.] Robert Adams, Edith Ella Adams; [m.] Darren Christopher, July 16, 1988; [ch.] Ella Sandra February 23, 1995; [ed.] Nicholas Chamberlaine Comprehensive School; [occ.] Licensed House Manager; [memb.] Nuneaton and District Society of Artists '84 - '87; [hon.] NVQ 3 Catering and Hospitality Supervisory Management/ Personal Art Exhibition - Nuneaton Art Gallery October 1986; [pers.] To make someone laugh, cry or even to think can only be an inspiration.; [a.] Aldridge, West Midlands, WS9 0QR

KEEGAN, JONATHAN
[b.] November 13, 1966, Birkenhead; [p.] Pam and Dennis Smith; [ed.] Rock Ferry High School, Wirral; [occ.] Manager for Agricultural Liming Firm; [hon.] Wayfair Williams Prize for English; [oth. writ.] Publications in various magazines.; [pers.] My thanks to English Teacher Helen Ash for teaching me to put into words what I really see.; [a.] Ledbury, Herefordshire, HR8 2LJ

KEELER, BETTY EDNA
[b.] February 15, 1920, London; [p.] William Charles, Christina Margaret Dyre; [m.] Eric Keeler, July 5, 1941; [ch.] John Eric Keeler B. Tech. Brunel U., Ronald Chas Keeler B. S. (Maths) 1974, Patricia Maryfair Child (Nee' Keeler), "Whitelands" College Educ. Putney; [ed.] Whitefriars Senior School, Wealdstone, Harrow, Middx, and Business Training College, Harrow; [occ.] Retired; [memb.] Pinner Organ Society, American Theatre Organ Society; [hon.] Sundry items.; [oth. writ.] 'Pantos' for children, A Nativity Play - distant past. Short stories for small children, and (currently) a collection mainly about people's pets, gleaned from friends and relations many of which are written in rhyme.; [pers.] I write in a 'happy vein', to please the young and young in heart - my young grandchildren in particular, deriving pleasure from their re-actions, and portrayal of the characters in the stories. I find that writing for little folk is a very nice thing to do!; [a.] Pinner, Middx, MA5 1EP

KELLY, JAYNE BELINDA
[b.] September 26, 1958, Crickowell, Wales; [p.] Irene Walker, Peter Walker; [m.] James John Kelly, April 26, 1986; [ch.] Lee, Simon and Rachael; [ed.] Ryland Bedford High School, Walsall College of Art, Walsall College of Technology, Bournville College, B'Ham; [occ.] Physiotherapy Helper; [oth. writ.] Many unpublished poems, which no one has yet seen.; [pers.] I thrive on creativity. Whether writing, painting or embroidery. Reading poetry to my children enhanced laughter and made them question the stories. These are my inspirations my stubbornness is my determination; [a.] Darlaston, West Midlands, WS10 8EQ

KELLY, JEAN
[b.] November 2, 1958, Lambeth Hospital; [p.] Joan and William Cherry; [m.] Tony, April 3, 1976; [ch.] Anthony; [ed.] Vauxhall Manor for Girls; [occ.] Data Entry Operator/Accounts Clerk; [oth. writ.] Although I like writing poems, this is the first one that I have ever sent anywhere for publication, apart from Memoriam's for my father and my niece that was published in local papers.; [pers.] I write poems, to show the people I have wrote about, how very special they are to me. I think of a particular subject, it only takes me about ten minutes to actually get the basic outline of the poem. Then I changed it around, to smooth it out, and get the maximum impact that I want from it.; [a.] Welling, Kent, DA16 2BW

KELLY, NEIL P. J.
[pen.] Neil Kelly; [b.] January 23, 1974, Chelmsford; [p.] Valerie and Adrian Kelly; [ed.] Rainsford High School, Chelmsford College and Liverpool Hope University College; [occ.] Training to become a primary school teacher; [memb.] "Hope" Musical Society, Student Nut and Nasuwt; [hon.] Studying for B.ED. (Honours) degree - qualify in 1998; [oth. writ.] This is my first published poem; [pers.] My poems often reflect my moods, thoughts and feelings. My greatest influence and support comes from my mum, dad and close family.; [a.] Chelmsford, Essex, CM1 2DP

KENDALL, GLODAGH
[b.] March 10, 1969, Limerick; [p.] Kevin Gray, Gemma Gray; [m.] Stuart Kendall, August 27, 1994; [ch.] Thomas Philip Kendall; [ed.] Parkstone Girls Grammar School; [occ.] Registered Nurse; [pers.] My writing has always been influenced and encouraged by my mother.; [a.] Stevenage, Herts, SG2 9QJ

KENDALL-BUSH, JANE
[pen.] For novels - Lyle Defreece; [b.] December 17, 1964, Manchester; [p.] Irene Huish, Ian Huish; [m.] Kimberley Kendall-Bush, January 16, 1993; [ed.] Portsmouth College of Art and Design, South Devon College of Arts and Technology; [occ.] Artist/Writer; [hon.] Interior Design (O.N.D.), Environmental Design (H.N.D.); [oth. writ.] 2 Novels (as yet unpublished). A 'Nest' of poems written over many years.; [pers.] I tell in words and pictures that which I cannot express in life, therefore, I am nothing without them.; [a.] Bristol, Avon, BS3 1SL

KENNEDY, MRS. MARY
[pen.] M. S. S. Kennedy; [b.] May 31, 1943, Glasgow; [p.] Carol and Fred Stoddart; [m.] Gilbert, May 3, 1960; [ch.] Drew, Ian, David; [ed.] Kinning Park Primary Vale of Leven Academy (at age 50 Kirkwall Grammar) open learning.; [occ.] Domestic Assistant in Local Hospital; [memb.] Rhyme Arrival Magazine; [hon.] Open Learning passed O level English then English poem published by Poetry Institute British Isles. Poem published by poets of Scotland; [oth. writ.] Poem published in Local Vintage Magazine verse for local advertisement.; [pers.] At age 50 I decided to go back to school to take my English O levels and highers to prove that life was not passing me by. There I got the poetry bug.; [a.] Kirkwall, Orkney, KW15 1QF

KENRICK, FRED
[b.] October 28, 1930, Dalton-in-Furness; [p.] Stanley Kenrick, Elizabeth Kenrick; [m.] Margaret Elizabeth Kenrick, July 24, 1954; [ed.] Dowdales Secondary School leaving at 14 years of age; [occ.] Retired; [memb.] B.K.V.A.; [hon.] No academic qualifications; [oth. writ.] Fist book of poems published 1996 B's Avon books plus one poem published in "The Morning Calm" British Korean Veterans Acc., Journal book title "The World I See"; [pers.] My attempt at poetry didn't start till about 1992 as my writing ability was very low; [a.] Dalton-in-Furness, Cumbria, LA15 8QB

KERR, PAUL CAMPBELL
[b.] July 25, 1972, Greenock; [p.] Richard Kerr, Morag Kerr; [m.] Keri McDonough, June 17, 1996; [ed.] Cowdenknowes High School, James Watt College; [occ.] Surface Mount Technician, Motorola Easter Inch; [memb.] The Institution of Electronics and Electrical Incorporated Engineers; [pers.] I am fascinated by the many and varied facets to man's character and hope to be able to capture at least a few of them in my writing.; [a.] Greenock, Inverclyde, DA16 0QE

KERRIGAN, JAMES JOHN
[b.] August 29, 1930, Glasgow, Scotland; [p.] Michael and Alice Kerrigan; [m.] Yvonne, January 1, 1972; [ch.] Eileen and Michael; [ed.] Marist Brothers Dumfries Scotland Regent Street Polytechnic London Strawberry Hill Teacher Training College London University; [occ.] Retired teacher, presently working in special education unit; [oth. writ.] Several unpublished poems unpublished auto biography of first 40 years of my life.; [pers.] Anything I have written has been done solely for pleasure. I hope someday perhaps to publish some work and dedicate it to my grandson Jack. My taste in literature is very catholic. I am also a great lover of classical music.; [a.] Handsacre Nr Litchfield, Staffordshire, WS15 4EH

KESZEG, MR. MICHAEL CHARLES
[pen.] K.C.M.; [b.] October 8, 1960, Mexborough; [p.] Karoly Keszeg, Yvonne Keszeg; [ed.] Mexborough Secondary School; [occ.] H.GV Driver; [oth. writ.] Jessica - Anchor Books, Despair, My Wife, Simple Sounds; [pers.] I write from the heart, involving my own personal experiences, and subject that appeal to me. Giving the readers of my work a spark of hope, proving maybe? The words not such a lonely after all.; [a.] Barnsley, S. Yorks, S71 5AA

KEYNAN, HASSAN A.
[pen.] N.D.C.E.; [b.] July 7, 1955, Dolow; [p.] Abdi Keynan and Habibo Keynan; [m.] Amina Hassan, April 6, 1992; [ch.] 1 girl; [ed.] Studied at the Univeristy of California at Los Angeles (UCLA) and the University of Sydney, Australia; [opp.] Researcher / Consultant; [oth. writ.] other poems; [a.] Osla, D376

KHWAJA, NOMANA YUSUF
[b.] February 18, 1974, Birmingham; [p.] Father: Mohammed Yusuf Khwaja, Mother: Khalida Parveen Khwaja; [ed.] Hodge Hill Girl's School, Josiah Mason College, Sutton Coldfield College of Further Education; [occ.] Legal Secretary; [oth. writ.] Several articles for Hodge Hill Girl's School monthly magazine; [pers.] My poems have derived from my personal life experiences and the greatest influence is reading romantic and tragedy literature since I was a child; [a.] Birmingham, West Midlands, B8 1RL

KING, FRANK
[b.] March 22, 1943, Leicester; [p.] Charles Francis King (Deceased), Winifred Mary King; [ed.] Lancaster Boys Secondary Modern; [occ.] Warehouse man; [memb.] Maidstone and District and East Kent Bus Club, Membership Secretary 154 Preservation Society (This being a 1950 all Leyland PD2 Open Platform Bus) double deck.; [pers.] Poets are unknown within the family but I just compose to please myself. They say many people have hidden talents, I just hope that mine will continue for the foreseeable future.; [a.] Leicester, Leics:, LE4 6HB

KING, GERALD M.
[b.] February 17, 1935, London; [p.] Leonard King and Emily Smith; [m.] Marie O'Regan, August 19, 1959; [ch.] Patrick, David, Anne, Eve-Marie; [ed.] Henry Maynard Jr., S.W. Essex Technical College; [occ.] Retired; [memb.] Brighton and Hove Philatelic Society; [oth. writ.] "Alice Through The Pillar Box", A Philatelic Fantasy. (1979) Deutsal, various cartoons, Philatelic articles, Snark Island (1985); [a.] Brighton, E. Sussex, BN2 4DP

KIRBY, RAYMOND PAUL
[b.] June 6, 1920, Leicester; [p.] John Kirby, Amanda Kirby; [ed.] Holy Cross School, Leicester; [occ.] Retired; [memb.] Performing Right Society. Mechanical Copyright, Protection Society. British Academy of Songwriters, Composer's and Authors. International Songwriter's Association. Guild of International Songwriters and Composers; [hon.] Mostly in music, the latest, in 1992. 1st Prize in Songwriters of Wisconsin Gospel Contest, in the U.S.A. Until a few years and was Gardening Expert for 'The Vegetarian' magazine; [oth. writ.] Articles on Gardening, Songwriting, Local History, Graphology and a Book on it. Personal Theology, Book of songs also published from an American Musical I wrote for, 6 poems in 6 Anthologies in last 12 months, short story on Radio, hymns published, song recorded.; [pers.] Influenced by musical family in my music, by a great friend, a Benedictine Monk, for 38 years in my Theology, and by Alfred Tennyson, and Percy Bysshe, Shelley, especially the latters 'Ozymandias', in my poetry. Completed Autobiography, the moving finger, recently.; [a.] Wigston Magna, Leicester, LE18 2GA

KIRK, ANDREW
[pen.] Andrew Kirk; [b.] February 14, 1981, Kettering; [p.] Jeanette and Stephen Kirk; [ed.] The Ferrers School, Higham Ferrers, Northants; [occ.] Pupil; [memb.] Oakley Hunt West Pony Club, Northants and Bedfordshire Mounted Games Teams, Mounted Games Association of Great Britain, Corporal in 858 Squadron Rushden Air Training Corp.; [hon.] Academic Achievement Award for 1995 for 858 (Rushden) Squadron A.T.C., numerous championship Rosettes for Mounted Games (Horse riding).; [pers.] My poem is a protest against the home meal trade. And dedicated to "Charlie" my first mounted games pony who is now 21 yrs. old and still taking part in competitions.; [a.] Rushden, Northants, NN10 9HA

KITCHING, RICHARD GORDON
[pen.] Mandrake; [b.] January 19, 1966, Beverley; [p.] Jean and Arthur Kitching; [m.] Samantha Caroline Kitching, October 31, 1992; [ed.] Malet Lambert High School, Hull; [memb.] The Fane; [pers.] In the fullness of time, hold sacred that which you touch, not in folly.; [a.] Kingston upon Hull, East Yorkshire, HU8 0JE

KNIGHT, JOE-LEE-ANN
[b.] February 1, 1980, Portsmouth; [p.] Sherrilee Margaret Knight; [ed.] I am home educated.; [pers.] I like writing because it helps me express my feelings.; [a.] Alton, Hampshire, GU34 2EU

KNOX, THOMAS
[pen.] Knox Johnston; [b.] March 18, 1933, Belfast; [p.] George and Marth Knox; [m.] Margaret Winifred Victoria, March 18, 1993; [ch.] Two (step sons); [ed.] Military - G.C.S.E., University, Gottingen; [occ.] H.G.V.I., "P.K.V.", "Unemployed; [hon.] Hutt River Citizen of the Year, Ambassador for Said County for 1 Year; [oth. writ.] Have written one hundred poems of many aspects of life.; [pers.] I try to reflect the goodness and evil of mankind. Plus the beauty of this world.; [a.] Dundonald, Co. Down, Northern Ireland, BT16 0PW

KRISHNAN, ANUJA
[pen.] "Dinju"; [b.] March 29, 1983, Trivandrum; [p.] R. Krishnan; [m.] Dr. V. Sobha (Head of the Dept. Kerala University); [ed.] School Student (VIII Std.) Holy Angel's Convent School, Trivandrum; [occ.] Studying in VIII Standard, Holy Angel's Convent School; [memb.] Kerala Kaumudi Reader's Club, Pettah Trivandrum; [hon.] Won 1st prize for Science Exhibitions and was honoured by Sri.Chithra Triunal Institute and seaweed Research Association, Madras for dance competitions; [oth. writ.] Some poems published in local Magazines (English and Malayalam); [pers.] I have been influenced by my mother's character. I want to reflect her character through this poem. Writing poems make me happy.; [a.] Trivandrum, South India, India, 695 001

KRZALIC, ADNAN
[b.] April 11, 1989, Sunderland; [p.] Fuad and Lesley Krzalic; [ed.] Currently attending shiny Row Infant School; [occ.] Student; [oth. writ.] This is my first attempt at poetry, and my nana and grandad Rochester said we should enter the competition as it wasn't too bad for a first try.; [pers.] I am very proud to have my poem in a book. My teacher, Mrs. Baines has helped me a lot as I am registered disabled and am hyperactive. But she is patient and encourages me.; [a.] Sunderland, Tyne and Wear, DH4 4XA

KUMAR
[pen.] Ashok; [b.] February 3, 1954, Punjab, India; [p.] Mr. D. D. Kumar Mrs. Kesra Devi; [ed.] Graduate in Humanities from Delhi University, India Post graduate in P.R. and Journalism; [occ.] Apparel Export Business; [memb.] Lions Club, New Delhi, India; [hon.] Several National Awards for Social Service by Lions Club International; [oth. writ.] Published in two Hindi Poetry books. The English translation of the book titles are 1. The Pangs of Past 2. The Lunar Eclipse; [pers.] A poem is not merely a thought but most beautiful way of expression of the finest human feelings and strong enough to create clouds in the clear blue sky. Poetry must be respected and loved.; [a.] New Delhi, India, 110 027

LADKIN, ROBIN
[b.] March 3, 1947, Uganda; [ch.] Ben and Sam; [ed.] Brunel University; [occ.] Management Consultant; [oth. writ.] As yet unpublished book of Rune poems; [pers.] My poems are a reflection of inner meeting outer, the worlds of psyche and gala meeting expressed in jazz rhythms; [a.] Kingsbridge, Devon, TQ7 3QD

LAKE, MAUREEN
[b.] October 26, 1937, Southend-on-Sea; [p.] George Brown, Dorothy Brown; [m.] Denis Lake, March 22, 1958; [ch.] Janette Bean, Kevin Lake; [ed.] Hethersett National Comprehensive. Passed the Scholarship but not enough places to fit everyone.; [occ.] Housewife, Formerly Shop Assistant; [memb.] Ladies Ten, Pin Bowling Team; [oth. writ.] I have written nine more poems, since entering the contest, but have not yet presented any more for publication; [pers.] I have been greatly encouraged by my family in my writing and they are my strongest critics.; [a.] Norwich, Norfolk, NR6 5RQ

LAKEHAL, SAMANTHA
[pen.] Annoushka Goldenhind; [b.] August 7, 1967, York; [p.] John Stocken - Avile Stocken; [m.] Abdel Lakehal, March 9, 1991; [ed.] South Devon College Torquay; [occ.] Veterinary Assistant (Ex Railway Worker); [oth. writ.] Several others poems about the railway and passengers. Short, descriptive story about a typical summer at British Rail. None of which have been shown for publication; [pers.] Thanks to Jo, Dave and Paul for inspiring me. The people from the north are out symbol of summer, "Jot It Me Down".; [a.] Torquay, Devon, TQ1 3JH

LAKEY, BERTHA HAZEL
[pen.] Hazel Munnick; [b.] October 30, 1933, South Africa; [p.] Jacobus and Isabelle Munnick; [m.] Nealer (Rod) Lakey, May 5, 1956; [ch.] Estelle (39) and Denis (32); [ed.] Matriculation at Livingstone High School, Claremont, Cape Town South Africa, Secretarial Courses and Language Courses in England, BA Degree (Open Univ.) in Social Sciences; [occ.] Retired - last occupation: Secretary for a Manager in Energy Command - DTI; [memb.] Retired Fellowship and Benevolent Societies; [oth. writ.] Many articles for church magazines and competitions eg. Limericks at work once; [pers.] I care about underprivileged people therefore support and work for several charities - have done: A 'Pianothon', 'Swimathon', 'Slimathon' and a 36-hour Fast for Oxfam; [a.] London, SE15 3PX

LAMB, ANDREW
[b.] June 19, 1944, Glencraig, Fife; [p.] Martha; [m.] Mary "Nee Armstrong", March 3, 1963; [ch.] Margaret, Ricky, Alex, Andrew; [ed.] Ballingry Secondary School; [occ.] Former Coal Miner; [hon.] First prize certificate for creative scots writing in Dunfermline Arts Festival 1995; [oth. writ.] Works in various anthologies, by Anchor Books Peterborough, and the P.I.B.I.; [pers.] Aye keep yir feet upon solid terrain, an aye look efter yir ain.; [a.] Ballingry, Fife, KY5 8PU

LAMBERT, SHIRLEY ANN
[b.] February 17, 1952, Stratford-upon-Avon; [p.] Albert Wilkins, Irene Wilkins; [m.] Steven Lambert, August 17, 1982; [ch.] Joanna; [ed.] Shottery Grammar; [occ.] Matron, Almshouses Stratford-on-Avon; [memb.] MSSCH (Member of the School of Chiropody); [oth. writ.] Poems written for family occasions or just for fun.; [pers.] I try to reflect life is general and I am influenced by the people I care for; [a.] Stratford-upon-Avon, Warwickshire, CV37 8NX

LAMBTON, CATHERINE
[b.] July 2, 1959, Gateshead; [p.] George and Audrey Smith; [m.] Stephen Lambton, August 31, 1985; [ch.] Two (left from four); [ed.] Roseberry Comprehensive, Pelton, Chester-le-Street; [occ.] Shop Assistant; [oth. writ.] Childrens Books - not yet published - The Christmas Fairy - it - Harry Gets His own Back and Sally Saves the Day. A small selection of poems.; [pers.] My stories and poems are always inspired by events in my life. A jigsaw made in heaven was the death of my oldest child from cancer and my father within a year of each other; [a.] Chester-le-street, Durham, DH2 2PW

LANCETT, PHYLLIS
[b.] September 19, 1944, Hereford; [p.] Percy and Mary Beaumont; [m.] Dennis Lancett, January 23, 1971; [ch.] Jayne Elizabeth, Richard John; [ed.] Bluecoat School for Girls, Hereford; [occ.] Registered General Nurse in Elderly Care; [memb.] Due to irregularity of working hours, I am unable to be a regular member of any societies, but have many interests, including music, theatre, literature, art, and of course country walks.; [hon.] Best Pre-Nursing Student. Silver medal in nursing exams.; [oth. writ.] I have written several other poems and adapted children's plans, but have not had anything published.; [pers.] I never cease to be enchanted by the wonders of mother nature, if only more people would pause to capture the beauty she creates, the world may be a more peaceful place in which to live. I have been greatly inspired by (18 poets and artists who have portrayed the beauty of pastoral life.; [a.] Hereford, Herefordshire, HR4 9XP

LANE, DAVID JOHN
[b.] July 5, 1960, Kettering; [p.] John and Florence Lane; [m.] Denise Ann Lane, September 2, 1944; [ch.] Michael Jow (4 months of age); [ed.] Westham Secondary Modern Southampton Institute of Higher Education, OWC and HNC Civil Engineering; [occ.] Highways Inspector; [memb.] Member of the Institute of Highways Incorporated Engineers; [oth. writ.] Poem published in Anthology entitled 'Lift the Veil', short story published in book entitled 'Shorts from the West Country.'; [pers.] All art forms emanate from the soul, to touch the soul of its audience.; [a.] Portland, Dorset, DT5 2DJ

LANE, DEE-DEE
[pen.] Dee-Dee Lane; [b.] June 23, 1943, Devon; [p.] Florence and William; [m.] John, happily living in sin for 11 years; [ch.] Lorraine and Stepdaughter Nicola; [ed.] Secondary Modern and Harrow School of Art to degree level; [occ.] Dress Designer and Foster Carer.; [memb.] Involved with Arab and Quarter Horse Racing.; [oth. writ.] I am at present writing my first novel. I also write lyrics for a local pop group.; [pers.] Through laughter and fun and warmth of the sun. To everyone, spread the word. Surely they have heard. Life is for living, when all's said and done.; [a.] Wembley, Middlesex, HA0 3PE

LANGLEY, MRS. BERYL
[pen.] Mrs. Beryl Langley; [b.] May 15, 1939, Ilford; [p.] Elsie and Burt Richardson; [m.] Martin, September 17, 1960; [ch.] Joanne and Susan; [ed.] Downshall, Seven Kings Ilford, Essex; [occ.] Nursery Woman; [memb.] Vintage Car Clubs; [oth. writ.] Car Club Magazines and Personal Birthday and Christmas Cards.; [pers.] I prefer my poetry to be humorous, or light-hearted observations of day to day life.; [a.] Upminster, Essex, RM14 3PA

LAPLAIN, PATRICIA
[b.] May 24, 1956, London; [p.] Jack and Jean Bird; [m.] Trevor, January 25, 1975; [ch.] Trevor (Jnr) Daniel; [ed.] Catford County, Waltham Forest College; [occ.] "Just a housewife"; [hon.] Certificate in counselling; [oth. writ.] I am currently working on my life story.; [pers.] I am a spiritualist and I have dealing ability. I am currently studying to become a counsellor, so that I may help people overcome their problems; [a.] South Woodford, London, EI8 2QJ

LARTER, FREDA
[b.] March 1, 1924, Reepham (Lincs); [p.] Joseph Massey, Ruth Massey; [m.] Harold George Larter (Dec.), September 19, 1942; [ch.] Timothy Roy, Kathryn Elizabeth; [ed.] Left school at 14; [occ.] (Housewife - Widow), writing poetry - a hobby; [memb.] Lincoln Breast Cancer Support Group; [oth. writ.] Several published in a magazine called "Lincolnshire Poets". (A Platform for Poets), one in a book called "Why War" by Triumph House (publ.), one in a book called "Poetic Landscape" by Anchor Books (all to help amateur poets); [pers.] I like to write about things which effect me emotionally. Or about someone close to me. As in "The Deep" have had cancer twice 1984 and 1995 this resulted in a mastectomy each time. This prompted me to write poems about this to help others. I belong to the Lincoln Breast Cancer Support Group.; [a.] Lincoln, Lincolnshire

LAVERTY, DELIA
[b.] April 25, 1928, Co. Tyrone; [p.] William J. Laverty, Brigid Larkin; [ed.] Mt. St. Michael's, Lurgan, Our Lady's Grammar School, Teacher Training College, Wolverhampton; [occ.] Retired Primary/Secondary Teacher, now painting and writing; [memb.] Down Arts Society, Newcastle Senior Choir, Spent five years teaching in S. Africa (in a voluntary capacity); [hon.] Distinction in art received a number of prizes for painting. Calligraphy and cooking, poems published in local weekly; [oth. writ.] Christmas Carol, Of Terrorism, A Happy Family, Tommy Lives On, Granyee, The Cobbler; [pers.] The beauty and wonder of God's Creation, inspires me to express my experiences in poetic form with reflections too on mans inhumanity to man.; [a.] Cookstown, Tyrone, BT80 8DY

LAW, THERESA C.
[b.] August 25, 1951, Barking; [p.] Violet Plant, Fred Plant; [m.] Alexander Law, July 10, 1971; [ch.] Theresa Anne, Jason Paul; [ed.] Erkenwald Comprehensive, Havering College; [occ.] Medically retired, Secretary; [memb.] EGG Crafters Guild of Great Britain, Barking and Dagenham Disablement Monday Club; [hon.] R.S.A. English and Typing; [pers.] My writing is what I see and feel at the time, it helps me to express myself and I hope it gives everyone who reads it enjoyment.; [a.] Dagenham, Essex, RM9 4SS

LAWRENCE, DORIS A. M.
[b.] August 25, 1935, Birmingham; [p.] My mother is still living; [ed.] The Oratory S. M. Birmingham, Further Education, Pitman's College Gosta Green Technical College; [occ.] Retired; [memb.] Member of the Medical Secretaries Association; [hon.] Shorthand, typing, computer, English, music and Catechetical Certificates; [oth. writ.] The parables of Our Lord, Is the Prodigal Sun, The 10 Bridesmaids, The Unscrupulous Judge etc. "The Yard", "Curley Clan."; [pers.] Through my poetry I hope in some small way able to create minds for a higher plane.

LAYCOCK, MICHAEL LAWRENCE
[pen.] Rocky; [b.] October 26, 1934, S. Wales; [p.] Lawrence Laycock and Caroline Laycock; [ch.] One, boy named Mark; [ed.] Manorside Secondary Modern School Finchley Central London; [occ.] Retired (I'm on invalidity benefit) was security guard; [memb.] I'm a member of The Royal National Lifeboat Institution (RNLI) (Shoreline); [oth. writ.] None tho' I have wrote several poems just for a pasttime.; [pers.] I look back on the good-times and try to reflect that in my poetry, I'm keen on the works of Dylan Thomas. I'm separated from wife. I live with my lady friend Doreen Margaret Nasia.; [a.] Kidbrooke, London, 8EL

LEARMOND, WAYNE
[b.] March 12, 1963, Liverpool; [ch.] Gregory Mark Learmond; [ed.] St. Martin's de Porres, Secondary Modern; [occ.] Unemployed; [hon.] C.S.E. (English Science); [oth. writ.] I have a huge amount of work as yet unpublished; [pers.] My aim in everything I write is to try and bring my words to life for the reader.; [a.] Liverpool, Lancs, L17 8TS

LEE, VERA W.
[b.] September 17, 1924, Oregon, USA; [p.] James and Catherine Hulme; [m.] Gordon Lee, June 10, 1944; [ch.] Rodger and Graham; [ed.] Basic; [occ.] Retired Clerical Officer; [memb.] WI. R.B. Legion, W. Section, Methodist Church, W.R.V.S. Arkwright Society (meals on wheels), Local Historical Society; [oth. writ.] Evening Out (Poetry now) (Orton Graphic), Near To Home (Nature's Nation) (Anchor), If I Won The Lottery (Winning Dreams) (Anchors Boder), Wistful Thinking; [pers.] We moved into Montana where my father died of war wounds 1926. Later with my mother and two brothers came to England and settled in Derbyshire. I like John Betjeman's poetry.; [a.] Ambergate, Belfer, Derbyshire, DE56 2GR

LEEDEN, WILLIAM J.
[pen.] Old Bill, A.G.; [b.] January 3, 1926, Tottington; [p.] George and Alice; [m.] Deceased, February 26, 1944; [ch.] Norman and Christopher; [ed.] Sec. Modern; [occ.] Old Age Pensioner; [memb.] Swaffham Exservicemen's Club; [oth. writ.] Have 17 poems as this is my first attempt I have no idea how to get the others looked at. Have sent them to R.A.F. magazine to look at.; [pers.] Memories of war the poem the new man is based on my personal experiences in world war II. I was a rear gunner in Lancaster Bombers. My other poems are all part of my memories when flying missions. No 5 Bomber Group.; [a.] Swaffham, Norfolk, PE37 7LF

LEES, MICHELLE
[b.] December 24, 1983, Liverpool; [p.] John and Gill Lees; [ed.] Robert Blair Primary, E.G.A.; [oth. writ.] None published; [pers.] I have always enjoyed poetry since I was little. I love writing poems and hope to make a success out of my poetry and gain great knowledge from other poets and show people my talent.; [a.] London, N1 0DR

LEIGH, WINIFRED E.
[b.] Abbey Wood, London; [p.] English; [ed.] Greenock High School, laterly trained at Morley College Theatre School under Rupert Doone; [oth. writ.] Write poems since childhood.

LEVEY, JENNY
[b.] November 23, 1957, Bristol; [p.] Desmond Levey, Mary Levey; [ed.] Page School for Girls Bristol and Soundwell Technical College; [occ.] Secretary Bristol City Contract Services; [oth. writ.] My poem has brought me my first publication and I am delighted.; [pers.] I should like the opportunity to write more material in the future now that a hidden talent has bene discovered.; [a.] Bristol, Avon, BS16 1JQ

LEWIN, MRS. GILLIAN
[pen.] Gillian Stovell; [b.] July 24, 1953, Redhill; [p.] Arthur Stovell, May Stovell; [ch.] Jennifer Lewin, April Lewin; [ed.] Bishop Simpson, Redhill Crawley College; [occ.] Single Parent; [memb.] Yoga Classes; [oth. writ.] Two poems about to be published in two poetry books: "Poet of 96" and "Up and Running."; [pers.] I am a deep thinker and write about things that I feel, or that have happened to me. I try to be positive in my outlook and take great pride in my daughters, whom I have raised single handedly.; [a.] Crawley, Sussex, RH10 7YL

LEWINGTON, JOAN
[pen.] Joan Lewington; [b.] Yorkshire; [p.] Florence and Maurice Bradley; [m.] Stanley R. Lewington, June 1988 (Widow Re-married); [ch.] Joan Diane Jones; [ed.] Business College (Diploma), Bible College, Ret. Social Worker formerly University Secretary; [occ.] Salvation Army (Local Officer), League of Mercy Secretary (and over 60s Club Secretary. Free-lance journalist (two newspapers), written 3 plays 4th in progress.; [hon.] Several "Editor's Choice" poems published in hardbacks by Dickins Publishing Company. Editor's choice Award National Library of Poetry 1995 (North America).; [oth. writ.] Poems, children's stories, articles published here and overseas. Author of two books of poetry one currently on sale in Westcountry; [pers.] My father, who was an official of the War Office (UK) wrote poetry and scripts for radio. It was he who inspired me to read and write poetry.; [a.] Brixham, Devon, TQ5 9QR

LEWIS, ANDREW
[b.] September 6, 1955, Cyprus; [m.] Helen Lewis, March 27, 1975; [ch.] Jayson, Olivia, Marios; [ed.] Downhills Park Comprehensive Tottenham; [occ.]

London Bus Driver; [memb.] Royal Society for the Prevention of Accidents, Institute of Advanced Motorists; [oth. writ.] Many written - none published; [pers.] I always try to mean what I say, and say what I mean, then I will never be sorry for what I have said.; [a.] Cambridge, Cambridgeshire, CB1 3QY

LEWIS, BRONWEN
[pen.] Bronwyn Lewis; [b.] September 14, 1970, Abercarn, Gwent; [p.] Ronald Lewis, Jane Lucas; [ed.] Newbridge Comprehensive School; [occ.] Factory Worker at Nortel Cwmcarn; [oth. writ.] Several poems published in anthologies.; [pers.] For years after I've tried and gone I'll die my words live on I place my soul in all I write immortality in black and white; [a.] Newport, Gwent, NP1 5ML

LEWIS, DAVID
[pen.] Ginnici/David St. Louis; [b.] January 10, 1962, Wales; [p.] Ralph and Jean Lewis; [ed.] St. Richard Gwyn High School Flint; [occ.] Freelance Photographer, One P.R. Officer; [hon.] National B-Tech in Media Studies; [oth. writ.] Professional Journals, Scripts for Promotional Videos; [pers.] I believe that beauty and love will one day bring mankind to it's senses.; [a.] Chester, Cheshire, CH1 4HL

LEWIS, MAUREEN
[b.] February 10, 1953, Eastleigh; [p.] Ellen and Charles Williams; [ch.] Dee, Kym and Richard; [occ.] Housewife and Mother; [pers.] Poet a nascitur, non fit "The Poet is Born, Not Made."; [a.] Eastleigh, Hampshire, SO50 5AE

LIAS, A. T.
[b.] March 5, 1972, Poole; [p.] Edwin Lias, Jeannette Howieson; [ed.] St. Edward's School, Poole College; [pers.] The poem 'Beautiful' is dedicated to a man who has given inspiration to every aspect of my life. My love and eternal thanks to Jools.; [a.] Poole, Dorset, BH12 4DH

LIDDELL, THOMAS ANTHONY
[b.] November 23, 1933, York; [p.] Thomas and Eileen Liddell; [m.] Divorced; [ed.] Nunthorpe Grammar; [occ.] Retired Instrument Maker; [memb.] Exmember York Chess Club, Exmember York Railway Institute Boxing Section, Exmember York Boys Club; [hon.] Two awards won at chess, Kirkby open, 1973, York Schools boxing champion, (7-2-7-12), 1949, Member of York youth boxing team, 1950.; [pers.] I try to learn from the all time greats, started writing poetry after listening to Sir John Betjamin.; [a.] York, Yorkshire

LIDDIARD, PAUL
[pen.] Paul Thomas; [b.] October 15, 1964, Singapore; [p.] Paula Liddiard (Mother); [ch.] (Son) Jamie Paul; [pers.] My inspirations, love and literate. "It is not true that we have only one life to live, if we can read, we can live as many more loves and as many kinds of lives as we wish" - S.I. Hayakawa.; [a.] Greenwich, London

LIGHT, URSULA
[pen.] A. Hag; [b.] October 1, 1920, Berlin; [p.] Ernst Frankel, Herta F.; [m.] Ivan Light, July 1958; [ch.] Alison Barnes; [ed.] Camden School for Girls, Chelsea Polytechnic, King's College London; [occ.] Retired; [memb.] Ashford Adult Education Centre; [hon.] M. Sc-Thesis on Potato Diseases; [oth. writ.] Time Lag - (A Paradigm Shift from Spacetime to Timespace) unpublished; [pers.] A theban play was the eye opener; [a.] Ashford, Kent, TN24 8HL

LILLIE, TOWNER DIANA
[pen.] Diana Simon; [b.] January 18, 1925, London, Stepney Green; [ch.] Two; [occ.] Retired; [hon.] Festival of Spoken Arts, 2 Certificates - Curtain Theatre (Drama Centre) 1978/9 - 1st Class Certif. Grade 4 Sub. Oral Communication.; [oth. writ.] Short story - 2 poems Polytechnic Magazine (Internal); [pers.] I enjoy writing from the heart. Deep feelings to be expressed to help others.; [a.] London, SW12 9SJ

LLOYD, SHELLEY LOUISE
[b.] May 12, 1976, Ashton; [p.] Ann Nigel Lloyd; [ed.] Mossley Hollins High and Tameside College of Technology; [memb.] Wild Life Association; [hon.] G.C.S.E. and City and Guilds - 356; [pers.] As I write I am not influenced by any particular person I just write what I see and feel.; [a.] Mossley, Lancs, OL5 9DN

LLOYD-WILLIAMS, JEAN
[b.] Droitwich Spa; [pers.] Being the eldest of three sisters, I have been a lover of nature, the country side, and gardens for years. I use to paint with oils once upon a time, and I hope to start again, because it's a wonderful pass time. As for poetry - I have been writing poems since I was a school girl, and I think my school gave me that urge to do it. I loved the English lessons. I never thought I would get one of my poems in a book, and I feel very proud of myself. I hope who ever reads my poem will enjoy reading it.

LOADER, ALAN CHARLES
[pen.] Leo, King; [b.] March 25, 1943, Watford; [p.] Fredrick and Gladys Loader; [m.] Joan, Iris, Loader, October 21, 1961; [ch.] Richard, Paul, Marilyn, Jane; [ed.] Saint Andrews Barton Road Secondary Modern; [occ.] Communications; [memb.] The Human Race; [hon.] A prize for art; [oth. writ.] My Father's Memorial Tribute on 16th May 1995; [pers.] What of our world if a good man lives, and of a man if not honest and true, what will this man know of the meaning of life.; [a.] Dover, Kent, CT17 0QQ

LOCKWOOD, DEBORAH
[pen.] Deborah Lockwood; [b.] October 31, 1944, Aldershot; [p.] Mildred (Nee' Blandamer) and Sidney 'Constant' Taylor; [m.] Rod Lockwood B.E.M., March 28, 1964; [ch.] Michaela and Mark; [ed.] Newport Rd. St. Michael's Sec. Mod. Farnham Art Farnborough Tec. Manor Park Adult.; [occ.] Cashier Aldershot Benefits Agency; [memb.] Genealogical Research, Homeopathy Assoc.; [hon.] Current doing NVQ level 2 Admin.; [oth. writ.] Poetry now. Regional Anthologies London 1993 'Holy Orders' Edited by Pat Wilson Peterborough (Hard Back), New Fiction, Shorts from Hampshire 1993 'The Rising Sun' Edited by Suzi Blair. Peterborough (Hard Back); [pers.] Ancestor of Benjamin Constant Born October 10, 1767. Writer, poet and politician. Traced back at 50 and along with the computer, blossomed!; [a.] Aldershot, Hants, GU12 4SF

LODGE, RONALD VICTOR
[pen.] Marron; [b.] September 6, 1936, Roxwell, Essex; [p.] Harry Lodge, Daisy Lodge; [m.] Margaret Irene Anne Lodge, November 4, 1964; [ch.] Dawn, John, Raymond and Peter; [ed.] Rainsford Secondary Modern Chelmsford Essex, Mid Essex Tech; [occ.] Postman; [memb.] West Bergholt Social Club, West Bergholt Cricket Club; [hon.] Diploma in Salesmanship Course taken at Loughborough College Leicestershire; [oth. writ.] Articles for village magazines and post office newsletters also short history of current post office for inclusion in welcome to new residents of West Bergholt Village published by church; [pers.] I try to include all past advises passed on to me by my late father and mother who have given me great strength in all decisions made by me; [a.] Colchester, Essex, CO6 3LH

LONG, STELLA RUTH
[pen.] Stella R. Long; [b.] July 8, 1926, Worcester; [p.] Biddy and Arthur Heaton; [m.] John Long (Deceased), September 9, 1969; [ed.] Ledbury Grammar School, Herefordshire; [occ.] Retired from College Administration; [memb.] Othery and Street W.I.'s, Somerset; [oth. writ.] I have written poetry since a child but never entered competitions. I have publications in the church magazine.; [pers.] Most of poetry has evolved from emotional or true stories; [a.] Street, Somerset, BA16 0DU

LOUGHREY, PAUL
[b.] May 28, 1976, Boksburgh, R.S.A.; [ed.] Bingley Grammar School; [occ.] Insurance Underwriter, Bradford Insurance Brokers; [oth. writ.] "Isolation" published in anthology "Fireside Verse." "Take These Matches" published in anthology, "Sunlight and Shadows."; [pers.] My writing helps me to deal with the myriad of emotions inside us all. I can only hope that in sharing my reaction to the questions life poses, others are able to find the answers they crave.; [a.] Keighley, W. Yorkshire, BD22 9NL

LOUGHRIDGE, KAREN
[pen.] Karen Loughridge; [b.] August 25, 1976, Belfast; [p.] Eleanor and Oliver Loughridge; [ed.] Carrickfergus Grammar School, Belfast College of Business Studies.; [occ.] Student, Bifhe; [hon.] 2 A levels HCIMA Certificate, Certificate in Japanese and Japanese Studies.; [oth. writ.] Personal collection of poems and short stories.; [pers.] Life - we enter through a window of happiness and leave through a back door of sorrow.; [a.] Carrickfergus, Atrim, BT38 9HE

LOVELL, DAPHNE DAWN
[pen.] Daphne Porter-Lovell; [b.] September 15, 1937, Oxfordshire; [p.] Winifred F. Porter and Arthur W. Porter; [m.] Divorced, June 13, 1979, October 25, 1958; [ch.] Jane Emma, Sally Cecilia, Simon Keith and Jonathan Douglas; [ed.] Boxhill GE., Abingdon CFE; [occ.] Secretary; [memb.] Drayton Players Amateur, Dramatic Society; [pers.] Life never ceases to amaze me: It is full of doors opening and closing, guiding us through the journey of life.; [a.] Abingdon, Oxon, OX13 6LY

LOWE, NORMAN
[pen.] Newol; [b.] April 15, 1929, England; [m.] Madge, June 25, 1949; [ch.] Large Family; [ed.] Primary Only, Left School at 14 years old; [occ.] Retired; [oth. writ.] I've had six poems published in various books of verse; [pers.] I write for the pleasure of myself and others, I hope but at times my works are a little spiky; [a.] Middleton, Lancs, M24 2NY

LUCAS, GAEL
[b.] May 2, 1980, Ireland; [p.] Guy Lucas, Joanna Lucas; [ed.] Bedgebury School, Goudhurst, Bethony School, Goudhurst; [occ.] Student; [memb.] BEWL Water Sailboarding Club; [hon.] Lamda Grade 8 Acting Distinction, Headway Art Competition High Commendation for 3D piece, Scholarship for Trombone and Drama; [oth. writ.] A poem entered into under sixteens Dyslexics competition (Awaiting Result) "Death is A Birth".; [pers.] I write from my heart and from my philosophy of life and experiences so far.; [a.] Gillingham, Kent, ME7 5PY

LUCAS, PAUL
[occ.] Retired; [hon.] Design Management Award, The Royal Society of Arts, Liveryman, The Worshipful Company or Furniture Makers; [a.] St. John's Wood, London, NW8 0JX

LUKE, HOLGATE
[b.] June 15, 1968, Hull; [p.] Marlene and Alexander; [m.] Julie, August 25, 1990; [ch.] James Luke, Jessica Rae; [ed.] David Lister School Hull; [hon.] Inclusion into the other side of the mirror; [oth. writ.] Amused BC (unpublished) subject of progress and spiritual transformation. A book of approx 35 poems (illustrated) including a Shamans Quest; [pers.] Listen to the wise men and take heed, for the truth lies between the lines and hard to read. (Amused BC).; [a.] Hull, Yorkshire/East, HU9 4SU

LYNCH, DAPHNE CAROL
[b.] December 22, 1951, Epsom; [p.] Irene and Joe Hill; [m.] Divorced; [ch.] Three girls and one grandchild; [ed.] No formal education, but I achieved R.S.A. and pitmans in English in 1990; [occ.] Porter Driver for the Royal Hospital for Nero - Disability.; [memb.] Michael Jackson's fan club.; [oth. writ.] I have six poems published to date. Two in Poetry now and four by Arrival Press. All are in proper anthologies.; [pers.] I am a R.C. christian an in much of my writing I try to reflect this. However life is so diverse and much of it connical that I can write on most things. My pets, family and friends are a great source of inspiration for me.; [a.] Chessington, Surrey, KT9 2QT

MACDONALD, ADELINE
[b.] December 14, 1983, Inverness; [p.] Marie and Brian MacDonald; [ed.] Plockton High School; [occ.] First year in Plockton High School; [hon.] Winner of the National Oxford Poetry Competition; [a.] Kyle of Lochalsh, Ross-shire, IV40 8BT

MACDONALD, ALEXANDER
[pen.] A. MacDonald-Cheeseman; [b.] February 22, 1936, Scotland; [p.] Angus MacDonald and Alice Cheeseman; [m.] Grace Ann MacDonald, September 15, 1961; [ch.] Amanda Claire; [ed.] Scottish Higher Leaving Certificate of Education; [occ.] Administrator; [oth. writ.] Collections of poems and prose not yet submitted for publication; [pers.] Influenced by a presbyterian upbringing in N.W. Scotland, by army and police service and by a lifelong admiration for the works of Shakespears, the English poets and Robert Service.; [a.] Inverness, Inverness, IV2 3LS

MACDONALD, JOAN M.
[b.] March 16, 1922, Grimsby; [p.] Anne and Cyril Hayden; [m.] Hugh MacDonald, December 23, 1942; [ed.] Elementary; [occ.] Retired; [memb.] Wander Lust Rambling Club RSPB; [hon.] None - I'm afraid; [oth. writ.] Heart seeds - Book of Poems 'Nessie' children's stories Witch of Kiltality - short story past editor of hospital magazine sharing and caring husband's war-time encounter with Humphrey Bogart; [pers.] I mostly write for my own pleasure as I love the written word. I think deeply of important issues and have a great love of my family and friends.; [a.] Grimsby, NE Lincs, DN37, 0RG

MACDONALD, SUSAN J.
[b.] June 17, 1954, Hull; [p.] George Wilby, Barbara Wilby; [m.] John MacDonald, November 3, 1973; [ch.] Nichola Elisa; [ed.] Aimthorpe High; [occ.] Office Administration Hornsea Freeport; [memb.] Worldwide Fund for Nature Whales and Dolphins Conservation Society; [hon.] Champion for Animals Award.; [oth. writ.] Many poems written, mainly on animal and environmental issues. None of which have been previously submitted for publication or competition.; [pers.] I get great satisfaction from putting down on paper my thoughts and feelings. I hope 'snake' will be the first of many, to succeed.; [a.] Cowden, East Yorkshire, HU11 4UL

MACFARLANE, DEBORAH
[b.] February 24, 1960, Camberley; [p.] Arthur Fosh, Joyce Fosh; [ch.] James William, Amy Louise; [ed.] France Hill Secondary Modern, - Access Course Spelthorne College - Ashford - hope to go on to University; [occ.] Housewife/single parent; [oth. writ.] Several short stories and poems awaiting publication; [pers.] Life is full of choices and decisions, always listen to your inner-self, follow your natural instincts and you won't go down a wrong pathway.; [a.] Feltham, Middx, TW14 9NR

MACFARLANE, MARY H.
[pen.] Mo; [b.] May 10, 1950, Edinburgh; [p.] Kathreen and William Thomson; [m.] Albert K. MacFarlane, March 30, 1968; [ch.] Two boys, James and Paul; [ed.] General; [occ.] Domestic Cleaner; [oth. writ.] Book, Heavens Harmony (Poems also published in local papers); [pers.] My ambition is to let all read my poems, and feel the need of a creator.; [a.] Dalkeith, Midlothian, EH22 2JD

MACLEAN, DUNCAN
[b.] August 4, 1961, Inverness; [ed.] 8 different schools - left with know certificates.; [occ.] Hospital Porter; [hon.] I have a Scotec Certification for Greenkeeping and Groundsmanship; [pers.] I boxed for Scotland at International level at Middleweight.; [a.] Dalry, Ayrshire, KA24 5EA

MACLEAN, RODERICK
[b.] November 22, 1961, Surrey; [p.] Iain and Jean MacLean; [m.] Susie MacLean, September 18, 1993; [ed.] Ravensbourne School for Boys, Bromley, Kent; [occ.] Assistant Transport Manager; [memb.] Institute of Advanced Motorists, Scottish Piping Society of London, Scots Guards Association; [oth. writ.] Own collection of own poems written since 1990. None published.; [pers.] I can only create poetry when gripped by inspiration. This comes of rare moments, usually late at night. Without inspiration my pen is sterile.; [a.] London, SW17 7QQ

MACLEOD, MARY
[pen.] Bunty MacLeod; [b.] March 17, 1950, Fort William; [p.] Archie Cameron, Alice Cameron; [m.] Iran MacLeod, April 5, 1969; [ch.] Kevin Ian, Brian; [ed.] Lochaber High School; [occ.] (Mature Student), Studying Child Psychology; [oth. writ.] This is the first; [a.] Fort William, Inverness-Shire, PH33 7AN

MACNELL, ROMA
[pen.] Annie Bayes; [b.] June 14, 1936, Northampton; [p.] Albert Carter, Sarah Carter; [m.] Albert MacNell, (2nd marriage children by 1st one); [ch.] Bernard Sylvia Hazel and Aileen; [ed.] Local Village Schools, Gt. Billing and Earls Barton; [occ.] Care Assistant; [oth. writ.] Purely for pleasure in my own little book; [pers.] I write what I see, and feel so others may understand the thoughts of anothers way of life.; [a.] Newport Pagnell, Bucks, MK16 0HP

MADLE, PETER RICHARD
[b.] August 8, 1930, Strood, Kent; [p.] Sidney Stephen and Kathleen Mary Madle; [m.] Audrey Joan Medhurst, May 24, 1958; [ed.] Rochester Technical School and H.M. Dockyard Chatham College; [occ.] Retired, Ex-Diagnostician Gunnery and Missile System M.O.D.N.; [hon.] Honour in Mathematics; [oth. writ.] Several poems published in local papers. Several poems written for my friends. Some poems written for people retiring to raise monthly for a local hospice.; [pers.] I strive to write funny poems or verse to my friends and about my friends to bring laughter into their lives. My have been influence by a poem my father wrote to me for my sixth birthday (started writing when recovering from heart attacks and cancer); [a.] Rochester, Kent, ME1 2VA

MAHER, MICHAEL
[pen.] Timothy Cameron; [b.] June 8, 1945, Birmingham; [p.] Patrick and Mary Maher; [ed.] The Oratory School Royal College of Surgeons, Dublin; [occ.] Retired Doctor; [memb.] Plymouth Literary Society; [pers.] I call on my past knowledge to inspire the future.; [a.] Plymouth, Devon, PL4 9QD

MAHON, THREASA ELENOR MARTH
[b.] September 30, 1977, Portlaoise; [p.] Rita and John Mahon; [ed.] Scoil Aongusa, Stradbally, Co. Laois 1983-1990. Scoil Criost Ri, Portlaoise, Co. Laois 1990-1995. Vocational School Co. Carlow 1995-1996; [occ.] I am currently a student at the V.E.C. in Co. Carlow; [memb.] I am a member of many local clubs, Macra na Feirme, Timahoe Football Club, Stradbally Camogie Club; [hon.] I was awarded a certificate for participation in a project competition and reached the finals. I also received a certificate of achievement regarding the project.; [oth. writ.] I have wrote many poems as a past time as I enjoy as a past time as I enjoy writing them. This is the first time something I wrote has ever been published.; [pers.] Most of my poems may reflect what I may be thinking and are meaningful to me. I enjoy writing poems. I feel I can express myself in my poetry.; [a.] Stradbally, Laois

MALINDINE, MARGARET
[pen.] Margaret Malindine; [b.] April 11, 1936, Hammersmith; [p.] James and Rose Malindine; [ch.] Michael and Susanna; [ed.] Coston Sec. Hod School, Greenford; [occ.] Masseuse/Reflexologist Reiki Healer; [hon.] Itec Qualification International Therapy Examination Council; [oth. writ.] I have written many poems, unpublished also a children's story; [pers.] I sing with slough philharmonic soc. and broadheath singers, meditate, attend taichi classes, am unmaterialistic, dreamy, creative, spiritual, my poetry is freely expressed from my soul; [a.] Slough, Berks, SL2 5NF

MALTBY, NIGEL LLOYD
[pen.] Nigel Lloyd Maltby; [b.] November 16, 1947, Woodhall Spa, Lincs; [p.] Dick Maltby, Jessie Maltby; [m.] Yvonne Denise Gossage, September 29, 1984; [ch.] Vincent James; [ed.] Gartree School, Tattershall, Charles Keane College, Leicester; [occ.] Postal Officer; [memb.] Association of Accounting Technicians; [oth. writ.] Several poems in local news media; [pers.] I enjoy sharing my feelings and life's experiences through my writing.; [a.] Boston, Lincs, PE21 9RP

MANNING, FRED
[b.] May 4, 1932, Devon; [p.] Hilda (mother); [m.] Denise, 1950; [ch.] Three; [ed.] Grammar Totnes Sch; [occ.] Retired from Running Retirements Home; [memb.] R.A.F.A., R.B.L.; [oth. writ.] Many, three published; [a.] Teignmouth, Devon, TQ14 9TH

MAPLETOFT, WINNIE
[b.] September 6, 1926, Hinckley; [p.] Jack and Olive Buckingham; [m.] Jack Mapletoft, June 19, 1948; [ch.] Kevin, Paul, Hilary, Elaine, Tony Michael; [ed.] Secondary Modern; [occ.] Retired Auxiliary Nurse; [memb.] St. Johns Ambulance Society; [oth. writ.] Spiritual poems for church quarterly magazine. Family verses for birthday, anniversary and other greetings cards.; [pers.] I am inspired to write my poems hoping to help someone along life's, way, and that inspiration comes from the heart.; [a.] Hinckley, Leicester, LE10 2RN

MARGERUM, DAVID SAMUEL
[pen.] Margerum David; [b.] July 20, 1932, Fulham, London; [p.] Daisy and Samuel Margerum; [ed.] Various Elementary Schools, as I was evacuated during the war - finished at Fulham Central School; [occ.] Unemployed; [oth. writ.] Crown Imperial off the Rails, Sixty Something, Published in three separate books, by anchor books of Peterborough; [pers.] I have occasional outbursts of inspiration mainly due to anchor books accepting my works as I am a beginner in this field.; [a.] Swindon, Wilts, SN3 1EY

MARSHALL, ALASTAR
[pen.] Alan Mars; [b.] September 24, 1963, Hatton Ceylon; [p.] Bruce and Rosamund Marshall; [ed.] Cargilfied (Prep. School), Trinity College, Glenarmond (Public school). L'Institut'eas etudiants Estrangers, L'Universite D' Ax Marseiller III. (1 year.); [occ.] Writer; [memb.] Member of Local Amateur Dramatic Society; [hon.] Winner of a daily telegraph crosswords competition in 1995. Entry to 'Tears in the Fence' Pamphet Comp. 1995 was 'Commended' by the adjudicator. Two Prep. School prizes - Junior Art, Senior French. Advanced Certificate in Proof - Reading.; [oth. writ.] Many poems published in 'Psychopoetica' (Dept. of Psychology, Hill University). Also published in 'Understanding' (Edin.), in Poetry Nottingham, and in 'Arrival Press' anthologies.; [pers.] Greatly influenced by the life and writings of Samuel Beckett. Favourite Poets are C. C. Cummings and Robert Frost.; [a.] West Linton, Peeblesshire, EH46 7EA

MARSHALL, BRENDA
[b.] September 14, 1939, Harpendon; [m.] Derek Marshall, September 14, 1957; [ch.] Wendy, Richard, Darren; [ed.] Dearham School Cumbria; [occ.] Self employed outside caterer; [oth. writ.] "Scribbles On Scraps" but nothing published; [a.] Carlisle, Cumbria, CA5 1AD

MARSHALL, ELAINE
[b.] March 6, 1955, Mancot, Deeside; [p.] Kathleen and Lawrance Morris; [ed.] Joanne and Colin Marshall; [occ.] Comprehensive School Queensfolly Deeside; [pers.] I just write poems when inspired by something, I used to write short stories for my children, when they where small. Put a few words together, make up little songs for them "I'm one of life's dreamers."; [a.] Connah's Quay, Flintshire, CH5 4UY

MARSHALL, RENEE
[b.] Brynmawr, S. Wales; [p.] Albert Charles Williams, Gertrude Williams; [m.] John Stuart Marshall, February 20, 1960; [ch.] Chris - Jane - Lynne - Diane - John and Joy Marshall (6 children); [ed.] Girls - Rugby High School Boys - Ashlawn Grammar; [occ.] Retired; [oth. writ.] Several poems printed in "Muse of poetry" and "Mainly for children" also in the local paper about the village green in Bilton; [pers.] I write for Sheer Joy - about life - my children and nature.; [a.] Rugby, Warwick, CV23 9DJ

MARSTON, ALAN
[b.] 1960, Lambeth; [m.] Janette; [ch.] Two Girls, Alana and Maisie; [ed.] Glenbrook Infants, Clampham, SW4; [occ.] Part-time at Sainsbury's; [oth. writ.] Entries in a few anthologies, an abominable poetry quarterly and the January 1995 edition (page fourteen), of the socialist standard.; [pers.] The best trip I ever had was on a bus to Streatham back in the sixties.; [a.] Wellingborough, Northants, NN8 3NN

MARTIN, STEPHEN
[b.] November 21, 1970, Cookstown, Co. Tyrone, N. Ireland; [p.] Brian and Patsy Martin; [m.] Rhona Henry (Girlfriend); [ed.] St. Patrick's High School, Cookstown, Co. Tyrone; [occ.] Factory Worker, Newark, Notts.; [pers.] I write to remind me of Ireland and how I miss its' people, its' culture, its' good and its' bad.; [a.] Lincoln, Lincolnshire, LN5 8DW

MARYAN, MRS. JOAN ESTHER COO
[pen.] Joan Maryan; [b.] December 26, 1924, Pottespury, Bucks; [p.] Mr. and Mrs. William and Edna Cooper; [m.] Mr. James Albert Maryan, January 26, 1946; [ch.] Paul, Susan, Mark, Robert, Emelie; [ed.] St Mary's Convent Np'ton Technical Art School, Northampton "Park School" Park Avenue Denver Colorado - USA Switch Board Operator; [occ.] Retired - A.T.S 42 yrs Sales Ass. for U.S.A. "Avon" Ambulance Driver - married since 1946; [memb.] A.T.S Life Member British Railway - spouce of late employee - Life Member Ladies Club - A.T.S; [hon.] Medals Awarded A.T.S. active service 1941 - 1945 W/93123 Joan Esther Cooper home address "Road Main Garage" Ltd., Roade, Northamptonshire; [oth. writ.] "Winter Time" "Summertime" "Tomorrow" "Day by Day" "Rocky Mountains" - Colorado - "Strangers in the Night" "Dead of Night" "The Way of Life" "Precious Year"; [pers.] I've painted in oil many pictures - rolled them up and given to anyone for rindness to my family and also personal painting of myself and my parents all three, I was pleased with - they have since been removed - James never read my poems - they survived.; [a.] Northampton, Np'tonshire, NN4 8AY

MASON, MARY
[b.] June 24, 1928, Hartlepool; [p.] Kate and John Oliver; [m.] Raymond, 1951; [ch.] Anthony, Marianne, Paul; [ed.] St. Joseph's F.C.J., Convent School Endsleigh Training College Hull; [occ.] Retired - Primary School Head - Teacher; [memb.] Friends of Lourdes H.C.P.T. - Handicapped Children's Pilgrim Trust (Lourdes); [hon.] L.A.M.D.A. Gold Medalist Reader of the Poetry Society.; [oth. writ.] Many poems unpublished! Youngest son Paul Shakespearian actor) Paul Breunau - has had radio written plays accepted by the B.B.C. and has appeared in various TV series.; [pers.] Down many a by way we may often stray and in our folly hide ourselves away in shame but sleep awake and watch the dawn of each new day.; [a.] Harttepool, TS25 3TB

MASTERSON, RITA
[pen.] Rita Masterson; [b.] Kilkenny; [m.] Edmon Masterson; [ch.] Eight; [ed.] Primary; [occ.] Homemaker; [oth. writ.] Just write for pleasure never entered other competitions; [a.] Clones, Monaghan

MATREAUX, JULIANA JOSEPH
[pen.] Juj; [b.] June 16, 1955, St. Lucia; [ch.] Son 23 yrs, daughter 21; [occ.] Student/community worker; [memb.] South East London Labour Party, Southwark Women's Action Group, Student Union, Sub-Committee member Hexagon Hsing Ass. Matrix Hsing Co-op; [hon.] Formal and informal counselling RSA, Community Leadership (RSA diploma); [oth. writ.] Written from age of 11 onwards consistently to date.; [pers.] I am involved at present in a growth process which enables me to partake in the giving and receiving of love for and from my fellow humans - through inner peace. My heart concern lay with the children with broken wings and tired eyes with no knowledge on how to begin their flight.; [a.] Peckham, London, SE15 5AY

MATTHEWS, C.
[pen.] Matt; [b.] September 14, 1930, Gloucester; [p.] Orphaned aged 3; [ed.] Central Secondary School Glos, Technical School Glos; [occ.] Retired; [oth. writ.] Coloured spectacles doesn't help. (Unpublished story of my childhood).; [pers.] The urge to record the harsh up bringing in my orphanage in the 1930-45 years.; [a.] Newton, Ayclife, Durham, DL5 7HY

MATTHEWS, MRS. JOAN Y.
[b.] November 3, 1940, Birmingham; [p.] Edward and Violet Crook; [m.] Derek George Matthews, March 29, 1958; [ch.] Jacqueline, Annette and Philip; [ed.] Sec/Modern School; [occ.] Registered Disabled, Worked from 15 to 50 years, Retired Sales Consultant; [memb.] Patron of Opera Society, and Member of Local Womens Institute, Suffers with Cervical Spondylosis and stays at home most of the time.; [hon.] School Diplomas in: Art/Design, Handwriting, 'Speach Choir' Elocution, School Reporter, Head Prefect, House Captain etc.; [pers.] I hope that whoever reads my poems will gain some sort of wisdom and understanding, as they are mostly abut the 'Trials of Life'; [a.] Swansea, Glam., SA7 9RZ

MATTHEWS, MAUREENE
[pen.] Maureene Matthews; [b.] February 17, 1939, Middlesex; [p.] Michael and Beatrice McLoughlin; [m.] June 20, 1959; [ch.] John and April Matthews; [ed.] Ealing Technical College; [occ.] clairvoyant and Counsellor - (Weekend Resident at The Galleria Shopping Centre, Hatfield, Hertfordshire - Private Bookings 0181-423-1460). Legal and Personal Executive; [oth. writ.] Numerous letters published in National Newspapers and Magazines: Poems published in competitors Journal and the 1991 Arrival Press book 'Winter Gold.'; [pers.] Communication relieves stress, love creates understanding, and the written word brings consolation.; [a.] Greenford, Middlesex, UB6 0SS

MAYNE, EDWARD
[b.] October 15, 1936, Redhill, Surrey; [p.] Edward Mayne, Marjorie Mayne; [m.] Mab's Mayne, second marriage April 28, 1979; [ch.] Gary, Paul, Keith; [ed.] Secondary Modern, Banstead, Surrey; [occ.] Stock Control; [hon.] Higher certificate Wines and Spirits; [oth. writ.] Short stories for children, not published. Personal observations, of the human race.; [pers.] Awareness of the beauty of nature and its forces, in all its forms.; [a.] Telscombe Cliffs, East Sussex, BN10 7DY

MCANULTY, PETER
[pers.] I like poems of the little people and folk love.; [a.] Dromara, Down

MCCAIG, AGNES
[b.] June 28, 1943, Glasgow; [p.] William and Susan Donnelly; [m.] James McCaig, October 1, 1965; [ch.] James, John, Susanne, Stephen; [ed.] Primary C Secondary School, Education Left School at Age 15; [occ.] Housewife; [oth. writ.] Various other unpublished poems.; [pers.] My favorite poet is Rabbie Burns as I feel he had a great insight into human nature.; [a.] Glasgow, Strathclyde, G32 9XQ

MCCALLION, DOMINIC
[pen.] Dominic McCallion; [b.] May 8, 1962, Omagh; [p.] Tommy McCallion (Dead) and Ruby McCallion; [m.] Ann McCallion, May 5, 1984; [ch.] Nadine; [ed.] Glebe P.S. and St. Colmans High, Strabane; [occ.] Manager Winemark, N.I. and Photographer; [oth. writ.] A large but as yet unshown collection of poems on a wide range of subjects.; [pers.] Not everyone can be the poet. But we can all be part of the poem.; [a.] Strabane, Tyrone, BT82 9BZ

MCCANAAN, OLIVE B.
[pen.] Ollie B.; [b.] May 21, 1959, Scunthorpe; [p.] John F. Brady - Olive M. Brady; [m.] Kenneth McCanaan; [ch.] Kavan John, Kathryn Jane; [ed.] Sir Frederick Gough (Comp) Bottesford; [occ.] Housewife/Mother; [memb.] Kukkiwon Tae-kwon-do Club Thurnscoe/Red belt; [oth. writ.] Lots of poems for myself and family only; [pers.] Always strive to see the 'good' in others.; [a.] Thurnscoe, Rotherham, S. Yorks, S63 0NR

MCCANN, VALERIE
[b.] April 4, 1939, Bradford, W. Yorks; [p.] Walter Tose, Annie Tose; [m.] Brian McCann, July 27, 1963; [ch.] John Brian, Steven Paul, Ian Patrick; [ed.] Bolling Girls Grammar School; [occ.] housewife, P/Time Domestic; [oth. writ.] A few poems not published; [a.] Bradford, W. Yorkshire, BD15 7LF

MCCARTHY, CHRIS
[b.] Cork (Rep. of Irl); [p.] Eddie and Betty McCarthy; [m.] Divorced; [ch.] 1 boy - David August 6, 1978; [ed.] Patrician Academy Mallow Co Cork Irl., Blackpool Term. and C.D.T. London.; [occ.] Sales Executive; [hon.] Lonxsdaale Trust Award for thesis at CDT London.; [oth. writ.] Many poems not yet published; [pers.] While I feel helpless to physically right the wrongs is this ever changing world we live in, if my poetry can convey some message, it maybe a start.; [a.] St. Leonard's-on-Sea, East Sussex, TN38 0JL

MCCLUSKEY, MARTIN
[b.] March 12, 1969, Port Glasgow; [p.] Annie Mitchell, Hugh McCluskey; [ch.] Christopher (8 yrs); [occ.] Cook and Publisher; [oth. writ.] With Courtesy and Colour, The Morning Mirror, Choose and Haunt It, The Necropolis Dream, Sleeper, Calmer Storms Will Break; [pers.] I wrote this stuff because its the only time I can speak honest and openly without some bugger, beneath me, criticizing me and my way of thinking nothing to do with - romance at all.; [a.] Port Glasgow, Renfrew

MCCORMICK, HELEN
[b.] September 1, 1923, Chorley; [p.] Clara Ellen and Owen Hope; [m.] Frank McCormick (Mac), August 18, 1945; [ch.] A son - Jed (educated at Plus Xth Prep Sch Preston College); [ed.] Duke Street Primary School, Chorley Grammar School Life; [occ.] Writer and Wife (Agent) Sal Keegan; [memb.] Chorley Hospital Crusade, C.A.B.; [hon.] One poetry award; [oth. writ.] Various articles in "She" "Woman" and on local radio. Had work turned down by every major publisher.; [pers.] My writings are diverse. Humour (mainly light Lancashire), Romantic and anything I feel strongly about. Was influenced by my own feelings, but admire and respect Rudyard Kipling.; [a.] Chorley, Lancashire, PR6 8ES

MCCOY, JEAN
[b.] April 23, 1942, Royton; [p.] Wilfred Bartram, Ivy Bartram; [m.] Bernard McCoy, October 17, 1987; [ch.] Step Daughter, Allison Wilson; [ed.] St. Anne's Cofe, Secondary Modern; [occ.] Medically Retired Social Worker; [oth. writ.] Have written childrens stories with illustrations. But as yet have not tried to have them published. Letters published in our local paper. Paint and frame my own pictures, and for other people.; [pers.] I like to express the reality of everyday life in my poetry, and in the reading of it, so that people get a message from it, and I hope enjoyment.; [a.] Oldham, Lancashire, OL8 3BJ

MCCULLOUGH, AMELIA PRUDENCE ROSE
[pen.] Prue McCullough; [b.] April 22, 1951, Ballymones, Co. Antrim; [p.] Frances Adeline MacLean - (the late) Reginald Welb MacLean; [m.] Martin Dominic McCullough, October 9, 1971; [ch.] Margaret Amelia Frances, Heather Elizabeth Rosemary; [ed.] Coleraine High School, Coleraine Technical College, College of Business Studies Belfast, West Midlands Retraining Centre.; [occ.] Housewife and mother of austistic adopted daughter (aged 21 yrs); [memb.] Had to drop most memberships when husband lost job in 1991. Also travel over to N.I. to see mother in Coleraine Co-Londonderry several times a year, (so really not fair to belong to organizations unless I can give them total commitment); [hon.] City and Guilds 4460 Hotel Reception; [oth. writ.] Have had various letters published in newspapers and magazines entered several writing competitions before. Although I've never won, I've been highly commended, twice this is the first poetry competition which I've won!; [pers.] I hope that my writing, whether prose or poetry will make people happier in a world where there are too many pessamists, and not enough optimists). I hope my writings will make the world a happier place!; [a.] Northfield, Birmingham, West Midlands, B31 1DY

MCCULLOUGH, COLETTE
[b.] September 23, 1953, Liverpool; [p.] Colin and Mabel Russell; [m.] Divorced; [ch.] Lee Sharon and Andrew William; [ed.] Stanley Park Comprehensive Liverpool.; [occ.] Dermatology Nurse; [oth. writ.] None Published; [pers.] Re-started writing poetry after break up of marriage.; [a.] Liverpool, Merseyside, L12 8QG

MCDONAUGH, LYNDSAY
[b.] October 27, 1981, Edinburgh; [p.] James McDonaugh, Gillian McDonaugh; [ed.] I am currently attending Broxburn Academy and have been since 1993; [memb.] South Queensferry and District Pipe Band, Westmuir Riding Centre, Redwings Horse Sanctuary; [hon.] I have 6 Horse Riding Diplomas, 11 Rosettes for participating in Horse Riding Events, I have a short Tennis Certificate, a Scottish Schools Hockey Certificate, a Scottish Schools Football Certificate and many Scot Vec Modules; [oth. writ.] This will be my first recognized poem and hopefully more of my other poems will do as well if not better than this one.; [pers.] I base my poetry on reality and personal experiences.; [a.] Broxburn, West Lothian, EH52 5LU

MCEWAN, MIKE
[b.] October 11, 1939, Glasgow; [ed.] Professional RMN, REN, RNT, DNA, M Phil, FRSH, Graduate of Dundee College of Technology Mediploma in Nurse Administration (DNA), Graduate of University of Glasgow (M Phil EDST); [occ.] University of Lecturer in Health Studies University of York; [memb.] Fellow of the Royal Society of Health Member of General Council University of Glasgow; [hon.] Territorial Decoration (TD) and Clasp, Gulf Medal, Saudi Arabian Medal, Kuwait Liberation Medal; [oth. writ.] A number of papers on military subjects presented at conversions/courses etc., thesis on stress as a curriculum development 1995 dissertation of nursing schemes 1988.; [pers.] Poetry used as a method of personal expression sometimes to express feeling or reaction to events or experiences and sometimes just for a bit of amusement.; [a.] Scarborough, N. Yorks, YO12 4TP

MCFADDEN, PATRICK
[b.] January 18, 1950, Co. Donegal, Eire; [p.] Neil McFadden, Cassie McFadden; [occ.] Carpenter; [oth. writ.] My Lovely Isle, The Wayward Farmer, several others none published.; [a.] Kennington, London, SE11 4JF

MCGOUGAN, WILLIAM
[pen.] Bill McGougan; [b.] September 25, 1939, Kilmarnosis, Ayrshire; [p.] Duncan and Margaret; [m.] Patrica Laura, May 16, 1959; [ch.] William, Jackie, Sean; [ed.] Secondary Modern Royal Navy H.E.T. twenty three years service (1956-1979); [occ.] Naval Area Communities Plymouth (Bar's Manager); [memb.] Robert Burn's Club Plymouth; [hon.] Serving with H.R.H., Prince of Wales Hms Norfolk (1971-73) Great Honour; [oth. writ.] Poems and an unfinished novel of service life (One Day); [pers.] Never look back unless to go forward influenced by Robert Burn's and Scottish Heritage.; [a.] Plymouth, Devon, PL2 1EF

MCGRATH, HANNAH BERNADETTE
[pen.] Bernadette Kennedy; [b.] January 5, 1925, Ballyferriter, Co. Kerry, Eire; [p.] Michael and Mary Brigid Kennedy; [m.] Patrick Joseph McGrath, December 28, 1954; [ch.] Four; [ed.] National School Ballyferriter, Presentation Convent Dingle Co. Kerry Eire; [occ.] Housewife, occasional Agency Nursing; [hon.] Registered Nurse (Gen), Registered Midwife, B.A. Open University, Registered Reflexologist; [oth. writ.] Some poems and short story at a creative writing class Kingsway College Homes Road London; [pers.] I hope to leave the world a better place because I had lived.; [a.] London, NW5 1UA

MCILHATTON, JAMES
[b.] October 10, 1941, Ballymowey, Co Antrim; [p.] William McIlhatton, Elizabeth McIlhatton; [m.] Margaret, April 25, 1969; [ch.] Maureen, James, Wendy, Jennifer, Junior; [ed.] Limited education was gained in the school of life's experience; [occ.] Janitor at Ballymena Academy; [oth. writ.] Poet. Author. Historian. Public Speaker. Written two books on history. Several poems. Published in local newspapers; [pers.] My greatest reward is when people get pleasure and enjoyment from reading my poems.; [a.] Ballymena, Antrim, B743 6LJ

MCINTYRE, ANGUS JACKSON HEWITT
[b.] April 11, 1966, Glasgow; [p.] James and Sarah McCormack Hewitt; [ch.] Carol-Ann; [ed.] Victoria Drive Secondary School Clydebank College; [hon.] Three O'Levels, Environmental Improvements Projects, City and Guilds in Carpentry and Joinery, Scottish Building Scheme; [oth. writ.] Suicide, Evolution (parts 1 and 2), Mushroom Wars (parts 1 and 2), Lost, Zephyr Through Time, The Felled Tree, The Confused Dove, Threads, Pep Talk, The Children's Plea, Inbetween The Lines, Tale of Caution, Strange Feeling; [pers.] Shine-on-Terry and June Maxwell for both pushing me to show my expressions in words for the first time to the outside world to my mother, Andrea and Jim for being there through my dark time. For the memory of my father; [a.] Glasgow, G14 9SZ

MCINTYRE, RUTH
[b.] July 9, 1950, Ormskirk, Lancashire; [p.] Robert Barrett and Christine Barrett; [m.] William McIntyre, May 23, 1970; [ch.] Pauline, Ruth and Alec (Twins); [ed.] Bourne School Kuala Lumpur, Malaysia, Queens Upper Secondary Modern-Germany, Primary school Clune Park Port Glasgow; [occ.] Housewife; [oth. writ.] Several poems printed by Triumph House, Peterborough; [pers.] Poetry is a heartfelt inspiration. Though Gone from This Earth was written with Robert Burns in mind, he is and always will be an inspiration to us all.

MCKAY, ANTHONY STEPHEN
[b.] April 13, 1955, Marston Green; [m.] Lorraine Ellen McKay, June 28, 1980; [ch.] Nicole Amanda; [ed.] Ryland Bedford High School (Sutton Coldfield);

[occ.] Decorator; [hon.] City and guilds craft certificate, distinguished; [oth. writ.] 'The Meaning of Easter' for Triumph House Christian Yearbook and 'A Friend for Life' for the Anthology 'Close Harmony'; [pers.] We live on through our words and actions and are also remembered by the same.; [a.] London, E12 6DF

MCKEARNEY, JAMES A.
[b.] October 24, 1957, Dungannon; [p.] Marylouise and James Joseph McKearney; [m.] Gail Lorraine McKearney, June 2, 1990; [ch.] Nicole, Louise and James; [ed.] Bishop Challoner Rlc; [occ.] Sales Engineer; [hon.] Diploma in travel and tourism; [oth. writ.] None other than 2 books that I have wrote for my own pleasure; [pers.] I have been writing ever since I can remember. I have not been influenced by any one writer. I tend to express my emotions on life, the good, the bad and the anguish we experience.; [a.] Kings Heath, Birmingham, B14 5BD

MCKECHNIE, WILLIAM
[pen.] Bill McKechnie; [b.] March 16, 1959, New Cumnock; [p.] Ian McKechnie, Mary Carson; [m.] Elaine Ann McKechnie, October 13, 1984; [ch.] Martyn John, Afton Louise; [ed.] Cumnock Academy (High School); [occ.] Team Worker, British Nuclear Fuels; [memb.] Assistant Scout Leader with the 6th Blackpool; [oth. writ.] Several poems published in anthologies, work magazines; [pers.] I write poetry for the fun of it. I like to see the pleasure other people gain from my work. Like Al Jolson use to say "you ain't seen nothing yet"; [a.] Blackpool, Lancs, F74 4PQ

MCKINNEY, JANET
[b.] July 28, 1936, Dorset; [m.] Francis Niall McKinney, March 30, 1964; [ch.] Joanne, Martin and Andrew; [ed.] Swanage Grammar, Bournemouth College of Commerce and Technology; [occ.] Partner in Architectural Technologist Firm; [oth. writ.] At present working on an illustrated Anthology of Verse, and an a Children's Story in conjunction with my Husband which we hope to publish.; [pers.] My writings have been influenced by events in everyday life and local history.; [a.] Bournemouth, Dorset, BH6 4DQ

MCLEISH, JENNIFER JACQUELINE
[b.] August 2, 1984, Dundee; [p.] Jack and Jacqueline McLeish; [ed.] Harris Academy, Dundee; [pers.] I enjoy writing and hope one day I will get to write a novel, I hope others will enjoy reading it.; [a.] Invergowrie, DD2 5AU

MCLINTOCK, ANDREW
[b.] December 16, 1969, Lanark; [p.] Robert McLintock, Dorothy McLintock; [ed.] Wishaw High School; [occ.] Personnel Administrator; [memb.] Kelso Loyal Rangers Supporters Club; [pers.] Inspired by the works of Richie James.; [a.] Alnwick, Northumberland, NE66 1BY

MCMAHON, LESLEE
[b.] August 8, 1963, Liverpool; [p.] Margaret Howelie; [m.] Thomas McMahon, November 27, 1993; [ch.] Mick Peers, Thomas Peers, Joseph Peers; [pers.] Dedicated to a very special Lady (my Mother) who sadly died, after long illness, age 47 yrs., where ever you maybe, in the rain, the snow, the stars at night, we know your beside us, to light up our life.; [a.] Liverpool, Merseyside, L14 2DR

MCMONAGLE, WILLIAM
[b.] March 5, 1962, Glasgow; [p.] Margaret Jackson; [m.] Christine McMonagle, June 12, 1987; [ch.] Scott Joseph, Shannon Alexandria; [ed.] Bankhead Primary School, Victoria Drive Secondary School; [occ.] Omnibus driver, tram driver; [oth. writ.] (For own pleasure) no other published works, although I have a small personal collection; [pers.] This is a personal dream fulfilled, although I never imagined I would ever be published. I feel very humbled by it all.; [a.] Blackpool, Lancs, FY4 3BZ

MCNAB, ISABEL
[b.] January 7, 1952, Inverness; [p.] Michael and Margaret Quigley; [m.] Dave Nicolson (Partner); [ch.] Alasdair, Janine and Stuart; [ed.] Oban High School, Logan and Johnston College; [occ.] Civil Servant, Stirling; [oth. writ.] Various poems and short stories written for family and friends. This is my first publication.; [pers.] I endeavour. To capture the highs and lows of life's learning process and transcribe the experiences, circumstance and emotion into verse. The resilience and compassion of the human race never cease to amaze me.; [a.] Alva, Clackmannanshire, FK12 5HS

MCNALLY, ROGER RENANDO
[b.] July 16, 1967, Wellingborough; [p.] Ricardo McNally, Loveen McNally; [ed.] Wellingborough Tresham College; [hon.] English Literature, English Language, Diploma in Information Technology; [pers.] I love to write with great feeling and sensibility, to express my words in a different way a poetic way inspired by what I hear and read.; [a.] Wellingborough, Northants, NN8 3DZ

MCONNACHIE, JOHN D.
[pen.] John Donald; [b.] February 24, 1942, Dingwall Rosshire, Scotland; [p.] Annie and Alec McNaught; [m.] Ellen Ruane Henderson, March 27, 1965; [ch.] 2 boys - Tom and John; [ed.] Newmains Junior Secondary School, Newmains Strathclyde Scotland; [occ.] Unemployed; [oth. writ.] Other poems written about things that happened.; [pers.] Always like poetry and sometimes take the time to try and write something entertaining.; [a.] Carluke, Strathclyde, ML8 4NG

MEDHURST, JAMES
[b.] June 4, 1968, Chatman, Kent; [p.] Norman Medhurst, Joan Medhurst; [ed.] Mid Kend College; [occ.] Civil Servant; [pers.] When I write I'm influenced by things that go on around me, the memories I have and the dreams that I hope will someday come true. I don't believe I have a talent, I just write about what I'm feeling inside.; [a.] Gillingham, Kent, ME7 1JJ

MEDLEY, MAUREEN SYLVIA
[pen.] Mo; [b.] December 16, 1943, Bradford; [p.] Fostered at the age 4; [m.] Widowed, December 24, 1977; [ch.] 2 boys, Paul, Stephen; [ed.] Secondary School; [occ.] Windowed housewife; [memb.] I am a member of the Daniel O'Donnell Fan Club; [oth. writ.] I have my own book and have written about 40 poems over a period of 15 years.; [a.] Bradford, Yorkshire, BD4 6EW

MELLOR, JOANNE
[b.] July 5, 1978, Newcastle, Staffs; [p.] Derek Mellor, Ann Mellor; [ed.] Cheadle High School, Leek College of Further Education; [occ.] Student; [pers.] Inspired by life, death and love, these are the things I try to express in my writings.; [a.] Cheadle, Staffordshire, ST10 1JT

MELMOTH, TARAH
[pen.] Tarah Melmoth; [b.] August 30, 1974, Devon; [p.] Janice Melmoth; [ch.] Expected June 1996; [ed.] Tiverton Comprehensive; [oth. writ.] Personal; [pers.] I like to express different angles with my poetry. Most of my poetry gives emotion and an element of peace.; [a.] Devon, EX16 9JH

MERCER, TIMOTHY DAVID
[b.] December 23, 1966, Knaresborough; [p.] Stan and Gillian; [m.] (Intended) Catherine Gardiner, 1997; [pers.] York City F.C. are my constant inspiration - I admire their constant striving for excellence against a tide of ineptitude.; [a.] Slough, Berkshire, SL1 1SW

MERRITT, MS. JILLIAN GEORGINA
[b.] June 7, 1958, Peckham, London; [p.] George Merritt, Eva Merritt; [m.] Separated; [ch.] 4 sons, Kevin, Paul, Simon, John Owen; [ed.] Millvale Secondary School Luton; [occ.] Cleaner; [pers.] I love to write poems in my space time, mainly romantic one's for my partner, Keith. This is the first I've sent and had published.; [a.] Dunstable, Beds, LU5 5QF

MERRY, NICOLETTE
[pen.] Nikki Merry; [b.] November 8, 1953, London; [p.] Herbert Johnson, Iris Johnson; [m.] John Derek Seaman; [ch.] Paula Karen, Stuart Thomas; [occ.] Care Worker; [pers.] My poem is dedicated to great Ormond St. Hospital for saving my grandson's Alfie Lee Holloway, life and to the many children who have not been as fortunate as he.; [a.] London, E6 3EF

METCALFE, BETTY GWENDOLINE
[b.] November 1, 1931, Ferndale; [p.] Winifred and Evan Lloyd Enoch; [m.] Robert Ives Metcalfe, July 10, 1954; [ch.] Kerry Lynne (daughter); [ed.] Primary Newton Junior 1936-42, Bridgend Girls Grammar School 1942-1948; [occ.] House wife and career for my mother who is 95 in June and has always lived with me; [memb.] I was a member of the Porthcawl Little Theatre which has now been disbanded.; [hon.] Centra Welsh Board (Equivalent to London Matriculation). 12 D Levels. In 1948 S2 in Chemistry in 1950, I was a Laboratory Assistant, from 1950 to 1960 when my daughter was born.; [pers.] I try to see beneath the surface of life's large and small drama's and being a scorpio I always put myself in the position of the other person in any conflict.; [a.] Porthcawl, Mid Glamorgan, S. Wales, CF36 5TP

MICHAEL, ANDREA
[pen.] Jodie Goldberg; [b.] May 23, 1981, Sandwell; [p.] Demi and Costas Michael; [ed.] Still at school (Leasowes High and Community College); [occ.] Student; [oth. writ.] Have written many poems and songs which have yet to be published.; [pers.] I try to make my writing as realistic as possible and always put all my effort into producing my best work. I have been greatly influenced by the Beatles.; [a.] Halesowen, B62 8RA

MICHANICOV, CHRIS
[pen.] Michanics; [b.] September 21, 1960, London; [p.] Demitrios Michanicov, Dora Michanicov; [ed.] Minchenden Comprehensive School, South Gate London N 14, Barnett College of Further Education; [occ.] Unemployed at present; [memb.] Swimming club; [oth. writ.] I have written quite a few poems which I have not yet published; [pers.] Every poem I write takes you on a journey through life. Where is mankind heading? And also about God's love to his people. I have been influenced by the singer song writer Cat Steven's songs.; [a.] London, N13 4AJ

MILLER, LINDA
[b.] October 7, 1956, Kent; [p.] Florence Wickham and Robert Wickham; [m.] Leslie Miller, February 1, 1975; [ch.] Daniel William and David Matthew; [occ.] Housewife and Aspiring Writer.; [oth. writ.] Many poems written for various anthologies.; [pers.] I endeavour to discover the magic in life, and to illuminate it in my work.; [a.] Dartford, Kent, DA2 7LJ

MILLGATE, PATRICIA
[b.] January 22, 1946, Woolwich; [p.] George Heyburn, Elizabeth May; [m.] Roger Millgate, November 9, 1980; [ch.] Jane, Lindsay, Robert Collis; [pers.] My first poem. I was compelled to write it after the death of my friend Doris (NE 'Winkle') after her death on 30-12-95; [a.] Longfield, Kent

MILLS, ALEXANDRA BURNESS BO
[b.] April 28, 1944, Rutherglen, Scotland; [p.] Thomas and Elsie Young; [m.] Divorced; [ch.] 3 Adult - Andrene, Peter, Susan; [ed.] Rutherglen Academy; [occ.] Retail Manageress Shoes; [memb.] Aberdeen, Genealogical Research and Family History Society. (Collector of old books and maps pertaining to Scotland), Antique Book Club - Aberdeen.; [oth. writ.] Poetry, short stories and the beginnings of my first book. Even a screen play all unsubmitted I just love to write.; [pers.] I am inspired to write by strong emotions, from love to sadness by observation of mankind, and the inspirational works of burns - a great observer.; [a.] Poncaster, S. Yorks, DN9 3PR

MILNE, ANDREW
[pen.] A.E.L. Milne; [b.] October 31, 1960, Corby; [p.] Jean Bennett, Robert Milne; [m.] Lesley Milne, July 31, 1993; [ed.] U.S. High School Graduation Diploma; [occ.] Safety Technician Cosalt International Aberdeen; [oth. writ.] None published a small collection of poems; [pers.] Exploring how I feel in my heart allows me to uncover the meaningful things I can say.; [a.] Portlethen, Kinkardinshire, AB1 4RG

MILTON, PAULINE WENDY
[b.] September 29, Aberdare, South Wales; [m.] Divorced Twice; [ch.] Sons and Daughters; [ed.] Totton Grammar/VI Form; [occ.] P/T Amateur Poet/Writer P/T Public Relations Officer; [memb.] Antique and Royal Doulton Colleges Club, Night Club, Women's Health, Promotion, Tennis Club, Assisting Army/Ex-Forces Club, some charity clubs, too numerous to mention, Social Pleasure Club, as forever optimistic with a love of life and men; [hon.] Seven O levels Basic Auxiliary Nursing, Basic Auditing and Merchandising, I hope the honesty of this profile reflects a serious yet optimistic approach to my life and writing - every day life in the raw; [oth. writ.] In process of writing a novel, fictional, with added life experiences, touching, raw, in the hope of evoking emotions with the reader. Several poems published in papers. Also several short stories, more requested, amateur level only; [pers.] I strive to ensure my poetry reflects life experiences, both comical and sad, in the hope the reader can relate to it personally. My stories/novels, are fictional I endeavour to approach subjects experienced by both large and small factions of our society.; [a.] Southampton, Hampshire, SO45 2NG

MINTON, LEESA
[pen.] Lisa Minton; [b.] September 3, 1968, Australia; [p.] John Minton, Shirley Knight; [ed.] University of Waikato, N-2 Morley College, London; [occ.] Counsellor; [memb.] British Association for Counselling; [pers.] Quality of relationship is something I value highly, people close to my heart: Friends, lovers, family, clients, teachers inspire me to write.; [a.] London, SW18 3BG

MITCHELL, MISS CHRISTIAN S.
[pen.] Nil; [b.] March 6, 1939, Caldercrulx Lanark's; [p.] David and Helen Mitchell; [m.] (To be) Mr. George Wothers Poon of Airdrie who greatly encourage me, 1998; [ed.] Comprehensive Non Denomination Leaving at 15; [occ.] Retired due to (Hearing) Disability; [memb.] Petersburn Airdrie Library, Writers Workshop, Librarian Ms Lindsay McKrell, Tutor Ms. Valerie Thornton; [hon.] 3 highers 1 "O" level and Various Scotvecs gained on Returning Adult Education 1986-1991 and Academic Achievement Award Re-R-education Higher "A".; [oth. writ.] 5 poems Anchor Press Triumph House Poetry now (all Peterborough) 4 and 1 short story in our writers GRP Anthology published in 1993 "Wummins Words Classy Burds" ISBN. 0-9522648-0-3; [pers.] Being a happily committed Christian I love to write about nature and do believe Goodness and Kindness will always ultimately win over evil. Though this may not be often obvious in Today's World; [a.] Airdrie, Lanarkshire, ML6 7AX

MITCHELL, E. MHAIRI
[pen.] Mhairi Mitchell; [b.] January 10, 1981, Glasgow; [p.] Charles and Eileen Mitchell; [ed.] Eastbank Academy, full-time student, presently sitting exams; [occ.] School student; [memb.] Youth Fellowship Church of Scotland; [hon.] Have not attained any of these as yet; [oth. writ.] None published various other poems; [pers.] Very much interested in religious studies history and life after death. My poetry tends to be based on these subjects; [a.] Glasgow, G32 0PP

MITCHELL, ELIZABETH MAY
[pen.] Elizabeth M. Mitchell; [b.] April 30, 1940, Alyth; [p.] Elizabeth and Alexander Byars; [m.] David Mitchell, September 19, 1958; [ch.] Three sons, one daughter; [ed.] Alyth Junior Secondary School; [occ.] Housewife; [memb.] Alyth Musical Society, Alyth Parish Church Millennium Committee; [oth. writ.] Poem published in poetry now 1994; [pers.] I love to hear about other people's escapades and I try to see the funny side of any situation.; [a.] Alyth, Perth, PH11 8AR

MITCHELL, MR. GRAHAM
[b.] May 14, 1960, Derby; [p.] Emma Alan; [ed.] Hardwick Infants Juniors Willington Juniors. Hatton Secondary, Comprehensive Weston-Mere Comprehensive; [occ.] Print Finisher; [memb.] Poetry Digest, Leics Anchor Books Peterborough, The International Society of Poets.; [hon.] BTEC Diploma in Cobol Computer Programming, 5 GCE's, 2 CSE's.; [oth. writ.] A number of poems featured on books. Local press and on local radio.; [pers.] If you cannot do anybody a good turn, never do them a bad one knowingly!; [a.] Derby, Derbyshire, DE22 2HD

MITCHELL, J. S.
[b.] March 29, 1912, Merriott, Somerset; [occ.] "Retired"; [oth. writ.] "Sleepy Valley", "Bridge Over the Forth", "Tempest of the Waves", "Betrayal", "The Green Grass", "Falling Leaves", "The Broken Wall", "Beyond the Mountain Range", "The Angry Sea"

MITCHELL, NIGEL TROY
[b.] November 24, 1964, Redruth; [p.] Frank Mitchell, Terena Mitchell; [ed.] Camborne Comprehensive School; [occ.] Lorry Driver/Cutter West Country Metals Ltd; [pers.] I write my poetry on things that spark my imagination, be it love, life or nature. I have been writing them since I was thirteen, this is my first contest, and my first publication.; [a.] Camborne, Cornwall, TR14 7HQ

MITCHELL, STANLEY
[b.] December 15, 1906, Onneley, Shropshire; [p.] Charles Edward Mitchell, Anastasia Mitchell; [m.] Mary (Nee Biddulph Mitchell, May 23, 1973 in St. Paul's O.B.E. Chapel; [ed.] Orme Boys High School Newcastle-under-Lyme. (Famous old boy-Novelist Arnold Bennett, St Paul's College, Cheltenham (Headman in Final year); [occ.] Retired Headmaster. Poplar drive, Blurton, Stoke-on-Trent School; [memb.] Member of the Order of the British Empire; [hon.] M.B.E. in the Queen's Birthday Honours List 1964; [oth. writ.] Several poems published in local magazines. An article on "Music in Youth Clubs" in "The Boy" magazine.; [pers.] I believe in the paramount importance of kindness of others as being the highest virtue advocated by St. Paul.; [a.] Leek, Staffs, ST13 8DW

MITCHELL, STELLA
[pen.] Stella Mitchell; [b.] October 1, 1945; [ch.] Two sons - four grandchildren; [oth. writ.] Several poems plus one compete story in Prose called "He Can Do It For You" which tells of the saving and healing power of God in the lives of wounded and abused people.; [pers.] My poetry comes from the reality of the world about me, and then a desire to reflect God's loving intervention into the chaos of this world.; [a.] Thetford, Norfolk, IP24 3QE

MOFFAT, ELIZABETH
[pen.] A. C. Jordan; [b.] March 5, 1980, Dumfries; [p.] Audrey Moffat and James Moffat; [ed.] Dalbeattie High School; [oth. writ.] A few poems and several short stories unpublished; [a.] Dalbeattie, DG5 4DZ

MOIR, EMMA JOYCE
[b.] October 26, 1984, Aberdeen; [p.] Greame Moir and Brenda Moir; [ed.] Foveran Primary School; [occ.] School girl; [oth. writ.] Article in local paper on Greece; [pers.] "Be excellent to one another and kind to animals."

MONAGHAN, MRS. MAY
[b.] May 6, 1939, Bexley Heath; [p.] Walter Millett, Dora Rose Millett; [m.] Divorced 1980; [ch.] Six; [ed.] Left School 1954 could not read or write (self taught); [occ.] Home Carer; [oth. writ.] None published many written; [pers.] My poems come from within. Writing is astress release. I write of things I believe, I've seen and done. I hope they give as much pleasure to the reader as they have to me the writer.; [a.] Dinnington, South Yorkshire, S31 7LA

MONK, SUZANNE
[b.] July 9, 1959, Rustington; [p.] Edith Groves, Leslie Grove; [m.] Barry Monk, April 7, 1977; [ch.] 3; [ed.] St. Edmunds Salisbury; [occ.] Care Worker; [oth. writ.] Several poems published in local papers, one published last year by Anchor books, book called the Spice of Life; [pers.] Poetry is a big part of my life. Its usually just one line that forms in my mind and flows from that, I people watch a lot and that gives me a lot of ideas. It has also in the past helped me to cope with lifes ups and downs.; [a.] Arundel, West Sussex, BN18 9ED

MONTEITH, JEAN
[pen.] Lucy; [b.] September 1, 1937, Carrickadartans; [p.] Ruby and Alex Sproule; [m.] Kenneth, December 12, 1956; [ch.] Six sons, 2 daughters and five grandchildren; [ed.] Small country school; [occ.] Housewife; [memb.] St. John Ambulance Sunday School Teacher C.E.F. helper; [hon.] St. John Ambulance public First Aid Exam. award and Caring for the Sick (Level I); [oth. writ.] Three poems published I am working on a children's story; [pers.] I enjoy putting my thoughts in rhyme. I get great satisfaction when folk enjoy my work.; [a.] Castlederg, Tyrone, BT81 7BD

MOODY, SIRE
[b.] October 23, 1946, Southampton; [p.] Len and Sylvia Cooc; [m.] Ray Moody, October 12, 1968; [ch.] Donna and Richard; [ed.] Secondary Modern, 3 CSE; [occ.] Admin. Assistant; [memb.] Volunteer with Children 20 years, "Southampton Children's Play Association"; [hon.] Special Award by Mayor of

Southampton 17/4/96 for my voluntary work in Southampton; [oth. writ.] Lots had on other poem published not this one; [pers.] Never be afraid to show love to those who matter to you, I would be nothing without my children and the strength of my husband; [a.] Southampton, Hampshire, SO18 1NJ

MOORE, LOUISE
[b.] November 6, 1967, Hampstead; [m.] Andrew Moore, March, 22, 1993; [ch.] Ryan John, Carley Jean; [ed.] Bentley Wood; [occ.] Housewife; [oth. writ.] Poem read out on T.V. am.; [pers.] I get my inspiration from observing not just the material world but also my inner self.; [Tn.] Potters Bar; [a.] Herts, EN6 2PS

MOORE, VIOLET M.
[b.] July 17, 1915, Ferryhill, Co Durham; [p.] Mr. and Mrs. F. Harrison; [m.] October 8, 1939; [ch.] Three; [ed.] Church of England School, Leeholme Co Durham; [occ.] R Pensioner Widow Last 13 Years of Fepow in Singapore; [oth. writ.] Quite a few more poems only done since 9 sent you my poem. "I gave you life a long time ago" last year. Ref your letter after I recovered from a almost fatal heart attack on 11-11-95 "God gave me another chance to survive at age of 79 1/2 years old."; [pers.] When 4 was 75 year old I wrote annual book called "Bouquet of memories" published and payed for oat of my small savings by myself. All monies have been donated to our chospice also save the children, blind, Great Ormond St. Eye.; [a.] Bury St. Edmunds, Suffolk, IP32 3ER

MOORHOUSE, JEAN
[b.] April 4, 1938, Salford; [p.] Olga and Bill High; [m.] Divorced; [ch.] Deborah, Robert, Bruce and Amanda; [ed.] Broughton High School Girls; [occ.] Unemployed; [oth. writ.] First attempt; [pers.] Romantic dreamer locked in the past. Disenchanted with present day selfish society. Long for old style community spirit.; [a.] Baltasound, Unst, Shetland, ZE2 9DU

MORELAND, MRS. L. J.
[pen.] Linda Joy; [b.] December 22, 1950, Urpeth Hall, Beamish; [p.] Mr. Cyril Slater, Mrs. Joan Slater; [m.] Mr. James Moreland, July 9, 1994; [ch.] 2; [ed.] North Heaton Secondary School; [occ.] Home Carer; [oth. writ.] Just the ones I have at home.; [pers.] Many times when I'm sitting along, I put pen to paper and write a poem. I spend my life caring for others, I get satisfaction making people smile and their days brighter feel. I was made for this job.; [a.] Killingworth, Newcastle, NE12 0DJ

MORGAN, MR. DANIEL ROMAN
[b.] August 3, 1968, Cardiff; [p.] Ms. P. C. Morgan; [ed.] Cedars Upper School Manchester School of Sound Recording; [occ.] Student (of music) Sound Engineer; [oth. writ.] Some personal poetry and contribution to lyrics whilst composing within a band setting; [pers.] It is my greatest ambition to combine music and words in my own style. My poetry is very heavily constructed the subjects concern the inner and outer self.; [a.] Buckingham, Bucks, MK18 1EW

MORGAN, THOMAS FREDERICK
[pen.] Tom Morgan; [b.] October 15, 1982, London; [p.] Frederick Kingsley Morgan and Bernadette Susan Tovell; [ed.] Loyola Preparatory School Buckhurst Hill, Essex, St Davis College, Llandudno; [occ.] School boy; [a.] Chingford, London, E4 8SR

MORRIS, GRAHAM
[b.] March 11, 1939, Chester; [occ.] Retired Lecturer; [pers.] I can sense life more comfortably through poetry!; [a.] Willaston, South Wirral, L64 1SQ

MORRIS, MRS. V. R. E.
[pen.] Green Fingers; [b.] March 5, 1920, Tile Barn Farm Hoo; [p.] Ernest and Florence - Harris; [m.] Ronald Jack Morris, July 28, 1951; [ch.] 1954 Son Paul - Deceased 1989; [ed.] School for Girls - Greenwich; [occ.] Retired - Exp Office; [memb.] IFAW; [oth. writ.] First try

MORRISON, ALYSON MARIE
[b.] September 20, 1979, Middlesbrough; [p.] Michael and Sandra Morrison; [ed.] Rosecroft Secondary School, Loftus; [occ.] Student; [memb.] Loftus Gym, Cross-Country Team for School, Middlesbrough Football Club Follower; [hon.] Trophy for 1st place in cross-country, records of achievement from school; [oth. writ.] The "Feline Spirit" was my first attempt at publishing my poetry.; [pers.] Thank you for publishing my poem, it was influenced by my two cats "Merlin and Gizmo."; [a.] Loftus, Cleveland, TS13 4LJ

MORRISON
[pen.] Alistair, John; [b.] February 25, 1946, Irvine; [p.] Angus Morrison, Jessica Giffen; [m.] Alexandra Guiney, March 2, 1970; [ch.] Kevin Morrison, Paul Morrison; [ed.] St. Mary's Primary, St. Peter's Secondary, eldest of seven children, left school at 15, help Mum finance.; [occ.] Unemployed at the moment owing to Lymphoma (Cancer), I am at present on the mend.; [memb.] Annick, and Noah's Ark, Spiritualist Associations; [hon.] Highland Dancing, Bronze, Silver, Gold Medal Tests plus Associate Teachers.; [oth. writ.] Very small parts in magazines.; [pers.] Very keen in music - all types, would love to song write, short stories, T.V. scripts etc.; [a.] Saltcoats, Ayr, KA21 5PL

MUNN, PETE
[b.] August 23, 1963, Perth; [p.] Isabella Munn, Alex Munn; [m.] Gillian Munn, May 29, 1993; [ch.] Jamie Andrew; [ed.] Auchterderran Junior High; [occ.] Packer-Apricot Computer Ltd-Glenrothes; [memb.] Delegate Official of Cardenden Amateur Boxing Club, Fife Flyers 3 'D's Ice Hockey Supporters Club; [hon.] Represented Scotland both home/abroad for club and country at Amateur Boxing - winning senior titles plus gold medal at Twintown Olympiad in 1984; [pers.] Never thought I'd ever get my poem published as I've never done anything like it before - shows what could be achieved with a bit of effort through boredom; [a.] Cardenden, Fife:, KY5 0EQ

MURPHY, ELAINE
[b.] December 4, 1945, Newcastle; [p.] Bill and Ella Stephenson; [m.] Joe, October 2, 1965; [ch.] Joseph, Stephen, and Susan; [occ.] Housewife; [oth. writ.] No work publishing but have written about 40 poems.; [pers.] Writing poems has become a hobby. Family and friends receive a poem for different situations Birthdays anniversaries etc., my poems come from love, I have had a lot of sadness in my life lately, people identify with my poems and if I bring pleasure, this makes me happy.; [a.] Birtlom, Durham, DH3 1NF

MURPHY, MISS MARIAN
[b.] March 11, 1961, Nottingham; [p.] Rita and Christopher Murphy; [m.] Divorced; [ch.] One son; [ed.] Cottersmore School Nottingham; [occ.] Housewife, Mother; [oth. writ.] This is the time I have presented one of my poems; [pers.] I started to write poetry when my sister lost her husband. It seemed easer to express the sort of feelings you couldn't say in conversation. I was greatly influenced by Kahlil Gibran, and Lord Tennyson.; [a.] Nottingham, NG8 1PB

MURPHY, THOMAS
[pen.] Prince Cavich; [b.] November 11, 1942, Bellshill; [p.] Margaret and Charles Murphy; [m.] Elinor Mary Murphy, October 25, 1968; [ch.] Thomas and Tracey Murphy; [ed.] Mossend Primary School, New Stevenson Secondary School; [occ.] Cellarman; [hon.] Royal Life Saving Teachers Award, Award of Merit - Bronze Medallion; [oth. writ.] Several poems, none published as this is the first time I have entered a contest. I write as a hobby really.; [pers.] I have always loved literature, be it poems or novels, especially the works of Oscar Wilde. I never imagined I'd have some of my own work published; [a.] Edinburgh, Midlothian, EH16 6SJ

MURRAY, JAMES G.
[b.] July 26, 1933, Durham; [p.] Martha, Andrew Murray; [m.] Josephine Murray, May 4, 1957; [ch.] Jean, Lynn, Julie; [ed.] Army 1st Class; [occ.] Retired; [memb.] Korean Vets Assn., Durham Light Infantry Assn., The British Legion; [hon.] (B.E.M.) British Empire Medal, (M.I.D.) Mention in Dispatches; [oth. writ.] Several unpublished stories and poems about my life's experiences; [pers.] My father loved poetry especially Burns, Scott, maybe something rubbed off.; [a.] Colchester, Essex, CO2 0DY

MURRAY, REV. THOMAS
[b.] December 30, 1924, Liverpool; [p.] Thomas and Margaret (Connolly); [ed.] Univ. College Dublin, Univ. College Calcutta; [occ.] Catholic Priest (Retired); [oth. writ.] A poem for each Sunday of the Three Year Cycle (in preparation).; [pers.] If reading my poems helps others as much as writing it helps me, my reward is great indeed.; [a.] Whalley, Lancs, BB7 9RR

MYATT, JENNIFER MORBEY
[b.] November 21, 1940, Marlborough, Wiltshire; [p.] Amy Amelia and Karl Ludvic Melsom; [m.] Bernard Edward Myatt, August 11, 1973; [ch.] Karl John; [ed.] Riland Bedford Secondary Modern and Kingsbury RD Continuation College; [occ.] Activity Carer and voluntary helper at Sutton Stroke Club; [oth. writ.] One poem: Eastern England Poets, one poem: Perceptions, two poems: Poetry Now, one poem: Local Newspaper, two poems: kept by S/ Coldfield College and RSA Examiner; [pers.] I find you can "lose yourself" for a while when reading poetry, it is a very pleasurable experience I wrote my "Kristopher" poems (three) as a record of my grandson, as when my son Karl asked me when, where and how he first achieved things I found it difficult to recall after twenty odd years.; [a.] Sutton, Coldfield, West Mids, B74 4LJ

NASH, MRS. ELIZABETH ANN
[pen.] Liz; [b.] January 5, 1954, Gosport; [p.] Mrs. Eva Rosana Briggs (My mother); [m.] Separated; [ch.] Five children, five grand children; [ed.] Primary School in Gosport; [occ.] Housewife, unable to work; [memb.] I sometime's collect and sale for Alzheimer's Disease Society; [hon.] Still waiting (ha ha) I have written another poem. When I got your letter I was so pleased. I know I can write more and earn a living from them. But I need someone like you to help, my mother poem is called discoved at last.; [oth. writ.] Now I know I am good enough, I will carry on writing, as it is something I enjoy, I write how I feel, and things just come together, maybe if I won I would love to buy some books to give me the joy the bring.; [pers.] I would love one of your books, but as you see I don't work, I would of enjoyed it very much, but. Thank-You, Whitehill; [a.] Bordon, Hants, SE35 9ED

NEL, KELVIN C.
[b.] October 7, 1962, Romford; [p.] David and Dinah; [m.] Shanie, August 27, 1988; [ch.] Jodie and Tatum; [occ.] Cinema Manager; [memb.] Electricity Consumer's Council, Lay Inspector Essex Social Services; [hon.] UCI Manager of the Year 1994-95. British Government and Politics English Language and Literature; [oth. writ.] Completed Daily Diary for the BFI "Chronicle of British Cinema 1995-96". Was published in "Diary of a Day in World Cinema"; [pers.] All my writings preach and reflect equality and racial tolerance.; [a.] Southend-on-Sea, SS1 2SN

NEWMAN, SHEILA
[b.] October 16, 1975, Wembley; [p.] George K. Newman, Beatrice Newman; [ed.] Claremont High School, Thames Valley University; [occ.] Student; [oth. writ.] Several poems published in other poetry anthologies; [pers.] I want my poems to express the innermost parts of my being as well as my faith in God. I hope that in reading my poetry I can show the beauty and triumph of the human spirit.; [a.] Wembley, Middlesex, HA9 6LS

NICHOLS, EDWARD
[b.] September 29, 1914, London; [p.] Thomas Nichols, Ada Nichols; [m.] Elizabeth Nichols, December 25, 1937, Died October 4, 1988, Remarried Avis Nichols, October 28, 1989; [ch.] Two boys, three girls, by my late wife.; [ed.] Craven Park (local school), Hackney Technical College, Bolt Court School of Art and Printing; [occ.] Retired Commercial Artist and Graphic Designer. Chief Artist Associated Newspapers, Publicity Studio.; [memb.] Retired President Pepping Forest Mentally Handicapped Society. The Aircrew Association, war service R.A.F. Coastal Command, demobbed with rank of Flt./Lt.; [oth. writ.] Several poems during war service none published. Wrote articles and produced The Daily Mail Motor Cycling Guide for many years. Have written a book, title "We Held The Key" a story based on my war service flying with R.A.F. Coastal Command, now in the last stages before publication.; [pers.] Poems written during the war were inspired by the tremendous spirit of self sacrifice and comradeship. I believe life is about people not material possessions.; [a.] Roydon, Essex, CM19 5JB

NICHOLS, WINIFRED
[b.] September 18, 1987, Wigan; [p.] Lilian Barton, Thomas Barton; [m.] Brian Nichols, February 18, 1987; [ch.] Anne Marie, Janet; [ed.] Up Holland Grammar, Wigan Technical Collage; [occ.] Co. Director; [hon.] RSA Business Management; [oth. writ.] Write purely for own and dialect plus romantic writings.; [pers.] The whole of life can be seen through poetry.; [a.] Wigan, Lancs, WN2 1LD

NICKLIN, TERENCE
[b.] April 11, 1934, Sheffield; [p.] Joseph Nicklin, Annie Nicklin; [m.] Ada Nicklin, March 2, 1957; [ch.] Jayne Elizabeth, Richard Terence; [ed.] Coleridge Road Grammar School; [occ.] Retired Coal Miner; [memb.] Secretary for the Royal British Legion, Honorary Poppy Organizer; [pers.] I dedicate my poem "The Tree" to my daughter Jayne Elizabeth Fairest; [a.] Sheffield, S. Yorks, S12 2BJ

NOEL-CEPHISE, JEAN MARIE
[b.] December 22 1944, Mauritius; [p.] Benjamin and Anne Noel-Cephise; [m.] Marie Paule Suzy Noel-Cephise March 1, 1969; [ch.] Only child Jean-Paul Noel-Cephise; [ed.] Educated in Mauritius Convent School Belle Rose Remy Olier Qautre-Bornes; [hon.] One of the winner of Immigrant Poet's Association founded in May 1995 supported by Southampton City Council; [oth. writ.] Over seventy poems twenty five in French, Les Saisons De La Vie, Mes Souvenir, Le Sentier. Wine, My Eden, Dreams, Music, The Price, Strange, Killing Time, England, Spirit ect ect; [pers.] Having been born poor an Island where many lives for peace and justice many of our questions remain unanswered why should so many dies of starvation why should so many innocents looked in prison by those who believes in freedom.; [a.] Andover, Hants, SP10 3PE

NOONAN, RICHARD M.
[pen.] Richard M. Noonan; [b.] March 25, 1971, Scotland; [p.] Phyllis Rosemary Noonan; [m.] To be married to Nicole Maatkamp, November 29, 1996; [ed.] West Cumbria Catering College, Tranei Chef de Cusine; [occ.] Head Chef Alhambra Hotel, Jersey; [oth. writ.] No other publication's, I have written many songs and poetry over the years, but had no publication; [pers.] Over a period of six years I have written about happenings and subjects of interest in my life and close to my heart I have been resident of the Island of Jersey for 2 years. I am also the head of a Motel on the Island; [a.] St. Helier, Jersey, JER 4LD

NORRIS, KATHLEEN
[pen.] Louise Roe; [b.] October 25, 1934, Burton-on-Trent; [p.] Samuel Roe, Edith Roe; [m.] Reginald Norris, December 25, 1954; [ch.] Gary, Tracey; [ed.] Secondary Modern Girls School; [occ.] Retired (recently undergone triple heart by-pass surgery); [oth. writ.] Several poems written. But this is the first one to be put into prints, as I've never submitted my work before.; [pers.] My feelings of injustice in this world. Influence my writing, a great deal.; [a.] Burton-on-Trent, Staffordshire, DE13 0NS

NOTHVON, ALEXANDER DRUMMOND
[b.] May 10, 1969, Stirling; [ed.] High School of Stirling; [occ.] Kitchen Porter Gleneagles (True Care Agency); [hon.] Quarter Semi Finalist for Fencor Stirling High Award 1981, Boy's Brigades; [pers.] I have never won anything in my life before but this would be a great benefactor as I am partially disabled I also enjoy Chinese confucius of Derek Waloors; [a.] Britt and Scot

NOTT, ROBERT ERNEST
[pen.] J.C.B.; [b.] November 30, 1933, North Shields; [p.] Joseph Williams and Florence Nott; [ed.] Elementary; [occ.] Retired from British Gas.; [memb.] Disabled Ex Service Club, Local Darts and 53 teams; [hon.] Honour receiving a reply from International Poets Soc. at my first attempt the award hopefully comes seeing a poem of mine in print (No pun intended); [oth. writ.] Just beginning to write lots of thoughts on the subject, at the moment I am moving house, from 18 Banbury Way, North Shields, Tyne and Wear.; [pers.] Eat English Beef and give up smoking use a condom live in peace. God save the queen.; [a.] North Shields, Tyne and Wear, NE29 6AW

NYE, BRIAN JOHN
[pen.] Brian John Nye Tattooist; [b.] April 6, 1950, London; [p.] Horace and Irene Nye; [m.] Carol Hedges, April 18, 1970; [ch.] Brian, Kirstie, Gary, Dannye, and Jemma Karma Leeta; [ed.] (John Dunne), (Thomas Calton) Sec. Modern; [occ.] Tattooist; [memb.] A.P.T.A. Ass., Pro, tattooists; [hon.] Winner of best individual tattoo on a woman 86/87 gold, silver, and bronze medals in county match target shooting; [oth. writ.] Verses from the valley's Christian poets of wales Valentine verse. Hog fever, light and enlightenment, onward Christian poet of Wales.; [pers.] A fool needs help to become a wiseman. A wiseman needs no help to become a fool. B. NYE. 87; [Tn.] Brigend; [a.] Mid-Glam, CF35 6ED

OATES, SYDNEY
[b.] December 5, 1926, Cleckheaton, West Yorkshire; [p.] James George Oates, Hannah Ellen Oates; [m.] Jean Oates, August 7, 1954; [ch.] Stephen James, Martin Frank, Julie Ellen, Vincent Sydney; [ed.] Whitcliffe Mount Grammar, Cleckmeaton Technical College, Bradford; [occ.] Retired; [memb.] Fellow, The Chartered Institution of Water and Environmental Management (FCIWEM), Incorporated Engineer, The Engineering Council (I. Eng.); [oth. writ.] Poems, short stories.; [pers.] The spiritual world endures.; [a.] Crowborough, East Sussex, TN6 2BJ

O'BOYLE, LUCY
[b.] September 27, 1945, Co. Clare; [p.] James J. McGrath, Mary McGrath; [m.] Robert O'Boyle, February 1970; [ch.] Mary Grace, Robert, Joseph; [a.] Stratford, London, E15 1AU

O'DONNELL, JASON
[b.] September 24, 1970, Luton; [p.] Olive O'Donnell, Edward O'Donnell; [ed.] Lea Manor High, Marsh Farm, Luton, Beds; [occ.] Unemployed, was production operator; [oth. writ.] Three poems published by editor David Foskett of - Anchor, books, Book titles - inspirations from Central England Poetic Justice, Addictive Poetry.; [pers.] For better or worse, I put life's emotions into verse. My influences are of the song genre and of motion pictures and themes that reflect on reality in our times.; [a.] Luton, Beds, LU4 8PH

O'DOWWELL, JEAN
[b.] January 28, 1935, Farnborough, Hants; [p.] Mr. and Mrs. Wap Fisher; [m.] Michael O'Dowwell; [ch.] Four; [ed.] Boarding School; [occ.] Housewife; [pers.] Always question.; [a.] Sarratt Rickmansworth, Herts, WD3 6BQ

OGDEN, G. A.
[pen.] George Alfred; [b.] January 11, 1925, Widnes; [p.] Charles and Victoria May Ogden; [m.] Elizabeth Peach (Deceased), 1948; [ch.] 6 children-4 daughters, 2 sons; [ed.] C of E Grammar; [occ.] Retired pensioner 18 years; [memb.] Fleet Air Arm HMS Victorious 1834 Sqdn, HMS Illustrious 1833 Sqdn War Service, Med: Indian Ocean Pacific Ocean, Atlantic Ocean.; [hon.] 1939-45 - Defence, The Atlantic Star, The Burma Star, The Pacific Star, Russian Medal. For now I can only send $20 as required. Later on I will send for book; [oth. writ.] My author is God I obey implicitly. My witness is of Jesus Christ I seek not reward for freely I receive, freely do I give.; [pers.] Post recorded writings to the Pope, Rev. AK Runcie, HM Elizabeth II, Cardinal B. Hulme, Rt Hon Margaret Thatcher, Neil Kinnock, Ian Paisley, David Steel I strive to reflect the goodness of God to mankind in my writings. If you want these writings you can have them to use as you wish no copyright needed.; [a.] Northwich, Cheshire, CW8 1JP

OKEEFFE, BERNARD
[pen.] Barney; [b.] November 17, 1963, The Curragh; [p.] Barney and Ber Okeeffe; [m.] Wendy McBride, September 21, 1991; [ch.] Sally and Anna; [ed.] Brownstown Primary and Kildare Post Primary Schools; [occ.] Electrician; [oth. writ.] Several poems of historical interest (local); [pers.] I would like my poems to increase people's awareness in local history and folklore; [a.] Brownstown, The Curragh, Kildare

OLDFIELD, ROGER
[pen.] Roger Oldfield; [b.] February 10, 1952, Bath; [p.] Arthur Oldfield, Mary Grace Oldfield; [m.] Andrea Oldfield, June 22, 1974; [ch.] Kerry Louisa, Rebecca Jane, Andrew Christian James; [ed.] Wellsway Comprehensive, Keynsham, Bath College of higher education, Bath University; [occ.] U.K.

Sales Manager for Engineering Testing Services; [memb.] Fellow of Institute of Quality Assurance; [oth. writ.] Editorials in various Engineering Magazines. Song lyric compositions for hobby. Poems published in local quarterly magazine - "Corstonian"; [pers.] I strive to reflect the spiritual aspects of life in my literary and the beauty of nature around us. I have been inspired by personal circumstances and philosophical outlook.; [a.] Bath, N. Somerset, BA2 9BY

OLDHAM, MOIRA MARGARET CARLY
[b.] February 16, 1949, Dartford, Kent; [p.] Thomas and Eileen Carlyle; [m.] Richard Jeffrey Oldham, November 30, 1968; [ch.] Tracey, Kelly, and Donna; [ed.] Secondary Modern School for girls; [occ.] Housewife - Ex Community Nurse now unable to work due to disabilities; [memb.] Congleton Country Music Club, ME Society; [oth. writ.] Poems and short stories nothing published as yet.; [pers.] I write poetry because there have been many times in my life where words can cheer a person or bring comfort to someone sick or in pain. I like to think that people who read my work, have a better understanding of "Life" seen through the eyes of an ordinary wife and mother, who's faith is her strength.; [a.] Rainow, Macclesfield, Cheshire, SK10 5UE

OLEGHE, GRACE
[pen.] Grace Izegbuwa Oleghe; [b.] November 19, 1970, Britian, Benin City, Nigeria; [ch.] 2 boys (sons); [ed.] O'Level Electronics, Computer Literacy Math English, Literature passed with high grades; [occ.] Mother and writer; [hon.] Honoured only with certificates of distinctions both in computers and electronics; [oth. writ.] Many other writings yet to be published. This I am working on at this moment.; [pers.] Life is short there is much to be discovered. Different is beautiful, every human being has walked a different path in life we all have some things to express to represent the key to life is to open your mind, and listen carefully; [a.] London, SE15 3UB

O'NEILL, EDWARD
[b.] Bootle (Liverpool); [p.] Edward and Sarah O'Neill; [m.] Stella Wilkinson, October 26, 1968; [ch.] Richard and Sylvia; [ed.] Bootle Grammar School, left at 15 (top boy) to assist family resources; [occ.] Semi-Retired Company Secretary; [memb.] F.I.A.C. F. Inst. Freight Forwarders. Past President of the Bootle Rotary Club (Mr. Noel Le Mare owner of Red Rum was a founder member.) Several Orchestral Societies.; [hon.] Founded the Bootle Dramatic Society; [pers.] Beware of prejudice. We have two ears to listen to both sides. Recreation - Music. Play Piano and Violin. Parents musical. Memories of setting on wooden benches up in the 'God's' at the Shakespeare Theatre listening to Wagner's Tannhauser and Tristan and Isolde. Price 1/-(5p)! Dame Eva Turner was Elizabeth in Tannhauser I remember as a young boy. Opera was very popular in Liverpool in those days Early 1920's); [a.] Pensby, Wirral, Merseyside, L61 8TE

ORD, JOHN L.
[b.] May 19, 1937, Pontefract; [p.] John Cairns Ord, Charlotte (Nee Hill); [ed.] Secondary Education..; [occ.] Decorator - Paperhanger; [oth. writ.] Ten poems published entitled Wings Of Love.; [pers.] I feel I try to write on the more beautiful aspects of life, as someone long ago wrote, it is still a beautiful world.; [a.] Pontefract, West Yorkshire, WF8 4SF

OSBORNE, MARY
[b.] January 29, 1935, Reading; [p.] George and Doris Annand; [m.] Eric Osborne, April 23, 1960; [ch.] Helen Louise; [ed.] The Abbey School, Reading; [occ.] Retired; [memb.] Stanton Guildhouse Trust, North Cotswold M.S. Soc.; [oth. writ.] Prose and poetry in local papers.; [pers.] I have suffered with M.S. for many years and find writing helps to widen my horizon's and interests.; [a.] Cheltenham, Glos, GL54 5LQ

O'TOOLE, KEITH
[b.] January 9, 1974, Amersham, Bucks.; [p.] Mr. O.P. and Mrs. M.B. O'Toole; [hon.] The Duke of Edingburghs Award; [oth. writ.] Other poems and short stories.; [pers.] Dedicated to those who we will never know but who fought. For us.; [a.] High Wycombe, Bucks, HP13 7QS

OTTLEY, JANICE MAY
[pen.] Jo Charles; [b.] June 30, 1937, Grimsby; [p.] Jack and Ivy Iggo; [m.] Denis Ottley, March 26, 1960; [ch.] Steve Jonathan and Claire Louise; [ed.] Wintringham Grammer School Grimsby; [occ.] Medical Photographers Assistant; [memb.] Grimsby Yarborough Ladies Choir, Cantabile Choir (Grimsby); [oth. writ.] Several Adult and Children's Short Stories (none published); [pers.] My aim is to entertain when I write. I write with feeling more than intellect.; [a.] Grimsby, N.E. Lincs, DN33 3NJ

OVERFIELD, HEATHER MARY
[b.] December 27, 1950, Trowbride, Wiltshire; [p.] William Pepler, Edna Pepler; [m.] Anthony Glenn Overfield, April 10, 1972; [ch.] One daughter, Melanie; [ed.] Nelson Haden Girls School, (Secondary Modern). Trowbridge, Wiltshire; [occ.] Market Trader, Flowers and Plants; [memb.] Parrot Society; [hon.] Brook Bond Travel Scholarship, both the Junior and Senior prizes for the school and county short stories. Book called 'Aberfan', contains a poem I wrote.; [oth. writ.] Poems read on radio Humberside, a couple of poems and articles published in local newspapers.; [pers.] My writing reflects anything I emotionally have experienced, and I can capture that moment with my pen. Sometimes the mood is sad, but often jolly. That's life.; [a.] Cottingham, East Yorkshire, HU16 5EU

OWEN, SUE
[b.] January 17, 1959, Hull; [p.] Annie and Jack Cooh; [m.] Stuart Owen, March 25, 1977; [ch.] Donna, Niki, Gemma; [ed.] Burton Stone Lane School, York College of further education; [occ.] Agency care worker; [memb.] Barbican Health Centre; [hon.] City and guild family community care. A level coohiny, R.S.A. in counselling; [oth. writ.] Several poem published in poem mags; [pers.] Everybody life reflected in my poems about living loving and life and my family. They get written from my heart; [a.] York, YC2 3CT

OWEN-SMITH, MRS. C. S.
[pen.] Sue Owen-Smith; [b.] April 28, 1957, Leamington Spa; [p.] Michael and June Blythe (Deceased); [m.] Divorced April 1990, June, 1976; [ch.] Elaine 17, Simon 16, Thomas 12; [ed.] High School education Knowle, Solihull; [occ.] Office work career, Recently resigned Building Society Agency cashier's post due to financial status as a single parent and am now in the privileged position of donating more time to writing; [memb.] Arrow Spiritual Church; [hon.] This will be my first published piece of work but...watch this space!; [oth. writ.] Personal including stories for children, poems for special friends, spiritual writing some having been read at local church meeting, etch.; [pers.] Mankind must become more spiritually aware to reach the conclusion of a peaceful world. As I learn so do I wish to teach. I am an "ordinary mum" with an extraordinary passion for writing.; [a.] Alcester, Warwickshire, B49 6QU

OWENS, JANET PATRICE
[pen.] Jan Patrice; [b.] April 18, 1962, Liverpool; [p.] James and Patricia Owens; [m.] Neil Winn; [ch.] Paul and Josh; [ed.] Stockbridge Ifant and Junior and Woolfall Senior; [occ.] Housewife and Mother; [hon.] I have had two poems published before the life of Racheal Brown and Insanity; [oth. writ.] The life of Racheal Brown, insanity, the better side of life, free spirits, the birthday party, red light, thoughts love affair, lots more.; [pers.] I have been writing poetry for as long as I can remember, it is very much a part of my life.; [a.] Liverpool, L14 6UX

OWENS, RUTH
[b.] August 5, 1941, Lancashire; [p.] Margaret-English, Tadauze-Polish; [m.] I am a widow (since February '87), March 18, 1972; [ch.] One daughter, aged 17 Emma; [ed.] Primary, Grammar in Cheshire then Saffron Walden College in Essex; [occ.] Drama Teacher (part-time) at Mossley Hollins High School; [oth. writ.] I am presently writing more poems and children's stories, plus a novel entitled "Middle Aged Wives" and a booklet entitled "Half a Century".; [pers.] I try to see the humorous side where applicable and reflect this in my work. I endeavour to emphazise with all situations in life.; [a.] Stockport, Cheshire, SK6 1RU

PAGE, PAMELA
[pen.] Pan Page; [b.] April 25, 1919, Tonbridge; [p.] MacBurn Page, Marjorie Page; [ed.] Boarding School (Godophin School) Dalford College of Physical Education London School of Economics, Institute of Group Analysis; [occ.] Retired; [memb.] Catehan Art Group, Cantiun Art Group, ARP 050; [hon.] None for writing.; [oth. writ.] Wrote poems as a child. How a few articles published about three decades ago! Have taken several courses with the open college of arts. At present and taking their advanced level poetry course.; [pers.] Am enjoying enormously the opportunity to develop interests (eg. Poetry, Paste Painting, Photography) for which there was little time while working. My aim is to extend my creative capacities as far as I am able for as long as I am able.; [a.] Caterham, Surrey, CR3 6RX

PALMER, SARAH
[b.] January 15, 1976, Greenwich, South London; [p.] Pat and Trevor Palmer; [ed.] Grammar School for Girls, Wilmington University of Luton; [occ.] Student; [hon.] Studying for BA Hons Women's studies; [pers.] It may sound naive, but, sometimes the troubles that we have prevent us from seeing the power and wonder of this world. It's braver to be happy.; [a.] Dartford, Kent, DA2 7EA

PARIS, LEE
[p.] Pearl R. and W. Munro Paris; [ch.] Shayne Andrew Munro Paris; [occ.] Self-Employed; [oth. writ.] Songwriter (Lyricist), children's series (books), true stories (magazines), non-fiction.; [pers.] Reality is our future. When one looks in the mirror and sees him/her self for who they really are, making the necessary changes to improve him/her self, only then will our world be a better place to live. We ask ourselves, what can we do to better a bad situation? What can I do?; [a.] Northwich, Cheshire, CW8 2JB

PARK, WILLIAM F.
[b.] April 16, 1976, Glasgow; [p.] William Park (Deceased), Agnes Park (Deceased); [m.] Martha (Deceased 1979), December 15, 1949; [ch.] Fred, Gary, Jan; [ed.] Gavinburn School, Old Kilpatrick, Dun Bartonshire; [occ.] Retired; [memb.] Bearsden Bowling Club, (President) Clydebank Indoor Bowling Club; [oth. writ.] Poems for Personal Pleasure Romantic and Humorous.; [pers.] I feel words used to reflect strong emotions in poetry are special as a way of expressing our inner selves.; [a.] Clydebank, Dunbartonshire, G81 3EP

PARKER, ZENA R.
[pen.] Zena; [b.] 1925, London; [m.] November 25, 1950; [occ.] Retired Business Woman with considerable knowledge of holticulture; [memb.] Eastbourne Artists Association, Pevensey Bay Art Group, National Federation of Spiritual Healers, A life long practice as a spiritual healer, with numerous successful cures, both with humans and animals, an artist with a growing local reputation; [oth. writ.] Many poems printed in local press of topical interest for local readership. Also many verses to suit recipients of personalized greetings cards which I have painted for them; [pers.] I have always loved painting I use pencil ink and wash oils and watercolour. Verse also, all of which are inspirational; [a.] Pevensey Bay, East Sussex, BN24 6BP

PARKIN, DEAN
[pen.] Dean Bardini; [b.] December 3, 1968, London; [p.] Sergio, Sandra; [occ.] Student at Arts Educational Drama School; [memb.] International Fund for Animal Welfare, World Society for Protection of Bears; [oth. writ.] Articles for boxing outlook magazine.; [pers.] God bless the people of Ireland and Italy whose blood cascades in me like mountain torrents, purifying my soul and filling me with the passion for righteousness.; [a.] Ealing, London, 4LR 1WS

PARRY, ANN-MARIE
[b.] October 2, 1973, Kidderminster; [p.] Mrs. Linda Watson; [ed.] Bredenbury Primary School, Bromyard Queen Elizabeth School, Church Stretton Secondary Modern School; [occ.] Deceased January 11, 1994 suddenly aged 20; [oth. writ.] Various other poems and thoughts unpublished; [pers.] Hoped that one day man would again live in harmony and become, once more, part of the nature cycle, not the destruction of it. Her poetry was greatly influenced by her own personal experiences.; [a.] Kidderminster, Hereford and Worcester, DY10 2NA

PARRY, JANET
[b.] December 22, 1957, Billinge, Wigan; [p.] Phyllis and Ernest Erlam; [m.] James Parry (Ex-spouse); [ch.] Gillian, Andrew (Deceased - December 31, 1985); [ed.] Wigan Girls High School; [occ.] Housewife; [memb.] Radis Bible Class; [hon.] GCE's, CSE's, Technical College Certification; [oth. writ.] Poem 'The Asking Price' in a Sparrows Worth. Poetry in Church Magazine's Fiction (as yet unpublished) Poetry book, (looking for publisher).; [pers.] I record the messages the Lord gives to me, in the most simplistic form, so anyone can understand. My talent comes from him alone and is something I wish to pursue, for his glory.; [a.] Wigan, Lancs, WN3 5TT

PARRY, WILLIAM CUTHBORT
[pen.] W. C. Parry; [b.] July 29, 1947, Middlesbrough; [p.] Edith and Henry; [m.] Susan; [ch.] Maria, June, Amanda, William; [ed.] Bertram Ramsey Sec/Mod.; [occ.] Salesman; [hon.] Duke of Edinburgh award Camping/Survival 1963; [oth. writ.] Some Published Stories and Poems Local Papers and Magazines; [pers.] Poetry to me are words which should make the heart flutter, I search for those words to create my poems.; [a.] Middlesbrough, Teesside, TS1 4EF

PASSMORE, LINDA
[b.] September 9, 1950, Barrow; [p.] Stanley and Marjorie Higgin; [m.] Dr. Derek A. Passmore, September 17, 1974; [ed.] Alfred Barrow School for Girls; [occ.] Housewife; [memb.] Redwings Horse Sanctuary; [hon.] Swimming Medals Duke of Edinburgh Award, Arctic Circle Expedition Certificate; [pers.] I believe animals should live in their natural environments, and that killing animals for sport should be banned.; [a.] Wrexham, Clwyd, LL13 9XD

PATRICK, MRS. MARGARET ELLEN
[pen.] Mitz Dyson; [b.] January 31, 1931, Sandle Heath, Cheshire; [p.] Leonard and Beatrice Phillips; [m.] Deceased, March 5, 1975; [ed.] Village School, Nether Alderley; [occ.] Housekeeper; [memb.] International Song Writers Association; [hon.] Bronze, Silver and Gold Medal and Empire Emblem Ballroom for Dancing; [pers.] Country lover, hate towns love caring for the aged, enjoy painting and drawing music lover, deplore cruelty to all animals; [a.] Bolton, Lancs, BL5 1AY

PAWSEY, KENNETH ARTHUR
[pen.] Arthur James; [b.] March 28, 1928, Portsmouth; [p.] William I. Pawsey, Madeline Pawsey; [m.] Pamela Lilian Pawsey, September 25, 1954; [ch.] Stephen, Victor, Susan Kay Pawsey; [occ.] Retired Technician, Highbury College of Technology Cosham Portsmouth Hants; [memb.] British Horse Society (Life Member), Meon Riding Club Hampshire, Portsmouth City and Solen District Unison Retired Members Group; [oth. writ.] Retired members group Unison.; [pers.] My writing is the verbalisation of my minds perception of love and life.; [a.] Portsmouth, Hants, PO3 6NJ

PEARS, JUNE
[b.] July 26, 1941, London's East End; [m.] April 4, 1964; [ch.] Two Sons; [ed.] Secondary School; [occ.] Housewife; [oth. writ.] The Toy Room At Night published by Arrival Press, The Life Boat Men, X'mas, A Friend, published by, Poetry Cavalcade.; [pers.] I write on inspiration, about every day life, things that make me laugh and things that make me sad, things that happen to most people at some time in there life's.

PENNEY, LOTTIE ROSEMARY
[pen.] Rose; [b.] January 20, 1936, Ashford, Kent; [p.] Mr. and Mrs. Harry Swadling; [m.] Mr. Arthur Penney, July 6, 1957; [ch.] Jennifer, Susan, Jeffrey, Mary-Ellen; [ed.] Ashford, North Girls School Sec; [occ.] Domestic Assistant; [a.] Ashford, Kent, TN24 0HW

PERCIVAL, FRANCES
[b.] January 8, 1915, London; [p.] Elizabeth and Arthur Reader; [m.] Arthur Percival (Deceased), March 2, 1940; [ch.] Terrence, Richard, Kathleen; [ed.] Grove Vale Elementary, East Dulwich, London Borough Polytechnic Elephant and Castle, London; [occ.] Retired; [memb.] Stoney Stratford Methodist Church, Bucks, British Legion (Womens Section); [hon.] Scholarship; [oth. writ.] New writer of short stories, good reviews by friends and advised to submit to women's magazine; [pers.] I have always enjoyed reading well written books and also doing cross words and quizwords.; [a.] Milton Keynes, Bucks, MK8 8HA

PHAIR, MARK
[pen.] Mark; [b.] July 16, 1969, Enniskillen; [p.] Kathleen and Ivan; [m.] Patricia Duffy-Phair, August 27, 1994; [ch.] Paul (son); [ed.] Enniskillen High School; [occ.] Mechanic; [oth. writ.] Several personal poems; [pers.] I have been greatly influenced by my wife and son; [a.] Enniskillen, Fermanagh, BT74 6EU

PHILLIPS, GEOFFREY H.
[b.] December 1, 1947, York; [p.] Hayden and Jean Phillips; [m.] Susan Anne, March 24, 1989; [ch.] Craig Neil, Andrew Stephen; [ed.] Archbishop Holgates Grammar School York, Tech Coll Yorks; [occ.] Retired, Ill Health; [memb.] Mensa Society; [oth. writ.] Various poems and children's stories, not published. Verbal written caricatures for various people, birthdays/occasions, etc.; [pers.] I write many for my own amusement as a hobby due to my health I must adhere to a fairly secretly life. I am a Menson and enjoy mind games.; [a.] York, N. Yorks, YO2 5NL

PHIPPS, LORRAINE SUSAN
[b.] November 20, 1960, Weymouth; [p.] Robert Everest, Maureen Riggs; [m.] Ian Phipps, June 27, 1987; [ch.] Jade Cora Parsonage, Dawn Katie Parsonage; [ed.] Weymouth Grammar School; [memb.] Legion of Dreams, things that should not be.; [pers.] Dedicated to my husband whose favorite poem this is.; [a.] Stadhampton, Oxon, OX44 7UB

PIMBLETT, DOROTHY
[pen.] Dorothy Pimblett; [b.] August 26, 1922, Eckington; [p.] Mr. and Mrs. E. Hobbs; [m.] William L. Pimblett, October 4, 1974; [ch.] Christopher W. Robinson; [ed.] Camms C/E School (Left age 15) Chesterfield Technical College taking 10 subjects including Secretarial Training; [occ.] Retired now disabled with transverse myerlitis; [memb.] Conservative Party; [hon.] Russel cup for being the best branch in Bolton. Was chairman for 25 years until being disabled (Hulton Womens Conservative Ass.); [oth. writ.] Only poetry, which have many poems of spiritual, love, despair, friendship, loss of loved ones etc.; [pers.] Had spiritual healing from Helen Hill. She brought to me a wonderful poem from Leonardo de Vinei. Since then have written poems. Have put pen to paper even when too tired. Would like Helen's name mentioned. She was a wonderful person; [a.] Bolton, Lancashire, BL5 1BN

PINNOCK, MR. IAN ROY
[pen.] Bunny; [b.] January 8, 1966, Bradford; [p.] Daphnne and Michael Pinnock; [m.] Miss Jennifer Ruddock; [ch.] Dickisha, Sabrina and Leon; [ed.] Bellevue-Boys School; [occ.] Car valeter; [pers.] My inspiration comes from listening and playing reggae music. Inspirations. The late and great Bob Marley the late Garnett Silk who sang about real life.; [a.] Bradford, W. Yorkshire, BD3 9DY

PLANT, JOAN
[b.] January 6, 1923, Grimsby; [p.] Mr and Mrs Albert Busby; [m.] Sidney Plant (Deceased), August 4, 1958; [ed.] Elementary; [occ.] Retired; [memb.] Belong to a local writers group. That's all; [oth. writ.] I write occasionally for "challenge" a christian newspaper printed in worthing. I have work published in rhyme arrival poetry now and also some Women's Mass. one or two anthologist and two in Pyramid Press.; [pers.] I had two strokes in 1979. I weak a caliyer and do my shopping in an electric wheelchair. I hadn't realized there was so much kindness, until I became disabled I live alone and writing is a blessing and my passion.; [a.] Grimsby, NE Lincs, DN32 7HG

PLATT, MARGARET
[b.] London; [p.] Reg. E. Hale and Doris M. Hale; [m.] Ernie G. Platt, November 22, 1975; [ch.] Carol and Ian; [memb.] Cheshunt Chimes Handbell Ringing Team, Handbell Ringers of Great Britain; [oth. writ.] Several poems one in each book published. One written for 'D-Day', published in local newspaper, Cheshunt and Waltham Mercury; [a.] Cheshunt, Herts, EN8 8TQ

PLUCINSKI, MRS. MARY
[pen.] Mary Bennett-Plucinski; [b.] September 16, 1937, Leicester; [p.] Isaiah Bennett, Celia Bennett (Nee Bradwell); [m.] Kazimierz Adam Plucinski, November 25, 1961; [ch.] Alan 33, Anya 28, Richard 18; [ed.] Holy Cross Catholic School, Alderman Newton's Girls' Grammar; [occ.] Housewife; [hon.] 4 GCE O'Levels English Language, English Literature, Latin, Mathematics; [oth. writ.] "My Dad" - published, "War" - published, - Many other poems not submitted. Trying to write a Mills and Boon book. I write Limericks; [pers.] Always do your best with what you have and be happy.; [a.] Leicester, Leics, LE2 9DD

PLUCK, DEREK J.
[pen.] Derek J. Pluck; [b.] March 5, 1951, Bristol; [p.] John George Pluck and Margaret Dorothy Pluck; [m.] E. Janet Pluck Nee Wiggins, April 5, 1975; [ch.] Rachel Heather; [ed.] Merrywood Grammar School, Bristol, Westfield College, University of London, Garnett College, University of London; [occ.] H.O.D - Mathematics and Science, Preston College; [memb.] Institute of Biology Wild Fowl and Wetlands Trust WWF (World Wide Fund for nature) Hebridean Whale and Dolphin Trust; [hon.] 1st Class Degree - Biological Science Doctor and Philosophy Degree Graduate Certificate of Education with Distinction featured in ABI's Men of Achievement' Volume 6; [oth. writ.] Collection of Poetry "Escape from the Chrysalis" (Hub publications, 1979), many poems in poetry magazines, articles a tropical fist and Philatelic subjects.; [pers.] Poetry mainly about natural history and landscapes. Landscapes seen as a loving thing and described frequently with religious and sexual imagery.; [a.] Preston, Lancs, PR2 3FU

PORT, CECIL ANDREW
[pen.] Cecil Andrew; [b.] September 7, 1923, Gravesend; [p.] William and Olive Port; [m.] Elizabeth Ann, December 26, 1945; [ch.] Raymond, Paul, Peter; [occ.] Retired; [memb.] Meopham Art Group; [pers.] Am a founder member of Meopham Art Group, and have several paintings exhibited locally and at Westminster; [a.] Gravesend, Kent, DA12 5SH

POSNER, MS. BARBARA
[b.] November 13, 1940, Hemel Hemstead, Herts; [p.] Russians Imigrants; [m.] Divorced, January 25, 1962; [ch.] Son (33); [ed.] Pitman's Secretarial College, King's Mead Bording School, Herts. Royden; [occ.] Caring for stray animals, Opening Cattery in very near future; [memb.] Member of Jonthan Clifford National Poetry foundation; [hon.] One poem on display at Keats Memorial Library, Keats Museum in Hamstead. Title: Keats Last Good Bye; [oth. writ.] 3 other poems published in Women's magazines plus romantic Story Of the Month.; [pers.] One day we shall know only great happiness, Never grow old, Only more beautiful as time goes on, Know only love, Eternal life with snowflakes falling, For tomorrow's dream, God will smile.; [a.] London, W9 3AS

POULSEN, JANET
[b.] July 3, 1945, Oxford; [p.] Mrs. Phyl, Mr. E. Seamons (Deceased); [m.] Divorced, August 5, 1972; [ed.] Tewin Water School for the Partially Deaf, Welwyn Herts; [occ.] On Incapacity Benefit due to prefound deafress and Meruere's disease and Tinnitus; [memb.] Various Associations for Hearing Disability Timmitus Association; [oth. writ.] When I was young. Published in Rhyme. Reason Editor Kerric Peteman Page 72. Rushson Village Church Page 16 Anchor Poets from the South.; [pers.] I believe in peace and all in all is good in people. I worked for as long as I was able, and now leave time to think of all the things I could have learnt at school but didn't bother to do so.; [a.] Blandford Forum, Dorset, DT11 7RJ

POULTER, CAROL
[b.] November 12, 1955, Erith, Kent; [p.] Margaret Mary and Leslie Bristo; [m.] Christopher Michael Poulter, October 13, 1973; [ch.] Samuel and Sullivan; [ed.] Plumstead Manor for Girl's, Southwark College; [occ.] Nursery Teacher Gad's Hill School; [hon.] N.N.E.B.; [pers.] Dedicated to Leslie Bristo my father; [a.] Rochester, Kent, ME2 1EJ

POWELL, PEARL
[b.] Swindon; [oth. writ.] Book - poetry now South 1984 poem title - Evening Into Night (30 lines) Book - Poetry now 1995 poem title - Waterfall to Sea (30 lines) book - South West 1996 poem title - Schoolboy (30 lines) book - Poetry Seeds poem title - Magic of Winter (30 lines) book - Poets in Protest poem title - Joyrider (30 lines) book - Addictive Poetry poem title - Drunken Man (30 lines); [pers.] My favorite pastime is writing for pleasure. I am fascinated by words, and I get inspiration from scenes, paintings, and photographs. My personal ambition is to publish a book of poetry on various themes.; [a.] Swindon, Wilts, SN5 8NT

PRATT, FREDRICK
[b.] March 30, 1941, Reading; [p.] Mr. and Mrs. Pratt; [m.] Mrs. Kathleen Pratt, April 18, 1970; [ch.] Nill; [occ.] Warehouse Assistant in Grocery Firm; [oth. writ.] A wise old owl lived in an oak, the more he heard, the less he spoke, use he spore, the more he heard, why call we, be live that old bird.; [pers.] I like all poems. As they quite often cheers you up if you are a bit down.; [a.] Andover, Frankshire, SP10 5OR

PRESTON, JACK
[pen.] Preston Walds; [b.] May 14, 1940, Burnley-Lanc's; [p.] John Irwin and Doris; [m.] Margaret Ann, November 14, 1959; [ch.] Tina Louise, and Sharon; [ed.] Secondary Modern, and (The Science of Life); [occ.] Aerospace Fabrications Fusion Welder; [memb.] M.S.F., Members Representative May Day Festival Organizer; [hon.] First Poem to be published; [oth. writ.] Poems, both political and General Speech Writer; [pers.] A poem can compliment life, I strive for the perfection of Shelley, but only find myself.; [a.] Burnley, Lancashire, BB12 6JH

PRICE, ANNIE L.
[pen.] Annie L. Price; [b.] April 3, 1914, Wales Rhonoda; [p.] William Stankey, Elizabeth; [m.] John Price (Deceased), June 10, 1936; [ch.] 3 grandchildren, greats 21; [ed.] State school left at 14, no further education reading and life educated me.; [occ.] Retired; [memb.] Brew House Workshop they Prose Plays. Musical Evenings, Opera S. Showing Othell D. this week 17 April; [oth. writ.] Mostly for people who ask me. Like shop mobility wheel chair charity. Home alert. For D.H.P's published in local. Other poems, papers, also in two books.; [pers.] Keep calm. I myself have a very unemotional nature. My poetry is mostly inspirational flashes. That come into my head from somewhere. I write them at once or I will forget them.; [a.] Burton on Trent, Staffs, DE15 9NE

PRICE, BETTY
[b.] February 24, 1943, Neath; [p.] John Williams, Violet Williams; [ch.] Ryan Alexander; [pers.] To be healthy and happy.; [a.] Neath, Glam., SA11 5PH

PRICE, JOHN F.
[b.] August 9, 1938, Bristol; [p.] John J. Price, Helen H. Price; [m.] Sandra S. Price, July 24, 1985; [ch.] I daughter, Kerry Anne; [ed.] Ashton Gate Sec/Mod Bristol; [occ.] Lorry driver; [oth. writ.] None published; [pers.] My writing reflects the current feelings that influence me during long lonely hours behind the wheel, of peace and daily frustrations.; [a.] Birmingham, W. Mids, B32 2ND

PRIME, DONNA
[b.] September 3, 1973, St. Asaph, Clwyd; [p.] Stan Prime, Marion Prime; [ed.] Prestatyn Comprehensive School; [occ.] Student and P/T Music Tutor; [memb.] 1, Direct Analysis Society (Graphology), 2, Mensa, 3 Bungee Club; [hon.] Gold medallist award from the Victoria College of Music, London (Electronic Organ), Associate of the Victoria College of Music (Piano A.V.C.M.).; [oth. writ.] A number of poems published by Peterborough based poetry now, Anchor Books and Arrival Press - in both magazines and various anthologies. A couple of short stories too.; [pers.] Mine in the darkness chilling. Fantastical. Fatalistic.; [a.] Prestatyn, Clwyd, LL19 8EN

PRINCE, OPAL VANESSA
[b.] June 17, 1962, London; [p.] Byron Prince, my mother deceased; [ed.] Alperton High Comprehensive School Plus Various London Colleges including Harrow College of Higher Education; [occ.] Personnel Assistant; [oth. writ.] I've won prizes in two writing competitions 'Look Now' magazine as a child and more recently 'The Voice' newspaper; [pers.] My debut poem "Why Die" represents a true life event. I would like to continue to write stories and poems based on my own personal experiences, both happy and sad. I am inspired by such writers as Maya Angelou, Terry McMillan and Bebe Moore; [a.] Neasden, London, Campbell, NW10 0AL

PRINCE, OPAL VANESSA
[b.] June 17, 1962, London; [p.] Father - Byron Prince, Mother - deceased; [ed.] Alpection High Comprehensive School plus various London colleges including Harrow College of Higher Education; [occ.] Personnel Assistant; [oth. writ.] I've won prizes in two writing competitions - 'Look Now' magazine as a child and more recently 'The Voice' newspaper; [pers.] My debut poem "Bitter Sweet Memories Of Mum" represents a true life events I would like to continue to write stories and poems based on my own personal experiences, both happy and sad I am inspired by such writers as Maya Angelou, Terry McMillan and Bebe Moore Campbell; [a.] Neasden, London, NW10 0AL

PROSSER, FRANK
[b.] August 13, 1916, Chatham; [m.] Rosie Jean Prosser, December 11, 1948; [ch.] Two; [occ.] Retired from British Railways, 1981; [hon.] Five Long Service Awards St. John Ambulance Defence Medal Air Ministry, Aircraft Production Award for Bravery, British Railways; [oth. writ.] Casualties, Flying Boat Days, I Saw Them Fly; [pers.] My first competition I've written 104 poems towards my book Lifetime of Memories had 14 published. I hope I'm not too old for this Comp.; [a.] Fairway, Rochester, Kent

QUINN, JEANNE E.
[pen.] Jennie Johns; [b.] June 17, 1932, London; [p.] Albert and Ellen Guinchard; [m.] John Anthony Quinn, March 7, 1953; [ch.] 3 Sons, 1 Daughter; [ed.] Varied went to 42 Schools as my father was a cowman, and was always moving, my education was very varied.; [occ.] Personel Assistant; [memb.] Poetry now; [hon.] Won the Brixton poetry competition several years ago. Letters of thanks received from John Betseman, Ronald Reagan, Margaret Thatcher, The Pope, Ken Livingston on my poems written for them.; [oth. writ.] Several poems published in magazines and books and poems of dedication to special people.; [pers.] I have been writing poetry since I was twelve, I have written over four hundred, my poems usually have a kind of meaning or message, such as my latest about the Dunblane tragedy and Leah Betts, my favorite poet is Byron. I like romantic verse.; [a.] London, 9DP

QUINN, WILLIAM
[b.] October 11, 1971, London; [p.] Irish Immigrants; [ed.] Dropped out of the all boys Catholic Comprehensive I'd attended before G.C.S.E's were sat; [occ.] Unemployed; [oth. writ.] Sixteen poems published in 'The Big Issue' magazine; [pers.] My poetry is largely founded in an unashamedly bleak perspective on existence both general and personal and in insights and perspective on the descent of Western Civilization into soul-less bread and circus' Nihilism, all of which is occasionally underpinned by a powerful attraction to christianity and an occasional expression, founded in cultural and racial pride, of my feelings as an albeit dislocated member of the Irish Diaspora.; [a.] London, 4BU

RACE, LINDA
[b.] July 5, 1949, Hartlepool; [p.] John Ernest A. Isabella; [memb.] Swimming; [pers.] I wrote this poem from my grief. I felt the frustration and isolation of man's disablement I love you mam. I never told you.; [a.] Hartlepool:, TS24 8QZ

RAE, ALAN J.
[b.] March 28, 1951, Irvine, Scotland; [p.] Samuel Rae, Margaret Rae; [m.] Elizabeth Rae, September 4, 1971; [ch.] Sammy, Christine-Ann, Denise; [ed.] Hurlford Junior Secondary; [pers.] Poetry floods my soul and trickles through my pen; [a.] Ayr, Strathclyde, KA8 9SE

RALL, JOHN
[b.] July 1, 1955, Wigan; [p.] John Rall and Mrs. Rall; [m.] Angela Rall, March 31, 1979; [ch.] Claire, Catherine, Christopher; [ed.] Abraham Guest Orrell, Wigan Technical College, Royal Air Force Regiment; [occ.] Shop owner; [memb.] Rugby League (coach), B.A.S.C., F.P.O.C., C.C.; [hon.] G.S.M. numerous sporting certificates and trophies; [oth writ.] Several military poems and cartoons published in Visor Military Magazine; [pers.] Politicians remind me of magnetic poles. Positive comments attract negative comments. But if two positive comments are made this creates an argument.; [a.] Doncaster, S. Yorks, DN3 1LQ

RAMM, SABRINA JAYNE
[b.] April 25, 1983, BMH Rinteln, Germany; [p.] Andrew Ramm, Corinne Ramm; [ed.] Langtoft CPS, Bourne Grammar School; [occ.] Pupil; [memb.] South Lincs Youth Theatre; [oth. writ.] One poem published - the Sea in Young Writers "Write and Shine" book (Lincolnshire and Humberside Edition).; [pers.] Aim high and do your best.; [a.] Peterborough, PE6 9LY

RAY, NICOLA HELEN ANN MAR
[b.] November 20, 1980, Chiswick, London; [p.] Eileen and Peter Ray; [ed.] Full time school; [occ.] School Girl; [memb.] Library; [hon.] Another poem printed. In Wot Not Poems through school. 3rd in cake competition, part of GNVQ in Health and Social Care.; [oth. writ.] My Journey to School; [pers.] I enjoy listening to music and see what's in the charts, I love to ride my bike, I write what I see and feel about life.; [a.] Ipswich, Suffolk, IP3 0HA

RAYNES, BRENDA
[b.] August 17, 1939, Sheffield; [p.] George William and Elizabeth; [m.] Thomas, many years; [ch.] Mary (33), Tim (30), Joanne (21); [ed.] Dinnington Technical College; [occ.] Housewife; [pers.] This poem is dedicated to my dear husband Tom for his understanding, strength and unwavering love during a very traumatic time.; [a.] Saltburn, Cleveland, TS12 2PR

REDHEAD, ALISON JANE
[pen.] A. Redhead; [b.] March 8, 1966, Rugby; [p.] Mr. and Mrs. E. McCauley; [m.] Mark Redhead, August 17, 1985; [ch.] Three; [occ.] Housewife; [oth. writ.] Lots of various poems.; [pers.] I am so pleased my poem was chosen. A friend kept saying to enter my poems.; [a.] Hillmorton, Rugby, CV21 4PG

REEVE, TREVOR
[b.] July 7, 1947, Cambridge; [p.] Claude Reeve, Miriam Reeve; [m.] Christine Reeve, October 16, 1971; [ch.] Karen, Paul, Claire; [ed.] Keysoe Secondary Modern; [occ.] Sales/Purchasing Clerk; [pers.] Always remember to step back and think before you speak out and regret.; [a.] Kempston, Beds, MK42 8NT

REEVES, COLIN
[b.] December 10, 1960, London; [p.] Len (Deceased and Margaret; [occ.] Supermarket Assistant; [memb.] RSPB; [oth. writ.] Several poems published in various anthologies; [pers.] Life is one big inspiration for my poems, the good, the bad, the humorous and the serious.; [a.] Huntingdon, Cambs, PE18 6JP

REID, PHILIP
[pen.] Philip Reid; [b.] May 24, 1973, Aberdeen; [p.] Catherine Reid and Charles Reid; [ed.] Speyside High School, Aberlour, The Robert Gordon University, Aberdeen; [occ.] Marketing Manager, Gordon Hotel, Tomintoul; [memb.] RSPB, Chartered Institute of Marketing (student member); [hon.] BA Hospitality Management; [oth. writ.] Several published poems, personal collection; [pers.] I hope my work will be a source of inspiration to others.; [a.] Glenlivet, Banffshire, AB37 9AN

RENDALL, JOHN HENRY ELLIS
[pen.] The Bard of Umberleigh; [b.] May 10, 1922, Twickenham, Middx; [p.] Henry Edward Rendall, Nora Katherine; [ed.] Hampton Grammar School; [occ.] Retired Civil Servant; [oth. writ.] 101 Nights of John Rendall (Dream stories), "Weecabix in the Nursery"; [pers.] My poems are statements of my views on certain aspects and life; [a.] Umberleigh, N. Devon, EX37 9AR

RENDELL, BERT
[pen.] Bert Rendell; [b.] July 7, 1926, Cardiff; [ed.] Left school 1939; [occ.] Retired (Chef at Sea and Hotels); [memb.] Aberaero Yacht Club R.A.O.B.; [oth. writ.] I have several unpublished poems.; [pers.] I have never had time to write while working as a Chef. But I have read Keats Longfellow ect.; [a.] Aberaeron, Dyfed, SA46 0DL

RENDLE, ALFRED DOUGLAS
[b.] June 21, 1919, Devon Port; [p.] William Rendle, Annie Voss; [ed.] Basic but never stops learning; [occ.] Retired; [oth. writ.] No other been submitted for publication.; [pers.] I greatly admire the early poets. Especially Keats.; [a.] Plymouth, Devon, PL6 5SN

RHYS, MAGDALEN
[pen.] Rather Fancy Magdalen; [b.] January 13, 1921, Brynaman, S. Wales; [p.] John William Rees, Annie Rees; [m.] Keri Rhys, January 13, 1947; [ch.] Gerionedd (Glan), Ingrid; [ed.] Both Started Comprehensive School, Banen School now Ysgol-y-Glyn then, son Served Apprenticeship in Welding. Daughter Ingrid went and passed with Shorthand, Typing, Contometer and Gen. Office Work; [occ.] (Myself) Retired Housewife. Small part in Brynaman Operatic Society, which has now disbanded; [memb.] Spiritualist's National Union. Healer's Guild (Founder Member in Wales) G.C.G. Silver Band (Now Brass Band) Brynaman Operatic Society. Ebenezer Independent Chapel, Brynaman; [hon.] Long Service Award with SNU (Spiritualist's National Union (C.S.N.U.) quite well known in Welsh TV and Radio did a lot of Public Work on Spiritualist's and General Platforms, Speaking, Demonstrating, also Healing. Principal, Soloist (Mezzo Sop.) with Gwaun-Cae-Gurwen Brass Band for many years, self-taught. Due to failing eyesight, have now learn to use word, process-self taught, when 73 years of age.; [oth. writ.] Have written in Autobiography, but as yet have not been lucky, although one publisher tried to get a grant for it but was unlucky. It is written in English title 'Black Diamond'. This poem "treasures." I paid 8 pounds or something to Tudor press to get it into their book the spirit writes in 1992, the book did not impress me at all. I think anything would have been accepted.; [pers.] When people receive cards, letters from me they derive great comfort from them. Many become dog-eared and torn, because the people carry them around with them. I have abundance of love which bubbles over onto others. Acts like a magnet. I write Welsh verses too. Maybe I have a little touch of my several times removed ancestor of Hymnist Pantycelyn.; [a.] Brynaman, Nr. Amanford, Dyfed, SA18 1TG

RICHARDSON, MR. WILLIAM
[pen.] The North Boy, Billy 2; [b.] March 26, 1949, Preston Hospital, North Shields, England; [ed.] St. Edmunds All Age, Roman Catholic School, Shiremoor, Tyne and Wear; [occ.] Recently Privitised Civil Servant (DSS Long Benton Newcastle on Tyne); [oth. writ.] Miscellany of poems and approx 400 songs, pieces of music (as yet unpublished); [pers.] Interested in people and with an introspective nature I am drawn to conclusion that there exists a much greater power behind and within the universe we live in. (God the author of all authorships); [a.] Whitley Bay, Tyne and Wear, NE25 9HG

RICKMAN, DAVID HOWARD
[b.] December 3, 1947, Everton, Hants; [p.] Cecil and Susan Rickman; [m.] Joyce (Divorced), December 14, 1968-1995; [ch.] 3 boys - Lee, Roy, Paul; [ed.] Ashley Secondary School - Hants HMS Ganges. Chichester Technical College (Further Education - Quality Control); [occ.] Quality Assurance Manager Sims Simcare Led; [memb.] Vice Chairman: Lancing Naval Old Comrades Association. Member HMS Ganges Association; [hon.] Bronze Medal Physical Training Blake Division 1993 HMS Ganges; [oth. writ.] Novel "Tudor Commando" - not published - seeking acceptance for publication.; [pers.] Spare Time for others. There are so many lonely people. A friendly smile, a sympathetic ear and a kind word are priceless. Time is life's most precious gift. It is running out for us all, second by second.; [a.] Lancing, West Sussex, BN15 8AN

RIDDELL, MARGARET
[b.] June 16, 1925, Chester; [p.] Hugh and Dorothy Jones; [m.] Rodford Riddell, July 20, 1949; [ch.] (Two) boy and girl; [ed.] Sale Grammar, Salford School of Physiotherapy; [occ.] Retired Physiotherapist; [pers.] I like classical poetry best, thought I also like some modern poetry; [a.] Sale, Cheshire, M33 3LD

RIGNALL, SHEILA ANN
[b.] June 30, 1934, Manchester; [p.] Ellen and Charles Royle; [m.] Divorced; [ch.] Karen and Gregory; [ed.] Secondary Modern; [occ.] Retired hairdresser; [oth. writ.] Poems and short stories. None published as yet,

only started writing poetry in September 1995.; [pers.] A near death experience in 1991 altered my conception of life as a whole, and I had the urge to set down my thoughts and analyse them. Creative writing was the result. I feel I have been given a new lease of life in more ways than one.; [a.] Walkden, Worsley, Lancs, M28 3WP

RILEY, EILEEN
[pen.] Patsy Adele; [b.] August 3, 1953, Wolverhampton; [p.] Winnifred and Noah Norton; [m.] John Riley, August 5, 1989; [ch.] Carl Grove, daughter in law Alison, grandson Joshua; [ed.] Northicote High School Bushbury Wolverhampton; [occ.] Medical Illustration Assistant; [pers.] My love and thanks to my family for their encouragement and belief.; [a.] Willenhall, West Mids, WV13 2HG

RITCH, GRACE MARIE
[b.] August 27, 1934, Orkney; [p.] Thomas Manson and Maggie Manson; [m.] Stanley Ritch, December 6, 1950; [ch.] Sylvia, Josephine, Olive, Gracie and Hazel; [ed.] Stromness Academy, Orkney; [occ.] Retired Farmers; [hon.] 6 credits for local history studies from Aberdeen University Distance Learning Courses.; [pers.] I enjoy writing and now have more time due to being retired.; [a.] Stromness, Orkney, KW16 3LL

RITCHIE, GARY
[pen.] Gary Ritchie; [b.] January 26, 1971, Kirkcaldy; [p.] Maureen and Peter Ritchie; [m.] Heather Brywes, not married; [ed.] West Wemyss Primary and Buckhaven High School; [occ.] General Labourer; [oth. writ.] Have had several poems published in high school magazines.; [pers.] To cheer people up even a little, when reading my poems.; [a.] Thornton, Fife, KY1 4BA

ROBERTS, CHARLES
[pen.] Charles Roberts; [b.] April 17, 1944, Calcutta, India; [occ.] Retired as a Chartered Accountant at the age of fifty one to become a songwriter; [memb.] He is a member of B.A.S.C.A. (British Association of Songwriters and Authors); [oth. writ.] Several of his songs have been released by a famous pop singer. He has also written fifty-three poems which are mainly in ballad format and could be set to music as songs. However, some of his poems are too intellectual or otherwise unsuitable to be released as songs.; [pers.] Charles Roberts is now trying to establish a name for himself, in the world of poetry.

ROBERTS, CLAIRE
[b.] November 8, 1959, Liverpool; [p.] Evaline Owens (Late William Chilcott); [m.] Nicholas Steed, July 6, 1996; [ed.] Liverpool, Ellergreen Comprehensive School; [occ.] Temporary work as receptionist/Administrator; [memb.] INC Star Trex Club (I am very interested in Science Fiction with a positive future for mankind); [oth. writ.] Personal poetry - some unpublished stories, etc.; [pers.] I believe in the creativity in the minds of each individual - an as yet untapped source of powerful positive energy.; [a.] Deeside, Clwyd, CH5 4NL

ROBERTS, LAWRENCE R.
[pen.] Larry Roberts; [b.] April 30, 1928, Plymouth, Devon; [p.] Jack (John) Roberts (Deceased), Margaret Annie (Deceased); [m.] Pelagia (Deceased), April 1950; [ch.] Helen Dianne; [ed.] II plus failure, Volunteered Royal Navy 1994 for life career as my father invalided from service after active service in Far East WW2; [occ.] Retired Civil Servant; [memb.] Royal British Legion and Royal Naval Association; [hon.] War Disability Pension and Campaign Medals including the King's Badge for Loyal Service, (King George V); [oth. writ.] Various articles and poems in anthologies magazines etc. (and Broadcast, Radio Wales).; [pers.] That the pretentiousness of modern materialism is vanity and not truth - is garish and the opposite of reality perse, reality... which tends to beauty in all its aspects, and is the higher spiritual reality.; [a.] Bristol, Somerset, BS8 4NH

ROBERTS, MARIE
[b.] July 2, 1935, Halesowen; [p.] Albert and Esther Shilvock (Deceased); [m.] John Leslie Roberts (Died Uganda '69), July 23, 1960; [ch.] Geoffrey and Michael; [ed.] Halesowen Grammar Southlands College, Wimbledon; [occ.] Retired teacher and smallholder; [memb.] Stourport Marina Cruiser Club Wilden Art School; [oth. writ.] Church Magazine; [pers.] The local church plays an important part in my life, helping to sustain a faith which stands the test of time. Living in the depths of the Wyre Forest, its beauty is the main inspiration of my work.; [a.] Bewdley, Worcs, DY14 9UT

ROBERTS, MARY
[b.] November 15, 1930, Glasgow; [p.] John and Jane Walker; [m.] James Roberts, September 6, 1952; [ch.] Five - Jean, Mary, Maureen, Lynn and James, all married I have eight grandchildren.; [occ.] Housewife; [oth. writ.] Poetry, Single End, Strathclyde Region; [a.] Airdrie, ML6 8TQ

ROBINSON, LESLEY
[b.] September 2, 1978, Manchester; [p.] Vincent and Pearl Robinson; [ed.] Wright Robinson High School and Stockport College of Further Education; [occ.] Training in Finance at Manchester Airport; [memb.] Lees Street Amateur, Musical and Dramatic Society; [pers.] I have always looked at poetry as a personal desire, but it would give me great pleasure if someone enjoyed my work.; [a.] Gorton, Manchester, M18 8GW

ROBINSON, NIGEL
[b.] December 14, 1963, Nottingham; [ed.] Adult Education Teacher Art, Pottery, 'A' Level Standard Qualifications, 'O' Level English Literature; [occ.] Unemployed; [pers.] "Creativity is the desire to win approval and aim to please with utmost satisfaction."; [a.] Nottingham, Notts, NG5 9HW

ROCHE, RISS ANNE
[pen.] Sarah Fairhead; [b.] July 14, 1948, London; [p.] Winifred and Jeremiah Roche; [ed.] Catholic Convent; [occ.] Voluntary Services Co-ordinator; [oth. writ.] Currently writing first novel; [pers.] Never betray a confidence; [a.] London, SW13 9BP

ROLFE, MAUREEN
[pen.] Mo Rolfe; [b.] January 18, 1966, Shropshire; [p.] Jenny Porter and Ray Porter (Deceased); [m.] Andrew Rolfe, July 21, 1990; [ch.] Sophia, Craig, Stuart and Chantel; [ed.] Sir John Talbots Grammar Whitchurch, Shropshire; [occ.] Forecourt Cashier; [pers.] My family mean everything to me. They give me the inspiration to write the things I want to express but can't speak about.; [a.] Chalgrove, Oxford, OX44 7SQ

ROSE, CORAL
[pen.] Coral Rose; [p.] Ron and Daphne Archer; [m.] John, March 18, 1967; [ch.] Celest, Samantha, Elizabeth; [oth. writ.] Currently writing a children's book, and re-arranging some earlier written poetry.; [pers.] Dedication - his faith has never faltered mine has all but disappeared, he urged me to keep writing I withdrew into my fears. But braver pens than I have bared all to go on, so 'the fox' is dedicated to my love, my life, my John.

ROSE, JULIAN
[b.] May 29, 1985, Reading; [p.] Judith, Stephen Rose; [ed.] Primary School, Pentrepoeth; [memb.] Brooke Hospital for Animals.; [a.] Newport, Gwent, NP1 9JF

ROSS, EDDIE
[b.] October 10, 1938, Jamaica; [p.] Henry Ross, Agatha Ross; [m.] Lucille Ross, July 17, 1960; [ch.] Michael, Ronald, Janet, Patrick, Peter, Diane; [ed.] Comprehensive; [oth. writ.] One poem published in National Voices one in the weekly. Gleaner 'UK' LTD; [pers.] I look I listen I learn everything to do with mankind I'm concerned.; [a.] Kilburn, London, NW6 5SX

ROSSINGTON, DAVID
[b.] February 14, 1951, Sleaford; [ed.] Lincoln Grammar, Sheffield University, Open University; [occ.] Unemployed; [memb.] Shepton Mallet Theatre Group; [oth. writ.] Several poems published in anthologies, co-writer of pantomimes for local group.; [pers.] Personal experiences and observations are the basis of my poems.; [a.] Shepton Mallet, Somerset, BA4 5DX

ROWAN, KEVIN
[b.] March 19, 1962, Liverpool; [p.] Brian Rowan, Catherine Rowan; [m.] Teresa Rowan, August 9, 1985; [ch.] Mark; [ed.] St. Kevin's Comprehensive, Kirkby, Teesside Polytechnic; [occ.] Marketing Assistant; [hon.] B.A. Business Studies; [pers.] My writing is an emotional release. I hope it provokes thought and provides pleasure.; [a.] Upton, Merseyside, L49 6PS

ROWE, DENNIS ROBERT
[pen.] Dennis R. Rowe; [b.] February 21, 1929, Northampton; [p.] George Rowe, Gertrude Rowe; [m.] Evelyn Ann Rowe, February 10, 1943; [ch.] Geraldine Ann; [ed.] Northampton Campbell Square Intermediate School Northampton Technical College; [occ.] Retired Manager; [memb.] Cornwall Family History Society Northampton Shire County Cricket Club Oxfordshire and Buckinghamshire Light Infantry Regimental Ass. The Royal Berkshire Regimental Ass. Normandy Veterans Association, The Parachute Regiment Association; [hon.] 2nd World War Record 1939-45 Europe Star. Defence Medal - French Campaign Medal France and Germany Star Palestine 1945-1948 French Medallion D Day French Award 1944-1989 Sporting Awards - Football - Cricket - running and shooting; [oth. writ.] 'Pegasus Journal' - articles and poems - central England poets - poem published - poems published in "Anchor Books" "Poetry now" True Life Story published in local press 'Voices on the wind' the International Society of poets; [pers.] I try to express the hopes and fears experiences in bloody battle. The relief and gratitude of survival to appreciate the miracle of God's land and its beauty to behold.; [a.] Northampton, Northants, NN3 3DH

ROWE, HAZEL J.
[b.] January 12, 1926, Lerryn; [p.] John and Ivy Collins; [m.] W. G. Daniel, August 17, 1946 (Divorced December 3, 1986); [ch.] Three sons and three daughters; [ed.] C.Of.E. Down End School, Bridgend Lostwithiel; [occ.] House Keeper

ROWE, RITA
[b.] December 14, 1958, Stevenage; [p.] Sylvia and Frank Hewitt; [ch.] Three (Daniel, Clare, Emily); [ed.] Left School at sixteen due to problem's at school no qualifications; [occ.] Carer for disabled daughter (Emily); [oth. writ.] Nothing published but alway's writing for my self. But my poem's come from within from pain to mixed feelings of life that we all experience at one time or another.; [pers.] My goal in life is to have a book published, I have never had anything in life to be proud of I would like to have something to be remembered by. I have even tried writing a story I was told it was very good.; [a.] Chesham, Bucks, HP5 3NA

ROWELL, STEVEN
[pen.] Ashley Rowell; [b.] February 18, 1975, York; [p.] Mrs. Cheryl Stather; [m.] Samantha Rowell, December 23, 1995; [ed.] Oaklands Secondary, York 6th Form College, York College of Arts and Technology; [occ.] Unemployed; [hon.] 'A' Levels, English, English Literature, Psychology; [oth. writ.] One poem published in anthology 'between the lines' title 'so happy now' editor Kerry Pateman.; [pers.] My poetry thrives on the high and low points of love and bitterness respectively. It enables me to roam between freedom and entrapment, worshipping the delicate and detesting negative energies. I admire the works of Denise Leverton.; [a.] York, N. Yorks, YO1 1EX

RUSSELL, LAURENCE
[b.] July 19, 1961, Wolverhampton; [p.] Frank and Marjorie; [ed.] St. Judes Infant School and Whitmore Secondary Modern School of Wolverhampton; [occ.] Duty Station Manager at Birmingham International; [memb.] Military and Aviation Book Society; [hon.] General, Service, Medal, with clasp for active service in Northern Ireland G.S.M.; [oth. writ.] Very many poems none of which I have ever entered in competitions because I never felt they would be understood or appreciated without knowing me personality.; [pers.] I have always loved poetry and have written at a particular time in my life where I have been downhearted. My poetry is my escape from the adversity that life can bring.; [a.] Wolverhampton, West Mids, WV9 5SA

RUSSELL, LYNNE
[b.] March 20, 1971, Hillcrest, Alnwick; [p.] Kenneth Graham Russell, Anne Taylor; [ch.] Joseph James Russell; [ed.] Coquet High Amble, University of Northumbria at Newcastle; [occ.] Local Government Officer Alnwick District Council; [hon.] LLB (Hons); [pers.] This poem reflects my fears for the future of our children. I often wonder what kind of world my son will have to grow up in.; [a.] Amble, Northumberland, NE65 0PX

RUSSELL, TERESA
[b.] September 24, 1959, Kettering; [p.] Mr. Robert Russell; [ch.] Sarah and Natarsia; [ed.] Secondary Education; [occ.] Machine Operator; [pers.] The personal effect on my fathers life touched my heart strings and inspired my poetic thoughts to send signal express to you.; [a.] Corby, Northants, NN17 2QU

RYAN, STEPHEN
[b.] July 18, 1971, Liverpool; [ed.] Liverpool City College, St. Christopher's Primary; [occ.] Student; [oth. writ.] Poems such as "My Divine Muse", about a young man's preference for the spiritual ecstasy of the non-physical realm, over that of the mundane and physical; [pers.] I write, by turns, with a sense of loss and desolation, of hope and fulfillment, depending on road, believe in Keats's view of the world as a "Vale of Soul-Making."; [a.] Liverpool, Merseyside, L26 0SU

RYAN, VALERIE
[b.] November 18, 1958, St. Helier's Hospital, Carshalton, Surrey; [p.] Eddie and Margaret Norman; [m.] Louis Ryan, May 22, 1993; [ed.] Cheam High School, Chatsworth Road, Cheam, Surrey; [occ.] Children's Nanny; [memb.] Downs and Weald Rambling Group/Cheam Social Club; [hon.] English Literature Award for Walking, 30 miles; [oth. writ.] Sutton Town Grandmother (poetry) had published in two books. (Life in Poetry) (Home Counties Poets); [pers.] The beauty of countryside and people inspires me to write poetry, I have been influenced by a love of nature.; [a.] Cheam, Surrey, SM3 8DN

SANTER, LYNN
[b.] July 18, 1961, London, England; [p.] Clare and Neville Santer; [ed.] Claremont (North London), Royal Melbourne Institute of Technology (Australia); [occ.] Financial Consultant, I.T. Industry.; [memb.] British Film Institute, Writers Guild of Great Britain, National Film Theatre, Australian Film Institute, Australian Society of Authors, Copyright Agency Limited.; [hon.] Writing Award for Marketing Presentation of the Year, American Chamber or Commerce, 1993. (Australian Chapter); [oth. writ.] Several feature screenplays - one in pre-production at Pinewood Studios. One unpublished novel "Sins of Life" adapted for screen and optioned by Scorpio Productions, Pinewood Studios.; [pers.] My love of writing, and life, lead me to write on a wide range of subjects, in many genres. My greatest joy is breathing life into the spark of idea and seeing others take pleasure from what I produce.; [a.] Harrow on the Hill, Middlesex, HA2 0HZ

SANVITI, DORIS
[pen.] Doris Sanviti; [b.] January 11, 1965, Islington, London; [p.] Luigi and Celestina Sanviti; [m.] Enzo Antoniazzi, April 20, 1996; [ed.] La Sainte Union Convent School, Highgate, London; [occ.] Civil Servant, Marketing; [pers.] As a deep reflector I portray in writing descriptive inner emotions including viewpoints from various perspectives that from time to time each one of us experiences.; [a.] Wood Green, London, N22 6JE

SARGEANT, BRIAN JOHN
[b.] November 24, 1946, Clapham, London; [p.] John and Lily; [m.] Margaret, July 1, 1977; [ch.] Two sons; [ed.] Tennyson Secondary Modern; [occ.] Sales Manager, Ex H.G.V. Driver; [oth. writ.] More poems.; [pers.] I can look at any subject, and be inspired by it, to put it in verse.; [a.] London, SW8 3TP

SARGEANT, MALCOLM
[pen.] Malcolm Sargeant; [b.] December 1, 1953, Brighton; [p.] John and Margaret; [m.] Marian, October 11, 1980; [ch.] Fitzherbert Secondary Modern; [oth. writ.] Many poems written; [pers.] I try to base many poems on life past and present; [a.] Brighton, Sussex, BN2 2ZN

SAVAGE, CLARE FRANCES
[b.] July 26, 1978, Sheffield; [p.] Michael and Christine Savage; [ed.] Westfield Secondary School, Stradbroke College; [occ.] Art and Psychology Student; [memb.] Whales and Dolphin Conservation Society; [hon.] 'Worthy of Commendation' award in National Poetry Competition; [oth. writ.] Poem published in poetry magazine; [pers.] Human emotions and the forces of nature fascinate me. In my writing and my art I try to reflect both sides of these, the dark and the light, the beautiful and the ugly.; [a.] Sheffield, Yorkshire, S19 6HD

SAVAGE, JACQUELINE
[b.] January 30, 1931, Manchester; [p.] Thomas and Lilian Slater; [m.] Douglas Savage (2nd marriage), November 29, 1978; [ch.] James, Stuart, Janine, Julie Weston; [ed.] Fairfield High for Girls Droylsden Nr Manchester; [occ.] Housewife Retired; [oth. writ.] Poem published in the 1994 Midlands anthology. Also voices in the wind 1996. And in various women's magazines.; [pers.] Help others but also live life to the full. As long as you don't harm others in doing so.; [a.] Derby, Derbyshire, DE24 0UB

SAXON, PATRICIA
[b.] August 4, 1947, Poplar (London); [p.] Eric John Dean and Johanna Dean; [m.] Peter Charles Saxon, October 25, 1980; [ch.] Lynn Michell, Paul Thomas, Corinne Joyce; [ed.] Lucton Girls Secondary Modern; [occ.] Night Care Assistant and School Midday Assistant; [pers.] I aim to write a friendly and beguiling simplicity that may be understood and enjoyed bu the young and old alike.; [a.] Buckhurst Hill, Essex, IG96HN

SCARBOROUGH, KATHLEEN
[pen.] Kathleen Scarborough; [b.] July 12, 1947, Grimsby; [p.] John Williams and Lillian May Reynolds; [m.] Divorced; [ch.] One daughter Deborah; [ed.] Havolock Comprehensive Grimsby; [occ.] Retired Nanny to English diplomat son; [memb.] A&C, R.d.A., A.C.; [oth. writ.] Several poems published started to write X'mas 1995.; [pers.] Give all mankind freedom. Give them love and joy. Give them good health. Give them time to live, to know all these things. Give them Peace on Earth.; [a.] Grimsby, S. Humberside, ON34 5TP

SCHOFIELD, MARGARET
[b.] March 15, 1936, Manchester; [p.] Edith and Tommy Brogan; [m.] Ken, October 12, 1957; [ch.] Steven, Ali and Liz, 5 grandchildren; [ed.] Brisoe Lane, Brookdale park S.M.; [occ.] "Blackpool Landlady"; [pers.] As I have not a good imagination I can only write about actual events.; [a.] Blackpool, Lancs, Uk, FY2 9SB

SCOFFHAM, OLIVE
[pen.] Olive Scoffham; [b.] February 23, 1929, Chasetown, W. Midlands; [p.] Mildred and Harry Postings; [m.] Ralph Scoffham, December 3, 1947; [ch.] Three boys, two girls; [ed.] Infants, Junior, and Senior Elementary Schools, left at 14 yrs, went into Domestic Service, then Chilminder; [occ.] Housewife, retired; [oth. writ.] This is my first poem; [pers.] I met my husband at 16 yrs, waited while he was away in the army, when he came home in 1947 we married, spent 22 yrs in married quarters, then he became a driving instructor till retiring.; [a.] Gorleston, Gt. Yarmouth, Norfolk, NR31 8AF

SCREEN, DAVID ROBERT
[b.] January 28, 1934, Nottingham; [p.] Arthur Screen, Hilda Screen; [ed.] Trent Bridge Secondary Nottingham; [occ.] Warehouse Returns Checker; [memb.] Boots Social and Sports Club Theatregoers Club; [hon.] Academia not a strong point.; [oth. writ.] To be published this summer. Entitled "Averting the Elements" this is only my second attempt. So its now two out of two.; [pers.] An avid theatregoer, I aim always to make life as simple as a nursery rhyme.; [a.] Nottingham, NG11 8AS

SCURR, DAVID
[b.] August 30, 1964, Leeds; [p.] John and Pauline Scurr; [m.] Michaela Scurr; [ch.] Charlotte and Joseph; [ed.] Leeds Metropolitan University; [occ.] Salesman; [oth. writ.] Short stories and poems; [pers.] I

write it as I feel it, with a slight touch of surrealism. My poetry is 99% emotion, 1% art.; [a.] Winsford, Cheshire, CW7 2DN

SELWAY, RONALD
[b.] April 19, 1931, Blaina; [p.] Helen Hole, David Selway; [m.] Thelma Eileen Rice, March 29, 1958; [ch.] Pauline, Teresa, Julie; [ed.] Glan y Avon Blaina; [occ.] Retired Factory Supervisor; [memb.] Abertillery and District Museum Society; [oth. writ.] "Mam, Mam, Who's My Father", Under Condensed Milk; [pers.] My writings is to try and reflect the warmth and deep feelings of the Welch Pit Valleys of South Wales and its Quiscotry ways of its people.; [a.] Llanhilleth, Gwent, NP3 2HS

SHADBOLT, MARTIN D.
[pen.] Terry Gowers; [b.] October 8, 1952, Sutton, Surrey; [m.] Terri McLeod, October 6, 1986 (Common Law); [ch.] Martin Paul Shadbolt 9 yrs, Amy Marie 6 yrs; [ed.] Winchcombe Road Secondary School for Boys Carshalton Surrey; [occ.] General Hand. SEM (Small Electric Motors) Lower Syenham SE26; [oth. writ.] Made in Who's Image? Why children, Our Christian Church, Your Country Needs You, "Amy Marie", "Martin Paul", "Elena Jayne"; [pers.] Through poetry I can express my feelings for the world and the people in it; [a.] Downham Bromley, Kent, BR1 5PT

SHAH, NISHA
[b.] December 2, 1980, London; [p.] Girish Shah, Jaya Shah; [ed.] At present: Connaught School for Girls (Secondary), Leytonstone, London; [occ.] Student; [oth. writ.] Poems and articles published in school magazine.; [pers.] Writing both poems and short stories is something which I thoroughly enjoy doing as it allows my imagination and the imagination of the reader to run free; [a.] Leytonstone, 4PX

SHARP, DOREEN
[b.] September 6, 1936, Northampton; [m.] Victor Sharp, October 1, 1960; [occ.] Housewife; [oth. writ.] Never had any writing published.; [pers.] I love all animals, Victor and I help injured wild animals. We find on the road.

SHARPE, DANNATT ROBERT
[b.] April 6, 1943, Portsmouth; [p.] Le Robert Sharpe RN, Winifred Dorothy nee Norton; [m.] Jennifer Ursula, December 28, 1978; [ch.] (Son) Christopher James Alexander, (Daughter) Nadine Ursula May; [ed.] St. John's College Southsea Hants, University of Leicester BSC, University of Southampton Dip Ed., Lady Spencer Churchill College Oxford (Cert. Ed. for Deaf); [occ.] Head of Unit for Hearing Impaired Children Hugh Christie Technology College Tonbridge; [memb.] Chartered Biologist Member Institute of Biology. Fellow of Zoological Society of London, Royal Observer Corp. Association No 1 group. Radio Society of Great Britain, Royal Naval Amateur Radio Society, Royal Air Force Amateur Radio Society; [hon.] Long Service Medal Royal Observer Corps 1988. Lord Lieutenants Meritorious Service Certificate by Lord Lieutenant East Sussex 1989; [oth. writ.] University of Southampton Biological Bulletin 1964-65. School Science Review. Several poems published local magazines, poetry now, up and running.; [pers.] Nature with its humour and pathos is my guide. I have been influenced by writers like Gerald Durrell and Carly Poets.; [a.] Uckfield, East Sussex, TN22 2BA

SHAW, IAN
[b.] March 6, 1967, Heywood; [p.] Tony and Brenda Shaw; [ed.] Sutherland Road High School; [occ.] Set Builder; [oth. writ.] Some poems published in various anthologies.; [pers.] I strive to explore the emotional ties that we all share. If just one reader can associate and draw something from it. Everything I've written has been worthwhile.; [a.] Bury, Lancs, BL9 7BT

SHAW, JUNE M.
[b.] June 28, 1947, Halifax; [p.] Herbert Whitworth-Irene Whitworth; [m.] John, November 26, 1966; [ch.] David Andrew and Michael John; [oth. writ.] "Easter" (Anthology of the Cross), currently working on a book of poems for children; [pers.] I would like children to grow up appreciating the arts. By writing simple poetry I hope to introduce them to an enjoyable past time.

SHAWKET, S. L.
[pen.] Deborah Lea; [b.] March 24, 1953, Davyhulme; [p.] Sylvia and Richard Howarth; [m.] Talib A. Shawket, January 8; [ch.] Deborah, Daniel, Deyn, (Grandchildren) David, Ryan, Naomi; [ed.] Hope Hall Comprehensive School Salford 6; [occ.] Housewife; [memb.] IFAW, W.W.F., The Kennel Club; [oth. writ.] Other work published includes poems: "The Memory" and "Time And Distance"; [pers.] Experiences throughout my life have influenced me to divulge into a deeper sense of heart felt emotions. Hobbies: My three standard poodles, canaries, reading and poetry.; [a.] Manchester, Lancashire, M28 1SN

SHEARING, T. J.
[b.] May 13, 1944, Barton on Sea, Hampshire; [p.] Mr. Reginald And Mrs. Betty Shearing; [m.] Vivienne Barnes; [ed.] To GCE 'O' Level Standard at Regents Park Boys' School, Southampton 4 'O' Levels in English, Maths, Technical Drawing, Physics; [occ.] Medically retired due to a back injury 2 years ago.; [oth. writ.] I write poems for my own personal enjoyment, really, but I do have one hanging in the Galley of A Frima's Hoseboat.; [pers.] This poem, Xmas on a Scottish Isle, is, in fact, a true story of my trip up to see my mother last Christmas. I, actually, write it on the plane from Gatnick to Glasgow airport and finished it on the ferry from Wemyss Bay to the Isle of Bute.; [a.] Southampton, Hampshire, SO18 1LQ

SHEEHAN, MARC
[b.] April 13, 1979, Hanover; [ed.] Hampton Grammar School; [occ.] A-Level Student; [memb.] National Starfleet Alliance, Curry Club; [oth. writ.] Other poems in the same style as "The River of Life"; [pers.] I aim to write poetry which appeals to as wide a range of readers as is possible by considering issues which are both stimulating and central to life.; [a.] Twickenham, Middlesex, TW2 7JG

SHEFFIELD, BARRY
[b.] April 2, 1939, Leicester; [m.] Jennifer Sheffield, May 13, 1995; [ch.] Three; [ed.] Intermediate School, Avid Reader, Love of Words Retentive Memory; [occ.] Retired Taxi Driver (32 years); [memb.] Relent Application to Join Mensa (Confident); [oth. writ.] None sent for publication except many letters to the "Leicester Mercury" 70's and 80's all published. Inprompts limericks humours writing for self and friends pleasure; [pers.] Distaste for inherited titles, wealth or power, handed down from mediaeval murderous robber barons. Time has brought "Respectability", (rather like the mafias present day invasions into legitimate business); [a.] Batley, W. Yorks, WF17 8AH

SHEPHERD, GAIL ELAINE
[b.] June 21, 1947, London; [p.] Ron Mackey and Pam Mackey; [m.] Michael Dudley Shepherd, April 25, 1992; [ch.] Pamela Lise Burn; [ed.] Coloma Convent Grammar, Croydon Nene College, Northampton; [occ.] Full-time Career; [memb.] Salvation Army; [oth. writ.] Several poems published in various anthologies.; [pers.] Any success that I have achieved through my writing has been due to a talent give to me by my creator - the Lord Jesus, the triune God. I give him the glory.; [a.] Leighton, Buzzard, Bedfordshire, LU7 7ST

SHIELDS, HAIDEE
[pen.] Dee Shields; [b.] August 12, 1917, Wiltshire; [p.] Albert Stacey, Mabel Stacey; [m.] Jack Shields (Deceased), September 11, 1976; [ch.] Sidney Bruce, Haidee Penelope; [ed.] Aldbourne C of E School Educated until the age of fourteen at this Village School; [occ.] Retired; [memb.] Berkshire Blind Society; [oth. writ.] Several poems published in local magazines. Interview and reading of a poem on tape for berkshire blind society.; [pers.] I began writing poetry as an expression of my inner thoughts when losing my sight restricted many activities.; [a.] Thatcham, Berks, RG13 4PQ

SIMMS, JONATHAN
[b.] July 8, 1972, Wordsley; [p.] Janice and Derek Simms; [ed.] Buckpool School, Dudley College, Stourbridge College; [occ.] Part-time Student, Stourbridge College; [oth. writ.] Seven poems published so far, and one self-published book of poems - with a friend, Sophie Tomlinson; [pers.] To seek the truth.; [a.] Stourbridge, West Midlands, DY8 5HT

SIMMS, MRS. MAUREEN
[pen.] Faith Hope; [b.] February 19, 1944, Oxfordshire; [p.] Bernard and Phyllis Weatherley; [m.] Silvester Simms, August 30, 1979; [ed.] St. Mary's Secondary Modern, Old Welwyn, Herts; [occ.] Housewife; [oth. writ.] A series of children stories. Each one about the adventures of Molly and Milly Mouse. (Unpublished). Also a few unpublished poems.; [a.] Arlesey, Beds, SG15 6RL

SIMPSON, LARRAINE
[b.] February 4, 1955, Croydon; [m.] October 13, 1973; [ch.] Daniel, David, Matthew and Jonathan; [ed.] Studying Psychology attending Selhurst College Croydon (195-1996); [occ.] Mother/Carer; [oth. writ.] Unpublished writings and poetry; [pers.] I have encouraged myself to write and doing so, I have expressed my feelings and my torment. To me this is my therapy for my emotional distress, and writing has given me inner strength as I look to the world of dreams that could be also sweet. I try not to be blinded by the dullness which surrounds me.; [a.] Croydon, Surrey, CR0 0TB

SIMPSON, MARY
[pen.] Mary Porter; [b.] July 17, 1973, Atherstone; [m.] Edward James Porter, forth coming November 9, 1996; [ch.] Bryan, Amy, Marijane plus stepdaughter called Laura; [ed.] Hartshill High Secondary School; [occ.] Housewife and mother; [pers.] It was my partner, Edward, who made me put pen to paper so most of my poems concentrate on the feeling of love which have bounded us both together.; [a.] Nuneaton, Warwickshire, CV10 9LX

SIMPSON, PAULINE
[b.] July 11, 1946, Northumberland; [p.] Noel and Dorothy Simpson; [m.] Divorced (Thank God); [ch.] Claire; [ed.] Secondary Education; [occ.] Secretary, University of Newcastle; [pers.] Look for the rainbow not the "Pot of Gold".; [a.] Newcastle, Tyne and Wear, NE12 9EA

SIMPSON, PAUL
[pen.] Lord Paul; [b.] August 31, 1953, Derby; [m.] Janine Sharon Church Hill, January 15, 1977; [ch.] Chase Ivor Robert, Sierra Lueze; [ed.] Rose Hill Secondary Mod, Allenton Sec Mod; [occ.] Bed Bound Paraplegic; [memb.] Founder Member, Disabled Authors Society; [hon.] Self taught a licensed amateur; [oth. writ.] Poems in local paper poems written for Celebrities digger (children's stories) articles for the disabled "So What Now" operations guide for novice radio amateurs; [pers.] Imagination defies disability; [a.] Derby, Derbyshire, DE23 7RB

SINCLAIR, PAMELA
[b.] January 19, 1970, Edinburgh; [p.] Mabel and Robert Sinclair; [m.] Partner - Alan Dawson; [ch.] Catherine Rose; [occ.] Housewife; [pers.] My family changed my "Sunless Days" thank you, you are all worth your weight in gold.; [a.] Galashiels, Selkirkshire, TD1 1QZ

SLARK, PIPPA DAWN
[b.] July 25, 1973, Harrow; [p.] Philip Slark, Julia; [ed.] Rooks Heath High School, Greenhill College; [oth. writ.] Large collection of poems as yet unpublished. Various poems shown displayed at conferences.; [pers.] I find writing a great way to get my emotions out and if I can reach anyone or help them through my writing it's a bonus.; [a.] Edgware, Middlesex, HA8 7TE

SMALL, MRS. ANNE
[b.] October 2, 1955, Cheshunt, Hertfordshire; [ch.] Caroline, Robert and Clementine; [ed.] North London Comprehensive School. I left school at 15 years of age and never had the opportunity to continue with my education.; [occ.] Housewife and Mother; [oth. writ.] This is my first poem I have sent to anyone. They are normally for myself and very special friends.; [pers.] Poetry has always interested me and is a comfort in times of stress and emotional turmoil. I express myself best in this form.; [a.] Wickford, Essex, SS12 0ET

SMALL, SUSAN
[b.] June 21, 1959, Bristol; [p.] Reginald Pottinger Lucas and Dorothy Lucas; [m.] Colin Small, July 21, 1984; [ch.] Marc Small, Joanne Worley (step children); [ed.] Broadoak Comprehensive School, Weston-super-Mare; [occ.] Housewife; [memb.] English Heritage, R.S.P.B.; [pers.] I am concerned for the welfare and well-being of wildlife and the countryside. If my writing can help in a small way to stop man's inhumanity to animals, it gives me the inspiration to continue.; [a.] Totnes, Devon, TQ9 5PB

SMITH, ALAN FREDERICK
[pen.] Alan Frederick-Smith; [b.] June 26, 1935, Lytham, Lancashire, England; [m.] Twice Married; [ch.] Rachel, Cathy, Caroline, Bella; [ed.] King Edward VII Grammar, Lytham Selwyn College, Cambridge University Dept. of Education, Oxford University, Centre for Contemporary Cultural Studies, Birmingham University; [occ.] Freelance Lecturer/Writer; [memb.] The Poetry Society, London 1990, East Finchley Labour Party, entry in 'International Who's Who in Poetry' since 1972 (pub. Melrose Press, London); [hon.] MA Hons English Literature (Cantab), Open Exhibition in history to Selwyn College, Cambridge, Fellow of the Salzburg Seminars in American Literature, Diploma of Merit Universita' Della Arti. Salsomaggiore Terme Pr - Italy (for poetry); [oth. writ.] Several poems published in local magazines, The Gulf Times Review (English Edition), Collection of poems in 'London and Meander' (published E.S. Smith), Broadcast of poetry on Riyadh Radio, Literature, Prefaces on Conrad Hawthorne, Scott-Fitzgerald and Blake (Academia Pubs.); [pers.] My ambition is to communicate directly through poetry to as wide an understanding readership as possible, whilst avoiding platitude or cliche and striving to keep language alive, expressive and thought provoking.; [a.] London, N2 9AE

SMITH, CAIN
[b.] June 17, 1986, Oldham; [p.] Kevin and Angela Smith; [ed.] Attending St. Josephs R.C. Primary School; [memb.] Press Park Newsround BBC1; [pers.] Reaching almost any sort of literature, writing and watching man UTD. I would like to be a barrister and a journalist.; [a.] Tameside, Lancs, OL5 0BG

SMITH, DAVID JAMES
[pen.] Dave J. Smith; [b.] February, 22, 1947, Southend; [p.] Mr. G. J. Smith, Mrs. E. C. Smith; [ed.] Rayleigh Sweyne Grammer Tech; [occ.] Taxi Driver; [memb.] Anglers Co-operative Ass.; [hon.] Matchfishing trophies Kart Racing trophies; [oth. writ.] Four different poems published in four different books by 'Poetry Now' all poems submitted have been published.; [pers.] My poems frighten me sometimes. I don't know where they come from. I only write when in a 'Certain frame of mind.'; [a.] Canvey Island, Essex, SS8 9DE

SMITH, EILEEN RAEBURN
[pen.] E. R.; [b.] July 10, 1954, Edinburgh; [p.] Peter and Irene; [ch.] Three Daughters, Five Grandchildren; [occ.] M. E. Sufferer for nearly 15 years now; [hon.] Best Mum Awards and I have lots of them. The only awards though; [oth. writ.] Weep No More, Hush My Darling, Your Born To Live and Your Born To Die.; [pers.] I write what I am feeling at that time my problem is I never seem to have time, to sit and write, which I love doing.; [a.] Livingston, W. Lothian, EH54 5LA

SMITH, ELIZABETH SPENCER
[b.] October 21, 1943, Spalding; [p.] John Spencer Beaumont, Elizabeth Sarah Beaumont; [m.] Trevor Smith, February 9, 1963; [ch.] Belinda, Julian, Soma; [pers.] This poem is dedicated to you my beautiful mummy. Each word tells you how much I love you and miss you dearly.; [a.] Spalding, Lincs, PE11 4DB

SMITH, GLENDA
[b.] February 5, 1956, Jamaica; [p.] Mr. and Mrs. Grace; [m.] Mr. Earl Smith, May 31, 1984; [ch.] Lee, Deon, Sapphire; [ed.] Silverthorne Secondary South Thames College; [occ.] Secretary Studying Ilex Part 2; [hon.] Diploma - Tort Litigation; [oth. writ.] Several poems written over the years. One song, have never thought of having them published; [pers.] I have always been able to put myself in other people's situation. I just put into words what I feel in my heart a said moment time; [a.] London, SW16 5AR

SMITH, MR. JAMES MCCOLL
[pen.] John Brown; [b.] July 15, 1937, London; [p.] Deceased; [m.] Mrs. Margaret Rose Smith, March 31, 1962; [ed.] St. Michales and Comprehensive, Haverstock Hill London N.W.5; [occ.] Medically Retired but still painting, drawing, writing; [memb.] Labour Party (New Labour) member; [hon.] Courages Brewery, man of the year, year centenary award, for my work in the East London, Barough of Hackney, E.9. for twenty five years; [oth. writ.] (In The Box.) Read out at the Hackney poetry Society Competition, some year's ago.; [pers.] There is alway's some one worse off than me. I have been to Tenisen Down's on the Isle of white, Tenison, being my favorite poet, with Worslsworth; [a.] St. Osyth, Clacton-on-Sea, Essex, CO16 8RS

SMITH, JEAN A.
[pen.] 'Pandora'; [b.] May 12, 1933, The Lee, Bucks; [p.] Arthur and Betty Sharp; [m.] Reg Smith, October 31, 1953; [ch.] 7, 4 girls and 3 boys; [ed.] Coope School, Wendover Bucks, Aylesbury Technical College Pre Nursing, Student Nurse Royal Free London; [occ.] Retired disabled arthritic; [memb.] British Legion Cookham Branch; [oth. writ.] Passing Years Passing Thoughts, How Much I Love You, My Own True Love, The Beyond. Many other poems none published small vanity book, private Lim edition 1990; [pers.] I am inspired by the world around me, by the love of my God and fellow man, by what my passage through life has shown me and what I have learned from it.; [a.] Cookham, Maidenhead, Berks, SL6 9DU

SMITH, JOHN WILLIAM
[b.] September 17, 1921, Longnor, Staff; [p.] Moses Smith, May Smith; [m.] (Wife) Blanche Smith, November 9, 1946; [ch.] (One - Daughter) Gloria, Jean, Smith; [ed.] Longnor, Staffs, Village School; [occ.] Retired, Formerly Works Cashier with Imperial Chemical Industries; [memb.] 1. Technics Plus - The Technics Keyboards Club. 2. Formerly a member of the British Astronomical Society; [hon.] Mentioned in Despatches in recognition of gallant and distinguished Services in Italy. (War Office 24/8/24) Recommended for a Commission in Regular Army - did not accept; [oth. writ.] Poetry written solely for recitation by my Granddaughter at Speech and Drama competition, with success.; [pers.] Six years Army service. 4 years overseas. Eight Army - Western Desert, Invasion of Sicily and Italy. Through Italian campaign from Reggio to Trieste. Now full time Carer for my wife who is severely handicapped with osteoarthritis.; [a.] Winsford, Cheshire, CW7 3NL

SMITH, MARIANNE
[pen.] Louise Wood; [b.] November 16, 1962, Chelmsford; [p.] Leslie Wood (Dec) Shirley Wood; [m.] Malcolm Smith, May 28, 1983; [ed.] Hylands School, Chelmsford; [occ.] Administrator Part Time; [oth. writ.] None First Attempt; [pers.] I am influenced by events a people around me. Normal every day life has a way of providing my material.; [a.] Chelmsford, Essex, CM1 3PD

SMYTH, EILEEN
[hon.] Studied law at Liverpool John Moores University: BA (Hons); [oth. writ.] I have written a number of poems, but this is my first submission for publication.; [a.] Chester, Cheshire, CH2 2BJ

SNEDDON, JENNIFER LOUISE
[b.] September 9, 1985, Glasgow; [p.] Eunice Sneddon, John Sneddon; [ed.] St. Leonard's Primary School East Kilbride; [occ.] School Girl; [memb.] East Kilbride Youth Choir 6th A East Kilbride Guide Company Sean Gavin Irish Dancing School.; [oth. writ.] Articles published in annual school magazine; [pers.] I thank God for the talents I have been blessed with. May He continue to inspire me throughout my life.; [a.] East Kilbride, Sov, G74 3SQ

SNOW, A. G.
[b.] April 27, 1919, London, West Ham; [p.] Arthur and Louie Snow; [m.] Janet Snow, December 31, 1943; [ch.] Leonard, Roberta and 5 Grandchildren; [ed.] Ramelagh Elementary School; [occ.] Retired for 12 years; [memb.] Ilford Labour Party; [hon.] 4 certificates of highly recommended and one second prize for short stories.; [oth. writ.] Poem printed in Anchor Book 1995. Short stories in book entitled "So Many Stories".; [pers.] I just love writing, picking the high lights of my life as subjects of my stories.; [a.] Ilford, Essex, IG6 2RR

SOPER, ROY JOHN
[b.] October 20, 1938, London; [p.] William Soper, Dorothy Soper; [m.] Wendy Danahar, February 4, 1967; [ch.] Jeremy Richard, Paula Marie, Nicola Jane; [ed.] Archbishop Temple Secondary School, Central School of Arts and Crafts; [occ.] Silversmith; [memb.] National Geographic Society; [hon.] Freeman of Goldsmiths Society, Freeman of the City of London; [oth. writ.] Other poems not published.; [pers.] I write purely for pleasure and relaxation.; [a.] London, E6 4EQ

SPALDING, BRYAN
[pen.] Breon Sales; [b.] June 25, 1935, Mansfield; [m.] Tate - Thelma, September 8, 1953; [ch.] Five; [ed.] St. Johns Mansfield Tech. College Ar. School; [occ.] Retired; [oth. writ.] Song corporations, Developing Children, New Nursery Figure, Letters on World Peace, Natural Balance; [pers.] I seek the true balance of life and to transmit same to others; [a.] Mansfield, Notts, NG18 3AN

SPANOS, MARGARET
[pen.] Gleeson Spanos; [b.] February 14, 1941, Tippereary Eire; [p.] Mother only now 86 yrs; [m.] Antoine, (Retired), June 1971; [ch.] (Two sons) Nicholas, Emmanuel; [ed.] St Mary's Convent, Nenegh SRN Whittington, ENT Grays Inn Rd, retired Unit High Sister; [occ.] Retired; [memb.] Poetry now mag. Anchor Books; [hon.] None but printed verse; [oth. writ.] 1st written, 1st poem published 1991. About 18 since in anthologies. ("Haunt of Terror", "Think Feeling", "It's a Hearts Delight") oneself pub. books and are on tape in Prince Michael of Kent Free top Library for the blind, ("I Cried with Joy in Tapes); [pers.] I don't even know what words I use, that why when they come they must be written the beauty of the earth is what makes me gulf. Its with sight I see it and try to share it in my extra gift of verse; [a.] Putney Vale, London, SW15 3EF

SPICER, RITA JOYCE
[pen.] Rita Spicer; [b.] February 21, 1942, Leicester; [p.] Eileen and Frederick Shaw; [m.] Percy Spicer, March 3, 1964; [ch.] Deborah and Sarah Spicer; [ed.] Various Secondary Modern Schools; [occ.] Steward II; [oth. writ.] Poetry in magazines and books.; [pers.] I find the writing of poetry my personal slate I show the world.; [a.] Waddington, Lincoln, LN5 9QX

SPRAGGS, ANITA
[b.] July 24, 1963, Kent; [p.] Mr. and Mrs. Martin; [m.] Paul Timothy Spraggs, August 29, 1995; [ch.] Mark, Anthony, Daniella; [ed.] Bennett Memorial School for Girls Tunbridge Wells Kent; [occ.] Office Clerk for children world Torquay; [pers.] This is my first poem to be entered into a competition, I have alway's put my feelings on paper, rather than express vocally.; [a.] Brixham, Devon, TQ5 0EB

STAMMERS, DORICE
[pen.] J. D. Jarome; [b.] January 6, 1949, Nottingham; [p.] Joan and Tom Harrison; [m.] Anthony Stammers, May 19, 1973; [ch.] 2 - boys and girl; [ed.] Secondary School; [occ.] Housewife; [oth. writ.] I have many poems that I've written but never submitted any.; [pers.] I write poems from things that touch my heart, my mum as pleaded to get me to send my poems for years, I never felt they were good enough till now.; [a.] Nottingham, 9G5 5FS

STANNARD, GILLIAN
[b.] September 12, 1956, Grimsby; [p.] Christine Holmes and Arthur Holmes; [m.] Divorced; [ch.] Four; [occ.] Housewife and writer; [memb.] National Poetry Foundation; [oth. writ.] I have had published two poems in anthology's by Anchor Books 1. Parents Grand and Great, 2. In From The Cold Royalties donated to Wood Green Animal Shelter; [pers.] As we live in sorrowful times with hunger wars and destruction, try to make the world a better place, the world can be a better place, if only we all tried and work together then we can live in peace.; [a.] Grimsby, S. Humberside, DN33 1RN

STANTON, HAYDEE SERON
[b.] March 14, 1961, Philippines; [p.] Natividad and Leodigario Seron; [m.] Richard Stanton, September 15, 1992; [ch.] Criztian Dantes; [ed.] Walsall College of Arts And Technology (Administration 2 NVQ); [occ.] Cashier/Sales Assistant; [memb.] Sea Cadets; [pers.] There are so many ways to show love of God and one of them is through writing an inspirational poem.; [a.] Birmingham, Warwickshire, B43 5ET

STANTON, MALCOLM
[b.] August 18, 1974, Minster Sheppy; [p.] C. R. Stanton, R. B. King; [ed.] Faversham Abbey School English City and Guilds and G.C.S.E. Maths City and Guilds. Studied Mech Eng. At Cant College; [occ.] Security Officer; [memb.] Weight Training Faversham; [hon.] Parents Full names are as follows, Carla Rose Stanton and Roger Bary King; [pers.] I wish to express what is going on and around me in my life.; [a.] Faversham, Kent, ME13 7ER

STANTON, SAMANTHA
[pen.] Sam; [b.] December 3, 1975, Norwich; [p.] Angela Pardon and David Pardon; [m.] Andrew, November 20, 1993; [ch.] Stacey Paige, awaiting next arrival; [ed.] Cromer High School; [occ.] Housewife (normally a Care Assistant); [hon.] Have many running award, medals, etc. Won Miss Cromer 1995 award for Local Carnival; [pers.] I enjoy using my imagination and writing seems the easiest way to express this, I get great influence from my partner.; [a.] Cromer, Norfolk, NR27 9DS

STARCK, MARGARET
[b.] January 18, 1923, Newmillerdam, Wakefield; [p.] Harry and Greta Midgley; [ch.] Franklin (educated at Rudolf Steiner School, Kerfeld); [ed.] 1) Scholarship to Wakefield Girls High School, 1993 2) 1941-43 Bingley Training College (Junior and Infants Training.); [pers.] Apart from 2 periods of voluntary service in German refugee camps, 1949-1951, taught at schools in the Wakefield area, British School, Hamburg and B.F.E.S. school Krefeld 1943-1961; [a.] Krefeld, Germany, 47809

STEELE, JAMES HAROLD DALTON
[pen.] Dalton-Steele; [b.] July 5, 1947, Manchester; [p.] Harold Dalton Steele, Dora Steele; [m.] Elaine Anne Steele; [ch.] Karen Anne and Mark James Dalton Steele; [ed.] Secondary School to GCE Std, Loughborough College: Vindiculture Various Business Study Courses; [occ.] Retired Businessman, (Retired Through Ill Health); [memb.] International Child Sponsorship Via Plan International; [hon.] Currently Studying in Computer Science at College Hoping to enrol on a degree course at Manchester University next year. I am awaiting acceptance of application.; [oth. writ.] "The Magical Adventures of Young Bumble" - a series of childrens stories in rhyme (as yet unpublished) "The Warriors of Wraak" - a sci-fi novel in the process of writing. Poems of various kinds.; [pers.] Enjoyment is in the minds perception of the moment but only the open minded can perceive what is actually there to enjoy. Life consists of many experiences both good and bad how good it is depends on how badly you want it.; [a.] Manchester, Lancashire, M41 9DR

STEPHEN, ROBERT
[b.] June 24, 1947, Rhynie, Aberdeenshire; [p.] John McGregor, Isabella Stephen; [m.] Wendy Eileen, June 21, 1969; [ch.] Lorna, Marianne; [ed.] Forgue School Huntly Grammer School; [occ.] Mobile Crane Driver, Rosyth Royal Dock Yard; [memb.] Lochbelly Golf Club; [oth. writ.] Many others unpublished poems (this is my first publishing attempt).; [pers.] I try to write the truth as I see it. I read a lot of burns.; [a.] Dunfermline, Fife, KY11 4AL

STEPHENS, SAMANTHA
[b.] February 9, 1970, Ipswich; [ed.] Hollywells High School; [occ.] Secretary; [pers.] My poems are generally about life and love. I tend to draw from my own personal experiences. I find writing poems a great comfort as well as a release for all my thoughts and feelings.; [a.] Felixstowe, Suffolk

STEVENS, MRS. KAREN
[b.] November 29, 1970, Carshalton, Surrey; [p.] Ian Winchester, Florence Winchester; [m.] Mark Stevens, March 25, 1995; [ed.] Rowan High School, Merton Tech. College; [occ.] Management Accounts Assist.; [memb.] Association of Accounting Technicians; [pers.] This poems was written in the memory of my grandfather, Walter MacDonald, who will live on in our hearts forever.; [a.] Sutton, Surrey, SM1 3ND

STEVENSON, JOHN DAVID
[pen.] Leicester Fox; [b.] October 3, 1959, Leicester; [p.] Desmere E. Lacht; [ed.] Average; [occ.] Cower; [pers.] In the memory of the spirit of Des

STEVENSON, ROSALYN C.
[pen.] Rosalyn C. Ellis; [b.] November 28, 1916, Beckenham; [p.] Mr. and Mrs. A. E. Virgo; [m.] Mr. Arther N. Stevenson, August 19, 1963; [ed.] Secondary School; [occ.] Retired; [memb.] Queenspark Books; [hon.] Small prize for art age 8 years also one oil painting chosen amount 200 for hanging in Gallery out of 8,000 also - good references; [oth. writ.] 34 poems letters to politicians and royalty am now writing a book; [pers.] Interested in my fellow countrymens welfare and the welfare of animals a lover of music; [a.] Seaford, E. Sussex, BN25 1SB

STIRTON, GRAEME
[b.] January 18, 1954, Ballater; [p.] Graham and Catherine; [m.] Maureen Stirton, October 10, 1993; [occ.] Self Employed Joiner; [memb.] Part time student, Aberdeen Music College Rutherstone Centre; [hon.] Graded Theory Guildhall School of Music and Drama; [oth. writ.] Several songs not yet published; [pers.] I write on personal experiences and true emotions, I hope in some way it may reach other people who have experienced similar events in their lives and be of some comfort. Influences life; [a.] Aberdeen, Grampian, AB1 7HD

STONE, MR. D.
[pen.] Don Stone; [b.] April 15, 1926, Leeds; [p.] Albert F. Stone and Jeannie Stone; [m.] Divorced - Jean, April 2, 1956; [ch.] Anne Maria and Michael David Ian; [ed.] Ellerby Lane Elementary Leeds; [occ.] Retired - Ex Painter and Decorator, Wartime-merchant Navy; [hon.] Wartime Medal 1939-1945; [oth. writ.] Several unpublished poems.; [pers.] Life is a school of learning, study wisely. Even mistakes are beneficial providing we don't repeat them.; [a.] Leeds, W. Yorks, LS14 2BQ

STOTT, LISA MARIE
[pen.] Lisa Marie; [b.] May 26, 1971, Atherton; [p.] Kenneth Stott, Sandra Stott; [ed.] Hesketh Fletcher C of E High School Atherton; [occ.] Sewing Machinist, and Greeting Card Verse Writer; [hon.] Poems published in the following books "The Way It Is" (Anchor Books) "Absent Friends (Poetry Nau) "The Other Side Of The Mirror" (The International Society of Poets; [oth. writ.] My aim is to make readers really think of what is happening in the world today, and face up to every day tasks, to give them hope.; [pers.] I am putting together my first book of my own which I hope will be successfully published based on every day things we all take for granted; [a.] Tyldesley, Manchester, M29 8BY

STUART, ELIZABETH
[pen.] Ginn; [b.] April 10, 1921, Whithorn; [m.] James Stuart, October 17, 1945; [ch.] 6; [ed.] Whithorn Higher Grade School; [occ.] Retired; [memb.] W.R.I. Guilds A.D.C.; [a.] Whithorn, Wigtownshire, DG8 8QN

STUART, JAMES
[b.] February 1, 1962, Greenoch; [p.] Janet and James (Deceased); [m.] Joan Deegan (Fiancee); [occ.] Project Manager of In Work Landscaping Ltd; [memb.] Guild of Master Craftsmen The Environment Council; [hon.] Environmental Coucillor "Glasgow Year of Culture Poetry Competition 1990" B.T. Conservation Awards 95-96; [oth. writ.] Working Class Hero, The Man, Crime-Time, Shadowlands.; [pers.] I don't try to say anything clever in my poetry. It is simply a vehicle which I use to highlight aspects of life on today's housing estates.; [a.] Greenoch, PA16 8UA

STUBBERFIELD, MARTIN
[b.] April 17, 1953, Trowbridge; [p.] Fredick and Joan Stubberfield; [ed.] The University of Wales College of Cardiff; [occ.] Yoga Teacher; [memb.] The British Wheel of Yoga; [hon.] English Literature; [oth. writ.] Poems and short stories.; [pers.] Happiness is to be found only in what moves and develops.; [a.] Bath, Banes, BA1 2RJ

SUDDELL, PAULINE-MARIAM
[b.] February 1, 1948, England; [p.] Lawrence and Levy; [m.] Peter John Suddell, January 6, 1981; [ch.] Debbie (6-8-69), Patsy (16-10-89); [ed.] Secondary Modern School, Bow London E3; [occ.] Housewife; [a.] London, Middlesex, E3 4JF

SULLIVAN, G. M. M.
[pen.] Gladys Margaret Mary; [b.] December 29, 1927, Hereford; [m.] Widow, March 29, 1950; [ch.] 3 grown up; [ed.] Salisbury Wiltshire St Elizabeth Roman Catholic Convent; [occ.] Packer; [a.] Tottenham, 3 AD

SURMAN, DAVID PAUL
[b.] December 6, 1968, Wolverhampton; [p.] Tony and Pearl; [ed.] Predominantly Secondary; [occ.] Civil Servant; [oth. writ.] A small number of poems published in a small number of books, plus my opinions regarding extraterrestrial intelligence published by Contact international.; [pers.] In everyday life - I frequently wonder, about the concept and reason - regarding our intelligence - within the great and infinite order - of the Cosmos. And I try, to reflect this curiosity, through my writing.; [a.] Amesbury, Wiltshire, SP4 7RG

SUTTON, ANTHONY
[b.] May 23, 1953, Ashingdon, Essex; [p.] Len Sutton, Gladys Sutton; [ed.] South Church Hall High School for boys Southend-on-Sea; [occ.] Factory Charge Hand; [memb.] (ASS) Member Royal British Legion, and member of the R.S.P.B.; [oth. writ.] Poem published in the Haverhill Echo (Local paper); [pers.] If everybody was kind and understanding in everything they say the world would be a better place than it is today.; [a.] Haverhill, Suffolk, CB9 7NF

SUTTON, HELEN MARIE
[b.] November 5, 1975, West Midlands; [p.] Graham and Susan Sutton; [ed.] Perryfield High School, Oldbury Sandwell College, West Midlands; [occ.] Care Assistant, Gables Nursing Home; [hon.] BTEC National Diploma in Social Care, 8 Distinctions, 3 Merits - 1993, Award for Highest Overall Achievement at College - 1993; [oth. writ.] I write various poetry and short stories although have never entered them for previous publication. Whilst at college, I co-wrote a play about the second world war entitled "Love Through The Blitz"; [pers.] Writing poetry and short stories is, for me, a manner in which I can express my personal feelings without having to disclose them verbally, my inspiration is my own creativity.; [a.] Oldbury Warley, West Midlands, B68 0RJ

SYKES, DRYDEN
[b.] May 8, 1976, Huddersfield; [p.] Stuart Sykes and Rose Sykes; [ed.] Colne Valley High School, Linthwaite Huddersfield; [occ.] Car Dismantler at local scrapyard (6 months); [oth. writ.] Various notepads, journals and rough bits of paper amounting to approx. 800 pages of poetry and song material; [pers.] I reflect teenage consciousness in my writings rock and roll being my main influence, my thoughts, views, and daily happenings fall into verse at intervals thru a normal life; [a.] Huddersfield, W. Yorkshire, HD7 5NN

TAFFETSAUFFER, DOROTHY
[pen.] Dorothy Taffetsauffer; [b.] August 25, 1939, Yorkshire; [p.] James, Esther Simm; [m.] Erich Taffetsauffer, March 21, 1960; [ch.] Andrew, Erich, Sharon, Martin; [ed.] Sec. Modern; [occ.] Housewife; [oth. writ.] Nothing published.; [pers.] One should not build a wall of fence around the past, only you can make good or bad thing last.; [a.] Llanelli, Dyfed, SA15 5HJ

TAHID, NAZIA KHATUN
[b.] June 8, The Royal Hospital, London; [p.] Abdul Tahid and Azizun Nessa; [ed.] Student of secondary school (year 8); [occ.] Student Mulberry School for girls (secondary)

TAMMAS, JEAN
[pen.] Jeanne Martin-Tammas; [b.] October 3, 1921, Co Armagh, NI; [p.] James and Sarah Martin (Deceased); [m.] Reginald Burt Tammas, September 18, 1943; [ch.] Four daughters (all married); [ed.] Milford, P.E. School, Armagh Girls High School; [occ.] Retired School Matron; [memb.] W.I., Parish Councilor, Sailing Club, London Crusader Choir, (Mostly Suspended because of illness); [hon.] Serve in Women's Land Army and also in the RAF during the war (1939-45); [oth. writ.] Poems published Autumn - (Nature's Voices), My Love and I (Valentine Poets), Sun Setting Over Evesham, (Candle in the Wind), Winter Changes (Winter Thoughts), The Wooly Flook (West Country Anthology) (All amateur books); [pers.] Although I know I will never be famous like Chritina Rosetta I would just like to think that long after my death I might be remembered for my poems, hopefully with affection.; [a.] Evesham, Worcs, WR11 5LP

TAWS, EVELYN
[pen.] Evelyn Prenvis; [b.] October 23, 1915, London; [p.] Not known (lost at birth); [m.] Widow, July 1942; [ch.] Two very dear daughters; [ed.] Lincoln Girl's, High School; [occ.] Very retired, Nurse; [memb.] S.R.N., Trained Nottingham City Hospital, 1934-1938; [oth. writ.] A Nurse in Time, A Nurse in Action, A Nurse in Parts, A Nurse Near By, A Turn for the Nurse, Handbecks Hutchusire, Peperbecks Arrow (1977-1981); [pers.] I simply like words; [a.] Hillingdon, UB10 0JA

TAYLOR, CAROLE MARIAN
[b.] May 6, 1944, Winchester; [p.] Joan and Percy Flux; [m.] Michael Richard Taylor, March 28, 1964; [ch.] Samantha and Justin; [ed.] Danemark Secondary School Winchester; [occ.] Catering Supervisor; [memb.] Body Souwn Health Club; [oth. writ.] Poems; [pers.] My poems reflect mainly on things that have personally affected my life; [a.] Chandlersford, Hants, SO53 2FT

TAYLOR, GABRIELLE
[b.] February 11, 1945; [m.] Bob (Frank Robert Taylor), May 27, 1961; [ch.] Dean (36), Martin (33), John (29); [ed.] Kibworth Beauchamp Grammar School; [occ.] 'At home' writing and painting I owned a residential home from 1983-1993 which I managed myself; [oth. writ.] Lots of poetry, including 'Grandpa's Chair' and 'Anne' also book recently completed but not yet in publication 'Last Night At The Frog and Basket'; [pers.] I enjoy amateur dramatics, and writing stories and poetry. I also paint with oils. Several poems in local 'Link' magazine. Although I have written on various subjects I find that it is easier for me to humanous than serious.; [a.] Bulby, Bourne, Lincs, PE10 0RU

TAYLOR, MRS. JULIE
[b.] June 16, 1938, Birkenhead, Cheshire; [p.] Mr. and Mrs. Morris; [m.] Mr. Peter Taylor, April 30, 1980; [ch.] One boy Robert Taylor; [ed.] Secondary School; [occ.] Housewife; [hon.] I have had poems published in papers and magazines on different occasions for my family and friends.; [oth. writ.] Song recorded in America called Day-by-day. Waiting to hear news its going to be released world wide, already have LP my self and tapes and music sheets; [pers.] I always find a lot of pleasure writing songs and poems. Mostly very sentimental sometimes its the way I feel.; [a.] Bexelyheath, Kent, DA6 8JT

TAYLOR, SHAUN ALEX
[b.] April 16, 1975, Kettering; [p.] Janice Taylor and Barry Taylor; [ed.] Lodge Park School (Comp); [occ.] Product Technician Rhophase Microwave Ltd; [memb.] The Writers Bureau; [pers.] Life is a valuable and special experience which poetry helps to capture its essence. Thomas Hardy was a greet inspiration for my writing.; [a.] Corby, Northants, NN17 2BJ

TERRY, LAVINIA CHRISTINE
[b.] February, 2, 1962, Manchester; [p.] James Fredrick Terry, Ellen Bernadette Terry; [ch.] Shadia, Sophia, Khalid, and Jake; [ed.] (Manchester Duice High School,) South Trafford College, Sale; [occ.] Housewife; [memb.] Reader's Digest Book Club, Gardening World Book Club; [hon.] Nursery Nursing Course; [oth. writ.] None except this competition; [pers.] I wish to dedicate to this poem to my children Shadia, Sophia, Khalid, and Jake with all my love. I would also like to say that I was greatly influenced by the Amnesty Political Prisoner's when I wrote this poem at the age of (15) and their plight.

THOMAS, ANDREA SELINA
[pen.] Andrea Selina Thomas; [b.] April 2, 1961, Ellesmere Port, Cheshire; [p.] Frederick W. Price, Evelyn Price (nee Harris); [ed.] Stanney County Comprehensive School E. Port, Mabel Flether College of

Drama and Dance Liverpool; [oth. writ.] Poetry published in England and America many short stories published and Broadcast on BBC Radio. Won the Halloween short story competition held by the liverpool daily post and echo newspaper; [a.] Whitby, Ellesmere Port, Cheshire, L66 2YX

THOMAS, PATRICIA ANNE
[b.] April 15, 1936, Huddersfield; [p.] Charles William and Frances Margaret Kaye; [m.] Sammy Thomas, October 5, 1985 (2nd Marriage); [ch.] Gregory James, Maria Theresa and Marcus Benedict Duffy; [ed.] St. Patrick's RC School, London College of Music, College of Technology, Huddersfield, Huddersfield University; [occ.] Legal Assistant, Kirklees Metropolitan Council; [memb.] Principal Small Academy of Combined Arts (Halifax); [oth. writ.] Various (including songs), unpublished; [pers.] The poet sings an ancient song which modulates only to reflect the times in which he lives.; [a.] Skelmanthorpe, Huddersfield, W. Yorks, HD8 9DH

THOMAS-SYMONDS, NICKLAUS
[b.] May 26, 1980, Griffitstown; [p.] Pamela M. Symonds, Jeffrey Symonds; [ed.] St. Felix R.C. Primary School, St. Alban's R.C. High School; [occ.] Student; [memb.] The Hansard Society, Liverpool F.C. International Supporter's Club; [hon.] Highly commended in the Free Press 'Young Journalist of the year' competition 1993, commended in the guardian 'Young Political Writer of the Year' competition 1994, Bronze Award for Mathematics from the Nat. West. Bank; [oth. writ.] Several poems published in local parish magazine, three poems published by triumph house.; [pers.] Poetry is a form of expression central to our very being.; [a.] Blaenavon, Gwent, NP4 9PZ

THOMPSON, IAN JAMES
[b.] October 17, 1971, Barking, Essex; [p.] James, Christine Thompson; [ed.] Fryerns Secondary School, Basildon. Thurrock Technical College, Grays; [occ.] Currently unemployed; [hon.] National BTech Diploma, Art and Design, Certificate in Environmental Studies; [oth. writ.] Poems, songs and short stories.; [pers.] At best poetry should only hope to inspire personal interpretation.; [a.] Basildon, Essex, SS14 3RQ

THOMPSON, LESLIE CHARLES
[pen.] Leslie Charles Thompson; [b.] November 1, 1929, Liverpool; [p.] Tom and Rose Thompson; [m.] Fay, September 12, 1953; [ch.] Stephen and Bernadette; [ed.] Local Grammar School; [occ.] Gardener handy man; [memb.] Halifax Cow Ass. Halifax R.U.F.C. Heart Research, we are Keen followers of Local Dramatics and Musicals; [oth. writ.] Christmas wish, will no-one help a stranger, hope, upon the Straight and narrow path, (Hymn); [pers.] I am a committed christian, much of my writings were inspired during friends of family trials, my wife and I are been supporters of local charities and we finally believe that acts speak louder than words.; [a.] Halifax, W. Yorks, HX3 0LA

THOMPSON, ROBERT
[b.] February 11, 1936, London; [p.] Deceased; [m.] Divorced 1983, May 17, 1966; [ch.] (Two) Son and daughter; [ed.] Secondary Modern Coppermill Lane Walthamston London; [occ.] Unemployed; [oth. writ.] Poem - The Future Now The Future, book - (Poetic Landscape), book - (Closet Poets), poem - The Invader.; [pers.] I have been writing poetry now for nearly twenty years, I have many pieces, as yet unpublished, most of my work is topical. I enjoy writing.; [a.] Dovercourt Harwich, Essex, CO12 3PA

THOMPSON, MRS. SHEILA
[pen.] S. Thompson; [b.] November 11, 1942, London Area; [p.] Agnes and Robert Stewart; [m.] Andy Thompson, July 12, 1972; [ed.] Nil- well, a private school for girls, which prepared you a little for life, but not scholastically; [occ.] House-wife, dog-owner, song-writer, boat owner; [memb.] The Wherry Trust, B.T.C.V., Friends of the Bure Valley Railway, etc. Birmingham Canal Society. Take mags. associated with Inland, Waterways; [hon.] I won a song competition out of 90 songs very proudest moment! Have had letters, articles published in various magazines perhaps it would be of interest to know how "Dion's War" came to be written. The radio was on as I wrote letters, and it came on as a news item, Dion's death at the age of 18 at the start of the gulf war. It is a song, and the tune came about occidentally, doodling with my keyboard, while was plugged through to a tape recorder. ("Young Son of Mine" ends despairingly on H7, a short of everlasting question work!); [oth. writ.] Have always written verse, stories etc. Am now working on 40 short poems, mainly about (English) rivers, including 6 appropriate photos.; [pers.] A favorite mis-quote! "You are nearer to God by a river, than anywhere else on Earth!"; [a.] Dunbor, E. Lothiam, EH42 1SA

THOMPSON, SHERYL
[pen.] Sheryl Roach; [b.] December 8, 1971, Norwich; [p.] Christopher Roach, Monica Roach; [m.] Steven Robert Thompson, June 15, 1996; [ed.] Norwich Comprehensive, The Norfolk College of Arts and Technology, Norwich School of Art and Design; [occ.] Artist; [oth. writ.] Poems published in anthologies by Arrival Press: 'Fur, Coats and Feathers' and 'Animals Forever'; [pers.] The inspiration for my poems come from my fears, my dreams, my deepest feelings and ambitions but most of all from life experience.; [a.] Norwich, Norfolk, NR3 4TE

THOMSON, MARGARET JEAN
[pen.] Greta; [b.] May 20, 1933, Rumbling Bridge, Kinross-shire; [p.] Alexander and Rosaline Wood (Nee Gray); [m.] James Spalding Thomson (Deceased March 1990), April 31, 1952; [ch.] 5 girls and 1 boy; [ed.] Crook of Devon, Fossoway, Kinross-shire-Primary, Kinross-Secondary; [occ.] Retired; [pers.] I have only recently been writing poetry mostly reflecting the peace of my surroundings. This has helped me greatly, adjust to my life without my husband. Ease the pain of my loss.; [a.] Morar by Mallaig, Inverness-shire, Scotland, PH40 4PB

THOMSON, VIRGINIA
[pen.] Ginnie Thomson; [b.] October 14, 1979, Bath, Avon; [p.] Gill and Andrew Thomson; [ed.] Home Education; [occ.] Student, Trowbridge Technical College; [oth. writ.] Village correspondent for "The Wiltshire Times"; [pers.] Have been greatly influenced by works of Jane Austen and William Shakespeare; [a.] Broughton, Gifford, Wiltshire, SN12 8PL

THORNTON, JOHN
[b.] August 23, 1930; [m.] Mary, August 28, 1961; [ch.] Catherine, John, Anthony, Simon, Grandchildren: Catriona, Iain; [ed.] St. Josephs College, Stoke-on-Trent, Hull University, Open University; [occ.] Retired Physics Teacher; [memb.] (1) Merseyside Open University Graduates Association, (2) Association of Open Univ. Graduates; [hon.] BA (Hons), BSC; [oth. writ.] 'Gas-Laws for All Seasons' - published in school Science Review, March '93.; [pers.] A strong belief in a personal God and an after-life sustains me and gives my present life meaning. Favourite poets: Francis Thompson, John Nasefield, Rupert Brooke.; [a.] Liverpool, L23 8SH

TIBBE, MRS. DORIS MARIE
[pen.] Billie; [b.] May 13, 1905, Bootle, Liverpool; [p.] Irish-Swedish; [m.] Dutch Minicaptain (Deceased), May 3, 1945; [ed.] Scanty, but good Commercial School, (Machine and Harpers); [occ.] Retired. But big house and garden's to keep.; [hon.] None - but deserve a lot - (my view entirely); [oth. writ.] Lot often a woman of 91 years (May 1996) can sit and read exercise book written at 10 years. Writing good steel nibs and ink pots then - must.; [pers.] Always have been an odd ball even when young - the last of a big family - another Swedish, father Irish - then I go Dutch. Life like a crazy quilt.; [a.] Liverpool, Lancs, L19 3PE

TILLEY, GWYNETH
[pen.] Gwyneth Tilley; [b.] February 16, 1920, Bargoed, Wales; [p.] Lily and Evan Bartlett; [m.] William John Tilley, August 5, 1939; [ch.] Douglas, Derek, David; [ed.] Elementary Schooling at Tynywern School, Trethomas, Gwent South Wales; [occ.] Retired; [hon.] Poetic Achievements Award Presented by Bedwas, Trethomas and Machen Community Council; [oth. writ.] Many poems, some short stories. Some of the poems have been published in anthologies.; [pers.] My writing has been inspired by my childhood in a mining village, where there was little money but much love and by encouragement from my family and friends.; [a.] Trethomas, Gwent, NP1 8DH

TIMMINS, ANN
[pen.] Ann Timmins; [b.] December 21, 1943, Blackburn; [p.] Lester and Edna Winstanley; [m.] Keith Timmins, 2nd marriage February 6, 1976; [ch.] Handicapped daughter, Sharon; [ed.] Notre Dame Grammar Blackburn; [occ.] Retired nurse, S.R.N. (due to ill health) R.N.M.S.; [memb.] Country and Western Line Dancing Club; [oth. writ.] Several poems published in local paper; [pers.] I describe real-life events, occurrences and people in my poems eg. "Winter Scene" is the view from my living room.; [a.] Blackburn, Lancs, BB6 7TB

TIMMINS, MARALYN
[b.] September 3, 1960, London; [p.] Lilian and Arthur Parsons; [m.] Philip Timmins, June 1, 1985; [ch.] Aron and Melissa; [oth. writ.] Publication of two further poems: 'Holding On', 'A Vow for Life', children stories for pleasure.; [pers.] Since early childhood my mother has encouraged my love of writing poetry and children's stories. Without the encouragement of my dearest friend no words could have been written.; [a.] Stevenage, Herts, SG2 8TD

TOMKINS, MRS. NOREEN
[b.] January 30, 1946, Gateshead; [p.] Douglas and Nora Haig; [m.] March 4, 1967; [ch.] One daughter Jane 24 yrs; [ed.] Secondary School, Hillhead at Lobley Hill, Gateshead; [occ.] Head of Care Furrowfield Boys School, Gateshead; [memb.] My work is very demanding but I love my work and I am dedicated to the boys who I look after, I collect for the blind with the boys.; [hon.] Open University Diploma in Child Care; [oth. writ.] None to date but I'm thinking about it, practice every week; [pers.] I love my husband and daughter very much, we have always been a great team, and I like nothing more than being with them; [a.] Gateshead, Tyne and Wear, NE10 8NG

TRANTER, KAREN MANDY
[b.] June 4, 1967, Coventry; [ed.] Coventry University - BSC Honors Degree in Computer Science; [occ.] Technical Support; [memb.] Local Fitness and Health Club; [oth. writ.] This is the first piece of poetry that I written. However, I do intend ti explore the world of writing further. Did write a poem called "The Bracken" which was quite successful at school.; [a.] Coventry, Warwickshire, CV4 9AT

TRAVIS, BRIAN
[b.] August 19, 1940, Uttoxeter; [ed.] Uttoxeter Grammar School, St. Peters College, Birmingham; [occ.] Head Teacher; [hon.] Dip. Ed., Cert. Ed.; [oth. writ.] Short stories and poems published in anthologies; [a.] Derby, Derbys, DE22 1EZ

TRUMAN, VERONICA
[pen.] Veg; [b.] January 2, 1948, Leicester; [p.] Arnold Granger and Florence Granger; [m.] John Truman, May 29, 1982; [ed.] Ravenhurts Road Junior, Market Bosworth Dixie Grammar School.; [occ.] Housewife; [memb.] Midland Golden Retriever Club: Vice Chairman Coalville Canine Society: Pat Dogs Mensa.; [a.] Groby, Leicestershire, LE6 0EZ

TUCKER, EDNA FLORENCE
[b.] March 5, 1920, Birmingham; [p.] A. H. Lawson, E. M. Lawson; [m.] Robert Joseph Tucker, June 10, 1939; [ch.] Pamela Florence, Christine Edna, Robert Edward, Valerie Margaret; [ed.] Secondary Modern; [occ.] Housewife; [oth. writ.] Poems not published; [pers.] Poem's about life

TUCKEY, BRIAN G.
[b.] August 15, 1928, Watton, Norfolk; [p.] Gerald and Winifred Tuckey; [m.] Daphne Mavis, October 10, 1953; [ch.] Sandra Ann and Keith Gerald; [ed.] General; [occ.] Avionics (Military) Data Controller, New Retired; [memb.] Western Front Association, The Great War, (Historical Research and Commemorative); [oth. writ.] Short Stories and Essays; [pers.] Where possible, to contribute to the collective quality of life, and to ensure that my participation is not to the detriment of others.; [a.] Maidenhead, Berks, SL6 2TE

TURNER, ATIR
[b.] December 1, 1976, London, Lewisham; [p.] Rita Kedge (Mother); [m.] Giles Turner, February 3, 1996; [occ.] Sales Assistant, Westminster; [pers.] I write what I feel inside my heart and mind. I'm influenced not by any poets I read, but from songs, hear and friends around me.; [a.] Woolwich, London, SE18 5RA

TURNER, MR. JOHN KEITH
[b.] November 12, 1939, Beeston, Notts; [m.] Eleanor, October 1, 1981; [ch.] Paul, Pamela, Shelana, Gareth; [ed.] Nottingham Bluecoat School; [occ.] Probate Executive (Solicitors); [memb.] Upton Park Bowling Club, Torquay, Club Champion, County Secretaries Winner 1994; [oth. writ.] Poetry review 1994 Teddy Bears and tears two mote published this year 'Cavalier' and 'Strange but true' (Rivacre Publications); [pers.] Greatly influenced by the beauty of Devon and Wales; [a.] Torquay, Devon, TQ1 4LD

TURNER, LILLIAN MAY
[pen.] Lady Hill Walker; [b.] April 11, 1945, Mansfield; [p.] Sheila and Albert Marland; [m.] Widowed; [ch.] Michelle Denise and Dawn; [ed.] Germany and Malaysia Armed Forces Boarding Schools; [occ.] Upholstery Machinist; [oth. writ.] I have a collection of poems, but never sent any for a review until now.; [pers.] Most of my poems reflect what has happened within my own personal life. Up to the present time.; [a.] Long Eaton, Notts, NE10 3ND

TURNER, MAGGIE
[pen.] Margaret Ross; [b.] July 17, 1945, England; [ed.] BA (Honours), Creative Writing, Film/TV at Bolton Institute of Higher Education; [occ.] Writer/T.V. Research; [memb.] Romantic Novelists Association, New Play Wrights Trust Authors Foundation Networking; [oth. writ.] Anthology of Poetry on AIDS/HIV. (Part Published), In Development: Winning, Diamonds, hysteria, (Screen plays). Second chances - a novel, Film - Cloned in Pre-Production.; [pers.] This poem is a response to the devastation that AIDS and HIV have brought into my life.; [a.] Manchester, Lancashire, M40 3RG

TUSEL, MRS. JENNY CATHRINE
[pen.] Jenny Wren; [b.] September 18, 1959, Singapore; [p.] Cathrine Carey, James Carey; [m.] David Josef Tusel, May 23, 1981; [ch.] Mark Antonee, Katie Emma Marie, Rebecca Jenny; [ed.] Wrockwardine Wood Comprehensive School; [occ.] Housewife, parent carer; [memb.] Wrekin Writer Group; [hon.] Swimming, Ballroom Dancing; [oth. writ.] Poems, children stories, short stories; [pers.] I write purely for the pleasure and satisfaction of it. But I believe that when a person writes something they often put something of themselves and what they feel into what they write.; [a.] Telford, Shropshire, TF2 6PS

TYLER, THERESA
[pen.] Mick Terri; [b.] August 16, 1945, Coventry; [p.] Bill and Kathleen Hirons; [m.] Divorced; [ch.] Three 2 boys 1 girl; [ed.] None very sick child until 16 then I taugh myself. I became Care Asst. Aromatherapist/Reflexologist; [occ.] Now disabled.; [oth. writ.] Poems published in inspirations S.F. writing now on 2nd book.; [pers.] I would like to thank Pam who cares for me. And is also my friend. Also Dr. Alan Done. Who without I would have given up. For both of you thank you.; [a.] Wootton, Beds, MK43 9SS

UNSWORTH, STEVEN
[b.] October 17, 1972, Horwich; [p.] Frank Unsworth, Maureen Unsworth; [ch.] St. Cuthberts R.C. School, Bolton, Seljord Folk High School, Norway. University of East Anglia; [ed.] Language Student; [pers.] Looking back at this poem four years after having written it, I feel that I stumbled upon answers to questions about my life which, at that time, I was unsure how to ask.; [a.] Bolton, Lancs, BL6 5PZ

VALK, MARGARET A.
[b.] March 15, 1908, Surrey; [m.] November 25, 1941; [ed.] Haberdasher's Aske's Girls School, Oxford University; [occ.] Retired (formerly social work teaching administration); [memb.] Ver Poets, The Guild of Pastoral Psychology; [hon.] OBE; [oth. writ.] Occasional inclusion of poems in anthologies published by Ver Poets.; [pers.] Believing in the therapeutic value of poetry, I ran a poetry group in a Geriatric hospital. We published a small booklet of our work now out of print.; [a.] Exeter, Devon

VINALL-BURNETT, MARGARET
[b.] October 3, 1913, Haslemere; [p.] Arthur, Francess Benneyworth; [m.] Albert Vinall (Deceased), 1940-42, Robert Burnett (Deceased), 1945 widowed (1975); [ch.] Nancy, Albert, Carolina, Rosalind, Robert, Dorothy, Jeffrey, Kenneth; [ed.] Cross in hand sy village school left at 14 to enter Domestic Service; [occ.] Writing, help with disabled committee work; [memb.] Limless Disabled, London, Surrey branch N.A.L.D. access disabled; [oth. writ.] Several poems published disabled mgs, Sussex poems, Anchor Books, Devon Poetry Club (70's) two put to music, 1939, published, Garasmart and Donavan Maejo, 1995 Island Moods, Pite, write from everyday life, real happenings; [pers.] Lost leg in 1942. Write to keep me some when I can't sleep.; [a.] Eastbourne, Sussex, BN22 7DE

WAITE, JACQUELINE CYNTHIA
[b.] July 4, 1964, Andover; [m.] Michael John William Waite; [ch.] Lucy, Hazel, Susan Waite (age 13); [ed.] The Winton Grammar School; [oth. writ.] Although I have been writing for many years, this is my first official entry.; [pers.] I have always admired the works of Robert Louis Stevenson and patience strong, and in teenage years the wit of Pam Ayres. Although, my own writings always fluctuate from sober to fun.; [a.] Andover, Hampshire, SP10 5HT

WALKER, EMILY
[b.] March 26, 1913, Blackley; [p.] Ann Eugene Spooner, G. A. Low; [m.] William Edward Walker, July 26, 1934; [ch.] Two sons, William and Robert; [ed.] Blackley Municipal, Manchester, Lancs England; [occ.] Mother, grand and great grandmother; [oth. writ.] Various poems; [pers.] I believe in honesty, trust, respect, love of family, love of country, and believe in a higher being.; [a.] Adelaide, Southern Australia, Australia, 5035

WALKER, GREIG
[pen.] Wee Brother; [b.] October 5, 1975, Sauchie; [p.] John and Valerie Walker; [ed.] Lornshill Academy; [occ.] Apprentice Joiner; [memb.] Ashburn House Burnsclub, Dunfermline District Accordion Band, Alloa Bowmar Pipe Band; [oth. writ.] Poem included in "Poetry now Anthologies Scotland 1996"; [pers.] I write what I feel, how I feel it.; [a.] Sauchie, Clackmannan, FK10 3LL

WALKER, JUSTIN IVAN
[b.] December 10, 1956, England; [ed.] Middlesex University, Salisbury College (Wiltshire); [occ.] Further Education Tutor; [memb.] Middlesex University Alumni; [oth. writ.] Full length novel 'The Mirrabelle Letters' (Mystery Thriller as yet unpublished) more poems and short stories.; [pers.] 'The Mirrabelle Letters' is a cross between Wilkie Collins and Kafka! - I love Georgian Poetry (The Edwardian Kind).

WALKER, MS. MAEVE
[b.] April 5, 1943, Cheshire; [p.] Miriam and Thomas Allen; [m.] Partner - Idris Owen, January 4, 1964; [ch.] 2 daughters - Karen and Rebecca; [ed.] Pear Tree Secondary Modern School for Girls, Derby; [occ.] Part Owner of Residential Home for the Elderly; [memb.] Of Rhyme Arrival currently involved in a correspondence writing course.; [hon.] City and Guilds in Catering, further Education; [oth. writ.] A poem printed in Christian poets in Wales "Tears".; [pers.] To achieve something worthwhile and work within one's limitations. To observe life. We pass this way but once!; [a.] Penysarn, Gwynedd, LL69 9UF

WALKER, MISS SHEILA
[pen.] Sheila Walker; [b.] February 1, 1939, Almondsbury, Nr. Bristol; [p.] Staney Walker, Doris Walker; [m.] Divorced; [ch.] Joanne Marie, Ian Lindsay, Lindsey Marie; [ed.] Filton Secondary Modern Bristol; [occ.] Receptionist (Chiropody); [pers.] Writing poetry extends the imagination and gives me a sense of tranquility; [a.] Ealing, Middx, W5 4BA

WALL, TERENCE
[b.] January 2, 1956, Southport; [p.] Dennis Wall and Isabella Wall; [m.] Caroline Wall, June 13, 1992; [ch.] David, Russell, Dionne, Peter, Michael, Jade, Shannon; [ed.] Farnborough Rd Christ Church School; [occ.] Martial Arts Instructor; [pers.] I can only write a poem, when I feel strongly about the subject.; [a.] Southport, Lancs, PR8 6AY

WALL-HAYES, JULIAN F.
[b.] October 10, 1969, Aldershot, Beryl, Greenhalgh; [p.] Frederick Wall-Hayes; [ed.] Courtmoor Secondary School Fleet; [occ.] Forte PLC M3 Service Area; [memb.] Fleet Broadway Club, Joe Bananas, Camberley; [oth. writ.] "Looking By Myself" in poetry now - Regional Anthologies London 1993.; [pers.] Love yourself before you can love others. Always try to

be happy, enjoy the good things in life and just experience the bad things, without bad times there cannot be good times.; [a.] Fleet, Hampshire, GU13 9QP

WALLACE, CLAIRE
[b.] March 3, 1984, London; [p.] Julia and Christopher; [ed.] Brentwood Ursulino Convent High School Essex; [occ.] School girl; [pers.] Would I love do write short stories, songs and poems; [a.] Ongar, Essex, CM5 0DR

WALLACE, GINA
[b.] August 6, 1986, London; [p.] Julia and Christopher; [ed.] Moreton C of E Primary School in Essex; [occ.] School girl; [pers.] Look forward to writing more poems and maybe stories too.; [a.] Ongar, Essex, CM5 0DR

WALT, MRS. ELLEN
[pen.] E. Walt; [b.] August 6, 1932, Bearpark; [p.] Ethel and Thomas Jally; [m.] John Walt, August 4, 1951; [ch.] Judith, Gillian, Neil; [ed.] Bearpark Mixed School; [occ.] Housewife; [oth. writ.] Poem published in book called Fir, Boats and Feathers (1995); [a.] Durham, DH7 7BD

WANDLESS, SHARON JOY
[pen.] Sharon Joy Wandless; [b.] October 16, 1959, Castleford; [p.] Edward, Jean Wandless; [ed.] Castleford High School; [memb.] Woman Center Castleford; [pers.] When I write I do it all from my heart, to try and express my feelings as well. To show that life is pressure to all.; [a.] Castleford, West Yorkshire, WF10 5DD

WARD, JOAN
[pen.] Joan; [b.] September 4, 1947, England; [p.] K. and E. Nunn; [m.] John Ward, June 24, 1967; [ch.] 3; [ed.] Secondary Modern; [occ.] Housewife; [pers.] For Johnny; [a.] Kings Lynn, Norfolk, PE31 7QE

WARD, PETER KENNETH
[b.] October 21, 1965, Jersey, CI; [p.] Yes Alvina Ward; [ed.] Le Squez Primary, Le Rocquier Highlands College 3 yrs.; [occ.] Painter all aspects of trade.; [hon.] Certificate from the Prince's Trust 1991. Because of published book.; [oth. writ.] Yes a book of verse published in 1991. "A Series of Words". Arthur. Stockwell Ilfrancombe Devon.; [pers.] "Well I am at best with the world when the rush of energy makes me laugh, cry, jump around. When I write, sing, compose, my material it's so uplifting. To be happy is life.

WARD, MR. SEAN
[b.] July 29, 1929, Chelsea; [p.] Mr. and Mrs. C. Ward; [ed.] St. Giles Special School in South Croydon, Cotswold College in Streatham and South London College in South Norwood; [occ.] Unable to work because of my severe disability.; [hon.] CSE grade 2 in Art City in Guilds in Gen. Edu. C.P.V.E. in media Studies.; [oth. writ.] Several poems I have wrote and I am making a collection of these. One of which I have had entered into the semi-finals of a competition. The others I do hope to have published in the near future.; [pers.] It is only recently that I realized I have the ability to write poems. I owe this to Christine Rouse, another poet who has influenced me.; [a.] Mitcham, Surrey, CR4 3EY

WARDLE, LYN
[b.] Wolverhampton; [p.] Thomas and Rose Hawkins; [m.] David; [occ.] Material Controller; [oth. writ.] Several short stories, one romantic novel (unpublished); [pers.] Like everyone, I wonder what happens to us when we die. Is that the end of us? Or do our souls go on, to be reunited with loved ones, maybe even be reborn. I like to think so. It is a subject of endless possibilities, and if reading my work makes someone take the time to consider those possibilities, it will have been worthwhile.; [a.] Willenhall, West Midlands, WV12 4BS

WARDLE, PAULINE M.
[b.] September 24, 1944, Birmingham; [m.] Mike, March 9, 1968; [ch.] Ann Peter Richard; [occ.] Housewife; [memb.] Member of Age Concern; [oth. writ.] Poem published in local magazine. Poem to be published water this year in a book called "Closet Poets" by poets now; [pers.] My poetry is based on my experiences and view of life; [a.] Newton Longville, Bucks, MK17 0HR

WARING, MARCUS
[pen.] Marcus Waring; [b.] June 1, 1974, Chichester, W. Sussex; [p.] Susan and Patrick Waring; [ed.] Westbourne House Prep School, Seaford College, South Devon College, Worcester College of H.E.; [occ.] Temporarily Working at Selfridges, London; [memb.] Bosham Sailing Club; [hon.] Diploma of H.E. in "Life and Literature in Shakespeare's England" B.A. (Huns) English studies; [oth. writ.] A collection of other poems (unpublished); [pers.] After studying Conrad's "Heart of Darkness" and forster's "A Passage to India." And "Howard's end, I am fascinated by the modernist's search for self, and plan to commence a career in writing by starting on a novel concerning a young man's psychological quest.; [a.] Fulham, London, SW6 5EB

WARREN, LESLIE
[b.] January 10, 1920, Horsham, W. Sussex; [p.] Ada and James Warren; [m.] Sylvia Warren, January 25, 1964; [ch.] Olive Warren; [ed.] Handeross School West Sussex; [occ.] Retired radio and tv engineer

WARREN, PAULINE
[pen.] Felicity Wells; [b.] May 9, 1947, Bromley, Kent; [p.] Percy Walker, Margaret Walker; [m.] Leslie Warren, September 4, 1971; [occ.] Housewife and 'Resting' typist; [oth. writ.] Poems used by two previous employers as company Christmas card insert and recruitment advertisement, plus poem published in the latter employer's internal magazine.; [pers.] I endeavour to write from the abundant wealth of experiences my sense and emotions are daily privileged to absorb, creating from all the creator creates.; [a.] Croydon, Surrey, CR2 6HT

WATKIS, MRS. ADLIN
[pen.] Shirley May; [b.] May 26, 1938, St. Ann, Jamaica; [p.] Osborne Williams and Florence Williams; [m.] 1956; [ch.] Five; [ed.] Comprehensive School St. Ann Jam.; [occ.] Catering Assistant; [memb.] Watch Tower Bible Society U.S.A.; [hon.] Diploma of Typing 1966; [oth. writ.] Several unpublished. Poems.; [pers.] I have been greatly blessed by having my attention directed to the Writings of the Poets' of Antiquities. I see in their Writings Enduring belief in a Supreme Being a Creator, Capable of undoing all the Suffering of Humanity, even their Hope of Waking up again from Sleep to a "God Reclaimed Restored Earth." This I expressed in my poems.; [a.] Ealing, London, W13 9TQ

WATSON, PAT
[b.] August 7, 1952, Burnley; [p.] Eric Barker and Florence Barker; [m.] Graham Watson; [ch.] Scott Paul; [ed.] Burnley High School for Girls, Municipal College, Bly.; [occ.] Investment Administrator; [pers.] Words are borne of feeling.; [a.] Honiton, Devon, EX14 8FY

WATSON, WENDY
[b.] March 10, 1955, Wellington, Somerset; [p.] Jack and Joyce Kittow; [m.] Kenny Watson, June 14, 1995; [ch.] Rachael; [ed.] Uffculme Secondary Modern, East Devon College, Tuerton; [occ.] Civil Servant/housewife; [oth. writ.] Other poems written over the last 20 years.; [pers.] Same beliefs as those in the verse 'Desiderate'; [a.] Postbridge, Devon, PL20 6SZ

WATTS, MICHAEL ALAN
[pen.] Mike Watts; [b.] December 12, 1937, Marton-in-Cleveland; [p.] Lt. Col. Alan Watts, Marian Watts; [m.] Philippa Watts, September 15, 1962; [ch.] 2 and one Grandchild; [ed.] Denstone College, Uttoxela Staffs; [occ.] Chartered Accountant and Composer; [memb.] Institute of Chartered Accountant, Chartered Institute of Toxelion, Licentiate Trinity College of Music London, Associate Member British Guild of Composers, Society to Promotion of New Music, Astrological Society.; [hon.] Only qualifications and a Number of Music Competition first prizes.; [oth. writ.] "Five Crystals" (includes this entry, no. 2) "Mike Doodlebug" (poems and short stories) from the ridiculous to paranormal), "Black Ether" (Horror), Sketches for the Ansaphone, "The Isle of the Dead" (after Arnold Bocklin and Rahmeninor). My time encounter with the late Sir Arnold Bax (Composer).; [pers.] I am not interested in fiction. My subject is reaching into the mind, searching the crystal, seeking truth and answers through prayer, the paranormal. And as a contrast, happy madness and the ridiculous (lead "My New Song").; [a.] Bourneyouth, Dorset, BM1 1JA

WAUDBY, GILBERT H.
[b.] August 20, 1917, Louth; [p.] Samual Waudby, Ethel Waudby; [m.] Megan Waudby, September 21, 1939; [ch.] Richard Colin; [ed.] Bottesford C. E. School; [occ.] Retired Factory Worker; [oth. writ.] Poems published in the Grantham citizen, 1 poem published in Eastern England Poets, 1 poem published in Poetic Places, 1 poem published in Poet's Favourites, published own book titled Sunshine and Showers, one hundred and one poems and a few limericks; [a.] Bottesford, Nottingham, NG13 0BT

WEATHERS, CECILIA
[b.] October 18, 1952, Scotland; [p.] Mary and Bernard Sarson; [m.] Timothy Weathers, September 7, 1974; [ch.] Matthew, Lisa, Fiona, Kristian and Gemma; [ed.] Hugh Faringdon Reading. Reading Technical College, Swansea Institute; [occ.] Student Art and Design; [oth. writ.] I have written poetry since I was ten. This is the first time I've entered a poetry competition and it has encouraged me to write a book of my own poetry.; [pers.] To me poetry is an emotional response to something I've seen or felt, it seems to be the best way of expressing my feelings.; [a.] Swansea, W. Glamorgan, SA1 4JN

WEBSTER, ALFRED BELT
[b.] August 29, 1925, Cheadle Hulme, Cheshire; [p.] George Webster, Sarah Webster; [m.] Jean Mary Webster, June 6, 1953; [ch.] Karen Janet; [ed.] Woods Lane Sec. Mod., Cheadle Hulme Cheshire; [occ.] Ex. Motorcycle Speedway Rider and Sportsman now East Hill Garage St. Austell Cornwall Employee; [pers.] Trying for a better world through poetry; [a.] St. Austell, Cornwall, PL25 4DP

WEITMAN, MAUREEN MAY
[b.] May 17, 1937, Southgate; [p.] George Greenwell, May Greenwell; [m.] Cyril Weitman, July 4, 1979; [ch.] Peter George; [ed.] Southgate County Grammer Bloomsbury Photographic College; [occ.] Free Lance Artist, Free Lance Photographic Restorer; [hon.] R.A.D.A Vere Speaking; [oth. writ.] Poem published in local book, article in the book. "Happy and Glorious".; [pers.] The tranquility of the English countryside promotes serene thoughts, inspiring conception for my writing.; [a.] Cheshunt, Hertfordshire, EN7 6QX

WELLAND, CHRISTINE
[pen.] Christine Oldacre; [b.] February 25, 1941, Guildford; [p.] William and Renee Biddle; [m.] Colin Welland, July 9, 1982 (2nd Marriage); [ch.] Simon (30), Carol (28); [ed.] Farnham Girls' Grammar 1952-1957; [occ.] Bookkeeper/Secretary; [memb.] Institute of Advanced Motorists, Elstead Afternoon Womens Institute; [oth. writ.] "Fur Appeal" as yet unpublished. A book about the cats who have accompanied me through life.; [pers.] Cats are my inspiration. Treat a cat as kindly as you would wish to be treated and the rewards will enrich your life tenfold.; [a.] Elstead, Godalming, Surrey, GU8 6DW

WELLER, AMELIA
[b.] January 2, 1980, Rochford; [p.] Nigel Weller, Barbara Weller; [ed.] Crowstone Preparatory School, Westcliff High School for Girls; [occ.] Student; [memb.] Focus Youth Theatre, Pamela Freedman School of Dance; [hon.] Bronze Medal L.A.M. verse and prose; [a.] Southend, Essex:, SS0 8NN

WELLS
[pen.] Isabel Christine; [b.] July 7, 1939, Willsden; [p.] James and Elizabeth Briggs; [ch.] Nicole, Lorraine; [ed.] Secondary Modern, Amble., Northumberland; [occ.] SNR Residential Social Worker; [oth. writ.] Just for pleasure; [pers.] Turning my own thoughts into poetry gives me great satisfaction, an insite, a reflection of the joys, the sadness within the world, within myself.; [a.] Abingdon, Oxon, OX14 5QE

WEST, HARRY
[b.] July 31, 1940, Scunthorpe; [p.] John West, Glady's Hilda West; [m.] Ann Marie West (2nd wife), July 25, 1973; [ch.] Tracy Anne, David Anthony, Richard James; [ed.] Duke of York's Royal Military School (Dover), University of Central England, Wolverhampton Technical Teachers' College; [occ.] Senior Lecturer Engineering, Science and Mathematics; [hon.] Bachelor of Science (Eng.) Certificate of Education; [oth. writ.] Four poems accepted for publication.; [pers.] My writing is at its stage. In one lifetime I will not achieve perfection but I will die trying!; [a.] Alverchurch, Worcs, B48 7PB

WESTLEY, FREDERICK WILLIAM
[b.] March 26, 1909, Enfield; [p.] Mr. and Mrs. J. Westley; [m.] Daisy, when 23 years of age; [ch.] Two sons, one daughter; [ed.] At four years of age, began at St. James Infant School, at Eleven having passed exam, finished education at George Spicer School, Enfield at 15 yrs. old; [occ.] Retired Blacksmith and Fitter; [oth. writ.] At the age of 70, decided to write my own quotations regarding the aspects of life as I see it. A philosophy or analysis you may call it. A book with over 500 phrases (Book has not been published) cynical, realistic humorous. Also several poems.; [pers.] I find that the creative spirit is a sedative to the restless mind, and no expedition into the world of knowledge has resulted in failure, when looking in the mirror of life, how easy to ignore the flaws in one's image; [a.] Middx, N21 2EA

WESTWOOD, PATRICIA
[pen.] Patricia Westwood; [b.] January 24, 1947, West Bromwich; [p.] Albet William Bradbury and Clara Jane Bradbury; [m.] Gerald Westwood, September 23, 1967; [ch.] 1 child, boy named Gerald age 10; [ed.] Hill Top, Girls School Sec. Modern. Also in Art Rylands Memorial School of Art; [occ.] Housewife; [hon.] First in class, at Hill Top School, position at Rylands School of Art and 7 out of 7 CSE's in English Lang, English Lit, Art, Arithmetic, Commerce, Typewriting, Religious Education; [oth. writ.] I have been writing poetry since I was a very young child.; [pers.] Poetry is so peacefully, it is nature.; [a.] Tipton, West Midlands, DY4 7RP

WHARRY, NORMAN
[b.] February 19, 1923, Nr Holsworthy; [p.] Dr. Robert Wharry and Margaret Harriot; [ed.] St. Petroc (Bude) Newton College; [occ.] Retired; [memb.] R.B. Legion, Newton Abbot Twinning Asc., Local Organizations, National Trust; [hon.] Two war medals and Burma star; [oth. writ.] Several poems published in anthologies, etc. Approx. 100 more waiting publication. Several short stories (under construction); [pers.] 5 years army war service, radiographer, teacher, interests, theatre (all angles) and a lot more, eg. people, travel, humour, "service to others"; [a.] Chudleigh, Devon, TQ13 0JT

WHITE, ALAN DAVID
[b.] August 22, 1966, Crawley; [p.] David White, Veronica White; [m.] Divorced; [ch.] Ashley David; [ed.] I Field Comprehensive; [occ.] Production Operative Team Leader; [oth. writ.] None Published; [a.] Crawley, W. Sussex, RH11 8LG

WHITE, JOHN
[b.] December 5, 1942, Sutton, Surrey; [p.] Both Deceased; [m.] Pauline, March 3, 1962; [ch.] Andrew 33 yrs., Tracy 32, Jonathan 24 yrs.; [ed.] Very Little Secondary Modern due to much time spent in Hospital as a child; [occ.] Education Welfare Officer (Enfield, Middlesex); [oth. writ.] 1 other published, "The Lord and I", Open Door (Pub. Triumph House) plus many others on varying subjects; [pers.] The response received from those who have read my poems has given me great joy. We all, I'm sure have some talent which I feel is our duty to share. Some, more gifted than I, have been "touched", the tragedy of our age is that so many are not touched, be it by things around us on the talents of others.; [a.] Enfield, Middlesex, EN1 4HB

WIGGINS, TRACEY
[b.] August 25, 1961, Liverpool; [p.] Iris and John Ennis; [m.] Richard Wiggins, December 19, 1987; [ch.] Terri, Richard and Tyler; [ed.] Forest of Needwood High and College, Certificate and 8 points diploma in Information Technology; [occ.] House wife; [oth. writ.] Publication in poetry now, Midlands 1996, Regional Anthologies; [pers.] Enjoy, reading, writing and Supporting Blind Club in North Warwickshire.; [a.] Burton-on-Trent, Staffs, DE13 9EN

WILDE, JON
[b.] November 8, 1953, Kidderminster; [p.] Peter Wilde (BBC Actor), Gwendoline (Nee Smith); [m.] Divorced; [ch.] Peter Anthony Wilde, Simon James Wilde, Kelly Wilde (Daughter-in-law); [ed.] Brighton, Hove and Sussex Grammar, Wallasey Grammar, Norwich City College, University of East Anglia; [occ.] Self employed in horticulture; [oth. writ.] Several poems for a possible future published collection. In the process of writing and researching for a book on North American Indian Creation Mythology.; [pers.] I strive to portray a transition to a higher level of spiritual consciousness within my poetry. I have also been influenced by the romantic poets and by the writings of Ben Okri.; [a.] Norwich, Norfolk, NR3 1NE

WILKINSON, ELIZABETH ANN
[b.] February 22, 1935, Runcorn Cheshire; [p.] Mr. and Mrs. H. W. Chimes; [m.] John Wilkinson, Died December 1989, March 9, 1956; [ch.] Three sons and two daughters; [ed.] All St Parish Church Girls School Runcorn.; [occ.] Now Retired; [hon.] Swimming awards when joung Red Cross. Gained my state Enrolled Nurse Certificate 1955 at Dulton Hospital Dulton Cheshire worked at St Helens Hospital Chester City Crossley hospital Dulton Recovery Hospital last Halton General Hospital; [oth. writ.] Several poems published in my maiden name chimes. Poems in Poetry now and arrival press. Poem in your book passage of time, waiting for this book.; [pers.] I'm a widow with 5 children and 5 grandchildren. Now retired after 42 yrs in the N. H. Service last past was night nurse on a busy surgical ward at Halton General Hospital Runcorn. I enjoy writing poems and reading love people; [a.] Runcorn, Ches, WA7 2DE

WILLIAMS, BRIAN
[pen.] B. K. Williams; [b.] September 17, 1937, London; [p.] Maude Williams, Sydney Williams; [m.] Wanda Morey, January 1, 1994; [ch.] Rebecca, Shannon; [ed.] Dormers Wells, Southall Middlesex Trinity College of Music London; [occ.] Human Resources Manager; [memb.] Institute of Personnel Development; [oth. writ.] Poems published in anthologies - magazines.; [pers.] I have been influenced by my experiences of life and strive to reflect them in my writing.; [a.] Pencoed, Mid-Glamorgan, CF35 6UT

WILLIAMS, CAROLE MAUREEN
[b.] October 5, 1943, Luton, Bedfordshire; [p.] Albert Edwards and Kathleen Edwards; [m.] Henry John, Williams, August 9, 1969; [ch.] Clifford John, Anna-Jone, Andrew Roy; [ed.] Harlington Comprehensive School and Challney Girls School; [occ.] Housewife, mother, dog walker, helping with elderly Lady's Sunday School Teacher.; [memb.] Church Fellowship group, Academy of Children's Writers, Cambridge, Silsoe Writers Group; [oth. writ.] Articles for Silsoe Village monthly magazine, poems published in local magazine, children's story's short story's in village magazine.; [pers.] I like my story and poems is to be humorous but with a moral to them and to leave the reader feeling happy and uplifted.; [a.] Silsoe, Bedfordshire, MK45 4DU

WILLIAMS, DIANA
[pen.] Harriett Turner; [b.] September 17, 1945, Newport, Gwent; [p.] Harry Balchin, Alice Balchin; [m.] Divorced; [ch.] Kevin Michael, Mark Clifton, Sandra; [ed.] Secondary Modern (St Andrews); [occ.] Disabled due to Arthritis; [hon.] One poem previously published in 'First Time' magazine; [oth. writ.] Story published in magazine; [pers.] I write to prove that the body may be disabled - but the brain is not; [a.] Eyemouth, Berwickshire, TD14 5DL

WILLIAMS, IRIS
[pen.] Iris Williams; [b.] April 2, 1932, Seaham; [p.] Joseph and Elizabeth Ritchie; [m.] Divorced; [ch.] Bany H. Robson (Lecturer); [ed.] Campdon Square Modern Secondary left at 14 yrs. always interested in art writing sculpture.; [occ.] The Art Studio, Voluntary working people with problems (Mental Health); [hon.] Many 1st in Art Barclays Vaux Sunderland Echo, Work Exhibited Sunderland, Middlesbrough Newcastle Burmingham Poland London, etc.; [oth.

writ.] Greed, currently published by you. Many letters, articles, etc. City Challenge North, The Big Picture Preparation East - End Carnival currently book exhibition.; [pers.] As an elusive asthmatic to live my life without self pity my art depicts sculptures from World Mythology.; [a.] Sunderland City, SR3 2HH

WILLIAMS, JAMIE NICHOLAS
[b.] May 26, 1976, Bradford, W. Yorkshire; [p.] Richard Williams, Mary Williams; [ed.] Dunbar Grammar School, East Lothian; [occ.] Since Leaving School in '93, I've been almost constantly unemployed; [memb.] Greenpeace; [pers.] I have found life can be exceptionally cruel and relentlessly unforgiving, while the world is destroyed around us each of us must remember improvements are only made and limited by our own actions and attitudes.; [a.] Edinburgh, Midlothian, EH4 2NW

WILLIAMS, JUNE MARCIA
[b.] June 12, 1958, Jamaica, W.I.; [p.] Mr. and Mrs. F. Townsend; [ch.] Jeanette and Lorraine; [ed.] Walford High School and Hammersmith and West London College; [occ.] Housewife (normally Admin. Assistant); [oth. writ.] Won first prize in local poetry competition in 1992; [pers.] Writing poetry is my way of expressing my deep innermost feelings. "The Curtain Closes" was read by myself at my fathers funeral in January 1995.; [a.] London, W3

WILLIAMS, LILIAN MAY
[pen.] Lilian May; [b.] January 30, 1913, St. Pancras, London; [p.] Deceased; [m.] December 26, 1938; [ch.] Three - Evelyn, David, Keith; [ed.] Comprehensive; [occ.] Retired; [hon.] One letter printed in Hertfordshire magazine; [oth. writ.] An biography of my early life (Girl From The Buildings), book of poems, never sent in small items in newspapers, and magazines.

WILLIAMS, MAIR ELUNED LYNE
[pen.] Elin Cairiag or Lynne Waterloo; [b.] May 11, 1921, Clawddnewydd Nr Ruthin; [p.] William David Roberts (Deceased) Mary Margaret Roberts; [m.] Ellis Williams (Deceased), August 18, 1969; [ch.] 2 nice step children and grandchildren; [ed.] Primary, County School, Grammar School Courses, etc.; [occ.] Retired esc-nurse, dental nurse and sec-register B. Mare: and Deaths; [memb.] Women's Institute, Mother's Union, Camera Club, Choral Society, Esp: Soc. London Welsh Ass. Theatre Arduduy, etc; [hon.] R.D.S.A. not a competitive type, usually; [oth. writ.] Articles, poems, 1 small book (Biography of a singer). Also, many, many things, begun, never finished - too many other interests at the time. (Lead a quiet life now adays.; [pers.] I believe in the Christian way of life - in honesty, compassion, pity, disliking foul language, I I'm somewhat old - fashioned but not old hat!); [a.] Penrhyndeudraeth, Gwynedd, LL48 6AH

WILLIAMS, MARGARET MARY
[pen.] M. Mary Williams; [b.] February 22, 1931, Scarisbrick; [p.] John and Edith Mary Bowerbank; [m.] Henley Ronald Williams, April 3, 1968; [ch.] Rachel Margaret, Deborah Ann, Jonathan Henley; [ed.] Ormskirk Grammar, Oakworth College; [occ.] Church Vestment Embroiderer; [hon.] Editor's Choice Award The Poetry Guild; [oth. writ.] Several poems published in anthologies and local press plus short stories in National Magazines.; [a.] Scarisbrick, Lancashire, L40 9RS

WILLIAMS, MR. PETER R.
[b.] October 30, 1953, Wales; [pers.] This poem is not intended to promote casual sex, or to lower moral standards, it is about two people genuinely in love.; [a.] Resolven, Neath, W. Glam

WILLIAMS, NICOLA ELIZABETH
[pen.] Nic; [b.] April 13, 1966, Bridgend; [p.] Nicholl and Jean Williams; [m.] Peter Williams, May 28, 1983; [ch.] Peter, Kirsty, Michael, Cory, Tyrone; [ed.] Queens Elizabeth Cambria Grammar School, Johnstown, Carmarthen, Dyfed; [occ.] Housewife and mother; [oth. writ.] Personal poetry relating to family members and personal events.; [pers.] I try to reflect my own personal feelings. "The ever open door" is dedicated to my late father in law" Robin who suffered with his health after working in the Welsch Coalmines for many years.; [a.] Llanelli, Dyfed, SA14 6LA

WILLIAMS, SHEILA MARY
[pen.] Sheila Mary Williams; [b.] June 11, 1935, Holyhead; [p.] Henry Lynch and Gwladys Lynch; [m.] Douglas Williams, November 2, 1957; [ch.] Sandra, Denise, Tracy, Gary, (Grandchildren) Mikayla and Charlie; [ed.] Holyhead County Secondary School; [occ.] Partner with Husband in Ice Cream Retail Business (Mobile); [hon.] 8 O - Locals, N.N.E.B. Certificate; [oth. writ.] To amuse family - none printed.; [pers.] Prefer to write humorous poetry and amusing and one formative poems for children.; [a.] Holyhead, Gwynedd, LL65 1DT

WILLIAMS, SUE
[b.] January 21, 1949, Cinderford; [p.] Raymond Mills, Muriel Mills; [m.] Michael Williams, December 19, 1970; [ch.] Jason Francis, Michelle S. Elizabeth; [ed.] Ryardean Woodside Primary. Abenhall Secondary Modern. Royal Forest of Dean College R.F.D.C.; [occ.] Housewife/Career; [oth. writ.] Review the citizen circles in the sand. - Anchor Books West Country Voices. - Anchor Books Lighting the Way - Triumph House Within Us All - Triumph House Feels Like Heaven - Triumph House; [pers.] 'Go for it' anyway, that's what my friends say.; [a.] Royal Forest of Dean, Glos, GL17 9DH

WILLIAMS, SUE
[b.] January 21, 1949, Cinderford; [p.] Raymond Mills and Muriel Mills; [m.] Michael Williams, December 19, 1970; [ch.] Jason Francis and Michelle S. Elizabeth; [ed.] Ryardean Woodside Primary, Abenhall Secondary Modern, Royal Forest of Dean College, R.F.D.C.; [occ.] Housewife/carer; [oth. writ.] Review/The Citizen Circles in the Sand - Anchor Books, West Country Voices - Anchor Books, Lighting the Way - Triumph House, Within Us All - Triumph House, Feels Like Heaven - Triumph House; [pers.] 'Go for it' anyway, that's what my friends say.; [a.] Royal Forest of Dean, Glos, GL17 9DH

WILLIAMSON, ROSEMARY
[b.] Belfast; [p.] Robert Dowling and Lettie Dowling; [m.] Rev. Samuel Edward Williamson, May 31, 1990; [ch.] 4 step children - 9 step grandchildren; [ed.] Bloomfield Collegiate School, Belfast (Girls Voluntary Grammar School), Extern: Trinity College, London; [occ.] Retired - formerly Educational Administrator and P/T drama teacher; [memb.] Belfast Unesco Club (Cofounder), Art Clubs - Monday Club Belfast, Bloomfield Art Club, Amateur Artist - water colours, exhibit periodically and sell work; [hon.] ATCL speech and drama (teacher), L.T.C.L. speech and drama (teacher) also Commonwealth Fellowship 1987, (Toured India - presented to Queen Etc.); [oth. writ.] 1. Worked for girls clubs movement and wrote plays and poems for the children, 2. Poetry - for journal of pres. church in Ireland, 3. Poetry and stretches for concerts, 4. History pageant for local church, 4. Articles for Teachers Union Journal, 5. Roving reporter for Civil Service Journal in earlier years; [pers.] Plant the seeds of love at every opportunity (the Beatles said "All you need is love" and testament said "Whosoever loveth fulfilleth the law"); [a.] Belfast, Down, N. Ireland, BT5 6NQ

WILLIS, PAUL
[b.] October 26, 1966, Eastleigh; [p.] Peter Willis, Rosemary Willis; [ed.] Romsey Secondary, Eastleigh College; [occ.] Warehouse Manager; [memb.] West Grimstead Badminton Club; [hon.] English Literature; [pers.] I enjoy the imagery and feelings poems can create, so my hope is for you to see all I have seen and feel all I have felt.; [a.] Totton, Hants, SO40 8FH

WILLS, FREDERICK
[b.] January 9, 1920, Dublin; [p.] Mr. and Mrs. Wills; [m.] Heather Wills, December 3, 1988; [ch.] One; [ed.] Ilford College, South East Essex College of Technology; [occ.] Retired Civil Engineer; [memb.] Active member of the Hertford Dramatic and Operatic Society, R.A.F. Seven Squadron Association, The Stirling Aircraft Association, East Herts Golf Club; [hon.] King George VI awarded me with the R.A.F. Distinguished Flying Medal in 1943 at Buckingham Palace; [oth. writ.] Prepared and Lectured on R.A.F. Bomber Command during the Last World War II. Writings of a Musical of the Life and Style from the beginning of the last century to the present day in the Hawaiian Islands.; [pers.] I have always been interested in writings of modern Poems, Drama, and more so Musicals, that are authentic.; [a.] Hoddesdon, Herts, EN11 0BH

WILLSHIRE, JAMES
[pen.] J.P. MacMurphy; [b.] August 17, 1963, Paulersbury; [p.] Margaret, Ronald; [ed.] Kingsbrook Comprehensive, Deanshanger, Milton Keynes; [occ.] Civil Engineer; [memb.] Pury Rangers F.C.; [oth. writ.] Many poems several short stories (none published).; [pers.] A wish to live out a hedonistic existence, at a very slow pace.; [a.] Towcester, Northants, NN12 8JP

WILSON, ANTHONY CHARLES
[pen.] T.C.; [b.] July 14, 1956, Suffolk; [ed.] Basic; [occ.] Beef Quality Controller; [oth. writ.] Travelling Love is a book of Poems telling of our 7,000 miles and 7 months tour of Europe in a Camping Car built for two after falling madly in love with life and each other, There are 84 Poems that are Inspired by and Totally Dedicated to my one and only D.D. Also helping D.D. to edit a story of her own writing.; [pers.] My D.D, Inspired me to be happy!!! To be happy is to be Loved, To be Loved is to be Alive, To be Alive is to be Happy to be Loved; [a.] Skegness, Lincs, PE25 1QR

WILSON, ARCHIE
[b.] May 23, 1947, Lowestoft; [p.] Archie And Rosina Wilson; [m.] Irene Wilson; [ch.] Darren, Jenny Wilson; [ed.] Kirkley RD Comprehensive Lowestoft, Ipswich Civic College; [occ.] Logistics Manager; [memb.] Director Eqous Theater Company, Member Widmer End Players; [oth. writ.] Stories in writings magazines poetry in local newspaper. Theatre critic for local paper.; [pers.] I write to entertain from personal experience and to demonstrate the beauty of the English Language.; [a.] High Wycombe, Burks, HP15 6BU

WILSON, DINO
[pen.] Dino Wilson; [b.] October 18, 1948, Sunderland; [p.] Thomas Wilson, Gladys Wilson; [m.] (Ex-wife) Christine/Anne, Divorced April 27, 1996; [ch.] Andrew, Deborah, Steven; [ed.] Bede Grammar (Sunderland); [occ.] Company Director; [oth. writ.] "Drug Run" look novel; [pers.] I have been to hell and back more times in life than most people, but enjoy what I have and live with an open mind; [a.] Dunston, Gateshead, U, NE11 9BN

WILSON, MICHELLE
[b.] October 11, 1973, Bradford; [p.] June Wilson and Richard Wilson; [m.] Will Marry, Adam Lee Wood, July 27, 1996; [ed.] Bingley Grammar School; [occ.] Order Entry Clerk, Grattan, Bradford; [memb.] I am a fully qualified Hairdresser (N.V.Q.); [oth. writ.] Many poems and short stories, also 2 novels. None ever submitted for publishing.; [pers.] Never read a book by its cover nor the contents - always read between the lines.; [a.] Bradford, W. Yorks, BD13 5DQ

WINDRIDGE, VIOLET ROSINA
[pen.] Rosina Ward; [b.] February 1, 1925, London; [p.] Ethel and Thomas Perry; [ch.] David, Linda, Jane; [ed.] West Ham High School for Girls, Stratford, London; [occ.] Retired; [oth. writ.] Many short poems and children's stories, none published as yet.; [pers.] I try always to put my feelings into my writing and give thanks for whatever the subject is about ie., End of War, beautiful things, Love and children.; [a.] Croydon, Surrey, CR0 7NF

WINN, MR. NICHOLAS
[pen.] Nick; [b.] December 10, 1949, Bristol; [p.] Mrs. Joyce Winn; [m.] Partner Sheila; [ch.] Mahtola (Sheila son, not mine); [ed.] Secondary Education in Bristol; [occ.] Nurse; [oth. writ.] I have had a few poems published in various anthologies, and local magazines. I possess a lot of material.; [pers.] I try to do something positive every day. (Getting 'gentle' published stemmed from this!); [a.] Midsomer, Norton, Somerset, BA3 2JZ

WINTERS, MARLENE
[b.] September 30, 1943, Portsmouth; [p.] Barnardos Child; [m.] Divorced; [ch.] Teresa Norton and Daniel Clare; [ed.] Parkside Annexe Secondary Modern, London S. W. 4.; [occ.] Voluntary Public Relations Consultant and Fundraiser for Newhammind; [memb.] A.M.I.S.M., Member of Institute for Supervision and Management; [hon.] N.E.B.S.M. National Education Board for Supervision and Management; [oth. writ.] Short stories I have never tried to get them published.; [pers.] Poetry is a statement of expression, I strive to find warmth and humour in mankinds. My poems often reflect another side of "The Simple Things We Do in Our Lives". I admire the artistic works of Victoria Wood.

WITHERINGTON, AVERIL
[b.] October 17, 1944, Northampton.; [p.] Violet and Frederick Hunter; [m.] Frederick Witherington; [ch.] Raymond, Stephen and Raclel, all grown up. I also have four grandchildren, from my son's; [ed.] General Secondary in London; [occ.] Medical Co-Ordinator for outpatients clinic's at King's College Hospital, London; [pers.] I have never entered a poetry contest before. I write for my own enjoyment, about the life around us.; [a.] Crofton Park, SE4 1RH

WOOD, LAWRENCE
[pen.] John Parr Brisbane Australia; [b.] April 15, 1948, Leeds; [p.] Marjorie Tomlin, Lawrence Wood; [m.] Divorced, 1973; [ch.] Two 1 boy, 1 girl; [ed.] Secondary Modem; [occ.] Pneumatics Hydraulic Sales; [oth. writ.] Poems; [pers.] There is too much, stress in the world, too much rush, too much anger, but there is also peace and love all around. In the natural world of nature, lays truth and reality, and calm. Be patient!!!; [a.] Leeds, Yorkshire, LS14 5PA

WOOD, MRS. KITTY CLARA
[pen.] Kate Johns; [b.] December 7, 1932, Newington, Kent; [p.] Edward and Evelyn Cox (Now Deceased); [m.] Albert Wood, March 3, 1962; [ch.] Daniel Anthony Wood (now married); [ed.] I was educated at several schools as my parents moved around. They worked on farms. My last school was Snodland Secondary. Now Hormsdale; [occ.] Just housewife; [oth. writ.] I have written several poems. Far too many to list here. Ranging from a few lines to fourteen verses. Have to write when I get the inspiration.; [pers.] I am now sixty-three years old. Wrote my first poem looking out over my first poem looking out over the South Downs in Hampshire. I am the eldest of a family of eight children. Four in Australia the other in England. Married to Albert Wood.; [a.] Aylesford, Maidstone, Kent, ME20 6RG

WOOD, RICHARD
[pen.] "Lena Ricardo", "Tex", "Madera"; [b.] August 3, 1914, Lisbon, Portugal; [p.] Anglo-Scottish (Clan MacDonald); [m.] Jennie Wood, January 27, 1939; [ch.] Son/daughter/3 grandsons; [ed.] Burnley Grammar School, Chester College, London University (External), Royal Naval College Greenwich; [occ.] Author/Artist (Retired Headmaster/Lecturer (Spanish); [memb.] Ark Royal (3) Survivors Assoc., Freemasonry International lapsed Baptist now Unitarian, Patron of various charities; [hon.] Double Victor Ludoreem (School), 3 College Colours (Soccer Raising Athletics) war medals. Honorary memberships of several organizations; [oth. writ.] "Abandon Ship" 1985, "Falcons Fear No Frontier" 1995 novels. "Village Tapestry" (Local History) hymns. Several local histories. Poetry-press articles. Brochures. Translations from Spanish poetry and lectures (e.g. Garcia Lorea etc). 2 novels ready for print.; [pers.] Baiting bumbling bureaucrats and M.P.'s past and present; [a.] Burnley, Lancashire, BB12 9AA

WOOD, RON
[b.] July 30, 1950, Christchurch; [p.] Stan Wood, Mary Wood; [m.] Marcia Randall, June 19, 1971; [ch.] Zarra Victoria and Karn Robert; [ed.] Somerford Secondary Modern Christchurch; [occ.] Working owner of local hair salons.; [memb.] Captain of local pool team, former chairman of Andover Youth Football Club, former committee member of Andover Sunday Football League.; [hon.] Several football and pool trophies.; [oth. writ.] More than a dozen poems published in paper back books by various publishers.; [pers.] I try to make my poetry easily readable but full of everyday happening and occasions to which most people can relate.; [a.] Andover, Hampshire, SP10 3PE

WOOD, SAMANTHA JANE
[b.] January 29, 1973, Hertforshire; [p.] Dorothy Grange, Albert Wood; [pers.] I wish to honour all of the people who have touched my life in every way. I hope through my writing that I touch theirs.; [a.] Hemel Hempstead, Herts, HP2 6EU

WREN, CAREY
[pen.] Carey Wren; [b.] April 10, 1971, Detroit, USA; [p.] Lesley Ann, Anthony James Good; [m.] Piers, July 27, 1991; [ch.] Jack; [ed.] Royal Latin Grammar, Oxford College of F.E.; [occ.] Branch Manager Travel Agency; [memb.] Leighton Buzzard Fencing Club; [oth. writ.] Many but still seeking publication including childrens poetry; [pers.] S**t happens; [a.] Newport Pagnell, MK16 0EA

WRIGHT, SYLVIA
[pen.] Clinton-Neels; [b.] August 11, 1933, Littleham, Exmouth; [p.] Doris Clark, Harold Clinton-Neels; [m.] Bevan Winston Wright, November 24, 1973; [ch.] One son - Kingsley Bevan Wright; [ed.] Cofe St. James Secondary Modern. I am self taught Dyslexic I could not read or write when I left school, "very backward". I put myself in service a manor house to earn money in my evenings and days off I taught myself.; [occ.] Retired but no pension. I am a Littlewoodspools collector spare time.; [memb.] I do not have any memberships I do not belong to any clubs. "Would like to".; [hon.] I wish I did have who knows I might achieve one through poetry. "I am a poet from nowhere" if you new my life history, you would understand the comment it is a great honour for me alone that you even, read my poem let alone like it. I have been writing poems for years I have always been nothing, a nobody.; [oth. writ.] One book and 1/2 of poems and verse unpublished, unread, my own thoughts all my own work. I am now writing my life story.; [pers.] I do portrait painting in oils picture collage. Stenciling doll making rag and plaster cast. But a lass I taught myself. I am a romantic by nature I love people I see the good in others, I don't dwell to much on card (I make my own) or others. Poetry in case their thoughts impede my thoughts and brain.; [a.] Rugeley, Staffs, WS15 1JJ

YARD, JOHN BRIAN
[b.] September 22, 1984, Lambeth; [p.] Carol and Barrie Yard; [ed.] Townsend Primary; [occ.] School

YARDLEY, MICHELLE LOUISE
[b.] June 24, 1981, Douglas; [p.] Charles and Monica; [ed.] Douglas Primary, Lanark Grammar; [occ.] Still attending School; [hon.] Winner of school competitions for poetry.; [oth. writ.] I have written many more poems. But this is the first comp. out with school that I have entered.; [pers.] I write my poems to express the way I am feelings at the time of writing.; [a.] Lanark, South L/Shire, ML11 8QY

YARWOOD, MICHAEL
[b.] December 8, 1948, Liverpool; [p.] Betty Yarwood; [m.] Jean Yardwood; [ch.] Peter James Yardwood; [occ.] Short story writer; [memb.] South West Circle of short story writers; [oth. writ.] Numerous short stories in books and collections. Poetry included in anthologies; [pers.] The Season's Change, The People Change, The World - Never.; [a.] Plymouth, Devon, PL6 6AR

YOUNG, JOANNE
[b.] December 1, 1976, Berkshire; [p.] David Young and Carol Young; [ed.] Maiden Erlegh School, University of East Anglia; [occ.] Student of history and law; [oth. writ.] Several poems written when at school; [pers.] I see poetry as a means of expressing personal thoughts, feelings and emotions. As I am 19, I look forward to the future which I hope will provide such inspiration for my poetry.; [a.] Reading, Berkshire, RG1 5PP

ZARSADIAS, PRIZZI
[b.] February 10, 1985, London; [p.] Rafael and Phoebe; [ed.] A junior at St. Mary's Roman Catholic School, London; [occ.] Student; [memb.] Wants to be a Brownie or a girl scout.; [hon.] 1. Ballet Primary - Honours Royal Academy of Dancing 2. Tap Primary - Highly Commended Imperial Society of Teachers of Dancing 3. Grade 2 Piano - Associated Board; [oth. writ.] Several poems and short stories with excellent remarks and high grades; [pers.] Great minds think alike. Kudos to my parents and teachers.; [a.] East Acton, London, W3 7NQ

Index of Poets

A

Abram, Aubrey 85
Abson, C. 336
Acheson-Crow, Charles 17
Achilleos, Elias 252
Acock, T. P. 381
Acres, Marian 266
Adam, Florence 242
Adams, Faye 37
Adams, Jim 351
Adams, Lorraine 291
Adams, M. W. 313
Adams, Mary-Ann 410
Adams, Steven 151
Adamson, Corraine 258
Addiman, David Geoffrey 190
Adeyemi, Sammy A. 45
Adeyemi, Yinka 324
Adkins, Karen Ann 420
Ainsworth, A. Colam 236
Ainsworth, Marjorie M. 315
Aiton, Susan 148
Akpokomua, Clara 188
Akridge, Paul 283
Alcock, Raymond 122
Alder, Frances 366
Aldridge, Amanda 367
Aldridge, Ian 258
Aldridge, Jean 26
Aldridge, Marie 276
Alexander, Joanne 213
Alexander-King, Jan 247
Ali, Sansel 236
Ali, Stephen 264
Alison, Claire 78
Allan, John F. 189
Allan, Kenneth M. 123
Allan, R. H. 300
Allan, Shirley Jane 397
Allcock, Wendy Ann 393
Allen, J. 291
Allen, Jennifer 350
Allen, John 31
Allen, Patricia 381
Allen, Stuart 401
Allen, Zoe-Michelle 222
Allison, Julie 368
Allison, Kerry 149
Alltoft, Richard 110
Allum, Kay 181
Allum, Vicki 135
Almond, Barbara 259
Almond, David 15
Almond, Noreen 175
Alston, Fred 22
Ambridge, A. 328
Ambury, Thea S. E. 155
Amy 150
Andersen, Mary 282
Anderson, Catherine S. 77
Anderson, D. 395
Anderson, David 426
Anderson, Glenda Mary 213
Anderson, Ian 354
Anderson, John 354
Anderson, Lucy 121
Anderson, Ruth 143
Andrew, Cecil 104
Andrews, Ena 84
Andrews, Joan 366
Andrews, Richard 220
Angell, Sara 393
Angus, Anne 258
Angus, Minette 405
Annis, Lorna 178
Anthony, Peter Charles 402
Appleby, H. J. 119
Arbon, M. M. 402
Archbold, Kevin 404
Archer, Linda 117
Archer, Melita 169
Archibald, James 358
Arditi, Oliver 65
Armbruster, Becky 8
Armstrong, David 79
Armstrong, Esther J. 3
Armstrong, Michelle 164
Armstrong, Scott 240
Armstrong-Braun, Klaus 422
Arnott, B. J. 388
Arnott, Maria 265
Ash, Pauline 416
Ashman, Sheila 299
Ashmore, K. 271
Ashok, Kumar 381
Ashton, Brendan 425
Ashwood, Keith 392
Ashworth, Jean 351
Askew, Lillian 391
Askey, Glyn D. 143
Askey, V. 423
Astley, Lynn M. 230
Aston, Arthur 20
Aston, Vivian 221
Atherley, Rosemary 42
Atherton, Ivy 362
Atkin, Angela 378
Atkins, Gaynor 9
Atkinson, Heather 3
Atkinson, Michelle 224
Attia, Kostas Nektarios 407
Austin, Ann 102
Austin, Gladys 87
Austin, Joanne 35
Austin, Kim L. 235
Austin, Patricia 396
Austin, S. 264
Austin, Shirley 220
Avery, Robert 122
Ayers, Sylvia 337
Ayesh, Aladdin 77
Ayre, C. 220

B

Bach, Adrian 244
Bachu, Soroya 302
Bacon, Kerry 274
Bacton, Andrew Brady 192
Bagge, Tom 266
Baggs, W. J. R. 323
Bagley, G. 301
Bagley, Gwen 18
Bailey, Anthea Diane 212
Bailey, Frances 214
Bailey, Frances V. 22
Bailey, Mary 417
Bailey, Molly 144
Bailey, Vicas L. 289
Bailey, Pamela Theobalds 401
Baillie, Alan 243
Bain, John 94
Bainbridge, Keith 235
Baker, C. P. 112
Baker, Charles 32
Baker, Edward John 254
Baker, Ivy E. 107
Baker, Joanne 189
Baker, Joyce M. 255
Baker, Karen 297
Baker, Margaret 406
Baker, Mick E. 385
Baker, Moira 126
Baker, Paul 225
Baker, Stephen 231
Baker-Moore, S. 152
Bakewell, R. J. G. 314
Baldwin, Clive A. 350
Balfour, D. I. 271
Ball, Anne E. 24
Ball, Leonora 291
Bamford, Paul 267
Bamford, Raye 56
Bamforth, Pauline 322
Banbury, Gwen 215
Bandy, Keith 225
Banks, Jean 366
Banks, Kathleen M. 172
Banks, William 141
Banner, Christine 22
Baptist, L. 221
Barclay, Margaret A. 236
Bardsley, Jayne 350
Bareham, Edna Louisa 320
Barger, Graham 208
Barker, Jennie 102
Barley, M. S. 328
Barlow, Barbara 373
Barnes, Andrew 243
Barnes, Annabel F. 92
Barnes, Dorothy 21
Barnes, L. 121
Barnes, Nicola 312
Barnes, Una 114
Barnett, Gordon 259
Barnett, Mollie 104
Barnett, W. 338
Barney, M. F. 401
Baron, Harry 309
Baron, M. J. 416
Barr, Tommy 177
Barrass, James H. 72
Barrenger, Maureen A. 127
Barrie, G. 113
Barrie, Helen 204
Barron, M. J. 384
Barrow, E. S. 226
Barrow, Sophie 292
Barson, Danny 184
Bartley-Berry, Dorothy 345
Barton, Constance 307
Bass, B. R. 112
Bass, Lucy 48
Bassett, Pamela 339
Bastiani, Angela 242
Bate, I. 121
Bate, L. G. 326
Bateman, John Montgomery 370
Bates, E. D. 117
Bates, Samuel Harry 284
Bathgate, Tracy 117
Batson, Jennifer 367
Battey, Arthur S. 199
Batty, D. E. 264
Battye, M. 155
Baulcombe, Gill 247
Bawden, Matthew 263
Baxter, Barbara A. 245
Bayliss, Janet 91
Bayliss, R. F. 330
Beall, Tom 147
Beall, Tom 226
Bean, Diana 3
Beard, C. A. 128
Beard, J. 180
Beaupierre, J. 389
Beck, Cynthia 107
Bedford, J. 220
Bedford, L. 338
Bedi, A. T. 341
Beech, Alan 30
Beech, Patricia 12
Beecham, I. 404
Beeching, R. C. 139
Belfield, S. M. 338
Belgin, Olivia 53
Bell, Alan 255
Bell, Clive Ayton 246
Bell, David 203
Bell, Janet 37
Bell, Rose 396
Bell, Sarah Jane 398
Belly 357
Bence, Susan Kaye 173
Benham, P. J. 232
Bennett, Becky 80
Bennett, Gary 252
Bennett, Ivan 93
Bennington, Deborah 24
Benson, Dawn 29
Benson, Karin 313
Bentley, J. B. 337
Beresford, Augustus 347
Berg, Jason 212
Bergin, J. M. 133
Berritta, R. 386
Berry, R. C. 165
Bertorelli, Dante 365
Best, Jim 247
Best, R. M. A. 142
Betteridge, M. 304
Bevan, Kate 385
Bevans, Lynne Michelle 142
Bicknell, Marion 382
Biddle, V. 326
Bidwell, Joan A. 351
Biggart, Mary M. 228
Biggins, Kim 274
Biggs, David 376
Bigwood, Reece 289
Billington, W. H. 153
Binnie, Roberta 411
Binns, Ruth A. 294
Birch, Hazel M. 7
Birch, Sheila M. 393
Birchmore, E. 226
Bird, Chris 77
Bird, Sandra 268
Bird, Wendy R. 157
Birkett, John H. 15
Birkin, Bonnie 209
Birrell, Samuel McKay 424
Biscoe, Pat 390
Bishenden, Maia 404
Bishop, Kenneth 42
Bishop, Mandy 276
Bizley, Roy 228
Bjelic-Rados, Gordana 239
Black, Jonathan 242
Blackford, Josephine 375
Blackham, Douglas 101
Blackmore, Andrew T. 420
Blackwell, D. R. 109
Blackwell, Sarah H. 400
Blaikie, Nancy Craig 392
Blain, Ursula A. 301
Blaker, Abigail E. 365
Bland, Nichola 338
Blease, Sarah 41
Blewer, Simone A. 176
Blight, Margaret R. 315
Bliss, M. 218
Blissett, E. A. 420
Blissett, Graham F. 310
Blockley, Philip George 171

Bloxham, Lucy-May 409
Blyth, Barbara Josephine 349
Boal, Millicent 287
Bockmann, Ingrid 103
Boden, Tony 300
Bolderbergs, Betty 7
Bolton, Gillian 185
Bolton, John M. L. 87
Bolton, Linda 231
Bond, R. H. 331
Bonel, Paul 265
Bonney, K. V. 303
Boocock, Nick J. 288
Boon, Barbara C. 197
Boone, Debbie J. 370
Booth, A. 50
Booth, Martin 298
Booth, Martin 379
Borge, Daisy Anne 101
Borland, Ishbel 206
Borley, Christina 27
Borwick, E. G. 405
Bos, Marilyn Anne 151
Bossen, Winifred M. 294
Botterill, H. 150
Bowden, Ray 151
Bower, Caroline 378
Bowers, Beryl 428
Bown, June 262
Boyce, Janina 90
Boyle, Jamie Keith 5
Boyle, Jennifer 5
Brace, Elizabeth 12
Bracey, Denise 96
Bracey, N. W. 232
Bradbury, Jane E. 242
Bradley, Brenda G. 216
Bradley, Catherine 190
Bradley, David W. 101
Bradley, John J. 417
Bradley, Malcolm E. D. 318
Bradley, Richard J. 176
Brady, Art B. 29
Brain, Angie 250
Brain, Warren 416
Bramall, Tom 237
Brammah, Alan 33
Brathwaite, Poet 273
Brattan, Hilary 354
Bray, C. 141
Brazier, Sylvia L. 409
Bredee, Pat 382
Breden, D. J. 145
Breeden, P. D. 138
Brennan, Angela 250
Brewin, Patricia D. 118
Brice, Kathleen 136
Bridgeman, Alison 201
Bridgeman, Barbara Ann 202
Bridger, Catherine 217
Briggs, James Andrew 254
Bright, Barrie-Jaine 308
Brind, Amanda 186
Broad, Eric 33
Brockie, Lindsay 272
Brocklesby, Margaret 386
Brodie, Marian 132
Bromidge, Ian 360
Brooker, Samantha 170
Brookes, Albert Charles 104
Brookes, Annette 4
Brooks, M. 324
Brooks, Sheila 329
Brooks, Sylvia 273
Brookshaw, Jim E. 187
Broomhall, Felicity Janet 83

Broomhall, Margaret J. 327
Brother, Wee 244
Brown, Christopher 208
Brown, D. W. 154
Brown, Iain R. 91
Brown, Irene Isabell 347
Brown, Iris J. 34
Brown, Katherine 222
Brown, Mary Crawford 397
Brown, Matthew 428
Brown, Mike 277
Brown, Nadine 339
Brown, R. F. 111
Brown, Shirley 122
Brown, Vanessa 167
Browne, Rosamund 313
Browning, Janet 239
Browning, Stella 399
Browning, V. 183
Bruce, E. M. 235
Bruce, Eugene 241
Bruce-Leggett, Sandra 236
Bruford, Ken 169
Brumby, E. J. 328
Brumwell, Dominic 86
Bryan, Catherine 60
Bryan, Hazel 23
Bryant, Margaret O. 328
Bryceland, M. 336
Bryceland, Vicky 262
Buchanan, Tom 222
Buckland-Evers, Gerald 251
Buckley, Anne E. 308
Buckley, Louise 417
Buckley, Peter 228
Buckley, Sarah 426
Buckmaster, John 212
Buckwell, Janine 256
Bull, L. 235
Burch, Carolanne 32
Burgess, B. 171
Burgess, Michael P. 71
Burnell, Amy 347
Burnett, Frances Mary 215
Burnett, Victoria 116
Burns, George B. 3
Burns, Linda Ann 327
Burns, Mary 236
Burns, Ruth 262
Burrell, Esther F. 372
Burroughs, P. 46
Burton, Peter 221
Burton, Sarah 389
Burton-Pye, Sheila J. 141
Burtonshaw, Shirley Jean 108
Bush, Gillian 193
Bush, Jane 188
Bush, Mary 237
Bush-Payne, Stella 164
Bushell, Danny 202
Buss, Peter 228
Bussey, Hilda 190
Butchart, Yvonne 39
Butcher, Sue 286
Butler, R. E. 270
Butler, Sue 287
Butt, Alan 207
Buzzle, Ronald John 379
Byerley, D. J. 270
Byne, Eileen P. 5
Byrne, J. 130
Byrom, Kathleen 295

C

Caddy, Beryl 197
Cahill, Deirdre 248

Cain, Ian 78
Cairns, Colin J. 267
Cairns, Gary S. T. 92
Cairns, Nora 318
Cairns, Wilma 389
Calder, E. B. 334
Calderwood, Edna 245
Caldwell, Eric A. 353
Caldwell, Julie 239
Calland, Lorraine 414
Callow, Jackie 347
Callow, K. J. 152
Calton, M. 403
Calvert, Dennis 187
Cambridge, V. 169
Cameron, Brenda 364
Cameron, Flora 199
Cameron, W. A. 413
Cameron, Wayne 229
Camp, George 87
Campbell, Catherine 256
Campbell, Denise 81
Campbell, E. 237
Campbell, Janette 255
Campbell, Sandra 305
Campbell, Veronica 164
Candler, Marvyn B. 229
Canning, Valerie 318
Cannings, Dennis James 309
Capaldi, Peter Vincent 166
Cape, Pete 136
Capper, J. 267
Cardwell, Sonia 421
Carey, Dorothy 97
Carey, Gillian 377
Carley-West, Lloyd 226
Carlin, W. 330
Carman, John 27
Carmichael, Jan P. 30
Carmichael, Margaret-Anne 119
Carmicheal, D. 276
Carnon, Alison 4
Caroline 189
Carpenter, Kym Adrian 164
Carr, June 257
Carr, Kathryn 218
Carr, M. D. 218
Carr, Matthew 251
Carr, Patricia Margaret 157
Carre, Gladys 420
Carrozzino, Vince 54
Carson, Mark 179
Carter, Eddie 106
Carter, Irene V. 201
Carter, Janet 179
Carter, Lesley 402
Carter, P. 226
Carter, Tim 384
Cartledge, Jonathan A. W. 239
Carvell, Adrian 214
Casey, Elizabeth 207
Cashford, Joan 107
Castle, Gillian 185
Castleton, Soo 217
Catlow, Mavis 228
Catterall, Jeannette A. 374
Cave 58
Cave, Doreen 19
Cave, Stephanie 127
Cavie, James E. 251
Cerbelli, Iride 91
Chalmers, Julie 250
Chambers, E. 267
Chambers, G. 41
Chambers, G. 218
Chambers, Pauline 146

Chana, Poonam K. 226
Channon, Tony 228
Chaplin, A. H. 143
Chaplin, Don 74
Chapman, Joseph 78
Chapman, R. 379
Chapman, Richard 379
Chapman, Tarany 230
Chappell, Barbara 191
Chappell, Jean Mary 357
Chappell, Leanda 294
Charles, Gina 362
Charlesworth, R. J. 64
Charlton, Tony 165
Charters, Tracy 223
Cheema, Priya 235
Cheetham, Sonny 341
Chester, Helen 248
Chesters, Catherine 217
Chetwynd, Elaine 211
Childs, A. F. 53
Childs, Janet 192
Chilton, Laura 333
Chisholm, J. 285
Chisholm, J. D. 415
Chiswell, Tony 272
Choat, Sandie 180
Christie, Donna Maria 365
Christie, Stuart 174
Churchyard, Hazel R. 183
Ciceri, Avis 260
Cirino, Joan 374
Clacy, Geoff 361
Clamp, Gillian B. 140
Clancey, John 239
Clancy, Eddie 350
Clapham, R. Ingrid 265
Clapham, Sheila 220
Clark, Bryan 250
Clark, G. M. 396
Clark, John 102
Clark, Kate 234
Clark, Kerri-Anne 410
Clark, Tom E. 313
Clarke, Anthony 103
Clarke, Anthony 250
Clarke, J. E. 268
Clarke, James 192
Clarke, Margaret 123
Clarke, Sarah 334
Clarke, T. 399
Clay, Jeanette 355
Claydon, Michelle 279
Clayton, Bill 424
Clee, Y. 181
Clegg, Kurt 297
Clegg, Sarah-Louise 334
Clegg, Timothy M. 279
Clelland, Moira 390
Clement, David 260
Clevett, Marilyn 63
Clifford, Pamela 146
Clifton, Tracy Kay 410
Clinton, John H. 369
Clough, Constance 417
Coast, Frances 340
Coates, Sandra 130
Coats, Jeanette 211
Cobb, Lillie Janet 333
Cocker, R. 384
Cockerill, Wilma 400
Cockett, Sharon 154
Codd, T. 394
Coe, M. D. 139
Coffey, Lisa 266
Cogan, Alison 259

Cogan, Margaret 147
Cohen, Estelle 251
Cohen, N. 390
Colbourne, Stephen D. 171
Cole, F. S. 133
Cole, Robert 285
Colella, M. 178
Colledge, Kelly 408
Collier, Kirsty 234
Collier, L. 318
Collier, R. 225
Collingwood, Mrs. Evelyn 341
Collins, Ann 251
Collins, D. M. 158
Collins, Emma 13
Collins, K. 169
Collins, Peggy 222
Collison, William F. 182
Colson, Edward 213
Colton, Wayne 167
Comis, Stephanie 337
Compston, H. 46
Compton, Leslie Anthony 138
Condron, Elizabeth Ann 357
Congleton, Sandra 128
Connelly, Roseanne 272
Connolly, Amy 261
Connolly, Marian 181
Connolly, Nora 233
Conolly, Nick 379
Coode, Peter S. 225
Cook, Alison 217
Cook, E. 303
Cook, Kathryn 281
Cook, Lynn 409
Cooke, Clare 246
Cooke, Paul 181
Cooke, Phyllis 170
Cooper, B. W. Tyas 223
Cooper, David 81
Cooper, Diane 91
Cooper, Hadrian 356
Cooper, Ian K. 90
Cooper, Kevin 112
Cooper, Nora Kathleen 229
Coote, V. M. 124
Cope, Jane 376
Coppen, P. E. 233
Corbett, Peter 155
Cordell, R. 137
Cornish, P. 388
Cotterell, T. W. 341
Cottle, Deborah 252
Couchman, Sarah 160
Counihan, James 417
Cousins, Norma 158
Coventry, Moira 269
Cowan, Heather 345
Cowan, May 326
Cox, Charmian 350
Cox, Gary J. 415
Cox, J. 403
Cox, Neil 138
Cox, Sara 169
Coyle, Greg 361
Cracknell, Katrina 155
Cramp, Diana 255
Cramp, Richard 415
Crane, Patricia 267
Cranfield, E. J. 397
Crawford, Betty 103
Crawford, James C. 371
Craythorne, Janette 250
Criddle, Evelyn 212
Crisp, Cynthia M. 6
Critchley, Adam 83

Crocker, Joyce 217
Crocker, P. T. 49
Crocker, Susan 236
Cromer, Laura 280
Cromwell, K. L. 334
Cropper, Arthur John 241
Cross, Brian 418
Cross, Charlotte 196
Cross, Janet 34
Crossan, Marian 154
Crossley, Hilary M. 104
Crouch, Vera 136
Crownshaw, Joanne 364
Crutcher, Kate 159
Cruz, Valerie 221
Cudd, Wendy A. 281
Cull, Marian 386
Cullen, Debi 183
Cullingford, Diana 195
Cummins, Angela 75
Cummins, Peggy 421
Cummins, Yasmin 418
Cunningham, James Ferguson 83
Cunningham, Moreen 233
Curran, Margaret F. 45
Curtis, David 246
Curtis, Iris 30
Cutting, John B. 210
Czuba, David 78

D

Dalby, Margaret J. 237
Dalby, Sue 139
Dale, Christine 215
Dale, J. 130
Dale, K. 229
Daley, Emma 206
Dallas, Karen 269
Dallimore, R. 69
Dalton, A. C. 378
Dalton, James H. 97
Dalton, Jane 210
Daly, Catherine 254
Dance, Barbara Helen 355
Dance, Buzzy V. 258
Dance, Eunice 360
Daniels, Christine 247
Daniels, Joanne 375
Darby, Rita 383
Darbyshire, Norah 316
Darwood, P. M. 155
Das, Anela 7
Davenport, Alan 241
Davenport, Pauline 149
Davidson, John Francis 348
Davidson, Mary 383
Davidson, Paul 262
Davies, Barbara 23
Davies, D. N. 224
Davies, David W. 307
Davies, Dawn 242
Davies, G. 235
Davies, G. R. 67
Davies, L. S. 419
Davies, Richard 56
Davies, S. P. 328
Davis, A. 283
Davis, Amanda Jayne 186
Davis, Doreen 19
Davis, Howard 88
Davis, Matthew 50
Davis, N. J. 222
Davis, S. P. 63
Davison, Amanda 12
Daw, Hannah 377
Dawes, Lily 418

Dawkins, Gemma 3
Dawson, P. N. 317
Dawson, R. J. 178
Day, Brian 353
Day, Christine 194
Day, Ellen M. J. 199
Day, Jennifer 239
Daynes, Steven 314
Deacon, Laura Elizabeth 224
Deacon, Valerie 168
Deal, Ian 197
Deans, Billie 187
De Artin, P. T. 299
Deeks, James 372
De Graft-Hayford, John E. S. 270
Dennison, Margaret 140
de Quincey, Gemma 369
Derbyshire, J. L. 176
Derrien, Christina 428
Derx, Harry C. 10
de Sanchez, Jennifer 257
Develin, Martin J. P. 231
Devine, H. P. 223
Devitt, Josie 367
Devonshire, Hazel 201
Dewey, Jane 363
Diabira, Bak 95
Dick, Chris 361
Dick, Malcolm P. 305
Dickeson, Tim 134
Dickinson, G. 56
Dimmock, A. 400
Dines, Yvonne 334
Dinham, Angela 84
Ditchman, Dee 244
Dixon, Cynthia Joy 377
Dixon, Tony 136
Dixon-Jones, Patricia 56
Dobbie, Alan 86
Dobinson, Patricia 292
Dobson, G. W. 144
Docherty, Gavin J. 241
Dodd, Julian Crichton 35
Doggett, Sylvia 180
Doherty, B. D. Jr. 322
Doig, Brian 207
Doig, Gillian 417
Dolbear, Jamie D. 90
Dolbear, Jim 18
Dolman, Elizabeth Jayne 92
Dolman, Sandra D. 146
Donaghue, Jean 84
Done, John 25
Donoghue, Audrey 371
Donovan, Angela 81
Donovan, Toni 268
Doolan, Lydia 406
Doran, Margaret 317
Doron, Marjorie Rose 132
Dorrian, Elizabeth 256
Douglas, Barbara 212
Douglas, Paddy 151
Dove, Margaret 52
Dover, Joan M. 358
Dowd, Lucy 276
Dowding, Ann 203
Dowding, Margaret 219
Dowle, Betty 248
Dowles, Ronald F. 231
Dowling, Sheila 128
Downing, Tommy 269
Doyle, C. 414
Doyle, George 16
Doyle, Russell W. 278
Dragoonis, Peter 408
Drake, Jacqueline 85

Drake, Sue 238
Dray, Sadie 387
Drayton, Brenda 243
Drewett, David 27
Drinkhill, J. M. 222
Driscoll, Juliet Ann 368
Drummond, Helen 19
Drury, Rosina 304
Dudley, S. M. 225
Duff, E. 159
Duffy, R. J. 127
Dugmore, Emma 13
Duke, Christopher 209
Duncan, L. 387
Dungate, Bill 90
Dunkley, Joan 308
Dunleavy, Geraldine 356
Dunlop, Josephine 21
Dunn, I. 174
Dunne, Richard 278
Dunning, J. W. 166
Dunton, Theresa 167
Durham, Valerie 291
Durrant, Dorothy 261
Dutton, Irene 373
Dutton, Jade E. 197
Dutton, S. 132
Dye, Denise Alison 34
Dyer, Alice 30
Dyer, Sandra 44
Dyka-Gerard, Rozarya 419
Dyke, Arthur H. N. 96
Dymond, N. 222
Dyson, Justin J. 22

E

Eames, Michael C. 271
Earl, Dennis 82
Earley, E. J. 409
Easingwood, Stephen 423
Easthope, Rebecca 270
Edgar, Charlotte 85
Edge, Emma 17
Edment, Isobel 425
Edmonds, Elizabeth A. 252
Edwards, Barry D. 201
Edwards, Brian 184
Edwards, Brian 361
Edwards, Dave 211
Edwards, Eileen Lawton 21
Edwards, Jessie 31
Edwards, Nicholas 43
Edwards, Peter 117
Edwards, Sheila 278
Eldridge, Jacqueline M. 92
Eley, Kerry 293
Elliot, Lorraine 234
Elliott, Carol 423
Elliott, Georgina 251
Elliott, Josephine Teresa 5
Elliott, Thomas 312
Ellis, Jo 199
Ellis, R. C. 268
Elsworthy, Martin S. 228
Elvery, Brenda (Folkestone) 351
Elvidge, Lindsey 277
Emery, Jennifer 428
Empson, George 427
Emsden, Richard 168
Emslie, Moira 393
England, N. G. 270
Englert, Ann 198
Ennis, Joe 348
Enticknap, Donna 309
Epton, Katrina 232
Erskine, J. A. 233

Esgate, Pam 340
Etherington, Philip 157
Ettles, J. 415
Evans, Abigail 187
Evans, B. 232
Evans, B. 293
Evans, B. 382
Evans, Brett James 202
Evans, John M. 257
Evans, Joyce 74
Evans, Marion 414
Evans, Mary Eileen 333
Evans, Sheelagh E. 306
Evers, John 375
Evers, Michael John 306
Ewart, Brenda 377
Ewers, Vera 141

F

Fabo, Michelle 331
Facchini, E. C. 335
Fagan, John 196
Fagan, R. M. 328
Fagan, Shaun 236
Fahy, Catherine 424
Fairchild, Joy 251
Falloon, P. 162
Fardell, M. 317
Farnworth, Elaine 363
Farr, K. 136
Farrell, William E. 411
Farrow, Linda 408
Farrow, Susan K. 404
Faulds, Andrew 28
Faulkner, Carla 244
Faulkner, Michael 264
Fauré, Emma 375
Fay, Doreen 89
Fears, T. C. 287
February, Patricia 209
Fee, Carole 252
Feeley, Michael 292
Fegan, Aimee 74
Fellowes, Anita 31
Felstead, Denise 374
Ferguson, Mary 408
Ferguson, Seumas Neil 341
Fiddes, M. 329
Field, D. G. 428
Field, Joanne 372
Fillery-Handzic, Jeanne 245
Finch, Maria 108
Findlay, Ronald 287
Finneran, H. 344
Finneran-Dinsdale, Helen 375
Firth, Anna Louise 27
Fish, Victoria 325
Fisher, Brian 193
Fisk, P. 296
Fitch, Valerie 165
Fitzgerald, H. 221
Fitzpatrick, J. 157
Fitzpatrick, John 104
Fitzsimmons, Kevin 171
Flaherty, Barbara M. 249
Flaherty, John 88
Flanagan-Quirke, Mary 182
Fleck, Fay 7
Fleetwood, Irene E. 240
Fleitz, Jason 368
Fleming, Karen 393
Fletcher, G. 171
Fletcher, Rhoda 383
Fletcher, Rita 160
Flood, Maralyn 232
Flynn, Mary 159

Fooks, Edwina 186
Fooladi, F. 229
Ford, Grace Brown 260
Ford, M. A. 168
Ford, Margaret 319
Ford, S. 285
Foreman, J. R. 160
Forrest, Marlene 163
Forrest, Susan M. 234
Fossett, Gemma 35
Foster, Danny Gordon 80
Foster, E. 332
Foster, Marie 175
Foulsham, Terry 72
Fountain, Peggy 306
Fountain, Phyllis 60
Fowler, Anne-Marie 74
Fozzard, T. B. 127
France, Ellen May 17
France, Hilda 189
Francis, J. 365
Francis, Joan 212
Francis, Patricia 262
Francis, Steven P. 155
Frank, Jacqui 23
Frankel, Rachel 162
Franklin, Dean 354
Fraser, Cecilia G. 197
Fraser, Keith 148
Fraser, Paul 134
Frazer, Brian 82
Frederick-Smith, Alan 96
Freeman, Chris 359
Freeman, G. 132
Freeman, Patricia M. 128
French, Jean 376
French, John 215
Fretwell, P. T. 169
Freudenberger, K. L. 50
Frew, Derek 213
Fricker, R. M. 129
Friel, Karen 284
Friskney, Anita 374
Frogson, T. K. 270
Frost, Denise 328
Frusher, Stella 277
Fryers, Diane Louise 364
Fulham, Janet 358
Fuller, B. M. 266
Furber, B. M. 163
Furber, B. M. 394

G

Gadeke, Jean E. 309
Gahan, K. 294
Galbraith, Margaret 343
Gales, Marc David 344
Galey, Richard 233
Gallagher, John 260
Gallagher, John 418
Galway, Miriam 327
Gamage, A. E. S. 120
Games, J. S. 55
Ganderson, Robert John 332
Garcia, Edith 188
Gardiner, Mary 280
Gardner, Chris 23
Gardner, Paul Richard 379
Gardner, R. A. 281
Garlinge, Cheryl 259
Garner, B. 225
Garner, Florence Clara 261
Garner, P. M. 386
Garraway, Linda Jane 344
Garrett, Sarah 227
Garvey, Ben T. 200

Garvey, Lisa M. 343
Gatehouse, Derek 20
Gates, J. 144
Gaunt, Philip 47
Gaunt, Wilfred 386
Gentry-Evans, Maureen 427
George, Linda 313
George, Margaret 325
Ghosh, Amitav 190
Gibbins, Steve 69
Gibbons, Chris 35
Gibbons, E. 284
Gibbs, Howard Wallace 196
Gibson, Charlene 73
Gibson, Coral 100
Gibson, Frances 73
Gibson, J. M. 317
Gibson, Peter John 119
Giddings, A. T. 303
Gilbert, Nancy 113
Gilbert, Philip C. 314
Giles, J. C. 283
Giles, J. W. 335
Giles, Mike 264
Giles, Vicky 306
Gillen, M.J.J. 49
Gillies, Jacqui 373
Gilliland, C. 407
Gillingham, Jacqui 23
Gillings, R. 58
Gilroy, John A. 36
Giordano, Dolores 74
Givnan, Anthony C. 259
Gizzi, Jessie L. 247
Glendinning, Alan 89
Glover, Frank 239
Glover, Helen 188
Gocher, Karen C. 403
Goddard, Jean 23
Goddard, Paul 43
Goddard, V. J. 108
Godley, David 261
Going, Bill 289
Golding, Ann 242
Golding, Evelyn 88
Goldsmith, Evelyn 261
Goodall, Kedra 383
Goode, Barbara 34
Goode, Ruth 238
Goodfellow, Carol 98
Goodman, Darren James 190
Goodman, M. 282
Goodman, Rachel Ellen 379
Goodwin, Lara 113
Gordon, Erica 82
Gordon, Paul S. 419
Gorman, Sheila 62
Gould, Liz 265
Gould, Neil 288
Goulding, Pamela 146
Gower, V. T. S. 170
Gowers, Terry 273
Goymer, N. P. 114
Grace, Gearoid 205
Grace, Sybil 312
Gracey, John 189
Grady, Christine 364
Grainger, Janice 252
Grainger, Joyce 252
Grainger, Mark 428
Grant, B. 218
Grant, Candida 254
Grant, Daphne J. 33
Grant, Frank 25
Grant, Irene 33
Grant, Janet 216

Grant, Patrick 126
Grant, Stuart 218
Grant, Vera E. 298
Graves, L. A. 312
Gravett-Pollicino, Esther 353
Gray, A. 414
Gray, A. A. 49
Gray, Doreen 204
Gray, Judith 245
Gray, Julie 18
Gray, Lisa 233
Greaves, Lindsey 304
Greaves, S. A. 116
Green, Helen 244
Green, Adrian 185
Green, Donna 199
Green, John 37
Green, Leonard R. 171
Green, Thomas D. 53
Green, F. O. 403
Greenfield, Veronica J. 57
Greenwood, S. 238
Gregory, Joan 239
Gregson, Debbie 11
Gregson, Derek 248
Grierson, Helen 92
Grieve, Freda 29
Griffin, Sharon 16
Griffith, Joshua 422
Griffiths, Colwyn 208
Griffiths, Ray 115
Griffiths, Shirley 219
Grimwood, H. K. 407
Grogan, P. 263
Groom, Valerie 384
Groome, June 5
Groundsell, J. D. 295
Groves, E. A. 340
Grundy, Janet 251
Guest, James 260
Guidery, V. D. 182
Gunner, Stephen 272
Guntrip, Margaret 316
Gurney, Tom 396
Gutteridge, Susan D. 396
Guy, Tom 118
Gwynn, Anne S. M. 99

H

Haddon, Marjorie 282
Hadley, Brenda M. 36
Hadley, G. 299
Hagger, J. 285
Haile, Christine 255
Haines, Phyllis 110
Hainie, Margaret N. 270
Hale, I. D. M. 297
Halferty, Annora 358
Hall, John A. 248
Hall, Richard 165
Hall, T. 345
Hall, W. G. 115
Hall, Yvonne 263
Hallam, S. D. 380
Halliwell, Leonard 272
Hallmann, Robert 391
Halls, Michelle E. 136
Hamblett, Cari Sophia 205
Hamill, David 214
Hamilton, Gillian 260
Hammond, Christine 195
Hammond, K. 280
Hammond-Kaines, F. 380
Hampshire, Lionel James 57
Hampton, Roger 267
Hancock, Mark W. 321

Handel, Patricia Anne 163
Hanson, Jacqueline 21
Hanson, Katie 148
Hanson, Sean 342
Hardcastle, Anita 310
Hardie, Catherine 4
Hardiman, Rebecca 268
Hardy, Paul 267
Hargreaves, R. 176
Harkcom, Dorothy 194
Harkness, Ronald 275
Harley, Colleen 356
Harper, Lyn 55
Harper, Sue 289
Harries, Elizabeth 177
Harrington, Doreen 246
Harris, Audrey 97
Harris, Brian 36
Harris, C. L. 271
Harris, Edward 38
Harris, J. 232
Harris, Jaki 249
Harris, Jean 248
Harris, Josh 246
Harris, Kate 316
Harris, Kenneth 63
Harris, Kirk 390
Harris, Marjorie 417
Harris, Miki Fingret 118
Harris, Susan 156
Harris, T. 117
Harrison, A. 264
Harrison, Barbara 88
Harrison, Bob 78
Harrison, F. J. 117
Harrison, Karen 393
Harrower, J. 225
Harry, Robert J. 390
Hart, A. W. 379
Hart, Julie 260
Hart, Kevin 121
Hartley, Duncan 416
Hartley, Margaret 282
Hartley, Maureen 167
Hartley, Valerie 156
Harvey, David John 89
Harvey, Dawn 184
Harvey, James 84
Harvey, Joan D. 357
Harvey, Pamela 319
Harvey, Rachel 238
Harvey, Roland 113
Harwood, J. M. 402
Harwood, Louisa 422
Haslam, M. C. 266
Hassell, Anja 205
Haswell, Fiona 14
Hatham, Katherine 383
Hatherley, Colleen 198
Hauser, John Robert 363
Haverty, G. 49
Hawkins, Marie J. 337
Hawkins, Shirley 324
Hawkridge, E. 331
Haycock, Lilian 388
Haydock, Paul A. 112
Haye, Emil 371
Hayes, Jonathan 261
Hayes, Linda 277
Hayfield, Vikki 231
Haynes, Barbara 79
Hayton, M. 167
Hayward, Frederick G. 33
Hayward, J. A. 161
Hayward, J. R. 47
Hayward, P. G. 279

Head, Peter 286
Head, Wendy 394
Headen, Olive 391
Hearn, Andrew 7
Hearn, Caroline 370
Heath, Brenda 351
Heenan, Catherine 195
Heibner, Errol 18
Heller, R. 273
Helps, Edna Hay 193
Hembry, Charmian 217
Hemingway, Denise 417
Hemmings, Claire 73
Hemmings, E. 408
Hemmings, May 42
Hemsley, M. 380
Henderson, Amanda 26
Henderson, Charles J. 76
Henderson, Colin 349
Hendrie, Jean 30
Henly, D. M. 228
Henn, Shirley 238
Henny, Michael William 385
Henstock, Aubrey 36
Henstock, Simon 318
Heppel, Pat 134
Hersh, Alan L. 195
Hesketh, Beverley 8
Hewitt, Millicent 157
Hewitt, Sally A. 159
Hewlett, Marion 72
Hibberd, Diane 201
Hickford, Pauline 123
Hickman, C. 178
Hickman, Pamela J. 110
Higgins, Fiona 22
Higgins, Martin 41
Higginson, Anthony 248
Higginson, Gary 91
Higginson, Sue 279
Higgs, Susan Ann 391
Higham, Brenda 189
Higham, Christine Atkinson 12
Higham, Susannah 123
Hill, Alexander 88
Hill, Ann 11
Hill, Doreen M. 28
Hill, Hazel 100
Hill, J. E. 392
Hill, Nadine Tanya 398
Hill, Yvonne 341
Hillen, Sheila M. 181
Hilton, Philip 136
Hinchliffe, Hannah 204
Hinks, Kerry 173
Hirons, Kieth R. 230
Hoad, Hilda 3
Hoare, Irene 347
Hoare, J. P. K. 263
Hobbs, B. 153
Hodge, S. 295
Hodgetts, Mary F. 148
Hodgkins, Kerry Ann 45
Hodgson, Edna 194
Hodgson, P. 392
Hodkinson, W. H. 142
Hogg, P. 291
Hoggard, Ros 266
Hogwood, K. V. 279
Holdaway, C. A. 293
Holden, Philip 224
Holder, Mary Y. 154
Holgate, Katie 128
Holgate, Louise 125
Holgate, Luke 329
Holgate, Sarah 129

Holhmerr, Gina 212
Holland, Doris 246
Holland, P. M. 339
Holland, Paul 229
Holleran, Martin James 301
Holley, V. B. 70
Hollins, Susan 406
Holloran, John 81
Holloway, Jane 399
Holloway, Ronald H. 101
Holloway, S. 162
Holmes, Arthur Eric 365
Holmes, Elizabeth G. 75
Holmes, Jacqui 256
Holmes, Louise Ann 158
Holt, A. P. 151
Holt, Dinah 100
Holt, Jason 185
Holt, Kristina 418
Homer, K. 142
Homewood, Cliff 14
Hood, Emma 257
Hooper, Gavin 256
Hooper, Wendy S. 226
Hope, Julie 84
Hopkins, James Thomas 75
Hopkins, Joyce 5
Hopton, Samantha 39
Hopwood, Barbara 93
Horsey, Jane 357
Horsfield, Marion 233
Horslen, Peter 226
Hossain, Nilofar 230
Hough, Rita 398
Houghton, Ruby A. 388
Houlton, Dorice 261
Hounsome, Marilyn A. 287
Hover, B. 394
Howard, Barry 91
Howard, Carol 187
Howard, Diane 376
Howard, Harrydan 376
Howard, J. T. 182
Howard, James 360
Howard, Maurice W. 290
Howarth, Elizabeth 242
Howarth, Peter 170
Howarth, Susan 117
Howarth, W. H. 272
Howe, P. R. 317
Howe, T. M. 129
Howell, Margaret 378
Howells, Belinda J. 353
Howells, Dave 106
Howells, Sharon 224
Howroyd, Paul S. 320
Howse, Dorothy 7
Hoyle, D. 128
Huber, C. 232
Huber, C. 238
Hudsmith, Annisse 272
Hudson, A. J. 114
Hughes, Caroline E. 346
Hughes, Catherine 205
Hughes, Eileen 16
Hughes, Elizabeth M. 98
Hughes, Gina 32
Hughes, James Carl 244
Hughes, Patsy 395
Hughes, Robert 288
Hulme, Derek D. 104
Hume, John 247
Hume, Leanne 157
Hume, Sylvia 120
Hunnaball, Elizabeth J. 359
Hunt, Gean 366

Hunt, Hayley 367
Hunt, Patricia 337
Hunter, Jean 188
Hunter, John 187
Hunter, Roy 312
Huntley, Joanne 241
Hurl, Malcolm 233
Hurley, Maryann 320
Hurley, S. J. 323
Hurrell, Paul James 296
Hutchin, D. 173
Hutton, Sheila 178
Hyde, D. C. 263
Hydon, D. H. 68
Hyland, Anthony S. 347
Hymas, Doris E. 253

I

Iachetta, Hayley 424
Ibolo, Maria 115
Ilsley, Henry 261
Ince, Gina 260
Ingham, Nellie 138
Ingram, Audrey 196
Ingram, Geraint 250
Ingram, James E. 19
Ingram, Wayne 164
Irvine, H. G. 266
Irving, R. A. 124
Isaac, Jodie 97
Isherwood, Christine 426
Isherwood, Janet Elizabeth 366
Ives, Linda 110
Ives, Paul 180

J

Jack, Winifred 115
Jackman, Ann 196
Jackson, D. Mark 236
Jackson, Gloria 349
Jackson, Hilary 350
Jackson, M. 61
Jackson, Marian 283
Jackson, Mona 264
Jackson, Nancy 126
Jackson, Sylvia 268
Jacob, Terence 302
Jacobs, Cornell W. 29
Jagmohan, Chandanee 361
Jagoe, Thomas 228
James, B. E. 399
James, Derek 4
James, Fred O. 353
James, Gerard Steven 352
James, Lisa Marie 65
James, Richard Ian 298
James, Sylvia E. 62
Jamieson, Garry Steven 352
Jarman, Pippa 115
Jarome, J. D. 220
Jarvis, Anne 254
Jasper, Sarah 265
Jay, Tony A. 298
Jeacock, Helen 346
Jebb, Pearl 239
Jeffcott, Christopher 208
Jefferies, Frances 76
Jeffrey, Leonie 336
Jeffries, L. J. 296
Jenkins, Charlene 350
Jenkins, Greg 255
Jenkins, Jay McClellan 373
Jenkins, L. W. 135
Jenkins, T. G. 297
Jenkins, T. P. 398

Jenkinson, Fay 182
Jennings, M. 340
Jennings, Paul 305
Jesson, Patricia 140
Jewkes, Benjamin 358
Jindra, Fenn 244
Johnson, Alfred 305
Johnson, Dee 357
Johnson, Helen M. 23
Johnson, John A. 34
Johnson, Kimberley 387
Johnson, Lavinia 137
Johnson, Stan 175
Johnson, Susan C. 49
Johnston, Brian D. 8
Johnston, Deborah 362
Johnston, Gordon S. 248
Johnston, Jean M. 258
Johnston, Knox 263
Johnstone, George S. 199
Joiner, Janet 258
Jolliffe, Gaelyn 106
Jones, A. M. 109
Jones, Alison C. 216
Jones, Angela 209
Jones, B. L. 284
Jones, C. R. 126
Jones, David Kendall 80
Jones, Diane 241
Jones, E. D. 332
Jones, G. F. S. 332
Jones, J. G. 408
Jones, Janet Robertson 102
Jones, Jean 37
Jones, Jeanne 32
Jones, Kerry 284
Jones, Kevin 150
Jones, Liz 262
Jones, Marshall 149
Jones, Maureen 224
Jones, Pauline 59
Jones, Peter A. 288
Jones, Philip David 233
Jones, Raymond 410
Jones, Roger 278
Jones, Sarah 135
Jones, Sheila Yvonne 294
Jones, Victor 332
Jones, W. 333
Jordan, Aileen Andrews 105
Jordan, Denise 253
Jordan, Jacqueline 247
Jordan, Tim 182
Joyce, Mary 342
Judd, Jean M. 5
Jude, Phillip D. 135

K

Kadkol, K. R. 235
Kandinsky, Stella 108
Kaur, Jasvinder 255
Kavanagh, Carol 372
Kay, Robert P. 224
Kayley, Eunice 259
Keach, Debbie J. 36
Keegan, Jonathan 94
Keeler, Betty Edna 87
Keeling, Ivan 10
Keightley, Carol 413
Keller, Richard 330
Kelly, A. C. 219
Kelly, Alistair James 28
Kelly, Daphne 354
Kelly, Jayne B. 365
Kelly, Jean 79
Kelly, Lilian Mary 110

Kelly, Neil 290, 336
Kelsey, Martin 427
Kempton, Pamela 427
Kendall, Clodagh 198
Kendall-Bush, Jane 255
Kendon, Anne 249
Kendrew, Mildred T. 425
Kendrick, C. 59
Kennedy, Bernadette 361
Kennedy, Louise 329
Kennedy, M. 380
Kennedy, Ruby E. 149
Kennedy, Ruth 286
Kenrick, F. 389
Kent, John Millar 428
Kenyon, Barry 97
Kernot, Edwina Ann 96
Kerr, Anne 206
Kerr, Paul 262
Kerrigan, J. 326
Keszeg, Michael 330
Key, Karena J. 182
Keynan, Hassan Abdi 411
Keyworth, Brian H. 119
Khamis, Tashmin Kassam 338
Khwaja, Nomana Yusuf 114
Kilcommins, A. M. 126
Kinch, Kerry 286
King, Anna 346
King, Caron 243
King, Edward 75
King, Frank 249
King, Gerald M. 37
King, Henry J. 200
King, Jean 210
King, Susan 226
King, Susan 295
Kingham, Jackie 377
Kingsbury, Violet 170
Kinshott, Margaret 316
Kirby, Raymond Paul 265
Kirk, Andrew 195
Kirk, Shirley Thornycroft 175
Kirk, Tammie 414
Kirkwood, Bill 243
Kirtland, Pat 311
Kitchener, Barbara 76
Kitching, Jean Ann 256
Knight, Joe 88
Knight, Valerie 325
Knowles, Carole 32
Knox, George W. 15
Krzalic, Adnan 243
Kunzlik, Margaret 148

L

Ladkin, Robin 164
Laffan, Matthew 231
Laird, Alex 247
Laird, J. R. 116
Laird, K. F. 294
Laity, S. 300
Lake, Maureen 132
Lakehal, Samantha 269
Lakey, Bertha 370
Lally, C. E. 399
Lamb, Andrew 309
Lamb, Ann 250
Lamb, Annamarie C. 203
Lambert, Shirley 417
Lambord, R. W. 124
Lambourne, Elsie 352
Lambton, Catherine 363
Lammas, Gwen 8
Lamont, Charles 418
Lampard, Avril D. 108

Lancaster, Linda 322
Lancett, Phyllis 265
Lane, David J. 247
Lane, Dee-Dee 200
Lane, Edward Lawrence 211
Lane, John William 176
Lane, Mary 416
Lane, W. K. 231
Lane-Cilmeri, Carol Lesle 372
Langford, Anne 98
Langley, B. M. 332
Lansdown, Diana 143
Lapham, Peter 171
Laplain, Pat 223
Larkin, Kathleen 382
Larsen, Eva 90
Larter, Freda 101
Lattimore, B. 299
Launchbury, H. 112
Laurence, Hilda E. 26
Laurence, Mary 181
Laverse, Georgina 3
Laverse, Mary 145
Laverty, Delia 246
Law, Theresa 396
Lawrence, D. 71
Lawrence, Royston 236
Lawreniuk, J. A. 180
Lawrie, Gavin 204
Lawson, Alison 95
Lawson, Gracie 369
Lawson, H. T. 122
Lawson, W. G. 223
Laycock, Michael L. 342
Leach, Harry Hartland 413
Leahey, Linda 238
Leahey, Ryan 295
Leamon, Colin John 20
Leathem, Cain 368
Leaver, D. G. 227
Ledley, V. J. 120
Lee, June 199
Lee, L. J. 162
Lee, Paul A. 121
Lee, Ronnie 403
Lee, Vera 152
Leech, Samantha 236
Leigh, P. W. 399
Leigh, V. 425
Leigh, Vernon A. 405
Leigh, W. E. 174
Leigh-Spencer, Margaret 133
Leisk, Janice 346
Lemon, Caroline 100
Leonard, Jason 256
Leslie, E. 303
Leslie, Teresa 162
Levey, Jenny 307
Levine, Emily 247
Lewin, G. 137
Lewington, Joan 250
Lewis, A. 295
Lewis, Andrea 6
Lewis, Bronwyn 378
Lewis, David 246
Lewis, Dorothy Jane 74
Lewis, Maureen L. 271
Lewis, Stan 296
Lias, A. T. 44
Liddell, David 371
Liddell, Thomas A. 388
Liddiard, Paul 264
Liddle, Thomas Allan 145
Lidster-Wood, Carol 73
Light, Ursula E. K. 221
Lightfoot, E. 123

Limbrick, A. 333
Linley, Mike 220
Linnecar, D. R. 163
Lister, Josephine 38
Litterick, Julia 85
Little, George 352
Little, H. A. 221
Little, Jean 30
Little, M. 64
Livesey, Harry 202
Lloyd, Ann 13
Lloyd, Graine 15
Lloyd, Natalie 392
Lloyd, Shelley Louise 299
Lloyd-Williams, Jean 368
Loader, A. C. 140
Lochead, Mandi J. 290
Locke-Hart, Christine 16
Lockwood, Deborah 28
Lodge, Penny 227
Lodge, Ronald V. 339
Loe, Michael John 399
Loft, Olive 179
Loftus, Debbie 98
Logie, Bertha 85
Lomas, Paul Andrew 67
Long, Stella R. 238
Lord, Eileen 203
Lord, G. 231
Loughrey, Paul 319
Loughridge, Karen 179
Lowe, N. 129
Lower, Kay 138
Lownds, Martin S. 48
Lowther, Sylvia 121
Lucas, Gael 253
Lucas, Paul 343
Luckin, Clare 194
Lumley, Penelope 219
Luscombe, M. 237
Luton, David 353
Luxford, Ann 348
Lycett, Gwen M. 99
Lynch, Daphne C. 207
Lyons, Paul 392

M

Maben, R. 428
MacBean 416
MacDonald, Adeline 188
MacDonald, Andrea C. 241
MacDonald, Don 248
MacDonald, Joan 346
MacDonald, Johanna M. 259
MacDonald, Mairianna 263
MacDonald, Susan J. 383
MacFarlane, D. B. 158
Macfarlane, Mary 227
MacGregor, Alexandrina D. 103
Machon, Irene 82
Mackay, Beatrice 34
Mackay, Karen 323
Mackay, Laura 144
MacLean, Duncan 206
MacLean, Roderick 301
Macleod, Bunty 109
MacMillan, Sarah 267
MacMurphy, J. P. 279
MacNab, James 33
MacNell, Roma 153
MacSweeney, David 372
MacTaggart, C. H. 270
Madle, P. R. 168
Maguire, Rosaleen 168
Maher, Michael D. 391
Maher, Thomas 218

Mahood, Diane E. 345
Mailer, Mark 423
Main, George 97
Main, Julie 309
Malindine, Margaret 330
Mallabone, Danielle 207
Mallard, David J. L. 198
Mallinson, Jacqueline 202
Maloney, Nicholas 133
Maltby, Nigel Lloyd 263
Manchip, Christopher 310
Mangan, Lisa 222
Manley, David F. 80
Mann, Pamela 277
Manners, Benita 214
Manning, Fred 27
Manning, Phillip S. 179
Mansfield, Alan 30
Mapletoft, Winnie C. 410
Maqbool, Balall 31
Marchant, J. A. 232
Mardel, J. H. 229
Margerum, D. S. 339
Marks, Simon 311
Marley, B. 408
Marsden, Sandra 386
Marsh, Joanna 355
Marsh, Stephen Russell 111
Marsh, Steve 142
Marshall, Alastair 261
Marshall, David Stephen 311
Marshall, Elaine 28
Marshall, Lorraine 332
Marshall, M. 152
Marston, Alan 94
Martin, Bessie 22
Martin, Catherine 414
Martin, E. E. 281
Martin, John 361
Martin, Lewis 422
Martin, Stephen 66
Martyn, Nikki 227
Maryan, Joan Ester 201
Maskell, Kerry 411
Mason, Brenda 109
Mason, Jo 32
Mason, Mary 340
Mason, Pat C. M. 161
Massey, J. 137
Massey, Sarah 382
Masterson, Rita 141
Mather, John Cord 93
Mathers, David 77
Matreaux, J. M. J. 385
Matthews, Barbara M. 254
Matthews, Gwen 211
Matthews, Joan Yvonne 8
Matthews, Matt 112
Matthews, Mauréene 343
Matthews, R. T. S. 236
Maunders, C. J. 386
Mawdsley, Cyril J. 253
Maxwell, June 253
May, Ella 93
May, Jean L. 371
May, Joyce 80
Mayers, C. P. 134
Mayfield, Terry 289
Maynard, Julie 29
Mayne, E. S. 303
Mayne, Lorna 333
Mayson, Shelagh 230
Mcall, Julia 6
McAnulty, Peter 381
McAusland, Bill 83
McCabe-Smith, Joseph 257

McCaig, Agnes 365
McCaig, James 358
McCallion, Dominic 76
McCanaan, Olive 116
McCann, Valerie 341
McCartan, Toni 278
McCarthy, Chris 245
McCarthy, D. 148
McCarthy, Kevin 231
McCarthy, P. M. 173
McCluskey, Martin 172
McComick, Norah 69
McConaghey, F. W. 120
McConnachie, John D. 102
McCormack, Mary 338
McCormick, Helen 258
McCormick, Kitty 387
McCoy, J. 222
McCran, Janet 13
McCrudden, Philomena 270
McCullough, Colette 11
McDonagh, L. 118
McDonnell, Eileen 189
McFadden, Patrick 268
McFall, Tracy 290
McGannan, Barbara 38
McGibney, Gavin 213
McGoff, Lisa 218
McGougan, W. 427
McGrath, Brendan 247
McGrath, Marjorie 67
McGrath, Patrick 304
Mcgriele, Marcia 277
McGuffie, Frances 367
McGuigan, Rosemary 271
McGuinness, E. M. 330
McHugh, W. 297
McIlhatton, James 89
McIlhatton, Rosemary 298
McIntyre, Angus Jackson 215
McIntyre, Ruth 313
Mckay, A. S. 154
McKay, Peter 142
McKechnie, William 235
McKee, Laurence 285
McKendrey, Samantha 177
McKenna, David 370
McKenzie, John 355
McKeon, Kathleen 338
McKinney, Janet 12
McKinnon, Sandra 263
McLeish, Jennifer 107
McLellan, Jamie D. 195
McLintock, Andrew 79
McMahon, Leslee 428
McManus, Breda 253
McManus, Kathleen 285
McMillan, Isabel 425
McNab, Isabel M. 255
McNally, R. 322
McNamara, Gwen 217
McNamara, Pamela 227
McNeeney, Laura 51
McNeish, Margaret 397
McPhail, Emma L. 355
McPhee, Anne 184
McPhee, Raymond 223
McPherson, Catherine 376
McPike, Jill 259
McQueen, Lyn 409
McSorley, Donna 79
Mead, Robert Philip 268
Mead, W. E. 264
Meadows, Christopher 90
Meakin, Elaine 207
Mears, Robert H. 403

Meazza, Dean Francis 262
Medcalf, N. F. 108
Medhurst, James 258
Medley, Maureen Sylvia 125
Meek, Margaret 174
Meiklejohn, Shona 264
Meldrum, Kate 60
Melham, Valerie J. 111
Melia, Sue 133
Mellor, Joanne 200
Melmoth, Tarah 113
Menhenitt, Linda 234
Meninsky, Philip 409
Menzies, Robin 230
Mercer, Tim 148
Meredith, Mary 282
Merrick, John Andrew 105
Merritt, J. G. 334
Merritt, Kathleen N. 220
Merry, Nikki 132
Metcalf, June 12
Metcalfe, B. G. 313
Metcalfe, Nicola J. 231
Mew, Norman 411
Michael, Andrea 426
Michanicou, Chris 344
Michaux, Stephen J. 143
Midgley, Terri 291
Miele, V. 333
Mifsud, Laurence 156
Millar, Betty 79
Miller, Bernard 367
Miller, Graham 370
Miller, H. R. 314
Miller, Linda 166
Miller, S. 401
Millership, Audrey 76
Mills, Alexandra Burness 369
Mills, Gemma 258
Mills, Graham 95
Milne, A. G. L. 131
Milnes, A. J. 174
Milnes, Winnie 232
Milton, P. W. 334
Mimms, June 24
Minton, Lisa M. 396
Mistry, J. 271
Mitchell, Christian S. 81
Mitchell, Elizabeth M. 7
Mitchell, Graham 240
Mitchell, J. S. 300
Mitchell, J. S. 327
Mitchell, Janet A. 29
Mitchell, Ley 269
Mitchell, Mhairi 44
Mitchell, Patricia A. 331
Mitchell, Stanley 330
Mitchell, Stella Clare 109
Mitchell, V. R. 59
Mochrie, Steven M. 137
Moffat, Yvonne 183
Moggach, C. A. 280
Moir, Emma 251
Monaghan, May 395
Monday, Martha 219
Monk, Angela 369
Monk, Rita 406
Monk, Suzanne 389
Monteith, Jean 370
Moody, Sue 406
Mooney, Amanda 375
Moonie, Margaret 127
Moore, James 243
Moore, Jennifer 308
Moore, Louise M. 396
Moore, V. M. 219

Moran, Angela 191
Moran, Dorothy 191
Moreland, L. J. 330
Moreland, Winifred E. 265
Moreno, A. P. 177
Moreton, B. 61
Morgan, Anne 106
Morgan, Betty 246
Morgan, Daniel 200
Morgan, Gail 35
Morgan, Gaynor Alison 254
Morgan, Thomas F. 288
Morlham, Lilian 179
Morris, D. 243
Morris, Graham 11
Morris, Jodie C. 242
Morris, Laura 157
Morris, Rose 300
Morris, V. 326
Morris, Vera R. 139
Morrison, A. J. 39
Morrison, Alyson 7
Morriss, Peter 231
Morse, Sasha Lianne 153
Morse, Stephen 160
Mortimer, Brian F. G. 349
Morton, B. 402
Moss, D. S. 120
Moulds, G. S. 164
Mountcastle, Maria 131
Mudie, Spencer Jay 303
Muir, Donis R. 198
Mulchay, Brenda 253
Mulford, Harry 363
Mulhern, Sean 139
Mullen, Kristie 113
Mullings, Dalsie 365
Mullins, Y. L. D. 122
Mulroy, Sheenagh Rose 161
Mulvaney, P. 161
Mundy, Darryl 210
Munn, Pete 126
Munro, Margaret 239
Murphy, Annie T. 193
Murphy, Elaine 362
Murphy, Jean D. 261
Murphy, M. 274
Murray, Alison 77
Murray, Clement 187
Murray, J. G. 315
Murray, Patricia 52
Murray, Thomas F. 130
Muter, P. 147
Muxworthy, Enyd 243
Myatt, Jennifer Morbey 19
Myers, Ernest 84
Myles, Mary 406

N

Nankivell, Sheila 280
Nash, E. 393
Nash, J. R. 291
Nash, Jill 253
Neal, John 187
Neale, Catherine 10
Neale, Doreen 250
Neill, Charlene 419
Neill, Diana 311
Nevins, E. M. 66
Newby, Joyce 98
Newell, Leslie 145
Newell, Royston 321
Newitt, A. 314
Newman, Sheila 225
Newton, D. M. 327
Newton, Ross 230

Nichol, Mollie 220
Nicholls, W. 224
Nichols, Edward William 99
Nichols, Winifred 325
Nicklin, Terence 335
Nicklinson, Michael J. 124
Ninnis, R. 61
Nixon, Sheila 327
Noël-Céphise, J. M. 384
Nolan, Chris 91
Nolan, Patricia 343
Noonan, Richard M. 274
Norfolk, Gill 79
Norgate, Cheryl 254
Norman, Charlotte Anne 106
Norman, Elizabeth 257
Norman, Ken 167
Norman, Wendy 228
Norris, Kathleen L. 153
Norris, R. 317
Nott, Robert E. 337
Nugent, Linda 172
Nunn, Lesley 174
Nutt, Catherine 13
Nutt, Edna A. 213
Nye, Brian John 19

O

Oakley, Simon 425
Oates, Sydney 160
O'Boyle, Lucy 153
O'Brien, Christine 90
O'Brien, Katie 133
O'Brien, Samantha 46
O'Connor, Robert 324
Odger, Ann 257
O'Donnell, Jason 96
O'Donnell, Jean 31
O'Dowd, John 93
Ogakwu, Vincent Oluonye 166
Ogden, G. A. 328
O'Grady, Barbara 202
Oishi, Ken 400
Oldbury, Doreen 349
Oldham, Moira 275
Oleghe, Grace 6
Oliver, K. 175
Oliver, Kelly 322
Ollier, Winfred 119
O'Malley, Elizabeth R. 374
O'Malley, Kieran D. 325
O'Neil, Janice Mary 96
O'Neill, Edward 35
O'Neill, Lawrence 159
O'Neill, Stella 114
O'Neill, Tim 51
Ord, Michael E. 219
Orde 131
O'Reilly, Joan 347
O'Reilly, Michael 298
Organ, Leigh 233
O'Rourke, Michael 266
O'Rourke, Rita 149
Orpwood, Roy 63
Orr, Peter 173
Osborne, David 184
Osborne, Jean Mary 13
Osguthorpe, Jackie 250
O'Sullivan, Gerardine 309
Oswell, Tracey 229
O'Toole, Keith 427
Ottley, Brenda 376
Ottley, Janice M. 83
Overfield, Heather 98
Overton, Emma 81
Owen, I. M. 390

Owen, Muriel Edna 283
Owen, Sue 223
Owen-Smith, C. S. 318
Owens, Janet Patrice 256
Owens, Margaret Mawson 228
Owens, Ruth 156

P

P., Catherine Nimmo 424
Padgham, R. 395
Page, Elizabeth 199
Pain, W. 415
Painter, A. V. 67
Palmer, Jack 374
Palmer, Lawrence Harold 227
Palmer, Mary 321
Palmer, Sarah 384
Pardoe, A. 230
Parfitt, Dorothy 364
Paris, Lee 342
Park, May 144
Park, William F. 299
Parker, Barbara C. 24
Parker, C. 174
Parker, Elizabeth 75
Parker, Eva 22
Parker, H. 294
Parker, Jeannette Anne 252
Parker, Kevin 421
Parker, M. 118
Parker, Patricia 324
Parker, Peter R. 164
Parker, Tanya 268
Parker, Yvonne 422
Parker, Zena R. 235
Parkin, Dean 18
Parkinson, Sandy 237
Parrington, Merlin 286
Parry, Janet 359
Parry, W. C. 68
Parsons, Amy 75
Parsons, Dorothy 94
Parsons, Yvonne 45
Partington, C. J. 290
Partlett, Rebecca 109
Partridge, Irene 6
Passey, Sue 229
Passfield, W. 312
Passmore, Linda 326
Patel, Vishal 147
Pateman, Robert S. (Margate) 316
Paterson, James 255
Paterson, K. 323
Patrick 277
Pattinson, Valerie 150
Pattwell, Michael 131
Paul, Joan 257
Paul, Shirley June 226
Pawsey, A. J. 305
Pawsey, Ka 134
Payne, Leslie 340
Payton, P. I. 235
Peachey, T. A. 229
Peacock, Patricia-Ann 282
Peacock, Vilma 159
Peacock, W. 134
Pearce, Douglas W. J. 241
Pearce, Jayne 36
Pearce, Margaret 272
Pearce, Selena 110
Pears, June Thelma 105
Pearson, Colleen 310
Pease, B. 304
Peck, Jill 191
Pelton, F. C. 119
Penney, L. 305

Pepper, P. 345
Percival, Frances 33
Perkins, Glenis 5
Perkins, Jodi 34
Perks-Hartnell, Lola 404
Perrot, J. M. 135
Perry, E. M. 289
Perry, Laurence Winston 278
Pescodd, M. 398
Pettitt, R. J. 231
Phair, Mark 38
Phillips, Adrian 191
Phillips, Celia 104
Phillips, Geoff H. 16
Phillips, Kitty D. 265
Phillips, M. 145
Phillips, Roger 135
Philp, H. 170
Philpott, Kelly 70
Philpott, Sandra 274
Phipps, Lorraine 336
Pickard, Nicola 225
Pickering, Lyn 282
Pickering, T. R. 339
Pickles, Janine 10
Pierce, Carole 349
Pigney, Teresa M. 321
Pike, Nicola 178
Pike, Robert Steven 219
Pilbeam, R. 315
Pilfold, L. 274
Pilsel, Mary Ann 130
Pimblett, Dorothy 15
Pinniger, E. 327
Pinnington, Marie 342
Pinnock, Ian 252
Piper, Rachael 147
Plant, Joan 428
Platt, Harold 10
Platt, Margaret 151
Platts, Sonia 319
Pleasance, Connie 203
Plucinski, Mary 122
Pluck, Derek J. 363
Pobihun, Roman 53
Poliak, Diana L. 351
Pollitt, Marion 221
Pollock, Alexandra 73
Polya, Lisa 380
Pope, Daphne 99
Porteous, Jenny 88
Porter, P. 297
Porter-Lovell, Daphne 31
Porthouse, M. 160
Posner, Barbara 346
Potter, Barbara 420
Potter, Damian 362
Potter, Gabrielle Louise 350
Poulsen, Janet 105
Poulter, Carol 374
Povey, Raymond H. 383
Powell, Pearl 150
Powell, Roger 131
Power, Jean 415
Power, June P. 89
Pratley, Sarah 120
Pratt, Claire Olite 95
Pratt, F. T. H. 64
Precious, Jennifer 359
Prentis, Vera 410
Preston, Jack 216
Price, A. L. 388
Price, Anne-Marie 356
Price, Betty 249
Price, Geoff 249
Price, John 377

Price, Megan 54
Priddle, Angela 373
Priest, Rodney George 166
Priestley, D. G. 234
Prime, Donna 197
Prince, Donna 256
Prince, Opal Vanessa 276
Prior, Steven 334
Proctor, J. 135
Prosser, Frank 82
Prout, Shelagh 70
Pruden, Tina 331
Pryke, D. E. 271
Pugh, Dan 85
Pugh, Spencer 422
Purbrick, J. 152
Purbrick, Peter D. 300
Purse, W. G. 219
Purser, Caroline 78
Purser, Patrick 322
Pursglove, Ivy 369
Purton, Wilfred 114
Purvis, Rachael 235
Pusey, Jackie 192

Q

Quarry, Paul 229
Quilt, H. 266
Quinn, Jeanne E. 209
Quinn, Larry 155
Quinn, William 428
Quirke, Gerard 244

R

R.A.M. 273
Race, L. 412
Radlett, Daniel J. 257
Rae, Alan J. 240
Rae, Sammy J. 137
Rafferty, Allan J. 251
Raheem, Areej 107
Rajendram, Edward 85
Rall, John 245
Ralston, Jennifer 362
Ramsay, Peter 263
Ramzan, Mohammed 218
Randle, Michael R. J. 149
Randle, Stephen 316
Rank, F. 158
Ransom, Elizabeth M. 28
Ratcliffe, Graham F. 95
Ratliffe, Joan G. 38
Rawlings, Andrew 259
Ray, Carol 357
Ray, Nicola 266
Raymond, Benn 246
Rayner, Joanna 76
Raynes, Brenda 364
Rea, Rosemary 262
Read, Barbara 78
Read, C. A. 311
Reade, Paul 225
Reda, P. 395
Redfern-Mason, Rebecca 380
Redhead, A. 305
Redpath, James 99
Rees, Elizabeth Ann 249
Reeve, Margarita 54
Reeve, Trevor 302
Reeves, Colin 209
Reid, Ellie Gibson 207
Reid, Philip 267, 398
Reid, V. 281
Relf, Katrina 275
Remmington, John 243

Rendall, John H. E. 17
Rendell, A. E. 329
Renwick, Billy 194
Renwick, Norman 123
Reynolds, Alice M. 307
Reynolds, M. J. 233
Reynolds, Paul 139
Rhodes, T. 385
Rhys, Magdalen 146
Rhys-Davies, Norma 265
Richards, Helen 80
Richards, Sue 61
Richards, W. 426
Richardson, A. G. 238
Richardson, Anne 184
Richardson, Christopher 201
Richardson, D. C. 40
Richardson, Glenda 200
Richardson, J. A. 300
Richardson, Phyllis 221
Richardson, S. 342
Richardson, William 267
Rickard, Julie 205
Rickman, David 240
Riddell, Margaret 116
Riddell, Thomas 416
Rider, Sheila 224
Ridge, Lynne 384
Riding, Lynda 270
Riggs, Janine 89
Riley, Dorothy 11
Riley, Eileen 240
Riordan, Nell Ferguson 400
Ripley, Dereck 206
Ritch, Grace M. 371
Ritchie, Brooke 208
Ritchie, Neil 163
Rivers, Julie 35
Rivers, Lorraine 115
Roach, Sheryl 71
Roberts, Allison 240
Roberts, Barbara E. 75
Roberts, Carl A. 214
Roberts, Charles 237
Roberts, Claire 26
Roberts, Gillian S. 360
Roberts, I. 175
Roberts, Jean 86
Roberts, Kelly 239
Roberts, Marie 161
Roberts, Mark 272
Roberts, Mary 345
Robertson, A. G. 336
Robertson, A. Scott 268
Robertson, D. 269
Robins, Sheila M. 141
Robinson, B. 156
Robinson, Fred 197
Robinson, James 30
Robinson, James Oliver 78
Robinson, John Barry 241
Robinson, Lesley 109
Robinson, Marjorie 329
Robinson, Nigel 131
Robinson, Victoria 226
Robson, Carolyn 251
Robson, Duncan 358
Roche, Anne 208
Roche, P. M. 288
Rock, Emma 360
Rodger, Mavis 166
Rogers, Elizabeth D. 425
Rogers, Jenny 346
Rogers, Louise 264
Rolfe, Maureen 144
Rook, Sylvia M. 237

Rose, Julian 247
Rose, M. Edith 178
Rosewell, Anne 342
Ross, Colin 302
Ross, Eddie 426
Ross, Lesley-Ann 306
Rossington, David 259
Rothwell, Jayne M. 411
Round, Delma 272
Routledge, Peter 331
Rowan, Kevin 172
Rowe, D. R. 272
Rowe, Giselle 37
Rowe, Hazel 361
Rowe, R. 397
Rowe, Sharon Lydia 59
Rowell, Ashley 196
Rowlands, Christopher 210
Rowley, Michelle 300
Rowney, M. 387
Ruck, G. 130
Ruddy, Alice 302
Rugg, Emma Jane 240
Rugg, Isabella 32
Rumgay, Earl 215
Rusbridge, P. 264
Ruse, Marilyn A. 283
Rush, Thomas C. 318
Russell, Laurence 419
Russell, Lynne 163
Russell, Pat 125
Russell, Rebecca 281
Russell, Sylvia 409
Rutherford, Carrie 214
Rutter, A. M. 156
Ryan, Claude (John) O'Donnell 360
Ryan, Martin 283
Ryan, Stephen 389
Ryan, Valerie 423
Ryder, Jason 255
Rysdale, Brian 414

S

Sadd, C. M. 276
Sadler, Alan G. 316
Sadler, Eleanor 214
Saele, Sheila 69
Sallis, W. 391
Sallows, Elizabeth 421
Salter, B. 222
Salter, E. 128
Samson, David J. M. 359
Sanders, C. 271
Sanders, M. 152
Sanderson, Eleanor Haydon 93
Sandford, Joyce 257
Sangers, John 248
Santer, Lynn 273
Sanviti, Doris 81
Sargeant, B. J. 165
Sassi, Rick 72
Satur, E. 423
Saum, Barbara 210
Saupe, Glynis 4
Savage, Clare 25
Savage, Jacqueline 17
Sawyer, Anne Prudence 354
Sawyer, Kevin 134
Saxon, P. 344
Scarborough, Kathleen 270
Scarisbrick, Henry 27
Schofield, Margaret 337
Schofield, Michael 325
Schofield, Wendy L. 131
Scholes, Maxine 172
Schurmann, F. E. 48

Scicluna, Patricia A. 315
Scoffham, Olive 129
Scott, Clarice 353
Scott, George V. 183
Scott, J. G. 47
Scott, Jane 307
Scott, Marie 284
Scott, Miriam 181
Scott, R. 162
Screen, David Robert 366
Scriven, Maria I. 155
Scully, Heather 245
Scurr, David 76
Sears, Emma 95
Sears, M. 413
Segal, Jeffrey 356
Sellars, Dee 373
Sellers, Cheryl Audrey 20
Selway, Ron 381
Sempey, Louise 238
Senior, Jean M. 77
Serbert, Charles 10
Shailer, Tom 331
Shand, George Livingston 421
Sharkey, Doug 359
Sharma, Arun 190
Sharman, E. J. 415
Sharp, D. 286
Sharp, Doreen 6
Sharp, Emma 27
Sharp, G. D. 418
Sharp, L. G. 395
Sharp, Nancy 322
Sharpe, D. R. 236
Shaw, Bernadette 183
Shaw, Christine 9
Shaw, June H. G. 9
Shaw, Ken 423
Shaw, P. J. 127
Shea, Margaret O. 227
Shearing, T. J. 407
Sheehan, M. 110
Sheffield, Barry 89
Shelvock, F. 151
Shenton, W. T. 277
Shepherd, Andrew 198
Sherwin, D. 281
Shine, J. E. 175
Shiner, Finlay 188
Shipley, Ann 351
Shipman, Beryl 310
Shipman, Brenda J. 24
Shires, Leeanne 288
Shorland, Craig Nicholas 192
Short, Mandy 51
Shorten, A. 220
Shotter, Luke 153
Shuter, W. F. 389
Shuttlewood, Jennifer 258
Sibbald, Robert 132
Sibbert, P. S. 412
Siddons, Iris E. 249
Silverlock, Karen 279
Simister, Jean 204
Simmons, Beryl 21
Simms, Jonathan 248
Simms, Kelly 237
Simms, M. 400
Simms, Pamela 223
Simpson, I. 296
Simpson, James 86, 249
Simpson, Joseph 352
Simpson, Larraine 382
Simpson, Mary 221
Simpson, Norah R. 216
Simpson, Paul 269

Sims, George 37
Sinclair, Michael 420
Sinclair, Pamela 40
Sisterson, Elisabeth 367
Skelton, C. R. 237
Skerrett, Carole 213
Skillington, F. J. 317
Skinn, H. 401
Skinn, Robin Nicholas 326
Slade, Heather 38
Slark, Pippa Dawn 218
Slater, Helen 25
Slater, Marion 405
Slaughter, M. 234
Slee, Angela 79
Slim, John 216
Slinn, Richard 296
Small, Anne 372
Small, Dorothy J. 239
Small, Susan E. 292
Smallridge, Dora May 335
Smart, F. H. 318
Smeaton, Kevin 232
Smiles, Barbara Jean 99
Smissen, Clifford 124
Smith, A. 110
Smith, Anna-Marie 185
Smith, Antony 422
Smith, Barry Harold 245
Smith, Bryan 24
Smith, Cain 254
Smith, Clarence A. 25
Smith, Craig J. 366
Smith, David James 203
Smith, Doreen 245
Smith, Dorothy 17
Smith, E. A. 218
Smith, Edith M. 202
Smith, Eileen 356
Smith, Elizabeth 364
Smith, Elizabeth Spencer 364
Smith, George 94
Smith, Gill 311
Smith, Glenda 14
Smith, Gwendoline 249
Smith, Hilda 368
Smith, Iris 355
Smith, J. D. Mant 412
Smith, J. M. 227
Smith, J. R. 176
Smith, James Ferri 245
Smith, Jane 254
Smith, Jean A. 16
Smith, Jennifer 193
Smith, Jillian 192
Smith, Joan S. 93
Smith, Joanne L. 38
Smith, John W. 354
Smith, Karen 62
Smith, Kathlees 230
Smith, Laura 273
Smith, Laura A. 324
Smith, Lorraine 148
Smith, M. L. 115
Smith, Margaret 116
Smith, Margaret Butter 167
Smith, Margaret Joyce 154
Smith, R. M. 68
Smith, S. M. 43
Smith, Sandra 275
Smith, Sarah 170
Smith, Vivian A. 275
Smith, Walter G. 394
Smith, Yvonne 275
Smithdale, Suzanne 419
Smyter, Beryl 240

Smyth, Eileen 189
Smyth, N. J. 233
Snaize, Julian Alan 380
Snell, L. G. 154
Snelling, S. A. 320
Snow, A. G. 394
Somerville, Gertrude Arbuthnot 15
Somerville, P. R. A. 180
Southwood, Peter E. 269
Souza, Ana Maria De Carter 17
Sowden, C. B. A. J. 140
Spalding, Bryan 6
Sparkes, Ivy 377
Sparks, William 388
Spence, Melanie 344
Spencer, Peter 266
Spencer, Susan E. 12
Spencer-Moore, B. 407
Sperring, Diane 349
Spicer, Jane 103
Spicer, Rita 124
Spiers, Emily 353
Spiller, John 310
Spilsbury, Teresa 228
Spraggs, Anita 99
Squires, Geraldine 246
Squires, L. M. 226
Squires, L. M. 412
Squires, Stephen 123
Staines, Denise 261
Stainsby, Helen 366
Standard, G. P. 57
Standring, R. I. 321
Staniford, Margaret 163
Stanton, F. 405
Stanton, Haydee 15
Stanton, Samantha 115
Starck, Margaret 295
Stead, Anne 4
Steel, Irene 307
Steele, Edith 98
Steele, Janice 205
Stell, D. M. 315
Stephen, Robert 129
Stephens, Allison 214
Stephens, Dennis G. 363
Stephens, Jenny G. 86
Stephens, K. J. 223
Stephens, Samantha 339
Stephenson, Doreen Beverley 310
Stevens, C. A. 114
Stevens, E. M. 402
Stevens, Karen 235
Stewart, Bill 100
Stewart, John 206
Stewart, John 209
Stewart, Malcolm 112
Stiles, Leslie G. 108
Stirton, Graeme 3
Stockham, Barbara 369
Stockley, Lesley 230
Stocks, C. 159
Stokes, Jane 210
Stokes, Lane 165
Stokes, R. E. J. 320
Stokes, W. L. 118
Stone, Debra 105
Stone, Eileen M. 262
Stone, Odele 223
Stoneman, Alyson 185
Stones, D. W. A. 271
Storey, Lynne 390
Stothard, Kimberley Ellen 306
Stott, Carla 371
Stott, Gavin 240
Stott, Lisa Marie 173

Stow, David A. 308
Strawbridge, David J. 206
Strong, Mary Greenway 303
Stuart, James 412
Stuart, Ron 143
Stubberfield, Martin 305
Stubbs, Christine 206
Stubbs, Sarah 285
Studd, A. E. 324
Suddards, David 87
Suleyman, Pembe 143
Sullivan, G. M. M. 172
Surman, David Paul 254
Sutton, A. L. 293
Sutton, Helen 259
Sutton, Vera 137
Swales, Dawn 92
Swann, Margaret 293
Sweet, Sonia 169
Sweetenham, S. 385
Swords, M. 306
Sykes, Dryden 36
Sykes, Shavon 418
Symons, Sarah 412
Synott, Julie 26

T

Tabor, Brenda 355
Taffetsauffer, Dorothy 16
Tagg, H. J. 320
Tahid, Nazia 297
Tait, H. 311
Tammas, Jeanne Martin 95
Taplin, Ron 314
Tarbuek, Ann 375
Tasker, Colin 251
Tate, Robert 381
Tattersdill, Arthur 128
Taylor, A. 397
Taylor, A. J. 267
Taylor, Ms. A. M. 238
Taylor, Beryl 14
Taylor, D. C. 319
Taylor, Gabrielle Anne 101
Taylor, H. 344
Taylor, Hartley 413
Taylor, J. 284
Taylor, Julie 9
Taylor, Julie 260
Taylor, Mary Durant 312
Taylor, Michael L. 319
Taylor, Michelle 315
Taylor, Rita 39
Taylor, Shaun A. 166
Teakel, David 348
Teasdale, Anne 21
Tebbutt, Joan A. 185
Tees, Elizabeth 307
Teiwel, E. 428
Telford, R. 406
Temple, Nicola 179
Terry, John 256
Terry, Christine Lavinia 368
Theedam, Victoria Joan 395
Thew, R. 225
Thirkettle, Sandra 280
Thirlaway, Eve 368
Thirlwell, Margaret 397
Thomas, Andrea Selina 186
Thomas, Ian 100
Thomas, J. M. 146
Thomas, J. R. 276
Thomas, Jean 14
Thomas, Patricia Anne 171
Thomas, V. K. 150
Thomas-Symonds, Nicklaus 235

Thompson, Beatrice 253
Thompson, Brenda 91
Thompson, David George 204
Thompson, Gail 260
Thompson, George 192
Thompson, Helen 257
Thompson, Helen E. 244
Thompson, Ian James 245
Thompson, Julie 186
Thompson, P. 378
Thompson, Pauline 400
Thompson, Robert 275
Thomson, Ann 254
Thomson, Ginnie M. 4
Thomson, S. 293
Thorn, Teresa Jane 42
Thorneloe, Muriel B. 64
Thornton, John 203
Thorogood, Ian Charles 205
Thorogood, J. R. 403
Thurlby, R. J. 125
Tibbitts, Gordon 8
Tilley, Gwyneth 82
Timmins, Ann 244
Timmins, Maralyn 125
Tinkler, Lynn 420
Tinsley, Heidi L. 352
Titley, Kathleen 177
Toal, Teresa 297
Todd, Hugh 80
Todd, Marilyn 177
Todd, Patricia 279
Tombs, Tom 392
Tomkinson, Maureen 413
Tomlinson, Kathleen 269
Tomlinson, N. 394
Tomlinson, Sharon 331
Toms, Emma 252
Tong, Alison 191
Toon, A. L. 386
Tooth, Florence 15
Tooth, G. 158
Totten, T. S. 150
Tovell, Carole 309
Tovell, Tov 234
Towers-Clark, David 308
Towner, Diana L. 193
Townsend, Bruce 352
Townsend, Joannah 19
Townsend, Maureen 158
Townsend, S. 123
Tranter, Martin 286
Travers, Kathy 234
Travis, Brian 28
Trayford, Christine 20
Treadwell, C. 181
Treuge, Gordon 94
Triggle, D. 232
Trotman, Heather 254
Trow, Hayley 21
Trubarac, Milan 344
True, Joan 311
Truman, Jill 184
Truscott, F.N.M. 107
Tucker, Edna F. 204
Tuckey, Brian G. 348
Turberfield, Diane C. 362
Turk, Robin P. 301
Turnbull, Jane 87
Turnbull, Meg 145
Turner, Andrew 250
Turner, F. C. 403
Turner, I. 41
Turner, John K. 215
Turner, L. M. 398
Tusel, J. C. 152

Twyning, Sid 264
Tydeman, Marion 219

U

Unsworth, Steven 269
Ursula Atkins 168
Usher, Lewey 219

V

Valk, Margaret A. 290
Vann, Sylvia 221
Vardy, Karlene 119
Vellam, Doris 106
Veltom, Audrey J. 357
Verdant, Earl E. 257
Vesti-Nielsen, Anita 347
Vesti-Nielsen, Rebecca 271
Vickers-James, Wendy 319
Villagran, Michelle 227
Vinal-Burnett, Margaret 387
Voller, Franie 242
Von, Sigvard Brevern 142

W

Waddington, J. 161
Wadeson, James 242
Wagner, Beryl 191
Waite, J. C. S. 18
Waite, Karen Jane 287
Wakelin, Carole 241
Walkden, E. V. 301
Walker, Barry Lee 194
Walker, Emily 253
Walker, Gary 256
Walker, Maeve 315
Walker, Raymond 111
Walker, Rebecca 226
Walker, Sheila 394
Walker, Vivien 323
Wall, Terence 415
Wallace, Barbara 352
Wallace, Claire 246
Wallace, Gina 359
Wallace, Keith M. 336
Waller, Abi 16
Waller, Andrew W. 249
Waller, H. 401
Walmsley, G. B. 295
Walmsley, Laura 141
Walsh, Paula Wendy 237
Walt, Ellen 20
Walters, M. A. 133
Walton, Amy 248
Walton, Jean E. N. 373
Wambeek, Edmund G. 77
Wandless, Sharon 301
Warbey, Karen Elizabeth 381
Ward, Ej 240
Ward, Joan 252
Ward, Mary L. 162
Ward, Maxine 274
Ward, Peter K. 335
Ward, Sally 382
Ward, Sean 387
Ward, Stella Rosemary 327
Ward, Tony 156
Wardle, L. 48
Wardle, P. M. 224
Wareing, G. M. 147
Waring, Josephine Ann 18
Waring, Peter 165
Warner, O. 407
Warren, Bernie 258
Warren, Janet 87
Warren, Joe 92

Warren, L. N. 323
Warren, Maria 412
Warren, P. M. 312
Warrington, Jacqueline 4
Warsza, Agatka 183
Waters, Penny 146
Waters, Sharyn 117
Wates, Polly 59
Watkis, Adlin 211
Watson, Alison Linklater 356
Watson, Charlotte R. 101
Watson, Dennis P. 103
Watson, Jean 208
Watson, P. 320
Watson, Pat 111
Watson, Robert James 304
Watson, Wendy 44
Watson, Wendy 143
Watson, William 292
Watts, M. 125
Watts, Mike 335
Waudby, Gilbert H. 84
Wearing, Wendy J. 292
Weaver, Daphne 102
Weaver, Tracy 112
Webb, A. 135
Webb, Ernest 9
Webb, J. 66
Webster, A. B. 343
Webster, Amanda 177
Weekly, S. 111
Wegehaupt, Ann-Marie 103
Weightman, Jill V. 100
Welland, Christine 374
Welland, Steve A. 145
Wellband, Sarah 236
Weller, Amelia 345
Wells, Elspeth 98
Wells, I. C. 150
Welsford, Alan 253
Wenstrom, Irene 308
Wesson, D. 407
West, Eleanor 186
West, Harry 29
West, James 101
West, Thomas Robert 299
Western, Jessica 26
Westley, Frederick William 186
Westney, Violet 161
Westwood, Patricia 230
Westwood, Sheila H. 139
Whale, Peter 320
Wharry, Norman 405
Wharton, Robert Edward 224
Whatmore, P. A. 178
Wheatley, Gerald 244
Wheelans, S. 237
Wheeler, Jan 94
Whelan, Christophe J. 102
Whelan, T. W. 314
Whetnall, Gillian 241
White, Alan David 9
White, John 73
White, K. M. 234
White, Mary 238
Whitehouse, M. 404
Whitfield, Louise 65
Whitmarsh, Pat 227
Wickers, Adam 242
Wiggins, Tracey 387
Wilde, Jon 13
Wilding, Janet 390
Wiley, Paul 141
Wilkinson, Elizabeth A. 9
Wilkinson, J. 229
Wilkinson, M. 55

Will, Pauline 280
Willett, Elisha Jane 193
Willett, R. 337
Williams, Anne 105
Williams, Brian Kenneth 14
Williams, D. 40
Williams, D. 224
Williams, Fiona 204
Williams, Iris 375
Williams, Ivor 424
Williams, Jamie 74
Williams, Jean 424
Williams, June 73
Williams, Lilian M. 321
Williams, M. C. 138
Williams, Margaret Mary 173
Williams, Michael Patrick 180
Williams, N. E. 340
Williams, Pamela Frances 149
Williams, Pearl 65
Williams, Peter R. 302
Williams, Sheila Mary 391
Williams, Sue 302
Williamson, Noel Egbert 139
Williamson, Penny 140
Williamson, Rosemary 160
Willingham, C. V. 293
Willis, Ann 308
Willis, Paul 265
Willmott, E. 41
Willmott, H. C. 220
Willoughby, Margaret 342
Wills, Federick T. B. 107
Wills, Julie 416
Wills, Sheila Lucy 51
Wilshaw, Andrew J. 360
Wilson, A. J. 313
Wilson, B. 111
Wilson, B. 273
Wilson, Iain 428
Wilson, J. 43
Wilson, Judith 94
Wilson, Lesley Ann 274
Wilson, Marilyn 278
Wilson, Michelle 44
Wilson, Norman 323
Wilson, Oriel 52
Wilson, Shelley 132
Wilson, Sidney 225
Winchester, J. D. 343
Windridge, V. 317
Winn, Nicholas 292
Winters, Marlene 336
Wiseman, Jill 194
Witherington, Averil 196
Withers, Maureen 154
Withers, Tammy 405
Wixon, Jean Valerie 243
Wlodarz, Robert 31
Womack, Hilda 10
Wones, Caroline 242
Wood, Ann 86
Wood, K. C. 137
Wood, Kelly-Marie 291
Wood, Laurence 289
Wood, R. 116
Wood, Ron 268
Wood, Samantha Jane 282
Woodcock, M. 287
Woodcraft, Tracy 382
Woodfield, Cora 106
Woods, Jeffrey 11
Woods, Louise 116
Woods, Paul Anthony 42
Woodward, A. R. 325
Woodward, James 298

Woollard, George E. 86
Wootten, Beatrice 25
Worbey, R. A. 50
Wozencroft, Grace 420
Wray, John 421
Wray, Laurence Peter 296
Wren, Carey 190
Wright, Gordon A. 348
Wright, Isabelle 241
Wright, Jennifer 83
Wright, Lucie 222
Wright, M. 180
Wright, Margaret-Jean 399
Wright, Marjorie 168
Wright, O. 120
Wright, Paula 406
Wright, Philip Robert 383
Wright, Sylvia 113
Wyatt, Patricia 389
Wynn, John 82

Y

Yard, John 253
Yardley, Michelle 385
Yates, Margaret Jean 290
Yeoman, Christine 240
York, Christopher J. 349
Young, Allan 378
Young, Christopher 192
Young, F. V. 321
Young, Gillian A. 427
Young, Joanne 201
Young, S. C. 335
Young, Vivienne 427
Youngs, S. 124

Z

Zambelli, Joan 194
Zarrabi, Angela 105